EDITORIAL BOARD

ROBERT C. CLARK
DIRECTING EDITOR
Distinguished Service Professor and Austin Wakeman Scott
Professor of Law and Former Dean of the Law School
Harvard University

DANIEL A. FARBER
Sho Sato Professor of Law and Director, Environmental Law Program
University of California at Berkeley

HEATHER K. GERKEN
J. Skelly Wright Professor of Law
Yale University

SAMUEL ISSACHAROFF
Bonnie and Richard Reiss Professor of Constitutional Law
New York University

HERMA HILL KAY
Barbara Nachtrieb Armstrong Professor of Law and
Former Dean of the School of Law
University of California at Berkeley

HAROLD HONGJU KOH
Sterling Professor of International Law and
Former Dean of the Law School
Yale University

SAUL LEVMORE
William B. Graham Distinguished Service Professor of Law and
Former Dean of the Law School
University of Chicago

THOMAS W. MERRILL
Charles Evans Hughes Professor of Law
Columbia University

ROBERT L. RABIN
A. Calder Mackay Professor of Law
Stanford University

CAROL M. ROSE
Gordon Bradford Tweedy Professor Emeritus of Law and Organization and
Professorial Lecturer in Law
Yale University
Lohse Chair in Water and Natural Resources
University of Arizona

UNIVERSITY CASEBOOK SERIES®

SENTENCING LAW AND POLICY

JOHN F. PFAFF
Professor of Law
Fordham Law School

The publisher is not engaged in rendering legal or other professional advice, and this publication is not a substitute for the advice of an attorney. If you require legal or other expert advice, you should seek the services of a competent attorney or other professional.

University Casebook Series is a trademark registered in the U.S. Patent and Trademark Office.

© 2016 LEG, Inc. d/b/a West Academic
    444 Cedar Street, Suite 700
    St. Paul, MN 55101
    1-877-888-1330

Printed in the United States of America

ISBN: 978-1-60930-296-2

To Molly, and to C, N + N.

ACKNOWLEDGMENTS

Thank you, first of all, to my wife Molly, for her unflagging support. And to Nestor Davidson and the rest of the administration at Fordham Law School, who consistently provided me with all the resources I needed (and then some) to complete this book. And thank you to all who helped with the research: Larry Abraham, Alissa Black-Dorward, and Todd Melnick in the law library, and those who worked on this project as RAs: Arielle Buss, Christie Falco, Samantha Gillespie, Allison Job, Jason Kosek, Emily Lee, Ruben Magalhaes, Emad Maghsoudi, Hannah McFarland, Colleen Powers, Alexandra Sadinsky, Paul Skydel, Brittany Taylor, Gilberto Vargas, Alyssa Wanderon, and Minning Yu.

SUMMARY OF CONTENTS

ACKNOWLEDGMENTS V

TABLE OF CASES XIX

PART 1. WHO, WHY, AND HOW WE SENTENCE

Chapter 1. Who We Sentence 5
A. A Simple Model of Human Behavior 6
B. Risk Factors for Criminal Behavior 13
C. The Proper Use of Social Science Evidence 34

Chapter 2. Why We Punish 37
A. The Normative Goals of Punishment 37
B. Positive Theories of Punishment 70

Chapter 3. The Competing Actors of the Criminal Justice System 81
A. Introduction 81
B. Police Officers 84
C. Prosecutors and Defense Attorneys 89
D. Judges 103
E. Governors and State Attorneys General 114
F. Parole Boards and Officers 116
G. Legislatures 121
H. Sentencing Commissions 129
I. Discretion and Actuarialism 131
J. Conclusion 141

PART 2. SENTENCING LAW AND PROCEDURE

Chapter 4. Factors Relevant to Sentencing: Offense Traits 145
A. Offense Severity 145
B. The Role of Motive 170
C. The Victim and Victim Impact Statements 177

Chapter 5. Factors Relevant to Sentencing: Offender Characteristics 189
A. Prior Criminal History 190
B. Immutable Characteristics 209
C. More Mutable Characteristics 242

Chapter 6. Procedures and Rights at Sentencing 249
A. Procedural Protections at Sentencing 249
B. Substantive Rules: A Silent Federal Court, More Active State Courts, Highly Active State Legislatures 253
C. The Supreme Court's Foray into Sentencing Law 300

Chapter 7. The Death Penalty 375
A. The Law of the Death Penalty 375

B. Is the Administration of the Death Penalty Broken?..........................407
C. The Death Penalty and the Theories of Punishment.........................417
D. Some Additional Issues 426

Chapter 8. Plea Bargaining 433
A. The Substantive Law of Plea Bargaining..434
B. The Debate over Plea Bargaining..454
C. Pulling It All Together..474

PART 3. SENTENCES AND RE-ENTRY

Chapter 9. Sentencing Policy and the Rise of the Prison................479
A. The Basic Theories of Prison Growth 481
B. The Politics of Crime 498
C. United States and Europe: A Comparison 527

Chapter 10. The Effects of Incarceration..537
A. Life Inside Prison..537
B. The Impact of Incarceration on an Inmate and His Family 548
C. Impact of Incarceration on Communities...569
D. Incarceration and Crime 574

Chapter 11. Alternatives to Incarceration...587
A. The Standard Alternatives: Probation, Fines, Community Service, Asset Forfeiture, and Boot Camps..588
B. Controlling Sex Offenders and Domestic Batterers 618
C. Shame, Restorative Justice, and Drug/Alternative Courts................649

Chapter 12. Parole and Re-Entry 697
A. The Challenges of Re-Entry 698
B. The Process of Parole...707
C. Violating Parole 752
D. The Other Ways Out of Prison: Commutations and Pardons.............768

Appendix. Statistical Glossary 773

INDEX 779

TABLE OF CONTENTS

ACKNOWLEDGMENTS V

TABLE OF CASES XIX

PART 1. WHO, WHY, AND HOW WE SENTENCE

Chapter 1. Who We Sentence 5
A. A Simple Model of Human Behavior 6
   A.1. The Rational Actor Model 6
      Gary Becker, Nobel Lecture: The Economic Way of Looking at
         Human Behavior 7
   A.2. "Behavioralist" Critiques 10
B. Risk Factors for Criminal Behavior 13
   B.1. Early Risk Factors 15
      David P. Farrington and Brandon C. Welsh, *Saving Children
         From a Life of Crime* 15
      Questions 20
   B.2. Lifecycle Trends in Offending 21
      Question 1: The Causes of the Trends 23
      Question 2: Can We Predict Who Will Be on What Path? 25
      Question 3: Do Criminal Justice Systems Properly Account for
         the Age Profile of Offending? 26
   B.3. The Importance of Place and Situation 27
      David Weisburd, *Place-Based Policing* 27
      Jon Hanson and David Yosifon, *The Situation: An Introduction
         to the Situational Character, Critical Realism, Power
         Economics* 31
      Questions 33
C. The Proper Use of Social Science Evidence 34

Chapter 2. Why We Punish 37
A. The Normative Goals of Punishment 37
   A.1. Utilitarian Theories 37
      A.1.a.   Deterrence 38
              Daniel S. Nagin, *Deterrence in the Twenty-First
                 Century* 40
              Questions 43
      A.1.b.   Incapacitation 44
              Questions 47
      A.1.c.   Rehabilitation 48
              Francis T. Cullen, *Rehabilitation: Beyond Nothing
                 Works* 48
              Questions 55
   A.2. Just Deserts/Retributivism 57
      Questions 61
   A.3. The Lack of Consensus 63
      Richard S. Frase, *Punishment Purposes* 66
      Questions 69

B. Positive Theories of Punishment 70
      James Q. Whitman, *The Comparative Study of Criminal Punishment* 71
         Questions 74
      David Garland, *Punishment and Modern Society, Ch. 6: "Punishment and the Technologies of Power: The Work of Michel Foucault"* 74

Chapter 3. The Competing Actors of the Criminal Justice System 81

A. Introduction 81
B. Police Officers 84
      Dan Richman, *Institutional Coordination and Sentencing Reform* 84
      Questions 89
C. Prosecutors and Defense Attorneys 89
    C.1. Prosecutors 89
        Questions 91
        Daniel C. Richman and William J. Stuntz, *Al Capone's Revenge: An Essay on the Political Economy of Pretextual Prosecution* 94
        Questions 98
    C.2. Defense Attorneys 99
        Amy Bach, *Ordinary Injustice: How America Holds Court* 102
        Questions 103
D. Judges 103
      Jeffrey J. Rachlinski, Sheri Lynn Johnson, Andrew J. Wistrich, & Chris Guthrie, *Does Unconscious Racial Bias Affect Trial Judges?* 106
      Timothy Griffin and John Wooldredge, *Sex-Based Disparities in Felony Disparities Before versus After Sentencing Reform in Ohio* 110
      Questions 113
E. Governors and State Attorneys General 114
F. Parole Boards and Officers 116
      Questions 121
G. Legislatures 121
      Thomas D. Stucky, Karen Heimer, and Joseph B. Lang, *Partisan Politics, Electoral Competition and Imprisonment: An Analysis of States Over Time* 124
      Questions 128
H. Sentencing Commissions 129
I. Discretion and Actuarialism 131
      Eric S. Janus & Robert A. Prentky, *Forensic Use of Actuarial Risk Assessment With Sex Offenders: Accuracy, Admissibility and Accountability* 132
J. Conclusion 141

PART 2. SENTENCING LAW AND PROCEDURE

Chapter 4. Factors Relevant to Sentencing: Offense Traits 145
A. Offense Severity 145
    A.1. Qualitative Assessments of Offense Severity 146
        Questions 155
    A.2. Quantitative Offense Severity 155
        Questions 165
        Questions 169
B. The Role of Motive 170
        Additional Questions 177
C. The Victim and Victim Impact Statements 177
        Questions 187

Chapter 5. Factors Relevant to Sentencing: Offender Characteristics 189
A. Prior Criminal History 190
    A.1. Theoretical Justifications 190
        Richard Frase, *Prior Conviction Sentencing Enhancements: Rationales and Limits Based on Retributive and Utilitarian Proportionality Principles and Social Equity Goals* 190
        Questions 198
        Problem: The Effect of a Prior Record in Minnesota 199
        Questions 202
    A.2. The Special Status of Prior History, and Its Reliability 202
        Questions 205
    A.3. Habitual-Offender and Three-Strike Laws 206
        Questions 208
B. Immutable Characteristics 209
    B.1. Developmental Genetic, and Neurological Factors 210
        B.1.a.   The Connection Between DGN and Crime 211
                 David P. Farrington, *Individual Differences and Offending* 211
                 Questions 217
        B.1.b.   The Normative Importance of DGN Evidence 217
                 Joshua Greene and Jonathan Cohen, *For the Law, Neuroscience Changes Nothing and Everything* 218
                 Questions 225
        B.1.c.   The Use of DGN Evidence in Court 226
                 Deborah Denno, *Courts' Increasing Consideration of Behavioral Genetics Evidence in Criminal Cases: Results of a Longitudinal Study* 226
    B.2. Sex and Offending 230
    B.3. Age and Offending 233
        Questions 241
C. More Mutable Characteristics 242

                    Questions 244
                    Problem: Aggravators and Mitigators in North Carolina 245

Chapter 6. Procedures and Rights at Sentencing 249
A. Procedural Protections at Sentencing 249
    Alan C. Michaels, *Trial Rights at Sentencing* 249
    Questions 253
B. Substantive Rules: A Silent Federal Court, More Active State
    Courts, Highly Active State Legislatures 253
    B.1. Federal and State Judicial Limits 254
         Richard Frase, *Limiting Excessive Prison Sentences Under*
              Federal and State Constitutions 256
         Questions 260
    B.2. Legislative Developments: The Rise of Structured
         Sentencing 260
         John F. Pfaff, *The Continued Vitality of Structured Sentencing*
              Following Blakely: *The Effectiveness of Voluntary*
              Guidelines 260
         B.2.a. Guidelines and Determinate Sentencing Laws 264
                 Problem: Guidelines in Practice 266
                 Questions 272
                 Questions 275
                 Questions 279
                 David Yellen, *Reforming the Federal Sentencing*
                      Guidelines' Misguided Approach to Real-Offense
                      Sentencing 282
                 Questions 287
         B.2.b. Mandatory Minimums 288
                 Michael Tonry, *The Mostly Unintended Consequences*
                      of Mandatory Penalties: Two Centuries of
                      Consistent Findings 291
                 Questions 295
         B.2.c. Truth in Sentencing and Parole Abolition 296
                 Questions 299
         B.2.d. The Untouched Prosecutor 299
C. The Supreme Court's Foray into Sentencing Law 300
    C.1. Introduction: The Element/Sentencing Factor Divide:
         Mullaney, Patterson, and *Almendarez-Torres* 301
         Questions 307
    C.2. Narrowing the Options: *Apprendi, Ring,* and *Harris* 309
         Apprendi v. New Jersey 314
         Questions 321
         Questions 327
    C.3. The Hammer Falls: *Blakely* and *Booker* 327
         C.3.a. The Apex of *Apprendi*: *Blakely v. Washington* 328
                 Blakely v. Washington 328
                 Questions 336
                 Questions 339

		Questions 341

          Problem: New York State's Persistent Felony
             Offender Law 342
          Questions 344
     C.3.b. *Blakely's Patterson: United States v. Booker* 344
          United States v. Booker 345
          Problem: Appellate Review in a *Booker* World 353
          Questions 356
  C.4. State Responses to *Blakely* 358
  C.5. The Federal Guidelines: *Rita*, *Gall*, and Beyond 362
       Questions 367
  C.6. The Final Cases (for Now): *Oregon v. Ice* and *Alleyne v. United States* 368
       Questions 373

Chapter 7. The Death Penalty 375
A. The Law of the Death Penalty 375
  A.1. The Supreme Court 376
       Gregg v. Georgia 380
       Questions 384
       McCleskey v. Kemp 387
       Questions 396
  A.2. Legislative Rules 397
     A.2.a. Types of Crimes (and Abolition) 397
     A.2.b. Standards for Execution 398
     A.2.c. Federal Rules 400
  A.3. The Executive Role in Executions 406
B. Is the Administration of the Death Penalty Broken? 407
    James S. Liebman, Jeffrey Fagan, and Valerie West, *A Broken System: Error Rates in Capital Cases* 407
    James S. Liebman, Jeffrey Fagan, and Valerie West, *A Broken System II: Why There Is So Much Error in Capital Cases, and What Can Be Done About It* 414
  Questions 417
C. The Death Penalty and the Theories of Punishment 417
  C.1. Retribution 417
      Susan Bandes, *The Heart Has Its Reasons: Examining the Strange Persistence of the American Death Penalty* 418
  C.2. Deterrence 421
      John J. Donohue and Justin Wolfers, *The Death Penalty: No Evidence of Deterrence* 422
D. Some Additional Issues 426
  D.1. Capital Cases, Non-Capital Cases, and Years of Life Lost 426
  D.2. County Variation, and the Prohibitive Costs of the Death Penalty 427
       Questions 429
  D.3. Current Political Support for the Death Penalty 430

Chapter 8. Plea Bargaining 433
A. The Substantive Law of Plea Bargaining..434
   A.1. The Supreme Court's View of Plea Bargaining...........................436
       Stephanos Bibas, *Regulating the Plea Bargaining Market:
From Caveat Emptor to Consumer Protection* 440
       Questions 441
   A.2. Non-Judicial Regulation of Plea Bargaining................................442
       Kate Stith, *The Arc of the Pendulum: Judges, Prosecutors, and
the Exercise of Discretion* 449
B. The Debate over Plea Bargaining..454
       Frank H. Easterbrook, *Criminal Procedure as a Market
System* 454
       Questions 459
   B.1. Plea Bargains and the Shadow of the Trial 459
       Questions 466
   B.2. Plea Bargains and Externalities 467
   B.3. Plea Bargains and Information..470
   B.4. Plea Bargains and Structured Sentencing 471
   B.5. Is Plea Bargaining Unavoidable? An International
Comparison..472
C. Pulling It All Together..474

PART 3. SENTENCES AND RE-ENTRY

Chapter 9. Sentencing Policy and the Rise of the Prison 479
A. The Basic Theories of Prison Growth 481
       John F. Pfaff, *The Empirics of Prison Growth: A Critical Review
and Path Forward* 481
   A.1. Our Limited Empirical Understanding of Prison Growth 486
   A.2. The Importance of Prosecutors to Prison Growth.......................487
       Questions 491
   A.3. The Role of Crime...491
   A.4. The Surprisingly Minimal Role of Drug Offenses.......................493
   A.5. The Deinstitutionalization of the Mentally Ill 496
B. The Politics of Crime 498
       John F. Pfaff, *The Micro and Macro Causes of Prison Growth*...........498
   B.1. "Nothing Works" and the End of Modernity 504
       Questions 506
   B.2. State Interest Groups, Fiscal Capacity, and Balanced Budget
Provisions 507
   B.3. Politicians, Sentencing Commissions, and Wariness About
Being Tough on Crime 511
   B.4. Politicians, the Census, and Rural Welfare 513
   B.5. Race, Geography, and Diffuse Responsibility 517
   B.6. The Public's Actual Punitiveness...523
       Questions 526
C. United States and Europe: A Comparison 527

James Q. Whitman, Book Review, *The Prisoners' Dilemma: Political Economy and Punishment in Contemporary Democracies* 530

Chapter 10. The Effects of Incarceration 537
A. Life Inside Prison 537
   Norval Morris, *The Contemporary Prison, 1965–Present* 538
      Questions 547
B. The Impact of Incarceration on an Inmate and His Family 548
   B.1. The Collateral Costs of Incarceration on the Inmate 549
      B.1.a. Prison and Labor Outcomes...549
      B.1.b. Prison and Health 552
         Questions 558
      B.1.c. Mental Health in Prison 559
      B.1.d. Drugs and Alcohol in Prison 562
   B.2. Prison and Family Life 565
C. Impact of Incarceration on Communities 569
D. Incarceration and Crime 574
   D.1. Incarceration's Total Effect 574
   D.2. General Deterrence and Incapacitation 578
   D.3. Individual (Specific) Deterrence and Incapacitation (and Rehabilitation)...581

Chapter 11. Alternatives to Incarceration 587
A. The Standard Alternatives: Probation, Fines, Community Service, Asset Forfeiture, and Boot Camps 588
   A.1. Probation 588
      Joan Petersilia, *Community Corrections: Probation, Parole, and Prisoner Re-Entry* 589
      Example: Probation in California 596
      Questions 598
   A.2. Fines and Fees..602
      R. Barry Ruback and Mark H. Bergstrom, *Economic Sanctions in Criminal Justice: Purposes, Effects, and Implications* 602
      Questions 606
      Questions 608
   A.3. Asset Forfeiture..608
      Problem: Asset Forfeiture in Two States..610
      Questions 611
      Questions 615
   A.4. Boot Camps..616
B. Controlling Sex Offenders and Domestic Batterers 618
   B.1. Controlling Released Sex Offenders: Civil Confinement.............619
      Kansas v. Hendricks 627
      Stephen J. Morse, *Fear of Danger, Flight From Culpability* 633
      Questions 643
   B.2. Domestic Restraining Orders..644

		Jeannie Suk, *Criminal Law Comes Home* 644
C.	Shame, Restorative Justice, and Drug/Alternative Courts 649	
	C.1. Shaming Sanctions 649	
	United States v. Gementera 652	
	Dan Kahan, *What's Wrong With Shaming Sanctions* 656	
	Questions 660	
	C.2. Restorative Justice 661	
	Mark S. Umbreit, Betty Vos, Robert B. Coates, & Elizabeth Lightfoot, *Restorative Justice in the Twenty-First Century: A Social Movement Full of Opportunities and Pitfalls* 661	
	Lawrence W. Sherman & Heather Strang, *Restorative Justice: The Evidence* 667	
	Questions 677	
	C.3. Drug and Other Therapeutic Courts 677	
	Allegra M. McLeod, *Decarceration Courts: Possibilities and Perils of a Shifting Criminal Law* 680	
	Daniel Richman, *Professional Identity: Comment on Simon* 691	
	Questions 695	

Chapter 12. Parole and Re-Entry 697

A. The Challenges of Re-Entry 698
    A.1. The Basic Problem 698
    A.2. What Seems to Work 699
        National Research Council, *Parole, Desistance From Crime, and Community Integration* 701
        Questions 707
B. The Process of Parole 707
    B.1. A Brief History of Parole 708
        Joan Petersilia, *Parole and Prisoner Re-Entry in the United States* 708
    B.2. Rights and Procedures at Parole 711
        B.2.a.   The Parole Board 712
                Susan C. Kinnevy & Joel M. Caplan, *National Surveys of State Paroling Authorities: Models of Service Delivery* 714
                Questions 717
        B.2.b.   Granting Parole 718
                B.2.b.i. Constitutional and Statutory Protections 718
                        Greenholtz v. Inmates of Neb. Penal & Corr. Complex 719
                        Questions 725
                B.2.b.ii. What Parole Boards Consider 727
                        Joel M. Caplan, *What Factor Affect Parole: A Review of Empirical Research* 727
    B.3. Conditions of Parole 730
        Lawrence F. Travis, III, and James Stacey, *A Half Century of Parole Rules: Conditions of Parole in the United States, 2008* 731

	Questions	748
	Questions	752
C.	Violating Parole	752
	C.1. Rights and Procedures at Violation Hearings	752
	Morrissey v. Brewer	753
	Questions	761
	C.2. Technical Violations	761
	C.3. The Impact of Parole Violations on Prison Growth	763
	John F. Pfaff, *The War on Drugs and Prison Growth: Limited Importance, Limited Legislative Options*	764
D.	The Other Ways Out of Prison: Commutations and Pardons	768
	Rachel E. Barkow, *The Politics of Forgiveness: Reconceptualizing Clemency*	768
	Questions	772

Appendix. Statistical Glossary **773**

INDEX 779

TABLE OF CASES

The principal cases are in bold type.

Allen v. Illinois 631
Alleyne v. United States 322, 370, 371, 372, 373
Almendarez-Torres v. United States 203, 307
Anglemyer v. State 360
Apprendi v. New Jersey 202, 203, 313, **314**
Atkins v. Virginia 255, 395
Beck v. Alabama 386
Bennis v. Michigan 610
Berger, State v. 257
Besser v. Walsh 343
Bible, State v. 361
Black, People v. 359
Blackledge v. Perry 438
Blakely v. Washington 203, **328**
Booker v. United States 65, 203
Booker, United States v. **345**
Booth v. Maryland 182
Bordenkircher v. Hayes 438, 470
Brady v. United States 437
Brimage, State v. 442
Brown v. Board of Education 304
Brown v. Plata 555
Bullock, People v. 258
Carachuri-Rosendo v. Holder 205, 233
Coker v. Georgia 377, 384
Conner v. State 257
Craig v. Boren 139
Crosby v. State 257
Cunningham v. California 359
Davis, State v. 257
Enmund v. Florida 386
Ewing v. California 206, 207, 255
Foster, State v. 359
Furman v. Georgia 376, 407
Gagnon v. Scarpelli 759, 760
Gall v. United States 362, 365, 366
Gaskins, People v. 257
Gault, In re 235
Gementera, United States v. **652**
Gideon v. Wainwright 99
Godfrey v. Georgia 386
Gomez, State v. 360
Graham v. Florida 26, 255
Graham v. West Virginia 309
Green, United States v. 328
Greenholtz v. Inmates of Neb. Penal & Corr. Complex **719**
Gregg v. Georgia 378, **380**
Guthrie v. Evans 545
Guy, State v. 360
Hamling v. United States 308
Hammoud, United States v. 344
Harmelin v. Michigan 254
Harris v. United States 322, 323, 324
Hayes, State v. 258
Humphrey v. Wilson 258
Hutto v. Davis 254
Jackson, United States v. 436
Jones v. United States 310, 312, 313, 325
Jurek v. Texas 378, 380
Kansas v. Hendricks 623, **627**
Kennedy v. Louisiana 255
Kimbrough v. United States 366, 367
Koch, United States v. 344
Lagares, State v. 442
Lent, People v. 597
Lockett v. Ohio 384, 386
Lockyear v. Andrade 255
Louisiana v. Kennedy 398
Lynch, In re 56
McCleskey v. Kemp 377, **387**, 394
McMillan v. Pennsylvania 305
Medas, United States v. 280, 345, 356
Miller v. Alabama 233
Monge v. California 312
Morrissey v. Brewer **753**
Mullaney v. Wilbur 302, 303
Natale, State v. 360
Nelson v. United States 367
North Carolina v. Pearce 438
Oregon v. Ice 368, 370
Padilla v. Kentucky 439
Patterson v. New York 303, 304
Payne v. Tennessee 182
Penry v. Lynaugh 386
Pineiro, United States v. 344
Portalatin v. Graham 343, 344
Proffitt v. Florida 378
Reggans v. Owens 726
Ring v. Arizona 322, 327, 396
Rita v. United States 362, 363, 364
Rivera, People v. 343
Roberts v. Louisiana 378
Robinson, People v. 361
Rompilla v. Beard 396
Roper v. Simmons 233, 255, 395
Ruiz, United States v. 470
Rummel v. Estelle 254
Rutherford v. State 259
Smylie v. State 360
Solem v. Helm 254
Spears v. United States 367
Specht v. Patterson 309
Stanford v. Kentucky 386

Strickland v. Washington 441
Thompson v. Oklahoma 386
Tison v. Arizona 386
Vasquez, State v. 442
Vernier, United States v. 285
Walton v. Arizona 325
Weems v. United States 254
Wiggins v. Smith 396
Williams v. Illinois 740
Williams v. New York 334, 376
Williams v. Taylor 396
Wilson v. State 257
Winship, In re 235, 301
Woodson v. North Carolina 378
Workman v. Commonwealth 258

UNIVERSITY CASEBOOK SERIES®
SENTENCING LAW AND POLICY

PART 1

WHO, WHY, AND HOW WE SENTENCE

A surprising feature of sentencing law in the United States is how traditionally *lawless* it has been. Both substantive criminal law and criminal procedure are regulated by a dense forest of constitutional doctrines designed to protect defendants from the power criminal law places in the hands of federal, state, and local governments. But punishment has generally been left unregulated. Prosecutors are free to pick among a wide range of potential charges, and to construct almost any sort of plea bargain, subject to no real executive or judicial oversight. Legislatures face no real constitutional limits on the sorts of sanctions they can devise, nor parole boards on how they decide who to parole or the sorts of conditions they can impose on parolees. And judges have traditionally been granted nearly limitless authority when imposing sentences; to the extent that power has been restricted in recent years, it is by legislative decree, not by any sort of constitutional protection.

Furthermore, even when the legislature creates statutory rules to regulate punishment, other actors frequently figure out ways to evade them. State supreme courts declare binding sentencing guidelines voluntary, or prosecutors work closely with defense attorneys and trial judges to circumvent tough sentencing laws. As we will see in the chapters ahead, criminal justice in the United States is fractured across multiple jurisdictional lines, leaving no one in charge to ensure that rules are followed. Local police report to commissioners appointed by city mayors, prosecutors are directly elected at the county level, judges may be elected or appointed at county or state levels, governors are elected at the state level while legislators are state officials elected in often-hyperlocal districts. As a result, upstream actors often have little to no actual authority over downstream ones.

As a result of all this discretion—either explicitly or implicitly granted or emerging from a lack of centralized oversight and control—sentencing law is much more a study in policy than in black-letter law. When asking "what can an actor do?" we are generally less interested in the constitutional or statutory rules that govern behavior and more concerned with the practical limitations on authority and with the actors' motivations. Often there are few rules regulating behavior at all, and those that exist are often easy to circumvent—which isn't to say they are irrelevant, but their impact is often more indirect that one might expect.

Given that policy concerns are central to sentencing law, this book will start by looking at how people, offenders and enforcers alike, respond to policy changes. Chapter 1 thus examines some basic models of human behavior to shed light on when we expect people to commit crimes. Without a basic understanding of the models of human behavior, we cannot determine whether a particular punishment advances goals such as deterrence or rehabilitation, nor can we accurately assess a defendant's culpability.

Thus I wait until Chapter 2 to turn to the normative theories of punishment that should help legislators, prosecutor, judges, parole officials, and everyone else determine what sentences are proper. After all, understanding the causes of behavior does not necessarily tell us how to use that information. Consider, for example, a judge facing two defendants convicted of the same sort of aggravated assault who differ only in age. Knowing that younger people are more violent and impulsive, should he impose a different sentence on the younger defendant? It depends: a judge focused on moral culpability may think the younger defendant deserves a *shorter* sentence, while another focused on the objective harm caused may think age irrelevant, and a third judge concerned with deterrence or incapacitation may think the younger—and thus riskier—defendant needs a *longer* sentence. This chapter also briefly touches on some of the positive theories of punishment. Regardless of what we think criminal punishment *ought* to try to accomplish, it is important to also understand what *in fact* it is trying to do—not just, say, deter or incapacitate, but also to regulate the unemployed or to advance broader political goals.

Chapter 3 then turns its attention to the wide array of criminal justice actors, examining both their roles in the sprawling, often poorly designed criminal justice "system" and the goals, incentives, and motives that drive their decisions. Some of the restrictions on their behavior are legal in scope, but many are more normative or ideological: judges might adhere to presumptive guidelines in part because they are afraid of reversal, but also because they may view themselves as morally obliged to do so or because they agree with the basic normative goal of the guidelines themselves.

One important overarching takeaway from Chapter 3, which will be a theme running throughout the book, is that there is really no such thing as the "criminal justice system." The word "system" seems to suggest a coherent entity attempting to advance some set of relatively well-defined goals. This grossly misstates how the "system" operates. Police, prosecutors, judges, parole boards, etc., are all often working at cross purposes and advancing different goals based on differences in constituencies, incentives, and normative values. And alliances across actors are fluid: prosecutors may work with legislators to restrain judicial discretion in one area while working with the judiciary to evade legislative rules in another. Put differently, punctuation matters: we will never talk about the "government's actions," but only about the "governments' actions."

CHAPTER 1

WHO WE SENTENCE

Whatever goals criminal sentencing seeks to achieve—and as we will see in Chapter 2, there are many—it is impossible to accomplish any of them without a rigorous understanding of how and why an offender makes the choices he[1] makes. How can we know if a particular policy deters or effectively incapacitates or even punishes culpable behavior for its moral wrongness without knowing how people respond to the incentives before them or how much control people in fact have over their behavior in different situations? Our discussion of sentencing law thus starts with an analysis of offender behavior.

It is important to note, though, that we should always be careful not to overly reify "the offender." The world is not neatly divided into those who commit crimes and those who do not: many who commit offenses might not have had they found themselves in difference circumstances, and likewise many who do not offend may have had their lives played out slightly differently. But in any context there are those who offend and those who do not (or those who are more or less likely to), and there are some regularities that separate the two groups. Furthermore, we can identify specific contexts that increase the propensity to offend; identifying such environments can help us craft the most appropriate sanction as well.

For example, men, and younger men in particular, are more likely to offend than women or older men. Not all young men offend, but being young and male increases the risk of criminal behavior. Similarly, intense financial pressure can reduce people's ability to control their anger. Again, not all people under financial stress lash out aggressively, but finding oneself in such a context increases the risk of violence.

So do not think of this chapter as "defining the traits of criminals," but more as highlighting the cognitive, physiological, and environmental factors that can increase the risk that any person engages in criminal behavior. Once we understand these risk factors, we can think more clearly about how to account for them when designing effective or morally appropriate punishments.

This chapter starts by defining the **rational actor model**, which is a convenient point of departure. Broadly speaking, the rational actor is someone who accurately accounts for all the various incentives he faces and establishes a plan of action intended to maximize his overall well-being. Though easy to reduce to a caricature, it actually has a significant amount of predictive power. Yet it also has its limitations: there are

---

[1] Given that approximately 75% of those arrested are male, I will generally use the male pronoun throughout this book when referring to offenders or defendants.

systematic errors in how people generally process information, and we turn to those (grouped under the term **behavioralism**) next.

We then consider the role hormonal, genetic, and other biological and psychological factors play in shaping the risk of offending. These factors in turn lead to the **life-cycle trajectory of offending** theory, which predicts that the risk of offending varies predictably over someone's life, in no small part due to changes in various biological and social restraints on improper behavior.

The chapter then pivots from looking at biological factors to environmental or **situational** ones: to what extent does a person's social context—where they live, where they work, who they live with, etc.—influence their behavior? Crime is densely concentrated (geographically, socially, etc.), in large part because certain environments are simply more likely to permit, or even *encourage*, offending. Obviously it is impossible to assess the right deterrent or moral sanction without understanding how these externals pressures shape conduct.

Finally, the chapter concludes with a brief discussion of the limits of social science evidence. This chapter, like the book as a whole, relies heavily on social science research. But sentencing law is a difficult *policy* field, and policy decisions involving bringing together empirical evidence and normative policy goals. So it is helpful to appreciate not just what issues in sentencing law empirical work can answer, but which ones it *cannot*—or *should not*.

A. A SIMPLE MODEL OF HUMAN BEHAVIOR

This section starts by providing a brief overview of the rational actor model, particularly as it applies to criminal behavior, and then turns to its "behaviorialist" extensions.

A.1. THE RATIONAL ACTOR MODEL

The core claim of the rational actor model is very straight-forward: people make choices with the goal of maximizing their happiness (or "utility"). It is easy to reduce this argument to caricature, in which people are thought to be rigorous calculators processing vast amounts of data to make precise, accurate decisions. Used properly, though, the model is much more modest, simply asserting that people try to maximize their utility as best they can, subject to a complicated set of values and desires, embedded within social institutions that shape their actions, and with only limited information and cognitive skills. One of the leading developers of the RAM was the economist and Nobel laureate Gary Becker. The excerpt below from his Nobel Prize lecture provides a good overview of how to think about the rational actor model and its relationship to criminal punishment.

Gary Becker, Nobel Lecture: The Economic Way of Looking at Human Behavior
101 J. Pol. Econ. 385 (1993)

My research uses the economic approach to analyze social issues that range beyond those usually considered by economists. [T]he economic approach I refer to does not assume that individuals are motivated solely by selfishness or material gain. It is a method of analysis, not an assumption about particular motivations. Along with others, I have tried to pry economists away from narrow assumptions about self-interest. Behavior is driven by a much richer set of values and preferences.

The analysis assumes that individuals maximize welfare as they conceive it, whether they be selfish, altruistic, loyal, spiteful, or masochistic. Their behavior is forward-looking, and it is also assumed to be consistent over time. In particular, they try as best they can to anticipate the uncertain consequences of their actions. Forward-looking behavior, however, may still be rooted in the past, for the past can exert a long shadow on attitudes and values.

Actions are constrained by income, time, imperfect memory and calculating capacities, and other limited resources, and also by the opportunities available in the economy and elsewhere. These opportunities are largely determined by the private and collective actions of other individuals and organizations. Thus wants remain unsatisfied in rich countries as well as in poor ones.

<u>Crime and Punishment</u>

I began to think about crime in the 1960s after driving to Columbia University for an oral examination of a student in economic theory. I was late and had to decide quickly whether to put the car in a parking lot or risk getting a ticket for parking illegally on the street. I calculated the likelihood of getting a ticket, the size of the penalty, and the cost of putting the car in a lot. I decided it paid to take the risk and park on the street. (I did not get a ticket.)

As I walked the few blocks to the examination room, it occurred to me that the city authorities had probably gone through a similar analysis. The frequency of their inspection of parked vehicles and the size of the penalty imposed on violators should depend on their estimates of the type of calculations potential violators like me would make. Of course, the first question I put to the hapless student was to work out the optimal behavior of both the offenders and the police, something I had not yet done.

In the 1950s and 1960s, intellectual discussions of crime were dominated by the opinion that criminal behavior was caused by mental illness and social oppression, and that criminals were helpless "victims." A book by a well-known psychiatrist was entitled *The Crime of Punishment*. . . . Such attitudes began to exert a major influence on social policy, as laws changed to expand criminals' rights. These changes reduced the apprehension and conviction of criminals and provided less protection to the law-abiding population.

I was not sympathetic to the assumption that criminals had radically different motivations from everyone else. I explored instead the theoretical and empirical implications of the assumption that criminal behavior is rational . . . , but again "rationality" did not imply narrow materialism. It recognized that many people were constrained by moral and ethical considerations, and they did not commit crimes even when these were profitable and there was no danger of detection. However, police and jails would be unnecessary if such attitudes always prevailed. Rationality implied that some individuals become criminals because of the financial and other rewards from crime compared to legal work, taking account of the likelihood of apprehension and conviction, and the severity of punishment.

The amount of crime is determined not only by the rationality and preferences of would-be criminals but also by the economic and social environment created by public policies, including expenditures on police, punishments for different crimes, and opportunities for employment, schooling, and training programs. Clearly, the types of legal jobs available as well as law, order, and punishment are an integral part of the economic approach to crime.

One reason why the economic approach to crime became so influential is that the same analytic apparatus can be used to study enforcement of all laws, including minimum wage legislation, clean air acts, insider trader and other violations of security laws, and income tax evasions. Since few laws are self-enforcing, they require expenditures on conviction and punishment to deter violators. The U.S. Sentencing Commission has explicitly used the economic analysis of crime to develop rules to be followed by judges in punishing violators of federal statutes.

The Rational Actor Model and Criminal Offending

Oversimplifying slightly, the rational actor model says little more than this: when the "price" of crime increases (the fine, the years in prison, the foregone income or lost relationships from going to prison, etc.), potential criminal offenders will commit fewer criminal acts, and vice versa. To today's student, such a claim may sound almost trivial. But as Becker notes, at the time he put forth his theory, it was a relatively controversial assertion. As one intellectual history of Becker's work puts it:

> In many ways, Becker's seminal work on the economics of crime can be seen as a restoration: by emphasizing the rationality of potential offenders, Becker brought the ideas of Beccaria and

Bentham back to criminology. Between the classical era of Beccaria and Bentham and its revitalization under Becker, models of criminal behavior had been shaped by various flavors of deterministic positivism, theories which left little room for individual decision-making. Biological determinists such as Ferri, Goring, and Lombroso looked to physiological factors; psychological determinists such as the Gluecks to mental states; and sociological determinists such as Shaw and McKay and Merton to social disorder and social strains. Becker's key insight was to return to the forefront the criminal as an autonomous decision-maker.[2]

The strength of the RAM comes from its testable implications: if the criminal sanction rises, or if other costs of engaging in crime go up (including increased returns on non-criminal behavior), we should see fewer people decide to engage in crime.[3] Chapter 10 will look what evidence we have of this in more depth; in short, though, the evidence is mixed.

A Few, Final Thoughts on Rationality and Utility Maximization

Before moving from the RAM, I want to take a moment to make sure three points are particularly clear.

1. The RAM is a positive, not normative, idea. The RAM does not argue that people *ought to* behave rationally or try to maximize their utility, nor does it say that rational decisions or utility maximization are inherently good things. All it states is that, as an *empirical* matter, people try to maximize their utility, and that a large fraction of the population (perhaps excluding children and the mentally handicapped) does so in a rationally-based way.[4]

2. The definition of "rationality" is fairly narrow. Social scientists and philosophers generally view rationality as meaning that a particular actor tries to select the most

---

[2] John F. Pfaff, *Gary Becker's Contributions to Law and Economics*, in PIONEERS OF LAW AND ECONOMICS 152 (Joshua Wright & Lloyd Cohen, eds., 2009) (CESARE BECCARIA, ON CRIMES AND PUNISHMENTS AND OTHER WRITINGS (1995); JEREMY BENTHAM, THE RATIONALE OF PUNISHMENT (2004); JEREMY BENTHAM, AN INTRODUCTION TO THE PRINCIPLES OF MORALS AND LEGISLATION (1970); ENRICO FERRI, CRIMINAL SOCIOLOGY (1897); SHELDON GLUECK & ELEANOR T. GLUECK, UNRAVELING JUVENILE DELINQUENCY (1950); CHARLES GORING, THE ENGLISH CONVICT (1919); CESARE LOMBROSO, CRIME: IT'S CAUSES AND REMEDIES (1918); CLIFFORD R. SHAW & HENRY D. MCKAY, JUVENILE DELINQUENCY AND URBAN AREAS (1942); Robert K. Merton, *Social Structure and Anomie*, 3 AM. SOC. REV. 672, 672–82 (1938)).

[3] This is carefully worded for a reason: if the sanction is incarceration, then we should expect crime to fall as the punishment increases simply because more potential offenders—whether coldly rational or utterly irrational—are behind bars and thus incapable of offending.

[4] Or, at the very least, their decision-making process is one that can be adequately modeled *as if* they are behaving rationally. The discussion of developmental, genetic, and neurological evidence in Chapter 5 below paints a far more complicated picture of how people *in fact* make decisions, but despite any complicated underlying mechanics the resultant behavior often *appears* to track that predicted by some variant of a rationality-based model.

valuable outcome from the set of feasible choices.[5] It is not a particularly bold claim, given that scientists have observed rats and pigeons adhering to this concept in lab tests—increase the relative cost of food X compared to food Y and their demand shifts away from X toward Y. It would be shocking if humans had evolved *away* from acting rationally. Which is not to say that we are *perfectly* rational: far from it.

3. What do we mean by "utility maximization"? All this means is that people try to make choices that make them as happy as possible, subject to a whole host of financial, emotional, psychological, institutional, and other constraints. In fact, the model is often referred to as one of "constrained maximization" in order to emphasize the importance of these constraints.

In summary, the RAM asserts each person has a relatively stable utility function, and that he tries to maximize that utility as best he can, subject to a wide range of financial, physical, mental, and institutional constraints. The RAM thus predicts that a potential criminal is trying to maximize something—wealth, excitement, etc.—and that he compares the benefits of the crime (including direct financial gain, the rush of excitement, any sort of acclaim from his peers) to its costs (including guilt, the expected state sanction, lost future income, social stigma imposed by neighbors, and so on) and decides whether it makes sense to commit the act.

Problem: What to Maximize: How important is it to understand *what* it is that people are trying to maximize? In other words, if a social scientist credibly said "I have incontrovertible evidence that people are rational," would we know how to design criminal policy if, say, the goal was to deter people from committing crime?

The RAM is a powerful model, but it is not a perfect one. So we will turn now to one of the major, broad-scale attacks on the RAM, **behavioralism**.

A.2. "BEHAVIORALIST" CRITIQUES

The "behavioralist" movement in the social sciences focuses on ways in which people act in *systematically* "non-rational" ways. The RAM does not require that people make flawless calculations about the relative costs and benefits of various actions, but it does generally assume that whatever errors people make are roughly random—some people may overestimate the risk of getting caught, others may underestimate it, but

---

[5] See, e.g., JON ELSTER, *Introduction*, in RATIONAL CHOICE: READINGS IN SOCIAL AND POLITICAL THEORY (Jon Elster, ed., 1986).

the average prediction is fairly spot-on. Behavioralists disagree, arguing (as one book is titled) that people are "predictably irrational," i.e., they make certain predictable, systematic errors when calculating costs or benefits.[6] This section starts with a brief overview of the types of rationality-failures that social scientists have identified, and it then turns its attention to evidence about when we expect these problems to be most pronounced.

Behavioralists have identified a host of systematic cognitive errors. Some of the ones that we will see in the chapters ahead include:

- **Availability.** Once something happens, people overestimate the likelihood of it happening again: we are much more afraid to fly the day after a plane crash, and we might buy flood insurance after reading about flooding along the Mississippi River even if we live on a hilltop in Brooklyn. **Question:** What does this suggest about the need to impose even-harsher punishments on repeat offenders if our goal is to deter future bad behavior? What does this tell us about our ability to deter first-time offending?

- **Salience.** Salience is a form of "magnifier" for availability: the more shocking—or salient—something is, the more likely we think it will happen again. Thus car accidents cause more deaths than plane accidents, but we fear the latter more because plane crashes are more salient. **Question:** A large fraction of violent crimes are committed by people known to the victim. Does our criminal policy necessarily reflect that? If not, what role does salience play?

- **Anchoring.** Our perceptions of the "right" answer to a question can be heavily shaped by irrelevant factors. Menus, for example, sometimes include a very expensive dish on the upper-right corner (where the eye first hits the page). This "anchors" the eater in a way that makes other less-expensive but still-overpriced dishes seem reasonable. **Question:** How might this bias affect our confidence in people's statements about the "morally correct" sentence for a specific crime? What concerns does this raise about granting judges wide discretion when setting sentences?

- **Various systematic misassessments of probabilities.** There are often predictable biases in the ways in which we take uncertain events into account. Heuristics such as **optimism** and **overconfidence bias** lead us to overstate the probability of succeeding or understate that of failing. The **neglect of probability bias** is a more general one

---

[6] DAN ARIELY, PREDICTABLY IRRATIONAL (2009).

that leads us to assume that low-probability events are basically zero-probability events. In other words, if something is unlikely, we treat it as impossible. **Question:** How do these biases effect a policy such as deterrence, given that punishment is almost always uncertain? Note that the probability a murder results in an arrest is about 65%, while the probability an auto theft results in an arrest is closer to 10%.

- **Confirmation Bias.** Once we make a decision, we tend to look for evidence that validates it, and we tend to discount or ignore evidence that cautions against it. Once we decide to buy an iPhone instead of an Android phone, we seek out articles praising the iPhone and ignore those criticizing it. **Question:** In some high-crime neighborhoods, as many as one in three young black men will find themselves in prison at some point in their lives. What sort of limits might confirmation bias place on the effectiveness of certain criminal justice policies?

- **Cognitive dissonance and affective forecasting.** Our predictions about future happiness or unhappiness tend to be overstated, as we adapt fairly quickly to our circumstances: things we thought would upset us rarely prove to be as upsetting in the long-run as expected, and likewise for things we thought would make us happy. Aesop's fable of the fox and the grapes is the classic example. A fox spends a long time trying to get some grapes that are just out of reach, and when he finally gives up and walks away he states "I bet those grapes were sour anyway!" **Question:** How do you think affective forecasting affects those contemplating crime for the first time? How about those who have already been to prison?

Note that these biases apply to offenders and enforcers alike. Legislators, for example, may target rare, salient crimes at the expense of more common but less available offenses. And many a case of prosecutorial misconduct likely arose at least in part from confirmation bias: sure that he had the right guy, the prosecutor would ignore, hide, etc., exculpatory evidence. So keep these in mind in Chapter 3 as well, when we discuss the incentives of various criminal justice actors.

That these biases exist does not mean they apply with equal force in all situations. In fact, we can also predict *when* these biases are more likely to plague decision-making. The general finding is that the more we are outside our comfort zone the more vulnerable we are to these errors. Or, put differently, the better we understand an issue, the better choices we make.

A classic study of anchoring demonstrated that the price MBA students assigned to a bottle of wine could be strongly influenced by having them first write down the last few (random) digits of their social security numbers: those with higher digits priced the bottle systematically higher. Yet when the same experiment was run using sommeliers as subjects, the effect went away. Unlike the MBA students, the sommeliers were experts in pricing wine and thus less vulnerable to the (irrelevant) anchor.

> **Question:** Are there certain categories of offenders or offenses—or even places where crimes occur—where we should expect the offender to be acting in a more-rational way? Or in a predictably less-rational way?
>
> **Question:** Are there certain legal actors more or less vulnerable to these biases? What does this tell us about the optimal way to, say, allocate cases across judges?

One last complication to keep in mind is that these heuristics can be tricky to use in practice since they often contradict each other. Availability, for example, states that when an event happens we overstate the likelihood it will happen again soon. But the **gambler's fallacy** states that when something hasn't happened for a while we think "it's due."[7] Both effects are real, both hold in different contexts, but they are mutually exclusive, and there is no theoretical way to predict which will apply in what context. So keep these heuristics in mind at all times, but also remain open to the possibility that other biases may be at work than the ones that initially come to mind.

B. Risk Factors for Criminal Behavior

The rational actor model acknowledges that people have different tastes and preferences, but it also tries to avoid simply positing "tastes" for observed behavior, since doing so reduces the model to a tautology with no predictive power. Assume we observe that Sam commits a crime while Joe does not; if we simply say that Sam has a stronger "taste" for crime or anti-social behavior,[8] we can never make any general predictions about who will commit crimes and when or where they will do so. What will Paul or Sam do in a different situation? If all we do is assert "tastes," we can never say. We need to understand what it is about

---

[7] It's called the "gambler's fallacy" due to the fact that people at, say, a roulette wheel will say "red is due!" if red hasn't hit recently, even though the probability of red coming up on any spin is equally random, regardless of the past history of hits.

[8] Some have argued that it is impossible to have any sort of "preference" to engage in crime, since "crime" is a social construct: murder or arson or insider trading is a crime only because the legislature or the courts say it is. At a literal level, this is perhaps true. But it is quite fair to say that people can differ in their levels of anti-social behavior, which readily translate into crimes: aggression (murder), destructiveness (arson), impulsiveness or greed (insider trading). Such conduct feels less socially constructed, even if the resulting crimes are.

Sam and his environment that explain his behavior, so we can predict what others will do in his environment or what he will do elsewhere.

Over the years, criminologists have developed an extensive list of risk factors that predict who is more likely to engage in criminal behavior, and when over the course of their lives they are more likely to do so. As this section explains, some of these factors are genetic or biochemical, others are developmental, and still others are environmental. It is impossible to design effective sentencing policies, no matter the normative goal, without understanding what drives people to engage in criminal behavior. Sadly, it will also quickly become clear that many of our current policies are not based on such an understanding.

When thinking about these factors, a few important caveats should be kept in mind:

1. "Predictive" does not mean "strongly predictive." That a trait is identified as a risk factor does not mean that those who possess the trait are almost certainly, or even necessarily more likely than not, to commit a crime. It could just be that those who possess a certain trait are, say, 10% more likely to commit a crime than those who don't, but those with the trait may still be unlikely to commit the crime at all. For example, those without the trait commit a certain crime 10% of the time, vs. 11% for those with the trait (which is 10% more).

2. Risk factors often do not work alone. In many cases, risk factors do not work in isolation, but interact in complicated ways with other risk factors. For example, the low monoamine oxidase A (MOMA) activity allele is thought to be a genetic risk factor, but only in men, and only men who come from broken homes.[9] Thus, in this case, "MOMA," "male," and "broken childhood home" are all risk factors, but no one alone is enough.

3. Correlation does not imply causation. Risk factors are, at some level, simply correlations: we observe that people with trait X are more likely to commit crimes than those without trait X. That two factors are correlated does not immediately mean that one causes the other. Of course, it could actually be that X actually causes crime. Or it could be that X does *not* cause offending, but X often occurs alongside trait Y, and Y *does* cause crime.[10]

---

[9] Giovanni Frazzetto, et. Al., *Early Trauma and Increased Risk for Physical Aggression during Adulthood: The Moderating Role of MAOA Genotype*, 2(5) PLoS ONE (May 2007), available at http://www.ncbi.nlm.nih.gov/pmc/articles/PMC1872046/.

[10] An apparent-but-non-causal correlation between two factors is called a **spurious correlation**. For example, those who commit crimes smoke at higher levels than non-offenders,

This section starts by looking at the factors present in youth that predict future criminality. As we will see, predicting future offending in young children may be particularly important, since interventions are most effective on younger individuals. Moreover, many of these factors are relatively constant over a person's life and may thus provide information about the relative risks of offending throughout adulthood. This section then looks at how (and why) the risk of engaging in criminal behaviors changes in predictable ways over the course of a person's life. And it concludes by examining the complicated ways in which environmental factors influence a person's willingness to engage in crime as well.

B.1. Early Risk Factors

In a comprehensive review of the early risk factors for criminal conduct, David Farrington and Brandon Welsh divide the traits into three broad categories: individual factors; family factors; and socioeconomic, peer, school, and community factors. The following excerpt summarizes their basic findings.

David P. Farrington and Brandon C. Welsh, *Saving Children From a Life of Crime*
(2007)

Individual Factors

- Low Intelligence and Attainment. To Farrington and Welsh, the key issue here is the "ability to manipulate abstract concepts." Low intelligence impedes this ability, which can lead to offending either by making it hard for people to account for the consequences of their behavior or by hindering their ability to empathize with potential victims.

  The effect is durable and starts young. Studies indicate that measures of low IQ at age three can predict offending through age 30; in one study the average IQs of frequent offenders (four or more offenses) were about 20 points lower than those of non-offenders, 88 to 101. And the converse holds as well, with the risk of offending falling as intelligence rises. **Question:** Should we sanction low-intelligence offenders more (because they pose more of a persistent risk) or less (because at some level their criminal conduct feels more "inevitable" and thus less culpable)?

---

but it is unlikely that smoking causes crime. Instead, something else (as we will see, impetuousness and a lack of future-thinking) causes both crime and smoking.

- Personality and Temperament. Farrington and Welsh again: "Antisocial behavior is remarkably consistent over time; or, to be more precise, the relative ordering of individuals is remarkably consistent over time. Psychologists assume that behavioral consistency depends primarily on the persistence of underlying tendencies to behave in particular ways in particular situations."

  One aspect of personality is temperament. Temperament manifests itself quickly, and its impact is, again, durable. Children viewed as "difficult" by their mothers at age 6 months are more likely to be viewed by their mothers—and, importantly, also their teachers—as difficult at ages 3 to 8. And one study found that children rated as "uninhibited" at 21 months were much more likely to be identified in self-reports and by parents as "aggressive" at age 13.

- Empathy. The intuition here is clear: the lower a person's ability to empathize, the less he appreciates the harm he causes his victim. While the evidence base is not particularly strong, several studies do suggest that lower levels of empathy are correlated with higher levels of aggressive behavior. Some studies indicate, however, that the effect of empathy can be shaped in important ways by intelligence and socioeconomic status.

- Impulsiveness. Farrington and Welsh put it bluntly: "Impulsiveness is the most crucial personality dimension that predicts offending." They point to wide number of studies linking hyperactivity in relatively young children (around age 11) to future offending into their 20s; one study found that restlessness at age 5 predicted delinquency at age 14. A representative study, conducted in Sweden, found that males with motor restlessness and concentration difficulties at age 13 were five times more likely to commit an act of violence by 26 than those without either trait (15% to 3%).

  There are several explanations for the impulsiveness-criminality link. One theory points to possible neurophysiological defects in the brain that lead to an inability to control behavior. Another looks to hormones, suggesting that impulsive people have low cortical arousal levels and thus engage in higher-risk behavior in search of greater stimulation.

  Another impulsiveness theory, advocated by James Q. Wilson and Richard Herrnstein as well as by Michael

Gottfredson and Travis Hirschi,[11] focuses on the timing of the costs and benefits of offending. Impulsive people, almost by definition, tend to put more emphasis on the present than on the future, and with criminal conduct the benefits are generally immediate and clear, while the costs are distant and to some extent uncertain: If I rob this person now, I will get his iPhone for sure, but I don't know if I'll get arrested, and if I am I don't really know what the punishment will be, and regardless it will be far in the future.

<u>Family Factors</u>

- Familial Offending. Having family members who engage in criminal acts is a predictor of future offending. In one large study, children with criminal parents or relatives were more than twice as likely to offend (63% vs. 30%). There are at least six causal explanations for this correlation:

    1. The children are exposed to the same risk factors as the parents (poverty, etc.)

    2. Male offenders tend to establish relationships with female offenders, and children of two criminal parents are distinctly anti-social.

    3. Direct and mutual behavioral influences: children like to imitate their parents, for example.

    4. Indirect ("mediating[12]") effects: male offenders may use child-rearing methods that do not instill strong consciences in children, for example, or they may live in neighborhoods that are conducive to juvenile offending.

    5. Some (perhaps weak) evidence based on identical-and-fraternal twin studies points to genetic links.

    6. To some extent, the police may concentrate on the children of known offenders, leading those children to have longer official records compared to the actual differences in behavior with similarly-situated children of non-offenders.

- Large Family Size. Children of larger families are consistently at greater risk of offending, perhaps because of reduced parental involvement and attention. Household

---

[11] JAMES Q. WILSON & RICHARD J. HERRNSTEIN, CRIME AND HUMAN NATURE (1985); MICHAEL GOTTFREDSON & TRAVIS HIRSCHI, A GENERAL THEORY OF CRIME (1990). The Gottfredson and Hirschi book is one of the most widely-read and widely-cited criminology books.

[12] See the Statistical Appendix for more discussion of mediating and moderating factors.

crowding can also lead to increased levels of stress and conflict.

- Child Rearing Methods. Differences in child-rearing practices can shape children's future proclivity to offend. The strongest risk factor is poor parental supervision; discipline, warmth, and involvement can matter as well. The effects are long-lasting: one study found that supervision predicted offending through at least age 45. The effects, however, need not be consistent across populations. In the US, for example, physical punishment has a much greater effect on future offending by whites than by blacks, perhaps due to different social meanings that attach to such discipline in different racial communities.[13]

- Child Abuse and Neglect. Numerous studies have established a link between abuse and future offending. Psychologists have posited several causal theories to explain the link. Some of these are that abuse may cause direct injury to the brain or may cause other bodily harms (such as reduction in the ability to feel pain), that abused children adopt impulsive coping strategies or learn to imitate their parents' behavior, or that abuse leads to changes in self-esteem that are linked to future violence.

- Parental Conflict and Disrupted Families. Children from broken homes have higher rates of offending, although studies suggest that the causal link may not be the brokenness itself but rather the parental conflict that led to the family breaking up. Instability—a changing cast of parental-role figures—is also a risk factor for future offending. The most empirically validated theory explaining this link appears to be the "life-course" theory, which Farrington and Welsh describe as "the effect of a sequence of stressful experiences, . . . such as parental conflict, parental loss, reduced economic circumstances, changes in parent figures, and poor child-rearing methods."

Socioeconomic, Peer, School, and Community Factors

- Socioeconomic Deprivation. That poverty and crime are linked is well-accepted, but the causal mechanism is complex. Farrington and Welsh, for example, point to an intriguing puzzle: when delinquents entered their peak offending years (about 17 to 18), they were actually better paid on average than their non-delinquent peers. In fact,

---

[13] In one study, whites who were physically punished were four times more likely to engage in violent behavior than those who were not (32% to 8%), while blacks who were physically punished showed no real difference in future violent behavior (32% to 28%).

their peak offending years coincided with their peak affluence years. **Question:** Can you think why this might be? What are delinquent-but-employed people doing at age 18 compared to their non-delinquent peers?

Note that poverty actually hits potential offenders twice. Growing up in poverty predicts future offending, but currently living in poverty does so as well. Some researchers argue that the link between childhood poverty and future offending is an indirect one: childhood poverty induces other conditions, such as poor parenting, that lead to offending.

- Peer Influences. It is well established that many juvenile offenses are committed by small groups of children, not lone actors. The causal story, however, is complex. To start, juveniles tend to do *most things* in small groups. Moreover, the causal story appears to be reciprocal (or endogenous[14]): hanging out with other delinquents increases the risk of delinquency, but being a delinquent results in stigma that induces delinquents to associate only with each other. That said, one study indicated that a key predictor for desistence among 19-year old recidivists was the decision to stop associating with groups of male friends.

As this reading makes clear, a person's risk of engaging in criminal behavior takes shape at a very early age. So it should not be surprising that evidence suggests interventions targeting the young tend to be the most successful. Early-age interventions are the most effective for two reasons. First, and easiest to understand, youthful brains are simply more physically adaptable. Think about how someone who learns a language at a young age never has an accent, while any adult learner always will.

Second, early interventions benefit from something called **cumulative advantage**: early advantages tend to lead to more advantages in the future, like a "snowball" effect. A child with a slight edge in reading in kindergarten will get more teacher attention and thus be even more ahead in first grade, leading to more attention . . . and on and on. Or a child with better impulse control early on will receive reinforcement that will help with impulse control in the future. So if we can strengthen a child's impulse control early on, we can put him on a more stable path going forward.

Note that cumulative effects can work in the opposite direction as well, as **cumulative disadvantage**. Think of two teen-agers, Bob and

---

[14] See the Statistical Appendix for more on endogeneity.

Mike, who steal from a store, but only Bob is caught. Bob suffers the disruption of detention, not to mention the stigma and collateral costs of being a felon (like difficulty securing a job). These disadvantages can accumulate and push Bob deeper into criminal conduct, not because he is any more innately "anti-social" than Mike, but because of a random negative shock.

QUESTIONS

1. **Imperfect correlates.** It often seems that the "real" risk factor is harder to observe than an imperfect correlate: poor parenting may be a risk factor, but it may be easier to observe that the defendant came from poverty. Poverty and poor parenting are correlated, but not perfectly. What are the risks of letting courts and other sentencing agencies (parole boards, say) use the easier-to-observe correlate? What are the risks of forcing them to uncover the "true" risk factor? What does this tell us about the ability to use social science evidence in sentencing?

2. **Too little, too late?** As noted above, early interventions are the most effective, yet children rarely have contact with the criminal justice system until their early teens at the earliest. What does this tell us about the options available to the criminal justice system? In particular, keep this question in mind when thinking about rehabilitation programs—but also when thinking about the moral culpability of adult offenders.

3. **Cumulative disadvantage and baselines.** Assume we see two offenders, Bob (from the Bob-and-Mike example above) and Joe. Both have committed a serious violent crime. Joe is simply dispositionally violent, while Bob has turned to a life of violence in part due to cumulative disadvantage (tellingly, Mike, who avoided detection, never committed a crime again). At one level, it seems like Bob is somehow less culpable. But is he? And even if he is, how can a judge observe the cumulative disadvantage? Bob and Joe might have similarly long records, albeit for different reasons. Does this render cumulative disadvantage an interesting but practically-useless concept?

4. **Too imprecise?** Farrington and Welsh note that offending and low IQ tend to be correlated; more precisely, some studies have shown a more U-shaped relationship, with offending lower at both extremes of the IQ distribution. But no study has derived a concrete relationship: "each one-point reduction in IQ results in a 2.3% increase in the risk of offending." So how should a judge take IQ into account? How useful is a general "lower IQ increases the risk of offending" statement?

As Farrington and Welsh point out, the differences in the likelihood that two people engage in crime can appear to be relatively stable over time: if Joe is more likely to commit crime than Bob when Joe and Bob are 18, the same is likely true when Joe and Bob are 45. However, it is not true that Joe is just as likely to commit a crime at 18 as at 45. In fact, criminal behavior tends to follow one of several empirically-documented age-profiles, as the next section discusses.

B.2. Lifecycle Trends in Offending

A person's proclivity to engage in crime is not constant over his life. Obviously, a toddler is less capable of theft than a teenager, and an eighty-year old man is less capable of assault than someone who is thirty. But more meaningfully, social scientists have observed that even between teenage years and middle-ages, a person's probability of offending follows a rough general profile.

The figure below provides a representative example of the lifecycle model of offending. In general, people do not commit many crimes when young; they start committing crimes in their early- to mid-teens, and they generally desist by their twenties or thirties (note that only 7.5% of the offenders in the graph belong in the two highest chronic groups). Moreover, teenagers tend to specialize in property crimes, with those who end up committing violent crimes starting to do so in their late teens or early twenties.

Figure 1–1: Age Profiles in Offending[15]

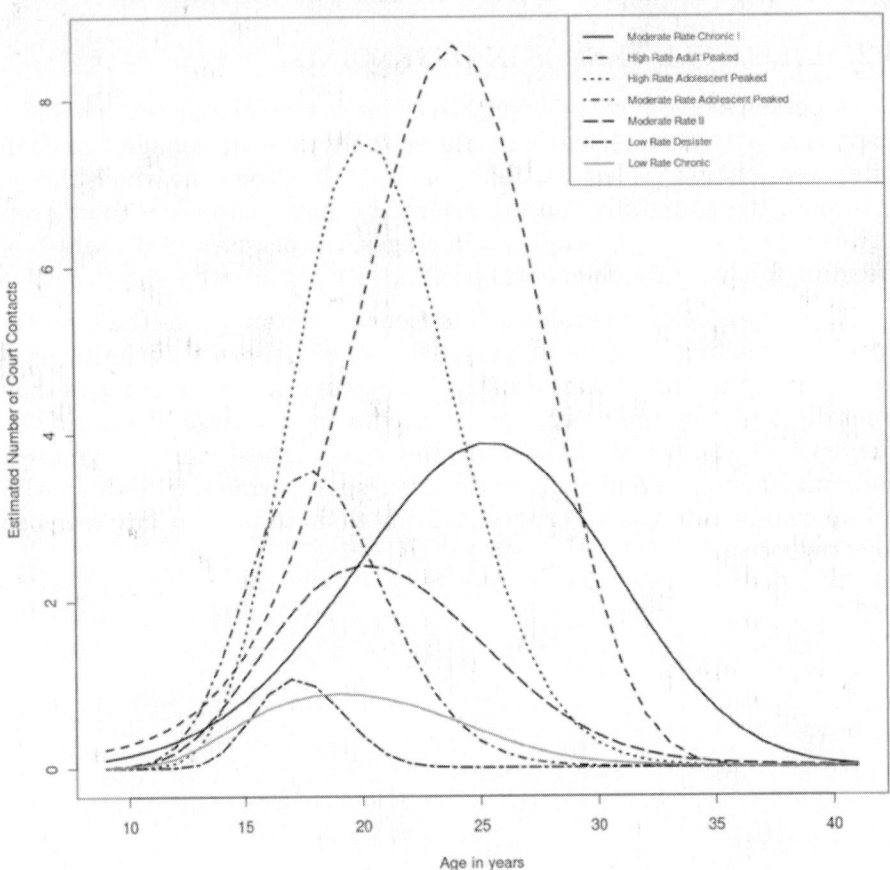

The data here come from a well-known study of 500 Boston youths who were identified as delinquent at age 7 and then interviewed periodically until they were 70. Other studies of other populations—such as delinquents in California, Holland, and England—yield qualitatively similar results. The shapes of the curves differ slightly, as do the number of different trajectory "groups," but the general patterns hold.[16] The one exception is that the Dutch data identifies a small group (about 2% of a 5,000-person sample) of "persistent" offenders who do not show any meaningful decline in offending, especially for property crime, even into their 70s.

---

[15] http://www.publicsafety.gc.ca/cnt/rsrcs/pblctns/djdctd-ntr-yth/index-eng.aspx

[16] In fact, such "group based" analyses are known to be very sensitive to small changes in the data: change the years observed, for example, and the exact number of groups and their shapes can shift. So you don't want to view the curves in Figure 1–1 as conclusive, but they are representative of the general *types* of curves these studies consistently produce.

The lifecycle trend immediately raises three important questions:

1. What causes these trends? As we will see, there are both innate physiological explanations as well as more complex social ones.

2. Can we identify which trajectory an offender belong to? The benefit to being able to do so is clear, since it would allow us to better target our sanctions. Unfortunately, the answer at least for now is "not really."

3. Does the criminal justice system take this profile into account at all? This, too, appears to be another question where the answer is "no."

We will look at the first two questions in more depth here. The third is one that we will come back to several times later in the book when we look at the specific design of the US criminal justice system.

QUESTION 1: THE CAUSES OF THE TRENDS

There are two core explanations for bell-shaped lifecycle offending curves. The first is biochemical and physiological. There are numerous hormones and other chemicals that regulate human behavior, including aggression, and the levels of these chemicals in the body vary predictably over the course of a person's life.[17] Tellingly, trends in criminal behavior track these chemical variations. Take testosterone, which is highly correlated with aggressive behavior: higher average levels of testosterone in men helps explain why men are substantially more likely than women to commit crimes, and violent crimes in particular.[18] But *trends* in testosterone levels in men also explain some the *trends* we see above. Until puberty, males and females alike have low testosterone levels. Starting in puberty, male testosterone levels increase, peaking around age 17—which is the age at which many of those men who will engage in violent behavior begin to do so.[19] Testosterone levels then begin to fall in the late 30s or early 40s, by which time all but the most persistent of offenders are starting to age out of crime.

Other biochemical levels exhibit similar correlations with trends in aggressive behavior. Serotonin, for example, regulates aggression, and studies indicate that serotonin levels tend to increase with age and thus mitigate aggressive behavior in middle-aged adults—and they decrease in the very old, which may partially explain why some elderly people revert to

---

[17] The discussion here draws heavily on Raymond E. Collins, *Onset and Desistance in Criminal Careers: Neurobiology and the Age-Crime Relationship*, 39 J. OFFENDER REHABILITATION 1 (2004).

[18] Men comprise about 80% of those arrested for violent crimes and 63% of those arrested for property crimes, for a total of 74% of all those arrested. See the data from 2011 available here: http://www.albany.edu/sourcebook/pdf/t482011.pdf.

[19] Of course, we do not want to be too reductionist. Hormone shifts alone surely do not explain all behavior: an eighteen-year old may be more willing to engage in violent crime simply because he is bigger than he was at thirteen, and so violent behavior is less risky and more likely to be successful.

aggressive behavior. Conversely, higher dopamine levels in the blood are correlated with more aggression, and dopamine levels appear to naturally drop as people transition from youth to middle-aged. Similar correlated patterns exist for other chemicals as well, such as norepinephrine and acetylcholine.

But physical processes are not the only ones that both regulate aggressive behavior and vary over the life-course; there are important social constraints that do so as well. Robert Sampson and John Laub have written extensively on these factors, focusing in particular on two: marriage and employment. Using the Boston data described above, they find, for example, that marriage is correlated with a 35% reduction in the probability of offending, and they identify at least five plausible causal explanations for this effect:

> (1) a "knifing off" of the past from the present; (2) opportunities for investment in new relationships that offer social support, growth, and new social networks; (3) forms of direct and indirect supervision and monitoring of behavior; (4) structured routines that center more on family life and less on unstructured time with peers; and (5) situations that provide an opportunity for identity transformation and that allow for the emergence of a new self or script, . . . [i.e.], the "movement from a hell-raiser to a family man."[20]

The importance of marital and employment constraints on criminal behavior is a particularly important issue, because unlike a person's biochemical makeup, criminal law enforcement can directly influence the effectiveness of these controls. For example, going to prison reduces an offender's employability: not only does a conviction alone reduce employability by labeling the offender as "untrustworthy," but the isolation of prison weakens the social ties that are important for finding work, and human capital[21] skills generally decay in prison as well. As a result, prison can incapacitate an offender today, but at the (often overlooked) cost of weakening non-state controls over behavior tomorrow. Chapter 10 examines these long-run costs in more depth.

Note, though, that some caution is needed here when looking at the effect sizes. There is an obvious statistical challenge here: those who are most likely to stop engaging in crime may be the ones most likely to find a job or a spouse. So while marriage and employment may reduce criminal behavior, a reduction in criminal behavior certainly increases someone's prospects in the marriage and job markets. While Sampson and Laub attempt to control for this endogenous feedback loop, it is unlikely that they eliminated it completely; if that is the case, then the effect sizes they report are too large, though by how much it is hard to say.

---

[20] Robert J. Sampson and John H. Laub. *A Life-Course View of the Development of Crime.* 602 ANNALS OF AMER. ACAD. OF POLITICAL AND SOC. SCI. 12 (2005).

[21] "Human capital" refers to a person's stock of skills: his education, intelligence, job-related skills, and so on. Like physical capital, human capital can decay. If someone does not use a particular skill-set for a while, his ability in that area declines.

QUESTION 2: CAN WE PREDICT WHO WILL BE ON WHAT PATH?

It would be great if we could predict what trajectory a delinquent would follow. Imagine if a judge had before him two 17-year old defendants, Adam and Bill, each convicted of the identical crime; and also imagine that the judge had a model that allowed him to predict, with a fair amount of accuracy, that Adam was a "classic desister" and Bill was a "moderate-rate persister." He could adjust his sanctions accordingly, perhaps giving Adam probation (since he likely is transitioning out of offending anyway) while giving Bill a prison sentence, but perhaps not one as long as that he would give a "high rate chronic" offender. Prison space could be used quite efficiently (assuming, of course, that is the normative goal of incarceration).

Unfortunately, it is remarkably hard to predict in advance what trajectory a juvenile is on. Using the Boston data, Robert Sampson and John Laub try to make these very predictions and repeatedly fail.[22] They develop a risk index using thirteen variables, which measure cognitive abilities, personality traits, and childhood behaviors. Restricting themselves to data from when the men in the sample were juveniles, they classify the men into high-risk (top 20% of the index) and low-risk (bottom 80% of the index) groups, and then examine whether those in the group predicted to be higher risk in fact engage in more crimes as adults.

The results are striking. First, both groups have very similar trajectories, peaking and desisting at the same point in the life cycle for violent, property, and drug crimes.[23] Second, while the levels of violent and property crime were somewhat higher for the high-risk group (at the peaks, the predicted probabilities of committing a violent offense were 0.07 for the high risk and 0.045 for the low risk, and of committing a property crime 0.3 for the high risk and 0.2 for the low risk), the levels of committing a drug offense were actually *higher* for the *low*-risk group (0.10 to 0.13 at the peaks).

Other approaches that took into account the interaction between offender and "familial" risk (i.e., environmental factors also thought to influence offense trajectories, such as low parental supervision and poverty) likewise failed to yield useful forward-looking predictions. Sampson and Laub are forced to conclude: "Clearly . . . the data are firm in signaling that persistent and frequent offending in the adult years is not easily divined from zeroing in on juvenile offenders at risk." In other words, juvenile factors can help us understand who is more likely to commit more crimes, but they provide little insight into the path they will take in committing them.

> **Question:** Does our inability to predict what path a particular defendant is on render the life-course data useless for judges and other sentencing authorities? Even if these results provide little guidance to a judge in a specific case, might they help the legislature craft more efficient sentences—and if so, how? And does

---

[22] Robert J. Sampson and John H. Laub. *Life-Course Desisters? Trajectories of Crime Among Delinquent Boys Followed to Age 70*, 41 CRIMINOLOGY 555 (2003).

[23] While the peak age varied across crimes (property crimes peaked in the late teens, violent crimes in the mid-20s, and drug crimes in the early 30s), the timing of the peak for each type of crime was the same for both groups.

your answer to this question perhaps suggest a way that these results could help a judge in an individual case as well? What are the various error costs a judge needs to consider when deciding between a shorter and longer sentence?

The inability to identify trajectories in advance, at least at young ages, is clearly disappointing. It suggests that interventions and incarceration need to be used cautiously and be subject to frequent re-evaluations. That we cannot predict trajectories in advance does not mean we cannot gain a better sense of an offender's trajectory later in his life; we should just be careful not to foreclose too rashly our ability to use such information as it becomes available.

QUESTION 3: DO CRIMINAL JUSTICE SYSTEMS PROPERLY ACCOUNT FOR THE AGE PROFILE OF OFFENDING?

I only want to briefly touch on this question here—we will return to it numerous times in the chapters ahead, particularly in Chapter 5, which looks at the role prior criminal history plays in sentencing. The short answer, basically, is "no." In the adult criminal justice system, sentences are generally determined by two factors, the offense and the offender's prior criminal history. The "offense" part of the sentence never makes any reference to age: if the sentence for murder is 20 years, it is 20 years for someone who is twenty-one or fifty-one. The criminal history part similarly makes no reference to the age of the offender, but in practice it actually increases the sentences on older—and thus *sooner*-to-age-out—offenders. It takes some time to generate a lengthy list of prior convictions. So offenders with longer records, who face elevated sentences, tend to be older, and thus substantially more likely to be close to aging out of crime (or at least aging into less crime).

That is not to say that age plays no role at all. Most obviously, the juvenile justice system exists in part to treat the young substantially differently, although it should be pointed out that a dominant trend recently has been to try to move juveniles charged with serious violent crimes into the adult system, where they face substantially longer sentences, possibly even life without parole for non-homicide crimes (until *Graham v. Florida*[24] foreclosed that possibility in 2010). Given the difficulties in predicting future offending at young ages and the significant likelihood of aging out of crime, such long sentences are troubling if efficient incapacitation is our goal.[25]

And sentencing guidelines do refer to age at times. Maryland's guidelines, for example, aggravate sentences based on sufficiently extensive youthful (under 23 years old) offending.[26] Conversely, § 5H1.1 of the Federal Sentencing Guidelines state that judges can take into account age as a mitigating factor. The primary focus of the federal provision is on older

---

[24] 560 U.S. 48 (2010).

[25] They are also troubling if deterrence is our goal, since younger offenders are less sensitive to long sentence lengths.

[26] See page 21 at http://www.msccsp.org/Files/Guidelines/MSGM/guidelinesmanual.pdf.

defendants and the challenges of being incarcerated when old, but the provision does note that youth, too, can mitigate. But sentencing regimes frequently ignore the well-documented age profile of offending. Consider, for example, three-strike laws, which impose severe sentences on defendants with long records. If applied too indiscriminately, they will rope in many defendants shortly before they would naturally start to desist.

B.3. THE IMPORTANCE OF PLACE AND SITUATION

So far we have looked at factors that are outside the control of the defendant, such as innate biological traits, parenting styles, or familial poverty. We now want to turn our attention to an important factor that, at least at first, is more within the defendant's control: his location. A growing body of research indicates that crimes generally occur in very specific locations, and that the locations in some ways contribute to the crimes that occur there: a person who commits a crime in one specific neighborhood might not in another. These findings are consistent with a school of thought in the social sciences called **situationalism**, which posits that someone's overall environment (both geographic and social) exerts a powerful influence on his behavior, often in imperceptible ways.

That environmental conditions influence criminal behavior is not a new idea. Perhaps most famously, in 1942 two University of Chicago sociologists, Clifford Shaw and Henry McKay, argued that crime rates in neighborhood on the southside of Chicago remained relatively constant, even as the populations in those neighborhoods changed.[27] Some recent work has followed in McKay and Shaw's footsteps and sought to explain persistent differences in criminal offending across neighborhoods, while other studies have taken an more micro-level approach to reveal that even *within* high-crime neighborhoods there are persistent pockets of higher and lower crime. The next reading discusses this micro-level research and explores the reasons why crime is so densely concentrated.

David Weisburd, *Place-Based Policing*
9 IDEAS IN AMERICAN POLICING (2008)

In the case of places, basic research has pointed to a tremendous concentration of crime at place. The first major study to point this out was conducted by Lawrence Sherman in the late 1980s. Sherman examined crime calls to the police at addresses in Minneapolis and found that about 3.5 percent of the addresses in Minneapolis in one year produced about 50 percent of the crime calls. More recently, my colleagues and I have shown not only that a similar level of crime concentration exists at street segments in Seattle, but also that the

---

[27] CLIFFORD SHAW AND HENRY MCKAY, JUVENILE DELINQUENCY AND URBAN AREAS: A STUDY OF RATES OF DELINQUENTS IN RELATION TO DIFFERENTIAL CHARACTERISTICS OF LOCAL COMMUNITIES IN AMERICAN CITIES (1942).

concentration of reported crime incidents at micro places is stable over a fourteen-year period (see Figure 3).

There are, in turn, a series of studies that suggest that significant concentration of crime at micro levels of geography exists, regardless of the specific unit of analysis defined. This concentration seems to be even greater for specific types of crime. For example, my colleagues and I found that 86 street segments out of 29,849 account for one third of the total number of juvenile crime incidents in Seattle.

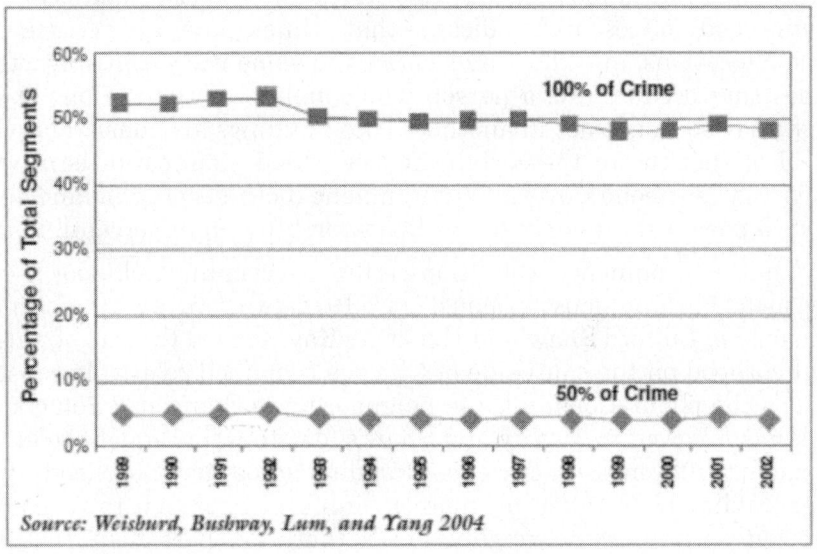

Figure 3: Concentration of Crime Incidents Across 30,000 Street Segments in Seattle, Washington

Source: Weisburd, Bushway, Lum, and Yang 2004

It is important to note that such clustering of crime at small units of geography does not simply mask trends that are occurring at a larger geographic level, such as communities. Research has shown, for example, that in what are generally seen as good parts of town there are often streets with strong crime concentrations, and in what are often defined as bad neighborhoods, many places are relatively free of crime. The extent to which crime at micro units of place varies from street to street is illustrated in a recent study of hot spots of juvenile crime. Using geographic statistics that identify spatial independence, [the study] show[s] that street segments right next to each other tend to have very different levels and patterns of crime over time.

Having said that crime is concentrated at place, it is important to note that crime is also concentrated among offenders. Is crime more concentrated at places than among offenders? We tried to make this comparison using crime incidents from Seattle over the 1989 to 2002 time period. Our results suggest that when using targets as a criterion, places are indeed a more efficient focus than offenders. Using this approach, we found that on average about 1,500 street segments accounted for 50 percent of the crime each year during this period. During the same period, 6,108 offenders were responsible for 50 percent of the crime each year. Simply stated, the police have to approach four times as many targets to identify the same level of overall crime when they focus on people as opposed to places.

[Unlike with offenders, who age into and out of crime, the] developmental patterns of crime at place . . . suggest much stability in crime incidents over time. In our Seattle study of crime trends at places, we found not only that about the same number of street segments were responsible for 50 percent of the crime each year, but also that the street segments that tended to evidence very low or very high activity at the beginning of the period of study in 1989 were similarly ranked at the end of the period in 2002. . . . While there are developmental trends in the data, what is most striking is the relative stability of crime at place over time.

There are at least two explanations for the observed stability in the location of offending: the "routine activities theory" and ecological theories of "social disorganization." In a separate paper, David Weisburd and some coauthors describe the two theories:[28]

> The main assumptions of [the routine activities theory] are that specific characteristics of places such as the nature of guardianship, the presence of motivated offenders, and the availability of suitable targets will strongly influence the likelihood of criminal events. Studies examining the factors that predict crime at micro places generally confirm this relationship.
>
> Routine activities theory does not necessarily predict stability of crime at place over time. Indeed, the theory was originally developed to explain changes in crime rates that were observed over long periods and that were related to changes in routine activities. But most scholars advocating hot spots approaches have argued that the routine activities of places are likely to be fairly stable over relatively shorter periods of time such as the 14 years in [Weisburd et al.'s study of Seattle discussed above]. The availability of suitable targets, of capable guardians, and the presence of motivated offenders in this context are not expected to change rapidly under natural conditions in the urban landscape, though they are likely to change over longer

---

[28] David Weisburd, Shawn Bushway, Cynthia Lum, and Sue-Ming Yang. *Trajectories of Crime at Places: A Longitudinal Study of Street Segments in the City of Seattle*, 42 CRIMINOLOGY 283 (2004).

periods as routine activities of offenders, victims and guardians change as well. Accordingly, the overall stability of crime at place we observe in our data is consistent with routine activities theory.

While routine activities theory has been a central feature of recent interest in crime hot spots, it is important to note that other theoretical approaches might also be consistent with our findings. Ecological theories of social disorganization used to explain the stability of crime patterns in communities, for example, might also be applied to micro crime places. In this case one might expect a stability of crime patterns because there is an underlying social and demographic stability at places. Conversely, relatively stable high crime rates at places may be explained by continuous social change that prevents the establishment of strong social bonds and community controls at the micro place level. Relatively high numbers of increasing and decreasing trajectories (representing on average higher overall rates of crime) in the urban center of Seattle are consistent with this perspective, as are the low rate stable trajectories showing higher concentrations in the less densely populated and more affluent northern parts of the city.

The increasing focus on location can be seen as a subset of a broader development, namely the study of situation more generally. The "Situationist" school in the social sciences argues that we overstate the extent to which our behavior is shaped by our innate dispositions and understate the important role of external—and often unnoted—pressures.

Perhaps the most famous example of situational pressures came from the Milgram electroshock experiments from the 1960s.[29] The following excerpt describes the experiment well:

> In 1961, Yale University psychology professor Stanley Milgram placed an advertisement in the *New Haven Register*. "We will pay you $4 for one hour of your time," it read, asking for "500 New Haven men to help us complete a scientific study of memory and learning."
>
> Only part of that was true. Over the next two years, hundreds of people showed up at Milgram's lab for a learning and memory study that quickly turned into something else entirely. Under the watch of the experimenter, the volunteer—dubbed "the teacher"—would read out strings of words to his partner, "the learner," who was hooked up to an electric-shock machine in the other room. Each time the learner made a mistake in repeating the words, the teacher was to deliver a shock of increasing

---

[29] See, e.g., STANLEY MILGRAM, OBEDIENCE TO AUTHORITY (1974)

intensity, starting at 15 volts (labeled "slight shock" on the machine) and going all the way up to 450 volts ("Danger: severe shock"). Some people, horrified at what they were being asked to do, stopped the experiment early, defying their supervisor's urging to go on; others continued up to 450 volts, even as the learner pled for mercy, yelled a warning about his heart condition—and then fell alarmingly silent. In the most well-known variation of the experiment, a full 65 percent of people went all the way.

Until they emerged from the lab, the participants didn't know that the shocks weren't real, that the cries of pain were pre-recorded, and that the learner—railroad auditor Jim McDonough—was in on the whole thing, sitting alive and unharmed in the next room. They were also unaware that they had just been used to prove the claim that would soon make Milgram famous: that ordinary people, under the direction of an authority figure, would obey just about any order they were given, even to torture.[30]

As Jon Hanson and David Yosifon explain, the Milgram experiment demonstrates clearly how important situational pressures are.

Jon Hanson and David Yosifon, *The Situation: An Introduction to the Situational Character, Critical Realism, Power Economics*
152 U. PA. L. REV. 129, 151–153 (2003)

We humans do not understand ourselves well.

Milgram's expectations matched those of the college students and psychiatrists who he surveyed beforehand. But out of the first forty teacher subjects he tested, twenty-six of them (sixty-five percent) went all the way to 450 volts. And that was only the beginning of a long series of studies revealing the disturbing "banality of evil."

[T]he reason for the experimental results should be clear: situation, like an invisible hand, moves us. Milgram performed this experiment hundreds of times using many different variations. By manipulating the situation, Milgram was able to increase or decrease conformity on the part of the teachers. For example, when it was not the teacher administering the shock himself, but rather a peer operating at the teacher's instruction, more than ninety percent of subjects administered the maximum shock. When an ordinary person rather than a scientist was demanding that the shocking continue, however, far fewer teachers went to 450 volts. The sixty-five percent full compliance observed

---

[30] Cari Romm, *Rethinking One of Psychology's Most Infamous Experiments*, available on-lone at http://www.theatlantic.com/health/archive/2015/01/rethinking-one-of-psychologys-most-infamous-experiments/384913/.

repeatedly at Yale shrunk to forty-eight percent when the study was moved off campus and purportedly run by "Research Associates of Bridgeport."

The vast discrepancy between ex ante predictions about the likely behavior of subjects in these experiments and their actual behavior reveals a central lesson of social psychology—namely, the profound ways in which situation influences our behavior. The naive predictions themselves reveal the gross extent to which we underestimate the power of the situation and wrongly presume that behavior is motivated by disposition.

The argument here is not that disposition does not matter—after all, even in the most "controlling" scenario at least 35% of the "teachers" refused to apply the full 450 volts.[31] But Milgram's experiments demonstrate the strong power that perhaps-consciously-imperceptible situational cues can have on our behavior. In most of these cases, the various cues caused people to behave in ways that they had just moments before claimed they would never do, and variations in these cues altered the results, even though the subjects would never have identified them as mattering.

The connection to crime is clear. One explanation for the micro-geographic concentration of crime is that certain blocks are simply more consciously conducive to crime: more dark alleys in which to lurk or in which to conduct illicit business, say, than another nearby block. But some of the difference could be explained by the way in which the block's environment shapes behavior in ways that are less perceptible, even to the offender. This is the theoretical logic that undergirds Broken Windows policing, which is premised on the idea that conditions of disrepair—broken windows, litter, graffiti, etc.—encourage crime, either by suggesting that surveillance is low (which is perhaps a more

---

[31] Recent evidence suggests that Milgram overstated his results. A reanalysis of his data suggests that a majority of his subjects did not actually believe they were administering dangerous shocks, and of those who did as many as two-thirds refused to apply the most-dangerous shocks. And a subsequent replication was able to capture the general gist of Milgram's results, but with most participants refusing to go past about 150 volts, one-third the maximum dose Milgram claimed to have observed. See http://www.psychologytoday.com/blog/fulfillment-any-age/201301/the-secrets-behind-psychology-s-most-famous-experiment.

Furthermore, recent interviews with some of the participants in Milgram's studies reveal that some of them were in fact testing *Milgram*. Some participants claimed they realized they were not really shocking people and kept going, just to see if Milgram would force them to. This points to a unique challenge of running experiments on people (as opposed to, say, animals or cancer cells): people, once aware they are part of an experiment, often change their behavior in response.

dispositionalist take) or by changing the cues a potential offender processes (a more situationalist perspective).[32]

But we need not limit ourselves to geography. Think about the context of corporate crime. Different corporations have different corporate "cultures"—compare, say, the descriptions of how Google operates compared to Enron—and these differences in cultures can influence behavior in situational ways as well. A wide range of situations—where we are, who we are there with, the outside pressures from family or work—can shape our behavior in ways that are often hard for us to perceive in ourselves, much less in someone else (such as when a judge is trying to determine the right sentence for a defendant).[33]

QUESTIONS

1. **Aggravating or mitigating factor?** If we believe that the goal of sentencing law is to punish moral wrongness, is someone more or less culpable if he commits a crime in a high-crime area? What if we think criminal law should deter?

2. **Avoidable situation?** Assume Bob commits a crime in a high-crime area. Even if we think imperceptible situational cues are mitigating, could we argue that Bob *chose* to be in a high-crime area and thus shouldn't benefit from any mitigation? Can we argue that even if Bob isn't aware of *what* cues matter, he should be aware that *something* about this area causes people to misbehave? At the same time, might there be *other* situational pressures that put Bob in that area in the first place?

3. **The challenge of applying situation.** Assume we think situational pressures should matter; whether as aggravators or mitigators is irrelevant for now. A young black man from a poor, high-crime neighborhood is about to be sentenced for an assault that arose during a street fight by an older, white female judge from a wealthy suburb. What concerns might we

---

[32] The available empirical evidence suggests that broken windows policing has had little to no effect on crime rates. See, for example, BERNARD HARCOURT, ILLUSIONS OF ORDER (2001); and Steven D. Levitt, *Understanding Why Crime Fell in the 1990s: Four Factors that Explain the Decline and Six that Do Not*, 18 J. ECON. PERSPECTIVES 163 (2004). But that does not mean that the theoretical concerns about the effect of street-level conditions on behavior are wrong. It could just mean that local officials did not respond optimally: perhaps they focused on too wide an area and thus stretched resources too thinly, or perhaps they ignored the way in which situational cues interacted with other relevant factors. Some have also argued that places like New York City didn't really engage in "broken windows" policing at all, instead using the term as a politically effective way to justify other policing tactics.

[33] In fact, behavioralists have coined the term **fundamental attribution error** to refer to the idea that we overstate the dispositional explanations for other people's behavior: when Joe gets in a fight, we rarely try to think about the situational factors that could have shaped his behavior but simply assume he is dispositionally aggressive. The cognitive shortcut here is obvious: assigning blame to someone's disposition is much easier to do than trying to gain an understanding on their whole social situation. Which also explains why we are more situationalist when it comes to our own failings. We understand our own context much more easily. Consider, for example, any tough-on-crime politician caught committing a crime himself: he rarely simply says "I'm a bad person," but instead offers up an array of situational explanations. That said, the Milgram experiment indicates we still evaluate situational pressures poorly even for ourselves.

have with this set-up? What does this tell us about when we can better take situation into account? Or about how we should structure our various criminal justice bureaucracies?

Whatever concerns the above questions raise, it is undeniable that situational cues influence our behavior in important ways, and ignoring them because they are challenging to assess impoverishes sentencing law. In the chapters ahead, we will want to consider how and when we can take into account these sorts of factors.

C. THE PROPER USE OF SOCIAL SCIENCE EVIDENCE

This section has provided a wide-ranging discussion of how people make decisions, including the decision to engage in criminal conduct, and the factors that shape those choices. I want to conclude by briefly pointing out the limits on how such evidence can and should be used. In particular, I want to discuss the importance of keeping positive and normative analyses separate.[34]

Social science evidence cannot tell us what we *ought* to do, only what we *can* do. The challenge of not blurring "is" and "ought" has long been acknowledged—the issue was famously raised by David Hume over 250 years ago—but it is an easy trap to fall into. A simple problem can illuminate the issue:

Problem: Assume that you are a judge, and you face two defendants convicted of the exact same crime, aggravated assault, and the only meaningful difference between them is age: one (Sam) is 17 and the other (Tom) is 29. Should you give them the same prison sentence?

A few stylized social science facts should immediately come to mind: the age profile in offending, for example, and the hormonal and other developmental trends that partially explain it. But what should you do with these facts? Do they mean you should lock up Sam for more years than Tom? For fewer?

The short answer is this: these facts cannot answer the question. First, we have to ask why we should punish (which is the topic of the next chapter). Is our goal to incapacitate or, say, impose the morally just sentence? Sam, who is younger and entering his peak offending years, may be more in need of incapacitation, while Tom, who is older and likely to start aging out of crime, requires less time behind bars. But, similarly, Tom may be more morally culpable (and thus deserving of more time in

---

[34] There is another important discussion we could have here, namely how to properly use social science evidence when the evidence base is confusing or incomplete, as is often the case in criminology. I will return to it throughout the book when discussing issues related to institutional design and competence.

prison) because he is less subject to the hormonal and developmental limitations that Sam faces. But the social sciences cannot tell us whether incapacitation or moral sanction is the "right" approach. This is a normative, philosophical question, not an empirical, positive social scientific one.

But let us limit ourselves just to moral sanction ("just deserts," to use the term we will define in Chapter 2). Does the age profile in offending answer the question here? Even in this narrow context, the answer is no. Whether the physiological differences between Sam and Tom are relevant to the moral wrongness of their conduct is *still* a moral question, not a positive one. That some factor *x* explains behavior does not *automatically* mean that we must take *x* into account when imposing punishment. As Stephen Morse, a neuroscientist and law professor, puts it, "Although neuroscientific evidence may surely provide assistance in performing [an] evaluation [of "self-control"], neuroscience could never tell us how much control ability is required for responsibility. That question is normative, moral, and, ultimately, legal."[35]

One way to think of social scientific evidence is as a form of cartography or navigation. A map cannot tell you whether you *should* drive from New York City to Chicago or to Miami. Nor can a map tell you if you *should* drive on I-80 or I-95. But a map can tell you that *if* you wish to go to Chicago, *then* you should take I-80, or that *if* you want to drive on I-95 *then* you're going to end up in Miami, not Chicago.

Same with the social sciences. They cannot tell us what we *should* do. But they can help us to understand that *if* we want a particular outcome, *then* we need to adopt a particular policy; or *if* we adopt a particular policy, *then* we will end up a particular outcome. Ignoring the age profile of crime means that we will overincarcerate older defendants relative to what is optimal from an incapacitation perspective (but perhaps optimal from a just deserts one), or conversely that if we take the age profile of offending into account we will end up with outcomes that appeal to incapacitationists but trouble just desert theorists.

---

[35] Stephen J. Morse, "New Neuroscience, Old Problems," in BRENT GARLAND, ED., NEUROSCIENCE AND THE LAW 179 (2004)

CHAPTER 2

WHY WE PUNISH

Now that we have examined *who* offends and *why* they do so, we can turn our attention to *how* to punish offenders, from both a normative and positive perspective. Normatively, we want to look at the arguments about what goals punishment *ought* to advance: should it deter, or incapacitate, or rehabilitate, or impose the morally correct sanction? And positively, we want to consider what punishment *in fact* seeks to do at a broader social level: is it designed to reduce crime, or regulate the underclass, or advance some other goal?

Note that to examine these normative theories of punishment we still some positive analysis. It is impossible, for example, to design an optimal incapacitation regime without understanding how people age into and out of crime. Nor can we decide if two people are equally morally culpable without an appreciation for how their different environments impact or impede their judgment. So while the results discussed in Chapter 1 cannot tell *what* the normatively correct goal of punishment is, they are of utmost importance for deciding *how* to best accomplish whatever goal we set.

While reading this chapter, keep the following overarching questions in mind: What theory of punishment should we follow? Do we want to follow just one, or do different theories apply for different offenders, or for different offenses? And—anticipating somewhat Chapter 3's discussion of criminal justice bureaucracies—if we want to adopt different goals in different contexts, who should get to decide: legislators, prosecutors, judges, parole boards, etc.?

A. THE NORMATIVE GOALS OF PUNISHMENT

Over the years—centuries, really—theorists have advanced numerous normative goals for criminal punishment, which we can divide roughly into two categories, utilitarian and retributivist. The utilitarian theories can then be further divided into deterrence, incapacitation, and rehabilitation. This section starts by considering each of the utilitarian theories, and it then turns to the retributivist perspective. It concludes by seeking common ground between the two broad camps.

A.1. UTILITARIAN THEORIES

The core utilitarian theories are **deterrence**, **incapacitation**, and **rehabilitation**. The basic goal of each theory is quite straightforward:

1. **Deterrence**. The goal of criminal punishment is to discourage offenders from breaking the law in the first place.

2. **Incapacitation**. The goal of criminal punishment is to prevent offenders, or potential offenders, from committing their crimes.

3. **Rehabilitation**. The goal of criminal punishment is to (re)form those who break the law into law abiding citizens.

The devil, as always, is in the details, and each of these theories faces serious practical and normative critiques. Each of the next three parts will present the basic contours of each theory and then ask several questions to probe their weaknesses.

Before continuing, it is worth pointing out that none of these theories is *inherently* utilitarian: one could justify deterrence, incapacitation, or rehabilitation as a moral necessity in and of itself. But, in practice, those who favor these theories generally do so for utilitarian or consequentialist reasons, and thus it makes sense to discuss them in that context.

A.1.a. DETERRENCE

When we talk about deterrence, the goal is not simply to prevent crime. After all, the path to little or no crime is, intuitively, quite clear: simply rely on brutally severe sanctions and arrest and conviction rates of 100%.[1] But such an approach, beyond its impracticality, is morally, fiscally, and policy-wise repugnant. So our focus is more on **optimal** deterrence, on how to best balance any reduction in the costs of crime with the attendant increase in the costs of enforcement—which includes not just the obvious financial costs (hiring more police, spending more on prisons), but the collateral financial and emotional harms to family-members and communities, and so on.

Of course, this balance can reflect either utilitarian or non-utilitarian attitudes, or even just different (utilitarian) ways of weighing the various costs and benefits. Consider the following simple example:

Problem: Look at the felony murder statutes from California and Colorado.

Cal Pen Code § 189: "All murder . . . which is committed in the perpetration of, or attempt to perpetrate, [a list of felonies] is murder in the first degree. All other kinds of murders are of the second degree."

Colo Rev Stat § 18–3–102(1)(b): "A person commits the crime of murder in the first degree if . . . he or she commits or attempts to commit [a list of felonies] and, in the course of or in

---

[1] Note, for future reference, that we already need to start thinking about the fractured nature of criminal justice bureaucracies. The severe sanctions are set by the state legislature, but the arrest rate is determined by the actions of local police—who are funded from local taxes—and the conviction rate is shaped by county-funded prosecutors. **Question:** Even if the state legislature wants a 100% arrest and conviction rate, how can it make sure that the more-local police and prosecutors do their part?

furtherance of the crime that he or she is committing or attempting to commit, or of immediate flight therefrom, the death of a person, other than one of the participants, is caused by anyone."

How do the utilitarian calculations in California and Colorado differ? Do they assign different weights to the value of different people's lives?

When crafting a sentencing regime with deterrence in mind, policymakers have two levers they can manipulate, namely the probability of arrest and conviction, and the sanction that is imposed when that conviction is secured. These form the expected penalty: if a defendant faces a 50% chance of a $100 fine, then his expected punishment is $50. So, in theory, the defendant then asks if committing the crime is worth at least $50, and he goes forward with it if it is. Each of these components of deterrence—the probability of arrest, the probability of conviction, the punishment imposed—is costly (in financial and other ways), and each influences the behavior of potential offenders differently. So part of the task of the state is figuring out how to balance them. After all, the state could also achieve an expected penalty of $50 with a 10% chance of a $500 dollar fine, or perhaps a 1% chance of 6 months in jail. These sanctions require fewer police and DA resources than a 50% arrest and conviction rate, but may have higher costs elsewhere (maintaining the jail, or trying to get payment from poor defendants).

> **Question:** From what we read in Ch. 1, which do you think will deter potential offenders more: a 75% chance at 2 years in prison, or a 25% chance at 6 years in prison? What does this tell us about the optimal way to focus on police vs. prisons? Do you think this is how US policy operates in practice?

There are two general flavors of deterrence: **specific** and **general**. Specific deterrence looks at a specific individual, asking how well punishing someone today for a crime he committed keeps him from committing a crime again. General deterrence takes a more global view, asking how we should structure the law to discourage *all* potential law-breakers from engaging in illegal acts, including those who have never offended before. When people talk about "deterrence" they are generally referring to general deterrence, but both sorts matter.

The following reading summarizes the current state of our understanding of how deterrence works.

Daniel S. Nagin, *Deterrence in the Twenty-First Century*
43 CRIME & JUSTICE 199, 200–205 (2013)

The criminal justice system dispenses justice by apprehending, prosecuting, and punishing individuals who break the law. These activities may prevent crime by three distinct mechanisms: incapacitation, specific deterrence, and general deterrence. Incapacitation concerns crimes averted by their physical isolation during the period of their incarceration. Specific and general deterrence involve possible behavioral responses. General deterrence refers to the crime prevention effects of the threat of punishment. Specific deterrence concerns the aftermath of the failure of general deterrence—the effect on reoffending, if any, that results from the experience of actually being punished.

My aim is to provide a succinct summary of the current state of theoretical and empirical knowledge about deterrence. . . . My main conclusions are as follows: First, there is little evidence that increases in the length of already long prison sentences yield general deterrent effects that are sufficiently large to justify their social and economic costs. Such severity-based deterrence measures include "three strikes, you're out," life without the possibility of parole, and other laws that mandate lengthy prison sentences.

Second, I have concluded that there is little evidence of a specific deterrent effect arising from the experience of imprisonment compared with the experience of noncustodial sanctions such as probation. Instead, the evidence suggests that that reoffending is either unaffected or increased.

Third, there is substantial evidence that increasing the visibility of the police by hiring more officers and allocating existing officers in ways that materially heighten the perceived risk of apprehension can deter crimes. This evidence is consistent with the perceptual deterrence literature that surveys individuals on sanction risk perceptions and relates these perceptions to their actual or intended offending behavior. This literature finds that perceived certainty of punishment is associated with reduced self-reported or intended offending.

Thus, I conclude, as have many prior reviews of deterrence research, that evidence in support of the deterrent effect of various measures of the certainty of punishment is far more convincing and consistent than for the severity of punishment. However, the certainty of punishment is conceptually and mathematically the product of a series of conditional probabilities: the probability of apprehension given commission of a crime, the probability of prosecution given apprehension, the probability of conviction given prosecution, and the probability of sanction given conviction. The evidence in support of certainty's deterrent effect pertains almost exclusively to apprehension probability. Consequently, the conclusion that certainty, not severity, is the more effective deterrent is more precisely stated as certainty of apprehension and not the severity of the legal consequence ensuing from apprehension is the more effective deterrent. This more precise statement has important policy implications; the empirical evidence from the policing and perceptual deterrence literature is silent on the deterrent effectiveness of policies that mandate incarceration after apprehension. These include policies such as mandatory minimum sentencing laws or sentencing guidelines that mandate incarceration. Thus, this revised conclusion about the deterrent effect of punishment certainty should not be construed as implying that policies mandating severe legal consequences have been demonstrated to achieve deterrent effects.

Together these conclusions have a range of policy implications, particularly as they relate to the United States. First, it is clear that lengthy prison sentences cannot be justified on a deterrence-based, crime prevention basis. Thus, the case for crime prevention benefits of measures requiring lengthy prison sentences such as California's three-strikes law must rest on incapacitation. Another implication is that crime prevention would be enhanced by shifting resources from imprisonment to policing or, in periods of declining criminal justice system budgets, that policing should get a larger share of a smaller overall budget.

While accumulation of knowledge about deterrence in the past four decades has been impressive, much remains to be learned. There are [several] major theoretical and related empirical gaps. The first concerns the deterrent effect of the certainty of apprehension. There are two distinct mechanisms by which the police may deter crime. One stems from their effectiveness in apprehending perpetrators of crimes; by definition this activity involves occurrences in which deterrence has failed. Thus, police effectiveness in successfully apprehending criminal perpetrators can have a deterrent effect only on others or on the perpetrator's future behavior. The second mechanism involves the effect of the intensity of police presence in creating a perception that apprehension risk is sufficiently high that no crime is committed in the first place. I speculate that this second mechanism is the primary source of police effectiveness in deterring crime. . . .

The second gap concerns the distinction between specific and general deterrence. The two are inextricably linked because the experience of punishment is a consequence of the failure of the threat of punishment to deter crime, yet no theory of deterrence explicitly addresses how the experience of punishment influences the deterrent effect of the threat of punishment. Relevant issues include how the experience of punishment affects the proclivity to commit crime due to potential stigma effects, sustained contacts with criminals in a prison setting, or participation in rehabilitative programs as well as the effect of the experience of punishment on perceptions of the certainty and severity of sanctions.

The [final] theoretical and empirical gap involves sanction risk perceptions. . . . Deterrence is the behavioral response to the perception of sanction threats. Establishing the link between risk perceptions and sanction regimes is imperative; the conclusion that crime decisions are affected by sanction risk perceptions is not sufficient to conclude that policy can deter crime. Policy cannot directly manipulate perceptions. It can affect only the variety and severity of sanctions legally available in the sanction regime and the manner of their administration. Unless perceptions adjust, however crudely, to changes in the sanction regime, the desired deterrent effect will not be achieved.

In another review of the deterrence literature, Nagin explains why the risk-of-apprehension effect may be the strongest:

> One explanation for what I call the certainty effect comes from criminological theory, which places at least as much emphasis on the deterrent effect of informal sanction costs as formal sanction costs. Informal sanction costs include costs that are separate from those that attend the imposition of formal sanctions, such as loss of freedom or fines, and include censure by friends and family and loss of social and economic standing. Importantly, the magnitude of informal costs may be largely independent of the severity of legal consequences. Merely being arrested for committing a crime may trigger the imposition of informal sanctions.[2]

In many cases, not only might the informal sanction be independent of the formal punishment, but it may be *larger* as well. Nagin's discussion of informal sanctions is an important reminder that criminal punishment does not operate in a vacuum, but interacts with—and depends critically on—the social environment in which the offender acts and lives. Keep this point in mind when Chapter 3 considers the haphazard way in which discretion is allocated across local, county, state, and federal actors. Not all these actors are as aware of, or as capable of responding to, the offender's social setting.

We now turn to a series of questions that shed more light on the challenges faced by a policymaker trying to implement a deterrent criminal code.

---

[2] Daniel S. Nagin, *Deterrence: A Review of the Evidence by a Criminologist for Economists*, 5 ANN. REV. ECON. 83, 85 (2013).

QUESTIONS

1. **Marginal deterrence.** Perhaps we think that the best way to reduce bank robberies is to set the sanction really, really high: we hire a lot of police officers to protect banks and investigate robberies, and the sanction for robbing a bank is set to the maximum possible (assume we are in a non-death penalty state, so life without parole). Once Jack decides to rob a bank, what are his incentives about shooting the bank guard to elude capture? Or, phrased differently, what is the incremental sanction he faces for escalating his offense? Does your answer help explain one reason why we often have different degrees of crimes, such as multiple levels of drug crimes based on the weight in possession? Does it justify punishing attempt crimes less than completed ones?

2. **Deterrence and impulsiveness.** Traditional economic models of punishment have argued that a 50% chance of spending two years in prison should be just as effective a deterrent as a 10% chance of 10 years in prison: in either case, the expected sanction is one year ($2 \times 0.5 = 10 \times 0.1 = 1$). Look back, though, to our discussion in Chapter 1, particularly the work of Gottfredson and Hirschi. Do their results push us toward the 50%/two-year sanction or the 10%/ten-year sanction? Does your answer suggest that states should focus more on imposing tougher sentences or increasing the probability of apprehension and punishment?

3. **Highly localized knowledge.** In another review of the literature on deterrence, Raymond Paternoster considers how well people know the law.[3] After all, changes in the law can't deter people if they don't know about the changes. He cites a phone survey of 1,500 respondents in fifty-four large, urban counties that found people do not know the law, and these results are consistent with previous work.[4] By showing that people do not generally know the law, these studies are thought to undermine claims that deterrence works. Take as a given that these results are accurate. Do they necessarily undermine general deterrence? Are these studies talking to the right people? Does the data from Seattle and Minneapolis given in Chapter 1 provide a valuable hint? Does it help to know that not only are criminal acts geographically concentrated, but that most offenders commit their crimes close to where they live?

4. **Highly localized effects.** Some evidence indicates that internal social controls—and a community's willingness to enforce social control over its members—turn to some degree on the perceived legitimacy of the law itself and how it is enforced. Given that these sorts of informal controls are likely far more important than formal sanctions in regulating behavior, what does this tell us about how criminal sanctions should be structured, and who should decide how to impose them? How relevant is the fact that crime "hot

---

[3] Raymond Paternoster, *How Much Do We Really Know About Deterrence*, 100 J. CRIM. L. & CRIMINOLOGY 765 (2010).

[4] Gary Kleck, Brion Sever, Spencer Li, and Marc Gertz, *The Missing Link in General Deterrence Research*, 43 CRIMINOLOGY 623 (2005). See also Paul H. Robinson & John M. Darley, *The Role of Deterrence in the Formulation of Criminal Law Rules: At Its Worst When Doing Its Best*, 91 GEORGETOWN L. J. 949 (2003).

spots" are generally disproportionately poor and minority? What sort of informational or political constraints does this impose on the criminal justice system?

5. **Displacement.** Assume that the police crack down on crime at Main Street and First Avenue, a known "hot spot" in the city. Citizens who live at Main and First will be happy. How about those who live at Main and Second Avenue? How relevant is the fact that Main and Second was not a "hot spot" earlier? Does your answer help explain why we see interstate task forces targeting drug crimes but not domestic violence? An article several years ago pointed out that the NYPD was a more effective anti-terrorism force than the FBI: is this concerning to New Yorkers? Chicagoans?[5]

6. **More or less punishment?** Joe is a much more impulsive person than Bob, so a five-year prison sentence may be enough to deter Bob from stealing from a store, but it isn't necessarily enough to deter Joe. Does this mean that we should increase the sanction that Joe faces, or perhaps counter-intuitively does it suggest that we should *reduce*, or at least not elevate, Joe's sanction (assuming we can differentiate the Joes of the world from the Bobs)?

7. **Informal sanctions and normalization.** As Nagin notes, informal sanctions play an important deterrent effect. What impact does highly-concentrated large-scale incarceration have on these informal controls? Might an overly aggressive *formal* sanction regime undermine the effectiveness of the *informal* regime? How do we want to balance these?

8. **What limits on punishment?** Is there anything in deterrence theory that prevents the state from punishing an innocent man if it knows that doing so will efficiently reduce crime? Or if it appears that the optimal way to deter jay-walking is to set the sanction at death or life without parole, must a deterrence theorist accept such a sanction? Conversely, must a prosecutor decline to charge a clearly-guilty person if he knows that it will not reduce crime at all? Put more generally, where in deterrence theory do ideas of "guilt" and "innocence" appear? *Do* they appear at all? And do the principles of deterrence provide any limits on how large or small a sanction can be?

9. **Deterrence and behavioralism.** People are deterred in part by their perceptions of the risk of punishment. From a specific deterrence perspective, how does a prior arrest and punishment influence the sort of sanction we need to use to deter the recidivist (assuming nothing else is changed by the conviction)?

A.1.b. INCAPACITATION

As with deterrence, the goal of incapacitation is simple: To restrict an offender's behavior so he cannot offend again. When we talk about incapacitation, we are almost always thinking of **incarceration**, of physically isolating the offender in some sort of penal institution so he

---

[5] William Finnegan, *The Terrorism Beat: How is the N.Y.P.D. Defending the City?*, THE NEW YORKER July 25, 2005.

cannot commit other crimes (at least against those outside the institution). But physical incapacitation is not the only sort that exists. Chemical castration incapacitates a rapist from raping again, and disbarring a lawyer incapacitates him from engaging in further legal malpractice.

Incapacitation need not even be imposed by the state. Consider the claim made in Chapter 1 that marriage and employment are pathways out of crime. In some ways, these can be seen as a form of incapacitation: if an offender is spending time with his spouse or at his job, he is physically isolated from hanging out on the street corner and getting into trouble with his friends.

In many ways, incapacitation is the easiest sanction to deploy. As long as the offender is securely confined, he cannot commit crimes against the broader public.[6] Yet, as with deterrence, the goal isn't just "to incapacitate," but "to *optimally* incapacitate." And this latter approach is a much more nuanced, and much trickier, endeavor. The challenge is to move beyond simply saying "lock this offender up for a very long time to keep us safe!" to asking "at what point does additional time being incapacitated cost more than whatever benefits society is getting from it?"

Trying to design an optimal incapacitation regime faces several major challenges. Many of these are raised in the questions below, so here I just want to focus on a few. First, the most obvious issue that demands attention is how long should someone be incapacitated, and how securely? Do we need to lock a particular offender in a secure prison for fifty years, or is it enough to impose probationary restrictions on him (no drinking, no associating with known felons, must find a job) for three years? States with guidelines have generally addressed this question by essentially looking at the defendant's prior criminal history and the severity of his offense; non-guideline states have left the question to the discretion of the sentencing judge (within the confines of statutory minimums and maximums).

Some jurisdictions have attempted to develop more sophisticated means of determining how much time an offender should spend in prison by developing models of **selective incapacitation**, which seek to predict who needs to be locked up, and for how long. If these models work well, then prisons will contain only the most serious offenders, and only during the times that they pose threats. The discussion in Chapter 1 of age-trajectories in offending, however, highlights the challenges such models face. Despite a growing understanding of offender behavior and

---

[6] Of course, this requires him to be more than just physically locked up. A senior-level member of a drug gang can still coordinate criminal activities if he, say, has access to a cell-phone.

motivations, it is still quite difficult to predict a specific person's offending profile in advance.[7]

As criminologists Alex Piquero and Alfred Blumstein point out, however, prediction may not always be necessary.[8] High-volume offenders are more likely to be caught just by chance, since they commit crimes more often and thus "roll the dice" of arrest and imprisonment more frequently. Piquero and Blumstein call this effect **stochastic incapacitation**. Note that stochastic incapacitation does not automatically mean that efforts at more sophisticated selective incapacitation models have no value: if high-volume offenders are also more adept at avoiding detection, we may need to still detain them longer to offset the lower probability of apprehension. But the presence of stochastic incapacitation certainly reduces the marginal benefit of investing in selective incapacitation techniques.

Second, when thinking about incapacitation, and incarceration in particular, it is important to keep in mind both short- and long-term effects. One concern with prisons is that they can serve as training grounds for future criminality, since young offenders can learn from older inmates how to commit crimes more effectively, or they can find themselves acculturated to a more criminal worldview. Thus the short-run reduction in crime from locking up the offender could be off-set, at least partially if not fully, by worse behavior upon release.

Or consider the implications of Sampson and Loeb's work on marriage and employment. Marriage and jobs act as forms of long-run incapacitation, but incarceration (and conviction more generally) undermines an offender's ability to secure either of these. And the longer and more severe the sanction, the more these options are reduced—but of course, at least in theory, the more serious the threat posed by the offender (correct?).

Question: How do these crime-causing ("iatrogenic" is the jargon word for this) effects of prison exposure interact with age-profiles in offending?

And third, think also about the supply-side question: what policies will politicians in fact be willing or able to supply? Are there, for example, structural reasons why politicians will favor harsh sentencing, besides just a desire to pander to "tough on crime" voters? The questions below will flesh out some of these concerns. Think about this issue in particular when you reach the false-positive/false-negative question.

As a policy matter, incarceration has been the most prominent tool of US penal policy over the past thirty to forty years. As we will discuss

---

[7] Parole boards, however, are getting better at developing models to predict recidivism risk *upon release*. So while it may be hard to determine the optimal sentence at sentencing, it may be possible to better craft sentences via rigorous parole release models.

[8] Alex R. Piquero and Alfred Blumstein, *Does Incapacitation Reduce Crime*, 23 J. QUANT. CRIMINOL. 267 (2007)

in more detail in Chapter 9, the US incarceration rate has soared from a middle-of-the-road 100 per 100,000 in the 1970s to nearly 750 per 100,000 today—the highest rate in the world. With 5% of the world's population, the US is home to over 20% of its prisoners. That said, prison inmates comprise only about 1.6 million of the 8 million people under criminal justice observation on any given day: prison is the most high-profile, but not the most widely used, method of punishment used today.

Let's now consider a few questions to flesh out some of the complicating details of incapacitation:

QUESTIONS

1. **Incapacitation beyond incarceration.** Incarceration is the most obvious form of incapacitation, but it is not the only one. Above we considered chemical castration and disbarment. Can you think of any other forms of incapacitation? What are the upsides of these? The downsides?

2. **Incapacitation and age.** Consider the following unsurprising fact: defendants with longer records tend to be older than those with shorter records. Data from a sample of felony criminal cases taken from the 75 most populous counties suggest the average age of defendants facing felony convictions with no prior felony convictions is about 28.4 years, while that of those with one prior is about 30.2, with two priors 31.2, and so on; those with ten or more priors have an average age of 36.2.[9] This should not surprise us, since it takes time to accumulate a long criminal record. But what does this tell us about the efficacy of three-strike laws and other sentencing provisions that enhance sentence length for repeat offenders? Are repeat offender laws necessarily targeting the right factor? On the other hand, what if we made youthfulness an aggravating factor, imposing harsher sanctions on younger offenders? Does the graph of age-offending profiles in Chapter 1 above caution against that as well, or at least highlight some important risks?

3. **Incapacitation and age, again.** The previous question is perhaps somewhat leading. But we can reframe it this way: with what information, and at what age for the offender, should we be increasingly confident that we have indeed convicted a "persistent" offender in need of long incarceration?

4. **Incapacitation and replacement.** To the extent the goal of incapacitation is to reduce crime, it does so only if no one fills in for a now-incapacitated offender. This has often been an argument against the War on Drugs, that locking up one street-level dealer should have no effect on drug markets since there is always another person waiting in the wings to take over the job. For what other sorts of crimes do you think this holds true? Would it apply to aggravated assaults arising from drunken late-night bar brawls? Domestic abuse? And even within the drug context, do you

---

[9] These results come from the State Court Processing Statistics dataset, which surveys a subset of the 75 most populous counties in the United States. These data are the average ages across all years of SCPS data (1990–2004).

necessarily think that the replacement rate is 1.0, i.e., for every ten dealers removed from the street, a full ten more step in to take their places?

5. **The false positive/false negative problem.** When talking about incarceration, a "false positive" is someone who is incarcerated but would not have committed a subsequent crime had he been free. Conversely, a "false negative" is someone who is not incarcerated but could have been and commits a crime while free.[10] Is it possible for the public—or anyone, for that matter—to observe how many false positives there are? How about false negatives? How does a false negative manifest itself, compared to a false positive? Which is riskier for a politician? Do other types of punishments suffer from similar problems?

6. **The limits of incapacitation.** Does incapacitation theory necessarily suffer from the same normative problem of deterrence, that it cannot suggest any *a priori* limits on what constitutes proper punishment?

A.1.c. REHABILITATION

The final consequentialist theory we will consider is rehabilitation. As with the other two consquentialist approaches, the goal of rehabilitation is straight-forward: the criminal justice system should use its resources to try to modify the offender's behavior so that he does not offend again. Rehabilitation was the dominant justification for the American penal system from the construction of the first prison, on Walnut Street in Philadelphia in 1790, through the 1970s—at least in theory, if not always in practice. The 1970s saw a shift from rehabilitation to punishment, even though rehabilitative prison programs never completely disappeared. Recent years have seen at least a partial revival of rehabilitation, particularly with the rise of problem-solving courts and better-designed prison therapy programs.

The following excerpt by Francis Cullen, a criminologist and former President of the American Criminology Society, summarizes the appeal of, and trends in, rehabilitation as a goal of punishment.

Francis T. Cullen, *Rehabilitation: Beyond Nothing Works*

42 CRIME & JUSTICE 299, 308–359 (2013)

[T]he rehabilitative ideal draws its power from its nobility and its rationality—from the promise that compassionate science, rather than vengeful punishment, is the road to reducing crime. Rehabilitation allows us to be a better and safer people—a bargain that an aspirational and utilitarian nation finds hard to turn down. Still, two potential weaknesses lie within the rehabilitative ideal. One is that the ideal is a

---

[10] The terms come from medicine: a false positive is someone incorrectly diagnosed as having a disease (here, engaging in criminal conduct), while a false negative is someone falsely diagnosed as being disease-free.

lie; we promise to save offenders but in reality intend often only to control and coerce them. The second is quackery; we claim to have the expertise to cure offenders but often do not.

Americans' public embrace of rehabilitation extends back more than 200 years. It was perhaps first evident prominently in the 1820s, when reformers in New York and Pennsylvania invented the "penitentiary." The name penitentiary is instructive because it expresses the aim to create an institution that would be an instrument of reformation, not punishment.

[Over the next 150 years, rehabilitation evolved. Perhaps its most durable development came during the Progressive Era at the start of the 1900s.] During this period, probation, parole, [and] indeterminate sentencing . . . went from the exception to close to the rule. These reforms constituted a coherent effort to implement the rehabilitative ideal. Thus, individual offenders would be assessed case by case; those judged less risky in a presentence report would be placed on probation where they would be supervised and counseled by a probation officer. If sent to prison, offenders would serve an indeterminate length until a parole board judged them cured, at which time they would come under the watchful and helpful eye of a parole officer. These justice system components remain with us nearly a century later and are invariably involved in discussion of policy and practice reforms.

[Support for rehabilitation began to decline in the latter half of the Twentieth Century.] The decline of support for the rehabilitative ideal was sudden and qualitative. By the mid-1970's, it had become common to ask, "Is rehabilitation dead?" [This attitude was eventually succinctly summarized by the claim "nothing works."] How could this occur?

Critics articulated a number of reservations about the rehabilitative ideal, but three were so fundamental as to render the treatment enterprise fully illegitimate. First, prisons . . . were not places in which reform either would be given priority or could be accomplished. Custodial goals—the need to maintain order and to prevent escapes—would always trump the therapeutic. Those in charge might give lip service to rehabilitation, but their jobs hinged on keeping prisons quiet, not curing offenders. They would use whatever methods it took to maintain control.

The second criticism focused on abuse of discretion. Under the rehabilitative ideal, correctional officials were given virtually unfettered discretion to diagnose and treat offenders. [In theory, judges and parole boards would use this discretion carefully.] In reality, the decision to send an offender to prison or release one from prison was not based on careful assessment and scientific expertise but on a hunch as to who might, or might not, be dangerous. Worse still, officials were suspected not simply of ignorance but of malice—of engaging in unjust decisions. Research on so-called extralegal factors suggested that racial stereotypes shaped sentencing and subsequent decisions.

The third criticism was that the treatment was "enforced." Many suspected that offenders could not be helped against their will and thus that a system of coerced cure was a futile enterprise. But the more significant concern was that in the name of rehabilitation, those state officials claiming to help offenders . . . could do almost anything they wanted to their charges. Unlike medical treatment, correctional treatment was not a choice. For those incarcerated, the price of refusing rehabilitation was a denial of freedom. But more than this was feared. This was the era of Stanley Kubrick's 1971 film *A Clockwork Orange* and Ken Kesey's *One Flew over the Cuckoo's Nest*. Commentators worried that new behavior and drug technologies would provide insidious means for dehumanizing mind control.

[Rehabilitation was also criticized by conservative politicians.] First, by focusing on the causes of behavior, such as poverty or family conflict, it provided excuses—readily available techniques of neutralization—for irresponsible choices. Second, and more important, state officials used their discretion to create a revolving door of justice. Judges were placing dangerous predators not in prison but back on the streets, and kindhearted or duped parole boards were being conned into releasing career criminals prematurely.

Perceptive readers will recognize that liberals and conservatives in the 1970s were calling for similar policies—purging state officials' discretion justified by rehabilitation through determinate sentencing—but for different reasons. Liberals believed that rehabilitation allowed for coercive practices that victimized offenders; conservatives believed that rehabilitation allowed for permissive practices that victimized innocent citizens. Liberals were interested in doing justice; conservatives were interested in controlling crime.

[Yet even while its support plummeted, rehabilitation] did not vanish from the nation's prisons; most institutions continued to offer some combination of substance abuse treatment, educational programs, and vocational training. In part, treatment survived because of the correctional staffs' continued support of offender treatment and in part because prison programming kept offenders busy. But even if the status quo tended to persist, the commitment to building therapeutic communities virtually evaporated. Punitive goals ascended in importance and created a context that was unsupportive, if not hostile, to treatment advocates.

[The push back against the "nothing works" was led by the development of sophisticated meta-analysis techniques that synthesized the findings of many studies in rigorous ways.* A leading "meta-analyst" was Mark Lipsey.]

---

* *Ed. note*: Please see the statistical abstract for a longer definition of **meta-analysis**.

Lipsey's meta-analyses, conducted on interventions with juveniles, yielded three findings. First and most important, the view that nothing works in treatment is wrong. Thus, in a study coauthored with David Wilson, he computed the overall effect size to be [6 percentage points: if the control group had a recidivism rate of 50%, those in rehabilitation programs had a recidivism rate of 44%.] This reduction is modest but not inconsequential, especially when dealing with high-risk offenders. More importantly, this overall effect size covered a grab bag of programs, including some with a primarily punitive orientation. But what if different types of interventions had different effects? Might not some programs work better than others?

This question leads to the second conclusion that can be drawn from Lipsey's work: The effects of interventions are heterogeneous, not homogenous. Lipsey found that the most effective interventions used modalities that were clearly rehabilitation-oriented, including counseling, interpersonal skills, cognitive-behavioral, and multi-model. Lipsey and Wilson noted that the overall [6] percent[age point] figure was "not representative of the impact achieved by the best programs." Indeed, the most effective interventions "were capable of reducing recidivism rates by as much as [20 percentage points], an accomplishment of considerable practical value in terms of expense and social damage associated with the delinquent behavior of these juveniles."

The third finding involves the other end of the effectiveness continuum: What does not work? A key finding of Lipsey and Wilson is that "deterrence programs," such as shock incarceration, are ineffective. There is now substantial evidence that interventions with a punitive focus (e.g., scared straight programs, control-oriented intensive supervision programs) are ineffective. Recent evidence also suggests that giving offenders a sentence of imprisonment compared with a noncustodial sanction has either a null or slightly criminogenic effect.* Similar results are found when inmates experience more, rather than less, painful conditions while incarcerated. In short, placing offenders in prison, especially harsh ones, or in punitively oriented correctional programs, has no specific deterrent [or rehabilitative] effects.

For [decades], the United States has been in the grip of what [one criminologist] calls "the penal harm movement." In the past decade, however, cracks in this movement have appeared and widened. Most recently, the financial crisis and strained state treasuries have fostered the view that mass incarceration, at least at current levels, is "not sustainable." State prison populations have declined for the first time in four decades. The punitive paradigm appears to have exhausted itself. As

---

* *Ed. note*: This does not mean that incarceration is counter-effective as a whole. It means that incarceration is no better than, and sometimes worse than, non-prison based options, though still perhaps better than nothing at all.

crime has receded as a political issue, officials have little to gain from looking tougher than their electoral opponents.

This has created an opportunity for another "new penology." Advocates of rehabilitation have an opportunity to design an agenda that specifies how best to conduct the correctional enterprise. [The rising appeal of rehabilitation can be seen in changing political rhetoric, in an increased focus on re-entry issues, on the rise of specialty treatment courts, and so on.]

[W]e would do well to recognize that rehabilitation's appeal is fundamentally rooted in its claim of utility. Correctional treatment comes with the promise that a human services response will not only improve offenders' lives but also enhance public safety. For this reason, it is essential that treatment programs work—that they reduce recidivism. Much as in medicine, interventions that provide comfort but not cure—and that cost a fair amount—will lose their legitimacy. And in corrections, the alternative to effective treatment has been the embrace of harsh punishment, including the fallback position that incapacitating the wicked will at least keep them off the streets for a while. Much is at stake.

As faith in rehabilitation declined sharply heading into the 1970s, an article published by Robert Martinson in 1974 is credited with with galvanizing the argument that "nothing works." But as Cullen and Paul Gendreau explain, the real lesson from Martinson's study was less "nothing works" than "what we are currently doing doesn't work":

> In 1974, Robert Martinson published his celebrated assessment of the effectiveness of correctional treatment, "What Works? Questions and Answers About Prison Reform"—an article that would have both substantive and symbolic significance. Martinson presented the results of an analysis of 231 program evaluation studies conducted between 1945 and 1967. "With few and isolated exceptions," he pessimistically concluded, "the rehabilitative efforts that have been reported so far have had no appreciable effect on recidivism." Importantly, Martinson then went on to pose a provocative question. "Do all of these studies," he asked, "lead irrevocably to the conclusion that *nothing works* [italics added], that we haven't the faintest clue about how to rehabilitate offenders and reduce recidivism?" He refrained from answering in the affirmative, but it was clear what he was suggesting. Soon after, it became a criminological wisdom that "nothing works" in the correctional system to change offenders.
>
> [Had criminologists been more skeptical,] they might have noticed that the Martinson review covered only 138 measures of recidivism—not 231—and that in these studies, fewer than 75

of the evaluated interventions could be called "treatments." They also might not have chosen to ignore Martinson's admission that his review did not include a category for behaviorally oriented programs—even though readily available literature at this time showed that this treatment modality had achieved promising results with other problem populations and had demonstrated successes in some correctional settings.

The technical finding of "no appreciable effects" [should] have been treated as regrettable and then used as evidence that correctional treatment was still based on faulty theories of crime, was using scientifically inappropriate intervention technique, and/or lacked quality in its implementation.[11]

In other words, the problem was less that inmates were inherently irredeemable, but that the programs being used weren't effective. Since then, social scientists have developed a much clearer sense of what in fact works. One dominant paradigm:

> argues that, while illegal behavior may have unique features, it occurs largely by the same processes as do other forms of human conduct, whether antisocial or prosocial. In a sense, this theory argues that behavior is, in the end, behavior, and that it is altered—including criminal behavior—by standard rather than by exotic means. Interventions based on this approach focus on creating learning experiences for offenders in which new (prosocial) cognitions and behaviors replace old (antisocial) ones.[12]

This approach focuses on positively reinforcing good behavior and sanctioning bad behavior ("operant conditioning"), on modeling prosocial behavior, and on "cognitive restructuring" to alter antisocial attitudes. As the Cullen reading above points out, the evidence indicates that these tactics tend to be more effective the less punitive the regime in which they are used.

Over time, psychologists, criminologists, and other social scientists have developed a comprehensive list of empirically-validated risk factors that rehabilitation efforts must target. These include:

> antisocial attitudes and values, antisocial peer associations, personality factors (e.g., lack of self-control and self-management skills, aggression, impulsivity), dysfunctional family/marital relationships, substance abuse, lack of education and employment skills, and poor use of leisure time. In contrast, other factors that were once thought to be important—such as

---

[11] Francis T. Cullen and Paul Gendreau, *From Nothing Works to What Works: Changing Professional Ideology in the 21st Century*, 81 PRISON J. 313, 321–322 (2001).

[12] Francis T. Cullen & Paula Smith, *Treatment and Rehabilitation*, in THE OXFORD HANDBOOK OF CRIME AND CRIMINAL JUSTICE 156, 168 (Michael Tonry, ed., 2011).

low self-esteem and fear of official punishment—have not been found to be related to recidivism.[13]

Analysts have also determined that resources should be aimed at the those who pose the greatest risk: they tend to need the most interventions, and the returns on modifying their behavior are the largest.

There are two major challenges that even these more-successful interventions face, one conceptually simple to address (if still difficult in practice), the other more generally difficult to manage. The conceptually straight-forward concern is that even effective programs will fail if they are not properly implemented. Pilot programs are often well-funded and staffed with well-trained, highly-motivated practitioners; as these programs get rolled out more widely, the quality of treatment may decline as budgets get stretched and prisons find themselves hiring lower-quality therapists and other clinicians. A tool designed to measure "treatment integrity" by assessing how closely actual treatment programs adhere to an "ideal" model has found that as many as 60% of evaluated programs do not receive passing grades, and only about 6% receive high grades. Not surprisingly, integrity scores and recidivism rates are negatively correlated: well-run programs see high reductions (on the order of 20%), while low-quality programs see next-to-none.[14]

The more confounding conceptual problem relates to human capital development. **Human capital** refers to a person's stock of education, knowledge, skills, health, moral values and other personal attributes. The term "capital" is used because people invest in these skills like any other sort of capital: they go to school, learn skills on the job, eat healthier food, go to church. It is also referred to as capital because just like with physical capital, it depreciates without constant re-investment: skills—whether employment skills or social skills—decay when unused. That human capital clearly suffers while in prison should be clear, and we will return to this point more in Ch. 10. Here, I want to focus on the implications of the well-established fact that investments in all forms of human capital are increasingly more productive the younger a person is.

There are several reasons for this observation. One is simply biological. Younger brains are more impressionable. There is also a rich-gets-richer, cumulative advantage effect at play as well. Someone who develops more skills at age two can make faster advances at age three, and he can then keep building on this initial head start, so earlier investments continue to pay off later in life. Writing specifically about the need to target anti-crime prevention strategies at children, David Farrington and Brandon Welsh state:

---

[13] *Id.* at 170.
[14] *Id.* at 172–173.

Developmental theory postulates that the early years of life are most influential in shaping later experiences. Greg Duncan and Katherine Magnuson . . . note: "Principles of developmental science suggest that although beneficial changes are possible at any point in life, interventions early on may be more effective at promoting well being and competencies compared with interventions undertaken later in life." They further say: "early childhood may provide an unusual window of opportunity for interventions because young children are uniquely receptive to enriching and supportive environments. . . . As individuals age, the gain the independence and ability to shape their environments, rendering intervention efforts more complicated and costly."[15]

As a general rule, the penal system does not get its hands on an inmate until later in life, at least by human capital investment standards. In this case, even an 18-year old is somewhat "old." So while Cullen and other are right to point out that a lot "works," it remains likely (subject to a few important caveats raised in the questions below) that the same dollar investment would have a much greater return if it targeted children instead.

But that raises a difficult coordination problem. Prison rehabilitation programs are managed by prisons and funded from the criminal justice line-item in the state budget (unless they are being run by jails or probation offices, in which case they are funded by county budgets). Early childhood interventions, however, come from education budgets at the state, county, and local levels. Thus there is an obvious externality: if the early childhood intervention both improves test scores (which is the metric by which the educational bureaucracy is judged) and reduces long-run risks of offending (which is not just a distant result but one on which the educational system is not judged), these sorts of programs will be under-provided.

Yet integrating the two is not straight-forward, even putting aside any sort of expected bureaucratic turf-protection and infighting. There are real risks to just focusing on the crime-reducing aspects of early-intervention programs. If policymakers were, say, to start justifying Head Start funding partly on the grounds that it could reduce crime as well, **labeling theory** warns that participants could come to view themselves as being at risk and thus (causally) more likely to offend.

QUESTIONS

1. **The challenge of evaluation I.** Assume that one hundred prisoners sign up a rehabilitation program, and of those one hundred only thirty recidivate. Meanwhile, if we look at the population of prisoners who

---

[15] DAVID P. FARRINGTON AND BRANDON C. WALSH, SAVING CHILDREN FROM A LIFE OF CRIME 8 (2007).

did not participate in the program, sixty out of every one hundred recidivate. Can we say that the program successfully cuts recidivism by 50%?

2. **The challenge of evaluation II.** Assume again that one hundred prisoners enter an in-prison rehabilitation program, but this time the recidivism rate is the same for both participants and non-participants. Does this mean the program doesn't work? Does your answer change if I add that both types of inmates are released back to the same communities under the same parole conditions?

3. **Targeting resources.** The readings above seem to suggest that rehabilitation resources should be targeted at the higher-security level prisons, since they hold the riskiest offenders. Are there pragmatic reasons *not* to do this? Would your answer change if it turns out that prisoners tend to be older in more-secure prisons? If time served tends to be longer in those prisons?

4. **Targeting children or offenders.** Targeting future offenders when they are young (i.e., pre-offending) is more effective than working with them when they are older (i.e., post-conviction). But identifying at-risk offenders is harder the younger they are. Recall the difficulty of determining life-time trajectories in advance, or consider the fact that diagnosing psychopathy in young children is profoundly difficult, if not nearly impossible.[16] And while perhaps as many as 1/3 of all Americans have a criminal record (at least an arrest, though not necessarily a conviction, and not necessarily for a felony), the number of *serious* offenders is much smaller. What problems does this pose for an aggressive effort to target serious offenders in advance? What sort of net would you need to cast? What costs are associated with it?

5. **Is rehabilitation punishment?** Does the provision of educational and social services to offenders—but often not to victims, at least not on the same scale—offend your basic notion of how those who break the law should be handled? If so, under what types of conditions are you more or less inclined to support rehabilitation, or what types of treatments seem more normatively appealing? Would you be more or less open to rehabilitation as the proper punishment for someone who, say, had a well-diagnosed impulse-control problem as compared to someone without such a condition?

6. **What limits exist for rehabilitation?** We asked this question with deterrence and incapacitation, and we can ask it here as well: does a theory of rehabilitation impose any clear limits on the nature of punishment? Consider the California case of *In re Lynch*.[17] John Lynch was convicted of second-degree indecent exposure twice, first in 1958 and again in 1967. California law at the time allowed the judge to impose an indeterminate sentence of one year to life on Lynch for his second offense, which the judge did. The indefinite detention had a rehabilitative goal. Just as we do not release someone from a hospital until he is healthy, likewise we should not

---

[16] If nothing else, two of the major diagnostic traits of psychopathy—narcissism and impulsivity—are simply defining traits of childhood. See, e.g., Jennifer Kahn, "Can You Call a 9-Year Old a Psychopath?" NEW YORK TIMES SUNDAY MAGAZINE MM32 (May 11, 2012).

[17] 8 Cal. 3d 410 (1977).

release a prisoner from prison until we think he is "cured"—and who knows how long that will take. Is such a long potential sentence at all justified? If not, do the limits come from rehabilitation theory itself or somewhere else?

And obviously we can—and do—target people for rehabilitation before they even offend. Is this morally problematic? Does it matter if the crime-reducing effect is just a collateral benefit of a broader early-intervention program, such as Head Start? Putting aside concerns about labeling (which is a major issue), would it be okay to intervene with high-risk kids solely from an anti-crime goal?

A.2. Just Deserts/Retributivism

The consequentialist theories we have considered so far are all united by a common thread, that the goal of punishment is to advance an overarching sense of the "public good" based on people's utilitarian perceptions. The primary alternative to these theories is a non-consequentialist effort to impose the "morally just" sanction on a defendant, regardless of its social-utilitarian costs. Within criminal law, this approach is referred to interchangeably as **Retributivism** or **Just Deserts**.[18] The goal of retributivism is to determine what this morally correct sanction is, regardless of its deterrent, incapacitory, or rehabilitative effect.

The classic statement of the retributivist perspective comes from Immanuel Kant, who wrote in *The Philosophy of the Law* that:

> Juridical punishment can never be administered merely as a means of promoting another good either with regard to the criminal himself or to civil society, but must in all cases be imposed only because the individual on whom it is inflicted *has committed a crime*. For one man ought never to be dealt with merely as means subservient to the purpose of another. . . . The penal law is a categorical imperative; and woe to him who creeps through the serpent-windings of utilitarianism to discover some advantage that may discharge him from the justice of punishment. . . .

The biggest challenge, of course, is determining what the "proper" punishment should be. The obvious point of departure is *lex talionis*, or an eye for an eye, which is a clear and straight-forward rule. But Heidi Hurd, a criminal philosopher, points out the problems that quickly arise with *lex talionis*:

> [N]o retributivist would embrace the claim that the state ought generally to be in the business of perpetrating the horrors on offenders that match in kind the horrors that they perpetrated

---

[18] Perhaps somewhat confusingly, an archaic definition of "desert"—which today refers only to arid wastes—is "what someone deserves." That said, many people still spell it "just desserts," seemingly referring to the idea of being served what you have earned.

on their innocent victims. No one in today's academy believes that the state ought to satisfy the demands of retributivism by torturing the torturer, raping the rapist, or flashing the flasher. And what would it even mean to be treasonous to the traitor?[19]

Hurd isn't entirely right that we reject *lex talionis*, as evidenced by support for the death penalty. But she is right in general that we find such eye-for-an-eye approaches unappealing, at least officially.[20] Moreover, *lex talionis* provides little to no practical guidance at all for victimless crimes. What is the proper punishment for a drug dealer, for a prostitute or her john, or for an environmental crime?

A leading alternative is the idea of "equality and proportionality," that more-blameworthy offenses should be punished more, and less-blameworthy offenses should be punished less, and similar offenses should be punished similarly.[21] Michael Tonry explains this idea well:

> Andrew von Hirsch has . . . shown how a punishment system can be devised and justified that has equality and proportionality as central elements. For many people, there is a strong intuitive appeal in [such] a punishment system. . . . Public opinion surveys have repeated demonstrated strong public support for the maxim "treat like cases alike and different cases differently."
>
> [Von Hirsch] distinguishes between ordinal and cardinal magnitudes of punishments. The cardinal magnitude is the unknowable, single deserved penalty. Ordinal magnitude indicates a crime's seriousness relative to other crimes. In von Hirsch's scheme, cardinal magnitudes can be approximated or negotiated for use in setting the "anchoring points" of a punishment scale, the most and (possibly) the least severe punishments that can appropriately be imposed on offenders. Within these anchoring points, punishments can be scaled in terms of relative severity of offenses. Thus, the combination of cardinal anchors with ordinal rankings celebrates equality (all level 8 offenses receive similar punishments) and proportionality (less serious offenses receive less severe punishments . . .). Some subsidiary issues remain a bit vague, including specification of anchoring points, the step problem

---

[19] Heidi M. Hurd, *Expressing Doubts About Expressivism*, 2005 U. CHI. LEGAL FORUM 405, 415 (2005).

[20] In many cases, politicians and other commentators suggest that some of the violence, including sexual violence, that persists in prisons constitutes an acceptable form of punishment; such views reflect a *lex talionis* perspective, even while official policies—such as the federal Prison Rape Elimination Act—seek to minimize such harms.

[21] Note that proportionality is often embraced by consequentialists as well: a proportional system may be seen as being more just, and just systems are thought to be more effective, since people appear to be more willing to voluntarily comply with a system's rules the more they think those rules are fair.

(how many severity categories), and the interval problem (are the severity differences between offense levels the same throughout the scale . . . ?).

The overall premise of von Hirsch's argument is that punishment is an exercise in blaming, and proportionality is a necessary implication. Persons committing relatively more severe offenses are relatively more blameworthy and deserve relatively more severe punishments.[22]

Proportionality is not the only standard, however. Others, for example, have argued for "parsimony." One of its leading proponents was the late Norval Morris, who:

> argued that desert is a limiting, not a defining, principle of punishment and that policy should prescribe imposition of the least severe "not undeserved" sanction that meets legitimate policy ends. Within these outer bounds of "not undeserved" punishments Morris has consistently argued for observance of a principle of parsimony.[23]

As support for rehabilitation faded in the 1970s, that for retribution (along with elements of deterrence and incapacitation) rose, and it remains one of the leading justifications for punishment today. Rehabilitation fell from favor as part of a much broader loss of faith in technocratic expertise in general, even well outside of criminal justice circles. Such an attitudinal shift privileged more-emotional responses to solving problems, including crime.

A key challenge that retributivism faces, though, is that everyone might have a different sense of what is morally just. In fact, an irony of just deserts is that many of its original proponents, such as Andrew Von Hirsch, saw it as a way to *reduce* what they perceived in the 1970s as overly-harsh punishments. Yet it was ultimately embraced, at least by American policymakers, as one way to justify increasingly *severe* sanctions.

John Kleining ably discusses the challenges that retribution has faced as a policy matter:

> A review of the philosophical literature from 50 years ago and before leaves the strong impression that an earlier generation had . . . consigned the notion of desert . . . to the dustbin of history. Indeed, for much of the previous two centuries, various forms of "forward-looking" consequentialism had gained the ascendancy . . . and . . . the "backwards-looking" idea of desert was often asserted to express a gut reaction to wrongdoing, no more than a primitive response to serious . . . wrongdoing.

---

[22] Michael Tonry, *Proportionality, Parsimony, and Interchangeability of Punishments*, in WHY PUNISH? HOW MUCH? 222–223 (Michael Tonry, ed., 2010).

[23] *Id.* at 232.

During the 1960s and 1970s, however, desert underwent something of an academic revival, as various liberal theorists sought to disentangle it from its emotivist associations and to articulate its connections with important dimensions of justice. [Yet fairly quickly] desert began to sink again into liberal desuetude. Those who had advanced desert as an appropriate and morally critical "gauge" for penal justice had trouble shaking it loose from powerful populist expressions of revenge or a retaliatory "getting back and getting even." Even when desert's connections to proportionality were acknowledged, its practical determinations were often beholden to conservative tough-on-crime policies. A good number of liberally-inclined writers, appalled by the punitiveness of—especially—American culture . . . gradually migrated back to rehabilitative approaches or [towards restorative justice techniques].

And yet desert has refused to go away quietly. . . . In a moral and institutional environment whose theorizing has been largely governed by consequentialist thinking . . . desert's . . . implicit proportionality constraint[ ] has seemed to provide an important check on the potential for an oppressive open-endedness associated with results-oriented thinking.[24]

Michael Tonry echoes these concerns. He notes that politicians often pay lip-service to retributivism, but they are not embracing its core principles when they do so:

> Some policy entrepreneurs used retributive-sounding language—"Do the time, do the crime [sic]" or "Adult time for adult crime"—but they did not typically mean that punishments should be apportioned in a consistent way to the gravity of the offenses and the culpability of offenders. Instead, they meant that offenders should receive whatever punishments policy makers specified, whether or not these sentences respected retributive principles or ideas about proportionality. . . .[25]

He then points out that this is a problem on both the severe and lenient ends of the scale. Laws such as life without parole, three-strike laws, and mandatory minimums all run the risk of being systematically disproportionate. But so too do more-lenient interventions such as drug courts, re-entry programs, and restorative justice programs.

The following questions flesh out retributivist theories in a bit more detail and address a few remaining questions with the approach.

---

[24] John Kleining, *What Does Wrongdoing Deserve?* In RETRIBUTIVISM HAS A PAST: HAS IT A FUTURE? 46, 47–48 (Michael Tonry, ed., 2011).

[25] Michael Tonry, *Preface*, in RETRIBUTIVISM HAS A PAST: HAS IT A FUTURE? vii, vii (Michael Tonry, ed., 2011).

QUESTIONS

1. **Objective vs. subjective retributivism.** There are two sources of blameworthiness: the magnitude of the harm and the culpability of the offender. We can think of these as "objective" and "subjective" branches of retributivism, depending on whether we prioritize the objective harm or the subjective intent. Though often correlated, these two approaches can cut in opposite directions. Is an intentional aggravated assault, for example, worse than a reckless murder? How should we balance these competing interests when they are not aligned? Is there a principled approach we can adopt?

Moreover, does your answer shape the factors you are willing to consider at sentencing? Consider two defendants who commit the same simple assault and are identical to each other in all relevant ways except that Mike is 18 and Paul is 28. Should they receive the same punishment?

2. **Subjective experiences of punishment.** Should sentencing regimes take into account the subjective experience of punishment? Prison, for example, will be a much more dangerous experience for a weaker inmate or for one unaffiliated with any gangs before arriving. Should such inmates receive shorter sentences to offset the greater deprivation prison entails? If so, what would the deprivation-duration "exchange rate" look like, and who would be qualified to calculate it?

3. **Can retributivists be non-consequentialists?** There are three (inter-related) goals that are central to retributivism: (1) all guilty individuals should be punished, (2) all guilty should receive the proper punishment, and (3) no innocent person should be punished. Does the fact that we live in a world of limited resources force retributivists to think along consequentialist lines? Can a government with only $1 million to spend on the criminal justice system fully accomplish all these goals? Even if you feel that retributivists cannot be purely non-consequentialist, does this mean that they must adopt a utilitarian or utilitarian-like consequentialism?[26]

4. **Can utilitarians be non-retributive?** Consider the following rough, stylized fact: people are more likely to voluntarily obey the law the more they respect it. To what extent does this claim impose limits on technocratic, consequentialist approaches and necessitate a more emotional, retributive response to crime control?

5. **Where is the victim?** Much of retributive theory focuses on ensuring that the offender receives his just punishment. But does such an approach overlook the moral rights of (abstract) victims? Assume that the optimal consequentialist theory results in 100 murders per year, but the correct retributive theory produces 125 murders per year.[27] Those additional twenty-five murders reflect true moral wrongs, although it is impossible to identify which twenty-five victims died as a result of adopting non-

---

[26] For a fuller discussion of this idea, see LOUIS KAPLOW & STEVEN SHAVELL, FAIRNESS VERSUS WELFARE (2002).

[27] Note that we do not care if we are, say, deterrence theorists or retributivists if we are suggesting the same sanctions (and thus the same outcomes). The theories only matter when they make different recommendations, which by definition will result in different crime rates.

consequentialist policies. Is this a serious limitation to just deserts? Can we adjust the theory accordingly?

Pushing further, is it possible for a retributivist theory to result in *fewer* murders? If so, what are the consequentialists taking into account that the retributivists are not and vice versa?

6. **Who decides 1: Democracy or elites?** A pluralistic society like ours will not have a common definition of the "morally just" sanction. So the question of who should decide what is just arises immediately. Paul Robinson raises a concern with simply letting the democratic process select the proper sanction (what he calls "empirical desert"):

> The community's shared views of justice may simply be wrong. Consider the lessons of slaveholding Southerners before the Civil War and the treatment of Jews in prewar Germany. Only a transcendent notion of justice, derived independently from principles of right and good . . . can assure that the law accords with moral principles. Accordingly, from a retributive perspective, empirical desert might sometimes seem a poor proxy for, or even a subversion of, a scheme based on a proper moral conception of desert.[28]

Put aside any concerns with Godwin's Law.[29] Is Robinson's concern legitimate? If we can't trust the public to decide, who do we trust? How do we choose these people? From where does their legitimacy come? Is there anything unique to criminal sentencing that allows it to remove itself from traditional democratic constraints?

7. **Who decides 2: Localness.** As noted in Chapter 1, crime is geographically dense. How localized should sanctioning be? If the moral values of high-crime urban neighborhoods differ from those of low-crime urban neighborhoods, and if cities differ from suburbs, and if cities in industrialized states differ from those in less-industrialized states, etc., etc., at what level should sentencing decisions be made?

Keep this question in mind in the next chapter, which examines the often-chaotic way in which responsibility is allocated across city, county, state, and federal agencies. Might some of the various pockets of discretion exist in part to allow more-local authorities to make decisions that conform to local morality? Are you comfortable with, say, police choosing what crimes to pursue based on precinct-level (or city-level, or county-level) views of what matters most?

8. **Anchoring effects and fragile moral intuitions.** As noted in Chapter 1, one powerful heuristic is the anchoring effect. People who observe higher random numbers may price a given bottle of wine more expensively than people who see a lower random number simply due to that number

---

[28] Paul H. Robinson, CRIMINAL LAW 98 (2012).

[29] There are two versions of Godwin's Law, the positive and normative. The positive holds that if any debate on the Internet goes on long enough, the probability that someone will be compared to Hitler approaches one. The normative version is that invoking Hitler to make a point generally means the invoking party automatically loses the debate.

"anchoring" them at a high value. Does this raise any concerns with asking people—whether the person on the street or the criminal philosopher in his office—what they think the morally "right" sanction is? Is this such a concern for proportionality-based regimes?

9. **Different concepts or different goals.** Retributivists criticize deterrence theorists (among others) for violating proportionality's requirement that if crime X is worse than crime Y, it should be punished more severely. Are deterrence theorists necessarily unconcerned with proportionality? Or are they focused on proportionality, just using a different goal as their baseline?

A.3. THE LACK OF CONSENSUS

That we have multiple theories of punishment wouldn't matter if each theory reached the same conclusion about how to punish a particular offender. And while in many cases the various theories may all make the same general recommendation, there are many issues where they may disagree. Consider the significance of the defendant's age:

> **Problem:** Sam and Thomas are each convicted of separate aggravated assaults. Both acts are basically identical, and Sam and Thomas as effectively identical to each other with one exception, that Sam is 18 and Thomas is 34. Who should be punished more severely if the goal is incapacitation? deterrence?[30] rehabilitation? retribution focused on the objective harm? on the subjective culpability?

Given that the theories can all cut in different directions, it would helpful if criminal codes provided guidance on how to approach difficult sentencing situations. Consider, however, the following examples:

New York Penal Law § 1.05: General Purposes:

The general purposes of the provisions in this chapter are:

4. To differentiate on reasonable grounds between serious and minor offenses and to prescribe proportionate penalties therefor;

6. To insure the public safety by preventing the commission of offenses through the deterrent influence of the sentences authorized, the rehabilitation of those convicted, and their confinement when required in the interests of public protection.

Colorado Criminal Code § 18–1–102.5: Purposes of Code with Respect to Sentencing:

The purposes of this code with respect to sentencing are:

---

[30] This is perhaps the trickiest of the ones, so a hint could help. Younger people are more impulsive, so a given sentence length deters less (since care less about future costs). The easy answer is "make sentences longer." But can you see an argument for "make sentences *shorter*"?

a. To punish a convicted offender by assuring the imposition of a sentence he deserves in relation to the seriousness of his offense;

b. To assure the fair and consistent treatment of all convicted offenders by eliminating unjustified disparity in sentences, providing fair warning of the nature of the sentence to be imposed, and establishing fair procedures for the imposition of sentences;

c. To prevent crime and promote respect for the law by providing an effective deterrent to others likely to commit similar offenses;

d. To promote rehabilitation by encouraging correctional programs that elicit the voluntary cooperation and participation of convicted offenders;

e. To select a sentence, a sentence length, and a level of supervision that addresses the offender's individual characteristics and reduces the potential that the offender will engage in criminal conduct after completing his or her sentence. . . .

Georgia Statutes § 16–1–2:

The general purposes of this title are:

4. To prescribe penalties which are proportionate to the seriousness of crimes and which permit recognition of differences in rehabilitation possibilities among individual criminals.

Minnesota Statutes § 609.01:

[The criminal section] shall be construed according to the fair import of its terms, to promote justice, and to effect its purposes which are declared to be:

1. to protect the public safety and welfare by preventing the commission of crime through the deterring effect of the sentences authorized, the rehabilitation of those convicted, and their confinement when the public safety and interest requires. . . .

Federal Government: 18 U.S.C. § 3553(a): Factors To Be Considered in Imposing a Sentence:

The court shall impose a sentence sufficient, but not greater than necessary, to comply with the purposes set forth in paragraph (2) of this subsection. The court, in determining the particular sentence to be imposed, shall consider—

2. the need for the sentence imposed—

    a. to reflect the seriousness of the offense, to promote respect for the law, and to provide just punishment for the offense;

    b. to afford adequate deterrence to criminal conduct;

c. to protect the public from further crimes of the defendant; and

d. to provide the defendant with needed educational or vocational training, medical care, or other correctional treatment in the most effective manner;

As is immediately clear, these statutes consistently embrace almost every theory of punishment—and in doing so effectively embrace *none*. In a recent sentencing case, *Booker v. United States*,[31] Justice Scalia made this very argument in a blistering dissent. The majority had weakened the binding effect of the federal sentencing guidelines but argued that the impact of its opinion would be slight because 18 U.S.C. § 3553(a) would still provide judges with guidance about how to sentence defendants. After pointing out that § 3553(a) lists all major theories of punishment, Scalia continues:

> The statute provides no order of priority among all those factors, but since the three just mentioned [deterrence, incapacitation, and retribution] are the fundamental criteria governing penology, the statute . . . authorizes the judge to apply his own perceptions of just punishment, deterrence, and protection of the public. . . . [D]istrict courts have discretion to sentence anywhere within the ranges authorized by statute. . . .[32]

In other words, § 3553(a) is too vague and all-encompassing to impose *any* restrictions on judicial sentencing behavior.

In this section I consider two efforts to impose some structure on this unwieldy mess of normative options. The first, developed by Norval Morris, is the idea of **limiting retributivism**, that retribution provides upper and lower bounds on sentences, but within those ranges consequentialist theories dominate. The second, made by Paul Robinson, attempts to separate out retributive from consequentialist punishment. Robinson argues that the criminal law should only impose retributive punishments, and more-consequentialist sanctions should be handled by a separate preventative system.

It is worth noting that at the same time that Robinson attempts to separate out retributive and consequentialist theories, he also raises an interesting path for *unifying* them. As the Robinson reading below demonstrates, he argues that the most effective consequentialist sanctions are the ones that are (viewed as) morally just: the issue is less, say, deterrence *or* retribution but more deterrence *through* retribution. But first let's start with limiting retributivism.

---

[31] 543 U.S. 220 (2005). We will examine this case in much more depth in Chapter 6.
[32] 543 U.S. at 287.

Richard S. Frase, *Punishment Purposes*
58 STANFORD L. REV. 67, 75–79 (2005)

[N]o jurisdiction in the United States or elsewhere has ever adopted . . . a one-dimensional approach. Instead, almost every system has adopted some form of what Norval Morris called "limiting retributivism". . . . Under this widely endorsed and adopted model, the offender's desert defines a range of morally justified punishments, setting upper and lower limits on the severity of penalties that may fairly be imposed. . . . These upper and lower limits also promote the utilitarian benefits of uniformity and proportionality. Within the range of deserved penalties, case-specific incapacitation, rehabilitation, deterrence, and other sentencing goals may be pursued, but only to the extent that they are needed in a given case.

Morris argued that desert can only define a range of penalties because the very concept of desert is inherently imprecise. In any given case there will be widespread agreement that certain penalties are clearly undeserved (because they are either excessively severe or excessively lenient). But there may be little political or philosophical consensus on the offender's precise deserts, even relative to other offenders committing the same crime.

But if a range of morally permissible penalties exists, why not sentence all offenders at the top of the range, or at least use that as the starting point in order to maximize crime-control effects? Morris's opposite presumption, in favor of the least severe penalty in the range, is based on both moral and practical grounds. The moral arguments are analogous to those that underlie the requirement that guilt be established by elaborate trial procedures and proof beyond a reasonable doubt: punishment intrudes on physical liberty and other very important rights, and the crime-control benefits of punishment are uncertain. Thus, the burden should be on the state to justify each additional increment of punishment severity.

The practical arguments for preferring sentences less severe than the offender's maximum desert flow not only from efficiency concerns (less severity is often adequate to achieve all utilitarian goals) but also from the pervasive need to encourage and reward cooperation from those accused of crime. [Also, i]ncarcerated defendants sent to prison or jail must have an incentive to cooperate with institutional rules and programs. Sentences must also leave room for backup sanctions—subsequent tightening of control (e.g., by revocation of probation or parole) if the defendant fails to cooperate—even if that failure is not, in itself, very blameworthy.

For all of these moral and practical reasons, limiting retributivism has been widely endorsed by scholars, model code drafters, legislators, sentencing commissions, judges, and practitioners. Some version of limiting retributivism has also been the basis for most contemporary sentencing laws. Indeterminate systems (still the most common sentencing regime) reflect a very loose version of this approach; most American sentencing guidelines systems embody a more precise and structured form of limiting retributivism. A range of allowable sanctions is provided for each case. The limits of sanction severity (tops and bottoms of the ranges) are scaled according to offense severity and prior conviction record, with the former usually having greater weight.

The Minnesota Sentencing Guidelines, in effect since 1980, represent a good example of limiting retributivism in operation. The modified just deserts sentencing philosophy adopted in Minnesota sets desert-based upper and lower limits on sanction severity, recognizes the principle of parsimony, leaves substantial scope for the application of non-desert sentencing purposes, retains substantial case-specific flexibility, and tailors overall sanction severity levels to available resources. Minnesota's guidelines have achieved a stable and workable balance between the conflicting purposes and limitations of punishment.

Paul Robinson is unpersuaded by the arguments for limiting retribution, arguing that while Morris "conceives of desert as having only vague requirements . . . To those who study the demands of desert, its requirements are not so vague or flexible."[33] Instead he proposes separating out the punitive function of detention from its protective part. Robinson's primary concern is that the US penal system has moved from backwards-looking retributivism to forward-looking prevention without changing its rhetoric. We still claim to "punish," but Robinson argues that one cannot "punish dangerousness":

> [I]t is impossible to "punish dangerousness." To "punish" is "to cause (a person) to undergo pain, loss, or suffering for a crime or wrongdoing"—therefore, punishment can only exist in relation to a past wrong. "Dangerous" means "likely to cause injury, pain, etc."—that is, dangerousness describes a threat of future harm. One can "restrain," "detain," or "incapacitate" a dangerous person, but one cannot logically "punish" dangerousness.

Robinson points out that unemployment, youthfulness, and growing up without a father are all predictors of future dangerousness, and thus their presence should result in a longer sentence were "dangerousness" the driving theory of sanctioning. Yet, he argues, it would be clearly (to whom?) un*just* to rely on these factors, whatever their preventative effect.

---

[33] Paul H. Robinson, *Punishing Dangerousness: Cloaking Preventive Detention as Criminal Justice*, 114 HARV. L. REV. 1429 (2001).

To Robinson, the unjustness of using these preventative factors is twofold. To start, their use is simply morally unjust. But he also argues that people are more likely to comply with laws they view as just, so relying on unjust terms in the name of prevention might actually *aggravate* offending:

> The justice problems resulting from the conflict between incapacitation and desert are significant not only because doing justice is an important value in its own right—the nonconsequentialist, retributivist view—but also because doing justice can have important crime-prevention effects—the consequentialist, utilitarian argument. [T]he moral credibility of the criminal law, built on community perceptions that the criminal justice system distributes liability and punishment justly, gives the criminal law crime-control power. Requiring the criminal justice system to distribute punishment according to predictions of future dangerousness rather than blameworthiness for past crimes can only undercut the system's moral credibility. As criminal liability is increasingly disconnected from moral blameworthiness, the criminal law can exercise less moral authority to change norms or to cause the internalization of norms. In the long run, then, using the criminal justice system as a mechanism for preventive detention may undercut the very crime prevention goal that is offered to justify such use.

Instead, Robinson proposes separating out the punitive from the preventative. This would entail a specific prison sentence for the backwards-looking punishment part, and more open-ended civil commitment for the forward-looking protective part. Not only would this be more morally just, and thus more widely respected, but it would allow the preventative part to focus on what really matters rather than having to mask its decisions in seemingly backwards-looking choices. As he points out:

> For example, instead of examining each offender to determine the person's actual present dangerousness, the current system uses prior criminal record as a proxy for dangerousness. Prior record has some correlation with dangerousness . . . [b]ut prior record is only a rough approximation of actual dangerousness, and its use in preventive detention guarantees errors of both inclusion and exclusion.

Robinson then points out how a preventive system would differ from a punitive one. Dangerousness would be subject to periodic review, conditions should be better than those used for punishment, detention should be for as short a period of time as necessary, and treatment should be offered if at all effective. He argues that cloaking preventive detention as "punishment" saves the criminal justice system from having to implement such changes.

As Robinson concludes:

> [T]here are understandable concerns about creating a broader system of explicit preventive detention: the Gulag Archipelago potential for governmental abuse is real. But if the alternative is the present system of cloaked preventive detention, the risk is worth taking. An explicit system of post-criminal commitment would better serve both the community and potential detainees.

A broader question worth considering is *why* states fail to nail down a specific sentencing goal in their statutes. One possible answer is that we do not actually *want* to be guided by one theory of punishment: we want to invoke different theories for different situations. For some crimes we may favor a deterrent-based system—perhaps corporate and drug crimes, where we think the actors are more calculating, rational, and aware of the law—while for others we may embrace sanctions even if we know they have no crime-reducing impact at all (think of some support for the death penalty). We may want to incapacitate a younger (and thus riskier) offender while favoring diversion for active-duty combat veterans suffering from PTSD (who may need to be *more* deterred but are also viewed as less morally culpable).

Thus the more important question, and one that seems to be generally unasked in the literature, may be less *what* theory should we follow or *how* should we integrate them but more *when* does *each theory* apply and, perhaps just as important, *who* should get to decide which theory is in effect. There's no good answer to these questions, but they are ones you should keep in mind throughout the course of this book.

QUESTIONS

1. **Prevention and justice.** Robinson argues that a law's "justness" leads to its crime-reducing effectiveness. Might causation run the other way? Robinson never explains *why* a law is seen as just and thus obeyed. Do you think a law's perceived justness is independent of its crime-reducing impact? Think of this another way: Robinson doesn't ask *why* the criminal law has moved towards focusing on future dangerousness (if it really has changed that much anyway).

2. **Historical concerns.** Robinson argues that we have shifted from looking at past culpability to future dangerousness. Think back to Cullen's writings on the history of punishment. Is Robinson's claim consistent with Cullen's history?

3. **Youth, broken homes and justice.** Robinson argues that factors like youthfulness or coming from a broken home are irrelevant to justice. Is

that true? If youthfulness makes a person more likely to commit a crime, is that irrelevant to his moral culpability? But if it matters, *how* does it alter his blameworthiness?

4. **Who decides?** If Robinson is right that people obey a law more because they view it as just than because they are likely to be punished for violating it, what does this tell us about who should determine what punishments look like? How relevant is the fact that crime is geographically quite concentrated? Keep in mind that even when the state legislature sets the official sentence, other actors (police, prosecutors, defense attorneys, judges, etc.) can shape what that sentence ultimate is.

B. POSITIVE THEORIES OF PUNISHMENT

So far this section has considered normative questions of how we *ought* to punish. And it goes without saying that these theories often influence the design of actual sentencing regimes. But sociologists, criminologists, and other social scientists have also pointed out that the criminal justice system is frequently used to advance other goals that may be only tangentially related to crime and punishment.

In fact, some commentators go so far as to argue that punishment, incarceration in particular, actually *fails* as a form of crime control but persists because it advances other social goals. It helps regulate the underclass, it replaces the mental health system, it regulates people's overall behavior in ways unrelated to offending, it is used to roll back advances in civil rights and instill a "new Jim Crow" regime, it helps politicians win elections. Whatever the normative appeal (or the normative failings) of these goals, the arguments go, these are the reasons for why prisons in fact exist and are supported.

In this section I want to focus on two of these explanations: that prison is used to regulate the underclass and the mentally ill, and that prison is used to shape behavior in the name of "power." The former argument is associated with socialist academics such as Georg Rusche and Otto Kirchheimer, while the latter is made most forcefully by the hugely influential but quite controversial scholar Michel Foucault. For now I put aside the New Jim Crow and election-winning theories, since we will consider those in more depth in Chapter 9.

To start, the following excerpt examines theories about punishment and the regulation of the underclass (with a brief initial discussion of Foucault as well), noting both that we use prisons to control the underclass, but also that prisons increasingly seem to serve as part of the social welfare state, providing medical and other services to underserved, at-risk populations.

James Q. Whitman, *The Comparative Study of Criminal Punishment*
1 Ann. Rev. L. & Soc. Sci. 17 (2005)

Much of [the] most interesting literature [on the sociology of punishment] explores the structural relationships between the criminal punishment and other forms of social discipline. The widest-ranging effort of this kind is the most famous modern study of punishment, Foucault's 1975 *Surveiller et Punir*, which aimed to show that the forms of nineteenth-century criminal punishment were intimately related to the forms of discipline in the workplace and the schools. Foucault saw the same forms of regimentation and surveillance appearing in a wide range of nineteenth-century social institutions. Criminal punishment, Foucault argued, could only be understood if we recognized its structural affinities with broader patterns of disciplinary behavior.

Although few studies are as ambitious as Foucault's, many have taken a similar tack, analogizing the structure of criminal punishment to other social practices of discipline. Scholars have put particular emphasis on the analogy between criminal punishment and the discipline of low-status workers. . . . [S]everal historians have demonstrated that the nineteenth-century American penitentiary borrowed its practices, in large measure, from the slave plantation. American prisoners were disciplined like slaves, and indeed they had the technical status of "slaves of the state" into the late twentieth century. Other studies have related the treatment of criminal offenders to the treatment of nonenslaved low-status workers. The implication of these studies is much the same: The way we punish criminals is often closely related to the way we discipline low-status workers, whether free or unfree. Criminal punishment borrows its structures, at least in part, from the structures of labor discipline.

There are also other studies that relate practices of criminal punishment to the treatment of low-status laborers. In particular, scholars have seen important connections between the management of prisons and the management of the low-wage economy. Some of those connections follow directly from the fact that prisons remain institutions of labor. Inmates work, in most modern prisons. . . . But the place of prisons in the economy of low-wage labor goes beyond that. Indeed, some powerful arguments have been made by scholars who believe that the deep structures of criminal punishment have to do precisely with the economics of low-wage labor and unemployment.

The pioneering effort to link criminal punishment to the dynamics of the low-wage labor market was made in the 1930s by Georg Rusche and Otto Kirchheimer. [Their argument], which assumed the truth of a Marxist theory of economics, described the relationship between prison and the economic opportunities of the least advantaged workers in society. If conditions in prison were insufficiently harsh, workers might have no incentive not to commit criminal offenses. Such a situation would be intolerable in a capitalist economy, which could maintain low wages only so long as a large number of workers were seeking employment rather than accepting incarceration. The logic of capitalism thus demanded that conditions of imprisonment be at least somewhat harsher than the conditions of civilian life for the average unemployed or low-wage worker.

Rusche and Kirchheimer's argument is very elegant. [Their] core claim . . . is clearly correct, and it remains provocative: Prisons are not just institutions in which punishment is administered. They are also institutions that distribute social resources, including food, shelter, medical care, and more. This means that there is always some possibility, in every society, that imprisonment may serve in part as means of providing social support and social services to disadvantaged segments of the population.

Some of the most important recent literature has pursued exactly that insight. David Garland . . . emphasized the structural connections between imprisonment and the social welfare state. Prison administrators tend to think of themselves as in the business of providing social services to a population of inmates made up of poorly integrated and poorly socialized individuals. Although punishment, of course, plays some role in prison, it does not necessarily dominate in the way one might expect. A similar argument has recently been made by Loïc Wacquant, who sees modern prisons as institutions increasingly devoted to housing the desperately poor in societies that have given up on maintaining a social welfare state. As Wacquant presents it, prisons are playing an increasingly important role: From being one of many institutions oriented toward the management of the lowest social orders, the prison is gradually evolving into the primary institution serving that purpose. This does not necessarily mean, however, that they have lost their punishment function. On the contrary, it may be that, in our use of prisons, we have substituted punishment for the provision of social services. In a dire and depressing return to the world of early modern Europe, our prisons are once again becoming workhouses.

Kindred arguments have been made about the relationship between the management of prisons and the treatment of one disadvantaged population in particular: the mentally ill. Early modern prison/workhouses also served as insane asylums, and scholars have often seen a connection between penal and mental institutions. Foucault began as a student of insanity before moving to the related topic of criminal punishment. In an influential argument, Erving Goffman related criminal punishment to the social structures of the insane asylum. And today some reformers, such as Human Rights Watch, observe that a stunning proportion of incarcerated persons in the United States is mentally ill. This suggests that American prisons are becoming the institution of last resort, or in many localities the only available institution, for the confinement of the mentally ill. Again, one fears that we are experiencing a dire and depressing return to the world of early modern Europe.

Criminal punishment is only one aspect of a much larger realm of social life: the realm of the management of low-wage, low-status, and disadvantaged populations.

As we will see in Chapter 10, prisons increasingly provide services to inmates the inmates otherwise would not get, such as dental exams, medical check-ups, mental health evaluations, drug treatment, and education. Some of these services, like education and drug treatment, may fall within the ambit of traditional "rehabilitation," but many, such as the medical services, do not. Obviously the state is not running prisons *in order to* provide these services. But to the extent that correctional spending reduces budgets for other, more general public health and educational programs—a widely made, but empirically quite complicated, claim—prisons (or other criminal justice agencies such as drug courts) *in effect* become key service providers.

Question: An obvious criticism of this approach is that a person shouldn't need to get a felony conviction in order to receive many of these services. Non-felons deserve these services as well, treatment is more effective and less costly outside of correctional facilities, and so on. But try to think of possible justifications for this approach. To focus the analysis, concentrate on mental health and drug addiction issues. Most mentally ill people and most users of drugs do not engage in serious crimes. So how does a prison-based service provision system allocate scarce treatment resources? In a world of limited governmental budgets is this a justifiable distribution? What challenges would a more widely-applied, non-prison based system face?

Stephen Raphael provides some evidence on the relationship between prions and mental health treatment. We will look at this issue in more detail in Chapter 10, so I just want to briefly touch on it here. Starting in the 1950s, the United States experienced a dramatic "deinstitutionalization" movement that resulted in the number of people in mental hospitals falling from about 500,000 in the 1950s to under 100,000 by the 1990s. Some of this reduction came about from the rise of pharmaceutical treatments that simply rendered institutionalization unnecessary. But that wasn't the only causal factor, and Raphael produces results suggesting that somewhere between 5% to 14% of the prison population in 1996, or somewhere between 48,000 and 148,000 inmates, can be attributed to a lack of mental hospital beds for these offenders. For these inmates, we are at some level using the prison as a substitute for the asylum.

QUESTIONS

1. **Can the criminal justice system really regulate the underclass?** Whitman focuses on Rusche and Kirchheimer's statement that prisons are a locus for providing services to the poor, but the two also argue that authorities would adjust prison populations in response to labor market conditions. As labor became more plentiful, prison populations would be raised to absorb some of the excess labor and thus minimize social agitation. Is this a realistic theory? How coherent is the criminal justice "system"? Which of its actors would need to coordinate with each other to accomplish this? And what is their incentive for doing so—and with what other political actors would they need to work?

2. **Will incarceration rates still rise as the economy declines?** Put aside the obvious answer to this, that if crime rises as the economy declines (an empirically weak effect, it turns out), then we should expect incarceration to rise with weakening economies. But assume that the crime rate stays flat as unemployment rises. Might we still see incarceration rates rise without any explicit, or even implicit, coordination? As a hint, consider the following: North Carolina's sentencing guidelines list as a mitigating factor that the defendant "has a positive employment history or is gainfully employed."

Shifting gears somewhat, one of the most influential sociological perspectives on the social justifications for prisons, at least within academic circles, is the one developed by Michel Foucault in his *Discipline and Punish*. David Garland does a good job summarizing Foucault's complex theories.

David Garland, *Punishment and Modern Society,* Ch. 6: "Punishment and the Technologies of Power: The Work of Michel Foucault"
(1990)

The opening section of *Discipline and Punish* sets up the problem which the book will unravel by presenting the reader with a startling juxtaposition of two very different styles of punishment: [the brutal, public execution of a regicide in Paris in 1757 by hanging and drawing and quartering, and a detailed timetable minutely regulating the lives of French prisoners, behind prison walls and away from public view, eighty years later.]

Foucault takes each of these measures to be definitive of the penal style of its period and ... he sets himself ... to explain the disappearance of punishment as a public spectacle of violence against the body, and to account for the emergence of the prison as a general form of modern punishment.

This change in penal technology—from the scaffold to the penitentiary—signifies for Foucault a deeper change in the character of justice itself. In particular the new concern—which the prison introduced—to know the criminal, understand the sources of his criminality, and to intervene to correct them whenever possible, had profound implications for the whole system of criminal justice. The result of these changes is a system dealing with offenders that is not so much punitive as corrective, more intent upon producing normal, conforming individuals than upon dispensing punishment. . . .

On a wider scale, these developments represent illustrative models of how power operates in a modern society. Open physical force, the apparatus of violence, and the ceremonies of might are more and more replaced by a mode of power based upon detailed knowledge, routine intervention, and gentle correction. The idea now is to regulate thoroughly and at all times rather than to repress in fits and starts, and by this means to improve troublesome individuals rather than to destroy them.

Foucault's [theory of] punishment [is] founded upon three major and interrelated concepts . . . : namely power, knowledge, and the body. Systems of production, of domination, and of socialization fundamentally depend upon the successful subjugation of bodies. More specifically, they require that bodies be mastered and subjugated to training so as to render them docile, obedient, and useful. . . . [Some institutions] aim to have their commands internalized, producing an individual who habitually does what is required without need of further external force.

"Power," for Foucault, is not to be thought of as the property of particular classes or individuals who "have" it, nor as an instrument which they can somehow "use" at will. Power refers instead to the various forms of domination and subordination and the asymmetrical balance of forces which operate whenever and wherever social relations exist. In this conception power is a pervasive aspect of social life and is not limited to the sphere of formal politics or of open conflict. It is also to be thought of as productive in effect rather than repressive in so far as power shapes the actions of individuals and harnesses their bodily powers to its ends. In this sense power operates "through" individuals rather than "against" them and help constitute the individual. . . .

This relationship between forms of power and the bodies which are caught up in them involves a third element, that of "knowledge." Foucault uses this [term] to describe the "know-how" upon which techniques and strategies depend and to point to the cognitive aspects which are inherent in all policies or programmes of action. Any exercise of power relies, to some extent, upon a knowledge of the "target". . . . The successful control of an object—whether it is an object in nature or a human object—requires a degree of understanding of its forces, its reactions, its strengths and weaknesses.

Taking these concepts as a framework of study, the history of punishment . . . is thus conceived of, at base, as a set of developing relationships between power, knowledge, and the body.

[Foucault concludes by describing] how the frontiers between judicial punishment and the other institutions of social life, such as the school, the family, [and] the workshop . . . came increasingly to be blurred by the development of similar disciplinary techniques in all of them, and the frequent transfers which take place from one institution to another. According to Foucault, there exists a kind of carceral continuum which covers the whole social body, linked by the pervasive concern to identify deviance, anomalies, and departures from regular norms. Foucault's description of Western liberal democracy as a society of surveillance, disciplined from end to end, is deliberately reminiscent of a totalitarianism which is usually ascribed to others.

To return, finally, to punishment once more, all this has some specific consequences for the way we think about penal practice. Within this overall framework, the process of punishing is not essentially different from that of educating or curing and it tends to be represented as merely an extension of these less coercive practices. This has two important results. First of all legal punishments come to be regarded as more legitimate and less in need of justification than when they were previously seen as forms of harm or coercion. Secondly, the legal restriction and limitations which once surrounded the power to punish—tying it to specific crimes, determining its duration, guaranteeing the rights of those accused, etc.—tend to disappear. [Penal law's] jurisdiction is thus extended so that it now sanctions not just "violations of the law" but also "deviations from the norm."

Discipline and Punish is a complex, wide-ranging book, but a core argument Foucault is making is that "the 'technical' and avowedly 'apolitical' concerns of conventional penology [are] precisely the areas of most interest to anyone wishing to discover how power operates (and disguises itself) within modern society."[34] In other words, to understand modern punishment, it is essential to understand the quotidian routines by which it manifests itself. They are all efforts to "train" the body to conform to (inchoately-defined—more on that in a moment) social norms.

Furthermore, the means by which we regulate behavior in prison change as our understanding of human nature and behavior changes more widely. In the era before modern psychology (and modern policing), the government relied on the shock-and-awe of rarely-imposed but highly-salient spectacular punishments to try to scare people into compliance. The rise of social work in the late 1800s and early 1900s and

---

[34] *Id.* at 153.

of Freudian psychology in the post-War era both influenced the sorts of rehabilitation programs run in prisons. The rejection of rehabilitation in the 1960s and 1970s was a symptom, not a cause, of a widespread rejection of modern scientific expertise, and the adoption of more cognitive-behavioral treatments and actuarial models in recent years is again reflective of changes taking place in medicine, psychology, and other non-penal professions.

There are, of course, important limitations to Foucault's argument. He believes, for example, that power is the *only* explanation for what motivates penal practices, and this clearly can't be the case. As Garland explains:

> [The] trend towards normalizing, disciplinary sanctions and an administrative mode of dispensing them has never successfully banished the punitive, emotive character of the penal process. Throughout the twentieth century, the condemnatory rituals of criminal courts and the humiliating routines of penal institutions have retained a clear concern with expressing punitive passions and moral censure, even in the years when the treatment ethos was at its zenith.[35]

Our goals are always complex, focusing not just on rehabilitation and deterrence, but on "justice, economy, vengeance, forgiveness, charity, evangelism, and so on."[36] If by "power" we mean regulating behavior to induce future compliance, whether via internalized values (rehabilitation) or external threats (deterrence), then power is certainly *an* aspect of punishment, but it is by no means the only one, and in many cases perhaps not even the dominant one.

The other major failing of Foucault's work, at least for our purposes here, is that he never really defines what "power" is and, more seriously, never defines *who* is wielding it. Garland again:

> [W]e still need to know who are the people in positions of power and how they came to be there. On these crucial questions, Foucault is notoriously reticent. Sometimes he uses the abstractions of Marxist terminology ("the dominant class," "the state," "the bourgeoisie"), occasionally he mentions "the judges," "psychiatric experts," or "the administration," but more often he simply avoids the issue altogether by using passive grammatical constructions which do not name subjects.[37]

As we will see in Chapter 3 and beyond, this is a major oversight. Power in the criminal justice system is widely and chaotically diffused, spread across multiple agencies and jurisdictions: local police, county

---

[35] *Id.* at 161.
[36] *Id.* at 163.
[37] *Id.* at 170.

prosecutors, state or county judges, state legislators elected by local constituencies, parole boards appointed by state-elected governors, etc., etc. Quite often these agencies are responding to different constituencies with different goals and incentives: police respond to the mayor,[38] who is elected by urban voters, while the county district attorney for that city may be more beholden to more-conservative, more-white, wealthier suburban voters. It is thus impossible to speak about "power" in the abstract. It is also impossible to conceive of power as a monolithic thing, given the wide variety of incentives, goals, constituencies, etc., that run through the criminal justice system.

That said, there is much in Foucault that is useful to keep in mind. Prison and punishment do not exist outside of "normal" life but likely do reflect one edge of an ever-changing continuum of control—it is perhaps not surprising that states adopted three-strike laws for crimes and zero-tolerance policies for schools at roughly the same time. And the policies we adopt, whether in prisons or schools or hospitals, reflect and adapt to our always-changing knowledge of what does and doesn't influence human behavior. And much of that control, in prisons, schools, and elsewhere, is about shaping people's behavior to conform to certain social norms.

Consider, for example, anger-management training. We've come to better understand how people regulate their moods, and that has changed the way in which we focus on anger management. Our knowledge about how the body works has changed, and so our regulatory regimes have shifted in response. And what is the goal of anger management but to make sure people respond to certain stressful situations in the "correct" way, ideally at a subconscious level?

Note that this need not be a bad thing. Controlling anger rather than lashing out violently is likely a social good. But it does reflecting prioritizing one response over another and training people to take the preferred steps.

I want to conclude this chapter by briefly looking at two other sociological arguments that we will look at in more depth in Chapter 10: the relationship between punishment and race and between punishment and politics. Regarding race, many commentators have suggested that punitive criminal policies in the United States, the War on Drugs in particular, have either been intentionally implemented as means for rolling back minority gains from the Civil Rights movement, or at least tolerated because they disproportionately destabilize minority as opposed to white communities. And it is inarguable that race and

---

[38] Of course, it is even more complex than that. The top echelons of the police force respond to city-level incentives, but line officers are harder to observe and regulate—what exactly are they doing as they drive around?—and so they may respond to a different set of incentives and constituencies: their fellow officers, their sergeants, their precinct residents (or a specific subset of them).

punishment interact in troubling ways in the United States: blacks make up about 12% of the population but 38% of state prisoners.

Not surprisingly, the complete story is actually fairly complicated. While blacks are overrepresented in prison populations, they are also overrepresented among crime victims and offenders. Blacks, for example, comprise approximately 48% of all murder victims and 52% of all murderers—and about 50% of all people in prison for murder. Thus some, though by no means all, of the disparity reflects underlying differences in offending. Of course, those *offending* differences are in no small part the product of racial discrimination and other structural barriers faced by poor, minority Americans, and they may even be aggravated by race-neutral enforcement decisions. So even a system whose racial breakdown for incarceration perfectly tracks that for offending—which is certainly not the case in the US, the example of murder aside[39]—may not really be a race-neutral system.

In recent years, crime has also become an effective electioneering device. One leading explanation for this move was put forth by Theodore Caplow and Jonathan Simon, who argued that in an age of identity politics, there are few issues that allow politicians to court voters from the other party: issues like abortion and gay rights do not lend themselves to compromise.[40] But appearing tough on crime was an issue that received bipartisan support and thus provided a valuable "wedge" topic to bring in additional votes. Thus tough-on-crime policies were implemented as part of a broader effort to remain in political power.

The key question, however, is *why* crime became so potent an electoral issue, since other issues surely could have been effective wedges as well. A likely answer was the concurrent rise in crime. Fig. 2–1 plots the property and violent crime rates in the US since 1960. A strikingly steady thirty-year rise quadrupled violent crime rates and doubled property crime rates by 1991. It is thus not surprising that appearing tough on crime was politically effective.

---

[39] As crimes become less serious, the data on racial breakdowns on offending become less clear, and the police have more discretion about which cases to pursue. So murder—clear offending/victimization data, little police discretion—is likely an outlier case, though by how much is unclear.

[40] Theodore Caplow & Jonathan Simon, *Understanding Prison Policy and Population Trends*, 26 CRIME & JUSTICE 63 (1999).

Figure 2–1: Crime in the United States, 1960–2010

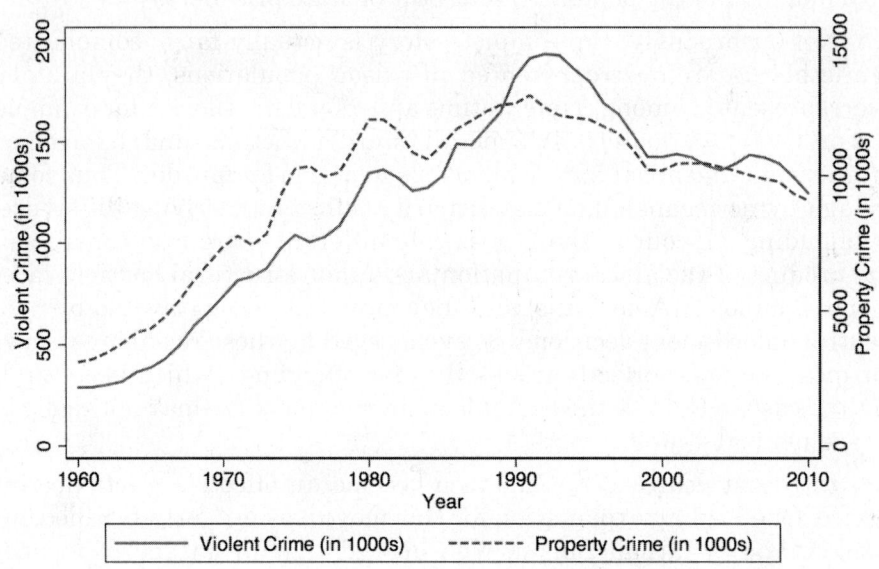

Tellingly, being tough on crime has become politically less effective in recent years—years in which crime has remained quite low, at least when compared to the 1980s and 1990s (note, though, that violent crimes rates are still twice as high as in 1960). That tough-on-crime rhetoric worked when crime was high and faded with declining crime rhetoric suggests that its effectiveness is less inherent to crime in general—although fear of crime has always been used by politicians to scare up votes—and more a reflection of and reaction to uniquely high and persistent levels of crime, violent crime in particular.

CHAPTER 3

THE COMPETING ACTORS OF THE CRIMINAL JUSTICE SYSTEM

So far we have examined the causes of criminal behavior and the criminal justice system's competing goals about how to respond to criminal acts. We now want to turn our attention to the behavior and incentives of those charged with accomplishing those goals. We often refer to the criminal justice "system" as if it is a coherent entity striving, at least in some rough way, to accomplish a specific goal. But this is a deeply problematic misconception.

A. INTRODUCTION

This so-called "system" consists of least ten different institutions—police, prosecutors, defense attorneys, juries, trial judges, appellate judges, parole boards and governors, legislators, and sentencing commissions—all of which operate at different levels of government, respond to different constituencies, and face different internal and external incentives. Responsibilities are spread across these various actors somewhat haphazardly, and no one institution or person has ultimate control, or thus responsibility, for what other upstream and downstream bureaucracies are doing.

It is, of course, possible to oversell the fractured nature of criminal justice administration in the United States. If nothing else, all prosecutors, most judges, and many governors, legislators, and sentencing commissioners are law school graduates and thus may develop relatively similar worldviews over time. But quite often the various criminal justice agencies are pursuing different, if not always inimical, goals, and so it is essential to understand what motivates the actors at each level of the system.

To see how the various pieces do and don't fit together, consider the following problem:

> **Problem:** A state has two grades of robbery: first degree, which requires the use of a firearm and carries a sentence of four to seven years, and second degree, which covers all other robberies and carries a sentence of two to five years. One day Bob pulls a gun on Joe and steals his wallet, but he is arrested the next day. Who determines how much time Bob will spend in prison?

There are a lot of possible answers here. Is it the legislature, which set the range of sanctions? Is it the prosecutor, who determines which degree of robbery to charge? Or the defense attorney, who may be able to cajole an aggressive prosecutor to choose the lesser charge? Is it the judge, who determines where in the given range to punish (and who could give Bob four or five years either way)? Is it the police, who could render first degree impossible if they search Bob's house without a proper warrant and thus get the gun excluded as evidence? Is it the parole board—if the state still has parole—that determines how much of the judge's sentence Bob has to serve?

Obviously, all play a role. And the interactions can be even more complex that this suggests. If the legislature revises the code so that first degree robbery carries a sentence of seven years to life and second degree of three years to life, then the legislature removes a lot of power from the prosecutor and hands it to the judge. Conversely, if the ranges are narrowed to seven-to-eight year vs. three-to-four years, the judges lose almost all discretion (as do parole boards) to the benefit of the prosecutors (or police).

What is most important to note is that all the various actors here respond to different constituencies. Police are city officials whose ultimate boss, the police chief, is appointed by the mayor.[1] Prosecutors, on the other hand, are elected at the county level, and outside of a few states subject to no higher-level oversight. And county-elected district attorneys will generally be more responsive to whiter, richer, more conservative, and less victimized suburban voters than urban mayors, implying that police and the prosecutors are often not on the same page.[2] And on it goes: governors, who appoint parole boards, are elected at the state level, while legislators are technically state officials but represent sometimes-hyperlocal districts. Judges are chosen at either the state or county level, and they may be appointed or elected (and, if elected, elected in partisan or non-partisan elections, which surely shapes their responsiveness to political parties and their machines).

The time ultimately served by a prisoner or a probationer, or the fine imposed on an offender, is determined by the quality of the evidence gathered by the police, the charge chosen by the prosecutor, the charges made available to the prosecutor by the legislature (perhaps in consultation with a state sentencing commission), the resistance raised by the defense attorney, the sentence imposed by the judge (which may

---

[1] Of course, even *within* the police (or prosecutors' offices, or parole boards, etc.) there are competing incentives and constituencies. Line officers respond to the pressures imposed by their sergeants, sergeants respond to precinct commanders, and precinct commanders to higher-up commanders who ultimately report to the chief. So even if the mayor says "do x" and the chief agrees, there is no immediate guarantee that the line officers will follow the directive (or at least implement it effectively or enthusiastically).

[2] Tellingly, a New York Times article recently bore the title "In *Unusual Collaboration*, Police and Prosecutors Team Up to Reduce Crime" (emphasis added, available on-line at http://www.nytimes.com/2014/06/05/nyregion/in-unusually-close-partnership-police-dept-and-district-attorney-team-up-to-reduce-crime.html). And that is in New York City, the one city where the district attorney (in this case, for Manhattan) covers a smaller jurisdiction than the police.

be shaped by restrictions established by guidelines and by the guideline-relevant evidence that prosecutors and defense attorneys decide to present), and the release decisions of the parole boards. And these choices are all influenced by personal and administrative views on the goals of punishment, by political pressures and electoral threats, and by complex webs of budgetary limits and free-riding opportunities (often shaped by powerful but underappreciated local, county, state, and federal intergovernmental transfers).

Perhaps most troubling is that this splintering of authority and responsibility is not the product of careful thinking about how to rationally allocate punishment discretion, but simply appears to have emerged with little thought over time. And as a result, important cracks and fissures can appear. Consider two examples we will look at in more depth below:

Example 1: Harry Connick, Sr., when elected as district attorney for New Orleans, vowed to abolish plea bargaining. But to do that, he needed the police to bring cases of a certain quality, and the New Orleans Police Department simply refused to do so. So, out of necessity, Connick, Sr., was forced to continuously dismiss a large volume of cases.

Example 2: Prosecutors are elected at the county level, and their offices are often funded by the county government. Probation is likewise a county expense, as are jail costs. But prisons are state-level institutions and thus are paid for out of state, not county, funds. If a prosecutor could convict a particular defendant of a misdemeanor (probation or jail) or a felony (prison), which will he choose if he's otherwise indifferent?

Complicating this issue is the fact that there is no one optimal level of responsibility. Crime tends to be geographically concentrated, even within areas such as cities or neighborhoods. But enforcement can displace crime to other areas or create other negative externalities. Imagine if one police precinct commander decided to stop enforcing drug laws because his constituents opposed drug interdiction efforts (think Hamsterdam from HBO's *The Wire*). The more-open drug markets in his jurisdiction would surely increase drug use (and related ills) in nearby areas which may have different policy preferences. Making things all the more complicated, the importance of these spillovers vary from crime to crime, as the following question indicates:

Question: What level (local, county, state, national, international) of enforcement and punishment should be responsible for domestic violence? For drug crimes? For terrorism? Why?

Understanding how responsibility is allocated across various criminal justice bureaucracies and the various (perhaps often poorly aligned) incentives these agencies face is essential for the "supply side" question of criminal justice. Much of the work on criminal justice focuses on what can be thought of as the "demand side" of policy: what sort of behavior or outcomes should we *demand from* these actors? Do we want them to lower crime? To improve social justice outcomes? To impose the morally just sanction? And so on. But never take your eyes off the supply-side question of what in fact *can (or will) these agencies do*? Telling a judge that he ought to ignore the crime-reducing effects of sentences and hand down "morally correct" punishments—that's the demand side—is fairly useless if the judge is elected in closely-contested elections by an electorate that insists crime rates be kept low. Whatever the validity of the demand-side argument, it simply cannot be supplied.

With that introduction, let's turn to look at the various bureaucracies in more depth.

B. POLICE OFFICERS

It may initially seem unusual to think of police as "sentencing actors," since their primary task is simply to arrest defendants and gather the evidence needed for conviction. But as noted above, the actions of police officers shape the options available to prosecutors. Consider the following example from New Orleans:

Dan Richman, *Institutional Coordination and Sentencing Reform*
84 TEX. L. REV. 2055, 2057–2061 (2006)

In [a] fascinating ... Stanford Law Review article,[3] Ron Wright and Marc Miller presented and assessed the efforts of New Orleans District Attorney Harry Connick[*] to take on a system in which, he claimed, "lazy" prosecutors were using the plea-bargaining process to " 'move' cases and avoid trial." Connick "instructed his prosecutors not to engage in plea bargaining—particularly charge bargaining[**]—except under very limited circumstances." What interested Wright and Miller, however, was that Connick coupled this promulgation with a move calculated to reduce the incentives that drive deeply discounted plea offers: a significant commitment of resources to the screening of cases presented by the police for prosecution.

Attorneys in the screening unit ... would review each investigative file from the police, speak to all the key witnesses and victims, and generally assess the strength of the case. Office policy then required them—if they decided to go forward—to charge the most serious crimes

---

[3] Ronald Wright and Marc Miller, *The Sentencing/Bargaining Tradeoff*, 55 STAN. L. REV. 29 (2002).

[*] *Ed. note*: This is Harry Connick, Sr., the father of the more-famous Harry Connick, Jr.

[**] *Ed. note*: "Charge bargaining," which we will talk about more in Chapter 8, is when prosecutors agree to drop or downgrade the charged offense as part of a plea bargaining: downgrading attempted murder to aggravated assault, or first degree arson to second degree arson. This is in contrast to sentence bargaining, in which prosecutors do not change the charged offense but agree to recommend a specific sentence for that offense.

that the facts would support at trial. And office policy made it extraordinarily difficult for the assistants handling the case thereafter to retreat from the charges thus specified. The result, as intended, was that the office declined a relatively high number of cases—a fact it blamed on poor police work—and that bargaining played an extraordinarily limited role in the disposition of cases that it did pursue. Wright and Miller thus found that "[t]he data mostly support . . . Connick's claims to have implemented a screening/bargaining tradeoff over the last thirty years." The lesson, they noted, is "that a committed prosecutor can implement the screening/bargaining tradeoff even without the conscious support of other actors in the system."

Wright and Miller were careful to note that "[a] prosecutor who shifts to stronger screening risks more strained relations with the local police." They optimistically suggested, however, that at least in theory, "an intense screening policy should encourage better police work," particularly if the police insisted on "feedback from the prosecutor's office both during and after the screening process" and "raise[d] the political cost for recalcitrant prosecutors who continue to decline cases that the police give a high priority."

In March 2002, after twenty-eight years in the post (five terms), Connick announced that he would not seek reelection. His successor, Eddie Jordan, took office in January 2003 and soon commissioned an "Operations and Needs Assessment" that was conducted by national consulting firm Linder & Associates under the auspices of the New Orleans Police Foundation. The team's report is a portrait of an utterly dysfunctional system, with the District Attorney's office at least acquiescing in and perhaps contributing to this dysfunctionality.

The consultants' report noted the lack of coordination between the D.A.'s office and the police and bluntly set out the consequences of unilateral action. The conviction rate for cases actually pursued hovered between 89.9% and 96.6% between 2002 and 2004 and, of the defendants who pleaded guilty, between 82.2% and 94.8% pleaded as charged. But only 40.3% of the Part I (FBI index) crime cases* presented by the police were accepted for prosecution in 2002 and only 38.2% in 2004. It is difficult to put these acceptance rates in a precise comparative perspective. But in California, in 2004, 60.7% of violent felony arrests and 76.4% of property arrests ended in convictions (not simply acceptances), with a 69.8% figure for all felony arrests. While one cannot easily quantify the point, the New Orleans acceptance rates were extraordinarily low.

The New Orleans police evidently were not responding to rigorous prosecutorial screening by bringing stronger cases. They were just

---

* *Ed. note*: Part I crimes are the most serious violent and property offenses: murder, aggravated (but not simple) assault, forcible rape, robbery, burglary, theft/larceny, auto theft, and arson.

continuing to bring weak ones and willing to suffer a refusal to prosecute. [T]he episode offers a powerful reminder that transcends both the city's idiosyncratic approach to criminal justice and the rationale behind D.A. Connick's demand for more rigorous screening: for better or worse, the police are critical actors in the sentencing process.

Once one sees a casefile not as a given but as an artifact of a fact-gathering process that is primarily dominated by the police and that incorporates prosecutorial decision-making only to the extent that some political or bureaucratic mechanism mediates between the two coordinate entities, one sees the limitations of a sentencing literature that focuses on the results of the plea bargaining or formal adjudicative process. Before we get too caught up in sentencing differentials across the defendants who are actually prosecuted, we ought to give some thought to the defendants who get away because investigative or adjudicative resources are not expended on them. And, of course, it is also helpful to get all murderers off the streets.

Without pointing fingers at D.A. Connick—who after all may have been making the best of a bad situation—one can use the breakdown in relations between his office and the New Orleans Police Department to raise some larger questions. Where prosecutors and police have independent sources of authority and stand in a coordinate, not hierarchical relationship, what mechanisms ensure that each agency internalizes, or at least strongly considers the policies and preferences of the other? One might model the relationship as a bilateral monopoly and assume that some degree of negotiation occurs between the two parties necessary to the prosecution of a criminal case. The validity of this assumption, however, turns on the degree to which the two are trying to maximize their joint output, or to which each is judged by a performance measure that implicates the other.

One could imagine an administrative mechanism that would prevent a prosecutor's office from shifting costs to the police (for however laudable a reason), prevent the police from shifting its costs back to the public (in the form of unprosecuted offenders), or both. [But state] systems . . . generally lack even [a] small degree of structural coordination, because police chiefs report to mayors and because district attorneys are directly elected. The degree to which alternative mechanisms will develop is ultimately a matter of politics.

Bill Stuntz and I have argued that electoral accountability can play an important role in ensuring the health of state systems . . . since voters can easily grasp and track the prosecutions of murders, rapes, and robberies that are staples of those systems. But political accountability will not always do the trick—either because so many elections are largely uncontested or because of deeper democratic failures. The New Orleans report noted that although the city had the highest homicide rate among the nation's seventy-one largest cities in 2002 and 2003, the vast majority of homicides reported and screened in those years did not end in convictions. Indeed, in 2002, only 14.3% of the 258 homicides reported and only 15.0% of the homicide cases screened ended in conviction. Why was this tolerated? Perhaps the rule is that (1) prosecutors are more likely to be held politically accountable than the police where there is a dysfunctional relationship between the two agencies—which would make sense, given that police chiefs are politically accountable only through elected mayors, and mayors have responsibilities (and sources of popularity) that go far beyond the criminal justice system; and (2) prosecutors will not always be held so responsible, either because they are held blameless or because of some larger failure of electoral accountability.

In short, Harry Connick's efforts to change punishment practices in the prosecutor's office were hampered by recalcitrance from the notoriously-problematic New Orleans Police Department. Without any direct, formal control over the police, the DA can only attempt to use moral suasion and his bully pulpit, but it is unclear how effective these tools are.

Of course, haphazard federalization does not *ensure* that this sort of dysfunction occurs. I once heard a retired district attorney of a major American city say that the greatest accomplishment of his career was teaching the police to bring him the exact sort of cases he needed. But the county (and thus the city) in which this district attorney worked was much more homogenous than New Orleans, so the police and prosecutors likely came from more-similar backgrounds and represented more-similar interests. Understanding how these bureaucracies interact is important, but often difficult.

So what sort of incentives and goals drive police? Three scholars have created a three-category taxonomy of police forces, looking at how police departments are organized.[4] As they explain:

> [O]rder maintenance is the operating philosophy of departments exhibiting the watchman style. Officers in these departments are encouraged to ignore certain types of criminal behavior, such as minor traffic violations and juvenile indiscretions, and to invoke laws only deemed important by citizens and local politicians. Not surprisingly, officers in these departments are subject to corruption and allegations of excessive force by minorities. Because of a lack of emphasis on professionalism, officers in watchman-style agencies tend to be working class,

---

[4] Allison T. Chappell, John M. McDonald, and Patrick W. Manz, *The Organizational Determinants of Police Arrest Decisions*, 52 CRIME & DELINQUENCY 287 (2006).

locally recruited, and low paid. They are poorly trained and seldom rewarded for seeking further education. These departments have flat bureaucratic structures, low budgets, little specialization . . . , and few rules. The penal law is but a device that empowers police to maintain order and protect citizens.

In contrast to watchman-style departments, legalistic-style and service-style agencies are highly professional but vary in their level of administrative complexity. Enforcing the law is the main strategy in legalistic organizations. Officers will issue a high rate of traffic citations, arrest a high proportion of juvenile offenders, and act vigorously against illicit enterprise. They act as if there is a single standard of acceptable behavior based on the law. Officers operate autonomously from the communities they serve, and all citizens are treated equally and impersonally. Legalistic departments are highly complex bureaucratic agencies that rely on central administrative authority and extensive rules and procedures. These police organizations have stiff entrance requirements and incentives for continuing education and training. Tasks and roles are specialized (e.g., there are often separate gang units and vice units), and there are strict evaluation processes.

In contrast, service-style agencies are highly professional but have less hierarchical structure and control. Service organizations are decentralized in command structure with many station houses or precincts presiding over individual beats. They are specialized, formalized, and professional. They employ civilians and embrace diversity. The emphasis on community relations is reflected in officer training and evaluations. The main goal of service-style agencies is to protect the common definition of public order. Service departments usually exist in more affluent and homogeneous communities, and they are concerned with public relations, problem solving, and deferral to community needs. Decisions whether to deal with offenders formally rest on assumptions about peace and order in the community and the future conduct of the offender. As a result, formal use of arrest powers is reserved only for serious crimes.

One of the more powerful recent efforts to adjust police behavior has been the adoption of CompStat or similar programs, which track offending and arrests at the block-by-block level, conceivably allowing senior leadership to hold precinct commanders and their subordinates accountable for crime trends in their districts. Of course, no policy is cost-free, and a central criticism of CompStat is that it encourages police to focus on those offenses and disruptions which can be most easily counted and evaluated by CompStat; these need not be the most pressing issues. It may also cause local commanders to favor policies that have immediate impacts on crime but which may be less effective in the long run.

Punishment at both the micro (offender) and macro (broad social outcomes) levels is initially determined by the police. The evidence that the prosecutor has in an individual case is shaped by the care of the investigating officers—like Richman says, the case file, which plays a significant role in determining what the defendant is charged with and either convicted of or pleads to, is largely under the control of the police. The police decisions about who to arrest similarly shape macro-level outcomes. If the police were to simply refuse to arrest people guilty of certain immigration offenses—a policy adopted in many so-called "sanctuary cities"—then they cannot be punished, no matter the retributivist or consequentialist justifications.

QUESTIONS

1. **Policing and theories of punishment.** Do all the typologies given by Wilson share a common theory of punishment? If so, what is it? What would policing look like if police adhered to a different theory of punishment—would it make a difference?

2. **Upstream and downstream control.** The example from New Orleans suggests that police actually have a decent amount of control over what the DA does: they can hamstring a DA by either refusing to make arrests or by bringing in weak cases (though they have little control over what the DA does with a strong case). The New Orleans case also suggests that the DA does *not* have comparable control over the police. Is there anything that could be done to give the DA more power over what the police do?

3. **CompStat and our theories of punishment.** What normative theories of punishment does CompStat seem to advance the best? What effect, if any, do you think it has on the positive goals of punishment, such as regulating the underclass or minorities, or allowing politicians to use fear of crime as an electioneering tool?

C. PROSECUTORS AND DEFENSE ATTORNEYS

C.1. PROSECUTORS

Prosecutors are arguably the most important actors in the criminal justice system, and they play a particularly critical role in sentencing. To start, prosecutors have almost unfettered discretion over the decision to file charges in the first place,[5] and they also have wide discretion over

---

[5] Angela Davis, for example, points out how hard it is to successfully make an equal protection case against seemingly-discriminatory prosecutorial decisions. Angela J. Davis, *Prosecution and Race: The Power and Privilege of Discretion*, 67 FORDHAM L. REV. 13, 38–50 (1998).

what charges to bring. This latter discretion has been amplified by legislatures, which continue to pass a dizzying array of overlapping statutes, many of which carry different sentencing implications. Consider the following problem:

Problem: Reckless Endangerment in Illinois

720 Ill. Comp. Stat. § 5/12–5:

a. A person commits reckless conduct when he or she, by any means lawful or unlawful, recklessly performs an act or acts that:

1. cause bodily harm to or endanger the safety of another person; or

2. cause great bodily harm or permanent disability or disfigurement to another person.

b. Sentence. Reckless conduct under subdivision (a)(1) is a Class A misdemeanor. Reckless conduct under subdivision (a)(2) is a Class 4 felony.

720 Ill. Comp. Stat. § 5/12–5.02:

a. A person commits vehicular endangerment when he or she strikes a motor vehicle by causing an object to fall from an overpass in the direction of a moving motor vehicle with the intent to strike a motor vehicle while it is traveling upon a highway in this State.

b. Sentence. Vehicular endangerment is a Class 2 felony, unless death results, in which case vehicular endangerment is a Class 1 felony.

720 Ill. Comp. Stat. § 12–5.1a

a. A person commits aggravated criminal housing management when he or she commits criminal housing management and:

1. the condition endangering the health or safety of a person other than the defendant is determined to be a contributing factor in the death of that person; and

2. the person recklessly conceals or attempts to conceal the condition that endangered the health or safety of the person other than the defendant that is found to be a contributing factor in that death.

b. Sentence. Aggravated criminal housing management is a Class 4 felony.

In Illinois, a Class A misdemeanor carries a punishment of no more than one year in jail, a Class 4 felony a sanction of one to three years in prison, a Class 2 felony a sanction of three to seven years, and a Class 1 felony a sentence of four to fifteen years in prison. And note that any violation of §§ 5/12–5.02 and 12–5.1a also violates § 12–5. So by the choice of charge, the prosecutor can determine whether a defendant, say, faces a maximum of one year in jail or fifteen years in prison (or at least a maximum of seven years in non-death cases, where the prosecutor may have more charging discretion).

QUESTIONS

1. **Justifiable?** Can we justify the overlap seen in the Illinois code? What could explain why the legislature did not define the crimes so that they did not overlap? Is this an acceptable delegation of authority? Who should have the discretion to determine what provision applies? Why?

2. **How will these statutes be used?** How do you think prosecutors will use this overlap? In a case where a more-specific (and thus more severe) provision applies, when do you think they will use the more-general one? What sort of factors do you think may influence this decision? And when *should* they use the more-generic provision?

It could be that such overlap is just the product of sloppy drafting: after all, legislators could write in provisions that require prosecutors to charge the more-specific offense whenever possible. However, in some cases it may not be clear what provision is the more specific.

> **Question:** Imagine a state that has a grand theft statute that criminalizes theft of anything worth at least $10,000 and a horse-theft statute that criminalizes stealing a thoroughbred horse. Which is the "more specific" statute when someone steals a thoroughbred horse worth $100,000? Would your answer change if all thoroughbred horses were worth at least $50,000?

Regardless, enforcing a "charge the more specific offense" provision in a world of plea bargains would be quite difficult. After all, the famous "Ashcroft Memo" issued by the US Department of Justice when John Ashcroft was Attorney General attempted to force federal prosecutors to always charge the most-serious charge, but its actual impact is unclear. If an Illinois DA accepts a plea to endangerment from a defendant guilty of vehicular endangerment, who will appeal? The victim may not even know about the various options (nor necessarily have standing to appeal even if he did), and certainly neither the DA nor the defense attorney will appeal the bargain they just made.

The more important question, however, is who we should trust with charging discretion. If legislators wrote highly precise, non-overlapping codes, then they would be the ones with discretion over who is charged with what. Do we want state-level officials, disproportionately drawn from lower-crime communities and viewing criminal punishment in the abstract, to wield that much authority? Perhaps we are better off giving more discretion to more-local actors dealing with specific cases. Maybe: it's a difficult empirical question, and one that should always be kept in mind.

Whatever the normative issues, the fact is that prosecutors have significant charging discretion. And prosecutors are likely the most powerful and important actors in the criminal justice area. A simple observation demonstrates their centrality. Between 1994 and 2008, crime rates were cut in half, and arrests for violent, property, and non-marijuana drug offenses fell by about 10%.[6] Yet during that same time, annual admissions to prison rose by about 40% and total prison populations by approximately 45%. How did this happen? Because felony filings—a decision that rests solely in the hands of the prosecutor—rose by about 40% as well. The data suggest that this increase in filings could explain *almost all* the growth in prisons during that time.[7]

Given the major role prosecutors play in driving sentencing outcomes, it is important to think carefully about what factors shape their decision-making. In this section I want to touch on two issues concerning prosecutors. First, exactly how autonomous are they: to what extent do political pressures constrain their decisions? And second, how important is it that prosecutors are county officials with the power to send defendants to state-funded prisons—a potentially-important source of moral hazard? It would be interesting to probe even more deeply into prosecutorial incentives, but unfortunately prosecutors are rarely studied, despite their power.

Let's start with autonomy and accountability. Almost all district attorneys in the United States are elected, and elected at the local level (city, county, or small-circuit-of-counties); only in Alaska, Connecticut, and New Jersey are local district attorneys appointed, and even in those states an electoral check remains, since they are appointed by (generally) elected state attorneys general.[8] The logic behind electing prosecutors is that elections should force district attorneys to respond to local concerns. Ronald Wright, however, is skeptical about how well this works in practice. In an article tellingly titled *How Prosecutor Elections Fails Us*, he cautions:

---

[6] The focus here is on non-marijuana drug arrests since a vast majority of marijuana arrests do not result in prison (as opposed to jail) terms. Only about 1% of prisoners are in prison for marijuana.

[7] People are often quick to argue that longer sentences played a key role in prison growth, but there is no real evidence of this in the data. We will discuss this more in Chapter 9. These results are from John F. Pfaff, *The Centrality of Prosecutors to Prison Growth: An Empirical Assessment*, available on-line at http://papers.ssrn.com/sol3/papers.cfm?abstract_id=1884674.

[8] In New Jersey, the state attorney general is appointed by the governor, so the electoral check is still present, but even further removed. Federal prosecutors are appointed as well, but the federal system handles only about 5% of all criminal cases and thus plays only a minimal role in criminal justice in the United States. As Ronald Wright and Marc Miller point out, Los Angeles County alone handles two-thirds as many felony cases as the entire federal system (64,000 to 91,000 in 2008). Ronald Wright and Marc Miller, *The Worldwide Accountability Deficit*, 67 WASH. & LEE L. REV. 1587, 1605 (2010).

> [T]he reality of prosecutor elections is not so encouraging. A national sample of outcomes in prosecutor elections . . . reveals that incumbents do not lose often. [C]hallengers do not come forward very often, far less often than challengers in state legislative elections. Uncontested elections short-circuit the opportunities for voters to learn about the incumbent's performance in office and to make an informed judgment about the quality of criminal enforcement in their district.
>
> Even in those exceptional campaign settings when the incumbent prosecutor faces a challenge and is forced to explain the priorities and performance of the office, elections do not perform well. The themes that incumbents and challengers invoke in their campaign speeches represent a lost opportunity to judge whether the prosecutor has applied the criminal law according to public values.
>
> [P]rosecutor elections fail for two reasons. First, they do not often force an incumbent to give any public explanation at all for the priorities and practices of the office. Second, even when incumbents do face challenges, the candidates talk more about particular past cases that about the larger patterns and values reflected in local criminal justice.[9]

Along with Marc Miller, Wright later argues that elections create an "accountability deficit": these elections fail to provide voter with meaningful information about how prosecutors make their decisions, which "contribute[s] to . . . turmoil and dissatisfaction" about how prosecutors exercise their discretion when it comes to declinations and diversion, charge selection, plea bargaining, and sentencing.[10]

Note, however, that neither Miller nor Wright argues that prosecutors are actually acting as unfaithful agents for the electorate. In fact, they say the exact opposite:

> This is not to say that prosecutors everywhere violate the law and the wishes of the people. A few do; most don't, or at least they don't most of the time. Prosecutors . . . pay careful attention to the power that goes with their everyday decisions—whether to decline or to charge, how to choose among available charges, whether to enter plea negotiations, what sentence to recommend, and so forth. Most prosecutors, in our experience, are conscientious public servants. This restraint, however, is based on individual virtue. Because *individual* responsibility is the origin of good behavior among prosecutors, it does not generate the level of public trust that one might expect in a

---

[9] Ronald F. Wright, *How Prosecutor Elections Fail Us*, 6 OHIO. ST. J. CRIM. L. 581, 582–583 (2009).

[10] Wright and Miller, *Accountability Deficit*, supra note 8 at 1598–1599.

government of laws. Both in the United States and elsewhere in the world, *institutional* strategies to guarantee prosecutor accountability all fall short of the mark.[11]

That prosecutors are generally unchallenged but nonetheless relatively faithful agents could mean that we have been lucky in who we elect, or it could mean that political and other pressures actually constraint prosecutors to the point that there is little of the discontent that prompts challenge. In an essay about the problem of pretextual prosecutions in the federal system, Daniel Richman and William Stuntz take the latter tack, suggesting that tight budgets and political pressure force local state prosecutors to focus on the serious cases that the electorate likely wants them to in the first place.

Daniel C. Richman and William J. Stuntz, *Al Capone's Revenge: An Essay on the Political Economy of Pretextual Prosecution*
105 COLUM. L. REV. 583, 600–608 (2005)

[Several] key features of [state] system[s] push against . . . pretextual prosecutions. First, a small but important part of state criminal codes are politically mandatory. Local prosecutors do not have the option of ignoring violent felonies and major thefts. The same is true, at least in some measure, of distribution of hard drugs. No district attorney can ignore these crimes in order to go after particular targets or pursue some personal agenda—at least not if she wants to keep her job. It is important to understand why that is so: These crimes are politically mandatory both because they are important to voters and because local prosecutors are politically accountable for dealing with them. Other provisions of state criminal codes give prosecutors options; these provisions create obligations.

Second, there are enough of these politically mandatory crimes to occupy all or nearly all of local prosecutors' time and manpower. This has not always been true; there have been periods in American history when district attorneys' offices had a good deal of slack. But any slack has long since disappeared, as the following data suggest. In 1974, there were 17,000 local prosecutors in the United States. By 1990, that number had grown to 20,000. During those same years, the number of felony prosecutions more than doubled. Crime has fallen since the early 1990s, but dockets (and hence prison populations) have continued to grow, and prosecutors' offices have not caught up with the earlier increase. Extreme docket pressure characterizes DAs' offices, particularly in the large cities where crime rates tend to be highest. It follows that criminal litigation must be rationed not only based on political necessity but also based on cost. "Detours" themselves may be cheap, but the investigations that give

---
[11] Id. at 1589.

rise to them are expensive, and district attorneys cannot afford expensive investigations. That is why high-end white-collar crime is (with a few rare exceptions) a federal preserve; only the feds have the manpower to deal with the long, intricate paper trails, and only the feds can afford to initiate and pursue major investigations without being certain that those investigations will turn up evidence of serious crimes.

Third, district attorneys are subject to performance measures that reinforce their tendency to concentrate on a small list of politically important crimes. The FBI's crime index measures the incidence of nine offenses: murder, manslaughter, rape, arson, kidnapping, aggravated assault, robbery, burglary, and auto theft. The FBI publishes reports about the number of index crimes nationwide; there is a good deal of publicity attached to these numbers in local jurisdictions. Responsibility for these numbers falls heaviest on police forces.... But as the primary and often the only source of the local district attorney's cases, the local police are also a potentially loud source of information about a given DA's performance, and they ensure that any district attorney not already fixated on these reports will soon become so.

That combination of political accountability and an independent performance measure matters in several different ways. Local prosecutors would go after violent crimes and major thefts even without the crime index. Pressure by victims and the sheer obviousness of a body lying in the street, a destroyed building, or a hospitalized citizen would see to that. But the index—specifically, the publicity that it brings to crime statistics—focuses even more attention on those offenses, since local voters will hear about whether their number is rising or falling, and by how much. Beginning in the 1990s, many prosecutors' offices followed [the] pattern [established by police departments engaged in "community" policing] of greater involvement with local communities, more "say" in charging practices by crime victims, [and] greater attention to "quality of life" offenses....

[T]he biggest effect of community policing and prosecution is to encourage prosecutors to enforce allegedly "minor" crimes.... That means more docket pressure—recall the data that show caseloads rising while crime was falling through the 1990s—leaving prosecutors less time for "detour" prosecutions. Greater community involvement in prosecution also generally means that local prosecutors must pay more attention to crime victims.

State codes remain full of "crimes" that invite strategic prosecution. Overcriminalization is a problem at the state and federal levels alike. But it matters much less at the state level, because the prosecutors who enforce those overbroad state codes have little time or incentive to exploit the opportunities those codes give them. The data generally support that proposition. [D]ata suggest that, at least in high-crime cities and counties, "truth in charging" is a fairly strong norm and that district attorneys in those high-crime jurisdictions prefer to charge serious crimes and lose than to charge unrelated lesser crimes and win.

There may be a partial exception in drug cases.... No good external measures of drug crime exist; there is no way to know how many sales of cocaine or heroin occurred in a given jurisdiction over a given period of time.

As the drug example suggests, this system is far from perfect. But at least for core crimes, meaning violent felonies and major thefts, the legal and political systems seem to reinforce one another. The law functions as law: These core crimes seem to be defined nonstrategically and in rough accord with public definitions. Prosecutors generally charge the crimes they believe defendants have committed, even when that practice poses a significant risk of acquittal. And voters know how large or small the gap is between the crimes their jurisdictions suffer and the criminal charges their prosecutors file.

Although relatively optimistic, Richman and Stuntz are careful to point out that the system remains flawed, and it is important to not lose sight of the risks that exist. There is some evidence, for example, that federal prosecutors are more willing to aggressively pursue complex white collar cases, in part because they provide trial prosecutors with the opportunity to impress the high-paying defense firms against whom they are arguing—and perhaps for whom they wish to work in the future; similar goals might motivate local prosecutors as well.[12] And Angela Davis, among many others, has pointed out the troubling role that race can play in prosecutorial decision-making.[13] Stuntz himself seemed less optimistic just a few years later, arguing that beginning around the 1950s "prosecutors . . . grew more politically insulated," and "voters began to treat local district attorneys as something akin to civil servants, routinely reelecting them in high- and low-crime times alike. . . ."[14]

Of course, bureaucratization is not necessarily a bad thing. The use of electoral control is a distinctly American phenomenon. In civil law countries, prosecutors are appointed bureaucrats, and these systems rely on internal and external bureaucratic controls to regulate prosecutorial behavior. In fact, it could be that the best system lies somewhere in between elections and bureaucracy, and as Wright and Miller point out, the differences between American and European prosecutors have shrunk over time. As American offices have become more bureaucratic, they have started to adopt more European-style formal internal control mechanisms. And as European prosecutors find themselves facing

---

[12] See, e.g., Richard T. Boylan & Cheryl X. Long, *Plea Rates and the Career Objectives of Federal Prosecutors*, 48 J. L. & ECON. 627 (2005).

[13] See, e.g., Davis, *Prosecution and Race*, supra note [6] at 31–38 (1998).

[14] WILLIAM J. STUNTZ, THE COLLAPSE OF AMERICAN CRIMINAL JUSTICE 250 (2011).

mounting caseloads—and thus forced to make more discretionary choices about how to choose among competing cases—they are increasingly subject to new, democratic checks.

It thus appears that prosecutors are subject to some meaningful electoral accountability. But that brings up the second issue, namely accountability to *whom*. The prosecutor's constituency is generally the county electorate, which raises some concerns. First, it creates a moral hazard problem. Prosecutors are county officials whose budgets are often set by county,[15] but prisons are paid for by the state. When a prosecutor seeks a felony conviction, he is seeking to spend someone else's money, providing him with a strong incentive to "overuse" prison. David Ball, for example, has produced evidence that county-level incarceration rates in California do not seem to vary with county-level violent crime rates (i.e., counties with higher violent crime rates do not systematically send proportionally more defendants to prison), but rather seem to respond to other, county-level political preferences.[16] Prosecutors may over-respond to local punitive attitudes because they can do so for free—especially since the local county government *does* have to foot the bill for misdemeanor jail sentences and probation.

Prosecutorial ability to free-ride on the state dime can distort other agency decisions, such as police hiring. For example, between 1982 and 2007, real expenditures on police rose by 125% while those on prisons rose by 255%,[17] despite evidence that a dollar spent on policing could be as much as 25% more effective at reducing crime than a dollar spent on prisons.[18] That we ended up over-relying on prisons could be due in part to the moral hazard problem: rather than incur the expense of policing themselves, local governments capitalized on the moral hazard problem to get the state government to fund local law enforcement via incarceration.[19]

(And to indulge in a moment of foreshadowing, this disconnect between local and state crime control introduces other distortions that we will consider elsewhere in the book. For example, state legislators may pass draconian sentencing laws in order appear "tough on crime" to suburban constituents while relying on local prosecutors to use their discretion during the plea process to circumvent these sentences, which

---

[15] Often, but not always, or at least not entirely. In Oregon, for example, the district attorney's salary is set and paid by the state, while the rest of his budget (along with a discretionary "bonus" counties can choose to add to the district attorney's salary) is paid for by the county. This gives both the state and the county some control over what the prosecutor chooses to do.

[16] W. David Ball, *Tough on Crime (on the State's Dime): How Violent Crime Does Not Drive California Counties' Incarceration Rates—And Why It Should*, 28 GA. ST. L. REV. 987 (2011).

[17] TRACEY KYCKELHAHN, JUSTICE EXPENDITURES AND EMPLOYMENT, FY 1982–2007, STATISTICAL TABLES Table 2 (2011).

[18] Steven D. Levitt, *Understanding Why Crime Fell in the 1990s: Four Factors That Explain the Decline and Six That Do Not*, 18 J. ECON. PERSPECTIVES 163 (2004).

[19] See, e.g., STUNTZ, COLLAPSE, supra note 14.

would drive up prison costs significantly. In doing so, legislators rely on the fact that the local constituencies in high-crime counties to whom the prosecutors respond often have less draconian views on crime control.

It is thus perhaps not surprising that in the wake of the financial crisis starting in 2008, state governments have finally started to attack this moral hazard problem. Most notably, the linchpin of California's recent efforts to rein in its unconstitutionally-overcrowded prison population is a program called "Realignment." Under Realignment, county jails must now incarcerate certain categories of low-level offenders who previously would have been sent to state prisons. The goal is clear: force local governments to bear the costs their prosecutors are imposing. It is unclear whether California will design the system properly—it is still in its infancy and in constant flux—but the underlying logic reflects a clear-headed effort to directly target moral hazard.

The other major concern raised by selecting prosecutors at the county level points in the opposite direction: not at the tension with state-level budgets, but at the tension with local-level crime trends, particularly in urban counties. Urban counties generally consist of two distinct regions, namely the urban core itself, and a ring of wealthier, whiter suburbs. One concern that William Stuntz has raised is that like state legislators (as noted above), prosecutors are likely more responsive to the disproportionately politically powerful suburbs—although these are the areas where crime rates tend to be *lower*. Thus the district attorney may face pressure to focus more on crimes that scare suburban voters (say, drugs) than on the crimes that actually disrupt the lives of urban residents (say, more-routine violent crimes).

QUESTIONS

1. **What is a good prosecutor?** In order to hold prosecutors accountable, we need a metric of "goodness." What should that be for a prosecutor? Clearly framing the innocent or engaging in discriminatory charging practices due to racial- or other-impermissible animus is "bad." But what is "good"? Simply responding to popular demands? Does that depend on how homogenous the district is—and if so, homogenous with respect to what traits? How relevant is the fact that crime, violent crime in particular, is quite geographically concentrated, even within local prosecutorial districts—and that other factors (minority presence, low income) tend to be concentrated there as well?

2. **Falling crime, rising prosecutions.** In arguing that time- and budget-constraints limit prosecutorial discretion, Richman and Stuntz state that "Crime has fallen since the early 1990s, but dockets . . . have continued to grow, and prosecutors' offices have not caught up with the earlier increase." Is there anything troubling about this statement? If prosecutors were wholly constrained by time, what would we expect the relationship

between crime rates and docket pressures to be? Do we observe this? If not, what lessons can we take away from that?

3. **No institutional controls?** Wright and Miller are concerned that the US system relies on individual controls, not institutional ones, to regulate prosecutorial behavior. Is this right? Does there seem to be some sort of institutional control in effect? Does the fact that Wright and Miller find that most prosecutors are relatively faithful agents imply something about institutional control methods?

C.2. DEFENSE ATTORNEYS

The defense attorney plays a more reactive role than the prosecutor, but she can still be a critical actor when it comes to sentencing outcomes. The defense attorney has no direct control over the charges a prosecutor brings, but a prosecutor may charge less aggressively when facing a more-aggressive defense attorney. And more-zealous and more-effective advocacy can help secure a more favorable plea, ensure that legitimate defenses are actually raised, and may be able to exclude evidence which triggers mandatory minimums or which aggravates sentences.

Criminal defendants have been entitled to defense counsel, regardless of ability to pay, since *Gideon v. Wainwright*, 372 U.S. 335 (1963). But *Wainwright* did not explain *how* state and local governments were to ensure that indigent defendants had adequate representation, and state and county governments have ultimately developed three methods to provide such representation: public defenders offices, assigned counsel systems, and contract attorney systems, with some states or counties relying on more than one of these approaches. A BJS report from 2000 summarizes these programs:

> Under a public defender system, salaried staff attorneys render criminal indigent defense services through a public or private non-profit organization or as direct government employees. In 1994, 68% of State court prosecutors reported that a public defender program was used to defend indigents in cases they prosecuted.
>
> In an assigned counsel system, courts appoint attorneys from a list of private bar members who accept cases on a judge-by-judge, court-by-court, or case-by-case basis. About 63% of prosecutors in State criminal courts reported an assigned counsel program in their jurisdiction.
>
> In contract attorney systems, private attorneys, bar associations, law firms, groups of attorneys, and nonprofit corporations provide indigent services based on legal agreements with State, county, or other local governmental units. Approximately 29% of prosecutors indicated that in their

jurisdiction contracts were awarded to attorney groups to provide indigents with legal representation.[20]

Most criminal defendants rely on state-provided counsel—approximately 80% in 1992 and 1996, and 86% of those with prior records (who face more-severe sentencing outcomes and thus may benefit more from experienced counsel).[21] Given the central importance of indigent defense, it is worth asking what turns on the type of lawyer available.

As Michael Roach points out, lawyers for the indigent tend to fall into one of two categories, namely public defenders or assigned counsel.[22] The differences in how such lawyers are paid can strongly shape their behavior:

> Public defenders are typically salaried employees whose full-time job is representing the indigent. Assigned counsel are typically private attorneys who self-select onto a panel of attorneys available to represent indigent defendants. Unlike public defenders, assigned counsel are usually paid on a case-by-case basis, and handling indigent matters is not their full-time occupation. These different systems potentially provide complicated incentives that can lead to agency problems, in particular adverse selection and moral hazard. I show that in state courts, assigned counsel generate significantly less favorable defendant outcomes than public defenders across a number of measures and that this differential is particularly sensitive to [agency problems].
>
> These agency problems take the form of either adverse selection or moral hazard. The potential for adverse selection comes from the part-time, self-selected nature of assigned counsel work, which theoretically allows attorneys to adjust their decision to join the panel in response to changing labor market conditions. Moral hazard issues stem from the notion that flatter fee structures could potentially induce assigned counsel to resolve cases more quickly than structures that pay a fixed hourly rate.

The concern with adverse selection is that as outside opportunities improve, better lawyers will decide that relatively low-paying assigned counsel work is not worth the time. The problem raised by moral hazard is that the less the lawyer is paid by the hour, the more likely he to quickly resolve the case via plea bargain.

---

[20] CAROLINE WOLF HARLOW, DEFENSE COUNSEL IN CRIMINAL CASES 4 (2000).

[21] That repeat offenders rely more heavily on provided counsel is at least partially the result of the financial costs of the earlier punishment: as we will see in Chapter 10, conviction, and especially incarceration, reduces subsequent income, making it harder to hire private counsel.

[22] Michael Roach, *Explaining the Outcome Gap Between Different Types of Indigent Defense Counsel: Adverse Selection and Moral Hazard Effects*, available on-line at http://papers.ssrn.com/sol3/papers.cfm?abstract_id=1839651

Roach's empirical results indicate that public defenders consistently outperform assigned counsel:

> Specifically, assigned counsel are significantly more likely to generate a guilty outcome for a client [by about 2.3 percentage points]. Assigned counsel are also significantly more likely to generate a conviction on the most serious offense category [by approximately 4.8 to 6.0 percentage points], generate a longer expected sentence (estimates range from 3.0 to 3.3 months), and lengthen time from arrest to adjudication [by approximately 26.3 to 26.6 days].*

In general, Roach's results suggest that the moral hazard problems are not too pronounced but the adverse selection ones are: lawyers work hard when they take an assigned case, but the quality of that lawyer depends on what other options he has available. Roach suggests that at the very least:

> The committees involved in approving candidates for this kind of work could benefit from simply being aware of these connections between outside labor market fluctuations and assigned counsel panel quality and outcomes. Perhaps additional institution controls and standards could be put in place to mitigate these effects.

Roach is not alone in finding that public defenders tend to outperform appointed counsel. Radha Iyengar finds that federal defendants represented by public defenders are less likely to be found guilty and receive shorter sentences when convicted than those with appointed counsel.[23] She also reports that public defenders tend to have better credentials (quality of law school, for example) and more experience, and she finds an adverse selection effect similar to Roach's—the outcome gap between public defenders and appointed counsel narrows the better compensated appointed counsel are. And in an analysis of murder cases in Philadelphia, James Anderson and Paul Heaton report that public defenders reduce conviction rates by 19%, life sentences by 62%, and overall time served by 24% when compared to appointed counsel.[24]

---

* *Ed. note*: As Roach points out, whether longer time to adjudication is good or bad is ambiguous. To a defendant out on bail, longer time to adjudication is a good thing: any negative outcome is delayed, and the probability of acquittal rises with time (since evidence decays, witnesses forget, etc.). For a defendant who doesn't make bail, the desire for promptness is greater. Roach further argues that from a system-wide perspective, speed is probably a good thing, though if we are trying to measure how good defense attorneys are *for their clients*, then what is best for the *system overall* seems irrelevant.

[23] Radha Iyengar, *An Analysis of the Performance of Federal Indigent Defense Counsel*, NBER Working Paper 13187 (2007).

[24] James M. Anderson and Paul Heaton, *How Much Difference Does the Lawyer Make? The Effect of Defense Counsel on Murder Case Outcomes*, National Institute of Justice (2011).

Regardless of quality, however, a pressing issue for indigent defense counsel is resources. As William Stuntz points out, the slight nominal increase in budget allocations for indigent defense over time has been swamped by the increase in caseloads: he estimated that real spending per case on indigent defense fell by half between the late 1970s and early 1990s.[25] The following excerpt, about Robert E. Surrency, the public defender in rural Greene County, Georgia, provides a representative example of the intense time and money pressures under which many public defenders now operate. The position is part-time. Surrency has a private practice on the side, but it does not pay enough, so he also works as the county's one public defender. He initially obtained the position in 1987 when he offered the lowest bid for the job: $15,000 plus $75 an hour for major cases.

Amy Bach, *Ordinary Injustice: How America Holds Court*
(2010)

In his first year, he represented forty defendants while maintaining a private practice. "It was a good side job," Surrency said. In the fourteen years that followed, his public caseload multiplied tenfold, while the amount of time he devoted to each case inevitably shrank. In 2001, the year I first met him, 1,359 people were arrested and held in the Greene County jail. Because the vast majority of criminal defendants nationwide are too poor to afford a lawyer, many of those arrested in Greene County would become his clients. During the same fourteen years, Surrency's pay rose only to $42,150.

I had come on the first day of "trial week," the term of court when this rural court attempts to resolve cases that have built up over the previous quarter with jury trials. The label is a misnomer. In four years, Surrency had taken only fourteen cases to trial out of 1,493; he won five. The rest of the cases he managed during that period—more than 99 percent—he plea-bargained. In this particular session no cases went to trial. People either pleaded guilty or had their cases rescheduled, a drill that took only two days. There were 142 defendants on the court calendar and 89 were Surrency's. In a flash, it seemed, forty-eight of his clients rose from the rickety dark wooden benches, one after the other, to plead guilty. After the first day I spent in court observing him, he announced, "We have successfully done a ten-page calendar in one day!" For Surrency, speed meant success.

Surrency had little time to talk in detail to his clients, and so he often had limited information to use in their favor. It was thus difficult for him

---

[25] STUNTZ, COLLAPSE, supra note 14. Real spending on indigent defense rose by 60% during the time. But the *fraction* of cases with appointed counsel rose from under half in the late 1970s to 80% in 1992—and this during a time when the *total number* of cases rose sharply as well.

to bargain with prosecutors to secure a more lenient sentence, nor could he produce the ultimate trump card: a willingness to go to trial when his clients claimed innocence. Many of them risked losing their homes, children, and livelihoods if they pleaded guilty, and yet his actions remained the same: His caseload often made it hard for him to clarify the facts—for example, whether his client had been the ringleader or had acted without intent or was guilty of a lesser crime—which is the kind of information that can mitigate the severity of a sentence or get charges dropped in negotiation. Part of Surrency's problem was that his contract did not fund investigations or expert witnesses.

QUESTIONS

1. **Case selection.** A Bureau of Justice Statistics study reported defendants with public defenders were incarcerated at a higher rate than those with private attorneys (71% to 54% in state courts). Does this necessarily imply that while better than appointed counsel, public defenders are inferior to retained counsel?

2. **Biting the hand that feeds?** Is there another potential source of moral hazard for appointed counsel that Roach's study does not discuss? The attorneys who volunteer for the panel are clearly lawyers who wish to be appointed now and (it is reasonable to assume) in the future. Besides the quality or urgency issues that Roach identifies, how might the desire for future appointment negatively impact the performance of appointed counsel?

D. JUDGES

Alongside prosecutors, judges are perhaps the most important actors when it comes to sentencing. Traditionally, judges have had tremendous power when setting sentences, as indeterminate statutes granted them wide discretion. The existence of parole meant that the judge's power was not absolute, but the imposed sentence often defined when a defendant would first be eligible for parole, ensuring that the judge's choice played a central role in determining time served.

In recent years, however, legislatures have sought to restrict the discretionary power of judges through sentencing guidelines, mandatory minimums, and other structured sentencing policies.[26] These developments, however, are not the focus of this section, and will be considered in Ch. 6. Instead, this section considers what it is that judges seek to accomplish from the bench, whatever the particular legal rules that may constrain their options.

---

[26] Legislatures have also tried to rein in parole boards, either by abolishing discretionary parole altogether, or by passing truth-in-sentencing laws, which require violent inmates to serve large percentages of their sentences before qualifying for parole. They have also developed actuarial release models that limit the discretion of parole boards in determining who to release and who to keep in prison.

The range of theories is wide. As Chris Guthrie, Jeffrey Rachlinski, and Andrew Wistrich point out:

> Legal scholars representing various schools of thought have long argued that judges do not merely find facts or apply legal principles in a completely accurate and unbiased fashion. Legal realists have argued that judges make choices that reflect their political ideology; proponents of critical legal studies have complained that judges favor the existing power structure; critical race and feminist scholars have argued that race and gender heavily influence judicial decisions; and law-and-economics scholars have asserted that judges make self-serving decisions designed to advance their political fortunes.[27]

Guthrie and his co-authors go on to point out that beyond these explicit factors, judges are often the victim of various biases as well. In this section, we will examine three forces that may shape how judges behave at sentencing: politics and ideology, race, and behavioral heuristics.

Start with political controls. Unlike federal judges, state judges do not receive lifetime appointments (except in Rhode Island). Some states employ partisan elections, others non-partisan elections, still others retention elections[28] following appointment by the governor or a merits commission (or the governor advised by such a commission).

Evidence suggests that selection methods influence sentencing decisions. Consider the following results:

- In Washington State, imposed sentences grow 10% longer as a trial judge approaches his or her next election.[29]

- In Kansas, trial judges elected in partisan elections are 16% to 23% more likely to impose incarceration than trial judges in that state who face only retention elections.[30]

- In Pennsylvania, judges approaching elections impose sentences approximately 24% to 37% longer than a recently-reelected judge, and a one standard-deviation increase in proximity to elections yields a 7% to 10%

---

[27] Chris Guthrie, Jeffrey Rachlinski, & Andrew Wistrich, *Inside the Judicial Mind*, 86 CORNELL L. REV. 777, 779–780 (2001).

[28] Under a retention election system, voters vote simply on whether to retain each judge whose term is expiring. Any judge who fails to receive enough favorable votes is removed from the bench, and whoever is in charge of appointments names a replacement. There is no head-to-head competition in these system: each candidate is simply competing against a favorable-vote cutoff line (such as 60% in Illinois).

[29] Carlos Berdejó and Noam Yuchtman, *Crime, Punishment, and Politics: An Analysis of Political Cycles in Criminal Sentencing* (2010), available on-line at http://faculty.haas.berkeley.edu/yuchtman/Noam_Yuchtman_files/Berdejo_Yuchtman_April_2012.pdf.

[30] Sanford C. Gordon & Gregory A. Huber, *The Effect of Electoral Competitiveness on Incumbent Behavior*, 2 Q. J. POLITICAL SCI. 107, 121 (2007).

increase in sentence length (so the effect operates over time, not just in an election year).[31]

- Politics appears to matter at higher levels as well. A study of Supreme Court decisions in Wisconsin suggests that justices who are initially appointed[32] rather than elected are more likely to vote against criminal defendants, and at least some (though not all) justices appear to have changed their behavior as elections neared (two became less defendant-friendly, one more so).[33]

These results indicate that whatever judges are maximizing, it is not exactly the desires of their constituents, or at least not all the time. In particular, judges appear to be somewhat more lenient than the electorate desires—or at least than they *think* the electorate desires. Unfortunately, the studies that examine this issue do not provide explanations about why judges are generally less severe when less (immediately) accountable. It's worth noting that one driving force behind the adoption of sentencing guidelines and other structured-sentencing rules was the perception that judges were too lenient.

One possible explanation for these trends is that criminal justice matters are generally viewed as being "low information, high salience" topics. What this means is that voters do not really pay attention to the day-to-day goings on, but make their decisions based on non-representative, high-profile cases. As elections near, then, judges become more concerned about high-profile mistakes, encouraging them to be more severe: voters will never know if a judge "over-incarcerates" someone, but if she gives a short sentence and the offender commits a horrible crime after release, that one case could determine the election.

Question: In the "low information, high salience" situation, is the judge a more faithful agent closer to, or further from, elections?

There is thus some "slack" to judicial behavior. Many commentators have raised the concern that judges will take advantage of such slack to satisfy racial and other biases by sentencing, say, minorities or women in systematically different ways. We start by looking at evidence of racial basis, and then we will turn our attention to gender bias.

---

[31] Gregory A. Huber & Sanford C. Gordon, *Accountability and Coercion: Is Justice Blind When It Runs for Office?*, 48 AM. J. POLITICAL SCI. 247, 255 (2004).

[32] All Supreme Court justices face retention elections, but some start via appointment, others via elections.

[33] Jason J. Czarnezki, *Voting and Electoral Politics in the Wisconsin Supreme Court*, 87 MARQ. L. REV. 323 (2003).

Jeffrey J. Rachlinski, Sheri Lynn Johnson, Andrew J. Wistrich, & Chris Guthrie, *Does Unconscious Racial Bias Affect Trial Judges?*
84 Notre Dame L. Rev. 1195, 1196–1197, 1221–1226 (2009)

Justice is not blind.

Researchers have found that black defendants fare worse in court than do their white counterparts. In a study of bail-setting in Connecticut, for example, Ian Ayres and Joel Waldfogel found that judges set bail at amounts that were twenty-five percent higher for black defendants than for similarly situated white defendants. In an analysis of judicial decisionmaking under the Sentencing Reform Act of 1984, David Mustard found that federal judges imposed sentences on black Americans that were twelve percent longer than those imposed on comparable white defendants. Finally, research on capital punishment shows that "killers of White victims are more likely to be sentenced to death than are killers of Black victims" and that "Black defendants are more likely than White defendants" to receive the death penalty.

Understanding why racial disparities like these and others persist in the criminal justice system is vital. Only if we understand why black defendants fare less well than similarly situated white defendants can we determine how to address this deeply troubling problem.

Two potential sources of disparate treatment in court are explicit bias and implicit bias. By explicit bias, we mean the kinds of bias that people knowingly—sometimes openly—embrace. Explicit bias exists and undoubtedly accounts for many of the racial disparities in the criminal justice system, but it is unlikely to be the sole culprit. Researchers have found a marked decline in explicit bias over time, even as disparities in outcomes persist.

Implicit bias—by which we mean stereotypical associations so subtle that people who hold them might not even be aware of them—also appears to be an important source of racial disparities in the criminal justice system. Researchers have found that most people, even those who embrace nondiscrimination norms, hold implicit biases that might lead them to treat black Americans in discriminatory ways. If implicit bias is as common among judges as it is among the rest of the population, it might even account for more of the racially disparate outcomes in the criminal justice system than explicit bias.

In this Article, we report the results of the first study of implicit racial bias among judges. We set out to explore whether judges hold implicit biases to the same extent as the general population and to determine whether those biases correlate with their decisionmaking in court.

Our research supports three conclusions. First, judges, like the rest of us, carry implicit biases concerning race. Second, these implicit biases can affect judges' judgment, at least in contexts where judges are unaware of a need to monitor their decisions for racial bias. Third, and conversely, when judges are aware of a need to monitor their own responses for the influence of implicit racial biases, and are motivated to suppress that bias, they appear able to do so.

Our first conclusion was perhaps the most predictable, though it is still troubling. Given . . . the frequency with which white Americans display at least a moderate automatic preference for white over black, it would have been surprising if white judges had failed to exhibit the same automatic preference. Similarly, the black judges carry a more diverse array of implicit biases, just like black adults generally: some exhibit a white preference just like the white judges; others exhibit no preference; and some exhibit a black preference. Overall, like adults, most of the judges—white and black—showed a moderate-to-large degree of implicit bias in one direction or the other. If ordinary adults carry a "bigot in the brain," as one recent article put it, then our data suggest that an invidious homunculus might reside in the heads of most judges in the United States, with the potential to produce racially biased distortions in the administration of justice.

It is worth noting, however, that the research on so-called "chronic egalitarians" suggests that this result was not inevitable. Some whites with longstanding and intense personal commitments to eradicating bias in themselves—chronic egalitarians—do not exhibit the preference for whites over blacks on the IAT [the Implicit Association Test, the primary test used by psychologists to test for implicit bias] that most white adults show. Despite their professional commitment to the equal application of the law, judges do not appear to have the same habits of mind as the chronic egalitarians. The proportion of white judges in our study who revealed automatic associations of white with good and black with bad was, if anything, slightly higher than the proportion found in the online surveys of white Americans. Thus, a professional commitment to equality, unlike a personal commitment to the same ideal, appears to have limited impact on automatic racial associations, at least among the judges in our study. Alternatively, the overrepresentation of black Americans among the criminal defendants who appear in front of judges might produce invidious associations that overwhelm their professional commitment.

[T]he research on judges . . . raises serious concerns about the role that unconscious bias might play in the criminal justice system. Jurors are drawn from randomly selected adults, and a majority of white jurors will harbor implicit white preferences. If police, prosecutors, jurors, judges, and defense attorneys all harbor anti-black preferences, then the system would appear to have limited safeguards to protect black defendants from bias. Based on IAT scores alone, both black judges and black jurors seem to be less biased than either white judges or white jurors, because black Americans show less implicit bias than white Americans. But even considerable numbers of blacks express implicit biases. Perhaps the only entity in the system that might avoid the influence of the bigot in the brain is a diversely composed jury.

That said, the rest of our results call into question the importance of IAT scores alone as a metric to evaluate the potential bias of decisionmakers in the legal system. Our second and third conclusions show that implicit biases can translate into biased decisionmaking under certain circumstances, but that they do not do so consistently.

Implicit associations influenced judges—both black judges and white judges—when we manipulated the race of the defendant by subliminal methods. [T]he subliminal processes triggered unconscious bias, and in just the way that might be expected.

The story for the explicit manipulation of race is more complicated, however. We believe that the data demonstrate that the white judges were attempting to compensate for unconscious racial biases in their decisionmaking [when the race of the defendant was explicitly addressed]. These judges were, we believe, highly motivated to avoid making biased judgments, at least in our study. Codes of judicial conduct demand that judges make unbiased decisions, at least in our study. Moreover, impartiality is a prominent element in almost every widely accepted definition of the judicial role. Judges take these norms seriously. When the materials identified the race of the defendant in a prominent way, the white judges probably engaged in cognitive correction to avoid the appearance of bias.

The black judges responded somewhat differently to the overt labeling of the defendant's race. Like the white judges, the black judges in our study also reported being aware of the subject of the study, yet they showed a correlation between implicit associations and judgment when race was explicitly manipulated. Among these judges, a greater white preference produced a greater propensity to convict the African American defendant.

We do not conclude, however, that black judges are less concerned about avoiding biased decisionmaking than white judges. We have no doubt that the professional norms against bias concern the black judges just as deeply as their white counterparts—if not more so. And we are mindful that research on the effect of race on judges' decisions in actual cases demonstrates no clear effects. We believe that both white and black judges were motivated to avoid showing racial bias.

Why then did the black judges produce different results? We can only speculate, but we suspect that both groups of judges were keen to avoid appearing to favor the white defendant (or conversely, wanted to avoid appearing to disfavor the black defendant). Black judges, however, might have been less concerned with appearing to favor the black defendant than the white judges. Those black judges who expressed a white preference, however, behaved more like their white counterparts in this regard, thereby producing a correlation between verdict and IAT score among black judges.

Given our results, we cannot definitively ascribe continuing racial disparities in the criminal justice system to unconscious bias. We nevertheless can draw some firm conclusions. First, implicit biases are widespread among judges. Second, these biases can influence their judgment. Finally, judges seem to be aware of the potential for bias in themselves and possess the cognitive skills necessary to avoid its influence. When they are motivated to avoid the appearance of bias, and face clear cues that risk a charge of bias, they can compensate for implicit bias.

Whether the judges engage their abilities to avoid bias on a continual basis in their own courtrooms, however, is unclear. Judges are subject to the same significant professional norms to avoid prejudice in their courtrooms that they carried with them into our study. But courtrooms can be busy places that do not afford judges the time necessary to engage the corrective cognitive mechanisms that they seem to possess. Control of implicit bias requires active, conscious control. Judges who, due to time pressure or other distractions, do not actively engage in an effort to control the "bigot in the brain" are apt to behave just as the judges in our study in which we subliminally primed with race-related words.

Furthermore, judges might be overconfident about their abilities to control their own biases. In recently collected data, we asked a group of judges attending an educational conference to rate their ability to "avoid racial prejudice in decisionmaking" relative to other judges who were attending the same conference. Ninety-seven percent (thirty-five out of thirty-six) of the judges placed themselves in the top half and fifty percent (eighteen out of thirty-six) placed themselves in the top quartile, even though by definition, only fifty percent can be above the median, and only twenty-five percent can be in the top quartile. We worry that this result means that judges are overconfident about their ability to avoid the influence of race and hence fail to engage in corrective processes on all occasions.

Gender, too, is thought to influence sentencing outcomes. As the next reading indicates, the means by which it can do so are varied.

Timothy Griffin and John Wooldredge, *Sex-Based Disparities in Felony Disparities Before versus After Sentencing Reform in Ohio*

Scholars have posed several explanations for sex-based disparities in the treatment of criminal defendants, most of which involve predictions of more lenient treatment of women relative to men. One such perspective is the chivalry hypothesis, which states that male judges, who dominate the courts, may believe that they are protecting a woman when seeking greater leniency. Similarly, preferential treatment of women with children might also reflect the court's interest in protecting families from hardships caused through the incarceration of mothers. Women may receive favorable treatment if judges count the protection of children among their focal concerns. By contrast, married fathers may be treated more severely by the courts if these men are perceived as irresponsible parents. A slightly more critical perspective underlies the paternalism hypothesis, which postulates that women receive more lenient treatment as part of an implicit arrangement in larger society where women "trade" their status for favored consideration in social institutions such as the justice system. A competing perspective to these other ideas is the evil woman hypothesis, which proposes that women who commit crimes are at risk of being perceived as violating prescribed gender roles. This results in a disproportionately more punitive reaction from criminal justice decision makers, who may seek to reaffirm traditional gender roles for women through legal sanctions.

Further complicating the question of disparate treatment by a defendant's sex is whether any chivalrous treatment is equally shared by African American women, or by women who stray from the prescribed roles of "good mother" and "good wife." [One scholar] suggested that, because of entrenched stereotypes about the supposed incivility of African American women, judges may be less likely to perceive these women as responsible spouses and mothers and thus might deny them leniency. Some argue that patriarchy-chivalry is inherently racist, structured to protect "respectable" (that is, middle-class and white) women only, and thus minority female offenders, who disproportionately come from disadvantaged backgrounds, will fail to occupy this respectable female role.

Similarly, employed women might be more likely to receive punitive treatment by the courts if they are viewed as stepping outside their expected gender roles. Also, sentencing judges might disregard gender in assessing the severity of drug offenses because they perceive male and female drug offenders as being equal in their risk for recidivism. Women convicted of serious drug crimes also might not enjoy any benefit of chivalry if judges view their involvement with drugs as a particularly irresponsible lifestyle that could jeopardize children. In this sense, the evil woman and chivalry perspectives could be seen as opposite predictions stemming from the same basic phenomenon: preferential or punitive treatment is meted out based on the degree to which court actors perceive a female defendant as fitting the stereotype of either a good or a bad woman.

Some scholars have argued that the empirical link between a defendant's sex and case outcomes is more modest than others believe, once controls are introduced for legally relevant criteria such as the nature of the offense and criminal record, though women may still receive some leniency because of perceptions that they are more amenable to rehabilitation or because of court actors' concerns for children. Evidence to date is mixed regarding the applicability of any one of these perspectives. Perhaps some of the ambiguity can be attributed to differences across studies in controls for severity of offense and criminal record (assuming that, relative to men, female defendants tend to cluster at the lower ends of offense severity and criminal history).

As a final note, even lunch-time can influence judicial decisions. Shai Danzinger and others discovered that Israeli judges become increasingly less favorably inclined toward potential parolees the hungrier (or at least the more tired or bored) they get.[34] The figure below plots the likelihood of ruling in favor of the parolee over the course of the day; the effect of food breaks is clear and unambiguous.

---

[34] Shai Danzinger, Jonathan Levav & Liora Avnaim-Pesso, *Extraneous Factors in Judicial Elections*, 108 PNAS 6889 (2011).

Figure 3–2: Time of Day and Parolee-Favorable Decisions

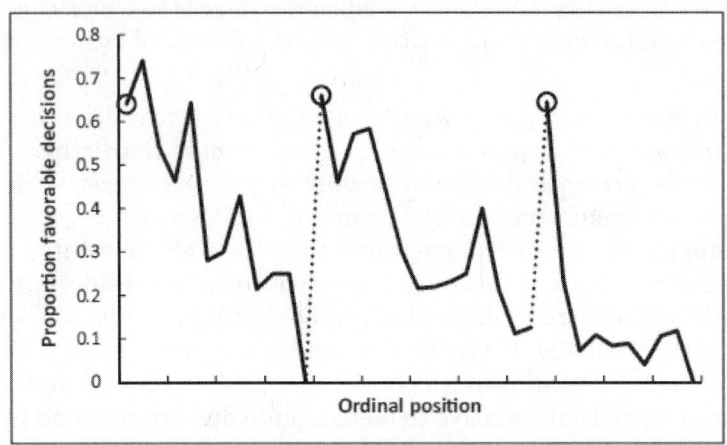

Fig. 1. Proportion of rulings in favor of the prisoners by ordinal position. Circled points indicate the first decision in each of the three decision sessions; tick marks on *x* axis denote every third case; dotted line denotes food break. Because unequal session lengths resulted in a low number of cases for some of the later ordinal positions, the graph is based on the first 95% of the data from each session.

Since the 1970s, states have taken various steps to try to rein in such abuses of discretion. Reforms such as guidelines, however, raise as many questions as they answer. Discretion, for example, is a weaselly thing: taking discretion away from judges has the effect of putting more in the hands of prosecutors (who can effectively determine the guideline sentence by choosing what charges to file). Do we trust prosecutors more than judges to be free of these biases? And seemingly-neutral provisions can often have racially- or gender-disparate impact. Increasing the sanction for offenders with increasingly longer prior records is something that all structured sentencing regimes do, and on its face this seems racially neutral. Yet blacks tend to have longer records than whites, perhaps because they objectively offend more (though if true, one must ask why), or perhaps because their neighborhoods—and neighborhoods remains racially stratified to this day—are subject to more aggressive policing, so more of their offenses are detected and punished.

So far, our discussion has focused on trial judges as opposed to appellate judges, which reflects the relative historical importance of trial judges. Under the indeterminate sentencing regimes that prevailed in the US until the 1970s, there was very little, at times almost nothing, for appellate courts to review when it came to sentencing: trial court discretion was large and generally unreviewable.[35] The rise of structured

---

[35] See John F. Pfaff, *The Future of Appellate Sentencing Review:* Booker *in the States*, 93 MARQ. L. REV. 683 (2009).

sentencing expanded the importance of appellate review, since in states with guideline systems appellate courts were now called upon to assess whether trial courts were properly adhering to the guidelines.

There is no reason to assume that appellate judges behave in ways that differ in any important respect from trial judges. Judge Richard Posner famously answered the question "What do [appellate] judges maximize?" with the answer "The same thing everybody else does."[36] The only possible restriction on appellate behavior is that the range of issues they consider is substantially more limited. In general, it appears that (state) appellate judges primarily ask whether the trial judge has a sufficient factual basis for the various aggravating and mitigating factors he used to justify the sentence imposed. Although appellate judges often have the statutory ability to review the substantive merits of a sentence, they do not appear to use this authority with any regularity.[37] Such circumscribed review likely restricts the extent to which appellate judges can indulge their policy preferences.

QUESTIONS

1. **The leniency of judges.** Why do you think judges are more lenient than their constituents? Does it have to do with demographics of the judge vis-à-vis her constituents? With docket pressure? With knowledge—and if so, what sort? Judges are "closer" to the world of crime than their (average) constituents, and thus more aware of the costs and effectiveness of offending, but also of victimization.

2. **Staggered elections.** Is it better or worse for different judges to be up for election in different years? What would the overall distribution of sentences look like over time if all judges are elected in the same year? in staggered years? Which outcome is more normatively appealing?

3. **Facially neutral but biased.** As noted above, some sentencing restrictions, like requiring harsher sanctions for repeat offenders, can appear racially neutral but operate in a racially disparate way. Assume that two defendants, one white and one black, have identical offending histories, but the black defendant has a longer official criminal record due to the increased presence of policing in his neighborhood (and thus the increased risk of arrest). If a judge imposes a tougher sentence on the black defendant, solely due to his longer record (as prescribed by the guidelines), is she acting in a biased manner? Should she correct for the underlying reason in prior-record disparities? *Can* she?

4. **Implicit bias.** What sort of steps can courts take to fight implicit bias? As a hint, note that implicit racial bias among referees in the NBA (who generally called fouls on black players more than on white ones) appears to

---

[36] Richard A. Posner, *What Do Judges Maximize? (The Same Thing Everybody Else Does)*, 3 SUP. CT. ECON. REV. 1 (1993).

[37] See examples in Pfaff, *Future of Appellate Sentencing Review*, supra note 35.

have almost completely vanished just a few years after an academic paper identifying the bias in their foul calls gained widespread attention.

5. **The proper role of appellate courts.** How hands-off should appellate courts be? Do various theories of punishment suggest different degrees of deference to trial-court fact-finding? Are some theories of punishment more fact-intensive or fact-specific than others?

E. GOVERNORS AND STATE ATTORNEYS GENERAL

The role of the governor (as well as the state attorney general) is fairly limited in sentencing law. In many states, the governor's most important criminal justice job is selecting the members of the parole board, whose incentives we discuss next. Governors also have the ability to grant pardons and other acts of clemency, although as we will see in Chapter 12, they use such clemency powers rarely. It is perhaps not surprising, then, that a recent empirical study found no real connection between a governor's political affiliation and that state's prison population.[38]

The lack of direct gubernatorial influence is perhaps somewhat troubling. The governor, after all, is the only truly state-level official involved in the criminal justice system. Even state legislators, whose offices are nominally state-level, are elected at the district level. With a state-wide constituency, the governor is uniquely capable of solving the various moral hazard and agency problems that infest disaggregated state criminal justice systems. In fact, since the start of the financial crisis in 2008 governors have increasing released prisoners early in order to rein in prison budgets; with state fiscal capacity severely constrained, governors are playing a more active role in protecting the state budget, since prosecutors generally lack any such incentive.

Moreover, there is at least one way governors can exert some authority, perhaps an important amount: the bully pulpit. Joseph Davey argues that "the political views of US governors concerning the proper reaction to criminal offenders should be considered one of the most significant factors in determining interstate variations in the rate of imprisonment."[39] To develop this point, he examines pairs of states (such as Missouri and Kansas, or North and South Carolina) which went from having similar to dissimilar incarceration rates shortly after one of the states elected a tough-on-crime conservative governor.

The causal story here, however, is tricky. Davey says, for example, that the then-newly elected conservative governor of Maine, Judd Gregg, "recently revised" various mandatory minimum laws. That is not quite correct: the *legislature* revised the laws, and Gregg signed the changes

---

[38] Thomas D. Stucky, Karen Heimer, and Joseph B. Lang, *Partisan Politics, Electoral Competition and Imprisonment: An Analysis of States Over Time*, 43 CRIMINOLOGY 211 (2005).

[39] JOSEPH DILLON DAVEY, THE POLITICS OF PRISON EXPANSION: WINNING ELECTIONS BY WAGING WAR ON CRIME 47 (1998).

into effect. Had the legislature balked, Gregg could not have changed the laws. And we have to ask: if the voters in Maine suddenly elected a much more conservative governor, did they also elect more conservative legislators, or did the incumbents who survived realize that they needed to adopt similar positions? Or—consistent with Davey's claim about gubernatorial importance—do governors have sufficient powers of political suasion to ram through legislation of this sort? It seems likely that they have *some* power, but it is indirect. And the findings by Stucky above caution against assuming it is particularly strong, which given the amount of discretion downstream actors have should not be surprising.

Furthermore, the governor's power, such as it is, is asymmetric. By encouraging legislatures to repeal or weaken state laws, he can deny prosecutors power. If the statutory maximum for assault drops from ten to five years, prosecutors cannot threaten ten year sentences during plea bargain negotiations. But the governor cannot force prosecutors to take advantage of tough-on-crime legislation that he pushes through. Consider the following example from New York State. Governor Nelson Rockefeller was sufficiently influential in advocating for the tough drug laws New York adopted in 1972 that they are referred to as the "Rockefeller Drug Laws." Yet Fig. 3–3 plots the number of drug offenders in New York State prisons, and look what happens in the years after 1972. They rise slightly, and then they *drop*. Local prosecutors didn't care about the new laws and declined to use them, taking advantage of them only when the crack epidemic (which arrived around 1984) motivated them to do so. It is also interesting to note that the number of drug offenders in New York prisons started dropping well before the Drug Laws were reformed, first toothlessly in 2004 and then more substantively in 2009.

Fig. 3–3: Drug Offenders in New York State Prisons

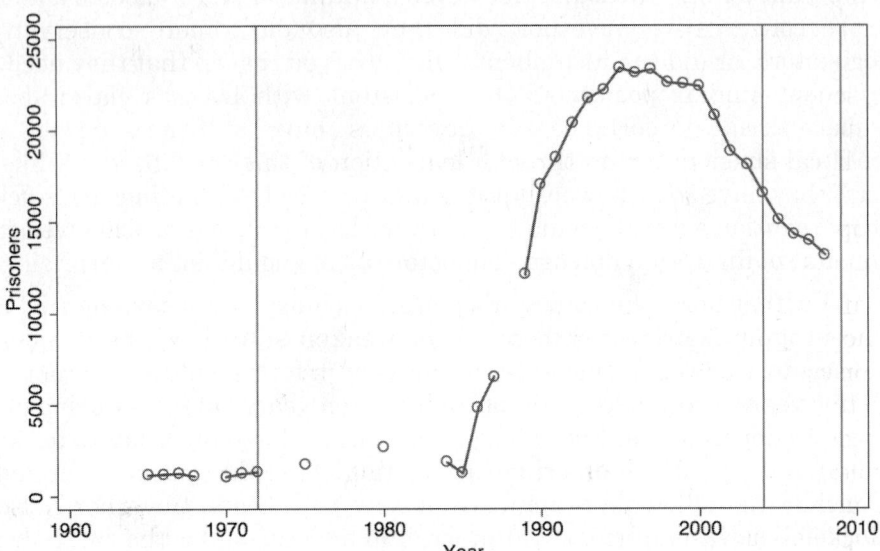

Note: The first line is 1972, the second 2004 and the third 2009. Data from the New York State Statistical Yearbook, various years.

The governor, however, is not the only state-level actor who can matter. In some states, the state attorney general has statutory power to act as a coordinating official over local prosecutors, which seems like a possibility for centralized control. As Rachel Barkow demonstrates, however, whatever nominal authority such attorneys general have, they rarely exert it, often due to court opinions that interpret such authority narrowly.[40] In some smaller states, like Alaska, Delaware, or Maine, state attorneys general have more direct control—in Delaware, the state attorney general appoints all local district attorneys, and in Maine the attorney general has exclusive authority to bring homicide charges—but Barkow rightly points out that, population-wise, these states are more akin to smaller localities in bigger states (Delaware is not even as large as any of the ten largest cities in the United States). As with the governor, one of the few government officials with authority over criminal justice issues and a true state-wide constituency fails to play much of a role in the day-to-day administration of criminal justice.

F. PAROLE BOARDS AND OFFICERS

The last actor with direct control over a prisoner's sentence is the parole board. The first parole board was established in 1876, and as state criminal justice systems increasingly embraced a therapeutic model of

---

[40] Rachel E. Barkow, *Federalism and Criminal Law: What the Feds Can Learn from the States*, 109 MICH. L. REV. 519 (2011).

rehabilitation, parole boards and parole releases spread: by 1940, 40% of all prisoners were released via parole, and by 1977 that number peaked at 72%. The connection between rehabilitation and parole is clear. Prisoners should not be released until they are rehabilitated, but they also should not be detained after such time, and it is impossible for a judge to know at sentencing exactly when that key transitional moment will occur. Thus parole boards would periodically examine prisoners before the expiration of their sentences to see if early release was appropriate.

By the 1970s, as faith in rehabilitation declined, so too did that in parole. By 2000, sixteen states had completely abolished parole, and by the early 2000s over forty states had restricted it in some way.[41] Yet we don't want to overstate the decline in parole. As of 2001, parole boards in fifteen states had full release powers, and those in nineteen more that had limited release powers still retained significant discretion (i.e., only releases for murder were restricted by statute). All told, in a majority of states the parole system continues to play an important role in prisoner supervision.[42]

My goal here is not to discuss the mechanics of the parole system; much of Chapter 12 is dedicated to that issue. In this section I simply want to briefly touch on the incentives faced by parole boards (who decide whether to release inmates) and parole officers (who supervise those who are released).

We will start with parole boards. A recent survey of parole board appointment policies makes it clear that states vary widely on the prerequisites for being on a parole board, and many do not require much in the way of criminal justice experience. In most states (43), vacancies are filled by gubernatorial appointments, while in the remaining states appointments were made by the director of corrections (a gubernatorial appointee himself), or jointly by executive and judicial authorities. Terms range from 4 to 7 years, though in one state the term is indefinite and in another permanent; salaries vary from $40,000 to $100,000. Only eleven states specified any educational requirements, and five more had vaguer educational qualifications; eight required at least a BA. Slightly under half of all states required work experience, and only fifteen required prior criminal justice or social work experience. Almost three-fourths of all states did not require any sort of in-service training.[43]

As that summary makes clear, parole board members are often not particularly well-trained or well-prepared for their jobs. Efforts to professionalize parole boards can be difficult. One governor appointed a

---

[41] See John F. Pfaff, *The Continued Vitality of Structured Sentencing Following* Blakely: *The Effectiveness of Voluntary Guidelines*, 54 UCLA L. REV. 235, 241–247 (2005).

[42] JOAN PETERSILIA, REFORMING PROBATION AND PAROLE 138 (2002).

[43] Mario M. Paparozzi & Joel M. Caplan, *A Profile of Paroling Authorities in America: The Strange Bedfellows of Politics and Professionalism*, 89 PRISON J. 401 (2009).

psychologist to the board, only to face criticism for that decision from law enforcement and victims'-rights groups. Perhaps not surprisingly, then, there are concerns that relatively unskilled and politically-dependent parole authorities are perhaps overly responsive to shocking crimes by parolees and highly vulnerable to political pressure. The authors of the parole-board survey give an example:

> A[n] . . . example sheds light on the direct political link between paroling authority members and the politicians who appoint them and how this linkage ignobly permeates the administration of parole. At the height of the Iowa caucus primary elections [in 2008], former Arkansas governor and Republican candidate for president Mike Huckabee was blamed by some for the 1997 parole of a rapist who, once paroled, raped and killed a woman in Missouri. . . . Huckabee denied involvement in the parole release decision of the rapist and stated that "governors don't parole people in Arkansas." In 1996, the parole board had voted not to grant parole to the convicted rapist. [I]t was reported that . . . then[-]governor Huckabee met with the parole board about the unduly harsh sentence that the convicted rapist had received. Subsequent to the meeting with the governor, the board's chair, who was appointed by a previous governor and later reappointed by Huckabee, arranged for a reconsideration of parole release hearing; . . . parole was granted. One of the members of the parole board who was involved in the 1997 reconsideration . . . came forward and declared that he felt pressure from . . . Huckabee to grant parole. Later, at least two additional board members added to the chorus of claims that they too were pressured into making a decision that they might otherwise not have made.
>
> The comments of one of the parole board members involved in the allegations of gubernatorial influence over the parole of the rapist is illustrative of a political skeleton in parole's professional closet: "We are not talking rocket science here. The board jobs are known to some degree [to be] political patronage, and they're not the most difficult jobs for the pay."
>
> The Arkansas Times reported that in 2002, members of the Board of Pardons and Parole earned $70,000 a year. The median income in Arkansas in 1999 was $32,182.[44]

The Huckabee example points to a significant problem parole boards and other actors with discretionary authority face, what I will call the "false positive" problem. Parole boards are in charge of making risk assessments, predicting both who will reciviviate and who will not. Sometimes—perhaps often—the board will make a mistake: it will parole

---

[44] *Id.*

someone who will recidivate (a false negative) or not parole someone who will not recidivate (a false positive).[45] Ideally, the board should seek to balance both types of errors, but in practice board members face highly asymmetric incentives. A false negative is publicly visible, but a false positive is almost completely invisible. It is easy to observe the parolee who reoffends, but it is very hard to see the non-parolee who would not have reoffended—no one questioned Huckabee about all those who were detained for *too long*. This suggests that parole boards have an incentive to be unduly harsh.

Their harshness, however, may not be unbiased. Stéphane Mechoulan and Nicolas Sahuguet, for example, provide evidence that blacks released via discretionary parole are generally 10% more likely to recidivate than whites.[46] These results imply that parole boards are not making color-blind decisions. The implications of Mechoulan and Sahuguet's intriguing results are discussed more in the questions below.

The parole board, however, only exerts partial control over the release of an inmate. While the parole board decides who gets released, parole officers help determine whether the now-released inmate remains free. And the revocation of parole, at least at a superficial level, has played an important (and perhaps increasingly important) role in prison growth over the past several decades. About 28% of prisoners admitted each year are coming in off parole; this is up from 15% in 1978.[47] (In California, an outlier, that percent peaked at nearly 70% in 2001, though it dropped precipitously from 62% to 23% in 2012 due to the particularities of Realignment.) Parole officers possess significant discretion in this process, so it is useful to understand their incentives as well.

After being paroled (by a parole board) or put on probation (by a judge), the defendant is supervised by a parole or probation officer (PPO). Like the police, prosecutor, and parole boards, PPOs have widespread discretion in how to handle the offenders they supervise when they run afoul of the various restrictions placed on them. A recent study of PPO behavior noted that very little work has been done to understand the how-and-why of PPO decision-making. The authors did note one set of ethnographic studies from the 1970s that pointed to the importance of institutional and organizational—but extra-legal—factors to PPO decisions:

---

[45] The use of "negative" and "positive" is somewhat arbitrary here. I am using "positive" to refer to someone identified as likely to recidivate.

[46] Stéphane Mechoulan & Nicolas Sahuguet, *Assessing Racial Discrimination in Parole Release*, available on-line at http://papers.ssrn.com/sol3/papers.cfm?abstract_id=1874251 (2011).

[47] That parolees make up a sizable share of entering admissions cohorts is clear; less clear is what this implies. It could be that prosecutors use parole violations as a speedy way to dispose of cases involving parolees committing new, substantive offenses, and it seems inappropriate to count such cases as examples of "parole violations driving growth," Chapter 9 discusses this in more depth.

[A] PPO's personal preferences were as likely to inform decision making as were standard structural or organizational factors. In an effort to maintain a positive reputation and appear credible to their superiors, parole officers reported pressure to underreport violations; they also believed that high revocation hearing rates might suggest that a given parole officer was unable to properly handle cases. In addition, caseload size may affect the officer's tendency to report minor violations. [The author] noted that large caseloads may cause officers to underreport minor violations; conversely, reduced caseloads may increase the officers' rate of reporting for rule violations by probationers and parolees. . . .[48]

In their own survey of 332 PPOs, from a survey mailed to 1,845 current members of the American Probation and Parole Association, the authors found the following PPO traits to be correlated with increased punitiveness, which they measured as a preference for formal proceedings (possibly leading to revocation) over internal administrative remedies which would avoid the risk of revocation: being female, being a racial minority, being in a smaller agency, and the absence of internal rules restricting violations back to prison due to technical violations; education, years of experience, geographic location (i.e., being Southern) and urbanization all did not seem to influence behavior much (although urban agencies are likely larger in size).

That larger caseloads seem to be correlated with more-punitive responses initially surprised the authors. Their focus was on technical violations, so they had assumed that as caseloads increased, PPOs would dispose of technical cases through faster, more informal means in order to focus on more serious violators. But their findings are consistent with a concern that is often expressed about PPOs and caseloads. In many ways, PPOs face a somewhat contradictory job: they are tasked both with providing support and directing offenders to services (such as employment training, job search assistance, as well as drug and other treatments) as well as with punishing offenders for violating any of the conditions of release they face. There is growing concern that increased caseloads and always-longer lists of release restrictions are pushing PPOs to favor enforcement over social support.

Of course, caseload pressure is not the only force pushing PPOs towards enforcement over service provision. As Mark Kleiman notes, programs may simply not be effective enough to be cost-benefit justifiable, especially in a time of tight budgets like today:

> The literature on recidivism reduction via service delivery—the "reentry" literature—for the most part, makes for fairly

---

[48] John J. Kerbs, Mark Jones & Jennifer M. Jolley, *Discretionary Decision Making by Probation and Parole Officers: The Role of Extralegal Variables as Predictors of Responses to Technical Violations*, 25 J. CONTEMP. CRIM. J. 424, 426–27 (2009).

depressing reading; a program that moves the 3-year return-to-prison rate from 66% to 60% counts as a success. Given that the total annual prison budget is only $60 billion, the potential savings from reduced incarceration can hardly finance major increases in social-service budgets or fuel major upsurges in neighborhood economic activity, even if spent in ways that lead to respending within the affected neighborhoods.[49]

Kleiman then argues that improved supervision techniques, relying on properly-designed sanctions (which favor short, immediate detentions over delayed formal revocations), can be much more effective, at least for preventing future offending. We will look at such programs in later chapters.

QUESTIONS

1. **A benefit to gubernatorial appointment?** Is there something to the fact that parole boards are appointed by the governor—as opposed to more-local authorities—that might force them to better balance false negatives and false positives? Would your answer be the same before and after the economic crisis of 2008?

2. **Truly invisible?** Is it true that false positives (people kept in prison who would not have reoffended) cannot be seen? Admittedly, false negatives manifest themselves in completed crimes, while identifying false positives requires us to observe that which did not (and could not) happen. But are such counterfactuals truly invisible? Even if not invisible, however, does the design of the parole board and the types of political pressures governors and parole boards face still render such evidence unusable?

3. **Racial bias in releases.** At first blush, Mechoulan and Sahuguet's results suggest that parole boards are more generous to black inmates than to white ones, since they "overrelease" blacks relative to whites. But is there an interpretation of these results that points to anti-black biases? How important is the fact that neighborhoods in the United States still remain relatively homogenous? And what do you think the geographic/demographic profile of paroles boards tends to be?

G. LEGISLATURES

So far, we have looked at the government officials with direct control over each step an offender takes in the criminal justice system: arrest (the police), prosecution (the lawyers), admission and time imposed (the judges), and release (the governor and the parole board). Presiding over this system is the legislature, which operates from a position both of

---

[49] Mark A. R. Kleiman, *Justice Reinvestment in Community Supervision*, 10 CRIMINOLOGY & PUB. POL'Y 651, 651 (2011).

power and weakness. On the one hand, the legislature[50] sets the rules: it defines crimes and the sentences that attach to them, establishes any guidelines or mandatory minimums (or creates a sentencing commission to do so), and controls the prison system's budget and wields extensive control over local budgets as well.[51] On the other hand, the legislature has no direct ability to ensure that the downstream actors actually obey the rules it sets. It cannot meaningfully prevent prosecutors from bargaining around mandatory minimums, or from even declining to prosecute entire categories of crimes, and it may often find itself disagreeing with how courts choose to interpret various guideline provisions.

The legislature thus faces a tricky strategic situation, since the downstream actors are not *entirely* free to do whatever they want, but they do have a significant amount of discretion. Recall the claim by Richman and Stuntz above that local prosecutors face some political pressure to avoid pretextual charging. This suggests that there are limits to the extent prosecutors can alter charges to circumvent legislative decrees; legislatures can capitalize on this friction to shape prosecutorial behavior. In other words, prosecutors may not have the political freedom to charge all murders as manslaughters to avoid what they perceive to be too-harsh punishments for murder. But if legislatures overreach, downstream actors will eventually seek ways to evade extreme rules. Consider the following example, which examines the use of drug courts in New York State:

> [O]ne must . . . appreciate a somewhat unique fact about New York City drug courts: they welcome drug dealers. In fact, . . . drug dealers comprised the overwhelming majority of all participants—an astounding 95 percent in the Bronx drug court and 90 percent in the Brooklyn drug court. Indeed, in the Bronx, practically all of the participants were charged not just with sale, but with B-felony sale—the highest level felony charge that was eligible for drug court.
>
> Why did the city's felony drug courts so readily accept drug dealers, and, conversely, why did they include so few drug possessors? Over the past two decades, institutional players of various stripes came to see the one-dimensional incapacitation model as unsustainable and inefficient. [E]ven some of the most hardened drug warriors had grown weary of harsh sentences as the lone drug-war weapon. On the surface of it, the drug-court model seemed to provide a third way—a politically-feasible

---

[50] And, less directly, the governor, via his veto- and agenda-setting powers, as well as his bully pulpit and any (informal) authority he has over members of his own party in the legislature.

[51] About one third of local revenue comes from intergovernmental transfers from the state government. See John F. Pfaff, *The Micro and Macro Causes of Prison Growth*, 28 GA. ST. L. REV. 1237 (2012).

middle ground that promised a little bit of something for everyone. For the therapeutic community, drug courts provided much-needed alternatives to incarceration. . . . For drug warriors, drug courts promoted expeditious case processing, required rigorous treatment, ensured traditional incapacitation for failing participants, and also deflated calls for more radical legislative change.

Drug courts, then, are experimentalist institutions born of incremental compromise. [T]he city's drug courts were intended, at least partially, as a response to (or an end-run around) the unpopular and draconian Rockefeller drug laws. As indicated by a New York State Commission (made up of prosecutors, defense attorneys, judges, and academics) that endorsed statewide drug-court expansion: "The courts, of course, do not write the state's drug or sentencing laws. . . . The issue is thus whether there is anything—consistent with their adjudicatory role—that our state courts can do."

Historically, for felony possession cases, drug courts were not needed to circumvent unwelcome application of the Rockefeller drug laws. Instead, prosecutors would commonly reduce felony possession charges to misdemeanor charges. Conversely, prosecutors had no readily available statutory option to reduce sale charges. In any event, prosecutors were unwilling to do so; they might have disliked aspects of the Rockefeller drug laws, but they still believed that drug sales were best handled as felonies, not misdemeanors. As such, drug courts offered a way to "draw a distinction," where the law as written had failed to do so, "between an addicted drug user or low-level seller, on the one hand, and a drug trafficker, on the other." Consequently, drug courts came to welcome many drug dealers because the preexisting sentencing options were undesirable, and the courts came to handle so few felony drug possessors, because this defendant population already comprised such a small pool.[52]

The experience in New York State demonstrates well both the friction—prosecutors were either unwilling or unable to avoid filing felony charges against drug dealers—and the slack: eventually prosecutors and judges worked together to circumvent the disliked Rockefeller Drug Laws.

I want to consider two questions about legislative incentives here. First, how do electoral pressures and political ideology influence legislative behavior? And second, is there any explanation for why legislatures seem to pass laws that are more severe than what prosecutors themselves (and perhaps even the public) desire? Answering

---

[52] Josh Bowers, *Contraindicated Drug Courts*, 55 UCLA L. REV. 783, 794–797 (2008).

these questions will provide a broad overview of legislative decision-making; Chapter 9 will examine the politics of punishment in much more depth.

To start, the following reading maps out the relationship between partisan politics and state penal policies.

Thomas D. Stucky, Karen Heimer, and Joseph B. Lang, *Partisan Politics, Electoral Competition and Imprisonment: An Analysis of States Over Time*
43 CRIMINOLOGY 211 (2005)

[T]hree recent quantitative studies have assessed the association between Republican party politics and imprisonment in states over time . . . [and] have produced somewhat inconsistent results. [Two studies find that incarceration rates rise with the percent of the legislature that is Republican, with the effect growing stronger over time, and one finds no effect of legislative conservatism.]

[One reason for the discrepancy could be different measures of "Republican-ness."] Second, and more important for our study, the association between Republican strength and imprisonment rates may not be as straight-forward as proposed by previous research. Specifically, it may be that the relationship between Republican strength and imprisonment is conditional on the political situation in voting districts. Indeed, political science research on state politics and public policy suggests that political competition at the district level can influence the orientation of legislators with regard to social policies.

[R]ecently, several researchers have suggested that . . . state and district-level competition are conceptually and empirically distinct. Thus, it is possible to have perfect competition at one level and none at the other. Hypothetically, all state legislative elections could be won by one party based on 51 percent of the votes or the state legislature could be narrowly controlled by one party (fifty-one to forty-nine seats), but no legislators would face meaningful competition on election day; these situations are likely to have very different policy consequences.

Indeed, recent researchers have begun to suggest that the politics-policy association may be conditional on district-level competition for votes. . . . As Barrilleaux and his colleagues . . . note, previous research has generally considered either the party in power or the macrolevel balance of power between the two parties. Barrilleaux and his colleagues suggest that one must consider both the party in power and the micro-level competition in a state. When there is close competition within a district, legislators must be truer to the preferences of core constituents, so as not to alienate core voters. Thus, Democratic and Republican legislators will each be expected to produce policies more in line with their respective party preferences when they face greater electoral competition. When the level of electoral competition goes down, however, there is less incentive for legislators to adhere to preferences of core voters because their seats are safe.

Following this logic, we would expect imprisonment rates to increase most when Republicans control the state legislature and face stiff competition. Under circumstances of high competition, Republican legislators should be most likely to vote closer to their core constituency preferences on law-and-order issues.

[*Ed. note*: Stucky's paper does not provide concise data on the extent to which state elections are competitive or contested. In a study of 30 states in the years 1994 and 1996 (the tail end of Stucky's study, which examined the years 1977 to 1996), Robert Hogan reports that, on average, 67% of state legislative races are contested and 28% competitive, where Hogan defines "contested" to mean that the losing major-party candidate received at least 10% of the vote and "competitive" to mean that the winning candidate received no more than 60% of the vote.[53] Stucky uses slightly different definitions: "uncontested" means the winner ran without opposition, and "competitive" means that the margin of victory was less than 20%, but Hogan's findings should be fairly consistent with Stucky's.]

[W]e find that the effect of the proportion of Republican seats in the legislature on the odds of admission (hereafter, the "Republican effect") indeed depends on both competition for seats and time. In any particular year, the Republican legislature effect increases as competition increases. Also, at any particular level of competition, the Republican legislative effect increases over time.

[Stucky et al. then provide an example which essentially demonstrates that the impact of a 10% increase in the number of Republicans in the state legislature doubles when moving from the least-competitive states to the middle-of-the-pack states, and then grows by another 20% when moving from those moderate states to the most competitive.]

The effect of Republican strength in the legislature also increases over time.... [L]oosely speaking, the Republican legislature effect starts out negligible, and becomes significantly positive over time. [And] although there is indeed a general tendency for the Republican legislative effect to become stronger over time, we demonstrate that the Republican legislative effect also depends on level of electoral competition.

There are a few limitations to our research, which must be appreciated. First, like previous studies of politics and imprisonment, we are assuming that Republican dominance is associated with an emphasis

---

[53] Robert E. Hogan, *Institutional and District-Level Sources of Competition in State Legislative Elections*, 84 SOC. SCI. Q. 543, 552 (2003).

on law-and-order that translates into criminal punishment. There may of course be important variations within party that are missed by this approach.

Another caveat is that our research, like other studies of imprisonment rates, considers only one stage in the criminal justice process. The complex interconnections between politics, imprisonment, and other parts of the criminal process, such as charging decisions, likelihood of indictment, and sentencing, need to be considered by future research.

Stucky's finding that punitiveness increases with political threat is supported in an interesting way in a paper by Rachel Barkow and Kathleen O'Neill. They find that a state legislature becomes more likely to establish a sentencing commission the smaller the majority party's margin of power. As they explain:

> A narrow partisan margin in the legislature has a strong relationship with the formation of sentencing commissions, and the correlation is most readily explained by the fact that, in the absence of the commission, each party would face enormous pressure to engage in a race to appear tougher than the other but would ultimately suffer the consequences of a strained budget when it was the party in power.[54]

And so, in such situations, the parties opt to delegate responsibility to a less-politically accountable institution. This again highlights the fact that politicians do not actually wish to be as tough on crime as their constituents demand, or that they fear entering into an "arms race" with the other party that results in policies that may be more punitive than what anyone desires.

> **Question:** Why do you think this is so? Is it just some sort of failure in the democratic process? How important a role do you think (political) salience plays here? Crime policy is surely more salient than, say, highway funding. Might this explain why a politician who perfectly shares his constituents' views on crime control might still be less punitive than they are? Will the relative difference in punitiveness vary with the type of crime? How relevant is the fact that state legislatures are often subjected to various forms of balanced-budget provisions?

While legislators may appear to often be less punitive than their constituencies, our earlier discussions suggested that other elected officials—prosecutors and judges in particular—may be less punitive

---

[54] Rachel E. Barkow & Kathleen M. O'Neill, *Delegating Punitive Power: The Political Economy of Sentencing Commission and Guideline Formation*, 84 TEX. L. REV. 1973, 1976 (2006).

than the legislators. We have seen evidence of prosecutors systematically pleading around tough sentencing laws, and one justification for mandatory minimums and some sentencing guidelines is the legislative perception that judges use their discretion to be too soft on crime. This brings us to our second question: What explains this upstream-downstream disconnect?

William Stuntz provocatively argues that this disconnect is the product of suburban overrepresentation in state legislatures. As Stuntz explains:

> As the United States grew richer and as its nearly all-white suburbs . . . mushroomed in the years following World War II, crime grew steadily more concentrated in cities, and especially in urban black neighborhoods. Thanks to sheer numbers, the political clout exercised by residents of high-crime neighborhoods declined; the power of safer, mostly white neighborhoods in cities and suburbs alike grew. White suburbanites had little to lose from crime in black ghettos. Throughout the 1950s and early 1960s, as violence in northern cities rose, crime remained a nonissue for suburban voters and a small matter for residents of the safer parts of those cities. . . . Beginning with the urban riots of the mid-and late 1960s, indifference turned to fear, then anger. The early and mid-1970s saw falling prison populations bottom out; by 1976, imprisonment was rising steeply.
>
> The core reason is simple. With respect to crime and criminal punishment, residents of *all* neighborhoods, safe and dangerous alike, have two warring incentives. On the one hand, they want safe streets on which to go about their business. . . . On the other hand, they are loath to incarcerate their sons and brothers, neighbors and friends. The desire for order and the longing for freedom, anger at crime and empathy for the young men whom police officers arrest and prosecutors charge—both forces are powerful, and they push in opposite directions. Local political control over criminal justice harnesses both forces without giving precedence to either.
>
> The balance between those dueling incentives looks different when power over criminal punishment is given to voters and officials outside the communities where crimes happen and punishments are imposed. Anger and empathy alike are weaker forces when they come from voters who see crime on the evening news than when they flow from voters' lived experiences. When both forces are weak, small changes in either can produce large

systemic consequences: no countervailing force checks the trend toward more or less punishment.[55]

The suburbanization of law enforcement priorities could help explain why the war on drugs garnered so much support, at least rhetorically (as we will see in Chapter 9, its impact on punishment and prison populations is often overstated). Unlike violent and property crime, drug crime feels like the sort of offense better able to "reach" the suburbs. Suburban voters were scared of drugs coming into their communities, but also more empathetic to the costs of enforcing laws against their own children. They are likely substantially less empathetic towards the targets of urban drug enforcement. Michael Tonry, in fact, has argued that the motivating spirit of the war on drugs is "malign neglect": the war's racially disparate impact was not the product of overt racial animus but rather an almost-immoral indifference to the impact it would have on heavily-policed, poor black neighborhoods in nearby cities.[56]

In short, those not victimized by crime and—perhaps more important—those not targeted by police are generally overrepresented in state legislatures.[57] Downstream prosecutors and judges are elected by constituencies more closely located to crime, although even at that level the geographic concentration of offending dilutes the political voices of those who bear most of the costs of crime and punishment. This results in a complex strategic game, which highlights again some of the important costs—but also benefits—of our decentralized system.

QUESTIONS

1. **Explaining downstream non-punitiveness.** Prosecutors and judges appear to be less punitive than legislators. Does Stuntz's analysis shed light on this lenient behavior? Can the relatively lenient behavior of prosecutors and judges in turn *explain* the punitiveness of legislators?

2. **The benefits of decentralization.** Does the discussion above point to any benefits to the decentralized criminal justice system(s) that we have? Might there still be better ways to allocate responsibilities across various regions?

3. **Controlling downstream actors.** What sort of steps can legislatures take if they want to better control judges, prosecutors, or police? What would be the costs and benefits of increasing state-level control of this sort?

---

[55] STUNTZ, COLLAPSE, supra note 14 at 35–36.

[56] MICHAEL TONRY, MALIGN NEGLECT (1995).

[57] This over-representation effect is strongest in Congress, especially in the Senate. At the state level, it may be less pronounced, but it is still problematic. In New York State, for example, New York City contributes 45% of the state's crimes, 46% of its prisoners, and 43% of its lower-house legislators, all of which seems fairly balanced. But recall that crime is highly concentrated, so most of that crime in New York City is coming from a limited number of blocks (and thus from the districts of a much smaller number of representatives).

4. **Constituents who vote.** Stucky argues that state representatives facing close elections will be more likely to represent the values of their core constituents. At first, this sounds like a positive view of the democratic check: tight elections lead to more-faithful agents. But are there reasons to be concerned? Who comprise this "core constituency" to which a representative in a tight race must be particularly faithful? Does it depend on whether the state legislative race is in a major federal election year or not? And is there another source of electoral pressure that Stucky is ignoring but which has become increasingly important in many races in recent years?

5. **Rehabilitation and punitiveness.** Recall the reading in Ch. 2 by Francis Cullen and others which argued that the American electorate has always favored rehabilitation more than tough-on-crime politicians seems to assume. Are politicians simply misreading the electorate, or is there a structural problem that leads politicians who want to be faithful agents to nonetheless feel the need to be tough on crime, even when they know their constituents want more-rehabilitative policies?

H. SENTENCING COMMISSIONS

Starting with Minnesota in 1978, as both crime and prison populations started to grow, states started to establish sentencing commissions to provide expert advice on how to design better sentencing regimes. As of 2011, at least twenty-two states have commissions; several other states have had commissions in the past but later abolished them.[58] In many cases, commissions were established to help the state design sentencing guidelines, though not all states with commissions have guidelines, and not all guideline states relied on (or retained) commissions. Chapter 6 discusses these developments in more depth, and in this section I just want to briefly highlight a few salient features of these commissions.

One key motivation for establishing commissions was to isolate sentencing policy from day-to-day political pressures. The "politics of crime" are often dysfunctional in important ways, so by removing some sentencing decision-making to more politically independent commissions, politicians could avoid some of the political incentives to over-punish. Yet Rachel Barkow argues that commissions are most successful when they are not *entirely* independent:

> [T]he unique politics of criminal law distinguish [sentencing commissions from other regulatory agencies] in several important respects. To begin with, sentencing commissions regulate most directly the behavior of judges[,] who are not

---

[58] According to the National Association of Sentencing Commissions, the states with commissions are Alabama, Alaska, Arkansas, Connecticut, Delaware, Washington (DC), Illinois, Kansas, Louisiana, Maryland, Massachusetts, Minnesota, Missouri, New Mexico, New York, North Carolina, Ohio, Oregon, Pennsylvania, Utah, Virginia, and Washington (state). The federal government has a sentencing commission as well. See http://thenasc.org/aboutnasc.html.

traditional regulated entities. Indirectly, sentencing commissions regulate criminal defendants. Neither group has the lobbying ability or power of a traditional regulated entity. Moreover, almost all of the powerful interest groups in this context support harsher sentences and less flexibility for judges—and that view tends to resonate with voters. The political landscape therefore creates strong incentives for legislatures to exercise close oversight of commissions to ensure that the commissions promote policies that appeal to these powerful groups and to voters. As a result, one would expect the traditional means of insulation to be largely ineffective at deterring political control.

[T]wo attributes . . . can enable the sentencing commission to better negotiate the highly politicized world of criminal sentencing. First, the agency must have strong connections with the relevant political actors. This can be achieved informally through contacts between the commission's members and the political branches, or it can be formalized by having legislators serve on the commission in some capacity. Although it may seem counterintuitive that having a legislator serve on a commission gives the agency more power, the experience of many state commissions shows that this can be an asset. These legislative members alert the commission to political concerns and provide ready-made advocates for the commission's conclusions when the legislature as a whole debates its proposals.

The second key characteristic involves the information generated by the agency. When sentencing commissions make persuasive policy arguments grounded in political concerns, legislators are more likely to defer to their judgment. And the arguments that have held the greatest sway are those that identify the costs of various sentencing policies. When agencies have shown that increased severity would strain existing prison resources and require new construction and financial outlays, state legislators have often been willing to compromise on their tough-on-crime proposals. This success is not surprising. Many states established sentencing commissions because they were facing prison overcrowding and believed sentencing commissions could help them control their use of penal resources. When the commissions then report that specific legislative changes will exacerbate already stretched prison resources, legislatures often opt to forego their proposals or enact alternatives that are less severe. Sentencing commissions in these circumstances thus provide the type of sober second thought that is often associated with the agency model. But their power does not derive from independence; it comes from the ability to generate politically salable information.

In other words, the successful sentencing commission acts, in effect, as an interest group for rational sentencing policy. When the sentencing commission is charged with focusing on the costs and benefits of sentencing, it may provide the legislature with a more measured assessment of what is needed than can law enforcement lobbyists. And like any other interest group, a politically savvy and well-connected agency is more likely to wield influence than one that is aloof from political pressures. Consequently, the structural features that enhance independence may cut against an agency's effectiveness when it needs to operate as an interest group to have its greatest influence.[59]

Barkow then goes on to demonstrate that some states developed more effective commission regimes than others.

Perhaps an important role for commissions is not just to provide expert advice, but also to provide political *cover*. Commission recommendations can become law in one of two ways: by default, unless the legislature actively rejects them, or only if the legislature actively affirms them. Some evidence suggests that the former approach produces more-rational sentencing regimes. It is politically less risky for a politician to fail to reject something than to openly approve it.

Question: Why do you think that politicians need to "hide" behind sentencing commissions? What risks does a politician face from approving a law weakening a sentence? from not weakening that sentence?

I. DISCRETION AND ACTUARIALISM

One question running through this chapter is whether all the various actors in the criminal justice system use the discretion they have properly, or whether problematic factors shape their decisions: do judges pay too much attention to race, say, or prosecutors to financial incentives? In recent years legislatures have sought to regulate the discretion of downstream actors via devices such as sentencing guidelines and parole instruments. Legislatures are, of course, partly motivated by the desire to reduce what they see as agency problems, but the push for guidelines also reflects a broader concern with how people use their discretion in general.

A growing social science literature highlights the fact that clinicians of all stripes—not just judges and parole boards, but doctors, psychologists, etc.—often make systematic, predictable errors when attempting to make any sort of "diagnosis," be it of a disease or the risk of recidivism. And this literature has gone beyond simply pointing out the problem to proposing a solution as well: the actuarial model.

---

[59] Rachel E. Barkow, *Administering Crime*, 52 UCLA L. REV. 715, 718–721 (2005).

The idea behind the actuarial model is simple. Impressionistic human judgment is replaced by a mathematical model that uses objectively observable traits as its inputs. Multiple studies have demonstrated that these models consistently perform as well as or outperform even highly-skilled and experienced clinicians when it comes to making predictions. Though developed initially in medicine, their applicability to criminal justice is clear: don't rely on a parole board member's or a judge's "sense" about whether someone will recidivate, but use an actuarial model to make this prediction instead. Over time, such models have become increasingly popular in criminal justice bureaucracies. The Virginia legislature, for example, codified the use of a specific actuarial model for assigning risk classifications to sex offenders.[60]

The following reading provides a relatively optimistic take on actuarial models. Such models, however, are not without their critics, and we will consider some of these counter-arguments afterwards.

Eric S. Janus & Robert A. Prentky, *Forensic Use of Actuarial Risk Assessment With Sex Offenders: Accuracy, Admissibility and Accountability*
40 Am. Crim. L. Rev. 1443 (2003)

The clinical method is ubiquitous in judicial settings. In a typical, well-done clinical evaluation, the expert examines the individual, gathers and reviews as much other information (e.g., medical and institutional records, court records and other documents pertaining to criminal history) as possible, and applies his expertise to produce an opinion.

The actuarial method of risk assessment is relatively new in the judicial context, though it has been used rather extensively in other settings. [A]ctuarial scales are developed using statistical analyses of groups of individuals . . . with known outcomes during a "follow-up" period (either arrested for or convicted of a new . . . offense, or not identified as having committed a new . . . offense). These analyses tell us which items ("predictor variables") do the best job of differentiating between those who reoffended and those who did not reoffend within a specified time period. Since some of these variables inevitably do a better job than others, these analyses also help us to determine how much weight should be assigned to each item. The variables are then combined to form a scale, which is tested on many other groups of offenders (cross-validation). At this point, it is possible to develop a "life" or "experience" table that provides probabilistic estimates of reoffense for each score, or range of scores, for different time frames. . . .

---

[60] Va. Code § 37.2–903(b) requires the parole board to use an actuarial model called Static-99 or a "comparable, scientifically validated instrument" to assess sex offender recidivism risk.

The "experience table" then becomes the focus in risk assessments. The individual to be assessed is scored on the factors, which are combined according to the formula, and the resultant risk score is compared to the table, which yields a probability representing the proportion of the reference group that reoffended. Speaking precisely, we can say that an individual with a particular score has characteristics that place him in a group of persons with the same score who were observed (over the follow-up period) to have a given probability, or frequency, of . . . recidivism.

In 1954, Paul Meehl wrote a seminal paper, arguing that actuarial methods provide more accuracy than do clinical methods. The empirical support for Meehl's thesis has been demonstrated repeatedly over the ensuing decades, with recent contributions noteworthy for their clarity and persuasiveness. A recent paper reported on a meta-analysis of 136 studies in which predictions by both human judges and "mechanical-prediction schemes" had been compared. In all instances . . . the clinician and the actuarial expert had access to the same predictor variables and made their predictions on the basis of the same criterion.

In only eight out of the 136 studies was clinical prediction superior to actuarial prediction. In 128 studies, either the results were comparable or actuarial prediction was superior. Actuarial prediction was found to be superior in 33% to 47% of the studies, depending on the type of analysis used. Across all of the studies, whether the clinician had access to more data did not significantly alter the superiority of actuarial prediction. Moreover, in those instances in which the clinician had access to a clinical interview, the superiority of actuarial prediction was even greater. The authors concluded:

> Even though outlier studies can be found, we identified no systematic exceptions to the general superiority (or at least material equivalence) of mechanical prediction. It holds in general medicine, in mental health, in personality, and in education and training settings. It holds for medically trained judges and for psychologists. It holds for inexperienced and seasoned judges.

Two recent meta-analyses further support the conclusion that actuarial assessments of risk are generally superior to clinical assessments [in criminal contexts as well].

Based on this, and similar, empirical evidence, many scholars have concluded that the predictive efficacy of actuarial methods of risk assessment is superior to clinically derived assessments of risk. [A] recent article notes, "In literally hundreds of comparisons over many domains including the prediction of recidivism, clinical judgment has essentially never been found to be superior to actuarial methods, whereas the converse has most often been demonstrated." In commenting on the demonstrated superiority of actuarial over clinical judgment, Meehl remarked, "I do not know of any controversy in the social sciences in which the evidence is so massive, diverse, and consistent." In sum, actuarial methods should be considered, at this point, to represent an "upper bound" in our ability to predict the risk of . . . recidivism.

Clinical risk assessment is, by definition, an exercise in human judgment. The susceptibility of human judgment to error has been the subject of considerable empirical scrutiny. Although by no means exhaustive, the following sources of error in clinical judgments have been noted: (1) ignoring or using incorrect base rates, (2) assigning suboptimal or incorrect weights to information (e.g., over-weighting "high profile" but relatively non-predictive information), (3) failing to take into account regression toward the mean, (4) failing to properly take into account covariation, (5) relying on illusory correlations between predictor variables and the criterion (i.e., basing decisions upon the presence or absence of information that is unrelated or only weakly related to the criterion), (6) failing to acknowledge the natural bias among forensic examiners toward "conservative" judgments, defined as an increased potential for incorrect judgments of dangerousness associated with a reluctance to find someone not dangerous, and (7) failing to receive, and thus benefit from, feedback on judgment errors.

In large measure, the superiority of actuarial risk assessment arises from the elimination or reduction of these and other sources of error. As Professors Will Grove and Paul Meehl observe, "[T]he clinician's brain is functioning as merely a poor substitute for an explicit regression equation or actuarial table. Humans simply cannot assign optimal weights to variables, and they are not consistent in applying their own weights." To be sure, [actuarialism] has faults, and some [actuarial] tools are better than others. Yet, even the weakest of the actuarial assessment methods appears to be systematically better than clinical judgments. [A]ny problems present in a poorly designed actuarial method are likely to be equaled or exceeded in clinical assessments.

Given the courts' routine reliance on clinical risk assessment to support long-term liberty deprivation, it is illogical to exclude demonstrably more reliable . . . tools. In making determinations with serious implications for individual liberty, courts must adopt state-of-the-art methods. As the above discussion indicates, a corpus of empirical evidence demonstrates the predictive superiority of [actuarial] over clinical judgments.

As Janus and Prentky explain, the difference between clinical and actuarial assessment is ultimately more one of computational power than of approach. Both clinical and actuarial judgments are attempting to measure how "far" some particular observation is from some relevant benchmark. The choice between using human judgment or a mathematical model is a choice over who can make that observation better, not over what sort of observation to make. Given how multi-dimensionally complex these sorts of "distance" questions can be, it should not necessarily surprise us that computer programs can answer them better than humans.

That said, the superiority of actuarial assessments to personal judgment is often hard for people to accept. Part of that reason is surely pride: it is difficult to admit that we are simply not as good at making decisions as we like to think. But one of the more intuitively appealing—if ultimately incorrect—attacks on actuarialism is the "broken leg" problem. The critique focuses on the fact that humans can take into account new factors faster than models can. Assume there is a model that predicts who will go to see movies on Friday nights, and the model predicts that Joe will go. But Joe stays home because he broke his leg earlier in the day, and the model—lacking any sort of "broken leg" question—is blind to that development. A human, of course, would have taken one look at Joe's leg and made the right call.

But the discretion that allows the human to incorporate the broken leg into her analysis is a double-edged sword. It enables her to take into account relevant factors, but it also permits her to rely on irrelevant factors or to include appropriate factors incorrectly. Ultimately, the evidence consistently suggests that this discretion does more harm than good. For every case where the human sees the broken leg and makes a better call there is more than one case in which the human takes into account something *ir*relevant that the model ignores and thus reaches a worse conclusion.

That said, the broken leg scenario does point to one important role human observers will continue to play in an actuarial world, at least in the short- to medium-run: as observers. Models are excellent at assessing *how* relevant various factors are, but they have a much harder time detecting *what* factors matter in the first place. So, in the broken leg example, a human observer would note that perhaps the model should include a "broken leg" variable and add that to the model, but she should still defer to the model in assessing its importance.

Nonetheless, there are several serious limitations to actuarial models that are important to acknowledge:

1. **The baserate problem.** Assume that we have a highly accurate actuarial model to assess whether potential parolees will recidivate within five years. It has a false positive rate of 1% (only 1% of those who in fact would not recidivate in the next five years are tagged as future recidivists) and a false negative rate of 0% (if someone is going to recidivate, the model will correctly identify him every time). The model classifies Joe as a recidivist. Should we give this result a lot of weight?

At first blush, the answer seems like an easy "yes!" But, in fact, it is impossible to answer the question with the information you have so far. You also need to know the baserate of offending in the population. Assume that we have 100,000 potential parolees, and only 0.1% of them (100) will recidivate. Under our assumption, our model will correctly identify all 100 future recidivists as such. But it will misclassify 1% of the remaining 99,900 non-recidivists (or 999 inmates) as recidivists. Thus only 100 out of 1099, or 9.1%, of all parolees identified as recidivists would actually have recidivated, and 999 inmates see their detentions extended incorrectly.

This problem declines as the baserate rises. If the recidivism rate is 1%, then there are 1,000 true positives and 990 false negatives, so now a positive result implies a 50.3% chance of recidivism. If the baserate is 10%, there are 10,000 true positives for 900 false negatives; now a positive results implies a 91.7% probability of recidivism. Knowing the relevant baserate is very important.

Question: What does the baserate problem tell us about the effectiveness of predictive models for first-time offenders vs. recidivists? Consider the following findings from a 2010 study by the Bureau of Justice Statistics on recidivism rates of over 400,000 inmates released in 2005: 28% of all releasees were rearrested within one year, and 77% within five (ranging from 48% of all murderers to 84% of all those convicted of larceny or auto theft). Moreover, 55% were reconvicted within five years, and 50% returned to prison (28% for a new offense).

Slightly Tangential Question: Why do you think the five-year recidivism rate for murderers released in 2005 is so much lower than the general average? How would such offenders differ demographically from other released inmates?

2. **Adaptive behavior.** In a wide-ranging critique of actuarial models, Bernard Harcourt points out that models can be self-fulfilling in a self-defeating way.[61] Consider racial profiling in highway car stops targeting drug couriers, which can be thought of as a form of actuarialism (with race as the primary entry in the model). Assume that race is predictive, i.e., black drivers are more likely to carry drugs than white drivers, so targeting based on race is efficient (whatever its other normative problems). If the

---

[61] See BERNARD HARCOURT, AGAINST PREDICTION (2006).

racial profiling is known, two competing effects will take place: fewer blacks will smuggle drugs, but more whites will start smuggling drugs. What will the net effect be?

Harcourt demonstrates that it is *possible*, though by no means guaranteed, that overall drug smuggling will go up. It's a question of responsiveness. In order to increase the number of stops of blacks, the police must reduce the number of stops of whites by the same number (assuming no increase in resources). What if the increase in enforcement causes black offending to drop by 8%, but that same reduction in enforcement against whites leads to a 12% increase in white offending? In this situation, overall smuggling goes up. And such asymmetric responses are not implausible. We must ask ourselves why it is that blacks had higher smuggling rates to start with. If it is at least partially because they have fewer legitimate outside opportunities, then they may be less responsive to changing enforcement patterns, as Harcourt's model assumes.

3. **Self-Reinforcing Models.** The IRS has an actuarial model, the Discriminant Function (DIF), that flags suspicious returns for further examination and, possibly, audit. One concern with the model is that it can become self-reinforcing. Assume, for example, that the model identifies those who are generally paid in cash as being more likely to evade their taxes. As the model starts to flag such returns, auditors are likely to uncover more violations in such returns, which in turn only emphasizes the need to audit more and more such returns. But as the example above indicates, as cash-based jobs are audited more intensely, other sorts of earners will begin to evade more, since their risk of detection falls. And the model can't, on its own, figure out where to look for the new evaders.

The IRS is acutely aware of this problem, and so it has also developed the Taxpayer Compliance Measurement Program (TCMP), which *randomly* selects thousands of returns for audit. By casting a wide net over *all* returns, the TCMP can detect where malfeasance is moving in response to the DIF, and it can update the DIF accordingly.

Of course, one can immediately see the problems that can arise. While the DIF is grudgingly accepted (since it is targeting the more-likely-to-be-guilty), the TCMP is widely detested, since it has to audit a lot of innocent people to find the evaders. Moreover, if evasion rates are low enough, we cannot ignore the real costs to large numbers of innocent people who have to be audited to detect offending patterns in the general population. Not surprisingly, efforts on the part of the IRS to expand the scope of the TCMP have faced serious Congressional resistance.

4. **Atheoretical investigations.** The primary focus of actuarial model development has been to design tools that predict the risk of recidivism. As these tools have become more sophisticated, sentencing commissions and parole and probation offices have increasingly redefined their missions as trying to minimize the risk of recidivism.

This raises a tricky question: are these agencies adopting risk assessment tools because they help them accomplish their desired goals, or are they defining their goals to fit the tools available? After all, there are issues beyond just "recidivism" that could motivate these institutions. Ideally, we should set our goals and look for the tools that advance them rather than defining our goals to fit what we can do, but it sometimes seems like we do the latter. The move in the 1970s away from rehabilitation and towards retribution, for example, was likely due at least in part to the sense that rehabilitation simply could not be operationalized. And it seems unlikely to be coincidental that the shift back toward rehabilitation or risk-reduction coincides with better actuarial tools and evidence-based processes.

Again, the normative implications are unclear. It may be better to do the second-choice goal well rather than the first-choice goal poorly. But we should be cautious about letting technological advances blindly shape our normative goals: simply because we have a tool does not mean we should necessarily use it, or use it to the exclusion of other options.

As actuarial models have become more widely accepted for making decisions at the back-end of sentencing, i.e., for parole, there has been a push to use them more at the front end as well, when the judge initially imposes the sentence. In a recent article, however, Sonja Starr raises several major concerns with using actuarial models at sentencing.[62] Part of her concern is constitutional, that these models impermissibly rely on suspect classifications. But her fears are also pragmatic, and she points out that the models being used are often answering the wrong question and thus may be leading to worse sentencing outcomes than not using them at all.

---

[62] Sonja B. Starr, *Evidence-Based Sentencing and the Scientific Rationalization of Discrimination*, 66 STANFORD L. REV. 803 (2014).

On the constitutional front, Starr notes that actuarial models often take into account the defendant's sex, age, and socio-economic status. And the Supreme Court has frequently invalidated laws that rely on broad statistical generalizations based on these categories, even if the generalizations are highly predictive. In *Craig v. Boren*, 429 U.S. 190 (1976), for example, the Court held that states could not impose a higher drinking age on men compared to women, even though young men were arrested for drunk driving at ten times the rate of young women. So while defenders of actuarial tools argue that excluding gender from the model would force women to serve disproportionately long sentences, the Court is fairly unsympathetic to such assertions. Starr points to similar concerns with the use of age and socio-economic status.

Starr also notes that while the tools never include race as a predictive factor explicitly, they may do so implicitly:

> [T]he socioeconomic and family variables that [the tools] include are highly correlated with race . . . , so they are likely to have a racially disparate impact. Given widespread de facto residential segregation and the concentration of crime in urban neighborhoods of color, the neighborhood crime rate variables found in some instruments are particularly disturbing. Rather than requiring specific information on neighborhood crime rate, for example, Pennsylvania's new [evidence based sentencing] instrument simply assigns extra risk points to Philadelphia County and Allegheny County (Pittsburgh) while treating "rural counties" as lowest risk and "smaller urban counties" as medium risk. The likely racial impact of this decision is obvious.[63]

Starr's (and the Court's) concern isn't necessarily with actuarial models in general, just with the use of "generic" or aggregate differences. In other words, basing decisions on broad generalities such "men are different than women," or "young are different than old," or "rural people behave differently than urban people" is constitutionally suspect, if not simply impermissible. The standard rebuttal to this argument by proponents of actuarial models is that clinicians—here, judges—are going to use these factors anyway, so let's at least make sure they use them correctly. But labeling a certain group as being "at risk" can cause members of that group believe they should act in that risky way—here, committing crimes.

This labeling may reinforce problematic stereotypes in other groups as well. For example, while men are more likely to commit crimes than women, most men will not commit crimes. But including "male" as a risk factor could encourage people to view all men as risky, not to make the more *comparative* claim that men are *more* risky than women albeit at a

---

[63] *Id.* at 838.

relatively low baserate. So while judges may rely on impermissible factors, it may be less harmful for judges to use them less accurately but less explicitly.

Question: While men are more likely to offend than women, the Court holds that punishing someone based on sex is likely insufficiently "individualized." But punishing based on prior criminal history is fine. Assume that prior criminal history is in fact a useful predictor of offending. What does it mean to say that prior criminal history predicts offending? Is that any more "individualized" a factor than sex? If there is no methodological difference, is there at least any sort of normative one?

Question (extreme version): Is there any such thing as individualization? If a witness says "I saw him do it," is that an individualized accusation, or is that an accusation because it rests on a host of assumptions about population averages?

Starr then points out that the argument for using such suspect factors is made even weaker by the fact that they are not particularly useful. Models that do not rely on them are about as accurate as those that do. Given this marginal contribution, the cost to public safety of not using them—if there is any cost at all—is slight, suggesting that even constitutional pragmatists would likely be willing to avoid using such categories.

Starr's final point is perhaps the most important. She points out that judges are likely using the wrong sort of tool. The tools judges currently use tell them how much of a recidivism risk the defendant poses *at that moment*, not *once the sentence has been served*. But if a judge is debating between a three and a five year sentence, she wants to know the risk of offending in the future, and how the choice of sentence *affects* that risk:

> Incarceration's effect on an individual's subsequent offending has two components. First, there is an incapacitation effect: while behind bars, he cannot commit crimes that he would have committed outside. If the incapacitation effect were the only effect that incarceration had on subsequent crime, then it would be logical to assume that the state's incarceration resources are best targeted at the highest-risk offenders. But the situation is not that simple because of the second component: the effect on the defendant's postrelease crimes. I will refer to this as the "specific-deterrence" effect, but it is really more complicated; it includes on the one hand specific deterrence (fear of reincarceration) plus any rehabilitative effect of prison programming, and on the other hand potentially criminogenic effects of incarceration (interference with subsequent employability, establishment of criminal networks, and so forth). There is no intuitive reason to assume that the specific-deterrence effect is determined by, or even correlated with, the

defendant's recidivism risk level. It is very possible that higher-risk defendants (or some of them, anyway) might be more inelastic to specific deterrence and rehabilitation and might be more vulnerable to the possible criminogenic effects of incarceration. If so, lengthening high-risk offenders' sentences might be more likely to increase the risk they pose after they get out, or at least to lower net risk less than would locking up some low-risk offenders.[64]

Starr then points out that the current tools are even less appealing once we take into account other goals, such as general deterrence or the "expressive effect on social norms."

Actuarial devices are useful only if they are designed to address the correct question. Time spent in prison is relatively unimportant for parole guidelines (except, perhaps, to the extent that time in prison predicts how well an inmate will adapt once released) but critical to sentencing tools. Failure to think carefully about what the real question is, and to use of tools designed for similar but clearly distinct issues, can lead to troubling results.

Though Starr frames her piece as a critique of evidence-based sentencing, proponents of actuarial models can reframe it in more optimistic terms. First, the constitutional defects in current models are not too practically problematic if less-tainted tools yield similar results. And second, while the use of devices designed for back-end parole decisions at front-end sentencing can be problematic, the solution could be to "just" produce models that better incorporate factors that more relevant to front-end decision-making, such as ones that account for the iatrogenic effects of incarceration—though one does not want to understate the challenges that might arise in trying to design such models.

J. CONCLUSION

To understand how criminal justice is administered in the United States, it is essential to appreciate how power and responsibility are allocated across a wide array of criminal justice bureaucracies. The term "criminal justice system" is dangerously misleading, since it implies a commonality of purpose and a centralization of authority that is simply lacking in the United States. It is possible that many of those in competing bureaucracies hold similar values or subscribe to similar policy goals. But the lack of meaningful direct downstream control, combined with the fact that each bureaucracy is generally beholden to a different electorate (if electoral pressure has any effect at all), implies that there is a significant amount of room for each agency to follow its own path, perhaps much to the consternation of upstream actors.

---

[64] *Id.* at 856–858.

So it should not be surprising that we see police departments refuse to bring prosecutors clean cases, or observe prosecutors, judges, and defense attorneys working to circumvent harsh drug laws. The laws on the books are not necessarily the laws on the ground. So to understand what punishment in the United States really looks like, we have to appreciate both the incentives of the various agencies and the amount of discretion they ultimately wield.

PART 2

SENTENCING LAW AND PROCEDURE

Having looked at who we punish, why we punish them, and who imposes the punishment, we now want to turn to the laws that guide how those punishments are imposed. Traditionally, there has been very little law at all when it comes to sentencing. In an indeterminate regime, which was the dominant form of sentencing until the 1970s, judges had basically unfettered discretion about what sentences to impose, limited only by statutory minimums and maximums, and by the ability of parole boards to grant early release.

Since the 1970s, however, much more law has crept into sentencing. States have adopted sentencing guidelines to regulate judicial behavior, for example, and they have constrained parole boards through "truth in sentencing" laws that require certain violent inmates to serve at least 85% of their sentences. So it is useful to look at the rules that are now in place, as well as how the Supreme Court has viewed this rise of true sentencing law.

Chapter Four start the analysis by looking at what aspects of the *offense* are given more weight. These include differences in offense severity, both quantitative (100 grams vs. 1 kilogram of cocaine, or five vs. twenty child pornography files on a hard-drive) and qualitative (simple vs. aggravated assault), the motivation behind the offense (i.e., hate crime statutes), and the impact of the crime on the victim. Offense severity is a universally accepted aggravating (or mitigating) factor, though one that is a bit more complicated to properly take into account than it initially seems. The other two factors—hate crimes and victim impact—are increasingly common, but remain quite controversial.

Chapter Five then turns from the offense to the offender, asking what aspects of the *offender* should matter for sentencing. The chapter starts with the most commonly used offender trait, his prior criminal record. As with some many other aspects of sentencing law, while popular and politically uncontroversial, the way in which we use it raises numerous troubling questions. We then move to the importance of traits that are beyond the offenders control, such as genetics, age and sex: to what extent should these be aggravating or mitigating factors? And finally, we turn to factors that fall more within the offender's control, such as drug and alcohol use, or even just exposure to certain situational cues (based on where he chooses to be).

In Chapter Six we confront the Supreme Court's long, confusing effort to regulate the new rules that started appearing in the 1970s. When sentencing regimes were indeterminate, the Supreme Court took a hands-off approach, since there wasn't much law to interpret, and the Constitution is fairly silent when it comes to punishment (especially since the Court has essentially cabined the Eighth Amendment's protection against cruel and unusual punishments to death penalty cases). As states began to adopt guidelines and other structured sentencing regimes, however, the Court found itself trying to carefully police what sorts of criminal facts had to be found by a jury vs. by a judge. The result is a string of frustrating, and often contradictory, cases that span more than thirty years and which nearly derailed guideline sentencing in the early 2000s (though the impact ultimately proved relatively minor for everyone but the federal government).

Chapter Seven briefly addresses the death penalty. Entire courses can be taught on the dense, complicated law that governs the death penalty, so the focus here is more high-level. We start with a survey of the Supreme Court rules that govern how the death penalty must be administered, as well as some of the laws Congress has passed to accelerate its imposition. We then touch on the issue of innocence and reversals to ask if, as one famous paper asserted, "the system is broken." Finally, we consider the evidence about the deterrent effect of the death penalty.

Chapter Eight concludes as something of a rebuttal to the Court cases in Chapter Six. While the Court has focused extensively on how structured sentencing implicates jury trial rights, the simple fact is that very few cases are resolved by jury—sentences, by and large, are determined via the plea process, which is the focus on this chapter. We start by looking at what law governs the plea process, including the scant attention the Court has paid to the issue as well as the effort, at least in New Jersey, to create *plea bargaining* guidelines to regulate *prosecutors*. Then we consider the normative debate over plea bargaining: is it just the market at work, with both sides reaching a deal that makes everyone better off, or is it a much more inherently coercive process? We also examine several pragmatic concerns that plea bargaining raises, such as whether changes in jury rights influence plea outcomes, negative externalities for those not involved in the process, and concerns about access to information.

CHAPTER 4

FACTORS RELEVANT TO SENTENCING: OFFENSE TRAITS

Those imposing sentences can look to traits of both the *offense* and the *offender*. Offense traits obviously refer to the nature of the offense, such as how much was stolen, how injured was the victim, what was the motivation for the offense, etc. And offender traits are demographic details such as the defendant's prior record, his age and sex, history of drug use, and so on.

Constitutionally, not much turns on the classification, since the burden of proof remains the same for all aspects of the offense, although offense characteristics may be less likely to be held constitutionally suspect as a class than offender traits.[1] From a policy perspective, however, it still makes sense to think about each factor separately. There may be systematic differences, say, in who can best assess various offense or offender characteristics, which may shed light on how discretion and responsibility should be allocated among police, prosecutors, judges, and other actors.

This chapter focuses on offense traits, looking at three in particular. First, we will examine the role of offense severity, considering both qualitative and quantitative differences among offenses. Second, we will discuss the extent to which the motive behind the offense should matter, specifically in the context of hate crimes. And third, we will look at what role the specific nature of the victim, and the subjective harm experienced by that victim, should play in setting the sentence.

A. OFFENSE SEVERITY

It seems obvious to argue that more serious offenses should be punished more severely. But that statement's superficial obviousness actually betrays its circularity. How do we measure severity? Do we look at objective harm or subjective intent? Are the things we can measure (kilograms of cocaine, dollars stolen) sufficiently correlated with whatever true harm we are trying to prevent or punish? Do our theories of punishment emphasize different margins of severity, and how do we resolve any conflicts that arise among the theories? In the end, the

---

[1] When states started to adopt more-structured sentencing regimes in the 1970s and 1980s, the courts drew an awkward line between "elements" and "sentencing factors": the former had to be found by a jury beyond a reasonable doubt, while the latter could be found a judge at a lower standard of proof. Some academics suggested that a defensible distinction would be to consider offense factors "elements" and offender traits "sentencing factors." As we will see in Chapter 6, the Supreme Court's decision in *Blakely* completely eliminated the distinction between element and sentencing factor, but it is still conceptually useful to draw the distinction.

statement "punish more severe crimes more severely" begs the questions "what is severity?" and "what is the true harm we are trying to punish?"

We will start our discussion by looking at how to broadly rank offenses qualitatively: is murder worse than assault (almost certainly) or is fraud worse that drug dealing (much harder to say)? For many offenses there is a rough consensus about how to prioritize, but that starts to break down the more specifically we define offenses and the more we move away from *malum in se* to *malum prohibitum* crimes. We will then turn to quantitative distinctions within offenses. Sometimes the analysis is trivial: trafficking ten kilograms of cocaine is likely worse than trafficking one. But sometimes we have to ask if we are counting the right thing. In a child pornography case, for example, is the number of images (which often plays an important role in grading) really the relevant metric for the harm we are concerned with? And is it normatively appealing that offenses with less quantifiable elements are punished in a "lumpier" fashion: it is okay to have four or five degrees of theft or drug trafficking since dollars and grams of heroin are easy to count, but just two degrees of assault (simple and aggravated) since it is harder to quantify pain?

A.1. QUALITATIVE ASSESSMENTS OF OFFENSE SEVERITY

Over the years, many studies have sought to measure the extent to which people agree about how to rank crimes, and to understand what factors explain any observed disagreements. Interestingly, despite purporting to examine offense seriousness, the studies frequently do not bother to establish a precise definition of what "serious" meant. A literature review by Stelios Stylianou in 2003 noted that "[t]he adjective 'serious' and the noun 'seriousness' have been used . . . without formal specification of meaning. In fact, most studies are based on the assumption that such definition is not necessary."[2] Perhaps the most effective definition of "seriousness" breaks it down into two components: *wrongfulness*, which focuses on the moral dimension of the crime, and *harmfulness*, which considers the more objective costs to the victim.

Stylianou then summarizes the basic findings of the literature:

> The most important characteristic associated with perceived seriousness of an act is the act's perceived consequences: violent behaviors . . . are generally perceived as the most serious, followed by property offenses. . . . This conclusion has been confirmed by virtually all studies and acknowledged by all summaries of findings of seriousness perceptions research. . . .
>
> White-collar violations are subject to the same rule: their perceived seriousness varies with their consequences. [One study] found that perceived seriousness is greater for

---

[2] Stelios Stylianou, *Measuring Crime Seriousness Perceptions: What We Have Learned and What Else Do We Want to Know*, 31 J. CRIM. JUST. 37, 38 (2003).

organizational crimes involving physical harm than for those involving economic harm; that physical harm and economic harm are separate factors in the ratings of organizational crimes; and that organizational crimes and common crimes with comparable impact are rated similarly.

Many behaviors without negative consequences are still negatively sanctioned. Victimless crimes are still crimes and they can be judged as more or less serious based on the extent to which they violate the moral standards of society. Victimizing behaviors too, are perceived as less or more serious based not only on their victimizing consequences, but also on the extent to which they are wrong in a moral sense.

[One study that attempted to distinguish the relative importance of wrongfulness and harmfulness to perceptions of seriousness found that people fell into one of two groups.] The first group was labeled "nondiscriminators" and it included 25 percent of the total usable sample. These respondents expressed their "principled disagreement with the proposition that crimes vary in their moral gravity." In this group, seriousness was highly correlated with harmfulness (wrongfulness was constant). Analysis of data from the rest of the respondents (labeled "discriminators") yielded three empirical categories of behaviors: crimes that are more harmful than wrong, crimes that are more wrong than harmful, and crimes that are equally wrong and harmful. For this group, seriousness depended on wrongfulness more than on harmfulness for crimes that were perceived as more wrong than harmful and on harmfulness more than on wrongfulness for crimes that were perceived as more harmful than wrong. [The study's author] concluded that "[r]ather than combining wrongfulness and harmfulness in some manner, these respondents [discriminators] appear to attend to the dominant feature of the crime—either its wrongfulness or its harmfulness—in judging seriousness."[3]

Stylianou then reports that respondents usually rank offenses similarly, especially the more serious the offenses: violent crimes are consistently ranked in similar orders, victimless crimes much less so. In other words, everyone agrees that murder is worse than assault, but there is less agreement about how to order gambling and prostitution. There is some evidence that demographic factors such as "age, gender, education, social class, urbanness, and religiosity" can explain some of the variation in results, although the magnitude of the effects varies across studies. There may be less consensus in general when it comes to

---

[3] Id. at 42–43.

cardinal rankings (i.e., not whether murder is worse than assault but how bad, in an absolute sense, is murder or assault).

It is worth noting that all these results are based on surveys, and survey data can be especially tricky to use. There is an extensive literature on the methodological short-comings of many of these studies—surveys are often accused of not providing a sufficiently wide range of offenses, results can be sensitive to very small differences in survey design,[4] and the regression models used to assess the relative importance of various differences between crimes often suffer from omitted variable bias.[5] But while care should be taken when using the results, care too should be taken not to dismiss them out-of-hand. Even if flawed, these results can be useful in some aspects. First, the more studies that return similar results—and many of the findings above have been replicated multiple times—the more likely it is that they are picking up something real. Second, even if the precise rankings are not entirely reliable, these studies do suggest that people pay attention to multiple aspects of crimes when ranking them, indicating that some of the disagreement we see relates to the major theories of punishment. And third, the studies highlight some important intergroup differences. The rest of this part considers these three points in turn.

Unidimensional or Multidimensional?

Many of the studies analyzed by Stylianou assume that crime rankings are "unidimensional": severity is defined as a concept with just one, single—albeit somewhat amorphous—component. This allows for easy ranking. There is no challenge in being asked to put the numbers "1 4 2 7 8 3 5" in order. But what if I asked you to put the following pairs of numbers in order: (2, 4) (3, 3) (0, 5) (5, 0)? Is there any coherent way to do so? Unlike the first set of numbers, these pairs are multidimensional, and it is hard to say which set is "largest" or to rank them.

And as Stylianou and others have noted, people appear to take a multidimensional view of crime severity. Stylianous focuses primarily on wrongfulness and harmfulness. Other studies have identified at least three dimensions: harmfulness, "deprivation," and "recklessness," where deprivation refers to the somewhat-libertarian idea that the seriousness of a crime relates to the extent it infringes on personal autonomy, and

---

[4] Perhaps the most interesting is the "fill in the blank" problem: if a crime is described too simply, respondents appear to add in details that the researcher cannot observe. Thus people rank the crime "A man stabs his wife. She dies." as more severe than "A woman stabs her husband. He dies." This likely results from the answerer adding in unstated details, like the woman was more likely to be acting in self defense. See Deirdre Golash & James P. Lynch, *Public Opinion, Crime Seriousness, and Sentencing Policy*, 22 AM. J. CRIM. L. 703 (1995).

[5] For example, a study that purports to show a racial difference in harm perceptions but does not include data on income or wealth may really be identifying a wealth effect, given that race and wealth are correlated. See the Statistical Appendix for a brief explanation of omitted variable bias.

recklessness to the (unrealized) additional harm that the offense could have brought about.[6]

An example from one study makes clear how hard it is to rank multidimensional variables. The following figure is taken from a paper by Jeremy Blumenthal which breaks "seriousness" down into harmfulness, deprivation, and recklessness; here, Dimension 1 refers to harmfulness, Dimension 2 to deprivation (with recklessness omitted from the analysis).[7]

Figure 1. Two-Dimensional Plot of Dimension 1 and Dimension 2

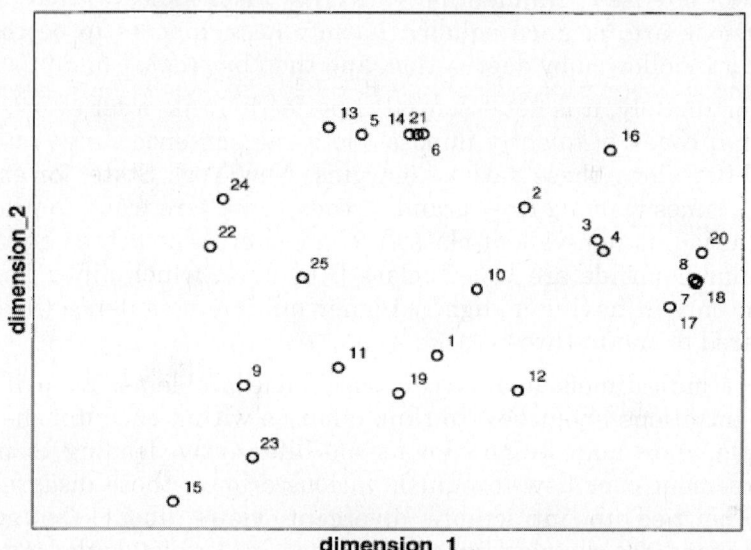

1 adultery	10 drunk driving	19 prostitution
2 arson	11 drug dealing	20 rape
3 assault	12 drug possession	21 robbery
4 battery	13 embezzlement	22 shoplifting
5 blackmail	14 extortion	23 speeding
6 burglary	15 jaywalking	24 tax evasion
7 child abuse	16 kidnapping	25 vandalism
8 child molestations	17 manslaughter	
9 civil disobedience	18 murder	

As is clear, some rankings are easy, but others are quite hard. For example, it is clear that kidnapping (offense 16) should be punished more severely than drug dealing (offense 11), since it is considered more severe along both dimensions. But should embezzlement (offense 13) be punished more severely than child abuse (offense 7)? Child abuse scores

---

[6] See, e.g., Jeremy A. Blumenthal, *Perceptions of Crime: A Multidimensional Analysis with Implications for Law and Psychology*, 38 MCGEORGE L. REV. 629 (2007).

[7] *Id.*

more highly along the harm dimension, but embezzlement more highly along deprivation. (Note that this is somewhat of a peculiar result, that embezzlement imposes a greater imposition on personal autonomy than child abuse: as I warned, some caution is needed when reading these reports.)

The Stylianou reading suggests one way people handle this: when one offense seems much more extreme along a particular dimension, that dimension is given priority. In other words, murder (offense 18) exhibits slightly less deprivation than tax evasion (offense 24), but it is much more harmful, so the difference in harm would drive the relative rankings of the two offenses. Blumenthal's results also indicate that not all dimensions are weighed equally: harmfulness appears to be the most important, followed by deprivation, and then by recklessness.

Fortunately, it is not essential to perfectly rank-order every offense. Criminal codes frequently impose the same sentence range on crimes that differ along these various margins. New York State, for example, lumps crimes ranging from grand larceny to welfare fraud to promoting prostitution as non-violent class B felonies; crimes such as aggravated vehicular homicide are violent class B felonies, which differ from non-violent only in having a slightly higher minimum sentence (five years, compared to one-to-three years).

Yet multidimensionality can pose some problems. Even if people share intuitions about how to rank offenses within each dimension, for example, they may weigh dimensions differently, leading to political disagreement over how to punish various crimes; these disagreements could be tied to intractably divergent views about the goals of punishment (see the next two discussions). It also clouds the signal sent by sanctions: in the end, a sentence is a one-dimensional encapsulation of a multidimensional idea, which always entails a loss of information. Why are two crimes punished the same, or differently?

One effort to generate a uniform ranking of offenses is to ask how much people would be willing to pay to eliminate a crime: such a monetized number should capture all the various dimensions in one result. One study reported that people would be willing to pay over $12 million to eliminate one murder, nearly $300,000 to eliminate one rape, slightly less than that to eliminate one armed robbery, about $87,000 to eliminate one aggravated assault, and about $35,000 to eliminate one burglary.[8]

> **Question:** How trustworthy are these results? Is it useful to ask people how much they would be willing to spend (which means, of course, how much would they like the government to spend)? Do you think we'd get different answers if the question wasn't

---

[8] Matt DeLisi, Anna Kosloski, Molly Sween, Emily Hachmeister, Matt Moore and Alan Drury, *Murder by Numbers: Monetary Costs Imposed by a Sample of Homicide Offenders*, 21 J. FORENSIC PSYCHIATRY & PSYCH. 501, Table 2 (2010).

"how much should we spend to eliminate one crime?" but rather "how many teachers should we fire/hospitals should we close/taxes should we raise to eliminate one crime?" Are these the same questions? Does the choice of question matter?

Question: DeLisi et al. do not provide a breakdown of how results vary across various demographic groups. What do you think such an analysis would likely indicate?

Severity Rankings and Theories of Punishment

It is worth considering the relationship between offense rankings and theories of punishment, both in terms of what (if anything) the rankings tell us about what theories people subscribe to in practice, and in terms of whether different perspectives on punishment would treat the rankings differently.

First, which theories of punishment would put the most weight on these rankings? Assume, at first, that we are in a world where resource limitations are not important; obviously this is unrealistic, and we will reintroduce budget limits shortly. To start, it seems like the rankings would be relatively unimportant to proponents of the consequentialist theories. These theories are focused much more on the *offender* than on the *offense*. So if it is easy to deter murder but really hard to deter insider trading, a deterrence theorist would be okay with setting the sanction for murder below that of insider trading. And incapacitation and rehabilitation are likewise concerned with the lifetime offending patterns of the offender far more than the particular offenses he is committing; to the extent that rehabilitation cares about the offenses in order to craft the right "treatment," that concern is unrelated to popular perceptions of severity, just like doctors determine the correct treatments for cancer and heart attacks without asking which is the "worse" ailment.

For retributivists, these rankings many matter more. Retributivists of a more natural law bent, who believe that there is some sort of extrinsic moral wrongness to offenses, may be relatively indifferent to popular perceptions of wrongness or severity. But those who take a more pluralistic, democratic perspective that our assessment of moral wrongness must come from the polity would view these rankings as essential for setting proportional (if not absolute) sentences.

Once we concede that resources are limited, however, even consequentialists may take these rankings into account, for essentially the same reasons that retributivists who favor democratic choices on "wrongness" would. Consider a prosecutor or judge who faces two defendants, a murderer and a burglar; each is just as likely to reoffend and each is equally amenable to rehabilitation, but the prosecutor or judge can send only one to prison (due, say, to a lack of capacity). One obvious way to determine which defendant gets prison, as compared to, say, probation, would be to ask which offense poses the greatest costs on people. (Of course, that assumes that the proper measure of "most severe" is the utilitarian "greatest cost on people," which is likely an assumption most consequentialists accept, but which is not essential for a consequentialist policy.)

The second major point to consider is what the observed rankings tell us about the theories of punishment people in fact subscribe to. Blumenthal's results indicate that people focus most on the harm caused, then on the imposition on the victim, then on the general risk created by the offense; Stylianou's point to the fact that some people simply prioritize harmfulness over wrongfulness, while others vary depending on which factor is more extreme/salient.

> **Question:** Does a focus on harmfulness suggest that a respondent is prioritizing one of the theories over the rest? How about a focus on wrongness? Do you expect the non-discriminators to generally subscribe to a different theory of punishment than discriminators (to use Stylianou's specific definition)?

Differences Across Groups

That a relative consensus exists for most crimes, and increasingly so for increasingly-severe crimes, should not be surprising: it is unlikely that many people would rank murder and arson differently. Perhaps more interestingly, there also appears to be a fair amount of consensus about the absolute seriousness of offenses, not just their relative position. Even across racial and gender lines, Americans are often similarly punitive.

But it is important not to overstate the extent of the agreement. As one study points out:

> [B]lacks and whites may hold similar attitudes on punitiveness and crime seriousness but for different reasons, reflecting their disparate positions in the social and economic order. [Evidence indicates that the] tendency of non-whites toward punitiveness results from a greater fear of criminal victimization while whites tend toward punitive attitudes as a result of political conservatism.[9]

The study then examines data from the 1987 General Social Survey which suggests that black punitiveness is in fact driven by fear of being victimized while that of whites is more closely tied to racial bias (which itself may be linked to conservatism).

These black-white differences reflect a deeper divide that runs through the American polity. In a recent study, two criminologists defined three competing theories to explain why Americans tend to be so punitive:

---

[9] Steven F. Cohn, Steven E. Barkan, & William A. Halteman, *Punitive Attitudes Toward Criminals: Racial Consensus or Racial Conflict*, 38 SOCIAL PROBLEMS 287, 289 (1991).

[1.] **Escalating Crime-Distrust Model.** [T]his model argues that support for getting tough on crime resides within two coexisting sentiments. People are most willing to support getting tough on crime because they perceive that crime is increasing and are concerned that rising crime rates will disrupt their way of life and because they have lost faith in the government, especially the courts, to protect them from the injurious effects of crime.[10]

[2.] **The Moral Decline Model.** [Two social psychologists,] Tyler and Boeckmann[,] contend that support for harsh crime-control policies is most likely to reside among those who feel uncertain about their place in the world. This relational concern—this prevailing angst—is associated with the feeling that core institutions within the society are in decline; society, in short, is in a state of moral decay. As Tyler and Boeckmann argue, "people are concerned about the symbolic harms that develop from the lack of a clear, shared set of moral values as well as from declining social ties among people. Those citizens who feel that the moral and social consensus that holds society together is declining are more supportive of punitive public policies."

Notably, Tyler and Boeckmann identify why perceptions that society is in a state of moral decay should predict greater punitiveness. They argue that people who believe "that there are fewer moral and social ties among people also think it is harder to rehabilitate criminals." They also believe that other lesser forms of punishment, such as shaming the offender, will not restore the social cohesion they desire. The ineffectiveness of these "softer" approaches to crime to shore up the moral boundaries of a society causes individuals to endorse more punitive approaches such as the three-strikes initiative and capital punishment. Tyler and Boeckmann thus argue that people who feel that society is in a state of moral decline support these symbolic policies not for instrumental reasons (e.g., deterrence) but as a conduit for reestablishing a sense of social cohesion.

[3.] **The Racial-Animus Model.** [T]he racial-animus model proposes that punitiveness in the United States, if not cross-culturally, is buoyed by negative feelings and views of minority group members. It suggests that race and racism are thus integral to any understanding of why Americans endorse get-

---

[10] A more expansive version of this explanation is the "instrumental" theory, which simply posits that people become more punitive as they increasingly fear being victimized themselves. See, for example, Tom R. Tyler & Robert J. Boeckmann, *Three Strikes and You're Out, but Why? The Psychology of Public Support for Punishing Rule Breakers*, 31 L. & SOC'Y REV. 237 (1997).

tough policies. . . . A relatively large body of research supports this claim.[11]

Using the 2000 National Election Survey, the authors attempt to unpack the relative importance of these three theories by examining predictors of pro-death penalty sentiments and the prioritization of punishment over more social solutions (such as anti-poverty programs). They find support for all three theories, with racial animus playing a significant role. Unfortunately, their models do not isolate group-specific explanations (i.e., blacks are more instrumental, whites more moral decay), although the Cohn et al. results indicate these surely exist.

That similar attitudes about the need to control crime can arise from substantially different normative perspectives forces us to think once more about our awkwardly-federalized criminal justice system. What if the motivations of those imposing the rules differ from those of the people the rules most affect? Suburban whites, for example, appear to motivated more by fears of decay and by animus, while blacks have a more instrumental view. And the suburban white vote is much stronger at the legislative level, where laws are passed, but (relatively) much weaker (even if still disproportionately powerful) at the city and county levels, where they are disproportionately enforced.

This disconnect does not necessarily lead to problems in all cases. Suburban white voters may wish to be tough on burglars and robbers because they see them as agents of moral decay, or visualize them as frightening young black men, and urban black voters may wish to be tough on the same group since they are disproportionately their victims. But the non-crime aspect of moral-decay punitiveness likely leads its proponents to prioritize anti-crime efforts that instrumentalists would not. The most obvious candidate is, of course, the war on drugs. There is ample evidence that blacks often take particularly harsh views of drug dealers as well, and have frequently been at the forefront of campaigns to toughen drug laws;[12] but suburban white voters are likely inclined to embrace policies that are less directly effective but more symbolically satisfying,[13] while urban black voters likely focus more on functionality.

Question: Does the potential disconnect between urban and suburban voters point to a flaw with or a benefit to how powers are allocated across jurisdictions? Urban laws will disproportionately reflect suburban interests, but urban enforcement is more in the hands of urban actors. Given the sorts of crimes that urban jurisdictions primarily focus on—

---

[11] James D. Unnever & Francis T. Cullen, *The Social Sources of Americans' Punitiveness: A Test of Three Competing Models*, 41 CRIMINOLOGY 99 (2010).

[12] See James Forman, Jr., *Racial Critiques of Mass Incarceration: Beyond the New Jim Crow*, 87 NYU L. REV. 21 (2012).

[13] This is reinforced by the fact that these voters do not bear the direct enforcement costs, nor do they bear the indirect costs of unimproved conditions due to the use of unsuccessful policies.

serious violent and property crimes—should we be concerned that the state criminal code will be inadequate?

Taken to its logical extreme, the variation in priorities across *groups* could argue for devolving criminal codification to more-local *areas*. Our neighborhoods, towns, and counties are increasingly politically homogenous and remain quite racially segregated, so group-based differences readily translate into regional differences. Obviously, there are several limits to devolution. First, one immediate problem would be defining the relevant jurisdictions and what laws would operate in areas too small to craft an entire criminal code of their own.

But second, and more important, not all crimes are equally "local," as we've discussed before. A bar brawl does not affect anyone outside the particular bar, and patrons are unlikely to choose where to live and drink based on the assault laws in various towns. But such concerns are surely at play when dealing with, say, drug trafficking. Not only do people from Community X buy drugs in Community Y and bring the drugs, and their attendant social ills, back to X, but if Y imposes tougher laws against drug trafficking then drug markets might just move directly to X. Excessive localism can lead to significant externalities, though there is no reason to assume that our current approach has struck the right balance between local control and displacement costs.

QUESTIONS

1. **The obvious question:** Do you agree with the ranking that people appear to generally share? Do you think the dimensions of severity discussed above capture the relevant aspects of what we are talking about when we discuss "severity," or are there important ones that were missed?

2. **Indifference to rankings.** Are you troubled by the fact that most consequentialist theories care about the rankings only as a concession to triage in a world of limited resources? If so, does that tell us anything about our perceptions of what punishment should be seeking to accomplish and how to balancing the various goals we have?

3. **Local vs. state issues.** The reading above suggested that local law creation could help address variations in group priorities, but it also notes that that introduces the very real risk of localized externalities. But aren't these externalities also present when we allow—as we do—for the local *enforcement* of state-level laws? If you are troubled by the possibility of externalities with codification, should you also be concerned about externalities with enforcement?

A.2. QUANTITATIVE OFFENSE SEVERITY

Ranking across offenses requires a qualitative approach: as the discussion above indicates, the multidimensional nature of severity makes it hard to assign a single numeric "score" to each crime. But for a particular type of crime, it is much easier to take a quantitative approach. It may be hard to quantify the difference between drug dealing and fraud, but it is easy to see the difference between trafficking 1 kilogram of cocaine compared to 10 kilograms, or embezzling $1,000 versus $1,000,000.

But while easy to operationalize and perhaps intuitively appealing, tying sentencing outcomes to quantitative factors does raise some interesting questions. The first and more important question is whether the easily-measured factor is in fact the right one to use in sentencing: are we basing sentencing on this factor because it is the most relevant or simply because it is the easiest to use?[14] The second question is whether the discontinuous cutoffs that define quantitative measures are defensible.

Start with the first question. Consider the following three pairs of statutes: theft in Texas and Ohio, drug offending in Alabama and New Jersey, and child pornography in Alaska and Connecticut.

Theft Statutes: Texas and Ohio

Texas Penal. Code § 31.03: Theft

e. Except as provided by Subsection (f), an offense under this section is:

1. A Class C misdemeanor if the value of the property stolen is less than:

    A. $50. . . .

2. A Class B misdemeanor if:

    A. the value of the property stolen is:

        i. $50 or more but less than $500. . . .

    B. the value of the property stolen is less than:

        i. $50 and the defendant has previously been convicted of any grade of theft; . . . .

3. a Class A misdemeanor if the value of the property stolen is $500 or more but less than $1,500;

4. a state jail felony if:

    A. the value of the property stolen is $1,500 or more but less than $20,000, or the property is less than 10 head of sheep, swine, or goats or any part thereof under the value of $20,000; . . .

    C. the property stolen is a firearm, as defined by Section 46.01;

---

[14] There is an old joke about a drunk man looking for his keys under a streetlight. A passerby asks him what he is doing, and the drunkard points halfway down the block and replies "I'm looking for my keys, which I dropped back there." The passerby asks why the man is looking under the light, since it is not close to where he dropped his keys. The man replies, "Because it's brighter here." Might this joke apply here? Are we looking at the easily-quantifiable factor simply because it is "brighter"?

5. a felony of the third degree if the value of the property stolen is $20,000 or more but less than $100,000, or the property is [various amounts of animals].

6. a felony of the second degree if:

    A. the value of the property stolen is $100,000 or more but less than $200,000; or

    B. the value of the property stolen is less than $200,000 and the property stolen is an automated teller machine or the contents or components of an automated teller machine; or

7. a felony of the first degree if the value of the property stolen is $200,000 or more.

f. An offense described for purposes of punishment [above] is increased to the next higher category of offense if it is shown on the trial of the offense that:

1. the actor was a public servant at the time of the offense and the property appropriated came into the actor's custody, possession, or control by virtue of his status as a public servant; . . .

3. the owner of the property appropriated was at the time of the offense:

    A. an elderly individual; or

    B. a nonprofit organization. . . .

5. during the commission of the offense, the actor intentionally, knowingly, or recklessly:

    A. caused a fire exit alarm to sound or otherwise become activated;

    B. deactivated or otherwise prevented a fire exit alarm or retail theft detector from sounding; or

    C. used a shielding or deactivation instrument to prevent or attempt to prevent detection of the offense by a retail theft detector.

Sentences in Texas:

1. First degree: Life or 99 years
2. Second degree: two to twenty years
3. Third degree: two to ten years
4. State jail felony: 180 days to 2 years in state jail
5. Class A misdemeanor: Jail of no more than a year

6. Class B misdemeanor: Jail of no more than 180 days
7. Class C misdemeanor: Just a fine (max of $500)

<u>Ohio Rev. Code. § 2913.02(B):</u>

2. Except as otherwise provided . . . , a violation of this section is petty theft, a misdemeanor of the first degree. If the value of the property or services stolen is one thousand dollars or more and is less than seven thousand five hundred dollars . . . , a violation of this section is theft, a felony of the fifth degree. If the value of the property or services stolen is seven thousand five hundred dollars or more and is less than one hundred fifty thousand dollars, a violation of this section is grand theft, a felony of the fourth degree. If the value of the property or services stolen is one hundred fifty thousand dollars or more and is less than seven hundred fifty thousand dollars, a violation of this section is aggravated theft, a felony of the third degree. If the value of the property or services is seven hundred fifty thousand dollars or more and is less than one million five hundred thousand dollars, a violation of this section is aggravated theft, a felony of the second degree. If the value of the property or services stolen is one million five hundred thousand dollars or more, a violation of this section is aggravated theft of one million five hundred thousand dollars or more, a felony of the first degree.

3. [I]f the victim of the offense is an elderly person, disabled adult, active duty service member, or spouse of an active duty service member, [all the degrees in the preceding section are raised one degree, except that theft of $1.5M or more is still first degree].

4. If the property stolen is a firearm or dangerous ordnance, a violation of this section is grand theft. Except as otherwise provided in this division, grand theft when the property stolen is a firearm or dangerous ordnance is a felony of the third degree. . . . If the firearm or dangerous ordnance was stolen from a federally licensed firearms dealer, grand theft when the property stolen is a firearm or dangerous ordnance is a felony of the first degree.

5. If the property stolen is a motor vehicle, a violation of this section is grand theft of a motor vehicle, a felony of the fourth degree.

6. If the property stolen is any dangerous drug, a violation of this section is theft of drugs, a felony of the

fourth degree, or, if the offender previously has been convicted of a felony drug abuse offense, a felony of the third degree.

7. If the property stolen is a police dog or horse or an assistance dog and the offender knows or should know that the property stolen is a police dog or horse or an assistance dog, a violation of this section is theft of a police dog or horse or an assistance dog, a felony of the third degree.

8. If the property stolen is anhydrous ammonia, a violation of this section is theft of anhydrous ammonia, a felony of the third degree.[15]

Drug Offenses: Alabama vs. New Jersey

Ala. Code § 13A–12–231:

1. [The code first defines marijuana trafficking If the quantity of cannabis involved:
   a. Is in excess of one kilo or 2.2 pounds, but less than 100 pounds, the person shall be sentenced to a mandatory minimum term of imprisonment of three calendar years. . . . [*Ed. note*: all offenses in § 13A–12–231 are Class A felonies, which means the maximum is 99 years or life.]
   b. Is 100 pounds or more, but less than 500 pounds, the person shall be sentenced to a mandatory minimum term of imprisonment of five calendar years. . . .
   c. Is 500 pounds or more, but less than 1,000 pounds, the person shall be sentenced to a mandatory minimum term of imprisonment of 15 calendar years . . .
   d. Is 1,000 pounds or more, the person shall be sentenced to a mandatory term of imprisonment of life without parole.

2. [The code defines cocaine trafficking as requiring at least 28 grams of cocaine. Like marijuana, the category minimums are three years, five years, fifteen years, and life, with ranges of 28–500 grams, 500–1000 grams, 1 kilo–10 kilos, and more than 10 kilos.]

3. [The code defines heroin trafficking.] If the quantity involved:

---

[15] This may sound like a random provision, but anhydrous ammonia is used in the production of crystal meth, which is likely why it is singled out in this way.

a. Is four grams or more, but less than 14 grams, the person shall be sentenced to a mandatory minimum term of imprisonment of three calendar years. . . .

b. Is 14 grams or more, but less than 28 grams, the person shall be sentenced to a mandatory minimum term of imprisonment of 10 calendar years. . . .

c. Is 28 grams or more, but less than 56 grams, the person shall be sentenced to a mandatory minimum term of imprisonment of 25 calendar years. . . .

d. Is 56 grams or more, the person shall be sentenced to a mandatory term of imprisonment of life without parole.

6. [The ranges and sentences for ecstasy are identical to those for cocaine.]

7. [The ranges and sentences for MDA are identical to those for cocaine as well.]

8. [The ranges and sentences for PCP are identical to those for heroin.]

9. [The ranges and sentences for LSD are identical to those for heroin as well.]

10. [The ranges and sentences for amphetamines are identical to those for cocaine.]

11. [The ranges and sentences for methamphetamines are identical to those for cocaine as well.]

NJ Stat. § 2C:35–5(b):

1. [The statute defines heroin and cocaine trafficking.]

2. A substance referred to in paragraph (1) of this subsection, in a quantity of one-half ounce or more but less than five ounces . . . is guilty of a crime of the second degree;

3. A substance referred to in paragraph (1) of this subsection in a quantity less than one-half ounce . . . is guilty of a crime of the third degree . . . ;

4. A substance classified as a narcotic drug in Schedule I or II other than those specifically covered in this section . . . in a quantity of one ounce or more . . . is guilty of a crime of the second degree;

5. A substance classified as a narcotic drug in Schedule I or II other than those specifically covered in this

section . . . in a quantity of less than one ounce . . . is guilty of a crime of the third degree . . . ;

6. [The statute defines LSD and PCP trafficking.]
7. [LSD] in a quantity of less than 100 milligrams . . . , or [PCP] in a quantity of less than 10 grams . . . , is guilty of a crime of the second degree;
8. Methamphetamine . . . in a quantity of five ounces or more . . . is guilty of a crime of the first degree.
9.
    a. Methamphetamine . . . in a quantity of one-half ounce or more but less than five ounces . . . is guilty of a crime of the second degree;
    b. Methamphetamine . . . in a quantity of less than one-half ounce . . . is guilty of a crime of the third degree. . . .
10.
    a. [The statute defines marijuana, marijuana-plant, and hash trafficking]. Marijuana in a quantity of 25 pounds . . . , or 50 or more marijuana plants, regardless of weight, or hashish in a quantity of five pounds or more . . . , is guilty of a crime of the first degree.
    b. Marijuana in a quantity of five pounds or more but less than 25 pounds . . . , or 10 or more but fewer than 50 marijuana plants, regardless of weight, or hashish in a quantity of one pound or more but less than five pounds . . . , is guilty of a crime of the second degree;
11. Marijuana in a quantity of one ounce or more but less than five pounds . . . , or hashish in a quantity of five grams or more but less than one pound . . . , is guilty of a crime of the third degree . . . ;
12. Marijuana in a quantity of less than one ounce . . . or hashish in a quantity of less than five grams . . . , is guilty of a crime of the fourth degree. . . .

Child Pornography Statutes

Alaska Stat § 11.61.127:

a. A person commits the crime of possession of child pornography if the person knowingly possesses or knowingly accesses on a computer with intent to view [pornographic material] knowing that the production of the material involved the use of a child under 18 years of age who engaged in the conduct or a depiction of a part of an actual child under 18 years of age who, by manipulation, creation, or modification, appears to be engaged in the conduct.

    c. Each film, audio, video, electronic, or electromagnetic recording, photograph, negative, slide, book, newspaper, magazine, or other material that visually or aurally depicts conduct described [as pornography] that is possessed or accessed in violation of (a) of this section is a separate violation of this section.

    d. In a prosecution under (a) of this section, it is an affirmative defense that the person

        1. possessed or accessed fewer than three depictions described in (a) of this section; and

        2. without allowing any person other than a law enforcement agency to view the depictions, either took reasonable steps to destroy the depictions, or reported the matter to a law enforcement agency and allowed the agency access to the depictions.

    g. Possession of child pornography is a class C felony [which carries a maximum sentence of five years].

<u>Alaska Stat § 12.55.127: Concurrent and Consecutive Sentences</u>

    d. If the defendant is being sentenced for two or more crimes of . . . possession of child pornography under AS 11.61.127, . . . , a consecutive term of imprisonment shall be imposed for some additional term of imprisonment for each additional crime or each additional attempt or solicitation to commit the offense.

<u>Conn. Gen. Stat. § 53a–196d:</u>

    a. A person is guilty of possessing child pornography in the first degree when such person knowingly possesses fifty or more visual depictions of child pornography.

    b. Possessing child pornography in the first degree is a class B felony and any person found guilty under this section shall be sentenced to a term of imprisonment of which five years of the sentence imposed may not be suspended or reduced by the court. [Class B felonies carry a maximum sentence of forty years.]

[Conn. Gen. Stat. § 53a–196e defines the possession of twenty to forty-nine images as a Class C felony (maximum of ten years in prison), for which at least two years cannot be reduced or suspended, and Conn. Gen. Stat. § 53a–196f defines the possession of fewer than twenty images as a Class D felony (maximum of five years), for which at least one year cannot be reduced or suspended.]

Conn. Gen. Stat. § 53a–196g:

In any prosecution for a violation of section 53a–196d, 53a–196e or 53a–196f, it shall be an affirmative defense that (1) the defendant (A) possessed fewer than three visual depictions of child pornography, (B) did not knowingly purchase, procure, solicit or request such visual depictions or knowingly take any other action to cause such visual depictions to come into the defendant's possession, and (C) promptly and in good faith, and without retaining or allowing any person, other than a law enforcement agency, to access any visual depiction or copy thereof, took reasonable steps to destroy each such visual depiction or reported the matter to a law enforcement agency and afforded that agency access to each such visual depiction, or (2) the defendant possessed a visual depiction of a nude person under sixteen years of age for a bona fide artistic, medical, scientific, educational, religious, governmental or judicial purpose.

In each case, the code draws a line at an easily-quantifiable point. How should we set about assessing the appropriateness of these lines? We can decompose the question into three pieces:

1. How closely does the quantifiable factor track the relevant social harm?

2. How important is that assessment of the social harm to the relevant theory of punishment?

3. If the factor is relevant to harm and the theory of punishment, is the cutoff point a logical one? Or might it just be an arbitrary focal point (like $100, or $1,000, or $10,000)?

The Social Harm. The easiest case might seem to be embezzlement, with the social harm equal to the amount taken. But is this necessarily correct? If Joe has $100 and Bob takes it, what is the *net harm* to *society*? Joe is worse off, but Bob is better off by the same amount. And what if Bob is poorer than Joe, so the $100 is actually more valuable to him? Of course, if Joe knows that he could lose his $100, he may take steps to protect it, and the costs of those steps are social losses: the $20 he spends on, say, a small safe is a net social loss.

So here we are in the seemingly easy case, and the story is already getting complicated. It is perfectly reasonable to argue that Bob's gain shouldn't count—society does not generally subscribe to such strictly utilitarian perspectives. But that's an important normative assumption:

the seemingly objective classification of harm as equal to the amount taken actually hides some normative work (and there are certainly some social scientists, economists in particular, who *are* willing to take the criminal's gain into account). And if we take the hyper-strict utilitarian perspective, we have to ask if various self-protection costs are correlated with the amount taken. A $40 safe may be able to protect $100 as well as $100,000, so the social harm of the two thefts may not be all that different. Or perhaps not—maybe we will go to greater lengths to protect more, so the grading picks up the correct trends, even if not for the right reasons.

Not surprisingly, the analysis does not get easier as we move to drug weights. Again, weight is a proxy for the real harms, but what exactly are the harms? There are the direct physiological costs to the users, as well as the emotional, psychological and sometimes physical costs to their family members; and there are the costs associated with drug markets, such as increased violence directly tied to the markets (enforcing territorial control, say) as well as indirectly resulting from the greater social disorder such markets create in their communities. At one level, weight is likely a proxy for these harms, since more weight translates into more doses, more addicts, and likely more disorder. But note that there are already separate offenses that handle many of the disorders that take place (murder, assault, robbery, and so on), and a weight-based line ignores all the other environmental factors that shape the level of harm—one kilo of cocaine trafficked into an open-air inner-city drug market may have greater social costs than that same kilo finding its way to a suburban community.

The harm analysis is trickiest for the child pornography case. Again, the number of images is a proxy for the real harm, but this is a far less obvious one than drug weight. Think again about the social harms we are trying to prevent. The most obvious harm is that to the minor. At a very rough level, perhaps there is a correlation here: an abuser may subject a child to greater abuse the more pictures he takes. But it seems likely that in most cases the cost of abuse is fairly independent of the number of images taken. Plus, we punish for the number of images *possessed*, not *taken*, when we sanction for possession: a person with one images from a set of one hundred faces a lesser sanction that a person with thirty from the same set, even though the harm to the minor is the same in both case.[16] Note, too, that the code do not distinguish between five images of five children versus five images of one child, despite the fact that the total harm caused to produce images of five children is likely greater than that to produce five images of the same child. It feels like we are moving a bit more towards looking under the streetlight.

---

[16] Though note that we know that only because I said it. Perhaps we punish thirty more than one because we think it is probative of the number of pictures taken. But is this a valid assumption? Do we have any data either way?

The Theories of Punishment. All theories care about the social harm of the offense: retributivists use it to assess moral culpability, and utilitarian consequentialists use to it balance the costs and benefits of punishment. But the theories may put different weights on the importance of these quantitative distinctions. In particular, a retributivist may view these distinctions as more essential than a consequentialist. For the latter, the social harm is just one element that goes into her utilitarian calculus: numerous other factors, particularly ones that are offender-specific (as opposed to offense-specific) matter as well. Which is not to say that retributivists are united in their use of quantifiable harms. To an objective-harm retributivist, such a factor is likely key, while to a subjective-intent retributivist the size of the harm desired is highly relevant, but (like the consequentialist) such a retributivist will likely also want to see more weight given to offender traits.

Logical Lines. Note that in all the examples above, each state draws its lines in different places. This could reflect different considered policy distinctions, but it is also consistent with there being a fair amount of arbitrariness at play. Note, too, that especially with drugs, state statutes create all sorts of "exchange rates" across drugs. The most famous such rate, of course, is the federal 100-to-1 cocaine/crack ratio. But consider the following from the New Jersey's drug sentencing statute. All of the following are first degree crimes (which generally face sentence ranges on the order of 10 to 20 years):

> 5 ounces of heroin, 5 ounces of cocaine or crack, 5 ounces of ecstasy, 5 ounces of methamphetamine, 100 mg of LSD, 10 grams of PCP, 25 pounds of marijuana, 50 marijuana plants, or 5 pounds of hash.

There are about 28 grams in an ounce. So while New Jersey has a 1-to-1 ratio for crack and cocaine, it also has a 1400-to-1 ratio for LSD to heroin/cocaine/crack/meth, but only an 80-to-1 ratio for those drugs to marijuana, and a 5-to-1 marijuana/marijuana-hash ratio. Are these logical ratios, even within a state? Do they properly account for all the various different harms different drugs entail?

QUESTIONS

1. **Various sliding scales.** Each of the statutes above imposes a sliding scale for each offense, but the scales differed widely in severity as well as granularity. For theft, for example, Texas has seven cutoff points with a final category of $200,000-or-more; Ohio has six cutoffs with a final category of $1.5 million-or-more. And, as noted above, the sentencing implications vary greatly as well. Do you think these differences reflect rational policy differences?

2. **Quantifiable vs. unquantifiable.** Not all crimes lend themselves to objective quantification. Aggravated assault, for example, is more severe

than simple assault, but that severity cannot be objectively quantified. Thus the line between aggravated assault and simple assault is always more subjective and thus more discretionary. Can we justify using objective lines for some offenses and not for others solely based on the quantifiability of the harm? Could you make an argument for replacing the cutoffs for, say, theft with "a little amount of money," "a fair amount of money," and "a lot of money"?

3. **Quantification and cliffs.** If something is quantifiable, why don't we punish it continuously, if we think that the quantity is the relevant harm. In other words, why in Alabama does the sanction for cocaine jump from 0 to 3 years at 28 grams, from 3 years to 5 years at 500 grams, from 5 to 15 years at 1 kilogram, and from 15 years to life at 10 kilograms? Why not have a sentencing policy that states that each 100 grams of cocaine translates into 6 more months in prison? Why do we have cliffs?

4. **Quantification and discretion.** Does the use of objective cutoffs constrain or expand prosecutorial power? Do you think it increases discretion or accountability?

Case Study: The 100-to-1 Crack/Powder Difference

One of the most controversial quantitative distinctions in recent years was the 100-to-1 crack/powder ratio. Until 2011, the federal statute that criminalized the manufacture or distribution of cocaine, 21 USC § 841, imposed a 5-year mandatory minimum on anyone convicted of manufacturing or distributing 500 grams of powdered cocaine or just 5 grams of crack cocaine ("cocaine base"), and a 10-year mandatory minimum for 5 kilograms of cocaine or 50 grams of crack cocaine. In 2011, Congress reduced the 100-to-1 ratio to 18-to-1, raising the crack cutoffs to 28 grams and 280 grams, respectively.

The standard was highly controversial, due in large part to two points. First, crack and powder cocaine are for all intents and purposes chemically identical. And second, convictions for crack and powder exhibit strong racial differences: in 2010, for example, 78.5% of all people convicted of a crack violation were black, 7.3% white and 13.1% Hispanic, while for powder only 26.8% were black, with 16.8% white and 54.7% Hispanic.[17] The standard argument, then, was that the drug sold disproportionately by blacks was punished much more severely than a drug sold disproportionately by non-blacks, despite no relevant pharmacological difference.

Yet the "crack and powder are identical" argument is much more complicated than this. First, while chemically identical (at least with respect to the narcotic element), crack and powder may in practice have significantly different pharmacological effects. Consider the following

---

[17] See http://www.albany.edu/sourcebook/pdf/t5392010.pdf.

testimony that Glen Hanson, then-Acting Director of the National Institute on Drug Abuse, gave to the US Sentencing Commission in 2002:

> Cocaine comes in two basic forms, either as a hydrochloride salt [*Ed. note*: this is "powder" cocaine] or as a neutralized or alkalinized form, which is sometimes referred to as free-base, and crack would fit into this latter group.
>
> The form of administration or the type of administration depends on the form of the cocaine. The hydrochloride salt typically can be administered either orally, internasally or by IV administration; whereas, the neutralized or alkalinized form makes the drug volatilizable when exposed to heat and then can then be smoked.
>
> [The impact differs based on how the drug is administered.] The more rapid onset are the smoked and intravenous forms of administration; whereas, the intranasal is in between, and the oral form is the slowest onset, being in the neighborhood of about 30 to 40 minutes.
>
> The duration of action is also dependent on the form of administration, with the intravenous and smoking being fairly short, a matter of 10 to 20 minutes duration of action; the longest being after oral, in the neighborhood of about 1 to 2 hours, and then intermediate being the nasal form of administration, which is about 45 to 60 minutes.
>
> Now the potency of the drug, although the drug itself doesn't change regardless of how it's administered, the potency is dependent on the concentration; that is, how high the drug gets inside the body.
>
> After intravenous and smoking, you tend to get higher levels, so that has a more potent effect; whereas, after oral administration, the levels tend not to be as high, so the effect is going to be less potent, and then in between that would be your intranasal administration.[18]

Dr. Hanson then points out that intravenous use and smoking generally have very similar responses, which leads to the following colloquy with one of the commissioners:

> **Commissioner O'Neill:** So then early on the evidence that was suggested that said that crack cocaine is somehow pharmacologically worse than powder cocaine in terms of its effect on the body just isn't substantiated by additional research?

---

[18] US Sentencing Commission Hearing, 2/25/02: *Cocaine Pharmacology, "Crack Babies," Violence,* 14 FED. SENT. RPT'R 191 (2002).

Dr. Hanson: It wouldn't be substantiated if you're talking about intravenous administration.

Commissioner O'Neill: That's what I mean . . . given the fact that the delivery systems are the same.

Dr. Hanson: They're very similar.

Dr. Hanson also notes that addictiveness is correlated with the speed on onset, and thus that "intravenous administration and smoking are more likely to be addicting or severely addicting than the other forms." He estimates that approximately 50% to 60% of those who take cocaine have done so intravenously, and he concludes by agreeing a commissioner who suggests that a better rule would focus on delivery, not substance.

The crack-cocaine disparity was not just premised on the different effects crack and cocaine may or may not have on the users, but also on the broader social effects of the drugs. Crack was a seminal drug in that it "democratized" cocaine: a drug that had traditionally been quite expensive could now be sold in individual $5 to $10 rocks, and it spread rapidly through poor communities, both as a drug to use as well as one that was relatively easy but profitable to manufacture. Of course, profitability invites competition, and that led to a significant upsurge in violence. It also led to a range of social pathologies among its users. As several economists point out:

> Between 1984 and 1994, the homicide rate for Black males aged 14–17 more than doubled and homicide rates for Black males aged 18–24 increased almost as much. . . . In stark contrast, homicide rates for Black males 25 and older were essentially flat over the same period. By the year 2000, homicide rates had fallen back below their initial levels of the early 1980s for almost all age groups.
>
> Homicide was not the only outcome that exhibited sharp fluctuations over this time period in the Black community. [S]tarting in the late 1980s or early 1990s[,] [t]he fraction of Black children in foster care more than doubled, fetal death rates and weapons arrests of Blacks rose more than 25 percent, and Black low birth weight babies increased five percent. Among Whites, there is little evidence of parallel adverse shocks. The poor performance of Blacks relative to Whites represents a break from decades of convergence between Blacks and Whites on many of these measures. [These increases are then followed by offset declines in later years.][19]

The question these authors then ask is to what extent the rise of crack in the 1980s explains these trends. Their results suggest that crack did play a significant role exacerbating many of these social ills in the

---

[19] Roland G. Fryer, Jr., Paul S. Heaton, Steven D. Levitt, & Kevin M. Murphy, *Measuring Crack Cocaine and Its Impact*, 51 ECON. INQUIRY 1651 (2013).

late 1980s, but that crack's effect declined in the early 1990s. The decline in crack-related violence does not appear to come from a decline in crack *use*, but rather from the stabilization of crack markets; the decline in crack's effect on poor birth outcomes appears to reflect changing distributions in the age-profile of crack users (older abusers aged out of child-rearing years, and younger people did not consume crack as extensively).

Thus there does appear to be a difference between crack and powder: crack is more likely to be administered in a more-potent way, and the social costs of the crack market were, at least for several years, substantially greater than those of powder cocaine. But such a statement raises a host of questions:

QUESTIONS

1. **Delivery methods.** How would you design a system that punishes based on delivery methods, not substance? Could you design equally effective systems for possession offenses as well as distribution offenses?

2. **Dosage 1.** A single "hit" of crack—the amount placed in the pipe that a user smokes at one time—is about 0.1 g to 0.5 g. And because of the intense but short high provided by crack, the average user would smoke crack about 3.3 to 16.5 hits of crack per day. Given these numbers, do the cut-offs at 5 grams and 50 grams make sense?[20]

3. **Dosage 2.** The typical internasal dose of cocaine is about 100 mg to 150 mg, so the 500-gram trigger for the 5-year mandatory minimum consisted of about 3,000 to 5,000 doses. Users do approximately 13 to 20 doses a month. What does this suggest about the crack/powder divide? Is this the right way to think about it?

4. **Drugs as proxies.** To the extent that much of the harm with crack was related to the markets for the drug, not the drug itself, can we justify using drug weight as the right proxy to target the real social harm? Could there be more effective ways to structure sentencing law to get at the real social harm? To start, ask what *is* (or *are*) the relevant social harm(s) here in the first place.

5. **Cocaine as drug or ingredient.** Powder cocaine is the key ingredient in crack cocaine, and 10 g of cocaine can produce something on the order of 9 g of crack. Theoretically, how should we sentence someone who is arrested at the airport with 500 grams of cocaine, which could be converted into crack or sold straight?

6. **Lack of Information.** The Fryer et al. paper, which was published in 2013, first appeared as a working paper in 2005, yet the 100-to-1 ratio was adopted in 1986, at the height of the crack epidemic and years before we had enough empirical evidence to clearly understand the causal implications of

---

[20] Use data is elusive, but the numbers given here come from a report generated by the Justice Department, relying on DEA Intelligence reports. The report, from 2002, is on-line here: http://www.justice.gov/archive/olp/pdf/crack_powder2002.pdf.

crack. Even though the Fair Sentencing Act of 2010 cut the ratio to 18-to-1, the legislators in 1986 faced a more violent world and less information about how to respond to it. How should they make such decisions in the presence of empirical uncertainty?

7. **Crack-heroin ratio.** Although § 841 is (in)famous for the crack-cocaine ratio, it also established (and maintains) a five-to-one ratio for heroin to cocaine (the 5-year trigger for heroin is 100 g, the 10-year one kilogram). Note that this also means that there was a 20-to-1 ratio for crack to heroin. Is it practical to design a rational sentencing regime that takes all the various differences into account? Can we still justify such an approach? And why did the crack-heroin ratio get no attention?

B. THE ROLE OF MOTIVE

In general, most criminal statutes focus on the what, not the why: what was stolen, not why the defendant stole it. Sometimes the "why" creeps in, particularly with doctrines such as duress. But by and large motive is legally irrelevant: it may be useful to bring up during the trial—it is easier to prove that a murder was committed intentionally rather than recklessly if the prosecution can convince the jury that the defendant truly hated the victim—but it is not an element of most crimes.

The leading exceptions to this rule are hate crime provisions. Since Washington and Oregon adopted the first hate-crime statutes in 1981, at least forty-five states have adopted statutes that aggravate sanctions for crimes that are committed due to some sort of pernicious motive. A few examples:

Idaho Code § 18–7902:

It shall be unlawful for any person, maliciously and with the specific intent to intimidate or harass another person because of that person's race, color, religion, ancestry, or national origin, to:

a. Cause physical injury to another person; or

b. Damage, destroy, or deface any real or personal property of another person; or

c. Threaten, by word or act, to do the acts prohibited if there is reasonable cause to believe that any of the acts described in subsections (a) and (b) of this section will occur.

For purposes of this section, "deface" shall include, but not be limited to, cross-burnings or the placing of any word or symbol commonly associated with racial, religious or ethnic terrorism on the property of another person without his or her permission.

Mass. Gen. Laws Ch. 265 § 39:

a. Whoever commits an assault or a battery upon a person or damages the real or personal property of a person with the intent to intimidate such person because of such person's race, color, religion, national origin, sexual orientation, gender identity, or disability shall be punished by a fine of not more than five thousand dollars or by imprisonment in a house of correction for not more than two and one-half years, or by both such fine and imprisonment. The court may also order restitution to the victim in any amount up to three times the value of property damage sustained by the owners of such property.

b. Whoever commits a battery in violation of this section and which results in bodily injury shall be punished by a fine of not more than ten thousand dollars or by imprisonment in the state prison for not more than five years, or by both such fine and imprisonment. Whoever commits any offense described in this subsection while armed with a firearm, rifle, shotgun, machine gun or assault weapon shall be punished by imprisonment in the state prison for not more than ten years or in the house of correction for not more than two and one-half years.

There shall be a surcharge of one hundred dollars on a fine assessed against a defendant convicted of a violation of this section; provided, however, that moneys from such surcharge shall be delivered forthwith to the treasurer of the commonwealth and deposited in the Diversity Awareness Education Trust Fund. . . . In the case of convictions for multiple offenses, said surcharge shall be assessed for each such conviction.

A person convicted under the provisions of this section shall complete a diversity awareness program. . . .

<u>N. J. Stat. § 2C:16–1</u>:

a. A person is guilty of the crime of bias intimidation if he commits, attempts to commit, conspires with another to commit, or threatens the immediate commission of an [enumerated] offense

1. with a purpose to intimidate an individual or group of individuals because of race, color, religion, gender, disability, sexual orientation, gender identity or expression, national origin, or ethnicity; or

2. knowing that the conduct constituting the offense would cause an individual or group of individuals to be intimidated because of race, color, religion, gender, disability, sexual orientation, gender identity or expression, national origin, or ethnicity; or

3. under circumstances that caused any victim of the underlying offense to be intimidated and the victim,

considering the manner in which the offense was committed, reasonably believed either that (a) the offense was committed with a purpose to intimidate the victim or any person or entity in whose welfare the victim is interested because of race, color, religion, gender, disability, sexual orientation, gender identity or expression, national origin, or ethnicity, or (b) the victim or the victim's property was selected to be the target of the offense because of the victim's race, color, religion, gender, disability, sexual orientation, gender identity or expression, national origin, or ethnicity.

b. Permissive inference concerning selection of targeted person or property. Proof that the target of the underlying offense was selected by the defendant, or by another acting in concert with the defendant, because of race, color, religion, gender, disability, sexual orientation, gender identity or expression, national origin, or ethnicity shall give rise to a permissive inference by the trier of fact that the defendant acted with a purpose to intimidate an individual or group of individuals because of race, color, religion, gender, disability, sexual orientation, gender identity or expression, national origin, or ethnicity.

c. Grading. Bias intimidation is a crime of the fourth degree if the underlying offense referred to in subsection a. is a disorderly persons offense or petty disorderly persons offense. Otherwise, bias intimidation is a crime one degree higher than the most serious underlying crime referred to in subsection a., except that where the underlying crime is a crime of the first degree, bias intimidation is a first-degree crime and the defendant upon conviction thereof may . . . be sentenced to an ordinary term of imprisonment between 15 years and 30 years, with a presumptive term of 20 years.

d. Gender exemption in sexual offense prosecutions. It shall not be a violation of subsection a. if the underlying criminal offense is a violation of [New Jersey's sexual assault provisions].

e. Merger. A conviction for bias intimidation shall not merge with a conviction of any of the underlying offenses referred to in subsection a. of this section, nor shall any conviction for such underlying offense merge with a conviction for bias intimidation. The court shall impose separate sentences upon a conviction for bias intimidation and a conviction of any underlying offense.

f. Additional Penalties. [A] court may order a person convicted of bias intimidation to one or more of the following:

1. complete a class or program on sensitivity to diverse communities, or other similar training in the area of civil rights;
2. complete a counseling program intended to reduce the tendency toward violent and antisocial behavior; and
3. make payments or other compensation to a community-based program or local agency that provides services to victims of bias intimidation.

Miss. Code § 99–19–307:

In the event it is found beyond a reasonable doubt that the offense was committed by reason of the actual or perceived race, color, ancestry, ethnicity, religion, national origin or gender of the victim, then the penalty for the offense may be enhanced by punishment for a term of imprisonment of up to twice that authorized by law for the offense committed, or a fine of up to twice that authorized by law for the offense committed, or both.

At first blush, the appeal of hate crime statutes is clear. Hating something about a person generally appears to be inappropriate and blameworthy. But upon closer inspection, several concerns quickly materialize:

1. **Including one group excludes another:** Compare the statutes from Idaho and Mississippi to those from Massachusetts and New Jersey: the former two do not aggravate offenses motivated by hatred of homosexuals, while the latter two do. And New Jersey's protects those victimized because of their gender identity, while even fairly-liberal Massachusetts's does not.

   Are we okay with a given state deciding which groups should be protected and which should be not? Is the fact that different states criminalize different types of hate an example of federalism at work, or is it something more troubling? One defense of hate crimes is that they make it clear that hate is unacceptable. But the message is actually substantially more ambiguous, since by penalizing some types of hate these statutes indirectly condone (or at least refuse to condemn) other sorts.

   That said, are we concerned that there are issues beyond sexual orientation and gender identity that will result in much interstate variation? All states include religion, and none include, say, obesity—though many, but not all, cover disabilities. How much room for disagreement is there really?

2. **When is the victim's characteristic a *motivating* factor?** When we think of hate crimes, the types of cases that immediately comes to mind are those like the killing of James Byrd, Jr., in Jasper, Texas, in 1998. Byrd, a black man, was beaten by three white men, who subsequently chained him to the back of their truck and dragged him for three miles, resulting in his eventual decapitation. His perpetrators, two of whom were known white supremacists, dumped his body in front of an African-American church and desecrated his body. There was no reasonable explanation for the crime's motive besides hate.

   But many cases are much tougher. Consider the situation in which Joe, a white man, decides that he is going to rob someone. It would be equally easy to mug Adam (who is white) or Bob (who is black), and Joe chooses to mug Bob due to mild racism. Did he "intentionally select[ ]" Bob "because of race," as the Wisconsin hate crime statute requires? What if Joe is in a state that allows people to carry concealed weapons, and he chose to mug Bob because he thinks blacks are less likely to carry concealed guns? Or what if Joe and Bob get into a fight over who starting pulling into a parking space first, but in the middle of the fight Joe hurls several racial epithets at Bob?

   In a broad (and skeptical) survey of hate crimes laws and the arguments both for and against them, James Jacobs and Kimberly Potter develop a 2x2 matrix to highlight when we should care more about hate as a motive.[21] One axis focuses on the degree of prejudice, the other on the extent to which that prejudice fuels behavior ("causes" the conduct). This taxonomy yields the following four categories:

   - High-Prejudice/High-Causation: This is the easy-to-define case, such as the Byrd murder. Prejudice is high, and it is central to the decision to offend.
   - High-Prejudice/Low-Causation. As an example this type of crime, they cite the case of David Dawson, a member of an Aryan Brotherhood gang who killed a black woman during a burglary. Dawson was highly prejudiced, but that prejudice played only a small role in the murder.
   - Low-Prejudice/Low-Causation. These are situational flare-ups, like the dispute between Joe and Bob over the parking space.

---

[21] JAMES B. JACOBS AND KIMBERLY POTTER, CRIMINAL LAW & IDENTITY POLITICS (1998).

- Low-Prejudice/High-Causation. Jacobs and Potter claim that these constitute the bulk of hate crime cases today. These are cases that involve offenders who "are not ideologues or obsessive haters" but rather individuals whose prejudices are "to some extent unconscious." An example of this category is Steven Vawter who, in a drunken spree, spray-painted "Hitler Rules" on a synagogue and a satanic symbol on a church; he argued that his behavior was aberrant, and many members of the community echoed that sentiment.

To what extent does it matter if we are dealing with Byrd's attackers or Steven Vawter? If the "causation" is high in the attack, why is it relevant whether it is part of a pattern of explicit hate or an aberrant expression?[22] What theories of punishment care, and what theories do not? And we can extend this analysis to all four categories: for each theory of punishment, which categories are treated similarly, and which different?

3. **What is the additional harm?** If we are punishing hate-motivated crimes more severely, it must be because they are more harmful (for some definition of harm). Jacobs and Potter point out that this is a narrow claim: it must be that they are more harmful *within* a category of offense. In other words, the code already distinguishes between simple and aggravated assault, so a hate-crime enhancement must mean that a hate-motivated aggravated assault is more severe than one not motivated by hate—*not* that hate-motivated assaults are disproportionately likely to be aggravated than simple.

Jacobs and Potter then point out that it is hard to identify evidence of such additional harms. Some studies report that victims of hate crimes suffer emotional harms, but this is true of all victims: they find no evidence of *additional*, marginal harm.[23] In fact, being the victim of a hate crime could be psychologically *protective*. Evidence indicates that some of the psychological cost of victimization comes from the sense of being disrespected by your community. But with a hate crime, that sense of being violated by your own community is absent, or it is at least attenuated.

---

[22] Note that it is unlikely that Vawter's *anti-Semitism* was unusual for him, just its open and aggressive expression. It is possible that he was so drunk that despite not harboring anti-Semitic impulses he thought it would be funny to engage in anti-Semitic acts. But the more likely story is that the drunkenness led him to state more openly what he felt internally.

[23] Note, though, that this is a case of absence of evidence, not evidence of absence.

Jacobs and Potter consider some of the other additional harms as well. One is third-party harms. After all, intimidation accounted for almost 45% of all violent hate crimes reported to the FBI in 2010, and nearly 29% of all reported hate crimes overall that year. Jacobs and Potter argue that the generally low-level nature of hate crimes suggests that the magnitude of third-party harms is slight, although they do not provide empirical evidence to back up this claim.[24]

Another possible harm is the risk of retaliation: if Joe beats up Bob because he is black, does that increase the chance that Bob or his friends will retaliate (compared to that risk had Joe beaten up Bob for a different reason)? Jacobs and Potter point to a disturbing implication of such a justification, that a defendant's punishment could turn not on his behavior but on that of his community (if we are afraid of group-retaliation). This is true. But don't we take such community-level concerns into account elsewhere? If our goal is optimal incapacitation, is it irrelevant if the defendant is released into a high-crime or low-crime environment? If our goal is optimal deterrence, shouldn't we take into account whether the offender's environment encourages or discourages offending? There are clearly differences between these examples and Jacob and Potter's concern, but are they meaningful ones?

4. **How serious a problem do we face?** According to the FBI, there were 7,699 hate crimes in 2010, of which 4,970 were violent; a significant majority of these (79%) were intimidation (2,231) or simple assault (1,681). For perspective, there were 1,246,248 violent index crimes in 2010—and neither simple assault nor intimidation rise to the level of an Index offense. Counting crudely, though, hate crimes comprise 0.4% of violent crimes (at least of all *reported* violent crimes, assuming that many simple assaults go unreported each year) and 0.07% of all Index violent and property crimes (of which there were over 10 million in 2010).

Admittedly, reporting for these types of crimes is spotty, so reported hate crimes likely understate the number of actual hate crimes, perhaps significantly. However, the reported hate crimes are likely the most hateful, or at least the most obviously and unambiguously so—and these tend to be low-level offenses. That said, is the fact that such crimes are

---

[24] It is not immediately clear that low-level necessarily implies few third-party effects. Spray-painting a swastika on a synagogue is vandalism, another low-level crime, but its psychological effect on congregants, and the wider Jewish community, could be great.

rare really an argument against punishing them more severely? Are there any real costs to having such a statute to use whenever needed?

Overall, Jacobs and Potter raise several serious concerns with criminalizing hate as a motive. But, to be clear, these concerns are not necessarily limited to hate crimes, but are present any time we try to criminalize motive. Why this motive and not that motive? What is the additional harm, or the additional need for deterrence, that comes from this motive? And so on. We focus here on hate crimes because these are the primary way in which we criminalize motive, but there is no reason that hate is the only motive to criminalize.

ADDITIONAL QUESTIONS

1. **Hate crimes and gender.** Some have argued that all rapes and sexual assaults are hate crimes. If we accept this, does this mean that they all should face aggravated sentences as a result?

2. **The additional harm.** Many if not most crimes are motivated by some sort of hate or animosity; at best, malignant indifference. So, as Jacobs and Potter point out, it is important to think carefully about what additional harm we are trying to target with hate crime laws: what makes certain types of hate worse than others? That, in and of itself, is an important question. And consider the role that the theories of punishment play in answering it—do certain types of hate matter differently for different theories?

But settling on the particular set of additional harms that merit additional punishment only raises a second question: is targeting motive the best way to get at these harms? For a given theory of punishment, what is the sanction intended to target? Does the motive matter directly? Or is it just a proxy for some other factor (like risk of recidivating)—and if a proxy, how good a proxy, especially when compared to the alternatives?

We can flip this question around as well: to what extent does the design of hate crime statutes shed (possible[25]) light on the harms that troubled the drafters as well as the theories of punishment to which they subscribed?

C. THE VICTIM AND VICTIM IMPACT STATEMENTS

Another way of thinking about the severity of crime is not just to look at its (nominally) objective harm—stealing $1,000 is worse than stealing $500, or trafficking five kilograms of cocaine is worse than trafficking one kilogram—but also at its subjective impact on the victim. A given crime will affect different victims differently, and in recent years a growing movement has argued that these subjective experiences of victimization should also be taken into account at sentencing. As a result, since the 1980s states have started to introduce **victim impact**

---

[25] To be clear, that you can detect views about harms and theories of punishment does not mean that these were actually in the drafters' minds at the time they wrote the statute.

statements at sentencing hearings, which provide the victim or the victim's family and friends an opportunity to address the offender, the judge, and the jury to explain the impact the crime has had on their lives. As Paul Cassell, a former federal judge and strong advocate for such statements, explains, support for victim impact statements spans the political spectrum:

> "Law and order" conservatives decried the seemingly single-minded focus of the judicial system on the rights of criminal defendants and inattention to countervailing interests. But concern was by no means limited to the political right. For example, advocates for the poor condemned the fact that the government did nothing to ameliorate the financial consequences of crime on indigent victims. The civil rights movement worried about the victims of racial violence in the South and the inability of those victims to force effective criminal prosecutions. And feminists criticized the treatment of rape victims, who were often themselves placed on trial during rape prosecutions.[26]

All fifty states have passed either a law or constitutional amendment allowing victims to be heard at sentencing. And the move toward greater victim involvement in sentencing has spread beyond the United States, as other common law countries such as the United Kingdom, Canada, Australia, and New Zealand have adopted such provisions as well.

Not surprisingly, states vary in how they use victim impact statements. The statutes below give a sense of the range of options and procedures available to victims: some speak before sentencing, others after; some in open court, some just to probation officers writing up a pre-sentence report; and so on.

<u>Tex. Code Crim. Proc. Ann. § 42.03(b)</u>:

> The court shall permit a victim, close relative of a deceased victim, or guardian of a victim . . . to appear in person to present to the court and to the defendant a statement of the person's views about the offense, the defendant, and the effect of the offense on the victim. The victim, relative, or guardian may not direct questions to the defendant while making the statement. The court reporter may not transcribe the statement. The statement must be made:
>
> 1. after punishment has been assessed and the court has determined whether or not to grant community supervision in the case;
>
> 2. after the court has announced the terms and conditions of the sentence; and

---

[26] Paul G. Cassell, *In Defense of Victim Impact Statements*, 6 OHIO ST. J. CRIM. L. 611, 612 (2009).

3. after sentence is pronounced.

Utah Code § 77–38–4(7):

1. The victim of a crime, the representative of the victim, or both shall have the right:

   a. to be present at the important criminal or juvenile justice hearings. . . . ;

   b. to be heard at the important criminal or juvenile justice hearings. . . . ;

   c. to submit a written statement in any action on appeal related to that crime; and

   d. upon request to the judge hearing the matter, to be present and heard at the initial appearance of the person suspected of committing the conduct or criminal offense against the victim on issues relating to whether to release a defendant . . . and, if so, under what conditions release may occur.

6. In all cases where the number of victims exceeds five, the court may limit the in-court oral statements it receives from victims in its discretion to a few representative statements.

7. Except as otherwise provided in this section, a victim's right to be heard may be exercised at the victim's discretion in any appropriate fashion, including an oral, written, audiotaped, or videotaped statement or direct or indirect information that has been provided to be included in any presentence report.

8. If the victim of a crime is a person who is in custody as a pretrial detainee, as a prisoner following conviction for an offense, . . . or who is in custody for mental or psychological treatment, the right to be heard under this chapter shall be exercised by submitting a written statement to the court.

Ky. Rev. Stat. § 421.520:

1. The attorney for the Commonwealth shall notify the victim that, upon conviction of the defendant, the victim has the right to submit a written victim impact statement to the probation officer responsible for preparing the presentence investigation report for inclusion in the report or to the court should such a report be waived by the defendant.

2. The impact statement may contain, but need not be limited to, a description of the nature and extent of any physical, psychological or financial harm suffered by the victim, the victim's need for restitution and whether the victim has applied for or received compensation for financial loss, and the victim's recommendation for an appropriate sentence.

3. The victim impact statement shall be considered by the court prior to any decision on the sentencing or release, including shock probation, of the defendant.

Ark. Code § 16–90–1112:

a.1. Before imposing sentence, the court shall permit the victim to present a victim impact statement concerning the effects of the crime on the victim, the circumstances surrounding the crime, and the manner in which the crime was perpetrated.

2. The victim may present the statement in writing before the sentencing proceeding or orally under oath at the sentencing proceeding.

b. The court shall give copies of all written victim impact statements to the prosecuting attorney and the defendant.

c. The sentencing court shall consider the victim impact statement along with other factors, but if the victim impact statement includes new material factual information upon which the court intends to rely, the court shall adjourn the sentencing proceeding or take other appropriate action to allow the defendant adequate opportunity to respond.

That victim impact statements are fairly new suggests that they are also controversial. Cassell does a good job laying out the arguments in favor of such statements, pointing to four key justifications:[27]

1. **Information to the sentencer.** As Cassell states, "[v]ictim impact statements provide information about the full harm of the defendant's crime." He argues that the victim can shed light on the magnitude of the injury caused, such as "bodily injury" vs. "serious bodily injury" or the amount stolen. They can also provide information for restitution (like the cost of funeral expenses in a murder case).

   Note, however, that this claim likely reflects Cassell's former job as a federal district court judge, where factors like the amount stolen frequently came in at the sentencing phase, not the guilt phase. In state codes, the magnitude of harm or amount stolen is generally an element of the crime itself and thus must be established at trial, and victim testimony at trial to establish an element of the crime (which is routine) is not a victim impact statement. Look back at the theft statutes in Part A.2 above. How much extra information will a victim impact statement provide, beyond what the prosecutor would need to establish at trial to secure a conviction for a given degree of theft?

---

[27] Cassell, *In Defense*, supra note 26 at 619–625.

2. **Benefiting the victim.** Noting that victim statements may be "both a right and rite," Cassell suggests that there "may be therapeutic aspects to a victim giving a victim impact statement," and points to at least one study suggesting that the evidence favors such an assumption. He acknowledges that some victims could be harmed by the process, but adds that participation is voluntary: self-selection as self-protection.

3. **Explaining the harm to the defendant.** When a victim gives his statement in open court in front of both the judge and defendant, such a statement may help the defendant better appreciate the harm he caused, a potentially important step in the rehabilitative process.

4. **Improving the perceived fairness of sentencing.** Cassell quotes a Presidential Task Force on Victims of Crime for this point: "[w]hen the court hears, as it may, from the defendant, his lawyer, his family and friends, his minister, and others, simple fairness dictates that the person who has borne the brunt of the defendant's crime be allowed to speak." This is not a tit-for-tat argument to Cassell, but one of legitimacy. He states: "We allow defendants to speak at sentencing to 'assure the appearance of justice and to provide a ceremonial ritual at which society pronounces it judgment.' By the same token, allowing victims the same opportunity assures perceived fairness." And there is a fair amount of evidence indicating that perceptions of fairness often matter as much as if not more than the outcome. To feel like one was heard but suffer a less-favorable outcome often feels better than to experience a better outcome while feeling ignored.

Although Cassell provides a strong defense for victim impact statements, they are not without controversy. Among the key concerns:

1. **Who is the victim?** At one level, this is a trivial question: the person actually victimized is clearly the victim. But who else are we willing to include? Families seem obvious, but how do we draw the line—how distant is too distant? Friends complicate the picture further, since a close friend could be more affected than a not-as-close sibling ("she was like a sister to me"). Moreover, one reason for punishing many crimes is because of their third-party and social-destabilizing effects; it is difficult to immediately see who should speak for these harms. Who, for example, are the victims of a crack dealer?

2. **Why does the victim matter for blameworthiness?** That victim impact statements are controversial is made

evident by the Supreme Court's jurisprudence on the issue. In 1987, in *Booth v. Maryland*, 482 U.S. 496 (1987), the Court held that such statements violated the Eighth Amendment; just four years later it reversed itself in *Payne v. Tennessee*, 501 U.S. 808 (1991).[28] The majority in *Booth* was concerned in part that impact statements "could divert the jury's attention away from the defendant's background and record, and the circumstances of the crime." The majority in *Payne* replied:

> [*Booth* held] that only evidence relating to "blameworthiness" is relevant to the capital sentencing decision. However, the assessment of harm caused by the defendant as a result of the crime charged has understandably been an important concern of the criminal law . . . in determining the appropriate punishment.

Though neither opinion engages deeply with the theories of punishment, it is possible that the majorities were each favoring different theories of punishment. Would an objective-harm retributivist favor *Booth* or *Payne*? How about a subjective-intent retributivist? A consequentialist?

3. **Problematic variation.** One key purpose of a victim impact statement is to influence the sentence—to help the factfinder understand why this particular case differs from another. But not all sources of variation are equal. One long-running criticism of impact statements is that they will cause the sentence to turn on the worthiness of the victim: jurors will punish those who kill people of higher "social worth" more severely, even though such worth may be irrelevant in the law's eyes.[29] It is also possible that details about the race, sex, or class of the victim could matter as well.

It is easy to think about various theoretical ways impact statements could be misused by jurors, but the proof is in the pudding: do we observe such misbehavior in the data? Using data from 241 interviews with jurors who sat on death penalty cases in South Carolina between 1986 and 2001, two legal academics and a statistician reported that

---

[28] It is worth noting that both *Booth* and *Payne* are death penalty cases, and a theme of "death is different" certainly runs through *Booth*, if implicitly.

[29] The claim that such worth is irrelevant is often asserted, but rarely if ever supported—is this necessarily true? Obviously ranking harms by the victim's social worth could quickly introduce quite disturbing race, class, sex, and other problematic biases into sentencing. But are there any margins of social worth that might matter? If your answer is "no," however, does this mean that mitigating evidence about the worth of the defendant—common in capital cases in particular—is equally impermissible?

they could detect no effect of victim admirability on a jury's decision to impose the death penalty.[30] Another study indicated that defendants charged with harming higher-status victims were more likely to face the death penalty, but the study was not examining victim impact statements and thus does not explain whether such statements increase the *marginal* risk of death.[31] Other studies have shown that victim status appears to influence mock jurors' views about the defendant, but these studies did not examine whether such views would have changed the sentence imposed.[32] And there is some evidence—though the question is perhaps surprisingly understudied—that the effect of impact statements can vary along race and sex lines, or interactions of the two (such as some evidence that black women in particular face tougher sanctions following victim impact statements).

In short, the evidence of troubling variation appears weak, but this could be due more to the thinness of the evidence base: this is absence of evidence, not evidence of absence. Little work has been done in this area, and what work there is has relied—perhaps in no small part due to necessity—on mock jury pools, the reliability of which is sometimes unclear.[33]

4. **Inflammatory statements.** Impact statements can be, and likely often are, emotional, and that emotion may sway jurors. A key question is whether it sways them *improperly*. This question was a key fissure running through *Booth* and *Payne*. The majority in *Booth* opposed impact statements on the grounds that they would lead to emotionally-driven decisions that were unconstitutionally "arbitrary and capricious," while the majority in *Payne* acknowledged the risk but held that the impact information was probative and that overly-prejudicial instances could be handled on a case-by-case basis; the dissent in *Payne* (comprised of the

---

[30] Theodore Eisenberg, Stephen P. Garvey, and Martin T. Wells, *Victim Characteristics and Victim Impact Evidence in South Carolina Capital Cases*, 88 CORNELL L. REV. 306 (2002).

[31] J. C. Beck, & R. Shumsky, *A Comparison of Retained and Appointed Counsel in Cases of Capital Murder*, 21 L. & HUM. BEHAVIOR 525 (1997).

[32] See, e.g., Bryan Myers & Edith Greene, *The Prejudicial Nature of Victim Impact Statements: Implications for Capital Sentencing Policy*, 10 PSYCH., PUB POL'Y, & L. 492 (2004).

[33] Such jurors are often handed written descriptions of cases, which are by necessity somewhat artificial, and they are called to make decisions that they know are not binding on real people. Some improvements, such as having the jurors watch videos rather than read statements, move mock jury decision-making towards real jury decision-making, but the artificiality is inescapable.

three justices from the *Booth* majority left on the Court) disagreed with the majority's optimism.

Unfortunately, although not unexpectedly, neither the majorities nor the dissents in both *Booth* and *Payne* marshal any empirical data to substantiate their claims.[34] And it turns out that the issue of emotion and judgment is complicated and still poorly understood. As several psychologists explain, there are three primary ways in which emotion influences decision-making (including juror decision-making):

- *Affect-as-Information*: "[E]motions inform us as to how we feel about things, and this allows us to make judgments based on those feelings without resorting to more effortful cognitive processing. Emotions serve as cognitive shortcuts. . . ." And, as behavioralism has shown us, these "heuristic" approaches can be problematically biased.

- *Mood-Congruency Effect*: People "tend to reach judgments that are consistent with their emotional state. . . . Consequently, if we are in a negative mood, we judge the target more negatively than if we are in a positive mood." Problematically, "we may misattribute the source of our negative emotions. That is, we may evaluate our target [i.e., the defendant or victim] more negatively if we are in a negative mood, regardless of whether the target influenced our negative mood in the first place."

- *Emotions and Attention*: "[E]motions may influence the kind of information we attend to, and this may in turn influence how we render judgments about the defendant or victim." One study, for example, reported that experimental subjects feeling angry were more likely to take more-dispositional views of the world, while those feeling sad were more likely to adopt more-situational perspectives.[35]

And the picture gets more complicated from there. To start, all these effects may be in play at any one time. Moreover,

---

[34] It is important to always pay attention to when the Court, or any court, does this, as it is a common occurrence. There is something ironic about justices debating whether jury decisions will be arbitrary and capricious when their own answers to that debate are themselves nothing more than arbitrary and capricious guesswork. For good discussions of this troubling behavior by courts, see, for example, Tracey L. Meares & Bernard E. Harcourt, *Forward: Transparent Adjudication and Social Science Research in Constitutional Criminal Procedure*, 90 J. CRIM. L & CRIMINOLOGY 733 (2000).

[35] Bryan Myers, Emalee Weidemann, and Gregory Pearce, *Psychology Weighs in on the Debate Surrounding Victim Impact Statements and Capital Sentencing: Are Emotional Jurors Really Irrational?*, 19 FED. SENT. RPT'R 13 (2006).

some emotions, like sadness, encourage *more* careful thinking, while others, like anger, encourage *less*. Furthermore, complicated moderating factors influence the role of emotion: in one study, impact statements increased the likelihood of mock jurors imposing the death penalty but only among those jurors who moderately supported that sanction; in another study, the sex of the defendant shaped the emotional influence of the impact statement. And most of these studies ask individuals how they would decide, rather than examining the interaction between emotion and group decision-making; one study suggests that "anger"—which appears to be the most problematic emotion[36]—does not appear to play an important role except *within* group deliberations.[37]

In the end, we seem to have a good sense of how complicated the issue is, but no good idea yet of how all the pieces fit together. Myers and his co-authors point out that "there has been little empirical study of what aspects of [impact statements] elicit emotional responses from jurors." And again, most of the studies that have been done have employed mock jurors operating under unusual lab conditions—yet, as Myers and his colleagues go on to point out, studies of real jurors would be plagued by numerous methodological challenges of their own, such as faulty recall by jurors about why they made the decisions they did.

Given how mixed the theoretical and empirical results are, it is useful to take a step back from looking at the micro-level trees to examine the macro-level forest: what overall effect do victim impact statements appear to have on sentencing outcomes? Julian Roberts provides the following summary:

Much of the research in the area has addressed the question of whether the introduction of victim impact statements (VIS) changes sentencing practices. Advocates of the instrumental approach to VIS assert that if they do not affect sentencing practices, victims will become disillusions. Critics respond that if sentencing practices do change as a result of the introduction of victim impact statements, the principle of parity in sentencing will be undermined. VIS are therefore criticized in both directions. . . .

Tests of the "impact" hypothesis has been conducted in a number of jurisdictions, and have generally found little effect on

---

[36] It is the one most likely to increase negative feelings toward the defendant, reduce cognitive processing, and push the juror into a more-dispositional worldview.

[37] See Ray Paternoster & Jerome Deise, *A Heavy Thumb on the Scale: The Effect of Victim Impact Evidence on Capital Decision Making*, 49 CRIMINOLOGY 129 (2011).

sentencing patterns. For example, [one study] found that victim input did not influence sentencing decisions in Ohio. [Another] report[ed] the results of an analysis of aggregate sentencing patterns in South Australia before and after the introduction of victim impact statements (in 1989). The results were clear: sentencing patterns did not become more severe in the post-reform phase. The researchers also concluded that the introduction of the VIS did not have any significant impact on the length of sentences of imprisonment. The same pattern has been replicated in other studies. In Canada, the introduction of victim impact statements had no discernable effect on the overall custody rate. Finally, interviews with legal professionals confirm the findings from empirical research. [One study] found agreement among legal professionals in South Australia that victim input had not increased sentence severity. This conclusion also applies to surveys of criminal justice professionals in other jurisdictions.

There are several explanations for this lack of effect of victim impact statements on sentencing patterns. First, . . . these statements appear in a small percentage of all cases appearing for sentencing, insufficient to affect the overall severity of sentencing patterns. Second, . . . the proliferation of mandatory and presumptive sentencing laws has restricted the influence of variables such as victim impact statements. The most likely reason that victim impact statements have little effect upon sentencing outcomes is that criminal justice professionals are able to protect the sentencing process from the influence of "extralegal" material. Prosecutors often exercise editorial control over the statements by excising material designed to enhance the severity of the statement, including allegations of prior misconduct by the defendant. . . . Judges—who are trained to ignore evidence with no probative value—appear unaffected by any appeals for severity from the crime victim. This conclusion is supported by surveys and interviews with prosecutors, defense counsel, and judges.[38]

Note that victims need not be upset if their statement does not affect sentencing, for at least two distinct reasons. First, how will they know that their statement had no effect? Unlike the judge, prosecutor, and defense attorney, the victim likely does not know what the "going rate" is for a particular crime. The prosecutor could inform him of this, but even then, if the defendant gets the going rate the victim won't know if that is because his statement was irrelevant or if the judge was likely to under-sentence but was pulled up to the going rate by what the victim

---

[38] Julian V. Roberts, *Crime Victims, Sentencing, and Release from Prison*, IN THE OXFORD HANDBOOK OF SENTENCING AND CORRECTIONS (JOAN PETERSILIA & KEVIN REITZ, EDS., 2012) at 111–112.

said. Second, there is an extensive literature on procedural fairness which makes it clear that feeling heard is often more important than getting the "right" outcome: victims may prefer the default sentence after being allowed to speak than a tougher sentence but without being heard.

Also, what is Roberts' normative position on VIS, and the goals of punishment more generally? He views judges as "protecting" the process from "extralegal" material given their training in ignoring evidence with "no probative value." If Cassell wrote the same summary of the literature, how would he spin the apparent judicial indifference to VIS?

QUESTIONS

1. **The role of punishment theory.** Which theory of punishment would support impact statements the most? The least? Which of the theories are most sensitive to potential changes in the empirical evidence given above? Least sensitive?

2. **Proper perspective?** A significant role of impact statements is surely comparative: they frequently attempt to tell the sentencer to punish the defendant *more* because the harm in the case was *greater* than usual. Does this raise concerns about the ability of juries—who, unlike judges, are not repeat players—to use these statements properly when they are called upon to impose the sentence? Jury sentencing is rare in non-capital cases but constitutionally required in capital cases.

3. **Troubling concerns?** Many discussions of victim impact statements talk about problematic variation in the evidence's use. How unique is this to VIS? Is there other evidence that has troubling implications? Even if so, is there anything uniquely concerning about impact statements?

4. **Loving families and punishment.** The Court in *Booth* notes that if impact statements matter, then the killer of a victim with a family (that is willing to make an impact statement) is more likely to face the death penalty than one without, and that such variation is impermissible. Assuming the Court's empirical claim is true, is that variation actually problematic? Can it be defended? If so, what normative assumptions are needed to do so?

5. **What were the various courts thinking about?** The majorities in *Booth* and *Payne* reach fundamentally different conclusions about the appropriateness of impact statements. At some level, this likely reflects different considerations of what constitutes the relevant "harm," and it may also reflect different overarching perspectives on the appropriateness of the death penalty.* But while the justices never talk about the various ways emotion can influence decision-making, might the *Booth* and *Payne* majorities have implicitly put greater weight on different emotion/decision-making relationships (mood congruency, for example)? If so, which?

---

* It is not inconceivable that justices generally opposed to the death penalty are naturally inclined to take a dim view of controversial evidence that makes the imposition of the penalty more likely; and vice versa for those justices who support the death penalty.

6. **Execution impact statements.** In capital cases, defendants can now introduce execution impact statements, which provide information about the impact the defendant's execution would have on his family and loved ones. In short, these are offender impact statements. If you agree that the impact on the victim is relevant for punishment, is it also true that the impact on the offender is relevant for punishment as well?

CHAPTER 5

FACTORS RELEVANT TO SENTENCING: OFFENDER CHARACTERISTICS

Chapter 4 examined the importance of *offense* traits in setting the proper sentence; this chapter turns its attention to *offender* characteristics. Although there is (almost) no legal significance to differentiating "offense" from "offender" traits,[1] there are useful theoretical and policy reasons for drawing the distinction. For example, different theories of punishment will put different weights on these factors: Objective retributivists may care primarily about offense characteristics, while consequentialists and subjective retributivists may focus more on offender traits.

This Chapter explores three categories of offender characteristics. The first is the offender's prior record. Though widely accepted as relevant to sentencing, under close inspection the arguments for its use—both retributivist and consequentialist—are fairly contestable. There may, for example, be consequentialist reasons to punish repeat offenders *less*, and for many philosophers there is little or no link between the morally just punishment for a given crime and the number of prior bad acts committed by the offender.

The second set of characteristics are traits beyond the offender's control, such as sex and age, as well as developmental, genetic, and neurological traits. These factors all shape the likelihood of committing an offense, the amenability to rehabilitation, and the culpability of the offender, but they are also traits that we are often uncomfortable considering. Many states, for example, forbid judges from accounting for a defendant's sex at sentencing, despite the fact that men are substantially more likely to commit crime, violent crime in particular. Why are we willing to explicitly account for some genetic and neurological differences (such as some mental illnesses) but not others (like sex)?

The third class of offender characteristics are those that are at least somewhat within an offender's control, such as social environment and drug or alcohol use. An offender's behavior can be strongly shaped by his situation, but he has some control over the situations in which he places himself; similarly, an offender who is on drugs at the time of his crime

---

[1] As we will see in Chapter 6, the Supreme Court's *Blakely* and *Booker* decisions, which determine the standards of proof at sentencing, treat offense and offender characteristics (other than prior criminal history) identically, despite academic efforts to convince them to do otherwise. See Douglas A. Berman, *Distinguishing Offense Conduct and Offender Characteristics in Modern Sentencing Reforms*, 58 STANFORD L. REV. 277 (2005).

may seem less culpable (or deterrable), but the decision to take the drugs in the first place may be seen as morally wrong (or deterrable). In each case, how willing are we to look past the offender's immediate context to the choices he made that put him there, and can we trust sentencing actors to properly evaluate these choices?

A. PRIOR CRIMINAL HISTORY

All sentencing regimes in the US take into account an offender's prior criminal history. This section examines the basic justifications for looking at prior criminal acts, the factor's unique constitutional status, and how we treat habitual offenders in particular.

A.1. THEORETICAL JUSTIFICATIONS

At first blush, it seems like defending the use of prior offenses as aggravating factors should be simple. After all, every state does this, and as we will see in Chapter 6, the Supreme Court views prior-record aggravation as so fundamental to sentencing policy that it exempts them from the constitutional limitations it places on the use of *all other* aggravating factors. Yet, upon closer inspection, such aggravation becomes harder to justify. The following reading examines the challenges repeat-offender rules pose for retributivists, and the discussion section afterwards considers those posed for consequentialists.

Richard Frase, *Prior Conviction Sentencing Enhancements: Rationales and Limits Based on Retributive and Utilitarian Proportionality Principles and Social Equity Goals*
JULIAN ROBERTS AND ANDREW VON HIRSCH, EDS., PREVIOUS CONVICTIONS AT SENTENCING: THEORETICAL AND APPLIED PERSPECTIVES (2010)

[Richard Frase discusses six different ways that just deserts theorists have evaluated the proper use of prior criminal history.]

1. The "Exclusionary" School

The "exclusionary" school is the term given . . . to the view of scholars who maintain that an offender's prior conviction record is unrelated to his desert and should have no bearing on the severity of his current sentence. Such a narrow view of desert may be correct in principle. . . . But when combined with a strict ("defining," not merely limiting*) view of desert, this approach is unworkable in practice because it seems to rule out any consideration of prior record, and thus encourages sentencing policymakers and practitioners to ignore desert principles entirely.

---

* *Ed. note*: Under a "strict" approach, desert theory is not simply placing limits on otherwise-consequentialist uses of prior records (like the limiting retributivism discussed in Chapter 1 above), but it is the sole source of justification for the use of prior records.

2. Diminished Culpability of First Offenders (and Second Offenders? Third? Fourth?)

This theory argues that first offenders can plausibly claim their offence was out of character, and that society should be somewhat less willing to fully convert its condemnation of the offender's criminal act into condemnation of the actor. This theory also asserts that we should give the first offender credit for his prior law-abiding life and, we hope, his ability to resume that life and learn his lesson. Under the narrowest version of this theory mitigation is limited to first offenders; a broader version, often referred to as progressive loss of mitigation, allows a lesser sentence reduction for second offenders, and some writers would continue to permit some mitigation for a third offence, or even a fourth, although the rationale for mitigation would seem to be quite strained at that point. Except for the last group, most variants of the reduced-desert theory reject the kind of steady escalation of penalties for each additional prior conviction which is found in the current sentencing laws and practices of many jurisdictions. These theories thus suffer (albeit to a lesser extent) from the weakness of the exclusionary approach—the theories (especially the narrower versions) would invalidate so much of current sentencing practice that policymakers and practitioners are likely to dismiss such theories. . . . Another problem with all reduced-desert theories is that they may lack widespread support; it seems that many people's moral intuitions tell them that criminal record is a matter of enhanced culpability for repeat offenders, not reduced culpability for first or second offenders.

On the other hand, reduced-desert theories do have one advantage over the desert-based rationales discussed below, all of which posit enhanced culpability for second and subsequent crimes—the reduced-desert approach has a clear upper limit, based on desert factors associated with the current offence(s), whereas the logic of enhanced-desert theories seems to permit an open-ended escalation of sanction severity. The idea that current offence(s) should set an upper limit on sanction severity finds support in sentencing guidelines systems, all of which recognize an offence-based "cap" beyond which criminal history no longer raises the guidelines recommended sentence.

3. The Recidivist's "Bad Character"

Character theories of enhanced punishment for repeat offenders seem to be based on the idea that such offenders have shown themselves, with each additional crime, to be more and more wicked and depraved, more antisocial and more indifferent to the rights of others. Julian Roberts has likened recidivism enhancements to the increased penalty and opprobrium attached to killing with premeditation—in both cases, he argues, we are more likely to ascribe the current offence to the offender, rather than to his surroundings or environmental factors. But premeditation is a particular mental state that is directly associated with the offender's criminal act; punishing bad character comes much closer to violating the fundamental principle that people are punished for what they have done (and with what intent), not for who or what they are.

There are also major practical problems in applying this approach—how much more blameworthy does the offender become with each additional crime, and is there any upper limit to penalty enhancements under this approach?

4. Heightened Notice and/or Defiance of Criminal Prohibitions

Another group of theories posits enhanced culpability for offenders who, after receiving formal condemnation of their prior criminal acts, ignore society's explicit warning and commit further crime in open defiance of these warnings. The notice theory may . . . assume some similarity between prior and current offences; . . . actual criminal-record enhancement rules[, however,] are much broader. Moreover notice theory does not explain further enhancements of punishment severity for a third, fourth or fifth offence.

As for defiance theories, some authors have questioned whether such a theory is acceptable in a liberal society where people are punished for their acts[,] not their attitudes and thoughts. One possible answer to this criticism would be to invoke an expressive theory under which offenders are punished to repudiate their false moral claim to act without regard to the rights of others or society; arguably, such false claims grow more offensive with each additional crime. But by how much and with what limits, if any?

5. Recidivism as Omission

This theory, recently proposed by Youngjae Lee, argues that the repeat offender's culpability is enhanced because he has failed to take appropriate action to control his criminal tendencies in light of his earlier crime, conviction, and punishment. Lee's theory seems to assume that, because of the prior conviction(s), the offender is or ought to be aware of his heightened risk of offending. From this actual or constructive awareness Lee derives a heightened duty on the part of the offender to rearrange his life in a way that ensures he will avoid further criminality.

Compared to the desert theories previously discussed, this theory has the potential to better explain rules that steadily escalate sentence severity as the number of prior convictions increases—the duty of the offender to control his criminal tendencies becomes steadily more important and obvious. But Lee's theory suffers from some of the defects of the other theories: it seems to apply mainly to offenders whose past and current crimes are similar, or at least caused by the same criminal impulses; the theory does not seems capable of generating a formula or useful guidelines for determining how much to enhance the repeat offender's sentence, and when to discontinue further enhancement for additional prior convictions; and this theory would seem to require courts to engage in difficult assessments of the extent to which the offender tried but was unable to control his criminal tendencies.

6. The Other Branch of Desert: Does Repeat Offending Create Broader "Harms"?

Most desert theorists probably agree that a person's desert depends on the harms he has caused or risked as well as his intent and other offender-based culpability factors. But thus far desert-based theories seem to have assumed that variations in harm do not explain or justify prior-record enhancements—the harm to the victim(s) of the current offence, say a burglary, is supposedly the same regardless of the offender's prior conviction record.

It can be argued, however, that an offender's prior record of crime affects how we view his most recent criminal acts, and that the total harm of repeat offending is greater than the sum of the harms of each offence viewed in isolation. The repeat offender's current burglary is more disturbing, to both the victim and society, in light of—and in proportion to—his prior crimes. We are forced to conclude that this offender poses a heightened threat to all of us (and heightened to a degree roughly proportional to his prior record). This conclusion makes us fearful, and reduces our level of trust in others; it forces us to take extra precautions against people like this, precautions which may be expensive or inconvenient; it also forces officials to take additional, more expensive measures to deal with the heightened levels of risk posed by this and similar offenders. These are all real and substantial harms, foreseeably caused by the offender's past and current crimes.

One problem with this theory is that it might be used to justify penalty enhancement based on our fear of what *other, similar* offenders may do; from a desert perspective, defendants are only accountable for the risks and harms which they or their criminal confederates have caused. Another problem with this theory is its potential to justify a limitless escalation of severity: our feelings of fear and distrust, and the extra precautions we and officials are forced to take, would if anything seem to accelerate with increases in the offender's prior record. Of course, such an accelerating effect could help explain severe habitual offender laws. But most desert theorists would probably agree that such laws cannot and should not be justified on desert grounds, and they would reject any desert theory that seemed to do this. Apart from the "no-upper-limit" problem, the increased-aggregate-harms theory does not suggest any practical formula or guidelines for deciding how much to enhance for each additional offence.

Consequentialist Concerns with Repeat-Offender Enhancements

In a wide-ranging examination of the consequentialist problems with repeat-offender enhancements, David Dana points out the flaws of several justifications for such laws.[2] To appreciate his arguments, however, it is helpful to first understand what he defines as the "economic" perspective on crime. Dana's focus is on optimal deterrence from a strictly utilitarian perspective. Two important points flow from this approach. First, if a crime imposes $100 in *social* harm,[3] then the sanction should be set equal to $100. If the criminal derives $101 in utility from the crime, he will commit it—and, to Dana, he *should*, since it is socially efficient to do so, and we certainly should not spend more than $100 to prevent $100 in social loss.[4] Second, the primary issue for the government is how to balance the probability of punishment vs. the magnitude of the sanction. Simplifying somewhat, a $100 penalty imposed with absolute certainty every time the criminal offends should deter roughly as much as a $200 penalty imposed every other time the offender offends. The optimal balance between the penalty (f) and the probability it is imposed (p) depends on the relative costs of each element: how much extra does it cost to hire additional police officers, prosecutors, etc. (which raise p) vs. imposing an extra year in prison or increasing the fine (which raise f)?

With this background, we can now look at Dana's discussion of the arguments for punishing recidivists more severely and whether they make sense from a deterrence perspective. He first notes that there are several reasons why we may not want to punish recidivists more, and in fact may want to punish them *less*.

1. <u>Extra information</u>: Police not only instinctively look to prior offenders first, but they have more information at their disposal for identifying their role: DNA records, fingerprint evidence, as well as information on family, friends, and

---

[2] David A. Dana, *Rethinking the Puzzle of Escalating Penalties for Repeat Offenders*, 110 YALE L. J. 733 (2001).

[3] By social harm, Dana means the *net* loss to society. If Tom simply grabs $100 out of Steven's hands, then there is very little social loss: Tom gains $100, Steven loses $100, but society as a whole basically breaks even (the only way there may be some social loss here is if the $100 was more valuable to Steven than to Tom—maybe Steven was poorer, or had some more immediately-pressing needs). If Steven fought back, though, the costs of those fights would be part of the social loss; or if Steven didn't go outside as much in order to avoid the risk of being mugged, the loss in utility from not going out would be a social loss; hiring police to deter Tom or prions cells to lock him up are social losses as well (since that money would be better spent hiring engineers or building useful products).

[4] A counter-argument might come to mind: what if we set the sanction at $1,000 and, as a result, no $100-crimes happen? We thus prevent the $100 in social loss at no cost, since we are never required to pay for the $1,000 sanction. Put aside the obvious rebuttal, that we will never get the crime rate to zero, so we will still occasionally incur the $1,000 cost. Even if we could get the crime rate to zero this way, Dana would oppose such a policy: from a strictly utilitarian perspective, we *want* the crime worth $101 to happen, since society is made $1 better off in the process (assuming the $100 social costs includes *all* costs, including, say, protection costs). If this seems like a problematic result, it is due to problems with strict utilitarianism, not with Dana's use of it.

residences. Thus p is higher for recidivists at no (or little) extra cost to the state, so we can maintain the same pf at less cost by reducing f—and Dana generally believes that pf, the total sanction, should remain constant, since it should equal the social cost of the crime, which is independent of whether it is committed by a first-time offender or a recidivist.

2. Heuristic biases: People tend to overweigh first-hand experiences, as well as those that are more salient and more recently-experienced. Thus recent releasees are likely to overestimate the probability of rearrest, and a higher (perceived) p means the state can save resources by imposing a smaller f. Note, too, that these heuristics argue *against* the practice of excluding sufficiently-old convictions from the prior-history score. (See why?)

3. Conservation of resources: Some economists have argued that we should not impose uniformly high sanctions on offenders but rather try to price discriminate: charge those who are hardest to deter the most. But we don't know who harder-to-deter offenders are, so we use prior history as a proxy. Dana replies that what matters is the social cost of the crime, not the benefits to the offenders. In other words, if the social cost of the crime is $100, then set the sanction at $100. The offender who derives $80 in utility won't commit the crime (which is good, since the net social loss would be $20), but those who value it at $200 or $2000 both will, and in both cases a strict utilitarian *wants* them to.

Dana then turns his attention to arguments that still may argue for enhanced sanctions for recidivists, though he is often skeptical of their reliability:

4. Learning by doing: If offenders become more skilled over time at evading capture, then we need to raise f to compensate for the declining p. But Dana is unconvinced that offenders learn much from crime to crime, or at least learn enough to offset the increased risk of capture discussed in point (1).

5. Declining error costs: We are very concerned about improperly convicting someone for the first time, so we impose a lesser sentence to hedge our bets (if we get it wrong, at least the sanction is not too severe). As the offender's record grows longer, we become less concerned that he may be innocent of this particular offense. Dana counters that it is not clear that the risk of error is all that great (though work by the Innocence Project and others may cast some doubt on his optimism), and that if this were

the justification we should see a big jump in sentence for the second conviction but not so much after that—but this is contrary to the design of many laws.

6. Social stigma: It is likely that a significant portion of the cost of conviction is not the state sanction, but the social stigma that attaches to that conviction. As an offender's prior record gets longer and longer, the amount of shame imposed might get smaller: for the first offense, he suffers $500 in shame, for the second only $200, for the third only $75, etc. In this case, the state sanction may need to rise to offset the decline in stigma to keep the total sanction constant. But if the *rate of decline* of stigma slows over time (in our example, the second sanction is $300 less than the first, the third sanction $125 less than the second, etc.), then the *rate of increase* in the state sanction should slow as well (it needs to offset a $300 decline after the first offense, but only a $125 decline after the second). But again, most repeat offender laws get *harsher*, not less severe, with more offenses. Moreover, Dana points out that the declining-stigma argument assumes that people don't use the state sanction as a signal about how much to shame—if they do, then as the state sanction increases, so too does the shame.

7. Respect for the law: If people obey the law the more they respect it, and if people demand that the sanction get tougher with each subsequent offense, then perhaps deterrence is most effective when it concedes to this psychological demand, even if it otherwise does not make sense. This is the one argument that Dana generally accepts as plausible, though it begs the question of *why* people feel that way.

Why Do We Look to Prior History?

The theoretical efforts to justify the use of prior history are all trying to answer the same question: what is it about a subsequent offense that makes extra punishment necessary, if the actual harm of the crime remains unchanged? As both Frase and Dana suggest, this can be a tricky question to answer. That said, there are some common themes that run through these articles; there are also a few justifications not raised by either author that deserve attention.

1. The risk of error. Frase talks about the "progressive loss of mitigation" and Dana about the "social interest in avoiding mistaken punishment." These concepts are not identical, since progressive loss of mitigation is concerned with errors by the defendant ("I'm not really that bad of a person") while mistake aversion is concerned with errors by the state ("did we lock up an innocent person?"). But

the two theories reflect a common theme, namely that prior convictions reduce our fears about getting things wrong this time.

2. The crime costs really are not the same. The notice, defiance, and omission theories all share the idea that a subsequent offense reflects a deeper moral failing; to the extent that just deserts seeks to set punishment equal to moral culpability, the culpability of a second offense is greater even if the harm to the victim remains the same. Frase's "broader harms" theory goes even further to argue that the actual harm from the crime is greater if the offender has a prior record, due to increased fearfulness, reduced trust, and more expenditures on protection. Dana's discussion of respect for legal rules (faintly) echoes this latter point: if we feel angry at people who repeatedly violate laws we feel are just, and if that anger grows with each violation, then the social cost of a crime rises with the offender's record, even if the general harm to the victim remains constant. In other words, perhaps the costs to the victim are not the only costs we need to consider.

3. Whither incapacitation? Just deserts and deterrence are not our only justifications for punishment, with incapacitation perhaps the dominant theory of the day. Does incapacitation better justify the aggravating use of prior records? Like a deterrence theorist, an incapacitationist could justify rising sanctions from an error-minimization perspective: our goal is to incarcerate someone just until he no longer poses a threat, and we do not know how long that is. So we impose shorter sentences up front, but as the offender reveals his continued propensity to offend, we use that information to justify longer and longer incapacitations. The analysis here is slightly different than Dana's, since Dana is trying to optimally deter a specific crime, while an incapacitationist is trying to optimally prevent a stream of crimes an offender may commit going forward. Our prediction about how many future crimes an offender is going to commit—and thus the need to lock him up for longer—grows with each subsequent offense, even if our prediction about the social cost per crime (which is what Dana cares about) does not change.

Question: Even if you accept this incapacitationist argument, is there any problem with laws like three-strike laws that impose significant enhancements later in an offender's career? What does our discussion of the lifecycle patterns in offending from Ch. 1 suggest?

4. Whither rehabilitation? Like incapacitation, rehabilitation is missing from the discussion as well. And the argument is the same: with limited resources, we want to concentrate our rehabilitative efforts on those who need them the most, and a longer criminal history indicates a greater need. But we are then forced to ask the obvious question of whether long prison sentences actually serve a rehabilitative role.

QUESTIONS

1. **Precise retributivist sanctions.** Frase frequently criticizes the various retributivist theories for not providing clear guidance on the exact penalty or schedule of sanctions that judges should use. Is this a fair critique of retributivist approaches? Is retributivism, which is inherently deontological, *capable* of providing precise punishments? Are retributive values of a sort that will vary from jurisdiction to jurisdiction, reflecting the different moral preferences of different jurisdictions?

2. **Recidivism and human capital.** Can we reconcile Lee's theory of "recidivism as omission" with human capital models? Returns on education of all sorts decline as a person gets older, and offenders generally start developing (adult) criminal records in their teens, if not early twenties. Moreover, does Lee's theory seem to "unfairly" reward older inmates who are aging out of crime? By blaming the 25-year old recidivist for not changing his ways, does his theory implicitly praise the 35-year old who stops recidivating, even though that cessation may be due less to choice and more to biochemical and other developmental changes?

3. **Recidivism and situation.** Continuing with Lee's theory, what role should prison and release conditions play in Lee's theory? The environments in which offenders are housed and into which they are released can play important roles in their post-prison success. How should a judge sentencing a recidivist under Lee's theory take into account such conditions, which are beyond the defendant's control? Is this concern relevant to the other retributivist theories which that Frase analyzes?

4. **The magnitude of recidivism.** Consider the following statistics: A Bureau of Justice Statistics study found that from a sample of over 400,000 inmates released in 2005, within five years over 75% had been arrested and over 55% had be reincarcerated (a BJS study of 200,000 paroles released in 1994 yielded similar numbers).[5] An earlier study by the Pew Center on the States found that approximately 45% of all inmates released in 1999 and in 2004 were reincarcerated within three years, with slightly under half returning for new crimes (as opposed to technical violations).[6] Do these high—and rather stable—recidivism rates argue in favor of tougher repeat offender laws, or against?

5. **Retributivism and unacceptable sanctions.** Frase warns that "desert theorists would probably agree that [strike laws and harsh habitual offender laws] cannot and should not be justified on desert grounds, and they would reject any desert theory that seemed to do this." If true, are desert theorists putting the cart before the horse? In other words, is it methodologically okay to say "I want outcome x" and then work to justify that outcome, rather than establishing the reasons for punishment first and then

---

[5] MATTHEW R. DUROSE, ALEXIA D. COOPER, AND HOWARD N. SNYDER, RECIDIVISM OF PRISONERS RELEASED IN 30 STATES IN 2005: PATTERNS FROM 2005 TO 2010 (2014).

[6] THE PEW CENTER ON STATES, STATE OF RECIDIVISM: THE REVOLVING DOOR OF AMERICA'S PRISONS (2011). Note that the "new crime" number is a lower bound on the number of readmitted prisoners who in fact faced charges for new crimes, since the new crime may have been dismissed as part of a plea bargain.

fleshing out their implications? The scientific method does not allow researchers to state their goal—"I want to show that chemical x causes cancer"—and then select the theory that gets them there. Is there a reason to handle things differently with philosophical issues?

6. **Philosophy vs. politics.** Several times Frase suggests that certain retributive theories about the role of prior history would be politically impossible. Does this suggest that there is a failure in our political markets, or that the theory is somehow flawed? If the theory reaches conclusions that run so afoul of popular intuitions, should we take that as at least partial evidence that the theory is likely overlooking or oversimplifying an important part of the problem?

7. **Prior acquittals.** Should we be allowed to increase a sentence based on prior *acquittals*? After all, acquittals can arise when the defendant in fact appears to have engaged in the relevant conduct but the state is simply incapable of proving this beyond a reasonable doubt. If a judge is confident that the defendant actually committed the prior act, why should he not take that into account? How about prior uncharged conduct? Which is more troublesome: prior acquitted conduct or prior uncharged conduct? How relevant is the fact that a trial has taken place in the former category but not the latter? We will return to this issue when talking about real offense sentencing in Chapter 6.

PROBLEM: THE EFFECT OF A PRIOR RECORD IN MINNESOTA

Figure 5–1 below is Minnesota's sentencing grid for non-sex offenses. The vertical axis gives the conviction offense, the horizontal the offender's criminal history score. As the grid makes clear, prior history can play a significant role in the sentence a defendant faces: a move from a score of 0 to a score 6, for example, more than doubles prison time for a Class-VIII felony; for felonies below Class VIII, a one-point change in score can turn a presumptively-stayed prison sentence into an unstayed one.

Fig. 5–1: Minnesota's Sentencing Grid for Non-Sex Offenses

IV. SENTENCING GUIDELINES GRID
Presumptive Sentence Lengths in Months

Italicized numbers within the grid denote the range within which a judge may sentence without the sentence being deemed a departure. Offenders with non-imprisonment felony sentences are subject to jail time according to law.

SEVERITY LEVEL OF CONVICTION OFFENSE (Common offenses listed in italics)		CRIMINAL HISTORY SCORE						
		0	1	2	3	4	5	6 or more
Murder, 2nd Degree (intentional murder; drive-by-shootings)	XI	306 *261-367*	326 *278-391*	346 *295-415*	366 *312-439*	386 *329-463*	406 *346-480[2]*	426 *363-480[2]*
Murder, 3rd Degree Murder, 2nd Degree (unintentional murder)	X	150 *128-180*	165 *141-198*	180 *153-216*	195 *166-234*	210 *179-252*	225 *192-270*	240 *204-288*
Assault, 1st Degree Controlled Substance Crime, 1st Degree	IX	86 *74-103*	98 *84-117*	110 *94-132*	122 *104-146*	134 *114-160*	146 *125-175*	158 *135-189*
Aggravated Robbery, 1st Degree Controlled Substance Crime, 2nd Degree	VIII	48 *41-57*	58 *50-69*	68 *58-81*	78 *67-93*	88 *75-105*	98 *84-117*	108 *92-129*
Felony DWI	VII	36	42	48	54 *46-64*	60 *51-72*	66 *57-79*	72 *62-84[2]*
Controlled Substance Crime, 3rd Degree	VI	21	27	33	39 *34-46*	45 *39-54*	51 *44-61*	57 *49-68*
Residential Burglary Simple Robbery	V	18	23	28	33 *29-39*	38 *33-45*	43 *37-51*	48 *41-57*
Nonresidential Burglary	IV	12[1]	15	18	21	24 *21-28*	27 *23-32*	30 *26-36*
Theft Crimes (Over $5,000)	III	12[1]	13	15	17	19 *17-22*	21 *18-25*	23 *20-27*
Theft Crimes ($5,000 or less) Check Forgery ($251-$2,500)	II	12[1]	12[1]	13	15	17	19	21 *18-25*
Sale of Simulated Controlled Substance	I	12[1]	12[1]	12[1]	13	15	17	19 *17-22*

☐ Presumptive commitment to state imprisonment. First-degree murder has a mandatory life sentence and is excluded from the guidelines by law. See Guidelines Section II.E., Mandatory Sentences, for policy regarding those sentences controlled by law.

▨ Presumptive stayed sentence; at the discretion of the judge, up to a year in jail and/or other non-jail sanctions can be imposed as conditions of probation. However, certain offenses in this section of the grid always carry a presumptive commitment to state prison. See Guidelines Sections II.C. Presumptive Sentence and II.E. Mandatory Sentences.

[1] One year and one day

[2] M.S. § 244.09 requires the Sentencing Guidelines to provide a range for sentences which are presumptive commitment to state imprisonment of 15% lower and 20% higher than the fixed duration displayed, provided that the minimum sentence is not less than one year and one day and the maximum sentence is not more than the statutory maximum. See, Guidelines Sections II.H. Presumptive Sentence Durations that Exceed the Statutory Maximum Sentence and II.I. Sentence Ranges for Presumptive Commitment Offenses in Shaded Areas of Grids.

Effective August 1, 2010

Among the rules that the Minnesota guidelines manual establishes for calculating the offense score are the following:

1. Each prior offense is assigned a certain number of points. As Figure 5–1 makes clear, non-sex offenses rise in severity from I to XI (the vertical axis in Figure 1 lists the sort of offenses that fall within each severity type); sex offenses in severity from H (failure to register as a sex offender) to A (violent sexual assault). The point scale is:

Severity Level	Points
I–II	1/2
III–V	1
VI–VIII	1-1/2
IX–XI	2
Murder 1st degree	2
A	2 (3 if current crime is sex offense)
B–E	1-1/2
F–G	1
H	1/2 (first offense), 1 (all subsequent)

2. Prior felonies or stays of imposition are not included in the score if there are more than fifteen years between the end of that prior sentence and the date of the current offense.

3. An additional point is assigned if the offender was on parole, probation, or other sort of conditional release when he committed the crime. But the point is not assigned if the offender was committed for treatment or (subject to a few exceptions) was on juvenile probation when he committed the crime.

4. Certain misdemeanors are effectively worth 1/4 point each, and no more than one point can come from all misdemeanors. If the instant crime relates to certain felony-level drunk driving charges, however, prior DUIs and related misdemeanors are worth 1/2 point each with no cap. Misdemeanors more than ten years old are not counted.

5. An offender receives one point for every two juvenile convictions for crimes committed after his fourteenth birthday but before his twenty-fifth, and only if each conviction was for a "separate behavioral incident" or "involved separate victims." With some exceptions, points from juveniles records are capped at one.

6. There is a no-double counting provision: if a prior misdemeanor causes a current crime to be charged as a felony rather than a misdemeanor, then that aggravating misdemeanor cannot also count toward the defendant's prior-history score.

QUESTIONS

1. **Retributivism.** Minnesota's sentencing commission from its inception has emphasized retributivism as one of its primary guiding principles. Does the guideline's approach to prior history adequately reflect a retributive philosophy? Which of the variants discussed by Frase appears dominant?

2. **Crime control.** Over time, the Minnesota sentencing commission has put increasing emphasis on crime control as well. Do these guidelines seem consistent with crime control goals?

3. **Diagonals.** We generally read sentencing guidelines either left to right (how the punishment for a given crime changes with prior history) or top to bottom (how punishment for a given prior history changes with currently offense severity). But what if we read the grid diagonally: are the differences in sanctions among a Class IX with two prior points, a Class VII with three, and a Class VII with four prior points justifiable?

4. **Differential history impacts.** Each additional point adds the same number of months to the sentence, although that additional amount varies across offense types. In other words, each extra point for a defendant convicted of a Class VIII offense adds ten months, but for a defendant convicted of a Class IV offense only three months. Are the offense-class differences justifiable? How about the consistent increase in sentence length within offense classes?

5. **Sex offenses.** For someone convicted of a sex offense, is it possible to justify treating a prior Class A sexual felony as worse than a prior first degree murder (3 points, vs. 2 for murder)? Class A sexual felonies apply to criminal sexual misconduct that involves "actual penetration" in situations such as when (1) the victim is under thirteen and the defendant more than three years older, (2) the victim is under sixteen and the defendant is more than four years older and is in a position of authority over the victim, (3) the victim has fear of bodily harm, or (4) a dangerous weapon is used.[7]

A.2. THE SPECIAL STATUS OF PRIOR HISTORY, AND ITS RELIABILITY

Prior criminal history has a special constitutional status among aggravating sentencing factors. To see how, consider a simple example. A state has two degrees of assault: second degree, which carries a statutory maximum of ten years, and first degree, which carries a statutory maximum of twenty years. The only difference between the two crimes is that first degree requires proof of an additional fact, x. In 2000, the Court held in *Apprendi v. New Jersey*, 530 U.S. 466 (2000), that *any* fact x required for the imposition of a greater sentence had to be found by a jury beyond a reasonable doubt—except for prior criminal history.[8]

---

[7] See Minn. Stat. § 609.342 for the full definition.

[8] Chapter 6 discusses *Apprendi*, and its history and ramifications, in much more detail.

That one fact could still be found by a judge by a preponderance of the evidence.

The Court provides very little justification for this exception. Two years before *Apprendi*, the Court held in *Almendarez-Torres v. United States*, 523 U.S. 224 (1998), that judicial (as opposed to jury) findings concerning prior criminal history did not violate a defendant's jury right, even when they were essential for raising a defendant's maximum sentence. The *Apprendi* majority's refusal to overturn *Almendarez-Torres* is half-hearted at best:

> Even though it is arguable that *Almendarez-Torres* was incorrectly decided, and that a logical application of our reasoning today should apply if the recidivist issue were contested, Apprendi does not contest the decision's validity and we need not revisit it for purposes of our own decision today to treat the case as a narrow exception to the general rule [that *Apprendi* establishes]. [530 U.S. at 489 (footnote omitted).]

The legitimacy of the prior-history exception weaken even more by Justice Thomas's concurrence in *Apprendi*. *Almendarez-Torres* was a 5–4 decision, with Justice Thomas voting with the majority. In *Apprendi*, however, Thomas admits that he thinks *Almendarez-Torres* was wrongly decided, and that prior history findings should be subject to the same constitutional rules *Apprendi* imposes on all other aggravating factors. The *Almendarez-Torres* and *Apprendi* majorities had defended treating prior history differently in part by looking to historical practice; in his long *Apprendi* concurrence Thomas examines sentencing practices from the Founding through the present to argue that those majorities' historical story was incorrect.

Yet subsequent cases have only reinforced the prior-history exception. In *Blakely v. Washington*, 542 U.S. 296, 302 (2004), which extended *Apprendi*'s reach to impose jury fact-finding on more classes of aggravating facts, the Court simply states that it is applying *Apprendi*'s rule that "other than the fact of a prior conviction, any fact that increases the penalty for a crime beyond the prescribed statutory maximum must be submitted to a jury, and proved beyond a reasonable doubt." The Court used nearly identical language the next year in *Booker v. United States*, 543 U.S. 220, 231–32 (2005), when it further extended *Apprendi*'s and *Blakely*'s reach. No further mention of the criminal history exception or its rationale is made in either opinion.

So the exception is now well-entrenched, but it is worth asking how justifiable it is from a policy perspective (whatever its possible historical origins). A key justification for requiring juries to find facts, and to find them beyond a reasonable doubt, is to ensure that the state has adequately proven its case, and to stack the deck against the state to prioritize personal liberty over crime enforcement. Perhaps prior records do not require such rigorous vetting: if all it takes to ascertain a defendant's prior history is a quick glance at his record in a well-maintained, easily accessed, nationwide database, then perhaps judicial fact-finding here can be pragmatically justified on efficiency grounds.

Unfortunately, such a well-maintained, easily accessed, nationwide database does not actually exist. Since 1995 the federal Department of Justice has spent hundreds of millions of dollars via the National Criminal History Improvement Program (NCHIP) to try to improve how states record, maintain, and share prior criminal records, and to develop centralized criminal history-, fingerprint-, and other databases. There is still much work to be done. In a 2006 report, for example, the Attorney General noted that a majority of the criminal records submitted to the FBI's nationwide Interstate Identification Index (III) were incomplete: half were missing information on final disposition, some included offenses not reported to the FBI, and others contained fingerprints whose quality is insufficient for use.[9] The Attorney General admitted that the III was "far from complete," but that it "is still the most comprehensive single source of criminal history information in the United States, and provides users, at a minimum, with a pointer system. . . ."[10]

The NCHIP program's efforts are laudable, and it should come as no surprise that a system of 48 million records spread across 50 states, the federal government, and numerous territories is hard to completely and comprehensively centralize. But the challenge NCHIP faces should raise serious questions about the policy wisdom of holding prior records to a lower evidentiary bar. The effect of prior history on a sentence can be substantial: in North Carolina, the expected sentence for a given felony class more than doubles when moving from the lowest criminal history score to the highest, and in Washington state such a move often more than doubles the sentence, and in some cases can septuple it![11] The Court's opinion in *Apprendi* holds facts with far less significant effects on sentencing outcomes to a high bar; it is not immediately clear why criminal history should be treated differently.

In fact, there is some evidence that Congress has had concerns about this very issue. For drug offenses, for example, 21 U.S.C. § 851 requires

---

[9] UNITED STATES DEPARTMENT OF JUSTICE, THE ATTORNEY GENERAL'S REPORT ON CRIMINAL HISTORY BACKGROUND CHECKS (2006). The report does note that more-recent records are better in quality.

[10] Approximately 10% of recidivists are arrested outside the state from which they were most recently released. See ALLEN J. BECK AND BERNARD SHIPLEY, RECIDIVISM OF PRISONERS RELEASED IN 1983 (1989) (12.5% of releases rearrested in a different state), PATRICK A. LANGAN AND DAVID J. LEVIN, RECIDIVISM IN 1994 (2002) (7.6% of releases rearrested in another state). Interstate coordination is thus not a minor issue here.

[11] In North Carolina, for example, a Class B1 felon with a criminal history score of 1 (the lowest possible) faces a default sentence range of 192 to 240 months, but a Class B1 felon with a criminal history score of 6 (the highest possible) faces a default range of 386 to 483 months. See FELONY PUNISHMENT CHART, available on-line at http://www.nccourts.org/Courts/CRS/Councils/spac/Documents/felonychartR_12_01_09min_max_sentences.pdf. In Washington, a Class X felon sees his default sentence rise from 12 years to 29 years as his prior history score rises from 0 (the lowest) to 9+ (the highest). For lower offenses, the effect is even larger: for a Class V felon, the sentence rises from 9 months to 7 years. See SENTENCING GUIDELINES COMMISSION, ADULT SENTENCING GUIDELINES MANUAL 2008, Table 1.

the US Attorney to prove the existence of aggravating prior offenses beyond a reasonable doubt (to a judge, though, not a jury). Congress is not entirely consistent here, since the Armed Career Criminal Act (ACCA) does not contain similar protections for recidivist felons who fall within its ambit, despite the fact that under the ACCA prior histories can increase the statutory maximum from, say, ten years to life (see 18 U.S.C. § 924(e)). But the drug law restrictions nonetheless suggest that legislatures are not always confident that criminal history is so easy to assess that a lower standard of proof is justifiable.

QUESTIONS

1. **General use of prior history.** Assume that Thomas's critique of the historical use of prior history is valid, and put aside questions about the reliability of prior-record evidence. Are there other reasons for treating prior records differently?

2. **Prior history detail.** Should our comfort with the *Almendarez-Torres* exception turn on the level of detail needed? Consider the following situation:[12] A legal immigrant, Joe, is convicted by California three different times on low-level drug charges. Later, after yet another drug conviction, the federal government attempts to deport Joe. In some situations, a defendant is eligible for a discretionary "cancellation of removal" if none of his prior felonies is an "aggravated felony." Joe's first drug conviction does not meet the definition of an aggravated felony; his second and third convictions count as aggravated felonies only if California explicitly charged him as a repeat offender. Thus the importance of Joe's prior record turns not just on the number of charges and convictions, but on detailed facts about those convictions.[13] Do you find it acceptable—either pragmatically or doctrinally—to subject such factfinding to a lower evidentiary and constitutional bar than, say, that for whether the defendant used a gun in the commission of the instant crime? If not, would you find it more acceptable if the statute simply denied cancellation if the state showed *any* prior conviction, not a specific sort of prior?

3. **"Inverting" prior record laws.** As we will see in Chapter 6, the Supreme Court's doctrine on jury factfinding is asymmetric: any fact that must be found before a judge can impose a *longer* sentence must be found by a jury beyond a reasonable doubt, but any fact required for a judge to impose a *shorter* sentence can be found by a judge by a preponderance of the evidence. Were the Court to eliminate the *Almendarez-Torres* exception, would we expect legislatures to "invert" their habitual offender laws, establishing default sentences that assumed the defendant had committed a lot of prior offenses and then allowing judges to mitigate based on a lack of

---

[12] These facts are drawn from *Carachuri-Rosendo v. Holder*, 560 U.S. 563, 130 S. Ct. 2577 (2010).

[13] Note that in the drug context, 21 U.S.C. § 851 applies and Joe's history, and its relevant facts, would need to be proven beyond a reasonable doubt. But that is not a constitutional matter, only a statutory protection, and one that does not exist for other, similar uses of prior records.

prior records? Would sentencing outcomes be the same—are the incentives to mitigate the same as those to aggravate?

A.3. HABITUAL-OFFENDER AND THREE-STRIKE LAWS

The most prominent form of recidivist provision is the three-strike law. About half of all states have a three-strike law, and other states (such as Kentucky and New York) have strike-like laws that go by different names. Most of the strike laws were adopted in the mid-1990s, after Washington State (1993) and California (1994) implemented the first official "three-strike" laws.

Despite their widespread adoption, however, such laws are rarely used outside of California. Frank Zimring and his coauthors suggest that nearly 90% of all strike sentences imposed in the United States have been imposed in California.[14] Nonetheless, the history of three-strike legislation can help shed some doctrinal and policy light on recidivist enhancements more generally. We will consider two points here in particular: the constitutionality of such laws, and their efficacy.

Much of the litigation and analysis of strike laws centers on California, which is not surprising: not only is it responsible for most strike sentences, but its strike law is viewed as being one of the harshest in the country. The Supreme Court addressed the constitutionality of California's law in *Ewing v. California*, 538 U.S. 11 (2003), in which it upheld the law against an Eighth Amendment challenge. Between 1984 and 2000, Gary Ewing was convicted of four felonies (all related to burglaries and robberies) and a string of low-level misdemeanors. In 2000, he stole three golf clubs worth $399 each; finding this to be Ewing's third strike, the court sentenced him to twenty-five years to life, and he challenged the sentence as grossly disproportionate under the Eighth Amendment for a $1,200 theft.

In a 5–4 decision, the Court upheld his conviction. The three-justice plurality opinion relied on a four-factor test based on: (1) deference to the legislature, (2) the need to respect multiple theories of punishment, (3) the need to respect federalism, and (4) the claim that the Eighth Amendment does not require proportionality between the offense and the sentence, just that it forbids "grossly disproportionate" sentences.

Regarding the first three points, the Court stated that "[w]hen the California Legislature enacted the three strikes law, it made a judgment that protecting the public safety requires incapacitating criminals who have already been convicted of at least one serious or violent crime. Nothing in the Eighth Amendment prohibits California from making that choice." 538 U.S. at 25. The plurality pointed to high levels of recidivism as justifying California's policy decision. For the proportionality point, the plurality argued that the proper comparison

---

[14] See FRANKLIN E. ZIMRING, GORDON HAWKINS, AND SAM KAMIN, PUNISHMENT AND DEMOCRACY: THREE STRIKES AND YOU'RE OUT IN CALIFORNIA (2003).

needed to balance the sentence against Ewing's lifetime criminal history, not just against his most recent offense. The plurality then held that his sentence was not grossly disproportional:

> Ewing's sentence is justified by the State's public-safety interest in incapacitating and deterring recidivist felons, and amply supported by his own long, serious criminal record. Ewing has been convicted of numerous misdemeanor and felony offenses, served nine separate terms of incarceration, and committed most of his crimes while on probation or parole. His prior "strikes" were serious felonies including robbery and three residential burglaries. To be sure, Ewing's sentence is a long one. But it reflects a rational legislative judgment, entitled to deference, that offenders who have committed serious or violent felonies and who continue to commit felonies must be incapacitated. [538 U.S. at 29–30.]

Justices Scalia and Thomas, concurring the decision, went even further and argued that non-capital sentences cannot be subject to proportionality review as a matter of principle.

The dissenters, in part, focused on a comparative question: what sentences are imposed by California and other states for similar conduct, and what sort of conduct is generally required in California and other states to impose so long a sentence? The dissenters noted that prior to the passage of California's strike law, a defendant in California like Ewing could not have received more than a ten-year sentence. The dissenters also pointed out that even murderers in California rarely serve sentences as long as the one Ewing was likely to serve, and that other states would likewise not impose such a long sentence on Ewing.

But the dissent's argument did not prevail, and so strike laws are clearly constitutional. But are they effective—do they sufficiently deter or incapacitate offenders? The empirical results, almost all of which again look to California, are mixed.[15] Zimring et al. argue that simple numbers imply California's law cannot have a big deterrent effect: only 10.6% of arrested adults in their three-city sample were second- or third-strike eligible. Joanna Shepherd counters that California's law appears to deter the *first* strike, since all offenders fear running up too high a record. So where Zimring et al. report a deterrent effect on the order of 1% to 2% over two years, Shepherd responds that the law appears to have prevented nearly 4,000 aggravated assaults, 11,000 robberies, and nearly

---

[15] The papers cited here are: Joanna Shepherd, *Fear of the First Strike: The Full Deterrent Effect of California's Two- and Three-Strike Legislation*, 31 J. LEGAL STUDIES 159 (2002); Eric Helland and Alexander Tabbarok, *Does Three Strikes Deter? A Nonparametric Estimation*, 42 J. HUMAN RESOURCES 309 (2007); Tomislav V. Kovandzic, John J. Sloan III, and Lynn M. Vieraitis, *"Striking Out" as a Crime Reduction Policy: The Impact of "Three Strike" Laws on Crime Rates in US Cities*, 21 JUSTICE Q. 207 (2004); and Thomas B. Marvell and Carlisle E. Moody, *The Lethal Effects of Three-Strike Laws*, 30 J. LEGAL STUDIES 89 (2001).

390,000 burglaries over its first two years (or two-year declines of roughly 1%, 6%, and 67%, respectively), although methodological concerns suggest that at least some of Shepherd's results are too high,[16] and she does note that larcenies increased by over 17,000 (a two-year increase of 1%). A more sophisticated approach by Eric Helland and Alexander Tabbarok estimated that strike laws reduce offending by those with two strikes by 17% to 20%, for an overall reduction in serious crime of about 31,000 crimes (or about 4%) per year. Tomislav Kovandzic, John Sloan, and Lynn Vieraitis, however, look beyond just California and find evidence that strike laws lead to increases in homicides (by 13% to 14% in the short run and by 16% to 24% in the long run) and no perceptible drop in crime otherwise. And Thomas Marvel and Carlisle Moody find some evidence that strike laws lead to slightly higher levels of police officer deaths—about one extra death per state every two years.

Of course, even if strike laws reduce crime, we want to consider whether they do so *efficiently*. And the results from Helland and Tabbarok are not particularly optimistic. Using some rough estimates, they find that California's strike law is cost-effective if each strike-affected prisoner would have committed crimes that cost about $148,000 each; given an estimated average crime cost of $34,000, California's strike inmates would have to be among the worst of the worst. Unlike most states' strike laws, however, which restrict the third strike to certain categories of severe felonies, California's is applicable to any felony[17]—which likely explains why Zimring et al. find a wide distribution of third-strike offenses: 3% homicide, 10% robbery, 7% assault, 22% burglary, 16% other thefts, 19% drugs, and 23% "other." Such a spread of offenses reduces the likelihood that third-strike inmates in California are truly the "worst of the worst." States with more restrictive strike laws, then, may have more efficient results.

Finally, note that strike laws are likely not the most important type of prior enhancement, despite their widespread notoriety. As Chapter 9 discusses, most offenders serve short sentences, on the order of six months to two years. Low-level mandatory minimums that require recidivists to be reincarcerated for short periods of time are probably doing much more "work" to drive up US prison populations than rarely-imposed-but-severe strike laws.

QUESTIONS

1. **Strikes and impulses.** Do strike laws make sense in light of our discussion in Chapter 1 about the above-average impulsiveness of many criminal offenders? Do any concerns you have with strike laws carry over to

---

[16] It is always a good idea to look at results to see if they seem plausible. In the mid-1990s California averaged approximately 300,000 burglaries per year, and it is unlikely that a single law could cut burglaries by two-thirds.

[17] See JOHN CLARK, JAMES AUSTIN, AND D. ALAN HENRY, "THREE STRIKES AND YOU'RE OUT": A REVIEW OF STATE LEGISLATION (1997), available on-line at http://www.ncjrs.gov/pdffiles/165369.pdf.

less-extreme recidivist enhancements as well? Or are strike laws relatively unique?

2. **Strikes over the lifecycle.** Do strike laws make sense in light of the lifecycle theory of offending discussed in Ch. 1? When thinking about this question, keep three stylized facts from that Chapter in mind: (1) offending generally rises from the teens to late twenties or early thirties and then declines over the rest of the person's life, and (2) interpersonal differences in the propensity to offend persist over people's lifetimes, and (3) it is hard to predict who will have higher lifetime levels of offending *ex ante*.[18] And again, can we differentiate strike laws from other recidivist enhancements?

3. **Old and new sentencing laws.** Is there anything potentially problematic with looking to a state's past sentencing practices to evaluate the legality of a new law? What if the new law is a response to new circumstances? In his dissent in *Ewing*, Justice Breyer notes that prior to the adoption of the three strike law, no defendant could have received a sentence of more than ten years of Ewing's crime. Justice O'Connor replies that this "is hardly surprising. . . . Profound disappointment with the perceived lenity of criminal sentencing (especially for repeat felons) led to passage of the three strikes law in the first place." Which Justice has the better argument? How relevant is the fact that between 1960 and 1993, California's violent crime rate rose from 238 per 100,000 to 1,077 per 100,000 (peaking in 1992 at 1,119 per 100,000)?

4. **Effectiveness of lesser enhancements.** That the Supreme Court upheld California's strike law seems to imply that it would surely uphold lesser enhancements (especially given the extreme nature of *Ewing*'s facts). But do the mixed results concerning the effectiveness of California's strike law imply that lesser enhancements will be even *less* effective? What if prosecutors are more willing to impose lesser sanctions more regularly? What if lesser sanctions are perceived as more just by the wider society?

B. IMMUTABLE CHARACTERISTICS

As we saw in Ch. 1, a person's proclivity to engage in criminal conduct is often shaped by traits generally not within that person's control, such as age, sex, and family upbringing when young. The next several sections will consider the challenging question of how to account for these factors at sentencing, if at all. Abstractly speaking, none of these factors should be treated any differently normatively: if you think that age is relevant at sentencing, then so too should sex, or genetic triggers, or home environment (at least when young and unable to relocate). Different normative theories may treat a given factor differently—retributivists may view youth as a mitigator, incapacitationists as an aggravator—but the question of *whether* to account for an immutable trait shouldn't turn on the trait.

---

[18] In other words, if person X is more likely than person Y to commit a crime when both are 18, then X is more likely than Y to commit a crime when both are 40, even though X is less likely at 40 to commit that crime than when he was 18.

But that's theory. In practice, the picture is much more complicated. Even if you accept that these traits should be taken into account, we should be concerned with judges and other sentencing actors "misusing" the trait, whether out of ignorance or (possibly implicit) bias, especially given how messy the evidence base is. So while much of this section will focus on *how* we should account for these traits, depending on the theory of punishment in question, we will also consider the risks of using such evidence in the first place.

In this section we will consider three key immutable traits: developmental, genetic, and neurological traits; age; and sex.[19] Before turning to these traits, however, I want to first briefly touch on arguments against using such evidence at all. In theory, all the consequential justifications for punishment—deterrence, incapacitation, and rehabilitation—would embrace their use, since such behavioral evidence allows us to craft more efficient sanctions.

> **Question:** Can you think of at least one major reason why even consequentialists would be concerned with using such evidence in the first place? What risk exists with saying, say, "men are more violent than women"? Or, conversely, "women are less violent than men"?

More resistance to the use of such evidence may come from retributivists, particularly those who focus on the harm from the crime as the primary metric of liability. The harm to the victim is, by and large, the same, whether the defendant is young or old, male or female. To the extent that retributivists are concerned with the subjective bad intent of the offender, such evidence becomes more relevant, although perhaps not automatically so.

I do not want to undersell the importance of such over-arching concerns. The bulk of this section will focus on *how* to use these factors and the risks that arise when using them. But keep these more-global concerns about *whether* to use them in mind, and ask whether some of the "as applied" concerns raised here may justify more "facial" bans on the use of such evidence.

B.1. DEVELOPMENTAL GENETIC, AND NEUROLOGICAL FACTORS

We start with developmental, genetic, and neurological (DGN) factors because the issues they raise apply with (almost) equal force to the other two categories of immutable traits examined below. For example, the question "is it him, or is it his genes?" lies at the heart of an argument Joshua Greene and Jonathan Cohen develop in a reading below about how the law should properly account for DGN evidence, and their answer is just as relevant if we replace "genes" with "sex" or "age."

---

[19] Technically, age is mutable, since it is constantly changing, but the offender has no control over his age, how it changes, or many of the behavioral regularities that attach to it.

Thus this section starts by examining the proper use of DGN evidence in depth, and then it considers how to apply these arguments to issues of age and sex.

Unlike a defendant's prior record, there is much less certainty about how to account for DGN evidence, and this section considers three open issues: First, what exactly do DGN results tell us? What are the behavioral implications of discovering that someone has a "genetic predisposition" for, say, violence? What does it even mean to say that? Second, how relevant is this evidence when determining how to punish a defendant? Is a defendant with a greater developmental, genetic or neurological predisposition for violence less culpable or more in need of incapacitation or deterrence? Or, perhaps counterintuitively, is the evidence ultimately immaterial? And third, how receptive have courts been to the use of such arguments in sentencing proceedings?

Note that throughout this section, we will move between developmental, genetic, and neurological issues without much distinction. Though biologically these are very different processes, the differences between them do not hold much legal significance: all three deal with innate (although often mutable) characteristics that shape behavior in ways over which the actor has no (or very little) control.[20]

B.1.a. THE CONNECTION BETWEEN DGN AND CRIME

Science's (or perhaps sciences') understanding of the DGN bases of behavior has been growing by leaps and bounds over the past few decades. The following reading provides an overview of what we know about the connections between DGN factors on the one hand and criminal and anti-social behavior on the other.

David P. Farrington, *Individual Differences and Offending*
MICHAEL TONRY, ED., THE HANDBOOK OF CRIME AND PUNISHMENT (1998)

Genetic Factors

There is no doubt that offending tends to run in families: criminal parents tend to have criminal children. For example, in the Cambridge Study in Delinquent Development, sixty-three percent of men with convicted biological fathers were themselves convicted up to age forty, compared with thirty percent of men with unconvicted biological fathers. However, the intergenerational transmission of criminality does not necessarily indicate any genetic transmission of criminal potential: this

---

[20] Technically speaking, "developmental" traits refer to those determined by how the body develops in utero, such as how various cell layers develop and fold in the brain; genetic traits to those shaped by one's genes; and neurological traits to those determined by the wiring of the brain. This section implicitly lumps biochemical and hormonal traits into these categories as well. These traits are not independent of each other and can interact in complex ways scientists are only beginning to fully understand.

transmission could equally be achieved through environmental influences [since parents and children tend to live in similar environments].

Special behavioral genetic designs are needed to disentangle genetic from environmental influences. The first involves the comparison of identical (monozygotic) and fraternal (dizygotic) same-sex twin pairs. Identical twins share 100 percent of their genes, whereas fraternal twins share about fifty percent of their genes. Arguably, however, the members of both types of twin pairs are exposed to the same shared family environmental influences. The results obtained with twin studies are quite consistent: identical twins are more concordant in their offending than fraternal twins. [R]esults from existing studies [have] found an average concordance rate of fifty-two percent for identical twins and twenty-one percent for fraternal twins.

The second design involves the study of children who were separated at birth from their biological parents and brought up by adoptive parents. According to the rationale of this design, these adopted children share genetic but not environmental factors with their biological parents, and they share environmental but not genetic factors with their adoptive parents. Again, the results obtained in adoption studies are quite consistent: generally, the offending of adopted children is significantly related to the offending of their biological parents. . . .

The third, most convincing, design involves comparing the concordance of identical twins reared together and identical twins reared apart. . . . Unfortunately, it is difficult to obtain large samples of identical twins reared in totally different environments from birth. At the present time, there appears to be no adequate study of offending using this method. However, the Minnesota Study of Twins Reared Apart retrospectively assessed the heritability* of childhood conduct disorder and adult antisocial personality disorder. [Researchers] found that heritability was forty-one percent for childhood conduct disorder and twenty-eight percent for adult antisocial personality disorder. Again, therefore, there are indications of some kind of genetic influence on antisocial behavior, although these heritabilities are lower than those obtained in the largest study of unseparated twins: fifty percent for violent crimes and seventy-eight percent for property crimes.

[One researcher, Raine,] concluded that there was some genetic influence on criminal potential, and that this might be greater for females than or males and greater for adult crime than for juvenile delinquency. However, little is known about the precise genes that might be involved, or about the precise individual factors related to criminal potential that might be genetically transmitted.

---

* *Ed. note*: Heritability measures the extent to which observed variation in traits (called "phenotypic variation") can be attributed to variation in genes, rather than in environment.

Psychophysiological Factors

Psychophysiology is concerned with the relationship between constructs such as arousal and emotion and physiological measures such as heat rate, skin conductance, and electroencephalographic (EEG) activity. Low arousal and low anxiety are key constructs measured by these psychophysiological variables. It is hypothesized that people with low arousal and low anxiety are particularly likely to become offenders. Low arousal and boredom lead to sensation seeking and risk taking to increase arousal. Individuals with low anxiety tend to have low internal inhibitions against offending and low guilt.

According to Raine, one of the most replicable findings in the literature is that antisocial and criminal people tend to have relatively low heart rates. This was true in the Cambridge Study, where heart rate was measured at age eighteen. More than twice as many of the boys with low heart rates were convicted for violence as of the remainder. [Furthermore,] Raine and his colleagues concluded that low cardiovascular, electrodermal, and cortical arousal all predicted offending, independently of academic and social factors.

Neurochemical and Hormonal Factors

Neurotransmitters are chemicals stored in brain cells that carry information between these cells. There are many neurotransmitters, but serotonin has been most replicably related to offending. The largest investigation of the relationship between serotonin and violence . . . found that men who were convicted for violence, and those who were high on self-reported violence, tended to have high blood serotonin levels. These relationships held up after controlling for socioeconomic status, intelligence, smoking, drinking, drug use, and other variables. Interestingly, the relationship between serotonin and violence was stronger for men from disharmonious, noncohesive families. Serotonin was not related to violence among the [study's] women.

Hormones, biochemical substances that carry information, are secreted into the bloodstream by endocrine organs located throughout the body. The hormone that has been studied most in relation to offending is testosterone. . . . Comparisons between violent and nonviolent male and female prisoners show significant and replicable associations between high testosterone levels and violence. In the Montreal longitudinal-experimental study, which is a follow-up of Montreal boys from age six, teacher ratings of fighting and bullying were associated with low testosterone levels at age thirteen but with high testosterone levels at age sixteen. These results suggest that high testosterone levels after puberty might be related to youth violence.

Neuropyschology and Brain Dysfunction

Neuropsychology is the study of the brain mechanisms that control behavior. To some extent, it is assumed that functions are localized in certain areas of the brain (although there are many exceptions to this). In particular, it is assumed that the "executive functions" of abstract reasoning, anticipation and planning, sustaining attention and concentration, and inhibiting inappropriate behavior are located in the frontal lobes. It follows that damage to the frontal lobes leads to impairment in abstract reasoning and concept formation, lack of foresight and insight, poor concentration, low anxiety, and uninhibited behavior. This "frontal lobe syndrome" is related to offending. Typically, offenders perform badly on neuropsychological tests. For example, in the Dunedin Study, male and female delinquents at age thirteen . . . showed significant impairment on verbal skills, auditory verbal memory, visuospatial analysis, and visual-motor integration.

Interest in the link between neurological functioning and offending has stimulated studies of the relationship between pregnancy and birth complications and later offending. In [a] Danish perinatal study, [researchers] . . . found that birth delivery complications predicted arrests for violence up to age twenty-two; eighty percent of violent offenders scored in the high range of delivery complications, compared with thirty percent of property offenders and forty-seven percent of non-offenders. Interestingly, delivery complications especially predicted violence when one or both parents were psychiatrically disturbed. In a later analysis of the same project, [researchers] showed that children who had neurological problems in the first week of life . . . together with family adversity (early maternal rejection, family conflict, family instability, a criminal parent) were particularly likely to be arrested for violent and nonviolent crimes.

However, the importance of delivery complications was not found in the Philadelphia Biosocial Project. . . . [P]regnancy and delivery complications did not significantly predict official or self-reported offending in the Cambridge Study. It may be that pregnancy and delivery complications predict offending mainly or exclusively when they occur in combination with other family adversities.

Psychological Influences on Offending

An extensive meta-analysis* . . . showed that low IQ and psychological factors such as hyperactivity, attention deficit, impulsivity, and risk taking were important predictors of later serious and violent offending.

Despite controversy about the merits of IQ tests, they have been used in numerous criminological studies. Taken together, the results show conclusively that offenders have significantly lower IQ scores than non-offenders. For example, in the Cambridge Study, one-third of the boys scoring ninety or lower on a nonverbal IQ test . . . at ages eight to

---

* *Ed. note*: A meta-analysis is a rigorous synthesis of results across numerous individual studies. By bringing together multiple studies, meta-analyses (if done well) are thought to yield more precise results. See the Statistical Appendix for more details.

ten were convicted as juveniles—twice as many as among the remainder. Low nonverbal IQ was highly correlated with low verbal IQ . . . and with low school attainment at age eleven; all of these measures predicted juvenile convictions to much the same extent. Furthermore, low nonverbal IQ predicted self-reported delinquency almost as well as convictions, suggesting that the link between low IQ and delinquency was not caused by the less intelligent boys having a greater probability of being caught.

Low IQ measured very early in life predicts later offending. For example, in a prospective longitudinal survey of Stockholm males, low IQ measured at age three significantly predicted officially recorded offending up to age thirty. Frequent offenders (those with our or more offenses) had an average IQ of eighty-eight at age three, whereas non-offenders had an average IQ of 101. All of these results held up after controlling or social class. Similarly, low IQ at age four predicted arrests up to age twenty-seven in the Perry Preschool Project and court delinquency up to age seventeen in the Collaborative Perinatal Project. [However, w]hile the relationship between low IQ and offending is not in doubt, the same cannot be said for the interpretation of it. The two most popular explanations focus on the executive functioning of the brain or on school failure as an intervening variable.

Impulsivity is the central construct in . . . [an] important criminological theor[y] . . . by Gottfredson and Hirschi.* Gottfredson and Hirschi castigated criminological theorists for ignoring the fact that people differed in underlying criminal propensities and that these differences appeared early in life and remained stable over much of the life course. The key individual difference construct in their theory was low self-control, which referred to the extent to which individuals were vulnerable to the temptations of the moment. People with low self-control were impulsive, took risks, had low cognitive and academic-skills, were self-centered, had low empathy, and had short time horizons.

Gottfredson and Hirschi argued that crimes were part of a larger category of deviant acts (including substance abuse, heavy smoking, heavy drinking, heavy gambling, sexual promiscuity, truanting, and road accidents), which were all behavioral manifestations of the key underlying theoretical construct of low self-control. They argued that between-individual differences in self-control were present early in life (by ages six to eight), were remarkably stable over time, and were essentially caused by differences in parental child-rearing practices.

In the Cambridge Study, boys nominated by teachers as lacking in concentration or restless, those nominated by parents, peers, or teachers as the most daring, and those who were the most impulsive on

---

* *Ed. note*: Gottfredson and Hirschi's theory is discussed in Chapter 1.

psychomotor tests all tended to become offenders. Later self-report questionnaire measures of impulsivity were also related to offending.

Temperament and Personality

Temperament even in the first few months of life predicts later behavior. In the Australian Temperament Project, children who were rated by then mothers at ages four to eight months as not amenable, irritable, and showing behavior problems tended to be rated aggressive-hyperactive at ages seven to eight. In the Dunedin Study, being under-controlled (restless, impulsive, with poor attention) at age three predicted aggression, impulsivity, and alienation at age eighteen and antisocial personality disorder and convictions at age twenty-one. Hence, the most important study of temperament in relation to offending essentially confirms the diagnostic importance of early impulsivity.

The Challenge of Using DGN Evidence

There are two clear takeaways from Farrington's article. First, DGN factors exert a strong influence on people's behavior, including their decisions to engage in criminal acts, but these influences are not absolute: identical twins behave similarly, but not identically. It may seem that this partial effect raises a tricky policy question—just how heritable must a behavior be for its heritability to serve as either a mitigating or aggravating factor? As the next reading shows, this question is actually both easier and harder than it initially seems.

Second, while DGN factors are significant, the means by which they influence behavior are extremely complex. For example, birth complications may increase a person's tendency to commit crime, but apparently only if that same person comes from an unstable family, and more so for men than for women. Genetic factors, on the other hand, seem to be more predictive for women than for men. And low IQ is correlated with offending, but whether this is an innate result of low IQ or the result of poor socialization by school systems ill-prepared to deal with such students is unclear. Thus even before we get to the question of whether such evidence *ought* to shape our views on deserved punishment, we confront the issue of what the evidence even *is*, and whether we trust judges and juries to understand it well.

The challenge complex scientific evidence poses to lay judges and jurors is well-known; even staunch defenders of jury deliberation acknowledge that sophisticated empirical and scientific evidence may be hard for jurors to handle.[21] We thus confront a tricky policy question: are the error costs of excluding DGN evidence greater than those of including it? That such evidence is a two-edged sword makes the question all the

---

[21] See, for example, Valerie Hans, *Judges, Juries, and Scientific Evidence*, 16 J. L. & POL'Y 19 (2007); Neil Vidmar, *Expert Evidence, the Adversary System, and the Jury*, 95 AM. J. PUB. HEALTH S137 (2005).

trickier. Even if one believes that evidentiary rules should tilt in favor of the defendant—a position that is admittedly stronger at the guilt phase than at the sentencing phase—it is unclear whether that argues for admitting or restricting DGN evidence. For example, evidence of genetic compulsion may lead a retributivist to argue for a reduced sanction, an incapacitationist to argue for an enhanced one, and a deterrence theorist to sit on the fence while trying to calculate the marginal benefits of more time. Thus generous admission rules, which increase the risk that jurors will use such evidence "incorrectly," may help a defendant in a retributive regime but hurt him in an incapacitationist one.

The Farrington article also indicates that it is not clear why we should treat DGN evidence any differently than environmental or situational evidence, since these two sets of factors often interact in important ways. While legal commentators often debate the importance of the "genetic revolution" or the "neurological revolution," far less attention is paid to any "situational revolution," even though these are not distinct ideas. And note that gene-environment interactions point to a further difficulty with using genetic evidence in court: a simple genetic test may tell us little if it is also important to know the exact environmental circumstances the offender was in at the time of his crime, and this latter evidence may be much harder to establish.

QUESTIONS

1. **Environmental interactions.** A key feature in the Farrington reading is the importance of environmental interactions: many traits that are predictive of anti-social behavior only manifest themselves in certain environments. While people have no control over their DGN make-up, can they control where go, and thus the environments in which they find themselves? And if so, does this lessen the extent to which DGN evidence should mitigate punishment? Or does it point to classes of offenders for whom the evidence should be given more weight? Keep your answers to these questions in mind when reading the next excerpt below.

2. **Understanding situation.** If you feel that greater defendant control over his environment undermines the mitigating impact of DGN evidence, there is a follow-up question to consider: can we trust judges and juries to properly determine when the environmental component is sufficiently important (somehow defined), and when the defendant had sufficient control over where he was (again, somehow defined)? If not, how should we structure the use of DGN evidence?

B.1.b. THE NORMATIVE IMPORTANCE OF DGN EVIDENCE

The Farrington article demonstrates that genetic and neurological factors are empirically important. So it may come as a bit of a surprise that it is less clear whether such factors are actually all that important normatively or doctrinally. The next reading argues that scientific advances in neurology will in fact revolutionize the law's views on responsibility, but it also explains the countervailing argument clearly. Although the article focuses on neurology, its arguments apply to all three aspects of DGN evidence—and to all immutable characteristics more generally.

Joshua Greene and Jonathan Cohen, *For the Law, Neuroscience Changes Nothing and Everything*
359 Phil. Trans. R. Soc'y London B 1775 (2004)

Given the law's . . . concern for mental states, along with its preference for "hard" evidence, it is no surprise that interest in the potential legal implications of cognitive neuroscience abounds. But does our emerging understanding of the mind as brain really have any deep implications for the law? [Many have] thought that it might. Some have argued, however, that new neuroscience contributes nothing more than new details and that existing legal principles can handle anything that neuroscience will throw our way in the foreseeable future.

In our view, both of these positions are, in their respective ways, correct. Existing legal principles make virtually no assumptions about the neural bases of criminal behavior, and as a result they can comfortably assimilate new neuroscience without much . . . conceptual upheaval: new details, new sources of evidence, but nothing for which the law is fundamentally unprepared. We maintain, however, that our operative legal principles exist because they more or less adequately capture an intuitive sense of justice. In our view, neuroscience will challenge and ultimately reshape our intuitive sense(s) of justice. Cognitive neuroscience, by identifying the specific mechanisms responsible for behavior, will vividly illustrate what until now could only be appreciated through esoteric theorizing: that there is something fishy about our ordinary conceptions of human action and responsibility, and that, as a result, the legal principles we have devised to reflect these conceptions may be flawed.

[In order to discuss the legal implications of neuroscience, the authors must first define three ways of thinking about free will.]

The first, known as "hard determinism", accepts the incompatibility of free will and determinism* ("incompatibilism"), and asserts determinism, thus rejecting free will. The second response is libertarianism (. . . no relation to the political philosophy), which accepts incompatibilism, but denies that determinism is true. [However,] there is not a shred of scientific evidence to support the existence of causally effective processes in the mind or brain that violate the laws of physics.

---

* *Ed. note*: "Determinism" refers to the theory that all action and thought is determined by material or physical relationships over which we have no independent control and which obey the laws of physics. This is in contrast to "dualism," which posits that not all mental states or decisions are physically (or materially) determined, i.e., that the mind is made of something more than—and outside of—the brain.

In our opinion, any scientifically respectable discussion of free will requires the rejection of what [one scholar] famously called the "panicky metaphysics" of libertarianism.

Finally, we come to the dominant view among philosophers and legal theorists: compatibilism. Compatibilists concede that some notions of free will may require indefensible, panicky metaphysics, but maintain that the kinds of free will "worth wanting" are perfectly compatible with determinism. Compatibilist theories vary, but all compatibilists agree that free will is a perfectly natural, scientifically respectable phenomenon and part of the ordinary human condition. They also agree that free will can be undermined by various kinds of psychological deficit, e.g. mental illness or "infancy." Thus, according to this view, a freely willed action is one that is made using the right sort of psychology—rational, free of delusion, etc.

The forward-looking—consequentialist approach to punishment works with all three responses to the problem of free will, including hard determinism. This is because consequentialists are not concerned with whether anyone is really innocent or guilty in some ultimate sense that might depend on people's having free will, but only with the likely effects of punishment. The retributivist approach, by contrast, is plausibly regarded as requiring free will and the rejection of hard determinism. Retributivists want to know whether the defendant truly deserves to be punished. Assuming one can deserve to be punished only for actions that are freely willed, hard determinism implies that no one really deserves to be punished. This leaves retributivists with two options: compatibilism and libertarianism. Libertarianism, for reasons given above, and despite its intuitive appeal, is scientifically suspect. At the very least, the law should not depend on it. It seems, then, that retributivism requires compatibilism. Accordingly, the standard legal account of punishment is compatibilist.

The title of a recent paper by Stephen Morse, "New neuroscience, old problems," aptly summarizes many a seasoned legal thinker's response to the suggestion that brain research will revolutionize the law. The law has been dealing with issues of criminal responsibility for a long time, Morse argues [, and] there is nothing on the neuroscientific horizon that it cannot handle.

The reason that the law is immune to such threats is that it makes no assumptions that neuroscience, or any science, is likely to challenge. The law assumes that people have a general capacity for rational choice. That is, people have beliefs and desires and are capable of producing behavior that serves their desires in light of their beliefs. The law acknowledges that our capacity for rational choice is far from perfect, requiring only that the people it deems legally responsible have a general capacity for rational behavior.

Thus, questions about who is or is not responsible in the eyes of the law have and will continue to turn on questions about rationality. [T]he argument goes [that] new science can help us figure out who was or was not rational at the scene of the crime, much as it has in the past, but new science will not justify any fundamental change in the law's approach to responsibility unless it shows that people in general fail to meet the law's very minimal requirements for rationality. Science shows no sign of doing this, and thus the basic precepts of legal responsibility stand firm. As for neuroscience more specifically, this discipline seems especially unlikely to undermine our faith in general minimal rationality. If any sciences have an outside chance of demonstrating that our behavior is thoroughly irrational or arational it is the ones that study behavior directly rather than its proximate physical causes in the brain. The law, this argument continues, does not care if people have "free will" in any deep metaphysical sense that might be threatened by determinism. It only cares that people in general are minimally rational. So long as this appears to be the case, it can go on regarding people as free (compatibilism) and holding ordinary people responsible for their misdeeds while making exceptions for those who fail to meet the requirements of general rationality.

In light of this, one might wonder what all the fuss is about. If the law assumes nothing more than general minimal rationality, and neuroscience does nothing to undermine this assumption, then why would anyone even think that neuroscience poses some sort of threat to legal doctrines of criminal responsibility? It sounds like this is just a simple mistake, and that is precisely what Morse contends. He calls this mistake "the fundamental psycholegal error" which is "to believe that causation, especially abnormal causation, is *per se* an excusing condition." In other words, if you think that neuroscientific information about the causes of human action, or some particular human's action, can, by itself, make for a legitimate legal excuse, you just do not understand the law. Every action is caused by brain events, and describing those events and affirming their causal efficacy is of no legal interest in and of itself. Morse continues, "[The psycholegal error] leads people to try to create a new excuse every time an allegedly valid new 'syndrome' is discovered that is thought to play a role in behavior. But syndromes and other causes do not have excusing force unless they sufficiently diminish rationality in the context in question."

In our opinion, Morse and like-minded theorists are absolutely correct about the relationship between current legal doctrine and any forthcoming neuroscientific results. For the law, as written, neuroscience changes nothing. The law provides a coherent framework for the assessment of criminal responsibility that is not threatened by anything neuroscience is likely to throw at it. But, we maintain, the law nevertheless stands on shakier ground than the foregoing would suggest. The legitimacy of the law itself depends on its adequately reflecting the moral intuitions and commitments of society. If neuroscience can change those intuitions, then neuroscience can change the law.

According to the law, the central question in a case of putative diminished responsibility is whether the accused was sufficiently rational at the time of the misdeed in question. We believe, however, that this is not what most people really care about, and that for them diminished rationality is just a presumed correlate of something deeper. It seems that what many people really want to know is: was it really *him*? This question usually comes in the form of a disjunction, depending on how the excuse is constructed: was it *him*, or was it his *upbringing*? Was it *him*, or was it his *genes*? Was it *him*, or was it his *circumstances*? Was it *him*, or was it his *brain*? But what most people do not understand, despite the fact that naturalistic philosophers and scientists have been saying it for centuries, is that there is no "him" independent of these other things.

Most people's view of the mind is implicitly *dualist* and *libertarian* and not *materialist* and *compatibilist*. Dualism, for our purposes, is the view that mind and brain are separate, interacting, entities. Dualism fits naturally with libertarianism because a mind distinct from the body is precisely the sort of non-physical source of free will that libertarianism requires. Materialism, by contrast, is the view that all events, including the operations of the mind, are ultimately operations of matter that obeys the laws of physics. It is hard to imagine a belief in free will that is materialist but not compatibilist, given that ordinary matter does not seem capable of supplying the non-physical processes that libertarianism requires.

So far as the law is concerned, information about the physical processes that give rise to bad behavior is irrelevant. But to people who implicitly believe that real decision-making takes place in the mind, not in the brain, demonstrating that there is a brain basis for adolescents' misdeeds allows us to blame adolescents' brains instead of the adolescents themselves. The fact that people are tempted to attach great moral or legal significance to neuroscientific information that, according to the letter of the law, should not matter, suggests that what the law cares about and what people care about do not necessarily coincide.

[The authors next develop a hypothetical about "Mr. Puppet," a man developmentally, genetically, and neurologically designed by malevolent scientists down to the very last atom and experience to kill a particular person in a particular way, which he does.]

[W]hat does the law say about Mr. Puppet? The law asks whether or not he was rational at the time of his misdeeds, and as far as we know he was. For all we know, he is psychologically indistinguishable from the prototypical guilty criminal, and therefore fully responsible in the eyes of the law. But, intuitively, this is not fair.

Thus, it seems that the law's exclusive interest in rationality misses something intuitively important. In our opinion, rationality is just a presumed correlate of what most people really care about. What people really want to know is if the accused, as opposed to something else, is responsible for the crime, where that "something else" could be the accused's brain, genes or environment.

The story of Mr. Puppet raises an important question: what is the difference between Mr. Puppet and anyone else accused of a crime? One obvious difference is that Mr. Puppet is the victim of a diabolical plot whereas most people, we presume, are not. But does this matter? The thought that Mr. Puppet is not fully responsible depends on the idea that his actions were externally determined. Forces beyond his control constrained his personality to the point that it was "no surprise" that he would behave badly. But the fact that these forces are connected to the desires and intentions of evil scientists is really irrelevant, is it not? What matters is only that these forces are beyond Mr. Puppet's control, that they're not really *his*.

Thus, it seems that, in a very real sense, we are all puppets. The combined effects of genes and environment determine all of our actions. Mr. Puppet is exceptional only in that the intentions of other humans lie behind his genes and environment. But, so long as his genes and environment are intrinsically comparable to those of ordinary people, this does not really matter. We are no more free than he is.

What all of this illustrates is that the "fundamental psycholegal error" is grounded in a powerful moral intuition that the law and allied compatibilist philosophies try to sweep under the rug. The foregoing suggests that people regard actions only as fully free when those actions are seen as robust against determination by external forces. But if determinism is true, then no actions are truly free because forces beyond our control are always sufficient to determine behavior. Thus, intuitive free will is libertarian, not compatibilist. That is, it requires the rejection of determinism and an implicit commitment to some kind of magical mental causation.

We have argued that, contrary to legal and philosophical orthodoxy, determinism really does threaten free will and responsibility as we intuitively understand them. It is just that most of us, including most philosophers and legal theorists, have yet to appreciate it. This controversial opinion amounts to an empirical prediction that may or may not hold: as more and more scientific facts come in, providing increasingly vivid illustrations of what the human mind is really like, more and more people will develop moral intuitions that are at odds with our current social practices.

People may grow up completely used to the idea that every decision is a thoroughly mechanical process, the outcome of which is completely determined by the results of prior mechanical processes. What will such people think as they sit in their jury boxes? Suppose a man has killed his wife in a jealous rage. Will jurors of the future wonder whether the defendant acted in that moment *of his own free will*? Will they wonder if it was *really him* who killed his wife rather than his uncontrollable anger? Will they ask whether he *could have done otherwise*? Whether he really deserves to be punished, or if he is just a victim of unfortunate circumstances? We submit that these questions, which seem so important today, will lose their grip in an age when the mechanical nature of human decision-making is fully appreciated. The law will continue to punish misdeeds, as it must for practical reasons, but the idea of distinguishing the truly, deeply guilty from those who are merely victims of neuronal circumstances will, we submit, seem pointless.

[I]t does not follow from the fact that free will is an illusion that there is no legitimate place for responsibility. As consequentialists, we can hold people responsible for crimes simply because doing so has, on balance, beneficial effects through deterrence, containment, etc. It is sometimes said that if we do not believe in free will then we cannot legitimately punish anyone and that society must dissolve into anarchy. In a less hysterical vein, Daniel Wegner argues that free will, while illusory, is a necessary fiction for the maintenance of our social structure. We disagree. There are perfectly good, forward-looking justifications for punishing criminals that do not depend on metaphysical fictions.

Regarding responsibility and punishment, one might wonder if it is humanly possible to deny our retributive impulses. This challenge is bolstered by recent work in the behavioral sciences suggesting that an intuitive sense of fairness runs deep in our primate lineage and that an adaptive tendency towards retributive punishment may have been a crucial development in the biological and cultural evolution of human sociality. If retributivism runs that deep and is that useful, one might wonder whether we have any serious hope of, or reason for, getting rid of it. Have we any real choice but to see one another as free agents who deserve to be rewarded and punished for our past behaviors?

For most day-to-day purposes it may be pointless or impossible to view ourselves or others in this detached sort of way. But—and this is the crucial point—it may not be pointless or impossible to adopt this perspective when one is deciding what the criminal law should be or whether a given defendant should be put to death for his crimes. These may be special situations . . . in which the counter-intuitive truth that we legitimately ignore most of the time can and should be acknowledged.

Rationality Versus Causation

The central tension between Morse on the one hand and Greene and Cohen on the other—between compatibilists and determinists in general—concerns the relative importance of rationality and causation.

Morse lays out the compatibilist position, and its focus on rationality, clearly in his paper *New Neuroscience, Old Problems*:

> If causation negated responsibility, no one would be morally responsible, and holding people legally responsible would be extremely problematic.... Virtually all legal responsibility and competence criteria depend on assessment of the agent's rational capacities in the context in question. For example, a person is competent in contract if he or she is capable of understanding the nature of the bargain; a person is criminally responsible if the agent was capable of knowing the nature of his or her conduct or the applicable law.[22]

Note that Morse's view of responsibility *can be* wholly consistent with a deterministic world. A person can be acting deterministically but still understand the wrongness (i.e., the social impermissibility) of his behavior. And there is a strong parallel between Morse's view and, say, the *McNaughten* standard for the insanity defense. *McNaughten* holds a defendant not liable by reason of mental defect if he cannot perceive the wrongness of his actions—if he is not rational. But it provides no relief to the defendant who knows what he is doing is wrong but cannot help himself.

The insanity defense actually sheds a fair amount of light on the debate between Morse and Greene/Cohen. Note that many states have moved away from the compatibilist-like *McNaughten* standard to a more causation-like irresistible impulse-style test. Under these latter standards, failure to appreciate the wrongfulness of one's actions remains a defense, but so too does the inability to *control* one's actions, even if one knows that the action is wrong. This suggests that people are concerned with more than just rationality, but with control as well.

Greene and Cohen's argument, then, is essentially that we *always* operate under irresistible impulses. In some cases we may feel like we are exerting control over our actions, while in others we may feel genuinely compelled to act. But, Greene and Cohen claim, in reality we are equally "not in control" in both instances (although, doctrinally, the irresistible impulse tests excuse only the latter actions). Neurology—along with development, genetics and behavioral fields like situationalism—are making it increasingly clear that our dualist intuitions do not align with our materialist nature.

The Implications of Determinism

A shift from a libertarian or compatibilist worldview to a deterministic one would not lead us to abolish punishment. It would, however, have at least two important implications. First, it would deal a profound blow to retributivism as a motivating ideology for punishment. Arguably, Greene and Cohen actually do not push this point far enough.

---

[22] Stephen J. Morse, *New Neuroscience, Old Problems*, in BRENT GARLAND, ED., NEUROSCIENCE AND THE LAW 177 (2004).

They argue that humans appear to be innately retributivist, and thus overcoming our retributive instincts may be quite hard. Yet an international perspective is useful here. There is absolutely no evolutionary difference between an American and, say, a Swede; to the extent that retributivism is "innate," it is equally innate in North Americans and in Scandinavians. Yet punishment in Sweden is substantially less punitive and retributive than it is in the United States, making it clear that social norms strongly influence any sort of "innate" retributivism. And these social norms are in turn shaped by changes in scientific knowledge, so our desire to be retributivist (or what we mean by retributivist) may change with our understanding of causation. The United States has gone through cycles of more- and less-retributive penal policy, with at least some of the change driven by shifts in our scientific views of the world.

Second, the shift toward determinism would force consequentialists to rethink their policies as well. Greene and Cohen state that determinism does not undermine consequentialist arguments *for* punishment, and they are correct about this. But it may force consequentialists to rethink *what* punishments are optimal. Some strands of consequentialist punishment take a rationality-centered approach: they assume that potential offenders are roughly rational and then ask how to adjust sanctions to discourage or prevent these rational actors from committing crimes. A more deterministic perspective should encourage consequentialists to try to better consider some of the more "automatic" responses that people may have and how those can be influenced.

So consider again the irresistible impulse test. From a dualist-deterrence perspective, the rule is easy to justify: if offender A is acting without free will but offender B is acting with free will, then only B can be deterred, and so criminal punishment should only be imposed on him. If Greene and Cohen are right, however, *all* criminal acts are equally irresistible, and there is no real free will distinction between A and B, even if A and B themselves *think* there is a difference. So while there may be pragmatic reasons for punishing different types of irresistible acts differently, there is no reason to believe that the lines the law currently draws will be the right ones, since their justification—based on A's and B's (misplaced) perceptions of differences in free will—is inconsistent with materialism.

QUESTIONS

1. **Environmental factors again.** Question 1 in Part B.1.a considered the fact that some DGN factors only matter in certain environmental situations and asked if people had control over where they are and thus more responsibility for these situational-contingent genetically-influenced responses. Does the Greene and Cohen reading change your answers at all?

2. **Deterrence.** How do we justify using deterrence principles in a deterministic world? Does determinism force us to embrace only incapacitation or rehabilitation as guiding principles?

3. **Situation.** The compatibilist/determinist debate seems to suggest that there is something unique about DGN evidence that forces us to rethink our fundamental justifications for punishment. But think back to our discussion of situationalism in Ch. 1: is situationalism any less significant in this respect than development or genetics or neurology? If not, why do you think DGN has received so much more attention than situationalism? Is it the nature of the evidence—striking images of brain scans versus dry regression results, or assumptions about the relatively reliability of "hard" versus "soft" sciences? Or is there a more substantive or legal reason for the difference?

B.1.c. THE USE OF DGN EVIDENCE IN COURT

As scientists make more and more discoveries about the effects of DGN factors on behavior, some commentators have raised concerns that such evidence will flood the courts and upend current penal jurisprudence. As the article below by Deborah Denno (which focuses on genetic evidence) makes clear, that has not been the case so far.

Deborah Denno, *Courts' Increasing Consideration of Behavioral Genetics Evidence in Criminal Cases: Results of a Longitudinal Study*
2011 MICH. ST. L. REV. 967 (2011)

[In 2009, Denno published an article reviewing the use of genetics evidence in 48 cases decided between 1994 and 2007. This paper updates that earlier work with 33 more cases decided between 2007 and 2011. The excerpt here summarizes her earlier work and her new findings.]

In 1994, defense preparations for *Mobley v. State* drew world-wide publicity because of Mobley's counsel's unprecedented efforts to gather behavioral genetics evidence to prevent Stephen Mobley's execution. According to some commentators at the time, the availability of such testing would prompt political and moral abuses of highly controversial information. Yet this Author's earlier survey of the forty-eight cases that had used behavioral genetics evidence during the thirteen years following Mobley (1994-2007) showed no apparent basis for these concerns. There were no abuses of the ilk that had been predicted and most courts still questioned the relevance of such evidence when attorneys attempted to introduce it at the penalty phase, a tact consistent with the Supreme Court's 2007 conclusions in *Schriro v. Landrigan*.

In essence, during the thirteen years between *Mobley* and *Landrigan*, there had been seemingly few changes in social and legal attitudes toward behavioral genetics. Moreover, the applicability of behavioral genetics evidence as mitigation in death penalty cases still seemed to baffle the press and public, thereby accentuating the controversy.

Consistent with *Mobley* and *Landrigan*, this Author's earlier study showed that courts articulated five major reasons for rejecting a defendant's submission of behavioral genetics evidence: (1) The mitigation evidence the defense had already submitted was sufficient and further information concerning the defendant's genetic attributes would most likely not have influenced the defendant's sentence; (2) behavioral genetics evidence is not as valid and reliable relative to other evidence introduced at trial, especially when there is conflicting testimony among the experts; (3) an association between a defendant's behavioral genetics and criminal behavior is "unorthodox" or "exotic"; (4) even if behavioral genetics evidence is accepted at trial, it can be detrimental to a defendant's case because it indicates that the defendant will commit further acts of violence and be a danger to society; and (5) behavioral genetics evidence collides with some courts' views of criminal responsibility, which may favor safeguarding the community rather than rehabilitation.

This Author's studies provide little support for any of these five rationales. For example, both studies have shown that behavioral genetics evidence can have a beneficial impact for some defendants in some cases, particularly when it bolsters or interacts with other kinds of mitigating evidence. There are also compelling arguments that behavioral genetics evidence is relevant and useful if applied in a limited way, such as to buttress other mitigating conditions, or to verify the existence of a condition that a court may question. Likewise, courts' rendering of behavioral genetic factors as "unorthodox" or "exotic" ignores the reality that such information has a long history in legal cases, even if that past was controversial or seemingly forgotten by more recent decisions, such as Mobley[309] and Landrigan.[310] Indeed, this Author's research uncovered eighty-one such cases over the past seventeen years.

The remaining rationales also lack support. While courts and commentators have long-stressed the double-edged-sword aspect of behavioral genetics evidence, this characteristic is inherent to many other mitigating factors. The Supreme Court's reliance on certain kinds of neuroscientific findings in *Roper v. Simmons* is an apt illustration. In *Roper*, the Supreme Court held that the Eighth and Fourteenth Amendments prohibited the execution of persons under age eighteen at the time their crimes were committed. The Court reasoned that relative to adults, juveniles are more immature and irresponsible, vulnerable to negative pressures from their peers and environment, and fragile and unstable in their identities. Although these disparities explained why juveniles may be less culpable, they also heightened the likelihood that juveniles would engage in impulsive thinking and criminality. The very factors that argued against juveniles' eligibility for the death penalty also made them more prone to misconduct, truly a double-edged sword. Likewise, the argument that behavioral genetics evidence conflicts with some courts' theories of criminal responsibility again reveals the confusion concerning the disparate standards relevant for the guilt-or-innocence phase of a trial as opposed to the penalty phase of a trial. The standard for mitigation evidence is far broader given the purpose that it serves.

Another aspect complicating these already difficult cases involves the apparent ignorance of some courts in dealing with the interactions among social, biological, and genetic variables. [S]uch variables are so intertwined it would be an artificial and misleading process to attempt to separate them for purposes of sentencing. Yet, the latest discoveries in behavioral genetics have not fallen on courts' deaf ears in more recent times. Indeed, the next Section's discussion of cases using behavioral genetics evidence during the last four years suggests that much of this judicial skepticism has ebbed if not disappeared entirely.

Courts during 2007-2011 seemingly quelled questioning whether sound behavioral genetics evidence should be admitted as mitigation at all during the penalty phase. Rather, the question now is whether sufficient evidence has been presented and, if so, how much weight it should be given. In all thirty-three of the decisions this Author examined, for example, courts appeared to at least consider behavioral genetics evidence in their analysis of mitigating factors and whether an attorney has rendered ineffective assistance. Likewise, none of the courts squarely rejected the introduction of behavioral genetics evidence nor referred to it as "exotic" or "unorthodox."

Courts' views of the weight such evidence ... take a variety of forms and, unsurprisingly, rely on case specific facts. Even when courts did not find that behavioral genetics evidence was likely to affect the outcome of the case or was outweighed by aggravating factors, they still addressed and acknowledged family history. Particularly striking over the last four years were arguments concerning defendants' genetic proclivities to alcohol and substance abuse—a far larger percentage than had previously been found. Again, regardless of whether such evidence positively affected the outcome of the defendant's sentence, courts did take it into account in the same way they would other kinds of mitigating evidence.

Even in cases where defendants' propensities for violence are not as marked, many courts remain unpersuaded by behavioral genetics evidence of substance abuse. Yet, again, the important point here is that the courts accept the validity of the evidence irrespective of whether it affects their decision about the sentence. Other courts in the last four years have tended to give behavioral genetics evidence (including alcohol or substance abuse) more weight—some to the point of considering it an error not to have a pretrial hearing on a defendant's genetic predisposition; others have made it grounds for vacating a death sentence.

One way to try to measure the potential effectiveness of behavioral genetics evidence in criminal cases is to provide a thorough sense of how the evidence is being used. In most of the thirty-three cases in this Author's Study, at least one of the defendants' claims alleged ineffective assistance of counsel for counsel's failure to adequately investigate or present mitigating evidence of behavioral genetic factors. Success in this arena depends on a wide range of factors. In general, both of this Author's studies show that, as would be expected, counsel's failure to present behavioral genetics evidence alone was often not enough to constitute ineffective assistance. But, when coupled with other factors, courts were less reluctant to grant evidentiary hearings or to vacate death sentences altogether for ineffective assistance.

This Article reports a number of new trends and arguments since 2007. The first trend concerns the changed role of behavioral genetics evidence in criminal cases. In this Author's original study of forty-eight cases, most cases employed behavioral genetics evidence in three primary ways: (1) to support a claim of ineffective assistance of counsel, (2) to provide proof and diagnosis of a defendant's mitigating condition, and/or (3) to indicate some likelihood of the defendant's future dangerousness. This Author's most recent study of thirty-three cases showed, however, that there was no third category and that no case applied behavioral genetics evidence to predict the defendant's dangerousness. Nor was the evidence ever used by the prosecution, much less as an aggravating factor. While this Author's original study did not report many cases in which the evidence was implemented detrimentally, the discovery that it has never been so used in the last four years is startling. After all, this finding contradicts the Supreme Court's view in *Landrigan* that such evidence could be submitted to enhance the perception of a defendant's level of dangerousness. Second, in light of the Court's 2002 decision in *Atkins v. Virginia*, behavioral genetics evidence now may play a larger role in defendants claiming a genetic predisposition to mental retardation and mental incompetence.

[T]he Author's 2007-2011 Study also revealed more cases in which courts incorporated behavioral genetics evidence to support defendants' claims of the inheritance of alcohol and drug dependency. This trend was particularly pronounced relative to other kinds of factors. Regardless, as these results make clear, courts seemingly no longer view any type of scientifically accepted behavioral genetics evidence as "exotic" in the same way that *Landrigan* did. Nor is there any overt indication that behavioral genetics evidence has reinforced concerns . . . that actors in the criminal justice system would increasingly and irresponsibly rely on distorted information in their decision making.

In short, courts appear to resist incorporating DGN evidence too readily into their decisions, despite the growing body of research showing strong—if sometimes complex and unclear—causal connections between DGN traits and criminal (or at least anti-social) behavior. The reasons for such resistance are unclear. It could reflect a natural conservatism of courts, it could reflect a perhaps-understandable unwillingness on the part of courts to incorporate complex scientific evidence when the evidence base itself remains somewhat unsettled, or it could reflect concerns about the normative implications of such evidence (as laid out by Greene and Cohen).

B.2. Sex and Offending

Criminal offending, particularly violent offending, is a predominantly male endeavor. In 2010, men comprised almost 75% of the 8.47 million people whose arrests were reported to the FBI. In particular, men were arrested for 89% of all murders, 77% of all aggravated assaults, and 87% of all robberies; the only crimes for which men were responsible for fewer than 70% of the arrests were larceny (56%), forgery (62%), fraud (57%), embezzlement (49%), and prostitution (29%).[23] Criminals tend to be men. And this patterns exists in other countries as well.[24]

There have been extensive efforts to try to explain this gender gap. Some theorists have pointed to innate differences, suggesting that men and women respond differently to a given criminogenic situation, while others have taken the more social perspective that men and women behave similarly in a given criminogenic situation but, due to various social forces, generally face different situations—it is more socially acceptable, for example, for a man to hang out on the street with his friends than for a woman to do the same.

The truth, as is so often the case, appears to lie somewhere in between. Consider the results from one study of adolescent delinquents.[25] The single best predictor of delinquency is associating with other delinquents. Using data from the National Longitudinal Survey of Youth, Daniel Mears and his co-authors demonstrate that males are more exposed to delinquent peers than women (pointing to the social hypothesis), but also that males are more responsive to those peers than

---

[23] Thus the remaining offenses where men were at least 70% of all those arrested were forcible rape (99%), burglary (84%), motor vehicle theft (82%), arson (83%), other assaults (73%), buying and receiving stolen property (80%), vandalism (81%), weapons charges (91%), sex offenses other than forcible rape (93%), drug offenses (80%), gambling (86%), offenses against the family (75%), DUI (76%), liquor laws violations (72%), drunkenness (83%), disorderly conduct (72%), vagrancy (80%), all other non-traffic offenses (76%), suspicion (80%), and curfew violations (71%).

[24] See, for example, ROSEMARY SHEEHAN ET AL., EDS., WHAT WORKS WITH WOMEN OFFENDERS, 2–3.

[25] Daniel P. Mears, Matthew Ploeger, & Mark Warr, *Explaining the Gender Gap in Delinquency: Peer Influence and Moral Evaluations of Behavior*, 35 J. RES. IN CRIME & DELINQ. 251 (1998).

females (pointing to the innate differences). This latter point begs the question: why are males more responsive? Here, again, the answers can be innate or social—many have argued that women are socialized to be less aggressive, etc., making them less responsive to delinquent peers, but there could be more innate differences as well. Sarah Bennett and her co-authors, for example, argue that "social cognition" skills, themselves a "complex interaction between the biological maturation of an individual and the environmental opportunities encountered," explain some of the gender gap in delinquency.[26]

Carissa Hessick provides an overview both of the arguments made by those advocating for taking gender or sex into account and of the serious concerns with the points they make.[27] She starts by noting that by the early 20th Century multiple states had explicitly adopted separate standards for women, in some cases housing them in different types of institutions or adopting different sentence maximums—at times higher than those for men, based on the belief that women were *more* amenable to rehabilitation than men and thus needed *more* time in prison to be thoroughly reformed.

Yet while these sex-specific policies were successfully attacked in the 1960s and 1970s and likely would not pass constitutional muster today, Hessick notes that scholars have continued to advocate for sex-specific differences at sentencing, perhaps with risky outcomes:

> [Advocates for treating women more leniently at sentencing] highlight that women tend to commit largely non-violent crimes, have lower offending rates, and lower recidivism rates. Many commentators highlight that imprisonment poses greater problems for female offenders who, as a group, tend to bear primary child care responsibility; thus, facially neutral policies that do not consider family responsibilities at sentencing are, in practice, disadvantageous for women. Some of the commentators also assert that many women offenders are less culpable—and should consequently receive shorter sentences—because male offenders led them into criminality. In effect, these commentators are criticizing the modern trend of gender-neutrality, arguing that such neutrality unfairly treats female and male offenders similarly despite salient differences between the two groups.
>
> The approach of these gender-effects commentators raises two concerns. First, they are endorsing some of the same gender stereotypes which historically supported not only leniency in

---

[26] Sarah Bennett, David P. Farrington, & L. Rowell Huesmann, *Explaining Gender Differences in Crime and Violence: The Importance of Social Cognitive Skills*, 10 AGGRESSION & VIOLENT BEHAVIOR 263 (2005).

[27] Carissa B. Hessick, *Race and Gender as Explicit Sentencing Factors*, 14 J. GENDER, RACE & JUST. 127 (2010).

judicial decision-making, but also greater severity for female offenders under the late nineteenth- and early twentieth-century reformatory model. The reformatory model was often justified by reference to the different offending patterns of women. The argument that female offenders are led into criminality by their male partners resembles the early twentieth-century view of the female offender as "childlike, wayward, and redeemable, a fallen woman who was more sinned against than sinner." Even the modern commentators' reference to female offenders' child-care responsibilities has resonance in the old reformatory model, which was sometimes justified on biological grounds. . . .

Second, and perhaps more troubling, is that some of the arguments the gender-effects commentators are making undercut arguments made by those who are concerned about the disparate racial impact of modern sentencing policy. In particular, many gender-effects commentators highlight female offenders' lower recidivism rates as a reason for them to receive lower sentences. But while women recidivate at a lower rate than do men, blacks and Latinos recidivate at a higher rate than whites.[28]

One could actually push Hessick's labeling theory argument even further: treating women differently not only reinforces domesticity norms in criminal justice settings, but in society more broadly. Sentencing does not take place in a cultural vacuum, and it both shapes and is shaped by the broader culture. Not surprisingly, states that have adopted guidelines have also frequently stated that judges are not allowed to take sex into account at sentencing.

That said, there is evidence that a defendant's sex still influences the sentence received. In indeterminate systems, judges have extensive discretion to rely on sex; even in structured regimes, sex can influence where in an approved range a judge sentences, or whether he aggravates or mitigates, or the types of charges selected by the prosecutors at the start of the process. The empirical literature generally suggests that women are treated more leniently at every stage of the process:

> In general, women offenders are more likely to be released prior to trial, receive downward departures from sentencing guidelines, less likely to be habitualized, sent to prison/jail, and more likely to receive leniency in sentencing if given a term of incarceration when compared to their similarly situated male counterparts.[29]

---

[28] *Id.* at 138–140.

[29] Cortney A. Franklin & Noelle E. Fearn, *Gender, Race, and Formal Court Decision-Making Outcomes: Chivalry/Paternalism, Conflict Theory or Gender Conflict?* 36 J. CRIM. JUST. 279, 279 (2008).

Note, though, that not all women are treated the same: some evidence suggests that white women are more likely to be treated leniently than similarly-situated black women. This could be due to explicit or implicit racial bias, or it could reflect the complicated biases surrounding paternalism towards women. Such paternalism may only attach to women perceived as "good," and minority women may in general be perceived as less "good," whether due to implicit racial bias or, say, the troubling interactions between race and class.

Question: Women Are Different. The proponents of treating women differently than men note that women commit less serious crimes, are less likely to recidivate, and are more likely pressured into their crimes by men. As a general matter, if the sentence is conditional on offense severity, do we need to explicitly account gender? What if there is a parole board with significant release oversight? How about the claim that women are pressured by men, assuming it is true?

B.3. AGE AND OFFENDING

The final immutable characteristic to consider is age. Unlike DGN factors, which are treated warily by courts, and sex, which is generally banned but still implicitly relied on by prosecutors and judges, age is often an explicit sentencing factor. In fact, there is an entirely separate parallel juvenile justice system that exists simply to handle young defendants. Interestingly, while DGN evidence is viewed with some suspicion, the justifications for treating juveniles differently are basically DGN claims: their brains are less well-formed, they are less capable of controlling their behavior or appreciating right from wrong, etc.

I want to start this section by briefly considering why we generally accept youthfulness as a mitigator but not other DGN-based factors and what that tells us about the goals of the criminal justice system. We will then turn to three policy issues: how we in fact treat juveniles, how judges take age into account in practice (outside the juvenile/adult divide), and—at the other end of the spectrum—the implications of the growing number of older offenders confined in US prisons.

The Acceptability of Age

Age is the one immutable characteristic that appears to be generally uncontroversial to invoke. The Supreme Court has held that young defendants—defined as those below the age of 18—cannot receive the death penalty, be sentenced to life without parole for non-homicide offenses, nor face mandatory life without parole sentences for murder.[30] Furthermore, states have developed entirely separate juvenile justice systems to handle younger defendants. As noted above, we used to treat

---

[30] *Roper v. Simmons*, 543 U.S. 551 (2005) (death penalty); *Graham v. Florida*, 560 U.S. 48 (2010) (non-homicide cases); *Miller v. Alabama*, 567 U.S. ___, 132 S. Ct. 2455 (2012) (automatic life without parole for murder).

women separately as well, but that immutability characteristic is no longer acceptable. What makes age different?

Part of it could be that age-related factors are more exogenous than sex-related ones. Many of the differences in behavior between men and women are thought to reflect social constructs more than innate differences: to base sentencing practices on these constructs is to reinforce them. Conversely, the population-average differences in behaviors between younger and older people are thought to be more the product of innate developmental differences. Of course, to excuse youthful misconduct on the grounds that children are more impulsive likely has labeling effects as well, but there is at least an implicit assumption that the material differences are more meaningful in this context.

There may also be an issue of equity. Sex (for most people) and race (for all people) remain fixed over the entire lifecycle, while everyone is younger and older. So taking sex into account means that we will always treat Mary different than Joe. But taking age into account does not: Mary and Joe will both be treated one way when young, and another way when old. So the rules are "the same" for everyone over the course of their lives.

The parallel system for juvenile offenders, as well as the reasoning behind the trio of Supreme Court cases limiting the punishment of juveniles, also point to the fact that for younger defendants rehabilitation remains the dominant theory of punishment—in part because of the sense that such defendants can mature and "age out" of crime, which the lifecycle model of offending supports. Thus while incapacitationists, and perhaps even deterrence theorists, could see youth as an *aggravating* factor, it is generally treated as a mitigating one in light of rehabilitative possibilities (especially since we cannot predict which juvenile offenders are destined to end up on more-persistent offender paths).

The Juvenile Justice System

Treating juveniles separately from adults has been a feature of American criminal justice for over a century. The first separate detention center for youths was established in New York City in 1825, and the first juvenile court was founded in Cook County, Illinois (home of Chicago) in 1899. Founded during the height of the Progressive Era, these courts purported to embrace the Progressives' rehabilitative ideal. As Barry Feld explains, this led legislatures to invest juvenile courts with tremendous discretion:

> The juvenile court's "Rehabilitative Ideal" envisioned a specialized judge trained in the social sciences and child development whose empathic qualities and insight would aid in making individualized dispositions. Social service personnel, clinicians, and probation officers would help the judge decide and pursue the "best interests" of the child. Progressives assumed that a rational, scientific analysis of the social

circumstances would reveal the proper diagnosis and prescribe the cure. Because the reformers acted benevolently, individualized their solicitude, and intervened scientifically, they saw no reason to circumscribe narrowly the power of the state. Rather, they maximized discretion to diagnose and treat, and focused on the child's character and lifestyle rather than on the crime.

By separating children from adults and providing a rehabilitative alternative to punishment, juvenile courts rejected both the criminal law's jurisprudence and its procedural safeguards such as juries and lawyers. Court personnel used informal procedures and an euphemistic vocabulary to eliminate stigma and any implication of a criminal proceeding. They conducted confidential, private hearings, limited access to court records, and adjudicated youths to be "delinquents" rather than criminals. Court personnel accorded only minor significance to a youth's offense because it provided, at most, only a "symptom" of his or her "real" needs. Because each child's circumstances differed, judges imposed indeterminate, nonproportional sentences that potentially continued for the duration of minority.[31]

Over time, however, concerns arose that this discretion was being abused, and gradually the courts were made more "adult-like." In *In re Gault*, 387 U.S. 1 (1967), for example, the Supreme Court held that various constitutional protections, such as the right to an attorney and the right to confront witnesses, applied in juvenile cases as well. And in *In re Winship*, 397 U.S. 358 (1970), it held that when a juvenile is charged with an offense that would be a crime for an adult, each element must be proven by the state beyond a reasonable doubt.

Perhaps, though, it would be more honest to say that juvenile courts were made more adult-like in *theory*. Things did not change so much in practice, at least in many areas of the country. Studies consistently find, for example, that decades after *Gault* large numbers of juveniles continue to appear in court without counsel—and those who have counsel are generally poorly represented. As always, the rhetoric of upstream actors—here, the US Supreme Court—does not guarantee compliance by the fairly autonomous, poorly-monitored downstream agents.

Over the course of the 1970s and 1980s, the tough on crime and anti-rehabilitative rhetoric that defined debates about adult punishment trickled down to juvenile justice as well. One manifestation of this was the increasing popularity of transfer law reforms. While the juvenile justice system was the default system for young offenders, it was not the only option: states had always adopted methods for transferring

---

[31] Barry C. Feld, *The Juvenile Court*, in MICHAEL TONRY, ED., THE HANDBOOK OF CRIME AND PUNISHMENT (1998).

particularly serious cases to adult court. And starting in the 1970s, the scope and nature of such laws changed dramatically.

In keeping with the individualistic, rehabilitative ideal, transfer had generally been handled on a case-by-case basis by juvenile court judges. Starting in the 1970s, however, numerous states started adopting "automatic transfer" laws which required that certain types of cases be tried in adult court for defendants above a certain age but below that of majority. As of 1970, only eight states had such laws, but by 2000 thirty-eight had them.[32] One can think of these laws as redefining the age of majority downward for certain categories of offenses. Some states also granted prosecutors the (almost unfettered) discretion to decide whether to file certain cases in juvenile or adult court. Other reforms that "toughened" juvenile justice include "once-an-adult" laws, which state that once a juvenile has been tried in adult court for one crime he was to be tried in adult court for any future offense (even if that offense otherwise would not require transfer).

The evidence suggests, however, that such tough-on-juvenile laws may actually be counter-productive. As Jeffrey Fagan and his co-authors state:

> Prior research has strongly suggested that prosecuting adolescents as adults leads to more, not less, crime. This is true for almost all studies asking this question, regardless of methodology. Our results add to what now is a consistent series of empirical studies showing that adolescents prosecuted and sentenced in criminal court are at significantly greater risk of rearrest for violent and felony property offenses, their risks accrue more quickly, and they are more likely to be subsequently incarcerated than matched samples of adolescents prosecuted in juvenile courts. That these results appear in studies that reflect a range of sampling and measurement conditions, as well as statutory and social structural contexts, suggests a robustness in these findings that demands policy attention. Despite repeated promises by politicians that being tough on crime by prosecuting children as adults will decrease crime and protect the community, we find that transfer to criminal court actually may increase the risk of violent and other serious crime by adolescents and young adults, increasing public safety risks for citizens while heavily mortgaging the possibility of reformation or prosocial development for many transferred offenders. The results suggest that policies facilitating "wholesale waiver," or categorical exclusion of certain groups of adolescents based solely on offense and age, are ineffective at specific deterrence of serious crime, despite political rhetoric insisting the opposite, and invite avoidable

---

[32] PATRICK GRIFFIN, SEAN ADDIE, BENJAMIN ADAMS, & KATHY FIRESTINE, TRYING JUVENILES AS ADULTS: AN ANALYSIS OF STATE TRANSFER LAWS AND REPORTING (2011).

public safety risks. We are confident that these results reflect systematic differences and are not the product of selection: the matching procedures used to construct this natural experiment and the inclusion of selection parameters in the analyses leave us confident that these results are valid and real.[33]

Fagan et al. go on to propose several explanations for the criminogenic effect of tougher sanctions, such as the fact that adult conviction may block employment and other opportunities that deter or prevent future offending, or that an adult conviction may lead a juvenile to identify (or "label") himself more strongly as a "criminal" and to act out accordingly.

Fagan's study, however, focuses on specific deterrence, namely how the recidivism rates of those juveniles locked up in adult prisons compare to those handled by the juvenile system. It does not address general deterrence: how many more juveniles in automatic-waiver states never commit a crime at all because of the risk of heightened punishment. Several studies have attempted to examine the effect of crossing over the age of majority on offending, and the results are mixed. A paper by Steven Levitt finds a strong effect, while two papers by Justin McCrary and another by Randi Hjalmarsson find no effect.[34] For methodological reasons, the no-effect results are likely stronger,[35] suggesting that the costs identified by Fagan et al. are not offset by reduction in crime driven by general deterrence.

Yet despite Fagan's argument that juvenile court is better than adult court, Feld provides a rather dour take on the juvenile justice system as well:

> During the last 30 years, judicial decisions, legislative amendments, and administrative changes have transformed juvenile courts from nominally rehabilitative social welfare agencies into scaled-down, second-class criminal courts that provide youngsters with neither therapy nor justice. Today, juvenile courts are a wholly owned subsidiary of the criminal

---

[33] JEFFREY FAGAN, AARON KUPCHIK, AND AKIVA LIBERMAN, BE CAREFUL WHAT YOU WISH FOR: LEGAL SANCTIONS AND PUBLIC SAFETY AMONG ADOLESCENT OFFENDERS IN JUVENILE AND CRIMINAL COURT at 69 (available on-line at http://papers.ssrn.com/sol3/papers.cfm?abstract_id=491202).

[34] Randi Hjalmarsson, *Crime and Expected Punishment: Changes in Perceptions at the Age of Criminal Majority*, 11 AM. L. & ECON. REV. 209 (2009); DAVID S. LEE AND JUSTIN MCCRARY, THE DETERRENCE EFFECT OF PRISON: DYNAMIC THEORY AND EVIDENCE (available on-line at https://escholarship.org/uc/item/2gh1r30h); JUSTIN MCCRARY AND SARATHA SANGA, YOUTH OFFENDERS AND THE DETERRENCE EFFECT OF PRISON (available on-line at http://papers.ssrn.com/sol3/papers.cfm?abstract_id=1980326). Steven D. Levitt, *Juvenile Crime and Punishment*, 106 J. POL. ECON. 1156 (1998).

[35] The Levitt paper relies on annual state-level data, while McCrary's uses individual data gathered at the daily level. As two criminologists point out, this difference suggests that Levitt's paper is likely blurring deterrence and incapacitation more than McCrary's. See Steven N. Durlauf and Daniel S. Nagin, *Imprisonment and Crime: Can Both Be Reduced?*, 10 CRIMINOLOGY & PUB. POL'Y 13 (2011). Moreover, McCrary has now replicated his findings using other datasets, an important—and, in the social sciences, all too infrequent—sign of confirmation.

justice system. Legislators and judges have manipulated the competing views of innocence and responsibility to maximize the control of young people who violate the law. At the "soft end" of juvenile courts' jurisdiction, state laws and courts have developed new strategies to deal with status offenses—the prohibited conduct of juveniles that would not be a crime if committed by an adult, such as truancy, runaway, curfew, and use of tobacco or alcohol. Many of these noncriminal minor offenders have been shifted out of the juvenile justice system into a hidden system of social control in private-sector mental health and chemical-dependency industries. At the "hard end," states transfer more juveniles to criminal courts for prosecution as adults, and they punish more severely those delinquent offenders who remain within the jurisdiction of the juvenile court. As a result of this "triage," juvenile courts have been transformed from a social welfare agency into deficient criminal courts for young offenders.[36]

Impact of Age on Sentencing

While age is formally taken into account through the juvenile justice system, it may also matter for those admitted to the adult penal system. In some regimes, courts are explicitly permitted to take age into account. Consider the following provision from the Federal Sentencing Guidelines, which generally try to restrain judicial discretion as much as possible:

> § 5H1.1. **Age (Policy Statement)**: Age (including youth) may be relevant in determining whether a departure is warranted, if considerations based on age, individually or in combination with other offender characteristics, are present to an unusual degree and distinguish the case from the typical cases covered by the guidelines. Age may be a reason to depart downward in a case in which the defendant is elderly and infirm and where a form of punishment such as home confinement might be equally efficient as and less costly than incarceration.

Admittedly, half of the provision is focused on older inmates, who we will discuss shortly; but youthfulness can matter as well. And, of course, judges in indeterminate regimes are always free to take age into account, at least implicitly (or quietly).

So it is worth considering how age in fact matters at sentencing. The empirical results are, again, mixed. Some studies find that older offenders receive longer sentences; others that they receive shorter; others that there is a curvilinear effect, with offenders in the "middle ages" of offending (around 30) receiving longer sentences than either those young or older; and others still find no effect one way or the other. Perhaps this ambiguity is not surprising. In a meta-analysis of the age-

---

[36] Barry C. Feld, *The Juvenile Court: Changes and Challenges*, 16 FOCUS ON L. STUDIES 1, 1 (2000).

punishment relationship, two criminologists, Jaejong Wu and Cassia Spohn, note that there is no theoretically clear, *a priori* way that age should affect sentencing. If younger offenders are thought more likely to recidivate, for example, they should be punished more, but if they are seen as more amenable to rehabilitation then perhaps punished less.[37] Or age may have little direct effect but may magnify the weight judges give to other factors, like race.[38]

Wu and Spohn's meta-analysis uncovered approximately sixty relevant studies on the age-punishment relationship. Of these, 40% reported a positive relationship between age and sentence (i.e., older offenders received longer sentences), 57% a negative relationship, and 3% no relationship. Their meta-analysis indicated that these differences were not due just to random variation in the data but to the importance of some moderator variables. Among their findings:

> the offender's age had a stronger effect on sentence length in federal courts than in state courts. Age had a negative relationship with sentence length in federal court but a positive relationship in state courts. Southern jurisdictions had a more pronounced disparity than did nonsouthern jurisdictions. In the South, older offenders received longer sentences than did younger offenders, but this relationship was reversed in states outside of this region.[39]

Wu and Spohn also reported that studies "without controls for criminal history, offense severity, and the mode of conviction generated greater sentencing gaps than those with appropriate controls for legally relevant and case processing factors." In other words, often the apparent effect of "age" was due to the omission of other factors correlated with it. Their overall conclusion was that age does not play that big a role in shaping sentencing length.[40]

The Problem of Older Prisoners

While most of the research on age has focused on juveniles, a new population that is receiving increased attention is that of older offenders. Between 1991 and 2010, the percent of prisoners over the age of 45 grew

---

[37] Jaejong Wu & Cassia Spohn, *Does an Offender's Age Have an Effect on Sentence Length?: A Meta-Analytic Review*, 20 CRIM. JUST. POL'Y REV. 379 (2009).

[38] Some criminologists, for example, talk about the "penalty" paid by young, black male defendants, suggesting that age may magnify the salience of race and sex. See, for example, Darrell Steffensmeier, Jeffery Ulmer, and John Kramer, *The Interaction of Race, Gender, and Age in Criminal Sentencing: The Punishment Cost of Being Young, Black, and Male*, 36 CRIMINOLOGY 763 (1998).

[39] Wu and Sphon, supra note 37 at 391.

[40] As an important aside, this finding indicates the general need to look beyond a single study to a rigorous synthesis of multiple studies. It is generally easy to find a paper with a strong result in one direction and another paper with an equally-strong result in the other. Does this imply weak methods? Noisiness around no effect? One strong paper and another weaker one? Simply viewing one paper by itself, or several papers at once but without some sort of effective synthesis, can often lead to incorrect conclusions.

from 10.6% to 27.3%; the total number increased 386%, from 87,000 to 423,000. Though this likely reflects in part the general graying of the American population, this growth rate exceeds that of those aged 45 and above, which grew by 103%, from 30.9% of the population (70 million) to 46% (142 million).

There are two ways that a prison population can age: long sentences can force people admitted when younger to grow old in prison, or states can simply start admitting more elderly offenders in the first place. Some recent research has pointed more to the latter effect than the former. An analysis of a large survey of prisoners taken in 2004 suggests that prison populations are getting older in part because there is a group of older offenders who are offending at higher rates than people their age did in previous cohorts. These offenders exhibit high levels of drug use and abuse, which could explain their elevated offending (and thus incarceration) rates.[41]

One of the biggest concerns with elderly inmates, besides the fact that they pose lower recidivism risks, is the cost. As a 2007 paper reported:

> The [Federal Bureau of Prisons] spends more than $400 million annually to imprison and care for elderly inmates [or about 6% of a $6.5B budget]. However, states also bear the burden of providing care for the aging inmate population. For example, Pennsylvania's spending on prison health services grew from $1.23 million in 1973 to $16.7 million in 1986, largely because of older inmate expenses such as eyeglasses, dentures, open-heart surgery, and care for the terminally ill. More than a decade ago, [one study] found the annual cost to incarcerate an inmate age 60+ in California to be about $69,000, compared to $21,000 for an inmate age 30. A 50-year-old person convicted in 1994 who serves a 25-year sentence at an average cost of $60,000 per year would cost the state of California about $1.5 million. More recently, a Georgia study found that inmates age 50+, who represent only 6% of the incarcerated population, consume more than 12% of the inmate health care budget. Consequently, the mean annual cost was $69,000 per older inmate.[42]

Prison life is also substantially harder for older inmates. A report on older inmates produced by Human Rights Watch lists some of the challenges faced by older inmates and those responsible for their incarceration. They need to be protected from younger, violent inmates, and they should not be forced to sleep on a top bunk. They may need more time to eat, more blankets to stay warm in cold weather, and age-

---

[41] See, e.g. Joe Palazzolo, *US Prisons Grapple with Aging Populations*, WALL STREET JOURNAL (January 28, 2015).

[42] R.V. Rikard & Ed Rosenberg, *Aging Inmates: A Convergence of Trends in the American Criminal Justice System*, 13 J. CORR. HEALTH CARE 150, 153 (2007).

appropriate educational and recreational options. Disciplinary standards need to reflect the reduced culpability of those with dementia, and older inmates with incontinence issues should not be forced to change in open bathrooms and suffer the resulting mockery, isolation, depression, etc. The report also notes that prison campuses are often scattered and poorly designed for those with reduced or limited mobility, including too few handicap-accessible bathrooms. The report then points out that retrofitting prisons to make them more accommodating to older inmates is "hampered by budget realities."[43]

For all these limitations, it is less clear whether older inmates are at significantly greater risk of victimization. Some prisons house older inmates in separate, age-specific locations, which minimizes the risk of victimization but increases the cost of maintenance. When asked by Human Rights Watch interviewers about older inmates in the general population, prison officials gave mixed reports, some claiming that older inmates were actually protected by younger prisoners, others that older inmates were disproportionately victimized at least for low-level offenses such as theft or harassment—though whether this is specifically because of age or because weaker inmates are often preyed upon and older inmates tend to be weaker is unclear.

QUESTIONS

1. **Juveniles and automatic waivers.** Fagan argues against automatic waivers on the grounds that they are criminogenic. But even if we abolished all automatic waivers, one de facto waiver still exists: the age of majority. In short, the juvenile justice system takes a very binary view of age. Is this defensible in light of Fagan's (and others') findings? If not, what would the alternative look like—how can we create a punishment scheme that treats age in a graded manner? *Can* we create such a system? What error costs would it introduce? To what extent do actuarial developments mitigate these concerns?

2. **The Supreme Court and legal cutoffs.** In *Roper*, *Graham*, and *Miller*, the Court effectively constitutionalized 18 as a major cut-off line: below that, defendants are considered too young to be fully culpable. But the day after one's 18th birthday, full adult liability attaches. The previous question addressed the wisdom of this. Assuming we have to draw the line, do we want the Court to be the one to draw it? Should it be a state or county decision—or even a judge-specific one?

3. **Age and prior records.** The Wu and Spohn results seem to suggest that once you control for, say, prior criminal history, age has little effect. Does that seem appropriate: should a 20-year old offender with 3 priors face the same sanction as a 30-year old offender with 3 priors? What concerns might you have?

---

[43] HUMAN RIGHTS WATCH: OLD BEHIND BARS: THE AGING PRISON POPULATION IN THE UNITED STATES 46–47 (2012).

4. **Experience of prison.** Prison is tougher for older inmates. How relevant should this be for setting a sanction? Independent of the implications of the age-profile of offending, should these factors be given weight, and if so how much?

C. More Mutable Characteristics

If you buy into an extreme form of hard determinism, then all traits are in a way immutable: a person obviously has no control over his genes, neurology, sex, or age, but he also doesn't have any real control over, say, where he lives or whether he drinks or takes drugs. The decision to relocate or drink may *feel* chosen, but it is actually the product of uncontrollable responses to a host of stimuli. Yet the evidence base does not yet indicate that hard determinism is correct; regardless, the legal system wholly rejects the idea (at least for now). So it is worth briefly considering the relevance of (seemingly?) more-mutable offender traits. We will focus primarily on the most obvious of these, namely the use of drugs or alcohol, and then touch on one or two other traits as well.

Alcohol and drugs play major roles in criminal offending. In the 2008 survey of crime victimization in the United States, about 24% of all victims of violent crime reported that their attackers were using alcohol or drugs at the time of the offense (and another 47% said they didn't know or couldn't tell); about 14% said alcohol, with the remaining saying drugs or both.[44] Similarly, in the 2004 Survey of Inmates in State and Federal Correctional Facilities, 56% of state prisoners admitted to using drugs in the month prior to their offenses, and 32% at the time of the crime; 17% of state offenders claimed their committed their instant offenses to get money for drugs.[45]

The only real normative wrinkle that mutability introduces is whether we should use the law to target the underlying behavior. In other words, taking a person's chemically altered state as a given, substance abuse mitigates culpability but increases the need for incapacitation and rehabilitation; the deterrent implications are unclear.[46] But what makes mutable traits different from immutable ones is that very "take as a given." We must take the offender's genes or sex or age as a given. But we need not take his drug abuse or drinking as a given.

Question: Reconsider the statement made somewhat blithely above, that substance abuse reduces culpability. Does it, necessarily? Where does the culpability now arise? Does that

---

[44] The data are available on-line in Table 32 at http://www.bjs.gov/content/pub/pdf/cvus08.pdf.

[45] These results are on-line at http://www.bjs.gov/content/pub/pdf/dudsfp04.pdf.

[46] **Question:** See why they are unclear? What effect will tougher sanctions have on the behavior of someone who is drunk or high? Can we determine what is optimal without more rigorous data?

fully negate any mitigating implications of intoxication? And what does it mean for deterrence?

The key question, then, becomes exactly how controllable are these factors: just how much control does someone have over being drunk or high on drugs? The more we view these behaviors as freely chosen, the less willing retributivists will be to mitigate, and the more consequentialists will focus their policies on trying to influence the first-stage behavior. Consider the points made in the following article from one of *Nature*'s journals:

> The aberrant behavioural manifestations that occur during [drug] addiction have been viewed by many as "choices" of the addicted individual, but recent imaging studies have revealed an underlying disruption to brain regions that are important for the normal processes of motivation, reward and inhibitory control in addicted individuals. This provides the basis for a different view: that drug addiction is a disease of the brain, and the associated abnormal behaviour is the result of dysfunction of brain tissue, just as cardiac insufficiency is a disease of the heart. . . . Therefore, although initial drug experimentation and recreational use might be volitional, once addiction develops this control is markedly disrupted. Although imaging studies consistently show specific abnormalities in the brain function of addicted individuals, not all addicted individuals show these abnormalities. This highlights the need for further research to delineate other neurobiological processes that are involved in addiction.
>
> Chronic exposure to drugs of abuse is required for drug addiction, and its expression involves complex interactions between biological and environmental factors. This might explain why some individuals become addicted and others do not, and why attempts to understand addiction as a purely biological or a purely environmental disease have been largely unsuccessful.
>
> Here, we summarize how new methodologies that allow us to study genes, molecular biology and the human brain are providing us with a greater understanding of drug addiction, and the implications of these findings for the prevention and treatment of addiction.
>
> Normal developmental processes might result in a higher risk of drug use at certain times in life than others. Experimentation often starts in adolescence, as does the process of addiction. Normal adolescent specific behaviours (such as risk-taking, novelty-seeking and response to peer pressure) increase the propensity to experiment with legal and illegal drugs, which might reflect incomplete development of brain regions . . . that

are involved in the processes of executive control and motivation. In addition, studies indicate that drug exposure during adolescence might result in different neuroadaptations from those that occur during adulthood. For example, in rodents, exposure to nicotine during the period that corresponds to adolescence, but not during adulthood, led to significant changes in nicotine receptors and an increased reinforcement value for nicotine later in life. Future research might allow us to clarify whether this is the reason that adolescents seem to become addicted to nicotine after less nicotine exposure than adults. Similarly, further studies might enable us to determine whether the increased neuroadaptations to alcohol that occur during adolescence, compared with those that occur during adulthood explain the greater vulnerability to alcoholism in individuals who start using alcohol early in life.[47]

The authors then note that "[i]t is estimated that 40% to 60% of the vulnerability to addiction is attributable to genetic factors," but that other factors such social status and mental illness can matter as well.

QUESTIONS

1. **First move.** Volkow and Li note that addiction requires extensive repeat use, and that the initial decision to engage in drug or alcohol use appears to be more rational, conditional on age-of-first-use. Does this suggest that certain categories of addicts can be thought to be more rationally culpable—or more able to be rationally deterred—than others? If so, what categories? Are you comfortable, normatively, drawing these lines? Do you think they can be accurately drawn?

2. **Rational addiction.** Several economists, particularly Gary Becker and Kevin Murphy, have put forth the theory of **rational addiction**, which argues that drug addictions generally behave quite rationally concerning their addictive behavior. Consider smokers who learn on June 1 that taxes on cigarettes are going to go way up on January 1 of the next year. The rational addiction model makes two predictions: smokers will hoard cigarettes in anticipation of the increase *and* they will *cut back* on smoking so that they will need to buy fewer (more-expensive) cigarettes once their stockpiles run out. Empirical evidence detects such behavior for smokers, which isn't too surprising: nicotine does not inhibit rationality. More surprisingly, some studies—but certainly not all—purport to similarly-rational behavior among those addicted to more-serious drugs. How does this shape our view of the immutability or mutability of addiction?

3. **Variation in outcomes.** How relevant is it that many of those who are intoxicated, whether by alcohol or drugs, end up not committing any crimes (other, in the case of drug consumption, than the drug offense itself)? Is it enough for the judge to know that the defendant was on cocaine at the

---

[47] Nora D. Volkow & Ting-Kai Li, *Drug Addiction: The Neurobiology of Behaviour Gone Awry*, 5 NATURE REVIEWS: NEUROSCIENCE 963, 963 (2004).

time of the crime, or does the judge also need to know what fraction of those on cocaine commit crimes? or perhaps commit the same crime as the defendant?

Obviously, drug use is not the only (seemingly) mutable trait that could be relevant at sentencing. Consider location. As the evidence on situational pressures presented in Chapter 1 indicates, a person's proclivity to offend is shaped in no small part by environment. And, at least in theory, people can move away from negative environments. There are, however, clear limits to this claim. Children, for example, have little say over where they live and what they are exposed to. And those in public housing may not have the ability to move to other public housing facilities, and in general the situational pressures may be the same across public housing facilities. More generally, movement to less-violent areas is constrained by the cost of moving: safer neighborhoods are more expensive and may be formally or informally hostile to those from higher-crime neighborhoods moving in. And as always, the persistent, impossible-to-answer question is whether we trust judges to try to account for these sorts of pressures and whether they are genuinely avoidable, or if we think the costs of misuse exceed any gains.

PROBLEM: AGGRAVATORS AND MITIGATORS IN NORTH CAROLINA

Below are the lists of aggravators and mitigators in the North Carolina guidelines. Read them through, and decide how the state approaches both mutable and immutable traits. Are they generally aggravators, mitigators, or both? Can we get any sense of what goal(s) North Carolina is trying to advance?

NCGS § 15A–1340.16(d): Aggravating Factors

1. The defendant induced others to participate in the commission of the offense or occupied a position of leadership or dominance of other participants.

2. The defendant joined with more than one other person in committing the offense and was not charged with committing a conspiracy.

2a. The offense was committed for the benefit of, or at the direction of, any criminal street gang, with the specific intent to promote, further, or assist in any criminal conduct by gang members, and the defendant was not charged with committing a conspiracy. A "criminal street gang" means any ongoing organization, association, or group of three or more persons, whether formal or informal, having as one of its primary activities the commission of felony or violent misdemeanor offenses, or delinquent acts that would be felonies or violent misdemeanors if committed by an adult, and having a common name or common identifying sign, colors, or symbols.

3. The offense was committed for the purpose of avoiding or preventing a lawful arrest or effecting an escape from custody.

4. The defendant was hired or paid to commit the offense.

5. The offense was committed to disrupt or hinder the lawful exercise of any governmental function or the enforcement of laws.

6. The offense was committed against or proximately caused serious injury to a present or former law enforcement officer, employee of the Division of Adult Correction of the Department of Public Safety, jailer, fireman, emergency medical technician, ambulance attendant, social worker, justice or judge, clerk or assistant or deputy clerk of court, magistrate, prosecutor, juror, or witness against the defendant, while engaged in the performance of that person's official duties or because of the exercise of that person's official duties.

6a. The offense was committed against or proximately caused serious harm . . . or death to a law enforcement agency animal, an assistance animal, or a search and rescue animal . . . , while engaged in the performance of the animal's official duties.

7. The offense was especially heinous, atrocious, or cruel.

8. The defendant knowingly created a great risk of death to more than one person by means of a weapon or device which would normally be hazardous to the lives of more than one person.

9. The defendant held public elected or appointed office or public employment at the time of the offense and the offense directly related to the conduct of the office or employment.

9a. The defendant is a firefighter or rescue squad worker, and the offense is directly related to service as a firefighter or rescue squad worker.

10. The defendant was armed with or used a deadly weapon at the time of the crime.

11. The victim was very young, or very old, or mentally or physically infirm, or handicapped.

12. The defendant committed the offense while on pretrial release on another charge.

12a. The defendant has, during the 10-year period prior to the commission of the offense for which the defendant is being sentenced, been found by a court of this State to be in willful violation of the conditions of probation imposed pursuant to a suspended sentence or been found by the Post-Release Supervision and Parole Commission to be in willful violation of a condition of parole or post-release supervision imposed pursuant to release from incarceration.

13. The defendant involved a person under the age of 16 in the commission of the crime.

14. The offense involved an attempted or actual taking of property of great monetary value or damage causing great monetary

loss, or the offense involved an unusually large quantity of contraband.

15. The defendant took advantage of a position of trust or confidence, including a domestic relationship, to commit the offense.

16. The offense involved the sale or delivery of a controlled substance to a minor.

16a. The offense is the manufacture of methamphetamine and was committed where a person under the age of 18 lives, was present, or was otherwise endangered by exposure to the drug, its ingredients, its by-products, or its waste.

16b. The offense is the manufacture of methamphetamine and was committed in a dwelling that is one of four or more contiguous dwellings.

17. The offense for which the defendant stands convicted was committed against a victim because of the victim's race, color, religion, nationality, or country of origin.

18. The defendant does not support the defendant's family.

18a. The defendant has previously been adjudicated delinquent for an offense that would be a Class A, B1, B2, C, D, or E felony if committed by an adult.

19. The serious injury inflicted upon the victim is permanent and debilitating.

19a. The offense is a violation of G.S. 14–43.11 (human trafficking), G.S. 14–43.12 (involuntary servitude), or G.S. 14–43.13 (sexual servitude) and involved multiple victims.

19b. The offense is a violation of G.S. 14–43.11 (human trafficking), G.S. 14–43.12 (involuntary servitude), or G.S. 14–43.13 (sexual servitude), and the victim suffered serious injury as a result of the offense.

20. Any other aggravating factor reasonably related to the purposes of sentencing.

NCGS § 15A–1340.16(e): Mitigating Factors

1. The defendant committed the offense under duress, coercion, threat, or compulsion that was insufficient to constitute a defense but significantly reduced the defendant's culpability.

2. The defendant was a passive participant or played a minor role in the commission of the offense.

3. The defendant was suffering from a mental or physical condition that was insufficient to constitute a defense but significantly reduced the defendant's culpability for the offense.

4. The defendant's age, immaturity, or limited mental capacity at the time of commission of the offense significantly reduced the defendant's culpability for the offense.

5. The defendant has made substantial or full restitution to the victim.

6. The victim was more than 16 years of age and was a voluntary participant in the defendant's conduct or consented to it.

7. The defendant aided in the apprehension of another felon or testified truthfully on behalf of the prosecution in another prosecution of a felony.

8. The defendant acted under strong provocation, or the relationship between the defendant and the victim was otherwise extenuating.

9. The defendant could not reasonably foresee that the defendant's conduct would cause or threaten serious bodily harm or fear, or the defendant exercised caution to avoid such consequences.

10. The defendant reasonably believed that the defendant's conduct was legal.

11. Prior to arrest or at an early stage of the criminal process, the defendant voluntarily acknowledged wrongdoing in connection with the offense to a law enforcement officer.

12. The defendant has been a person of good character or has had a good reputation in the community in which the defendant lives.

13. The defendant is a minor and has reliable supervision available.

14. The defendant has been honorably discharged from the Armed Forces of the United States.

15. The defendant has accepted responsibility for the defendant's criminal conduct.

16. The defendant has entered and is currently involved in or has successfully completed a drug treatment program or an alcohol treatment program subsequent to arrest and prior to trial.

17. The defendant supports the defendant's family.

18. The defendant has a support system in the community.

19. The defendant has a positive employment history or is gainfully employed.

20. The defendant has a good treatment prognosis, and a workable treatment plan is available.

21. Any other mitigating factor reasonably related to the purposes of sentences.

CHAPTER 6

PROCEDURES AND RIGHTS AT SENTENCING

For much of American history there has been little legislative, appellate-judicial, or constitutional oversight of sentencing outcomes. At the time the Constitution was drafted, sentences were fairly determinate (often death), so the Constitution is relatively silent when it comes to punishment. And as rehabilitation took over as the dominant justification for punishment (at least in theory), legislators vested wide, and generally unreviewable discretion in judges and parole boards. Starting in the 1970s, however, as discretion in general and rehabilitation in particular fell out of favor, states began to adopt more rigid sentencing policies that created more "law-based" sentencing regimes, transferring power away from courts and ultimately towards prosecutors. Over the course of the 2000s, the US Supreme Court handed down a series of confusing opinions that at least partially undermined a key part of these more-structured sentencing systems, but sentencing law in many parts of the country remains much more structured now than it was for most of our nation's history.

This chapter starts with an overview of what procedural, trial-like protections a defendant is entitled to at sentencing. It then considers what substantive protections defendants have against severe sanctions. The Court has refused to impose any real constitutional limits on punishment, but legislatures have restricted what judges can do, to both the benefit and detriment of defendants. This chapter then concludes by describing the Supreme Court's long and tortuous sentencing law jurisprudence that came about in the wake of these legislative innovations and culminated in the Court's *Blakely* and *Booker* opinions.

A. PROCEDURAL PROTECTIONS AT SENTENCING

The conventional wisdom concerning sentencing proceedings is that substantially fewer procedural protections apply there than at the guilt phase. As the following reading makes clear, it is true that defendants have fewer protections, but that does not mean they have none.

Alan C. Michaels, *Trial Rights at Sentencing*
81 N. C. L. REV. 1771 (2003)

Do constitutional trial rights apply at sentencing? *Williams v. New York* is often seen as the seminal case. [In *Williams*, the] Court concluded that Williams's sentence of death—concededly based on hearsay allegations that he was not given the opportunity to challenge prior to sentencing—did not violate the Due Process Clause of the Fourteenth Amendment. The Court justified its conclusion on the ground that looser evidentiary rules were necessary at sentencing to achieve the progressive goals of achieving rehabilitation and reformation through a process of individualized sentencing.

The half-century since *Williams* has seen a revolution in the constitutional rights governing criminal trials. Do these rights apply at sentencing? Judging by the Supreme Court's steady citation to *Williams* for the relative absence of constitutional procedural restrictions at sentencing, the drumbeat of commentators criticizing that same absence, and the calls for additional procedural rights at sentencing, one might conclude that the answer is a nearly uniform no. That conclusion would be wrong. More trial rights apply at sentencing than many have supposed.

Confusion about the extent of trial rights at sentencing undoubtedly traces from the Court's utter failure to articulate a consistent explanation for whether and when constitutional adjudication rights apply to sentencing proceedings. In deciding whether a particular right applies, the Court regularly decides individual cases without reference either to the larger procedural picture or to earlier decisions regarding the applicability of trial rights at sentencing. Moreover, the Court's proffered methodology in these cases is ad hoc. For example, depending on the case, the Court has justified its conclusions on the basis of the constitutional text, historical practice, considerations of due process, and the purposes of sentencing. The Court frequently fails to offer these justifications, however, when they do not support the Court's result.

There is[, however,] an explanatory principle that fits the law of trial rights at sentencing. According to this principle, the Constitution requires a balanced and thorough process for determining sentences following a criminal conviction. The vision is of a reasonably thorough process directed at getting the best estimate of the appropriate sentence with both prosecution and defense advancing their positions on equal terms. There is . . . no constitutionally mandated presumption of "sentencing innocence"; within the range of legislatively prescribed sentences for the crime, "too high" is neither better nor worse than "too low." In this vision, the defendant, by virtue of his conviction, has lost the constitutional entitlement to have errors resolved in his favor that protected him at trial. The defendant has also lost some autonomy interests that he had at trial. So long as a balanced approach is preserved, some tradeoffs of procedure for efficiency are acceptable.

Under this explanatory principle, called the "best-estimate" principle here for short, trial rights directed at ensuring a fair and balanced determination of the appropriate sentence do apply at sentencing. On the other hand, "special-protection" rights, those rights that are designed to give the defendant extra protections—particularly by insuring that errors will tend to be resolved in the defendant's favor, but also rights that provide extra protection against state oppression or otherwise champion the defendant's autonomy—do not apply.

The best-estimate principle is offered here as a descriptive explanation of which rights apply at sentencing, not as a normative justification. The suggestion here is not that this is how the constitutional mandates for sentencing procedures ought to have been conceived, but rather that this is the system that has been conceived. Having a firm idea of where we are should help courts and commentators figure out where we should go.

[Michaels then highlights three other theories that have some explanatory power, but which are not as accurate as the "best estimate" approach at predicting the Court's decisions:

- *Textualism.* "Perhaps rights that seem mandated by the text of the Constitution, such as the right to employ counsel, are more likely to apply at sentencing than rights, such as the right to appointment of counsel for indigents, that stand on weaker textual footing."

- *Historical Practice.* "[I]t could be that the descriptive explanation for whether a right applies at sentencing depends on whether the procedure generally governed sentencing proceedings at the time of the enactment of the Bill of Rights or, perhaps in the case of rights that are purely a matter of due process, at the time of the enactment of the Fourteenth Amendment."

- *Due Process Right.* "[I]t could be that the key distinction is whether the right is derived from the Due Process Clause on the one hand, or from the specifically enumerated rights of the Fifth, Sixth, and Eighth Amendments on the other. Sometimes the notion behind this distinction is that the Court can use different methods of constitutional interpretation for matters to which the 'Bill of Rights speaks in explicit terms' and those for which it does not."]

The following Table* provides a complete taxonomy of trial rights at sentencing. In addition, the Table describes how each of the rights questions would be resolved under the descriptive principles discussed above and how the undecided questions would likely be decided under each principle.

---

* *Ed. note*: The column titled "S. Ct." addresses whether the US Supreme Court has addressed the issue; "L. Ct." whether lower courts have considered it. A capital "Y" indicates that the relevant court has explicitly affirmed the right, a capital "N" that it has explicitly rejected the right. A "?" indicates silence or no clear answer. A lower-case "y" or "n" means that the court has given a sense of its views, but not as a firm holding. "Source" refers to the Constitutional amendment used to justify the holding. The four entries under "Principles" turn from the positive to the normative and indicate whether the particular right *should be* provided for the best estimate theory and the other three theories discussed above.

Table 1. Trial Rights at Sentencing.

Right	At Sentencing?		Source	Principles			
	S. Ct.	L. Ct.		Const. Text	Historical Practice	Due Process Right	Best Estimate
Counsel							
Use an attorney	Y	–	6th	Y	Y	N	Y
Appt. for indigent	Y	–	6th	N	N	N	Y
Effective assistance	y	Y	6th	N	N	N	Y
Counsel of choice	?	y/split	6th	n	y	N	n
Proceed pro se	?	split	6th	n	y	N	N
Bail							
Nonexcessive bail	y	?	8th	Y	y	N	y
Bail at all	n	n	5th	N	n	Y	n
Notice of Charges	?	y	5th/6th	y	N	?	Y
Trial by Jury	N	–	6th	n	n	N	N
Discovery (*Brady*)	y	Y	5th	N	N	Y	Y
Double Jeopardy							
No post-verdict adverse change	N	–	5th	y	N	N	N
Collateral estoppel	?	?	5th	n	N	N	y
Speedy Trial	?	split	6th	n	y	N	y
Public Trial	?	y	6th	n	y	N	N
Proof Beyond a Reasonable Doubt	N	–	5th	N	N	Y	N
Confrontation							
Use of hearsay	n	N	6th	Y	N	N	N
In court procedures	?	n	6th	Y	N	N	N
Right of presence	?	Y	5th/6th	N	?	y	Y
Present Evidence							
Speak	?	split	5th/6th	n	Y	?	Y
Rebut state's evidence	?	y	5th	n	?	Y	Y
Call witnesses	?	N	6th	y	?	Y	?
Remain Silent							
Not to testify	Y	–	5th	n/a	n/a	n/a	n/a
No use of compelled testimony	?	split	5th	y	y	N	n
No inference re: facts	Y	–	5th	N	N	N	N
No inference re: other	?	?	5th	N	N	N	N
Fit with Supreme Court Decisions				5–6	7–4	4–7	10–1

[O]ne can see that the principle corresponds nearly perfectly with the Court's decisions—even though those decisions have been split almost 50–50 between rights applying and not applying. Indeed, the fit was a perfect one until the Supreme Court's 1999 decision in *Mitchell v. United States* held the rule against drawing adverse inferences from a defendant's silence applicable at sentencing.

[Before continuing on, it is important to point out one entry in Michaels' chart that has changed since his article was published in 2003: as a result of *Blakely*, defendants are now entitled to jury factfinding at sentencing—at the beyond a reasonable doubt standard—for certain types of sentencing facts. As we will see in Part C.3 below, that this seems contrary to the "best estimate" approach is ultimately not surprising, since the 5–4 split in *Blakely* did not fall along the usual left-right lines but instead along a less-frequently seen doctrinal/pragmatic schism, with the doctrinalists coming out ahead.]

The difference between how evidence is handled at the guilt phase as compared to the sentencing phase points to how the goals of each stage differ. The guilt phase is highly adversarial, with a locally-elected executive official—the prosecutor—squaring off against a privately-retained advocate (or his publicly-appointed equivalent), and with the evidence gathered via direct testimony subject to immediate cross-examination. Sentencing could not proceed much more differently. The primary document, if there is one, is the pre-sentence report, which is a written file prepared not by dueling parties but by the probation office, which is often located inside the judiciary. The sentencing process is not wholly inquisitorial—defendants generally have the right to challenge what the report says[1]—but it is much less adversarial than the trial phase, suggesting (as Michaels points out) a different set of normative goals.

QUESTIONS

1. **Our primary concern.** Assume that Michaels is right that the Court either intentionally or inadvertently has adopted a "best evidence" rule for sentencing. Does this make sense? If we accept that the standard should be higher at the guilt phase, why not at the sentencing phase as well? *Why* do we want a high bar at the guilt phase? What exactly is the high bar at the guilt phase protecting defendants *from*? Just the conviction itself, or something more? *Why* are we concerned with wrongful convictions?

2. **Best estimators.** Do you agree with all of Michaels' assessments of what the best estimate approach requires (i.e., the last column of the table above)? Might some of the factors he lists as "no" actually advance the best-estimate theory, or some of those he lists as "yes" not play too big a role?

B. SUBSTANTIVE RULES: A SILENT FEDERAL COURT, MORE ACTIVE STATE COURTS, HIGHLY ACTIVE STATE LEGISLATURES

Perhaps the more interesting issue to consider is what sort of *substantive* protections does a defendant have at sentencing.[2] Such protections can come from two primary sources: legislatures can define sentencing ranges, and state and federal courts can place constitutional limits on what those ranges can be. Three broad patterns exist today. First, the federal judiciary imposes almost no substantive limits at all on non-capital sentences. Second, state judiciaries are more willing to find particular sentences constitutionally impermissible, although a quick

---

[1] See, e.g., Or. Rev. Stat. § 137.079.

[2] This chapter will just focus on non-capital protections. Capital cases are substantially different, and these were covered in Ch. 7 below.

survey of state sentencing laws makes it clear that these holdings only take place at the extreme margins. And third, state legislatures have spent the past three decades aggressively imposing substantive limits on the sentences judges can impose, in ways both favorable and (perhaps more often) unfavorable to defendants.

B.1. FEDERAL AND STATE JUDICIAL LIMITS

Any federal protection against excessive sanctions comes from the Eighth Amendment, which bans "cruel and unusual" punishments. While there is a vibrant jurisprudence on what constitutes "cruel and unusual" in the death penalty context, the Court has been relatively quiet when it comes to non-capital cases—and when it has issued rulings, they have been somewhat fractured and contradictory.

While the Eighth Amendment has been found to bar certain *types* of punishment,[3] the Court has almost never found it to bar a particular prison sentence. A prison sentence would be impermissible under the Eighth Amendment only if it is somehow "disproportional" to the crime. In *Rummel v. Estelle*, 445 U.S. 263 (1980), however, the Court noted that findings of disproportionality outside the capital context are "exceedingly rare"—in fact, it fails to cite a single instance of such a reversal,[4] all the while pointing to numerous counterexamples. Moreover, *Rummel* ultimately upholds Rummel's life sentence under a recidivist statute for the crime of stealing $120.75. And two years later the Court overturned an appellate decision that had reversed a 40 year prison sentence and $20,000 fine for marijuana possession and distribution on proportionality grounds, cautioning that defining punishments is a "basic line-drawing process that is properly within the province of legislatures, not courts."[5]

The next year came the one exception, *Solem v. Helm*, 462 U.S. 277 (1983), in which the Court reversed as disproportionate a recidivist sentence of life without parole for issuing a "no account" check. The Court laid out a three-pronged disproportionality test that looked at the gravity of the offense and punishment, the sentences imposed on offenders in the same jurisdiction, and the sentences imposed on similar crimes in other jurisdictions.

Solem, however, stands alone. A few years later, in *Harmelin v. Michigan*, 501 U.S. 957 (1991), the Court faced a first-time offender who

---

[3] According to *Harmelin v. Michigan*, 501 U.S 957, 990 (1991), the only case directly on point appears to be *Weems v. United States*, 217 U.S. 349 (1910), in which the Court held that incarceration at "hard and painful labor, with chains fastened to the wrists and ankles at all times," along with additional civil restrictions such as lifetime government surveillance and "deprivation of the rights of parental authority, guardianship of person or property, participation in the family council, etc." was so unheard of in American penology that it was both cruel and unusual.

[4] Its one example is *Weems*, but that case focused far more on the *type* of punishment rather than on its length.

[5] *Hutto v. Davis*, 454 U.S. 370 (1982) (internal quotation marks omitted).

received a mandatory life sentence without the possibility of parole for possessing 672 grams of cocaine. Two justices (Scalia and Rehnquist) argued that under the Eighth Amendment there was no proportionality test for non-capital offenses at all; and three (Kennedy, O'Connor, and Souter) claimed that while such a test did exist, and while the mandatory sentence in question could be cruel, it was not unusual. These five votes led the Court to uphold the sentence.

Since *Harmelin*, the Court has not found any non-capital case disproportionate.[6] The most obvious opportunities it had to do so were in *Ewing v. California*, 538 U.S. 11 (2003), and *Lockyear v. Andrade*, 538 U.S. 63 (2003), which challenged California's three-strike. Gary Ewing's final offense involved stealing three golf clubs worth $399 each; he had a long list of prior property, robbery, burglary, and drug convictions. Leandro Andrade's final offense involved stealing nine videotapes from two K-Marts; his prior offenses included petty theft, burglary, escape, and two federal marijuana-transportation charges. Ewing received a 25-years-to-life sentence, and Andrade *two* 25-years-to-life sentences (because he committed two separate K-Mart thefts). The Court held that both were consistent with the Eighth Amendment.

While the US Supreme Court has been reluctant constitutionalize non-capital sentencing, state supreme courts have been more willing to do so. The following reading highlights these developments, and it serves a powerful and important reminder that for all the attention the US Supreme Court receives, criminal policy is ultimately a state-law issue, and so state-constitutional decisions play a much more important role than they receive credit for, and in the aggregate may even be more important that those of the US Supreme Court.

---

[6] In *Graham v. Florida*, 560 U.S. 48 (2010), the Court held that, under the Eighth Amendment, juvenile defendants could not receive life without parole for non-homicide offenses. While *Graham* represents an Eighth Amendment restriction on sentencing, it is a very narrow exception: just as "death is different," so too is juvenile offending. Moreover, the majority—written by Kennedy—makes it clear that its decision is not based on the sort proportionality review that Kennedy argued for in *Harmelin*. The type of review envisioned by *Harmelin* is designed for evaluating individual sentences (as-applied challenges, one could say), while *Graham* involves a facial challenge to an entire category of sentencing. As a result, the majority relies on a completely different line of cases, ones narrowly tailored to special classes of defendants: mentally retarded capital defendants (*Atkins v. Virginia*, 536 U.S. 304 (2002)), juvenile capital defendants (*Roper v. Simmons*, 543 U.S. 551 (2005)), and capital defendants charged with non-homicide offenses (*Kennedy v. Louisiana*, 554 U.S. 407 (2008)). *Graham* thus does not reflect a departure from the Court's unwillingness to find sentences disproportionate, although Kennedy does spend several pages stressing that the "controlling opinion" in *Harmelin* held that proportionality review exists, despite the fact that *Graham* itself explicitly eschews any such analysis.

Richard Frase, *Limiting Excessive Prison Sentences Under Federal and State Constitutions*
11 U. Pa. J. Const. L. 39 (2008)

In other areas of constitutional litigation, it is now well-established that courts can and do grant broader protections to citizens under state constitutional provisions than are required by the federal constitution. [S]ince state court judges are either directly elected or appointed by locally elected officials, decisions invalidating excessive legislative and executive actions under state law raise fewer issues of democratic legitimacy than when federal judges engage in constitutional review. In addition, state constitutions are often worded differently than the Eighth Amendment, which gives state courts more leeway to adopt a different interpretation. Indeed, some state constitutions explicitly prohibit disproportional or "excessive" penalties.

Nevertheless, state court rulings invalidating criminal penalties on state constitutional grounds have thus far been rather infrequent. This may be at least partly due to defense attorneys being unaware of relevant state constitutional provisions and case law; the summaries below are an effort to begin to address that problem, and encourage litigators, courts, and scholars to be less "Fed-centric."

A. Survey of State Constitutional Provisions Limiting Punishment Severity

All fifty states have constitutional provisions related to sentencing. All but two states, Connecticut and Vermont, have provisions specifically limiting severe punishments of all kinds. But both of those states have provisions limiting severe fines, and Vermont courts interpret that state's "proportioned" fines clause to apply to all types of penalties.

The forty-nine states with express or implied all-penalties provisions fall into five categories:

1. Ten states have constitutions which either explicitly [eight] or by interpretation [two] require proportionate penalties.

2. Nineteen state constitutions prohibit cruel or unusual penalties, including two states . . . with proportionate-penalty clauses (category (1), above).

3. Six state constitutions prohibit cruel penalties (omitting the "unusual" element), including one state . . . with a proportionate-penalty clause.

4. Twenty-two state constitutions prohibit cruel and unusual penalties, including eight states . . . which also have a proportionate-penalty clause and/or one of the provisions in category (5), below.

5. Nine states, all of which are included in one of the four categories above, have additional state constitutional

provisions related to excessive penalties or treatment [such as prohibiting "unnecessary rigor," "abuse," or "euthanasia, ... torture, or ... cruel, excessive, or unusual punishment"].

To summarize: thirty-five states have constitutional provisions or case law standards that differ from the Eighth Amendment—expressly banning disproportionate penalties, cruel or unusual punishments, cruel punishments, and/or one of the forms of mistreatment described in category (5), above.

B. State Constitutional Case Law Favorable to Defendants

Cases construing the state constitutional provisions surveyed above are as varied as the provisions themselves, and do not always track differences in the constitutional text. Some courts cite such differences as grounds for recognizing broader state constitutional protection, while other courts ignore textual differences and apply federal constitutional standards. Courts in states from the first two categories above (those with proportionate-penalty clauses, or those that prohibit cruel or unusual punishment) seem to be somewhat more likely to grant broader protection, but many states in each category do not do so. The reluctance of state courts to grant broader protection against excessive penalties under state constitutions is surprising given the frequency with which expanded criminal procedure rights are recognized by state courts in other contexts. For example, many courts have given citizens greater protection from searches and seizures under state provisions worded similarly or even identically to the Fourth Amendment.

Whether or not the state constitution is worded differently, or is deemed more protective, numerous cases across a diverse group of states have invalidated sentencing provisions or specific sentences under state constitutional law.[7] Although most courts merely apply the *Solem* framework, some state courts have developed more precise proportionality analysis or state-law principles. The following are examples of some of these state court decisions.

In *Conner v. State* [626 N.E.2d 803 (Ind. 1993)], the Indiana Supreme Court held that the state's proportionate penalties clause grants more protection than the Eighth Amendment. The court further held that the defendant's six-year sentence for selling a harmless substance represented to be marijuana was unconstitutionally disproportionate because it was twice as severe as the three-year

---

[7] [The following footnote is from the article.] Some state cases have struck down sentences under the Eighth Amendment, without separate discussion of state constitutional provisions. E.g., *Crosby v. State*, 824 A.2d 894 (Del. Super. Ct. 2003); *Wilson v. State*, 830 So. 2d 765 (Ala. Crim. App. 2001); *People v. Gaskins*, 923 P.2d 292 (Colo. Ct. App. 1996); see also *State v. Davis*, 79 P.3d 64 (Ariz. 2003) (invalidating mandatory consecutive sentences totaling fifty-two years without possibility of release for statutory rape). But see *State v. Berger*, 134 P.3d 378 (Ariz. 2006), cert. denied., 127 S. Ct. 1370 (2007) (distinguishing *Davis* and upholding mandatory consecutive terms totaling 200 years without release for first-offense possession (downloading) of child pornography).

maximum penalty applicable to the sale of real marijuana. The court therefore vacated the sentence and remanded with instructions to impose a sentence of no more than three years.

The Kentucky Court of Appeals, applying that state's ban on "cruel punishment" in *Workman v. Commonwealth* [429 S.W.2d 374 (Ky. Ct. App. 1968)], invalidated sentences of life without parole given to two fourteen-year-old rape offenders. The court's decision was based in part on the principle . . . that a punishment is unconstitutionally excessive if it "[goes] beyond what is necessary to achieve the aim of the public intent as expressed by the legislative act [or] . . . exceeds any legitimate penal aim."

In *State v. Hayes* [739 So. 2d 301 (La. Ct. App. 1999)], the Louisiana Court of Appeal vacated a mandatory sentence of life without parole under that state's cruel or unusual punishment clause (but without emphasizing the differences between state and federal constitutional texts). The court found the sentence constitutionally excessive in light of the following facts: Hayes's current offense involved theft of approximately $1,000 from his employer; he admitted the crime and returned the $693 still in his possession; he had a second job, and that employer thought highly of Hayes and believed he could be rehabilitated; his prior crimes were mostly minor property offenses; his one "crime of violence" (required, to impose the life sentence) was a strong-armed robbery and theft of a bicycle committed when Hayes was a juvenile; and the presentence report recommended a sentence of ten years.

In *People v. Bullock* [485 N.W.2d 866 (Mich. 1992)], the mandatory life-without-parole penalty upheld by the Supreme Court in *Michigan v. Harmelin* was found to violate the Michigan Constitution, in part because that state's constitution forbids cruel or unusual punishments. The Michigan Supreme Court implicitly adopted a retributive theory, stressing the defendant's limited culpability in the absence of any proof of sale or intent to sell.

Sometimes courts cite the state constitution and reach results seemingly more generous than what would be expected based on the most recent U.S. Supreme Court decisions, but without expressly holding that the state constitution grants additional protection. For example, the Georgia Supreme Court has, in a series of cases, invalidated severe penalties under both the Eighth Amendment and the cruel and unusual punishment clause of the Georgia Constitution, based in large part on post-offense legislative changes substantially lowering penalties for the crime in question. In the most recent case, *Humphrey v. Wilson* [652 S.E.2d 501 (Ga. 2007)], the defendant was a seventeen-year-old high school student charged with having oral sex with a fifteen-year-old student. Applying the penalties in effect at the time of the crime, the trial court imposed a mandatory minimum sentence of ten years with no possibility of parole, along with required life-long sex-offender registration and public notification of the defendant's status. One year after the crime, the law was changed, making this offense a misdemeanor and eliminating the sex-offender registration requirement. In striking down these penalties, the state supreme court did not hold that the legislative change was retroactive, but rather treated it as an important factor in applying the federal and state "evolving standards of decency" and gross disproportionality criteria.

As Frase mentions in passing, while state courts are more aggressive than federal courts in enforcing proportionality requirements, they still do so infrequently. Indiana serves as a good case example here. Since 1970, Indiana Rule of Appellate Procedure 7(B) has allowed appellate courts to revise sentences that appear incorrect "in light of the nature of the offense and the character of the offender." At first, the sentence had to be "manifestly unreasonable," but in 2003 the rule was amended to a less-deferential "inappropriate" standard. Between 2003 and 2007, the Indiana Supreme Court heard twenty-two cases under Rule 7(B) and reduced eleven of them.[8] At first blush, that seems like a fairly aggressive review process, until you realize that between 2003 and 2007 Indiana's superior and circuit courts processed over 341,000 cases; twenty-two cases constitute 0.006% of all felonies cases in the state.[9]

It is also unclear going forward exactly how such proportionality review should take place. The Supreme Court's decisions in *Blakely* and *Booker*, which are not Eighth Amendment cases but rather Fifth and Sixth Amendment ones, should in theory make proportionality review trickier and costlier to perform. Whether they will do so in practice is less clear—at least in Indiana, for example, the post-*Blakley* proportionality review cases have made no mention of *Blakely*, and several recent post-*Blakely* cases handed down by the US Supreme Court (particularly *Ice v. Oregon*) suggest that the Court is not going to enforce *Blakely*'s requirements outside a narrow range of issues. Part C.6 below explains this issue in more detail.

Ultimately, substantive restraints on sentences have not come from the judiciary but rather from the legislature, in the form of structured sentencing. This is an important development, since legislatures are likely less friendly to defendants than judiciaries. In fact, structurally, the judiciary will always be more favorable to the defendant. A constitutional challenge can never leave a defendant worse off: the courts police only the upper ends of sentences, not the lower, so a defendant can never find his sentence suddenly impermissibly *lenient*. At worst he is no

---

[8] See *Rutherford v. State*, 866 N.E.2d 867, 873 (Ind. 2007).
[9] To be clear, that the state supreme court has reviewed only a small fraction of cases does not automatically imply that such review is unimportant: a small number of reversals could either *cause* lower courts to *ignore* the supreme court, or it could be the *effect* of the lower courts *paying close attention*. Such a small volume of appeals, however, is at least strongly suggestive that such review has little impact.

worse off. Legislatures, however, can manipulate the maximum *and* the minimum, and thus *can* make life worse for the defendant.

QUESTIONS

1. **What bothers state courts.** How significant is the fact that almost all the state cases cited by Frase involve life without parole, and in at least one case *mandatory* life without parole? Do you think parole-eligible life sentences would face similar scrutiny? If not, what does that indicate about at least some of the reasons why state courts invalidate sentences?

2. **What is proportionality?** State courts often focus on the question of proportionality. But what *is* proportionality? Or, put differently, who would have an easier time arguing that a fifty year sentence for a 35-year-old recidivist is "proportional" to the harm of the crime(s): an incapacitationist? retributivist? deterrence theorist? How concerning is it that courts use the term "proportional" without ever stating a clear definition of what they mean?

B.2. LEGISLATIVE DEVELOPMENTS: THE RISE OF STRUCTURED SENTENCING

Unlike the courts, state and federal legislatures have spent the past four decades developing a wide range of new sentencing regimes. The following excerpt defines the basic developments, and we will consider each in more depth below.

John F. Pfaff, *The Continued Vitality of Structured Sentencing Following Blakely: The Effectiveness of Voluntary Guidelines*
54 UCLA L. REV. 235 (2006)

The nature of criminal sentencing in the United States has undergone an important shift since the 1970s. At the start of that decade, sentencing was dominated by the indeterminate approach: Prisoners were sentenced by judges to wide ranges of years (in some states, such as California, a criminal could receive a sentence of one year to life), and parole boards determined when in fact prisoners were released. During the 1970s, however, indeterminacy was attacked on several fronts. First, and perhaps most important, judges and academics alike, led by Andrew von Hirsch and Judge Marvin Frankel, began to view indeterminate sentences as too arbitrary, as "law without order." Similarly situated defendants could receive dramatically different sentences based on which judge each faced or which day each appeared before a given judge. And there was a growing concern that, either consciously or unconsciously, judges were taking into account impermissible factors such as defendants' race and sex when meting out punishments. Second, to the extent that it was justified on reformative or psychotherapeutic grounds, indeterminacy became less appealing as people turned against the rehabilitative ideal. And third, conservative critics feared that indeterminate sentences undermined the deterrent power of the law. Under the weight of these assaults, the old system began to collapse.

The result was the fragmenting of correctional policy in the United States, with every state curtailing its indeterminate system to at least some degree, but with each state responding differently. From the 1970s through today, six general types of sentencing reforms gained popularity: (1) the creation of determinate sentencing systems; (2) the development of sentencing guidelines; (3) the imposition of mandatory minimums; (4) the passage of two- and three-strikes laws (which are essentially forms of mandatory minimums for repeat offenders); (5) the abolition of parole; and (6) the adoption of truth-in-sentencing laws. Table 1 shows the wide variation in policies adopted across the United States.

Under determinate sentencing, state legislatures establish either specific sentences or ranges of sentences that judges are required to impose. Though some discretion might remain with the judge, it is greatly limited. The most rigid of these systems [was]* California's, in which a judge [was] often given three possible sentences (say, four, six, or eight years) and [was] expected to impose the middle sentence unless mitigating factors suggest the lower or aggravating factors the higher. In the 1970s, Alaska, Arizona, California, Colorado, Indiana, Illinois, New Jersey, New Mexico, and North Carolina adopted such systems. Though seemingly popular in the 1970s, no state has adopted such an approach since 1980, and at least one state, North Carolina, ultimately replaced its determinate structure with presumptive guidelines.

Instead, like North Carolina, jurisdictions have favored guidelines and sentencing commissions. Minnesota adopted the first guideline system in 1980, and since then nineteen jurisdictions have adopted guidelines, though only seventeen currently employ them; nine use presumptive guidelines, eight voluntary.* Five other states currently use commissions though as of 2006 had yet to adopt guidelines. The central difference between the two types [of guidelines] is that under presumptive guidelines, judicial failure to adhere to the guidelines is appealable by both the defendant and the government, while no such appeal exists for voluntary guidelines. Besides their ability to rationalize sentencing, guidelines and commissions appeal to legislators for two central reasons: They allow a degree of coordinated policy planning not possible when judges and parole boards make case-by-case decisions, and

---

    * *Ed. Note*: As we will see in Part C.3, determinate regimes as they were initially designed are no longer constitutional in the wake of *Blakely*. The discussion here focuses on these regimes as they were first established, and we will consider how they have changed below. At the time this article was originally written, California's determinate regime had not yet been declared invalid.

    * *Ed. Note*: As we will see below, fewer states now employ presumptive guidelines due to *Blakely*, though most adapted their laws to conform with *Blakely*'s new rules. We will look at current laws in Part C.4 below.

they provide a measure of political insulation to (at least partially) shield criminal policy from sudden outbursts of public opinion.

Besides using guidelines, states have sought to restrain judicial discretion at sentencing through mandatory minimums. Despite trenchant theoretical and pragmatic attacks, repeat offenders often face elevated minimum sanctions, and mandatory minimums have also targeted violent offenders and those convicted of violating drug and firearm statutes. [All states employ some types of mandatory minimums.] The most high profile of these policies are the "three-strikes" laws adopted by twenty-five jurisdictions. These laws require that an offender serve a dramatically increased sentence following a third (or, for two-strikes laws, a second) conviction. In general, strike legislation has been used more for political gain than actual crime control: Of the twenty-five jurisdictions with such laws, only one uses them regularly, California, which is responsible for approximately 90 percent of all sentences under them. The lower-profile mandatory minimums are thus more important.

At the same time that legislatures have limited judicial discretion over sentence length at the front end of the process, they have also sought to constrain discretion, usually that of the parole board, at the back end. Two policies in particular have been implemented to limit discretion over the actual release date. The first is the abolition of parole. Starting with Maine in 1975, fourteen states and the federal government to varying degrees abolished parole boards and their ability to release prisoners early. All but three of these states eliminated discretionary parole release for all offenders. The second is the passage of truth-in-sentencing laws, which require inmates to serve a specific percentage of their sentences. Many truth-in-sentencing laws came into effect following the passage of the Violent Crime Control and Law Enforcement Act of 1994, which provides federal funds to states that adopt an 85 percent standard for violent offenders, the focus of most (though not all) state truth-in-sentencing laws. As of 1998, twenty-eight states had adopted the 85 percent level required for federal funds, and thirteen states had imposed other (generally lesser) standards. Though the financial incentives offered by the federal government are often extensive—in 1998, for example, the government awarded over $92 million to just eleven states in the South, including $32 million to Florida alone—many states have declined to adopt truth-in-sentencing laws due to prison capacity constraints.

The spread of structured sentencing has been wide, but it has not been universal. As shown in Table 1 below, which is taken from the Pfaff reading, as of 2006 eleven states had not adopted any sort of sentencing guideline regime, truth-in-sentencing law, nor strike law, nor had abolished parole; and only four states had done all four. And while every state has introduced mandatory minimums of one sort or the other, a slim majority (of about twenty-six states) does not systematically employ any sort of guideline or determinate system and thus allows judges to still sentence under relatively indeterminate rules.[10] But it is impossible to look at American sentencing today and not appreciate the fundamental limitations on discretion that legislatures have imposed over the years. I just want to spend a few pages highlighting some important aspects of the major structural reforms.

TABLE 1
STATE SENTENCING PRACTICES

State	Abolish Parole	Guidelines	Truth-in-Sentencing	Strike Laws
Alabama				
Alaska		1980		
Arizona	1994	1977	1994	
Arkansas		1994		1995
California		1976	1994	1994
Colorado		1979		1994
Connecticut			1995	1994
Delaware	1990	1987	1990	
District of Columbia			2000	
Florida	1983	1983, abolished 1998	1995	1995
Georgia			1995	1995
Hawaii				
Idaho				
Illinois	1978	1970s	1995	
Indiana	1977	1976		1994
Iowa			1996	
Kansas	1993	1993	1995	1994

---

[10] I say "systematically" to reflect the fact that some states classified as "non-guideline/non-determinate" may have a few pockets of determinacy in their sentencing code. New York State, for example, is predominantly an indeterminate state, but its drug code is now determinate. When sentencing a non-drug Class B felon, for example, the judge is authorized to impose a sentence of up to twenty-five years, with a minimum of one-third the maximum; for a drug Class B felon, the judge imposes a fixed sentence of between one and nine years.

State	Abolish Parole	Guidelines	Truth-in-Sentencing	Strike Laws
Kentucky				
Louisiana		1992, abolished 1995	1997	1994
Maine	1975		1995	
Maryland		1983		1994
Massachusetts				
Michigan		1999	1995	
Minnesota	1980	1980	1993	
Mississippi	1995		1995	
Missouri		1997	1994	
Montana				1995
Nebraska				
Nevada				1995
New Hampshire				
New Jersey		1978	1997	1995
New Mexico		1977		1994
New York			1995	
North Carolina	1994	1994	1994	1994
North Dakota			1995	1995
Ohio	1996	1996	1996	
Oklahoma			1998	
Oregon	1989	1989	1995	
Pennsylvania		1982	1911	1995
Rhode Island				
South Carolina			1996	1995
South Dakota				
Tennessee		1989	1995	1995
Texas				
Utah		1979	1985	1995
Vermont				1995
Virginia	1995	1995	1995	1994
Washington	1984	1984	1990	1993
West Virginia				
Wisconsin	1999	1985, abolished 1995, reinstated 2003		1994
Wyoming				

B.2.a. Guidelines and Determinate Sentencing Laws

The sentencing reform that represents the greatest departure from indeterminacy is the sentencing guideline or the determinate sentencing law (which are functionally identical).[11] Between 1970 and 2004, eight states adopted determinate sentencing laws (DSLs), ten presumptive guidelines, and eight voluntary guidelines; one state later changed from

---

[11] Both scholars and judges tend to ignore determinate sentencing laws when discussing guideline systems, but the two approaches impose limits on judicial discretion in the same general manner. The only real difference is that determinate sentencing laws are written directly into the state criminal code while sentencing guidelines are published in a separate document (and perhaps amended through slightly less formal means). Tellingly, the Court has refused to draw any distinction between determinate sentencing laws and sentencing guidelines in its *Blakely* opinions, nor has any state apparently sought to make this argument. All of which is to say that the difference is one of form, not function.

a DSL to presumptive guidelines, and one presumptive guideline state and one voluntary guideline state repealed their guidelines. As we will see in Part C.4 below, since *Blakely* the distribution has shifted to five DSLs, seven presumptive guidelines (amended to comply with *Blakely*), and twelve voluntary guidelines (although three perhaps only partially so). Not only do a lot of states use some form of guideline system, but these states tend to be those with a larger fraction of the nation's prisoners. In 2003, the last year before *Blakely*, the seventeen states with presumptive guidelines or DSLs held over 43% of all prisoners and were responsible for just a hair under 50% of all prison admissions. Thus the potential impact of guidelines (or their undoing) is greater than the number of states that employ them suggests.

At least at the state level, all guidelines and DSLs adheres to a common framework. While most substantive offenses carries wide sentencing ranges, guidelines[12] set much narrower default options. In Washington State, for example, second degree kidnapping carries a maximum sentence of ten years, but at the time of Blakely's crime the default range for an offender with a few prior offenses (like Blakely) was forty-nine to fifty-three months. In presumptive regimes (which include DSLs), the judge is required to impose a sentence within that default range unless he has sufficient evidence of various enumerated aggravators or mitigators. If aggravators dominate mitigators, he is allowed to impose a sentence in a higher range; if mitigators dominate, in a lower range. Failure to make adequate findings is grounds for appeal by either side. Voluntary regimes follow a similar structure except that failure to comply provides no grounds for appeal.

While the frameworks are similar, guidelines differ in the details. Some states use detailed grids, with multiple offense categories on one axis and prior history classes on the other (see, for example, North Carolina's guidelines in the upcoming problem, or Minnesota's in Chapter 5), while others rely on more narrative descriptions. In Ohio, for example, the pre-*Blakely* statutes established a range of sentences for each crime, and the guidelines essentially just said that the judge could only impose the longest sentence if she found that aggravators dominated mitigators or the shortest if mitigators dominated aggravators; otherwise, she was free to impose any other sentence in the range. And, of course, states opt for different numbers of offense and prior history classes, compute the relevant levels in different ways, and so on. But, overall, guideline states have much more in common with each other than they do with non-guideline jurisdictions.

---

[12] From here on, I will use "guidelines" to refer to both guidelines and DSLs, absent a compelling reason to draw a distinction.

PROBLEM: GUIDELINES IN PRACTICE

Consider the following hypothetical case: Joe shoots and wounds someone who he (correctly) believes to be an undercover police officer, hitting him in the leg. The injury is not very severe, and legally speaking hovers somewhere in the grey area between "bodily injury" and "serious bodily injury." Joe is a former member of the US Army, where he served three combat tours in Iraq and Afghanistan; he regularly sees a psychologist to deal with the stress and anxiety he feels as a result. In these tough economic times is now several months behind on child support payments to his ex-wife and child, though he is looking for a job.

We want to compare how Joe would be punished in North Carolina, a guideline state, and New York, an indeterminate state. Start with North Carolina. The prosecutor has at his disposal several assault statutes that could work in this situation:

§ 14–32: Felonious assault with deadly weapon with intent to kill or inflicting serious injury; punishments.

a. Any person who assaults another person with a deadly weapon with intent to kill and inflicts serious injury shall be punished as a Class C felon.

b. Any person who assaults another person with a deadly weapon and inflicts serious injury shall be punished as a Class E felon.

c. Any person who assaults another person with a deadly weapon with intent to kill shall be punished as a Class E felon.

§ 14–32.4: Assault inflicting serious bodily injury; strangulation; penalties.

a. Unless the conduct is covered under some other provision of law providing greater punishment, any person who assaults another person and inflicts serious bodily injury is guilty of a Class F felony.

§ 14–33: Misdemeanor assaults, batteries, and affrays, simple and aggravated; punishments.

a. Any person who commits a simple assault or a simple assault and battery or participates in a simple affray is guilty of a Class 2 misdemeanor. . . .

c. Unless the conduct is covered under some other provision of law providing greater punishment, any person who commits any assault, assault and battery, or affray is guilty of a Class A1 misdemeanor if, in the course of the assault, assault and battery, or affray, he or she:

1. Inflicts serious injury upon another person or uses a deadly weapon; . . .

4. Assaults an officer or employee of the State or any political subdivision of the State, when the officer or employee is discharging or attempting to discharge his official duties. . . .

§ 14–34.5: Assault with a firearm on a law enforcement, probation, or parole officer or on a person employed at a State or local detention facility.

a. Any person who commits an assault with a firearm upon a law enforcement officer, probation officer, or parole officer while the officer is in the performance of his or her duties is guilty of a Class E felony.

§ 14–34.7. Assault inflicting serious injury on a law enforcement, probation, or parole officer or on a person employed at a State or local detention facility; penalty.

a. Unless covered under some other provision of law providing greater punishment, a person is guilty of a Class F felony if the person assaults a law enforcement officer, probation officer, or parole officer while the officer is discharging or attempting to discharge his or her official duties and inflicts serious bodily injury on the officer. . . .

c. Unless covered under some other provision of law providing greater punishment, a person is guilty of a Class I felony if the person does either of the following:

1. Assaults a law enforcement officer . . . while the officer is discharging or attempting to discharge his or her official duties and inflicts physical injury on the officer.

North Carolina then computes the prior criminal history score by looking at prior offenses and weighting them according to the following chart:

Prior Offense Class	Weight
A felony	10
B1 felony	9
B2, C, D felony	6
E, F, G felony	4
H, I felony	2
A1, 1, DUI misdemeanors	1

Thus a defendant with one A-felony prior and two C-felony priors would have a score of 22 (10 x 1 + 6 x 2). Assume that Joe has a B1 prior, an E prior, and an H prior. North Carolina caselaw holds that if the prosecutors and defense counsel stipulate to a particular criminal history in writing the court may treat that as proof of that history.

The offense level and prior history score determine the starting point of our analysis. Taken together, they point the judge to a specific square on the sentencing grid, given below, which provides a range of minimum sentences for the judge to impose, with the maximum capped at 120% of the minimum.

FELONY PUNISHMENT CHART
PRIOR RECORD LEVEL

Offense Class	I 0-1 Pt	II 2-5 Pts	III 6-9 Pts	IV 10-13 Pts	V 14-17 Pts	VI 18+ Pts
A	Death or Life Without Parole						
B1	A 240 - 300 192 - 240 144 - 192	A 276 - 345 221 - 276 166 - 221	A 317 - 397 254 - 317 190 - 254	A 365 - 456 292 - 365 219 - 292	A Life Without Parole 336 - 420 252 - 336	A Life Without Parole 386 - 483 290 - 386
B2	A 157 - 196 125 - 157 94 - 125	A 180 - 225 144 - 180 108 - 144	A 207 - 258 165 - 207 124 - 165	A 238 - 297 190 - 238 143 - 190	A 273 - 342 219 - 273 164 - 219	A 314 - 393 251 - 314 189 - 251
C	A 73 - 92 58 - 73 44 - 58	A 83 - 104 67 - 83 50 - 67	A 96 - 120 77 - 96 58 - 77	A 110 - 138 88 - 110 66 - 88	A 127 - 159 101 - 127 76 - 101	A 146 - 182 117 - 146 87 - 117
D	A 64 - 80 51 - 64 38 - 51	A 73 - 92 59 - 73 44 - 59	A 84 - 105 67 - 84 51 - 67	A 97 - 121 78 - 97 58 - 78	A 111 - 139 89 - 111 67 - 89	A 128 - 160 103 - 128 77 - 103
E	I/A 25 - 31 20 - 25 15 - 20	I/A 29 - 36 23 - 29 17 - 23	A 33 - 41 26 - 33 20 - 26	A 38 - 48 30 - 38 23 - 30	A 44 - 55 35 - 44 26 - 35	A 50 - 63 40 - 50 30 - 40
F	I/A 16 - 20 13 - 16 10 - 13	I/A 19 - 23 15 - 19 11 - 15	I/A 21 - 27 17 - 21 13 - 17	A 25 - 31 20 - 25 15 - 20	A 28 - 36 23 - 28 17 - 23	A 33 - 41 26 - 33 20 - 26
G	I/A 13 - 16 10 - 13 8 - 10	I/A 14 - 18 12 - 14 9 - 12	I/A 17 - 21 13 - 17 10 - 13	I/A 19 - 24 15 - 19 11 - 15	A 22 - 27 17 - 22 13 - 17	A 25 - 31 20 - 25 15 - 20
H	C/I/A 6 - 8 5 - 6 4 - 5	I/A 8 - 10 6 - 8 4 - 6	I/A 10 - 12 8 - 10 6 - 8	I/A 11 - 14 9 - 11 7 - 9	I/A 15 - 19 12 - 15 9 - 12	A 20 - 25 16 - 20 12 - 16
I	C 6 - 8 4 - 6 3 - 4	C/I 6 - 8 4 - 6 3 - 4	I 6 - 8 5 - 6 4 - 5	I/A 8 - 10 6 - 8 4 - 6	I/A 9 - 11 7 - 9 5 - 7	I/A 10 - 12 8 - 10 6 - 8

DISPOSITION
Aggravated Range
PRESUMPTIVE RANGE
Mitigated Range

A – Active Punishment I – Intermediate Punishment C – Community Punishment
Numbers shown are in months and represent the range of <u>minimum</u> sentences

So, if Joe is convicted under § 14–32(a), a class C felony, and found to have a criminal history score of 15 (so prior record level of V), the sentencing grid indicates that the minimum sentence the judge can impose must fall in the range of 101–127 months, with associated maximums of 122–153 months.

Finally, North Carolina has lists of mitigating and aggravating factors that the judge can take into consideration. Prior to *Blakely*, the prosecution had to prove aggravators to the judge, and the defendant had to prove mitigators, both by a preponderance. Since *Blakely*, the burden remains unchanged for mitigators, but now the prosecutor must prove aggravators to a jury beyond a reasonable doubt (unless the defendant waives his jury rights for a bench trial, in which case the judge can find beyond a reasonable doubt). If the judge thinks aggravators outweigh mitigators, he *may* sentence in the "aggravated" range, and likewise in the "mitigated" if he thinks mitigators dominate. He cannot depart from the presumptive range without such findings, but need not depart when it is possible to do so. A fact cannot count as an aggravator if it is an element of the crime in question.

The aggravators and mitigators (which we also saw in Chapter 5) are given here:

NCGS § 15A–1340.16(d): Aggravating Factors

1. The defendant induced others to participate in the commission of the offense or occupied a position of leadership or dominance of other participants.

2. The defendant joined with more than one other person in committing the offense and was not charged with committing a conspiracy.

2a. The offense was committed for the benefit of, or at the direction of, any criminal street gang, with the specific intent to promote, further, or assist in any criminal conduct by gang members, and the defendant was not charged with committing a conspiracy. A "criminal street gang" means any ongoing organization, association, or group of three or more persons, whether formal or informal, having as one of its primary activities the commission of felony or violent misdemeanor offenses, or delinquent acts that would be felonies or violent misdemeanors if committed by an adult, and having a common name or common identifying sign, colors, or symbols.

3. The offense was committed for the purpose of avoiding or preventing a lawful arrest or effecting an escape from custody.

4. The defendant was hired or paid to commit the offense.

5. The offense was committed to disrupt or hinder the lawful exercise of any governmental function or the enforcement of laws.

6. The offense was committed against or proximately caused serious injury to a present or former law enforcement officer, employee of the Division of Adult Correction of the Department of Public Safety, jailer, fireman, emergency medical technician, ambulance attendant, social worker, justice or judge, clerk or assistant or deputy clerk of court, magistrate, prosecutor, juror, or witness against the defendant, while engaged in the performance of that person's official duties or because of the exercise of that person's official duties.

6a. The offense was committed against or proximately caused serious harm . . . or death to a law enforcement agency animal, an assistance animal, or a search and rescue animal . . . , while engaged in the performance of the animal's official duties.

7. The offense was especially heinous, atrocious, or cruel.

8. The defendant knowingly created a great risk of death to more than one person by means of a weapon or device which would normally be hazardous to the lives of more than one person.

9. The defendant held public elected or appointed office or public employment at the time of the offense and the offense directly related to the conduct of the office or employment.

9a. The defendant is a firefighter or rescue squad worker, and the offense is directly related to service as a firefighter or rescue squad worker.

10. The defendant was armed with or used a deadly weapon at the time of the crime.

11. The victim was very young, or very old, or mentally or physically infirm, or handicapped.

12. The defendant committed the offense while on pretrial release on another charge.

12a. The defendant has, during the 10-year period prior to the commission of the offense for which the defendant is being sentenced, been found by a court of this State to be in willful violation of the conditions of probation imposed pursuant to a suspended sentence or been found by the Post-Release Supervision and Parole Commission to be in willful violation of a condition of parole or post-release supervision imposed pursuant to release from incarceration.

13. The defendant involved a person under the age of 16 in the commission of the crime.

14. The offense involved an attempted or actual taking of property of great monetary value or damage causing great monetary loss, or the offense involved an unusually large quantity of contraband.

15. The defendant took advantage of a position of trust or confidence, including a domestic relationship, to commit the offense.

16. The offense involved the sale or delivery of a controlled substance to a minor.

16a. The offense is the manufacture of methamphetamine and was committed where a person under the age of 18 lives, was present, or was otherwise endangered by exposure to the drug, its ingredients, its by-products, or its waste.

16b. The offense is the manufacture of methamphetamine and was committed in a dwelling that is one of four or more contiguous dwellings.

17. The offense for which the defendant stands convicted was committed against a victim because of the victim's race, color, religion, nationality, or country of origin.

18. The defendant does not support the defendant's family.

18a. The defendant has previously been adjudicated delinquent for an offense that would be a Class A, B1, B2, C, D, or E felony if committed by an adult.

19. The serious injury inflicted upon the victim is permanent and debilitating.

19a. The offense is a violation of G.S. 14–43.11 (human trafficking), G.S. 14–43.12 (involuntary servitude), or G.S. 14–43.13 (sexual servitude) and involved multiple victims.

19b. The offense is a violation of G.S. 14–43.11 (human trafficking), G.S. 14–43.12 (involuntary servitude), or G.S. 14–43.13 (sexual servitude), and the victim suffered serious injury as a result of the offense.

20. Any other aggravating factor reasonably related to the purposes of sentencing.

NCGS § 15A–1340.16(e): Mitigating Factors

1. The defendant committed the offense under duress, coercion, threat, or compulsion that was insufficient to constitute a defense but significantly reduced the defendant's culpability.

2. The defendant was a passive participant or played a minor role in the commission of the offense.

3. The defendant was suffering from a mental or physical condition that was insufficient to constitute a defense but significantly reduced the defendant's culpability for the offense.

4. The defendant's age, immaturity, or limited mental capacity at the time of commission of the offense significantly reduced the defendant's culpability for the offense.

5. The defendant has made substantial or full restitution to the victim.

6. The victim was more than 16 years of age and was a voluntary participant in the defendant's conduct or consented to it.

7. The defendant aided in the apprehension of another felon or testified truthfully on behalf of the prosecution in another prosecution of a felony.

8. The defendant acted under strong provocation, or the relationship between the defendant and the victim was otherwise extenuating.

9. The defendant could not reasonably foresee that the defendant's conduct would cause or threaten serious bodily harm or fear, or the defendant exercised caution to avoid such consequences.

10. The defendant reasonably believed that the defendant's conduct was legal.

11. Prior to arrest or at an early stage of the criminal process, the defendant voluntarily acknowledged wrongdoing in connection with the offense to a law enforcement officer.

12. The defendant has been a person of good character or has had a good reputation in the community in which the defendant lives.

13. The defendant is a minor and has reliable supervision available.

14. The defendant has been honorably discharged from the Armed Forces of the United States.

15. The defendant has accepted responsibility for the defendant's criminal conduct.

16. The defendant has entered and is currently involved in or has successfully completed a drug treatment program or an alcohol treatment program subsequent to arrest and prior to trial.

17. The defendant supports the defendant's family.

18. The defendant has a support system in the community.

19. The defendant has a positive employment history or is gainfully employed.

20. The defendant has a good treatment prognosis, and a workable treatment plan is available.

21. Any other mitigating factor reasonably related to the purposes of sentences.

QUESTIONS

1. **The range.** What is the lowest minimum sentence that Joe could receive? What is the highest?

2. **Prosecutorial power.** How much control does the prosecutor have over what the sentence should be? How important is the choice of charge? the choice of aggravators? the choice of prior offenses to invoke?

3. **Consistency.** Guidelines are thought to improve consistency by helping make sure that "similar" defendants—defined as those charged with similar crimes and with similar prior histories—are sentenced more similarly. Does anything in the above example make you concerned about whether this is a fair measure of "consistency"?

4. **Multiple pathways.** Are there different ways to achieve basically the same sentence (i.e., the default range for crime X is similar to the aggravated range from crime Y, and Joe can plausibly be sentenced in the aggravated range)? Is this satisfying?

Now consider the situation if the story of Joe above took place in New York State. First, consider the possible charges a prosecutor could bring:

§ 120.00: Assault in the third degree.

A person is guilty of assault in the third degree when:

1. With intent to cause physical injury to another person, he causes such injury to such person or to a third person; or
2. He recklessly causes physical injury to another person. . . .

Assault in the third degree is a class A misdemeanor.

§ 120.05: Assault in the second degree.

A person is guilty of assault in the second degree when:

1. With intent to cause serious physical injury to another person, he causes such injury to such person or to a third person; or
2. With intent to cause physical injury to another person, he causes such injury to such person or to a third person by means of a deadly weapon or a dangerous instrument; or
3. With intent to prevent a . . . a police officer . . . from performing a lawful duty, . . . he or she causes physical injury to such . . . police officer . . . ; or
4. He recklessly causes serious physical injury to another person by means of a deadly weapon or a dangerous instrument. . . .

Assault in the second degree is a class D felony.

§ 120.08: Assault on a peace officer, police officer, fireman or emergency medical services professional.

> A person is guilty of assault on a . . . police officer . . . when, with intent to prevent a . . . police officer . . . from performing a lawful duty, he causes serious physical injury to such . . . police officer. . . .
>
> Assault on a peace officer, police officer, fireman or emergency medical services professional is a class C felony.

§ 120.10: Assault in the first degree.

A person is guilty of assault in the first degree when:

1. With intent to cause serious physical injury to another person, he causes such injury to such person or to a third person by means of a deadly weapon or a dangerous instrument; or
3. Under circumstances evincing a depraved indifference to human life, he recklessly engages in conduct which creates a grave risk of death to another person, and thereby causes serious physical injury to another person. . . .

Assault in the first degree is a class B felony.

§ 120.11: Aggravated assault upon a police officer or a peace officer.

> A person is guilty of aggravated assault upon a police officer . . . when, with intent to cause serious physical injury to a person whom he knows or reasonably should know to be a police officer . . . engaged in the course of performing his official duties, he causes such injury by means of a deadly weapon or dangerous instrument.

Aggravated assault upon a police officer or a peace officer is a class B felony.

§ 120.20: Reckless endangerment in the second degree.

A person is guilty of reckless endangerment in the second degree when he recklessly engages in conduct which creates a substantial risk of serious physical injury to another person.

Reckless endangerment in the second degree is a class A misdemeanor.

§ 120.25: Reckless endangerment in the first degree.

A person is guilty of reckless endangerment in the first degree when, under circumstances evincing a depraved indifference to human life, he recklessly engages in conduct which creates a grave risk of death to another person.

Reckless endangerment in the first degree is a class D felony.

In New York, the maximum sentence for a Class B felony must fall between three and twenty-five years, for a Class C felony between three and fifteen years, and for a Class D felony between three and seven years. The minimum for all three felony classes must be at least one year and no more than one-third the maximum imposed. Thus a judge could give a defendant convicted of a Class B felony a minimum/maximum of 8-1/3 to twenty-five years (the harshest sentence) to one to three years (the most lenient sentence). For class D felonies, if a judge thinks a wide range would be unfair to the defendant he is allowed to impose a single, fixed determinate sentence.

New York is not a guideline state, so prior history is not as rigorously incorporated into sentencing, except that it does have a persistent offender statute (§ 70.10), the relevant part of which states:

When the court has found . . . that a person is a persistent felony offender [i.e., two or more prior felony convictions], and when it is of the opinion that the history and character of the defendant and the nature and circumstances of his criminal conduct indicate that extended incarceration and life-time supervision will best serve the public interest, the court, in lieu of imposing [the default sentence] for the crime of which such person presently stands convicted, may impose the sentence of imprisonment authorized . . . for a class A-I felony [maximum of life, minimum of fifteen to twenty-five years]. In such event the reasons for the court's opinion shall be set forth in the record.

Joe has a sufficient number of prior felonies to trigger § 70.10; assume that his "history and character" are sufficiently inconsistent that whether the persistent offender statute should apply is an open question of fact for the prosecutor to argue and the judge to decide.

QUESTIONS

1. **Ranges.** What is the range of sentencing outcomes that Joe can face in New York? How does the scope of the range compare to that in North Carolina?

2. **Institutional power.** How does the power of the New York prosecutor compare to that of his North Carolina counterpart? And likewise for the judge? Consider all the various margins: choice of original charge, choice of how to use prior history, choice of how to invoke mitigating and aggravating factors.

3. **Allocation of power.** Which system's allocation seems more appealing to you? Why? Does your theory of punishment matter? Your views on institutional competence?

State vs. Federal Sentencing Guidelines

So far we have just looked at state guideline regimes, even though one of the earliest adopters of guidelines was the federal government. The federal guidelines, however, look nothing like state guidelines. For all the differences among state sentencing guidelines, any one state guideline system is more similar to that of any other state than any state guideline system is to that in the federal system. The US Sentencing Guidelines are truly an outlier. And this is not a compliment: after 1984, when the federal guidelines went into effect, some states interested in adopting guidelines found it politically expedient to not use the phrase "guidelines" lest the project be tainted by comparison to the federal version.

The North Carolina sentencing grid is fairly indicative of the sort of post-conviction adjustments that take place in state sentencing: the offense and prior history define the relevant "box," and the judge can generally move up or down by one box (or, in North Carolina, up or down *within* a box). Such is not the case in the federal system. Aggravators and mitigators are not qualitative factors to be weighed, but are instead assigned specific "points" that a judge uses to compute a seemingly precise "offense level." Consider the following (partial) example:

§ 2B1.1: Larceny, Embezzlement, and Other Forms of Theft; Offenses Involving Stolen Property; Property Damage or Destruction; Fraud and Deceit; Forgery; Offenses Involving Altered or Counterfeit Instruments Other than Counterfeit Bearer Obligation of the United States

a. Base Offense Level:
   1. 7, if (A) the defendant was convicted of an offense referenced to this guideline; and (B) that offense of conviction has a statutory maximum term of imprisonment of 20 years or more; or

2. 6, otherwise
b. Specific Offense Characteristics
    1. If the loss exceeded $5,000, increase the offense level as follows:

	Loss (Apply the Greatest)	Increase in Level
a.	$5,000 or less	no increase
b.	More than $5,000	add 2
c.	More than $10,000	add 4
d.	More than $30,000	add 6
e.	More than $70,000	add 8
f.	More than $120,000	add 10
g.	More than $200,000	add 12
h.	More than $400,000	add 14
i.	More than $1,000,000	add 16
j.	More than $2,500,000	add 18
k.	More than $7,000,000	add 20
l.	More than $20,000,000	add 22
m.	More than $50,000,000	add 24
n.	More than $100,000,000	add 26
o.	More than $200,000,000	add 28
p.	More than $400,000,000	add 30.

    5. If the offense involved theft of, damage to, destruction of, or trafficking in, property from a national cemetery or veterans' memorial, increase by 2 levels.
    8. (Apply the greater) If—
        a. the offense involved conduct described in 18 U.S.C. § 670 [theft of medical supplies], increase by 2 levels; or
        b. the offense involved conduct described in 18 U.S.C. § 670, and the defendant was employed by, or was an agent of, an organization in the supply chain for the pre-retail medical product, increase by 4 levels.
    10. If (A) the defendant relocated, or participated in relocating, a fraudulent scheme to another jurisdiction to evade law

enforcement or regulatory officials; (B) a substantial part of a fraudulent scheme was committed from outside the United States; or (C) the offense otherwise involved sophisticated means, increase by 2 levels. If the resulting offense level is less than level 12, increase to level 12.

12. If the offense involved conduct described in 18 U.S.C. § 1040 [fraud involving major disaster or emergency benefits], increase by 2 levels. If the resulting offense level is less than level 12, increase to level 12.

14. If the offense involved an organized scheme to steal or to receive stolen (A) vehicles or vehicle parts; or (B) goods or chattels that are part of a cargo shipment, increase by 2 levels. If the resulting offense level is less than level 14, increase to level 14.

15. If the offense involved (A) the conscious or reckless risk of death or serious bodily injury; or (B) possession of a dangerous weapon (including a firearm) in connection with the offense, increase by 2 levels. If the resulting offense level is less than level 14, increase to level 14.

16. (Apply the greater) If—

    a. the defendant derived more than $1,000,000 in gross receipts from one or more financial institutions as a result of the offense, increase by 2 levels; or

    b. the offense (i) substantially jeopardized the safety and soundness of a financial institution; (ii) substantially endangered the solvency or financial security of an organization that, at any time during the offense, (I) was a publicly traded company; or (II) had 1,000 or more employees; or (iii) substantially endangered the solvency or financial security of 100 or more victims, increase by 4 levels.

    c. The cumulative adjustments from application of both subsections (b)(2) and (b)(16)(B) shall not exceed 8 levels, except as provided in subdivision (D).

    d. If the resulting offense level determined under subdivision (A) or (B) is less than level 24, increase to level 24.

19. If the offense involved—

    a. a violation of securities law and, at the time of the offense, the defendant was (i) an officer or a director of a publicly traded company; (ii) a registered broker or dealer, or a person associated with a broker or dealer;

or (iii) an investment adviser, or a person associated with an investment adviser; or

b. a violation of commodities law and, at the time of the offense, the defendant was (i) an officer or a director of a futures commission merchant or an introducing broker; (ii) a commodities trading advisor; or (iii) a commodity pool operator, increase by 4 levels.

The federal sentencing grid is reproduced below. Compare the ranges available to federal judges to those in North Carolina. Note that unlike in North Carolina, the federal system is a determinate system: the judge will pick a number in the range, and that is the defendant's exact sentence (with the possibility of up to 15% time off for good behavior, but otherwise there are no minimums or maximums, just "the sentence").

SENTENCING TABLE
(in months of imprisonment)

Zone	Offense Level	I (0 or 1)	II (2 or 3)	III (4, 5, 6)	IV (7, 8, 9)	V (10, 11, 12)	VI (13 or more)
Zone A	1	0-6	0-6	0-6	0-6	0-6	0-6
	2	0-6	0-6	0-6	0-6	0-6	1-7
	3	0-6	0-6	0-6	0-6	2-8	3-9
	4	0-6	0-6	0-6	2-8	4-10	6-12
	5	0-6	0-6	1-7	4-10	6-12	9-15
	6	0-6	1-7	2-8	6-12	9-15	12-18
	7	0-6	2-8	4-10	8-14	12-18	15-21
	8	0-6	4-10	6-12	10-16	15-21	18-24
Zone B	9	4-10	6-12	8-14	12-18	18-24	21-27
	10	6-12	8-14	10-16	15-21	21-27	24-30
Zone C	11	8-14	10-16	12-18	18-24	24-30	27-33
	12	10-16	12-18	15-21	21-27	27-33	30-37
Zone D	13	12-18	15-21	18-24	24-30	30-37	33-41
	14	15-21	18-24	21-27	27-33	33-41	37-46
	15	18-24	21-27	24-30	30-37	37-46	41-51
	16	21-27	24-30	27-33	33-41	41-51	46-57
	17	24-30	27-33	30-37	37-46	46-57	51-63
	18	27-33	30-37	33-41	41-51	51-63	57-71
	19	30-37	33-41	37-46	46-57	57-71	63-78
	20	33-41	37-46	41-51	51-63	63-78	70-87
	21	37-46	41-51	46-57	57-71	70-87	77-96
	22	41-51	46-57	51-63	63-78	77-96	84-105
	23	46-57	51-63	57-71	70-87	84-105	92-115
	24	51-63	57-71	63-78	77-96	92-115	100-125
	25	57-71	63-78	70-87	84-105	100-125	110-137
	26	63-78	70-87	78-97	92-115	110-137	120-150
	27	70-87	78-97	87-108	100-125	120-150	130-162
	28	78-97	87-108	97-121	110-137	130-162	140-175
	29	87-108	97-121	108-135	121-151	140-175	151-188
	30	97-121	108-135	121-151	135-168	151-188	168-210
	31	108-135	121-151	135-168	151-188	168-210	188-235
	32	121-151	135-168	151-188	168-210	188-235	210-262
	33	135-168	151-188	168-210	188-235	210-262	235-293
	34	151-188	168-210	188-235	210-262	235-293	262-327
	35	168-210	188-235	210-262	235-293	262-327	292-365
	36	188-235	210-262	235-293	262-327	292-365	324-405
	37	210-262	235-293	262-327	292-365	324-405	360-life
	38	235-293	262-327	292-365	324-405	360-life	360-life
	39	262-327	292-365	324-405	360-life	360-life	360-life
	40	292-365	324-405	360-life	360-life	360-life	360-life
	41	324-405	360-life	360-life	360-life	360-life	360-life
	42	360-life	360-life	360-life	360-life	360-life	360-life
	43	life	life	life	life	life	life

QUESTIONS

1. **Ephemeral precision.** How ephemeral is the precision here? Note that someone who steals more than $400 *million* faces the same sentencing range as someone who steals half that but steals medical supplies, or as someone who steals one-fourth that amount but was an officer in a financial firm. Are these are equal degrees of offending?

2. **Theories of punishment.** Can you determine what theory of punishment, if any, the guidelines are attempting to advance? If no clear theory is apparent, how normatively appealing is it that judges generally sentenced within the presumptive range?

3. **Moving around the grid.** A two-point increase means different things at different offense levels (keeping criminal history scores the same), and different things at different criminal history scores (keeping offense levels the same). Does a rational pattern emerge?

The goal of the federal approach is to eliminate as much discretion as possible: ranges are narrow, and the guidelines dictate the exact implication of any aggravating or mitigating factor, with the substantive offense defining the starting offense level. The result is a sentencing regime that can be incredibly complex to operate. North Carolina's list of aggravators and mitigators is quite representative of what guideline states use. The federal system, however, requires a three-volume set of books of factors and points that runs for hundreds of pages—with all sorts of attendant caselaw interpreting it as well.

A clear example of the complexity can be seen in *United States v. Medas*, 323 F.Supp.2d 436 (E.D.N.Y. 2004). In the immediate post-*Blakely* confusion, US Attorneys were unclear what guideline factors had to be proven to a jury, so the AUSAs in *Medas* submitted a special verdict form to the jury to get it to find all the various sentencing factors, just to be safe. Here are a few examples of the questions asked:

F.

Do you find that the government proved, beyond a reasonable doubt, that the defendant engaged in narcotics-related offenses as part of the same course of conduct as the conspiracy to import charged in Count One of the indictment?

   Yes

   No

G.   ANSWER ONLY IF ANSWER TO F IS YES:

Which of the following substances, if any, do you find that the government *439 proved, beyond a reasonable doubt, were the subject of narcotics-related offenses engaged in by the defendant as part of the same course of conduct as the conspiracy to import charged in Count One of the indictment?

   ___Cocaine

   ___Marijuana

H.   ANSWER ONLY IF RESPONSE TO G INCLUDES COCAINE

Which of the following quantities, if any, do you find that the government proved, beyond a reasonable doubt, were the subject of narcotics-related offenses engaged in by the defendant as part of the same course of conduct as the conspiracy to import charged in Count One of the indictment?

   — 150 kilograms or more of cocaine

   — at least 50 kilograms but less than 150 kilograms of cocaine

   — at least 15 kilogram but less than 50 kilograms of cocaine

   — at least 5 kilograms but less than 15 kilograms of cocaine

— at least 3.5 kilograms but less than 5 kilograms of cocaine

— at least 2 kilograms but less than 3.5 kilograms of cocaine

— at least 500 grams but less than 2 kilograms of cocaine

— at least 400 grams but less than 500 grams of cocaine

— at least 300 grams but less than 400 grams of cocaine

— at least 200 grams but less than 300 grams of cocaine

— at least 100 grams but less than 200 grams of cocaine

— at least 50 grams but less than 100 grams of cocaine

— at least 25 grams but less than 50 grams of cocaine

— less than 25 grams of cocaine

A. Do you find that the government proved, beyond a reasonable doubt, that the defendant was an organizer *440 or leader in the importation charged in Count Two of the indictment and that the importation charged in Count Two of the indictment involved five or more participants or was otherwise extensive?

Yes

No

B. ANSWER ONLY IF ANSWER TO A IS NO:

If your answer to question A is no, do you find that the government proved, beyond a reasonable doubt, that the defendant was a manager or supervisor (but not an organizer or leader) of the importation charged in Count Two of the indictment and that the importation charged in Count Two of the indictment involved five or more participants or was otherwise extensive?

Yes

No

C. ANSWER ONLY IF ANSWER TO A AND B ARE NO:

If your answer to questions A and B are no, do you find that the government proved, beyond a reasonable doubt, that the defendant was an organizer, leader, manager, or supervisor of the importation charged in Count Two of the indictment and that the importation involved fewer than 5 participants?

Yes

No

These questions—which, again, were focused just on the post-conviction aggravators and mitigators—ran on for *twenty pages*. Something like this is simply inconceivable at the state level. No state prior to 1984 had a system so complex and, tellingly, no state since that has adopted guidelines has developed anything akin to the federal system.

Perhaps the most controversial aspect of the federal sentencing guidelines is their reliance on what is called "real offense sentencing." Real offense sentencing encourages or requires judges to consider evidence outside that proven at trial when setting sentences—perhaps even evidence about conduct for which the defendant was never charged, or even acquitted. Not surprisingly, it is a fairly controversial approach, and while the entire federal sentencing regime is[13] built around real offense sentencing, state guideline systems have universally rejected it, at least in the extreme form used by the federal guidelines.

David Yellen, *Reforming the Federal Sentencing Guidelines' Misguided Approach to Real-Offense Sentencing*
58 STAN. L. REV. 267 (2005)

Introduction

All sentencing systems make use of information beyond the elements of the offense of conviction. This practice, known generally as "real-offense sentencing," is necessary because of the complexity and variety of criminal behavior and the need to keep criminal statutes relatively simple. Two defendants convicted of violating the same statute may be very different in terms of amount of harm caused, levels of personal culpability, and degrees of dangerousness to the community.

One of the enduring challenges in sentencing policymaking is the need to identify the appropriate structure and scope of real-offense sentencing. What facts beyond the elements of the offense of conviction should have an impact on the defendant's sentence? Should consideration of such additional facts be systematized or left to the discretion of individual judges? Should certain types of information be excluded from sentencing decisionmaking, even if they are logically relevant? What process and burden of proof should apply to such fact-finding?

The United States Sentencing Commission adopted a radical policy that requires judges to consider, in a mechanistic way, a great deal of real-offense sentencing information. This policy helped make the Federal Sentencing Guidelines overly rigid and complex. . . .

I. What Is Real-Offense Sentencing?

Real-offense sentencing is easier to discuss than to define. In some ways, it is easier to identify what real-offense sentencing is not. It is not its polar opposite: charge-offense sentencing. Pure charge-offense sentencing involves setting a sentence or sentencing range based entirely on the statute of conviction. The consideration of any facts beyond the elements of the offense introduces "real-offense" elements. I will use the term in this broad sense: real-offense sentencing is the use in sentencing of any facts beyond those necessarily found by a jury in reaching a guilty verdict or admitted by a defendant as part of a guilty plea. Real-offense

---

[13] As we will see below, real offense sentencing survives *Blakely* and *Booker*, albeit in a slightly different form.

sentencing information can concern the offense or the offender. It can relate to the harm caused by the offense, the defendant's culpability, or background information about the offender.

The principal reason generally cited for employing real-offense sentencing information is that the facts necessary for conviction are generally quite limited. Even in jurisdictions with well-developed criminal codes, criminal statutes tend to be broad in scope. Two defendants convicted of violating the same criminal statute may present vastly different situations [whether one's focus on in retribution, deterrence, incapacitation, or rehabilitation, although what "real offense" information is most relevant will vary based on which of these goals the sentencer is seeking to advance].

When jurisdictions [adopt] . . . structured-sentencing systems, such as sentencing guidelines, they must confront . . . questions about real-offense sentencing head on. How should sentencing guidelines take account of facts beyond the offense of conviction? There are at least three possible approaches. First, drafters of sentencing guidelines could determine that some facts beyond the offense of conviction are important enough to be incorporated into the calculation of the applicable sentencing range. Second, the guidelines range could be determined largely or entirely based on the offense of conviction, but within the exercise of her discretion in choosing a particular sentence within the authorized range, a judge could be permitted to rely on real-offense factors. Third, judges could be authorized to deviate or depart from the applicable guidelines range based on real-offense factors determined at sentencing. Aspects of each of these approaches are apparent in sentencing guidelines systems in place today across the country.

[S]tructured-sentencing systems [also] raise particular issues regarding plea bargaining and prosecutorial influence on sentences. In a system of judicial discretion, the charges brought against a defendant determine the statutory maximum but otherwise have limited impact on the sentence imposed. Linking the sentence imposed more closely to the offense of conviction, as all sentencing guidelines systems do, increases the prosecutor's influence on sentences because prosecutors have broad authority to select or reject the charges that might be brought against the offender. In theory, then, a charge-based guidelines system shifts a great deal of sentencing authority to prosecutors. Sentencing commissions have considered whether it is possible and appropriate to counter this enhanced prosecutorial influence by utilizing some version of real-offense sentencing. As will be seen in the next Parts, the states and the federal system have diverged greatly on this key point.

A. State Guidelines Systems

State sentencing guidelines emphasize simplicity and do not attempt to incorporate much real-offense sentencing into their structures. Every state sentencing guidelines system, whether presumptive or advisory, determines the applicable guidelines range largely based on the offense of conviction.

This charge-offense approach does not mean that real-offense sentencing factors beyond criminal history play no role under state guidelines systems. Most guidelines result in a range of permissible sentences, within which the judge has broad discretion. Here, as in the traditional system, a judge can rely on virtually any factor she deems relevant. There may or may not be a requirement that the judge explain the choice of a particular sentence. In addition, most guidelines systems allow judges to depart from the guidelines in unusual cases. These departures are based on real-offense elements determined at sentencing.* On the whole, though, it is fair to say that state guidelines systems are largely charge-based and make only modest use of real-offense sentencing.

B. Federal Sentencing Guidelines

The Federal Sentencing Guidelines are dramatically different than all state systems. The U.S. Sentencing Commission adopted a model that incorporates far more real-offense elements than any other structured-sentencing system ever has. For example, each offense Guideline contains numerous "specific-offense characteristics," such as the amount of loss or drug quantity involved in an offense, or the possession or use of a dangerous weapon. In addition, "adjustments" that are applicable to all offenses include the defendant's role in the offense, the criminal's selection of particularly vulnerable victims, and behavior constituting obstruction of justice.

Most dramatically, for major categories of offenses such as fraud and narcotics, the Guidelines call for sentences to be based not just on offenses for which the defendant has been convicted but also on "alleged related" offenses, committed in the same course of conduct or as part of a common scheme or plan. In other words, if the judge concludes, by a preponderance of the evidence,* that the defendant committed other related offenses, those other offenses are included in the Guidelines calculation. This determination is true if those related offenses were never charged, if the charges were dropped as part of a plea agreement, or even if the defendant was acquitted of that conduct. Although judges in discretionary systems can take other alleged offenses into account, the federal approach is truly radical. The Federal Guidelines are a mandatory system; a judge applying the Guidelines must base the sentence on alleged related offenses. Further, the Guidelines consider

---

* *Ed. note*: These are the aggravators and mitigators, such as those given in North Carolina above. Here Yellen makes a slight error: *all* state guideline systems (not most) allow judges to depart from the default sentence if they find sufficient aggravating or mitigating factors.

* *Ed. note*: Yellen is somewhat unclear here. *Prior* to *Booker*, the standard was preponderance. As we will see, post-*Booker* the guidelines are at least nominally voluntary, so the standard is lower.

alleged related offenses just as much as charges that have resulted in conviction.

It is hard to understate the extent to which the federal guidelines allowed judges to look beyond the conviction offense. A striking example is *United States v. Vernier*, 152 Fed. Appx. 827 (11th Cir. 2005). Jonathan Lee Vernier pled guilty to the unauthorized use of a credit card and to transporting over $5,000 in stolen goods after he was arrested for stealing a van containing over $100,000 in jewelry and obtaining numerous cash advances on the driver's credit card. As a result of his prior criminal history and a few other aggravating factors from the crime itself (such as assaulting police officers during his arrest), he faced a presumptive sentence of 51 to 63 months in prison.

But there was one more issue at play. The government believed not only that Vernier stole from the driver, but that he killed him as well. Blood that matched the driver's DNA was found splattered all over the van, and the driver's DNA was found on a tire iron and camera tripod. The government, however, never charged Vernier with murder, something it would have had to prove beyond a reasonable doubt. Instead, it introduced the murder as an aggravating factor at sentencing, which (since this was a pre-*Blakely* case) would require it to only prove it by a preponderance. The judge ultimately imposed a 210-month sentence: clearly about 150 months of that sentence—12.5 *years*—was for the uncharged murder. The 11th Circuit ultimately upheld the sentence.

As Yellen notes, some state aggravators and mitigators do take on a "real offense" vibe, like "the offense was particularly cruel" or "involved the use of a firearm." But no state relies on real offense sentencing nearly to the extent that the federal system does, and several states have gone so far as to ban the use of conduct that would otherwise constitute a separate crime.[14]

Question: Look at the list of aggravators and mitigators for North Carolina above. Which ones, particularly among the aggravators, seem most like "real offense" elements? Are there ones that seem less so—and if so why? Does this tell us anything about the sort of real offense elements that bother us the most?

Note, though, that while the federal guidelines are almost universally disliked by academics and policymakers alike, even the federal system is not the most real-offense-like system out there. The most real-offense regime there is is an indeterminate one. Under indeterminacy, judges can consider *anything*, no matter how flimsy, and need explain *nothing*. Even the federal guidelines provided more limitations than this, restricting judges to a list of relevant sentencing

---

[14] See, e.g., Wash. Code § 9.94A.530(3).

factors, requiring them to find these factors by a preponderance, and to explain themselves. Yet a majority of states still use indeterminate regimes. This suggests that the concern with real offense sentencing is something more complex than just the fact that judges are considering offense-like traits after conviction.

> **Question:** How significant do you think it was that pre-*Blakely* the federal guidelines—again, unique among all guidelines—were *mandatory*, not *presumptive*? In other words, if the prosecution proved that a certain two-point increase applied, the judge was *compelled* to increase the defendant's offense score by two. Conversely, in the states, the judge could not aggravate unless the state proved that enough aggravators existed, but even if they did the judge did not *need* to aggravate.

The Impact of Sentencing Guidelines

States adopted sentencing guidelines for various reasons: in the 1980s the focus was on minimizing the importance of impermissible factors such as race or on pushing back against perceived judicial lenience. As we moved into the 1990s and 2000s, and as prison populations continued their unrelenting upsurge (from 300,000 in 1980 to 700,000 in 1990 to 1.3 million in 2000), states became increasingly concerned about resource management and began to view guidelines as a means to rein in costs. It is thus worth asking two questions: to what extent did guidelines reduce judicial reliance on "impermissible" factors such as race and sex; and to what extent were they able to manage resource use?

Unfortunately, most research on guidelines and their race-sex effects have focused on the federal guidelines. That which has focused on state guidelines has generally indicated that guidelines have reduced the impact of race and, at least in some contexts (depending perhaps in no small part on how much discretion the guidelines left in judges' hands) gender as well. But these results may be too optimistic, as Shawn Bushway and Anne Morrison Piehl explain:

> [Several current studies study race-based disparities by] focus[ing] not on the total amount of variation in the sentence length but rather on the variation from the recommendation of the guidelines and the end result—the length of the sentence. As judges in guideline systems start where the guideline recommendations end, this proposed approach can reasonably claim to focus on the actions at the "judging" stage (whether the resolution takes place in the courtroom or through a plea bargain).
>
> Studies of four jurisdictions using this type of empirical model have found little evidence of racial disparity on the part of judges in strict guideline systems . . . but evidence of substantial disparity in the voluntary guideline systems. These results are

largely consistent with the general claim that presumptive sentencing guidelines reduce judicial discretion and racial disparity.

But this conclusion presumes there is only one interesting stage in the sentencing process. The theory of hydraulic displacement of discretion proposes that legislatively-imposed requirements, such as guidelines and mandatory minimums, displace discretion to the prosecutor in the charging stage. Given that guidelines do not attempt to constrain prosecutorial discretion, perhaps it is no surprise that guideline data are not particularly useful at facilitating the study of prosecutorial discretion.[15]

Bushway and Piehl then provide data from Washington State suggesting that prosecutors take race into account when making charging decisions. Thus, at some level, judges "launder" racially biased charging decisions by imposing sentences that are race-blind *conditional on the charge*.

When it comes to resource management, there is even less to say. Measuring the impact of guidelines on prison size is difficult because guidelines were adopted for various reasons—some to increase punitiveness, others to rein in prison use—but empirical models of prison growth generally just define a state as "guideline" or "non-guideline" state, without any deeper examination into *why* a guideline state adopted them. So a finding that guidelines lead to larger populations on average does not necessarily mean that guidelines failed to reduce prison populations (or mitigated the rate of growth) in states that wanted that outcome, only that the impact of states with different, more punitive goals, dominated the statistical results. Sadly, like with race-sex analysis, most empirical work on guidelines has focused on the federal system (where the data is vastly better), despite the idiosyncratic nature of the federal guidelines.

QUESTIONS

1. **Fiscal impact and crime.** One empirical study argued that states with presumptive guidelines invalidated by *Blakely* saw a drop in crime, suggesting that guidelines reined in punishment. The author referred to this as *Blakely*'s "silver lining," claiming that states with guidelines were somehow saved from the harmful effects of their own guidelines.[16] Assume the observed effect is valid and causal: adopting guidelines causes crime to rise (at least on the margin). Does this mean that guidelines are net social losses?

2. **Real offense sentencing vs. indeterminacy.** In the end, *is* there any difference between real offense sentencing and indeterminacy?

---

[15] Shawn D. Bushway & Anne Morrison Piehl, *Social Science Research and the Legal Threat to Presumptive Sentencing Guidelines*, 6 CRIMINOLOGY & PUB. POL'Y 461, 464–65 (2007).

[16] Joanna Shepherd, Blakely's *Silver Lining: Sentencing Guidelines, Judicial Discretion, and Crime*, 58 HASTINGS L. J. 553 (2006).

3. **Real offense sentencing and prosecutorial power.** The ironic history of real offense sentencing is that it was intended to *reduce* the power of the prosecutor to protect against the very concern about biased charging decisions noted by Bushway and Piehl above, by allowing judges to consider all the various aspects of the offense a (biased) prosecutor might have left out, but ultimately transferred tremendous power to the federal prosecutor. How does ROS transfer power to the prosecutor? In the federal system, is it relevant that almost all ROS factors were aggravators, not mitigators?

4. **Guidelines and state size.** The states that adopted guidelines or DSLs tended to be large: 12 of the 15 most populous states adopted one of these approaches, although one (Florida) later repealed its guidelines.[17] Why might larger states be more likely to adopt guidelines than smaller? Some explanations may be immediately apparent, but there may be some more complicated reasons as well.

B.2.b. MANDATORY MINIMUMS

Mandatory minimums are perhaps the most prevalent of structured sentencing rules. The following table, taken from a Bureau of Justice Assistance report on structured sentencing, lists the types of mandatories that states had as of 1994; there is no doubt that the list has grown longer since then.[18] As is immediately clear, every state has some sort of mandatory sentencing policy, and most states impose mandatories on numerous types of offenses.

---

[17] The twelve states with guidelines or DSLs are California, Florida, Illinois, Pennsylvania, Ohio, Michigan, North Carolina, New Jersey, Washington, Arizona, and Indiana. Only Texas, New York, and Massachusetts never had guidelines.

[18] BUREAU OF JUSTICE ASSISTANCE, NATIONAL ASSESSMENT OF STRUCTURED SENTENCING, Table 3–3 (n.d.)

Table 6–1: Mandatory Minimums Across States, 1998

State	Repeat/ Habitual	Drunk Driving	Drugs	Weapons Possession	Sex Offenses	Other
Alabama	•	•	•	•		
Alaska	•		•	•		•
Arizona	•	•	•	•	•	
Arkansas	•		•	•		
California	•		•	•	•	•
Colorado	•	•	•	•	•	•
Connecticut		•	•	•	•	
Delaware	•		•	•		
DC			•	•		•
Florida	•		•	•		
Georgia	•	•	•	•	•	
Hawaii	•			•		•
Idaho	•	•	•	•	•	
Illinois	•	•	•	•	•	•
Indiana	•		•	•		
Iowa	•		•	•		
Kansas		•				
Kentucky	•	•		•	•	
Louisiana	•			•		
Maine		•		•		
Maryland	•		•	•		
Massachusetts		•	•	•		
Michigan	•	•	•	•		
Minnesota	•		•	•		
Mississippi	•		•	•		
Missouri	•		•	•		

State						
Montana	•	•	•	•		
Nebraska	•	•			•	
Nevada	•		•	•		
N. Hampshire	•	•		•	•	
New Jersey	•	•	•	•	•	
New Mexico	•	•		•		
New York	•					
N. Carolina	•	•	•		•	
N. Dakota		•	•	•		
Ohio	•	•		•		
Oklahoma	•			•		
Oregon		•				
Pennsylvania	•	•	•	•	•	•
Rhode Island	•	•	•	•	•	•
S. Carolina	•		•	•		
S. Dakota			•	•		
Tennessee		•				
Texas	•	•		•		
Utah	•				•	
Vermont	•				•	
Virginia		•		•		•
Washington	•				•	•
W. Virginia	•		•	•		
Wisconsin	•	•	•	•	•	•
Wyoming	•					

Despite their widespread use, mandatory minimums are generally disliked by academics and judges, and even by many prosecutors and police officers (who nominally benefit from the increased power they provide). The two major justifications for mandatory minimums are that they reduce disparity in sentencing outcomes and they reduce crime: disparity by, say, preventing a white defendant from getting probation while an otherwise identical black defendant gets prison time, and crime by either providing a clearer signal of the sanction being imposed or by limiting overly-lenient discretion. Yet they appear not to accomplish these goals, and they impose significant direct and indirect costs along the way. The following article by Michael Tonry, a vocal critic of mandatory minimum sentencing laws, lays out some of the problems with such laws.

Michael Tonry, *The Mostly Unintended Consequences of Mandatory Penalties: Two Centuries of Consistent Findings*
38 CRIME & JUSTICE 65, 65–70 (2009)

The greatest gap between knowledge and policy in American sentencing concerns mandatory penalties. Experienced practitioners, policy analysts, and researchers have long agreed that mandatory penalties in all their forms—from 1-year add-ons for gun use in violent crimes in the 1950s and 1960s, through 10-, 20-, and 30-year federal minimums for drug offenses in the 1980s, to three-strikes laws in the 1990s—are a bad idea. That is why the U.S. Congress in 1970, at the urging of Texas Congressman George H. Bush, repealed most of the mandatory minimum sentence provisions then contained in federal law. It is why nearly every authoritative nonpartisan law reform organization that has considered the subject, including the American Law Institute in the Model Penal Code (1962), the American Bar Association in each edition of its Criminal Justice Standards (e.g., 1968, standard 2.3; 1994, standard 18–3.21[b]), the Federal Courts Study Committee (1990), and the U.S. Sentencing Commission (1991) have opposed enactment, and favored repeal, of mandatory penalties. In 2007, the American Law Institute approved a partial second edition of the Model Penal Code that repudiated mandatory penalties. In 2004, an American Bar Association commission headed by conservative Justice Anthony Kennedy of the U.S. Supreme Court called upon states, territories, and the federal government to repeal mandatory minimum sentence statutes. The recommendations were overwhelmingly approved by the ABA House of Delegates.

Policy makers promoting mandatory penalties usually offer three justifications. Mandatory penalties are said to assure evenhandedness: every offender who does the crime will do the time. They are said to be transparent: mandatory penalty laws assure everyone, offenders, practitioners, and the general public alike, that justice will be done and be seen to be done. They are said to prevent crime: the certainty of punishment will deter would-be offenders. The insuperable difficulty with all these claims is that centuries of evidence show them to be untrue.

There is a fourth justification, but it is one that has no place in a society that takes human rights seriously. Enactment of mandatory penalties is sometimes justified in expressive terms, irrespective of their effects. Their enactment is said to acknowledge public anxiety and assuage victims' anger. They are a sign that policy makers are listening, and care, and are prepared to take action. This assumes, however, that offenders' interests in being treated justly and fairly do not warrant consideration. People may sometimes feel that way, but that cannot be a legitimate basis for making policy in a free society. In no other setting would the claim be allowed that harm may properly be done to individuals solely because doing so might give pleasure to other people.

Objections to mandatory penalties are well documented and of long standing. They are not mandatory, whatever the law may say, and they are not transparent. When mandatory penalty laws require imposition of sentences that practitioners believe are too severe, three things happen. Sometimes prosecutors sidestep the laws by not bringing charges subject to them or by agreeing to dismiss them in plea negotiations. Sometimes sentences are imposed that everyone involved believes are unjustly severe. Sometimes judges and prosecutors disingenuously evade their application. Because these things happen, mandatory penalties produce wide disparities between cases that are comparable in every way except how they were handled. And because practitioners often feel they must devise ways to circumvent their application, critical decisions are not made in court openly, transparently, and accountably. Laws ostensibly meant to produce consistent penalties on center stage produce inconsistent ones behind the scenes.

Nor does the evidence show that mandatory penalties provide effective deterrents to crime. From the accounts of pockets being picked at the hangings of pickpockets in eighteenth-century England to the systematic empirical evaluations of the past 30 years, similar conclusions emerge. Mandatory penalty laws have not been credibly shown to have measurable deterrent effects for any save minor crimes such as speeding or illegal parking or for short-term effects that quickly waste away.

Two separate claims are sometimes conflated. One is that mandatory penalty laws prevent crimes by means of their putative certainty of application. Relatively little research has been done on that question. When probabilities of suspicion, arrest, prosecution, and conviction are compounded and the time required to dispose of cases is taken into account, certainty is an unrealistic aim in any case. The second claim, sometimes referred to as the marginal deterrence hypothesis, is that increases to previously applicable penalties will prevent crimes by raising their prospective punitive cost. A few studies by economists have found marginal deterrent effects, but they have been refuted by other economists. Most other social scientists conclude that the hypothesis cannot be confirmed or that occasional findings of deterrent effects in studies of particular policies in particular places have no generalizable policy implications. The clear weight of the evidence is that the marginal deterrence hypothesis cannot be confirmed.

The decent thing to do would be to repeal all existing mandatory penalties and to enact no new ones. If that is politically impracticable, there are ways to avoid or ameliorate the foreseeable dysfunctional effects of mandatory penalties. First, make penalties presumptive rather than mandatory. Second, add "sunset provisions" providing that the laws lapse and become presumptive after 3–5 years, and include such provisions in any new mandatory minimum sentencing laws.

As Tonry mentioned, Justice Kennedy attacked mandatory minimums in a speech to the ABA in 2003, which led to the formation of the ABA's Kennedy Commission, which was charged with proposing ways to reform sentencing in the United States—and represented the first time since the Warren Commission's investigation into the assassination of President John Kennedy that a sitting member of the US Supreme Court allowed his name to be attached to a commission. The Commission touched on many issues, but among them were mandatory minimums. In particular, the Committee had this to say:

> [M]andatory minimum sentences (i.e., sentences which require a court to impose a minimum period of incarceration mandatory sentence regardless of the circumstances of a particular case or the characteristics of an individual defendant) should be avoided, so that sentencing courts may consider the unique characteristics of offenses and offenders that may warrant an increase or decrease in a sentence.
>
> Standard 18–3.21 (b) [of the ABA's Standards for Criminal Justice: Sentencing (3d ed. 1994)] provides that "[a] legislature should not prescribe a minimum term of total confinement for any offense." This means no mandatory minimum sentences. Such sentences would be inconsistent with the notion of individualizing sentences within a guided discretion regime. There should be no need for mandatory minimum sentences in a jurisdiction that insists upon four elements in sentencing: guidance to judges as to sentencing norms for offenses and repeat offenders, judicial discretion to vary from the norms, on-the-record explanations for any variance upward or downward, and judicial review of any variance from a sentencing norm. All of these elements are found in the Sentencing Standards and are reflected in our recommendations.[19]

---

[19] AMERICAN BAR ASSOCIATION JUSTICE KENNEDY COMMISSION, REPORT TO THE HOUSE OF DELEGATES 27 (2004).

In other words, like Tonry, the ABA's Sentencing Standards propose presumptive minimums, not mandatory ones: judges should be able to depart, but perhaps they initially need to make specific findings. At first blush, this seems eminently reasonable. But think back to our discussion in Chapter 3 about actuarial models. One of the core findings in actuarial research is that mandatory models work better than presumptive ones. In fact, a wide-ranging survey of actuarial-vs.-clinical studies notes the risk of "presumptive" actuarial regimes in which clinicians remain free to depart from the model's recommendation:

> The limited research examining this [option] . . . shows that greater overall accuracy is achieved when clinicians rely uniformly on actuarial conclusions and avoid discretionary judgments. Clinicians apparently identify too many "exceptions," that is, the actuarial conclusions correctly modified are outnumbered by those incorrectly modified.[20]

In many fields outside of criminal justice, there is a strong move *away* from discretion and towards more-mandatory-like guidelines. So why should criminal justice be any different?

After all, regardless of one's theory of punishment, sentencing is an actuarial process: the idea of (true) individualization is no less meaningless here than in any other area. Whether a particular offender deserves a particular sentence under retribution, deterrence, incapacitation, or rehabilitation requires comparing his offense and characteristics to some sort of representative baseline. So if criminal justice regimes are to reject mandatory minimums even as other areas of inquiry attempt to narrow discretion, it would be useful to figure out if there is a problem with *how* they are designed rather than *whether* we use them at all. There are two key possibilities to consider:

1. Too many factors. It could be that it is simply impossible, or at least infeasible, to design an actuarial model of sufficient "depth" to reach a satisfying conclusion. The sheer bulk of the federal guidelines indicates the challenge of trying to design a system that eliminates all discretion—and those guidelines *still* acknowledged the need for discretion. But does this necessarily imply that we cannot reasonably assert that, in some easy-to-define scenarios, a sentence below a certain line is actuarially impermissible?

2. Judges are better than legislators. A *well-designed* actuarial model consistently ties or beats clinical judgment, but a poorly-designed one would surely fare worse. As we saw in Chapter 3, Sonja Starr pointed out that most actuarial sentencing models rely on the same factors as parole models, even though the latter deal with exiting

---

[20] Robyn M. Dawes, David Faust & Paul E. Meehl, *Clinical Versus Actuarial Judgment*, 243 SCIENCE 1668, 1670–71 (1989).

offenders and the former with those who are entering. And even if tractable guidelines are possible, we may think that legislatures or commissions face political or other pressures that lead them to implement poorly-designed minimums. If we believe that judges are better isolated from these pressures and have sufficiently good judgment, we may favor judicial discretion over administrative guidelines.

Both the opponents and proponents of mandatory minimums are trying to reduce error costs: the opponents the costs of excessive severity, the proponents those of excessive leniency. Any debate over the efficacy of mandatory minimums has to take into account the relative institutional and political competencies of judges and legislators; too often, however, the debate simply focuses on moralizing outrage over shocking extremes (fifty years for a small crime, zero years for a big one) or broad, unsubstantiated claims about reducing crime.

QUESTIONS

1. **Too many options?** Tonry is right to highlight the fact that discretion is never eliminated, it is just reallocated to different parties. That said, to what extent would mandatory minimums become more appealing, at least on the margin, if legislatures streamlined statutes so prosecutors had fewer options to pick from for any given act? Recall Richman and Stuntz's point back in Chapter 3 that state prosecutors are generally trying offenses for which people have fairly clear intuitive senses of what constitutes the crimes.

2. **Theory vs. Practice.** Can we really oppose a mandatory minimum of one year for murder? On the other hand, given the realities of the political pressures faced by judges, what would be lost by making such a minimum just presumptive? Where do we think the shift to presumptive prison time will matter more? less?

3. **Actuarial models?** The argument that actuarial assessments outperform clinical has strong empirical support. But is that what is really happening here—is sentencing really an actuarial effort?

4. **Pro-defendant minimums.** Texas only recently passed a life without parole statute, and prior to its adoption prosecutors would push for the death penalty for murderers by arguing that they could be released in the future, even though no death-eligible murderer who received life had ever been paroled. Might some defendants who received death have been better off if the jury were convinced they would spend some minimum time in prison? For murder this minimum would have to be huge, but might the logic apply to lesser offenses as well? Would presumptive minimums provide sufficiently similar "protection"?

5. **Whither incapacitation?** Tonry says that mandatory minimums cannot be justified from a deterrent, crime-reduction perspective. But deterrence isn't the only way to reduce crime. If we take a protective incapacitation perspective (i.e., we lock up not to "punish," but to immobilize

until no longer a threat), does another argument for mandatory minimums arise?

B.2.c. Truth in Sentencing and Parole Abolition

States have sought to limit not just front-end judicial discretion via guidelines and mandatory minimums, but also back-end parole discretion via the abolition of parole or restrictive "truth-in-sentencing" laws, which require offenders (generally just violent offenders) to serve a significant portion of their sentences (generally 85%). I want to focus here on two issues related primarily to truth-in-sentencing laws. First, I want to consider the extent to which limits on back-end release policies shape the way front-end actors (prosecutors and judges) impose sentences. And second, TIS laws demonstrate the ambiguous effect of federal financial carrots. These carrots are one of the more interesting ways the federal government tries to shape state sentencing outcomes, though they are rarely studied.

First, to what extent do front-end actors alter their behavior in response to changes in back-end restrictions—just how hydraulic is discretion? When it comes to TIS laws, there is some adaptation, but its dynamics are complex.

Emily Owens reports that the adoption of TIS laws does not lead to much change on the part of prosecutors:

> I [do] not [find] evidence that TIS laws are subverted by charge bargaining or by changes in conviction rates. Specifically, I do not find evidence that enacting a TIS law changes the fraction of people who plead guilty to misdemeanors or are finally charged with felonies relative to people arrested for the same offenses in states where these crimes were not subject to TIS legislation. Similarly, I fail to find any evidence that TIS laws are associated with changes in conviction rates overall, or felony conviction rates. How could this be possible? Recall that defendants should be more willing to plead guilty to misdemeanors if they anticipated that the misdemeanor punishment was much better than the felony punishment. If TIS laws change sentences for felonies and misdemeanor punishments in a way that makes misdemeanor pleas less attractive, then this could explain the apparent lack of preadjudication maneuvering.
>
> [T]he data suggest that TIS laws are associated with convergence in punishment for felonies and misdemeanors. Passing a TIS law is associated with a large, but only marginally precise, increases in all sentences. . . . Individuals convicted of felonies receive sentences that are approximately two and a half times as long as those convicted of misdemeanors. The difference between felony and misdemeanor sentences,

however, falls by 40 to 50 percentage points when TIS laws are in place.

These estimates confirm that the large increase in sentences seen [in the data] is driven by punishments that TIS laws technically should not affect. To the extent that TIS laws reflect a desire by the legislature to make criminal justice sanctions tougher, judges appear to be behaving in accordance with such wishes. Those accused of committing TIS-eligible offenses are receiving longer sentences. This increase in sentence length, however, affects individuals who are convicted of misdemeanor offenses, a group that is technically not subject to the law. While TIS laws are not intended to influence the punishment of individuals convicted of misdemeanors, people who are arrested for, but not convicted of, TIS-eligible offenses end up being treated more harshly by the justice system.[21]

Note that Owens is looking at time *sentenced*, not time *served*. If imposed sentences remain fixed but the percent of those sentences that must be served increases, then TIS laws result in "more" severity than her results indicate.

It is worth noting, however, that at least one other paper using the same data as Owen reached somewhat different conclusions. Fusako Tsuchimoto and Libor Dusek, who looked at a wider sample of offenders than Owens,[22] argue that the adoption of TIS laws reduces the probability of conviction by 25% (through dismissal or acquittals), and that the imposed sentence drops by 14%—total time served increases, but judges appear to offset some of the severity.[23]Taken together, these results indicate that TIS laws are not wholly circumvented, but that front-end actors nonetheless appear to respond in ways that somewhat offset their impact.

Another aspect of TIS laws is that they highlight the often underappreciated potential importance of federal financial incentives. The federal government has little direct say over state penal policy, but it can offer powerful financial carrots (via grants) or wield powerful financial sticks (by threats to withhold financial assistance). The former played a major role in the adoption of TIS laws. Almost every state with a TIS law adopted it after 1994, in the wake of the Violent Crime Control Act (VCCA) of 1994, which set aside billions of dollars in federal aid for prison

---

[21] Emily G. Owens, *Truthiness in Punishment: The Far Reach of Truth-in-Sentencing Laws in State Courts*, 8 J. EMPIRICAL LEGAL STUDIES 239, 254–260 (2011).

[22] Owens restricts her analysis to violent offenders, since they are generally the subject of TIS laws. Tsuchimoto and Dusek look at all offenders, since some TIS laws apply to a small set of non-violent criminals. Neither study engages with the other, making it hard to know how much turns on this difference.

[23] FUSAKO TSUCHIMOTO AND LIBOR DUSEK, RESPONSES TO MORE SEVERE PUNISHMENT IN THE COURTROOM: EVIDENCE FROM TRUTH-IN-SENTENCING LAWS, unpublished manuscript (2009), available on-line at http://www.coll.mpg.de/economix/2010/paper/dusek.pdf.

construction, but only for states that met the 85% minimum for violent offenders.

The following chart from an Urban Institute report on TIS laws indicates the effectiveness of the VCCA's grant provision.[24] The chart shows how state TIS laws changed in the wake of the VCCA's passage. The vertical axis shows a state's pre-VCCA TIS law, the horizontal axis its post-VCCA law. So states along the main diagonal (the gray boxes) did not change their laws following the VCCA. But those to the left of the diagonal adopted harsher laws, those to the right more lenient ones. Thus, for example, prior to the VCCA New Jersey had no TIS law, but afterwards it adopted the tougher 85% standard (while retaining discretionary parole release).

Table A. Changes in state truth-in-sentencing legislation, as related to violent offenders, before and after the passage of the 1994 Crime Act[2]
States that received federal TIS grants at any time during 1996-99 are marked in bold uppercase letters. Other states are in lowercase letters.

			Truth-in-sentencing laws for violent offenders: Laws enacted after the Crime Act, January 1, 1995 through December 31, 1999				
			=85% of determinate or maximum sentence required by statute	Other specific percent (<85%) of determinate or maximum sentence required by statute	=85% of determinate or maximum sentence required by statute	Other specific percent of minimum or maximum sentence required by statute	No statutory TIS requirements
			No parole release (reflects determinacy in system)		Parole release allowed (reflects indeterminacy in system)		
Truth-in-sentencing laws for violent offenders: Laws enacted before the 1994 Crime Act	No parole release (reflects determinacy)	=85% of determinate or maximum sentence required by statute	AZ CA GA MN NC OR VA WA (8)				
		Other specific percent (<85%) of determinate or maximum sentence required by statute	FL IL KS ME (4)	aK DE (2)			
	Parole release allowed (reflects indeterminacy in system)	=85% of determinate or maximum sentence required by statute			MO (1)		
		Other specific percent of minimum or maximum sentence required by statute	DC MS NY TN wi (5)		CT ky LA (3)	ar co ma md MI ne nh nv PA tx (10)	
		No statutory TIS requirements	IA OH (2)	in (1)	NJ ND OK SC (4)	id mt (2)	al hi nm ri sd UT* vt wv wy (9)

Notes: Number of states in each cell is given in parentheses.
* Utah does not have truth-in-sentencing statutes but received federal grant funding on the basis of its truth-in-sentencing practices.

Two features stand out. First, there are *no* states to the right of the main diagonal. No state weakened its TIS law in the wake of the VCCA. Second, of the twenty-seven states that met the federal standards after the VCCA (the first and third columns), eighteen did not have such harsh

---

[24] WILLIAM J. SABOL ET AL., THE INFLUENCES OF TRUTH-IN-SENTENCING REFORMS ON CHANGES IN STATES' SENTENCING PRACTICES AND PRISON POPULATIONS (2002).

laws prior to the VCCA. As the chart makes clear, the VCCA did not induce *every* state to adopt the federal standard, and a report by the National Institute of Corrections indicated that many states were unmoved by the offer of federal aid.[25] But it still had a meaningful impact on the decisions of multiple states—many of which are high-population, high-crime, high-incarceration states.

QUESTIONS

1. **TIS and guidelines.** Would we expect the effect of TIS to be stronger in guideline or non-guideline jurisdictions? When do we think legislatures would feel more compelled to adopt both?

2. **Constant charging.** Is Owens' finding that prosecutors do not appear to significantly plead out TIS-eligible cases as non-TIS cases surprising in light of what Richman and Stuntz said above (in Chapter 3) about the inability of state prosecutors to engage in pretextual prosecutions? Would we expect her results to remain the same if TIS laws migrated from *malum in se* violent offenses to less intuitively-wrong *malum prohibitum* crimes?

3. **TIS, displacement, and budgets.** One economist, Amanda Ross, found evidence that the adoption of TIS laws displaced some violent crime from the adopting state into the border-counties of adjacent states.[26] What do you think she reported happened to local police budgets in the states that adopted TIS laws, in the wake of the observed displacement effect?

B.2.d. THE UNTOUCHED PROSECUTOR

Looking at the various structured sentencing regimes that have been implemented over time, at least one strikingly consistent fact stands out: at no point have meaningful—or, really, any—restrictions been placed on prosecutors (except for the *Brimage* guidelines in New Jersey restricting plea bargaining options in drug cases, which are discussed in Chapter 8 below). And this despite the significant budgetary moral hazard problem we have discussed before. Academics have certainly suggested numerous proposals for dealing with this problem, but, outside of California's somewhat-indirect approach via Realignment, no state has attempted to implement such controls. This could partly reflect the political power of prosecutors as well as their historical role as relatively autonomous local actors, even in jurisdictions where the state attorney general has some official power over local DAs. Entrenched acceptance of prosecutorial discretion may be relevant as well.

Question: Judicial discretion is no less a legal tradition than prosecutorial discretion, yet we have imposed severe

---

[25] NATIONAL INSTITUTE OF CORRECTIONS, STATE LEGISLATIVE ACTIONS IN TRUTH IN SENTENCING: A REVIEW OF LAW AND LEGISLATION IN THE CONTEXT OF THE VIOLENT CRIME CONTROL AND LAW ENFORCEMENT ACT OF 1994 (1995).

[26] Amanda Ross, *Crime, Police, and Truth-in-Sentencing: The Impact of State Sentencing Policy on Local Communities*, 42 REG. SCI. AND URB. ECON. 144 (2012).

restrictions on the former. Why do you think this is? Is judicial discretion inherently more problematic? simply more visible? How significant is it that guidelines were adopted in a period of rising crime? (Note, though, that not all guidelines were intended to increase severity!)

Some have also suggested that it would be too difficult to impose guidelines on prosecutors, since it is too hard to monitor what they do. Yet this is ultimately an unconvincing argument, given that it is clearly refuted—or at least complicated—by experiences in New Jersey. It is also hard to monitor what police do in the station-house and in interrogation rooms, but that has not kept the Court and legislators from attempting to regulate their behavior, and with some seeming success. It is not clear why the same attitude cannot be taken with regards to prosecutors.

It is thus well worth asking why the prosecutor has been given a free pass during the age of structured sentencing. In fact, not only was the prosecutor given a free pass, but structured sentencing actually increased his power by tying the hands of the other parties. Discretion is hard to eliminate—it simply gets moved. So by restricting judges and parole boards, legislatures ultimately delegated significant power to prosecutors. This has been a frequent criticism of the federal system, but it can be applied to the states as well. Reconsider the comparison between North Carolina and New York State above: how much more power does the prosecutor have in North Carolina?

> **Question:** Can you think of a way to redesign the guidelines in North Carolina to reallocate discretion away from prosecutors to some other set of actors? Which actors will end up with more power? How appealing is this?

That prosecutors have been given more power is not *per se* bad, but we should ask whether we want discretion in the hands of a partisan executive actor or an arguably less partisan (at least in most states) judicial actor. Or, perhaps better phrased, we should ask exactly how that discretion should be divided between the two.

C. THE SUPREME COURT'S FORAY INTO SENTENCING LAW

As cases such as *Williams v. New York* indicate, the Supreme Court traditionally refrained from involving itself in managing indeterminate sentencing regimes. In such systems, the legislature delegated tremendous discretion to courts, and outside of a few Eighth Amendment cases the Court was willing to let trial courts exercise that discretion however they saw fit. As legislatures started to impose limits on how trial courts could exercise that discretion, however, the Court began to pay more attention to sentencing regimes. In other words, while legislatures were free to grant courts almost-unfettered discretion, if they were going to fetter it they had to do so "correctly." This section works its way through the Court's often puzzling and frustrating structured-sentencing jurisprudence.

C.1. INTRODUCTION: THE ELEMENT/SENTENCING FACTOR DIVIDE: *MULLANEY*, *PATTERSON*, AND *ALMENDAREZ-TORRES*

Much of the constitutional wrangling over structured sentencing turned on trying to draw a coherent line between an "element of the crime" and a "sentencing factor." The Supreme Court made it clear in *In re Winship*, 397 US 358 (1970), that any element of a crime had to be proven to a jury beyond a reasonable doubt. But the standards for sentencing factors were lower: they need not be proven to a jury, and the standard of proof could be less than reasonable doubt, with the burden even placed on the defendant. Needless to say, legislatures had a strong incentive to try to classify as many offense characteristics as sentencing factors as it could. Unfortunately, the Court never clearly distinguished element from factor until it completely abolished the distinction (more or less) in *Blakely*.

The Court has long struggled with the distinction. Even before it invoked the concept of "sentencing factor" (a term first used in *McMillan v. Pennsylvania* in 1986), it had had a hard time stating what constituted an "element" of a crime. Consider the following sets of statutes and jury instructions (S1A, S1B, and J1 come from one state, S2A, S2B, and J2 from another state):

S1A: Murder: "Whoever unlawfully kills a human being with malice aforethought, either express or implied, is guilty of murder and shall be punished by imprisonment for life."

S1B: Manslaughter: "Whoever unlawfully kills a human being in the heat of passion, on sudden provocation, without express or implied malice aforethought, ... shall be punished by a fine of not more than $1,000 or imprisonment for not more than 20 years...."

JI1: "In all cases where the unlawful killing is proved beyond a reasonable doubt, and where there is nothing in the circumstances of the case to explain, qualify or palliate the action, the law presumes it to have been done with malice aforethought. And if the accused, that is the defendant, would reduce the crime below the degree of murder, the burden is upon him to rebut the inference which the law raises from the act of killing, by evidence in defense."

S2A: Murder: "With intent to cause the death of another person, he causes the death of such person ... ; except that in any prosecution under this subdivision, it is an affirmative defense that . . . [t]he defendant acted under the influence of extreme emotional disturbance for which there was a reasonable explanation or excuse. . . . Nothing contained in this paragraph shall . . . preclude a conviction of manslaughter in the first degree. . . .

S2B: Manslaughter: "With intent to cause the death of another person, he causes the death of such person . . . under circumstances which do not constitute murder because he acts under the influence of extreme emotional disturbance . . . The fact that homicide was committed under the influence of extreme emotional disturbance constitutes a mitigating circumstance reducing murder to manslaughter in the first degree and need not be proved in any prosecution initiated under this subdivision. . . .

J2: The defendant must prove extreme emotional disturbance by a preponderance of the evidence.

Question: In a moment of rage, Joe kills Bob. Is it any harder for Joe to knock down his charge to manslaughter in State 1 than in State 2? What does Joe have to prove in State 1? In State 2? Likewise for the prosecutor?

The language in these two sets of statutes differs, but that reflects when they were written, not their core substance. Both are effectively saying the same thing: killing someone dispassionately is murder, killing someone in the heat of the moment is manslaughter. And both put the burden of proving "heat of the moment" on the defendant (either by refuting dispassion in State 1 or affirmatively establishing passion, called "extreme emotional disturbance," in State 2).

Yet the Supreme Court held one set unconstitutional and, almost two years later to the day, the other set constitutional. In *Mullaney v. Wilbur*, 421 U.S. 684 (1975), the Court held that the first set, which came from Maine, violated due process by requiring the defendant to prove an element of the offense. Maine argued that "malice aforethought" was not an element of the crime because it "does not come into play until the jury already has determined that the defendant is guilty and may be punished at least for manslaughter. In this situation . . . the defendant's critical interests in liberty and reputation are no longer of paramount concern. . . ." The Court rebutted this claim, stating:

> This analysis fails to recognize that the criminal law of Maine . . . is concerned not only with guilt or innocence in the abstract but also with the degree of criminal culpability. Maine has chosen to distinguish those who kill in the heat of passion from those who kill in the absence of this factor. Because the former are less 'blameworth(y),' . . . they are subject to substantially

less severe penalties. By drawing this distinction, while refusing to require the prosecution to establish beyond a reasonable doubt the fact upon which it turns, Maine denigrates the interests found critical in *Winship*. [421 U.S. at 697–98.]

Whether you agree with it or not, the rule in *Mullaney* is straightforward. How, then, does the Court uphold the second set of statutes, which come from New York? In *Patterson v. New York*, 432 U.S. 197, 205–206 (1977) the Court stated:

> We cannot conclude that Patterson's conviction under the New York law deprived him of due process of law. The crime of murder is defined by the statute, which represents a recent revision of the state criminal code, as causing the death of another person with intent to do so. The death, the intent to kill, and causation are the facts that the State is required to prove. . . . No further facts are either presumed or inferred in order to constitute the crime. The statute does provide an affirmative defense that the defendant acted under the influence of extreme emotional disturbance . . . which, if proved by a preponderance of the evidence, would reduce the crime to manslaughter, an offense defined in a separate section of the statute. It is plain enough that if the intentional killing is shown, the State intends to deal with the defendant as a murderer unless he demonstrates the mitigating circumstances.

This justification seems to simply restate New York's provision without really explaining how it differs from Maine's. The majority[27] in *Patterson* attempted to distinguish the two:

> *Mullaney* surely held that a State must prove every ingredient of an offense beyond a reasonable doubt, and that it may not shift the burden of proof to the defendant by presuming that ingredient upon proof of the other elements of the offense. . . . It was unnecessary to go further in *Mullaney*. . . . As we have explained, nothing was presumed or implied against Patterson; and his conviction is not invalid under any of our prior cases. [432 U.S. at 215–216.]

Not surprisingly, the dissent is unconvinced:

> The Court today, without disavowing the unanimous holding of *Mullaney*, approves New York's requirement that the defendant prove extreme emotional disturbance. The Court manages to run a constitutional boundary line through the barely visible space that separates Maine's law from New York's. It does so on the basis of distinctions in language that are formalistic rather than substantive.

---

[27] *Mullaney* was a 9–0 decision, *Patterson* a 5–3 one, despite only one seat changing hands during that time (John Paul Stevens replaced William Douglas in 1975).

> The test the Court today establishes allows a legislature to shift, virtually at will, the burden of persuasion with respect to any factor in a criminal case, so long as it is careful not to mention the nonexistence of that factor in the statutory language that defines the crime. The sole requirement is that any references to the factor be confined to those sections that provide for an affirmative defense.
>
> With all respect, this type of constitutional adjudication is indefensibly formalistic. A limited but significant check on possible abuses in the criminal law now becomes an exercise in arid formalities. What *Winship* and *Mullaney* had sought to teach about the limits a free society places on its procedures to safeguard the liberty of its citizens becomes a rather simplistic lesson in statutory draftsmanship. [432 U.S. at 221–224.]

It is hard to see how to doctrinally distinguish the statutes in *Mullaney* and *Patterson*, but there may be a political story, one that repeats itself thirty years later in the *Apprendi*-to-*Blakely*-to-*Ice* line of cases. In *Mullaney*, the Court issued a clear, but sweeping rule. In *Patterson*, it realized the collateral costs may have been too high, and it appears to try to dial back its holding without directly admitting its error. The statute challenged in *Patterson* was one that New York had adopted when it revised its criminal code to follow the then-recently released Model Penal Code, whose basic framework would eventually be adopted by over two-thirds of all states. Had the Court invalidated New York's extreme emotional disturbance provision, it may have invalidated similar recently-adopted provisions in other states, and it may have undermined MPC-style codes even more deeply.

The Court's reticence at admitting error is understandable. The Court has no enforcement authority except for moral suasion: it has no financial carrots or sticks it can wave, and it has no police force it can dispatch.[28] To admit error so quickly could have undermined public support and thus the Court's effectiveness. On the other hand, partial-repeals-in-passing leave confusion in their wake; as we will see, this has certainly been the case with *Booker*'s partial-repeal-in-passing of *Blakely*, at least for the federal criminal justice system.

So, *Patterson* converted *Mullaney* into a formalist drafting rule . . . almost. As the dissent notes, after *Patterson* Maine's error was less that it shifted as essential aspect of the crime—dispassionate action—onto the defendant, but that it wrote that rule improperly. Yet *Patterson* did not

---

[28] The Court's opinion in *Brown v. Board of Education*, 347 U.S. 483 (1954), for example, was widely ignored in the Deep South, which did not integrate its schools until a decade later, when the Civil Rights Act of 1964—passed by a Congress with monetary power and signed into law by a President with various enforcement agencies—tied millions of dollars to integration. Interestingly, the Border States *did* integrate quickly after *Brown*, perhaps because the Court had more moral/political authority in those states, at least for this particular issue.

overturn *Mullaney*,[29] so it left open the possibility that the Court could intervene in the future if it felt that a defendant were forced to disprove something that felt "too much" like an element. After all, even the *Patterson* Court did warn that while "the Due Process Clause requires the prosecution to prove beyond a reasonable doubt all of the elements included in the definition of the offense of which the defendant is charged . . . , there are obviously constitutional limits beyond which the States may not go in this regard." Unfortunately, the *Patterson* opinion provided no guidance about what those limits are.

Nine years later, in *McMillan v. Pennsylvania*, 477 U.S. 76 (1986), the Court issued its first major opinion dealing with sentencing factors in a structured-sentencing regime. The case confronted the constitutionality of a mandatory minimum law. The challenged provision was the following:

> 42 Pa. Cons. Stat. § 9712: Sentences for offenses committed with a firearm:
>
> a. Mandatory Sentence: [A]ny person who is convicted . . . of a crime of violence . . . shall, if the person visibly possessed a firearm or a replica of a firearm, whether or not the firearm or replica was loaded or functional, that placed the victim in reasonable fear of death or serious bodily injury, during the commission of the offense, be sentenced to a minimum sentence of at least five years of total confinement notwithstanding any other provision of this title or other statute to the contrary.
>
> b. Proof at Sentencing: Provisions of this section shall not be an element of the crime. . . . The court shall consider any evidence presented at trial and shall afford the Commonwealth and the defendant an opportunity to present any necessary additional evidence and shall determine, by a preponderance of the evidence, if this section is applicable.

Question: Before looking at the Court's decision in *McMillan*, think about whether there are any reasons it should be invalidated under *Mullaney* (putting aside *Patterson*). Is this the type of situation that concerned the *Mullaney* Court? Would your it make a difference if the crime carried a statutory maximum of ten years or three years? Note that in the first case

---

[29] At least not explicitly, leading to more confusion. In 1986, for example, in *McMillan v. Pennsylvania*, the Court stated that "We believe that the present case is controlled by *Patterson*, our most recent pronouncement on this subject, rather than by *Mullaney*," which would suggest that *Patterson* supersedes *Mullaney*. But twelve years later, in *Almendarez-Torres v. US*, the Court went out of its way to distinguish *Mullaney* from *Patterson* rather than acknowledging that the latter reversed the former.

the minimum only raises the floor, but in the latter case it raises the ceiling as well.[30]

In *McMillan*, the Court upheld the mandatory minimum law and its holding that facts that raised the floor did not count as elements. It acknowledged the tension between *Mullany* and *Patterson*, but one of its justifications for supporting the law is that ultimately there was no *Mullaney*-like due process violation:

> The Court in *Mullaney* observed, with respect to the main criminal statute invalidated in that case, that once the State proved the elements which Maine required it to prove beyond a reasonable doubt the defendant faced "a differential in sentencing ranging from a nominal fine to a mandatory life sentence." In the present case the situation is quite different. Of the offenses enumerated in the Act, third-degree murder, robbery . . . , kidnaping, rape, and involuntary deviate sexual intercourse are first-degree felonies subjecting the defendant to a maximum of 20 years' imprisonment. Voluntary manslaughter and aggravated assault . . . are felonies of the second degree carrying a maximum sentence of 10 years. Section 9712 neither alters the maximum penalty for the crime committed nor creates a separate offense calling for a separate penalty; it operates solely to limit the sentencing court's discretion in selecting a penalty within the range already available to it without the special finding of visible possession of a firearm. The statute gives no impression of having been tailored to permit the visible possession finding to be a tail which wags the dog of the substantive offense. Petitioners' claim that visible possession under the Pennsylvania statute is "really" an element of the offenses for which they are being punished—that Pennsylvania has in effect defined a new set of upgraded felonies—would have at least more superficial appeal if a finding of visible possession exposed them to greater or additional punishment . . . but it does not.

The Court is surely right that there is a qualitative difference between raising the ceiling and lifting up the floor. The law in *McMillan* did not authorize a judge to impose a sentence he could not have otherwise given, it simply excluded a part of that range. So *McMillan* defines one sort of "sentencing factor": something that raises the floor but not the ceiling is not an element. The rule makes sense, but it raises some troubling questions (ones the Court would eventually return to in *Alleyne v. United States* twenty-seven years later), as we see here.

---

[30] To be clear, the mandatory minimum only applied to crimes that had maximums of more than five years, so the ceiling-raising issue did not apply in this particular case. But we will see examples later where the ceiling goes up as well.

QUESTIONS

1. **What is the sentence range?** Mandatory minimums surely raise the average sentence: judges were always free to impose at least five years in the cases implicated by § 9712, but the legislature likely passed the law because in some non-trivial number of cases they weren't. Is the Court thus right that a mandatory minimum does not "expose" the defendant to greater punishment? If you are a defendant, are you indifferent between the pre- and post-§ 9712 worlds?

2. **Where to draw the line.** Assume mandatory minimums expose defendants to tougher *de facto* punishments, even if not tougher *de jure*. If this is troubling, should it be so as a blanket matter, or is it more case-specific? What if we have evidence that judges already imposed sentences above five years in all cases where § 9712 ultimately applied? In 80% of the cases? 50%? 20%? Can we draw a line? Do we *want* a line?

3. ***Patterson* and mandatory minimums.** How comfortable is the *McMillan* Court with *Mullaney* or *Patterson*? Think back to the New York State statutes at issue in *Patterson*. In New York, murder is a Class A-I felony and manslaughter a Class B felony. The sentencing range for a Class A-I felony is eight to twenty years, for a Class B felony one to nine years. If we reconceptualize the defendant's failure to prove by a preponderance that he acted under extreme emotional disturbance as the court finding by a preponderance that he did not do so—and is that a fair reconceptualization?—then does the New York statute upheld in *Patterson* seem to trigger the Court's hypothetical concern in *McMillan* about exposure to greater sanctions?

The high-water mark for the Court's embrace of sentencing factors came in *Almendarez-Torres v. United States*, 523 U.S. 224 (1998). Hugo Almendarez-Torres had previously been convicted of three "aggravated felonies"[31] and deported from the United States. In the current case, he pled guilty to illegally re-entering the country pursuant to 8 U.S.C. § 1326. The relevant portions of § 1326 are:

8 U.S.C. § 1326: Reentry of Removed Aliens

a. In general: Subject to section (b) of this section, any alien who:

　1. has been denied admission, excluded, deported, or removed . . . , and thereafter:

　2. enters . . . the United States [without permission] . . . shall be fined under Title 18, or imprisoned not more than 2 years, or both.

b. Criminal penalties for removed aliens. Notwithstanding subsection (a) of this section, in the case of any alien described in such subsection:

---

[31] "Aggravated felony" is a term of art in the federal system, referring to a specific list of twenty-two types of felonies given in 8 U.S.C. § 1101(a)(43). The particulars are not relevant here.

> 2. whose removal was subsequent to a conviction for commission of an aggravated felony, such alien shall be fined under such title, imprisoned not more than 20 years, or both. . . .

Almendarez-Torres was indicted for violating § 1326(a), but the indictment said nothing about the aggravating felonies. When entering his plea, Almendarez-Torres did allocute to the aggravated felonies. At his sentencing hearing, however, he argued that the longest sentence he faced was two years, since the Court had held in *Hamling v. United States*, 418 U.S. 87 (1974), that an indictment must state all the elements of the crime, and the "aggravated felony" provision in § 1326(b)(2) constituted a separate element that was not in the indictment. The Court found itself forced to decide whether the "aggravated felony" was an element or a sentencing factor.

A five-justice majority held that the prior convictions were sentencing factors, not elements, and thus Almendarez-Torres could be sentenced under § 1326(b)(2) despite the defects in the indictment. The majority viewed the question as one of Congressional intent:

> An indictment must set forth each element of the crime that it charges. But it need not set forth factors relevant only to the sentencing of an offender found guilty of the charged crime. Within limits, see *McMillan v. Pennsylvania* . . . , the question of which factors are which is normally a matter for Congress.

The majority went on to examine "the statute's language, structure, subject matter, context, and history" to find that Congress did not intend (b)(2) to create a separate offense. Importantly for future cases, the majority put great weight on the nature of the factor in question, noting that "recidivism . . . is a traditional, if not the most traditional, basis for a sentencing court's increasing an offender's sentence." The majority also continued to argue—without admitting it—that *Mullaney* and *Patterson* created a drafting rule.[32]

The dissent, not surprisingly, was unpersuaded by this reasoning. It noted in particular the weakness of the majority's invocation of *McMillan*, arguing:

> The feebleness of the Court's contention that here there is no serious constitutional doubt is evidenced by the degree to which it must ignore or distort the analysis of *McMillan*. [T]hat opinion emphasized—and emphasized repeatedly—that an increase of the maximum penalty was not at issue. Beyond that, it specifically acknowledged that the outcome might have been different (i.e., the statute might have been unconstitutional) if the maximum sentence had been affected. . . . The opinion distinguished one of our own

---

[32] The majority asserted that the *Patterson* Court "said that *Mullaney* had considered (and held 'impermissible') the shifting of a burden of proof '*with respect to a fact which the State deems so important that it must be either proved or presumed.*' And the Court then held that similar burden shifting was permissible with respect to New York's homicide-related sentencing factor 'extreme emotional disturbance.' That factor was not a factor that the state statute had deemed 'so important' in relation to the crime that it must be either 'proved or presumed.' " (Emphasis in original.) But, of course, by making extreme emotional disturbance a defense to murder, the New York code clearly *presumed* its absence when convicting someone of murder.

precedents on this very ground, noting that the Colorado Sex Offenders Act invalidated in *Specht v. Patterson*, 386 U.S. 605 (1967) . . . increased a sex offender's sentence from a 10-year maximum to an indefinite term up to and including life imprisonment.

Furthermore, the dissent was unpersuaded by the emphasis on recidivism. It pointed out that the majority's key case in favor of treating recidivism differently, *Graham v. West Virginia*, 224 U.S. 616 (1912), predated *Mullaney* (by over 60 years), and that "[w]hatever else *Mullaney* stands for, it certainly stands for the proposition that what *Graham* used as the line of demarcation for double jeopardy and some due process purposes (the matter "goes only to the punishment") is not the line of demarcation for purposes of the right to jury trial and to proof beyond a reasonable doubt." It also argued that many common law cases made it clear that prior convictions *did* have to be charged in the indictment and proved to a jury beyond a reasonable doubt.

Almendarez-Torres marks the apex of the sentencing-factor/element distinction. It proved to be the only case in which the Court upheld as constitutional judicial fact-finding which elevated the statutory ceiling on the sentence a defendant could receive. In subsequent cases the Court would find such elevation impermissible—except, repeatedly, when it comes to recidivism. The recidivism carve-out is one without any real legal basis except for *stare decisis*—especially since one of the five justices in the *Almendarez-Torres* majority, Thomas, admitted in an opinion two years later that, given the chance, he would change his vote.

C.2. Narrowing the Options: *Apprendi*, *Ring*, and *Harris*

The outcome in *Almendarez-Torres*, along with its reading of *McMillan*, granted states significant latitude to reclassify aspects of offenses as "sentencing factors" rather than elements, or at the very least gave constitutional support to such classifications that had been taking place for a while. All presumptive guidelines effectively established ceilings that judges were able to surpass only by making additional findings. Such ceilings were below the official statutory maximum, but drawing a principled line between "guideline maximum" and "statutory maximum" is, as we will see in *Apprendi*, perhaps impossible.

Example: In Washington State, second degree kidnapping (a category-V offense on the state's guideline grid) is a Class B felony, which faces a statutory maximum sentence of ten years. Yet look at Washington's sentencing grid below. In the pre-*Blakely* world, the judge could not increase the sentence above the default maximum—but still below the statutory maximum—without making additional findings of fact. What is the "real" statutory maximum for, say, a defendant with a criminal history score of 2?

Sentencing Grid D: For Crimes Committed After July 24, 1999

"CURRENT"
RCW 9.94A.510

Seriousness Level		Offender Score								
		0	1	2	3	4	5	6	7	8	9+
	LEVEL XVI	LIFE SENTENCE WITHOUT PAROLE/DEATH PENALTY									
	LEVEL XV	280m / 240-320	291.5m / 250-333	304m / 261-347	316m / 271-361	327.5m / 281-374	339.5m / 291-388	364m / 312-416	394m / 338-450	431.5m / 370-493	479.5m / 411-548
	LEVEL XIV	171.5m / 123-220	184m / 134-234	194m / 144-244	204m / 154-254	215m / 165-265	225m / 175-275	245m / 195-295	266m / 216-316	307m / 257-357	347.5m / 298-397
	LEVEL XIII	143.5m / 123-164	156m / 134-178	168m / 144-192	179.5m / 154-205	192m / 165-219	204m / 175-233	227.5m / 195-260	252m / 216-288	299.5m / 257-342	347.5m / 298-397
	LEVEL XII	108m / 93-123	119m / 102-136	129m / 111-147	140m / 120-160	150m / 129-171	161m / 138-184	189m / 162-216	207m / 178-236	243m / 209-277	279m / 240-318
	LEVEL XI	90m / 78-102	100m / 86-114	110m / 95-125	119m / 102-136	129m / 111-147	139m / 120-158	170m / 146-194	185m / 159-211	215m / 185-245	245m / 210-280
	LEVEL X	59.5m / 51-68	66m / 57-75	72m / 62-82	78m / 67-89	84m / 72-96	89.5m / 77-102	114m / 98-130	126m / 108-144	150m / 129-171	230.5m / 149-198
	LEVEL IX	36m / 31-41	42m / 36-48	47.5m / 41-54	53.5m / 46-61	59.5m / 51-68	66m / 57-75	89.5m / 77-102	101.5m / 87-116	126m / 108-144	150m / 129-171
	LEVEL VIII	24m / 21-27	30m / 26-34	36m / 31-41	42m / 36-48	47.5m / 41-54	53.5m / 46-61	78m / 67-89	89.5m / 77-102	101.5m / 87-116	126m / 108-144
	LEVEL VII	17.5m / 15-20	24m / 21-27	30m / 26-34	36m / 31-41	42m / 36-48	47.5m / 41-54	66m / 57-75	78m / 67-89	89.5m / 77-102	101.5m / 87-116
	LEVEL VI	13m / 12+-14	17.5m / 15-20	24m / 21-27	30m / 26-34	36m / 31-41	42m / 36-48	53.5m / 46-61	66m / 57-75	78m / 67-89	89.5m / 77-102
	LEVEL V	9m / 6-12	13m / 12+-14	15m / 13-17	17.5m / 15-20	25.5m / 22-29	38m / 33-43	47.5m / 41-54	59.5m / 51-68	72m / 62-82	84m / 72-96
	LEVEL IV	6m / 3-9	9m / 6-12	13m / 12+-14	15m / 13-17	17.5m / 15-20	25.5m / 22-29	38m / 33-43	50m / 43-57	61.5m / 53-70	73.5m / 63-84
	LEVEL III	2m / 1-3	5m / 3-8	8m / 4-12	11m / 9-12	14m / 12+-16	19.5m / 17-22	25.5m / 22-29	38m / 33-43	50m / 43-57	59.5m / 51-68
	LEVEL II	0-90 days	4m / 2-6	6m / 3-9	8m / 4-12	13m / 12+-14	16m / 14-18	19.5m / 17-22	25.5m / 22-29	38m / 33-43	50m / 43-57
	LEVEL I	0-60 days	0-90 days	3m / 2-5	4m / 2-6	5.5m / 3-8	8m / 4-12	13m / 12+-14	16m / 14-18	19.5m / 17-22	25.5m / 22-29

While *Apprendi* is a important pushback against *Almendarez-Torres*, the Court had begun retreating from the latter opinion a bit sooner, in *Jones v. U.S.*, 526 U.S. 227 (1999). In that case, the Court faced a constitutional challenge to the federal carjacking statute, given here:

> 18 USC § 2119: Whoever, possessing a firearm as defined in section 921 of this title, takes a motor vehicle that has been transported, shipped, or received in interstate or foreign commerce from the person or presence of another by force and violence or by intimidation or attempts to do so, shall:
>
> 1. be fined under this title or imprisoned not more than 15 years, or both,
>
> 2. if serious bodily injury . . . results, be fined not more than 25 years, or both, and
>
> 3. if death results, be fined under this title or imprisoned for any number of years up to life, or both.

The question was whether the statute defined three separate crimes or one crime with two "sentencing factors." The implications of the options is clear: if three separate offenses, then "bodily injury" or "death" must be alleged in the indictment and proven to a jury beyond a reasonable doubt. But if those factors were sentencing factors, then they need not be in the indictment and could be found by a judge by a preponderance.

It is worth starting by asking whether there is any difference between 18 U.S.C. § 2119 and 8 U.S.C. § 1326, the re-entry statute under review in *Almendarez-Torres*. Is there any meaningful substantive difference? Any structural differences? Putting aside the "recidivism-is-unique" aspect to *Almendarez-Torres*, what is the expected outcome of this challenge to the carjacking statute?

Ultimately, however, the Court found that the carjacking statute defined three separate crimes—the opinion wouldn't merit inclusion in a casebook if all it did was confirm an earlier decision! The only difference in voting between *Almendarez-Torres* and *Jones* was one justice, Thomas, who had come to regret his decision in the former case.

The majority initially based its decision on detailed analysis of Congressional intent. But more importantly for our purposes here, it also invoked the doctrine of constitutional avoidance: it stated that to hold that the statute comprised one offense with two sentencing factors would be "to raise a genuine Sixth Amendment issue not yet raised." The majority explained its concern about the continuing tension between *Mullaney* and *Patterson*:

> The terms of the carjacking statute illustrate very well what is at stake. If serious bodily injury were merely a sentencing factor under § 2119(2) (increasing the authorized penalty by two thirds, to 25 years), then death would presumably be nothing more than a sentencing factor under subsection (3) (increasing the penalty range to life). If a potential penalty might rise from 15 years to life on a nonjury determination, the jury's role would correspondingly shrink from the significance usually carried by determinations of guilt to the relative importance of low-level gatekeeping: in some cases, a jury finding of fact necessary for a maximum 15-year sentence would merely open the door to a judicial finding sufficient for life imprisonment. It is therefore no trivial question to ask whether recognizing an unlimited legislative power to authorize determinations setting ultimate sentencing limits without a jury would invite erosion of the jury's function to a point against which a line must necessarily be drawn.
>
> The question might well be less serious than the constitutional doubt rule requires if the history bearing on the Framers' understanding of the Sixth Amendment principle demonstrated an accepted tolerance for exclusively judicial factfinding to peg penalty limits. But such is not the history. To be sure, the scholarship of which we are aware does not show that a question exactly like this one was ever raised and resolved in the period before the framing. On the other hand, several studies

demonstrate that on a general level the tension between jury powers and powers exclusively judicial would likely have been very much to the fore in the Framers' conception of the jury right. [526 U.S. at 243–244.]

In short concurrences, Justices Stevens and Scalia went even further, highlighting positions that would play important roles in *Arizona v. Ring* and *Blakely v. Washington*:

> Justice Stevens: Like Justice Scalia, I am convinced that it is unconstitutional for a legislature to remove from the jury the assessment of facts that increase the prescribed range of penalties to which a criminal defendant is exposed. It is equally clear that such facts must be established by proof beyond a reasonable doubt. That is the essence of the Court's holdings in *In re Winship*, *Mullaney v. Wilbur*, and *Patterson v. New York*. To permit anything less "with respect to a fact which the State deems so important that it must be either proved or presumed is impermissible under the Due Process Clause." This principle was firmly embedded in our jurisprudence through centuries of common-law decisions. Indeed, in my view, a proper understanding of this principle encompasses facts that increase the minimum as well as the maximum permissible sentence, and also facts that must be established before a defendant may be put to death. If *McMillan v. Pennsylvania* and *Walton v. Arizona** departed from that principle, as I think they did, they should be reconsidered in due course. It is not, however, necessary to do so in order to join the Court's opinion today, which I do. [*Id.* at 252–253.]

> Justice Scalia: In dissenting in *Almendarez-Torres v. United States*, I suggested the possibility, and in dissenting in *Monge v. California*,** I set forth as my considered view, that it is unconstitutional to remove from the jury the assessment of facts that alter the congressionally prescribed range of penalties to which a criminal defendant is exposed. Because I think it necessary to resolve all ambiguities in criminal statutes in such fashion as to avoid violation of this constitutional principle, I join the opinion of the Court. [*Id.* at 253.]

The dissent started by disagreeing with the majority's textual-interpretive decision. But then it turned to the constitutional issue. It asserted that "*McMillan* confirmed the State's authority to treat aggravated behavior as a factor increasing the sentence, rather than as an element of the crime," and that *McMillan* "rejected the claim that whenever a State links the 'severity of punishment' to 'the presence or

---

* *Ed. note*: *Walton* is a capital sentencing case that *Ring* reverses. See *Ring* below.

** *Ed. note*: 524 U.S. 721 (1998). *Monge* was a double-jeopardy case involving a retrial over a prior conviction in the context of California's three-strikes law.

absence of an identified fact' the State must prove that fact beyond a reasonable doubt." *Id.* at 265. It also stated that the majority's invocation of constitutional doubt was unnecessary, given the holding in *Almendarez-Torres*.

Finally, the dissent warned about another potential drafting rule issue. It suggested that Congress could achieve the exact same outcome as existed before *Jones* without running afoul of *Jones*:

> Congress could leave the initial paragraph of § 2119 intact, and provide that one who commits the conduct described there shall "be imprisoned for any number of years up to life." It could then add that "if the sentencing judge determines that no death resulted, one convicted under this section shall be imprisoned not more than 25 years" and "if the sentencing judge determines that no serious bodily injury resulted, one convicted under this section shall be imprisoned not more than 15 years." The practical result would be the same as the current version of § 2119. . . . [*Id.* at 266.]

The dissent cautioned, presciently, that if the rephrased version of § 2119 remains unconstitutional in the eyes of the majority then perhaps presumptive guidelines and some capital-sentencing statutes are constitutionally suspect as well (as came to pass in *Ring*, *Blakely*, and *Booker*).[33]

The Court continued to expand the logic behind *Jones* in *Apprendi v. New Jersey*, 530 U.S. 466 (2000). In *Apprendi*, the Court faced a statute similar to that in *Almendarez-Torres*.

The path the Court started down in *Jones* was taken to its next (but not final) stage in *Apprendi*. In *Apprendi v. New Jersey*, the Supreme Court faced a statute that was similar to the one it confronted in *Almendarez-Torres*. Charles Apprendi expressed his displeasure at the recent integration of his all-white neighborhood by firing several bullets through the window of the house occupied by his new, African-American neighbors. He went so far as to admit, and then retract, that he shot at his neighbors "because they are black in color and he does not want them in the neighborhood."

Apprendi pled guilty to various charges, including two counts of second-degree possession of a firearm for an unlawful purpose, which carried a statutory range of five to ten years. As part of the plea agreement, the prosecution reserved the right seek a higher sentence for one of the firearm possession charges under New Jersey's hate-crime statute:

---

[33] More accurately, the dissent warns that the federal guidelines may be unconstitutional, but it says nothing about state sentencing. This reflects a deeply problematic federal-only bias in the Court's sentencing jurisprudence that we will discuss in more depth when we get to *Blakely*.

NJ Stat § 2C:44–3(e): Criteria for sentence of extended term of imprisonment: The court shall . . . sentence a person who has been convicted of a crime, . . . to an extended term if it finds, by a preponderance of the evidence . . . [that] [t]he defendant in committing the crime acted, at least in part, with ill will, hatred or bias toward, and with a purpose to intimidate, an individual or group of individuals because of race, color, religion, sexual orientation or ethnicity.

NJS 2C:43–7(a)(3): Sentence of imprisonment for crime; extended terms: In the cases designated in section 2C:44–3, a person who has been convicted of a crime may be sentenced . . . to an extended term of imprisonment, as follows: In the case of a crime of the second degree, for a term which shall be fixed by the court between 10 and 20 years. . . .

Before reading the opinion in *Apprendi*, ask yourself if the aggravated sentence—when hate is found by a judge by a preponderance, not by a jury beyond a reasonable doubt—is permissible under *Mullaney*, under *Patterson*, and under *Almendarez-Torres* (or to the dissenters in that case). Then read the opinion below.

Apprendi v. New Jersey
530 U.S. 466 (2000)

■ JUSTICE STEVENS delivered the opinion of the Court.

New Jersey threatened Apprendi with certain pains if he unlawfully possessed a weapon and with additional pains if he selected his victims with a purpose to intimidate them because of their race. As a matter of simple justice, it seems obvious that the procedural safeguards designed to protect Apprendi from unwarranted pains should apply equally to the two acts that New Jersey has singled out for punishment. Merely using the label "sentence enhancement" to describe the latter surely does not provide a principled basis for treating them differently.

Any possible distinction between an "element" of a felony offense and a "sentencing factor" was unknown to the practice of criminal indictment, trial by jury, and judgment by court as it existed during the years surrounding our Nation's founding. The defendant's ability to predict with certainty the judgment from the face of the felony indictment flowed from the invariable linkage of punishment with crime. The substantive criminal law tended to be sanction-specific; it prescribed a particular sentence for each offense. The judge was meant simply to impose that sentence[, and this] practice at common law held true when indictments were issued pursuant to statute.

We should be clear that nothing in this history suggests that it is impermissible for judges to exercise discretion—taking into consideration various factors relating both to offense and offender—in imposing a judgment *within the range* prescribed by statute. We have often noted that judges in this country have long exercised discretion of this nature in imposing sentence *within statutory limits* in the individual case. As in *Williams,* our periodic recognition of judges' broad discretion in sentencing . . . has been regularly accompanied by the qualification that that discretion was bound by the range of sentencing options prescribed by the legislature.

The historic link between verdict and judgment and the consistent limitation on judges' discretion to operate within the limits of the legal penalties provided highlight the novelty of a legislative scheme that removes the jury from the determination of a fact that, if found, exposes the criminal defendant to a penalty *exceeding* the maximum he would receive if punished according to the facts reflected in the jury verdict alone. We do not suggest that trial practices cannot change in the course of centuries and still remain true to the principles that emerged from the Framers' fears "that the jury right could be lost not only by gross denial, but by erosion." But practice must at least adhere to the basic principles undergirding the requirements of trying to a jury all facts necessary to constitute a statutory offense, and proving those facts beyond reasonable doubt.

Since *Winship,* we have made clear beyond peradventure that *Winship's* due process and associated jury protections extend, to some degree, "to determinations that [go] not to a defendant's guilt or innocence, but simply to the length of his sentence." This was a primary lesson of *Mullaney v. Wilbur.* . . .

[The majority summarizes the holdings in *McMillan* and, particularly, *Almendarez-Torres.*] Finally, as we made plain in *Jones* last Term, *Almendarez-Torres* . . . represents at best an exceptional departure from the historic practice that we have described. Even though it is arguable that *Almendarez-Torres* was incorrectly decided, and that a logical application of our reasoning today should apply if the recidivist issue were contested, Apprendi does not contest the decision's validity and we need not revisit it for purposes of our decision today to treat the case as a narrow exception to the general rule we recalled at the outset. Given its unique facts, it surely does not warrant rejection of the otherwise uniform course of decision during the entire history of our jurisprudence.

In sum, our reexamination of our cases in this area, and of the history upon which they rely, confirms the opinion that we expressed in *Jones.* Other than the fact of a prior conviction, any fact that increases the penalty for a crime beyond the prescribed statutory maximum must be submitted to a jury, and proved beyond a reasonable doubt.

New Jersey's defense of its hate crime enhancement statute has three primary components: (1) The required finding of biased purpose is not an "element" of a distinct hate crime offense, but rather the traditional "sentencing factor" of motive; (2) *McMillan* holds that the legislature can authorize a judge to find a traditional sentencing factor on the basis of a preponderance of the evidence; and (3) *Almendarez-Torres* extended *McMillan's* holding to encompass factors that authorize a judge to impose a sentence beyond the maximum provided by the substantive statute under which a defendant is charged. None of these persuades us that the constitutional rule that emerges from our history and case law should incorporate an exception for this New Jersey statute.

New Jersey's first point is nothing more than a disagreement with the rule we apply today. [Second,] the State's reliance on *McMillan* is likewise misplaced. When a judge's finding based on a mere preponderance of the evidence authorizes an increase in the maximum punishment, it is appropriately characterized as "a tail which wags the dog of the substantive offense" [citing *McMillan*]. [And third,] New Jersey's reliance on *Almendarez-Torres* is also unavailing. [Its] reasons supporting an exception from the general rule . . . do not apply to the New Jersey statute. Whereas recidivism "does not relate to the commission of the offense" itself, New Jersey's biased purpose inquiry goes precisely to what happened in the "commission of the offense." Moreover, there is a vast difference between accepting the validity of a prior judgment of conviction entered in a proceeding in which the defendant had the right to a jury trial and the right to require the prosecutor to prove guilt beyond a reasonable doubt, and allowing the judge to find the required fact under a lesser standard of proof.

■ JUSTICE THOMAS . . . concurring.

[In a lengthy concurrence, Justice Thomas reviews criminal cases from the Founding to the present day to argue that not only was *Almendarez-Torres* wrongly decided, but so too was *McMillan*: "No doubt a defendant could, under [a mandatory minimum] scheme, find himself sentenced to the same term to which he could have been sentenced absent the mandatory minimum. The range for his underlying crime could be 0 to 10 years, with the mandatory minimum of 5 years, and he could be sentenced to 7. (Of course, a similar scenario is possible with an increased maximum.) But it is equally true that his expected punishment has increased as a result of the narrowed range and that the prosecution is empowered, by invoking the mandatory minimum, to require the judge to impose a higher punishment than he might wish. The mandatory minimum 'entitl[es] the government,' to more than it would otherwise be entitled (5 to 10 years, rather than 0 to 10 and the risk of a sentence below 5). Thus, the fact triggering the mandatory minimum is part of 'the punishment sought to be inflicted[;]'; it undoubtedly 'enters into the punishment' so as to aggravate it and is an 'ac[t] to which the law affixes . . . punishment,' Further, . . . it is likely that the change in the range available to the judge affects his choice of sentence."]

■ JUSTICE O'CONNOR, with whom THE CHIEF JUSTICE, JUSTICE KENNEDY, and JUSTICE BREYER join, dissenting.

Today, in what will surely be remembered as a watershed change in constitutional law, the Court imposes as a constitutional rule the principle it first identified in *Jones* [i.e., that any fact (other than a prior conviction) that increases the penalty for a crime beyond the prescribed statutory maximum must be submitted to a jury, and proved beyond a reasonable doubt.]

Our Court has long recognized that not every fact that bears on a defendant's punishment need be charged in an indictment, submitted to a jury, and proved by the government beyond a reasonable doubt. Rather, we have held that the "legislature's definition of the elements of the offense is usually dispositive." *McMillan v. Pennsylvania*; see also *Almendarez-Torres v. United States*; *Patterson v. New York*. Although we have recognized that "there are obviously constitutional limits beyond which the States may not go in this regard," and that "in certain limited circumstances *Winship's* reasonable-doubt requirement applies to facts not formally identified as elements of the offense charged," we have proceeded with caution before deciding that a certain fact must be treated as an offense element despite the legislature's choice not to characterize it as such. We have therefore declined to establish any bright-line rule for making such judgments and have instead approached each case individually, sifting through the considerations most relevant to determining whether the legislature has acted properly within its broad power to define crimes and their punishments or instead has sought to evade the constitutional requirements associated with the characterization of a fact as an offense element.

The Court . . . cites our decision in *Mullaney v. Wilbur* to demonstrate the "lesson" that due process and jury protections extend beyond those factual determinations that affect a defendant's guilt or innocence. The Court explains *Mullaney* as having held that the due process proof-beyond-a-reasonable-doubt requirement applies to those factual determinations that, under a State's criminal law, make a difference in the degree of punishment the defendant receives. The Court chooses to ignore, however, the decision we issued two years later, *Patterson v. New York,* which clearly rejected the Court's broad reading of *Mullaney*.

Although we characterized the factual determination under New York law as one going to the mitigation of culpability, as opposed to the aggravation of the punishment, it is difficult to understand why the rule adopted by the Court in today's case . . . would not require the overruling of *Patterson*. Unless the Court is willing to defer to a legislature's formal definition of the elements of an offense, it is clear that the fact that Patterson did not act under the influence of extreme emotional disturbance, in substance, "increase[d] the penalty for [his] crime beyond the prescribed statutory maximum" for first-degree manslaughter. *Patterson* is important because it plainly refutes the Court's expansive reading of *Mullaney*. Indeed, the defendant in *Patterson* characterized *Mullaney* exactly as the Court has today and we *rejected* that interpretation....

[T]he Court also fails to explain adequately why the Due Process Clauses of the Fifth and Fourteenth Amendments and the jury trial guarantee of the Sixth Amendment require application of its rule. Upon closer examination, it is possible that the Court's "increase in the maximum penalty" rule rests on a meaningless formalism that accords, at best, marginal protection for the constitutional rights that it seeks to effectuate.

For example, under one reading, the Court appears to hold that the Constitution requires that a fact be submitted to a jury and proved beyond a reasonable doubt only if that fact, as a formal matter, extends the range of punishment *beyond the prescribed statutory maximum*. A State could, however, remove from the jury (and subject to a standard of proof below "beyond a reasonable doubt") the assessment of those facts that define narrower ranges of punishment, *within the overall statutory range,* to which the defendant may be sentenced. Thus, apparently New Jersey could cure its sentencing scheme, and achieve virtually the same results, by drafting its weapons possession statute in the following manner: First, New Jersey could prescribe, in the weapons possession statute itself, a range of 5 to 20 years' imprisonment for one who commits that criminal offense. Second, New Jersey could provide that only those defendants convicted under the statute who are found by a judge, by a preponderance of the evidence, to have acted with a purpose to intimidate an individual on the basis of race may receive a sentence greater than 10 years' imprisonment.

Given the pure formalism of the above readings of the Court's opinion, one suspects that the constitutional principle underlying its decision is more far reaching. The actual principle underlying the Court's decision may be that any fact (other than prior conviction) that has the effect, *in real terms,* of increasing the maximum punishment beyond an otherwise applicable range must be submitted to a jury and proved beyond a reasonable doubt. The principle thus would apply not only to schemes like New Jersey's, under which a factual determination exposes the defendant to a sentence beyond the prescribed statutory maximum, but also to all determinate-sentencing schemes in which the length of a defendant's sentence within the statutory range turns on specific factual determinations (*e.g.,* the federal Sentencing Guidelines).

[Note, however, that u]nder ... discretionary-sentencing schemes, a factual determination made by a judge on a standard of proof below "beyond a reasonable doubt" often made the difference between a lesser and a greater punishment. [A] State may leave the determination of a defendant's sentence to a judge's discretionary decision within a prescribed range of penalties. When a judge, pursuant to that sentencing scheme, decides to increase a defendant's sentence on the basis of certain contested facts, those facts need not be proved to a jury beyond a reasonable doubt. Under the Court's decision today, however, it appears that once a legislature constrains judges' sentencing discretion by prescribing certain sentences that may only be imposed ... in connection with the same determinations of the same contested facts, the Constitution requires that the facts instead be proved to a jury beyond a reasonable doubt. I see no reason to treat the two schemes differently.

Consideration of the purposes underlying the Sixth Amendment's jury trial guarantee further demonstrates why our acceptance of judge-made findings in the context of discretionary sentencing suggests the approval of the same judge-made findings in the context of determinate sentencing. ... One important purpose of the Sixth Amendment's jury trial guarantee is to protect the criminal defendant against potentially arbitrary judges. [T]he concerns animating the Sixth Amendment's jury trial guarantee, if they were to extend to the sentencing context at all, would apply with greater strength to a discretionary-sentencing scheme than to determinate sentencing. In the former scheme, the potential for mischief by an arbitrary judge is much greater, given that the judge's decision of where to set the defendant's sentence within the prescribed statutory range is left almost entirely to discretion. In contrast, under a determinate-sentencing system, the discretion the judge wields within the statutory range is tightly constrained. Accordingly, our approval of discretionary-sentencing schemes ... demonstrates that the defendant should have no right to demand that a jury make the equivalent factual determinations under a determinate-sentencing scheme.

Whether one believes the determinate-sentencing reforms have proved successful or not ... the apparent effect of the Court's opinion today is to halt the current debate on sentencing reform in its tracks and to invalidate with the stroke of a pen three decades' worth of nationwide reform, all in the name of a principle with a questionable constitutional pedigree. Indeed, it is ironic that the Court, in the name of constitutional rights meant to protect criminal defendants from the potentially arbitrary exercise of power by prosecutors and judges, appears to rest its decision on a principle that would render unconstitutional efforts by Congress and the state legislatures to place constraints on that very power in the sentencing context.

■ JUSTICE BREYER, with whom the CHIEF JUSTICE joins, dissenting.

In modern times, the law has left it to the sentencing judge to find those facts which (within broad sentencing limits set by the legislature) determine the sentence of a convicted offender. There are many ... manner-related differences in respect to criminal behavior. Empirical data collected by the Sentencing Commission make clear that, before the Guidelines, judges who exercised discretion within broad legislatively determined sentencing limits . . . would impose very different sentences upon offenders engaged in the same basic criminal conduct, depending, for example, upon the amount of drugs distributed . . . , the amount of money taken . . . , the presence or use of a weapon, injury to a victim, the vulnerability of a victim, the offender's role in the offense, recidivism, and many other offense-related or offender-related factors. [I]t is [thus] important for present purposes to understand why *judges,* rather than *juries,* traditionally have determined the presence or absence of such sentence-affecting facts in any given case. And it is important to realize that the reason is not a theoretical one, but a practical one. It does not reflect (Justice Scalia's opinion to the contrary notwithstanding) an ideal of procedural "fairness," but rather an administrative need for procedural *compromise.* There are, to put it simply, far too many potentially relevant sentencing factors to permit submission of all (or even many) of them to a jury.

At the same time, to require jury consideration of all such factors—say, during trial where the issue is guilt or innocence—could easily place the defendant in the awkward (and conceivably unfair) position of having to deny he committed the crime yet offer proof about how he committed it, *e.g.,* "I did not sell drugs, but I sold no more than 500 grams." And while special postverdict sentencing juries could cure this problem, they have seemed (but for capital cases) not worth their administrative costs.

The source of the problem lies not in a legislature's power to enact sentencing factors, but in the traditional legislative power to select elements defining a crime, the traditional legislative power to set broad sentencing ranges, and the traditional judicial power to choose a sentence within that range on the basis of relevant offender conduct. Conversely, the solution to the problem lies, not in prohibiting legislatures from enacting sentencing factors, but in sentencing rules that determine punishments on the basis of properly defined relevant conduct, with sensitivity to the need for procedural protections where sentencing factors are determined by a judge (for example, use of a "reasonable doubt" standard), and invocation of the Due Process Clause where the history of the crime at issue, together with the nature of the facts to be proved, reveals unusual and serious procedural unfairness.

I am willing . . . to assume that the majority's rule would provide a degree of increased procedural protection in respect to those particular sentencing factors currently embodied in statutes. I nonetheless believe that any such increased protection provides little practical help and comes at too high a price. For one thing, by leaving mandatory minimum sentences untouched, the majority's rule simply encourages any legislature interested in asserting control over the sentencing process to do so by creating those minimums. That result would mean significantly less procedural fairness, not more. For another thing, this Court's case law, prior to *Jones v. United States,* led legislatures to believe that they were permitted to increase a statutory maximum sentence on the basis of a sentencing factor. And legislatures may well have relied upon that belief.

QUESTIONS

1. **Is *Apprendi* a drafting rule (the simple version)?** Is O'Connor correct in her dissent that *Apprendi* is little more than a drafting rule? As we will discuss in a moment, the majority expressly stated that its decision was not invalidating a murder statute for which death was the maximum but which allowed death to be imposed *only* if the judge made additional factual findings. Given this, would the New Jersey statute, rewritten as O'Connor foresaw, pass muster under *Apprendi*?

2. **Is *Apprendi* a drafting rule (the complex version)?** Revise the fact of *Apprendi* a bit. Assume that New Jersey has a hate-crime statute that allows a defendant to be sentenced for ten more years than he otherwise could be without the bad motive, a gun-enhancement statute that allows an additional five years to be added to any offense when a gun is used (other than one for which a gun is an element of the crime), and a school-safety enhancement that permits an additional fifteen years for any felony committed within 500 feet of an elementary or high school. Assume, too, it has an aggravated assault statute with a statutory maximum of twelve years, a stalking statute with a statutory maximum of seven years, and a drug trafficking statute with a statutory maximum of eighteen years. Make this statutory regime *Apprendi*-compliant per O'Connor's dissent. Is it as easy as O'Connor makes it seem? Does she overstate her case by focusing on just one crime and one enhancement?

3. **Zombie-*Mullaney*/Zombie-*Patterson*.** Had the Court in *Patterson* expressed overruled *Mullaney*, how would *Apprendi* have been decided? Would the case have even come up? Can you think of any reason why, given the tension between *Mullaney* and *Patterson* running through so many of these opinions, the Court did not simply overrule one or the other in the process?

4. **Determinacy and indeterminacy.** How compelling is O'Connor's claim that the very support for indeterminacy—which involves extensive, unregulated judicial fact-finding—means that determinate regimes should be constitutional as well? Even if you find it valid on its own terms, does it meaningfully engage with the core theoretical argument driving the majority's position?

5. **Reliance.** Breyer is concerned that legislatures may have relied on the Court's earlier unclear precedent. Is reliance a valid concern in this context? Even if it is, what—if anything—does the inescapable tension between *Mullaney* and *Patterson* imply about the reasonableness of that reliance?

Apprendi left two important questions open. First, it did not clearly explain why judicial factfinding was acceptable when required to impose a higher sentence within the statutory maximum but impermissible when required to impose a sentence (perhaps the same sentence) above the statutory maximum. In other words, was *Apprendi* just a drafting rule? And second, it created some lingering confusion about *McMillan*. As both Stevens and Thomas pointed out, mandatory minimums could be seen as raising the expected punishment and thus falling within the requirements set out by *Apprendi* (or *Mullaney*) that such facts be found by a jury beyond a reasonable doubt.

In two cases handed down two years (almost to the day) after *Apprendi*, the Court resolved both these questions—sort of. In *Ring v. Arizona*, 536 U.S. 584 (2002), the Court made it clear that *Apprendi* was *not* a drafting rule: *any* fact (besides, of course, prior convictions) required for a higher sentence—whether that sentence was above or within the statutory maximum—had to be found by a jury beyond a reasonable doubt. (*Ring* would prove to be the intellectual forebear of *Blakely*.) In *Harris v. United States*, 536 U.S. 545 (2002), a heavily-divided[34] Court held that *Apprendi* did not apply to mandatory minimums and thus did not overturn *McMillan*.

Taken together, *Ring* and *Harris* appeared to define a fairly clear rule about what constitutes an element versus a sentencing factor. Anything that raises the ceiling must be proven to a jury beyond a reasonable doubt, but something that raises the floor need not be. And this would be the rule that would persist for over a decade. Eleven years after *Ring* and *Harris*, however, the Court overturned *Harris* and *McMillan* in *Alleyne v. United States*, 133 S.Ct. 2151 (2013), creating another fairly coherent, but quite different, rule: anything that raises the ceiling *or* floor must be proven to a jury beyond a reasonable doubt.

We will look at *Alleyne* in a little bit. For now, start with *Harris*. The Court in *Harris* considered the constitutionality of a federal firearms statute:

> 18 USC § 924(c)(1)(A): [A]ny person who, during and in relation to any crime of violence or drug trafficking crime . . . uses or carries a firearm, or who, in furtherance of any such crime, possesses a firearm, shall, in addition to the punishment provided for such crime of violence or drug trafficking crime:
>
> 1. be sentenced to a term of imprisonment of not less than 5 years;
> 2. if the firearm is brandished, be sentenced to a term of imprisonment of not less than 7 years; and
> 3. if the firearm is discharged, be sentenced to a term of imprisonment of not less than 10 years.

---

[34] The vote was 4–1–4, with Breyer concurring only with some parts of the plurality's opinion.

In all instances, the maximum the judge could impose was life. The US Attorney and the trial court in Harris's case treated brandishment (which is what the judge found by a preponderance to be how Harris used a gun) as a "sentencing factor," not an element. Harris, not surprisingly, challenged this decision pursuant to *Jones*, arguing that clauses (1) through (3) defined three separate offenses, just like the three provisions in the carjacking statute considered in *Jones*.

A majority of the justices initially concluded that the factors here (brandishing, discharging) seemed less like traditional elements than those in *Jones* (serious bodily injury, death). A four-justice plurality—this is the one part of opinion that Breyer did not sign onto—then tackled the more general question of whether *Apprendi* overturned *McMillan*. The rationale was relatively straight-forward:

> *McMillan* and *Apprendi* are consistent because there is a fundamental distinction between the factual findings that were at issue in those two cases. *Apprendi* said that any fact extending the defendant's sentence beyond the maximum authorized by the jury's verdict would have been considered an element of an aggravated crime. . . . The same cannot be said of a fact increasing the mandatory minimum (but not extending the sentence beyond the statutory maximum), for the jury's verdict has authorized the judge to impose the minimum with or without the finding. As *McMillan* recognized, a statute may reserve this type of factual finding for the judge without violating the Constitution. [536 U.S. at 557.]

The plurality made it clear that this was a doctrinal and historical argument, not a pragmatic one:

> [Harris] argues, however, that the concerns underlying *Apprendi* apply with equal or more force to facts increasing the defendant's minimum sentence. Those factual findings, he contends, often have a greater impact on the defendant than the findings at issue in *Apprendi*. This is so because when a fact increasing the statutory maximum is found, the judge may still impose a sentence far below that maximum; but when a fact increasing the minimum is found, the judge has no choice but to impose that minimum, even if he or she otherwise would have chosen a lower sentence. Why, [Harris] asks, would fairness not also require the latter sort of fact to be alleged in the indictment and found by the jury under a reasonable-doubt standard? The answer is that because it is beyond dispute that the judge's choice of sentences within the authorized range may be influenced by facts not considered by the jury, a factual finding's practical effect cannot by itself control the constitutional analysis. The Fifth and Sixth Amendments ensure that the defendant "will never get *more* punishment than he bargained

for when he did the crime," but they do not promise that he will receive "anything less" than that. [536 U.S. at 565–566.]

The plurality then provided what was the Court's clearest definition of an "element" since the *Mullaney-Patterson* debates began: "Read together, *McMillan* and *Apprendi* mean that those facts setting the outer limits of a sentence, and of the judicial power to impose it, are the elements of the crime for the purposes of the constitutional analysis." Justice Breyer, who joined in the judgment but not the plurality's efforts to distinguish Harris's case from Apprendi's, noted that he could not see any real difference between the situation in *Apprendi* and *Harris* but joined in the judgment because he continued to think that *Apprendi* was the incorrectly decided case.

The dissent reiterated the argument that Thomas made in his *Apprendi* dissent:

> But to say that is in effect to claim that the imposition of a 7-year, rather than a 5-year, mandatory minimum does not change the constitutionally relevant sentence range because, regardless, either sentence falls between five years and the statutory maximum of life. . . . This analysis is flawed precisely because the statute provides incremental sentencing ranges, in which the mandatory minimum sentence varies upward if a defendant "brandished" or "discharged" a weapon. As a matter of common sense, an increased mandatory minimum heightens the loss of liberty and represents the increased stigma society attaches to the offense. [536 U.S. at 577–578.]

That last sentence sounds doctrinal, but it is potentially empirical. If judges imposed sentences of at least eleven years on defendants sentenced under any of the three prongs of § 924(c)(1)(A), the escalating mandatory minimums do not really seem to entail any "heightened loss of liberty." In this case it is a moot point, since the dissent noted that sentences under § 924(c)(1)(A) were almost always five, seven, or ten years, suggesting that federal judges imposed the minimum sentence that they could, which is consistent with other reports claiming that federal judges, chafing at the punitiveness of federal criminal law, have often sentenced at the lower ends of the available ranges.[35] But it is worth highlighting that the dissent fails to carefully discuss *where* the loss of liberty and stigma comes from: the *potential* sentence versus the *actual* sentence.

The majority's rule, however, avoided this issue altogether, by settling on a formalist definition of "element." An "element" was anything that raised the maximum *possible* sentence, not the effective sentence.[36]

---

[35] See, e.g., Frank O. Bowman III, *Fear of Law: Thoughts on Fear of Judging and the State of the Federal Sentencing Guidelines*, 44 ST. LOUIS U. L. J. 299 (2000).

[36] There is a potential irony here: the justices who made the formalist argument belonged to the Court's "pragmatic" wing, and those who made the functionalist argument its "doctrinal"

But unlike in *Apprendi*, the formalist definition employed in *Harris* did not yield a mere drafting rule, as the Court's decision in *Ring* made clear.

Ring confronted Arizona's death penalty statute, which the Supreme Court had previously upheld in *Walton v. Arizona*, 497 U.S. 639 (1990), a decision which the majorities in both *Jones* and *Apprendi* stated they were not overturning. The rule in place in Arizona at the time was the following: First degree murder could be punished either by life or death, but death could not be imposed unless the judge found, beyond a reasonable doubt, the existence of at least two aggravating factors from an enumerated list. Thus the Arizona statute directly implicated the formalist concern raised by O'Connor in her *Apprendi* dissent: was there something unique to the idea of "statutory" maximum as opposed to any other sort of presumptive (but rebuttable) limit *within* that maximum?

The Court had upheld Arizona's statute in *Walton*, a case that predated *Apprendi* by ten years. Quoting from an earlier case that had also upheld Arizona's statute, the controlling plurality in *Walton* stated:

> Aggravating circumstances are not separate penalties or offenses, but are "standards to guide the making of [the] choice" between the alternative verdicts of death and life imprisonment. Thus, under Arizona's capital sentencing scheme, the judge's finding of any particular aggravating circumstance does not of itself "convict" a defendant (i.e., require the death penalty), and the failure to find any particular aggravating circumstance does not "acquit" a defendant (i.e., preclude the death penalty). [497 U.S. at 648.]

Not surprisingly, in the string of cases it cites to justify this position, the plurality cited only *Patterson*, not *Mullaney*.[37]

The Court worked hard to avoid overturning *Walton*. In *Jones*, it stated that *Walton*:

> characterized the finding of aggravating facts falling within the traditional scope of capital sentencing as a choice between a greater and a lesser penalty, not as a process of raising the ceiling of the sentencing range available. We are frank to say that we emphasize this careful reading of *Walton*'s rationale because the question implicated by the Government's position on the meaning of [the carjacking statute] is too significant to be decided without being squarely faced. [526 U.S. at 251.]

(The dissent in *Jones* was unimpressed by the argument: "In distinguishing this line of precedent, the Court suggests *Walton* did not

---

wing (a point we will discuss more when looking at *Blakely*). This seeming contradiction can be resolved by noting that the formalist definition adopted by the *Harris* majority preserves modern sentencing techniques better than the dissent's less-formalist definition, and that appeared to be the goal of the majority.

[37] More accurately, the plurality *did* cite *Mullaney*, but only when discussing the separate issue of shifting the burden of proof for mitigators onto defendants.

'squarely fac[e]' the key constitutional question. . . . The implication is clear. Reexamination of this area of our capital jurisprudence can be expected.")

In *Apprendi*, the majority quoted *Almendarez-Torres* to distinguish *Walton*:

> [O]nce a jury has found the defendant guilty of all the elements of an offense which carries as its maximum penalty the sentence of death, it may be left to the judge to decide whether that maximum penalty, rather than a lesser one, ought to be imposed. . . . The person who is charged with actions that expose him to the death penalty has an absolute entitlement to jury trial on all the elements of the charge. [530 U.S. at 497.]

And like in *Jones*, the dissent (comprised of the same dissenters) was unpersuaded:

> If a State can remove from the jury a factual determination that makes the difference between life and death, as *Walton* holds that it can, it is inconceivable why a State cannot do the same with respect to a factual determination that results in only a 10-year increase in the maximum sentence to which a defendant is exposed.
>
> The distinction of *Walton* offered by the Court today is baffling, to say the least. The key to that distinction is the Court's claim that, in Arizona, the jury makes all of the findings necessary to expose the defendant to a death sentence. [T]hat claim is demonstrably untrue. A defendant convicted of first-degree murder in Arizona cannot receive a death sentence unless a judge makes the factual determination that a statutory aggravating factor exists. Without that critical finding, the maximum sentence to which the defendant is exposed is life imprisonment. . . . [T]he extent of our holding in *Walton* should have been perfectly obvious from the face of our decision. We upheld the Arizona scheme specifically on the ground that the Constitution does not require the jury to make the factual findings that serve as the "prerequisite to imposition of [a death] sentence," or "the specific findings authorizing the imposition of the sentence of death." If the Court does not intend to overrule *Walton*, one would be hard pressed to tell from the opinion it issues today. [530 U.S. at 537–538.]

The dissents in *Jones* and *Apprendi* were correct: *Walton* would be reconsidered, and seven justices would explicitly vote to reverse *Walton* (at least with regard to the *Apprendi* issue). This is *Ring*.

The majority's argument in *Ring* was straight-forward. First, it noted that its rule in *Apprendi*:

> "is one not of form, but of effect." If a State makes an increase in a defendant's authorized punishment contingent on the finding

of a fact, that fact—no matter how the State labels it—must be found by a jury beyond a reasonable doubt. [536 U.S. at 585–586.]

It then pointed out that the Arizona Supreme Court interpreted its death penalty statute as saying that the judge *had* to make certain factual findings before imposing death. As a result, the majority concluded, "we are persuaded that *Walton*, in relevant part, cannot survive the reasoning of *Apprendi*." 537 U.S. at 603. The dissent, written by O'Connor and joined only by Rehnquist, argued that if *Apprendi* and *Walton* were in tension it was *Apprendi*, not *Walton*, that should be reversed. (Breyer, whose dislike of *Apprendi* equaled O'Connor's, concurred (alone) in the judgment on *Eighth* Amendment grounds, looking at the particulars of capital sentencing to reach that decision.)

So the stage was now set for *Blakely* and *Booker*. *Harris* and *Ring* appeared to set out a relatively clear definition of what constituted an "element" for Fifth and Sixth Amendment purposes, and this definition appeared to ensnare all aggravating factors in presumptive guidelines. But *Ring* was a capital case, and sometimes "death is different." After all, the *Ring* majority wrote "we overrule *Walton* to the extent that it allows a sentencing judge, sitting without a jury, to find an aggravating circumstance necessary for imposition of the death penalty." The door was open, perhaps just a crack, to limit *Ring* to capital cases. *Blakely* shut that door convincingly.

QUESTIONS

1. ***Harris* and *Apprendi*.** The dissent in *Harris* stated that:

   Jones called into question, and *Apprendi* firmly limited, a related precept underlying *McMillan*: namely, the State's authority to treat aggravated behavior as a factor increasing the sentence, rather than as an element of the crime. Although the plurality resurrects this principle, it must do so in the face of the Court's contrary conclusion in *Apprendi*, which adopts the position taken by the dissent in *McMillan*: "[I]f a State provides that a specific component of a prohibited transaction shall give rise both to a special stigma and to a special punishment, that component must be treated as a 'fact necessary to constitute the crime' within the meaning of our holding in *In re Winship*."

   Was the dissent right in its interpretation of *Apprendi*?

2. **Inevitability.** Is *Blakely* inevitable given *Ring*? Do *Jones*, *Harris*, *Apprendi*, and *Ring* leave any room for a death-is-different argument to preserve presumptive sentencing?

C.3. THE HAMMER FALLS: *BLAKELY* AND *BOOKER*

Though the scope of the Court's opinion in *Apprendi* was unclear, that in *Ring* was fairly unambiguous: for the purposes of *Apprendi*, the relevant "maximum" is the highest sentence the judge can impose without additional fact-finding, even if that is below the statutory maximum for the offense. *Ring* thus cast a constitutional pall over all presumptive sentencing regimes that relied on judicial fact-finding.

In *Blakely v. Washington* and *United States v. Booker*, the Court made explicit what *Ring* implied. At least to some degree. For while *Blakely* applied *Ring*'s rule to all presumptive sentencing regimes, *Booker* (like *Patterson* before it) immediately started to push back against it. And later Court opinions, particularly *Oregon v. Ice*, constrained the scope of *Blakely* (as well as *Apprendi*) even more, albeit (again) opaquely.

Thus while *Blakely* is often discussed in dramatic terms—"a legal earthquake, a forty-car pileup, a bombshell, and a bull in a china shop"— its actual impact is harder to pin down.[38] The Court quickly began to limit its reach, and it appears that states adapted to its holding with little difficulty. This section examines *Blakely* and *Booker* in detail; Part 4 then looks at the Court's subsequent cases and Part 5 at how states have responded to these decisions.

C.3.a. THE APEX OF *APPRENDI*: *BLAKELY V. WASHINGTON*

In many ways, the outcome in *Blakely* was inevitable given the Court's holding in *Ring*. In fact, a week before the Court issued its *Blakely* opinion, a federal district judge in Massachusetts unknowingly anticipated that decision when he declared the federal sentencing guidelines unconstitutional under *Apprendi* and *Ring*.[39] Yet as the excerpts below make clear, the dissenters from *Apprendi* and *Ring* maintained their opposition in *Blakely*; this enduring resistance ultimately resulted in the confused, fractured outcome in *Booker*.

Blakely v. Washington
542 U.S. 296 (2004)

[The facts of the case: Ralph Blakely, Jr., pled guilty to second degree kidnapping with a firearm for the brutal abduction of his estranged wife and their thirteen year old son. The statutory maximum for second-degree kidnapping was ten years, but given his criminal history Blakely's "standard range" under Washington State's presumptive guidelines was 49 to 53 months. Though the prosecution recommended a sentence within this range, the judge imposed a sentence of 90 months, citing the "exceptional cruelty" of the crime; "exceptional cruelty" was an enumerated aggravator under Washington's guidelines, although Blakely had not allocuted to the necessary details in his plea. Blakely appealed his sentence.]

---

[38] Kevin Reitz provides these examples of alarmist language in *The New Sentencing Conundrum: Policy and Constitutional Law at Cross-Purposes*, 105 COLUM. L. REV. 1082, 1086 (2005). Also see Justice O'Connor's reaction in her *Blakely* dissent given below.

[39] See *United States v. Green*, 346 F. Supp. 2d 259 (D. Mass. 2004).

■ JUSTICE SCALIA delivered the opinion of the Court:

This case requires us to apply the rule we expressed in *Apprendi v. New Jersey*: "Other than the fact of a prior conviction, any fact that increases the penalty for a crime beyond the prescribed statutory maximum must be submitted to a jury, and proved beyond a reasonable doubt."

The State . . . contends that there was no *Apprendi* violation [in sentencing Blakely above the "standard range" but below the statutory maximum] because the relevant "statutory maximum" is not 53 months, but the 10-year maximum. . . . Our precedents make clear, however, that the "statutory maximum" for *Apprendi* purposes is the maximum sentence a judge may impose *solely on the basis of the facts reflected in the jury verdict or admitted by the defendant*. In other words, the relevant "statutory maximum" is not the maximum sentence a judge may impose after finding additional facts, but the maximum he may impose *without* any additional findings. When a judge inflicts punishment that the jury's verdict alone does not allow, the jury has not found all the facts "which the law makes essential to the punishment," . . . and the judge exceeds his proper authority. Because the State's sentencing procedure did not comply with the Sixth Amendment, petitioner's sentence is invalid.[40]

By reversing the judgment below, we are not, as the State would have it, "find[ing] determinate sentencing schemes unconstitutional." This case is not about whether determinate sentencing is constitutional, only about how it can be implemented in a way that respects the Sixth Amendment.

Justice O'Connor argues that, because determinate sentencing schemes involving judicial factfinding entail less judicial discretion than indeterminate schemes, the constitutionality of the latter implies the constitutionality of the former. This argument is flawed on a number of levels. First, the Sixth Amendment by its terms is not a limitation on judicial power, but a reservation of jury power. It limits judicial power only to the extent that the claimed judicial power infringes on the province of the jury. Indeterminate sentencing does not do so. It increases judicial discretion, to be sure, but not at the expense of the jury's traditional function of finding the facts essential to lawful imposition of the penalty. Of course indeterminate schemes involve judicial factfinding. . . . But the facts do not pertain to whether the defendant has a legal *right* to a lesser sentence—and that makes all the difference insofar as judicial impingement upon the traditional role of the jury is concerned. In a system that says the judge may punish burglary with 10 to 40 years, every burglar knows he is risking 40 years in jail. In a system

---

[40] The United States urges us to affirm. It notes differences between Washington's sentencing regime and the Federal Sentencing Guidelines but questions whether those differences are constitutionally significant. The Federal Guidelines are not before us, and we express no opinion on them.

that punishes burglary with a 10-year sentence, with another 30 added for use of a gun, the burglar who enters a home unarmed is *entitled* to no more than a 10-year sentence—and by reason of the Sixth Amendment the facts bearing upon that entitlement must be found by a jury.

But even assuming that restraint of judicial power unrelated to the jury's role is a Sixth Amendment objective, it is far from clear that *Apprendi* deserves that goal. Determinate judicial-factfinding schemes entail less judicial power than indeterminate schemes, but more judicial power than determinate *jury*-factfinding schemes. Whether *Apprendi* increases judicial power overall depends on what States with determinate judicial-factfinding schemes would do, given the choice between the two alternatives. Justice O'Connor simply assumes that the net effect will favor judges, but she has no empirical basis for that prediction. Indeed, what evidence we have points exactly the other way: When the Kansas Supreme Court found *Apprendi* infirmities in that State's determinate-sentencing regime in *State v. Gould* . . . , the legislature responded not by reestablishing indeterminate sentencing but by applying *Apprendi*'s requirements to its current regime. The result was less, not more, judicial power.

The judgment of the Washington Court of Appeals is reversed. . . .

■ JUSTICE O'CONNOR, with whom the CHIEF JUSTICE, JUSTICE BREYER, and JUSTICE KENNEDY join, dissenting:

The legacy of today's opinion, whether intended or not, will be the consolidation of sentencing power in the State and Federal Judiciaries. The Court says to Congress and state legislatures: If you want to constrain the sentencing discretion of judges and bring some uniformity to sentencing, it will cost you—dearly. Congress and States, faced with the burdens imposed by the extension of *Apprendi* to the present context, will either trim or eliminate altogether their sentencing guidelines schemes and, with them, 20 years of sentencing reform.

The "effect" of today's decision will be greater judicial discretion and less uniformity in sentencing. Because I find it implausible that the Framers would have considered such a result to be required by the Due Process Clause or the Sixth Amendment, and because the practical consequences of today's decision may be disastrous, I respectfully dissent.

Far from disregarding principles of due process and the jury trial right, as the majority today suggests, Washington's reform has served them. Before passage of the Act, a defendant charged with second degree kidnapping . . . had no idea whether he would receive a 10-year sentence or probation. After passage of the Act, a defendant charged with second degree kidnapping knows what his presumptive sentence will be; he has a good idea of the types of factors that a sentencing judge can and will consider when deciding whether to sentence him outside that range; he is guaranteed meaningful appellate review to protect against an arbitrary sentence. Criminal defendants still face the same statutory maximum sentences, but they now at least know, much more than before, the real consequences of their actions.

Washington's move to a system of guided discretion has served equal protection principles as well. Over the past 20 years, there has been a substantial reduction in racial disparity in sentencing across the State. The reduction is directly traceable to the constraining effects of the guidelines—namely, its "presumptive range[s]" and limits on the imposition of "exceptional sentences" outside of those ranges. To the extent that unjustifiable racial disparities have persisted in Washington, it has been in the imposition of . . . alternative sentences. The lesson is powerful: racial disparity is correlated with unstructured and unreviewed discretion.

The consequences of today's decision will be as far reaching as they are disturbing. Washington's sentencing system is by no means unique. Numerous other States have enacted guidelines systems, as has the Federal Government. [Here Justice O'Connor cites statutes from Alaska, Arkansas, Florida, Kansas, Michigan, Minnesota, North Carolina, Oregon, and Pennsylvania.] Today's decision casts constitutional doubt over them all and, in so doing, threatens an untold number of criminal judgments. Every sentence imposed under such guidelines in cases currently pending on direct appeal is in jeopardy.

The practical consequences for trial courts, starting today, will be equally unsettling: How are courts to mete out guidelines sentences? Do courts apply the guidelines as to mitigating factors, but not as to aggravating factors? Do they jettison the guidelines altogether? The Court ignores the havoc it is about to wreak on trial courts across the country.

What I have feared most has now come to pass: Over 20 years of sentencing reform are all but lost, and tens of thousands of criminal judgments are in jeopardy. I respectfully dissent.

■ JUSTICE BREYER, with whom JUSTICE O'CONNOR joins, dissenting:

The majority ignores the adverse consequences inherent in its conclusion. As a result of the majority's rule, sentencing must now take one of three forms, each of which risks either impracticality, unfairness, or harm to the jury trial right the majority purports to strengthen. This circumstance shows that the majority's Sixth Amendment interpretation cannot be right.

A first option for legislators is to create a simple, pure or nearly pure "charge offense" or "determinate" sentencing system. In such a system, an indictment would charge a few facts which, taken together, constitute a crime, such as robbery. Robbery would carry a single sentence, say, five years' imprisonment. And every person convicted of robbery would receive that sentence—just as, centuries ago, everyone convicted of almost any serious crime was sentenced to death.

Such a system assures uniformity, but at intolerable costs. First, simple determinate sentencing systems impose identical punishments on people who committed their crimes in very different ways. Second, in a world of statutorily fixed mandatory sentences for many crimes, determinate sentencing gives tremendous power to prosecutors to manipulate sentences through their choice of charges. Defendants, knowing that they will not have a chance to argue for a lower sentence in front of a judge, may plead to charges that they might otherwise contest.

A second option for legislators is to return to a system of indeterminate sentencing, such as California had before the recent sentencing reform movement. [Breyer then recounts the standard concerns with such a system.] Returning to such a system . . . would do little to "ensur[e] [the] control" of what the majority calls "the peopl[e,]" *i.e.*, the jury, "in the judiciary," since "the peopl[e]" would only decide the defendant's guilt, a finding with no effect on the duration of the sentence. It is difficult to see how such an outcome protects the structural safeguards the majority claims to be defending.

A third option is that which the Court seems to believe legislators will in fact take. That is the option of retaining structured schemes that attempt to punish similar conduct similarly and different conduct differently, but modifying them to conform to *Apprendi*'s dictates. Judges would be able to depart *downward* from presumptive sentences upon finding that mitigating factors were present, but would not be able to depart *upward* unless the prosecutor charged the aggravating fact to a jury and proved it beyond a reasonable doubt.

This option can be implemented in one of two ways. The first way would be for legislatures to subdivide each crime into a list of complex crimes, each of which would be defined to include commonly found sentencing factors such as drug quantity, type of victim, presence of violence, degree of injury, use of gun, and so on. A legislature, for example, might enact a robbery statute, modeled on robbery sentencing guidelines, that increases punishment depending upon (1) the nature of the institution robbed, (2) the (a) presence of, (b) brandishing of, (c) other use of, a firearm, (3) making of a death threat, (4) presence of (a) ordinary, (b) serious, (c) permanent or life threatening, bodily injury, (5) abduction, (6) physical restraint, (7) taking of a firearm, (8) taking of drugs, (9) value of property loss, etc.

This "complex charge offense" system . . . prejudices defendants who seek trial, for it can put them in the untenable position of contesting material aggravating facts in the guilt phases of their trials. [He notes that defendants may be essentially forced to argue "I did not sell drugs, and if I did, I did not sell more than 500 grams"]

The second way to make sentencing guidelines *Apprendi*-compliant would be to require at least two juries for each defendant whenever aggravating facts are present: one jury to determine guilt of the crime charged, and an additional jury to try the disputed facts that, if found, would aggravate the sentence. Our experience with bifurcated trials in the capital punishment context suggests that requiring them for run-of-the-mill sentences would be costly, both in money and in judicial time and resources. Indeed, cost and delay could lead legislatures to revert to the complex charge offense system. . . .

The uncomfortable fact that could make the system seem workable—even desirable in the minds of some, including defense attorneys—is called "plea bargaining." The Court can announce that the Constitution requires at least two jury trials for each criminal defendant—one for guilt, another for sentencing—but only because it knows full well that more than 90% of defendants will not go to trial even once, much less insist on two or more trials. [The] greater expense attached to trials and their greater complexity, taken together in the context of an overworked criminal justice system, will likely mean, other things being equal, fewer trials and a greater reliance upon plea bargaining—a system in which punishment is set not by judges or juries but by advocates acting under bargaining constraints.

Is there a fourth option? Perhaps. Congress and state legislatures might, for example, rewrite their criminal codes, attaching astronomically high sentences to each crime, followed by long lists of mitigating facts, which, for the most part, would consist of the absence of aggravating facts. But political impediments to legislative action make such rewrites difficult to achieve. . . .

For the reasons given, I dissent.

A Close Look at *Blakely*'s Arguments

At first blush, *Blakely* seems like a relatively straight-forward case that extended *Apprendi* and, more clearly, *Ring* to their logical conclusions. Examined a bit more closely, however, and some potential problems emerge from the opinion.

In many ways, the majority and dissent in *Blakely* seem to be carrying on almost completely separate conversations. This may be less surprising once we better understand the divide that ran through the Court. Since *Almendarez-Torres*, the Court's sentencing cases often tuned on a 5–4 split that did not adhere to the conventional left/right ideological divide: Ginsburg, Scalia, Souter, Stevens, and Thomas on one side, Breyer, Kennedy, O'Connor, and Rehnquist on the other. As Walter Dellinger points out, the apparent cross-party divide is actually a consistent party-line vote when we define the parties as "legalist" (or "doctrinal") and "pragmatist."[41] That doctrinal and pragmatic arguments exhibit little overlap is to be expected.

---

[41] http://www.slate.com/articles/life/the_breakfast_table/features/2004/a_supreme_court_dialogue/showtime_for_the_supremes.html.

So consider a remark made by two members of Ohio's Criminal Sentencing Commission in the wake of *Blakely*: "Did you hear the one about the defendant whose right to a jury trial was vindicated by giving judges more power?"[42] Ohio's Supreme Court responded to *Blakely* by declaring Ohio's guidelines wholly voluntary: a decision about jury rights ultimately expanded judicial power by removing a check on judges' discretion. To the sentencing commissioners, this was a troubling outcome.

But would the *Blakely* majority see it as such? The majority was concerned with a clear, simple doctrinal point: if the state creates a legally binding expectation, only a jury can make the necessary fact-finding to break that expectation. As Justice Scalia explained, "The Sixth Amendment is not a limitation on judicial power, but a reservation of jury power. It limits judicial power only to the extent that the claimed judicial power infringes on the province of the jury." In other words, the *Blakely* majority was not interested in any sort of power-balance between juries and judges, or between prosecutors and defendants, or any other of the many pairings that exist in the criminal justice system. It was focused solely on expectations.

So now return to Justice Breyer's complaint about the majority's position: "As a result of the majority's rule, sentencing must now take one of three forms, each of which risks either impracticality, unfairness, or harm to the jury trial right the majority purports to strengthen. This circumstance shows that the majority's Sixth Amendment interpretation cannot be right." Several questions immediately arise:

1. Was Justice Breyer engaging the majority on its own terms, or was he attacking an argument the majority was not making? Was the majority purporting to "strengthen" the jury trial right? In part of its opinion not excerpted above, the majority favorably cited *Williams v. New York*, 337 U.S. 241 (1949), which upheld a judge's use of "facts outside the trial record" when imposing the death penalty in an indeterminate sentencing regime. Is a majority that still follows *Williams* one that is necessarily concerned with strengthening juries or restraining judges?

2. Justice Breyer's point about unfairness was based on "real-offense sentencing" concerns, that offenders who commit similar offenses may not be punished similarly. Assuming that Breyer is right, that sentences will become more disparate in the wake of *Blakely*, does that necessarily mean that the outcome is *worse*?

Another fissure running through *Blakely*, conceptually tied to the doctrinal/pragmatist divide, concerned appellate judicial discretion and

---

[42] See David Diroll and Scott Anderson, "Felony Sentencing After *Foster*," available online at http://www.sconet.state.oh.us/Boards/Sentencing/resources/Publications/foster.pdf.

due process. The majority insisted on a bright line that eliminated any distinction between "sentencing factors" and "elements of a crime," stating any such distinction would require judges to ensure "that the law must not go *too far*—it must not exceed the judicial estimation of the proper role of the judge." Such analysis is too subjective, the majority held, because "the very reason the Framers put a jury-trial guarantee in the Constitution is that they were unwilling to trust government to mark out the role of the jury."

Justice Breyer responded to this claim with a due process argument: "Congress might permit a judge to sentence an individual for murder though convicted only of making an illegal lane change. But that is the kind of problem that the Due Process Clause is well suited to cure. *McMillan* foresaw the possibility that judges would have to use their own judgment in dealing with such a problem; but that is what judges are there for." In other words, the majority did not trust appellate judges to make subjective decisions about whether a "sentencing factor" looked too much like an "element," while Justice Breyer believed that this was the very type of decision the Due Process clause appears to trust judges to make.

One more margin of disagreement was historical. The *Blakely* majority's doctrinal argument did not emerge from thin air, but was built on a particular historical reading of the founders' intent. Justice O'Connor criticized the majority: "Because broad judicial sentencing discretion was foreign to the Framers . . . , they were never faced with the constitutional choice between submitting every fact that increases a sentence to the jury or vesting the sentencing judge with broad discretionary authority to account for differences in offenses and offenders." Sentences in the colonial and early post-Revolution period were tightly linked to the conviction offense. Was Justice O'Connor's concern convincing?

There is also a generally-unstated subtext to *Blakely*: in many ways, this opinion has very little to do with state sentencing, and quite a lot to do with federal sentencing. Consider the following two statements. The first comes from Justice Scalia's majority opinion in *Blakely*:

> This would mean, for example, that a judge could sentence a man for committing murder even if the jury convicted him only of illegally possessing the firearm used to commit it—or of making an illegal lane change while fleeing the death scene. Not even *Apprendi*'s critics would advocate this absurd result. [542 U.S. at 306.]

The second comes from Washington State's code at the time *Blakely* was issued:

> Wash Code Rev § 9.94A.530(3): In determining any sentence above the standard sentence range, . . . [f]acts that establish the elements of a more serious crime or additional crimes may not

be used to go outside the standard sentence range except upon stipulation or when specifically provided for in [provisions involving pattern offenses, such as allowing the court to acknowledge past domestic abuses when imposing sentence for the most recent instance].

In other words, the "tail wags the dog" concern that motivated the majority was *impossible* in Washington. In fact, such a result was impossible in almost all states that used sentencing guidelines, since almost all rejected so-called "real offense sentencing." The federal guidelines, however, were built on real-offense sentencing through-and-through.

The majority exhibited a federal-sentencing orientation elsewhere as well, such as when it relied on a federal sentencing statute for the claim that an "evaluation of *Apprendi*'s 'fairness' to criminal defendants must compare it with the regime it replaced, in which a defendant, with no warning in either his indictment or plea, would routinely see his maximum potential sentence balloon from as little as five years to as much as life imprisonment." State guideline regimes simply did not permit such dramatic changes; the federal system did. The dissents by Justices Breyer and O'Connor similarly referred to federal complexities that did not exist at the state level. Justice Scalia may have said that "The Federal Guidelines are not before us, and we express no opinion on them," but it is clear that they were forefront in the minds of the majority and dissents alike.

QUESTIONS

1. **Asymmetry.** *Blakely* exhibits an interesting asymmetry: facts required for a higher sentence must be proven beyond a reasonable doubt to a jury, but those required for a lower sentence can be found by a preponderance of the evidence by a judge. Can we justify this distinction? What is the jury designed to do, and is this task more important when the state is being increasingly severe than when it is being increasingly merciful?

2. **Conflicting constitutional goals.** The dissenters pointed out that the majority's opinion may lead to sentencing outcomes that put increased weight on constitutionally suspect factors, such as the defendant's race or sex. How should a doctrinal approach to the Sixth Amendment take such risks into account? In other words, how can a doctrinal approach balance competing doctrinal interests (here, between the jury-right clause and the equal protection clause)? Recall the point made by Kaplow and Shavell in Chapter 2, that even retributivists are forced to make consequentialist decisions in a world of limited resources. How applicable is their analysis here? Is the "doctrinal" majority effectively making a "pragmatic" choice between jury rights and equal protection, even if it doesn't acknowledge it?

3. **Appellate courts and due process.** Contrary to Justice Breyer, Justice Scalia expressed doubt about appellate courts' ability to prevent trial courts from violating due process if such courts had to draw the line between "sentencing factor" and "element." Is there something different about appellate courts reviewing lower *courts* for due process violations than reviewing executive-branch actors for such violations (which they do routinely)? Should we be concerned about appellate review of executive delegations to the judiciary (here, to draw the factor/element line) as opposed to that review of executive actions?

4. **Tail wagging the dog.** Can we reconcile the facts of *United States v. Vernier*, the 11th Circuit case involving the defendant who pled guilty to credit card fraud but had his sentence aggravated to account for an uncharged murder, with Justice Breyer's statement that "Congress might permit a judge to sentence an individual for murder though convicted only of making an illegal lane change[, b]ut that is the kind of problem that the Due Process Clause is well suited to cure"?

5. **The inevitability of *Blakely*.** The majority in *Blakely* claimed that it was just applying the rule in *Apprendi*. Was this right? Could the Court have reached the opposite conclusion in *Blakely* without overturning *Apprendi*? How analogous would such a situation be with the that which exists between *Patterson* and *Mullaney*? Even if an oppositely-decided *Blakely* could have been reconciled with *Apprendi*, however, could it have been reconciled with *Ring*? Or would an opposite conclusion in *Blakely* have necessitated reversing *Ring*?

6. **Greater includes the lesser?** How convincing is Justice O'Connor's greater-includes-the-lesser-point, that if a legislature can grant judges unfettered discretion via indeterminacy or highly cabined discretion via jury fact-finding of sentencing factors, then the legislature should also be able to create systems that fall somewhere in between? Are there any institutional concerns with her proposal?

7. **States vs. Feds.** As noted above, while nominally dealing with a state sentencing statute, the Justices seem to spend much of their time implicitly debating federal sentencing (clearly anticipating the debate to come in *Booker*). That said, had the Justices taken a more state-specific focus, do you think the opinion would have turned out any differently? If so, how?

8. ***Blakely v. Almendarez-Torres*.** Is the prior-history exemption as defensible under *Blakely* as under *Apprendi*? Does *Blakely* modify the logic of *Apprendi* in any way that would justify reversing *Almendarez-Torres*?

The Options That Remain

Justice Breyer's dissent lays out many (but not all) of the sentencing regimes that states can continue to use following *Blakely*. The primary options are:

1. Presumptive guidelines with juries finding aggravating facts.
2. "Uncapped" guidelines that consist only of mandatory minimums.
3. Voluntary guidelines.
4. Indeterminacy.
5. Strict determinacy or complex-charge systems

Since no state uses a strictly determinate system, we will not consider that option further. But let us look at the other choices in turn.

Justices Scalia and Breyer disagree strongly over the feasibility of sentencing juries. Justice Scalia notes that the only state to anticipate *Blakely*'s holding, Kansas, had adopted sentencing juries; Justice Breyer looks with alarm at the costs of sentencing juries in capital cases. Justice Scalia appears to have the upper hand in this debate. In Kansas, the average sentencing hearing takes approximately one hour, and it involves the same jury as the trial: the burden does not appear to be that great.[43] And of the thirteen states affected by *Blakely*, seven have chosen to adopt sentencing juries, contrary to Breyer's prediction. As for Breyer, capital cases are outliers in multiple ways, including the complicated nature of the sentencing phase: capital costs have very little in common with non-capital costs.

Two states—Michigan and Pennsylvania—have employed some form of "uncapped" guidelines (although the Michigan state supreme court recently weakened them in the wake of *Alleyne*[44]). Both implemented these systems prior to *Blakely*, and neither had found any *Blakely* defect with its guidelines. At the same time, no other state has opted to follow in Michigan's or Pennsylvania's footsteps since 2004.

It is perhaps surprising that nowhere in his dissent does Justice Breyer discuss voluntary guidelines, despite the fact that Washington, DC, and seven states—Arkansas, Delaware, Maryland, Missouri, Utah, Virginia, and Wisconsin—have chosen to use such guidelines.[45] Ohio has since decided to follow course in the wake of *Blakely*.[46] By only suggesting, but not requiring, judges to follow them,[47] such guidelines are clearly permissible under *Blakely*. The defendant has no *legal*

---

[43] See Adam Liptak, "Justices' Sentencing Ruling May Have Model in Kansas," NEW YORK TIMES, July 13, 2004.

[44] *People v. Lockridge* (July 29, 2015), available on-line at http://courts.mi.gov/Courts/MichiganSupremeCourt/Clerks/Recent%20Opinions/14-15-Term-Opinions/149073-Opinion.pdf.

[45] Wisconsin used voluntary guidelines from 1985 to 1995 and again from 2003 to 2009. Washington, DC, did not adopt its guidelines until 2004, the same year the Court handed down *Blakely*.

[46] See *State v. Foster*, 845 N.E.2d 470 (Ohio 2006).

[47] Parties cannot appeal if a judge fails to adhere to voluntary guidelines. See, for example, Va. Code § 19.2–298.01(F) and MD Code Crim. Proc. § 6–211(b).

expectation that he will receive the default guideline sentence, which is the condition at the heart of the majority's opinion.

And there is some evidence that voluntary guidelines can accomplish some, though not all, of what presumptive guidelines did.[48] In a study that primarily compared outcomes in Virginia and Missouri to those in presumptive- and no-guideline states, I found that the sentences imposed on similar offenders are more consistent in voluntary guideline states than in no-guideline states, but less consistent than in presumptive guideline states. Similarly, race and sex influence sentence length less in voluntary guideline states than in no-guideline state, but more than in presumptive guideline states. It should be stressed, however, that voluntary guidelines appear to be much more effective in Virginia than in Missouri. And while judges are elected in Missouri, they are appointed, retained, and promoted by the legislature in Virginia. So just how voluntary are the Virginia guidelines in practice?

Finally, like uncapped guidelines, the last option—indeterminacy—was in use before *Blakely* and remains in use following it. And like uncapped guidelines, no state with guidelines that violated *Blakely* has opted to go down that path. Unlike uncapped guidelines, however, indeterminacy remains the sentencing regime used in a majority of states.

QUESTIONS

1. **Voluntarily binding.** Are there reasons to be concerned about the constitutional permissibility of voluntary guidelines? As noted above, judges surely face (or at least feel) substantial pressure in Virginia to conform to the guidelines. And, not surprisingly, compliance rates are high: In 2010 the Virginia Criminal Sentencing Commission reported a compliance rate of 79.6%, with only 44.9% of the non-compliant sentences (or 9.2% of all cases) involving aggravators.[49] Do such high compliance rates, along with the identifiable political pressures that seem likely to encourage them, suggest that defendants could have a reasonable expectation of receiving an unenhanced sentence?

In other words, does the majority's solely-doctrinal focus on the legal threat of appellate reversal make sense? How important are other factors, such as the risk of losing one's spot on the bench, or evidence that judges may feel obligated to comply with voluntary guidelines due to internal, institutional pressures? However, even if the doctrinal line is normatively unappealing, how would courts set about determining when there is "enough" pressure on trial judges to create a sufficient expectation? Do they have the institutional competence to do so?

---

[48] Pfaff, *The Continued Vitality of Structured Sentencing Following* Blakely: *The Effectiveness of Voluntary Guidelines*, 54 UCLA L. REV. 236 (2006).

[49] VIRGINIA CRIMINAL SENTENCING COMMISSION, 2010 ANNUAL REPORT, available on-line at http://www.vcsc.virginia.gov/2010AnnualReport.pdf.

2. **State case, federal opinion.** To what extent is Justice Breyer's concern with a charge offense system driven by his experience with federal, as opposed to state, sentencing? Compare the following guidelines provisions concerning the use of guns in a crime:

From the federal sentencing guidelines:

U.S.S.G. § 2B3.1(b)(2): (A) If a firearm was discharged, increase by 7 levels; (B) if a firearm was otherwise used, increase by 6 levels; (C) if a firearm was brandished or possessed, increase by 5 levels; (D) if a dangerous weapon was otherwise used, increase by 4 levels; (E) if a dangerous weapon was brandished, or possessed, increase by 3 levels; or (F) if a threat of death was made, increase by 2 levels.

And from the North Carolina list of aggravators:

N.C. Stat. § 15A–1340.16(d)(10): The defendant was armed with or used a deadly weapon at the time of the crime.

How pressing is Breyer's concern in North Carolina (which is fairly representative of state guidelines) as opposed to in the federal system?

How Far Does *Blakely* Reach?

At one level, *Blakely* is a wide-reaching opinion that packed a powerful punch. Now that the dust has (more or less) settled, it has invalidated the sentencing guidelines of the federal government and in thirteen states: Alaska, Arizona, California, Colorado, Indiana, Minnesota, New Jersey, New Mexico, North Carolina, Ohio, Oregon, Tennessee, and Washington.[50] These jurisdictions represent almost all states that had presumptive guidelines in 2004 and a majority of all states with presumptive or voluntary guidelines that year.

Moreover, these fourteen jurisdictions had disproportionately large prisoner populations. In 2004, these states possessed over 425,000 prisoners, or about one-third of the 1.3 million inmates in state prisons; including the federal system, over 605,000 (or over 40%) of the nation's 1.5 million prisoners. Numbers such as these motivated Justice O'Connor's warning about the volume of appeals that *Blakely* could generate, and "the havoc it [would] wreak on trial courts across the country."

Yet despite all this, the overall impact of *Blakely* may ultimately be slight. Part C.4 fleshes this point out in more detail, but the basic story is simple: outside of federal sentencing, most sentences imposed in *Blakely*-violating states did not involve constitutionally-problematic aggravators. In some states, fewer than 5% of sentences involved aggravators, and many of these likely resulted from pleas in which the

---

[50] See John F. Pfaff, *The Future of Appellate Sentencing Review:* Booker *in the States*, 93 MARQUETTE L. REV. 683 (2009).

defendant (unlike Blakely) allocuted to the necessary facts (or could easily be induced to do so in a post-*Blakely* world).

Furthermore, O'Connor's lament that twenty years of sentencing reform has come to an end understates substantially the scope of reform that has taken place since the 1970s, and it overstates *Blakely*'s effect on it. Guidelines are just one type of reform, along with truth-in-sentencing and strike laws, parole abolition, sentencing commission establishment, parole guidelines, and expanded scope of mandatory minimums, to name just some of the structural changes states undertook. And by and large *Blakely* affects none of these. Thus the fears of Justices O'Connor and Breyer do not appear to have been realized: states have responded to *Blakely* with relative ease, and sentencing in the affected states does not appear to have been greatly affected.

QUESTIONS

1. **Appealable sentences.** In part of her dissent, Justice O'Connor discusses the potential volume of sentencing appeals at the federal level, noting that over 270,000 sentences had been imposed between *Apprendi* and *Blakely*. At the state level, between 2000 and 2004 the thirteen states affected by *Blakely* admitted over 1.2 million inmates to prison (with California alone responsible for over 630,000 admissions). How many of these sentences were likely constitutionally impermissible? And how important is the following fact: the median time spent in prison in many states is somewhere between six to twenty-four months?

2. ***Blakely*'s silver lining, redux.** In question 1 on page 303 above, we considered the claim that states with guidelines invalidated by *Blakely* would likely see incarceration rates go up and thus crime go down. Should we expect *Blakely* to lead to substantially different incarceration rates? Does Figure 6–1, which compares incarceration rates in states affected by *Blakely* to those unaffected by the decision, shed any light on the issue?

Figure 6–1: Per Capita Prison Populations

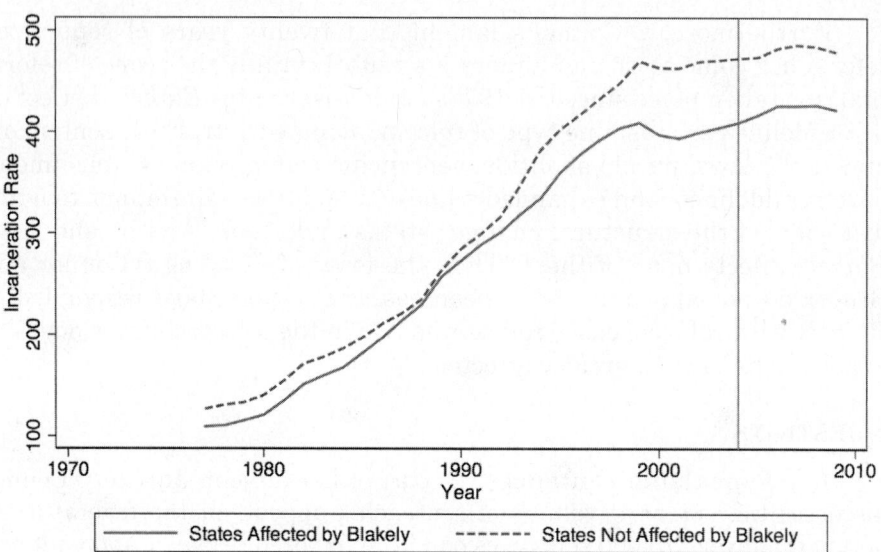

PROBLEM: NEW YORK STATE'S PERSISTENT FELONY OFFENDER LAW

Between 2004 and 2010, New York State's Persistent Felony Offender (PFO) Law, NY Penal Law § 70.10, was repeatedly challenged for requiring judicial fact-finding of the sort banned by *Blakely*. Does the law violate *Blakely*? Below is the statute as well as some of the caselaw surrounding it. The PFO law reads in part:

> 1. Definition of persistent felony offender. A persistent felony offender is a person . . . who stands convicted of a felony after having previously been convicted of two or more felonies. . . .
>
> 2. Authorized sentence. When the court has found . . . that a person is a persistent felony offender, and when it is of the opinion that the history and character of the defendant and the nature and circumstances of his criminal conduct indicate that extended incarceration and life-time supervision will best serve the public interest, the court, in lieu of imposing the sentence of imprisonment authorized [elsewhere] for the crime of which such person presently stands convicted, may impose the sentence of imprisonment authorized by that section for a class A-I felony [,which carries a maximum term of life and is the highest possible felony in New York State].

NY Crim. Proc. Law § 400.20 explains further how the "history and character" evidence should be determined:

> 2. Authorization for hearing. When information available to the court prior to sentencing indicates that the defendant is a persistent felony offender, and when, in the opinion of the

court, the available information shows that a persistent felony offender sentence may be warranted, the court may order a hearing to determine (a) whether the defendant is in fact a persistent felony offender, and (b) if so, whether a persistent felony offender sentence should be imposed. . . .

6. Burden and standard of proof; evidence. Matters pertaining to the defendant's history and character and the nature and circumstances of his criminal conduct may be established by any relevant evidence, not legally privileged, regardless of admissibility under the exclusionary rules of evidence, and the standard of proof with respect to such matters shall be a preponderance of the evidence. . . .

9. [When] the uncontroverted allegations with respect to the defendant's history and the nature of his prior criminal conduct do not warrant sentencing him as a persistent felony offender, or where the defendant has offered to present evidence to establish facts that would affect the court's decision on the question of whether a persistent felony offender sentence is warranted, the court may fix a date for a further hearing.

In *People v. Rivera*, 833 N.E.2d 194 (N.Y. 2005), and several other cases, the New York Court of Appeals (the highest court in New York State) held that the PFO did not violate *Blakely*. The court pointed to precedent holding that prior convictions alone are enough to trigger an A1 sentence under the PFO. The *Rivera* Court stated that:

> Criminal Procedure Law § 400.20, by authorizing a hearing on facts relating to the defendant's history and character, does not grant defendants a legal entitlement to have those facts receive controlling weight in influencing the court's opinion. The statutory language requiring the sentencing court to consider the specified factors and to articulate the reason for the chosen sentence grants defendants a right to an airing and an explanation, not a result. [833 N.E.2d at 68.]

In *Besser v. Walsh*, 601 F.3d 163 (2d Cir. 2010), however, a panel on the Second Circuit reversed *Rivera* (and other consolidated cases). The court said:

> In the briefs submitted by state authorities, it was suggested that a finding of two felony convictions alone locks in the Class A-I range, with life as a maximum. We disagree. The history/character/criminal conduct findings, which are subject to appellate review, are necessary to lock in the Class A-I range and, if such findings do not justify a Class A-I sentence, require the sentencing court to sentence the defendant in a lesser range, usually as a second felony (or violent felony) offender. [601 F.3d at 172.]

This decision by the panel was then itself reversed *en banc* by the Second Circuit in *Portalatin v. Graham*, 624 F.3d 69 (2d Cir. 2010). A majority of the panel deferred to the New York Court of Appeals' interpretation of the PFO statute. Three dissenting judges (including two of the judges who issued *Besser*) pointed out that the trial judges who imposed the contested sentences appeared to have explicitly relied on certain judicially-found facts, even if not required to do so, and that:

> [M]y colleagues have successfully defended the PFO statute against a facial attack by showing that the predicate felonies may alone justify a Class A-I sentence, while not addressing the claims before us that factfinding beyond the predicate felonies actually occurred and enhanced the sentences of the petitioners. [624 F.3d at 100.]

QUESTIONS

1. Is the *Rivera* Court's argument convincing, or does *Besser* have the upper hand? If prior convictions alone justify an A1 sentence under the PFO, are the findings about the history and character serving as aggravators or mitigators?

2. Even if the *Rivera* Court is correct, is the dissent in *Portalatin* still right about the need to permit as-applied challenges? In other words, even if PFO findings *can* be seen as mitigators, might they in some cases be *actually used* as aggravators? If you think this concern is a valid one, what would the effect of such a holding be? Would we expect the number of A1 sentences imposed under the PFO to fall, or would we just expect judges to change the way they write their opinions? Does your answer depend on whether you take a more institutionalist or realist view of judicial behavior?

C.3.b. *BLAKELY'S PATTERSON: UNITED STATES V. BOOKER*

As soon as the Court issued its opinion in *Blakely*, people's attention turned to its implications for federal sentencing.[51] Federal judges, prosecutors, and defendants quickly realized that *Blakely* quite likely invalidated the federal guidelines, although the various circuits split on that issue; those distinguishing the federal guidelines from Washington's focused primarily on the fact that the guidelines were not statutes, and so guideline limits did not equal "statutory limits."[52]

In many ways, *Blakely*'s implications for federal sentencing were greater than those for state sentencing. Aggravating facts were used relatively sparingly in state sentencing, but they were the very essence of the federal sentencing regime. As noted above, in one post-*Blakely*/pre-*Booker* case in the Eastern District of New York, prosecutors attempted

---

[51] See, for example, Adam Liptak, "Sentencing Decision's Reach is Far and Wide," NEW YORK TIMES (June 27, 2004); and Kate Stith and William Stuntz, "Sense and Sentencing," NEW YORK TIMES A27 (June 29, 2004)

[52] See *United States v. Pineiro*, 337 F.3d 464 (5th Cir. 2004); *United States v. Hammoud*, 381 F.3d 316 (4th Cir. 2004); and *United States v. Koch*, 383 F.3d 436 (6th Cir. 2004).

to cover their bases by submitting all the required fact-finding to a sentencing jury. The form ran over twenty pages![53]

In *Booker*, the Supreme Court explicitly confronted whether *Blakely* invalidated the federal guidelines. The result was one of the most fractured Court opinions issued in recent years. There were two majorities. The first—the same five-justice majority from *Apprendi* through *Blakely*—declared that the guidelines rely on unconstitutional judicial fact-finding. The second—the *Blakely* dissenters plus Justice Ginsburg, the only justice to sign on to both majorities—issued the remedy, which was to make the guidelines voluntary. Sort of. The two majorities do not mesh well, and as you will see in Part C.5, the Court has been forced to hand down at least ten opinions to date trying to define precisely how the two pieces fit together.

United States v. Booker
543 U.S. 220 (2005)

■ JUSTICE STEVENS, with whom JUSTICE SCALIA, JUSTICE SOUTER, JUSTICE THOMAS, and JUSTICE GINSBURG join, delivered the opinion of the Court in part.

The question presented . . . is whether an application of the Federal Sentencing Guidelines violated the Sixth Amendment. We hold that . . . the Sixth Amendment as construed in *Blakely* does apply to the Sentencing Guidelines. As the dissenting opinions in *Blakely* recognized, there is no distinction of constitutional significance between the Federal Sentencing Guidelines and the Washington procedures at issue in that case.

[O]ur holding in *Blakely* applies to the Sentencing Guidelines. We recognize, as we did in *Jones, Apprendi*, and *Blakely*, that in some cases jury factfinding may impair the most expedient and efficient sentencing of defendants. But the interest in fairness and reliability protected by the right to a jury trial—a common-law right that defendants enjoyed for centuries and that is now enshrined in the Sixth Amendment—has always outweighed the interest in concluding trials swiftly. As Blackstone put it:

> [H]owever *convenient* these [new methods of trial] may appear at first (as doubtless all arbitrary powers, well executed, are the most *convenient*) yet let it be again remembered, that delays, and little inconveniences in the forms of justice, are the price that all free nations must pay for their liberty in more substantial matters; that these inroads upon this sacred bulwark of the nation are fundamentally opposite to the spirit

---

[53] *United States v. Medas*, 323 F.Supp. 2d 436 (E.D.N.Y. 2004); see also Albert Alschuler, *To Sever or Not to Sever? Why* Blakely *Requires Action by Congress*, 17 FED. SENT. RPTR. 11 (2004).

of our constitution; and that, though begun in trifles, the precedent may gradually increase and spread, to the utter disuse of juries in questions of the most momentous concerns.

4 Commentaries on the Laws of England 343–344 (1769).

Accordingly, we reaffirm our holding in *Apprendi:* Any fact (other than a prior conviction) which is necessary to support a sentence exceeding the maximum authorized by the facts established by a plea of guilty or a jury verdict must be admitted by the defendant or proved to a jury beyond a reasonable doubt.

■ JUSTICE BREYER, with whom the CHIEF JUSTICE and JUSTICE GINSBURG, JUSTICE KENNEDY, and JUSTICE O'CONNOR join, delivered the opinion of the Court in part.

We here turn to the . . . question . . . that concerns the remedy. We answer the question of remedy by finding the provision of the federal sentencing statute that makes the Guidelines mandatory, 18 USCA § 3553(b)(1),* incompatible with today's constitutional holding. We conclude that this provision must be severed and excised, as must one other statutory section, § 3742(e),** which depends upon the Guidelines' mandatory nature. So modified, the Federal Sentencing Act makes the Guidelines effectively advisory. It requires a sentencing court to consider Guidelines ranges, but it permits the court to tailor the sentence in light of other statutory concerns as well. . . .

[Justice Breyer justifies severing the mandatory provisions instead of requiring jury factfinding by looking to legislative history, laying out 5 reasons why Congress would not have intended the Guidelines to require jury fact-finding of aggravating factors: (1) its particular use of the word "judge," (2) a real-offense sentencing scheme that limits disparity requires judicial fact-finding, (3) the resulting scheme would be far more complex than Congress intended, (4) plea bargaining in an increasingly disparate shadow would itself lead to more disparate outcomes, and (5) Congress would not have approved of the asymmetry in jury requirements between upward and downward departures by judges.]

[After severing the two mandatory provisions discussed above, the remedial majority continues:] The remainder of the Act function[s] independently. Without the "mandatory" provision, the Act nonetheless requires judges to take account of the Guidelines together with other sentencing goals. See 18 USCA § 3553(a).* The Act . . . requires judges to consider the Guidelines' "sentencing range established for . . . the applicable category of offense committed by the applicable category of defendant," the pertinent Sentencing Commission policy statements, the

---

* *Ed. note*: 18 USC § 3553(b)(1) reads, in part: "[T]he court shall impose a sentence of the kind, and within the range, referred to in [the guidelines]. . . ."

** *Ed. note*: 18 USC § 3742(e) reads, in part: "[T]he court of appeals shall review de novo the district court's application of the guidelines to the facts."

* *Ed. note*: USCA § 3553(a) instructs the courts to consider the deterrence, incapacitation, and retribution when setting a sentence. See question 3 on page 372 below.

need to avoid unwarranted sentencing disparities, and the need to provide restitution to victims. And the Act nonetheless requires judges to impose sentences that reflect the seriousness of the offense, promote respect for the law, provide just punishment, afford adequate deterrence, protect the public, and effectively provide the defendant with needed educational or vocational training and medical care.

Moreover, despite the absence of § 3553(b)(1), the Act continues to provide for appeals from sentencing decisions. We concede that the excision of § 3553(b)(1) requires the excision of a different, appeals-related section, namely § 3742(e), which sets forth standards of review on appeal. Excision of § 3742(e), however, does not pose a critical problem for the handling of appeals. That is because, as we have previously held, a statute that does not *explicitly* set forth a standard of review may nonetheless do so *implicitly*. We infer appropriate review standards from related statutory language, the structure of the statute, and the "sound administration of justice." And in this instance those factors, in addition to the past two decades of appellate practice in cases involving departures, imply a practical standard of review already familiar to appellate courts: review for "unreasonable[ness]."

Until 2003, § 3742(e) explicitly set forth that standard. In 2003, Congress modified the pre-existing text, adding a *de novo* standard of review for departures and inserting cross-references to § 3553(b)(1). In light of today's holding, the reasons for these revisions—to make Guidelines sentencing even more mandatory than it had been—have ceased to be relevant. The pre-2003 text directed appellate courts to review sentences . . . to determine whether the sentence "is unreasonable" with regard to § 3553(a). Section 3553(a) remains in effect, and sets forth numerous factors that guide sentencing. Those factors in turn will guide appellate courts, as they have in the past, in determining whether a sentence is unreasonable.

[W]e read the statute as implying this [i.e., "reasonableness"] appellate review standard—a standard consistent with appellate sentencing practice during the last two decades. Nor do we share the dissenters' doubts about the practicality of a "reasonableness" standard of review. "Reasonableness" standards are not foreign to sentencing law. The Act has long required their use in important sentencing circumstances—both on review of departures, and on review of sentences imposed where there was no applicable Guideline. Together, these cases account for about 16.7% of sentencing appeals. That is why we think it fair (and not, in Justice Scalia's words, a "gross exageratio[n]") to assume judicial familiarity with a "reasonableness" standard. And that is why we believe that appellate judges will prove capable of facing with greater equanimity than would Justice Scalia what he calls the "daunting prospect" of applying such a standard across the board.

Neither do we share Justice Scalia's belief that use of a reasonableness standard "will produce a discordant symphony" leading to "excessive sentencing disparities," and "wreak havoc" on the judicial system. The Sentencing Commission will continue to collect and study appellate court decisionmaking. It will continue to modify its Guidelines in light of what it learns, thereby encouraging what it finds to be better sentencing practices. It will thereby promote uniformity in the sentencing process.

Regardless, in this context, we must view fears of a "discordant symphony," "excessive disparities," and "havoc" (if they are not themselves "gross exaggerations") with a comparative eye. We cannot and do not claim that use of a "reasonableness" standard will provide the uniformity that Congress originally sought to secure. Nor do we doubt that Congress wrote the language of the appellate provisions to correspond with the mandatory system it intended to create. But, as by now should be clear, that mandatory system is no longer an open choice. And the remedial question we must ask here . . . is, which alternative adheres more closely to Congress' original objective: (1) retention of sentencing appeals, or (2) invalidation of the entire Act, including its appellate provisions?

■ JUSTICE STEVENS, with whom JUSTICE SOUTER joins, and with whom JUSTICE SCALIA [partially] joins . . . , dissenting in part.

Neither of the two Court opinions that decide these cases finds any constitutional infirmity inherent in any provision of the Sentencing Reform Act of 1984 (SRA) or the Federal Sentencing Guidelines. Specifically, neither 18 USCA § 3553(b)(1), which makes application of the Guidelines mandatory, nor § 3742(e), which authorizes appellate review of departures from the Guidelines, is even arguably unconstitutional. Neither the Government, nor the respondents, nor any of the numerous *amici* has suggested that there is any need to invalidate either provision in order to avoid violations of the Sixth Amendment in the administration of the Guidelines. The Court's decision to do so represents a policy choice that Congress has considered and decisively rejected. While it is perfectly clear that Congress has ample power to repeal these two statutory provisions if it so desires, this Court should not make that choice on Congress' behalf. I respectfully dissent from the Court's extraordinary exercise of authority.

[The remedial majority's opinion is] unique because, under the Court's reasoning, if Congress should decide to reenact the exact text of the two provisions that the Court has chosen to invalidate, that reenactment would be unquestionably constitutional. In my judgment, it is therefore clear that the Court's creative remedy is an exercise of legislative, rather than judicial, power.

[Moreover,] this Court is ill suited to the task of drafting legislation and that, therefore, as a matter of respect for coordinate branches of Government, we ought to presume whenever possible that those charged with writing and implementing legislation will and can apply the statute consistently with the constitutional command. The Government has already shown it can apply the Guidelines constitutionally even as written, and Congress is perfectly capable of redrafting the statute on its own. Thus, there is no justification for the extreme judicial remedy of total invalidation of any part of the SRA or the Guidelines.

[The] Court has [also] neglected to provide a critical procedural protection that existed prior to the enactment of a binding Guidelines system. Before the SRA, the sentencing judge had the discretion to impose a sentence that designated a minimum term "at the expiration of which the prisoner shall become eligible for parole." [I]t was the Parole Commission—not the sentencing judge—that was ultimately responsible for determining the length of each defendant's real sentence. Prior to the Guidelines regime, the Parole Commission was designed to reduce sentencing disparities and to provide a check for defendants who had received excessive sentences. Today, the Court reenacts the discretionary Guidelines system that once existed without providing this crucial safety net.*

Other concerns are likely to arise. How will a judge go about determining how much deference to give to the applicable Guidelines range? How will a court of appeals review for reasonableness a district court's decision that the need for "just punishment" and "adequate deterrence to criminal conduct" simply outweighs the considerations contemplated by the Sentencing Commission? What if a sentencing judge determines that a defendant's need for "educational or vocational training, medical care, or other correctional treatment in the most effective manner" requires disregarding the stiff Guidelines range Congress presumably preferred? These questions will arise in every case in the federal system under the Court's system. Regrettably, these are exactly the sort of questions Congress hoped that sentencing judges would not ask after the SRA.

I respectfully dissent.

■ JUSTICE SCALIA, dissenting in part.

The majority's remedial choice is . . . wonderfully ironic: In order to rescue from nullification a statutory scheme designed to eliminate discretionary sentencing, it discards the provisions that eliminate discretionary sentencing.

That is the plain effect of the remedial majority's decision to excise 18 USCA § 3553(b)(1). District judges will no longer be told they "shall impose a sentence . . . within the range" established by the Guidelines. Instead, under § 3553(a), they will need only to "consider" that range as one of many factors, including "the need for the sentence . . . to provide just punishment for the offense, to afford adequate deterrence to criminal

---

* *Ed. note*: The SRA abolished the Parole Commission.

conduct, [and] to protect the public from the further crimes of the defendant."

The statute provides no order of priority among all those factors, but since the three just mentioned are the fundamental criteria governing penology, the statute—absent the mandate of § 3553(b)(1)—authorizes the judge to apply his own perceptions of just punishment, deterrence, and protection of the public even when these differ from the perceptions of the Commission members who drew up the Guidelines. Since the Guidelines are not binding, in order to comply with the (oddly) surviving requirement that the court set forth "the specific reason for the imposition of a sentence different from that described" in the Guidelines, the sentencing judge need only state that "this court does not believe that the punishment set forth in the Guidelines is appropriate for this sort of offense." That is to say, district courts have discretion to sentence anywhere within the ranges authorized by statute—much as they were generally able to do before the Guidelines came into being. To be sure, factor (6) is "the need to avoid unwarranted sentence disparities among defendants with similar records who have been found guilty of similar conduct," but this would require a judge to adhere to the Guidelines only if all other judges had to adhere to the Guidelines (which they certainly do not, as the Court holds today) or if all other judges could at least be expected to adhere to the Guidelines (which they certainly cannot, given the notorious unpopularity of the Guidelines with many district judges). Thus, logic compels the conclusion that the sentencing judge, after considering the recited factors (including the Guidelines), has full discretion, as full as what he possessed before the Act was passed, to sentence anywhere within the statutory range. If the majority thought otherwise—if it thought the Guidelines not only had to be "considered" (as the amputated statute requires) but had generally to be followed—its opinion would surely say so.

As frustrating as this conclusion is to the Act's purpose of uniform sentencing, it at least establishes a clear and comprehensible regime—essentially the regime that existed before the Act became effective. That clarity is eliminated, however, by the remedial majority's surgery. . . . Until today, appellate review of sentencing discretion has been limited to instances prescribed by statute. Before the Guidelines, federal appellate courts had little experience reviewing sentences for anything but legal error. "[W]ell-established doctrine," this Court said, "bars [appellate] review of the exercise of sentencing discretion. [O]nce it is determined that a sentence is within the limitations set forth in the statute under which it is imposed, appellate review is at an end." When it established the Guidelines regime, Congress expressly provided for appellate review of sentences in specified circumstances, but the Court has been appropriately chary of aggrandizement, refusing to treat § 3742 as a blank check to appellate courts. Thus, in 1992, the Court recognized that Congress's grant of "*limited* appellate review of sentencing decisions . . .

did not alter a court of appeals' traditional deference to a district court's exercise of its sentencing discretion." Today's remedial opinion does not even pretend to honor this principle that sentencing discretion is unreviewable except pursuant to specific statutory direction.

As I have suggested earlier, any system which held it *per se* unreasonable (and hence reversible) for a sentencing judge to reject the Guidelines is indistinguishable from the mandatory Guidelines system that the Court today holds unconstitutional. But the remedial majority's gross exaggerations (it says that the "practical standard of review" it prescribes is "already familiar to appellate courts" and "consistent with appellate sentencing practice during the last two decades"[54]) may lead some courts of appeals to conclude—may indeed be designed to lead courts of appeals to conclude—that little has changed.

Bear in mind that one of the most significant features of the remedial majority's scheme of "unreasonableness" review is that it requires courts of appeals to evaluate each sentence *individually* for reasonableness, rather than apply the cookie-cutter standards of the mandatory Guidelines (within the correct Guidelines range, affirm; outside the range without adequate explanation, vacate and remand). A court of appeals faced with this daunting prospect might seek refuge in the familiar and continue (as the remedial majority invites, though the merits majority forbids) the "appellate sentencing practice during the last two decades." At the other extreme, a court of appeals might handle the new workload by approving virtually any sentence within the statutory range that the sentencing court imposes, so long as the district judge goes through the appropriate formalities, such as expressing his consideration of and disagreement with the Guidelines sentence. What I anticipate will happen is that "unreasonableness" review will produce a discordant symphony of different standards, varying from court to court and judge to judge, giving the lie to the remedial majority's sanguine claim that "no feature" of its avant-garde Guidelines system will "ten[d] to hinder" the avoidance of "excessive sentencing disparities."

Will appellate review for "unreasonableness" preserve *de facto* mandatory Guidelines by discouraging district courts from sentencing outside Guidelines ranges? Will it simply add another layer of unfettered judicial discretion to the sentencing process? Or will it be a mere formality, used by busy appellate judges only to ensure that busy district judges say all the right things when they explain how they have exercised their newly restored discretion? Time may tell, but today's remedial majority will not.

---

[54] Deciding whether a departure from a mandatory sentence (for a reason not taken into account in the Guidelines) is "unreasonable" . . . , or whether a sentence imposed for one of the rare offenses not covered by the Guidelines—though surrounded by *mandatory* sentences for related and analogous offenses—is "plainly unreasonable" . . . , differs *toto caelo* from determining, in the absence of *any mandatory scheme*, that a particular sentence is "unreasonable."

I respectfully dissent.

■ [JUSTICE THOMAS's dissent, which discusses issues of severability and the proper use of legislative history, is omitted.]

■ JUSTICE BREYER, with whom THE CHIEF JUSTICE, JUSTICE O'CONNOR, and JUSTICE KENNEDY join, dissenting in part.

The Court today applies its decisions in *Apprendi* v. *New Jersey* and *Blakely* v. *Washington* to the Federal Sentencing Guidelines. I continue to disagree with the constitutional analysis the Court set forth in *Apprendi* and in *Blakely*. But even were I to accept that analysis as valid, I would disagree with the way in which the Court applies it here.

[T]he Federal Guidelines are not statutes. The rules they set forth are *administrative*, not statutory, in nature. Members, not of Congress, but of a Judicial Branch Commission, wrote those rules. The rules do not "establis[h] minimum and maximum penalties" for individual crimes, but guide sentencing courts, only to a degree, "fetter[ing] the discretion of sentencing judges to do what they have done for generations—impose sentences within the broad limits established by Congress." The rules do not create a new set of legislatively determined sentences so much as they reflect, organize, rationalize, and modify an old set of judicially determined pre-Guidelines sentences. Thus, the rules do not, in *Apprendi*'s words, set forth a "prescribed *statutory* maximum," as the law has traditionally understood that phrase.

I concede that *Blakely* defined "prescribed statutory maximum" more broadly as "the maximum sentence a judge may impose solely on the basis of the facts reflected in the jury verdict or admitted by the defendant." But the Court need not read this language as extending the scope of *Apprendi*. *Blakely* purports to follow, not to extend, *Apprendi*. And *Blakely*, like *Apprendi*, involved sentences embodied in a statute, not in administrative rules.

At the same time, to extend *Blakely*'s holding to administratively written sentencing rules risks added legal confusion and uncertainty. Read literally, *Blakely*'s language would include within *Apprendi*'s strictures a host of nonstatutory sentencing determinations, including appellate court decisions delineating the limits of the legally "reasonable." (Imagine an appellate opinion that says a sentence for ordinary robbery greater than five years is unreasonably long unless a special factor, such as possession of a gun, is present.) Indeed, read literally, *Blakely*'s holding would apply to a single judge's determination of the factors that make a particular sentence disproportionate or proportionate. (Imagine a single judge setting forth, as a binding rule of law, the legal proposition about robbery sentences just mentioned.) Appellate courts' efforts to define the limits of the "reasonable" of course would fall outside *Blakely*'s scope. But they would do so, *not because they escape Blakely's literal language*, but because they are not *legislative* efforts to create limits. Neither are the Guidelines *legislative* efforts.

For these reasons, I respectfully dissent.

Booker's Controversial Remedy

The merits majority in *Booker* is a straightforward application of *Blakely*. The remedial majority, however, is a substantially more complicated creature. Rather than relying on sentencing juries, it holds that the federal guidelines are voluntary, but subject to "reasonableness review," although the remedial majority provides no real guidance as to what such review looks like. Reconciling the two majority opinions is difficult, if not impossible. The question is how (or even whether) an appellate court can reject a sentence as being "unreasonable" without implicitly creating the very required judicial factfinding that the merits majority and *Blakely* forbid.[55]

Two leading sentencing scholars have attempted to draw up a workable solution:

> [A]n appellate court could not reverse a sentence as unreasonably high ... because of a specific fact, as that would turn that fact into a jury issue. But it could reverse a sentence because under the totality of circumstances, no reasonable judge would impose this sentence. Appellate courts would reverse sentences without pinpointing exactly which facts and policies their reversals rested on. This vague approach would resemble the old but still constitutional model of unfettered sentencing discretion. Thus, there would be no Sixth Amendment violation.[56]

Is this a convincing argument? Consider the following problem:

PROBLEM: APPELLATE REVIEW IN A *BOOKER* WORLD

Assume that in some state, aggravated assault is defined as "knowingly or purposely causing serious bodily injury," and that the statutory maximum is ten years but the default guideline range is four to five years. The following three cases come down the line:

1. Adams is convicted of aggravated assault when the prosecutor proves that he beat his neighbor with a baseball bat, breaking his arm. The judge imposes a six-year sentence, and the appellate court reverses as unreasonable.

2. Brown is convicted of aggravated assault when the prosecutor proves that he shot his brother in the shoulder with a pistol,

---

[55] Justice Breyer's dissent from the merits majority itself touches on this problem. Can we interpret his concern as an implicit acknowledgement that if the majority's reading of *Blakely* sticks, his remedial remedy can lead to the very problems discussed here?

[56] Stephanos Bibas & Susan Klein, *The Sixth Amendment and Criminal Sentencing*, 30 CARDOZO L. REV. 775, 784 (2008).

causing serious blood loss and extensive hospitalization. The judges imposes a six-year sentence, and the appellate court upholds the sentence.

3. Chapman is convicted of aggravated assault when the prosecutor proves that he shot his cousin in the leg with a rifle, again causing serious blood loss, but requiring only minimal medical care. The judge imposes a six year sentence, and the appellate court reverses the sentence as unreasonable.

The appellate courts here adhere to Bibas and Klein's proposal: they do not pinpoint the specific facts that motivate their decisions, and the caselaw returns vague statements about what is and is not unacceptable. But are Bibas and Klein right that sentencing discretion remain unfettered? Consider a fourth case: Davis is convicted of aggravated assault for hitting his friend with a hammer, dislocating his shoulder. If you were a trial judge imposing a sentence, what would you impose? If you were an appellate court observing a six-year sentence for this crime, how would you respond? Does the fact that the appellate court never names a specific fact matter, either pragmatically or doctrinally?

The example given in the problem may seem to stack the deck against the Bibas and Klein proposal. As they say, the goal of reasonableness review may simply be to weed out those sentences that "no reasonable judge" could impose—to police the most extreme sentences. But it still remains unclear how even this minimal sort of enforcement does not raise *Blakely* concerns. Assume that the statutory maximum for a crime is twenty years but the default range is four to five years, and a judge imposes a twenty-year sentence on a defendant with no aggravating factors and a host of mitigating conditions. This feels like the exact situation where Bibas and Klein think reasonableness review can work. But if the appellate court reverses that sentence while upholding a separate twenty year sentence for a defendant with many aggravators and no mitigators, the appellate court is in effect stating—not even really implying—that at least some of those aggravators were ultimately required for the twenty years to be reasonable. And as Justice Scalia points out in his dissent, this is the very fact-finding the merits majority rejects.

And even if the Court were to eventually accept such a line—and as we will see below, the Court's post-*Booker* cases trying to figure out exactly what this fractured opinion means are confusing—is it an appealing one to rely on? As I have argued elsewhere:

> One of the key goals of structured sentencing is to inject greater transparency and objectivity into sentencing decisions. It is troubling to save such a system by imposing review that is

intentionally vague and ill-defined—after all, a well-defined reversal would be . . . unconstitutional.[57]

The distinction drawn by Bibas and Klein requires opacity and imprecision. What might be the collateral costs of such an approach?

On the other hand, in a limited way such review could have some upside. Perhaps it can be used to police particularly extreme sentences: fifty years for a minor theft, say, with a lot of mitigators and no aggravators. Technically such a review would create an implicit bar making it impossible to impose another fifty year sentence without additional jury fact-finding, but perhaps (almost by the definition of "particularly extreme") such cases are rare enough that the minor (?) constitutional defect is an acceptable cost (i.e., when a judge later imposes a fifty year sentence on a deserving offender and is not reversed).

Three states attempted to implement *Booker*, but as we will see below all three ended up with only procedural review: appellate courts will ensure that trial court followed the proper procedures, but if so they will not overturn the sentence on substantive grounds. Whether such review exerts any real influence is ultimately an empirical question, but one that does not as of yet appear to have an answer:

> Unfortunately, there is very little empirical evidence available to resolve this debate. We can, however, at least flesh out the questions that must be answered and consider what the few available findings suggest. The two central questions are: (1) Given the range of internal and external pressures that may induce trial judges to adhere to guidelines (such as personal senses of obligation, greater public accountability, institutional pressures, and so on), how important is appellate review in general?; and (2) What are the marginal benefits of substantive review over procedural review [which survives *Blakely*]? The more closely outcomes in voluntary guideline systems track those in presumptive guideline systems, and the more procedural review appears to be as effective as substantive review, the more states can use (truly) voluntary guidelines or procedural review to accomplish the goals of presumptive guidelines without having to risk the potential costs of the Bibas-Klein approach.

> There does not appear to be any research at all yet addressing the second question. A few studies, however, shed some light on the first. These explore the relative effects of voluntary and presumptive guidelines, and their evidence is mixed.[58]

---

[57] Pfaff, *The Future of Appellate Sentencing Review*, supra note 50.
[58] Pfaff, *The Future of Appellate Sentencing Review*, supra note 50.

QUESTIONS

1. **Invalidating everything?** Does the merits majority, as those dissenting from it argue, invalidate "the whole act"? Obviously this is false at a literal level—as the *Blakely* and *Booker*-merits majorities go to lengths to stress, all their decisions do is redefine the relevant fact-finder. But consider again the case of *United States v. Medas*, 323 F.Supp. 2d 436 (2004), in which federal prosecutors submitted a remarkably complex twenty-page special verdict form to the jury in order to be immune to any future federal-*Blakely* attack. Given the extensive fact-finding built into the federal (as opposed to state) guidelines, wouldn't *Blakley*-izing the Sentencing Reform Act effectively invalidate it?

2. **Extreme examples?** To what extent is the *Medas* situation typical? Justice Stevens notes that the problematic fact-finding in most cases involves issues like drug weight and the use of guns—relatively straightforward facts that are easily amenable to jury fact-finding. In fact, in his dissent from the remedial majority Stevens makes the following comment:

> [T]he Department of Justice already has instituted procedures which would protect the overwhelming majority of future cases from *Blakely* infirmity. The Department of Justice has issued detailed guidance for every stage of the prosecution from indictment to final sentencing, including alleging facts that would support sentencing enhancements and requiring defendants to waive any potential *Blakely* rights in plea agreements. Given this experience, I think the Court dramatically overstates the difficulty of implementing this solution.

How much should the challenge posed by complex, but rare, cases influence the Court's decision process? After all, while rare, these may also be the cases where guidelines are most important.

3. **Theories of punishment.** The remedial majority argues that 18 U.S.C. § 3553(a)(2) can guide "reasonableness" review. How much guidance does this section, given here, provide?

   (a) Factors To Be Considered in Imposing a Sentence.—The court shall impose a sentence sufficient, but not greater than necessary, to comply with the purposes set forth in paragraph (2) of this subsection. The court, in determining the particular sentence to be imposed, shall consider—

   (1) the nature and circumstances of the offense and the history and characteristics of the defendant;

   (2) the need for the sentence imposed—

   (A) to reflect the seriousness of the offense, to promote respect for the law, and to provide just punishment for the offense;

   (B) to afford adequate deterrence to criminal conduct;

(C) to protect the public from further crimes of the defendant; and

(D) to provide the defendant with needed educational or vocational training, medical care, or other correctional treatment in the most effective manner....

Could Congress amend this section to provide clearer instructions to district and appellate courts? Could it do so in a way that does not trigger *Blakely* concerns? Do we *want* it to?

4. **Regulations vs. Statutes.** How convincing is Breyer's point that the federal guidelines are administrative, not statutory? What (if anything) in *Blakely* focuses on the source of the required fact-finding? How relevant is it that Washington State's guidelines had been designed by an administrative body and then adopted by the legislature?[59]

5. **The scope of jury power.** Elsewhere in *Booker*, the merits majority notes that:

> The effect of the increasing emphasis on facts that enhanced sentencing ranges, however, was to increase the judge's power and diminish that of the jury. It became the judge, not the jury, that determined the upper limits of sentencing, and the facts determined were not required to be raised before trial or proved by more than a preponderance. As the enhancements became greater, the jury's finding of the underlying crime became less significant. And the enhancements became very serious indeed.

How compelling an argument is this? Did the enhancements in any way *reduce* the power of the jury? The sentencing regime challenged in *Apprendi* clearly reduced jury-power. But did an *Apprendi*-consistent guideline regime do so as well? Compared to indeterminacy, does a guideline regime reduce jury power? The majority seems to be trying to provide a pragmatic explanation for a doctrinal decision. Does it work well?

6. **Recusal.** How significant is the fact that Justice Breyer served as a lawyer for the Senate Judiciary Committee in the 1970s when it was developing the federal guidelines and then was a founding commissioner on the United States Sentencing Commission? Breyer contemplated recusing himself from *Booker* but ultimately decided against it.[60] Should he have done so?

Like *Patterson* after *Mullaney*, *Booker*'s efforts at a partial repeal of *Blakely* left courts and legislatures at both the state and federal level unsure of the exact nature of the legal regime they faced. The states handled the confusion relatively easily, while the federal system remains somewhat baffled by what *Booker* means. We will consider each in turn, and then

---

[59] See Washington State Sentencing Guidelines Commission, Powers and Duties of the Commission, available on-line at http://www.ofm.wa.gov/sgc/documents/historical.pdf.

[60] Tony Mauro, "Breyer Sought Advice on Whether to Recuse in Sentencing Case." LEGAL TIMES (January 18, 2005).

conclude with a few later Court cases wrapping up *Blakely*'s and *Booker*'s loose ends.

C.4. STATE RESPONSES TO *BLAKELY*

Blakely did not invalidate presumptive guidelines, but simply imposed additional restrictions on how they could be used. Recall the options that Breyer argued survived *Blakely*:

1. Sentencing juries for aggravating factors. Presumptive guidelines were valid so long as juries, not judges, made the relevant findings for aggravators, and did so beyond a reasonable doubt.

2. Uncapped guidelines. *Blakely* applied to aggravators, not mitigators. States could thus "uncap" their guidelines: the maximum value in any cell would be the statutory maximum, but judges would face presumptive minimums that they could not dip below absent compelling mitigating evidence.

3. Voluntary guidelines. The *Blakely* majority made it clear that as long as the fact-finding wasn't *required*, it didn't trigger the Sixth Amendment. No state with voluntary guidelines before *Blakely* faced any meaningful challenges afterwards. This points to a possible variant of uncapped guidelines: presumptive minimums, voluntary maximums.

4. Indeterminacy. The Court repeatedly made it clear that indeterminacy remains valid under its Sixth Amendment cases.

When *Blakely* was issued, seventeen states had determinate sentencing laws or presumptive guidelines: Alaska, Arizona, California, Colorado, Indiana, Illinois, New Jersey, and New Mexico employed DSLs; and Kansas, Michigan, Minnesota, North Carolina, Ohio, Oregon, Pennsylvania, Tennessee, and Washington employed presumptive guidelines. Four of these states had systems in place that ultimately did not run afoul of *Blakely*:

- Kansas's Supreme Court, racing ahead of the US Supreme Court, had required sentencing juries in the wake of *Apprendi*.
- Illinois's regime was structured in such a way that it had no presumptive aggravating factors.
- Michigan employed uncapped guidelines.
- Pennsylvania's Supreme Court had interpreted its guideline statutes in a manner that rendered them effectively voluntary.

But the remaining thirteen states had to amend their processes to align with *Blakely*. Eight—Alaska, Arizona, Colorado, Minnesota, New

Mexico, North Carolina, and Washington—opted to fully *Blakely*-ize their systems, requiring sentencing juries to find any aggravating factors beyond a reasonable doubt (except, obviously, when the defendant admitted to them during plea bargaining or waived the right to jury fact-finding for a bench trial). Minnesota attempted to reduce the potential cost of jury fact-finding by widening judges' discretionary ranges, thus militating against the need to make aggravated findings.

One state, Ohio, opted to make its guidelines wholly voluntary. In *State v. Foster*, 845 N.E.2d 470 (2006), the state supreme court relied on *Booker* for the proposition that supreme courts have the authority to engage in such statutory rewriting, but the state court otherwise ignored the approach adopted by the remedial majority in *Booker*. There is no "reasonableness review," and the guidelines are wholly voluntary: "we have concluded that trial courts have full discretion to impose a prison sentence within the statutory range and are no longer required to make findings or give their reasons for imposing . . . sentences." *Id.* at 498.

California also made its DSL voluntary, but only temporarily, and not without a serious fight. California's DSL employed a rigid "multiple-choice" structure for most offenses: for each offense the judge faced three possible sentences (for example, 6, 12, or 18 years), and the sentencing statute in place before *Blakely* (Cal. Penal Code § 1170) stated that "the court *shall* order imposition of the middle term, unless there are circumstances in aggravation or mitigation of the crime" (emphasis added). In *People v. Black*, 113 P.3d 534 (2005) the California Supreme Court appeared to almost willfully misread *Blakley* in upholding this sentencing regime:

> The mandatory language of section 1170 . . . does provide some support for defendant's position [that *Blakely* invalidates the DSL]. But, as the high court has emphasized, in analyzing the Sixth Amendment right to a jury trial, "the relevant inquiry is one not of form, but of effect" [citing *Apprendi*]. [I]n operation and effect, the provisions of the California determinate sentence law simply authorize a sentencing court to engage in the type of factfinding that traditionally has been incident to the judge's selection of an appropriate sentence within a statutorily prescribed sentencing range. Therefore, the upper term is the "statutory maximum" and a trial court's imposition of an upper term sentence does not violate a defendant's right to a jury trial under the principles set forth in *Apprendi*, *Blakely*, and *Booker*. [*Id.* at 543.]

The view taken by a majority of the California Supreme Court was consistent with O'Connor's concerns following *Apprendi*. But it is this exact sort of formalism, and focus on "traditional sentencing factors," that *Blakely* forecloses. The Supreme Court shot down this argument (and several others) in *Cunningham v. California*, 549 U.S. 270 (2007).

California responded by passing Senate Bill 40, which turned California's regime into a wholly-voluntary one, with a sunset provision set to expire on January 1, 2012; in 2011, Senate Bill 526 extended the sunset to January 1, 2014.

Perhaps more interesting is to look at what happened in the three states that attempted to follow *Booker* more than *Blakely*. Indiana, New Jersey, and Tennessee all introduced "reasonableness review," Indiana via a combination of legislative enactment and supreme court interpretation,[61] New Jersey via state supreme court opinions that closely tracked *Booker*,[62] and Tennessee via legislative enactment.[63] In all three states, however, what has emerged is not any sort of substantive "reasonableness review" at all, but rather just procedural review. In all three states, appellate courts simply ensure that the trial courts explain that they considered the relevant aggravators and mitigators, but they do not attempt to second-guess how those are weighed.

Though procedural, however, such review need not be completely formalistic. Two examples from Tennessee:

> The Tennessee case of *State v. Guy* [2008 WL 5130729] lays bare the hollowness of post-*Blakely* ["reasonableness" review]. In *Guy*, the appellate court struck two of the six aggravating factors found by the trial judge yet upheld the sentence, stating: "Although the court improperly applied two enhancing factors, we nonetheless conclude that the sentences imposed are appropriate. The record reflects that in determining the specific sentence length, the trial court considered [relevant sources of evidence], as well as the required principles of sentencing. . . ." In other words, as long as the trial judge jumps through the required procedural hoops—as long as he thinks about the necessary sources of evidence and theories of punishment—improper application of the guidelines generally results in the sentence being upheld.

---

[61] The state supreme court required sentencing juries in *Smylie v. State*, 823 N.E.2d 679 (Ind. 2005). The legislature responded by making the guidelines voluntary, but leaving the appellate courts unsure if they could engage in any review. In *Anglemyer v. State,* 868 N.E.2d 482 (Ind. 2007), the state supreme court made it clear that the guidelines had been *Booker*-ized and thus were subject to reasonableness review.

[62] *State v. Natale*, 878 N.E.2d 724 (N.J. 2005).

[63] While the legislature was still acting, Tennessee's state supreme court issued an opinion upholding Tennessee's presumptive guidelines that echoed the same sort of open defiance of *Blakely* seen in *Black* in California. In *State v. Gomez*, 163 S.W.3d 632 (Tenn. 2005), Tennessee's supreme court upheld its presumptive guidelines by saying they did not violate *Booker* since the federal guidelines were mandatory (i.e., if aggravators were found the judge was *required* to aggravate) while Tennessee's were just presumptive (i.e., a judge could not impose a higher sentence without finding aggravators, but he was not compelled to do so). Of course, *Blakely* drew no such distinction, and the mandatory nature of the federal guidelines played no role in the reasoning in *Booker*. The US Supreme Court would have surely reversed this case as it did *Black* had the actions of the Tennessee legislature not rendered it moot. But *Gomez*, along with *Black*, likely reflected a strong desire on the part of state supreme courts to try to avoid *Blakely* fixes.

That is not to say that review, at least in Tennessee, is wholly toothless. Even procedural review can have some punch. Consider *State v. Bible* [2008 WL 5234755], which appears to be the only available opinion to adjust a sentence since the [legislature *Booker*-ized the guidelines]. The appellate court held that the trial court had improperly used an aggravator, and it noted that the trial court had stated in its sentencing report that it had put great weight on that factor when deciding to aggravate the defendant's sentence. As a result of this error, the appellate court reduced the sentence, rather than remanding for resentencing. The appellate court was not saying that the invalid factor was required to impose a greater sentence. Instead, the appellate court took the trial court at its word that the invalid aggravator was critical to its decision and adjusted the sentence accordingly. Thus, the outcome in *Bible* has no implications for future cases—a subsequent case identical to *Bible* in every way except for a different sentencing statement would likely not result in resentencing—but it nonetheless exemplifies meaningful procedural review.[64]

Moreover, it is important not to denigrate procedural review, since we do not know what sort of indirect effects it may have. The very act of having to explain the sources and evidence considered may influence the decision that a judge reaches. There appears to be no empirical evidence about the magnitude of such an effect, but it certainly is a plausible one.

The one exception to procedural review is Indiana's continued use of Appellate Rule 7(B), which allows state courts to modify sentences when "justice" requires. This is explicit substantive review of the very sort that should trigger the concerns raised above with the Bibas-Klein proposal. But so far there is no evidence of constitutional challenge to Rule 7(B), and the Indiana Supreme Court has continued to use it post-*Booker*, albeit rarely.

So at least in the states, the hope of the remedial majority in *Booker* has not come to pass (outside of the narrow 7(B) exception in Indiana). State appellate courts, even in states like New Jersey—whose state supreme court adopted *Booker* using almost identical language—are not engaging in any real sort of "reasonableness" review.[65] The decision to engage in purely procedural review often seems to be reached implicitly, if not almost by accident: in New Jersey, for example, state court opinions

---

[64] Pfaff, *The Future of Appellate Sentencing Review*, supra note 50.

[65] To be fair, at the time I surveyed New Jersey's post-*Booker*, post-*Natale* opinions, in 2009, almost every single appellate case was considering the retroactivity problems of sentencing post-*Natale* defendants who committed their crimes pre-*Natale*. Only a handful considered "pure" post-*Natale* cases. But those that did adopted a purely procedural approach. Consider the following from *People v. Robinson*, 2008 WL 398299, at *8: "The trial judge properly reviewed the record, made findings regarding the applicable aggravating and mitigating factors, and then balanced those factors. The record supports the judge's conclusion that the aggravating factors substantially outweighed the mitigating."

continue to cite pre-*Blakely* precedents authorizing much more substantive review while engaging in procedural decision-making.

In short, O'Connor's nightmare of state sentencing collapse has simply not come to pass. States have adapted to *Blakely* with relatively little difficulty, perhaps in part because they did not rely that much of aggravators beforehand. Sentencing juries were thus not a serious challenge for most of the affected states to adopt. And those that followed in the footsteps of *Booker* accidentally ended up going down *Blakely*'s path instead and thus avoided the confusion that the federal system has wrestled with, and to which we turn now.

C.5. THE FEDERAL GUIDELINES: *RITA*, *GALL*, AND BEYOND

In *Booker*, the remedial majority introduced the idea of "reasonableness review" but did not provide any guidance for what that meant. Two subsequent cases, *Rita v. United States*, 551 U.S. 338 (2007), and *Gall v. United States*, 552 U.S. 38 (2007),[66] attempted to define more precisely what such review entailed. *Rita* considered whether appellate courts could treat within-guideline sentences as presumptively reasonable, and *Gall* whether they could treat non-guideline sentences as presumptively unreasonable. In *Rita*, the Court held that appellate courts *could* presume that within-guideline sentences were reasonable:

> [T]he presumption is not binding. It does not, like a trial-related evidentiary presumption, insist that one side, or the other, shoulder a particular burden of persuasion or proof lest they lose their case. Nor does the presumption reflect strong judicial deference of the kind that leads appeals courts to grant greater factfinding leeway to an expert agency than to a district judge. Rather, the presumption reflects the fact that, by the time an appeals court is considering a within-Guidelines sentence on review, *both* the sentencing judge and the Sentencing Commission will have reached the *same* conclusion as to the proper sentence in the particular case. That double determination significantly increases the likelihood that the sentence is a reasonable one.
>
> Rita points out that many individual Guidelines apply higher sentences in the presence of special facts. . . . In many cases, the sentencing judge, not the jury, will determine the existence of those facts. A pro-Guidelines "presumption of reasonableness" will increase the likelihood that courts of appeals will affirm such sentences, thereby increasing the likelihood that

---

[66] As evidence of the dangerous lives criminal tend to live, *Gall* was actually the second case to attempt to resolve the issue it confronted. The first was *United States v. Claiborne*. However, after oral arguments but before the Court issued its opinion, Claiborne was killed in drug-related violence, and the case was dismissed as moot.

sentencing judges will impose such sentences. For that reason, Rita says, the presumption raises Sixth Amendment "concerns."

In our view, however, the presumption, even if it increases the likelihood that the judge, not the jury, will find "sentencing facts," does not violate the Sixth Amendment. This Court's Sixth Amendment cases do not automatically forbid a sentencing court to take account of factual matters not determined by a jury and to increase the sentence in consequence. Nor do they prohibit the sentencing judge from taking account of the Sentencing Commission's factual findings or recommended sentences.

The Sixth Amendment question, the Court has said, is whether the law *forbids* a judge to increase a defendant's sentence unless the judge finds facts that the jury did not find (and the offender did not concede).

A nonbinding appellate presumption that a Guidelines sentence is reasonable does not require the sentencing judge to impose that sentence. Still less does it *prohibit* the sentencing judge from imposing a sentence higher than the Guidelines provide for the jury-determined facts standing alone. As far as the law is concerned, the judge could disregard the Guidelines and apply the same sentence (higher than the statutory minimum or the bottom of the unenhanced Guidelines range) in the absence of the special facts (say, gun brandishing) which, in the view of the Sentencing Commission, would warrant a higher sentence within the statutorily permissible range. Thus, our Sixth Amendment cases do not forbid appellate court use of the presumption. [551 U.S. at 347–353.]

In practice, the Court's subsequent analysis of the trial judge's conduct verged almost on procedural review. It noted that the judge listened to Rita's arguments for leniency and, in a brief statement, concluded that they were unpersuasive; that was sufficient. In his concurrence, Scalia went further and argued that "reasonableness review" could *only mean* procedural review in a post-*Blakely* world, for the same reasons given in my critique of the Bibas-Klein proposal above:

Nothing in the Court's opinion explains why, under the advisory Guidelines scheme, judge-found facts are *never* legally necessary to justify the sentence. By this I mean the Court has failed to establish that every sentence which will be imposed under the advisory Guidelines scheme could equally have been imposed had the judge relied upon no facts other than those found by the jury or admitted by the defendant. In fact, the Court implicitly, but quite plainly, acknowledges that this will not be the case.... Under the scheme promulgated today, some sentences reversed as excessive will be legally authorized in later cases only because additional judge-found facts are present.... The Court does not even attempt to explain how this is consistent with the Sixth Amendment.

No explanation is given because no explanation is possible. The Court has reintroduced the constitutional defect that *Booker* purported to eliminate. I cannot acquiesce in this course. If a sentencing system is permissible in which some sentences cannot lawfully be imposed by a judge unless the judge finds certain facts by a preponderance of the evidence, then we should have left in place the compulsory Guidelines that Congress enacted, instead of imposing this jerry-rigged scheme of our own. In order to avoid the possibility of a Sixth Amendment violation, which was the object of the Booker remedy, district courts must be able, without finding any facts not embraced in the jury verdict or guilty plea, to sentence to the maximum of the statutory range.... I would hold that reasonableness review cannot contain a substantive component at all. I believe, however, that appellate courts can nevertheless secure some amount of sentencing uniformity through the procedural reasonableness review made possible by the *Booker* remedial opinion. [551 U.S. at 369–370.]

Souter alone dissented, worrying about the gravitational pull of presumptive reasonableness:

But if sentencing judges attributed substantial gravitational pull to the now-discretionary Guidelines, if they treated the Guidelines result as persuasive or presumptively appropriate, the *Booker* remedy would in practical terms preserve the very feature of the Guidelines that threatened to trivialize the jury right. For a presumption of Guidelines reasonableness would tend to produce Guidelines sentences almost as regularly as mandatory Guidelines had done, with judges finding the facts needed for a sentence in an upper subrange. This would open the door to undermining Apprendi itself, and this is what has happened today. [551 U.S. at 390.]

The majority attempted to address Souter's concern by pointing out that the presumption is only for *appellate* courts. The trial court is not allowed to simply impose the guideline range without considering other potentially relevant factors. The Court stressed: "In determining the merits of these arguments, the sentencing court does not enjoy the benefit of a legal presumption that the Guidelines sentence should apply." 551 U.S. at 351. But it is not clear how meaningful a rebuttal this is: trial courts act in the shadow of appellate rules, so if appellate courts are going to presume within-range sentences are correct trial courts will take that into account.

The impact of the within-range presumption, however, turns in part on how outside-of-range sentences are handled: after all, a safe harbor is less important the calmer the seas outside it. The Court confronted this latter question in *Gall*, and it held that outside-range sentences could *not* be viewed as presumptively *un*reasonable. Despite a guideline recommendation of 30 to 37 months in prison, the trial judge had sentenced Gall to 36 months of probation, in light of substantial mitigating evidence. The appellate court reversed, holding that "a sentence outside of the Guidelines range must be supported by a justification that 'is proportional to the extent of the difference between the advisory range and the sentence imposed,'" and then finding several specific reasons why the facts in Gall's case were not sufficiently extreme to justify so extensive a departure.

The heart of the Court's decision in *Gall*, which overturned the appellate court's reversal, was this:

> both the exceptional circumstances requirement and the rigid mathematical formulation reflect a practice—common among courts that have adopted "proportional review"—of applying a heightened standard of review to sentences outside the Guidelines range. This is inconsistent with the rule that the abuse-of-discretion standard of review applies to appellate review of all sentencing decisions—whether inside or outside the Guidelines range. [552 U.S. at 49.]

The Court then laid out its basic definition of reasonableness review:

> Regardless of whether the sentence imposed is inside or outside the Guidelines range, the appellate court must review the sentence under an abuse-of-discretion standard. It must first ensure that the district court committed no significant procedural error, such as failing to calculate (or improperly calculating) the Guidelines range, treating the Guidelines as mandatory, failing to consider the § 3553(a) factors, selecting a sentence based on clearly erroneous facts, or failing to adequately explain the chosen sentence—including an explanation for any deviation from the Guidelines range. Assuming that the district court's sentencing decision is procedurally sound, the appellate court should then consider the substantive reasonableness of the sentence imposed under an abuse-of-discretion standard. When conducting this review, the court will, of course, take into account the totality of the circumstances, including the extent of any variance from the Guidelines range. If the sentence is within the Guidelines range, the appellate court may, but is not required to, apply a presumption of reasonableness. But if the sentence is outside the Guidelines range, the court may not apply a presumption of unreasonableness. It may consider the extent of the deviation, but must give due deference to the district court's decision that the § 3553(a) factors, on a whole, justify the extent of the

variance. The fact that the appellate court might reasonably have concluded that a different sentence was appropriate is insufficient to justify reversal of the district court.

Practical considerations also underlie this legal principle. The sentencing judge is in a superior position to find facts and judge their import under § 3553(a) in the individual case. The judge sees and hears the evidence, makes credibility determinations, has full knowledge of the facts and gains insights not conveyed by the record. The sentencing judge has access to, and greater familiarity with, the individual case and the individual defendant before him than the Commission or the appeals court. Moreover, district courts have an institutional advantage over appellate courts in making these sorts of determinations, especially as they see so many more Guidelines sentences than appellate courts do. [552 U.S. at 51–52. Internal quotes omitted.]

The Court then discussed how the trial court appeared to give serious consideration to various factors laid out in § 3553(a) and elsewhere, and that the appellate court gave "virtually no deference" to those considerations.

Justice Scalia grudgingly concurred:

Although I continue to believe that substantive-reasonableness review is inherently flawed, I give *stare decisis* effect to the statutory holding of *Rita*. The highly deferential standard adopted by the Court today will result in far fewer unconstitutional sentences than the proportionality standard employed by the Eighth Circuit. Moreover, . . . the Court has not foreclosed as-applied constitutional challenges to sentences. The door therefore remains open for a defendant to demonstrate that his sentence, whether inside or outside the advisory Guidelines range, would not have been upheld but for the existence of a fact found by the sentencing judge and not by the jury. [552 U.S. at 60.]

Souter was likewise resigned, admitting that "[m]y disagreements with [the] earlier cases are not the stuff of formally perpetual dissent. . . ." 552 U.S. at 60–61. Thomas dissented on the grounds that the *Booker* remedial opinion remained invalid, and Alito on the (opposite) grounds that the majority undermined effective substantive review too severely. But Thomas and Alito represent outliers here, and with *Rita* and *Gall* each securing seven-justice majorities, the parameters of *Booker* seem relatively fixed.

On the same day the Court handed down *Gall*, it also issued its opinion in *Kimbrough v. United States*, 552 U.S. 85 (2007). *Kimbrough* represented the federal government's last-ditch efforts to ensure that at least one part of the guidelines—ironically, perhaps, its most widely-disliked part—remained binding. The government argued that whatever *Booker* implied for the rest of the guidelines, the guidelines' 100-to-1 crack/cocaine ratio[67] deserved special deference. The same seven-justice majority from *Gall* was not convinced. In fact, it argued that the standard reasons for deferring to the guidelines at all were *absent* in this case, stating that "The crack cocaine Guidelines . . . present no occasion for elaborative discussion of this matter because those Guidelines do not exemplify the Commission's exercise of its characteristic institutional role." 552 U.S. at 89.

Thomas and Alito dissented from *Kimbrough* exactly as they did in *Gall*. There is really nothing more that need be said about *Kimbrough*, a peculiar case brought about the federal government's peculiar desire to protect a part of the guidelines that the Sentencing Commission itself had been trying to change for years. *Rita* and *Gall* are the cases that matter; *Kimbrough* is merely a sideshow.[68]

But while *Rita* and *Gall* define the main contours of the *Booker* remedy, they were not the Court's last word on the issue. In at least one more case, the Court found itself struggling to define exactly how the various presumptions work. So, in *Nelson v. United States*, 555 U.S. 350 (2009), the Court had to make it clear that the presumption of reasonableness was an *appellate* presumption, not a trial presumption. In *Nelson*, the sentencing judge asserted that "the Guidelines are considered presumptively reasonable," and that "unless there's a good reason in the [sentencing] factors . . . , the Guideline sentence is the reasonable sentence." The Court sent the case back to the trial court, stating that "[o]ur cases do not allow a sentencing court to presume that a sentence within the applicable Guidelines range is reasonable." *Id.* at 352. But the Court's *Booker* jurisprudence looks increasingly settled at this time.

QUESTIONS

1. **Voluntary guidelines and Justice Souter.** Would Justice Souter find Virginia's voluntary guidelines problematic for gravitational reasons? Would he find *any* effective voluntary guidelines problematic? What does it mean for non-binding guidelines to work?

2. **Gravity and *Gall*.** Does the outcome in *Gall* necessarily alleviate all of Souter's concerns? In the end, it isn't all that clear that *Booker* has changed much for the Federal system. In 2010 and 2011, about 55% of all

---

[67] Until the Fair Sentencing Act was passed in 2012, 21 U.S.C. § 841 mandated a five-year minimum sentence for anyone convicted of possessing five grams of crack or five hundred grams of power cocaine, and a ten-year minimum for anyone convicted of possessing fifty grams of crack or five kilos of cocaine. (The FSA reduced the ratio from 100-to-1 to 18-to-1.) The guidelines in turn adopted this ratio throughout its sentencing regime (i.e., beyond just the mandatory-minimum cutoffs).

[68] A few years later, in *Spears v. United States*, 555 US 261 (2009), the Court made it clear that trial courts were free to ignore the 100-to-1 ratio in its entirely. In that case, the trial court replaced the 100-to-1 ratio with its own 20-to-1 ratio, a decision upheld by the Court.

sentences were within the recommended guideline range—a decline from the pre-*Booker* level of 65%, but not by much, and still a majority of cases.

3. **Appellate presumptions.** How intelligible is the Court's distinction between appellate and trial-court presumptions?

C.6. THE FINAL CASES (FOR NOW): *OREGON V. ICE* AND *ALLEYNE V. UNITED STATES*

We have come, at last, to the end of this very long road, one that began in 1975 in Maine, and started ending, more or less, in 2009 in Oregon. In *Oregon v. Ice*, 555 U.S. 160 (2009), the Court addressed a challenge to the constitutionality of Oregon's law concerning the choice of consecutive vs. concurrent sentences. The majority in *Ice* described the statute well: "The controlling statute in Oregon provides that sentences shall run concurrently unless the judge finds statutorily described facts." 555 U.S. at 165. This seems like an easy *Blakely* case: a consecutive sentence is longer than a concurrent sentence, and that longer sentence cannot be imposed without additional factfinding, so such required factfinding must be done by a jury. This is the very heart of *Blakely*, and so this statute should have be quickly unconstitutional.

But a five-justice majority, led by Ginsburg, upheld the statute. The majority argued that:

> [H]istorical practice and respect for state sovereignty . . . counsel against extending *Apprendi*'s rule to the imposition of sentences for discrete crimes. The decision to impose sentences consecutively is not within the jury function that "extends down centuries into the common law" [quoting *Apprendi*]. Instead, specification of the regime for administering multiple sentences has long been considered the prerogative of state legislatures. [555 U.S. at 168.]

It further noted that:

> It bears emphasis that state legislative innovations like Oregon's seek to rein in the discretion judges possessed at common law to impose consecutive sentences at will. Limiting judicial discretion to impose consecutive sentences serves the "salutary objectives" of promoting sentences proportionate to "the gravity of the offense" [quoting *Blakely*], and of reducing disparities in sentence length. . . . All agree that a scheme making consecutive sentences the rule, and concurrent sentences the exception, encounters no Sixth Amendment shoal. To hem in States by holding that they may not equally choose to make concurrent sentences the rule, and consecutive sentences the exception, would make scant sense. Neither *Apprendi* nor our Sixth Amendment traditions compel straitjacketing the States in that manner. [555 U.S. at 171.]

That last paragraph is rather shocking. Ginsburg was right that *Apprendi* does not require such straight-jacketing (as O'Connor argued in her dissent from that case), but *Blakely* does. Or, at least, *Blakely* does *not* permit the sort of functionalist argument about "salutary objectives" that the majority put forth here. Neither does *Ring*, an opinion *written by Ginsburg*.

Not surprisingly, Scalia's dissent was blistering:

The Court's justification of Oregon's scheme is a virtual copy of the dissents in [our earlier] cases.

We have taken pains to reject artificial limitations upon the facts subject to the jury-trial guarantee. We long ago made clear that the guarantee turns upon the penal consequences attached to the fact, and not to its formal definition as an element of the crime.

There is no doubt that consecutive sentences are a "greater punishment" than concurrent sentences. For many defendants, the difference between consecutive and concurrent sentences is more important than a jury verdict of innocence on any single count: Two consecutive 10-year sentences are in most circumstances a more severe punishment than any number of concurrent 10-year sentences.

To support its distinction-without-a-difference, the Court puts forward the same (the very same) arguments regarding the history of sentencing that were rejected by *Apprendi*. Our concern here is precisely the same as our concern in *Apprendi*: What happens when a State breaks from the common-law practice of discretionary sentences and permits the imposition of an elevated sentence only upon the showing of extraordinary facts?

The Court protests that in this case there is no "encroachment" on or "erosion" of the jury's role because traditionally it was for the judge to determine whether there would be concurrent terms. Alas, this argument too was made and rejected in *Apprendi*.

The Court then observes that the results of the Oregon system could readily be achieved, instead, by a system in which consecutive sentences are the default rule but judges are permitted to impose concurrent sentences when they find certain facts. But the permissibility of that alternative means of achieving the same end obviously does not distinguish *Apprendi*, because the same argument (the very same argument) was raised and squarely rejected in that case. . . .

Ultimately, the Court abandons its effort to provide analytic support for its decision, and turns to what it thinks to be the

> "salutary objectives" of Oregon's scheme. The same argument (the very same argument) was made and rejected in *Booker* and *Blakely*. The protection of the Sixth Amendment does not turn on this Court's opinion of whether an alternative scheme is good policy, or whether the legislature had a compassionate heart in adopting it.
>
> Today's opinion . . . gives cause to doubt whether the Court is willing to stand by *Apprendi*'s interpretation of the Sixth Amendment's jury-trial guarantee. [555 U.S. at 173–178.]

Scalia and his fellow dissenters were not alone in taking this view. For example, in *State v. Foster*, the Indiana state supreme court case that applied *Booker* to its guidelines, the court held that required factfinding for consecutive sentences suffered from the same constitutional defect as the guidelines.

In *Ice*, we see another *Patterson*. A majority of justices, seemingly scared by what they saw as the potential reach of *Blakely*, decided to rein it in, but without the courage or, at least, the votes to explicitly reverse—or even explicitly cabin—*Blakely*. As a result, *Blakely* applies to guidelines but . . . nothing else? Not much else? Where exactly the line will be drawn will often be unclear (recall that it took six years for New York's Persistent Felony Offender law to extricate itself from *Blakely* review), but *Ice* indicated that the Court was unlikely to extend *Blakely*'s reach much further.

And that's how things were for four years, until somewhat unexpectedly the Court expanded the scope of *Blakely* once more, this time overturning *McMillan* and *Harris* in *Alleyne v. United States*, 133 S.Ct. 2151 (2014). Allen Ryan Alleyne was convicted of, among other things, robbery and using or carrying a firearm during a violent crime. The latter charge required a five year minimum, unless the firearm was brandished (seven year minimum) or fired (ten year minimum). Alleyne was convicted by a jury that found he used a gun, but said nothing on the verdict form about brandishing. Based on the presentence report, however, the judge found that he brandished the gun and imposed a seven-year sentence for the gun charge. Alleyne appealed.

Like so many other outcomes in this line of cases, *Alleyne* was a fractured opinion, 5–4 in some parts, 4–1–4 in others. The heart of the disagreement centered on what aspect of "punishment" the Sixth Amendment felt the jury must define. To the majority, led by Thomas, the punishment was the entire range of the potential sanction, floor and ceiling alike. Moving the floor was no different than moving the ceiling, and since *Apprendi* requires jury fact-finding for the latter, it must require it for the former as well:

> In *Apprendi*, we held that a fact is by definition an element of the offense and must be submitted to the jury if it increases the punishment above what is otherwise legally prescribed. While

Harris declined to extend this principle to facts increasing mandatory minimum sentences, *Apprendi*'s definition of "elements" necessarily includes not only facts that increase the ceiling, but also those that increase the floor. Both kinds of facts alter the prescribed range of sentences to which a defendant is exposed and do so in a manner that aggravates the punishment. Facts that increase the mandatory minimum sentence are therefore elements and must be submitted to the jury and found beyond a reasonable doubt.

It is indisputable that a fact triggering a mandatory minimum alters the prescribed range of sentences to which a criminal defendant is exposed. But for a finding of brandishing, the penalty is five years to life in prison; with a finding of brandishing, the penalty becomes seven years to life. Just as the maximum of life marks the outer boundary of the range, so seven years marks its floor. And because the legally prescribed range is the penalty affixed to the crime, . . . it follows that a fact increasing either end of the range produces a new penalty and constitutes an ingredient of the offense.

it is impossible to dispute that facts increasing the legally prescribed floor aggravate the punishment. Elevating the low-end of a sentencing range heightens the loss of liberty associated with the crime: the defendant's "expected punishment has increased as a result of the narrowed range" and "the prosecution is empowered, by invoking the mandatory minimum, to require the judge to impose a higher punishment than he might wish." Why else would Congress link an increased mandatory minimum to a particular aggravating fact other than to heighten the consequences for that behavior? This reality demonstrates that the core crime and the fact triggering the mandatory minimum sentence together constitute a new, aggravated crime, each element of which must be submitted to the jury. [133 S.Ct. at 2158–2161.]

The dissent, however, argued that the majority misstated the goal of the Sixth Amendment, shifting the jury right from something that protects defendants from judges to something that protects judges from legislators:

Suppose a jury convicts a defendant of a crime carrying a sentence of five to ten years. And suppose the judge says he would sentence the defendant to five years, but because he finds that the defendant used a gun during the crime, he is going to add two years and sentence him to seven. No one thinks that this violates the defendant's right to a jury trial in any way.

Now suppose the legislature says that two years should be added to the five year minimum, if the judge finds that the defendant used a gun during the crime. Such a provision affects the role of the judge—limiting his discretion—but has no effect on the role of the jury. And because it does not affect the jury's role, it does not violate the jury trial guarantee of the Sixth Amendment.

The Framers envisioned the Sixth Amendment as a protection for defendants from the power of the Government. The Court transforms it into a protection for judges from the power of the legislature. For that reason, I respectfully dissent.

As I have explained, *Apprendi*'s constraint on the normal legislative control of criminal procedure draws its legitimacy from two primary principles: (1) common law understandings of the "elements" of a crime, and (2) the need to preserve the jury as a "strong barrier" between defendants and the State. Neither of those principles supports the rule the majority adopts today.

First, there is no body of historical evidence supporting today's new rule. . . .

Nor does the majority's extension of *Apprendi* do anything to preserve the role of the jury as a safeguard between the defendant and the State. That is because even if a jury does not find that the firearm was brandished, a judge can do so and impose a harsher sentence because of his finding, so long as that sentence remains under the statutory maximum. The question here is about the power of judges, not juries. Under the rule in place until today, a legislature could tell judges that certain facts carried certain weight, and require the judge to devise a sentence based on that weight—so long as the sentence remained within the range authorized by the jury. Now, in the name of the jury right that formed a barrier between the defendant and the State, the majority has erected a barrier between judges and legislatures, establishing that discretionary sentencing is the domain of judges. Legislatures must keep their respectful distance.

I find this new rule impossible to square with the historical understanding of the jury right as a defense from judges, not a defense of judges. [133 S.Ct. at 2167–2171.]

The dissent then pointed out that two of the majority's key claims—that "because the legally prescribed range is the penalty affixed to the crime, it follows that a fact increasing either end of the range produces a new penalty and constitutes an ingredient of the offense" and that "criminal statutes have long specified both the floor and ceiling of sentence ranges, which is evidence that both define the legally prescribed penalty"—simply assumed what the majority was trying to prove, and did so without any additional support.

Perhaps the most compelling rebuttal by the dissent, though, is the following:

> [T]he majority offers that "it is impossible to dispute that facts increasing the legally prescribed floor aggravate the punishment." This argument proves too much, for it would apply with equal force to any fact which leads the judge, in the exercise of his own discretion, to choose a penalty higher than he otherwise would have chosen. The majority nowhere explains what it is about the jury right that bars a determination by Congress that brandishing (or any other fact) makes an offense worth two extra years, but not an identical determination by a judge. Simply calling one "aggravation" and the other "discretion" does not do the trick. [133 S.Ct. at 2172.]

Interestingly, neither the majority nor dissent drew attention to what could be a highly probative fact: federal judges frequently sentence at mandatory minimum lines, suggesting that in many cases the mandatory minimum *is* the sanction. Thomas alluded to this when he rhetorically asked why Congress would pass mandatory minimum laws but to push up imposed sentences, but in general both opinions are based on theoretical, historical, and doctrinal debates over what is "punishment," not on the pragmatic implications of mandatory minimums on sentencing outcomes.

QUESTIONS

1. ***Ice v. Blakely.*** Is there any principled way to preserve *Blakely* while reaching the same outcome as *Ice* does for concurrent/consecutive sentences? Is there anything doctrinally or pragmatically different about factfinding for one sentence vs. that for how to punish two convictions?

2. **Judicial discretion.** Upon remand from *Alleyne*, the trial judge remains free to impose the same sentence on Alleyne as he did before, only now from his own discretion, not due to legislative decree. How relevant is this, both to the majority and dissent, as well as from a broader policy perspective?

3. **Who threatens us more?** The dissent in *Alleyne* views juries as a form of protection *from* judges, not a form of protection *for* judges. But today, who is best able to protect defendants from state over-reach? Does protecting defendants from judges actually make defendants better off, or are defendants more protected by shielding judges from (aggressive?) legislatures?

CHAPTER 7

THE DEATH PENALTY

One theme that runs through this book is how relatively "lawless" sentencing is, especially when it comes to Constitutional oversight: states are free to allocate discretion among the police, prosecutors, judges, and parole boards as they see fit, and there are few restrictions on the sorts of sentences they can impose or how they go about imposing them. That changes, however, when it comes to the death penalty. At least over the past forty years, the Supreme Court has inserted itself much more aggressively into the death penalty process than it has into any other aspect of punishment. And while death row admissions and inmates comprise only a small number of the total penal population (about 100 to 150 admissions per year, out of an admissions cohort of around 650,000; about 3,000 inmates out of a prison population of 1.5 million and total correctional population of over 7 million), the administration of the death penalty receives more political and activist attention than any other aspect of criminal sanctioning. So it is worth spending a little time reviewing the law and policy of the death penalty.

The death penalty raises a host of complicated normative, legal, and policy issues, and entire textbooks have been written on this one topic. In this brief chapter we will focus on just four basic issues. First, we will examine the law that drives the death penalty, including Supreme Court doctrine, legislative enactments, and (more recently) executive cessations. Then we will look at the increasingly salient issue of error: how often are death penalty verdicts improperly imposed, how well does the court system correct these mistakes, and to what extent do these error rates tell us anything about the harder-to-observe error rate for non-death cases? We will then turn to justifications for the death penalty, focusing in particular on some of the trickier retributive aspects of it and whether it is an effective deterrent against murder. And finally, we will conclude by looking at a few smaller questions about how the death penalty is implemented (such as issues of costs).

A. THE LAW OF THE DEATH PENALTY

Except for the *Apprendi-Blakely-Booker* line of cases, the Supreme Court has generally not involved itself much in sentencing law. And that aloofness initially extended to the death penalty as well, until concerns about its administration grew strong enough that the Court started to regulate it more closely in the 1970s. In this section, we will review the Court's death penalty jurisprudence, the state and federal legislative responses, and recent executive actions in light of innocence concerns.

A.1. THE SUPREME COURT

Until 1972, the Supreme Court had little to say about the death penalty. The death penalty had been a central sanction from the beginning of the colonial period, even if its reach varied from colony to colony. And while a handful of states banned the death penalty in their state constitutions as early as the mid- to late-1800s, the legitimacy of the death penalty as a sanction was never doubted. And that view was supported by a Supreme Court that did not get involved in how it was implemented.

Perhaps the most vivid example of the Court's hands-off approach comes from its 1949 case *Williams v. New York*, 337 U.S. 241 (1949), in which it upheld a judge's decision to impose the death penalty after he reviewed all sorts of information he had received from the probation office and "other sources," and which the defendant never had a chance to rebut. And it did so by arguing that the criminal justice system's commitment to *rehabilitation* required that judges be allowed to consider a wide array of evidence when imposing sentence.

In the landmark case of *Furman v. Georgia*, 408 U.S. 238 (1972), however, the Supreme Court declared that the arbitrary way the death penalty was administered by all the states and the federal government violated the Constitution's Eighth Amendment ban on cruel and unusual punishment, ushering in a brief, four-year moratorium on executions in the United States. Presaging the challenges the Court would face trying to regulate the death penalty in the future, it's first major death penalty opinion—one of the longest Supreme Court opinions, at 232 pages—is fractured and confusing. The majority holding, in its entirety, is this:

> Petitioner in No. 69–5003 was convicted of murder in Georgia and was sentenced to death pursuant to Ga. Code Ann. s 26–1005. . . . Petitioner in No. 69–5030 was convicted of rape in Georgia and was sentenced to death pursuant to Ga. Code Ann. s 26–1302. . . . Petitioner in No. 69–5031 was convicted of rape in Texas and was sentenced to death pursuant to Vernon's Tex. Penal Code, Art. 1189. . . . Certiorari was granted limited to the following question: "Does the imposition and carrying out of the death penalty in (these cases) constitute cruel and unusual punishment in violation of the Eighth and Fourteenth Amendments?" The Court holds that the imposition and carrying out of the death penalty in these cases constitute cruel and unusual punishment in violation of the Eighth and Fourteenth Amendments. The judgment in each case is therefore reversed insofar as it leaves undisturbed the death sentence imposed, and the cases are remanded for further proceedings. So ordered.
>
> Judgment in each case reversed in part and cases remanded. [408 U.S. at 239–40.]

That's it. What followed were nine separate opinions, including five distinct opinions from the majority: one each from each justice, none with any co-signers. Each of the four dissenters wrote his own opinion as well, although there was a bit more co-signing among them. As two long-time scholars of the death penalty observe, the various majority opinions in *Furman* pointed to at least five reasons why the death penalty was unconstitutional:[1]

1. *Per se* cruel and unusual. Only two justices, Brennan and Marshall, made this argument. Not surprisingly, as soon as *Furman* was issued states with invalidated death penalties did not simply abandon the sanction but set about trying to amend them to comport with the less extreme concerns raised by the rest of the justices in the majority.

2. Failure of desert. The statutes were generally so broadly written, and often encompassed such a wide array of offenses, including crimes that did not result in death (a practice that would be effectively invalidated in *Coker v. Georgia*, 433 U.S. 584 (1977)), that the Court was concerned the statutes were over-inclusive. Without more guidance, there was too great a risk that people the community in general did not want executed would be executed.

3. Fairness. Although there was no rigorous empirical evidence before the Court in *Furman* about racial discrimination in the imposition of the death penalty—that could come later, with the famous Baldus study in *McClesky v. Kemp*, 481 U.S. 279 (1987)—Douglas raised concerns that death penalty statutes were "pregnant with discrimination" (both racial and economic).

4. Individualization. Brennan argued that "[t]he State, even as it punishes, must treat its members with respect for their intrinsic worth as human beings." Four years later, this argument would play a role in striking down mandatory death penalty statutes (i.e., the sole sanction for certain violent crimes was death), even though such statutes appear to address concerns about fairness and proportionality.

5. Heightened procedural reliability. Brennan also argued that, simply put, death was different: "Death, in its finality, differs more from life imprisonment than a 100-year prison term differs from one of only a year or two." As such, courts had to be much more sure that the death penalty applied to

---

[1] Carol S. Steiker & Jordan M. Steiker, *Judicial Developments in Capital Punishment Law* 79–83 (in JAMES A. ACKER, ROBERT M. BOHM, & CHARLES S. LANIER, EDS., AMERICA'S EXPERIMENT WITH CAPITAL PUNISHMENT, 3RD ED., 2014).

a particular case, and so additional procedures could be required.

In the wake of *Furman*, every state faced a moratorium on imposing the death penalty. So for the next few years, many worked quickly to adjust their death penalty statutes to comport with what they thought the key aspects of *Furman* were. Four years later, in 1976, five of those statutes ended up before the Supreme Court, which upheld three (in *Gregg v. Georgia*, 428 U.S. 153 (1976) *Jurek v. Texas*, 428 U.S. 262 (1976) and *Proffitt v. Florida*, 428 U.S. 242 (1976)) and invalidated two (in *Woodson v. North Carolina*, 428 U.S. 280 (1976) and *Roberts v. Louisiana*, 428 U.S. 325 (1976)).

The death penalty regimes in North Carolina and Louisiana were rejected by the Court because they imposed mandatory death sentences: in North Carolina, for example, anyone convicted of first degree murder was automatically sentenced to death. In the eyes of these states, that solved the problem of unfettered jury discretion by eliminating it altogether. The Court was not persuaded for three reasons. First, it argued that such mandatory sentences went against a broad historical movement away from mandatory death penalties that had started as early as the colonial era. Second, it pointed out that juries could evade the mandatory sentence by declining to convict for first degree and instead convict for a lesser degree, even when the facts strongly supported a first-degree conviction. So disparities could persist (based on how juries convicted defendants), in ways that would be even harder for appellate courts to police. And third, the Court held that mandatory death penalties were insufficiently individualized.

In contrast, Florida, Georgia, and Texas created additional rules to guide and regulate when juries could impose death. Georgia, for example, required that a jury must find one of ten aggravating factors beyond a reasonable doubt (except in cases of treason or an airplane hijacking, in which case no additional findings were needed):

> b. In all cases of other offenses for which the death penalty may be authorized, the judge shall consider, or he shall include in his instructions to the jury for it to consider, any mitigating circumstances or aggravating circumstances otherwise authorized by law and any of the following statutory aggravating circumstances which may be supported by the evidence:
>
> (1) The offense of murder, rape, armed robbery, or kidnapping was committed by a person with a prior record of conviction for a capital felony, or the offense of murder was committed by a person who has a substantial history of serious assaultive criminal convictions.

(2) The offense of murder, rape, armed robbery, or kidnapping was committed while the offender was engaged in the commission of another capital felony, or aggravated battery, or the offense of murder was committed while the offender was engaged in the commission of burglary or arson in the first degree.

(3) The offender by his act of murder, armed robbery, or kidnapping knowingly created a great risk of death to more than one person in a public place by means of a weapon or device which would normally be hazardous to the lives of more than one person.

(4) The offender committed the offense of murder for himself or another, for the purpose of receiving money or any other thing of monetary value.

(5) The murder of a judicial officer, former judicial officer, district attorney or solicitor or former district attorney or solicitor during or because of the exercise of his official duty.

(6) The offender caused or directed another to commit murder or committed murder as an agent or employee of another person.

(7) The offense of murder, rape, armed robbery, or kidnapping was outrageously or wantonly vile, horrible or inhuman in that it involved torture, depravity of mind, or an aggravated battery to the victim.

(8) The offense of murder was committed against any peace officer, corrections employee or fireman while engaged in the performance of his official duties.

(9) The offense of murder was committed by a person in, or who has escaped from, the lawful custody of a peace officer or place of lawful confinement.

(10) The murder was committed for the purpose of avoiding, interfering with, or preventing a lawful arrest or custody in a place of lawful confinement, of himself or another.[2]

Texas went a slightly different path. As the Court in *Jurek* explained:

> The new Texas Penal Code limits capital homicides to intentional and knowing murders committed in five situations: murder of a peace officer or fireman; murder committed in the course of kidnaping, burglary, robbery, forcible rape, or arson; murder committed for remuneration; murder committed while escaping or attempting to escape from a penal institution; and

---

[2] Ga. Code § 27–2534.1(b) (now Ga. Code § 17–10–30).

murder committed by a prison inmate when the victim is a prison employee.

In addition, Texas adopted a new capital sentencing procedure. That procedure requires the jury to answer three questions in a proceeding that takes place subsequent to the return of a verdict finding a person guilty of one of the above categories of murder. The questions the jury must answer are these:

(1) whether the conduct of the defendant that caused the death of the deceased was committed deliberately and with the reasonable expectation that the death of the deceased or another would result;

(2) whether there is a probability that the defendant would commit criminal acts of violence that would constitute a continuing threat to society; and

(3) if raised by the evidence, whether the conduct of the defendant in killing the deceased was unreasonable in response to the provocation, if any, by the deceased.

If the jury finds that the State has proved beyond a reasonable doubt that the answer to each of the three questions is yes, then the death sentence is imposed. If the jury finds that the answer to any question is no, then a sentence of life imprisonment results. [428 U.S. at 268–269.]

As the following excerpt from the opinion upholding Georgia's statute demonstrates, the Court felt that procedures such as these were sufficient to rectify its concerns about arbitrary and capricious enforcement.

Gregg v. Georgia
428 U.S. 153, 196–206 (1976)

We now turn to consideration of the constitutionality of Georgia's capital-sentencing procedures. In the wake of *Furman*, Georgia amended its capital punishment statute, but chose not to narrow the scope of its murder provisions.

Georgia did act, however, to narrow the class of murderers subject to capital punishment by specifying statutory aggravating circumstances, one of which must be found by the jury to exist beyond a reasonable doubt before a death sentence can ever be imposed. In addition, the jury is authorized to consider any other appropriate aggravating or mitigating circumstances. The jury is not required to find any mitigating circumstance in order to make a recommendation of mercy that is binding on the trial court, but it must find a statutory aggravating circumstance before recommending a sentence of death.

These procedures require the jury to consider the circumstances of the crime and the criminal before it recommends sentence. No longer can a Georgia jury do as Furman's jury did: reach a finding of the defendant's guilt and then, without guidance or direction, decide whether he should live or die. Instead, the jury's attention is directed to the specific circumstances of the crime.... As a result, while some jury discretion still exists, the discretion to be exercised is controlled by clear and objective standards so as to produce non-discriminatory application.

As an important additional safeguard against arbitrariness and caprice, the Georgia statutory scheme provides for automatic appeal of all death sentences to the State's Supreme Court. That court is required by statute to review each sentence of death and determine whether it was imposed under the influence of passion or prejudice, whether the evidence supports the jury's finding of a statutory aggravating circumstance, and whether the sentence is disproportionate compared to those sentences imposed in similar cases.

On their face these procedures seem to satisfy the concerns of *Furman*. No longer should there be "no meaningful basis for distinguishing the few cases in which [the death penalty] is imposed from the many cases in which it is not."

The petitioner contends, however, that the changes in the Georgia sentencing procedures are only cosmetic, that the arbitrariness and capriciousness condemned by *Furman* continue to exist in Georgia—both in traditional practices that still remain and in the new sentencing procedures adopted in response to *Furman*.

First, the petitioner focuses on the opportunities for discretionary action that are inherent in the processing of any murder case under Georgia law. He notes that the state prosecutor has unfettered authority to select those persons whom he wishes to prosecute for a capital offense and to plea bargain with them. Further, at the trial the jury may choose to convict a defendant of a lesser included offense rather than find him guilty of a crime punishable by death, even if the evidence would support a capital verdict. And finally, a defendant who is convicted and sentenced to die may have his sentence commuted by the Governor of the State and the Georgia Board of Pardons and Paroles.

The existence of these discretionary stages is not determinative of the issues before us. At each of these stages an actor in the criminal justice system makes a decision which may remove a defendant from consideration as a candidate for the death penalty. *Furman*, in contrast, dealt with the decision to impose the death sentence on a specific individual who had been convicted of a capital offense. Nothing in any of our cases suggests that the decision to afford an individual defendant mercy violates the Constitution. *Furman* held only that, in order to minimize the risk that the death penalty would be imposed on a capriciously selected group of offenders, the decision to impose it had to be guided by standards so that the sentencing authority would focus on the particularized circumstances of the crime and the defendant.

The petitioner further contends that the capital-sentencing procedures adopted by Georgia in response to *Furman* do not eliminate the dangers of arbitrariness and caprice in jury sentencing that were held in *Furman* to be violative of the Eighth and Fourteenth Amendments. He claims that the statute is so broad and vague as to leave juries free to act as arbitrarily and capriciously as they wish in deciding whether to impose the death penalty. While there is no claim that the jury in this case relied upon a vague or overbroad provision to establish the existence of a statutory aggravating circumstance, the petitioner looks to the sentencing system as a whole (as the Court did in *Furman* and we do today) and argues that it fails to reduce sufficiently the risk of arbitrary infliction of death sentences. Specifically, Gregg urges that the statutory aggravating circumstances are too broad and too vague, that the sentencing procedure allows for arbitrary grants of mercy, and that the scope of the evidence and argument that can be considered at the presentence hearing is too wide.

The petitioner attacks the seventh statutory aggravating circumstance, which authorizes imposition of the death penalty if the murder was "outrageously or wantonly vile, horrible or inhuman in that it involved torture, depravity of mind, or an aggravated battery to the victim," contending that it is so broad that capital punishment could be imposed in any murder case. It is, of course, arguable that any murder involves depravity of mind or an aggravated battery. But this language need not be construed in this way, and there is no reason to assume that the Supreme Court of Georgia will adopt such an open-ended construction. In only one case has it upheld a jury's decision to sentence a defendant to death when the only statutory aggravating circumstance found was that of the seventh, and that homicide was a horrifying torture-murder.

The petitioner also argues that two of the statutory aggravating circumstances are vague and therefore susceptible of widely differing interpretations, thus creating a substantial risk that the death penalty will be arbitrarily inflicted by Georgia juries. In light of the decisions of the Supreme Court of Georgia we must disagree. First, the petitioner attacks that part of 27–2534.1(b)(1) that authorizes a jury to consider whether a defendant has a "substantial history of serious assaultive criminal convictions." The Supreme Court of Georgia, however, has demonstrated a concern that the new sentencing procedures provide guidance to juries. It held this provision to be impermissibly vague . . . because it did not provide the jury with "sufficiently 'clear and objective standards.' " Second, the petitioner points to 27–2534.1(b)(3) which speaks of creating a "great risk of death to more than one person." While such a phrase might be susceptible of an overly broad interpretation, the Supreme Court of Georgia has not so construed it. The only case in which the court upheld a conviction in reliance on this aggravating circumstance involved a man who stood up in a church and fired a gun indiscriminately into the audience. On the other hand, the court expressly reversed a finding of great risk when the victim was simply kidnaped in a parking lot.

The petitioner next argues that the requirements of *Furman* are not met here because the jury has the power to decline to impose the death penalty even if it finds that one or more statutory aggravating circumstances are present in the case. This contention misinterprets *Furman*. Moreover, it ignores the role of the Supreme Court of Georgia which reviews each death sentence to determine whether it is proportional to other sentences imposed for similar crimes. Since the proportionality requirement on review is intended to prevent caprice in the decision to inflict the penalty, the isolated decision of a jury to afford mercy does not render unconstitutional death sentences imposed on defendants who were sentenced under a system that does not create a substantial risk of arbitrariness or caprice.

The petitioner objects, finally, to the wide scope of evidence and argument allowed at presentence hearings. We think that the Georgia court wisely has chosen not to impose unnecessary restrictions on the evidence that can be offered at such a hearing and to approve open and far-ranging argument. So long as the evidence introduced and the arguments made at the presentence hearing do not prejudice a defendant, it is preferable not to impose restrictions. We think it desirable for the jury to have as much information before it as possible when it makes the sentencing decision.

Finally, the Georgia statute has an additional provision designed to assure that the death penalty will not be imposed on a capriciously selected group of convicted defendants. The new sentencing procedures require that the State Supreme Court review every death sentence to determine whether it was imposed under the influence of passion, prejudice, or any other arbitrary factor, whether the evidence supports the findings of a statutory aggravating circumstance, and "[w]hether the sentence of death is excessive or disproportionate to the penalty imposed in similar cases, considering both the crime and the defendant." In performing its sentence-review function, the Georgia court has held that "if the death penalty is only rarely imposed for an act or it is substantially out of line with sentences imposed for other acts it will be set aside as excessive." The court on another occasion stated that "we view it to be our duty under the similarity standard to assure that no death sentence is affirmed unless in similar cases throughout the state the death penalty has been imposed generally...."

The provision for appellate review in the Georgia capital-sentencing system serves as a check against the random or arbitrary imposition of the death penalty. In particular, the proportionality review substantially eliminates the possibility that a person will be sentenced to die by the action of an aberrant jury. If a time comes when juries generally do not impose the death sentence in a certain kind of murder case, the appellate review procedures assure that no defendant convicted under such circumstances will suffer a sentence of death.

QUESTIONS

1. **Mercy.** In *Gregg*, the Court justifies continued discretion in terms of mercy: "Nothing in any of our cases suggests that the decision to afford an individual defendant mercy violates the Constitution." Thus inconsistencies that persist are framed as inconsistent acts of *mercy*. Is this the right way to frame the problem? Can "mercy" be used to perpetuate the very problems *Furman* was concerned with?

2. **Guidance.** Does your answer to Question 1 change your views on whether the Court was correct that the 10 factors provided by Georgia meaningfully cabin discretion and avoid arbitrariness?

3. **Judicial review and systemic problems.** The Court puts a lot of weight on the fact that state Supreme Courts review death cases for arbitrary enforcement (when death is imposed). First, how concerning are the state supreme courts' asymmetric power: they can decide if the death penalty is improperly imposed, but they cannot review cases for the improper *failure* to impose death. What concerns should this raise? Second, justices on the Georgia Supreme Court are elected in non-partisan elections: should the US Supreme Court have taken that into account when trusting judicial review to protect unpopular defendants?

4. **Mandatory death, judicial review, and bias.** Does your answer to question 3 change your views about the propriety of mandatory death provisions (regardless of the Court's official decree about them), especially if paired with automatic state supreme court review? Does our discussion of mercy suggest that the Court's concerns in *Woodson* and *Roberts* about the lack of individualization is incorrect?

In the years after *Gregg*, the Court limited the reach of the death penalty, at least to some extent. In *Coker v. Georgia*, 433 U.S. 584 (1977), the Court held that a rapist who did not kill his victim could not be executed; in effect, the Eighth Amendment appears to limit the death penalty to those who kill (although the Court has never stated that as a blanket rule). Citing *Gregg*, the majority pointed out that a sanction violates the Eighth Amendment if it "(1) makes no measurable contribution to acceptable goals of punishment, and hence is nothing more than the purposeless and needless imposition of pain and suffering; or (2) is grossly out of proportion to the severity of the crime." In this case, it held that execution was grossly disproportionate for rape.

Then in *Lockett v. Ohio*, 438 U.S. 586 (1978), the Court held that a defendant must be allowed to bring in any relevant mitigating evidence.

The law in Ohio at that time limited arguments for mitigation to three possible claims:

> (B) Regardless of whether one or more of the aggravating circumstances listed in division (A) of this section is specified in the indictment and proved beyond a reasonable doubt, the death penalty for aggravated murder is precluded when, considering the nature and circumstances of the offense and the history, character, and condition of the offender, one or more of the following is established by a prepondence [sic.] of the evidence:
>
> (1) The victim of the offense induced or facilitated it.
>
> (2) It is unlikely that the offense would have been committed, but for the fact that the offender was under duress, coercion, or strong provocation."
>
> (3) The offense was primarily the product of the offender's psychosis or mental deficiency, though such condition is insufficient to establish the defense of insanity.[3]

The Court overturned the statute on the grounds that it was too restrictive. Individualization required that a defendant be allowed to invoke any sort of mitigating factor he or she (*Lockett* was a rare case involving a female defendant: of the 1,408 executions since *Gregg*, only 15 have been of women) wishes to raise. As the Court explained:

> [W]e conclude that the Eighth and Fourteenth Amendments require that the sentencer, in all but the rarest kind of capital case [the Court deferred ruling on murder committed by those under a life sentence], not be precluded from considering, *as a mitigating factor,* any aspect of a defendant's character or record and any of the circumstances of the offense that the defendant proffers as a basis for a sentence less than death. We recognize that, in noncapital cases, the established practice of individualized sentences rests not on constitutional commands, but on public policy enacted into statutes. The considerations that account for the wide acceptance of individualization of sentences in noncapital cases surely cannot be thought less important in capital cases. Given that the imposition of death by public authority is so profoundly different from all other penalties, we cannot avoid the conclusion that an individualized decision is essential in capital cases. The need for treating each defendant in a capital case with that degree of respect due the uniqueness of the individual is far more important than in noncapital cases. A variety of flexible techniques—probation, parole, work furloughs, to name a few—and various postconviction remedies may be available to modify an initial

---

[3] Ohio Rev. Code § 2929.04.

sentence of confinement in noncapital cases. The nonavailability of corrective or modifying mechanisms with respect to an executed capital sentence underscores the need for individualized consideration as a constitutional requirement in imposing the death sentence.

There is no perfect procedure for deciding in which cases governmental authority should be used to impose death. But a statute that prevents the sentencer in all capital cases from giving independent mitigating weight to aspects of the defendant's character and record and to circumstances of the offense proffered in mitigation creates the risk that the death penalty will be imposed in spite of factors which may call for a less severe penalty. When the choice is between life and death, that risk is unacceptable and incompatible with the commands of the Eighth and Fourteenth Amendments. [438 U.S. at 604–605.]

Lockett invoked the common theme that "death is different." although it is worth asking how true that is. If nothing else, the costs per error in death cases may be greater, but the *number* of errors in non-death cases, which comprise well over 99.9% of all criminal convictions, surely dwarf those in death cases; the total error cost is harder to compare than *Lockett*'s individual-case perspective suggests.

The Court further restricted the scope of the death penalty over the next few years. Some cases focused on procedural protections, holding that the failure to include lesser-included (and thus non-capital) charges in capital cases risked arbitrary jury behavior (*Beck v. Alabama*, 447 U.S. 625 (1980)), as did including aggravating factors that were so open-ended as to provide no guidance (*Godfrey v. Georgia*, 446 U.S. 420 (1980), striking down the "wantonly vile" aggravator in Georgia's statute (number 7 above)). It also extended *Coker*'s concerns with proportionality to hold that a minor participant convicted of felony murder (the getaway driver of a robbery that unexpectedly resulted in murder) could not be executed (*Enmund v. Florida*, 458 U.S. 782 (1982)).

As the Court grew more conservative over the 1980s, however, its restrictions on executions waned. In *Tison v. Arizona*, 481 U.S. 137 (1987), the Court made it clear that *Enmund*'s limitation only applied to minor participants, and that it was not impermissible to execute someone convicted of felony murder who was a much more major participant in the crime and the killing. And while the Court held it unconstitutional to execute anyone under the age of 15 in *Thompson v. Oklahoma*, 487 U.S. 815 (1988), it sanctioned the execution of those 16 and older in *Stanford v. Kentucky*, 492 U.S. 361 (1989), allowing the US to become the world's leading executioner of juveniles. Finally, in *Penry v. Lynaugh*, 492 U.S. 302 (1989), it held that the execution of the mentally retarded did not violate the Constitution either.

Perhaps one of the more controversial opinions during this time, and one that focused on what has become a central issue in the administration of the death penalty, was *McCleskey v. Kemp*, 481 U.S. 279 (1987), which considered a challenge to the death penalty in Georgia on the grounds that it was administered in a racially biased manner.

McCleskey v. Kemp
481 U.S. 279, 282–342 (1987)

■ JUSTICE POWELL delivered the opinion of the Court.

This case presents the question whether a complex statistical study that indicates a risk that racial considerations enter into capital sentencing determinations proves that petitioner McCleskey's capital sentence is unconstitutional under the Eighth or Fourteenth Amendment.

[After being sentenced to death and completing his state appeals,] McCleskey next filed a petition for a writ of habeas corpus in the Federal District Court for the Northern District of Georgia. His petition raised 18 claims, one of which was that the Georgia capital sentencing process is administered in a racially discriminatory manner in violation of the Eighth and Fourteenth Amendments to the United States Constitution. In support of his claim, McCleskey proffered a statistical study performed by Professors David C. Baldus, Charles Pulaski, and George Woodworth, and (the Baldus study) that purports to show a disparity in the imposition of the death sentence in Georgia based on the race of the murder victim and, to a lesser extent, the race of the defendant. The Baldus study is actually two sophisticated statistical studies that examine over 2,000 murder cases that occurred in Georgia during the 1970's. The raw numbers collected by Professor Baldus indicate that defendants charged with killing white persons received the death penalty in 11% of the cases, but defendants charged with killing blacks received the death penalty in only 1% of the cases. The raw numbers also indicate a reverse racial disparity according to the race of the defendant: 4% of the black defendants received the death penalty, as opposed to 7% of the white defendants.

Baldus also divided the cases according to the combination of the race of the defendant and the race of the victim. He found that the death penalty was assessed in 22% of the cases involving black defendants and white victims; 8% of the cases involving white defendants and white victims; 1% of the cases involving black defendants and black victims; and 3% of the cases involving white defendants and black victims. Similarly, Baldus found that prosecutors sought the death penalty in 70% of the cases involving black defendants and white victims; 32% of the cases involving white defendants and white victims; 15% of the cases involving black defendants and black victims; and 19% of the cases involving white defendants and black victims.

Baldus subjected his data to an extensive analysis, taking account of 230 variables that could have explained the disparities on nonracial grounds. One of his models concludes that, even after taking account of 39 nonracial variables, defendants charged with killing white victims were 4.3 times as likely to receive a death sentence as defendants charged with killing blacks. According to this model, black defendants were 1.1 times as likely to receive a death sentence as other defendants. Thus, the Baldus study indicates that black defendants, such as McCleskey, who kill white victims have the greatest likelihood of receiving the death penalty.

[McCleskey claims] that the Georgia capital punishment statute violates the Equal Protection Clause of the Fourteenth Amendment. He argues that race has infected the administration of Georgia's statute in two ways: persons who murder whites are more likely to be sentenced to death than persons who murder blacks, and black murderers are more likely to be sentenced to death than white murderers. As a black defendant who killed a white victim, McCleskey claims that the Baldus study demonstrates that he was discriminated against because of his race and because of the race of his victim. In its broadest form, McCleskey's claim of discrimination extends to every actor in the Georgia capital sentencing process, from the prosecutor who sought the death penalty and the jury that imposed the sentence, to the State itself that enacted the capital punishment statute and allows it to remain in effect despite its allegedly discriminatory application. We agree with the Court of Appeals, and every other court that has considered such a challenge, that this claim must fail.

Our analysis begins with the basic principle that a defendant who alleges an equal protection violation has the burden of proving "the existence of purposeful discrimination." A corollary to this principle is that a criminal defendant must prove that the purposeful discrimination "had a discriminatory effect" on him. Thus, to prevail under the Equal Protection Clause, McCleskey must prove that the decisionmakers in *his* case acted with discriminatory purpose. He offers no evidence specific to his own case that would support an inference that racial considerations played a part in his sentence. Instead, he relies solely on the Baldus study. McCleskey argues that the Baldus study compels an inference that his sentence rests on purposeful discrimination. McCleskey's claim that these statistics are sufficient proof of discrimination, without regard to the facts of a particular case, would extend to all capital cases in Georgia, at least where the victim was white and the defendant is black.

The Court has accepted statistics as proof of intent to discriminate in certain limited contexts. First, this Court has accepted statistical disparities as proof of an equal protection violation in the selection of the jury venire in a particular district. Although statistical proof normally must present a "stark" pattern to be accepted as the sole proof of discriminatory intent under the Constitution, "[b]ecause of the nature of the jury-selection task, . . . we have permitted a finding of constitutional violation even when the statistical pattern does not approach [such] extremes." Second, this Court has accepted statistics in the form of multiple-regression analysis to prove statutory violations under Title VII of the Civil Rights Act of 1964.

But the nature of the capital sentencing decision, and the relationship of the statistics to that decision, are fundamentally different from the corresponding elements in the venire-selection or Title VII cases. Most importantly, each particular decision to impose the death penalty is made by a petit jury selected from a properly constituted venire. Each jury is unique in its composition, and the Constitution requires that its decision rest on consideration of innumerable factors that vary according to the characteristics of the individual defendant and the facts of the particular capital offense. Thus, the application of an inference drawn from the general statistics to a specific decision in a trial and sentencing simply is not comparable to the application of an inference drawn from general statistics to a specific venire-selection or Title VII case. In those cases, the statistics relate to fewer entities, and fewer variables are relevant to the challenged decisions.

Another important difference between the cases in which we have accepted statistics as proof of discriminatory intent and this case is that, in the venire-selection and Title VII contexts, the decisionmaker has an opportunity to explain the statistical disparity. Here, the State has no practical opportunity to rebut the Baldus study. "[C]ontrolling considerations of . . . public policy," dictate that jurors "cannot be called . . . to testify to the motives and influences that led to their verdict." Similarly, the policy considerations behind a prosecutor's traditionally "wide discretion" suggest the impropriety of our requiring prosecutors to defend their decisions to seek death penalties, "often years after they were made." Moreover, absent far stronger proof, it is unnecessary to seek such a rebuttal, because a legitimate and unchallenged explanation for the decision is apparent from the record: McCleskey committed an act for which the United States Constitution and Georgia laws permit imposition of the death penalty.

Finally, McCleskey's statistical proffer must be viewed in the context of his challenge. McCleskey challenges decisions at the heart of the State's criminal justice system. "[O]ne of society's most basic tasks is that of protecting the lives of its citizens and one of the most basic ways in which it achieves the task is through criminal laws against murder." Implementation of these laws necessarily requires discretionary judgments. Because discretion is essential to the criminal justice process, we would demand exceptionally clear proof before we would infer that the discretion has been abused. The unique nature of the decisions at issue in this case also counsels against adopting such an inference from the disparities indicated by the Baldus study. Accordingly, we hold that the Baldus study is clearly insufficient to support an inference that any of the decisionmakers in McCleskey's case acted with discriminatory purpose.

On the one hand, he cannot base a constitutional claim on an argument that his case differs from other cases in which defendants *did* receive the death penalty. On automatic appeal, the Georgia Supreme Court found that McCleskey's death sentence was not disproportionate to other death sentences imposed in the State.

On the other hand, absent a showing that the Georgia capital punishment system operates in an arbitrary and capricious manner, McCleskey cannot prove a constitutional violation by demonstrating that other defendants who may be similarly situated did *not* receive the death penalty. In *Gregg,* the Court confronted the argument that "the opportunities for discretionary action that are inherent in the processing of any murder case under Georgia law," specifically the opportunities for discretionary leniency, rendered the capital sentences imposed arbitrary and capricious. We rejected this contention. . . .

Although our decision in *Gregg* as to the facial validity of the Georgia capital punishment statute appears to foreclose McCleskey's disproportionality argument, he further contends that the Georgia capital punishment system is arbitrary and capricious in *application,* and therefore his sentence is excessive, because racial considerations may influence capital sentencing decisions in Georgia. We now address this claim.

To evaluate McCleskey's challenge, we must examine exactly what the Baldus study may show. Even Professor Baldus does not contend that his statistics *prove* that race enters into any capital sentencing decisions or that race was a factor in McCleskey's particular case. Statistics at most may show only a likelihood that a particular factor entered into some decisions. There is, of course, some risk of racial prejudice influencing a jury's decision in a criminal case. There are similar risks that other kinds of prejudice will influence other criminal trials. The question "is at what point that risk becomes constitutionally unacceptable." McCleskey asks us to accept the likelihood allegedly shown by the Baldus study as the constitutional measure of an unacceptable risk of racial prejudice influencing capital sentencing decisions. This we decline to do.

At most, the Baldus study indicates a discrepancy that appears to correlate with race. Apparent disparities in sentencing are an inevitable part of our criminal justice system. The discrepancy indicated by the Baldus study is "a far cry from the major systemic defects identified in *Furman.*" As this Court has recognized, any mode for determining guilt or punishment "has its weaknesses and the potential for misuse." Specifically, "there can be 'no perfect procedure for deciding in which cases governmental authority should be used to impose death.'" Despite these imperfections, our consistent rule has been that constitutional guarantees are met when "the mode [for determining guilt or punishment] itself has been surrounded with safeguards to make it as fair as possible." Where the discretion that is fundamental to our criminal process is involved, we decline to assume that what is unexplained is invidious. In light of the safeguards designed to minimize racial bias in the process, the fundamental value of jury trial in our criminal justice system, and the benefits that discretion provides to criminal defendants, we hold that the Baldus study does not demonstrate a constitutionally significant risk of racial bias affecting the Georgia capital sentencing process.

Two additional concerns inform our decision in this case. First, McCleskey's claim, taken to its logical conclusion, throws into serious question the principles that underlie our entire criminal justice system. The Eighth Amendment is not limited in application to capital punishment, but applies to all penalties. Thus, if we accepted McCleskey's claim that racial bias has impermissibly tainted the capital sentencing decision, we could soon be faced with similar claims as to other types of penalty. Moreover, the claim that his sentence rests on the irrelevant factor of race easily could be extended to apply to claims based on unexplained discrepancies that correlate to membership in other minority groups, and even to gender. Similarly, since McCleskey's claim relates to the race of his victim, other claims could apply with equally logical force to statistical disparities that correlate with the race or sex of other actors in the criminal justice system, such as defense attorneys, or judges. Also, there is no logical reason that such a claim need be limited to racial or sexual bias. If arbitrary and capricious punishment is the touchstone under the Eighth Amendment, such a claim could—at least in theory—be based upon any arbitrary variable, such as the defendant's facial characteristics, or the physical attractiveness of the defendant or the victim, that some statistical study indicates may be influential in jury decisionmaking. As these examples illustrate, there is no limiting principle to the type of challenge brought by McCleskey. The Constitution does not require that a State eliminate any demonstrable disparity that correlates with a potentially irrelevant factor in order to operate a criminal justice system that includes capital punishment. As we have stated specifically in the context of capital punishment, the Constitution does not "plac[e] totally unrealistic conditions on its use."

Second, McCleskey's arguments are best presented to the legislative bodies. It is not the responsibility—or indeed even the right—of this Court to determine the appropriate punishment for particular crimes. It is the legislatures, the elected representatives of the people, that are "constituted to respond to the will and consequently the moral values of the people." Legislatures also are better qualified to weigh and "evaluate the results of statistical studies in terms of their own local conditions and with a flexibility of approach that is not available to the courts," Capital punishment is now the law in more than two-thirds of our States. It is the ultimate duty of courts to determine on a case-by-case basis whether these laws are applied consistently with the Constitution. Despite McCleskey's wide-ranging arguments that basically challenge the validity of capital punishment in our multiracial society, the only question before us is whether in his case, the law of Georgia was properly applied. We agree with the District Court and the Court of Appeals for the Eleventh Circuit that this was carefully and correctly done in this case.

Accordingly, we affirm the judgment of the Court of Appeals for the Eleventh Circuit.

■ JUSTICE BRENNAN, with whom JUSTICE MARSHALL joins, and with whom JUSTICE BLACKMUN and JUSTICE STEVENS join [in part], dissenting.

The Court today holds that Warren McCleskey's sentence was constitutionally imposed. It finds no fault in a system in which lawyers must tell their clients that race casts a large shadow on the capital sentencing process. The Court arrives at this conclusion by stating that the Baldus study cannot "*prove* that race enters into any capital sentencing decisions or that race was a factor in McCleskey's particular case." Since, according to Professor Baldus, we cannot say "to a moral certainty" that race influenced a decision, we can identify only "a likelihood that a particular factor entered into some decisions," and "a discrepancy that appears to correlate with race." This "likelihood" and "discrepancy," holds the Court, is insufficient to establish a constitutional violation. The Court reaches this conclusion by placing four factors on the scales opposite McCleskey's evidence: the desire to encourage sentencing discretion, the existence of "statutory safeguards" in the Georgia scheme, the fear of encouraging widespread challenges to other sentencing decisions, and the limits of the judicial role. The Court's evaluation of the significance of petitioner's evidence is fundamentally at odds with our consistent concern for rationality in capital sentencing, and the considerations that the majority invokes to discount that evidence cannot justify ignoring its force.

The Court maintains that petitioner's claim "is antithetical to the fundamental role of discretion in our criminal justice system." It states that "[w]here the discretion that is fundamental to our criminal process is involved, we decline to assume that what is unexplained is invidious."

Reliance on race in imposing capital punishment, however, is antithetical to the very rationale for granting sentencing discretion. Discretion is a means, not an end. It is bestowed in order to permit the sentencer to "trea[t] each defendant in a capital case with that degree of respect due the uniqueness of the individual." The decision to impose the punishment of death must be based on a "particularized consideration of relevant aspects of the character and record of each convicted defendant." Failure to conduct such an individualized moral inquiry "treats all persons convicted of a designated offense not as unique individual human beings, but as members of a faceless, undifferentiated mass to be subjected to the blind infliction of the penalty of death."

The Court also declines to find McCleskey's evidence sufficient in view of "the safeguards designed to minimize racial bias in the [capital sentencing] process." It has now been over 13 years since Georgia adopted the provisions upheld in *Gregg*. Professor Baldus and his colleagues have compiled data on almost 2,500 homicides committed during the period 1973–1979. They have taken into account the influence of 230 nonracial variables, using a multitude of data from the State itself, and have produced striking evidence that the odds of being sentenced to death are significantly greater than average if a defendant is black or his or her victim is white. The challenge to the Georgia system is not speculative or theoretical; it is empirical. As a result, the Court cannot rely on the statutory safeguards in discounting McCleskey's evidence, for it is the very effectiveness of those safeguards that such evidence calls into question. While we may hope that a model of procedural fairness will curb the influence of race on sentencing, "we cannot simply assume that the model works as intended; we must critique its performance in terms of its results."

The Court next states that its unwillingness to regard petitioner's evidence as sufficient is based in part on the fear that recognition of McCleskey's claim would open the door to widespread challenges to all aspects of criminal sentencing. Taken on its face, such a statement seems to suggest a fear of too much justice. Yet surely the majority would acknowledge that if striking evidence indicated that other minority groups, or women, or even persons with blond hair, were disproportionately sentenced to death, such a state of affairs would be repugnant to deeply rooted conceptions of fairness. The prospect that there may be more widespread abuse than McCleskey documents may be dismaying, but it does not justify complete abdication of our judicial role. The Constitution was framed fundamentally as a bulwark against governmental power, and preventing the arbitrary administration of punishment is a basic ideal of any society that purports to be governed by the rule of law.

In fairness, the Court's fear that McCleskey's claim is an invitation to descend a slippery slope also rests on the realization that any humanly imposed system of penalties will exhibit some imperfection. Yet to reject McCleskey's powerful evidence on this basis is to ignore both the qualitatively different character of the death penalty and the particular repugnance of racial discrimination, considerations which may properly be taken into account in determining whether various punishments are "cruel and unusual." Furthermore, it fails to take account of the unprecedented refinement and strength of the Baldus study.

Finally, the Court justifies its rejection of McCleskey's claim by cautioning against usurpation of the legislatures' role in devising and monitoring criminal punishment. The Court is, of course, correct to emphasize the gravity of constitutional intervention and the importance that it be sparingly employed. The fact that "[c]apital punishment is now the law in more than two thirds of our States," however, does not diminish the fact that capital punishment is the most awesome act that a State can perform. The judiciary's role in this society counts for little if the use of governmental power to extinguish life does not elicit close scrutiny. . . .

A second dissent, written by Blackmun, raises a point that *Gregg* and its fellow cases seemed to have overlooked, namely that the jury isn't the only potential source of arbitrariness in the application of the death penalty. After all, a defendant cannot face death unless the prosecutor chooses to charge him with a death-eligible offense—and the array of statutes available to prosecutors ensures that they can always find a viable non-death charge to file if they so desire. As Blackmun explains:

> [McCleskey] submitted the deposition of Lewis R. Slaton, who, as of the date of the deposition, had been the District Attorney for 18 years in the county in which McCleskey was tried and sentenced. [Slaton] testified that during his years in the office, there were no guidelines informing the Assistant District Attorneys who handled the cases how they should proceed at any particular stage of the prosecution. There were no guidelines as to when they should seek an indictment for murder as opposed to lesser charges, when they should recommend acceptance of a guilty plea to murder, acceptance of a guilty plea to a lesser charge, reduction of charges, or dismissal of charges at the postindictment-preconviction stage, or when they should seek the death penalty. Slaton testified that these decisions were left to the discretion of the individual attorneys who then informed Slaton of their decisions as they saw fit. [481 U.S. at 357.]

It is important to be clear about what the Baldus study—and numerous subsequent replications—found. The primary source of disparity is not the race of the *defendant* but the race of the *victim*. As a recent review of the empirical literature explains:

> These empirical studies of racial disparities in death-charging and death-sentencing—done in different jurisdictions, with differing methodologies, covering a variety of time periods—produced results remarkably consistent with the Baldus study findings in Georgia a quarter of a century ago: 1) there is little or no disparity based on race of the defendant alone; 2) there is a statistically significant disparity based on race of the victim(s)

alone; and 3) there is an even greater disparity based on the combination of race of the defendant and race of the victim. While these numerous subsequent studies tend to confirm, if any confirmation were needed, the findings presented to the Court in *McCleskey*, they also validate Justice Powell's assumption that upholding McCleskey's Eighth Amendment claim would not have invalidated just Georgia death sentences, but would have led to successful challenges under every other post-Furman statute, i.e., that *McCleskey* would have become a second *Furman*.[4]

In other words, the bias appears to stem more (though by no means solely) from a devaluation of the life of a black victim rather than an increase in animosity towards a black killer.

Though the Court has taken no further significant steps to address racial imbalances in the application of the death penalty, in the 2000s it did impose a few more limitations on the sanction's reach, overturning two earlier cases in the process. In *Atkins v. Virginia*, 536 U.S. 304 (2002), the Court overturned *Penry* and held that executing someone who is mentally retarded violated the Eighth Amendment. The majority invoked "evolving standards of decency," pointing out that numerous states had adopted explicit bans on executing the mentally retarded in the wake of *Penry*. It also argued that executing the mentally retarded failed on both proportionality (less culpable, harder to deter) and procedural protection (harder to make mitigating arguments, more likely to falsely confess) grounds.

Then, three years later, in *Roper v. Simmons*, 543 U.S. 551 (2005), the Court reversed *Stanford* and held that executing anyone under the age of 18 at the time of the crime was a *per se* violation of the Eighth Amendment. The majority first pointed again to "evolving standards" at the state level. It then argued that three aspects of youthfulness—"a lack of maturity and an underdeveloped sense of responsibility," greater susceptibility to (negative) peer pressure, and less well-formed character—collectively "render suspect any conclusion that a juvenile falls among the worst offenders." Thus youth are less culpable and harder to deter, which the majority argued are the two primary penological justifications for the death penalty. The majority, like it also did in *Atkins*, also pointed to international law, highlighting the extent to which the United States' willingness to execute the young (and mentally retarded) truly stood out from world trends. Justice Scalia, in his dissent, attacked the majority for cherry-picking the empirical studies on which it relied. More broadly, Scalia argued—along the lines of *Furman* and *Gregg*—that the individualized nature of criminal justice proceedings obviated any need for a blanket ban. *Some* 17 or 18 year olds were likely

---

[4] Steven F. Shatz & Terry Dalton, *Challenging the Death Penalty with Statistics:* Furman, McCleskey, *and a Single County Study*, 34 CARDOZO L. REV. 1227, 1250–1251 (2013).

mature and culpable enough to merit execution, so we should trust the system to filter out those who are not from those who are.

Finally, death penalty cases were not immune to the *Blakely-Booker* line of cases: in fact, *Ring v. Arizona*, 536 U.S. 584 (2002), the case which made *Blakely* essentially inevitable, was a death penalty case. In *Ring*, the Court held that only juries could find whatever aggravating facts state law required for a defendant to qualify for the death penalty (and had to do so beyond a reasonable doubt); prior to *Ring*, many states had allowed judges to find these facts. That does not mean that juries necessarily had to *impose* the death penalty. In some states, juries could (and still can) make the required findings but the judge could (and still can) nonetheless decline to impose the death penalty. *Ring*, however, does foreclose the alternative, in which juries decline to find the aggravating factors but are overridden by the judge.

As the Steikers point out, the net effect of these opinions, plus several others that highlighted the need for competent capital defense work (*Rompilla v. Beard*, 545 U.S. 374 (2005), *Wiggins v. Smith*, 539 U.S. 510 (2003), and *Williams v. Taylor*, 529 U.S. 362 (2000)), has been to push the cost of capital cases significantly higher.[5] In some cases, this has caused local jurisdictions to forego seeking the death penalty; in a few others, to introduce special tax just to fund capital cases. We will turn to these financial issues at the end of the chapter.

QUESTIONS

1. **Prosecutor explanations.** The majority in *McCleskey* argued that the "wide discretion" granted prosecutors effectively precluded asking them to explain how they use that discretion. Can you justify that position? Moreover, how convincing was the Court's argument that the prosecutor didn't need to explain himself since McCleskey in fact committed a death-eligible offense? Was that responsive to the claim that McCleskey was raising?

2. **Fear of justice.** The majority in *McCleskey* warns that accepting McCleskey's argument would lead to a slippery slope that could undo the entire criminal justice system at ever step. The dissent mocks this as a "fear of too much justice." Is the majority's apprehension valid? The dissent then goes to point out that even if the majority's concerns are valid, nonetheless *racial* problems are uniquely deserving of judicial intervention. Is *this* a compelling argument?

3. **Legislative deference.** The majority in *McCleskey* then claims that resolving this sort of bias is the role of state legislators, not of courts. And the majority is correct that legislatures have access to many more sources of information than courts do. But is there anything in *Furman* that suggests that the Court can address only *certain types* of arbitrary application? Furthermore, look at the states whose death penalty laws keep

---

[5] Steiker & Steiker, supra note 1 at 96.

appearing before the Supreme Court: Georgia, Texas, Louisiana, Florida, Virginia, etc. Does this raise any concerns about deference to the legislature and the proper role of the courts, federal courts in particular?

4. **Evolving standards.** In both *Atkins* and *Roper*, the "evolving standards of decency" and "national consensus" to which the majorities point are both still minorities of death-penalty using states. In *Atkins*, the dissent points out that only 47% of states with the death penalty (18 out of 38) had abolished executions for the mentally retarded. The majority pointed out, though, that 16 of those 18 abolitions came *after Penry*, which held such sanctions permissible. For *Roper*, the dissent points out that the numbers are even less striking: only five states changed their views on juvenile death sanctions after *Thompson* gave them its constitutional blessing. At least when it comes to evolving national standards, who has the better argument in *Atkins*? *Roper*?

A.2. LEGISLATIVE RULES

As always, the Court simply sets the floor that states have to stay above; states remain free to adopt any additional rules that are consistent with those standards. So states vary in terms of the types of murders that trigger the death penalty, as well as the findings that are required for a defendant to be eligible for the death penalty. Moreover, even though the Court has maintained since *Gregg* that the death penalty is constitutionally permissible, since 1976 ten of the thirty-nine states (including DC) that had the death penalty in 1976 have abolished it, nine by legislative action, one by legislative inaction.[6]

A.2.a. TYPES OF CRIMES (AND ABOLITION)

One way in which states differ in the imposition of the death penalty is in the choices of eligible crimes, most importantly in how they treat felony murder.

As the Court made clear in *Tison*, punishing felony murder with death is permissible, even if the defendant never actually directly caused the death of anyone, although he needs to be a major participant and to have acted with reckless indifference to human life. Since 1976, at least ten states have executed someone for either felony murder (seven states, ten people) or for hiring someone else to kill (three additional states, ten more executions).[7]

Another variation is in how states view non-homicide offenses: it turns out that not every state restricts the death penalty to murder. Montana's criminal code, for example, still leaves open the possibility of death for aggravated kidnapping (Mont. Code Ann. § 45–5–303) or some

---

[6] New York State re-adopted the death penalty post-*Furman* in 1995, but the state's highest court held its statute unconstitutional under the state constitution in 2007. The state legislature has never bothered to fix the statute.

[7] http://www.deathpenaltyinfo.org/those-executed-who-did-not-directly-kill-victim.

forms of aggravated sexual assault (Mont. Code Ann. § 45–5–503), neither of which require death. Florida retains the crime of "capital drug trafficking" (Fl. Stat. § 893.135), which only requires that the importation of the drug would *probably result* in the death of someone. And Georgia defines hijacking an aircraft (though no other form of transportation), even if no-one dies, as a capital crime, as well as treason (Ga. Stat. § 16–5–44). The arguments that the Court made in overturning the imposition of the death penalty for (non-lethal) child rape in *Louisiana v. Kennedy*, 554 U.S. 407 (2008), such as the small number of states with such laws, suggest that the Court would view a death sentence under these statutes quite critically; tellingly, no one has been sentenced under them.

One final way that state legislatures can define the crimes eligible for death is by setting that number to zero: abolition. Ten states abolished the death penalty before 1976, starting with Wisconsin in 1853. Since the Court restored the death penalty in 1976, another ten states and the District of Columbia have also abolished the death penalty. And the speed of repeal has been picking up. Between 1981 and 1984, three states abolished the death penalty, and then no state followed suit until 2007. But from 2007 to 2015, six states have abolished the sanction, a rate of more than one every other year. The most recent, Nebraska, which abolished its death penalty in May 2015 when the (Republican-dominated) legislature overrode the (Republican) governor's veto of its repeal bill, caught significant national attention because it demonstrated that repeal was possible even in fairly conservative states.

A.2.b. STANDARDS FOR EXECUTION

Perhaps more important than who is made eligible for death are the rules the state adopts for how to impose it. Two scholars classify state death penalty statutes as falling into one of three regimes:[8]

1. **Balancing Schemes.** The core idea here is that the statute instructs the jurors to balance various aggravating and mitigating factors against each other. As Acker and Lanier explain:

   The statutes that rely on this balancing approach differ in important specifics. For example, some schemes limit the sentencer to consider only aggravating factors enumerated in the statute. Others provide that after finding at least one statutory aggravating circumstance, additional aggravating evidence—even if not linked to a statutory sentencing factor—may be considered. . . . Because the Constitution requires that all relevant mitigating evidence be admissible in a capital trial, proof cannot be limited to statutory mitigating factors. Nevertheless, several death-

---

[8] James R. Acker & Charles S. Lanier, *Beyond Human Ability? The Rise and Fall of Death Penalty Legislation* 119–122 (in JAMES A. ACKER, ROBERT M. BOHM, & CHARLES S. LANIER, EDS., AMERICA'S EXPERIMENT WITH CAPITAL PUNISHMENT, 3RD ED., 2014)

penalty laws include nonexhaustive lists of mitigating circumstances identified by legislatures as meriting the sentencer's consideration.

Acker and Lanier go on to explain that some balancing states are "permissive," while others are "quasi-mandatory." Permissive states hold that sentencers are not required to impose the death penalty, even when aggravators trump mitigators. Some states go further and forbid death when mitigators exceed aggravators. Quasi-mandatory states, on the other, hold that the sentencer *must* impose death when it finds at least one aggravator and no mitigator.

2. **Threshold Schemes.** Under a threshold scheme, a capital defendant becomes eligible for death as soon as the sentencer finds one aggravating factor. In these situations, the sentencer "typically is instructed to 'consider' other relevant aggravating circumstances, as well as mitigating factors.... The sentencer is not directed to weigh or balance aggravating and mitigating factors...." These statutes look quite similar to pre-*Furman* statutes, except that guilt and punishment are separated into distinct trials, and the critical "triggering" factor is expressly given in the statute.

3. **Special Sentencing Issues.** Only three states—Oregon, Texas, and Virginia—use these sorts of statutes, but Texas and Virginia are the nation's first and second states, respectively, when it comes to total executions. So while not widely used across *states*, they are widely used across *executions*. As Acker and Lanier point out, special sentencing statutes "distill the threshold judgment concerning an offender's death-penalty eligibility to a 'yes-no' answer, given in response to discrete, ostensibly fact-dependent special sentencing issues."

So, for example, in Texas and Oregon, the jury is asked "whether there is a probability that the defendant would commit criminal acts of violence that would constitute a continuing threat to society." A jury that votes yes is then instructed to consider whether mitigating evidence exists to mitigate to life. In Virginia, there are two special issues: future dangerousness and whether the offense was "outrageously or wantonly vile, horrible, or inhuman, in that it involved torture, depravity of mind or aggravated battery to the victim." An answer of yes to either renders the defendant death eligible (subject to consideration of mitigating evidence).

For all the work put into revising the death statutes to comply with *Furman* and *Gregg*, it is worth asking how much they have regulated discretion, and how much the choice of regime matters. Acker and Lainer are pessimistic. They first note that the complexity often confuses jurors, and evidence suggests that they frequently misinterpret the instructions they face. They then point out that, in the end, the rule might not matter at all:

> Most discouraging, perhaps, is the mounting evidence that the elaborate sentencing criteria and procedures mandated by statute are largely irrelevant to the actual deliberations and verdicts of juries. Life and death sentencing decisions in practice often continue to be made independently of balancing, threshold, or other statutory formulas. Many jurors appear to make up their minds about the appropriate sentence prematurely, during or immediately after the guilt phase of the trial, without even considering the evidence offered during penalty-phase proceedings.[9]

Question: Can you see any potential problems with the future-dangerousness factor that is at the heart of the special sentencing issue regimes? Recall that Texas and Oregon ask the jury to find beyond a reasonable doubt that there is a *probability* that the defendant will commit *an* act of violence in the future.

A.2.c. FEDERAL RULES

The federal system has its own death penalty statutes, but they are rarely used: the federal government has executed only three people since restoring the death penalty in 1988 (out of 1,408 executed nationwide since 1976), and its 62-inmate death row is in the middle of the national pack. Federal statutes matter much more when they impact state executions, which they do primarily by regulating federal habeas corpus procedures.

Federal habeas corpus has long been a tool by which state prisoners alleged defects in their convictions. As a Bureau of Justice Statistics discussion paper explains:

> State prisoners can petition Federal courts to review the validity of their convictions and sentences. They seek to relitigate collaterally Federal constitutional issues already adjudicated in State court. These petitions, commonly called habeas corpus petitions, allege that the criminal proceedings and the resultant convictions and or sentences involved violations of the prisoners' Federal constitutional rights by the police, prosecutor, defense counsel, or State court. If a prisoner's petition is successful, a Federal court can issue a writ of habeas corpus, ordering that the prisoner be released from custody, have the sentence

---

[9] *Id.* at 123.

reduced, or the case remanded for further proceedings such as retrial or resentencing.

These petitions . . . highlight the complex interrelationship between the State and Federal courts in a Federal system of government. Despite a State appellate court's having devoted considerable resources in determining whether reversible error occurred at the trial where a prisoner was convicted, lower Federal courts have the jurisdiction to review the State court criminal proceedings for possible violations of Federal constitutional provisions, based on both U.S. statute and subsequent Supreme Court decisions. Many commentators disagree over whether the Federal collateral review of State criminal proceedings is necessary to preserve national uniformity in individual constitutional rights. This conflict will never be settled completely because the disagreements reflect divergent positions on basic values, such as Federal oversight and individual liberty. Yet, systematic information on how Federal courts handle habeas corpus petitions can help reduce friction between the two sets of court systems by replacing inaccurate images or untested assumptions about the Federal review process.[10]

As Figure 7–1 indicates, the volume of habeas petitions spiked in the early 1960s and then rose with the number of inmates in state prison during the 1980s and, especially, the 1990s.[11] The dominant claim is ineffective assistance of counsel. A 1995 BJS study of 18 federal districts in 9 large states reported that 25% of the habeas cases were for (at least) ineffective assistance of counsel; this includes both capital and non-capital cases, with capital cases making up only about 1% of all habeas filings.[12] A subsequent study of a random sample of 368 capital habeas cases filed in 13 high-capital sentencing districts between 2000 and 2002 reported that over 81% of cases argued that assistance was ineffective.[13]

---

[10] ROGER A. HANSON & HENRY W. K. DALEY, FEDERAL HABEAS CORPUS REVIEW: CHALLENGING STATE COURT CRIMINAL CONVICTIONS 1–2 (1995).

[11] Figure 7–1 comes from FRED CHEESMAN, ROGER HANSON, BRIAN OSTROM, AND NEAL KAUDER, PRISONER LITIGATION IN RELATION TO PRISONER POPULATION 2 (1998).

[12] HANSON AND DALEY, supra note 10 at 14.

[13] NANCY J. KING, FRED L. CHEESMAN II, AND BRAIN J. OSTROM, EXECUTIVE SUMMARY: HABEAS LITIGATION IN U.S. DISTRICT COURTS 5 (2007).

Figure 7–1: Habeas Petitions in Federal Court Over Time

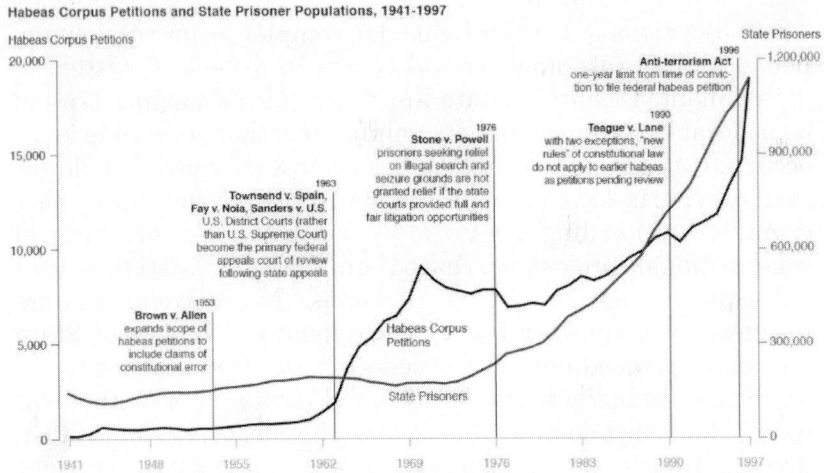

As habeas petitions rose, prosecutors, legislators, and both state and federal judges complained that the filings were taking up valuable court time, and impeding the finality of criminal cases by allowing prisoners to relitigate in federal court issues they had lost at the state level. So Congress repeatedly threatened to curtail the process, and it finally did so in 1996, when it enacted the Anti-Terrorism and Effective Death Penalty Act (AEDPA). As the name of the act makes clear, the habeas reforms were aimed at death penalty cases, even though those comprised only about 1%, at most, of habeas filings.

AEDPA reformed habeas appeals several ways, though two in particular deserve attention. As John Blume explains, AEDPA:

- Created a statute of limitations for habeas corpus cases. Prior to AEDPA, there was no set time limit on a habeas petitioner's ability to seek federal review of his state conviction or sentence. AEDPA contains a one-year statute of limitations with various tolling provisions.

- Placed extremely stringent restrictions on a habeas petitioner's ability to file a second (or subsequent) habeas petition. Federal courts must dismiss any claim raised in a previous petition. Claims not previously raised are subject to dismissal unless the petitioner is able to demonstrate either that the claim relies on a new retroactive legal rule, or that new facts have been discovered (which could not have been discovered previously), and that these facts establish by clear and convincing evidence that no reasonable factfinder would have found the petitioner guilty.

- Regulated the circumstances under which a federal district court is permitted to convene an evidentiary hearing in cases where the petitioner fails to take advantage of state court fact-development opportunities.

- Altered in several respects the exhaustion of state remedies requirement.
- Modified preexisting law regulating appeals in habeas matters.

But, the two big ticket items were:

- A new chapter, Chapter 154, which created a new set of procedures for capital cases in opt-in jurisdictions.
- A new section, § 2254(d), which limited the circumstances under which a federal court can grant the writ of habeas corpus.

I will discuss these two provisions in more detail.

A. The Opt-In Provisions

Chapter 154 of AEDPA provides a number of procedural advantages to qualifying states in federal habeas proceedings. Colloquially, these states are referred to as opt-in jurisdictions. Chapter 154's provisions are applicable to states that provide both a "mechanism for the appointment, compensation, and payment of reasonable litigation expenses of competent counsel in State post-conviction proceedings brought by indigent prisoners whose capital convictions and sentences have been upheld on direct appeal" and "standards of competency for the appointment of such counsel."

AEDPA provides opt-in states with a shorter statute of limitations period: 180 days as opposed to one year. It treats an untimely filed petition as a second habeas petition, and only permits a petitioner to amend a habeas petition after a response is filed if the prisoner can meet the rigorous standards for a second or successive petition. In most circumstances, Chapter 154 prevents a federal court from reviewing a claim that the state courts found to be procedurally defaulted. Finally, the opt-in provisions require the lower federal courts to decide habeas cases under relatively tight timelines: A federal district court must issue a final judgment in a habeas case within 180 days of the petition being filed, and the court of appeals must decide the case on appeal within 120 days of the briefs being filed.

B. Section 2254(d)

Section 2254(d), which, most agree, was the centerpiece of AEDPA, provides as follows:

> An application for a writ of habeas corpus on behalf of a person in custody pursuant to the judgment of a State court shall not be granted with respect to any claim that was

adjudicated on the merits in State court proceedings unless the adjudication of the claim—

(1) resulted in a decision that was contrary to, or involved an unreasonable application of, clearly established Federal law, as determined by the Supreme Court of the United States; or

(2) resulted in a decision that was based on an unreasonable determination of the facts in light of the evidence presented in the State court proceeding.

This statutory language had no habeas pedigree; for example, it was not taken from any Supreme Court decision, like other AEDPA provisions, nor was it part of any previous habeas reform proposal offered by Congress or a habeas scholar. The floor debates and the perfunctory conference report on AEDPA are also unilluminating regarding § 2254(d)'s intent. Thus, for the most part, the federal courts were forced to divine its meaning from scratch.

The Supreme Court, remarkably, has said little about how § 2254(d) works beyond that it limits a federal court's power to grant relief. And the Court has also said little about how § 2254(d) fits in with prior judge-made habeas doctrines. . . .

There are a number of interpretive questions that are currently percolating in the lower federal courts. By and large, however, the Court has not yet resolved many of the thornier questions.[14]

Blume then goes on to point out that the opt-in provisions have had no effect at all, with no states successfully opting in (while some have tried, courts have held that they failed). He also argues, contrary to many commentators (but with some empirics to back him up) that even § 2254(d) has had relatively minor effect. His explanation turns on a common theme running through this book, namely the constant tension between the various bureaucratic agencies involved in criminal justice, here the Supreme Court and Congress:

Why? Why, in spite of the AEDPA hype, has there been so little bite? The answer, or I should say answers, are certainly subject to debate. Some would say, and I would agree, that a significant contributing factor is that AEDPA is so poorly drafted. But poor drafting would be a simple story, and . . . I do not believe this particular story is quite so simple. Others would argue, and again I agree in part, that AEDPA's framers chose arcane statutory language, especially for § 2254(d), that had no prior habeas history or pedigree. The use of new statutory language combined with the speed with which Congress enacted AEDPA left the Supreme Court, and lower federal courts, with little

---

[14] John H. Blume, *AEDPA: The Hype and the Bite*, 91 CORNELL L. REV. 259, 270–74 (2006).

guidance regarding Congress's intent. That argument also has some force, but again, I do not think it is the complete story. Finally, some may even argue that the Court narrowly construed AEDPA in order to avoid any Article III or Suspension Clause problems with the statute. I find this even less likely, but not wholly out of the question.

The argument I advance . . . is that AEDPA's lack of bite is largely due to the fact that the Supreme Court, in the absence of congressional habeas reform throughout the 1960s, 1970s, 1980s, and 1990s, had already significantly curtailed the writ of habeas corpus. Furthermore, the Supreme Court and lower federal courts—but especially the Supreme Court—believe that it is ultimately up to the courts, not Congress, to decide how much habeas is "enough." While the Court maintains that the scope of the writ is primarily for Congress to determine, it does not, in my view, really believe that to be true. At the end of the day, the Court has assumed a fair share of the responsibility for determining the scope of habeas review, or how much habeas is enough. However, . . . the Court has a very narrow view of the great writ's scope.[15]

Overall, AEDPA does not appear to have had a big impact on the rate at which prisoners filed habeas cases. In fact, according to one BJS report, habeas filings actually *rose* in the wake of AEDPA, with state prisoners filings an additional 18,000 habeas cases above what would have been expected pre-AEDPA between 1996 and 2000, as shown in Fig. 7–2.[16]

---

[15] *Id.* at 261–62.

[16] This is Figure 4 from JOHN SCALIA, PRISONER PETITIONS FILED IN U.S. DISTRICT COURTS, 2000, WITH TRENDS 1980–2000 (2002).

Figure 7–2: Habeas Filings by State Prisoners, 1991–2000

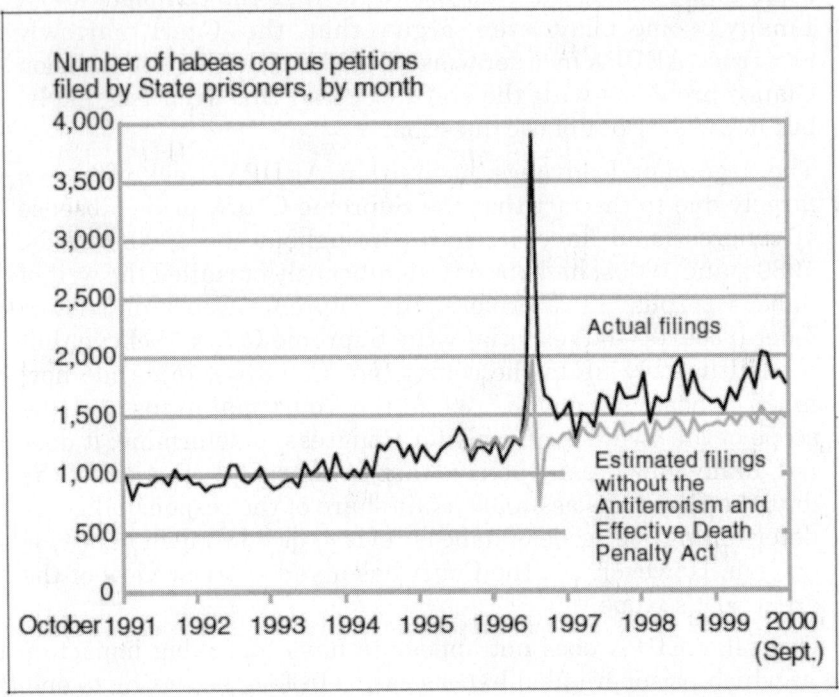

A.3. THE EXECUTIVE ROLE IN EXECUTIONS

Governors have a more-restricted role when it comes to the administration of the death penalty, limited primarily to commutations and moratoriums. As we will see, these powers can at times be used to effect significant change, but in general governors are likely among the weakest actors when it comes to the death penalty.

Since the death penalty was restored in 1976, governors have commuted 279 death sentences (out of more than 4,000 imposed, or about 7%), almost all to life or life without parole. This is true even in cases where the reason for the commutation was a concern by the governor over the very guilt of the inmate. It should be noted, though, that 181 of these commutation—65%—came about from just two mass commutations conducted by two Illinois governors, George Ryan in 2003 (due to concerns about how the death penalty was administered in Illinois) and Pat Quinn in 2011 (in anticipation of signing a bill abolishing the death penalty in Illinois). Another 8 were commuted by Gov. Jon Corzine of New Jersey on the eve of signing a bill abolishing the death penalty in that state as well.

Several other governors have introduced state-wide moratoriums on the imposition of the death penalty. Some of these moratoriums are officially announced by governors, others simply occur when the state fails to execute anyone of a long period of time—California, for example, has not executed anyone in almost ten years, despite having the largest death row population (over 740, which is more than 25% of all death row inmates).[17] Initially, these moratoriums were motivated by concerns over the administration of the death penalty and the risk of executing innocent people. In recent years, however, more governors have found themselves staying all executions over concerns about the specific three-drug "cocktail" that is used to execute people by lethal injection.[18]

B. Is the Administration of the Death Penalty Broken?

One of the biggest critiques of the death penalty is that it puts innocent people at risk of being killed by the state. Of the more than 4,000 sentenced to death since 1976, at least 131 have subsequently been exonerated: they were later acquitted of all charges, the prosecution dismissed all the related charges, or the governor pardoned them on the basis of innocence.[19] Moreover, several of the mass commutations discussed above, as well as the legislative repeals of the death penalty, have been motivated at least in part out of concerns about the risks of executing an innocent person.

In 2000, three academics released a groundbreaking report on the seeming deficiencies in the administration of the death penalty. Parts of the report are excerpted here, and we will flesh out the implications of the report in the questions that follow.

James S. Liebman, Jeffrey Fagan, and Valerie West, *A Broken System: Error Rates in Capital Cases*
1973–1995 (2000)[20]

In *Furman v. Georgia* in 1972, the Supreme Court reversed all existing capital statutes and death sentences. The modern death-sentencing era began the next year with the implementation of new capital statutes designed to satisfy *Furman*. Unfortunately, no central repository of detailed information on post-*Furman* death sentences exists. In order to collect that information, we undertook a painstaking search, beginning in 1991 and accelerating in 1995, of all published state

---

[17] See, e.g., http://www.deathpenaltyinfo.org/death-penalty-flux.

[18] Lethal injection, the leading form of execution since 1976 (at almost 90%), generally relies on a three-drug protocol to execute the inmate: a paralytic, an anesthetic, and a drug that stops the heart. In recent years, however, drug companies have started to refuse to supply the anesthetic to prison systems, forcing state departments of correction to look for alternative sources, ranging from trading with other states to the black market. Perhaps not coincidentally, these states have seen a rise in the number of botched or problematic executions. As a result, numerous states have declared moratoriums as they try to figure out the proper way to administer lethal injection, or pass laws bringing back or scaling up older approaches to execution, such as the firing squad or electrocution.

[19] http://www.deathpenaltyinfo.org/innocence-list-those-freed-death-row.

[20] All formatting is from the original report.

and federal judicial opinions in the U.S. conducting direct and habeas review of *state* capital judgments, and many of the available opinions conducting state post-conviction review of those judgments. We then (1) checked and catalogued all the cases the opinions revealed, and (2) collected hundreds of items of information about each case from the published decisions and the NAACP Legal Defense Fund's quarterly death row census, and (3) tabulated the results.

Nine years in the making, our central findings thus far are these:

- Between 1973 and 1995, approximately **5,760** death sentences were imposed in the U.S. Only **313 (5.4%; one in 19)** of those resulted in an execution during the period.
- Of the 5,760 death sentences imposed in the study period, **4,578** (79%) were finally reviewed on "direct appeal" by a state high court. Of those, **1,885 (41%; over two out of five)** were thrown out because of "serious error," *i.e.*, error that the reviewing court concludes has seriously undermined the reliability of the outcome or otherwise "harmed" the defendant.
- Nearly all of the remaining death sentences were then inspected by state post-conviction courts.

Our data reveal that state post-conviction review is an important source of review in states such as Florida, Georgia, Indiana, Maryland, Mississippi, North Carolina, and Tennessee. In Maryland, at least **52%** of capital judgments reviewed on state post-conviction during the study period were overturned due to serious error; the same was true of at least **25%** of the capital judgments that were similarly reviewed in Indiana, and at least **20%** of those reviewed in Mississippi.

- Of the death sentences that survived state direct and post-conviction review, **599** were finally reviewed in a first habeas corpus petition during the 23-year study period. Of those 599, **237 (40%; two out of five)** were overturned due to serious error.
- The **"overall success rate"** of capital judgments undergoing judicial inspection, and its converse, the **"overall error-rate,"** are crucial factors in assessing the effectiveness of the capital punishment system. The "overall *success* rate" is the proportion of capital judgments that underwent, and *passed*, the three-stage judicial inspection process during the study period. The "overall *error* rate" is the reverse: the proportion of fully reviewed capital judgments that were *overturned* at one of the three stages due to serious error. <u>**Nationally, over the entire 1973–1995 period, the overall error-rate in our capital punishment system was 68%**</u>.
- "Serious error" is error that **substantially undermines the reliability of the guilt finding or death sentence imposed at trial**. Each instance of that error warrants public concern. **The most common errors are (1) egregiously incompetent defense**

lawyering (accounting for **37%** of the state post-conviction reversals), and **(2) prosecutorial suppression of evidence that the defendant is innocent or does not deserve the death penalty** (accounting for another **16%—19%**, when all forms of law enforcement misconduct are considered). As is true of other violations, these two count as "serious" and warrant reversal *only* when there is a reasonable probability that, but for the responsible actor's miscues, the **outcome of the trial would have been different**.

- The seriousness of these errors is also revealed by what happens on retrial, when the errors are cured. In our state post-conviction study, an astonishing <u>82%</u> **(247 out of 301) of the capital judgments that were reversed** were **replaced on retrial with a sentence *less* than death, or *no* sentence at all**. In the latter regard, **7% (22/301) of the reversals for serious error resulted in a determination on retrial that the defendant was <u>*not guilty*</u> of the capital offense**.

- The result of **very high rates of serious, reversible error** among capital convictions and sentences, and **very low rates of capital reconviction and resentencing**, is the **severe attrition of capital judgments**. As is illustrated by the flow chart below:

  1. For every 100 death sentences imposed and reviewed during the study period, **41 were turned back** at the state direct appeal phase because of serious error. Of the 59 that got through that phase to the second, state post-conviction stage, **at least 10%—meaning 6 more of the original 100—were turned back** due to serious flaws. And, of the 53 that got through that stage to the third, federal habeas checkpoint, **40%—an additional 21 of the original 100—were turned back** because of serious error. All told, at least **68 of the original 100 were thrown out because of serious flaws**, compared to only 32 (or less) that were found to have passed muster—**after** an average of **9–10 years** had passed.

  2. And among the individuals whose death sentences were overturned for serious error, 82% (56 in our example) were found on retrial **not** to have deserved the death penalty, including **7% (5)** who were ***found innocent of the offense***.

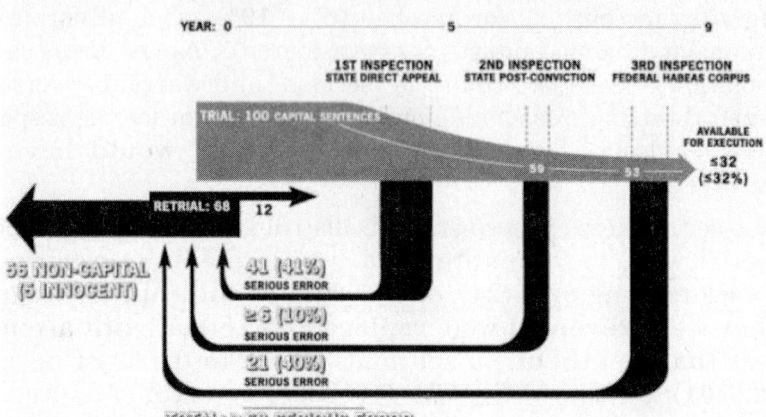

- High error rates pervade American capital-sentencing jurisdictions, and are geographically dispersed. Among the 26 death-sentencing jurisdictions with at least one case reviewed in both the state and federal courts and as to which information about all three judicial inspection stages is available:

    1. **24 (92%)** have overall error rates of **52% or higher**;
    2. **22 (85%)** have overall errors rates of **60% or higher**;
    3. **15 (61%)** have overall error rates of **70% or higher**.
    4. Among other states, Maryland, Georgia, Alabama, Mississippi, Indiana, Oklahoma, Wyoming, Montana, Arizona, and California have overall error rates of **75%** or higher.

- It sometimes is suggested that Illinois, whose governor declared a moratorium on executions in January 2000 because of a spate of death row exonerations there, generates "uniquely" flawed death sentences. Our data dispute this suggestion: **The overall rate of serious error found to infect Illinois capital sentences (66%) actually is slightly *lower* than the nationwide average (68%)**.

- High error rates have persisted for decades. **A majority** of all cases reviewed in **20 of the 23 study years**—including in 17 of the last 19 years—were found seriously flawed. In **half** of the years studied, the error rate was **over 60%**. Although error rates detected on state direct appeal and federal habeas corpus dropped some in the early 1990s, they went back up in 1995. The amount of error detected on state post-conviction has apparently *risen throughout* the 1990s.

- The **68% rate of *capital* error** found by the three stage inspection process is **much higher than the error rate of less than 15%**

found by those same three inspections **in *noncapital* criminal cases**.

- Appointed federal judges are sometimes thought to be more likely to overturn capital sentences than state judges, who almost always are elected in capital-sentencing states. In fact, state judges are the first and most important line of defense against erroneous death sentences. They found serious error in and reversed **90% (2,133 of the 2,370)** capital sentences that were overturned during the study period.

- Under current state and federal law, capital prisoners have a legal right to one round of direct appellate, state post-conviction and federal habeas corpus review. **The high rates of error found at *each* stage—including even at the *last* stage—and the persistence of high error rates *over time* and *across the nation*, confirm the need for multiple judicial inspections.** Without compensating changes at the front-end of the process, the contrary policy of cutting back on judicial inspection makes no more sense than responding to the insolvency of the Social Security System by forbidding it to be audited.

- Finding all this error takes time. Calculating the amount of time using information in published decisions is difficult. Only a small percentage of direct appeals decisions report the sentence date. By the end of the habeas stage, however, a larger proportion of sentencing dates is reported in one or another decision in the case. Accordingly, it is possible to get a good sense of timing for only the 599 cases that were finally reviewed on habeas corpus. Among those cases:

  1. It took an average of **7.6 years** after the defendant was sentenced to die to complete federal habeas consideration in the 40% of habeas cases in which reversible error was found.

  2. In the cases in which no error was detected at the third inspection stage and an execution occurred, **the average time between sentence and execution was 9 years**. Matters did not improve over time. **In the last 7 study years** (1989–95), **the average** time between sentence and execution *rose to 10.6 years.*

- High rates of error, and the time consequently needed to filter out all that error, frustrate the goals of the death penalty system. In general, **where the rate of serious reversible error in a state's capital judgments reaches 55% or above (as is true for the vast majority of states), the state's capital punishment system is effectively stymied—with its proportion of death sentences carried out falling <u>*below 7%*</u>**.

The recent rise in the number of executions is not inconsistent with these findings. Instead of reflecting improvement in the *quality* of death sentences under review, the rising number of executions may simply reflect how many *more* sentences have piled up for review. If the error-induced pile-up of cases is the *cause* of rising executions, their rise provides no proof that a cure has been found for disturbingly high error rates. To see why, consider a factory that produces 100 toasters, only 32 of which work. The factory's problem would not be solved if the next year it made *200* toasters (or added 100 new toasters to 100 old ones previously backlogged at the inspection stage), thus doubling its output of working products to *64*. With, now, 136 duds to go with the 64 keepers, the increase in the latter would simply mask the persistence of crushing error rates.

The decisive question, therefore, is not the *number* of death sentences carried out each year, but the *proportion*.

- In contrast to the annual *number* of executions . . . , **the *proportion* of death row inmates executed each year . . . has remained remarkably stable—and *extremely low***. Since post-*Furman* executions began in earnest in 1984, **the nation has executed an average of about 1.3% of its death row inmates each year**; in no year has it ever carried out more than **2.6 percent—or 1 in 39—** of those on death row.

- [These results] suggest[ ] that **executions are increasing, *not* because of improvements in the quality of capital judgments, but instead because so many more people have piled up on death row that, even consistently tiny *proportions* of people being executed—because of consistently prodigious error and reversal rates—are prompting the *number* of executions to rise**. As in our factory example, rising output does not indicate better products, and instead seems to mask the opposite.

To help appreciate these findings, consider a scenario that might unfold immediately after any death sentence is imposed in the U.S. Suppose the defendant, or a relative of the victim, asks a lawyer or the judge, "What now?"

Based on almost a quarter century of experience in thousands of cases in 28 death-sentencing states in the U.S. between 1973 and 1995, a responsible answer would be: *"The capital conviction or sentence will probably be overturned due to serious error. It'll take nine or ten years to find out, given how many other capital cases being reviewed for likely error are lined up ahead of this one. If the judgment is overturned, a lesser conviction or sentence will probably be imposed."*

As anyone hearing this answer would probably conclude as a matter of sheer common sense, all this error, and all the time needed to expose it, are extremely burdensome and costly:

- Capital trials and sentences cost more than noncapital ones. Each time they have to be done over—as happens 68% of the time—that difference grows exponentially.
- The error-detection system all this capital error requires is itself a huge expense—apparently *millions of dollars* per case.
- Many of the resources currently consumed by the capital system are not helping the public, or victims, obtain the valid death sentences for egregious offenses that a majority support. Given that nearly 7 in 10 capital judgments have proven to be seriously flawed, and given that 4 out of 5 capital cases in which serious error is found turn out on retrial to be more appropriately handled as non-capital cases (and in a sizeable number of instances, as non-murder or even *non-criminal* cases), it is hard to escape the conclusion that large amounts of resources are being wasted on cases that should never have been capital in the first place.
- Public faith in the courts and the criminal justice system is another casualty of high capital error rates. When most capital-sentencing jurisdictions carry out fewer than 6% of the death sentences they impose, and when the nation as a whole never executes more than 2.6% of its death population in a year, the retributive and deterrent credibility of the death penalty is low.
- When condemned inmates turn out to be *innocent*—an error that is different in its consequences, but is *not* evidently different in its causes, from the other serious error discussed here—there is no accounting for the cost: to the wrongly convicted; to the family of the victim, whose search for justice and closure has been in vain; to later victims whose lives are threatened—and even taken—because the real killers remain at large; to the public's confidence in law and legal institutions; and to the wrongly *executed*, should justice miscarry at trial, and should reviewing judges, harried by the amount of error they are asked to catch, miss one.

If what were at issue here was the fabrication of toasters (to return to our prior example), or the processing of social security claims, or the pre-takeoff inspection of commercial aircraft—or the conduct of *any other* private- or public-sector activity— neither the consuming and the taxpaying public, nor managers and investors, would for a moment tolerate the error-rates and attendant costs that dozens of states and the nation as a whole have tolerated in their capital punishment system *for decades*. Any system with this much error and expense would be halted immediately, examined, and either reformed or scrapped.

The question this Report poses to taxpayers, public managers and policymakers, is whether that same response is warranted here, when what is at issue is not the content and quality of tomorrow's breakfast, but whether society has a swift

and sure response to murder, and whether thousands of men and women condemned for that crime in fact deserve to die.

In a subsequent study, *Broken System II*, the same three authors sought to explain *when* the death penalty system was more likely to break down. Their basic findings:

James S. Liebman, Jeffrey Fagan, and Valerie West, *A Broken System II: Why There Is So Much Error in Capital Cases, and What Can Be Done About It*
(2002)

The higher the rate at which a state or county imposes death verdicts, the greater the probability that each death verdict will have to be reversed because of serious error.

- The overproduction of death penalty verdicts has a powerful effect in increasing the risk of error. Our best analysis predicts that:
  - Capital error rates more than *triple* when the death-sentencing rate increases from a quarter of the national average to the national average, holding other factors constant.
  - When death sentencing increases from a quarter of the national average to the highest rate for a state in our study, the predicted increase in reversal rates is *six-fold*-to *about 80%*.

In particular, the more often states impose death sentences in cases that are not highly aggravated, the higher the risk of serious error.

- At the federal habeas stage, the probability of reversal grows substantially as the crimes resulting in capital verdicts are less aggravated. For each additional aggravating factor, the probability of reversal drops by about 15%, when other conditions are held constant at their averages. Imposing the death penalty in cases that are not the worst of the worst is a recipe for unreliability and error.

Comparisons of particular counties' and states' capital-sentencing and capital-error rates illustrate the strong relationship between frequent death sentencing and error. For example:

- Among counties with 600 or more homicides and five or more death sentences during the study period, ten had the highest death-sentencing rates. . . . These counties had an average capital error rate of 71% at the first and last appeal stages, and eight of them put a total of 16 people on death row who were later found not guilty. The ten comparable capital counties with the lowest death-sentencing rates . . . had an average error rate of 41%, and none sentenced anyone to death during the study period or since who was later found not guilty.

- All but one of the 10 states with the highest death-sentencing rates during the 23-year study period had overall capital reversal rates at or above the average rate of 68%.

PRESSURES ASSOCIATED WITH OVERUSE OF THE DEATH PENALTY

Four disturbing conditions are strongly associated with high rates of serious capital error. Their common capacity to pressure officials to use the death penalty aggressively in response to fears about crime and regardless of how weak any particular case for a death verdict is, may explain their relationship to high capital error rates.

- **The closer the homicide risk to whites in a state comes to equaling or surpassing the risk to blacks, the higher the error rate.** Other things equal, reversal rates are twice as high where homicides are most heavily concentrated on whites compared to blacks, than where they are the most heavily concentrated on blacks.

- **The higher the proportion of African-Americans in a state—and in one analysis, the more welfare recipients in a state—the higher the rate of serious capital error.** Because this effect has to do with traits of the population at large, not those of particular trial participants, it appears to be an indicator of crime fears driven by racial and economic conditions.

- **The lower the rate at which states apprehend, convict and imprison serious criminals, the higher their capital error rates.** Predicted capital error rates for states with only 1 prisoner per 100 FBI Index Crimes are about 75%, holding other factors constant. Error rates drop to 36% for states with 4 prisoners per 100 crimes, and to 13% for those with the highest rate of prisoners to crimes. Evidently, officials who do a poor job fighting crime also conduct poor capital investigations and trials. Well-founded doubts about a state's ability to catch criminals may lead officials to extend the death penalty to a wider array of weaker cases—at huge cost in error and delay.

- **The more often and directly state trial judges are subject to popular election, and the more partisan those elections are, the higher the state's rate of serious capital error.**

ADDITIONAL FINDINGS

Heavy use of the death penalty causes delay, increases cost, and keeps the system from doing its job. High numbers of death verdicts waiting to be reviewed paralyze appeals. Holding other factors constant, the process of moving capital verdicts from trial to a final result seems to come to a halt in states with more than 20 verdicts under review at one time.

Poor quality trial proceedings increase the risk of serious, reversible error. Poorly funded courts, high capital and non-capital caseloads, and unreliable procedures for finding the facts all increase the chance that serious error will be found. In contrast, high quality, well-funded private lawyers from out of state significantly increase a defendant's chance of showing a federal court that his death verdict is seriously flawed and has to be retried.

Chronic capital error rates have persisted over time. Overall reversal rates were high and fairly steady throughout the second half of the 23-year study period, averaging 60%. When all significant factors are considered, state high courts on direct appeal—where 79% of the 2349 reversals occurred—found significantly more reversible error in recent death verdicts than in verdicts imposed earlier in the study period. Other things equal, direct appeal reversal rates were increasing 9% a year during the study period.

State and federal appeals judges cannot be relied upon to catch all serious trial errors in capital cases. Like trial judges, appeals judges are susceptible to political pressure and make mistakes. And the rules appeals judges use to decide whether errors are serious enough to require death verdicts to be reversed are so strict that egregious errors slip through. We study four illustrative cases in which *the courts approved the convictions and death sentences of innocent men* despite *a full set of appeals*. These case studies show that judges repeatedly recognized that the proceedings were marred by error but affirmed anyway because of stringent rules limiting reversals.

SUMMARY EXPLANATION

The lower the rate at which a state imposes death sentences-and the more it confines those verdicts to the worst of the worst-the less likely it is that serious error will be found. The fewer death verdicts a state imposes, the less overburdened its capital appeal system is, and the more likely it is to carry out the verdicts it imposes. The more often states succumb to pressures to inflict capital sentences in marginal cases, the higher is the risk of error and delay, the lower is the chance verdicts will be carried out, and the greater is the temptation to approve flawed verdicts on appeal. Among the disturbing sources of pressure to overuse the death penalty are political pressures on elected judges, well-founded doubts about the state's ability to convict serious criminals, and the race of the state's residents and homicide victims.

There is no reason to assume that things have gotten any better since these studies were written in 2000 and 2002. Seven states have abolished the death penalty since the report came out, often out of concerns about innocence and error. And since 2000, at least 62 death row inmates have been exonerated, a rate of more than four every year. Yet the report still raises several questions about how to think about the application of the death penalty in the United States.

QUESTIONS

1. **Broken or working?** The most obvious question, of course, is whether the findings here indicate a system that is broken or working. Yes, there are a lot of errors, but we know this because the *system* catches them (note that the authors' definition of error is one found by the courts, not an outside source). If we think the death penalty is morally important, how to do interpret the results here?

2. **What is the real cost of error?** The authors focus on the error rate of 68%, which includes both the number of cases reversed for improperly imposing the death penalty on a guilty defendant and improperly punishing an innocent person at all. Obviously the latter errors—which are about 7 percentage points of that 68%—are the far more serious. What are the real costs of the errors that come from misapplying the death penalty to guilty defendants, who still end up serving incredibly long sentences?

3. **Extrapolating the results.** Can we extrapolate either result—68% excessive sentencing, 7% convicting the innocent—to lesser offenses? In other words, can we use these results to argue that at least 105,000 inmates in our 1.5 million-prisoner system (i.e., 7% of them) are likely innocent? Or is death "different" in this respect to? And if different, in which direction: more likely to be erroneous, or *less* likely?

C. THE DEATH PENALTY AND THE THEORIES OF PUNISHMENT

It is unfair to point out the flaws of the death penalty without asking whether it accomplishes any of our goals of punishment as well. Obviously, the death penalty has little to offer a rehabilitationist, even though the Supreme Court invoked rehabilitation to justify letting a judge consult a wide array of information when imposing death in *Williams v. New York*, 337 U.S. 221 (1949). As for incapacitation, death obviously incapacitates, so the real question is does it do so *efficiently*; we'll look at this in the next section. Here, I want to focus on the two justifications for—and arguments against—the death that have received perhaps the most attention: retribution and deterrence.

C.1. RETRIBUTION

The deontological nature of retribution can lend itself to facile arguments: the death penalty is needed because it . . . just is morally right. Or should be banned because it . . . just is morally wrong. Susan Bandes, however, provides a much more sophisticated take on the nature of retribution and capital punishment.

Susan Bandes, *The Heart Has Its Reasons: Examining the Strange Persistence of the American Death Penalty*
42 Studies in L., Politics, & Soc'y 21 (2008)

Retributivists "seek to punish an offender because she deserves to be punished in a manner commensurate to her legal wrongdoing and responsibility. Not more, not less." What is interesting about standard retributivist arguments is that they present the need to punish the offender, as well as the ability to determine what punishment the offender "deserves," as bloodless and abstract philosophical questions. Retributivism is often portrayed as a way to avoid or civilize emotional reactions to crime, a means of determining the fair and just punishment from the community's point of view, rather than acquiescing to the punishment that the victim or the community might desire out of anger and vengeful feeling.

Indeed, retributivists tend to be especially eager to distance retribution from revenge. One defender of retributivism hastens to assure us that it "isn't just a fancy word for revenge . . . and is not the idea that it is good to have and satisfy [the emotion of vengefulness]." A similar aversion to the concept of revenge holds sway among jurors voting for death. Scott Sundby reports that a large proportion of jurors he interviewed identified the importance of their "desire to see justice done," though a very small proportion identified the importance of "feelings of revenge," and several were angered by the suggestion that revenge played a role in their decisions. He notes that similar results were found in a Gallup poll of the general population. As Frank Zimring succinctly observed: "Vengeance is an anachronism with a bad press."

To what extent can retributivism, without reference to emotional affect, explain how societal or individual notions of fair and just punishment are shaped, particularly when the death penalty is at issue? What motivates a polity, or a community, to determine that the death penalty is the just desert for certain crimes? My contention here is not that the institution is fueled solely by the thirst for vengeance, or that jurors who vote for death are motivated solely by vengeful impulses. [T]he emotional landscape is far more complex than that. Rather, I suggest that the traditional debate suffers for its insufficient attention to the emotional landscape in all its complexity. Without attention to emotion, retributive theory becomes circular, empty and indeterminate—we punish because it is the right thing to do, and we mete out the punishment that is right.

There are two separate but overlapping questions: first, why the United States—but no other Western country, and 38 of the states—but not the other 12, consider the death penalty the "just desert" for certain categories of murder. Retributive theory has no good answer to this question. "Modern notions of desert are ordinal rather than cardinal." (That is, they address where on the continuum punishment should fall, but not what types of punishment should bracket the continuum.) Second, there is the question of why some jurors, in some cases, determine that a particular capital defendant deserves to die. Capital punishment in its "idealized" form has always assumed the existence of a group of heinous offenders, the worst of the worst, for whom there should be consensus that death is a just desert. Perhaps such a consensus could exist in theory—the "McVeigh Factor" has become a shorthand for the notion of crimes for which such a moral consensus might, hypothetically, come to exist. However, the idealized form bears little resemblance to the actual decision-making process engaged in by those faced with life or death decisions. In practice, the decision is—and always has been—heavily influenced by a host of variables unrelated to the nature and circumstances of the crime.

As Jeffrie Murphy recently observed (or, more accurately, characterized Nietzsche as observing) "our abstract theorizing—at least in moral theory—cannot fully be divorced from its social setting and from our own personal human psychology, a psychology that may affect us in ways of which we are not fully conscious." Murphy's own work, in which he unsparingly examines his evolving retributivist impulses, is instructive. He at one point admitted to—and indeed defended—an attitude of "retributive hatred," but later became wary of the hardness and arrogance of that attitude. He remains a "reluctant retributivist;" the reluctance stemming from his awareness of the opacity of his own motives. We should be similarly cautious when evaluating the fervent, frequent claim that retributivist philosophy in general, and retribution in sentencing in particular, are all about morality and justice, and not at all about emotion.

In contrast to standard retributivism, Robert Blecker has argued for what he terms emotive retributivism. He argues that the death penalty is the just and even obligatory punishment for certain crimes, not as a matter of undifferentiated vengeance but as a means of giving voice to anger and rage toward the defendant and a way to show empathy for the victim's suffering. He argues that "moral desert can never be reduced strictly to reason, nor measured adequately by rational criteria: Forgiveness, love, anger, resentment are part of justice." Once these emotional wellsprings of the legal and moral calculus are thus acknowledged, a more clear-eyed debate about retribution's proper role in our capital punishment system can take place.

Both the retributive philosophy and the retributive impulse are better understood with reference to the emotional dynamics that help shape our intuitions of justice. These intuitions are affected by social and political context, for example by societal views of crime and what needs to be done to keep us safe. The attitudes of the populace might be better understood with reference to the constellation of emotional factors that influence moral reasoning, and specifically, those that influence our individual and collective experience of crime. Perceptions of crime level and the danger posed by crime are formed in light of pre-existing templates about how the world works. The perceptions are also highly influenced by portrayals (e.g. media coverage or official pronouncements) that evoke strong emotions, including outrage, fear, the urge to blame and—too often—racial animus. Indeed, as Markus Dubber argues, it is difficult to assess the justice of a regime of punishment without considering its ability to promote empathy and "counteract the natural tendency of antipathy toward the offender." The attitudes of individual capital jurors in particular might be better understood by examining all these same factors, as well as the anger, fear, compassion, empathy or prejudice elicited by capital defendants.

We might also gain a more dynamic understanding of how attitudes about what constitutes just punishment are communicated. Retributive theory is expressive: it assumes that punishment—via both its threat and its infliction—performs a signaling function, and thus is ostensibly concerned with the communication of norms and norm enforcement. Oddly, though, it pays little attention to how the signaling effect influences the measure of "just deserts." It fails to address how norms are communicated—both to the penal institutions and their actors, and to the populace.

It tends to assume a static model of top-down communication in which the signaling effect is achieved simply by the existence and enforcement of the law on the books. To put it another way, it tends to assume that the message is communicated in a vacuum, rather than in concert with other forces which might amplify or distort its meaning. It is doubtful that the dynamics of signaling are ever that simple, but we know that in the capital context, they are much more complex. Attitudes toward the appropriateness of the death penalty are not developed or passed along in a static, top-down manner. Positions on the death penalty both draw from and are aimed toward a broader, more unruly, more interactive pool of knowledge and misinformation.

The standard model fails to consider, for example, the "audience effect" on the punishment calculus: the notion that the presence of an audience increases the measure of moralistic punishment. This effect has been documented in the death penalty context, [with studies finding] that the prospect of running for re-election causes judges to render more—and more flawed—death sentences.

The "just deserts" calculus, when the death penalty is at issue, is influenced by media coverage, popular cultural representations of crime, elections and other political pressures and folk knowledge, all of which tend to traffic in fear, anger and prejudice. The measure of just punishment, in the real world of capital litigation, is taken not in a vacuum, but in light of intense public pressure, raw emotion and political ambition.

Emile Durkheim may be correct that our attempts to redefine the emotions underlying our penalogical impulses are merely cosmetic. At the very least, we mislead ourselves if we believe that the sanitized philosophical category of retribution does much work in explaining why we continue to execute.

The obvious question that Bandes' analysis raises is whether it is an argument for or against the continued use of the death penalty. On the one hand, she is right that a wholly top-down view of what is "just" misses the complexity of how those decisions are made by non-policymakers. On the other hand, those expressions at the top are not meaningless: they still shape more-popular perspectives. So were the government to abolish the death penalty, it would be saying, at least to some degree, that the sort of emotional elements at play in support for the death penalty were not entirely valid. Whether we want the government to make these sorts of decisions is an unanswerable (political) question, but it is a question that Bandes' analysis unavoidably raises.

C.2. Deterrence

The other major justification for the death penalty is that it effectively deters murders. A tremendous amount of empirical effort has been given to this question, but in the end the results are not particularly promising. Whatever effect there is, if there is one, is almost certainly quite weak, and given how the death penalty is administered in the US, it is almost impossible to detect this sort of effect in the first place.

In a widely-cited critique of the empirical literature on the deterrent effect of the death penalty, economists John Donohue and Justin Wolfers provide several figures that, right off the bat, cast serious doubt on the death penalty having a major impact on murders.[21] The first compares homicide trends in the US to those in Canada, two countries with fairly different legal histories when it comes to the death penalty.[22] Despite differences in capital policies, however, homicide trends in the two countries—which are culturally, politically, and economically quite

---

[21] John J. Donohue & Justin Wolfers, *Uses and Abuses of Empirical Evidence in the Death Penalty Debate*, 58 STANFORD L. REV. 791 (2005).

[22] *Id.* at 799, Fig. 2.

similar—track each other closely, strongly suggesting that something other than execution policy is driving these trends.

The second graph compares trends in homicides in states that had the death penalty with those in states that never had the death penalty, at least during the sample period.[23] Obviously, changes capital policy can't have any real effect in states that don't have the death penalty at all. Again, trends in both types of states are remarkably similar, casting further doubt on the centrality of executions to controlling homicide.

The rest of their paper is dedicated to a more technical examination of prior empirical work on the death penalty, demonstrating that much of it contains significant errors and, much more important, that the estimated impact of the death penalty can swing wildly, from preventing a lot of murders to *causing* a lot of additional deaths, by making small changes to the model. They summarize their findings in a shorter piece, excerpted here.

John J. Donohue and Justin Wolfers, *The Death Penalty: No Evidence of Deterrence*

The Economists' Voice 3.5 (2006)

As we show in a recent Stanford Law Review article and describe below, when one considers all the evidence the empirical support for the proposition that the death penalty deters is at best weak and inconclusive.

[A] recent study (by Dezhbakhsh, Rubin, and Shepherd, hereafter DRS) . . . finds that each execution saves on balance 18 lives. As we show in our recently published piece in the Stanford Law Review, however, these estimates are simply not credible.

An immediate problem is that DRS do not actually run the regression that they claim to run. The regression they claim to run actually yields the opposite result: each execution is associated with 18 more executions! (The different results turn on how they measure the key variable defined as "the percent Republican vote in the most recent Presidential election"). We do not suggest, though, that this specific result should be seriously entertained either, as the paper is far more fundamentally flawed.

Like [an earlier study], the DRS study mis-uses a sophisticated econometric technique—instrumental variables estimation. Statistically, the cleanest way to estimate the effect of the death penalty would be to run an (unethical and impossible) experiment, executing convicts more vigorously in randomly selected states, and then comparing the changes in homicide rates across states. DRS attempt to create econometrically a quasi-experiment by identifying a set of variables, "instruments," that

---

[23] *Id.* at 801, Fig. 3.

might cause changes in the execution rate but not otherwise affect the homicide rate.

Unfortunately, small mis-specifications in this technique can yield extremely misleading results. Instrumental variables estimation requires a valid instrument. However the instruments that DRS use are not valid, and it stretches plausibility to believe that they generate quasi-experiments in capital punishment policy, rather than simply reflecting changes in crime markets or social trends.

Their instruments are: 1) the statewide aggregate number of prison admissions; 2) total statewide aggregate police payrolls; 3) judicial expenditures (albeit not adjusted for inflation or state size) and 4) the statewide percent Republican vote in the most recent Presidential election. To be valid, they would have to influence executions and there would have to be no other link between these variables and the homicide rate.

This is not the case. For example, DRS tell us that Republicans tend to be tougher on crime. If true, that would imply that not only does the percent Republican vote correspond with executions (as DRS posit) but it is likely also related to other get-tough measures that might cause crime to fall (say, tougher sentencing laws or more vigilant policing.)

Indeed, all three authors of the DRS study have used these very same instruments in assessing the impact of other anti-crime measures, indicating that their own work is premised on the belief that there are other pathways from these instruments to the crime rate. If these alternative pathways are important then their estimates of the deterrent effects of capital punishment will be severely overstated.

We show that with the most minor tweaking of the DRS instruments, one can get estimates ranging from 429 lives saved per execution to 86 lives lost. These numbers are outside the bounds of credibility. With 1000 executions over the last 25 years, if we had saved 429,000 lives (against an actual murder toll of roughly 500,000 over that period), the impact of the death penalty would leap out of the data. Murders would have plummeted in death penalty states compared to non-death penalty states, or in the United States, compared with non-executing Canada.

In fact, when we make precisely these comparisons, the murder rates across treatment and control states seem to follow virtually identical paths.

A further important problem with the DRS study is that they [make a mistake estimating the error bounds on their estimate. Once fixed, the] confidence interval around their preferred point estimate . . . extends from 119 lives saved per execution to 82 lives lost! We are prepared to believe that this interval captures the true effect of each execution, but this provides little guidance to policymakers.

Other studies also claim to draw strong conclusions from noisy data. But they are also rife with coding errors and overstatements of statistical significance, or are not robust to small changes in sample, functional form, or control variables. The problem is simply that execution rates have varied too little over the last 30 years to admit any robust inference from data collected over this period.

[Furthermore, what we are trying to estimate is the marginal contribution of the death penalty to deterrence.] The penalty for committing a capital murder (if one is caught) is already extraordinarily high—being locked in a cage for the rest of one's life without possibility of parole. So what is the marginal deterrence of an infrequently administered additional sanction of death, many years later? Indeed, executions are so rare and appeals so lengthy that it is not even clear that being sentenced to death reduces the life expectancy of a criminal (especially given the high risks of death on the street). For instance, in 2004 there were 16,137 homicides, and only 125 death sentences were handed out; of the 3,314 prisoners on death row, only 59 were executed.

[Also, consider the results from] a key paper by Lawrence Katz, Steven Levitt and Ellen Shustorovich's (hereafter, KLS), which appeared in the same issue as DRS. KLS analyzed annual state homicide execution data from 1950–1990, publishing four models with a full set of controls. These models yielded the following alternatives estimates of net lives saved per execution: 0.6, 0.4, –0.8, and –0.5 (with the negative numbers suggesting net lives lost per execution).

We have updated KLS' data to include a longer time period, extending it to cover 1934–2000. Reliance on the death penalty was far greater 70 years ago than it has been in the past two decades and this greater variation is necessary to obtain reasonably precise estimates. The resulting four estimates for the longer data period: –1.5, –1.5, –1.7, –1.0, now uniformly suggesting no benefit from executions (an estimate of –1 implies that no murders were deterred and one life was lost by virtue of the execution). We also tried two further specifications. . . . Across each of these quite reasonable specifications, we find considerable variation in the estimated relationship between execution and murder rates. Our reading of these results suggests (weakly) that the preponderance of the evidence supports the view that increases in executions are associated with increases in lives lost, although further permutations of the full array of plausible models would be needed before strong conclusions could be reached.

One reason to believe that the KLS methodology yields unbiased estimates is that the focus of their paper is not on the deterrence effect: for them, capital punishment is only a control variable. Why is this better? Because it makes it less likely that they would be tempted to tailor their specification to generate a particular result concerning the impact of the death penalty. Our re-analysis of the existing literature suggested a tendency of many authors to only report results that were favorable to a particular political position.

Our guess is that estimating more models will only reinforce the lack of robustness of any particular finding, confirming the high degree of model-dependence in the estimated effects of the death penalty. Moreover, we should emphasize that these regressions merely highlight an association between executions and homicides, and the direction of the causal arrow remains an open question.

The view that the death penalty deters is still the product of belief, not evidence. The reason for this is simple: over the past half century the U.S. has not experimented enough with capital punishment policy to permit strong conclusions. Even complex econometrics cannot sidestep this basic fact. The data are simply too noisy, and the conclusions from any study are too fragile. On balance, the evidence suggests that the death penalty may increase the murder rate although it remains possible that the death penalty may decrease it. If capital punishment does decrease the murder rate, any decrease is likely small. In light of this evidence, is it wise to spend millions on a process with no demonstrated value that creates at least some risk of executing innocents when other proven crime-fighting measures exist? Even consequentialists ought to balk.

Donohue and Wolfers point to the lack of variation in the use of the death penalty as one reason why it is hard to estimate its deterrent effect, even when using county-level data. And it is important to appreciate the extent to which executions are concentrated not in states, but in counties: even in death-penalty states, there are many counties that have never executed anyone. Although there are 3,143 counties in the US, 30% of all executions have taken place in just 15 of them, and 9 of those are in Texas.[24] All told, all executions have taken place in just 20% of US counties.

Empirically, this is a significant problem. The studies Donohue and Wolfers consider all use variation across counties and time to try to identify any sort of deterrent effect of the death penalty. But almost all observations—all years for 80% of the counties, and some years even for the remaining 20%, which don't execute someone *every* year—are zeroes. Statistically, this raises certain technical problems that almost no studies account for, and which tend to make results much more sensitive to small changes in how the tests are designed.

Thus what we have is, in many ways, a "known unknown." The nature of the data is such that empiricists can say, with some certainty, that it is simply impossible to accurately estimate the deterrent impact

---

[24] See http://www.deathpenaltyinfo.org/executions-county.

of the death penalty on murder. But within that realm of uncertainty, the dominant trend has certainly been in the direction of saying that whatever effect there is is likely weak.

D. SOME ADDITIONAL ISSUES

The death penalty raises some other interesting, but smaller, issues, which we will consider here.

D.1. CAPITAL CASES, NON-CAPITAL CASES, AND YEARS OF LIFE LOST

Without any doubt, few if any sanctions receive as much attention as the death penalty, whether in terms of political debates or efforts by non-profits and other groups to reform or abolish the punishment. And this disproportionate attention is often justified on the grounds that the death penalty is a uniquely extreme punishment: it is one of the only instances in which the government can take someone's life. (That it also appears to be error-prone only amplifies the concern.)

But it is also important to appreciate the limited scope of capital punishment. In recent years, the United States has sentenced about 80 people to death per year, compared to prison admissions on the order of 650,000; death row admissions comprise only 0.01% of total admissions. When looking at total populations, the 3,000 inmates on death row make up about 0.2% of the 1.5 million people in prison, and about 0.04% of the 7 million people in prison or jail or on probation or parole. It is a serious punishment, but one that is almost never imposed.

So is it entirely true to argue that the death penalty is the most important sanction, even when it comes to state-imposed death? As we will see in future chapters, simply being sent to prison, even for relatively short periods of time, can lead to adverse experiences that, statistically speaking, increase the risk of dying at a younger age, such as increased poverty (which is in turn correlated with greater risks of death and sickness) and increased exposure to disease. So what if we think about the mortality costs of punishment less in terms of "people executed" and more in terms of "person-years of life lost"?

If a state executes a 30-year old man, it cuts short his life by about 30 or 35 years. Since 2000, the US has executed about 56 people per year, or taken about 1,680 person-years of life per year. During that time, we have also admitted on average more than 600,000 inmates per year to prison. If each incarceration results in the defendant living, say, just three months less than he otherwise would, then routine admissions would cost us 150,000 person-years of life per year, nearly 100 times the "costs" of executions. Executions are shocking and salient, but given how rarely they are imposed and rarer still they are performed, it seems like non-death sentences have a far greater impact on years-of-life lived, but get nowhere near the popular or legal attention.

Question: Is there something qualitatively different about taking someone's life actively, via execution, instead of passively, via worsening life outcomes? Even if so, is it one that we *should* put moral weight on, or should we, when possible, resist such instincts?

We can see the costs of this excessive focus on one sanction elsewhere as well. In his dissent from *Blakely*, for example, Breyer argued against sentencing juries by citing the fact that the punishment phase of capital trials can run to over $1 million. At no point does he acknowledge that Kansas had been using sentencing juries in routine non-capital cases for years at fairly low cost. So focused was Breyer on the high-profile capital case that he completely missed the lower-profile, but directly-on-point non-capital example.

D.2. County Variation, and the Prohibitive Costs of the Death Penalty

As we discussed above, the death penalty is applied very narrowly geographically, with all executions taking place in about 20% of the country's 3,134 counties. On the one hand, perhaps this shouldn't bother us. A constant theme in this book is that there is much to be said for local control over crime control and punishment decisions. And since the fiscal moral hazard problem isn't really at play here—as we will see shortly, most of the outsized costs of imposing the death penalty are prosecution and defense costs borne by the county—counties that seek to be tougher are forced to pay for that policy position. If neighboring counties have different perspectives on capital punishment, why should that bother us (more than any other difference in political views)?

On the other hand, we generally think of criminal codes as being *state* documents, so perhaps county variation within a state should trouble us. Texans or Virginians guilty of capital murder do not all face the same expected sanction: where *within* Texas or Virginia one commits a crime can matter a lot. If our insistence on defining most crimes at the state level reflects some sense that state-level uniformity is important, then the disparate imposition of the state's most powerful and high-profile sanction could be problematic.

Moreover, much of that variation could be driven by costs, which seems like a potentially unappealing explanation for intercounty variation. The death penalty is by far the most expensive sanction to impose, given that it requires two trials and that convictions are subject to long series of appeals. (Plea bargains generally require the defendant to waive any right to appeal, eliminating those costs, but defendants cannot plead guilty to death, so the option of appeal always remains and is almost always taken advantage of.) And most of those costs fall on county budgets, since the bulk of the costs aren't the confinement on death row and eventual execution—the state-funded costs that are at the heart of the prosecutorial moral hazard problem we've discussed at length—but the litigation and defense costs.

These costs can be prohibitive, and they can lead to some perverse actions. Consider the following examples:

While state and national politicians promote the death penalty, the county government is typically responsible for the costs of prosecution and the costs of the criminal trial. In some cases, the county is also responsible for the costs of defending the indigent. Georgia, Alabama and Arkansas, for example, provide little or no funding for indigent defense from the state treasury. In Lincoln County, Georgia, citizens have had to face repeated tax increases just to fund one capital case.

In Sierra County, California authorities had to cut police services in 1988 to pick up the tab of pursuing death penalty prosecutions. The County's District Attorney, James Reichle, complained, "If we didn't have to pay $500,000 a pop for Sacramento's murders, I'd have an investigator and the sheriff would have a couple of extra deputies and we could do some lasting good for Sierra County law enforcement. The sewage system at the courthouse is failing, a bridge collapsed, there's no county library, no county park, and we have volunteer fire and volunteer search and rescue." The county's auditor, Don Hemphill, said that if death penalty expenses kept piling up, the county would soon be broke. Just recently, Mr. Hemphill indicated that another death penalty case would likely require the county to lay off 10 percent of its police and sheriff force.

In Imperial County, California, the county supervisors refused to pay the bill for the defense of a man facing the death penalty because the case would bankrupt the county. The county budget officer spent three days in jail for refusing to pay the bill. A judge reviewing the case took away the county's right to seek the death penalty, thus costing the county the partial reimbursement which the state provided for capital cases. The County took the challenge all the way to the California Supreme Court and ended up costing the County half a million dollars. In the criminal trial, the defendant was acquitted.

In Mississippi, Kemper and Lauderdale Counties recently conducted a border survey battle to avoid responsibility for a capital murder trial. Faced with a case that could cost the county $100,000, Kemper County wanted to show that the scene of the murder was outside their border and conducted two surveys of the site. County Supervisor Mike Luke explained, "As much as we were talking about the taxpayers of Kemper County having to pay out, we believed we needed to be sure." Luke said that the decision to seek the death penalty was not his—he only had to come up with the money. Lauderdale County, where the trial was originally scheduled, has now sent a bill to Kemper County for expenses incurred while holding the defendant in jail for 19 months. Kemper County is considering how much it will have to raise taxes just to pay the initial costs of the prosecution.

In Yazoo City, Mississippi, the town is worried that it, too, might get stuck with an expensive death penalty case. "A capital murder trial is the worst financial nightmare any government body could envision," said the editor of the local paper.

There are three big points to take away from this. First, the likelihood of facing death appears to vary with factors that we think should be irrelevant to justice, like a county's fiscal health or tax rate. Second, given that the death penalty can consume such a big portion of local (as opposed to state) budgets, it is clear that we can't debate whether to use capital punishment within taking into account the *full* costs of the sanction: not just to the criminal justice budget, but also to the budgets for public health, infrastructure, etc.

And third, the examples above highlight the challenges that even more-local approaches to crime control face when trying to get the prosecutor to internalize the costs of his decisions. Prosecutors may be likely to over-incarcerate because they don't bear the costs of incarceration: those are state expenses, and they are county officials. But the examples here suggest that prosecutors are often indifferent to the impacts of their choices on *county* budgets as well. Note how one county supervisor stresses that he doesn't determine when to charge the capital case, he only has to find the money once the prosecutor—like him, a county official—files the charges.

The editorial from the Yazoo paper is somewhat perplexing along these lines. A capital cases is the "worse financial nightmare" that a county government "could envision," as if the capital case was imposed on it by forces beyond its control. Most capital cases are borderline cases, in which the prosecutor is not inevitably compelled by either politics or morality to charge the capital offense. So this "financial nightmare" is something imposed on the county *by a county official*. But an independently elected one, and one who is apparently remarkably independent of other county officials and pressures.

QUESTIONS

1. **Is punishment a state issue?** Although criminal codes are written by state officials, even outside the death setting do we really view them as *state* policies?

2. **Supreme Court and costs.** Should the Supreme Court think about these costs when establishing the rules it lays out for death penalty cases? If not, should it at least attempt to insist that more fiscally-stable actors, i.e., the state or federal governments, help offset the costs in the name of non-arbitrary enforcement?

3. **Costs and county variation.** If *all* prison costs were borne by the county, would the county variation in death penalty application be less problematic? Death is the only sanction where the county cost (litigation) is the dominant cost: should it be administered differently than the rest of the sanctions?

4. **Prosecutors and budgets.** Should the prosecutor pay attention to other county budget issues when deciding whether to prosecute a capital case? If she should, how can we get her to do so? Do we think the electoral check will work here?

5. **Incapacitation.** What does this discussion of costs tell us about the efficacy of imposing the death penalty from an incapacitation perspective?

D.3. CURRENT POLITICAL SUPPORT FOR THE DEATH PENALTY

In recent years, there's been a trend in states repealing the death penalty. It is worth asking whether that reflects changing attitudes on the part of the political elites or the public at large. According to a recent Gallup poll,[25] provided in Figure 7–5, while support for the death penalty is down from its mid-1990s high, about 2/3 of Americans still support the death penalty for murderers.

Fig. 7–5: Support for and Opposition to the Death Penalty

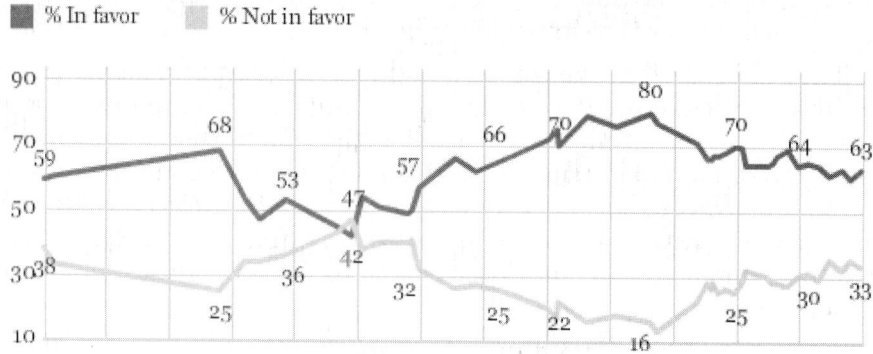

Tellingly, however, the drop was concentrated among Democrats (especially) and independents, as Figure 7–6 (from the same Gallup poll) demonstrates. It's not surprising, then, that outside of Nebraska recent repeals have been concentrated in fairly Democratic states.

---

[25] See: http://www.gallup.com/poll/178790/americans-support-death-penalty-stable.aspx?version=print.

Fig. 7–6: Political Parties and Support for the Death Penalty

Views of Death Penalty for Convicted Murderers, 1994 vs. 2014, by Political Party

	1994	2014	Change
	%	%	pct. pts.
DEMOCRATS			
In favor	75	49	-26
Not in favor	22	46	+24
INDEPENDENTS			
In favor	80	62	-18
Not in favor	14	32	+18
REPUBLICANS			
In favor	85	76	-9
Not in favor	12	22	+10

GALLUP

So while the trend line tentatively points towards a gradual repeal across the country, at least for now support remains high. The same poll, however, also indicated that when presented with the option of life without parole, just under half—45%—favor LWOP over death; only 50% favor death (with 5% undecided). So despite high support for death, it is not inconceivable that death could be generally replaced with LWOP sooner than later.

CHAPTER 8

PLEA BARGAINING

Having just worked our way through hundreds of pages of Supreme Court opinions about the exact structure of jury-trial rights, we are forced to confront an unpleasant fact: the jury trial is a rarity. A 2009 survey of case outcomes in large US counties reported that 66% of the nearly 50,000 sampled cases resulted in conviction within a year (54% of them felonies, 12% misdemeanors), with only 2% of the felony convictions resulting from trials—and that includes both bench and jury trials. Of the 35% of cases that resulted in no conviction,[1] 25% were dismissals with only 1% trial acquittals (again, including both bench and jury trials), and 9% were otherwise disposed (such as diversion or deferred prosecution). Yet despite the centrality of plea bargaining, trends are difficult to track, since data are not widely or consistently gathered, and defining the proper baseline for the rate can be tricky. Consider, for example, the following:

> **Question:** William Stuntz, citing a report by the Bureau of Justice Statistics, once wrote that in 1987 more 90% of all felony cases were resolved by plea bargains.[2] Yet the BJS report actually says the following: out of every 100 felony arrests brought to prosecutors, 5 were diverted or referred to diversion programs or other courts, 18 were rejected at screening, and 20 were dismissed in preliminary hearings. Of the remaining 57 cases that went forward, 54 (or 94.7%) were resolved by plea to either a felony or misdemeanor. And it gets more complicated than that. If we focus just on arrests that result in a felony indictment—the above example included felony arrests that later result in misdemeanor charges—out of every 100 arrests four are diverted or referred, thirteen are dismissed in court, and of the 83 carried forward 74 (or 89.2%) result in pleas.
>
> What is "the plea rate" according to this data? Should we look at all convictions or just felony convictions? Considering just the "all arrests" data, is the plea rate 54%, since 54 out of 100 arrests results in a plea? Is it 70%, since 54 out of the 77 cases not referred or screened result in pleas? Or is it 95%, since 54 out of 57 cases not referred, screened, or dismissed yield pleas? Note that screening and referral are acts of prosecutorial discretion, while dismissal appears more judicial—does this

---

[1] There's a rounding error in the data, which is why 66% of the cases result in conviction and 35% in non-conviction, for a total of 101% of all cases. See BRIAN A. REEVES, FELONY DEFENDANTS IN LARGE URBAN COUNTIES, 2009—STATISTICAL TABLES (2013).

[2] William J. Stuntz, *The Pathological Politics of Criminal Law*, 100 U MICH L REV 505, 566 n. 230 (2001), citing BARBARA BOYLAND ET AL., US DEP'T OF JUSTICE, THE PROSECUTION OF FELONY ARRESTS—1987 (1990).

influence your answer? And when thinking about "pleas for felonies," should we restrict ourselves to pleas for cases involving felony indictment, or pleas for cases involving felony arrests? After all, the felony arrest means that the prosecutor might be able to use the credible threat of a felony charge to induce a misdemeanor plea—isn't that still in some way a felony-based plea?

Putting aside the perhaps-surprising definitional difficulty, it seems pretty clear that plea rates have generally been fairly high, and perhaps have trended upwards, at least from the 1960s to the 1990s. Stuntz, for example, reports that plea rates climbed from 72% in a sample of counties in 1965 to 80% by the end of the 1970s to over 90% just for felonies by 1987. According to data from the State Court Processing Statistics, which looks at criminal justice outcomes in a shifting sample of the 75 largest counties in the US, however, the plea rate was high and stable between 1990 and 2004, ranging from 89% in 1990 to 93% in 2004, peaking at 95% in 1998.

It is thus inarguable that the plea is the primary means of disposing of cases in the United States; even if the upward trajectory identified by Stuntz is correct, pleas still constituted a majority of dispositions as far back as the 1960s. In this chapter, then, I look at the law of plea bargaining, and then consider the normative arguments for and against it and their implications for how (or whether) we should attempt to reform it.

A. THE SUBSTANTIVE LAW OF PLEA BARGAINING

In this section, we will discuss the substantive, as opposed to procedural, law of plea bargaining. The procedural rights are certainly important, but their effect on sentencing outcomes is at most indirect.[3] The substantive rights—what sort of deals can prosecutors offer, for example, either constitutionally or statutorily/administratively—have a much more direct impact on sentencing outcomes, and so it is on those that we will focus here. We will start with a brief summary of what exactly constitutes "plea bargaining" and then turn to the Supreme Court's jurisprudence on the issue, since that defines the rules all actors must follow. We will then examine more restrictive rules that individual states or agencies have adopted.

So, what is plea bargaining? In short, the prosecutor and the defendant reach an agreement in which the defendant agrees to plead guilty rather than contest the case trial in exchange for some sort of concession from the prosecutor. There are two broad types of bargains that occur: **charge bargains** and **sentencing bargains**. Under charge

---

[3] The Court has held, for example, that defendants are entitled to legal representation when they plead, that the state must uphold its end of the deal or the plea agreement is invalid, and that the *Strickland* ineffective-assistance-of-counsel standard applies to the plea process as well.

bargaining, the prosecutor agrees to drop or reduce some of the charges in exchange for the plea: a defendant initially charged with aggravated assault and illegal possession of a firearm may plead guilty just to the assault charge, or a defendant charged with first degree robbery may plead guilty to second degree robbery. Under sentencing bargaining, the defendant pleads guilty to the original (not a lesser) charge in exchange for the prosecutor being less aggressive at sentencing: the prosecutor may ask the judge to impose a lenient sentence, or agree not to raise certain aggravating factors, or at the very least not oppose the defendant's request for leniency. In exchange, the defendant most obviously gives up his shot at acquittal by pleading guilty. But there are often other collateral concessions that the defendant has to make as well, such as waiving any right to appeal, either directly or via habeas.

Looking at plea bargaining from the defendant's perspective—whose goal is to get the shortest sentence possible when conviction seems likely—which type of plea is more appealing depends on the sentencing system in place. In an indeterminate regime, charge bargaining may not really guarantee a shorter sentence. In Texas, for example, theft of $20,000 to $100,000 is a third degree felony, which faces a sentence of two to ten years; that of $100,000 to $200,000 is a second degree felony facing two to twenty years in prison. Pleading down from a second degree to third degree felony cuts the maximum in half but still leaves open the possibility of no real change in the sentence. Sentencing bargain, however, could be quite effective, especially in a courtroom with a culture of judges agreeing in general to go along with prosecutorial recommendations.

In a guideline regime, however, charge bargaining can be much more effective. Consider a defendant in Minnesota who is initially charged with a controlled substance crime in the first degree, but pleads guilty to a controlled substance crime in the second degree. Before looking at the guidelines, little turns on the plea: the statutory maximum for first degree is thirty years, for second degree twenty-five years. Yet look now at part of Minnesota's sentencing grid:[4]

---

[4] The top number in each box is the default sentence. The range underneath is the range from which the judge is permitted to choose without any additional fact-finding.

SEVERITY LEVEL OF CONVICTION OFFENSE (Example offenses listed in italics)		CRIMINAL HISTORY SCORE						
		0	1	2	3	4	5	6 or more
Murder, 2nd Degree (intentional murder; drive-by-shootings)	11	306 261-367	326 278-391	346 295-415	366 312-439	386 329-463	406 346-480[2]	426 363-480[2]
Murder, 3rd Degree Murder, 2nd Degree (unintentional murder)	10	150 128-180	165 141-198	180 153-216	195 166-234	210 179-252	225 192-270	240 204-288
Assault, 1st Degree Controlled Substance Crime, 1st Degree	9	86 74-103	98 84-117	110 94-132	122 104-146	134 114-160	146 125-175	158 135-189
Aggravated Robbery, 1st Degree Controlled Substance Crime, 2nd Degree	8	48 41-57	58 50-69	68 58-81	78 67-93	88 75-105	98 84-117	108 92-129

For every criminal history score, there is no overlap in ranges between first and second degree controlled substance crimes. By offering the defendant the plea to the lesser charge, the prosecutor effectively ensures that the judge *must* impose a shorter sentence. Guidelines thus give the prosecutor more leverage, since he can offer more credible sentencing commitments, and they make charge bargaining more effective than sentence bargaining.

A.1. THE SUPREME COURT'S VIEW OF PLEA BARGAINING

While plea bargaining has been with us for much of our nation's history—George Fisher has detailed its development since the early 1800s[5]—the first major Supreme Court case to address the substantive nature of plea bargaining was *United States v. Jackson*, 390 U.S. 570 (1968), which examined the constitutionality of the Federal Kidnaping [sic] Act, which made the death penalty available only if the defendant opted for a jury trial. Specifically, the statute, 18 U.S.C. § 1201(a), read:

> Whoever knowingly transports in interstate . . . commerce, any person who has been unlawfully . . . kidnaped [sic] . . . and held for ransom . . . or otherwise . . . shall be punished (1) by death if the kidnaped [sic] person has not been liberated unharmed, and if the verdict of the jury shall so recommend, or (2) by imprisonment for any term of years or for life, if the death penalty is not imposed.

The district court declared the statute unconstitutional, on the grounds that it put too heavy a burden on the defendant's constitutional right to a jury trial: to plead not guilty and insist on a jury trial was to introduce the risk of death. The Supreme Court agreed and severed the death provision from the statute.

Jackson appears to argue that undue pressure to plead is constitutionally impermissible. And while *Jackson* technically remains good law, the Court quickly but indirectly backed away from the full implications of its holding, in a *Mullaney-Patterson/Blakely-Ice*-type move that should be quite familiar by now. *Jackson* opened up the door

---

[5] GEORGE FISHER, PLEA BARGAINING'S TRIUMPH (2003).

to aggressive review of plea bargains, both facially—does this particular statute give the prosecutor too much leverage?—and as applied—did the prosecutor stack too many charges in an effort to coerce a plea in a specific case? Trial and appellate courts might have found themselves bogged down in reviewing a large fraction of pleas, undermining a major justification for the practice (namely its help in managing large dockets).

And so, just two years later in *Brady v. United States*, 397 U.S. 742 (1970), the Court quickly backpedaled. Robert Brady had pled guilty under the same Federal Kidnaping Statute invalidated by *Jackson* (prior to that case's resolution) and received a term of thirty years. He appealed, arguing that the risk of death imposed too great a burden. A unanimous Court, seven of whose members had agreed but two years earlier that the death provision of the statute was facially impermissible, found that Brady's plea was not unduly coerced by the death penalty threat. The Court, observing that to be valid pleas must be "voluntary" and "intelligent," stated:

> [E]ven if we assume that Brady would not have pleaded guilty except for the death penalty provision of § 1201(a), this assumption merely identifies the penalty provision as a "but for" cause of his plea. That the statute caused the plea in this sense does not necessarily prove that the plea was coerced and invalid as an involuntary act.
>
> We decline to hold . . . that a guilty plea is compelled and invalid under the Fifth Amendment whenever motivated by the defendant's desire to accept the certainty or probability of a lesser penalty rather than face a wider range of possibilities extending from acquittal to conviction and a higher penalty authorized by law for the crime charged.
>
> A contrary holding would require the States and Federal Government to forbid guilty pleas altogether, to provide a single invariable penalty for each crime defined by the statutes, or to place the sentencing function in a separate authority having no knowledge of the manner in which the conviction in each case was obtained. In any event, it would be necessary to forbid prosecutors and judges to accept guilty pleas to selected counts, to lesser included offenses, or to reduced charges. The Fifth Amendment does not reach so far. [397 U.S. at 750–753.]

The *Brady* Court's argument is clearly a strawman: there is a lot of room between a total ban on plea bargaining and complete acceptance of the volition of all pleas based on sentencing tradeoffs.[6] The Court could

---

[6] The Court does make it clear that there are limits to the types of pressure defendants can face:

> Of course, the agents of the State may not produce a plea by actual or threatened physical harm or by mental coercion overbearing the will of the defendant. But nothing

easily have said *"this pressure* is too much, even though *that amount of pressure* is okay." The Court's argument, therefore, is correct only if it is unwilling to engage in any sort of substantive review. Though it never admits this outright, this appears to be just what it is trying to avoid.

The Court reiterated its refusal to engage in substantive review in *Bordenkircher v. Hayes*, 434 U.S. 357 (1978). Paul Hayes was arrested in Lexington, Kentucky, for forging a check to the amount of $88.30 (which translates to about $310.78 in 2012). Hayes had several prior convictions and was thus eligible for Kentucky's harsh repeat-offender law, which at the time imposed a life sentence. The prosecutor offered him a deal of five years to plead guilty, but he said that if Hayes insisted on going to trial he would add the Habitual Offender violation to the charges, thus exposing Hayes to the risk of a life sentence. Hayes refused to plead guilty, was convicted, and was sentenced under the Habitual Offender Act.

In an opinion that makes it clear that the death penalty did not uniquely drive the outcome in *Brady*, the Court held that such a threat did not unconstitutionally chill Hayes's right to a jury trial. The five-justice majority first held that there was nothing "vindictive" about the prosecutor's charging approach (since the Court had held vindictive charging decisions impermissible in *North Carolina v. Pearce*, 395 U.S. 711 (1969), and *Blackledge v. Perry*, 417 U.S. 21 (1974)). And it then concluded:

> There is no doubt that the breadth of discretion that our country's legal system vests in prosecuting attorneys carries with it the potential for both individual and institutional abuse. And broad though that discretion may be, there are undoubtedly constitutional limits upon its exercise. We hold only that the course of conduct engaged in by the prosecutor in this case, which no more than openly presented the defendant with the unpleasant alternatives of forgoing trial or facing charges on which he was plainly subject to prosecution, did not violate the Due Process Clause of the Fourteenth Amendment. [434 U.S. at 365.]

The "limits" to which the majority refers, given the magnitude of the sentence imposed and its distance from the plea offered in the case, cannot be tied to the sentencing pressure, but must surely refer to something like the sort of physical coercion noted in *Brady*; unfortunately, the majority fails to say what might trigger the limits.

---

of the sort is claimed in this case; nor is there evidence that Brady was so gripped by fear of the death penalty or hope of leniency that he did not or could not, with the help of counsel, rationally weigh the advantages of going to trial against the advantages of pleading guilty.

Stuntz points out the danger of the rule handed down in *Bordenkircher*.[7] Legislatures have a strong incentive to pass tough sentencing laws. On the one hand, they receive all the upside from the law by getting to look "tough on crime."[8] On the other hand, they do not receive the downside when the law is used improperly: the overzealous prosecutor does. So legislatures pass excessively tough laws—laws likely tougher than what the legislators themselves think are just—and *Bordenkircher* grants prosecutors almost unfettered discretion to use them as hammers to pound out pleas. And as long as defendants continue to plead out, the public will generally be uninformed about how the process works.

Stuntz quickly demonstrates that the Court could have developed an easy way to regulate plea bargaining:

> Imagine an opinion that required that the government make one of two showings. First, the government could point to some reasonable number of factually similar cases in which the threatened sentence had actually been imposed, not just threatened. The number need not be large to have a substantial effect. Even if no such showing could be made, the government would have a second means of justifying the threat: require that the trial judge find that the sentence in question—the threatened one, not just the sentence actually imposed—was fair and proportionate given the defendant's criminal conduct.

But the Court declined to follow such a route. Instead, it effectively abandoned any effort at substantive oversight of the plea bargaining process.

At least, perhaps, until 2010. In a potentially-landmark case that year, *Padilla v. Kentucky*, 559 U.S. 356 (2010), the Court held that Hugo Padilla's attorney provided him with ineffective assistance by failing to disclose the immigration implications of pleading guilty (i.e., automatic deportation). Though generally thought of as an immigration-rights case, it also represents a rare instance of the Court directly regulating the plea bargaining process. Stephanos Bibas explains why the case could be so important:

---

[7] William J. Stuntz, Bordenkircher v. Hayes: *The Rise of Plea Bargaining and the Decline of Law*, in CRIMINAL PROCEDURE STORIES (Carol S. Steiker, ed., 2005).

[8] Or at least this has traditionally been the case. As we will see in Chapter 9, the sustained drop in crime over the past four decades has been changing the political dynamics of crime policy, making being "smart on crime" more politically astute than being "tough on crime."

Stephanos Bibas, *Regulating the Plea Bargaining Market: From Caveat Emptor to Consumer Protection*
99 CAL. L. REV. 1117 (2011)

Padilla is a landmark interpretation of the Sixth Amendment's right to effective assistance of counsel, but it is much more than that. The Court began to move beyond its fixation upon the handful of cases that go to jury trials. It recognized that the other 95 percent of adjudicated cases resolved by guilty pleas matter greatly, and began in earnest to regulate plea bargains the way it has long regulated jury trials. Though the Court's shift in emphasis is nascent, it is long overdue and welcome.

The Court's indifference to pleas reflected both practicality and principle. The judicial system had grown addicted to plea bargaining, relying on guilty pleas to resolve the vast majority of criminal cases, and could not afford to stifle this trade. Courts, assuming that innocent defendants would not plead guilty and that parties plea bargain in the shadows of expected trial outcomes, counted on jury trials as backstops to protect defendants. Additionally, the Bill of Rights provided no explicit protections for plea bargaining.

Much criminal procedure thus resembled a Potemkin village, a fine-looking facade inhabited by few. The Court trusted the shadows cast by trials to regulate plea outcomes, even though few defendants dared risk the huge penalties for going to trial. And because most guilty pleas waive defendants' rights to appeal, few typical guilty-plea cases ever reached the Supreme Court. The Court continued to filigree procedures for atypical jury trials, heedless of their effects on the overwhelming majority of cases resolved by plea.

Padilla is the Court's first case to treat plea bargaining as a subject worthy of constitutional regulation in its own right and on its own terms. By heeding plea-bargaining realities and evolving professional norms, the seven-Justice majority began to drag the law into the twenty-first century. One can at least hope that the Court will persist in this new direction. Plea bargaining is no longer an insignificant corner of the market reserved for indisputably guilty people who need no protection beyond caveat emptor. Over the protests of Justices Scalia and Thomas, a solid majority of the Court at last sees that plea bargaining is the norm; sets the going rate; and needs consumer regulation and competent counsel to make it intelligent, voluntary, and just. That is a welcome first step, but it will also require rulemaking and legislation to complete the consumer-protection analogy.

Not everyone agrees with Bibas that *Padilla* will prove to be a landmark case. Any potentially-sweeping Supreme Court decision carries with it the chance of a quick retraction; the *Patterson* to *Padilla*'s

Mullaney could be right around the corner. Darryl Brown also points out that *Padilla* doesn't really target the real source of the problem, namely under-funded indigent defense counsel:

> *Padilla* in effect mandates that criminal defense counsel be aware of immigration law, so that they can make their clients aware of deportation risks. But *Padilla* does not mandate or compel defense counsel to zealously and creatively represent their clients. *Padilla* remains a mere refinement of the ineffective assistance doctrine first defined in *Strickland v. Washington* [466 U.S. 668 (1984)], a doctrine under which state and federal courts have created a long track record of finding poor lawyering to be constitutionally adequate. There is no reason to think *Padilla* will change that judicial track record significantly. Quality defense representation depends much more on the resources that jurisdictions provide to their indigent defense systems (or that paying clients provide to their retained attorneys) than on the Supreme Court's specifications of minimal standards for constitutionally adequate counsel, especially a standard that the Court explicitly defines as one that is highly deferential to defense attorney performance. There is scant reason to think that courts will use *Padilla* any more than they have used *Strickland* to ensure that defense lawyers make optimal tactical use of the criminal or immigration law that they are now required to know.[9]

It thus remains unclear for now if *Padilla* represents a turning point in which the Court starts regulating plea bargaining like it does trials, or a one-time foray with very little follow-up. Regardless, it seems likely that significant plea bargaining reform is far more likely to come from the legislature and the executive than from the judiciary.

QUESTIONS

1. **Unintended consequences.** Might there be some risks to the defendant of a system like that suggested by Stuntz? What does it incentivize prosecutors to do? If the idea is that pleas which seem cruel *and* unusual are impermissible, how can the prosecutors make such pleas permissible? Is there any check on this?

2. **Political economy of substantive review.** What incentive do lower courts have to reverse plea bargains? Note that the famous "trial penalty"—the fact that defendants who insist on their jury right rather than opting for a bench trial appear to receive higher sentences if convicted—is imposed by judges, not by prosecutors. What does this tell us about the behavior or attitude of many judges?

---

[9] Darryl K. Brown, *Why* Padilla *Doesn't Matter (Much)*, 58 UCLA L. REV. 1393, 1407–1408 (2011).

3. **Proportional plea bargaining.** Why couldn't the Court impose some sort of proportionality rule: the offered sentence cannot be less than x% (one-half? one-third? one-fifth?) of the maximum sentence threatened. Could the prosecutor still evade this in ways that would be hard for the judiciary to detect? How exactly would this work in an indeterminate system?

A.2. NON-JUDICIAL REGULATION OF PLEA BARGAINING

While the US Supreme Court has declined to police plea bargaining closely—and has declined to require trial or appellate courts to play any role either—some states and municipalities have opted to create more-binding limits on the plea process. This section will briefly review these approaches and their results.

By far the most ambitious effort to regulate plea bargaining has taken place in New Jersey. The process started with respect to drug crimes, where the New Jersey Supreme Court eventually found that too much power had been vested in prosecutors. As Ronald Wright explains:

> The New Jersey Supreme Court recognized that . . . prosecutorial power over mandatory minimum sentences, combined with statutory restrictions on judicial sentencing power, created a regulatory imbalance. In the court's view, this imbalance amounted to a violation of the state's separation of powers doctrine because it removed from judges any meaningful part in sentencing, which is a traditional judicial function. The unrestricted prosecutorial power to select an enhanced sentence, in the view of the court, also violated the legislature's overarching purpose to promote uniform sentences for comparable drug offenders.[10]

The state supreme court thus required that the state attorney general—who, unlike many state attorneys general, has some regulatory oversight of all district attorneys in the state[11]—to create guidelines for plea bargaining drug offenses. These guidelines, which have been through numerous revisions (and currently run over 100 pages), are now known as the "Brimage" Guidelines,[12] and they instruct prosecutors about acceptable discounts, including aggravating and mitigating situations that permit lesser or greater discounts. Trial courts have the

---

[10] Ronald F. Wright, *Sentencing Commissions as Provocateurs of Prosecutorial Self-Regulation*, 105 COLUM. L. REV. 1010, 1030–1031 (citing *State v. Lagares*, 601 A.2d 698 (N.J. 1992) and *State v. Vasquez*, 609 A.2d 29 (N.J. 1992)).

[11] New Jersey is one of only three states, along with Alaska and Connecticut, whose local prosecutors are not directly elected but are appointed by the state attorney general. Delaware also does not have local elections for prosecutors, but that is because the state is so small that it contains just one (state-wide) prosecutorial district run by the state attorney general.

[12] After the case *State v. Brimage*, 706 A.2d 1096 (N.J. 1998), which focused on problematic plea bargaining and sentencing disparities across counties, such as those produced by the fact that almost all urban drug sales, unlike their suburban or rural counterparts, automatically qualified for the proximity-to-school enhancement solely due to the density of urban schools; that case led to the latest revision of the guidelines.

authority to review plea decisions under an "arbitrary and capricious" standard.

The primary goal of the guidelines is to ensure that mandatory minimums are not used problematically. Per the guidelines manual:

> These Guidelines are designed to channel the exercise of a prosecutor's discretion in formulating and tendering negotiated plea offers to resolve charges for offenses . . . that carry a mandatory minimum term of imprisonment and parole ineligibility that are subject to waiver and reduction. . . . These specified . . . offenses . . . are hereinafter referred to as "Brimage-eligible offenses."
>
> When a prosecutor has a factual and legal basis to charge a defendant with a Brimage-eligible offense, the prosecutor shall be required to charge the most serious provable Brimage-eligible offense, and the prosecutor shall not dismiss, downgrade, or dispose of such charge except in accordance with the provisions and requirements of these Guidelines. A prosecutor is not permitted to circumvent these Guidelines by instead charging a non-Brimage-eligible offense, . . . or by downgrading a provable Brimage-eligible offense to a non-Brimage-eligible offense.

Below is the list of aggravators and mitigators, as well as the range of plea offers available for first-degree distribution. According to the guidelines, absent other conditions, if the aggravator-mitigator "grand score" is greater than three, the DA must offer a sentence above the presumptive (middle) sentence in the relevant box of the grid; if above seven, the maximum (right-most number). If the grand total is less than negative three he must offer something below the presumptive; if below negative seven, the minimum (left-most number).

AGGRAVATING AND MITIGATING FACTORS
(Consult Brimage Guidelines 2 for definitions and rules regarding "double counting")

Defendant Name_____   Promis Number_____

AGGRAVATING FACTORS	Points	Yes	No	Insufficient Facts	Value
1. Community Impact.					_____
a. Children were present in premises; OR	2	☐	☐	☐	
b. Offense occurred in a drug-free park, public housing, or public building zone; OR	2	☐	☐	☐	
c. Offense occurred in a designated "Quality of Life" special enforcement zone	3	☐	☐	☐	
2. Bail Violation.					_____
Offense occurred while on bail or defendant has committed a bail violation after arrest in present case (3 points or 4 points if defendant was fugitive or failed to appear in court in present case)	3 or 4	☐	☐	☐	
3. Risk of Injury to Officers or Others.					_____
a. Offense involved threatened violence; OR	3 or 4	☐	☐	☐	
b. Resisting arrest; OR	3 to 5	☐	☐	☐	
c. Flight or Eluding; OR	4 or 5	☐	☐	☐	
d. Attempted destruction of evidence/hindering apprehension	3	☐	☐	☐	
4. Organization.					_____
a. Part of a sophisticated drug-distribution operation; OR	3 or 4	☐	☐	☐	
b. Defendant is involved in organized criminal activity; OR	3 or 4	☐	☐	☐	
c. Middle or upper-echelon participant in a drug-distribution scheme; OR	3 or 4	☐	☐	☐	
d. Defendant substantially influenced another person in committing the offense; OR	3	☐	☐	☐	
e. Defendant contributed special skills to the criminal conduct	3	☐	☐	☐	
5. Profiteering.					_____
a. Criminal conduct provided a substantial source (3 points) or primary source (4 points) of income or livelihood; OR	3 or 4	☐	☐	☐	
b. Offense involved actual distribution for money (2 points, or 3 points if sale to undercover officer or informant); OR	2 or 3	☐	☐	☐	
c. Defendant is eligible for anti-drug profiteering penalty	4	☐	☐	☐	
AGGRAVATING TOTAL					☐

SCHEDULE II

AGGRAVATING AND MITIGATING FACTORS
(Consult Brimage Guidelines 2 for definitions and rules regarding "double counting")

Defendant Name_____   Promis Number_____

MITIGATING FACTORS	Points	Yes	No	Insufficient Facts	Value
1. Non-Pecuniary Distribution. Offense involved distribution of CDS only to friends/relatives (other than minors)	3	☐	☐	☐	_____
2. Defendant's Role in Criminal Scheme. a. Defendant was only minimal (3 points) or minor (2 points) participant in the criminal conduct; OR	2 or 3	☐	☐	☐	_____
b. Defendant was substantially influenced by another person more mature (other person's identity must be known)	2	☐	☐	☐	
3. Voluntary Renunciation. Defendant voluntarily terminated participation in the scheme before arrest or police intervention	4	☐	☐	☐	_____
4. Drug Treatment. Defendant is enrolled and participating in an approved drug treatment program (Outpatient 2 points; Residential 3 points)	2 or 3	☐	☐	☐	_____
5. No Court Involvement. Defendant has no prior conviction, juvenile adjudication or adult PTI or conditional discharge	3	☐	☐	☐	_____
6. Youthful Offender. Defendant was less than 21 years old at time of offense (2 points); or defendant was at least 21 but less than 26 (1 point). (Do not use if defendant falls into Criminal History Category IV or V, has pending charge for N.J.S.A. 2C:35-6, or is subject to Special Application and Enhancement Feature A (street gang involvement)).	1 or 2	☐	☐	☐	_____

MITIGATING TOTAL ☐

GRAND TOTAL (Subtract Mitigating Total from Aggravating Total) ☐

TABLE 5
OFFENSES UNDER N.J.S.A. 2C:35-5 (1st DEGREE)*
(FIRST-DEGREE DISTRIBUTION OR POSSESSION WITH INTENT)

OFFENSE DESCRIPTION	TIMING	Criminal History Category				
		I Minor	II Significant	III Serious	IV Extended Term	V Enhanced Extended Term
A. 2C:35-5 (1st degree) no weapons	Pre-Indictment	24 30 36	30 36 42	36 42 48	48 54 60	54 60 66
	Initial Post-Indictment	30 36 42	36 42 48	42 48 54	54 60 66	60 66 72
	Final Post-Indictment	33 39 45	39 45 51	45 51 57	57 63 69	63 69 75
B. 2C:35-5 (1st degree) weapons	Pre-Indictment	30 36 42	36 42 48	42 48 54	54 60 66	60 66 72
	Initial Post-Indictment	36 42 48	42 48 54	48 54 60	60 66 72	66 72 78
	Final Post-Indictment	39 45 51	45 51 57	51 57 63	63 69 75	69 75 81
C. 2C:35-5 (1st degree) Substantial quantity no weapons	Pre-Indictment	48 54 60	54 60 66	60 66 72	72 78 84	78 84 90
	Initial Post-Indictment	54 60 66	60 66 72	66 72 78	78 84 90	84 90 96
	Final Post-Indictment	57 63 69	63 69 75	69 75 81	81 87 93	87 93 99
D. 2C:35-5 (1st degree) Substantial quantity weapons	Pre-Indictment	54 60 66	60 66 72	66 72 78	78 84 90	84 90 96
	Initial Post-Indictment	60 66 72	66 72 78	72 78 84	84 90 96	90 96 102
	Final Post-Indictment	63 69 75	69 75 81	75 81 87	87 93 99	93 99 105

*If the offense involves a school zone violation and a first-degree amount of methamphetamine or marijuana, use Row A or B. (See Special Offense Characteristic #3 in Section 7.3.)

What is most immediately obvious is how closely the Brimage guidelines mirror the sentencing guidelines that states have implemented for judges: offense severity on the vertical axis, prior criminal history on the horizontal. And they operate in almost the exact same way. Like with sentencing guidelines, the prosecutor has a list of aggravating and mitigating factors which, as shown above, are fairly similar to those used at sentencing. The guidelines are designed to make sure more-severe offenders do not receive overly lenient pleas and more-sympathetic defendants overly harsh ones. The guidelines also focus on *when* the plea is entered.

Question: Why do you think the timing of the plea has the effect that it does? Can you think of cases in which this structure could actually be *harmful* to the prosecution?

There are then a host of exceptions. One chapter covers particularly serious aggravating factors. Another provides direction on how a prosecutor can offer a below-guidelines plea if the case appears difficult to win. The guideline manual admits that such decisions are fact-intensive and hard to review, but, it continues:

> Under this system, all county prosecutors' offices will be making these fact-sensitive, case-by-case downward departures from uniformly determined starting points, in contrast to the plea negotiation system found by the New Jersey Supreme Court to be deficient in *State v. Brimage*, where county prosecutors could establish their own "standardized" plea offers that became the variable starting points for the application of upward and downward departures.

Moreover, prosecutors are required to publicly state when they are invoking the "hard to prove" provision, although they are not required to explain why. In some cases supervisors are required to sign off on the departure. Both aspects should inject more regularity and transparency into pleading.

All in all, New Jersey indicates that it is possible to create prosecutorial guidelines that operate much like sentencing guidelines. And while these guidelines just apply to one type of drug charge (albeit a serious one), there is no reason why they could not be extended to other charges. In fact, the New Jersey Attorney General has done just that, developing guidelines for sex offender registrations and other issues.[13] That other states have not adopted similar plea bargain restrictions thus reflects a lack of will, not feasibility.

While New Jersey represents the high-water mark for prosecutorial guidelines, its guidelines are not the only attempt; several other jurisdictions have attempted to regulate pleas as well. Washington State, for example, has had state-level prosecutorial guidelines since 1984. These guidelines, however, are much more impressionistic than New Jersey's. While New Jersey's guidelines currently span over 100 pages and involve numerous checklists, forms, and tables, Washington's law on charge selection reads, in its entirety, as follows:

---

[13] See Ronald F. Wright, *Prosecutorial Guidelines and the New Terrain in New Jersey*, 109 PENN. ST. L. REV. 1087, 1097 n.46 (2005), and http://www.state.nj.us/lps/dcj/agguide.htm.

> Wash Rev Code § 9.94A.411(2): Selection of Charges/Degree of Charge:
>
> i. The prosecutor should file charges which adequately describe the nature of defendant's conduct. Other offenses may be charged only if they are necessary to ensure that the charges:
>
>   A. Will significantly enhance the strength of the state's case at trial; or
>   B. Will result in restitution to all victims.
>
> ii. The prosecutor should not overcharge to obtain a guilty plea. Overcharging includes:
>
>   A. Charging a higher degree;
>   B. Charging additional counts.
>
> This standard is intended to direct prosecutors to charge those crimes which demonstrate the nature and seriousness of a defendant's criminal conduct, but to decline to charge crimes which are not necessary to such an indication. Crimes which do not merge as a matter of law, but which arise from the same course of conduct, do not all have to be charged.

Moreover, the guidelines do not have any enforcement mechanism. The Code explicitly states:

> Wash. Rev. Code § 9.94A.401: These standards are intended solely for the guidance of prosecutors in the state of Washington. They are not intended to, do not and may not be relied upon to create a right or benefit, substantive or procedural, enforceable at law by a party in litigation with the state.

As a result, the guidelines are not thought to have had much of an effect on prosecutorial behavior.[14]

Several jurisdictions have even attempted to simply ban plea bargaining entirely. Alaska abolished plea bargaining in 1975, as did El Paso, Philadelphia, and the Bronx to varying degrees at various times. But, in general, such bans have not persisted. They have not failed because they suddenly overwhelm the system with cases it cannot handle, an oft-cited concern, but rather because the political will to maintain them eventually subsides. As one commentator puts it:

> Efforts to simply ban most plea bargains have also repeatedly failed. . . . Almost all have been limited in major ways, such as to prosecutors alone or to certain stages of the adjudication process or to certain types of crimes. In each case, either the bargaining shifted to other stages in the adjudication process, the provision of bargains merely shifted from prosecutors to

---

[14] See, e.g., David Boerner & Roxanne Lieb, *Sentencing Reform in the Other Washington*, 28 CRIME & JUST. 71, 90 (2001).

judges, or prosecutors increasingly ignored the ban or subverted it through subterfuges. In the modern era no large city in the United States has gone for a long period without some form of widely practiced plea bargaining.[15]

Howe notes, among other things, that during the period of Alaska's ban—which lasted from 1975 to 1990 and eventually faded when a new state attorney general deemphasized its importance—average sentences at trial for violent crime were 445% longer than those for pleas,[16] and 334% longer for fraud offenses, suggesting that some sort of bargain was still being reached in plea cases. The results from the bans suggest they may be feasible from a docket-pressure perspective, but they are unlikely to be politically durable. If we want to reform plea bargaining, it is most likely going to require us to accept it, not eliminate it.

Finally, the federal government has often attempted to regulate the discretion of its prosecutors. Federal prosecutors are the most centralized prosecutors in the country—appointed by the President, they are expected to follow policies issued by the Department of Justice in Washington, DC ("Main Justice"). The following excerpts describe the current state of efforts to regulate how AUSAs and US Attorneys handle plea bargains.

Kate Stith, *The Arc of the Pendulum: Judges, Prosecutors, and the Exercise of Discretion*
117 YALE L. J. 1420, 1440–43, 1469–70 (2008)

Although it had never before sought to direct or monitor routine charging and plea decisions across the land, the Department of Justice in 1989 issued a new directive that sought to hold all federal prosecutors to the Guidelines' regime of "real offense" sentencing, and in particular sought to prohibit "fact bargaining" over sentencing enhancements. To be sure, the "Thornburgh Memorandum," as it came to be known after the Attorney General who issued it, was not the first step toward centralization of policies on prosecutorial charging discretion. As previously noted, in the final days of the Carter Administration, the Department had issued general "principles" to guide federal prosecutors.

But the Thornburgh Memorandum contained more specific and more prescriptive language concerning both plea bargaining and (unlike the 1980 Principles) sentencing bargaining. On charging and charge bargaining, it directed that "a federal prosecutor should initially charge the most serious, readily provable offense or offenses consistent with the defendant's conduct. Charges should not . . . be abandoned in an effort to

---

[15] Scott W. Howe, *The Value of Plea Bargaining*, 58 OKLA. L. REV. 599, 611–12 (2005).

[16] No state banned *pleas*, only plea *bargaining*. So defendants could still plead guilty in Alaska, but technically the prosecutor could not bargain with them to reach some sort of plea deal.

arrive at a bargain that fails to reflect the seriousness of the defendant's conduct." On sentencing, Main Justice went even further in its instructions to prosecutors than the Sentencing Commission had in its limitations on judges. Prosecutors were instructed "only to stipulate to facts that accurately represent the defendant's conduct" because Congress "could not have . . . intended the reforms [it] enacted to be limited to the small percentage of cases that go to trial." A slightly milder variant of this new national policy on bargaining of charges and sentences was reissued by Attorney General Janet Reno in 1993. The Reno Memorandum was left in place by the administration of President George W. Bush until after Congress enacted the Feeney Amendment in 2003.

We would do well to recognize that the Thornburgh Memorandum (and later, those of Attorneys General Reno and Ashcroft) sought to centralize the exercise of prosecutorial power essentially by delegitimating the exercise of prosecutorial discretion. The central command of these policies is that prosecutors must apply the criminal law severely by charging "the most serious, readily provable" offense in nearly every case. The federal criminal law is generally not designed to serve such severe purposes; it has lesser-included and overlapping offenses that are applicable to many sets of facts—and it fairly cries out for the exercise of informed prosecutorial discretion. Perhaps it is politically inevitable that if called upon to respond in one sentence to the question, "What should prosecutors charge?", officials at Main Justice must answer "the most serious charge available." (They can hardly answer, for instance, "about half the most serious charge.")

But until the Feeney Amendment in 2003, no one actually asked the Department this question, much less required it to issue a system-wide policy related to charging under the Guidelines. Main Justice itself chose to issue national policies on charging and sentencing, stimulated by the emergence of the Sentencing Guidelines. If all federal prosecutors had abided by the pronouncements from Main Justice, the result would have been a rigidity in law enforcement wholly incompatible with the flexible and variable substantive criminal law that Congress has enacted. Moreover, defendants in principle would have been denied the opportunity to urge anyone—court or prosecutor—to judge how the laws should be applied to the particular facts of their case. Finally, had prosecutors actually refused to exercise discretion in charging and plea bargaining, it is quite possible that discretion would have simply devolved to a lower (or earlier) stage in prosecution—law enforcement agents.

[In 2003, as part of the PROTECT Act, Congress enacted the Feeney Amendment which, among other things, required Main Justice to issue plea bargaining standards or face intense Congressional scrutiny over plea bargaining. Then-Attorney General John Ashcroft issued the "Ashcroft Memo" shortly after the Feeney Amendment went into effect.]

Attorney General Ashcroft issued a new Memorandum in July 2003 that, like the Thornburgh Memorandum and Reno Memorandum before it, sought to alter the behavior of individual prosecutors primarily by means of strict charging policies that were mandatory on their face. In order to reduce the incidence of fact bargaining, the July 2003 Ashcroft Memorandum not only expressly employed that term—"federal prosecutors may not 'fact bargain' "—but went on to explain the meaning of this requirement in practice: "[I]f readily provable facts are relevant to calculations under the Sentencing Guidelines, the prosecutor must disclose them to the court, including the Probation Office." In a September 2003 follow-up memorandum, which explicitly superseded the Reno Memorandum, Attorney General Ashcroft repeated the central requirement of both the earlier directives—that "federal prosecutors must charge and pursue the most serious, readily provable offense or offenses that are supported by the facts of the case"—but listed fewer circumstances in which local offices would have authority to deviate from this general rule absent the express approval of Justice Department officials in Washington. The September 2003 Memorandum of Attorney General Ashcroft repeated the strictures of his July memorandum on "fact bargaining" and sentencing advocacy.

The immediate effectiveness of these statements of policy, no matter how mandatory on their face and how few the expressly authorized exceptions, depended on the incentives and attitudes of U.S. Attorneys and their line prosecutors. No enforcement mechanism having been provided, and language being what it is—for example, what is "readily provable"?—there was operational and interpretive space in implementing these mandates. In any event, . . . there were not enough people in Main Justice to monitor and enforce "mandatory" charging policies in every U.S. Attorney's office. The mandatory-policy approach to controlling dispersed prosecutorial discretion can work (if it can work at all) only by altering the practice and norms of U.S. Attorneys' offices over time.

Question: In a world of overlapping offenses, what is the "most serious offense"? Is it just the sentence length—but if so, the maximum, the minimum, the expected sentence given guidelines or parole policies? And does criminal history matter if that has any impact? If drug trafficking carries a longer term than some degree of aggravated assault, is the drug charge really more serious than the violent offense? Is an offense with a seven-year maximum but a mandatory minimum of three years more severe than an offense with no mandatory minimum but a maximum of ten years?

Stith goes on to point out that *Booker* ultimately gutted the Ashcroft Memo and made oversight of plea bargaining tougher. To monitor potentially problematic pleas, the Ashcroft Memo required prosecutors to report to Main Justice any downward departure from the guideline sentence that "is not supported by the facts and the law." By rendering the federal guidelines voluntary, *Booker* effectively decreed that any downward departure is no longer "[un]supported by . . . the law," since all sentences are now legally permissible.

Perhaps the more important point in Stith's analysis, however, is that it highlights the importance of enforcement. Without adequate enforcement—present in New Jersey, absent in Washington State and Washington, DC—plea guidelines will likely fail.

> **Question:** If District Court judges were called upon to enforce the Ashcroft Memo like New Jersey trial courts enforced the *Brimage* guidelines, do you think enforcement would still have worked? Given the broad language used in the Memo and the federal judiciary's common antipathy toward the guidelines in particular and the punitiveness of federal criminal law more generally, how rigorously would these rules have been enforced? Does this tell us anything about the importance of New Jersey's detailed, grid-based approach?

The last point to consider here is simply this: just how big is the plea discount? After all, the "coercive" nature of plea, if there is any, stems entirely from the "too good a deal to pass up" effect of the discount. Even before providing a numeric answer, though, it is worth thinking about a matter of definition. Gerard Lynch, a federal judge and law professor, thinks the very term "plea bargain discount" is problematic:

> In a system where ninety percent or more of cases end in a negotiated disposition, it is unclear why the "discounted" punishment imposed in that ninety percent of cases should not rather be considered the norm. Where almost no one pays the "manufacturer's suggested retail price," and almost everyone buys the item at a "discounted" price, no one really gets a "bargain," and the product's real price is what is actually charged in the marketplace.

> This may pose a problem of transparency, and is hard on those few who for whatever reason find themselves paying retail, but there is no reason to assume that offenders who receive "plea bargained" dispositions are receiving any lower a sentence or charge of conviction than the system as a whole regards as appropriate for their case. We are predisposed to regard the pleading defendant as receiving a discount precisely because a fully litigated jury trial is theoretically normative, because its outcome therefore has greater legitimacy, and because we are constitutionally prohibited from recognizing that the system attaches a penalty to going to trial. Given the extreme severity

of sentencing in the United States by world standards, however, it is hard to take seriously the notion that ninety percent of those serving our remarkably heavy sentences are the beneficiaries of "bargains."[17]

Fair enough. But whether one views the trial sentence as the legitimate sentence and the plea as discount, or the trial sentence as a too-high starting point and the plea as the closer-to-accurate value, it is impossible to decide how overly-generous the plea is (in the first case) or how much better it is than the official sentence (in the second) without knowing the size of the actual discount.

Unfortunately, there is not a lot of solid data available on the size of the plea discount. The statistical problems with estimating it are significant. It is true that we could compare the sentences imposed on those convicted at trial for, say, second degree assault with those imposed on those who plead guilty to that crime, but it is unclear what that comparison tells us: what if prosecutors consistently take the more-serious cases within that category to trial, whether to send a clearer signal to more-serious offenders or for other, perhaps personal or career-advancing, reasons? To what extent is any discount due to savings from foregone trials vs. "probability bargaining" (i.e., offering a steeper discount as evidence becomes less clear cut)? Are those pleading to second-degree assault actually guilty of second-degree assault or would they have been charged with first-degree had the case gone to trial?[18] Perhaps because plea bargaining has often been treated as an embarrassing secret not to be discussed in polite company, we lack the sort of rigorous, detailed datasets that would allow us to really analyze exactly what sort of discounts are being offered.

A recent paper by two social scientists sums up the ambiguous state of knowledge on plea discounts:

> The literature is mixed as to whether significant trial penalties exist, and only a handful of studies examine how they might vary. Numerous studies focused on the sentencing effects of different modes of conviction show that those convicted by trial, especially jury trials, receive more severe sentences. . . . [O]ne recent analysis . . . even found significant "process discounts," or plea-trial sentencing differences[,] in five sentencing guidelines states. Numerous other studies not focused on the plea-trial sentencing issue found that trials are sentenced more

---

[17] Gerard E. Lynch, *Screening Versus Plea Bargaining: Exactly What Are We Trading Off?*, 55 STAN. L. REV. 1399, 1401–02 (2003).

[18] Even seeing the indictment offense doesn't necessarily help: if we observe that someone indicted on first-degree assault pleads to second-degree, we do not know if that charge reduction is an example of charge bargaining or the prosecutor realizing, with more investigation after the initial indictment, that the offense really was second-degree assault. The lesser charge in the first case is a "discount," but in the second it might just reflect the less-serious nature of the crime.

severely than guilty pleas when mode of conviction is treated as a control variable. . . .

Many studies suggest that the size of any plea-trial sentencing differences likely varies by jurisdiction. . . . Specifically, scholars have debated the relationship between trial penalties—plea rewards and court caseloads, with some arguing that heavy caseloads drive mode of conviction differences, and others that such differences are independent of caseload pressure. . . . Furthermore, trial penalties have been found to be stronger for defendants with more substantial criminal histories . . . , and to be stronger for blacks. . . .

Other studies fail to find significant plea rewards or trial penalties. . . . [One study] finds that the size of plea-trial sentencing differences varies by offense type, with meaningful differences in robbery cases but not assault, burglary, or larceny.

Overall, then, the literature shows mixed findings on (and approaches to studying) trial penalties—most studies find them, yet some important ones do not. The literature also suggests that plea-trial differences may vary by jurisdiction, with caseload being especially important in conditioning such differences. Finally, a few studies suggest that trial penalties may vary by offense type, prior record, or race-ethnicity.[19]

B. THE DEBATE OVER PLEA BARGAINING

While plea bargaining appears to be quite firmly established in the American criminal justice system, academics and policy-makers continue to debate its merits and how (or whether) it can be reformed or improved. In this section, we want to consider the arguments for and against plea bargaining, both normative and positive (the line between these blurs frequently), and ask what they mean for how we want to structure plea bargaining going forward.

The classic defense of relatively unstructured plea bargaining systems was put forth by Frank Easterbrook, whose argument is excerpted here:

Frank H. Easterbrook, *Criminal Procedure as a Market System*
12 J. LEGAL STUD. 289, 308–320 (1983)

Plea bargaining establishes the price for most crimes. It establishes price in the same way as bargaining in the market for goods and services. Many parties negotiate discrete sales over time. A seller of widgets will

---

[19] Jeffrey T. Ulmer & Mindy S. Bradley, *Variation in Trial Penalties Among Serious Violent Offenders*, 44 CRIMINOLOGY 631, 632–633 (2006).

accept a bid that exceeds the marginal costs of making more widgets and is as high as the price that would be offered by another buyer. Similarly, the prosecutor will accept a plea that exceeds the punishment his office could obtain by investing an equal amount of prosecutorial resources on other cases. The defendant, who buys the plea, pays by surrendering his right to impose costs on the prosecutor by demanding trial and by surrendering his chance of acquittal at trial.

Plea bargaining is a regular feature of criminal procedure. It is also a regular target of critics. The defenders of plea bargaining are rarely enthusiastic; they are more likely to describe it as a necessary evil than as a desirable feature of criminal procedure. Yet plea bargaining is desirable, not just defensible, if the system attempts to maximize deterrence from a given commitment of resources. It serves the price-establishing function at low cost. Constant plea negotiations will lead to rapid adjustments in penalties as conditions change. The parties save the costs of trials. Defendants presumably prefer the lower sentences to the exercise of their trial rights or they would not strike the deals. Prosecutors also prefer the agreements; they may put the released resources to use in other cases, thus increasing deterrence. If defendants and prosecutors (representing society) both gain, the process is desirable.

Market Failure Challenges to Plea Bargaining

One line of argument is to say that the process of bargaining is flawed. Prosecutors will take advantage of ignorant defendants, and there is sure to be some inequity, if only by chance, in the results of bargaining. Defendants' lawyers, who have a conflict of interest if working for a fixed fee, may use plea bargaining to hide sloth or even fraud.

These points are true but trivial. Conflicts of interest (agency costs) are as pressing throughout the criminal process as at the time of plea. Lawyers may cut corners at trial too. There is little reason to think people are systematically cheated by this. Lawyers acquire reputations, and their fees reflect both the anticipation of bargaining and the opportunity for sloth. Particular defendants may lack the information necessary to search intelligently, but in legal markets as in others search by even a few buyers may be sufficient for efficiency. Defendants represented by a public defender's office or a specialized criminal bar receive the gains of this search. The specialized bar or office also is able to obtain and use, at low cost, information about "the going rate" for particular offenses. Information and reputation effects create economies of scale in defense. At all events, if clients cannot distinguish very well among lawyers, the implications reach far beyond plea bargaining.

The most common and most powerful market-failure argument is that plea bargains are not voluntary sales by defendants of their rights but are instead coerced responses to threats by prosecutors and judges. Coerced agreements, like those induced by fraud, are not value maximizing and are not enforced at common law. So it should be with plea bargains, these critics maintain.

The coercion argument rests on the existence of a sentencing differential: one sentence if there is a plea, and a higher sentence if the defendant stands trial and is convicted. The higher sentence may be characterized as a penalty for the defendant's exercise of his right to trial (and the associated procedural rights). Make this penalty high enough and even the innocent will plead guilty; but high or low, any penalty on the exercise of the fundamental right to trial is illegitimate.

The problem with the coercion argument is that it begs the question. If plea bargains are honest compromises among the parties, in which defendants who might be acquitted surrender that possibility in exchange for a lower sentence, then there will be a [legitimate] sentence differential that is indistinguishable from the coercive threat of which the critics complain. Plea bargaining is "coercive" only if circumstances cause him to accept a higher sentence or if the risk of [higher trial] sentence would not exist but for the existence of plea bargaining. Because plea bargaining does exist, we cannot easily determine whether the [higher trial] sentence would exist in its absence.

Some indirect approach is necessary. I think the best chance for understanding whether the sentencing differential is coercive is to ask whether the size of the differential may be understood as a logical consequence of the bargaining process. If it can, then the differential is a function of an ordinary market; if it cannot, then the differential is coercive. Opponents of plea bargaining point out that the differential is quite large. [Large differentials are not inconsistent with non-coercive bargains.]

There are three principal sources of the sentencing differential in plea bargaining: (1) the defendant relinquishes his chance to be acquitted; (2) the defendant relinquishes procedural rights that impose costs on prosecutors; and (3) the defendant avoids perjuring himself by denying guilt. I take these up in turn.

[Easterbrook then demonstrates the following: First, if defendants heavily discount the future (i.e., a sentence of twenty-five years does not seem that much worse today than a sentence of fifty years, since offenders are present-minded and thus do not care much about the future*), then the prosecutor has to offer a lot to get a defendant to eliminate the chance of acquittal. Easterbrook provides a simple numeric example: if a defendant has a discount rate of 10% (which is not particularly high), then the present value of a 50-year sentence is 9.91 years.** If the probability of conviction is 0.75, then the expected sanction

---

* *Ed. note:* Recall that those who commit crimes tend to have relatively high discount rates in general.

** *Ed. note*: A 10% discount rate means that someone is indifferent between $1.00 today and $1.10 in the next time period (whenever that is: here, in a year). See the Statistical Appendix for a short explanation of present value.

from going to trial is 7.43 years. A sanction of 14.27 years imposed with certainty has the same present value, so this defendant would rationally demand 14.27 years instead of fifty, or else will go to trial. A sharp decline, but a rational—not coercive—one.

Second, the rational discount on the offer becomes even steeper when we account for the prosecutor's incentives. Trials are costly, and they grow most costly as trial rights expand. By pleading out one case, the prosecutor frees resources to process other cases and thus perhaps increases the deterrent (and incapacitative) impact of his office. This further increases the size of a rational, not-intended-to-be-coercive discount.

And third, at least in the federal system, defendants who spoke at trial and were convicted could see their sentence increased for the putative perjury they committed by improperly defending themselves. To Easterbrook, this increase in sentence length is a legitimate part of the "trial penalty" that comes from not pleading, justifying even larger gaps between trial and plea sentences.]

What remains is the argument that plea bargains . . . have perverse effects on third parties that more than offset the conservation of resources and increased deterrence I have discussed. John Langbein, for example, argues that plea bargains impair the exemplary function of the criminal law because they becloud valuable information, obtainable only from trials, about who is guilty and who is not.

Yet this value cannot be derived from the supposed clarity of information about guilt or innocence trial conveys. Most trials end in a verdict of guilt or innocence, but this is simply a way of suppressing uncertainty. Trials produce a verdict by rounding up to one (guilt) or down to zero (innocence) a probability that hovers in jurors' minds somewhere between 0.999 and 0.51. (The burden of proof requires probabilities less than, say, 0.90 to be rounded down.) Plea bargains reflect the probabilities case by case; trials disguise probabilities in individual cases and reflect them only over large populations of cases

The market failure objections to plea bargaining consequently are not compelling. And legal doctrines reflect this, treating plea bargains almost as part of the common law of contracts. The market approach to plea bargains explains features of the system that otherwise may be puzzling.

Unconscionable Pleas

Sometimes defendants plead guilty even while protesting their innocence. The courts uphold these pleas so long as the record contains some evidence from which a jury might have found guilt. They have been, however, a particular target of commentators, who maintain that the courts condone the punishment of innocent people.

From a market perspective, acceptance of such pleas is no mystery. Sometimes the evidence may point to guilt despite the defendant's factual innocence. It would do defendants no favor to prevent them from striking the best deals they could in such sorry circumstances. And if the probability of the defendant's guilt is indeed low even on the evidence that would be placed before the court—for example, if only one defendant in twenty would be convicted on such evidence—the sentencing differential will be correspondingly steep. There is again no reason to prevent the defendant from striking a deal that seems advantageous.

Easterbrook is not alone in taking a strongly contractual view of plea bargaining. In an article conveniently titled *Plea Bargaining as Contract*, Robert Scott and William Stuntz assert that the standard arguments used to invalidate private contracts do not convincingly argue against plea bargains.[20] For example:

- Duress: Scott and Stuntz point to the plea/trial differential as the main source of potential duress. But, they argue, this reduces to the strange claim that pleas and problematic because they are too *generous*. They then note:

  > To be sure, the plea favors the defendant only because the post-trial sentence is so high. But this is a complaint about background sentences, not plea bargaining. The problem of background sentences only implicates plea bargaining (as distinct from sentencing policy) to the extent that it suggests strategic manipulation by prosecutors.

  They also state that in standard contract theory, "coercion in the sense of few and unpalatable choices does not necessarily negate voluntary choice."

- Unconscionability: Scott and Stuntz argue that there is nothing substantively unconscionable about a plea bargain contract since the defendant gets exactly what he has bargained for (and in *Santobello v. New York*, 404 U.S. 257 (1971), the Supreme Court held that a plea could be revoked if the prosecution did not perform as promised). From a procedural perspective, plea bargains are performed case-by-case, so the common complaints about adhesion contracts do not apply. Nor does the generally "slapdash" nature of negotiations rise to the level of unconscionability.

  Furthermore, the bargaining process is not a unilateral monopoly, but a bilateral one: the prosecutor does not wield all the power, able to force the defendant to accept whatever

---

[20] Robert E. Scott & William J. Stuntz, *Plea Bargaining as Contract*, 101 YALE L. J. 1909 (1992).

he offers. Like Easterbrook, Scott and Stuntz argue that the defendant's right to force the prosecutor to engage in a costly trial gives him significant leverage in the negotiation process.

- Contracts of Enslavement. Contract law denies such contracts, but Scott and Stuntz point out, rightly, that plea bargains are not analogous to contracts of enslavement: "The defendant's liberty is not being traded for something else; rather, a *risk* of 'enslavement' (prison) is being traded for a *certainty* of somewhat less enslavement."

- Distributional justice. Finally, Scott and Stuntz argue that banning plea bargains would likely make things even worse for innocent defendants. To handle the increase in trials, states would have to adopt looser trial procedures; since these procedures are almost all intended to favor the defendant, the increase in errors would be borne almost entirely by the innocent. Furthermore, with more trials the expertise of defense lawyers would become more important, perhaps disadvantaging poorer defendants, who have access to lesser lawyers.

QUESTIONS

1. **Background sentences.** Are Scott and Stuntz right that our concerns about plea discounts perhaps reflects a more fundamental concern with the base sentences? If so, how do we fix *that* problem? Do we need to focus on prosecutors or legislators? What incentives do legislators currently have to *not* raise sentences?

2. **Unconscionability.** Think back to the reading in Chapter 3 about wholesale plea bargaining in a mid-sized Southern courtroom. Do these sorts of pleas start to raise concerns about unconscionability?

Though they admit that the bargaining process is imperfect, Scott and Stuntz conclude that standard contract solutions to standard contract problems can be a useful way to address plea bargaining reform. In the rest of this section, then, we want to consider the validity of this optimistic view of plea bargain as contract.

B.1. PLEA BARGAINS AND THE SHADOW OF THE TRIAL

A major question determining the normative appeal of plea-bargains-as-contracts is whether they operate in the "shadow of the trial": if the costs of going to trial change, do the associated plea bargains? In other words, if a new Supreme Court decision decreases the probability of conviction at trial (by, say, increasing a defendant's procedural protections), does the plea offer made by the prosecution shift commensurably in favor of the defendant? Easterbrook clearly assumes this is the case, stating that plea bargaining "serves the price-establishing function at low cost. Constant plea negotiations will lead to rapid adjustments in penalties as conditions change."

If pleas really do take place in the shadow of the trial, then the Supreme Court's focus on trial-outcomes and relatively hands-off approach to the substance of plea bargain is perhaps less concerning, since those trial rights "trickle down" to the plea process. Of course, the courts are not the only relevant shadow: if pleas respond to legislative shadows, then even if prosecutors rarely impose the really long sentences legislatures make available to them, they may be able to extract more—and more severe—pleas as legislatures become more punitive. If, however, pleas do not respond to judicial or legislative shifts, then the centrality of plea bargaining, and the Court's hands-off attitude towards it, raise some troubling normative implications. In effect, criminal justice rules are set by the prosecutors, in negotiation with defense attorneys, and with little meaningful indirect—and even less direct—participation by the other branches of government. Given the historical commitment in the US to checks and balances in government action in general, for such checks to breach down in criminal justice, where the government's power is often at its most powerful and invasive, would be concerning.[21]

Both William Stuntz and Stephanos Bibas have pointed to important reasons why the plea process may not respond to shadows as completely as we may hope. First, Stuntz—in an article written after his piece with Robert Scott—points out that the incentives of the prosecutor differ in a key way from those of a civil plaintiff:

> Prosecutors are not like civil plaintiffs: they are not paid by the conviction, with bonuses for each additional month the defendant spends in prison. [Thus] extra months in prison are not like marginal dollars in civil cases. Once the defendant's sentence has reached the level the prosecutor prefers . . . adding more time offers no benefit to the prosecutor. Indeed, prosecutors may actually value "extra" prison time negatively. Plea bargains do not always, maybe not even usually, involve haggling over a surplus as in negotiated settlements in civil cases. A civil plaintiff has the incentive to take every dollar he can, just as the defendant wishes to pay as little as possible. In criminal cases, one of the two parties is like that: the defendant

---

[21] The complete political economy story is significantly more complex, of course. If, for example, we think that legislatures suffer from well-defined agency problems that lead them to implement excessively harsh sentencing laws—where "excessive" is taken to mean even more extreme than they themselves personally desire—then we may want prosecutors to be somewhat nonresponsive to new legislative sentencing enhancement; William Stuntz has suggested that this very problem may exist. We turn to the politics of criminal justice in Chapter 9.

almost always prefers freedom to incarceration and less incarceration to more. The prosecutor's utility function, though, is much more complicated.[22]

Stuntz thus concludes that the goal of the prosecutor is to:

> [A]chieve the results that forces other than the law—her own preferences, her boss's electoral ambitions, local voters' priorities, and the like—suggest. The law serves only to define her opportunities. And she generally has more opportunities than she needs.

As a result, bargains may be somewhat unresponsive to judicial and legislative shadows, particularly increasingly punitive ones (since shadows that make conviction tougher benefit the defendant, the party who *is* bargaining like a civil litigant).

Bibas focuses much more extensively on the behavioralist limitations that may block criminal law's shadow from falling across plea bargains, examining the impact of several of the heuristics discussed in Chapter 1.[23] As he admits, the most he can do is speculate about the potential impact of such heuristics. First, "we do not know what the trial rate would be without these influences." Second, the magnitude of the impact of these biases are unknown, and some can often cut in contradictory directions or be offset by other heuristics. So it is useful to think about how and when these heuristics will matter, but it is also important to appreciate the limitations in our understanding of them so far. Here are some of the concerns Bibas raises:

- *Overconfidence and Self-Serving Bias*: If both sides are too optimistic about outcomes at trial, each has a weaker incentive to plead, and the probability of finding mutually agreeable terms declines.[24] Bibas notes that the impact of this bias depends on the sentencing regime in place: under an indeterminate regime, there is lots of room to be optimistic about the sentence that will be imposed, but

---

[22] William J. Stuntz, *Plea Bargaining and Criminal Law's Disappearing Shadow*, 117 HARV. L. REV. 2548, 2554 (2004).

[23] Stephanos Bibas, *Plea Bargaining Outside the Shadow of Trial*, 117 HARV. L. REV. 2463 (2004). I apologize for the confusing metaphor of blocking a shadow; it is unclear how exactly one would block the *absence* of light.

[24] For example, assume that the sentence if convicted after trial is ten years, and both the defendant and the prosecutor care about the total number of years in prison. If the defendant thinks he has a 75% chance of acquittal, he will not accept an offer of more than 2.5 years; if the prosecutor thinks he has a 75% chance of winning, he will not make an offer of fewer than 7.5 years. No deal is possible. If the two sides have the same expectations, then a deal can be struck: if the defendant thinks he has only a 25% chance of acquittal, then he will accept an offer of 7.5 years. And if both parties are relatively pessimistic, then a deal becomes even more likely. If, for example, the defendant thinks he has only a 25% chance of acquittal, he will accept any deal under 7.5 years, and if the prosecutor thinks he has only a 25% chance of winning, he will accept any offer of more than 2.5 years, so anything between 2.5 and 7.5 years is mutually agreeable.

guidelines narrow significantly the range of potential over-optimism.

> **Question:** Bibas is right that indeterminacy creates opportunity for relative optimism. But if the prosecutor, defense attorney, and judge are repeat players in a given courtroom, how true is this? And might indeterminacy also lead to pessimism?

- *Denial Mechanisms*: This one is straight forward: if someone comes to believe that he is not guilty when he in fact is, his willingness to strike a deal will decline. As Bibas states:

  > Denial takes many forms. Offenders often deny the facts, their deeds, their knowledge, or their culpability; or they minimize how harmful or wrong their actions were. These denials are not simply public-relations ploys. They reflect offenders' fears of admitting the truth to themselves. They flow from underlying attitudes and cognitive distortions that impede clear perception of the truth. For example, offenders who falsely claim innocence to others begin to deceive themselves and to distort what they remember and how they interpret those memories.

- *Discounting Future Costs*: As we discussed in Chapter 1, individuals who engage in criminal activity tend to put less weight on future outcomes than the average person across a wide range of situations. Bibas argues that offenders with high discount rates (i.e., ones who put less emphasis on the future, and who are thus more likely to recidivate) will have to be given *more*-generous pleas to compensate for their strong preference for "today": the defendant will demand more for the immediacy of certain punishment.

  Bibas is right to point out the importance of discount rates on the types of pleas offenders will take, but it quite possible that he got the effect backwards. It depends on what, exactly, Bibas means by "higher discount rate" (a term he does not precisely define). For Bibas to be right, if we say that Adam has a higher discount rate than Bob, we must mean that Adam values a unit of consumption today more than Bob does, so the prosecutor has to pay him more (via a lesser sentence) to give it up.

  This is not an implausible definition of "higher discount rate," but it is not how that phrase is typically used. To economists, if Adam has a higher discount rate than Bob, then Adam and Bob may value consumption equally today,[25] but Adam cares less about future costs and benefits than Bob does. In this case, the difference between a ten and fifteen year sentence matters less to Adam than to Bob, since Adam does not look into the future too much; that five year difference occurs beyond the range of his serious attention, but within range of Bob's. In this case, the prosecutor could extract a more favorable (to the prosecutor) plea from Adam than from Bob, the opposite of what Bibas claims.

This example points to a broader problem with behavioralist claims. Two plausible definitions of the same effect can lead to significantly different conclusions, and empirically assessing which is more accurate is quite difficult to do.

- *Risk Tolerance and Distribution*: A person's willingness to take a plea depends in part on his risk tolerance: the lower a person's tolerance for the risk, the more willing he is to take the certainty of a plea over the uncertainty of trial. As Bibas points out, however, risk tolerance varies with "sex; adolescence and age generally; wealth, social class, self-employment, and education; church attendance; and marital status." Thus different groups will accept different pleas, likely based on factors that have troubling distributional implications. In fact, Bibas argues that the group likely to receive the most favorable pleas (at least along this margin) are single, non-church-going men, perhaps particularly those on the wealthier and better-educated end.

- *Framing*: Recall that framing refers to the fact that our decision whether to be risk averse or risk loving turns on how a particular gamble is framed. If it is framed as a gain ("save 200 for sure, or gamble on saving 600"), we tend to be risk averse and lock in the gains (save the 200); if as a loss ("lose 400 for sure, or gamble on losing 0"), we tend to prefer the risk (shoot for losing none). At one level, plea bargaining seems like a loss frame—lose five years of freedom for sure, or gamble on losing none—which should encourage people to go to trial.

But there is one category of defendant for whom the frame is a gain-frame: those charged with relatively minor offenses who cannot make bail. For these defendants, the plea will almost certainly be for time served. So now they can gain release for sure or gamble on a delayed-release-

---

[25] To the extent that they do not, that has nothing to do with discount rates, but with utility more generally, independent of future discounting.

with-acquittal. Under this frame, the defendant is risk averse and thus more likely to take the plea.

From a normative perspective, framing is tricky, since there is no "absolute" baseline of comparison. It is impossible to present *any* choice without some sort of frame, so deciding which is "better" or "worse" is really hard, if not conceptually impossible, to do. But acknowledging the framing effect does help us understand how pleas will be distributed, as well as appreciate the collateral implications (maybe costs, maybe benefits) of more or less generous bail policies.

- *Anchoring*: Exposure to numbers, even irrelevant ones, can "anchor" our perceptions. Many restaurants, for example, often have highly-overpriced dishes on the top-right corner of the menu (where the eye first falls) to anchor our perceptions on the high-end of the scale, so the cheaper-but-still-expensive items seem cheap (compared to the anchor). And we have a hard time moving away from an initial (and perhaps subconscious) anchor. This could explain one reason prosecutors stack charges: not just for the purpose of charge bargaining, but to set the anchor at "severe punishment." Thus a prosecutor who starts with seven charges and bargains down to one will likely end up with a more favorable deal than the prosecutor who starts with two and ends up at the same, single charge in the exact same case. New defendants are likely to be more vulnerable to anchors than experienced felons (since the experienced felons expect to see the stack shrink during pleas, so the anchor isn't as strong).

Bibas then suggests that we should look to lawyers to act as debiasers: while lawyers themselves often suffer from these biases, they are trained, repeat actors, and the behavioralist literature does suggest that experts are less vulnerable to these biases than non-experts (although they are by no means immune). Debiasing, however, is not easy:

> Simply telling someone about a heuristic or bias does not counteract it, although drawing attention to someone's mood can offset that mood's influence. Telling people to try harder or concentrate more does not work, nor does offering monetary incentives to get the right result. Informing people about various risk factors and asking them to describe how those factors apply to them has no effect on overoptimism. Nor does it help much to ask people to compare their cases to best-case scenarios instead of to worst-case scenarios. Indeed, focusing attention on risk factors can exacerbate overoptimism because it allows people to emphasize selectively the facts favorable to

them. Likewise, giving people more information exacerbates overoptimism by facilitating selective recall.

But the story Bibas presents is not bleak, just challenging. And in telling it, Bibas implicitly points to the strong need for lawyers to understand the basic psychology of decision-making, without which they may not be able to serve their clients well. He also further demonstrates that the ways in which defendants obtain counsel can have unexpected consequences. Among the positive steps that lawyers can take, Bibas notes:

> By reformulating outcomes in [terms of expected values], lawyers can reduce risk seeking induced by loss aversion and mitigate framing effects. Indeed, lawyers have to be careful with their great power to frame. Clients may anchor heavily on lawyers' initial frames, so an initial forecast that is bleak or optimistic may be hard to revise later on. Lawyers can also educate clients about the many forces that are beyond their control at trial. Because overoptimism is especially severe when parties think they can control outcomes, lawyers can reduce overoptimism by reducing illusions of control. Lawyers can also perform detailed risk analyses, drawing attention to the temporal, emotional, and monetary costs of continuing litigation, as well as to its various risks. Prompting clients to give rationales for their choices reduces framing, and asking clients to quantify their certainty helps reduce overconfidence.

> By far the most successful debiasing technique is to have clients consider the opposite. Overoptimism, self-serving bias, denial, framing, anchoring, or loss aversion may prompt a defendant to count on acquittal at trial. In response, lawyers can make defendants focus on evidence and arguments that cut against their own position. Psychologists have repeatedly found that considering the opposite reduces overconfidence, biased information assimilation, biased hypothesis testing, and excessive perseverance of beliefs. Merely telling someone to consider the other side's arguments is no panacea, however. Subjects may find counterarguments so difficult to imagine and formulate that they may become even more convinced of their original positions. Rather, for this method to be effective, the lawyer should make the other side's strongest case forcefully and persuasively. This is exactly what mediators do in civil settlements.

> Interestingly, [two researchers, Russell Korobin and Chris Guthrie] found that the most influential step lawyers can take is to recommend a settlement without giving any reasons. Apparently, clients are more inclined to defer to a lawyer's judgment and authority than they are to assimilate and apply

debiasing instructions. In other words, lawyers exert a great deal of influence over clients' settlement decisions just by offering their opinions. Because appointed counsel meet with their clients later and less often than retained counsel, they have less time to cultivate and exercise this influence.

Not everyone, however, is as optimistic as Bibas is about lawyers as debiasers. Rebecca Hollander-Blumoff, for example, points to several possible heuristic limitations on the part of lawyers.[26] Prosecutors and defense attorneys may be psychologically inclined to find "closure" and operate under intense time-and workload-constraints, both of which favor the use of heuristical reasoning over the purely rational. Furthermore, group identity and adversarialism—"prosecutors" on this side, "defense attorneys" on that side—again push against level-headed rationality in favor of mental shortcuts (such as stereotyping). Like Bibas, Hollander-Blumoff admits she has no empirical evidence about how all these swirling heuristics ultimately interact, but she stresses that it is important not to be too optimistic too quickly about the debiasing power of lawyers.

In short, the shadow cast by trial rights is mediated by the psychology of the prosecutor, the defendant, and the defendant's lawyer. At this point, we lack clear empirical evidence about how all these various psychological biases net out and about how large these effects are in general or for particular sub-populations (older, first-time black female offenders, say, or younger, white male recidivists).

QUESTIONS

1. **Ambiguity aversion, Part I.** People don't like risk: that's risk aversion. People also don't like uncertainty: this is called ambiguity aversion. The classic example of ambiguity aversion is Ellsberg's Paradox: People are told that Urn A contains 50 white balls and 50 black balls, while Urn B contains 100 balls divided between white and black at an unstated ratio. When asked which urn they'd rather use when wagering on whether the next ball drawn will be white, people consistently prefer Urn A to Urn B, even though there is no principled reason to prefer one over the other (see why?). How does ambiguity aversion (which Bibas does not talk about) interact with, say, overconfidence?

2. **Ambiguity aversion, Part II.** Ambiguity aversion is a well-known heuristic, but Bibas never discusses it. This is not really a criticism of Bibas: the lists of heuristics are enormously long, so it is often impossible to discuss them all. All behavioralist studies suffer from Omitted Heuristic Bias. But does this sort of omission raise any concerns with Bibas's results?

3. **Lost in a sea of heuristics.** Even if the study mentioned all heuristics, it would be impossible to estimate the cumulative net effect of all of them taken together. So what does this mean about how to take these

---

[26] Rebecca Hollander-Blumoff, *Social Psychology, Information Processing, and Plea Bargaining*, 91 MARQUETTE L. REV. 163 (2007).

heuristics into account at plea bargaining? Should we just throw up our hands and ignore the results? Or is there a way to incorporate these complicated, at-times-contradictory findings into policy?

B.2. Plea Bargains and Externalities

There are three troubling externalities when it comes to plea bargains: there is that between the prosecutor and the public, that among defendants (a literal prisoners' dilemma), and a less-obvious externality between prosecutors and legislators. The effect of the first externality is unclear, but that of the latter two cuts in the same direction, with each leading to more punishment, and more severe punishment, than if it were not present.

First, the prosecutors. Putting aside any cognitive biases, prosecutors are not perfect agents for society. The optimal role of prosecutors is to maximize some sort of amalgam of public safety and justice. But while prosecutors certainly care about these, they also care about promotions, about getting home to see their families for dinner, etc., etc. In other words, they do not internalize the full social benefit or cost of their actions, and so they behave suboptimally (from a social perspective).

Of course, this agency problem exists whether we permit plea bargaining or not: prosecutors will decline to bring cases, or will conduct some trials poorly, and so on. So the question is not "are pleas imperfect because of agency slack?" but rather "does plea bargaining permit a certain sort of agency slack that is particularly troubling?" Or, phrased even more difficultly, "do the additional agency costs of plea bargaining more than offset any of its efficiency gains?" After all, for example, plea bargaining does allow prosecutors to concentrate resources on serious and difficult cases. But it also allows prosecutors to overprosecute minor cases to look "tough on crime." Plea bargaining may also facilitate over-ambitious conduct, like overprosecuting minor cases and pleading them out to look "tough on crime," or pleading out important but risky cases to avoid the risk of losing and hurting promotion possibilities.

In all these cases, we need to ask how often, and to what degree, these problems occur; for now, we have no data on this at all. Certainly, plea bargaining reduces transparency, making it harder for the public at large to monitor prosecutorial behavior and thus increasing the risk of agency problems. But at this point, it is hard to say more, beside the fact that these sorts of concerns should always be in the back of our minds.

Moreover, as you think about these issues more and more, they become harder and harder to grapple with. On the one hand, prosecutors may accept too-low pleas in complex cases. On the other hand, prosecutors have too strong an incentive to send people to prison due to the financial moral hazard problem. These effects cut in different directions; trying to estimate the net effect of all the various externalities is likely impossible. Which raises a tough issue: we may be able to think about how to solve (or at least mitigate) each of these externalities one by one, but unless we can eliminate them all, sometimes we are better off in a world with two offsetting defects than just one by itself (economists call this the "theory of the second-best"). Just because we can solve one of many problems does not automatically mean that we should.

Question: Sure, the prosecutor is not perfectly incentivized. But who else is imperfectly incentivized? If we want to understand the social optimality of case outcomes, as opposed to prosecutorial behavior (see why these are different questions?), who else's behavior do we need to model?

Second, the prisoner's dilemma. The core idea with the prisoners' dilemma is that two people, acting independently, would be better off if they could coordinate their actions, but without any formal way to coordinate they each take steps that make both of them worse off. Figure 8–1 provides an example of the classic version of the dilemma.

Figure 8–1: The Prisoners' Dilemma

		Player A	
		Silent	Confess
Player B	Silent	–2, –2	–10, 0
	Confess	0, –10	–8, –8

The basic idea is the following. Two people, A and B, are arrested for a serious crime. If they both stay silent, each is convicted of a minor offense (say, resisting arrest): these are the payoffs of –2 (the first number in each cell is what A receives, the second is what B receives). But if A agrees to confess and turn state's witness, then he walks free (payoff of 0) and B gets convicted of the more serious offense (–10); the opposite payoffs occur if B confesses and A stays silent. If both confess, then each receives a slightly-discounted sentence (for, say, admission of responsibility or saving the court's time).

What are the incentives of the parties here? Consider A's choices. If he knows that B is going to stay silent, then he is better off confessing (payoff = 0) than staying quiet himself (payoff = –2). And if he knows that B is going to confess, A is better off confessing (payoff = –8) than staying quiet (payoff = –10). In other words, no matter what B does, A wants to confess, either to betray B (when B stays quiet) or to mitigate the harm from B confessing as well. Since the payoffs are symmetrical, B's incentives are the same.

Thus both A and B will confess. But this is a surprising outcome, since both are better off if each remains quiet: –2 is better than –8! The problem is one of coordination: if A and B have no ability to credibly coordinate, their own private incentives will induce them to behave in suboptimal (for them) ways.

The example in Figure 8–1 demonstrates one simple type of prisoners' dilemma that exists in plea bargaining: at least in crimes with two or more people, a plea discount for confessing helps create the incentive for each party to sell out the other. Look back at Figure 8–1 and ask yourself how A's and B's incentives change in a world with no plea-bargaining—so the payouts in the (confess, confess) square were (–10, –10) (see why those would be the payoffs?).

But there is a more complex defendant externality that deserves some attention. As Stuntz and others have noted, trials are very costly for prosecutors, and so plea bargains increase the resources that prosecutors can apply to other trials, or to other plea sessions. Thus when defendant A pleads guilty, he increases the leverage that the prosecutor can bring to induce B—a defendant in a completely different case—to plead (since, for example, the threat to go to trial is now more credible). Thus there is another externality, not between co-defendants, but across all defendants.

The normative implications of this effect are ambiguous. Douglas Savitsky, for example, argues that if plea bargaining were restrained—which would limit the prisoners' dilemma effect—then "easily disposed of cases [would] become expensive, due to the need for trial . . . and [a prosecutor] would be incentivized to prosecute cases with greater social importance. . . ."[27] Perhaps. But the effect could run the opposite direction, too: cases of social import are likely more expensive to prosecute in general, so the prosecutor would have to think about whether to secure, say, ten drug convictions or one aggravated assault at trial. Our lack of understanding of prosecutorial incentives makes it hard to estimate what the "exchange rate" is across offense types. Savitsky makes the case too simple by comparing Enron and Bernie Madoff to small-time marijuana charges; the real challenge are low-profile-but-serious crimes which are hard to secure convictions for. What exactly are the prosecutor's incentives when deciding between a mid-level crack bust and a domestic violence case in which a repeatedly-battered spouse is wary of testifying?

The other externality problem relates back to the free-riding concern introduced by allowing county-funded prosecutors relatively unfettered access to state-funded prisons. This problem skews the incentives of prosecutors. But plea bargaining arguably skews the incentives of legislators as well. In looking at the post-*Bordenkircher* politics of criminal justice, William Stuntz notes that crime was rising steadily from the 1960s through the 1990s, and so:

---

[27] Douglas Savitsky, *Is Plea Bargaining a Rational Choice? Plea Bargaining as an Engine of Racial Stratification and Overcrowding in the United States Prison System*, 24 RATIONALITY & CHOICE 131 (2012).

[There] was an ongoing bidding war in legislative halls to see who could propose and pass the broadest criminal liability rules and the harshest sentencing statutes. Prosecutors were not required actually to apply those harsh laws across the board. So legislators had no reason to worry about the breadth and severity of the statutes that began to fill the criminal code.[28]

As a result, Stuntz argues, the nature of criminal law changed. The criminal law no longer "define[d] the conduct that leads to a prison term," since there were too many laws to enforce; and overlapping sentencing laws meant that no single sentencing law defined the specific consequences of a particular violation. Instead:

The *real* law, the "rules" that determine who goes to prison and for how long, is not written in code books and case reports. Prosecutors . . . define it by the decisions they make when ordering off the menus their states' legislatures have given them. The behavior that will lead to a stay in the local house of corrections varies from courthouse to courthouse, and from prosecutor to prosecutor. So do the sentences that attach to most crimes. Law does not govern criminal justice. The menu has grown too large; prosecutors have too many options.

In other words, plea bargaining made legislative toughness-on-crime cheaper: legislators could "purchase" tough laws at the plea-bargained discount.[29] And legislatures then took advantage of this discount in a way that transferred tremendous discretion and power to prosecutors. With plea bargaining creating externalities that run in multiple directions, responsibility is diffused in troubling ways.

B.3. Plea Bargains and Information

Plea bargains are made in an environment of limited information, particularly for the defendant, and there does not appear to be any constitutional guarantee to discovery. In *United States v. Ruiz*, 536 U.S. 622 (2002), the Court found no constitutional problem with a defendant waiving her right to impeachment evidence as part of the plea bargain. Pleas must be knowing and voluntary, but they need not be fair, and impeachment evidence goes to "fairness." There appear to be some potential loopholes in *Ruiz*, particularly the Court's favorable reference to the fact that the government had already agreed in the plea to turn over any evidence relating to the defendant's innocence. This, however, is just dicta; Bibas has argued that the logic of *Ruiz* applies as much to exculpatory evidence as to impeachment evidence, although some lower federal courts and some state appellate and supreme courts have

---

[28] Stuntz, Bordenkircher v. Hayes, supra note 7.

[29] The discount is even larger than this: Stuntz further argues that when prosecutors apply overly-tough laws in ways that are politically unpopular, the prosecutor pays the political price, as no one blames the legislature for providing him with that option.

disagreed and held that at least some materially exculpatory evidence must be turned over during the plea process.[30]

That, however, is simply the constitutional bar. Local DA offices remain free to set their own rules, and many do implement "open file" policies, in which defendants and their attorneys have free access to all non-work product information. In fact, more than forty states require some sort of pre-trial disclosure, and in general states (but not the federal system) have been expanding the scope of pre-trial discovery. To Bibas, this is a good thing, since it helps overcome the informational deficits that lead to over-optimism: a defendant has a better chance of properly (or at least more properly) assessing his true probability of conviction the more information he has.[31]

B.4. PLEA BARGAINS AND STRUCTURED SENTENCING

The impact of sentencing guidelines on plea bargaining is, like almost everything else in this chapter, ambiguous. On the one hand, Bibas argues that guidelines could reduce some of the cognitive biases that complicate bargaining. By sharply narrowing the implications of a plea, for example, they mitigate some of the risk of over-optimism bias (or ambiguity aversion). Both the defendant and the prosecutor have more room to be overly-optimistic in an indeterminate regime with a sentencing range of one to twenty years compared to a guideline regime with a range of eight to twelve (even though the means are the same). Guidelines can also alter anchoring. Sticking with our previous example, a defendant may anchor onto twenty years in the indeterminate regime (even if the usual sentence is more like ten) but only on twelve under the guidelines (or perhaps even ten, if judges are known to generally sentence at the midpoint).

Note that *Blakely* makes an appearance here. By eliminating presumptiveness, *Blakely* may undermine the over-optimism check, but perhaps not so much the anchoring effect. By eliminating the presumptive nature of some guidelines—or, in at least some of the jurisdictions that adopted jury fact-finding, by inducing the legislature to enlarge the presumptive ranges—*Blakely* provides more room for possibly-unwarranted optimism. But anchoring often comes about from various quantitative details, so the shift from presumptive to voluntary may not alter anchors too significantly if the numeric ranges remain relatively the same.

---

[30] For a list of such decisions, see Máximo Langer, *Rethinking Plea Bargaining: The Practice and Reform of Prosecutorial Adjudication in American Criminal Procedure*, 33 AM. J. CRIM. L. 223, 274 n. 201 (2006).

[31] Another collateral benefit of more generous discovery is that it compensates for underfunded defense attorneys, who now can spend more time evaluating the evidence rather than independently gathering it. See Darryl K. Brown, *The Decline of Defense Counsel and the Rise of Accuracy in Criminal Adjudication*, 93 CAL. L. REV. 1585 (2005).

On the other hand, guidelines and other forms of structured sentencing make sentencing much more "lumpy." Under an indeterminate regime, a prosecutor could offer a sentence of ten years to the defendant he thought he could convict 100% of the time, a sentence of 9.5 years to the defendant he thought he could convict 95% of the time, a sentence of 6.2 years to the defendant he thought he could convict 62% of the time, and so on. Structured regimes, by design, limit this sort of flexibility. Whether this is a good or bad, however, is an open question.

To Easterbrook, lumpiness would likely be a defect—for some defendants the prosecutor will not be able to offer a sufficient deal and will be forced to go through with a costly trial that otherwise could have been avoided. But to others, this is actually a good thing. Oren Bar-Gill and Oren Gazal Ayal, for example, argue that limited discounting options may benefit innocent defendants.[32] Assuming that innocence and probability of conviction are sufficiently correlated, the discount a prosecutor would have to offer an innocent defendant would be greater than that permitted by the sentencing regime, forcing him to either take a low-probability case to trial or to drop that case altogether.

Such lumpiness is not a perfect solution to the innocence problem. If nothing else, as Bibas points out, parties can still bargain around these limitations by "manipulating facts, guideline adjustments, and terms of cooperation."[33] It is also unclear what effect this would have on broad categories of crimes where factual guilt may be systematically more obvious than the ability to prove it: domestic violence, some non-stranger rape cases, certain types of complicated white-collar crime. In these cases, the plea discount may be an important way of securing a conviction in a case that is more legally/procedurally tricky than factually so. That said, in these sorts of cases it is worth asking whether excessive-sentences-plus-steep-discounts is the proper way to target such offenses, or if some deeper, more structural reform is preferable.

> **Question:** How big a practical concern is the lumpiness in a regime with multiple overlapping offenses—how limited will DAs really be? How normatively appealing are the implications of this question?

B.5. Is Plea Bargaining Unavoidable? An International Comparison

Many American commentators who want to reform plea bargaining have looked to Europe for guidance: European criminal justice systems rely much less on plea bargaining yet seem to function fairly well. It is thus worth asking what lessons, if any, we can learn from European experiences.

---

[32] Oren Bar-Gill & Oren Gazal Ayal, *Plea Bargaining Only for the Guilty*, 49 J. L. & Econ. 353 (2006). Bibas, *Shadow*, supra note 23 echoes this point as well.

[33] Bibas, *Shadow*, supra note 23 at 2536.

On the one hand, it should be immediately noted that while plea bargaining rates in Europe are lower than they are in the US—John Langbein, a prominent comparative law scholar, once referred to Germany as "the land without plea bargaining"[34]—plea-like behavior has been on the rise there, and countries have adopted laws and procedures that are more conducive to non-trial resolutions of cases. This is likely due at least in part to increasing case pressures during a period of slowly rising violent crime and steeply rising drug arrests (and flat or slightly-falling property crimes).[35] The European trends thus indicate that even in countries disinclined to plea bargain such an approach is increasingly popular. That, in turn, cautions that meaningful abolition in the US could be impossible. But plea bargain rates are nonetheless lower in Europe, and they do not suffer from some of the defects seen here; European practices may thus offer possible paths for reform, or at least lessons to learn.

In a survey of plea (or plea-like) practices in France, Germany, and Italy, Yue Ma highlights a few key differences between Continental and American approaches.[36] The biggest difference is the role of judicial oversight. The American criminal justice system views plea bargaining as essentially a private bargain between two parties; the judge's role is limited to making sure the contract is not improperly entered into. European judges, on the other hand, take on much more active roles, continuously monitoring and regulating the plea process. In France, for example, once a prosecutor decides to charge a defendant with a high-enough level offense (a *crime*),[37] he must refer the case to a magistrate judge, who then controls much of the subsequent process; the prosecutor cannot even drop a charge without the approval of the magistrate, making it tougher to stack charges. And while the prosecutor has discretion over whether to charge an offense as *crime* or something lower, he makes that decision unilaterally, not as part of bargain.

In Italy, judges play perhaps an even stronger role. Italy did not have any sort of plea bargaining system in place prior to 1989; frequent backlogs were dealt with via large-scale amnesties. Italy now has two approaches to plea bargains: party-agreed sentences and abbreviated trials. Under party-agreed sentences, the prosecution and defense can privately agree to any sentence under two years.[38] Such an agreement, however, is subject to judicial review, both to determine whether the

---

[34] John H. Langbein, *Land Without Plea Bargaining: How the Germans Do It*, 78 MICH. L. REV. 204, 224 (1979).

[35] Marcelo F. Aebi, *Crime Trends in Western Europe from 1990 to 2000*, 10 EUROPEAN J. CRIM. POL'Y & RES. 163 (2004).

[36] Yue Ma, *Prosecutorial Discretion and Plea Bargaining in the United States, France, Germany, and Italy: A Comparative Perspective*, 12 INTERNAT'L CRIM. JUST. REV. 22 (2002).

[37] In France, crimes fall in three categories: *crimes*, *délits*, or *contraventions* (in descending order of severity).

[38] This refers to the sentence actually agreed to, not the statutory maximum (which can be more than two years).

parties have correctly determined the nature of the offense and whether the sentence is appropriate. And the judge must explain every acceptance in writing, to prevent him from simply rubber-stamping defense/prosecution agreements. Moreover, while prosecutors must approve any such sentence agreement, they cannot refuse without good reason, they must explain any refusal in writing, and refusals are subject to judicial review as well. With abbreviated trials, defendants can ask for a quick, immediate trial based on the evidence gathered to that point; if the prosecution agrees, the trial is held promptly. The benefit to the defendant is that his sentence is set at one-third that had he gone to trial. Again, prosecutorial approval is required, but courts can review any refusal for unreasonableness, again restricting the power of the prosecutor.

Besides greater judicial involvement, European pleas differ because not only are sentences generally lower, reducing prosecutorial leverage, but at least France and Germany do not allow consecutive sentences. This reduces the coercive power of stacking lesser offenses, since one conviction or five generally has the same sentencing implication. Furthermore, that dropping charges often requires judicial approval makes it harder to charge bargain, and certainly makes it much more public.

Finally, victims play a bigger role in European systems, limiting prosecutorial discretion even further. Victims in France, for example, can appeal the prosecutor's decision to file lower-level (i.e., non-*crime*) charges, and German victims can likewise appeal, first to the chief prosecutor and then to an appellate judge, the failure to bring a prosecution for evidentiary (but not policy) purposes. Some victims' rights groups have argued for more victim participation in the plea process in the United States as well, although it does not appear that much actual progress has been made along these lines.[39]

C. Pulling It All Together

So, where does this leave us? Though long part of the criminal justice system in America, over the past several decades plea bargains have shifted from being fairly common to almost inevitable. The law currently treats them like it does most private contracts: the terms are generally unreviewable as long as the contract is entered into voluntarily and knowingly.

The defenders of plea bargaining point out that it allows prosecutors to allocate their resources more effectively and thus expand the crime-fighting effect of the law (whether through deterrence, incapacitation, or rehabilitation). It also allows them to concentrate on more difficult and more serious cases without letting lower-level cases slide altogether

---

[39] See, e.g., Michael M. O'Hear, *Plea Bargaining and Victims: From Consultation to Guidelines*, 91 Marquette L. Rev. 323 (2007).

unpunished. And it may even be optimal to innocent defendants by allowing them to mitigate their exposure to punishment.

The critics, on the other hand, point to several defects. Defendants are often forced to decide whether to take pleas early in the process when information is extremely limited. This increases the risk of bad choices on its own terms, but it also amplifies the risk that problematic heuristics will lead defendants astray. Furthermore, the presence of these heuristic biases means that changes in trial rights may not change plea offers with sufficient "tightness," implying that the Court's focus on trial rights rather than plea rights is misplaced. Plea bargains may also aggravate agency problems with both prosecutors and legislators. And the ability to stack numerous charges, add on severe sentences when pleas are rejected, and use various charging and sentencing options to finely determine the sentence gives prosecutors significant power; defendants are not powerless—their call on the prosecutor's time (and risk of professional embarrassment if there is an acquittal) is a real bargaining chip—but prosecutors are almost certainly bringing the bigger knife to the fight.

Some potential reforms seem relatively straight-forward, like increased pre-trial discovery. Such discovery solves some of the information asymmetries, helps reduce the reliance on heuristics, and partially offsets the funding differential between prosecutors and defense attorneys. And it seems to be the general direction in which states are moving.

Other defects seem harder to clearly reform. That plea bargaining permits legislators to pass tough sentencing laws that they do not really expect to be regularly enforced, for example, could be solved by limiting the percent discount that can be offered and thus pushing some of the political cost back onto the legislators.[40] Although given the current complexity and redundancy of state criminal codes—some states have more than a dozen versions of one type of crime—it is hard to see how fixed discounts could have much effect as long as charge bargaining is possible. And charge bargaining is hard to police without active judicial involvement—a solution that experiences in both Europe and New Jersey suggest is feasible, although no state has followed in New Jersey's footsteps, and New Jersey only has plea guidelines and judicial review for one category of drug offenses.

In general, the major concerns with the US plea bargaining system are a lack of information, minimal judicial oversight, and significant (arguably excessive) sentencing pressure at the disposal of the prosecutor. It does appear that these defects can be addressed, to varying

---

[40] In other words, if prosecutors can only offer a 20% discount and the legislature sets the sanction for aggravated assault at 20 years, expecting most sentences to be about five, then when the prosecutor is repeated forced by law to impose 16 year sentences, the legislature may suffer political costs and thus reduce the sentence.

degrees, without abolishing—or even severely constraining—the plea bargaining process. But the politics of crime control have, for whatever reasons, made such policies vanishingly rare.

PART 3

SENTENCES AND RE-ENTRY

So far, we have considered everything that takes place from the moment the judge or jury says "guilty"—or, far more often, the moment the defendant pleads guilty—through the imposition of the sentence. Now we turn our attention to those sentences themselves. We start with the most prominent punishment, incarceration. In 2010, over 1.5 million people were in state prisons and almost 750,000 more in local jails, a scale of imprisonment unseen in American history or around the world. Our 2013 incarceration rate of 496 per 100,000 (down from an all-time high of 527 in 2007) was almost four times our incarceration rate of 137 per 100,000 in 1978, and it was the highest rate in the world. Home to only five percent of the world's population, the United States houses nearly *one quarter* of its prisoners. It is thus essential to understand both the causes and consequences of this unprecedented use of incarceration.

Chapter 9 examines what we know about the causes of the remarkable growth in US incarceration rates (and punishment more generally) over the past four decades. The rapid increase in imprisonment that started in the mid-1970s caught most analysts unawares, and it occurred after at least fifty years of stable incarceration rates (back to the 1920s, when national prisons statistics were first gathered). Not surprisingly, a lot of ink has been spilled in efforts to explain the sources of this boom, although we do not really understand its causes very well. Chapter 9 fleshes out the basic theories scholars have put forth to explain prison growth and development, and it considers what little empirical evidence we have about their validity. It then focuses in a bit more detail on one theory in particular, namely that the "politics of crime and incarceration" are uniquely pathological. It also discusses how race, class, and geography all interact to shape both the size and racial distribution of prison populations. It then concludes with a brief discussion of international comparisons: despite having crime rates that are relatively similar to those in Europe and Canada, our incarceration rate is stubbornly, and significantly, higher, and it is worth asking if foreign experiences can help us understand why we imprison so much more.

Chapter 10 turns its attention to the consequences of incarceration. It looks first at incarceration's impact on inmates, both while they are inside the prison and once they are released, considering such issues as imprisonment's effect on employment, health, marriage, and familial development. It then examines the effect incarceration, and mass incarceration in particular, has on communities. The most pressing question is whether incarceration reduces a crime, a surprisingly tough question to answer well. The chapter then concludes by looking at some of the collateral costs of incarceration on communities: punishment, like crime, is geographically concentrated, so large-scale incarceration has the ability to alter how communities function.

Chapter 11 then moves away from incarceration to other sanctions. While imprisonment receives the most attention, and appears to be responsible for a large share of state expenditures on punishment, it is not the dominant sanction: the 1.5 million people in state prisons and 750,000 in local jails comprise only one-third of the slightly more than eight million people under some form of correctional observation each day. This chapter discusses numerous alternatives to incarceration, such as probation, fines and asset forfeitures, drug- and other therapeutic-courts, domestic violence protection orders, shaming sanctions, and the various restrictions we place on sex offenders (civil confinement, registries, residency requirements, and techno-corrections such as monitoring bracelets). It considers both the basic nature of these punishments as well as evidence about their effectiveness.

Finally, Chapter 12 concludes by moving away from sentences to what comes next: re-entry. With 650,000 to 700,000 inmates leaving prison each year, how we handle their return has become an issue of increasing importance. This chapter considers the goals of, and rules imposed by, parole, as well as what sorts of reforms could prepare inmate for re-entry even before they leave prison. The results are fairly disappointing: by and large, the policies in place do not seem well-designed for facilitating re-entry and desistance, although the sheer volume of returning prisoners may now be encouraging states and counties to think about how to implement more-effective programs.

CHAPTER 9

SENTENCING POLICY AND THE RISE OF THE PRISON

The United States currently houses over 1.5 million people in prison and nearly 750,000 in jail. Two figures succinctly demonstrate just how extreme and unprecedented these numbers are. First, Figure 9–1 plots the US incarceration rate (just prisons, not jails) over time. Between 1925 and 1972 the rate hovered around 100 per 100,000, peaking at 137 in 1939; from 1972 to 2013, that rate soared from 93 to 487 per 100,000, peaking at 527 per 100,000 in 2007 (though the total prison *population* peaked in 2009 at over 1.61 million). So unexpected was this explosion in imprisonment that in 1979 the preeminent criminologist Alfred Blumstein wrote that he and another criminologist:

> [H]ave hypothesized that it is not crime that is stable, but the level of *punishment*, and imprisonment rate per capita in particular, that the society maintains around a constant level. The existence of such a stable imprisonment rate suggests that, as a nation's prison population begins to fluctuate, pressure is exerted to restore the prison population to that stable rate.[1]

They went on to suggest that if prison populations get too large, police may reduce arrests, prosecutors filings, and judges prison admissions, while parole boards may become more generous. Blumstein and Moitra's article could not have been timed worse, published at the exact moment the US incarceration rate passed its previous high (set in 1939) and started its four-decade surge. That someone with as deep an understanding of penal policy as Alfred Blumstein got things so wrong indicates just how unique and unanticipated this growth was.

---

[1] Alfred Blumstein and Soumyo Moitra, An Analysis of the Time Series of the Imprisonment Rate in the States of the United States: A Further Test of the Stability of Punishment Hypothesis, 70 J. CRIM. L. & CRIMINOLOGY 376, 376 (1979).

Figure 9–1: United States Incarceration Rate, 1925–2013

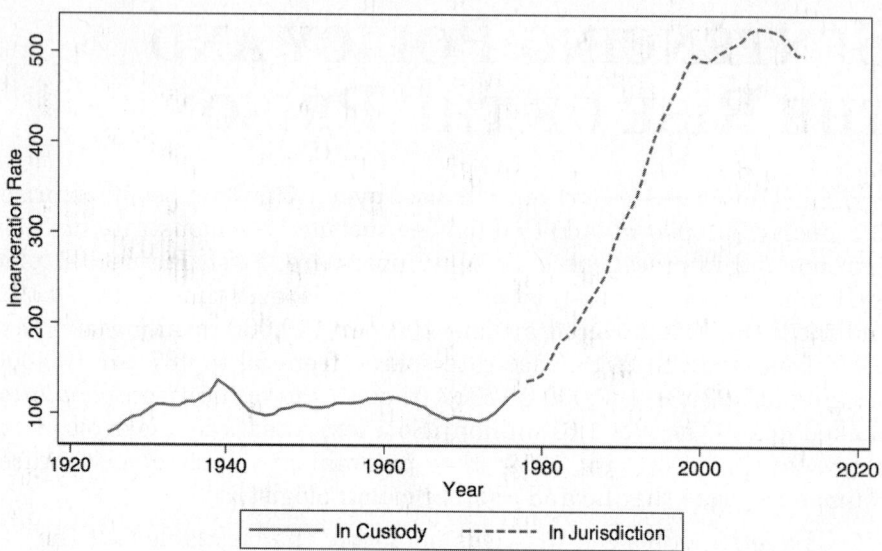

Figure 9–2 places the US prison population in a broader, international context, plotting the US incarceration rate alongside that from several other nations.[2] The US rate is the highest in the world, and the only countries with comparable levels of incarceration are not ones with which the US necessarily wishes to be associated. Our political allies all operate prison systems about three-and-half to seven times smaller than ours (on a per-capita basis)—and this despite the fact that violent crime is actually *higher* in Western Europe than in the US, and has been since about 1990.[3]

---

[2] Here the incarceration rate is that of prisons and jails combined. International comparisons have to use the combined prison-jail counts since not all countries run separate systems. The data come from ROY WALMSLEY, WORLD PRISON POPULATION LIST, 8th Ed. (2010).

[3] The relationship between crime and prison populations is quite complex, and we will look at it more closely in Chapter 10.

Figure 9–2: Select Incarceration Rates, 2008

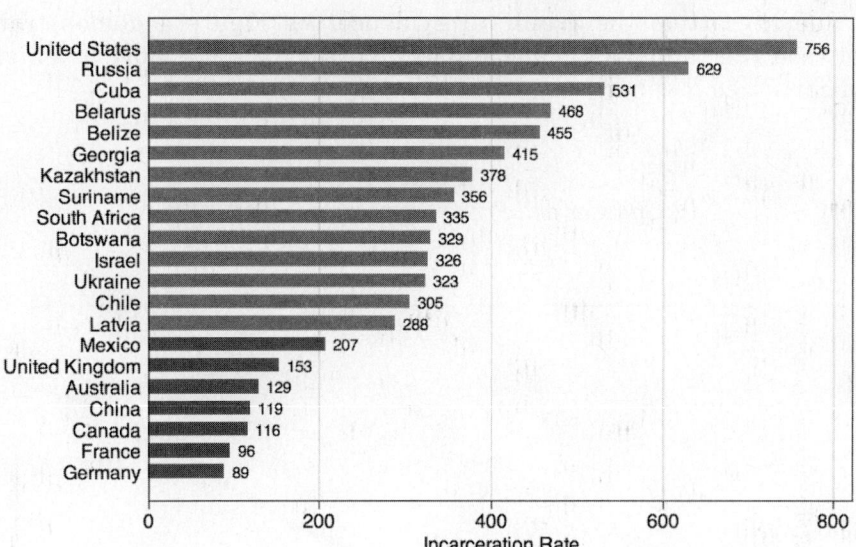

A. THE BASIC THEORIES OF PRISON GROWTH

So it is worth asking what has fueled this unique rise in US incarceration rates. The following reading summarizes the basic theories that numerous scholars have put forth over the years.

John F. Pfaff, *The Empirics of Prison Growth: A Critical Review and Path Forward*
98 J. CRIM. L. & CRIMINOLOGY 547, 552–565 (2008)

[Recent] efforts [to explain prison growth] fall into four broad schools of thought: the "crime theory," which links prison populations to crime rates; the "economic theory," to the importance of labor market and economic conditions; the "demographics theory," to shifts in race and age; and the "political theory," to changes in political ideology or manipulation by politicians seeking reelection. Four other, less overarching theories have been noted as well: the deinstitutionalization of the mental health system, the expansion of prison capacity, the imposition of population caps by federal courts, and the fiscal health of the states. Each of these theories also provides important insights into the mechanics of population growth. I will consider each in turn.

1. The Crime Theory

The crime theory posits that a powerful factor influencing incarceration rates is crime. Its simplest version is quite intuitive: rising crime rates should increase prison admissions and populations (and declines in crime should lead to corresponding reductions, perhaps with a lag). Yet this theory has often been viewed with suspicion. Perhaps this is due in part to the graphical evidence. As Figure 4 demonstrates, between 1960 and 2004 crime and incarceration did not move in a highly synchronized manner.

Figure 4
Offender and Prison Populations, 1960-2004

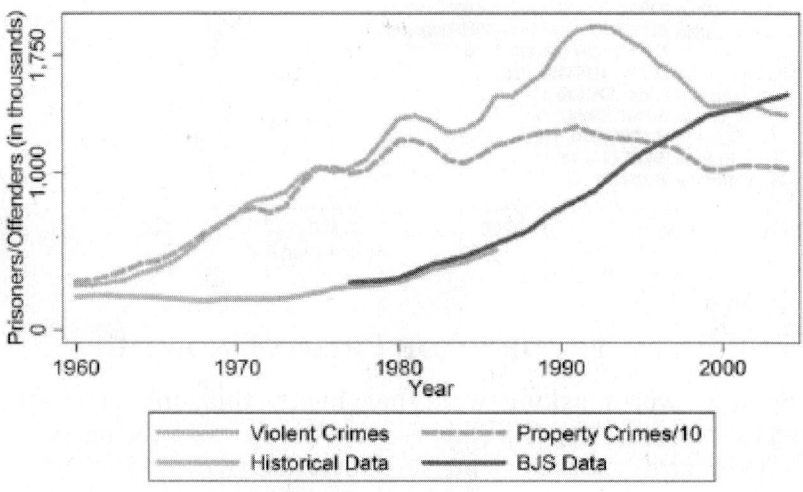

Source: BJS website: http://www.ojp.usdoj.gov/bjs.
Property crimes are divided by 10 to fit on same axes.

[Alfred Blumstein, though admitting that his stability-of-punishment hypothesis is incorrect,] has continued to argue that the relationship between crime and punishment is weak. In a recent article written with Allen Beck, he states that only 12% of the growth in state prison populations between 1980 and 1996 was tied to changes in offending (with the remaining 88% due to increased incarcerations and longer sentences). Nonetheless, [empirical studies indicate] that crime does in fact influence the incarceration rate.

2. The Economic Theory

The economic theory suggests that underlying economic conditions are powerful forces driving prison populations. [Georg] Rusche and [Otto] Kirchheimer's [1939] book [*Punishment and Social Structure*] is often considered the seminal work in this field. It argues that penal practices respond to labor conditions: the more abundant labor is, the less care the penal system shows to those who fall within its grasp. Rusche and Kirchheimer's theory, however, suffers from several shortcomings. . . . In particular, prisons often operate at a loss and thus not (as Rusche and

Kirchheimer claim) to the benefit of the state; penal practices often differ across states and countries with similar economic conditions; and ideology and politics surely play a role. Furthermore, such a theory over-anthropomorphizes capitalism. Penal practices can shape and control the labor market only if there is a high degree of coordination between police, judges, and non-legal actors in the business world.

Note, however, that even if Rusche and Kirchheimer and their successors failed to develop a convincing overarching theory, they are right to draw our attention to the potential importance of economic conditions. Judges may be more willing to sentence the unemployed, and to sentence them to longer sentences. And poverty can encourage crime and thus increase prison populations. In these cases, unemployment influences incarceration even though the judges are not involved directly in macro-level social control. When unemployment is higher, judges are simply more likely to face unemployed defendants at sentencing (and to give them longer sentences). Furthermore, greater income inequality may make the "underclass" appear more "different," leading judges—perhaps unconsciously—to sentence such defendants more harshly. Thus while theories of coordinated social control are problematic, it remains important to evaluate how economic factors operate in less direct, but still important, ways.

3. Demographic Theories

Given the interplay in American society among race, crime, and incarceration, it should come as no surprise that the theories linking race and prison populations are . . . complex. . . . Three strands in particular deserve attention. The first is the most direct, focusing on race's influence over day-to-day decisions concerning arrest, prosecution, and sentencing. This can be thought of as a theory of "institutional racism," with racial bias manifesting itself in the quotidian tasks that define the criminal justice system. Police may be more willing to arrest, district attorneys more willing to prosecute, juries more willing to convict, and judges more willing to incarcerate minorities (and to do so for longer terms). [Empirically, however,] the question of how institutional racism has influenced the size of the overall prison population remains relatively open.

The second strand [links] more punitive criminal policies to a strategic political backlash against the social changes of the 1960s, including the civil rights movement. Katherine Beckett provides a clear exposition of this position, arguing that political campaigns such as Barry Goldwater's 1964 presidential bid attempted to tie crime to political dissent, using attacks on the former to quash the latter. Randall Kennedy similarly notes that among the many roles race has played in criminal justice, one has been as a "thinly veiled code" to signal opposition to the social transformation started in the 1960s, especially with respect to civil rights.

The third strand is closely related to the crime theory. Advanced most strongly by Michael Tonry, it asserts that racial bias helped motivate (and continues to motivate) the war on drugs, and that this war has subsequently played a dominant role in the prison population surge. Tonry argues that changing arrest patterns fueled the growth in prison populations, with race playing an important role in these changes. Note, though, that Tonry's argument is equally consistent with racial indifference and with racial animus.

Though this nation's long-running problems with race have surely influenced prison populations, each of the three strands above suffers from important reservations. First, each theory, particularly that of institutional racism, has a hard time untangling the correlation between race and class. Not only may police, prosecutors, juries, judges, and parole boards treat whites better than blacks, but they may treat the rich better than the poor; even in the absence of any class bias, the rich may be better able to avoid prison (or longer sentences) because they can hire better lawyers. To the extent that race and class are correlated, isolating the effect of race may be difficult. . . .

Second, the actual effect of the political and rhetorical use of "crime" on prison populations is unmeasured. The route from political device to effective policy is long and complex. Not only is it often difficult for a legislature to pass a new law, but even once passed administrative intransigence can thwart meaningful implementation.

And finally, while it is undeniable that the war on drugs has had a disparate racial impact, two concerns with Tonry's argument deserve attention. First, . . . the impact of the war on drugs may have fallen disproportionately on the black population, but so too did the harms from the drug epidemics—crack in particular. Second, the effect of the war on drugs on overall prison populations is often overstated. Despite large numbers of arrests, relatively few drug offenders are sent to prison. Drug offenders make up only 20% of state prisoners;* property offenders comprise 20%, and violent offenders 50%. Even if every prisoner in 1998 whose primary offense was a drug charge were released, the total population would have been approximately 1 million instead of 1.3 million: that is still more than triple the population in 1977.

4. The Political Theories

[These will be discussed in Part B below.]

5. Four Other Important Factors

While the factors central to the four schools have received much of the attention, at least four other relevant variables have been contemplated as well. The first is the deinstitutionalization of the mentally ill that has taken place since the 1970s. Steven Raphael notes that mental hospital inpatient rates generally declined over the period

---

* *Ed. note*: Since this article was written, that percentage has dropped to 17%.

from 1971 to 1996, sometimes sharply (in Texas, for example, they fell from nearly 325 per 100,000 residents in 1971 to around 50 per 100,000 residents in 1996), and his results suggest that deinstitutionalization was responsible for between 48,000 to 148,000 of the prisoners incarcerated in 1996, or between 4.5% and 14% of the total prison population.

A second important factor is prison capacity. Some researchers have suggested that not only are new prisons built in anticipation of greater prison populations, but that defendants are more likely to be incarcerated the more cell space is available: capacity can induce incarceration. The central idea is that, on the margin, a judge is more willing to incarcerate—and to do so more severely—the more space he thinks is available. Such a theory assumes that judges are aware of prison capacity in their jurisdictions and that they have the discretion to adjust their sentencing accordingly. The first seems reasonable, since judges certainly have contacts with various relevant actors in the criminal justice system. The second depends on a state's sentencing regime.

The third factor is related to capacity, namely federal court orders imposing population caps and other restrictions in response to severe overcrowding. The 1965 case of *Talley v. Stephens* marked the first foray by a federal court into state prison oversight. Ultimately forty-seven states and the District of Columbia have found their prison systems subject to judicial orders, all but seven to a significant degree. Most important for the question here, approximately twelve states* have had their entire prison systems—rather than particular facilities—declared unconstitutional due (at least) to overcrowding and, as a result, have been subject to extensive federal judicial regulation; the subsequent population caps slowed population growth in those states.

The final important factor is the general financial and budgetary health of the state in question. Constructing and maintaining prisons is a costly endeavor, so wealthier states are in a better position to expand and maintain capacity. On the margin states are more likely to invest in the criminal justice system the better their economies and the more tax revenues they collect. Two recent studies by the Vera Institute of Justice indicate that states have recently begun looking for ways to slow, if not reverse, the growth of prisons in light of tighter post-2001 budgets. In 2002, for example, twenty-five states cut expenditures on corrections; only higher education spending was cut in more (twenty-nine). This is consistent with a positive relationship between a state's economic health and its incarceration rate.

---

* *Ed. note*: That number is now thirteen: since 2009, the entire California prison system has been declared unconstitutionally overcrowded and has been operating under the supervision of the federal judiciary.

A.1. OUR LIMITED EMPIRICAL UNDERSTANDING OF PRISON GROWTH

While the explanatory theories of prison growth are widely known and fairly well accepted, there is much disagreement about the absolute and relative impact each of them has had on prison growth. Unfortunately, the empirical studies that have been done on the issue are all deeply flawed, leaving us with little understanding of how the various factors matter. Here we want to look at two major conceptual problems with the current models that have implications for our broader understanding of how the criminal justice system operates.[4]

First, almost all the empirical work on prison growth uses state-level data; those that do not rely, even more troubling, on national-level data. Yet, as we have seen repeatedly before, and as we will see even more so in the pages ahead, criminal justice in the United States is less a state issue (and even less a national one), and more a county-level concern that interacts in poorly-understood ways with state-level institutions. Thus state-level analyses of, say, the impact of unemployment or inequality or racial distributions on prison populations overlook a lot of important county-level variations.

For example, the percent of the population that is black in New York State is roughly the same as that in Arkansas. But blacks in New York are densely concentrated in a few large urban areas, while those in Arkansas are spread more evenly across south-eastern half of the state. A state-level study would treat New York and Arkansas as being similar, since at a state-level of aggregation they *are* similar. But the county-level variation in concentration surely influences penal outcomes.

Second, and related, most empirical projects have not attempted to identify *where* in the criminal justice system growth is taking place. They attempt to estimate the effect of, say, crime rates or labor conditions or politics on "total prison population" or "total prison admissions." But total prison admissions are determined by choices made by criminals, police, prosecutors and defense attorneys, judges, sentencing commissions, and legislators; total population adds in parole boards and governors as well. There is absolutely no reason to assume that a factor like income inequality has the exact same influence on each of these institutions. So if a model reports that a 1% increase in income inequality increases prison admissions by 0.7%, we do not really know what that means—even if it is correct—since it is a complicated average of the effect of income inequality on each institution. In other words, most studies have

---

[4] A third major problem with many, if not all, of the studies is that they make numerous important statistical-methodological errors. While these errors are important from an empirical perspective, they are less relevant for our legal understanding of prison growth. For those who are interested in the methodological failings of these empirical papers, I discuss them at length in John F. Pfaff, *The Empirics of Prison Growth: A Critical Review and Path Forward*, 98 J. CRIM. L. & CRIMINOLOGY 547 (2008).

put the causal horse before the cart, attempting to understand "why" before narrowing down the question of "who."

So let's ask: who is responsible?

A.2. THE IMPORTANCE OF PROSECUTORS TO PRISON GROWTH

Prison growth can occur due to changes at one or more of six steps: increases in crime, in arrests per crime, in prosecutions per arrest, in convictions per prosecution, in admissions per conviction, and in time served per admission. Each step involves different actors at different levels of government. Police, for example, exert significant control over arrest decisions, although upstream actors can try to influence those choices (like when legislatures expand asset-forfeiture laws to try to induce police to go after more drug offenders). Prosecutions are, obviously, decided by prosecutors, although state legislators can give them more or less power through the criminal and sentencing codes, and police can limit prosecutorial options through the evidence they gather (or don't gather). And so on. It should be clear by now that teasing out a convincing causal story requires a significant amount of care.

So it is useful to try to understand, at least roughly, how responsible each stage is for prison growth, even if the outcome at each stage is the product of numerous institutional interactions. Surprisingly, at least since the mid-1990s, when the crime drop began, it appears that almost all the growth has taken place in exactly one stage: the prosecutor's decision to file felony charges against an arrestee. Our understanding of what happened prior to the mid-1990s is restricted by limitations in available data, although it is likely that the story during that time is more complicated, due to complex reactions to crime rates that rose steadily from 1960s to 1980, with an additional dramatic spike in violence from 1985 to 1991.

Focusing just on the post-1991 period, however, is quite useful, since it helps us understand what forces drive growth today, enabling us to think more clearly about how to structure policies going forward. The following results are generally taken from a study of thirty-four states, which form a reasonably representative sample of the country as a whole, between 1994 and 2009.[5]

1. Crime. Across all fifty states between 1994 and 2009, violent crime fell by 48% and property crime by 43%.

2. Arrests. Between 1994 and 2009, total arrests in the 34-state sample for serious violent and property crimes, as well

---

[5] The choice of states was determined by the availability of the data. These results all come from John F. Pfaff, *The Centrality of Prosecutors to Prison Growth: An Empirical Assessment*, available on-line at http://papers.ssrn.com/sol3/papers.cfm?abstract_id=1884674.

as non-marijuana drug offenses—since marijuana arrests rarely result in incarceration—fell by almost 10%.

3. Felony filings per arrest. While the total number of arrests fell by almost 10% between 1994 and 2009—from 3.74 million to 3.39 million—the total number of felony filings *rose* by 37%, from 1.39 million to 1.91 million. The fraction of arrests that turn into in felony filing rose thus from 0.37 to 0.57.

4. Admissions per filing. Here there was almost no change: the fraction of filings that led to admissions varied from 0.26 to 0.27 between 1994 and 2009. It is worth noting that admissions per filing does elide two steps: convictions per filing and admissions per conviction. Unfortunately, there is not enough reliable case-level data to get a good measure of convictions.

Thus felony filings have been the primary—at times seemingly almost the sole—driver of prison *admissions*, at least since the mid-1990s; filings have risen by 37% and admissions by 40%. But we can take this argument even further. Despite all the anecdotal examples and conclusory claims about "throwing away the key," there is no evidence of systematic increases in time served. Thus, since time served has remained relatively flat over this period, by driving admissions felony filings also are the main engine behind *total prison growth*.

Given how counter-intuitive this is, it is worth examining a bit more closely the claim that time spent in prison hasn't increased over the years. Figure 9–3, which plots the annual number of people admitted to and released from prison, provides an intuitive sense of why this result should not, in fact, be surprising. If sentences were getting tougher and tougher, we would expect that the number released to grow at an increasingly slower rate than the number admitted, but except for a few years in the late 1980s, we simply do not see that happening. In fact, since the late 1990s the two lines have converged, suggesting that our sentences have become more *lenient*. And more-rigorous studies back this intuitive story up.[6]

---

[6] See, e.g., John F. Pfaff, *The Myths and Realities of Correctional Severity: Evidence from the National Corrections Reporting Program*, 13 AM. L. & ECON. REV. 491 (2001); John F. Pfaff, *The Durability of Prison Populations*, 2010 U. CHI. LEGAL FORUM 73 (2010); Pfaff, *Centrality of Prosecutors*, supra note 5.

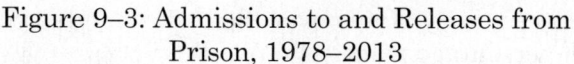

Figure 9–3: Admissions to and Releases from Prison, 1978–2013

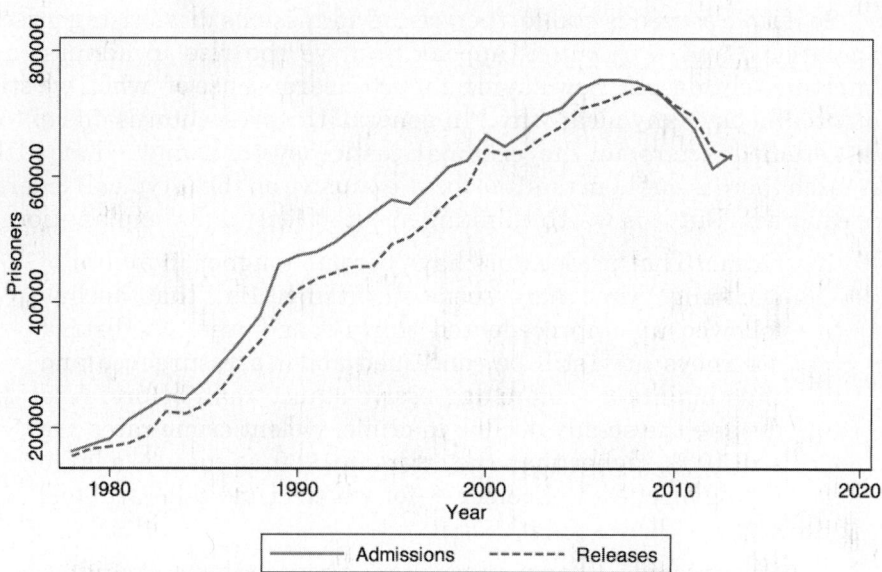

One potential concern to think about, however, is the role of parole practices. If a large number of inmates are paroled after a short time in prison but then quickly violated back, over and over again, then official "time served" statistics may look short, even though inmates are in effect serving long sentences on the "installment plan." Here's an example of just how problematic this effect *could* be: In State 1, a defendant is required to serve 100% of an 18-month sentence for a crime. In State 2, a defendant convicted of the same offense receives a 24-month sentence but is paroled after 12; three months later he violates parole and returned to serve out the last 9 months of his sentence. State 2 would appear to have more people being admitted for shorter stints than State 1, but in reality State 2 should be thought of as a *longer*-sentence state. In other words, *apparent* time served can fall even as *real* time served is growing, just given how the data are generally gathered.

Yet depending on the theoretical concerns, this effect does not appear to be that strong. Data from the National Corrections Reporting Program over the years 2000 to 2012 suggests that most inmates serve only one or two stints in prison: the door may be revolving, but it is not revolving a lot.[7] Furthermore, outside of California, which has traditionally relied more heavily on parole releases and violations than other states to manage its oversized prison population, parole violators comprise only about 30% to 40% of admissions; more important, that

---

[7] John F. Pfaff, The War on Drugs: Limited Impact, Limited Legislative Options, 52 HARV. J. LEGIS'N 173 (2015).

share has been relatively stable over the past ten or so years, rising by only about ten percentage points.

So if time served is stable, then rising admissions drive rising prison populations, and prosecutors appear to drive the rise in admissions. Unfortunately, despite now having a much clearer sense of "who," we still don't really have any idea "why." In general, the prosecutor is one of the least-studied actors in the criminal justice system, and what little research there is on them tends to focus exclusive on the (atypical) federal bureaucracy. But it is worth thinking about at least a few explanations.

1. Crime. That prosecutors have become tougher in an era of declining crime may seem surprising. But that decline followed an unprecedented thirty-year surge. So district attorneys may still be concerned about a resurgence and thus maintain a more aggressive stance than before. And despite the steady decline in crime, violent crime rates are still 100% higher than they were in 1960, so there is a large voting block—the Boomers—for whom crime rates still feel high.

2. Prior records. Even if prosecutors' attitudes haven't shifted, due to the crime boom they still face a pool of defendants will longer records than before: defendants in 1995 or 2005 are more likely to have a longer record than those in 1985 or 1975. If prosecutors are generally harsher towards recidivists, their increased toughness may just reflect the nature of defendants they face.

3. Budgets. It's important to never lose sight of the moral hazard problem of county prosecutors and state prison budgets. But that moral hazard problem is as prevalent today as it was fifty years ago, so why would that *change* prosecutor behavior? Perhaps the growth in federal grants to law enforcement, often tied to certain punitiveness benchmarks, has encouraged district attorneys to take even more advantage of it. If nothing else, the moral hazard problem at least provides prosecutors with the *ability* to cheaply become more aggressive, even if that increase in aggression is driven by other factors.

4. The next election. As we saw above, district attorneys do not usually face meaningful electoral threat. But what if they are more punitive because they now have greater political ambitions (perhaps because the crime boom made law enforcement experience a more-appealing trait on the campaign trail)? Thus the toughness isn't about winning another district attorney race, but rather about helping a run for state attorney general, governor, Congressperson, Senator (state or federal)?

At this point, we can only toss out hypotheses, since prosecutors' offices remain empirical black boxes: they are the only major institution in the criminal justice system that does not regularly report extensive statistics and data. So it is difficult to say more about why prosecutors act the way they do, or why their behavior appears to have changed over time. But it is nonetheless quite helpful to understand at least where the growth is taking place.

QUESTIONS

1. **Long records and prosecutors.** What does the age profile of offending imply about the effect of longer records due to the crime boom? How long should we expect such an effect to persist? How relevant are longer records due to the pre-1991 crime surge to filing and sentencing decisions in 2010?

2. **Reforming the prosecutor.** If it is true that prosecutors are the primary engines of prison growth, what types of reforms would someone looking to rein in prison growth propose? Are some more politically viable than others?

A.3. THE ROLE OF CRIME

Before looking at the role of politics in prison growth, it is useful to touch on the explanatory variable that seems to be the most obvious, but one of the harder ones to evaluate: crime. Roughly speaking, we should expect prison populations to rise when crime rates rise and fall when they fall. Figure 9–4 plots the incarceration rate and the index crime rate since 1960. Three trends emerge: between 1960 and 1973, the incarceration rate was flat or falling while crime grew; between 1973 and 1991, both the incarceration rate and the crime rate rose; and from 1991 to the present, the crime rate has fallen while the incarceration rate has continued to rise. In short, no clear pattern immediately emerges.

But Figure 9–4 is a difficult graph to interpret, because the relationship between crime and incarceration is complex. In particular, it is endogenous, which means that while crime rates influence prison populations, so too do prison populations influence crime rates. On the one hand, as crime goes up, more people are arrested and incarcerated, leading to a positive relationship between crime and incarceration. On the other hand, as incarceration goes up, crime goes down, leading to a negative relationship. Because of these dueling effects—plus the fact that incarceration rates are clearly shaped by more than just crime rates, and these other factors are changing all the time as well—the simple correlation shown in a graph cannot really tell us what the causal connection is between crime and incarceration, though many commentators frequently try to do just that.[8]

Figure 9–4: Crime and Incarceration, 1960–2010

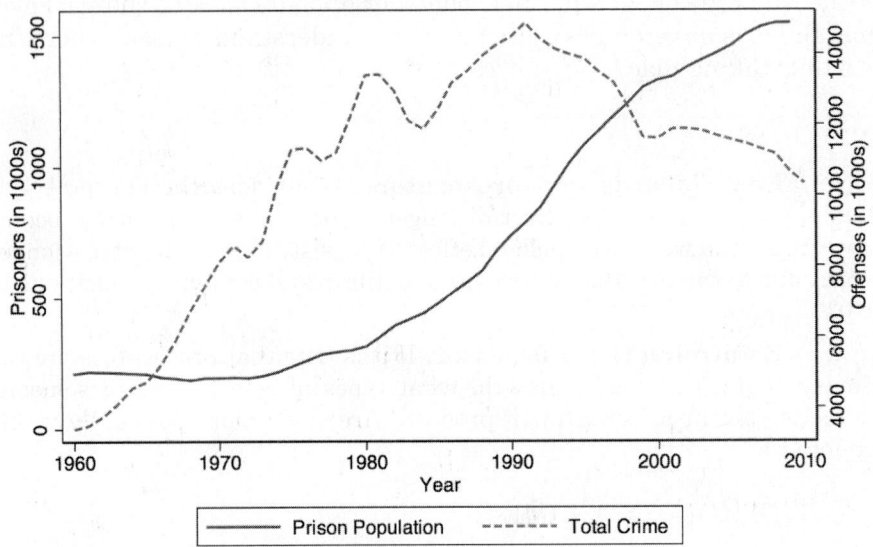

The best way to escape the problem of endogeneity is to run a randomized trial: choose twenty-five states at random and increase their crime rates and compare their subsequent prison populations to those in the twenty-five states that did not have their crime rates forcibly pushed up. (Or, to understand how prison populations shape crime rates, randomly increase the prison populations in twenty-five states and compare crime rates.) But such a proposal is clearly ludicrous. It is impossible for analysts to exogenously increase crime rates—and even if they could it would be completely unethical and political unpalatable to do so.

So we must rely on less direct, and thus noisier and less reliable, methods. Only one study, by Yair Listokin, has done so, using a popular but often controversial technique called instrumental variables.[9] Listokin's results suggest that, at least between 1985 and 1997, a 1% increase in crime led to a 1% increase in the prison population, once he controls for several other possible causal factors. This result should be treated with significant caution: the uncertainty around it is significant, and his approach likely suffers from some important-but-hard-to-

---

[8] The Statistical Appendix discusses endogeneity in more depth. It is worth stressing that these sorts of tricky, endogenous relationships are common in the criminal justice system, though they are often overlooked—at great cost—by the empirical projects that examine it.

[9] Yair Listokin, Does More Crime Mean More Prisoners? An Instrumental Variables Approach, 46 J. L. & ECON. 181 (2003).

measure methodological limitations.[10] But taking it at face value for a moment, two important implications flow from this result.

First, if correct, it implies that between 1973 and 1991 the increase in crime rates explains about half of the increase in incarceration rates. This means both that crime is the most important explanation for prison growth during the crime boom, but also that a lot of other factors played roles as well. Second, it suggests that the crime drop that started in 1991 acted as a major *brake* on prison growth since then, as violent crime fell by 48% and property crime by 43% between 1991 and 2010. That said, Listokin's data ends in 1997, and it could be that the relationship between crime and incarceration is different during a crime surge than during a crime drop, so we do not want to extrapolate his results to the present without more (currently-unavailable) data.

In short: rising crime appears to have been an important explanatory factor during the crime surge that peaked in 1991. And rising crime rates likely had indirect effects as well, such as by changing political attitudes towards punishment more generally. Since the crime drop began, however, the relationship between serious crime and prison populations is less clear.

A.4. THE SURPRISINGLY MINIMAL ROLE OF DRUG OFFENSES

Most empirical studies, such as Listokin's, focus on the relationship between prison population and serious violent and property crimes. But another major crime category frequently charged with driving prison populations is drugs, with many commentators pointing to the War on Drugs as a major engine of incarceration growth. The sheer number of people arrested for drug offenses certainly suggests that this could be an important factor. In 1980, 580,900 people were arrested for drug violations, comprising 5.5% of all 10.5 million arrests that year; in 2009, 1.66 million were arrested on drug charges, making up 12.2% of that year's 13.7 million arrests. In total, over 38.7 million drug arrests were made between 1980 and 2009 (or 9.5% of the total 407 million arrests). In fact, more people are arrested each year on drug charges than are incarcerated for all crimes.

Yet drug arrests ultimately have not been the primary engine of prison growth, at least not directly. Figure 9–5 plots the percent of all

---

[10] What comes next is a technical explanation aimed at those with some background in statistics; skipping over this will not have any impact for the rest of this discussion. Listokin uses abortion as an instrument for crime, building off the work of Steven Levitt and John Donohue. The problem is that it seems likely that it is only an imperfect instrument. Abortion works as an instrument if it is correlated with crime but otherwise uncorrelated with prison admission rates (Listokin's dependent variable). But it is plausible to assert that abortion influenced, say, women's earning power and thus state tax revenue, and that state tax revenue has shaped states' willingness to incarcerate. Unfortunately, it is the very nature of—and the very problem with—IVs that it is impossible to test empirically whether such indirect correlations exist, nor can the implications of their presence be easily quantified.

state prisoners who are serving time for drug offenses. While the share rises strikingly from 6.4% in 1980 to almost 22% by 1990, non-drug offenders always constitute at least 78% of all prisoners, even in 1990, when the share of drug offenders peaked (21.8%). In 2009 drug offenders comprised only 17.8% of all state prisoners. Including federal inmates, who are much more likely to be serving time for drug crimes, raises the 2009 value only to 21.8%.

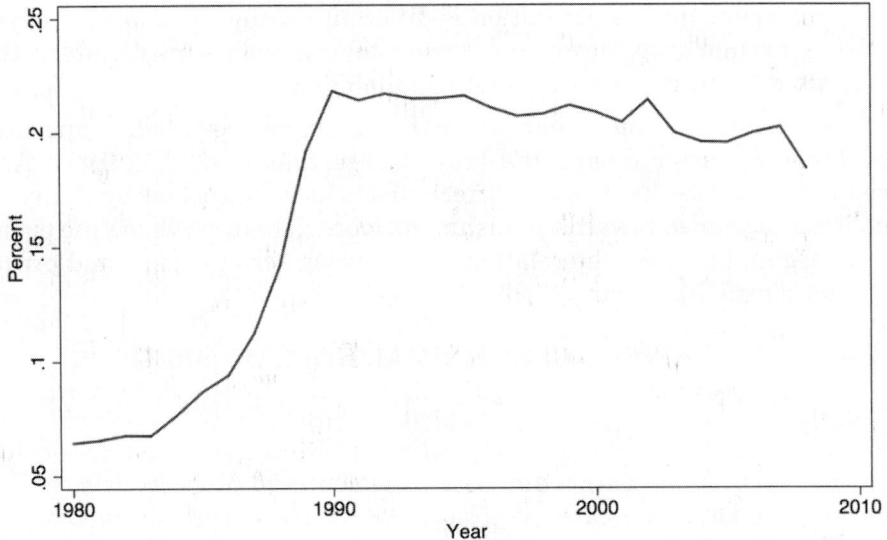

Figure 9–5: Percent of Prisoners Serving Time For Drug Offenses, 1980–2010

Given these relatively low percentages, why are people so quick to blame drug incarcerations for prison growth? Table 9–1 suggests a possible answer.

Table 9–1: Share of State Prisoners by Offense Type, 1980 and 2009

	1980	2009	% Change	% Contrib
Violent	173,300	724,300	318%	51%
Property	89,300	261,200	192%	16%
Drug	19,000	242,200	1175%	21%
Other	12,400	134,500	985%	11%

The *rate of growth* of drug prisoners dwarfs that of violent and property offenders: it is approximately 2.6 times that of violent crimes and 5 times that of property crimes. But base rates matter. In 1980 prisons held nearly ten times as many violent offenders as drug inmates and nearly five times as many property prisoners. So while the rate of growth for violent inmates was slower than that for drug inmates, the additional 551,000 violent offenders added to state prisons between 1980 and 2009 comprise 51% of the 1,068,200 total prisoners added during that time; violent and property offenders combined are responsible for more than two-thirds of that growth. Including Federal prisoners does not change these results noticeably. Overall, drug inmates contributed only about 20% to the growth in incarceration—not a trivial number by any means, but less significant than one often hears.

Table 9–1, however, does undersell the role of drug convictions slightly. Penal policy was not invariant between 1980 and 2009: priorities changed during that time. And if we recalculate Table 9–1 by breaking it into two periods, 1980–1990 and 1991–2009, we see that drug incarcerations did matter more in the early years (almost on a par with, but slightly less than, the incarceration of violent offenders)—but thus *even less so today.*

Table 9–2: Various Offenses' Contribution to State Prison Growth, 1980–1990, 1990–2009

	1980	1990	2009	% Contrib, 1980–90	% Contrib, 1990–2009
Total	294,000	681,400	1,362,000		
Violent	173,300	316,600	724,300	36%	60%
Property	89,300	173,700	261,200	22%	13%
Drug	19,000	148,600	242,200	33%	14%
Other	12,400	45,500	134,500	9%	13%

That's not to say that the War on Drugs is irrelevant, but whatever effect it has is more indirect than the conventional accounts suggest. Police may target those with drug (or other) priors more aggressively for non-drug offenses, and prosecutors may be more likely to charge such defendants, and to charge them with more-serious offenses. And to the extent that non-drug offenses are committed by those addicted to drugs or in furtherance of drug transactions, our insistence on treating drugs a criminal problem rather than a public health one may foreclose more-efficient treatment and legalization/decriminalization options. Furthermore, drug enforcement itself can undermine social capital in high-enforcement neighborhoods by removing relatively non-violent residents who make a net positive contribution to community stability.[11] All these effects surely matter, but their impact is indirect and difficult to measure empirically.

---

[11] These ideas are fleshed out more fully in Pfaff, *War on Drugs*, supra note 7.

A.5. THE DEINSTITUTIONALIZATION OF THE MENTALLY ILL

Another possible engine of prison growth has been the deinstitutionalization of the mentally ill. Between the 1950s and the 1990s, the number of people confined in mental hospitals fell by over 80%, from over 500,000 to under 100,000. Part of this trend reflected the rise of outpatient care and improved pharmacological options, and part of it changing attitudes about what constituted mental illness. But part of the decline likely reflected reduced access to mental health care. And while the mentally ill are much more likely to be the victims of crime than the perpetrators, the lack of access to hospitalization and other treatment options may lead some mentally ill to commits crimes they otherwise would not have, and thus to end up in prison.

Two scholars, Steven Raphael and Michael Stoll, looked at state-level data between 1971 and 1996 to estimate how many additional inmates were serving time in prison due to the deinstitutionalization of the mentally ill.[12] Acknowledging that any such model is going to be imprecise, they reported that somewhere between 28% and 86% of prisoners with mental illnesses would not have been in prison but for deinstitutionalization. This translates into 4.5% to 14% of the 1996 state prison population, or somewhere between 48,000 to 148,000 of the slightly more than 1 million inmates housed in state institutions that year. A later study that looked at prison and jail inmates, and limited itself to serious mental illness, estimated that nearly 310,000 of the 1.9 million people in either institution—or 16%, on par with Raphael's and Stoll's numbers—suffered from a disease such as severe depression, schizophrenia, bipolar disorder, etc.[13]

Perhaps one of the more provocative analyses of deinstitutionalization and incarceration is by Bernard Harcourt.[14] Defining "total institutionalized population" as those locked up *both* in hospitals and prisons, he notes that even by 2000 the rate of institutionalization remained *below* what it was in the 1950s, due to the number of people hospitalized in the earlier period; if we include jails, the total institutionalization rate reaches new highs in the late 1990s. In other words, the desire to lock people up that we saw in the 1980s and beyond was not something new, but a return to old practices, just via a different institution: the prison, not the hospital.

---

[12] Steven Raphael and Michael Stoll, *Assessing the Contribution of the Deinstitutionalization of the Mentally Ill to Growth in the U.S. Incarceration Rate*, 42 J. LEGAL STUDIES 187 (2013).

[13] H. Richard Lamb & Linda E. Weinberger, *The Shift of Psychiatric Inpatient Care From Hospitals to Jails and Prisons*, 33 J. AM. PSYCHIATRY & L. 529 (2005).

[14] Bernard E. Harcourt, *An Institutionalization Effect: The Impact of Mental Hospitalization and Imprisonment on Homicide in the United States, 1934–2001*, 40 J. LEGAL STUDIES 39 (2011).

Harcourt then goes on to produce a provocative graph, reproduced here, plotting murder rates (the dashed line) against total incarceration rates:

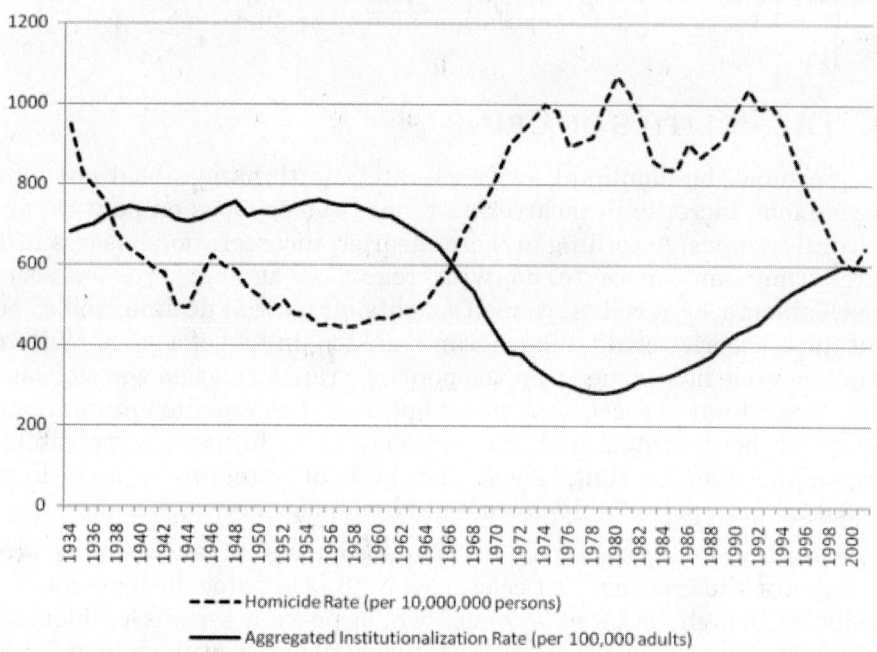

The basic point is this: when institutionalization in *either* a hospital or prison is high, homicide (the most reliably-recorded offense) is low, and when institutionalization goes down, homicide appears to rise. What makes this result so peculiar is that while we locked up people in the 1950s at similar rates as in the 1990s, the people themselves were quite different, namely older, whiter, and more female—all traits negatively correlated with homicide offending.

One possible explanation for this striking correlation is that some of the relationship between crime and incarceration may be spurious. Perhaps as people's attitudes towards crime get harsher, institutionalization goes up (due to harsher policies) and crime goes down—not due to the harsher policies themselves, but due to the *attitudes* that *drive* those policies. Or perhaps our tolerance for deviance is lower when society feels more stable (the 1950s or 1990s, compared to the 1960s and 1970s), leading to (proportionally) more people being locked up during lower-crime periods. The more powerful such attitudinal effects, perhaps the less important incarceration rates, and thus the less important who it is we are locking up.

Obviously, such attitudinal effects could explain only part of the story, and there is no clear answer yet to what Harcourt has revealed.

But it does force us to think a bit more carefully about how we define the "incarcerated" population and the complicated relationship between institutionalization and offending.

Question: Are there other groups we should include in the "total incarceration" population along the lines suggested by Harcourt?

B. THE POLITICS OF CRIME

Perhaps the dominant approach lately to thinking about our four-decade long increase in incarceration has been to focus on political and cultural changes. According to these theories, incarceration has less to do with crime and more to do with reactions against broader social developments: civil rights, women's rights, industrial decline, and so on. But these theories could tell too grand and too unified of a story; William Stuntz for one has argued that the political transformation was not some major, coordinated reaction to social upheaval but was the unintentional result of poorly-integrated institutions with diffused responsibility responding ineptly (but, given the lack of integration and direct accountability, predictably) to changes in demography and crime.

Stuntz's theory is likely the more compelling: as we have seen repeatedly, the criminal justice system in the US is too disaggregated to really be thought of as a "system," which poses a serious problem for coordinated-response theories. But these theories still yield a lot of important insights about how the criminal justice system operates—even if the various agencies are not coordinated, for example, they still may be (independently) responding in similar ways to similar political or ideological changes—so it is important to understand their insights as well as those of Stuntz.

The following passage briefly summarizes the basic themes of the current political theory of prison growth as well as some concerns with their arguments.

John F. Pfaff, *The Micro and Macro Causes of Prison Growth*
28 Ga. St. U. L. Rev. 1239 (2012)

Perhaps the most ambitious general [political] theory is that developed by David Garland in his book *The Culture of Control*. Simplifying somewhat, Garland argues that a wave of cultural and economic shocks during the 1960s and 1970s—the oil crisis, the decline of industrialization, changing gender roles, the Civil Rights movement—led citizens in the United States (and the United Kingdom) to fundamentally rethink the proper goal of government. Voters lost faith in the government's ability to *provide for* them via the welfare state, and instead asked the state to *protect* them *from* outside threats, crime in particular. This political reordering privileged retributivism and incapacitation over rehabilitation, and populist policies over more technocratic ones.

Another theory, advanced by Theodore Caplow and Jonathan Simon, suggests that politicians focused more on crime starting in the 1970s due to the rise of "identity politics." Issues such as abortion and civil rights are polarizing topics that provide little room for compromise, and thus little room for politicians to draw voters away from their opponents. But there was a strong national consensus about the need to be "tough on crime," so politicians used the issue to try to poach voters from the other party. There is some quantitative support for Caplow and Simon's theory. One paper, for example, has demonstrated that a state's prison admission rate appears to rise as the majority party's control of the legislature becomes more uncertain. This is consistent with politicians choosing to deploy "tough on crime" policies to attract voters in contested elections.

Katherine Beckett has put forth a more cynical argument, namely that politicians stoke people's fear of crime to scare them into voting for them—tough-on-crime rhetoric is less a response to the public's genuine fear of crime but rather an attempt to make the public fear crime in the first place. Her evidence for this is survey data suggests the public's fear of crime *lags* politicians' rhetoric about it instead of *leading* it.

A common theme ties these theories together. Whether due to the public's loss of faith in the government, to polarizing political issues taking on increased importance, or to efforts to literally "scare up" votes, these theories argue that by the 1970s politicians had begun to devote increasing attention to criminal justice issues. And there is no doubt that each of these theories has some merit to it. But it is worth asking whether these theories remain compelling today.

A key limitation to all these theories is that they pay too little attention to the spike in crime that started in the early 1960s. Though concurrent with broad social changes, the dramatic rise in crime between 1960 and 1991 [*Ed. note*: see Fig. 9.4 above] . . . surely influenced people's views about the proper role of government. In fact, [that] Figure . . . may understate why crime became so politically salient. Figure 11 plots what I will call the "effective" incarceration rate: not the number of prisoners per 100,000 people, but the number of prisoners per 1,000 violent and per 1,000 property crimes.

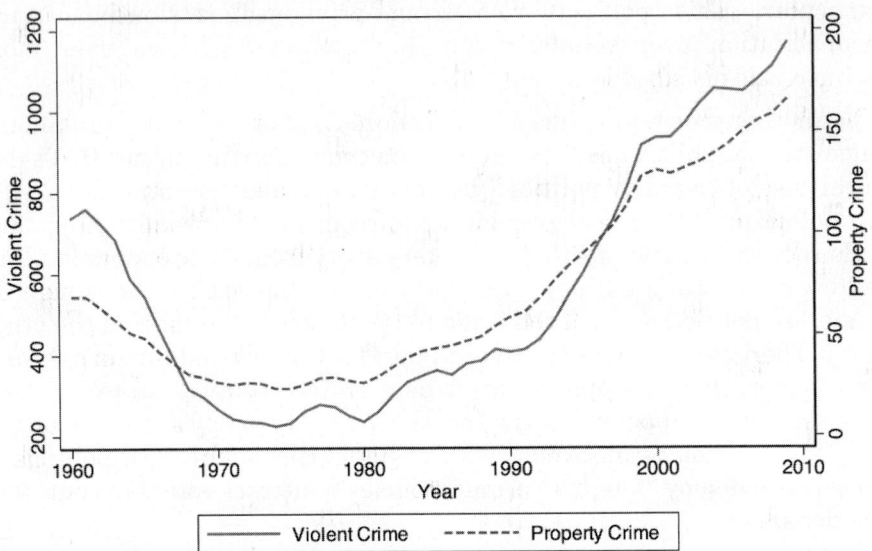

[T]he effective incarceration rate actually *declined* at the start of the crime boom and then remained flat into the early 1980s. Such an apparent "failure" of the criminal justice system likely amplified whatever concerns the crime wave was producing on its own. It thus seems unlikely that the punitive "turn" occurred independently of the crime boom, which then suggests that the "politics of crime" of the high-crime 1970s may be qualitatively different than those of the low-crime 2010s.

And at least at the national level, there is some anecdotal evidence consistent with this claim. Crime policy has not played an important role in the past several Presidential or Congressional elections. And it is worth noting that during the 2011–12 Republican Presidential primary race, no candidate opposing Newt Gingrich's bid for the party's nomination has raised the fact that he helped establish "Right on Crime," a conservative group committed to reducing prison populations.

Unfortunately, our understanding of local-level politics is much weaker. To start, the interest groups that are powerful at the state level are not necessarily the same as those that are powerful at the federal level; there are surely state/local differences as well, but these are even harder to uncover. Moreover, state and local politicians often face different electoral pressures as well. State legislative elections, for example, are often much less contested than those for Congress, and local elections may be less contested still. Given evidence linking punitiveness more to electoral vulnerability than to conservativeness, differences in contestation may be important. That said, county-level actors could be subject to similar political pressures or cultures as state- and national-level actors, and it certainly would be surprising if there were no correlation at all. But to the extent county-level actors are driving prison growth, we need a richer (any?) understanding of the particular political environments in which they operate.

Nonetheless, these theories still provide valuable insight into how local politicians may behave in the years ahead, and what policies may be more or less viable. For example, many reforms put forth these days are more technocratic in nature: actuarial risk scales, diversion courts, various forms of technocorrections. If these programs are scaled up too quickly, or implemented poorly, they could engender significant pushback. A public whose views are still more "protect from" than "provide for" may not have a great tolerance for technocratic error—although that tolerance may be higher during periods of lower crime.

More generally, the decline in crime suggests that crime is less politically salient overall these days, whether as a tool for reaching out to voters from the other party (as Caplow and Simon suggest) or as a means of playing on people's fears (as Beckett argues). The on-going financial and economic malaise surely plays a role in this. But relatively low crime rates have reduced crime's importance as well. This implies that politicians have room to experiment now that they did not have even a few years ago. Yet the work of Garland, Beckett, Caplow and Simon and others cautions against taking too many risks: if crime starts to rise again, its political salience may very well return.

A more specific branch of the political theory considers the extent to which some people have tried to use the criminal justice system to roll back gains that minorities made via the Civil Rights movement. Some, like Michelle Alexander, argue that arrests, incarceration, and post-release collateral restrictions are used as a form of political repression. Others, like Michael Tonry, make a more indirect claim, that the collateral costs of incarceration are politically tolerable because they fall disproportionately on minorities. Politicians thus reap the benefits of appearing tough on crime without facing the full political costs of their actions.

It is clear that race and punishment interact in troubling ways. Blacks make up approximately 12% of the US population, but by the late 2000s they comprised 28.3% of all arrests, 38% of all those convicted of felonies, and 38% of all prisoners. And even though blacks are over-represented among poorer Americans, these disparities (at least for convictions and incarceration) cannot be explained by class effects alone, since only 24% of American families earning under $20,000 self-identified as black. Moreover, it is undeniable that a sizeable number of whites resent the advances that blacks have made in recent decades, and Beckett and others provide evidence that tough-on-crime rhetoric is often used to signal resistance to the Civil Rights movement, affirmative action, etc.

Yet the connection between this resistance and prison growth is difficult to untangle. In this section I just want to touch on two of the leading concerns. First, some of the disparity in punishment reflects disparities in offending—although some of the racial differences in offending are likely themselves the product of earlier differences in punishment. Second, drug offenses, which are the offenses over which police and prosecutors have the most discretion, and which have been the focus of much of the writing on this topic, simply have not contributed significantly to prison growth, at least not directly.

Start with offense differentials. Some of the racial disparity in arrests, convictions, and incarcerations reflects underlying racial differences in offending. Blacks engage in higher levels of violent and property crimes, so a race-blind system would still arrest and convict blacks at a rate greater than their share of the population. For a particularly striking example, Figure 12 plots the murder rates for white and black males aged 18 to 24; since most murders are intraracial, racial differences in victimization correlate to racial differences in offending. Throughout the sample period, the homicide rate for young black men [follows the same trajectory as that for young white men, but it] is nearly ten times [higher]. More generally, between 1980 and 2008, blacks made up 47% of all murder victims and 52% of all murderers.

Similar patterns hold across other offenses. According to the 2008 National Crime Victimization Survey, blacks are disproportionately likely to be the victims of violent and property crime. For violent crimes, their victimization rate was 25.9 per 1,000 households, compared to 18.1 per 1,000 for whites; for property crimes, a rate of 158, compared to 130.2 for whites. And blacks are similarly over-represented among violent offenders: victims report that 22.8% of their attackers were black—which is actually not that far off from the overall arrest rate of 28.3%.[15] Thus at least some of the racial disparity in the criminal justice system is due to differences in offending (and thus also victimization) rates.[16]

---

[15] Henry Ruth and Kevin Reitz suggest that the punishment disparity for significant violent crimes—homicide, rape, robbery, serious assault—are roughly in keeping with disparities in offending; the imprisonment disparities for lesser offenses do not track offending differences nearly as closely. That a majority of all prisoners (52.4% overall, and 54.1% of black prisoners) are in prison for violent crimes suggests that differentials in serious offending do play an important role in explaining differences in incarceration rates.

[16] None of this discussion should be read as downplaying an important feedback loop between punishment and offending. Conviction and incarceration often bring with them significant collateral consequences: restrictions on housing, welfare benefits, employment options, and so on. And these limitations could themselves contribute to future offending—and thus to the racial disparity in offending. The criminal justice system is thus responding to offending differentials that it itself has helped to create, or at least magnify.

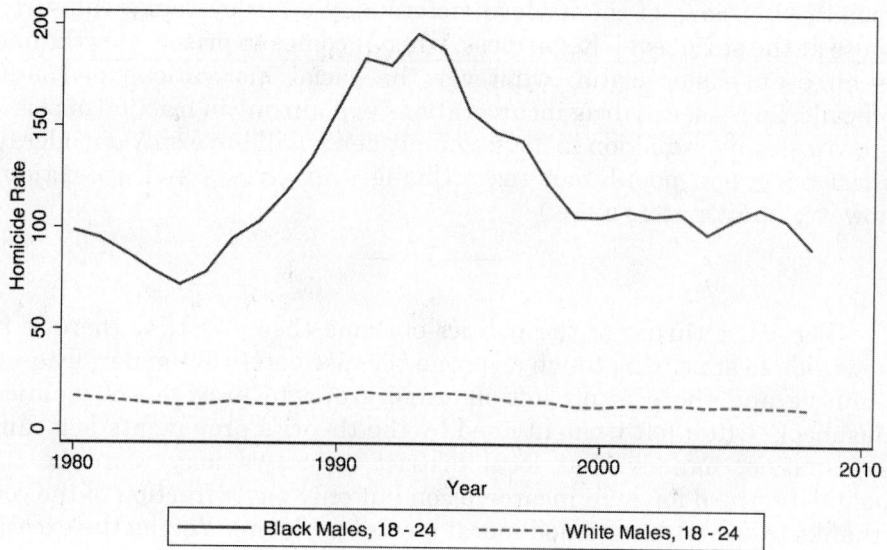

Unlike violent and property offenses, however, drug offenses provide much more room for discretionary responses, which is why many advocates of the anti-Civil Rights hypothesis focus on them. Their motivation is clear. Data indicate that blacks and whites *use* drugs at roughly similar rates, yet in 2008 blacks comprised 35% of all drug arrests, 44% of all drug convictions, and 45% of all prisoners serving time for drug convictions; note, though, that dealing is more likely to result in incarceration than using, and racial breakdowns on dealing are harder to come by. Moreover, the police have the ability to concentrate or distribute the racial impact of drug enforcement. Tracey Meares and Dan Kahan, for example, have argued that reverse stings, which would focus on buyers rather than seller, would have less-concentrated racial effects while still being as effective as the current supply-side approaches.

And it could very well be that the heavily reliance on supply-side enforcement is either motivated by, or tolerated because of, some degree of racial animus [, although minority groups often themselves lobbied for tougher drug laws, since minorities were disproportionately victimized by drug-related crime]. Yet even if true, this does not imply that the war on drugs has played a major role in prison growth. [*Ed. note*: see above for the explanation why.]

Finally, it is important to again return our focus to local actors. Consider, for example, the following two facts: New York State adopted its draconian Rockefeller Drug Laws in 1973, but as of the early 1980s only 5% of its inmates were serving time for drug offenses, a percent that would rise to over 30% by 1991. Just because state-level politicians had passed a punitive law did not mean that local officials immediately used it. And given that counties are more racially homogenous than states, the racial perceptions of county-level actors may differ systematically from those at the state level. Regardless, when it comes to prison growth there is an even easier claim: whatever the racial motivations of county officials, increases in drug incarcerations explain only a fraction of prison growth, so any reduction in drug commitments will have only a moderate effect on prison population size. (Changes in arrests and convictions, however, may matter more.)

The basic thrust of the politics-of-crime theory is that there is no downside to appearing tough on crime because voters are generally quite punitive and there is no soft-on-crime group to provide any political pushback. Often left unmentioned by the theory's proponents is a third explanation, namely that local district attorneys may reap the full political reward for each incarceration but only pay a fraction of the cost (thanks to the oft-mentioned moral hazard problem). Yet, as the excerpt above indicates, the complete picture is fairly complex. Here I want to flesh out some issues only briefly noted above and consider a few others that were not addressed at all.

B.1. "Nothing Works" and the End of Modernity

David Garland's theory is one of the more widely cited explanations for the rise of mass incarceration, so it deserves a little more attention. Garland's basic point is that the 1970s witnessed a sharp and wholly unexpected pivot in criminal justice policy away from a widely-shared set of norms about the proper role of government in society towards something much different, and much less stable. In response to a wide array of social shocks—the oil shocks, the decline of industrialization, changing marriage patterns and gender roles, increased suburbanization, the rise of the television, expanding civil rights, and growing moral relativism—people lost faith in the ability of the government to take care of them, a core aspect of "modernity." The public's expectation of the government shifted from "provide for" to "protect from": from providing services to protecting them from external threats. Although this change was a general attitudinal shift, Garland focuses on nine ways it shaped the nature of punishment in particular in the United States and the United Kingdom:

1. The decline of the rehabilitative ideal. Garland sees the fall of the rehabilitative ideal as a clear signal of the decline of modernist faith in the government's ability to provide services more generally. Shifting from rehabilitation to incapacitation is an indication that the goal now is just protection.

2. The re-emergence of punitive sanctions and expressive justice. To Garland, the rise of just deserts as a primary

justification for punishment reflected the return of "anachronisms that had no place within a 'modern' penal system." A state could have rejected rehabilitation without embracing the more punitive and shame-based aspects of punishment in the late 20th Century.

3. Changes in the emotional tone of criminal policy. As Garland puts it:

> Since the 1970s, the fear of crime has come to have new salience. What was once regarded as a localized, situational anxiety, afflicting the worst-off individuals and neighborhoods, has come to be regarded as a major social problem in and of itself, quite distinct from actual crime and victimization, and distinctive policies have been developed that aim to reduce fear levels, rather than to reduce crime.

In other words, our attention has shifted from reducing crime to reducing the *fear* of crime. And it is true that people's perceptions of crime are often not closely related to actual trends. But in the questions below we will consider whether Garland is missing something significant here.

4. The return of victim. Garland poses the victims' rights movement as essentially a zero-sum game in tension with defendants' rights: "Any untoward attention to the rights or welfare of the offender is taken to detract from the appropriate measure of respect for victims."

5. The reinvention of the prison. Prior to the incarceration boom that started in the late 1970s prison was increasingly viewed as a failed institution incapable of achieving its purportedly rehabilitative ideals. The boom, however, resulted from a growing sense that "prison works," given that the goal was incapacitation and retribution, not rehabilitation.

6. The transformation of criminological thought. Garland argues that modern penality viewed offending as deviant behavior that could be cured, while its successor "increasingly views crime as a normal, routine, commonplace aspect of modern society, committed by individuals who are, to all intents and purposes, perfectly normal."

7. The expanding infrastructure of crime prevention and community safety. Garland points to the rise of "[c]ommunity policing, crime prevention panels, Safer City programs, Crime Prevention through Environmental Design projects, Business Improvement Districts,

Neighborhood Watch, city management authorities" as a fundamental shift in enforcement priorities, away from "prosecution, punishment, and 'criminal justice' " and towards "prevention, security, harm-reduction, loss-reduction, fear-reduction."

8. Civil society and the commercialization of crime control. Garland asserts that policing services are increasingly administered by private actors and agencies. Note, though, that the focus on private prisons, at least, is generally overstated: only about 6% of all state prisoners are in private prisons, and only a handful of states use private prisons for any sizable share of inmates.

9. New management styles and working practices. Garland argues that police, prisons, and probation/parole have all become more managerial, affording less discretion to field agents and attempting to manage risks in a more cost-efficient manner. He states, for example, that:

> police now hold themselves out less as a crime-fighting force than as a responsive public service, aiming to reduce fear, disorder and incivility and to take account of community feeling in setting enforcement priorities.

Garland's argument is expansive, and it has been quite influential in shaping how people think about modern trends in enforcement. Any grand theory, however, especially of an institution as complex as criminal punishment, is likely to have some significant limitations or problems with it, as the following questions suggest.

QUESTIONS

1. **Whither crime, Part I.** Look at the list of the social forces that Garland points to explain the loss of faith in modernity in general, and in penal modernity in particular. How concerning is it that he doesn't refer to rising crime rates, focusing instead on oil shocks, familial changes, etc.?

2. **Whither crime, Part II.** According to Garland, when do the politics of crime "go national," along with a shift to managing the *fear* as much as the reality of crime? Was this a purely political shift, or was it tied to criminological fundamentals?

3. **Victim vs. offender.** Is the victim-offender relationship a zero-sum game? What would restorative justice theorists have to say about that? Furthermore, if Garland is right, why must a "modern" system ignore the costs to the victim? Rape shield laws were adopted to prevent a rape victim from being victimized a second time during trial—while detrimental to the rights of the defendant, was the motivation reactionary or anti-modern?

4. **Rehabilitation and harm reduction.** On the one hand, Garland seems to lament the decline of rehabilitation as a goal. On the other hand, he views the shift from "criminal justice" to "harm reduction" as problematic.

Are these consistent positions? If not, is there still any way to tie them together?

5. **Crime and fear.** What does Garland mean when he says police focus less on "fighting crime" and more on taking into account community interests when setting "enforcement priorities"? What types of communities is he thinking about?

B.2. STATE INTEREST GROUPS, FISCAL CAPACITY, AND BALANCED BUDGET PROVISIONS

Our popular view of how policy gets made is through the dueling actions of competing interest groups: industry and green group fight over environmental regulations, management and labor over wage laws, EFF and RIAA over copyright and the internet, and so on. But such head-to-head competition seemingly disappears when we get to criminal justice issues. There are plenty of groups in favor of tougher sentencing laws—prison guard unions, victims' rights groups, rural communities that are home to prisons, firms that service those prisons, and so on—but no one directly on the other side. Groups like the ACLU or New York State's Drop the Rock[17] may oppose particular criminal practices or policies, but there are no generalist "soft on crime" groups (although some might lump the nascent "smart on crime" groups as being so). This seems to imply that criminal justice should be a one-way severity ratchet.

But the head-to-head model is not the right way to think about things, at least not at the state level. Unlike the federal government, all but one state operates under some sort of balanced-budget provision, which makes state spending much more of a zero-sum game.[18] And unlike the federal government, states cannot print their own money, and they borrow at less favorable rates. Thus every dollar spent on a prison is a dollar not spent on a school, hospital, or road. So the opponents of tougher sentencing laws are not just some criminal justice groups, but everyone else competing for a somewhat fixed pot of money.

And many powerful groups at the state level have interests that do not favor increased incarceration. A 2002 survey of political observers and policymakers about the relative power of state-level interest groups found that the top ten groups were:

1. General business organizations (such as the chamber of commerce)

---

[17] Drop the Rock is an interest group that had sought to reform New York's historically draconian Rockefeller Drug Laws.

[18] The National Conference of State Legislatures points to three different sorts of balanced-budget requirements: some states (44) require the governor to submit a balanced budget, some(41) require the legislature to pass a balanced budget, and some (38) do not allow deficits to be carried over into subsequent years. Clearly, many states adopt two or three of these approaches. Only one, Vermont, adopts none. See http://www.ncsl.org/documents/fiscal/StateBalancedBudgetProvisions2010.pdf.

2. School teachers' organizations
3. Utility companies
4. Insurance companies (both general and medical)
5. Hospital and nursing associations
6. Lawyers ("predominantly trial lawyers, state bar associations")
7. Manufacturers
8. General local governments
9. Physicians and state medical associations
10. General farm organizations[19]

These results have been fairly stable over time: Seven of these ten groups were in the top ten in a 1985 survey as well, and two just outside it.[20] Of these ten groups, three likely are directly opposed to increased incarceration (schools, hospitals, physicians), and several others are likely not avid proponents: the chamber of commerce, for example, would likely prefer to have lower taxes than more prisons. None is a clearly tough-on-crime group, like gun associations (20th in 2002, 35th in 1985), the Religious Right (27th in 2002, 34th in 1985), or victims' rights groups (39th in 2002, unranked in 1985).

It is important, though, to not oversell the balanced-budget story. That a governor is required to submit a balanced budget does not imply that a state needs to pass one. And states often come up with creative ways to balance a budget in name only. New York State, for example, sold Attica prison to a state agency (i.e., to itself) and funded the sale with bonds, effectively allowing the state to circumvent its balanced-budget requirement.[21] While that may be an extreme case, it demonstrates that balanced budget provisions do not guarantee that budgets actually meaningfully balance—but they do make deficit spending *harder* and thus should not be dismissed as irrelevant.

We should therefore be skeptical that criminal justice spending is necessarily a one-way ratchet. Consider the following thought experiment: if tough-on-crime groups faced little to no political opposition, they should be effective at carving out ever-greater fractions of the state budget. Figures 9–6 and 9–7 indicate that this is not the case, certainly not recently.

---

[19] Clive S. Thomas & Ronald J. Hrebenar, *Interest Groups in the States*, in POLITICS IN THE AMERICAN STATES Table 4–1 (Virginia Gray & Russell L. Hanson, eds., 2004).

[20] In 1985, Bankers' associations, traditional labor associations, and individual bank and financial institutions were in the top ten, but by 2002 they had dropped to 11, 12, and 25, respectively. Their replacements were insurance companies (previously 13), hospitals (previously 17), and physicians (previously 11). So outside of individual banks, the changes were only slight.

[21] See http://www.nytimes.com/1997/04/02/nyregion/pataki-urges-new-york-undo-sale-of-attica-prison-to-itself.html.

Figure 9–6 plots the percent of all states' discretionary budgets that are spent on corrections and criminal justice more widely (corrections, state police, and judicial costs).[22] In both cases, a common pattern emerges. Corrections' share of the budget is flat from 1950 to the early 1970s, at around 1% of the budget and rising to about 3% by the early 1990s. (Note that this national average masks a lot of interstate differences.) This increase takes place during the time of both rising crime and incarceration, when increased spending on prisons likely made a certain amount of sense. Since 1991, when crime dropped but prison populations rose, *relative* spending on prisons has been fairly stable, hovering around its 1991 level.

Figure 9–6: Spending on Corrections and Criminal Justice as a Percent of State Budgets, 1952–2014

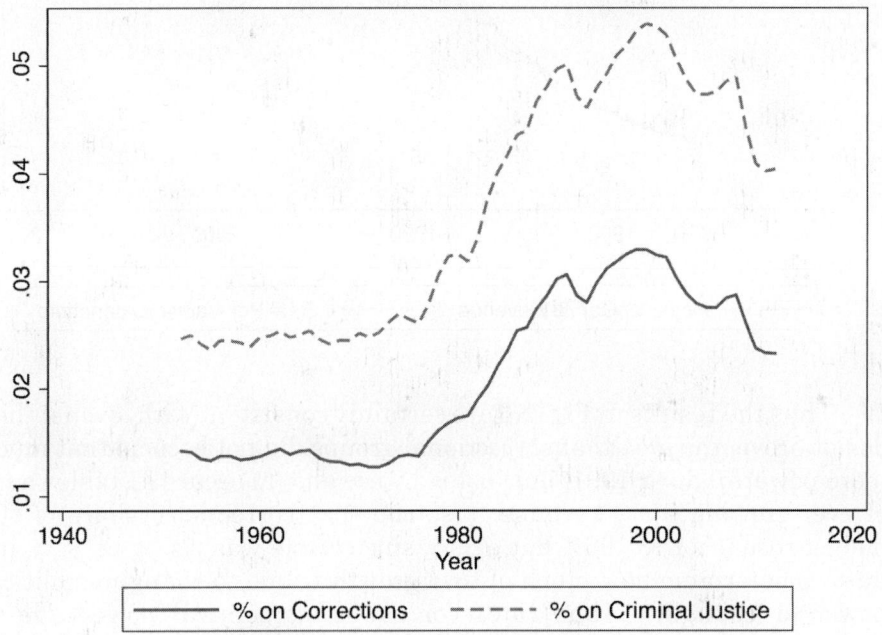

How is this possible? As Fig. 9.7 demonstrates, between 1950 and 2010, real per capita state revenues have surged, and spending has risen in close lock-step. Thus, once crime went into decline, the increased spending on prisons seems to be part of a widespread increase in *all types* of spending due to generally-rising revenues, not a prisons-specific increase at the expense of other programs. And, in fact, the data do not show any real of "crowding out": the budget shares of many programs, including higher education, remain relatively constant during the post-

---

[22] State law and federal mandates dictate how a significant portion of a state's budget must be spent. So the discretionary budget is the total budget minus spending on welfare, health and hospitals, highways, primary and secondary education, and interest on debt.

1991 era as well, lending more credence to a rising-tides-lifts-all-boats explanation.

Figure 9.7: Real Per Capita State Spending and Revenues, 1952–2014

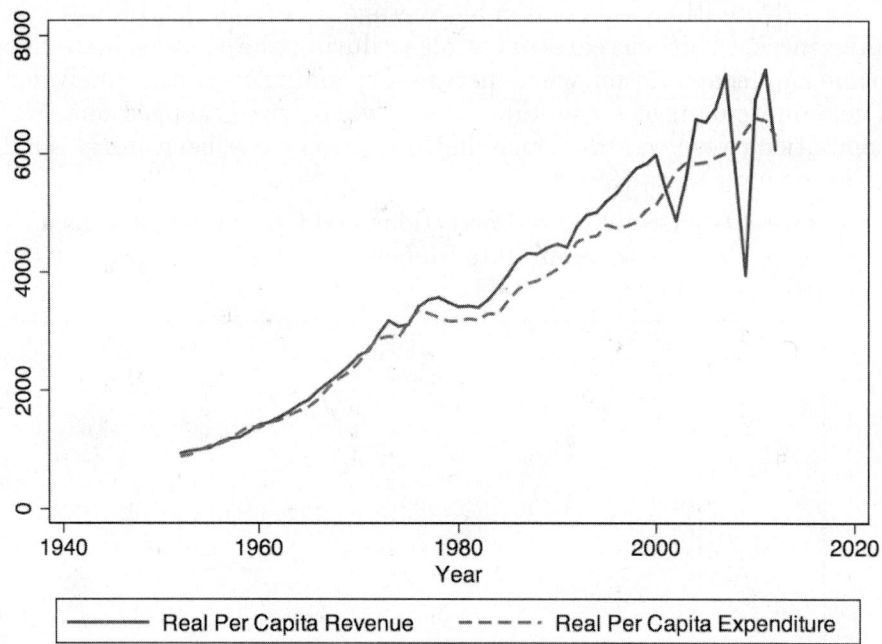

Thus the results in Fig. 9.6 are certainly consistent with, even if they do not prove, the idea that correctional groups did not become that much more powerful after 1991, but instead were able to secure a stable share of ever-growing state revenue. It's true that corrections' share of the budget rose prior to 1991, but again, since crime was rising as well, it's hard to determine how much of that growth is due to changing political power or changing crime rates—or changing political power *due* to changing crime rates as opposed to other social shifts. Unfortunately, no empirical study has examined this.

What then is the takeaway? The politics of crime are not necessarily all that much different from those in other areas. The lack of head-to-head interest group competition is mediated by the relatively zero-sum nature of state budget allocations. And trends in prison spending since the crime drop began suggest that increasing state fiscal capacity may be a more important explanation than changing political power.

Question: Since 1991, crime rates have fallen by nearly 40%, while the number of students in state universities and colleges have risen by 31%.[23] Given the stability of spending shares, does

---

[23] For education numbers, see http://nces.ed.gov/programs/digest/d10/tables/dt10_197.asp.

this fact shape your views about the accuracy of the claim that the political clout of prisons did not shift much over the 1990s and 2000s?

B.3. POLITICIANS, SENTENCING COMMISSIONS, AND WARINESS ABOUT BEING TOUGH ON CRIME

Consider the following two slightly-stylized facts:

1. Over the course of the 1980s and 1990s, the effect of the Republican-ness of a state legislature on prison admission rates grew stronger, but the magnitude of the relationship grew as more seats became contested.[24]

2. State legislatures are more likely to adopt sentencing commissions as prison populations increase, as the percent of the budget spent on corrections increases, and as the size of the majority party's majority shrinks.[25]

Question: Before reading on, stop and ask yourself: what do these two facts, taken together, tell us about politicians and their desire to be tough on crime?

The implications of the two facts above seem clear: politicians believe that being tough on crime wins votes, but they also often do not actually want to be tough on crime (or at least as consistently tough as we seem to think). If being tough on crime is electorally expedient, as Fact 1 implies, then it is somewhat surprising that, as indicated by Fact 2, politicians are more likely to tie their hands with respect to crime control when elections become more important—right when powerful electoral maneuvers are most essential!

This is not to say that being tough on crime is a purely cynical electoral move detached from any underlying ideological preferences. After all, Fact 1 points out that Republicans have become increasingly tough on crime independent of political pressures; none of this should be taken as contradicting David Garland's surely-correct claim that ideologies in the United States shifted to the right in the 1970s and 1980s. But these results do indicate that politicians are aware of the costs of being tough on crime, and as those costs rise (more overcrowded prisons, more money going to prisons rather than other projects) or as the benefits of toughness decline (less need to secure votes, less popular concern about crime as crime rates fall) we should expect to see political support for being tough on crime wane.

And that is exactly what we are seeing today. As far back as 2000, legislators started thinking about ways to roll back incarceration in the

---

[24] Thomas D. Stucky et al., Partisan Politics, Electoral Competition and Imprisonment: An Analysis of States Over Time, 43 CRIMINOLOGY 211 (2005).

[25] Rachael E. Barkow & Kathleen M. O'Neill, Delegating Punitive Power: The Political Economy of Sentencing Commissions and Guideline Formation, 84 TEXAS L. REV. 1973 (2006).

wake of recession that following the popping of the dotcom bubble. The fiscal pressures of the current credit crunch have only increased the incentive to constrain prison growth. In fact, 2010 was the first year since 1972 that the absolute number of prisoners declined nation-wide. It is not necessarily coincidental, for example, that California decided to implement its Realignment program to correct the prosecutorial moral hazard problem in the midst of a severe recession (rather than, say, building its way out of its overcrowding problem). And the late 2000s/early 2010s saw multiple governors commute sentences to rein in prison populations and save money, and at seemingly little political cost.

The desire to limit or roll back incarceration rates, however, appears to be more than just a short-run response to fiscal pressures. Instead, it is likely that we are witnessing a more fundamental shift in the "politics of crime." With offending rates down to levels not seen since the 1970s—although still substantially higher than those experienced in the 1950s and 1960s—crime simply lacks the political salience it had before. And as a result, politicians are moving away from "tough on crime" perspectives. Even conservative groups, such as "Right on Crime," are now dedicated to scaling back incarceration rates. It is telling that during the 2012 Republican presidential primary, when Mitt Romney was engaged in a tough fight with Newt Gingrich, of the myriad charges Romney's campaign launched at Gingrich it never once raised the fact that Gingrich was a foundational member of Right on Crime. Similarly, a 2011 poll of 800 disproportionately-older likely-voting Republicans in Florida—a state known for its penal toughness—found that a majority (65%) would vote for a "smart on crime" candidate over a "tough on crime" one.[26] Mindless "toughness" no longer packs its prior political punch, most likely due to a combination of low crime rates and serious economic distress.

In short, it is worth noting that the longest sustained increase in incarceration appears to have coincided—perhaps not coincidentally—first with a period of rising crime, and then with a long period of economic expansion. As that expansion has slowed down and reversed, so too has prison growth, at least as long as crime rates have remained low. When budgets are growing, the zero sumness of state budgetary processes are harder to detect (although it is still there: everyone is getting more, but some are not getting as much more as they otherwise would have). As budgets contract, the competition for scarcer dollars becomes more intense, and current outcomes indicate that the penal system is not as uniquely protected from cuts as commentators thought during the boom times.

---

[26] http://www.floridataxwatch.org/resources/pdf/SmartJusticePoll11912.pdf.

B.4. POLITICIANS, THE CENSUS, AND RURAL WELFARE

There are still at least two reasons why some politicians may continue to fight for tougher sentencing laws, even as budgets tighten and crime declines: the census and what we can loosely call "rural welfare." First, the census. In almost all states, prisoners are counted as residing where they are incarcerated, not where they lived prior to incarceration. Since many prisons are located in rural communities, and most prisoners come from cities, such counting effectively transfers voting power from urban to suburban and ex-urban districts—in troubling ways, since prisoners cannot vote while in prison (outside of Maine and Vermont).

Take New York State as an example. Like all states, New York has an equal representation law that requires all legislative districts to house roughly the same number of people. After the 2000 Census, seven upstate, Republican-controlled state senate districts satisfied the equal representation requirement only by counting the (non-voting, predominantly urban) prisoners held in their prisons: if prison populations shrunk noticeably, or if the state decided to count a prisoner's residence as his last pre-incarceration address, these seven senators would find their districts reshaped in a way that would shrink the representation of the more-conservative upstate residents in favor of the more-liberal urban residents.

In 2004, the New York State Senate was controlled by the Republicans, 37–24. That's a sizable majority, but all it would have taken would have been losing seven seats for control to flip back to the Democrats. Nonetheless, that year New York passed a seemingly major reform bill aimed at reducing the impact of the Rockefeller Drug Laws. Yet the reforms did not change things as much as they might appear.

For example, the legislation changed the sanction for the quite-common Class B drug felony. The original regime relied on an indeterminate sentence: the judge set a maximum of somewhere between 3 to 25 years, and the minimum was one-third the maximum. Under the 2004 reforms, the judge imposed a determinate sentence somewhere between 1 and 9 years (with minimal time off for good behavior). At first blush, this looks like a huge discount, with the maximum dropping from 25 to 9 years.

> **Question:** Assume a judge sentences Defendant Q to the Class B maximum under the old regime, and Defendant R to the Class B maximum under the revised regime. When is Q eligible for release? When is R?

Once you look closely, it becomes clear that the reforms were more superficial than meaningful, and that should come as no surprise: implementing meaningful reforms would have jeopardized the Republican's majority in the state senate, so as long as the Republicans maintained control of the Senate they would surely block substantial reform.

In 2008, the Democrats seized control of the state senate and proceeded to enact deeper cuts to the Rockefeller Drug Laws, finally eliminating some of the mandatory sentencing provisions, and thus granting judges the ability to use alternatives for low-level, non-violent drug offenders. Whatever the policy merits of such a decision, it was also good politics for the Democrats, since weakened Rockefeller laws would reduce Republican power. The Democrats later weakened the prison-census connection even more directly when they passed a law that required inmates to be counted as "residing" at their last home addresses rather than in their prisons.

Only a few other states count prisoners the same way.[27] Most states count prisoners as residing in their prisons, introducing distortion in representativeness, and creating a strong incentive for politicians with prisons in their districts—which tend to be poorer, more rural, and more conservative—to remain tough on crime in no small part for personal or party power.

The second effect that can lead politicians to oppose decarceration efforts is the perceived economic boost of prisons to relatively poor, rural communities. While most offenders come from urban areas, most prisons are located in more remote reaches of the state. Consider the maps below of the locations of New York's and California's prisons, and note how far most prisons are from New York City and Buffalo in New York, and from cities such as San Francisco, Los Angeles, and San Diego in California. Prisons are now viewed as a form of economic support, perhaps even as a type of socially-acceptable rural welfare. The head of the Corrections Corporation of America, a private-prison company, once said that the attitude toward prisons "used to be 'not in my back yard.' Now, they want it in the front yard." Competition among rural communities for new prisons has often been fierce, and some places have gone so far as to build prisons without any contract from the state in the hopes of lobbying for prisoners once the prison come on-line.

---

[27] For those interested, a list of laws and their implications can be found here: http://www.prisonersofthecensus.org/50states/.

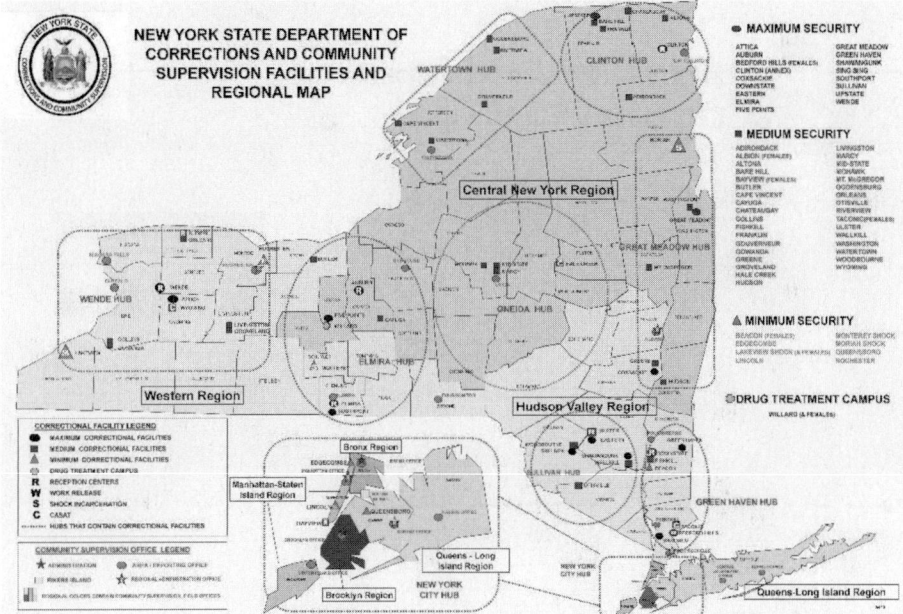

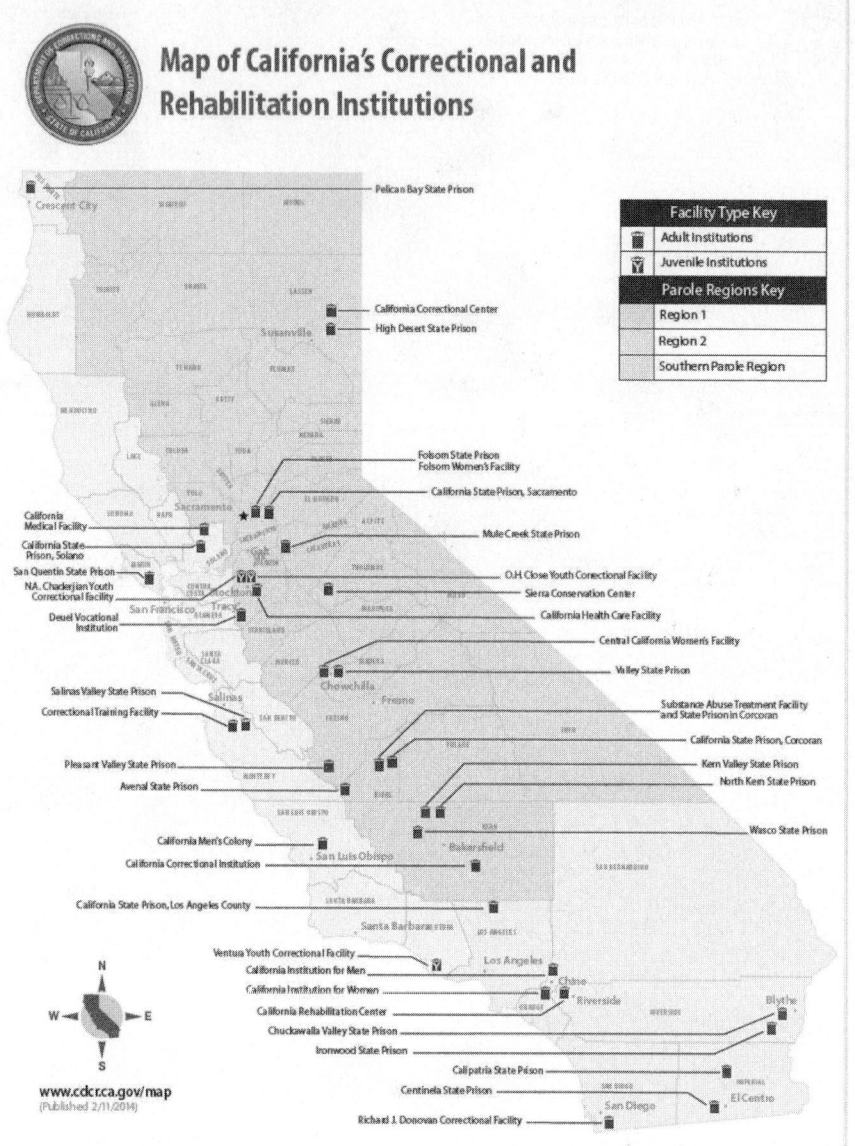

But it is worth checking empirically whether prisons bring with them enough jobs to really elevate the economies of the rural communities where they are located. Do they create enough jobs? Are those jobs filled by local residents or distant commuters? Do the prisons purchase their supplies locally or from afar? That a prison is in a county does not automatically imply it will bring much economic benefit.

Unfortunately, the evidence suggests that any such benefit is small. Amy Glasmeier and Tracey Farrigan, for example, compare fifty-five poor rural counties that acquired prisons between 1985 and 1995 to fifty-five similar counties that did not receive prisons, and they find that prison location did reduce poverty somewhat, but only in counties that started with relatively low poverty rates and workforces with above-average education.[28] Moreover, the economic improvements did not induce any structural, economy-wide changes or improvements.

Using roughly the same data as Glasmeier and Farrigan,[29] Gregory Hooks and his co-authors look at the period 1969–1994 and find that prisons are positively correlated with employment in urban counties from the 1970s and 1980s but negatively so in the 1990s.[30] Surprisingly, they find that for poor rural counties prison location appears to be consistently negatively correlated with employment. And in a more localized study of rural New York State between 1977 and 2000, Ryan King and his co-authors similarly find no real economic benefit.[31]

Thus whatever the intuitive appeal of prisons as a form of economic support, they do not appear to bring much actual economic benefit to the communities in which they are located. Moreover, whatever benefits they bring must be balanced against the costs. And among the relevant costs are not just the direct financial costs of maintaining a prison, but the perhaps-more-indirect costs of rural siting: placing prisons in rural communities makes it harder for predominantly-urban inmates to maintain already-weakened familial ties, and broken family ties make reintegration tougher when that inmate is released. None of this, however, is to say that politicians are incorrect in thinking that the *perception* of economic benefits—however ephemeral they prove to be in reality—makes lobbying for prisons *politically* savvy.

B.5. RACE, GEOGRAPHY, AND DIFFUSE RESPONSIBILITY

The next political theory to consider is one put forth by William Stuntz in his book, *The Collapse of Criminal Justice*, published shortly after his untimely death in 2011. Where theorists like Garland, Rusche and Kircheimer, Tonry, Beckett, and others often look to broad, social changes independent of crime, Stuntz (1) pays much closer attention to the importance of the crime boom that started in the 1960s and (2) focuses much more on the micro-level, bureaucratic imperfections that permeate our criminal justice system, particularly the diffusion of responsibility and control across agencies at various levels of

---

[28] Amy K. Glasmeier and Tracey Farrigan, *The Economic Impacts of the Prison Development Boom on Persistently Poor Rural Places*, 30 INTERNAT'L REGIONAL SCI. REV. 274 (2007).

[29] Ideally, replication of studies should be conducted with new data: test the pill on one sick population and, if it works, test it again on a different population. This is often impossible in the social sciences, since we do not have that many "populations" to test. But "replication" with the same data should be viewed with some skepticism, since it does not reflect a truly independent re-evaluation.

[30] Gregory Hooks, Clayton Mosher, Thomas Rotolo, and Linda Lobao, *The Prison Industry: Carceral Expansion and Employment in US Counties, 1969–1994*, 85 SOC. SCI. Q. 37 (2004).

[31] Ryan Scott King, Marc Mauer, and Tracey Huling, *An Analysis of the Economics of Prison Siting in Rural Communities*, 3 CRIMINOLOGY & PUB. POL'Y 453 (2004).

government. To paint his theory with an overly-broad brush, Stuntz ties the rise in incarceration to:

1. Rising crime in the 1960s
2. The growing concentration of blacks in violent, urban centers
3. The growing political power of wealthier, whiter suburbs
4. The increased, but by no means complete, centralization of criminal justice authority at the state (as opposed to local) level

Together, these forces led to an increase in incarceration, one that Stuntz argues—here adopting a position fairly unlike that of the other political theorists—none of the various politicians themselves actually wanted.

Stuntz's point of departure, however, is not the severity of punishment that defined the last two or three decades of the Twentieth Century, but the surprising leniency of the 1960s. Recall from Fig. 11 in the excerpt above that between 1960 and the mid-1970s, the effective incarceration rate—the number of people imprisoned per *crime committed*—actually *fell*. He argues that:

> The mid-twentieth century's lenient turn was the product of more detached police, more liberal prosecutors, and a political disconnect between a justice system that served one set of voters [increasingly black urban residents] but was governed by another [increasingly white [suburbanites]. [T]here was [not] any obvious political advantage to be gained by reducing criminal punishment . . . in the midst of steeply rising levels of criminal violence. [This] [l]enity was party the consequence of suburbanites' indifference to rising urban crime.[32]

Such leniency was, however, unsustainable—and, to Stuntz, immoral: "Whatever the line is between a merciful justice system and one that abandons all serious effort at crime control, the nation had crossed it."[33] Such a failure was bound to create a backlash, and it did. Here I want to focus on Stuntz's concerns about budgetary issues and diffuse political responsibility allowed the backlash to grow in strength.

We have already discussed the prosecutorial moral hazard problem in detail, and Stuntz raises it to explain both why urban communities face excessive punishments, but also why they are likely *under*-policed, since police come from the local budget and thus lack the implicit state subsidy that incarceration enjoys. Of course, this moral hazard problem had been around for decades, even during the 1960s and 1970s when crime rose and incarceration fell. So the moral hazard problem may be

---

[32] WILLIAM J. STUNTZ, THE COLLAPSE OF AMERICAN CRIMINAL JUSTICE (2011).
[33] *Id.*

an important cause, but it is not necessarily enough all by itself. What else was going on?

Stuntz's explanation:

> Once the punitive turn got rolling, it kept rolling; there was nothing to stop it. The justice system became the rough equivalent of a vessel with no one at the wheel, its course and speed set by forces that were opaque even to the government officials who were subject to them.
>
> The consequence was a failure of democratic governance. Where state and local officials alike were responsible for rising levels of imprisonment, neither was truly responsible. Neither [prosecutors nor legislators] fully controlled the process by which the prison beds [paid for by legislators, filled by prosecutors] were made and filled, so neither was able to slow or reverse the process. And the voters with the largest stake in that process—chiefly African American residents of high-crime city neighborhoods—had the smallest voice in the relevant decisions.
>
> These claims run counter to the growing academic conventional wisdom that politicians consciously used the criminal justice system as an alternative means of governing the nation's poor [here he cites, among others, Garland and Simon]. That conventional wisdom gives too much credit to the politicians, whose conduct offers little evidence that they were seeking to create a justice system like the one we have today. And if the politicians did consciously choose the system we have, their predecessors in the 1960s and early 1970s must have chosen the system *they* had: a justice system dominated by lenity, not severity. Absent a theory that explains why politicians' and voters' preferences changed so radically in such a brief period of time, it seems more likely that the various actors in the system did what came naturally. They followed their own preferences when the voters allowed, and made choices that conformed to short-term political incentives when the voters insisted on a different tack. Cumulatively, these choices changed the justice system radically: first in one direction, then the other. But neither the officials in charge of criminal justice—from Supreme Court Justices to state legislators, from prosecutors to police chiefs—nor the voters planned on such radical change, in either direction.

Though Stuntz distances himself from Garland, the passage above also shows the complementarity of the two theories. Garland would argue that he *did* provide a theory for why voters' preferences changed, and that that change took place around the time the prison boom started; at the very least, Garland suggests that voters did in fact start to demand a "different tack," and that politicians responded. But there are two immediate rebuttals that come to mind. First, as Stuntz argues, line police officers, line prosecutors, and some trial judges are relatively isolated bureaucracies, despite the political accountability of their chiefs or, in the cases of elected judges, their own accountability to the voters. Changing rhetoric among more voter-sensitive politicians higher up the food chain does not imply immediate policy shifts further down the line. And second, it is worth asking if whatever changes we saw in the 1970s were enough to explain the *magnitude* of the shift identified by Stuntz.

So the question remains as to why the incarceration rate has risen *so* high. Part of the explanation is tied to the crime boom. As Stuntz points out, during the crime surge of the 1970s and 1980s, prison populations grew by approximately 5% per year; during a similar surge in crime during the 1920s and early 1930s, they grew by about 4%. So some of the unprecedented growth in prison populations was clearly due to an *expected* rate of growth during an *unprecedentedly* long period of rising crime. In other words, it was simply the *durability* of the crime wave that explains some of our elevated incarceration rates.

But incarceration rates declined in the 1930s as post-Prohibition crime rates fell; in contrast, incarceration rates continued to rise in the 1990s, and into the 2000s, even as crime rates again fell. So *something* had clearly changed in how the criminal justice system operated during those two times. Though Stuntz does not make this argument, one explanation is simply that the crime drop was not immediately obvious: the decline in the early 1990s was indistinguishable from the brief leveling off of crime that took place in the early 1980s, just before the explosion in crack-related violence. And throughout the early 1990s several prominent criminologist, including John DiIulio, James Q. Wilson, and James Fox, were arguing—with much media support—that a wave of young "superpredators" were lurking just around the corner. Voters and criminal justice bureaucracies alike were thus unlikely to want to roll back punishment in the early- to mid-1990s until they were more sure that what they were witnessing was a real decline.

But that explanation alone cannot explain the durability of penal toughness, and Stuntz looks to uncover evidence of a deeper shift, which he finds in the changing relationship between offenders, victims, and enforcers. In the first half of the Twentieth Century, like today, crime was concentrated in cities. But Stuntz highlights two big differences between these eras. First, the demographics of who lived in high-crime urban neighborhoods changed, from European immigrants in the 1920s and 1930s, to blacks in the 1970s and 1980s. For various reasons (many if not all of them tied to our nation's deep racial problems), the immigrant communities were able to achieve greater political clout in the cities in the early 1900s than blacks were in the late 1900s. And not just in the cities: immigrant communities were also better able to secure state- and nationwide power than blacks too.

Second, the criminal justice system was less professionalized and bureaucratized during the 1920s and 1930s. Police positions were patronage-based, for example, and officers were often involved in local politics. By the 1970s, professionalization and bureaucratization had set in, one result of which was while immigrants dominated the police forces of the 1920s and 1930s, blacks often made up only 10% of urban police forces in the 1970s and 1980s, even in cities with large black populations. Stuntz argues that district attorneys offices likewise became more bureaucratic and politically isolated, and thus less responsive to community needs and desires from the 1970s on, especially when compared to the 1920s and 1930s. And to the extent that DAs *are* politically responsive, it is at the county level, where wealthier, whiter suburbanites have grown more powerful in the post-War era.

Thus the fundamental shift:

> By the late nineteenth century . . . working-class immigrants and their offspring largely governed the justice system that governed them. Even today, African Americans have no such power.[34]

As criminal justice agencies centralized, power was increasingly concentrated in the hands of white voters, despite the fact that crime disproportionately impacted black communities. The jurisdictions that governed crime had always included both cities and suburbs, and the post-War years saw the latter grow more powerful at the expense of the former.

This shift led to two effects. First, it contributed to the instability of the 1960s through the 1980s, and then to the resistance to change in the 1990s and 2000s. Start with the 1960s to 1980s. Stuntz explains:

> As the United States grew richer and as its nearly all-white suburbs . . . mushroomed in the years following World War II, crime grew steadily more concentrated in the cities, and especially in urban black neighborhoods. Thanks to sheer numbers, the political clout exercised by residents of high-crime city neighborhoods declined; the power of safer, mostly-white neighborhoods in cities and suburbs alike grew. White suburbanites had little to lose from crime in black ghettoes. Throughout the 1950s and early 1960s, as violence in northern cities rose, crime remained a nonissue for suburban voters and a small matter for residents of the safer parts of those cities: their own neighborhoods were peaceful enough, and the state of other neighborhoods was no great concern. Beginning with the urban riots of the mid-and late 1960s, indifference turned to fear, then anger. The early and mid-1970s saw falling prison populations bottom out; by 1976, imprisonment was rising

---

[34] *Id.*

steeply. The consequence was the most lenient criminal justice system in American history, followed by the most severe. As American criminal justice ceased to be an exercise in local self-government, stability and equilibrium disappeared. Volatility and extremism took their place.

Stuntz points to two warring incentives when it comes to crime control: we want our communities to be safe (safety), but we do not want to lock up the brothers and cousins of our neighbors (empathy). As the seat of power moves away from the location of crime, both forces grow weaker, leading to more instability; the continuing punitiveness since 1991 suggests that empathy is still the weaker of those two feelings and thus the one more likely to get short shrift.

These dynamics also explain why the punishment regime did not change much after 1991: the budgetary impact of prisons was too slight to overcome general suburban apathy about punishment's impact on poor communities. As the decline in crime more obviously became The Crime Drop, there were some reforms that tried to move away from incarceration, particularly a shift toward more policing. But then the economics of criminal justice intervened again. In the wake of the dotcom crash:

> Roughly half of the 1990s increase in the size of urban police forces has been undone. Meanwhile, the prison population continued to grow, albeit more slowly than before. So far, the crime-fighting strategy that depended most on state budgets has prevailed over the one funded by even more cash-strapped cities.[35]

It was only by 2010 that the fiscal pressures on the states had grown so great, and crime sufficiently non-salient, that prison populations dropped for the first time in almost forty years.

Stuntz also notes the trickiness of making causal inferences about declining crime and rising prison populations. To many, the crime decline seemed to *validate* large-scale incarceration. Stuntz cites the case of Fox Butterfield, the New York Times crime correspondent, whose puzzlement at rising incarceration and falling crime rates was criticized by conservatives who accused him of inverting the causal story: the falling crime rates were *due* to increased incarceration, and so the correlation made perfect sense.[36]

Where most of the political theories are top-down—politicians are seen as using criminal justice issues to directly control certain classes of

---

[35] *Id.*

[36] Ultimately, both sides in this debate are right, and thus both sides are in some ways wrong. Increasing incarceration reduces crime, but increasing crime rates increase incarceration. Theory alone cannot tell us which effect is stronger: it is an empirical question, and one that is devilishly hard to answer. So if we see falling crime and rising incarceration, it could be the system working rationally and stably, or it could reflect some sort of shift in punitiveness.

offenders—Stuntz's is more bottom-up, and thus perhaps a bit more in keeping with the disaggregated nature of our criminal justice system. It is a theory based on the cumulative impact of numerous small changes that were perhaps rational for each actor at each stage but which cumulatively added up to a radical shift, one that only now might just be starting to change again.

B.6. THE PUBLIC'S ACTUAL PUNITIVENESS

I want to conclude this section by asking whether politicians have been correct in assuming that voters have been unwaveringly tough on crime. It is true that in an international context Americans are distinctly punitive. James Q. Whitman has argued at length that when compared to Europeans Americans have always possessed less forgiving views of criminal offenders, something that reformers who point to Europe as a model to follow should keep in mind.[37] But taking a more localized perspective, are scholars like Jonathan Simon and Theodore Caplow correct when they say that "[i]t is widely accepted that political candidates for statewide office must establish themselves as favoring more severe punishments to stand a chance of election"?[38]

A naïve glance at survey evidence may suggest that Simon and Caplow are correct: two-thirds of Americans incorrectly believe that crime is getting worse, about 60% consistently report that courts are not treating offenders harshly enough, most respondents say that imprisonment is generally the right punishment, and about 60% favor the death penalty for murderers.

Yet, on closer inspection, the picture is more convoluted. Survey responses are often very fragile, sensitive to the order of the questions and—more important here—the options provided. For example, while 60% of Americans favor the death penalty for murder when asked "do you favor the death penalty for murder?", that share drops when other options, such as life without parole, are included. Furthermore, when punishment questions make up just one or two questions in a survey, respondents rely on stereotypes of "common offenders;" when given more details, their answers become more nuanced.

More-detailed surveys suggest that Americans continue to embrace rehabilitation as a penal goal, and that they increasingly dislike prison as the primary response to criminal conduct. Among the results national surveys have uncovered:

- There is widespread support for early intervention programs aim at young and career offenders.

---

[37] See James Q. Whitman, Harsh Justice: Criminal Punishment and the Widening Divide Between American and Europe (2005).

[38] Theodore Caplow & Jonathan Simon, *Understanding Prison Policy and Population Trends*, in PRISONS 70 (Michael Tonry & Joan Petersilia, eds., 1999).

- In a 2001 poll, 55% of respondents said the goal of incarceration should be rehabilitation, compared to only 25% in favor of protection and 16% in favor of punishment.
- In a 2006 poll about the best strategy for dealing with crime, 36% cited prevention (education programs), 22% rehabilitation (job training), 20% enforcement (police on the streets), and 19% punishment (more prisons, longer sentences).
- In a 2012 poll, 45% of respondents replied that "too many people are in prison in the United States," compared to only 13% who said "too few." (29% thought things were fine, and 14% didn't know.)

And in the survey of Florida Republicans discussed above, 81% favored evidence-based community alternatives over juvenile prisons for young offenders, 68% favored alternative sanctions for non-violent, young offenders given the costs of incarceration, 81% said they would vote for a candidate who advocated diverting defendants convicted of minor, non-violent crimes, and 60% agreed that even minor violent offenders should not necessarily be sent to prison. The results here may be somewhat contingent—the survey was sponsored by a tax policy group, so many of the questions focused on taxes and cost savings, issues that are particularly salient due to the current economic downturn, Tea Party tax protests, and continued low crime rates—but they nonetheless suggest that even a strongly-conservative segment of the population is not, or at least no longer remains, strongly tough-on-crime.

Taken together, these results suggest that politicians have space to be less punitive, particularly in a time of lower crime. Yet politicians do not win elections without a good understanding of their constituency. So if Americans are generally open to rehabilitations and alternatives to incarceration, why do politicians still favor such punitive policies? It could be because views may chance as we move from the abstract to the concrete. *In general*, Americans favor rehabilitation programs. But when a particular person in a particular program recidivates in a particularly violent way, the politicians may pay a price.

There is a critical asymmetry here: we directly observe every false negative (should not have recidivated, but does), but we cannot directly observe the false positives (would not have recidivated if released, but not released). We can count on our hands the number of parolees who commit crimes on release, but we can count the number of non-parolees who would not have committed a crime had they been paroled only indirectly through complicated statistical models. So a politician bears all the downside risk of less-punitive policies but has a much harder time securing the upside benefit of smarter incarceration policies.

Because of this, criminal justice is thought of as a "low information, high salience" topic. Voters are generally uninformed about how the criminal justice system operates on a day-to-day basis. But when something atypical and shocking happens—a parolee committing a double homicide—they base their voting decisions on that one, highly salient event. As a result, politicians have a strong incentive to be fairly cautious with reforms.

If nothing else, then, these results provide some support for the adoption of politically-independent sentencing commissions. Commissions may be more immune to the political shocks of high-profile false negatives, and so they may be better able than politicians to deliver to the public its long-run (as opposed to angry short-run) desires for a criminal justice system that focuses more on protection and treatment than on punishment.

* * *

So, to summarize this long, winding political story. The US has seen rising crime and rising incarceration in the past, but it has never seen anything like what we have gone through over the past four decades. It is thus important to understand how we got here and why, since it is impossible to figure out how to best move forward without understanding how we arrived here.

Many theories focus on broad political shifts, particularly a rightward drift in the American electorate induced by economic upheaval and displeasure at the civil rights and other social movements. And these theories are surely correct that the American public is more conservative today than it was in the 1960s—or at least that it demands policies that are more conservative than it did then. This is not a semantic difference: conditions today are not the same as they were in 1960, so even if policy preferences are stable, policy demands might not be. For example, despite the crime drop of the past two decades, both violent and property crime are still 100% higher than they were in 1960; it is not surprising that people who were alive in the 1960s would demand tougher punishment regimes today than they did back then, even if their values remained fixed.

But a challenge these top-down theories face is that they do not necessarily explain why downstream actors follow the lead of upstream ones. A good example of this problem is seen in the book *Plague of Prisons*, by Ernest Drucker. Drucker tries to argue that passage of New York's draconian Rockefeller Drug Laws in 1973 drove up the state's prison population. But Figure 9–8 points out a serious problem with his claim: neither drug-related incarcerations nor New York's prison population starts to rise until nearly a decade *after* the Rockefeller Laws are adopted (indicated by the first vertical line on the graph), and both rise in sync with those trends elsewhere in the nation.[39] In other words,

---

[39] John F. Pfaff, *Waylaid by a Metaphor: A Deeply Problematic Account of Prison Growth*, 111 MICH. L. REV. 1087, 1092 (2013).

despite efforts by New York's governor and legislature to crack down on drug crime, the local police and prosecutors ignored the laws until they found it privately rational to do so. Note, too, that reliance on the drug laws appears to decline well before the state's two reforms to the Rockefeller Laws were passed, in 2004 (the second line) and 2009 (the third), and that neither reform appears to have much of an impact on trends, again pointing the importance of local, not state, actors.

Figure 9–8: Inmates in New York Prisons for Drug Offenses, 1965–2013

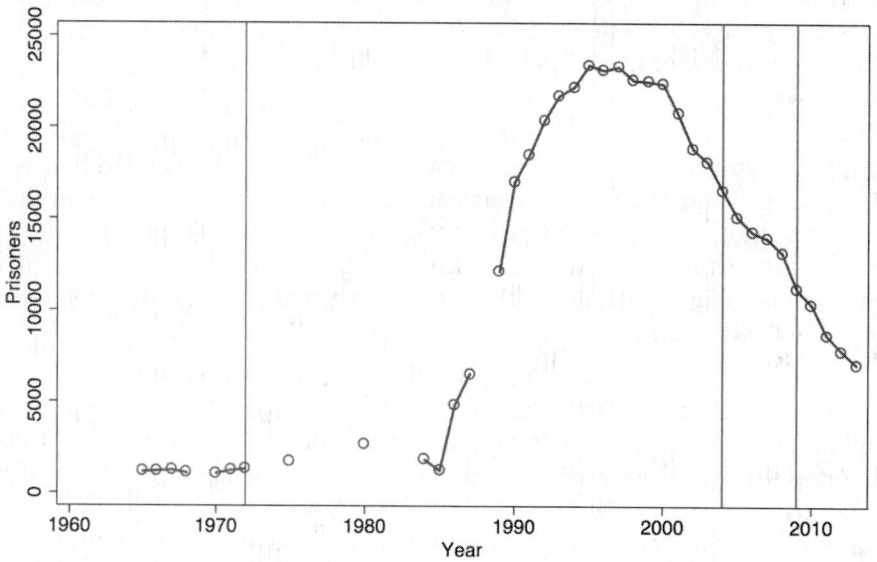

Thus the power of Stuntz's theory. By taking a more bottom-up perspective, it demonstrates how the private incentives of the downstream actors—the ones with the most discretionary control over criminal justice outcomes—shifted in response to changes that, in many cases, were either uncorrelated with or only indirectly tied to problems of crime (bureaucratization, the Great Migration, white flight to the suburbs). Stuntz's theory makes it clear that if we want to better regulate the use of incarceration in the United States, we need to have a good understanding not just of overarching ideological perspective, but also of the various institutional incentives, as well as the fissures and defects that plague the system.

QUESTIONS

1. **How to fix the system?** The most obvious question is this: if Stuntz is right, how do we fix the criminal justice system? Is the solution just local localism? This is clearly the route that California is heading down with Realignment, but can you think about why California is limiting itself to non-violent, non-sexual, non-serious offenders? Are there reasons we don't want

to completely localize enforcement—or, at least, are there certain types of crimes where localization makes more or less sense?

2. **Garland and democracy.** David Garland's theory points to a general loss of faith in government services and a resultant demand that the government protect us from crime. If Garland is right, does that mean our current level of incarceration is what is democratically desired, and so reforms aimed at reducing incarceration are somehow anti-democratic?

C. UNITED STATES AND EUROPE: A COMPARISON

In order to understand the causes of prison growth in the US, it may be helpful to look abroad, since Europe has not experienced the same surge in incarceration that we have. Figure 9.9 plots incarceration rates in the EU every three years from 1992 to 2010.[40] Two patterns emerge from this figure. First, like in the US, European rates have been trending upward; the sharp jump in 2004, caused by the entry of higher-incarceration Eastern European and Baltic countries, only changes the level (by about 10%) of a fairly steady, Europe-wide rise. Second, the European levels are still well below those in the United States, even when we account for the more-punitive former Warsaw Pact countries. What explains the difference?

---

[40] The graph plots three lines. The solid line plots the incarceration rate of those countries that belong to the EU in that year (so Lithuania, which joined the EU in 2004, is included in years 2004, 2007, and 2010 but not in any of the prior years). The short-dashed line plots the incarceration rate of those countries that joined the EU prior to 1992 (so Lithuania is not included in this line at all), and the long-dashed line the incarceration rate in every year of all countries that joined the EU by 2010 (so Lithuania is included in every year of this line).

Figure 9.9: European Incarceration Rates, 1992–2010

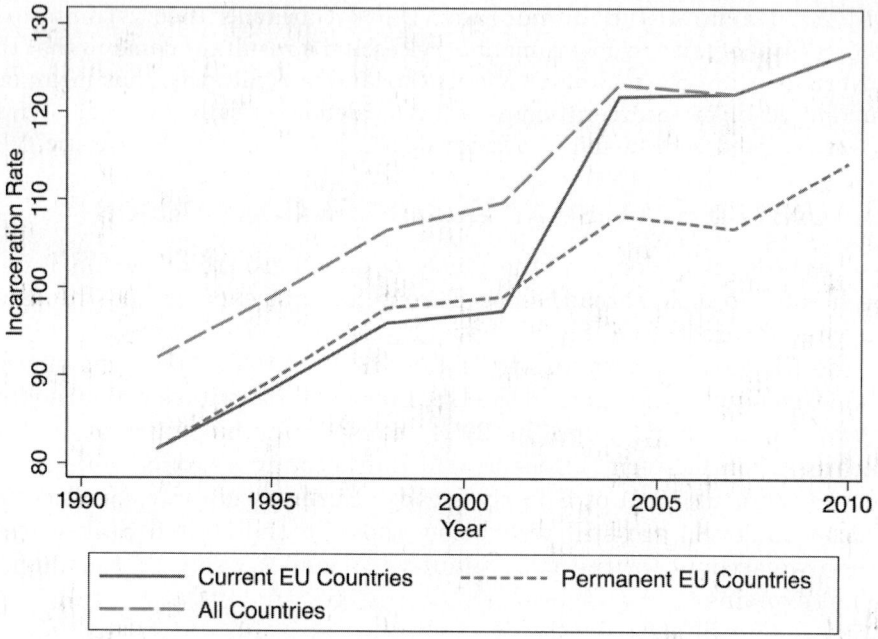

Part of the explanation is crime, but not just any crime. European crime rates are not much lower than those in the United States. In fact, crime rates in Europe now are actually higher now than those in the US, and they are continuing to rise.[41]

Yet while incarceration has risen in response to rising crime, why does it still remain lower than that in the US? Franklin Zimring and Gordon Hawkins, in their aptly-titled book *Crime is not the Problem: Violence in America*, argue that what sets the US apart is its level of *lethal* violent crime, which shapes Americans' views on how *all crimes* should be handled:

> To characterize concern about serious personal violence as the dominant image in public fear of crime may seem like an overstatement. [We] will document the relatively low levels of danger to life associated with residential burglary as a crime, but residential burglary is a crime that citizens greatly fear in California. Indeed, including residential burglary as a triggering felony in the California "three strikes" sentencing proposal was vigorously supported by the public even though it tripled the cost of the program. Is this not evidence that nonviolent threats are as salient to individuals as violent ones?

---

[41] See, e.g., PAOLO BUONNANO & ROBERTO GALBIATI, CRIME IN EUROPE AND IN THE US: DISSECTING THE "REVERSAL OF MISFORTUNES" (2010).

Probably not. Public fear of burglary is generated by images of the worst thing that could happen in the course of a housebreaking, rather tha[n] the kind of things that usually do happen when burglars appear. [Most burglaries are of unoccupied structures, and most burglars of occupied structures would react non-violently.] [B]ut the image of burglary that produces high levels of citizen fear finds the victim defenseless in bed and at risk of murder. It is the worst-case burglar that provokes those citizens who express high levels of fear regarding residential burglary.

[Zimring and Hawkins then note that people generally adopt a homogenous, composite view of "the criminal."] In an urban environment where armed robbery frequently leads to the death of victims, the purse snatcher and the burglar will acquire much of the threatening character of the robber because the composite generalized image of the criminal that conditions public fear acquires the characteristics of the armed robber.[42]

In other words, we fear all crime more than many other countries because we overestimate the risk it will end in lethal violence—but that is because our levels of lethal crime are substantially higher than they are in the rest of the developed world.

Zimring and Hawkins then continue, pointing out that a tough-on-crime response to violent crime will generally not increase the number of violent offenders locked up by much:

The dramatic increase in resources devoted to the punishment of crime in recent years provides a clinical case study of the impact of a general crackdown on crime on policy towards violent crime. The paradox of the crime crackdown is this: When penal resources are scarce, the priority given to more serious offenses means that life-threatening violence will receive a large share of the most serious punishments. No matter how small the prison, we tend to make room for Charles Manson and Willie Horton. But expanding punishment resources will have ore effect on case of marginal seriousness rather than those that provoke the greatest degree of citizen fear. The result is that when fear of lethal violence is translated into a general campaign against crime, the major share of extra resources will be directed at nonviolent behavior.[43]

But criminal justice is about more than crime, and the US and Europe differ in more than just their levels of lethal violence. The following excerpt, reviewing a book by the British criminologist Nicola Lacey, touches on the some of the economic, cultural, and political

---

[42] FRANKLIN E. ZIMRING & GORDON HAWKINS, CRIME IS NOT THE PROBLEM: LETHAL VIOLENCE IN AMERICA 12–13 (1997).

[43] *Id.* at 17.

differences between Europe and the US that may explain our divergent rates of incarceration, and in doing so may help us better understand how we got here and what solutions are possible.

James Q. Whitman, Book Review, *The Prisoners' Dilemma: Political Economy and Punishment in Contemporary Democracies*
13 NEW CRIM. L. REV. 625, 625–632 (2010)

American punitiveness is . . . quite literally off the comparative charts. How can we explain this ugly fact. . . ? The data collected by [two scholars] strongly suggest that the answer lies in political economy: they show that punishment regimes are generally most punitive in neoliberal, market-oriented countries like the United States and the United Kingdom, and less punitive in the countries that they classify under three other headings, "conservative-corporatist," "social-democratic," and "oriental corporatist."

What can account for these correlations between punitiveness and political economy? The first part of *The Prisoners' Dilemma* [by Nicola Lacey] offers Lacey's basic analytic account of the driving forces behind the punitiveness of the "market liberal" orders of which the United States is the most familiar, not to say most extreme, representative. [H]er principal focus is on two aspects of comparative political economy, labor economics and electoral institutions.

The relationship between labor economics and criminal punishment has been a subject of long-standing interest among scholars. . . . There is an older, broadly *marxisante* tradition, that starts from the recognition that the prison population is overwhelmingly drawn from the mass of laborers at the low end of the wage market. Many conclusions follow from the proposition that prisons house low-wage workers, and more broadly the poor: that prison labor may compete with free labor; that prison conditions must be unpleasant enough that workers do not prefer imprisonment to membership in the re-serve army of the unemployed (the "principle of less eligibility"); or that prisons may simply evolve . . . into holding pens for the impoverished and the low-caste. There is also a Foucauldian strand of argument . . . which links prison to practices of industrial discipline.

Lacey rings a significant change on these literatures, and one that offers a strong argument against the proposition that the American style of harsh punishment must inevitably spread to the rest of the capitalist world. Drawing on the "varieties of capitalism" scholarship . . . , she distinguishes the workforces of neoliberal economies like that of the United States from the workforces of coordinated economies like that of, for example, Germany. "Coordinated" market economies—those descended from the "organized capitalism" of the turn of the nineteenth century—are characterized by distinctive patterns of social and labor relations. They tend to have comparatively robust social welfare orders. Moreover, by contrast with liberal market economies, coordinated market economies depend heavily on a highly trained workforce, able to produce high-quality, high-unit-cost goods. These are workers with consider-able industry-specific and indeed firm-specific human capital, which implies that they are generally less mobile than workers in a liberal market economy like that of the United States, and more deeply integrated into their communities.

If, as so many scholars have believed, there is some intimate relationship between imprisonment and labor markets, then we might expect the differences between the labor markets of liberal market economies and those of coordinated market economies to lead to corresponding differences in their punishment practices. Exactly that, Lacey argues, is the case. Coordinated economies depend on skilled workers who are well integrated into society. The implication for punishment practices is fundamental: if coordinated economies need well-integrated workers, then it should be no surprise to discover that their punishment systems emphasize reintegration into society.

Thus we should not expect the prisons of coordinated economies to be in the classic Marxist business of holding the whip-hand over the "reserve army of the unemployed"—by contrast with liberal market economies.

This does not mean that coordinated economies have no ugly face to present: they can be quite tough on outsiders—particularly ethnic outsiders—who do not come across as easy candidates for integration. Nevertheless, it does help explain why they do not descend into the depths of punitiveness found in the American liberal market economy.

Labor market differences are only part of Lacey's political economy story, though. She also emphasizes differences in electoral systems. Scholars . . . have laid much of the blame for the harshness of criminal punishment in the United States on the extreme politicization of American criminal justice. Elected officeholders in America often run on tough-on-crime platforms—and those elected officeholders commonly include not only ordinary political representatives but also judges and prosecutors. At the same time, the views of criminal justice professionals carry much less weight than they do in northern continental Europe. The result is a nasty race to the political bottom, in which the competing parties try to outdo each other in proposing ever harsher criminal legislation.

Why do we not see the same pattern in countries like Germany? Lacey points to the mechanics of electoral representation, and in particular to the contrast between first-past-the-post representation of the kind used in the United States and proportional representation of the kind used in Germany. American elections are decided in a single round of voting, with victory going to the candidate who receives the largest number of votes in any given district. . . . Germany, by contrast, has a mixed system, in which only some candidates are elected to represent particular districts. Other representatives are drawn from party lists, with parties represented in proportion to their share of the vote. Germany thus uses a system of partial proportional representation, with representation by parties rather than by districts. Such systems of proportional representation, Lacey observes, are empirically associated with coordinated market economies.

Systems of proportional representation, Lacey contends, make for healthier electoral politics when it comes to criminal justice. This is primarily because the disciplined parties that dominate in coordinated economies with proportional representation remain tightly wedded to their established constituencies and their established programs. American politicians are constantly in the hunt for the votes of the "floating median voter": they are scrambling to find issues that will attract otherwise uncommitted votes. Crime is, of course, just such an issue. Politicians in countries like Germany, by contrast, can depend on committed voters, to a large extent; and German parties are always already associated with particular issues. The consequence is that systems of proportional representation of the kind we find in coordinated economies are broadly immune to the horrors of American-style politicization of crime. Instead, they show a salutary deference to the views of criminal justice professionals.

Lacey also makes use of the argument I offered in what she calls the "degradation thesis" of my 2003 book *Harsh Justice*. My book offered a claim about the historical development of social status over the last two and half centuries. Degradation, I argued, is indeed centrally important to the functioning of punishment; and the harshness of American punishment reflects a much grander American willingness to tolerate degrading practices. But why is there more toleration for degradation in America? The answer lies in a comparative history of that reaches back to the mid-eighteenth century. Historically, I argued, persons of different status were subject to different forms of criminal punishment in the Western world. Those of high social status were punished in relatively mild and nondegrading ways, whereas those of low social status were subjected to harsh and degrading punishments. Over the last couple of centuries, this now-forgotten premodern system of status distinctions has broken everywhere in the Atlantic world, but it is has broken down differently in America and northern continental Europe. Northern continental Europe has experienced a process of "levelling up," in which historically high-status punishments have slowly been generalized to the entire population. Continental Europe is marked by an egalitarian effort to guarantee dignity for all. By contrast, America has tended to level down, eliminating all forms of high-status treatment and establishing a kind of equality of low status. The result is that norms of degradation that been largely been abolished in countries like France and Germany have survived in the United States, with great consequent suffering for convicts.

Nevertheless, there is a core unclarity in Lacey's argument about labor markets that deserves some scrutiny. Lacey observes that coordinated market economies are "premised on incorporation." It is not clear whether she means this as a claim about the mechanics of their labor markets or about as a claim about their cultural values. If Lacey is making a claim about the mechanics of labor markets, I think her conclusions must be rejected. [Whitman then points out that coordinated economies often have persistently high unemployment rates, suggesting that not everyone is integrated into the economy.]

But perhaps that is not what she means when she says that coordinated market economies are "premised on incorporation." There is a more plausible way to read her argument; and that is to read it as an argument about cultural values. Not all workers in a country like Germany can be proud members of the skilled trades—perhaps least of all the small number of mostly violent and sorely maladjusted Germans who end up in prison. Nevertheless, admiration for skilled labor may have set the cultural tone in ways that have a real effect on incarceration practices. German culture, one might argue, assumes that the most normatively attractive state of affairs is one in which citizens are integrated into the economy on the basis of a strong command of professional knowledge. It assumes, that is, a norm of *Standesehre*, as Weber analyzed it—of the honor of belonging to a guild-like, profession-based, status group. If such is the cultural norm, if the measure of true integration into society is the kind of integration en-joyed by skilled laborers, then it may come naturally to make the effort to treat inmates as though they could easily be integrated—as though they could easily be transformed into persons with professional status honor.

It is not the case, I would suggest, that punishment in the coordinated economy of a country like Germany is more oriented toward integration because its workers all belong in fact to skilled trades, and certainly not because ex-convicts can in fact routinely be transformed into high-wage, high-status, well-integrated skilled workers. Punishment is more oriented toward integration because there is a deep cultural commitment to generalizing the *Standesehre* of skilled workers to the whole wage-earning population. There is here, as so often, a drive to level up, a drive to treat everybody, even prison inmates, as though they belonged to a relatively honorable and well-integrated status group. The economy of the labor market cannot explain the pattern. What can explain it is the economy of honor—in this case, the economy of Weberian *Standesehre*.

I believe that we can also profitably reflect on the cultural significance of Weberian *Standesehre* if we wish to make the best sense of Lacey's claims about electoral politics. In effect, Lacey's book makes two claims: first, that systems of proportional representation are inevitably less subject to the temptations of courting the median voter than are systems of first-past-the-post; and second, that in countries like France and Germany, there is more willingness to defer to the expertise of criminal justice professionals. The first of these claims represents a real, and convincing insight. The second, by contrast, is not argued by Lacey in a wholly satisfying way.

Lacey is absolutely right to say that there is more deference to professional expertise in France and Germany than there is in the United States. But why does this difference exist? The answer is not that politicians in these coordinated economies operate within a system of proportional representation in which they never try to appeal to the median voter by playing the tough-on-crime game. France does not have a system of proportional representation at all, and Germany has a mixed system. Most importantly, politicians in both countries do play the tough-on-crime game—though surely less often than their American counterparts. The deeper difference lies elsewhere. The deeper difference is that even when tough-on-crime politicians like Nicolas Sarkozy enter office, they must always negotiate their legislative programs with the professional experts in the relevant ministries. The deeper difference is that professional expertise commands social respect and political power in France and Germany, for reasons that manifestly go beyond the dynamics of proportional representation.

Those reasons are many. France and Germany both have deeply rooted bureaucratic traditions, for example. But we should note that, in part, the social power enjoyed by German and French criminal justice professionals reflects, once again, the high cultural value their societies place on *Standesehre*. Criminal justice professionals are professionals: they are members of a skilled, specialized, knowledge-based guild, and they operate in societies with deep-seated leanings toward deference and respect for professionals. Respect for professional knowledge belongs to the economy of honor in these continental countries. In the last analysis, the critical truth is that continental cultures remain very much oriented toward respect and deference—in contrast to the United States, where deference of all kinds tends to be suspect. The ultimate differences lie, to invoke the Weberian tradition once again, in the social structures of authority on either side of the Atlantic.

The broad takeaway from Zimring and Hawkins and from Whitman/Lacey is that America's exceptional incarceration rate did not arise in a vacuum, and thus addressing it will similarly require us to think about the broader cultural environment in which prisons, and those who shape their sizes, are situated. On the other hand, there remains a giant elephant in the room: the distinctions identified by Whitman/Lacey have been around, as Whitman notes, since the 1800s, if not earlier. Yet until the mid-1970s US incarceration was nothing exceptional. So clearly *something* changed, and something *comparative*. Perhaps Zimring and Hawkins point to the answer: perhaps the US became uniquely lethally violent, and underlying differences primed the US to respond in a much more punitive way.

CHAPTER 10

THE EFFECTS OF INCARCERATION

In this chapter, we turn from the "why" of incarceration to the "what": what does incarceration do to those who are incarcerated, their families, and their communities? As is so often the case in criminology, the answers are unclear. Prison can deter potential offenders and remove violent and disruptive individuals from the community. But it can also increase the risk of reoffending, weaken social ties, undermine future employment, destabilize already-weakened families, and lead to adverse physical and mental health outcomes. Measuring the magnitude of these effects, however, is difficult: those who end up in prison tend to come from already-weakened social settings, so simply comparing, say, the employment outcomes of ex-inmates to non-inmates overstates prison's impact on employment. Furthermore, the effects are highly contextual and thus vary over time. The impact on crime of rising incarceration during the low-incarceration/high-crime 1970s, for example, is surely different than that of rising incarceration during the high-incarceration/low-crime 2010s.

This chapter starts by looking at what life is like inside prisons. This is an important point on its own terms, since it forces us to ask to what extent should the conditions of confinement, and perhaps their differential impact across various types of inmates, be considered when deciding how to punish. We then look at the effects of incarceration on inmates, on their families, and on their communities, both during incarceration and following release. This chapter will not provide any clear or satisfying answers, because they do not exist. And this lack of answers raises tricky normative questions in and of itself: what is the optimal policy when we do not fully understand the costs and benefits? What sort of presumptions should we make? And who should bear the burden of that uncertainty?

A. LIFE INSIDE PRISON

Popular culture, such as television shows like *Oz*, portray prisons as violent, almost lawless, institutions. But while life in prison is a deeply unpleasant experience, in many ways it is more because of the boredom than the violence, as shown in the following excerpt, which is drawn from a diary kept by a prisoner in Illinois as part of a research project on prison conditions.

Norval Morris, *The Contemporary Prison, 1965–Present*

The Oxford History of the Prison
(Norval Morris & David J. Rothman, eds., 1994)

One Day in the Life of #12345

You asked me to keep a diary for one day. You told me I was not to tell that things were good or bad—just to tell you exactly what I did and what happened to me through one day. I have never done anything like this before. It is not easy to describe a day of monotony and boredom other than as monotonous and boring.

Before I start on the diary, let me say this: if you expect the usual prison tale of constant violence, brutal guards, gang rapes, daily escape efforts, turmoil, and fearsome adventures, you will be deeply disappointed. Prison life is really nothing like what the press, television, and movies suggest. It is not a daily round of threats, fights, plots and "shanks" (prison-made knives)—though you have to be constantly careful to avoid situations or behavior that might lead to violence. A sense of impending danger is always with you; you must be careful to move around people rather than against or through them, but with care and reasonable sense you can move safely enough. For me, and many like me in prison, violence is not the major problem; the major problem is monotony. It is the dull sameness of prison life, its idleness and boredom, that grinds me down. Nothing matters; everything is inconsequential other than when you will be free and how to make time pass until then. But boredom, time-slowing boredom, interrupted by occasional bursts of fear and anger, is the governing reality of life in prison.

So, here is my diary for yesterday:

<u>5:30 A.M.:</u>

I was awakened by the wake-up call for the kitchen detail. I am not on that detail, but the banging on the bars of the cell near me, to awaken a prisoner who is on the kitchen detail, wakes me every morning. I knew I could doze for the next half hour, half awake but careful not to think about where I was. I heard Tyrone stirring in the bunk beneath mine, but today he did not, as he often does, celebrate the new day with a loud and odorous fart.

<u>6:00 A.M.:</u>

As F House came to life, the noise began—radios, TVs, shouting from cell to cell—and so it would go on till night, with an occasional scream of rage or fear through the night.

Tyrone and I did our best to keep out of each other's way in the space of nine feet by six in our cell while we used our toilet and washed and dressed and pulled up the blankets on our steel bunks. We change our outer clothes sometimes twice a week, sometimes once a week, and our socks and underwear every other day. If you have money, or influence, or a friend in the laundry, you can do better than this. Our sartorial flourish is our sneakers, with Nike outranking Reebok and so on down the line; they cost a lot, but in this place they are worth it.

8:05 A.M.:

All the cells throughout the prison, ours included, were locked for "Morning Count." The count, usually four times a day but sometimes more, is a slow process. The early morning count and the last count around 11:30 p.m. do not interfere with the routine of the prison, since all prisoners are then locked in their cells and the count is easier to take. The other counts present more difficulty. Nothing goes on in the prison until the count is reported from every cell house and from everywhere that prisoners are supposed to be, nothing until the numbers reported reconcile exactly the numbers that are supposed to be there. It can go on for a long time. It is the central ritual of prison life.

10:30 A.M:.

I decided . . . to have a shower; I felt hot and smelly from [an earlier] workout. I took off my shoes and socks, rolled up my pants legs, slipped into my shower sandals, and grabbed my washcloth and towel and a green bar of state-issue soap. Many prisoners buy "commissary soap," some TV-advertised soap, on their weekly visit to the commissary; but I'm going nowhere special for some time, and state soap will do fine until I'm free. At this time all the cells were open in F House, so without having to signal the guard I walked down the three flights of stairs and along the paint-peeled ramp to the showers. Most prisoners shower "with security," that is, when there are guards about to watch the shower room. I prefer to shower "without security." The showers are dangerous places; gangs tend to shower together as protective measure; only a very few prisoners shower alone and without security, as I do. I am know as a loner and dangerous to cross and tend therefore to be left alone. The shower room seems designed for crazies. There are these buttons you push, and then the water comes out of for a couple of minutes, then is stops, and you push again. This is supposed to be for "water conservation," but of course everyone pushes all the buttons all the time so that the water is hotter and continuous. So much for saving water.

When you come to prison it is wise to leave all shyness behind. But I am not anxious for myself in the showers. Here in Stateville there aren't gang rapes or even rapes that I hear about, though they are reputed to take place occasionally, and they are certainly more frequent in the jails. Here, the gay community is largely left alone by both prisoners and guards, though there is a good deal of vulgarity directed their way. The old thing about "dropping the soap in the shower" is ancient history. Girlie magazines and a tacit acceptance of masturbation, including mutual masturbation, as well as of other relatively consensual homosexual relationships, minimize sex-related violence. And the fact that there are quite a few women guards at Stateville seems to help.

Prisoners taking showers need security from gang attacks, not from sexual attacks. Still, I suppose I am always a little anxious in the showers; I avoid being alone in the showers with any one or more who might have some particular reason to dislike me. Even if violence is not all that common, still there is often tension and anxiety and, I suppose, fear.

11:30 A.M.:

I looked for some semi-clean socks, got dressed, and started typing a letter. I was waiting for the call to lunch, though I hate the mess hall at lunchtime. It is chaos at lunch; the prisoners refuse to act "orderly," and the guards do not take the trouble to enforce order. The gang element is definitely in control. Nevertheless, to the sound of "Chow going out the door," I joined the mass of prisoners heading for the tunnel. We were kept waiting outside the mess hall. The noise built up. The guy in front of me yelled at one of his buddies, who stepped up and joined him in front of me. I made no complaint; it wasn't worth it, and in the confusion nobody took any notice of such matters.

The door to our segment of the dining room was finally opened, the guards stepped back, and everyone tried at once to squeeze through the twenty-inch opening, rushing for the soggy vegetables and limp pasta that awaited them. Once I got my food, after ten or fifteen minutes in the surging line, with the food servers shouting at one another, spraying the food, I sat down at a table and joined my regular lunchtime group, with conversation devoted to complaints about the food and discussions of TV programs. I found myself unusually dejected, waiting for the doors to be unlocked so that I could get back to the relative peace of my cell.

1:00 P.M.:

I joined the "school" detail with six others from F House and went off to a course on computers run in the school area. Unlike all but a few prisoners in Stateville, I am a genuine high school graduate. There are a few more who claim to be such, but the truth is that a majority of my fellow prisoners in Stateville are functionally illiterate, and only a handful have any sort of a record of high school academic achievement. In earlier years in Stateville I worked in the furniture factory and in the tailor shop, earning more than I can earn at school, but the computer course interested me, and I applied for it and got it. I have now been in it for three months and am beginning to be able to write programs. It fills my afternoons, three days a week, two hours each day.

The better-educated have the pick of the jobs in Stateville. Though it is poorly paid, the library, particularly the law library, is probably the best job, passing prison time more swiftly than other prison jobs, having influence in the prison, and being left alone by the guards; but the computer class seems to me in some ways even better. In the distant years when I am free I may be able to use what I am learning about computer programming, but I doubt it; the point is that it helps to keep me alive here.

3:30 P.M.:

Two guards escorted the school detail back to F House. I went back to my cell. Tyrone was showering, his work in the tailor shop finished. While he was away I turned on the TV. It is my set, but I cannot control what we watch, since his friends outside could afford to give him a set if he wanted it. So, if we are to share this cell, we have to strike some bargain about what we watch. I am fortunate; he mostly falls in with my preferences, and when he doesn't, I yield.

I've never watched so much TV as I do here. I turned on Channel 11/WTTW Chicago, "Your Window to the World," for me an ideal program. It's just what I want, a public television news commentary program; I wish I had money to give them a contribution—they ask for it frequently. The TV is on a little table we have rigged up beside the toilet; it is best watched by lying on one's bunk. Tyrone came in and lay down on his bunk without speaking. It's the best way; avoid useless chatter.

I got sleepy and dozed.

I was awakened by the mailman rapping on the bars of our cell and giving a small package of mail to Tyrone. Nothing for me; after a year or two in prison, incoming mail dries up to a trickle, even if you write regularly.

5:00 P.M.:

I watched the local news. It was depressing, much of it about the activities of people who are on their way here. I lay on my bunk, half listening to the news, half daydreaming of freedom. Like most other prisoners, I devote much of my waking thought, and all my dream time, to being out of prison.

5:25 P.M.:

The loudspeaker blared again, "Three and four galleries, get ready for chow." The food is often worse in the evening than at lunch, but it is better to go than to stay in what by now the thundering noise of F House, with TVs and radios blaring and, it seems to me, every prisoner shouting to another prisoner and nobody listening. The evening meal was a less-adequate replica of lunch, with more bread and less pasta; but the pushing and shoving was also less, and the gangs were less active.

* * *

There are, of course, the regular variations in our days. Regularly we go to the barbershop, where our apprentice-barber fellow prisoners practice their skills on us. There is the weekly visit to the commissary. There are Sundays, with their more relaxed regimen, more open yard and gym time, more sitting or walking about in groups talking. There are times to go to the library and to the law library for those of us still appealing our convictions or pursuing prisoners' rights litigation, which they tell me is a good way to "do time" but rarely produces any success in the courts. And then there are the hard-to-avoid confrontations with some of the guards—leading to tickets and segregation and loss of a "good time." Even worse are the collective punishments of the "lockdown," when cells are locked for all twenty-four hours, sometimes for months, with only one shower a week out of the cell; time moves even slower then.

Neither Tyrone nor I use prison hooch or drugs to get through the days and nights, but many prisoners do, and the disorder of prison, the frequency of punishments and of lockdowns, is increased because of it. Drugs, all drugs, are readily available at about twice their street price, payable inside or outside the prison. Some drugs come over the wall; some are brought in by guards; some make their way in with visitors, despite the administration's efforts; small quantities are hidden under the stamps or built into pockets in envelopes; one way or another, I am told, drugs are available in every large prison and jail, and they certainly are available here if you can pay for them.

Gang activity is another addiction of our prison. Gang membership is known to the prison authorities, but there is not much they can do about it. They try to move gang leaders about, from one prison to another, but this only briefly interrupts gang activity—new leaders promptly emerge. The gangs influence who moves safely in the prison and who gets into trouble with the prison authorities; they influence a great deal of life in prison. The influence of gangs in Stateville is much the same as it is on the streets, though mercifully they are not equipped with guns here, only with shanks.

I am not sure whether the average prisoner is safer physically in prison than on the streets, where most of us come from. In Stateville, we are less likely to be shot and killed but possibly slightly more likely to be knifed or injured seriously in a fight. Fights are not uncommon but they are always followed up by the prison authorities, and an effort is made to punish those responsible There are regular and intermittent shakedowns of all the cells and other areas for shanks and other contraband. It is a violent place, but most prisoners do their time without being victimized physically unless they are looking to prove something to themselves or unless they get it into trouble with betting, or hooch, or drugs, or with the gangs. Those who adhere to the main tenets of the prison culture—never "rat" on another prisoner, always keep your distance from staff, "do your own time"—have the best chance of avoiding violence.

I hope this diary is of use to you; it fails to capture the constant unhappiness of prison life and the constant sense of danger—you are never for a moment happy, except sometimes briefly on visitors days, and that is a bitter happiness. The letter misses the relentless, slow-moving routine, the dull repetitiveness, the tension mixed with occasional flashes of fear and rage; it misses the consuming stupidity of living this way. I am sorry; it is not easy. Probably prison was easier to describe many years ago when prison guards saw themselves as punishers, inflicting pain on prisoners, and prisoners joined together to resist them. Now, in prisons like Stateville, purposes are unclear, education is largely a token, idleness takes the place of work and industry, and keeping peace and safety between prisoner and prisoner is the prevailing aim. Anyhow, that is how it appears to this prisoner.

Let me know, when you will visit me. I hope soon.

Here we encounter the first complicated fact of this chapter. Prisons are clearly violent places. Yet if we look at homicide rates, which are likely the only really reliable crime rate we can consider,[1] the rate in prison in 2002 was actually lower than the national rate, 4 per 100,000 vs. 5.6 per 100,000. And, in practice, this implies that the homicide victimization rate for offenders is substantially lower than what they face in the outside world, since most violent crime is highly concentrated in the communities from which these offenders disproportionately come.

Sexual assault in prison, which perhaps better measures the sort of routine day-to-day violence that may permeate prisons and be only weakly correlated with homicide, has received significant of attention of late, especially since the passage of the Prison Rape Elimination Act in 2003. In 2007, there were 2,421 allegations of "inmate-on-inmate nonconsensual sexual acts," which is PREA's analog to the FBI's "forcible rape" category, of which 268 were confirmed. This translates into rates of 96 per 100,000 for the allegations and 11 per 100,000 for the confirmed cases. For comparison, in 2010 the rate of forcible rape for the nation was 27.5 per 100,000, although for men it was something closer to 4 per 100,000.[2]

Or consider assaults in prison. According to official statistics in the Census of State and Federal Correctional Facilities, there were 30,344 inmate-on-inmate assaults in 2000, which translates into a rate of 2,755 per 100,000 (which was up slightly from 2,561 per 100,000).[3] In an effort to account for almost-certain under-reporting in official statistics, several social scientists interviewed about one-third of all prisoners in a high-

---

[1] Homicides cannot be falsely reported by inmates, nor can they be ignored by prison officials, although officials may attempt to cover up some murders as natural deaths, suicides, or accidental deaths. At least since the passage of the Death in Custody Reporting Act of 2000, however, it seems reasonable to assume that reported and real homicide rates bear a reasonable relationship to each other. See http://bjs.ojp.usdoj.gov/content/pub/pdf/shsplj.pdf for more information on DiCRA.

[2] The rate of rape for women in 2010 was 54.2 per 100,000, and 93% of all rape victims were women. Since there are roughly as many men as women (155 million to 159 million), this translates into a rate of 4 per 100,000 for men. Of course, rape is widely under-reported, and it is likely that men under-report more so even than women.

[3] JAMES J. STEPHAN & JENNIFER C. KARBERG, CENSUS OF STATE AND FEDERAL CORRECTIONAL FACILITIES, 2000, v (2000).

incarceration mid-Atlantic state in 2005 and reported assault rates on the order of 7,500 per 100,000 to 20,500 per 100,000.[4] For comparison, in 2000 the aggravated assault rate nationwide was 324 per 100,000.

The comparison here, though, is not quite fair, since the prison surveys look at *any* assault, and the FBI just reports *aggravated assault*. The FBI does not provide offending data on simple assault, but in 2000 nearly three times as many people were arrested for simple assault as for aggravated assault; if arrests are equally proportional to offending for both types of crimes, then the overall assault rate outside of prison is about 1,200 per 100,000.

> **Question:** Looking just at official statistics, does this mean that someone in prison is about twice as likely to be assaulted in prison as outside of it (2,755 per 100,000 vs. 1,200 per 100,000)? Is the nationwide population really the correct comparison group? Comparing the survey results to the UCR statistics suggests that the risk of assault in prison is up to 20 times higher (20,500 per 100,000 to 1,200 per 100,000). But what (similar) concerns should we have with the *UCR* assault rate?

In short, we should be careful not to underestimate the magnitude of violence within prison, but we should also be careful not to forget the disproportionately violent environment from which prisoners are drawn.

All that said, the nature of prisons vary widely for institution to institution. Obviously, conditions in minimum security prisons will be less oppressive than those in a maximum-security institution. And conditions are likely better in jurisdictions with well-funded prison systems than in those that spend much less per-capita.[5] But even prisons with the same type of prisoners in the same state—even when physically close—can be quite different, as this report from New York State indicates:

> Another example of this variation is found in two neighboring prisons in the western region of the state, Gowanda and Collins Correctional Facilities. Although both are medium-security prisons for men located across the road from each other, their cultures are worlds apart. At Collins, inmates and staff refer to the prison as a "campus." The atmosphere is markedly peaceful; prisoners and staff reported few complaints when we visited. Everyone seemed invested in keeping the prison safe and calm. At Gowanda Correctional Facility, however, we received numerous reports from inmates, attorneys and family members

---

[4] Nancy Wolff, Cynthia L. Blitz, Jing Shi, Jane Siegel & Ronet Bachman, *Physical Violence Inside Prisons: Rates of Victimization*, 34 CRIM. JUSTICE & BEHAV. 588, 593 Table 1 (2007).

[5] In a 2001 study, for example, the BJS reported that state per capita expenditures ranged from $8,128 in Alabama (the only state to spend under $12,000 per year) to over $44,000 in Maine, with the national average at $22,650. http://bjs.ojp.usdoj.gov/content/pub/pdf/spe01.pdf.

before, during and after the visit about serious correction officer misconduct. Letters and phone calls about inmate abuse pointed to an unspoken policy of "might makes right," which appeared largely ignored by a detached administration. In explaining the different attitudes and styles among staff, correction officers at Collins said that security staff tends to seek positions at prisons where the culture supports their style of management.[6]

And while unpleasant, conditions have been even worse in the past. In a wave of cases starting across the South in the 1960s and 1970s, federal courts reversed a long-standing policy of remaining uninvolved with prison conditions and started to find that the conditions in many prisons violated the Eighth Amendment. By 2000, at least 26 states had had most or all of their correctional system under some sort of judicial oversight. And the impact has been significant, as Margo Schlanger explains:

> Although assessing the impact of the litigation is a complex topic . . . , it is clear that inmates gained much from the orders. For example, a case study of *Guthrie v. Evans* [93 F.R.D. 390 (S.D. Ga. 1981)], the Georgia State Prison case that ended in 1985, summarized its positive effects:
>
>> The inhuman practices and conditions at [Georgia State Prison] that the special monitor described in 1979 no longer exist. The reign of terror against inmates has ended. Today, guards do not routinely beat, mace, and shoot inmates. Inmates and guards no longer die from a lack of safety and protection. Guards can walk the cells without having to carry illegal knives and pickax handles to protect themselves. The medical, mental, nutritional, educational, and recreational needs of inmates are now provided for. . . . Those changes were the result, in large part if not solely, of the Guthrie litigation.
>
> Inmate memoirs and writings confirm the point. For example, a 1979 article by Wilbert Rideau, then the (inmate) editor of the Louisiana State Penitentiary's *Angolite*, gave credit to court-order litigation for reducing sexual violence:
>
>> While [rapes] used to be a regular feature of life here at the Louisiana State Penitentiary, they are now a rare occurrence. Homosexuality still thrives, but the violence and forced slavery that used to accompany it have been removed. In 1976, Federal District Court Judge E. Gordon West ordered a massive crackdown on overall violence at the prison, which paved the way for the allocation of money,

---

[6] PRISON VISITING COMMITTEE OF THE CORRECTIONAL ASSOCIATION OF NEW YORK, STATE OF THE PRISONS 10 (2002).

manpower, and sophisticated electronic equipment to do the job. Since then, any kind of violence at all between inmates elicits swift administrative reprisal and certain prosecution. This, more than anything else, has made Angola safe for the average youngster coming into the prison today.

Many—though by no means all—other sources concur. Moreover, the effects of court orders are by no means limited to the systems in which they are entered. As I have suggested elsewhere, "orders also cast a marked general deterrent shadow on systems hoping to avoid them. And they have a mimetic impact, as other systems imitate them not out of fear but rather out of a more positive interest."

Prison and jail officials were frequently collaborators in the litigation. If they did not precisely invite it, they often did not contest it. [T]he remedies in the cases, frequently designed at least in part by the defendants themselves, very much served what at least some of those defendants saw as their interests: increasing their budgets, controlling their inmate populations, and encouraging the professionalization of their workforces and the bureaucratization of their organizations. As one jail administrator put it:

> To be sure, we used "court orders" and "consent decrees" for leverage. We ranted and raved for decades about getting federal judges "out of our business"; but we secretly smiled as we requested greater and greater budgets to build facilities, hire staff, and upgrade equipment. We "cussed" the federal courts all the way to the bank.

Even when the litigation was not simply justification for a larger budget, it was useful to prison and jail administrators seeking to solidify their control over their organizations. A prison official in Kentucky, describing a major court-order case about conditions at the Kentucky State Reformatory, explained that the consent decree in the case

> Changed the whole system. It made the system unified. We had a cabinetwide policy and then institution policies clarified those. . . . That's the guideline by which you operate and function. . . . We have all this training. The training uses all the policies and procedures, explains the importance of the policies and procedures.

The decrees professionalized and bureaucratized by the terms they imposed, but also by their impact on who was interested in becoming or qualified to become an administrator. As an inmate involved in the same Kentucky litigation observed:

> But you know what? Guys like those old-time wardens can never be warden at LaGrange any more. That's the beautiful thing about that consent decree. It made that system so damn sophisticated that you just can't walk out of the head of a holler in Hazard, out of the logging woods, an' walk right in and be the warden.

In short, court orders had an enormous impact on the nation's jails and prisons by direct regulation, their indirect effects, and the shadow they cast. Among the areas affected were staffing, the amount of space per inmate, medical and mental health care, food, hygiene, sanitation, disciplinary procedures, conditions in disciplinary segregation, exercise, fire safety, inmate classification, grievance policies, race discrimination, sex discrimination, religious discrimination and accommodations, and disability discrimination and accommodations—in short, nearly all aspects of prison and jail life, with the notable (if not quite universal) exceptions of education, custody level, and rehabilitative programming and employment.[7]

Such oversight was undermined in 1996, however, when Congress passed the Prison Litigation Reform Act, which made it harder for federal district courts to maintain oversight of state prison systems, and for prisoners to file claims in federal court alleging improper conditions. The motivation behind the statute was a concern about the impact of frivolous lawsuits as the volume of confinement cases soared (from about 3,000 to 40,000 between the 1970s and the late-1990s). The impact of the PLRA on prison conditions is hard to observe, but it surely must have had some effect on the margin.

In short, prisons are unpleasant places, though today the boredom may be more harmful than the constant background violence. And while prison litigation and the resulting professionalization of departments of correction have improved conditions significantly, serious problems persist. For example, as we will see below, California's prison system has been under the control of the Ninth Circuit for several years now; the courts have held that as many as one inmate per day has "unnecessarily" died due to overcrowding and inadequate medical and mental health care.

QUESTIONS

1. **Subjective punishment, Part 1.** Prison is unpleasant, but identical conditions will impact different defendants differently: someone weak and claustrophobic will find a given term in a specific prison more punitive than someone strong and tolerant of confined spaces. This has led

---

[7] Margo Schlanger, *Civil Rights Injunctions Over Time: A Case Study of Jail and Prison Court Orders*, 81 N.Y.U. L. REV. 550, 561–564 (2006).

some academics to argue that we should take these subjective experiences into account, both from a retributivist and a consequentialist perspective. Others have replied that, at least from a retributivist perspective, subjective experience is relatively unimportant, since "punishment" is less about the punishment *experienced* by the offender and more about the *objective statement* about the wrongness of the conduct. Normatively, who has the more compelling argument?

2. **Subjective punishment, Part 2.** If we did take subjective experiences into account, who would "win," and who would "lose"? Are we okay with these distributive implications? And how would judges or correctional officials accurately assess that subjective experience, and should it be evaluated *ex ante* or *ex post*, i.e., at sentencing or parole?

B. THE IMPACT OF INCARCERATION ON AN INMATE AND HIS FAMILY

Here are some facts which, taken out of context, seem to suggest that going to prison severely weakens an inmate's life experiences:

- Unemployment rates are substantially higher: 62% of New York State parolees are unemployed, and as many as 80% of California's.[8]

- The wages of those who have been to prison are about 20% lower than those who never have, weeks worked are 45% fewer, and annual income is about 60% smaller.[9]

- HIV rates of prisoners are three times the national average, and prisoners are at elevated risks for diseases such as tuberculosis and Hepatitis.[10]

- The rate of mental health problems in prisons appears to be about five times that in the overall US population.[11]

- Similarly, drug use and abuse among inmates seems to be about five time the national average (and likely skewed more towards heavier, non-marijuana, drugs).

- Children of incarcerated parents are about 10% more likely to engage in antisocial behavior than similarly-situated peers.[12]

---

[8] https://www.parole.ny.gov/program_stats.html (last visited November 1, 2014); Mediha Fejzagic DiMartino, "Parolees Struggling to Find Jobs," The (San Bernardino) Sun Times, August 29, 2009 (citing the California Research Bureau).

[9] BRUCE WESTERN, PUNISHMENT AND INEQUALITY, at 116 Table 5.2 (2007).

[10] See, e.g., Andrew P. Wilper, Steffie Woolhandler, J. Wesley Boyd, Karen E. Lasser, Danny McCormick, David H. Bor, & David U. Himmelstein, *The Health and Health Care of US Prisoners: Results of a Nationwide Survey*, 99 AM. J. PUB. HEALTH 666 (2009).

[11] JAMES & GLAZE, MENTAL HEALTH PROBLEMS, supra note 7.

[12] Joseph Murray, David P. Farrington, & Ivana Sekol, Children's Antisocial Behavior, Mental Health, Drug Use, and Educational Performance After Parental Incarceration: A Systematic Review and Meta-Analysis, 138 PSYCH. BULL. 175 (2012).

The picture here is bleak, and it suggests that punishment continues long after the inmate is released from prison. But the implications of the above facts are somewhat difficult to unpack. Prisoners are not drawn from a random sample of the American population: they are disproportionately poor, sick, and addicted to drugs and alcohol *even before incarceration*. Thus to properly understand the *marginal* impact of incarceration on financial, social, and health outcomes, we need to compare those in prison not to the average American (as the above statistics do), but to other, *similar* individuals. Making such careful comparisons is challenging—the data are not readily available—but studies that do so indicate that prison exacerbates some of the ills identified above, but not all, and often to a smaller extent than the above facts suggest. This chapter will look at the collateral costs of incarceration on inmates and then on the communities from which they are disproportionately drawn. It then will conclude by looking at the relationship between incarceration and criminal offending, which is influenced in part by all the other collateral effects we will have considered.

B.1. THE COLLATERAL COSTS OF INCARCERATION ON THE INMATE

B.1.a. PRISON AND LABOR OUTCOMES

Compared to the average person, released inmates are less likely to find work, and the work they find is likely to pay less. But then inmates often had more checkered employment histories prior to their first incarceration; such difficulties perhaps contributed to the decision to commit crime in the first place, or some common factor—such as an untreated mental illness—both complicated the job search and led to greater risk of offending. So what is the *marginal* contribution of incarceration to diminished work-force outcomes?

One of the more rigorous treatments of this issue is by the sociologist Bruce Western.[13] He points to several ways in which incarceration can directly reduce employment options: direct restrictions (certain jobs are foreclosed to felons), loss of trust, loss of human capital, and loss of social (networking) capital. The first three are fairly intuitive; the fourth may need some explanation. **Social capital** is a nebulous word that takes on different meanings in different sociological contexts, but here it refers to the web of personal connections we all have, which can be very important in the job search. Despite the way it is often described, the labor market is not defined by formal arms-length transactions, since people frequently find jobs via contacts, friends, friends-of-friends, and so on. Incarceration undermines these networks: inmates are stigmatized, and

---

[13] BRUCE WESTERN, PUNISHMENT AND INEQUALITY, supra note 9.

they are often housed far from where they live, making it hard to maintain those ties that could have otherwise survived.

Comparing ex-inmates to a group of individuals who appear similar in many ways to the inmates but who had never been to prison, Western makes the following findings about those who have been to prison (by race/ethnicity of the inmate):[14]

% Reduction in:	White	Black	Hispanic
Weeks worked	9.7%	15.1%	13.7%
Hourly pay	16.3%	12.4%	24.7%
Annual income	35.8%	36.9%	32.2%

In other words, a white person sent to prison works 9.7% fewer weeks compared to a similarly-situated white person who hasn't been to prison, earns 16.3% less per hour, and has an annual income 35.8% smaller. The loss in income in particular can be severe. As Western states:

> A thirty-year old black high school dropout . . . earns on average nearly $9,000 annually, with incarceration resulting in a reduction of about $3,300. The parallel white earnings average $14,400, and the reduction about $5,200.

Tallied up, the lost income as a percent of total expected earnings runs to just over 40% for white, black, and Hispanic inmates alike.

Much of this effect is from ex-inmates being diverted to the "secondary labor market" of unsteady, part-time jobs with little security and no benefits. A defining feature of this market is a stagnation in wage growth. For workers who have not been incarcerated, wages rise between the ages of 25 to 35 by about 15% (for blacks) to 20% (for whites and Hispanics); for former inmates, from 0% (for whites and Hispanics) to 5% (for blacks).

Given the explanations for why incarceration reduces wages, such as loss of trust and displacement from the primary labor market, we should expect that the income effect of punishment is greater for wealthier defendants: their positions are more likely ones that require trust, are more likely to rely on human and social capital, and are more likely to face licensing restrictions. And there is some evidence consistent with this theory. Joel Waldfogel, for example, looked at defendants convicted of fraud and larceny in federal courts and found:

> large and significant effects of conviction on the employment probabilities and income of some federal fraud and larceny offenders, in particular those whose pre-conviction jobs apparently involve trust and those who go to prison. The pattern

---

[14] Id. at Fig. 5.1.

of income effects appears to be based on stigma rather than, say, stalled experience growth or job displacement.[15]

The effect of conviction is much less for those whose jobs do not require trust. John Lott similarly finds that the income effect on those convicted of federal drug offenses rises with the defendant's pre-conviction income.[16] Moreover, the income effect is often much greater than any fine imposed on the defendant.

A major problem that released inmates face is a host of restrictions on employment. In some cases, inmates are explicitly banned from jobs; in other cases, they are simply incapable of securing the necessary license from the state licensing agency, as the following passage describes:

> Licensing restrictions have generally been justified as essential "to foster high professional standards," while restrictions on employment opportunities are said to ensure that those hired have "good moral character." Employment-related sanctions have also been held out as preventive measures: "[s]ince organizations and employers are generally considered responsible for their employees, they must be allowed access to applicants' backgrounds and have the right to exclude those who present a danger to society as measured by their prior record." These restrictions are imposed not only for positions requiring specialized training, but for jobs typically held by workers with minimal educational and work experience. As the availability of low-skilled jobs declines, the economic consequences of collateral sanctions that restrict employment opportunities will escalate for ex-offenders, their families, and their communities.
>
> One of the primary employment restrictions facing ex-offenders is the prohibition against public employment. Alabama, Delaware, Iowa, Mississippi, Rhode Island, and South Carolina permanently deny convicted felons the right to public employment. The other forty-five states "permit public employment of convicted felons in varying degrees." Some states also impose or allow restrictions on hiring or licensing ex-offenders or parolees for particular professions (e.g., law, real estate, medicine, dentistry, engineering, pharmacy, nursing, physical therapy, and education).
>
> Many states further decrease ex-offenders' employment prospects through occupational licensing laws that contain character requirements that either bear no direct relation to the licensed occupation or that do not consider the individual circumstances of the crime for which the applicant was

---

[15] Joel Waldfogel, *The Effect of Criminal Conviction on Income and Trust "Reposed in the Workmen,"* 29 J. HUMAN RES. 62 (1994).

[16] John R. Lott, Jr., *An Attempt at Measuring the Total Monetary Penalty from Drug Convictions: The Importance of an Individual's Reputation*, 21 J. LEGAL STUDIES 159 (1992).

convicted. Licensing restrictions not only result in the loss of new employment opportunities, but also often act as a bar on reemployment in the profession in which the offender worked before she was convicted. Other ex-offenders find themselves unable to use skills they learned in prison occupational training programs.

Some employment restrictions are grounded in concerns for public safety, and may therefore be appropriate. As one commentator noted: "[I]t is clear why persons convicted of child molestation are not permitted to work in day care centers." However, there is a distinction between sanctions that are adopted with a goal of preventing future criminal activity and those that are essentially retributive, as is, perhaps, a bar on ex-offenders becoming licensed as barbers.

While some may see the benefit of allowing employers to discriminate against convicted felons, it is especially difficult to rationalize such discrimination on the basis of an arrest that did not even result in a conviction. Yet, this happens in a majority of states: "Thirty-eight states permit all employers (public and private) and occupational licensing agencies to inquire about and rely upon arrests that did not result in a conviction."[17]

The irony here can be painful. As the passage notes, New York State generally bans former inmates from working as barbers by denying them licenses. Yet what is the most popular training program in New York prisons? Barber school. While one state agency trains inmates to be barbers, another denies them the ability to practice.

Question: On-line access to criminal records has made it easier for employers to determine whether an applicant has a prior record or not (rather than relying on self-reports on job applications). What has this done for the employment opportunities for those with records? for those without records? Do you think there is one group of people without records who have particularly benefitted from on-line access?

B.1.b. PRISON AND HEALTH

Prisoners tend to be sicker than the population in general. Consider the following statistics from a 2009 article in the Journal of Epidemiology and Community Health (those unfamiliar with the concept of an "odds ratio" (OR) please see the next footnote):[18]

---

[17] Deborah N. Archer & Kele S. Williams, *Making America "The Land of Second Chances": Restoring Socioeconomic Rights for Ex-Offenders*, 30 N.Y.U. REV. OF L. & SOC. CHANGE 527, 535–537 (2006).

[18] Assume that there is a 10% chance people of type A will come down with a disease and a 20% chance that people of type B will contract it. Then the odds that an A-group person gets the disease is $O_A = (0.1)/(0.9) = 0.11$, and the odds a B-group person gets it is $O_B = (0.2)/(0.8) =$

Disease	Odds Ratio[19]	95% Confid. Interval[20]
Hypertension	1.12	1.03–1.22
Diabetes	1.06	0.92–1.23
Obese (vs. normal)	0.76	0.68–0.84
Overweight	1.19	1.09–1.29
Underweight	0.42	0.29–0.60
Angina	0.90	0.68–1.17
Heart attack	0.98	0.77–1.24
Asthma	1.31	1.19–1.45
Arthritis	1.49	1.36–1.63
Cancer	1.13	0.94–1.35
Cervical Cancer	3.94	2.91–5.34
Hepatitis	3.26	2.82–3.77

In other words, prisoners are at an elevated risk for a wide range of pathologies, generally to a statistically significant degree. Another study identified the rate of HIV infection among state prisoners at 1.7%, among federal inmates at 0.9%, and in the general population at 0.5%.[21]

These statistics suggest that prisoners tend to be sicker than the population as a whole. Unfortunately, as we saw with employment outcomes, this is not necessarily the right comparison group. Prisoners frequently come from communities that are disproportionately sick and have reduced access to medical care. It is thus hard to distinguish the *effect* of prison on health versus the population health from which

---

0.25. So the "odds ratio" for A-group people is (0.11)/(0.25) = 0.44, and for B-group people (0.25)/(0.11) = 2.27.

So, a few take-away points: (1) Always pay attention to the reference group. (2) If the odds ratio is less than one for the reference group, that group is less likely to experience the event. (3) Conversely, if the odds ratio is greater than one for the reference group, it is more likely to experience the event. (4) Clearly, if the odds ratio is one (or close to/indistinguishable from one), then the two groups are equally likely to experience the event.

[19] These results control for age, sex, race, education, USA-as-birthplace, marital status, alcohol consumption, and smoking.

[20] The "95% confidence interval" is a rough way of measuring the uncertainty of the effect. None of these studies looks at every person in the country or world, so the estimate is imprecise. But if the entire range of values is greater than or less than one, then we have some confidence in the fact that we have identified a true difference, not something that is just the product of who we randomly happened to sample.

[21] Wilper et al., *Nationwide Survey*, supra note 10.

prisoners are *selected*. A 2011 article in a leading medical journal, *The Lancet*, conceded that "The contribution of prisons to illness is unknown," though it added that "shortcomings in treatment and aftercare provision contribute to adverse outcomes."[22]

A recent study of Dutch prisons makes clear the importance of this selection effect.[23] Compared to the general Dutch population, the odds ratio of death within twenty-five years for a cohort of inmates incarcerated in 1977 was a quite-high 3.21, with a 95% confidence interval of 2.60–3.95.[24] But when compared to a cohort of criminals who were convicted in 1977 but not sent to prison, the odds ratio of dying drops to 1.47, with a 95% confidence interval of 1.14–1.89. And the number of causes of death that appear to be statistically significant drop as well, from eight (out of eleven) to three. The authors are careful to note, though, that incarceration rates were lower in the Netherlands in the 1970s and that prison sentences are much shorter than those in the United States. Nonetheless, their results do suggest that simply comparing inmates to the general population will tend to overstate the negative health implications of prisons.

But again, do not read that to mean that prisons are not unhealthy places. Studies looking at the National Longitudinal Survey of Youth, for example, which has tracked a large number of people over many years of their lives, find that incarceration is strongly linked to negative physical health outcomes at age 40, even when those who have been to prison are compared to similar ("matched") individuals who have not.[25] In 2005, the Vera Institute's Commission on Safety and Abuse in America's Prisons held several days of hearings about the conditions in American prisons, including access to health care. Among the more troubling points made by several experts were:

- All the doctors in Mississippi prisons had lost their licenses to practice medicine outside the prison.

- Many of the doctors in California prisons were retired "anesthesiologists, radiologists, pathologists," i.e., doctors whose primary practice had not been primary care.

---

[22] Seena Fazel and Jacques Baillargeon, *The Health of Prisoners*, 377 LANCET 956, 956 (2011).

[23] Anja Dirkzwager, Paul Nieuwbeerta, and Arjan Blokland, *Effects of First-Time Imprisonment on Postprison Mortality: A 25-Year Follow-Up Study with a Matched Control Group*, 49 J. RES. CRIME & DELINQ. 49 (2011).

[24] If the probably someone who didn't go to prison would die within the sample period was 15%, then the odds ratio of 3.2 implies that the risk of death of prisoners was 65%.

[25] See, e.g., Michael Massoglia, *Incarceration, Health, and Racial Disparities in Health*, 42 L. & SOC'Y REV. 275 (2008); Jason Schnittker & Andrea John, *Enduring Stigma: The Long-Term Effects of Incarceration on Health*, 48 J. HEALTH & SOC. BEHAVIOR 115 (2007).

- Doctors generally view their patients from an adversarial perspective, frequently assuming that they are malingering.[26]

And in one striking study, Rucker Johnson and Steven Raphael provide results indicating that a significant portion of the racial disparities in HIV infections are due to racial disparities in incarceration.[27]

Perhaps the most dramatic example of health care problems in prison comes from California. In 2005, a federal district judge appointed a receiver to oversee improvements in California's crumbling medical infrastructure in its prisons. In 2009, with little progress being made, a three-judge panel on the Ninth Circuit required the state to provide a plan for reducing overcrowding in order to improve the unconstitutional conditions. The state appealed the order, but the Supreme Court upheld it in *Brown v. Plata*, 131 S.Ct. 1910 (2011). The Court noted that:

> Prisoners suffering from physical illness . . . receive severely deficient care. California's prisons [which are operating at 200% capacity] were designed to meet the medical needs of a population at 100% of design capacity and so have only half the clinical space needed to treat the current population. A correctional officer testified that, in one prison, up to 50 sick inmates may be held together in a 12-by 20-foot cage for up to five hours awaiting treatment. The number of staff is inadequate, and prisoners face significant delays in access to care. A prisoner with severe abdominal pain died after a 5-week delay in referral to a specialist; a prisoner with "constant and extreme" chest pain died after an 8-hour delay in evaluation by a doctor; and a prisoner died of testicular cancer after a "failure of MDs to work up for cancer in a young man with 17 months of testicular pain." . . . Many . . . prisoners, suffering from severe but not life-threatening conditions, experience prolonged illness and unnecessary pain.
>
> The trial court found: "[I]t is an uncontested fact that, on average, an inmate in one of California's prisons needlessly dies every six to seven days due to constitutional deficiencies in the [California prisons'] medical delivery system."

Which isn't to say that all prison care is universally bad; there is a lot of heterogeneity across the country. As one expert at the Vera's Commission's hearing explained:

> I will just say in terms of some of the more chronic diseases, like diabetes, that in the better systems there will be chronic care programs set up so that people will be seen on a regular basis,

---

[26] See http://www.vera.org/project/commission-safety-and-abuse-americas-prisons.
[27] Rucker C. Johnson & Steven Raphael, *The Effects of Male Incarceration Dynamics on Acquired Immune Deficiency Syndrome Infection Rates among African American Women and Men*, 52 J. L. & ECON. 251 (2009).

that they will get their medications, that it's not dependent on the patient him or herself putting in a slip for those kinds of problems, but once they get enrolled in the program, then they're seen on a regular basis, the same as if you or I went to see our doctor and they said come back in three months.

Unfortunately, that's not true in a lot of systems. It's true in some and not true in others. It's what the direction things are moving, but I think a big problem still exists in facilities that I've seen with people getting their medications so that people who need Insulin or blood pressure medications are not routinely getting them all the time, that people who need to be seen and treated for their blood pressure aren't getting seen.[28]

New York State provides a concrete example of why providing adequate care is challenging:

During recent years, [the department of corrections] has improved several important areas of inmate health care. Offering the newest HIV medications, for example, has contributed to an 85% decline in the number of AIDS-related deaths since 1995. Aggressive testing and treatment of tuberculosis have helped produce a 66% decline in the number of inmates with active TB. The construction of five regional medical units (similar to hospitals) and the renovation of prison clinics throughout the system have generally improved services.

Still, medical care varies widely among facilities and in some prisons is woefully inadequate. The problem is largely due to noncompetitive pay rates for medical staff and hiring and performance standards that fall below those in the community. New York State prison physicians, for example, are not required to be board-certified. Because correctional health care providers are Civil Service employees, termination for poor performance is difficult to impose. . . .

At many facilities we visited, inmates spoke of a one-to-three-week wait to see a staff physician and cursory evaluations by nurses at sick call. Likewise, overworked nurses described the difficulties of working in understaffed clinics with minimal guidance from under-qualified or absentee medical directors. According to Department officials, for correctional facilities located close to New York City or within commuting distance from major hospitals, attracting qualified health care professionals is virtually impossible. . . .

Accessing decent health care in prison is also confounded by various Department rules that limit or deny certain treatments to inmates. A glaring example is [the department of corrections']

---

[28] Testimony of Goldenson at 68–69 of http://www.vera.org/files/public-hearing-2-day-2-panel-1-quality-of-medical-care.pdf.

requirement that an inmate be enrolled in or have completed a prison-based drug program in order to receive treatment for hepatitis C. Prison officials say that because hepatitis C is spread primarily through intravenous drug use, and because using drugs while on hepatitis C medication can have life-threatening side effects, drug education and treatment should precede medical treatment. The problem is, not every prison in the state system has a drug treatment program. [I]t is highly unlikely that a doctor in the community would require a patient to enroll in a drug program before he or she receives treatment for hepatitis C. While prisoners with hepatitis C should be made aware of the serious health risks associated with continued substance use, a more reasonable approach would be to require health care staff to counsel and educate inmates individually, rather than to mandate their participation in a program that is not readily accessible to every prisoner.

A related problem is that inmates cannot receive treatment for hepatitis C unless they have at least fifteen months left on their sentence or fifteen months until their scheduled parole board hearing. According to the National Institutes of Health, only people who can be available for a full year of intensive care should be treated, otherwise the treatment is ineffective. However, inmate attorneys say that correction officials use parole board appearances as a pretext for denying the costly treatment, knowing that the majority of inmates convicted of violent offenses are denied parole and will remain in prison for years. One remedy would be to use the expiration of an inmate's sentence, rather than the next parole board appearance, in deciding treatment.

These and other problems are related to the lack of a uniformly administered quality assurance program. . . . Most hospitals in the community have a quality assurance team that meets weekly, collects data and makes decisions based on that data to improve the quality of care. . . . On the majority of prison visits, however, we met medical staff whose knowledge of quality assurance as a concept, or of actual procedures for assessing quality, was vague. . . .[29]

The picture painted here seems to argue for improved medical care for inmates, and they are inarguably entitled to sufficient care. But there are still some tricky normative issues to consider:

---

[29] VISITING COMMITTEE, supra note 6, at 21–22.

QUESTIONS

1. **Improved access to care.** Prisoners are disproportionately drawn from the poor and under- or unemployed; these are people who lack stable medical insurance and likely get infrequent or no medical care. To the extent that prison health care is inadequate but better than what the inmate would have received were he not incarcerated, does this offset any anger or disappointment you may feel about inadequate prison healthcare?

2. **Who is more deserving?** The first, and most obvious, response to Question 1 is that the state has a special obligation to make sure that those subjected to its most intense punishment are treated sufficiently well. But this is not quite the easy answer as it may appear. Why should inmates, who have committed a crime, be entitled to greater care than similarly-situated law-abiding citizens? To the extent that incarceration is about protecting these similarly-situated law-abiding citizens (since crime is geographically concentrated), why does protecting them from crime impose on the state additional obligations to provide above-expected care to the victimizers?

3. **Best we can do, Part 1?** Is a collateral-benefit explanation appealing: it would be great to provide care to everyone, but that is not feasible. But here we have a sub-population that is notoriously sick and ill-cared for in the open world. At the very least we can take care of this group, even if they are not the most deserving. And in many cases, we can provide care more consistently than we could to people not confined in an institution. When thinking about this, put aside any social-health concerns (i.e., treating prisoners for TB may reduce its spread in the overall population for the benefit of offenders and non-offenders alike).

4. **Best we can do, Part 2?** Nonetheless, even if you accept the "treat those we can" argument, why does that advocate focusing on *prison* healthcare? Why not soup-kitchen/food-bank healthcare? Or at-risk public school healthcare? Is it a matter of baserates—the percent of inmates with poor healthcare is larger than that of homeless or at-risk students, so focusing on prisons is the most efficient means of provision? Even if this is true, is that a normatively satisfying answer?

5. **Health care vs. crime control.** The solution upheld in *Plata* was to reduce overcrowding by releasing almost 50,000 prisoners to mitigate the strain placed on California's prison-medical system. How do we properly balance a defendant's Eighth Amendment right to adequate medical care against the average citizen's (perhaps less clearly specified and thus perhaps less strongly defensible) right to be free from criminal victimization? Do you think your answer would be different now, a time of low crime and high incarceration, than in a period of high crime and low incarceration (like the 1960s and 1970s), since now there is a substantial body of low-level offenders who could be released with fairly low risk of recidivism, particularly violent recidivism?

It is clear that much could be done to improve patient care in prisons. And certainly for injuries incurred while in prison, the state may have a particular obligation to provide adequate care, as well as for the increased risk of mental and physical health problems. But broader questions about the level of care morally required are (genuinely) tricky. And they are compounded by our current ignorance about just how much prison life contributes to them.

B.1.c. MENTAL HEALTH IN PRISON

According to a 2006 report by the Bureau of Justice Statistics (the most recent of its kind), in 2005 56% of all state prisoners, 45% of all federal prisoners, and 64% of all jail inmates had suffered from *some* sort of mental health problem at some point in their lives; within twelve months of the survey, the numbers were 24%, 15%, and 21%, respectively.[30] For comparison's sake, the number of Americans in the general population in 2001–2002 reporting some sort of mental illness within the previous twelve months was around 11%, suggesting, at least at first blush, that the incidence of recent mental illness is about twice as high in prisons as in the population in general. And the incidence seems to be rising: a 1999 BJS report estimated that the mentally ill comprised 16% of state prisoners, 7% of federal prisoners, and 16% of jail inmates.

However, once again some care needs to be taken when comparing prisoners to the population at large. Mental health outcomes appear to be negatively correlated with socioeconomic status, so the fact that prisoners disproportionately come from poorer neighborhoods suggests that the proper comparative baserate should be higher than the national average.[31] Furthermore, reduced access to health care (including mental health care) in these lower-income communities likely leads to reduced diagnoses among those not incarcerated. Inmates, on the other hand, are widely screened, suggesting that even comparing rates between

---

[30] JAMES & GLAZE, MENTAL HEALTH, supra note 11.

[31] As one study explains:

> Low socioeconomic status (SES) is generally associated with high psychiatric morbidity, disability, and poor access to health care. In countries where comparable epidemiologic studies have been carried out, the lowest educational group had a higher prevalence of psychiatric morbidity. Poorer coping styles, ongoing life events, stress exposure, and weaker social support are some examples of psychiatric risk factors that are more prevalent in lower SES groups. For the same level of severity, lower SES groups faced more disabilities and a poorer prognosis. In countries providing less generous welfare support [such as the United States], lower SES groups also faced less favorable access to health care; whatever the welfare coverage, they were less likely to use specialized mental care.

V. Lorant, D. Deliège, W. Eaton, A. Robert, P. Phillippot, & M. Ansseau, *Socioeconomic Inequalities in Depression: A Meta-Analysis*, 157 AM. J. EPIDEMIOLOGY 98, 98 (2003).

prisoners and the communities from which they come may overstate the impact of prison.[32]

Furthermore, evidence about the impact of prisons *on* mental health is ambiguous. As one researcher, Craig Haney, explains:

> The empirical consensus on the most negative effects of incarceration is that most people who have done time in the best-run prisons return to the freeworld with little or no permanent, clinically-diagnosable psychological disorders as a result. Prisons do not, in general, make people "crazy." However, even researchers who are openly skeptical about whether the pains of imprisonment generally translate into psychological harm concede that, for at least some people, prison can produce negative, long-lasting change. And most people agree that the more extreme, harsh, dangerous, or otherwise psychologically-taxing the nature of the confinement, the greater the number of people who will suffer and the deeper the damage that they will incur.[33]

Haney then goes on to note that the group most at risk of increased mental illness due to incarceration are those who suffer from mental illness or developmental disability at the time of admission. He also points to the well-documented psychological harms that afflict prisoners incarcerated in so-called "supermax" prisons, ultra-secure facilities that severely restrain human contact and engage in other forms of "social deprivation," stating that "there are few if any forms of imprisonment that produce so many indices of psychological trauma and symptoms of psychopathology. . . ."[34]

Even if the mental illness rate in prisons is not exceptionally higher than that in the populations from which many prisoners come, the mentally ill still comprise a significant portion of the prison population. Furthermore, these are the mentally ill who have revealed themselves as ones who behave criminally, perhaps violently so.[35] So it is worth asking what steps prisons take to treat these individuals.

According to a 2000 BJS report (the most recent one on mental health services), 95% of all confinement (as opposed to community-based)

---

[32] Some studies which point to greater mental health illness in prisons also count anti-social personality disorder (ASPD) as a mental illness, despite the fact that ASPD is often "no more than a psychiatric label for criminal behavior," which artificially inflates the rate of mental illness in prison. See Virginia Aldigé Hiday & Padraic J. Burns, *Mental Illness and the Criminal Justice System*, in A HANDBOOK FOR THE STUDY OF MENTAL HEALTH, 2D EDITION 483 (Teresa L. Scheid & Tony N. Brown, eds., 2010).

[33] Craig Haney, *The Psychological Impact of Incarceration: Implications for Post-Prison Adjustment*, working paper prepared for the US Dep't of Health & Human Services and the Urban Institute (2001).

[34] *Id.* at 14.

[35] It is worth noting that, despite some conventional wisdom to the contrary, the mentally ill are rarely violent and are more likely to be the victims of crime than the perpetrators. Hiday & Burns, supra note 32 at 486.

facilities provided some sort of mental health services, with 84% providing therapy or counseling and 83% psychotropic medication; almost two-thirds also provided access to 24-hour mental health care (either on- or off-site).[36] It appears that about 79% of those classified as mentally ill were receiving therapy or counseling "on a regular basis." Of course, as is often the case, interstate variation was quite wide. Some states, for example, administered psychotropic medication to over 20% of their inmates (Hawaii, Maine, Montana, Nebraska, and Oregon) while others to less than 5% (Alabama, Arkansas, and Michigan); it is unlikely that the difference can be wholly explained by different rates of mental illnesses.

The BJS survey, however, is relatively silent as to the depth and quality of the services provided. A report by Human Rights Watch, however, suggests that mental health care services are generally underprovided.[37] Among its findings:

- Of the 17,640 people on prison mental health staffs, only 18.4% are psychiatrists or psychologists. "Counselors, who typically need no mental health degree or training[,] and 'others' accounted for 58.6% of the total."

- A report by the American Psychiatric Association recommended a caseload for prison psychologists of no more than 150 patients on psychotropic medication. Yet Washington State had a per-psychologist caseload of 200, and Arkansas a rate of 164 only because its official mental illness rate was half to a quarter that seen in the rest of the country.

- Staff turnover is high, positions often remain vacant, and funding for additional doctors is hard to find. The medical director for Iowa's prisons admitted that he need to more than double his number of psychiatrists (from three to eight) but lacked the necessary funding, particularly since "it's very hard to attract psychiatrists to the Department of Corrections."

- Counselors and psychologists are often underqualified. A 1988 survey found that 40% had less than a Master's degree.

These results all suggest that the mental health care provided in prison is likely inadequate. But, then again, so too is that provided in offenders' communities. Evidence indicates that lower socioeconomic status is correlated with reduced access to medical care—and thus likely mental

---

[36] ALLEN J. BECK & LAUREN M. MARUSCHAK, MENTAL HEALTH TREATMENT IN STATE PRISONS, 2000 (2001).

[37] HUMAN RIGHTS WATCH, ILL-EQUIPPED: US PRISONS AND OFFENDERS WITH MENTAL ILLNESS (2003).

health care as well.[38] And the questions asked of general health care apply to mental health care as well: should inmates be entitled to *better* healthcare than what they receive outside of prison?

However, psychological treatment is not the only factor to consider. Many offenders who are mentally ill at the time of their offense are also abusing drugs and/or alcohol, and it appears that it the interaction of illness and substance abuse, not just the mental illness alone, that plays a significant role in driving criminal behavior. In other words, drug and alcohol treatment of offenders can be seen not just as an important process on its own terms, but also as an important part of the effort to break the link between mental illness, offending, and incarceration. So we turn to that next.

B.1.d. DRUGS AND ALCOHOL IN PRISON

According to the 2008 National Crime Victimization Survey, 24.2% of violent crime victims reported that their assailants appeared to be under the influence of drugs or alcohol at the time of the offense, with 13.8% reporting alcohol, 5.1% drugs, and 3.9% both (with the remaining unclear).[39] A 2002 survey of jail inmates reported that 68% admitted to alcohol or drug abuse or dependence in the year leading up to the offense resulting in incarceration, with 47% reporting alcohol problems and 53% drug problems (which implies that 32%, or just under half, were abusing both alcohol and drugs).[40] A separate 2004 study of prison inmates reported that 56% of state inmates admitted to abusing drugs within a month of the incarcerating offense, and 32% to abusing drugs at the time of the offense.[41] Of that 56%, 40.3% reported using marijuana or hashish, 21.4% cocaine or crack, 8.2% heroin or opiates, 5.4% depressants (like Quaaludes), 12.2% stimulants (generally methamphetamine), 5.9% hallucinogens, and 1% inhalants.

For comparison purposes, in 2012, about 9.2% of the population aged 12 and above—or almost 24 million out of 260 million—used any sort of illegal drug in the month leading up to being surveyed.[42] Almost half of those people had used marijuana (or about 7% of the population), with only 6% using cocaine (or about 0.7% of the population) and 1% using heroin (or about 0.1% of the population).

---

[38] James B. Kirby & Toshiko Kaneda, *Neighborhood Socioeconomic Disadvantage and Access to Health Care*, 46 J. HEALTH & SOC. BEHAVIOR 15 (2005).

[39] MICHAEL R. RAND & JAYNE E. ROBINSON, CRIMINAL VICTIMIZATION IN THE UNITED STATES, 2008—STATISTICAL TABLES (2011).

[40] JENNIFER C. KARBERG & LAUREN J. JAMES, SUBSTANCE DEPENDENCE, ABUSE, AND TREATMENT OF JAIL INMATES, 2002 (2005).

[41] CHRISTOPHER J. MUMOLA & JENNIFER C. KARBERG, DRUG USE AND DEPENDENCE, STATE AND FEDERAL PRISONERS, 2004 (2006).

[42] http://www.drugabuse.gov/publications/drugfacts/nationwide-trends.

A recent article in the *Journal of American Medical Association* summarized the current state of drug treatment in prisons.[43] It noted that somewhere on the order of 80% of inmates who could use drug treatment do not receive it, which not only impedes recovery from addiction but increases the risk of future exposure to HIV, hepatitis C, and other diseases that are often associated with drug abuse. The article also points out that many interventions, though underutilized, appear to be effective:

> In a meta-analysis of 66 incarceration-based treatment evaluations, therapeutic community and counseling approaches were respectively 1.4 and 1.5 times more likely to reduce reoffending. Individuals who participated in prison-based treatment followed by a community-based program postincarceration were 7 times more likely to be drug free and 3 times less likely to be arrested for criminal behavior than those not receiving treatment.
>
> The benefits of medications for drug treatment were shown in a recent randomized trial in which heroin-dependent inmates began methadone treatment in prison prior to release and continued in the community postrelease. At 1-, 3-, and 6-month follow-up, patients who received methadone plus counseling were significantly less likely to use heroin or engage in criminal activity than those who received only counseling. The potential exists for immediate adoption of methadone maintenance for incarcerated persons with opioid addictions, but most prison systems have not been receptive to this approach.
>
> The cost of integrating volunteer-led self-help organizations such as Alcoholics Anonymous and Narcotics Anonymous into criminal justice settings is nominal and could provide support to the recovery efforts of addicted persons in the criminal justice system. One dollar spent on . . . prison-based treatment saves between $2 to $6. These economic benefits in part reflect reductions in criminal behavior.
>
> Drug education—not drug treatment—is the most common service provided to prisoners with drug abuse or addiction problems. More than one-quarter of state inmates and 1 in 5 federal inmates meeting abuse/dependence criteria participate in self-help groups such as Alcoholics Anonymous while in prison. However, though treatment during and after incarceration has been shown to significantly reduce drug use and drug-related crime, less than 20% of inmates with drug abuse or dependence receive formal treatment.

---

[43] Redonna K. Chandler, Bennett W. Fletcher, & Nora D. Volkow, *Treating Drug Abuse and Addiction in the Criminal Justice System*, 301 J. AM. MED. ASS'N 183 (2009).

The article then points out that there are many barriers to effective drug abuse interventions. Not only do prisons rarely provide the services, but there is very little post-incarceration follow-up, which not only increases the chance of relapse, but also the risk of post-release death from an overdose.

As the article notes, there may be a significant collateral benefit from drug treatment: it may directly reduce criminal offending. Defenders of treatment have generally argued that reducing drug use can reduce offending due to the causal link between drug abuse and criminal behavior. But a recent meta-analysis of drug treatment programs reported that the effect of treatment programs on offending was *greater* than their effect on drug use, which would be impossible if their effect on crime was wholly mediated by their effect on drug use.[44] The authors acknowledge that the effect could be partly due to differences in reporting errors—both reoffending and drug relapse are hard to estimate precisely. But these surprising results could also reflect the fact that behavioral effects of drug treatment programs may reach beyond just drug use.

One under-addressed issue with drug use and incarceration is the risk posed by re-entry from prison and the resumption of drug use. The *JAMA* articles notes that "[r]eturning to neighborhoods associated with preincarceration drug use places the addicted individual in an environment rich in drug cues," and—making matters worse—that "compulsive seeking of drugs when addicted individuals are reexposed to drug cues progressively increases after drug withdrawal." In fact, there is evidence that deaths by overdose spike significantly immediately after release from prison. A review of studies from several countries found that the relative risk (RR)[45] of dying from a drug overdose during the first two weeks after release compared to weeks three through twelve ranged from 3.1 (with a 95% CI of 1.3 to 7.1) to 8.4 (95% CI of 5.0 to 14.2).[46] When compared to weeks five through twelve, the RR range rose to 3.2 to 11.0. The review authors point to several explanations for these results:

---

[44] Ojmarrh Mitchell, David B. Wilson, & Doris L. MacKenzie, *Does Incarceration-Based Drug Treatment Reduce Recidivism? A Meta-Analytic Synthesis*, 3 J. Exp. Criminology 353 (2007).

[45] Relative risk, a concept roughly the same as the odds ratio, is defined as the $p(\text{event})/p(\text{not-event})$. In other words, if the probability a male commits a crime is 2% and that a female commits a crime is 0.5%, then the relative risk of offending for men $2/0.5 = 4$ (and for women is $0.5/2 = 0.25$). As with the odds ratio, the critical value is 1: a RR > 1 implies the group under question is more at risk than the control group, and a RR < 1 implies it is less at risk. Thus in our example men are more at risk, since $4 > 1$, and (necessarily) women are less at risk, since $0.25 < 1$.

[46] Elizabeth L. C. Merrall, Azar Kariminia, Ingrid A. Binswanger, Michael S. Hobbs, Michael Farrell, John Marsden, Sharon J. Hutchinson & Sheila M. Bird, *Meta-Analysis of Drug-Related Deaths Soon After Release from Prison*. 105 Addiction 1545 (2010). The two US studies had RRs of 3.1 (for New Mexico) and 8.2 (for Washington State). Two studies from the UK had RRs of 7.4 (for Scotland) and 7.5 (for England and Wales), and two studies from Australia had RRs of 4.4 (for Western Australia) and 4.0 (for New South Wales).

The increased risk of drug-related death may be explained by a decrease in tolerance to drugs as a result of being in prison where drug use is less frequent and the drugs may be of lower purity; and there could be a tendency for "celebration" on release. Across the six studies the RRs for weeks 1 + 2 are elevated to different extents, which is perhaps unsurprising given the possible variations in prisons' drug policies and in the nature of illicit drug use more broadly.[47]

The findings in the *JAMA* article also highlight again the importance of appreciating the jurisdictional fissures that run through the criminal justice system. Recall that the authors note that correctional treatment is often ineffective in the long run if there is no community supervision upon release. But these are two separate budgetary realms: the state prison system and the local probation or public health system—and even if there is state funding for the public health system, that is funding coming from the healthcare bureaucracy, not the criminal justice bureaucracy. So state correctional dollars may be wasted if state or local healthcare dollars are not allocated to follow-up care for drug addicts. Coordinating these disparate jurisdictions and bureaucracies is a challenge the criminal justice system has yet to solve.

Question: The *JAMA* article argues that $1 on some treatment programs can yield up to $2 to $6 in savings, especially when we include the savings from reduced crime. What institutional challenge does that raise for implementing such seemingly cost-effective programs?

B.2. PRISON AND FAMILY LIFE

Researchers have long observed that men who go to prison appear to be less likely to marry and more likely to divorce than men who do not. If incarceration is causing these effects, then these statistics point to important collateral costs that could offset some of whatever benefits incarceration provide. Scholars such as Robert Sampson and John Laub, for example, have shown that marriage, like stable employment, appears to play an important role in the desistance from crime; we have already seen that incarceration reduces employment opportunities, so if it also reduces marriage options, it could undermine another future anti-criminogenic force in the defendant's life. Moreover, children of unstable families are more likely to commit crimes themselves in the future, so if parental incarceration contributes to familial instability, then incarceration could contribute to the intergenerational "transmission" of criminal conduct by undermining already-disadvantaged families—and in 2007 over 1.75 million children under the age of 18 had a parent (generally a father) in prison.

---

[47] *Id.* at 1549.

In a study of marriage and incarceration, Bruce Western and Leonard Lopoo lay out some of the potential ways incarceration can destabilize an inmate's personal life.[48] If nothing else, while in prison it is hard (though not impossible) for an inmate to marry. Furthermore:

> [I]ncarceration also limits the participation of married men in their primary relationships. Incarceration separates men geographically and socially. Prisons are often located far from the poor urban communities that supply most of the inmates, so sustaining personal contact can be costly for the partners of incarcerated men. Only 40% of incarcerated fathers report having weekly contact with their families, mostly by mail or phone. Prisoners earn virtually no income and often accumulate child support arrears while locked up. The emotional and financial detachment of incarcerated men helps explain ethnographic reports that partners of incarcerated men often form new relationships. In short, the incapacitative effect of incarceration is likely to prevent marriage among those who are single and increase the risk of separation among married couples.
>
> Incapacitation describes how incarceration lowers the likelihood of marriage while a man is serving time, but incarceration may negatively affect marriage long after release. Incarceration carries a stigma that marks ex-offenders as dishonest or unreliable. The stigma of incarceration is often seen in labor market studies. . . . There is less evidence that prospective marriage partners are deterred, like employers, by the signal of a criminal conviction, but some field reports are suggestive. [One study], for example, reports that poor women in urban areas avoid men who are involved in crime, even if it is lucrative.
>
> The incarceration of a spouse may also stigmatize family members. As [Erving] Goffman observes, stigma is passed on through personal relationships, contaminating intimates and acquaintances. [Donald] Braman's fieldwork in Washington, DC, found that symptoms of depression and isolation from family and friends were experienced more by the wives of incarcerated men than the men themselves. By engendering feelings of shame among spouses and other family members, the stigma of incarceration during marriage may increase the risks of divorce or separation even after a man is released from prison.
>
> Finally, incarceration may reduce the likelihood of marriage by diminishing an ex-offender's economic fortunes. Because the wage gap between ex-inmates and non-inmates grows over the life course, incarceration's effect on marriage may also be quite

---

[48] Leonard M. Lopoo & Bruce Western, *Incarceration and the Formation and Stability of Marital Unions*, 67 J. MARRIAGE & FAMILY 721 (2005).

persistent. Under these conditions, a male partner will be unable to contribute adequately to the household finances after release, and his partner may be more inclined to refuse to marry him or to divorce him (if married).

The distance between prisons and prisoners' families can be quite striking. Consider the following example from New York State. In 2014, over 46% of New York's prisoners came from New York City, and a bit under two-thirds likely came from New York City, Long Island, Westchester, and Erie County (the home of New York's second largest city, Buffalo).[49] Yet look again at the map of where prisons are in the state (last seen in Chapter 9). The extent to which they are concentrated in the north and center of the state is striking, given how many offenders come from the southeast and the west.

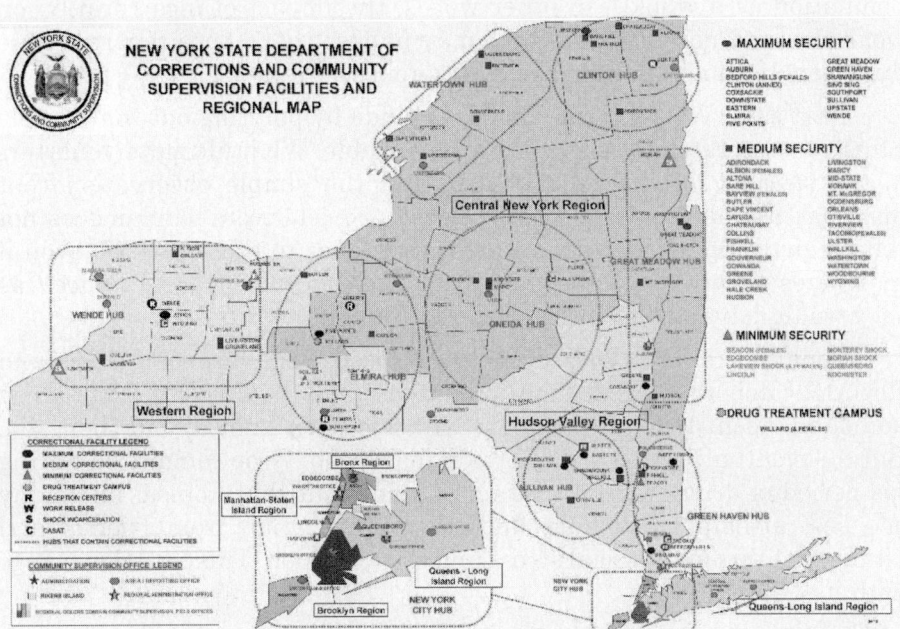

Yet despite the theoretical plausibility of these theories linking incarceration to marital instability, the empirical effect does not appear to be that strong. There is a noticeable immediate incarceration effect: while in prison, men are one-fifth as likely to marry as similar non-incarcerated men and three times more likely to get divorced. Upon release, however, there does not appear to be any sustained effect that either reduces marriagability or increases the risk of divorce, conditional

---

[49] For data on prison counts, see http://www.doccs.ny.gov/Research/Reports/2014/Under Custody_Report_2014.pdf. The report does not disaggregate by county, so the data that includes Long Island, Westchester, and Erie counties come from data on felony convictions. http://www.criminaljustice.ny.gov/crimnet/ojsa/nys-felony-process-report2010.pdf. Assuming that rates of incarceration track rates of filings, the extrapolation is permissible. Looking at New York City data, the two numbers are fairly close (48.3% of all prisoners, 40.6% of all filings).

on the already-low baseline marriage rates in their comparison populations (which are disproportionately poorer, more-minority communities that already have comparatively low marriage rates). Thus, Western notes, there does not actually appear to be any additional marital stigma attached to incarceration, despite its theoretical plausibility and its observed analog in the employment market.

Furthermore, Western and Lopoo note that their model may *overestimate* the negative effects of incarceration. First, it is impossible to control for all the relevant variables, so some selection bias persists.[50] Second, their study pays particularly close attention to at-risk minority communities, and "analysis of data for poor urban, mostly minority, couples suggests the individual and aggregate effects of incarceration may well be larger for [these] high-incarceration groups than in the U.S. population as a whole." In other words, the impact of incarceration on wealthier and non-black inmates may be less than those reported here due to environmental, social, etc., differences.

That said, Western and Lopoo conclude by pointing out that simple rates may not catch the most relevant variable. What ultimately matters is the *strength* of the relationship, and the simple observation that marriage and divorce rates post-release are relatively similar does not tell us anything about what incarceration does to those ties. So even if marriages survive incarceration, they likely do not operate *as well* as they would have had no one in the couple been incarcerated.

Donald Braman, for example, discusses the case of Louisa and Robert.[51] Robert served time in prison and, having kicked a drug addiction, spent three sober years with his wife, Louisa, and their son. But he eventually returned to prison for a robbery he committed during his period of drug addiction. Braman points out that Louisa, like many spouses, attempted to hide Robert's incarceration from friends and family, but this led to social stress and ostracization. This isolation brings with it serious costs:

> Low-income families often rely on extended networks of family and friends to cope with poverty and hardship. The fluid households and expansive exchange networks that these families maintain are, while not necessarily their own ideal image of family, adaptive necessities for making ends meet in the long run. Perhaps the most significant consequence of

---

[50] In other words, those who go to prison are not identical to those who do not: we do not randomly assign people to "commit a crime" and "get incarcerated." So if those unobserved factors—like impetuousness—are both more likely to lead to crime and to lead to lower probabilities of marriage or greater probabilities of divorce (which, at least in the case of impetuousness, seems plausible), then some of the difference in marriage or divorce rates between former inmates and non-inmates will be due to this unobserved factor, no matter how well we try to "match" similar people.

[51] Donald Braman, *Families and Incarceration*, in INVISIBLE PUNISHMENT: THE COLLATERAL CONSEQUENCES OF MASS IMPRISONMENT 131–134 (Marc Mauer & Meda Chesney-Lind eds., 2002).

stigma among families of prisoners, then, is the distortion, diminution, and even severance of these social ties. Stigma related to incarceration is powerful, in part, because the families know that the very same relationships on which they have come to depend can be turned 5against them, as social networks that provide resources are transformed into social networks of approbation. It is little wonder, then, that many family members carefully guard information about incarceration.

As a result, some family members are forced on a daily basis to choose between sacrificing the honesty of their relationships or the relationships themselves. The result can be draining and painful. For Louisa, in addition to her concern about potential labeling [of her husband and of herself] by the people she knows, she feels the pull of her evasion and deception at her own conscience. As Louisa describes herself lying, her voice quivers with disappointment in herself and she begins to cry. Although she does not want her husband to be branded a criminal, she does feel guilty about her lying.

Braman then notes that stigma is often greater for the innocent parties outside the prison than for those serving time inside them. First, stigma is often "contagious," with people assuming—often incorrectly—that family members of those in prison must be somehow blameworthy as well. Second, stigma is relative. So while Louisa in out in the world interacting with those *not* in prison and thus exposed to their "judgment and condemnation," Robert's peers are fellow inmates, for whom the stigma of prison is, obviously, much less. As Braman explains:

> Indeed, most of the participants in this study told no one outside of the immediate family about their relative's incarceration, and many were hiding the incarceration from extended family members. Accounts of nervous covering, public humiliation, and deeply felt stigma were common. Far from being unconcerned about criminality, familial integrity, or honesty, families of prisoners wrestle with each of these issues every day in an environment that they often perceive as hostile and unforgiving. They are not shameless but, rather, deeply stigmatized and often significantly injured.

These sorts of pressures surely shape spousal and parental relationships in harmful ways.

C. Impact of Incarceration on Communities

The scale of incarceration affects not just offenders and their immediate families but their communities as well. This is due in large part to the concentration of incarceration. Inmates are not drawn at random from the wider American polity, but rather come from a narrow range of communities. Some parts of New York City, for example, are home to "million dollar blocks," single blocks with so many residents in prison that the state is spending over $1 million per year to incarcerate them.[52] Moreover, these pockets of intense incarceration are geographically stable. Take one recent study of Chicago, which compared neighborhood incarceration rates in 1990-95 to those in 2000-05.[53] The high-incarceration neighborhoods in 1990-95 were almost always the high-incarceration neighborhoods in 2000-05 as well.

This dense concentration of incarceration thus concentrates its collateral costs as well—although this implies it concentrates any crime-reducing benefits as well. In this section I just want to briefly touch on incarceration's community-level effects on employment, health, drug and alcohol use, and family life.

Start with economic outcomes. Not surprisingly, the diminished economic opportunities of inmates spill over into the communities from which they come and to which they return. Todd Clear summarizes the basic literature well:

> The economic prospects of people who live in poor communities are linked. Family members earning money contribute to the welfare of their families, and this is true even when some of those earnings are from criminal activity such as drug sales. [One] study of poor mothers found that up to 91 percent of them reported that they had received money from members in their networks; 55 percent had received cash from their families, 32 percent from their boyfriends, and 41 percent from their child's father. Incarceration removes from the neighborhood many of the men who had provided support to these women. The concentration of formerly incarcerated men in poor neighborhoods may also damage the labor market prospects of others in the community. [Dorothy] Roberts points out that "the spatial concentration of incarceration . . . impedes access to jobs for youth in those communities because it decreases the pool of men who can serve as their mentors and their links to the working world . . . generating employment discrimination against entire neighborhoods." [Another study has] shown that, as county-level incarceration rates grow, so do unemployment rates for blacks who live in those counties.
>
> Ethnographies show how, in impoverished neighborhoods, a work-aged male generates economic activity that translates into

---

[52] Sort of. The million dollar number comes from multiplying average per-inmate spending on incarceration by the number of inmates from that block in prison. But the amount spent per year incarcerating those inmates is not the number of inmates times the average cost but the number of inmates times the *marginal* cost, and some research suggests that the marginal cost of incarcerating an inmate can be as little as half to one-fifth the average cost.

[53] These are Figures 2 and 3 from Robert J. Sampson & Charles Loeffler, *Punishment's Place: The Local Concentration of Mass Incarceration*, 139 DAEDALUS 20 (2010).

purchases at the local deli, child support, and similar expenditures. This economic value is generated in a variety of endeavors, including off-the-books work, intermittent illicit drug trade, theft, welfare, and part-time employment. Many, if not most, of those who engage in crime also have legal employment, so their removal from the neighborhood removes a worker from the local legal economy. In large numbers, incarceration raids supplies of local human capital and leaves a gap in employable residents. Even families that reap the individual benefit of newly available employment suffer the indirect costs of depleted neighborhood economic strength. One estimate holds that increases in incarceration since 1980 have reduced young black male labor force activity by 3–5 percent.[54]

It is worth remembering that these effects are taking place in neighborhoods that are already disproportionately poor.[55]

Concentrated incarceration can also have public health implications beyond just the inmates, but here the effects are ambiguous and the evidence limited. There is some evidence, for example, suggesting that the release of incarcerated inmates increases the risk of sexually transmitted diseases and tuberculosis among the non-incarcerated population to which the inmates return.[56] At the same time, incarceration removes violent offenders from the community and may thus reduce the direct health risks they pose, and prisons can provide some medical care to those who otherwise would not receive it, thus mitigating some health risks.[57] Unfortunately, a recent view noted that:

> Of [the] broader effects of mass imprisonment on population health, relatively few have been tested to date. [T]here has been some work on disparities in [sexually transmitted infection (STI)] rates at the individual and community levels. Yet aside

---

[54] Todd R. Clear, *The Effects of High Imprisonment Rates on Communities*, 37 CRIME & JUSTICE 97, 115–116 (2008).

[55] One of the more shocking examples of the aggregate effect of incarceration on labor market outcomes comes from BRUCE WESTERN, PUNISHMENT & INEQUALITY supra note 9. During the 1990s it appeared that the unemployment rate for young black males with no more than a high school diploma declined, a significant social achievement; at the end of his presidency Bill Clinton touted this fact as a key accomplishment of his time in office. Yet among those excluded from unemployment statistics are prisoners. So many poorly-educated young black men were incarcerated during the 1990s that it skewed their unemployment statistics. Extrapolating from evidence about inmates' immediate pre-incarceration employment status, Western demonstrates that had the incarceration rate for young black inmates with limited education not soared—to approximately 1 in 3—then their unemployment rate would have *risen* during the 1990s. The decline in young black male unemployment was a statistical artifact of their large-scale incarceration.

[56] See, e.g., the sources in Christopher Wildeman, *Invited Commentary: (Mass) Imprisonment and (Inequities in) Health*, 174 AM. J. EPIDEMIOLOGY 488 (2011). Note that not all the findings (like that linking incarceration to TB) are from the United States.

[57] See, e.g., Nicholas Freudenberg, *Jails, Prisons, and the Health of Urban Populations: A Review of the Impact of the Correctional System on Community Health*, 78 J. URB. HEALTH 214 (2001).

from STIs, we have little sense of what the broader health consequences of mass imprisonment may be.[58]

Yet the concentration of incarceration, poverty, poor health, and limited access to healthcare outside of prisons certainly suggests that there should be *some* effect, even if we do not yet know how big it is.

Concentrated incarceration also has the ability to alter social relationships outside pre-existing relationships as well. Consider its impact on the marriage market. In high-incarceration communities, the gender ratio is out of balance: one study of high-incarceration neighborhoods in Washington, DC, reported that there were 62 men for every 100 women.[59] The effects of this imbalance are wide-ranging:

> [A] shortage of men places women at a disadvantage in negotiating and maintaining mutually monogamous relationships, because men can easily find another relationship if they perceive their primary relationship to be problematic. Moreover, men who maintain multiple simultaneous partnerships may be confident that their primary partner will not end the relationship, because primary relationships are relatively difficult for women to attain. In focus groups conducted among black persons in rural North Carolina, both men and women believed that the scarcity of men and the extremely adverse socioeconomic plight of black women (and men) profoundly influence partner selection, the sexual availability of women, the type of male sexual behavior that women tolerate, and the participation of both sexes in high-risk sexual behaviors. Respondents reported extensive concurrent partnerships among unmarried persons, particularly men[.][60]

Other studies have returned similar results. Kerwin Kofi Charles and Ming Ching Luoh, for example, demonstrate that marriage markets operate within narrow race, age, and location ranges, implying that the concentration of incarceration concentrates its disruptive effects on marriage (i.e., women in high-incarceration communities cannot simply look to other, more advantageous markets).[61] They then generate empirical results suggesting that the women in high-incarceration areas are less likely to marry, and weak evidence that when they do marry they marry lower-quality men. They also find evidence that the marriages that do happen are less likely to result in divorce, likely *due to* the reduced options.

---

[58] Wildeman, *(Mass) Imprisonment*, supra note 56 at 490.

[59] DONALD S. BRAMAN, DOING TIME ON THE OUTSIDE: INCARCERATION FAMILY LIFE IN URBAN AMERICA (2003).

[60] Adaora A. Adimora & Victor J. Schoenbach, *Social Context, Sexual Networks, and Racial Disparities in Rates of Sexually Transmitted Diseases*, 191 J. INFECTIOUS DISEASES S115 (2005).

[61] Kerwin Kofi Charles & Ming Ching Luoh, *Male Incarceration, The Marriage Market, and Female Outcomes*, 92 REV. ECON. & STAT. 614 (2010).

Large scale concentrated incarceration also has the ability to alter the "collective efficacy" of a neighborhood. Collective efficacy refers to a neighborhood's ability to police itself—the extent to which informal social control regulates behavior. As Tracey Meares explains in a review of the relationship between collective efficacy and crime:

> In describing the . . . nature of community social organization, modern theorists look to two dimensions: (1) the prevalence, strength, and interdependence of social networks; and (2) the extent of collective supervision that the residents direct and the personal responsibility they assume in addressing neighborhood problems.[62]

As we will see in the next section, collective efficacy is an important tool in the war against crime. And it should be immediately clear that incarceration can interact with it in complicated ways.

On the one hand, violent crime can undermine social control by discouraging people from taking informal enforcement actions and developing social ties: will you reprimand a teenager if he may be carrying a gun? will you sit on your stoop talking to your neighbor if there is a non-trivial risk of getting hit by a stray bullet? Open-air drug markets can similarly weaken social control, not just because they increase the risk of violence, but because they make being outside less pleasant. Social ties fray, there are fewer eyes on the street to discourage crime, and less informal-but-effective punishment. To the extent incarceration reduces crime (and, as the next section demonstrates, that "to the extent" is an important qualifier), it can improve social control.

But it should also be clear now how incarceration can reduce social control as well. Incarceration weakens the offender's ties to the neighborhood and thus likely reduces the effectiveness of social controls: if the person is already stigmatized or shunned, how effective can additional stigmatization be in regulating his behavior? And even if the offender is not substantially stigmatized upon his return, his reduced ability to stabilize his life via meaningful employment and/or marriage further reduces his ability to participate in and be responsive to the neighborhood.

In addition, as Braman's work indicates, incarceration has the ability to stigmatize family members of the offender, thus reducing *their* involvement in community interactions, and thus their ability to monitor the neighborhood or shame those who violate its rules. Incarceration also contributes to more single-parent (generally mother) families—the 1.7 million children noted above with a parent in prison comprise about 2.3% of all children in the nation, although that number is 6.7% for black children—which reduces parental oversight and is strongly correlated

---

[62] Tracey L. Meares, *It's a Question of Connections*, 31 VAL. U. L. REV. 579, 581 (1997).

with subsequent juvenile delinquency, and thus reduced social cohesion in the community.

When it comes to collective efficacy, then, incarceration is like chemotherapy or radiation treatment: in an effort to purge the body of malignant cancerous cells, these treatments also kill off many healthy cells, and the hope is that the patient comes out ahead on balance. Likewise incarceration removes some threats to collective efficacy while creating others. But the evidence is much less clear about the circumstances under which the net effect is positive.

* * *

We have now covered many of the collateral costs of incarceration—and some benefits (access to drug treatment, perhaps some improved access to certain types of medical care). These consequences are important in their own right, but they also all contribute to our understanding of how incarceration affects the outcome that most concerns the criminal justice system: the crime rate. We turn to that now.

D. INCARCERATION AND CRIME

Broadly speaking, there are two ways that incarceration can shape the crime rate: via general deterrence, and via specific deterrence/incapacitation/rehabilitation. The first is the idea that fear of prison will prevent potential offenders from crossing that line between "potential" and "actual." The second is the idea that incarceration can deter a formerly-incarcerated offender from re-offending out of fear of returning to an unpleasant environment, can incapacitate an offender until he no longer poses a threat (such as by aging out of crime), or can reform an inmate so he has no desire to reoffend. These latter three approaches do not operate independently. For example, incarceration could simultaneously hold an offender until he has started to age out crime while training him (rehabilitating him) for a career outside of prison—or while eroding his human capital and thus his post-conviction employment opportunities, reducing the relative deterrent effect of incarceration. I want to start, however, by asking a higher-level question: what is the overall, net effect of increases in incarceration on the crime rate? Once we know this, we can ask the more specific question of what is driving this effect, and what that means for optimal policy design.

D.1. INCARCERATION'S TOTAL EFFECT

The effect of incarceration on crime is a widely-researched question. Unfortunately, our understanding of this relationship is not as strong as one might wish, thanks to a bedeviling statistical problem. The relationship between crime and incarceration is highly **endogenous**. An endogenous relationship is one where the causal arrow runs in both directions. An example of a non-endogenous relationship is that between rain and a backyard garden: the amount of rain drives how many flowers bloom, but the number of blooming flowers does not shape rainfall.[63] But the relationship between incarceration and crime runs in both directions. At least in the short run, more incarceration leads to less crime, but more crime leads to more incarceration. Oversimplifying somewhat, if we run a simple statistical model that doesn't explicitly (and correctly) account for this reciprocal relationship—and doing so is, for methodological reasons beyond the scope of this book, profoundly hard—then the results we see are basically net effect of two relationships, the negative effect of incarceration on crime and the positive effect of crime on incarceration.

And a quick survey of the evidence indicates that failing to take endogeneity into account has important implications on the effects reported. Table 10–1 summarizes the results given in a report on crime and prison produced by the Vera Institute of Justice,[64] which started by surveying the state of the literature about incarceration's impact on crime rates:

Table 10–1: Results from the VERA Survey

Studies that do not account for endogeneity		
Study	Sample	Elasticities[65]
Marvell & Moody (1994)	49 states, 1971–1989	–1.6 (index crimes)
Besci (1999)	51 states, 1971–1993	–0.46 (violent crimes) –0.91 (property crimes) –0.87 (index crimes)
Raphael & Winter-Ebmer (2001)	50 states, 1971–1997	~ 0 (violent crimes) –1.1 (property crimes)
Donohue & Levitt (2001)	50 states, 1973–1997	~0 (violent crimes) –1.6 (property crimes)
Levitt (2001)	50 states, 1950–1999	–1.3 (violent crimes) –0.76 (property crimes)

---

[63] **Question:** What if we replaced "how many flowers bloom" with "plant growth in the Amazon rainforest"?

[64] DON STEMEN, RECONSIDERING INCARCERATION: NEW DIRECTIONS FOR REDUCING CRIME, Table 1 (2007). The summary here drops two studies that the report includes. Both of these looked at national time series data rather state-level time series data. Incarceration rates vary so much across states that national-level data does not return particularly meaningful results, so I drop those studies here.

[65] Elasticity refers to percent effect on crime of a 1% change in incarceration. In other words, an elasticity of –0.4 implies that a 1% increase in incarceration reduces crime by 0.4%.

DeFine & Arvanites (2002)	51 states, 1971–1998	~0 (murder, rape, assault, robbery)
		−1.1 (burglary)
		−0.56 (larceny)
		−1.4 (auto theft)
Kovandzic & Sloan (2002)	57 FL counties, 1980–1998	~0 (index crimes)
WSIPP (2003)	39 WA counties, 1980–2001	−2.4 (index crimes)
Liedka, Piehl, & Useem (2006)	51 states, 1970–2000	−0.118 (index crimes, state with incarc. rates < 325)
		+0.05 (index crimes, states with incarc. rates > 325)
Kovandzic & Vieraitis (2006)	58 FL counties, 1980–2000	~0 (index crimes)
Studies that control for endogeneity		
Levitt (1996)	51 states, 1971–1993	−3.8 (violent crimes)
		−2.6 (property crimes)
Spelman (2000)	51 states, 1971–1997	−4.0 (index crimes)
Spelman (2005)	254 TX counties, 1990–2000	−4.4 (violent crimes)
		−3.6 (property crimes)

Two features stand out in Table 10.1. First, and less important to the discussion here, note that studies using similar data—same states, similar years—often return different results. This is a common problem in empirical social science work, since results can be very sensitive to seemingly minor methodological choices. One should therefore always be careful not to put too much weight on any one study's findings. Second, and more relevant to our analysis here, the studies that control for endogeneity consistently return results suggesting a stronger impact of incarceration on crime.

However, there are several caveats that one needs to take into account when thinking about these results, even for the studies that account for the endogenous relationship. First, these results are the *average* effect, not the *marginal* effect. In other words, they basically tell us how much higher crime would be were the incarceration rate set to zero—on average, how much of an effect does our prison system have?

But that is not what we care about: what matters is the *marginal* effect, the effect of incarcerating just one more prisoner.

Second, scale matters as well, wth the marginal effect of incarceration likely stronger the smaller the prison population. As the prison population grows, particularly in times of declining crime (as has been the case in the US since 1991), the criminal justice system is almost certainly imprisoning increasingly less-severe offenders, whose incarceration thus yields smaller reductions in crime.

A recent paper by Rucker Johnson and Steven Raphael attempts to address both these issues, estimating the marginal gains of one more person-year in prison, and separating out the effects between 1978 to 1990 (when prison populations were relatively small) and 1991 to 2004 (when populations were larger).[66] They find that from 1978 to 1990, each additional prison year resulted in thirty fewer index offenses; for 1991 to 2004, only eight fewer. At least one other paper, which does not properly control for endogeneity, returns similar findings that the effectiveness of incarceration declines with its scope.[67]

The economist John Donohue attempted to design a more comprehensive model to determine whether the marginal benefits of incarceration justify its marginal costs.[68] Noting that deriving cost-benefit values is fraught with peril—as we saw above, estimates of the elasticity of crime with respect to prison are all over the map, and that's before we get to tough normative questions like how to calculate the savings from one fewer assault or murder—he reports a wide range of marginal benefit values. His results suggest that for most estimates incarceration is (naively) cost-benefit justifiable, although the gap between cost and benefit shrinks between 1986 and 2005 (the years he considers), sometimes sharply—and in a few cases to the point that prison ceases to be justifiable by 2005.

> **Question:** Why do I insert the "naively" into the claim that prisons are cost-benefit justifiable. If spending one extra dollar on prisons reduce crime by $2.50, shouldn't we spend that dollar? What's naïve about saying that?

So that's the big story: incarceration appears to reduce crime, perhaps even in a cost-benefit justifiable way, albeit at a diminishing rate. It may now be useful to look at *why* it appears to be at least

---

[66] Rucker Johnson & Steven Raphael, *How Much Crime Reduction Does the Marginal Prisoner Buy?*, 55 J. L. & ECON. 275 (2012).

[67] Raymond V. Licdka, Anne Morrison Piehl, & Bert Useem, *The Crime-Control Effect of Incarceration: Does Scale Matter?*, 5 CRIMINOLOGY & PUB. POL'Y 245 (2006). That the paper fails to control for endogeneity means that its estimates of the size of incarceration's effects are likely too small, but that doesn't mean that the qualitative relationship it estimates *between* high- and low-incarceration states is incorrect.

[68] John J. Donohue III, *Assessing the Relative Benefits of Incarceration: The Overall Change Over the Previous Decades and the Benefits on the Margin*, in DO PRISONS MAKE US SAFER? THE BENEFITS AND COSTS OF THE PRISON BOOM (Steven Raphael & Michael Stoll, eds., 2009).

moderately effective: is it deterrence? incapacitation? rehabilitation? something else?

D.2. GENERAL DETERRENCE AND INCAPACITATION

The purpose of incapacitation is not just to lock up those who commit crimes, but to discourage people from committing crimes in the first place. Measuring this effect, however, is difficult. Simply looking at the relationship between aggregate incarceration rates and aggregate crime rates cannot separate the effect of general deterrence from specific incapacitation. But it is also impossible to conduct wide-ranging surveys that accurately capture how changes in sentencing law change the behavior of the random person on the street. So some sort of indirect attack is needed.

The standard approach for teasing out the general deterrent effect of sanctions is to look at new sentencing enhancements. Assume that the legislature raises the additional mandatory-minimum punishment for using a gun in a robbery from three years to five. Any short-run reduction in armed robbery can be attributed to deterrence: since the armed robber would have been in prison for at least three years before the rule change, increased declines in robberies during that time are due to deterrence (controlling, of course, for all other changing factors).

The results of these studies have been mixed, but generally weak. Several studies have looked at the impact of gun enhancements on offending, yielding ambiguous results.[69] Similar approaches looking at the enhancement effect of aging into majority status and thus facing adult rather than juvenile punishments have not uncovered significant effects.[70] But the results are not all negative. One of the most reliable

---

[69] Daniel Kessler and Steven Levitt found a significant deterrent effect for California's Proposition 8, which was passed in 1982 and increased the sentence for recidivists committing certain violent crimes, but their results have been attacked on methodological grounds by Steven Raphael and by Aaron Chalfin and Justin McCrary. A study by Jens Ludwig and Steven Raphael of Project Exile in Richmond, Virginia, which diverted ex-felons caught with firearms to the more punitive federal system, did not turn up significant results either. But a multistate study of gun enhancements by David Abrams finds that such laws reduce gun robberies by about 5% over the first three years, for a rough elasticity of –0.1. See Daniel Kessler & Steven D. Levitt, *Using Sentence Enhancements to Distinguish between Deterrence and Incapacitation*, 42 J. L. & ECON. 343 (1999); Steven Raphael, *The Deterrence Effect of California's Proposition 8: Weighing the Evidence*, 5 CRIMINOLOGY & PUB. POL'Y 471 (2006); AARON CHALFIN & JUSTIN MCCRARY, CRIMINAL DETERRENCE: A REVIEW OF THE LITERATURE (unpublished manuscript, 2014); Jens Ludwig & Steven Raphael, *Prison Sentence Enhancements: The Case of Project Exile*, in EVALUATING GUN POLICY: EFFECTS ON CRIME AND VIOLENCE (Jens Ludwig & Philip J. Cook, eds., 2003); and David S. Abrams, *Estimating the Deterrent Effect of Incarceration Using Sentencing Enhancements*, 4 AM. ECON. J.: APPLIED ECON. 32 (2012).

[70] Steven Levitt found that the response of juveniles to aging into the tougher adult system suggested an elasticity of –0.4, i.e., a 10% increase in sentence length reduced crime via deterrence by 4%, a large effect by the standards of the deterrence literature. See Steven D. Levitt, *Juvenile Crime and Punishment*, 106 J. POL. ECON. 1156 (1998). But replications by David S. Lee and Justin McCrary and by Randi Hjalmarsson have returned much weaker, and possibly no, effects; the latter studies are generally methodologically stronger. See DAVID S. LEE & JUSTIN MCCRARY, THE DETERRENT EFFECT OF PRISON: DYNAMIC THEORY AND EVIDENCE

studies looking at three-strike laws has found a moderate deterrent effect to the third strike, and a randomized trial looking at whether the increased threat of incarceration led to the payment of fines found a strong effect.[71]

The general weakness of a general deterrent effect should not necessarily surprise us. Those who commit crimes tend to heavily discount the future, so sentence enhancements likely do not change their calculus too much;[72] young offenders in particular exhibit such present-mindedness, which likely explains much of why the juvenile-to-adult-sanction transition does not appear to have a significant deterrent effect. Conversely, in the controlled experiment involving fines and incarceration, the threat of incarceration was immediate, and represented a shift from no time served to time served, something that is salient to even the most present-minded offender.

Another potential limitation to general deterrence is knowledge of the law. If potential offenders are unaware of the sentencing regime or changes in that regime, then changing sanctions will have no effect. How well informed, then, are those who are most likely to commit crimes? Perhaps somewhat shockingly, criminologists do not really know the answer to this question, but what little evidence there is suggests that correlation between actual risk and perceptions of risk are not particularly strong.

In a random phone survey of approximately 1,500 residents in major urban counties, for example, Gary Kleck and colleagues asked respondents about their perceptions of the certainty and severity of punishment for several serious crimes (homicide, robbery, aggravated assault, and burglary) and then compared the perceptions to official statistics from those counties.[73] Their results suggest that Americans *in the aggregate* have fairly accurate perceptions of sentences imposed (even erring on the side of thinking they are longer than they actually are), but significantly overstate the likelihood of going to prison. At a more local level, however, the results are less optimistic: those living in more-

---

(unpublished manuscript, 2009); and Randi Hjalmarsson, *Crime and Expected Punishment: Changes in Perceptions at the Age of Criminal Majority*, 11 AM. L. & ECON. REV. 209 (2009).

[71] Eric Helland & Alexander Tabarrok, *Does Three Strikes Deter? A Nonparametric Estimation*, 42 J. HUMAN RESOURCES 309 (2007), which is discussed above in Chapter 5; David Weisburd, Tomer Einat, & Matt Kowalski, *The Miracle of the Cells: An Experimental Study of Interventions to Increase Payment of Court-Ordered Financial Obligations*, 7 CRIMINOLOGY & PUB. POL'Y 9 (2008).

[72] Raymond Paternoster summarizes several studies looking at how changes in time served change perceptions in the disutility of punishment, and the results suggest high levels of discounting: one study found that a five year sentence is viewed as only twice as bad as a one-year sentence, and another that compared to a one-year sentence a ten year sentence is seen as only four times as bad and a twenty year sentence as only six times worse. Raymond Paternoster, *How Much Do We Really Know About Criminal Deterrence*, 100 J. CRIM. L. & CRIMINOLOGY 765, 805–806 (2010).

[73] Gary Kleck, Brion Sever, Spencer Li, & Marc Gertz, *The Missing Link in General Deterrence Research*, 43 CRIMINOLOGY 623 (2005).

punitive counties have similar perceptions of the risks of punishment as those living in less punitive counties. So we are right in general, but not in particular. Even more surprising, the correlation between actual and perceived severity was weaker among those self-identifying as having been arrested (who comprised about 10% of the sample). A follow-up study also rejected the idea of "wisdom of crowds": even if *individual* beliefs did not correlate strongly with county variations in punishment, might *county-average* perceptions be more correlated? The answer again appears to be no.[74]

As Kleck and his co-authors point out, this weak relationship may not be all that surprising. As they explain: "Few people, whether criminals or non-criminals, are consumers of criminal justice statistics, and even criminals have only limited personal experience with crime and punishment." And this effect is even stronger for potential offenders who have yet to commit a crime, since they have had *no* contact. Moreover, the media covers only a highly biased subset of all cases, providing little accurate systematic information.

That said, for deterrence to work we do not need everyone to perfectly understand the law all the time. As two economists, Tom Miles and Jens Ludwig, explain:

> For deterrence to operate requires that *some* members of the population of potential offenders respond to incentives and be aware of relevant changes in the incentives to commit crime. It is not necessary that all criminals be "perfectly rational" or avidly track the Federal Register for changes in sentencing rules. Evidence that many or even most people at risk for criminal behavior are drunk, ignorant, or dim is not sufficient to categorically dismiss the possibility of a deterrent effect.
>
> The notion that deterrence can be ignored in the evaluation of changes in sanction policy is also inconsistent with a large body of evidence suggesting that as a general matter, people respond to incentives at least in the aggregate. But is this true for crime prone people as well? As [Philip] Cook notes . . . , denying that criminals respond to incentives "is tantamount to claiming that potential criminals . . . are fundamentally different from everyone else, if indeed there is anyone who can be excluded from the 'potential criminal' category.'"[75]

And the perceptions literature does contain some positive results consistent with this claim. As we will see shortly, while the baseline risk perceptions of those who have been to prison are often inaccurate, offenders tend to be relatively good Bayesians: as they get more information, they update their perceptions fairly well. So while the

---

[74] Gary Kleck & J.C. Barnes, *Deterrence and Macro-Level Perceptions of Punishment Risks: Is There a "Collective Wisdom"?*, 59 CRIME & DELINQ. 1006 (2008).

[75] Thomas J. Miles & Jens Ludwig, *The Silence of the Lambdas: Deterring Incapacitation Research*, 23 J. QUANT. CRIMINOLOGY 287, 290–291 (2007).

evidence for general deterrence may be weak, that for specific deterrence is stronger. We turn now, then, to the offender-specific effects of incarceration on crime.

Question: What steps can various criminal justice actors take to increase or improve perceptions of sanction risks for potential offenders?

D.3. INDIVIDUAL (SPECIFIC) DETERRENCE AND INCAPACITATION (AND REHABILITATION)

By now, we should have a good sense of all the various factors that will shape how incarceration influences an offender's future conduct. On the one hand, the unpleasantness of prison should act as a deterrent, as should the extent to which the offender better appreciates the risk of getting caught and punished. This is the specific deterrent effect. Moreover, while the offender is in prison he is (obviously) aging, and so he leaves prison older than when he entered, and thus less likely on average to offend due to the age-profile of offending, at least for older offenders (what about the defendant admitted at 18 and released at 22?).

Yet there are clear countervailing effects as well. The offender generally leaves with fewer job prospects, weakened family ties—and perhaps stronger ties with criminal networks thanks to their concentrated exposure to them in prison—fewer social controls, lingering and perhaps aggravated health problems, and possibly unresolved drug and alcohol problems. And note that each of these factors aggravates the others: sickness makes it even harder to get a job, not being able to get a job (which is often thought to be a direct way of desisting from crime) may increase the risk of future drug use, reduces access to health insurance and thus health care, and is thought to reduce the ability to find a spouse—which is *another* path out of crime. Thus all these collateral costs undermine whatever specific deterrent effect incarceration has. Deterrence, after all, is not an absolute question but a relative one: what are the relative costs and benefits of committing the crime? By weakening legal options, incarceration increases the relative return on illegal choices. Likewise with incapacitation. Offenders may age out of crime, but employment, health, and other factors surely shape that proclivity as well.

So determining the net effect of all these conflicting factors is ultimately an empirical question, and a challenging one at that. In a review of studies, Francis Cullen and co-authors find little evidence of a specific deterrent effect.[76] Their primary conclusions are:

- *With some confidence, we can conclude that, across all offenders, prisons do not have a specific deterrent effect.*

---

[76] Francis T. Cullen, Cherly Lero Jonson, & Daniel S. Nagin, *Prisons Do Not Reduce Recidivism: The High Cost of Ignoring Science*, 91 PRISON J. 48S (2011).

Custodial sentences do not reduce recidivism more than noncustodial sanctions.

- *With less confidence, we can propose that prisons, especially gratuitously painful ones, may be criminogenic.* On balance, the evidence tilts in the direction of those proposing that the social experiences of imprisonment are likely crime generating.
- *Although the evidence is very limited, it is likely that low-risk offenders are most likely to experience increased recidivism due to incarceration.* From a policy perspective, it is essential to screen offenders for their risk level and to be cautious about imprisoning those not deeply entrenched in a criminal career or manifesting attitudes, relationships, and traits associated with recidivism.

Two points deserve additional attention. First, the authors are not arguing that incarceration has no specific deterrent effect, but that it has no *additional* effect when compared to non-custodial sentences such as intensive probation. After all, reformers are not proposing that we do *nothing* with criminal offenders, just that we rely on non-prison based punishments more. And there is evidence that offenders "are more likely to dread intensive and lengthy community-based punishments than shorter prison terms." We will discuss these alternatives in more depth in Chapter 11.

Second, their point about the criminogenic effect of incarceration refers to the fact that the costs of being in prison, such as the reduced pro-social ties and the increased connection with offender networks, outweigh whatever deterrent effects incarceration has. The authors, however, are quick to point out that the evidence base on prison's effect on crime is surprisingly thin for how many people are in prison. Thus, on the one hand, at least one paper has found evidence that harsher prison conditions do have a strong general-deterrent effect: Lawrence Katz, Steve Levitt and Ellen Shustorovich report that each additional death in prison (their proxy for tougher prison conditions more generally) reduces both violent and property crimes by about 30 to 100 per 100,000.[77] On the other hand, an innovative paper by Keith Chen and Jesse Shapiro suggests that moving an inmate from a lower-level prison to the next-highest security level generally raises the risk of recidivism.[78] So we face off-setting effects: the *threat* of tougher conditions appears to reduce recidivism, but *carrying through* with the threat when necessary increases the risk of recidivism by those put in tougher conditions. Chen and Shapiro run some calculations that suggest the latter effect trumps the former, which is consistent with the findings by Cullen and his co-

---

[77] Lawrence Katz, Steven Levitt, & Ellen Shustorovich, *Prison Conditions, Capital Punishment, and Deterrence*, 5 AM. L. & ECON. REV. 318 (2003).

[78] M. Keith Chen & Jesse M. Shapiro, *Do Harsher Prison Conditions Reduce Recidivism? A Discontinuity-Based Approach*, 9 AM. L. & ECON. REV. 1 (2007).

authors. But it is important to note the complex way in which this effect plays out.

Question: Can we reconcile the findings in Katz et al. with those in Chen and Shapiro? Are they necessarily measuring the same thing? What policy implications flow from their (joint) findings? Might we want to keep conditions harsher (putting aside normative concerns and focusing just on deterrence), but then invest more in reintegration of those incarcerated?

Even if incarceration does not have strong specific deterrent effects, however, it may still have an important incapacitory one. Even if offenders recidivate upon release, they are not committing crimes—at least against the non-incarcerated population—while in prison, and they may commit *fewer* crimes upon release as well. Incapacitation studies attempt to measure how many crimes per year certain types of offenders commit (referred to in the literature as "lambda") and then calculate how many crimes are prevented by locking up however many of these offenders we have in prison, taking into account what we know about lifecycle trajectories of offending.

Yet it is unclear just how much this literature tells us. Part of the problem is that it is really hard to calculate lambda. Studies generally have to rely on self-reports in surveys, and criminals are not entirely reliable. Moreover, interviews conducted in prison will generally overstate lambda, since analysts are more likely to interview long-serving inmates (since they are more likely to be there).[79] And estimating marginal effects of a policy change is difficult, since the distribution of lambdas in the population varies with the incarceration rate: the more people in prison, the more the additional people you arrest will have below-average lambdas (since on average the higher-lambda people are already more likely to be in prison).

On top of all this, incapacitation research ignores the **replacement rate**: to what extent does locking up Joe reduce Joe's offending but increase that by Bob, who sees a new niche to enter? Many have argued this is a problem with the war on drugs: every time a street dealer is arrested another person simply takes his place. Data suggest that replacement here is not one-for-one, but it points to serious limitation in incapacitation, at least for drug and perhaps some property offenses.

These problems have led some scholars to argue against studying "incapacitation" or "deterrence" effects and simply focusing on the total impact of a given policy change.[80] Yet this is an unappealing outcome, since it is quite hard to really understand the impact of a policy change

---

[79] Imagine a prison system in which at any given point ten people are serving ten-year terms and ten people are serving six-month terms. Over the course of a year, there will be ten long-serving inmates and twenty short-serving inmates, yet a survey on any given day will find the divide to be 50–50, overstating the average severity of offenders.

[80] Miles & Ludwig, *The Silence of the Lambdas*, supra note 75.

without understanding how it operates. Consider a change in the law that increases the sentence for a class of crimes by five years. The general deterrent effect starts immediately, while the specific deterrent and incapacitory effects do not start for five more years. Furthermore, isolating specific deterrence from incapacitation helps us better understand how much we should focus on conditions (since worse conditions undermine specific deterrence) or how much we should invest in developing sophisticated predictive models of lambda (if we think incapacitation is the key driver). Unfortunately, we simply lack much understanding at this point.

> **Question:** What does it mean that we know so little about how incarceration operates? If we're retributivists, is it immaterial—morality is, after all, non-empirical. But if we're consequentialists, how do we set up the error cost analysis: in what direction should we err? Does our weighing change in different circumstances, like during a crime boom vs. a crime decline?

> **Question:** Which institutions should be in charge of weighing these error costs? What does this tell us about how we should structure sentencing authority?

Yet despite our limited knowledge—and how we should act when knowledge is limited like this is an important normative question to consider—there are some broad points that appear to emerge from this discussion:

- Longer sentences likely buy little reduction in crime and may be counterproductive: they do not add much in the way of general deterrence, and whatever the gains from incapacitation appears to be offset at least somewhat by declines in specific deterrence.

- The proper comparison is prison vs. a different sanction, not prison vs. no prison, which likely leads current studies to overstate the positive impact of incarceration on crime.

- The collateral costs of incarceration are important in their own right, and they also point to a major way in which punishment can be self-defeating unless steps are taken to contain these costs.

- It is important, however, not to overstate the *marginal* contribution of incarceration to these costs: offenders are disproportionately drawn from relatively small communities whose social and environmental problems are often somewhat hidden in official statistics (which even at the city level are too high-level).

None of these results imply that we should have no one in prison, but they do suggest that it is quite likely we are over-incarcerating now. So it is worth considering what alternative sanctions may look like, which is the focus of the next chapter.

CHAPTER 11

ALTERNATIVES TO INCARCERATION

Although incarceration receives the bulk of media's and the commentariat's attention, it is not the primary form of punishment in the United States: in 2013, there were 1.57 million people in prison, 2.3 million in prison or jail, but over 3.9 million on probation and 850,000 on parole. Thus of the more than 7 million people under supervision, over 4.75 million, or more than 67%, are not locked up. And this percent rises even more when we include civil decisions, such as civil confinement or civil domestic restraining orders (of which perhaps almost one million are granted per year), which are non-criminal actions that are clearly used to advance criminal justice goals. Arguably we should refer to *prison* as the "alternative" sentence, given its minority status.

In this section, we will look at nine types of alternative sanctions. The first four are ones that have been in use for a long time: probation, fines, community service, and asset forfeiture. We will then briefly touch on boot camps, which were thought to be a strong alternative to imprisonment but which have faded in light of disappointing empirical findings. The next alternative is post-incarceration civil confinement, which has been widely adopted for managing sex offenders (other approaches for restricting sex offenders, such as registries, notification laws, and residency restrictions, will be discussed in Chapter 12, which looks at re-entry). We will consider whether civil confinement is justifiable (both positively and normatively) and briefly ask whether it can (and will) be extended beyond sex offenders to other types of criminals. The seventh alternative operates in a closely-related domestic field, namely civil domestic violence restraining orders, which are designed to incapacitate and deter without putting too much demand on scarce prison resources. The last two alternatives, shaming/restorative justice efforts and drug/alternative courts, reflect more fundamental efforts to move away from a punishment-based criminal justice system.

Before turning to the specifics, however, there is one general point to keep in mind thorough these sections. A common issue or concern raised with alternatives to incarceration is **net widening**. Alternatives are generally framed as "alternatives" because they are seen as a way to efficiently reduce prison populations without jeopardizing public safety. Thus the appeal of boot camps: intense, military-style training could be a politically viable alternative to incarceration that could also achieve similar reductions in crime at a fraction of the cost. But when boot camps are introduced, one of two things can happen. Judges may divert offenders who they otherwise would have sent to prison to boot camps, or judges may continue to send those inmates to prison and instead send offenders who would have received something even less invasive (probation, say, or even dismissal) to the camps. This latter effect is referred to as net widening, since instead of reducing the amount restrictive punishment the alternative actually increases it.

Whether net widening is normatively good or bad, however, is a tricky issue. *If* our goal is just to reduce the use of the most serious sanction, then net widening reflects a loss: prison use remains stable, but more people are punished more severely. For broader normative goals, however, the imposition of tougher sanctions need not be a loss. In fact, Joan Petersilia once referred to this effect in some contexts as "net *repairing*," on the grounds that more-granular alternatives expand the sentencing options available to judges in ways that may *advance* criminal justice goals. When discussing alternatives to incarceration, it is therefore always important to ask who you think will in fact be the likely "recipient" of the new option.

A. THE STANDARD ALTERNATIVES: PROBATION, FINES, COMMUNITY SERVICE, ASSET FORFEITURE, AND BOOT CAMPS

The five approaches considered here are likely what first springs to most people's minds when they hear the term "alternatives to incarceration."

A.1. PROBATION

The idea behind probation is simple: rather than sending lower-level offenders to prison, judges release them back into the community, subject both to numerous restrictions on what they are allowed to do and to supervision by a probation officer. Probation started informally in Boston in the mid-1800s, when prosecutors would agree to not file charges against defendants in exchange for them promising to not reoffend, and private individuals, in particular a bootmaker named John Augustus, would post the necessary bond to have the defendant released from jail. By 1878, Massachusetts codified this informal system, and all other states eventually followed suit.

Probation is now the primary form of punishment used in the United States. Figure 11–1 plots the number of people on probation as well as the percent of the correctional population they represent.[1]

---

[1] Data are taken from here: http://www.albany.edu/sourcebook/pdf/t612010.pdf.

Figure 11–1: Probation in the United States, 1980–2012

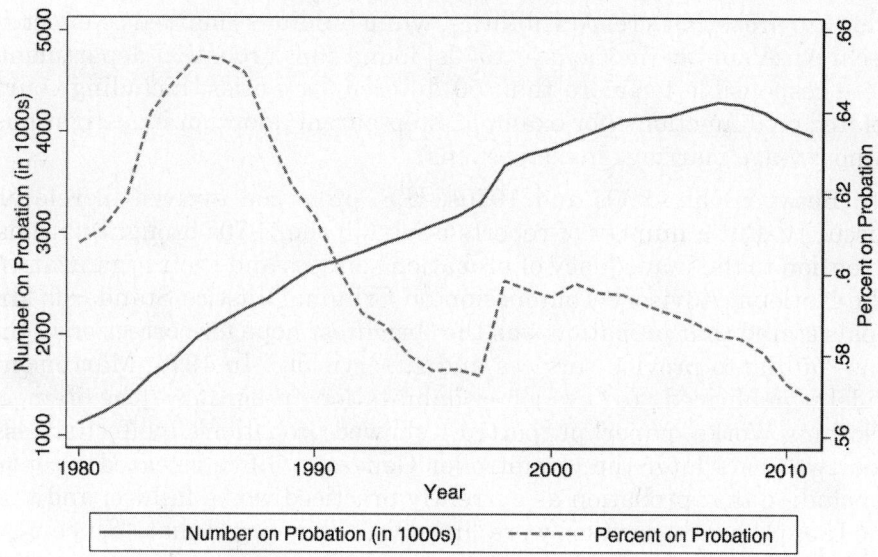

For the past three decades, probationers have comprised about 60% of all prisoners, parolees, and probationers. How successful a program probation has been, however, is an open question. Joan Petersilia, a leading scholar of probation and parole, provides a good summary of the issues and challenges faced by the probation system.

Joan Petersilia, *Community Corrections: Probation, Parole, and Prisoner Re-Entry*
CRIME & PUBLIC POLICY (James Q. Wilson & Joan Petersilia, eds., 2011)

Initially, probation officers were volunteers who, according to [John] Augustus [the bootmaker above], just needed to just have a good heart. Early probation volunteer officers were often drawn from Catholic, Protestant, and Jewish church groups. In addition, police were reassigned to function as probation officers while continuing to draw their pay as municipal employees. But as the concept spread and the number of persons arrested increased, the need for pre-sentence investigations increased; and the volunteer probation officer was converted into a paid-position. The new officers hired were drawn largely from the law enforcement community—retired sheriffs and policemen—and worked directly for the judge.

Gradually the role of court support and probation officer became synonymous, and probation officers became "the eyes and ears of the local court." As [David] Rothman observed some years later, probation developed in the United States very haphazardly, and with no real thought. Missions were unclear and often contradictory, and from the start there was tension between the law enforcement and rehabilitation purposes of probation. But most importantly, tasks were continually added to probation's responsibilities, while funding remained constant or declined. A survey [in the late 1970s] found that probation departments were responsible for more than 50 different activities, including court-related civil functions (for example, step-parent adoption investigations, minority-age marriage investigations).

Between the 1950s and 1970s, U.S. probation evolved in relative obscurity. But a number of reports issued in the 1970s brought national attention to the inadequacy of probation services and their organization. The National Advisory Commission on Criminal Justice Standards and Goals stated that probation was the "brightest hope for corrections," but was "failing to provide services and supervision." In 1974, Martinson's widely publicized review of rehabilitation programs [the famous "Nothing Works" paper] purportedly showed probation's ineffectiveness, and two years later the Comptroller General's Office released a report concluding that probation as currently practiced was a failure, and that the U.S. probation systems were "in crisis." They urged that, "Since most offenders are sentenced to probation, probation systems must receive adequate resources. But something more fundamental is needed. The priority given to probation in the criminal justice system must be reevaluated."

In recent years, probation agencies have struggled—with continued meager resources—to upgrade services and supervision. But there is no doubt that probation plays a critical role in justice system case processing. Anyone who is convicted, and many of those arrested, come into contact with the probation department; probation officials, operating with a great deal of discretionary authority, dramatically affect most subsequent justice-processing decisions. Their input affects not only the subsequent liberties that offenders will enjoy, but their decisions influence public safety, since they recommend (within certain legal restraints) which offenders will be released back to their communities, and judges follow their sentence recommendations 70 to 90 percent of the time.

When the court grants probation, probation staff have great discretion about which court-ordered conditions to enforce and monitor. For persons who violate probation conditions, probation officers are responsible for deciding which violations will be brought to the court's attention and what subsequent sanctions to recommend. And even when an offender goes to prison, the offender's initial security classification (and eligibility for parole) will be based on information contained in the probation officer's presentence investigation. Finally, when the offender is released from jail or prison, probation staff often provide his or her community supervision. In fact, it is safe to say that no other justice agency is involved with the offender, and his case as comprehensively as the probation department.

The Growth of Community Corrections Populations

As the U.S. population has grown, more citizens are being arrested and convicted, and all corrections populations (prisons, jails, probation, and parole) have grown simultaneously. The number of offenders in prison and jail reached 2.3 million and, for the first time, one in 100 adults was in prison or jail. With far less notice, however, the number of people on probation or parole has also skyrocketed to more than 5 million, up from 1.6 million just 25 years ago. This means that a stunning 1 in every 31 adults, or 3.2 percent, is under some form of correctional control in the United States.

It is important to note that the national picture of correctional populations is disproportionally influenced, or skewed, by relatively few states. Four states from four different regions in the United States dominate corrections: California, Texas, New York, and Florida. They account for about two-fifths of all offenders under correctional control.

Funding for Community Corrections

Despite wide usage and its essential role in supervising serious offenders, community corrections has often been the subject of intense criticism. It is often depicted as permissive, uncaring about crime victims, and committed to a rehabilitative ideal that ignores the reality of violent, predatory criminals. Americans have very low confidence in and little knowledge of probation and parole. [One] national survey conducted [in 1995] found that roughly 60 percent of those surveyed reacted favorably to the performance of the police, while only 25 percent expressed confidence in probation. In a 1996 national poll, 53 percent of the sample agreed that "community corrections programs are evidence of leniency in the criminal justice system." Citizen surveys repeatedly show that the public thinks that prisons and jails make people worse, but it does not believe that probation and parole make them better, hold offenders accountable, or protect the public.

However, a recent national public opinion poll by Zogby International found that Americans strongly support alternatives to prison for nonviolent, nonserious crimes (those where the loss of property was less than $400). Nearly 80 percent of respondents felt that the most appropriate sentence for a nonserious offender is supervised probation, with no prison or jail unless these alternatives fail. But, 60 percent of those polled felt that incarceration was necessary if violations of probation or parole were detected, even if no new crime was committed. It appears that the public favors community corrections for certain offenders but wants it to be a more credible sanction, where violations are detected and consistently punished.

Unfortunately, the current economic woes have left probation and parole agencies woefully underfunded, undermining their potential effectiveness. However, in the aggregate, community-based supervision has never been shown to decrease recidivism, contributing to their weak position to argue for increased funding. Despite the fact that community corrections populations have grown at a rate similar to that of prisons and jails, funding for prisons and jails has increased significantly while spending for probation and parole remains unchanged from what it was in 1977. [Michael] Jacobson wrote that, with few resources and growing caseloads, parole agents "experience constant pressure, including anxieties about whether someone on their caseload will be the next murderer of a Polly Klass. Indeed, a combination of high caseloads, few internal resources, and frequent political condemnation makes their job one of the most difficult and stressful in the criminal justice system."

* * *

Supervision Conditions, Caseload Size, Access to Services, and Civil Disabilities

Every probationer and parolee is required to sign a contract stating that they agree to abide by certain conditions. Conditions generally can be grouped into standard conditions applicable to all offenders, and special conditions that are tailored to particular offenders. Standard conditions are similar throughout most jurisdictions, and include payment of supervision fees, finding employment, not carrying weapons, reporting changes of address and employment, not committing crimes, and submitting to search by the police and parole officers. Special conditions are tailored to the offenders' particular circumstances, such as periodic drug testing for substance abusers and law enforcement registration for sex offenders.

Ironically, while caseloads have grown and funding has declined, the proportion of offenders subject to special conditions—particularly drug testing—has increased. The public's more punitive mood, combined with inexpensive drug testing (now about $5 per test) and a greater number of offenders with substance abuse problems, contributes to the increased number of conditions imposed. The Bureau of Justice Statistics reports that nearly half of all probationers had five or more conditions to their sentence required by the court or probation agency. A monetary requirement was the most common condition (84 percent), and more than 2 of every 5 probationers were required to enroll in some form of substance abuse treatment. Nearly a third of all probationers were subject to mandatory drug testing—43 percent of felons and 17 percent of misdemeanants.

Parole requirements are more stringent. [A study in 1991] found that 80 percent of parolees were required to have "gainful employment," 61 percent "no association with persons of criminal records," 53 percent "pay all fines and restitution," and 47 percent "support family and all dependents." It was estimated that more than a third of all U.S. probationers and parolees have court-ordered drug testing conditions in

1998. Surely the number is higher today, but there are no more recent statistics on the issue.

The problem, however, is that while many probationers and parolees have dozens of supervision conditions, the enforcement of those conditions is usually quite lax. Caseloads have risen and funding has remained stagnant or decreased, so that most conditions remain Unenforced. Mark Kleiman studied drug testing orders for probationers in California and concluded that, "infrequent testing and lax sanctioning make offenders confident that they can continue using drugs with impunity."

Many in the field agree that the "piling up" of supervision conditions has created unrealistic expectations and has hurt the credibility of community corrections. Carl Wicklund, executive director of the American Probation and Parole Association [APPA], advocates the "three R's" of supervision conditions: they should be realistic—few in number and attainable; relevant—tailored to individual risks and needs; and research-based—supported by evidence that they will change behavior and result in improved public safety and reintegration outcomes.

* * *

But what is the ideal caseload size? To some, this might seem to be a rather straightforward question, but in practice it is quite complex. [N]ot all offenders or court orders are alike, and the political and policy environments of jurisdictions provide services that vary greatly. The . . . APPA . . . urges agencies to adopt a "workload" rather than "caseload" approach, where time factors weigh into the case. For example, a case with a high priority would require 4 hours per month equaling 30 as a total caseload (if an officer has 120 hours per month to supervise offenders). But the APPA has also published "not to exceed" caseload standards.

Unfortunately, a large body of research now exists showing that smaller caseloads and stricter reporting requirements do not necessarily reduce recidivism. [A 1993 study] found that offenders on smaller [caseloads] (25 to 30 cases per officer versus 50 to 75 per officer) were no less likely to have new arrests but were more likely to have their parole and probation revoked because of technical violations (due to closer surveillance). But [that study] did find one positive finding from the evaluation: offenders who were on smaller caseloads *and* completed counseling, were employed, and paid restitution had lower rearrest rates. This suggests that interventions that focus on diminishing behaviors associated with criminality are more important to reducing recidivism than simply increasing contacts between officer and offender.

[A 2008 BJS study] reported that the average adult parole caseload was 38 active parolees for each officer, but the average does not really describe the experiences of most parolees. Two-thirds of adult offenders on parole are required to have face-to-face contact with their parole officer at least once a month, including 14 percent who are required to have weekly face-to-face contact. An additional 17 percent of paroled offenders are required to meet with their parole officers less than once a month or to maintain contact by mail, telephone, or other means. An additional 13 percent of paroled offenders are no longer required to report on a regular basis. In sum, this means that about 30 percent of all U.S. parolees are basically being supervised "on paper" with few services or active surveillance. This type of paper parole is becoming more popular because even though the parolee has no formal reporting requirements, they are still considered in the custody of corrections agencies and their legal rights are severely limited. Parolees can be visited in their homes and on the street and searched without a warrant by law enforcement or parole agents. If they are found to be in violation of parole conditions, they can be returned to prison as a parole violator without a criminal court proceeding. Parole board officials use the more lenient legal standard of "preponderance of the evidence," as opposed to the "beyond a reasonable doubt" standard that is required in criminal court convictions. This most lenient standard is deemed appropriate because a parolee is still in the legal custody of the state's prison system.

Many serious offenders are left unsupervised, and this undoubtedly contributes to high recidivism rates. [A 1992 report] found that nearly half of all probationers do not comply with the terms of their sentence, and only a fifth of those who violate their sentences ever go to jail for their noncompliance. It is also true that thousands of probationers and parolees abscond (that is, whereabouts unknown) from supervision. The BJS estimates that in 1990 just 1 percent of all adult probationers and parolees had absconded from supervision, but by 2007, 9 percent of adult probationers were on absconder status, and 7 percent of parolees were on absconder status. In California the figure is even higher. On any given day, 20 percent of all parolees had absconded supervision. While a majority of jurisdictions issue warrants for such violators, funding shortages mean that little is done systematically to locate absconders. It is also worth noting that probation and parole officers play a vital role to crime victims, providing them information about the offender's whereabouts, conditions of supervision, and other issues affecting victim safety. When offenders abscond, the victim's peace of mind and safety are threatened.

The justice system simply cannot afford to do much monitoring for the majority of offenders under supervision. Agencies are trying to deploy more staff and rehabilitative resources to higher-classified offenders and—because budgets are limited—spend correspondingly fewer dollars on lower-classified offenders. The New York City Department of Probation, for example, uses automated check-in kiosks for the city's low-risk probation population, a strategy that could be applied to low-risk parolees as well. The limited use of kiosks began in the 1990s, and by

2003 about 70 percent of all New York adult probationers were on kiosk supervision. After being trained on how to use the system, probationers assigned to kiosk supervision report to the kiosk and answer questions about their conditions (e.g., residence, updated contact information, employment, and new arrests). The kiosk system uses a biometric hand scanner that generates a receipt when used. A recent [2007] assessment of the city's kiosk system found that it helps improve compliance with reporting conditions without sacrificing public safely. Moreover, kiosks allow the department to allocate more resources to those who pose the greatest risk to public safety-probationers who are identified as high-risk for recidivism. Arrest rates for both low-risk and high-risk probationers are down.

As Petersilia suggests, the scope of the restrictions that can be placed on probationers seems nearly limitless. Some more examples:

> The greatest restraint on permissible probation conditions is limited imagination. Abundant appellate cases support the rule that, as long as conditions are sufficiently reasonable and specific, judges have broad latitude in designing them.
>
> Throughout the country, legislation imposes the standard condition that probationer not engage in any further criminal activity.
>
> Although the Fourth Amendment restricts conditions that can be placed upon probationers the same way it restricts conditions for parole, a probationer who has consented to being searched as a condition of probation has a reduced expectation of privacy; thus, a law enforcement officer may search the probationer's home upon reasonable suspicion that the probationer is engaging in unlawful activity.
>
> Turning to specific affirmative conditions, the following have been either statutorily authorized or validated on appeal: that probationer pay a fine; make restitution; forfeit property; perform community service; repay the costs of prosecution; surrender to a marshall for work-release; secure "satisfactory employment;"" submit to counseling; pass psychiatric tests; appear before a grand jury and disclose the source of his past supplier of drugs; submit to reasonably circumscribed searches of his person; that sex-offender inform his probation officer of any new intimate relationships so the officer may make sure such person is aware of the probationer's conviction status; that probationer inform immediate neighbors of his sex-offender status; requiring an ignition device on a drunk driver's automobile, prohibiting car from starting unless driver's breath is alcohol free.

Permissible negative conditions include the following: that offender not hold public office or leadership position in any labor organization; not participate in any federal or state political activity; refrain from consuming alcoholic beverages; abstain from using narcotic drugs and associating with drug users or dealers; avoid contact with a specified person; not engage in the automobile-repossession business; not teach for a year; surrender all obscene material, terminate his interest in a pornography company and not associate with known homosexuals; stay out of designated counties within the state; "associate only with law-abiding persons;" not gamble; not associate with any Irish-Catholic organizations or visit any Irish pubs; not protest abortions at women's health organizations for one year; and not sire any more children until demonstrating an ability to support them.[2]

EXAMPLE: PROBATION IN CALIFORNIA

It may be useful to see how probation operates in practice. This example works through the probation process, from imposition to revocation or success, as practiced in California. The primary provision governing probation is:

Cal. Penal Code § 1203.1:

a. The court, or judge thereof, in the order granting probation and as a condition thereof, may imprison the defendant in a county jail for a period not exceeding the maximum time fixed by law in the case.

b. The court shall consider whether the defendant as a condition of probation shall make restitution to the victim or the Restitution Fund.

c. In counties or cities and counties where road camps, farms, or other public work is available the court may place the probationer in the road camp, farm, or other public work instead of in jail.

d. In all cases of probation the court may require as a condition of probation that the probationer go to work and earn money for the support of his or her dependents or to pay any fine imposed or reparation condition, to keep an account of his or her earnings, to report them to the probation officer and apply those earnings as directed by the court.

e. The court shall also consider whether the defendant as a condition of probation shall make restitution to a public agency for the costs of an emergency response. . . .

h. The probation officer . . . shall consider whether any defendant who has been convicted of a nonviolent and nonserious offense

---

[2] ARTHUR W. CAMPBELL, THE LAW OF SENTENCING § 5.4 (2014).

and ordered to participate in community service as a condition of probation shall be required to engage in the performance of house repairs or yard services for senior citizens. . . .

j. The court may impose and require any or all of the above-mentioned terms of imprisonment, fine, and conditions, and other reasonable conditions, as it may determine are fitting and proper to the end that justice may be done, that amends may be made to society for the breach of the law, for any injury done to any person resulting from that breach, and generally and specifically for the reformation and rehabilitation of the probationer, and that should the probationer violate any of the terms or conditions imposed by the court in the matter, it shall have authority to modify and change any and all the terms and conditions and to reimprison the probationer in the county jail within the limitations of the penalty of the public offense involved.

The key clause here is (j), which allows the judge to impose "other reasonable conditions," a significant grant of discretion. The California courts have imposed the following guidelines for judges to follow when determining what conditions to impose:

A condition of probation will not be held invalid unless it (1) has no relationship to the crime of which the offender was convicted, (2) relates to conduct which is not in itself criminal, and (3) requires or forbids conduct which is not reasonably related to future criminality. . . .[3]

These standards are not toothless, but they are expansive. Courts have upheld conditions ranging from imposing abstinence from alcohol for someone convicted of drug sales, to mandating community service work, to even requiring that a purse snatcher wear tap shoes.[4] But courts do toss out some restrictions as being excessively punitive or too attenuated from the underlying offense, such as a case in which the probationer was required to give up his truck following a conviction for theft. Conditions that trigger constitutional rights—such as bans on having children or banishment from communities—are generally viewed with disfavor as well.

The standard of review, however, is abuse of discretion, which means that appellate courts are generally deferential to the trial court imposing the conditions. And the open-endedness of § 1203.1 and *Lent* means that these are very fact-intensive cases. Thus while the appellate court reversed a provision requiring a thief to forfeit his truck, it could conceivably uphold the exact same condition on someone who, say, committed a drive-by shooting.

The last major provision is, of course, revocation or modification of terms:

---

[3] *People v. Lent*, 541 P.2d 545, 548 (Cal. 1975).

[4] See KATHRYN SELIGMAN, KIMBERLY FITZGERALD, & GABRIEL TAMES, OVERVIEW OF PROBATION AND PROBATION REVOCATION LAW 7 (2003).

Cal. Penal Code § 1203.2:

a. At any time during the period of supervision of a person . . . released on probation . . . , if any probation officer, parole officer, or peace officer has probable cause to believe that the supervised person is violating any term or condition of his or her supervision, the officer may, without warrant or other process and at any time until the final disposition of the case, rearrest the supervised person and bring him or her before the court or the court may, in its discretion, issue a warrant for his or her rearrest. Upon such rearrest, or upon the issuance of a warrant for rearrest the court may revoke and terminate the supervision of the person if the interests of justice so require and the court, in its judgment, has reason to believe from the report of the probation or parole officer or otherwise that the person has violated any of the conditions of his or her supervision, has become abandoned to improper associates or a vicious life, or has subsequently committed other offenses, regardless whether he or she has been prosecuted for such offenses. . . .

b.1. Upon its own motion or upon the petition of the supervised person, the probation or parole officer, or the district attorney, the court may modify, revoke, or terminate supervision of the person pursuant to this subdivision. . . . The court in the county in which the person is supervised has jurisdiction to hear the motion or petition. . . . The court shall give notice of its motion, and the probation or parole officer or the district attorney shall give notice of his or her petition to the supervised person, his or her attorney of record, and the district attorney or the probation or parole officer, as the case may be. After the receipt of a written report from the probation or parole officer, the court shall read and consider the report and either its motion or the petition and may modify, revoke, or terminate the supervision of the supervised person upon the grounds set forth in subdivision (a) if the interests of justice so require.

QUESTIONS

1. **Appealing?** Is it normatively appealing to give judges so much discretion in setting conditions? Does it matter that probation is a relatively "minor" sanction? Note that in California probation can last for several years.

2. **Guidelines.** It is interesting to note that while California adopted a fairly strict determinate sentencing law, it allows judges tremendous freedom to tailor probation sentences. Can we justify this difference? Why regulate years-in-prison strictly, but not "external" conditions of confinement? Are there different risks of abuse? Is it just easier to think about how to regulate one margin (time in prison) vs. many (consumption limits, associative limits, etc., etc.)? Of course, if it is hard to create guideline

to regulate the imposition of probation, doesn't that also make us concerned that judges will use their discretion here improperly?

3. **What is recidivism?** A probationer (or a parolee) can be violated back for violating any of the terms of probation, including failure to get a job. What does this do to our definition of "recidivism"?

Probation is often criticized for not "really" being punishment. But it is certainly possible to design probation programs that are as punitive as prisons. As Joan Petersilia explains:

> [In Marion County, Oregon,] [s]elected offenders were given the choice of serving a prison term or returning to the community to participate in the Intensive Supervision Probation program, which imposed drug testing, mandatory community service, and frequent visits with the probation officer. About a third of the offenders given the option between Intensive Supervised Probation or prison chose prison. When Minnesota inmates and corrections staff were asked to equate a variety of criminal sentences, they rated three years of intensive supervision probation as equivalent in punitiveness to one year in prison.[5]

That said, the results for probation in general are somewhat disappointing. In perhaps one of the most of comprehensive studies of probationer recidivism, the Bureau of Justice Statistics tracked for three years 79,000 probationers sentenced in thirty-two counties across seventeen states in 1986.[6] The study found that of every 100 felony probationers, 62 had an arrest or other disciplinary hearing, and 26 ultimately ended up in prison within three years; 33 would successfully complete their terms (including 22 who never had any disciplinary actions), 10 would abscond, 28 would still be serving their probationary term without having yet failed, and 3 would be dead or deported.

> **Question:** The probability that someone violates the terms of his probation (or parole) decreases each year he remains free. In other words, those who violate their probation terms are most likely to do so in their first year, a bit less likely in their second year (if they make it that far), and so on. Does this necessarily mean that probation conditions "steer" probationers onto the "correct" path?

> **Question:** Does a 62% re-arrest/hearing rate mean that probation "doesn't work"? "works"? How do we measure "works"? Is the re-arrest/re-admission rate the only metric we can consider?

---

[5] JOAN PETERSILIA, REFORMING PROBATION AND PAROLE IN THE 21ST CENTURY 71 (2002).

[6] PATRICK A. LANGAN & MARK A. CUNNIFF, RECIDIVISM OF FELONS ON PROBATION, 1986–1989 (1992).

Often seen as unsuccessful, there have been numerous attempts to improve the design of probation, and some are bearing fruit. One of the most promising programs right now is the Hawaii Opportunity Probation with Enforcement (HOPE) program (which is spreading beyond Hawaii under the name "Swift, Certain, and Fair"). HOPE was motivated by a desire to overcome the "social trap" of low enforcement due to high caseloads:

> [The probation system was caught in a social trap.] Because violation rates were high (of probationers with scheduled monthly meetings with a probation officer, which included drug tests, roughly half tested positive for one or more illicit drugs and another 14 percent simply failed to appear at all) no probation officer had the time to write up every violation, and no judge would have had the time to hear all those cases had they been filed. That made it seem reasonable for probation officers to set priorities, giving multiple warnings and asking for revocation only once a probationer's file fairly bristled with violations.
>
> But that seemingly sensible approach had a perversely self-reinforcing consequence: Since the most likely result of a violation was a mere warning, there was little incentive for probationers to comply. They had no reason to believe a probation officer's "final warning," any more than they believed the previous warnings that had led to no action. The deferred, low-probability threat of a drastic sanction—probation revocation—was not an effective deterrent. As a result, violation rates remained high.[7]

HOPE attempted to overcome this trap by taking advantage of a behavioral regularity we saw back in Chapter 1: those who engage in criminal conduct tend to respond more to the certainty than the severity of punishment. HOPE relied on short sanctions administered quickly and with great certainty. As a result, the need to punish *fell*, since probationers were effectively deterred. As Angela Hawken explains:

> HOPE is a strategic new approach for managing probationers. The HOPE intervention starts with a formal warning, delivered by a judge or hearings officer in open court, that any violation of probation conditions will not be tolerated: Each violation will result in an immediate, brief jail stay. Each probationer with substance abuse issues is assigned a color code at the warning hearing. The probationer is required to call the HOPE hotline each weekday morning. Those probationers whose color is selected must appear at the probation office before 2 pm that day for a drug test. During their first two months in HOPE,

---

[7] Angela Hawken, *The Message from Hawaii:* HOPE *for Probation*, PERSPECTIVES: J. AM. PROBATION & PAROLE ASS'N 36, 40 (Summer 2010).

probationers are randomly tested at least once a week (good behavior through compliance and negative drug tests is rewarded with an assignment of a new color associated with less-regular testing). A failure to appear for testing leads to the immediate issuance of a bench warrant, which the Honolulu Police Department serves. Probationers who test positive for drug use or fail to appear for probation appointments are brought before the judge. When a violation is detected, the probation officer completes a "Motion to Modify Probation" form and faxes this form to the judge (a Motion to Modify form was designed to be much simpler than a Motion to Revoke Probation and can be completed very quickly). The hearing on the Motion to Modify is held promptly (most are held within 72 hours), with the probationer confined in the interim. A probationer found to have violated the terms of probation is immediately sentenced to a short jail stay (typically several days servable on the weekend if employed, but increasing with continued non-compliance), with credit given for time served. The probationer resumes participation in HOPE and reports to his or her probation officer on the day of release. Unlike a probation revocation, a modification order does not sever the probation relationship. A probationer may request a treatment referral at any time; but probationers with multiple violations are mandated to intensive substance-abuse-treatment services (typically residential care). The court continues to supervise the probationer throughout the treatment experience and consistently sanctions noncompliance (positive drug tests and no-shows for treatment or probation appointments).

Since probation officer time, court time, police officer time and jail space are all scarce, the feasibility of running HOPE at a large scale depends on low violation rates. The key operating assumption—amply borne out by the evaluation results—was that the program's demonstrated capacity and will for follow-through on threatened sanctions would lead to low violation rates. Reliability in sanctioning was achieved by starting small and growing the program sufficiently slowly so that the demand for sanctions never outstripped the supply. The program has grown from 34 probationers to more than 1,500 without adding courtrooms, judges, court clerks, probation officers, police officers or jail cells. . . .[8]

Because the threat of immediate punishment is credible and salient, HOPE does not need to use many of the punitive resources it threatens. As a result, HOPE is scalable in a way that, say, drug courts are not.

---

[8] *Id.* at 37–38.

Pilot programs are underway in Oregon and Washington to bring HOPE to the mainland.

A.2. FINES AND FEES

The criminal justice system has multiple economic sanctions and devices at its disposal, such as fines, restitution, costs and fees, and asset forfeiture. This section considers the first three; asset forfeiture is the subject of the next section. At first blush, economic sanctions have much going in their favor: they can be both backward looking (punitive) and forward (preventative), and they can be finely scaled to match the nature of the offense and the offender. Furthermore, they are cheaper to administer than incarceration, and they avoid many of the collateral costs of imprisonment that we looked at in Chapter 10. For these reasons fines are actually the dominant sanction in most Western European countries today. But they are not so widely used in the United States, although their use (particularly of costs and fees) is rising. This section will flesh out exactly what these sanctions look like and try to understand what limits their use as alternatives to incarceration in the United States.

We start with fines. Barry Ruback and Mark Bergstrom provide a succinct overview of the use of fines in the United States and Europe.

R. Barry Ruback and Mark H. Bergstrom, *Economic Sanctions in Criminal Justice: Purposes, Effects, and Implications*
33 CRIM. JUSTICE & BEHAVIOR 242 (2006)

In Western Europe today, fines are the primary criminal penalty, largely because of concerns about the negative effects of incarceration and beliefs that fines are effective at preventing recidivism. For example, in the Netherlands, Germany, and Sweden, fines are the legally presumptive penalty and are used in 80% to 90% of all sentences.

In Europe, there are two types of fines: prosecution diversion systems and day fines. As diversion devices, fines are used for conditional dismissal of charges. In Sweden, Germany, and the Netherlands, if the defendant agrees to pay a fine (often, the amount that would have been imposed had the defendant been convicted), the prosecutor will dismiss charges. The day fine is based on both the seriousness of the offense and the defendant's ability to pay. Day fines consist of two parts, an assessment of the degree of punishment needed (based on the severity of the offense) and a translation of this punishment into a monetary amount based on the individual's economic circumstances (typically, the offender's daily income). Thus, day fines make more equitable the punishment impact of a fine for rich and poor persons.

In the United States, in contrast, many judges are opposed to fines because many believe that fines cannot be enforced against the poor and have little effect on the wealthy, whom they perceive as buying their way out of punishment. Judges generally believe that fines by themselves cannot serve as an alternative to either probation or incarceration. Moreover, most model penal codes and sentencing standards are opposed to fines, which are assumed to have little correctional value and to be biased against the poor. In addition, flat fines and fines with absolute maximums may become ineffective when legislatures do not regularly update them to adjust for inflation. For some offenses, in which the fine is statutorily determined, fines are regressive and fail to meet the goals of individualized justice. As a result, fines are used primarily in courts of limited jurisdiction, especially traffic courts. [I]n lower courts, fines are used for minor offenses (e.g., shoplifting), particularly for first-time offenders who have enough money to pay the fine. Although the day fine was initially tested in Staten Island, New York in 1988–1989 and has been introduced in several other U.S. jurisdictions, it has failed to gain widespread support.

Nationally, fines are imposed in 25% of all felony convictions: 20% of violent offenses, 24% of property offenses, 27% of drug offenses, 19% of weapons offenses, and 27% of other offenses. Fines are often used in connection with probation to increase the likelihood of payment and the level of punishment. When they impose fines, judges in many state systems rarely have information about the offender's ability to pay. This lack of information may result in fines that are too high, especially because legislatively imposed sanctions are required and may themselves be beyond what some offenders can pay. But it is also possible that fines might be set too low, which means that the sentence will fail to fulfill its potential for retribution and deterrence. In the federal system, where judges might have better information than in many state systems, fines are strongly and positively related to ability to pay.

According to [two criminologists], within a jurisdiction judges usually apply the "going rate" for fines so that all violators of a particular offense are obligated to pay the same or similar amounts. Because judges tend to use this going rate for fines, however, they neglect to adjust the seriousness of the penalty to the particular defendant. And, because this going rate is usually low (to accommodate the poorest offenders), fines have little penalty value for affluent offenders. Rather than at initial sentencing, judges' adjustments to fines tend to be at the back end, when they often excuse the remaining unpaid portion or simply let the probation period expire without enforcing the fine. Research suggests that fines are more likely to be paid if the amounts and payment schedules are reasonable and take into account an offender's ability to pay, if the offender's payments are closely monitored, and if progressively more coercion is used in response to nonpayment.

Ruback and Bergstrom only indirectly touch on what many think is perhaps the biggest barrier to wider use of fines in the United States: their lack of moral condemnation. Dan Kahan lays out the concern clearly:

> Fines . . . are politically unacceptable not because the public perceives that they are insufficiently severe, but because it believes that fines are insufficiently expressive of condemnation. To be sure, it is unlikely that fines mean only one thing to all segments of American society. . . . But . . . fines do have a meaning that is sufficiently concrete, sufficiently widespread, and sufficiently at odds with appropriate condemnation, to rule them out as a serious alternative to imprisonment.
>
> What makes fines, when viewed as mere prices, unacceptable is that they fail to impose the condemnation that the offender deserves—however much disutility they impose. The expressive dimension of punishment also grounds the sensibility that it violates equality to fine the rich while imprisoning the poor. The white-collar offender who is fined might suffer as much as the common offender who is imprisoned, but against the background of social norms he clearly is not being condemned as much. That kind of inequality does matter because appropriate condemnation is what punishment is all about.[9]

Kahan goes on to point out that fines' inadequacy as a form of condemnation is borne out by casual observation (the common critique of fines as merely "the cost of doing business"), by the observed behavior of politicians (who refuse to rely exclusively on fines), and by survey data. He concludes:

> The meaning of fines in American society is no doubt the product of particular social and historical circumstances. In the abstract, fines could be viewed as sanctioning rather than merely pricing misconduct, just as, in the abstract, imprisonment could be viewed as merely pricing rather than sanctioning. Indeed, fines apparently are regarded as genuine sanctions in Western European nations, which use criminal fines much more extensively than do American jurisdictions.[10]

Kahan's argument indicates that for many offenses fines *alone* may be insufficient. But that does not mean that fines *along with* other sanctions cannot be politically viable, and that such joint sanctions may still be cheaper than incarceration alone, if the increased reliance on

---

[9] Dan M. Kahan, *What Do Alternative Sanctions Mean?*, 63 U. Chi. L. Rev. 591, 620–622 (1996).

[10] *Id.* at 624.

fines is offset by a reduction (but not elimination) of the incarcerative part of the sanction. This may be particularly true for monetary sanctions that are designed as restitution (payable to the victim, either directly, or indirectly by funding a general "victims' fund") rather than fines (payable to the state).

According to Ruback and Bergstrom, restitution is imposed in 13% of violent cases, 26% of property cases, 6% of drug cases, 6% of weapons cases, and 10% of other cases; this comes to 14% of all felony cases. This infrequent use of fines, despite all states having restitution programs, is generally blamed on bureaucratic and implementation problems:

> Restitution programs have generally been seen as unsuccessful for three reasons: (a) judges are reluctant to impose restitution on offenders who are assumed to be unable to pay it, (b) payment on restitution orders typically follows other financial obligations (e.g., costs, fines), and (c) there is often ambiguity about who is responsible for monitoring, collecting, disbursing, and enforcing restitution payments.

One challenge fines face, as Ruback and Bergstrom point out, is non-compliance, with offenders often not paying their fines. This is problematic for many reasons. As David Weisburd, Tomer Einat, and Matt Kowalski explain:

> For example, the offender may think that he or she "beat the system" in cases where the court-ordered financial obligation was not enforced. Also, the courts may be less likely to use financial penalties if they believe that such penalties are not being implemented. The community, in turn, may interpret failure to enforce monetary obligations as a more general indication of the inefficiency of the court administration system.[11]

Without some sort of enforcement mechanism, fines cannot work. But that enforcement mechanism is often incarceration, which defeats much of the savings goals of using fines. Weisburd and his coauthors discuss a program in New Jersey that was designed to increase probationer compliance with monetary sanctions through clearly communicated threats of probation violation and incarceration. And while the program did increase compliance, the costs to probation officers were sufficiently high that it was unclear if the program could "pay for itself." It was just how costly it would be to impose incarceration in those situations where needed to make sure the threat remained credible. None of which is to say that such programs cannot work, only that it is difficult to design ones that achieve high compliance in a relatively inexpensive way.

---

[11] David Weisburd, Tomer Einat, & Matt Kowalski, *The Miracle of the Cells: An Experimental Study of Interventions to Increase Payment of Court-Ordered Financial Obligations*, 7 CRIMINOLOGY & PUB. POL'Y 9, 12 (2008).

Thus, between the lack of condemnation and the difficulty in collection, fines and restitution are unlikely to become major components of the US criminal justice system anytime soon. In fact, it is quite telling that Congress initially relied extensively on fines when setting up the federal sentencing guidelines for many of the reasons articulated here, but over time started to impose more and more prison sanctions on top of the fines due to political pushback.

QUESTIONS

1. **Big speeding fines, Part 1:** Some European countries determine speeding fines based on the income of the driver. Thus in 2013 a Swedish millionaire had to pay about $130,000 for going about 77 kmph in a 50-kmph zone in Finland; and in 2010 a Swiss millionaire faced a potential fine of nearly $1 million for driving 180 mph, or 2.5 times the posted speed limit. If fines are this big, do they start to feel sufficiently punitive and less like the "cost of doing business"?

2. **Big speeding fines, Part 2:** In 2002, a senior Nokia executive, Anssi Vanjoki, faced a fine of over $100,000 for driving 75 kmph in a 50 kmph zone. The fine was based on his 1999 income, which had been inflated by his decision to sell a large number of options he held on Nokia stock. By 2002, Nokia's stock price had fallen to the point that Vanjoki could not sell his remaining options, and so his official income was much lower. On appeal, the fine was cut by about 95%. How concerning is it that calculating income can be tricky? That said, how often will the calculation be difficult? And should the fine be based on income (the annual flow) or wealth (the total stock of net assets)?

3. **Subjective experience.** Finland has day fines, but it doesn't have the equivalent for prison. In other words, if a crime carries with it a term of incarceration, there isn't some sort of calculator that accounts for how the offender will experience that sanction to determine how long he should spend in prison. Why are countries like Finland okay with subjective fines but not subjective imprisonment? How do the distributional impacts differ in the two regimes—compare the fine that Vanjoki would suffer compared to a Nokia factory worker, and then the prison sentence he would receive compared to that which the factory worker would get.

Unlike fines and restitution, costs and fees—which local and state governments throughout the country are increasingly relying on—are viewed less as punishment and more as a means of paying for probation, parole, court time (including the costs of defense counsel for indigent defendants), and other administrative fees. These fees can be quite steep, often running into the thousands of dollars, and like fines they are often fixed independently of income or ability to pay; even when tied to income, judges often administer them as if they are not. Such fees are thought to play a destabilizing role in re-entry, burdening parolees and probationers with costs they can't handle, undermining their ability to provide for themselves and their families, and adding to the daily levels of stress, which can be a meaningful risk factor for reoffending.

I want to consider here a major normative question these costs raise: to what extent should offenders be responsible for paying for their own punishment, alternative sanctions in particular? Two sociologists, Katherine Beckett and Alexes Harris, attack the idea of offender-funded punishments:

> Proponents of correctional and court fees argue that offenders—not taxpayers—should pay for the cost of punishing their misdeeds. The idea that offenders should foot the bill for criminal justice expenditures is a moral and political claim, one that likely has broad appeal. Nonetheless, this claim is in tension with at least two other important principles. First, public criminal law systems rest on the premise that crime is mainly a wrong against the state; violations of criminal law are thought to be significant enough to warrant the state's usurpation of the dispute resolution process. In such systems, the criminal law process wrests conflicts from private parties and renders them the responsibility of government. Compelling defendants to reimburse the state for its criminal justice expenditures is in tension with this principle. Moreover, unlike users of other services for which fees are assessed, penal targets are compelled to partake of these services; they cannot use fewer of them or look for an alternative provider of them. It can be argued that if the state compels penal targets to use (often expensive and ineffective) state "services," then the government is obligated to pay for them. Indeed, this fiscal obligation is an important check on government power.[12]

How compelling is Beckett's and Harris's argument? On the one hand, the state is forcing the defendant to pay for resources in a monopolistic setting. On the other hand, at some level the initial compulsion comes from the defendant, not the state: by committing the crime in the first place, the defendant "forces" the state to expend its limited resources to apprehend and punish him. Furthermore, not only is the state compelled to expend more of its resources on criminal justice, thus diverting them from other uses (schools, hospitals, lower taxes), but all court cases are now further delayed by the time it takes to process this case. Much of law and economics is concerned with internalizing externalities, so why are these any different, at least as a theoretical matter? (As a practical matter, ability-to-pay becomes a pressing issue, given the general poverty of criminal defendants.)

---

[12] Katherine Beckett & Alexes Harris, *On Cash and Conviction: Monetary Sanctions as Misguided Policy*, 10 CRIMINOLOGY & PUB. POL'Y 509, 510–511 (2011).

Does the fact that options such as probation, parole, electronic monitoring, and other sanctions that often result in the imposition of fees are used as alternatives to more-expensive incarceration make the argument against fees any stronger? In general, states do not charge defendants for time spent in prison.[13] But the states are now charging defendants for procedures intended in part to keep prison costs down and thus save the state money. This seems a bit more like "double-dipping" in a way, pushing the cost of cost-saving punishments onto those often least able to afford them. If prisoners are not expected to pay for the most serious sanction, can we justify making them pay for lesser, alternative sanctions—especially if these fees increase the risk that the offender will end up in prison, thus eliminating the cost savings of keeping him out?

QUESTIONS

1. **Reframing the question:** One can ask, "if prisoners don't pay for prison, why should they pay for alternatives?" Of course, the question can be reversed as well: "if those given non-incarceratory sentences have to pay, why shouldn't those in prison pay?" Which argument is more compelling?

2. **The moral hazard problem, Part ∞.** Why might we see fees for probation, electronic monitoring, etc., but not for prisons? Note, too, that the example of jurisdictions thinking about charging inmates for lockup in note 13 above focused on jails, not prison. What makes prisons different? Why might this explain why we see the fee structures we do? If those in charge of probation, electronic monitoring, etc., were not able to charge fees, how might they handle inmates?

3. **Fees and situation.** Does the government (which government?) bear any responsibility for a defendant's situational environment—either where he lives, or what the situational cues are there? How does that shape our sense of the fact that the defendant is "making demands" on state resources that he needs to repay?

A.3. ASSET FORFEITURE

Another traditional sanction, akin to a fine, is asset forfeiture, in which assets involved in criminal activity—say, the truck used to smuggle drugs across the border—are confiscated by the state. Though not used very often for most of our nation's history, asset forfeiture has become much more widely used, and criticized, as a tool in the war on drugs. Its defenders see it as a way to target the materiel needed to maintain an illegal drug operation, while its detractors fear that the search for high-dollar goods skews both the types of offenses and the types of offenders on which police focus. This section will sketch out the basics of forfeiture law and look at evidence about its effects on police behavior over the past few decades.

---

[13] Some county jails, however, have started to consider the idea, at least for defendants who can afford to pay. See, e.g., http://money.cnn.com/2011/11/09/news/economy/california_jail/index.htm?iid=HP_River.

Asset forfeiture, which can be administered by both the civil and criminal systems, has existed in the United States since the 18th century—and has existed in legal systems going back to antiquity. But its use prior to the 1980s, with one brief but telling exception, has been limited to narrow cases involving admiralty law and customs duties. The one exception? Its use grew significantly during Prohibition as a way of seizing the assets used in the manufacture and distribution of alcohol. It is thus not surprising that its resurgence occurred during another Prohibition-like police process, the war on drugs. It is on this contemporary manifestation, which began when the federal government started beefing up its civil forfeiture laws in the 1970s, that I want to focus here.

We will generally discuss civil (as opposed to criminal) forfeiture, since police use this approach far more widely, given that its rules are much more favorable to the prosecution. While criminal forfeiture cannot begin until after the defendant has been convicted, civil forfeiture does not even require an indictment. And criminal forfeiture can be used only against the defendant's property, while civil forfeiture can target property "derived . . . from a course of conduct," which casts a much wider net, often covering even third-party property.[14] There are some advantages to criminal forfeiture—the court can require forfeiture of innocent property if the defendant cannot pay a court-ordered monetary penalty, an option unavailable in civil forfeiture (which can only target property actually involved in or derived from in the criminal conduct)—but they do not seem to trump the benefits of civil forfeiture.

The basic debate can be summed up as follows:

Supporters of civil asset forfeiture, including law enforcement officers and prosecutors, argue that it is an essential tool for fighting crime, both by reducing the profitability of crimes and by removing the assets required for certain criminal activity. Forfeiture is especially important, proponents claim, for reducing the rewards of financially motivated crimes such as drug trafficking and sales, gambling and vice, and organized crime.

Proponents also argue that asset forfeiture protects the public's interest and promotes the social good by compensating individual victims, funding victim compensation funds, and, where allowed by law, funding schools, drug treatment and drug education programs. Finally, proponents argue that civil asset forfeiture makes additional funds available for important law enforcement activities. However, critics charge that the lure of potential financial rewards affects law enforcement activities and priorities. The combination of tremendous financial

---

[14] STEFAN D. CASSELLA, ASSET FORFEITURE LAW IN THE UNITED STATES, 2D ED. 19 (2012).

incentives and limited protections for property owners creates a situation ripe for abuse.[15]

It is thus worth looking at the nature of civil forfeiture laws in the United States. I want to focus on three aspects in particular: how much of the assets seized are returned to the police department, the burden of proof for seizing the property, and whether there is an "innocent owner" defense.

In all three aspects, most laws strongly favor the state. Twenty-seven states, for example, return 100% of the proceeds to the police, while only eight return none (instead contributing the money to general state funds). The remaining sixteen states return between 50% and 95% to the police, with most (ten) returning at least 75%. When it comes to burdens of proof, twenty use only the preponderance of evidence standard, while fourteen more use the even lower probable cause standard for some (four) or all (ten) civil forfeiture actions. Only three use the beyond a reasonable doubt standard, with the rest using clear and convincing either sometimes (three) or all the time (nine); one state uses a mix of clear and convincing and beyond a reasonable doubt.

The statistics skew even more strongly in the state's favor when it comes to the innocent owner defense. In the early years of the uptick in civil forfeitures, it was often no defense that a person's property was used in an illegal activity without his knowledge. The quintessential case was *Bennis v. Michigan*, 516 U.S. 442 (1996), in which the Supreme Court upheld forfeiture of a wife's car when her husband used it, without her knowledge, to transport drugs. Yet while the Court held that there was no constitutional right to an innocent owner defense, the federal government and all fifty states ultimately passed such laws, although in thirty-eight states the burden is on the defendant to prove his own innocence, and in only six is the burden on the government for all types of property.

PROBLEM: ASSET FORFEITURE IN TWO STATES

Consider the outcomes of a civil forfeiture case in two states. In Florida, the state must prove that the property was used for illegal activities by a clear and convincing standard, and the burden is on the state to rebut "innocent owner" claims by the property's owner by a preponderance of the evidence. Once the property is seized, the seizing police agency receives 85% of the assets. In Indiana, the state needs to prove that the property is seizable only by a preponderance, and the "innocent owner" defense is an affirmative defense, the burden of which is thus on the owner. However, none of the proceeds of the seizure go directly to the seizing police agency.

---

[15] MARIAN R. WILLIAMS, JEFFERSON E. HOLCOMB, TOMISLAV V. KOVANDZIC, & SCOTT BULLOCK, POLICING FOR PROFIT: THE ABUSE OF CIVIL ASSET FORFEITURE (2010).

In Florida, asset forfeiture is triggered as follows:

Fl. Stat. § 932.703(1)(a): Any contraband article, vessel, motor vehicle, aircraft, other personal property, or real property used in violation of any provision of the Florida Contraband Forfeiture Act, or in, upon, or by means of which any violation of the Florida Contraband Forfeiture Act has taken or is taking place, may be seized and shall be forfeited subject to the provisions of the Florida Contraband Forfeiture Act.

The trigger in Indiana is essentially the same.

So consider the following problem: Paul is driving south down a highway that is a well-known corridor for transporting drugs: cocaine moves northbound, the cash from the deals southbound. Police stop Paul as part of a routine traffic stop and, in a subsequent search, find $15,000 in cash in the trunk of the car. Paul is in his early 20s, does not have a steady job, and is dressed in clothes that the officers would later testify as being "consistent with membership in a criminal drug gang." The police attempt to seize the money as being the proceeds from a drug sale.

QUESTIONS

1. What is the likely outcome of a forfeiture proceeding in Florida? In Indiana?

2. Does your answer change in the amount in the car is $5,000? $500,000?

3. In which state is the stop more likely to happen in the first place, assuming that Paul was not driving in any distinguishable way (perhaps above the speed limit—thus the stop—but not more so than the cars around him)?

4. Assume that there is other evidence consistent with Paul being a drug courier, such as several prior convictions for drug trafficking. Can the police now seize his car as well? What if the car is owned by a friend with a similar criminal background? By a close friend, albeit one without such a record? By his elderly grandmother with whom he lives? By his elderly grandmother who lives three towns away from him? The "innocent owner" provisions are:

Fl. Stat. § 932.703(6)(a): Property may not be forfeited under the Florida Contraband Forfeiture Act unless the seizing agency establishes by a preponderance of the evidence that the owner either knew, or should have known after a reasonable inquiry, that the property was being employed or was likely to be employed in criminal activity.

Indiana's provision, Ind. Stat. § 34–24–1–5, is a bit more verbose, but essentially requires that an innocent owner not "know of the illegal use."

While each state has its own civil forfeiture law, it is worth looking at the federal law in a bit more detail, due to a provision it contains called "equitable sharing." Equitable sharing can take place under one of two approaches. **Joint investigative forfeitures** occur when the assets have been seized as part of operation involving both local officers (perhaps from multiple states) and federal officials. Centralization in the federal system in these settings can cut through a lot of knotty distributional/jurisdictional challenges. More controversial is **adoptive forfeiture**, in which local officials transfer assets seized solely by local officials to the federal government for forfeiture. In such settings, the government then returns about 80% of the assets to the local agency and keeps 20% for itself. The primary restriction on adoptive forfeiture is that the federal government can only adopt funds that come from criminal activity that could have been prosecuted under federal law (although no actual prosecution, state or federal, is required) and which would have been eligible for federal forfeiture. This limits equitable sharing primarily to drug cases, but these cases make up the significant share of civil forfeiture cases in general. The Department of Justice also has its own internal guidelines that impose minimums on the values of assets it is willing to adopt, denying states access to equitable sharing for low-level forfeitures.

While the justification for joint investigative forfeitures makes sense, that for adoptive forfeitures is harder to see immediately, as economists Jefferson Holcomb, Tomislav Kovandzic, and Marian Williams explain:

> Government officials and proponents of adoptive forfeitures frequently cite improved inter-agency coordination and cooperation, more efficient forfeiture processing, and tougher federal criminal penalties for many crimes (especially drug crimes). Critics note that these are rather superficial rationales and argue that the most reasonable explanation is that it is in the financial interests of many state and local agencies to process forfeitures through the federal government rather than using their own existing state legal framework to do so. In effect, adoptive forfeitures allow state and local law enforcement to circumvent their own state laws and utilize federal law for processing forfeitures.

> There are several reasons that state and local agencies would elect to use equitable sharing. First, different states may require different standards of proof to forfeit property. Some of these are more restrictive than the federal government's preponderance of the evidence standard.

> Second, while some state statutes require forfeiture funds to be used for non-law enforcement purposes, state and local agencies can enter into agreements with other agencies to coordinate and enhance forfeiture activities. The funds obtained through such

multi-agency agreements may be distributed consistent with the terms of these agreements and are generally exempt from the statutory restrictions on the use of forfeiture funds. Furthermore, the federal government requires that any funds distributed through equitable sharing arrangements be used solely to fund continuing law enforcement activities, even for agencies in jurisdictions where law enforcement receives none of the proceeds from state forfeitures. The federal government will discontinue equitable sharing agreements with an agency if it is discovered that funds are being used for non-law enforcement purposes—even if the state statute requires such use. In this manner, the federal government's asset forfeiture program helps state and local agencies avoid restrictions in state law that would increase the effort necessary to forfeit funds or diminish the incentives for law enforcement to engage in such activities in the first place.

Through equitable sharing, many law enforcement agencies are able to receive funds from assets that may not have been forfeited under state law, they may receive a larger percentage of the assets forfeited than state law allows, and they may be able to use those resources to fund activities and costs that would otherwise be prohibited.[16]

It is thus easy to see the appeal of adoptive forfeiture for police in, say, Ohio, where the burden of proof is clear-and-convincing and zero percent of the seized funds redound to the seizing agency. By handing over the property to the federal government, the standard drops to a preponderance, and the local police may get up to 80% of the funds. Not surprisingly, equitable sharing is popular with local police; over the course of the 2000s, local police received about $10 million per year from the federal program, while drug-related seizures in total were only slightly more than that.[17]

The volume of assets seized is significant, running into the hundreds of millions, if not over a billion, dollars per year; in the latter half of the 2000s, seizures by the federal government alone consistently topped $1 billion per year. The two federal accounts that hold either assets seized directly by federal agents or the remaining assets from joint or adoptive forfeiture after rebates are paid to the states held $1.4 billion in 2008.

But some perspective is needed here. A billion dollars a year is a lot of money, but state and local spending on policing is substantial—in 2006 it ran to about $76 billion. So that billion in seized assets comprised about

---

[16] Jefferson E. Holcomb, Tomislav V. Kovandzic & Marian R. Williams, *Civil Asset Forfeiture, Equitable Sharing, and Policing for Profit in the United States*, 39 J. CRIM. JUSTICE 273, 274–275 (2011).

[17] The data here are from WILLIAMS ET AL., POLICING FOR PROFIT, supra note 15. Unfortunately, data about the federal program are more detailed than those about the state program, so the comparisons here are only approximate.

1.3% of state and local policing budgets. Forfeitures thus comprise a somewhat small, albeit perhaps non-trivial, share of police spending.

It is thus worth asking to what extent such flows of cash alter how law enforcement officers allocate their time. At first blush, there is certainly potential for abuse. And there are certainly some compelling anecdotes of the temptation of a large forfeiture shaping police behavior poorly. Famously, David Scott was killed by local and federal police in an early-morning raid his ranch, where officials alleged he was running a large-scale marijuana operation. Scott was shot by officers as he came out of his bedroom with a gun, thinking he was being burgled. No marijuana was ever found on his property, and an investigation by the local district attorney concluded that the raid was motivated by a desire to seize the ranch via forfeiture. The local and federal governments eventually settled a $100 million wrongful-death suit for $5 million.

Yet as distressing as the Scott case is, vivid anecdotes ultimately tell us very little. After all, while civil forfeiture—particularly equitable sharing, which ensures that most of the funds must go to the police—has the potential to skew incentives, there is an important counter-balance. Money is fungible. While federal law requires that, say, the $100,000 it returns to local police must go to law enforcement activities, there is nothing in federal law that prevents the local government from then cutting the police budget by $100,000 in response. Thus when opponents of civil forfeiture point to facts such that forfeitures make up an average of 14% of law enforcement budgets for a random sample of 52 law enforcement agencies in Texas, the causal effect is not immediately clear.[18] If forfeitures were to decline, would other funds be released to offset the loss, and if forfeitures go up are enforcement funds further reduced? If that is the case, then the skewing effects of forfeiture start to fade. Admittedly, one study involving interviews with law enforcement officials suggested that they felt that forfeitures were a necessary part of their budgets, but survey results are often unreliable due to cynical and sincere problems with respondents. It is essential to look to more objective measures.

And empirical studies indicate such financial offsetting appears to take place. Two social scientists, Katherine Baicker and Mireille Jacobson, recount the following anecdote:

> [A] former San Jose police chief recalled one year when his department's new budget had no funds for equipment; when the chief asked the city manager why "he kind of waved his hand dismissively and said 'Well, you guys seized $4 million last year.'"[19]

---

[18] WILLIAMS ET AL., POLICING FOR PROFIT, supra note 15 at 12.

[19] Katherine Baicker & Mireille Jacobson, *Finders Keepers: Forfeiture Laws, Policing Incentives, and Local Budgets*, 91 J. PUB. ECON. 2113, 2117 (2007).

Using county-level data from 1991 to 2001, Baicker and Jacobson then demonstrate that county governments appear to offset nearly 100% of the funds the federal government returns to the local police via equitable sharing, and do so more aggressively the tighter the county's general financial condition. Counties divert about half the money to other criminal justice institutions, such as corrections and the judiciary; thus forfeitures do increase overall criminal justice budgets, but not necessarily in a way that strongly skews police behavior. Counties also use forfeiture money to augment social welfare spending, but only in times of financial distress.

Baicker and Jacobson also look at the impact of forfeitures under state law, focusing on a subset of five states. They again find offsets, but of a lesser degree: between 47 and 65 cents of each dollar seized is offset, as opposed to the nearly one-for-one offset of federal funds. In an earlier version of the paper, Baicker and Jacobson hypothesize that local governments may in part be trying to incentivize police to use state rather than federal forfeitures laws.[20]

Not surprisingly, police respond to the real, not statutory, financial incentives. Police focus on drug offenders is closely tied to the amount of funding that they actually get to keep, not what the statutes suggest they should receive. Roughly speaking, Baicker and Jacobson find that a 1% increase in the actual sharing rate increases drug arrests by about 0.66%; this is an effect almost seven times stronger than that from a change in the official (*de jure*, not *de facto*) sharing rate. When allowed to keep more assets, police reduce focus on marijuana, increase focus on cocaine and heroin, and reduce focus on robbery, larceny, and burglary. The substitution to heroin (a small but profitable market) from marijuana (a large but less lucrative market) provides some evidence that police really are focusing on the bottom line when making arrest decisions. But the impact of offsets on police decision-making indicates that the legislature nonetheless can exert some control over police behavior.

QUESTIONS

1. **No convictions.** Some statistics suggest that as many as 80% of civil forfeitures occur in the absence of any sort of criminal prosecution of the owner. Is this necessarily problematic? As we've seen before, and will see in Chapter 12 again, a host of collateral costs and consequences attach to a criminal conviction, many of them even if no prison time is served. If the prosecutor is confident he can get a plea—and recall that it appears that about 75% of all felony filings are resolved by plea bargains—might forfeiture-without-conviction actually be better *for the defendant*?

---

[20] KATHERINE BAICKER & MIREILLE JACOBSON, FINDERS KEEPERS: FORFEITURE LAWS, POLICING INCENTIVES, AND LOCAL BUDGETS, NBER Working Paper 10484 (2004).

2. **A twist on the moral hazard problem, Part 1.** In a civil forfeiture case, who gets the money? Who gets the money from a fine imposed as a result of a conviction? How does this shape the appeal of civil forfeiture?

3. **A twist, Part 2.** Does the fact that county governments appear to offset a chunk of asset forfeitures, thus freeing up money for other county-government programs, alter the answer you gave to Question 2 at all?

4. **Unintended benefits.** Increased asset forfeiture rates encourage police to shift from targeting marijuana to targeting heroin. Is this a good thing?

A.4. BOOT CAMPS

Starting roughly in the 1980s, states began looking more closely for **intermediate sanctions**, punishments that were less severe (and less expensive) than prison but at least seemingly more severe than probation, which was often viewed as little more than a slap on the wrist. Support for such sanctions came from both the left and the right. Those on the left hoped that offenders who otherwise would have been sent to prison—thus suffering the various collateral costs associated with being locked up—would be diverted to lesser punishments. Those on the right, whose views were more ascendant at the time, saw intermediate sanctions as a politically viable way to rein in some of the costs associated with expected prison growth.[21]

One intermediate sanction that was highly popular, at least for a while, was the boot camp, or "shock incarceration." Two criminologists describe how boot camps are organized:

> Correctional boot camps are short-term incarceration programs modeled after basic training in the military. Participants are required to follow a rigorous daily schedule of activities, including drill, ceremony, and physical training. They rise early each morning and are kept busy most of the day. Correctional officers are given military titles, and participants are required to use these titles when addressing staff. Staff and inmates are required to wear uniforms. Punishment for misbehavior is immediate and generally involves some type of physical activity like push-ups. Frequently groups of inmates enter the boot camps as cohorts, called squads. There is often an elaborate intake ceremony where inmates are immediately required to follow the rules, respond to staff in a subordinate manner, stand at attention, and have their heads shaved. Many programs have graduation ceremonies for those who successfully complete the program. Frequently, family members and others from the public attend the graduation ceremonies.

---

[21] See generally Francis T. Cullen, Kristie R. Blevins, Jennifer R. Trager, & Paul Gendreau, *The Rise and Fall of Boot Camps: A Case Study in Common-Sense Corrections*, in REHABILITATION ISSUES, PROBLEMS, AND PROSPECTS IN BOOT CAMP (Brent B. Benda & Nathaniel J. Pallone, eds., 2005).

While there are some basic similarities among the correctional boot camps, the programs vary in many aspects. For example, camps differ in the amount of focus given to the physical training and hard labor required in the program versus therapeutic elements, such as academic education, drug treatment, or cognitive skills building. Some camps emphasize the therapeutic programming, while others focus on discipline and rigorous physical training. Programs also differ in their points of departure from the justice system. Some are designed to be an alternative to probation; others as an alternative to prison. In some jurisdictions judges sentence participants to the camps; in others, participants are identified by department of corrections personnel from those serving terms of incarceration. Another difference among programs is the presence or absence of an aftercare or reentry program designed to assist the participants with adjustment to the community following the residential phase.[22]

Boot camps were appealing because they were less expensive than prisons but retained the controlling, punitive nature of such institutions. Boot camps also meshed well with declining faith in social-work based rehabilitation and increased focus on "personal responsibility." As Michael Tonry states:

> The reasons for boot camps' popularity are self-evident. Many Americans have experienced life in military boot camps and remember the experience as not necessarily pleasant but as an effective way to learn self-discipline and to learn to work as part of a team. Images of offenders participating in military drill and hard physical labor make boot camps look demanding and unpleasant, characteristics that crime-conscious officials and voters find satisfying.[23]

Francis Cullen and several co-authors provide some evidence that Tonry was correct in suggesting that Americans' familiarity with military boot camps would bolster their support for their correctional analogues. As they explain:

> [T]his common-sense commitment to boot camps could insulate its holders—at least for a time—from countervailing critical analysis and empirical data. Thus, when state officials in Georgia were presented with evaluation research revealing the ineffectiveness of boot camps, they responded in this illuminating way:

---

[22] David B. Wilson & Doris Layton MacKenzie, *Boot Camps*, in PREVENTING CRIME: WHAT WORKS FOR CHILDREN, OFFENDERS, VICTIMS AND PLACES 74–75 (Brandon Welsh & David P. Farrington, eds., 2006).

[23] MICHAEL TONRY, SENTENCING MATTERS 110 (1996).

Reacting to the study, a spokesman for Governor Zell Miller said that "we don't care what the study thinks"—Georgia will continue to use its boot camps. Governor Miller is an ex-Marine, and says that the Marine boot camps he attended changed his life for the better; he believes that the boot camp experience can do the same for wayward Georgia youth. . . . "Georgia's Commissioner of Corrections" . . . also joined the chorus of condemnation, saying that academics were too quick to ignore the experiential knowledge of people "working in the system" and rely on research findings.

The common-sense appeal of correctional boot camps drew strength from another factor: the unchallenged, almost hegemonic cultural belief that military boot camps "break a person down" and then "build 'em back up." When probed, most people have no specific idea what this means—that is, they cannot articulate what is being broken down and what is being built back up. Rather, they harbor only some vague notion that boot camps strip away a recruit's youthful immaturity, slovenliness, and general disrespect for authority and "turn them into a man."[24]

In the end, the evidence has generally not been favorable toward boot camps, and since the 1980s their use has faded. By 2000, the number of camps and the number of inmates enrolled in them had dropped by more than a third; subsequent data does not seem available. A meta-analysis of forty-three studies of boot camps reported almost no effect of boot camp admission on recidivism: the odds-ratio for boot camp attendees vs. a comparison group (that could have either received a lesser punishment like probation or a greater one like jail or prison) was 1.02,[25] implying almost no difference in outcome.[26]

Question: Is the fact that boot camps are no better than the alternatives a reason not to use them? Can we still justify their use?

B. CONTROLLING SEX OFFENDERS AND DOMESTIC BATTERERS

One area of law that has seen the extensive development of alternative sanctions—or perhaps in this case complementary sanctions, since they are often used in conjunction with incarceration rather than

---

[24] Cullen et al., supra note 21.

[25] Recall that an odds ratio of 1.0 implies that both the treatment and control groups in an experiment face the same odds of "failure" (here, recidivating). An odds ratio of 1.02 thus means that the treated group—those admitted to boot camps—actually were slightly more likely to recidivate, but not by any statistically significant degree.

[26] DAVID B. WILSON, DORIS L. MACKENZIE, & FAWN NGO MITCHELL, EFFECTS OF CORRECTIONAL BOOT CAMPS ON OFFENDING (2008).

as a substitute for it—is the regulation of sex offenders and domestic abusers. Over the years, states have developed three major approaches for handling sex offenders: registration and notification laws, residency restrictions, and civil confinement. In this section we will just look at the last one; we will save the first two for the chapter on re-entry (since they are less alternative sanctions and more efforts, perhaps misguided and even counterproductive, to prevent reoffending by paroled sex offenders). This section then turns to domestic abuse, where we will consider the impact of civil restraining orders and mandatory arrest laws.

B.1. CONTROLLING RELEASED SEX OFFENDERS: CIVIL CONFINEMENT

In many ways, questions about the propriety of civil confinement for sex offenders strike at the heart of the central debate in sentencing law: what is the goal of punishment? Is it backwards-looking retribution or forward-looking prevention and deterrence? The traditional prison sentence blurs the two together and thus saves us from having to address this question directly. But post-incarceration civil confinement for sex offenders forces us to confront it head-on, since civil confinement is purely forward-looking and consequentialist. And while our analysis here looks solely at civil confinement for sex offenders, there is no reason the justifications for confining sex offenders cannot be extended to cover other types of crimes—so always keep in the back of your mind the questions of whether we want these approaches to spread more widely, and whether there is any principled way to confine them to sex offenders.

To start, though, it is first worth asking why it is that civil confinement, and other policies such as registration lists and residency restrictions, have only targeted sex offenders. Are we in the midst of a serious wave of sex offenses, particularly those aimed at children, or is this more of a panic? Unfortunately, data from the 2010 National Crime Victimization Survey points towards the latter explanation.[27] As we see in Table 11–1 below, while sexual abuse rates appear to be higher among children than older people, sexual abuse rates among children are lower than all other major victimization rates (except robbery, which isn't that surprising).

Table 11–1: Victimization Rates in 2010

Violent Victimizations Per 1,000 (Per Age Group)					
Age	Sex Assault	Robbery	Tot. Assault	Agg. Assault	Simple Assault
12–14	2.7	0.7	24.1	5.8	18.3
15–17	1.7	2.7	18.6	3.9	14.7

---

[27] JENNIFER L. TRUMAN, CRIMINAL VICTIMIZATION, 2010, Table 5 (2011).

18–20	1.1	5.9	26.9	6.9	20.0
21–24	1.5	3.7	21.7	8.0	13.7
25–34	1.3	2.5	15.0	3.3	11.7
35–49	0.6	1.5	10.4	1.9	8.6
50–64	—	1.3	9.7	2.1	7.6
65+	0.1	0.6	1.7	0.2	1.5

A few points about Table 1. First, it should be pointed out that the estimated rates for sexual abuse, particularly abuse of children, are unreliable due to small sample sizes. And second, the population sizes aren't the same for each cell. So a rape/sexual assault rate of 2.7 per 1,000 for ages 12–14 translates into about 327 assaults (on a population of about 12 million), while a rate of 1.3 per 1,000 for ages 25–34 yields about 542 assaults (on a population of nearly 42 million).

Yet the results in Table 11–1 do not foreclose the possibility that sexual assault, particularly of minors, is of significant importance these days: perhaps sex offenses, those against children in particular, are disproportionately under-reported. But efforts to look beyond official reported data seem to confirm the story in Table 11–1, namely that the incidence of sexual abuse against children is low—and *falling*. According to one of the leading scholars on child crimes, David Finkelhor, substantiated cases of child sexual abuse dropped by 62% between 1992 and 2010, and a Minnesota study of sexual abuse of students reported 29% and 28% declines in reporting by non-family and family-member adults, respectively.[28]

Another possible explanation is that while the rates of victimization, do not appear to be significantly higher, perhaps those who commit sex offenses are uniquely hard to deter: the trope that sex offenders are especially unstoppable is widely invoked. Yet the data here are not quite so clear, either. In 1994, the Bureau of Justice Statistic tracked 262,420 paroled non-sex offenders and 9,691 paroled sex offenders, including 4,295 paroled child molesters.[29] Table 11–2 summarizes the basic findings:

---

[28] http://www.nytimes.com/2012/06/29/us/rate-of-child-sexual-abuse-on-the-decline.html.
[29] Patrick A. Langan, Erica L. Schmitt, and Matthew R. Durose, Recidivism of Sex Offenders Released from Prison in 1994 (2003).

Table 11–2: Recidivism Rates of Sex- and Non-Sex Offenders

	New Sex offense		New Non-sex offense	
	Rearrested	Reconvicted	Rearrested	Reconvicted
Child molesters	5.1%	3.5%	39%	20%
Other sex offenders	5.3%	3.5%	43%	24%
Non-sex offenders	1.3%	Unstated	68%	48%

These statistics seem to indicate that those convicted of a prior sex offense were less likely to commit a new non-sex offense, but substantially more likely to commit a new sex crime. Note, though, that baserates matter. While child molesters were more likely to commit new sex offenses, most new sex offenses were not committed by released child molesters. Simplifying somewhat, about 5% of the 9,691 paroled sex offenders committed new sex offenses, which translates into approximately 485 new sex crimes; the 1.3% sex offending rate of the 262,240 paroled non-sex offenders yields more than 3,400 new crimes. So sex offenders are four times as likely to recidivate, but nearly 90% of all sex crimes committed by parolees were committed by *non-sex* parolees.

It thus remains unclear why, objectively, sex offenses have received such attention. Keith Soothill explains some of the possible reasons for why we are in a sex offense "panic" these days:

> The reasons for a shift in public interest [in sex offenses] are complex. Certainly the new wave of the women's movement in the late 1960s and early 1970s began to embrace the crime of rape as a focus of concern and helped to develop an appreciation and understanding of the immense harm and trauma caused by sexual violence. Hence, sexual crime began to capture public interest and concern more widely as the serious nature of the offense of rape began to be recognized. However, the gradual discovery of child sexual abuse, which began in the 1960s, accelerated in the 1980s with the recognition of child sex abuse in the family. . . .
>
> Since the 1990s the focus has shifted from the family to "stranger-danger" with a series of high-profile cases of sexual murders involving children. In the United States, these included 12-year-old Polly Klaas in 1993 . . . and 7-year-old Megan Kanka in 1994. . . . Similarly, in the United Kingdom, high-profile cases included the murder of 8-year-old Sarah Payne in 2000 . . . and the murder in Soham in 2002 of two 10-year-old schoolgirls, Holly Wells and Jessica Chapman. . . .

These quite recent cases have aroused public interest and have led to definite policy changes [such as California's three-strikes law and various reporting regimes collectively known as "Megan's Laws," after Megan Kanka].

However, from the 1970s sex crime has increasingly been used to sell newspapers. Hence, the darker side of an increasing interest in child sex murder has been the media seeing much potential in exploiting the topic for marketing purposes. Recently, Monckton-Smith has argued that the analytically distinct crimes of homicide and rape are dangerously linked, particularly in media (mis)representations. The ready conflation by the media of sex crime with murder means that readers are getting an increasingly distorted view of sex offending. Public attitudes are molded in part by media representation. Media interest, in turn, partly explains the current discrepancy between public and professional perceptions of sex offending.

However, there are also dangers in stressing the comparative recency of an increasing public concern about certain kinds of sex crime. [Estelle] Freedman points to how "from the 1930s through the 1950s, the sexual psychopath provided the focus for public discussions of sexual normality and abnormality, while the state played an increasingly important role in defining sexual deviance and in prescribing psychiatric treatment." The sex crime panics described by Freedman began in the mid-1930s but declined during World War II. [She] notes that "although arrest rates for sexual offenses in general rose throughout the period, the vast majority of arrests were for minor offenses, rather than for the violent acts portrayed in the media."[30]

Another reason for the disproportionate attention sex crimes receive, particularly those against children, likely has to do with the victim. As social psychologists have demonstrated, being the victim of crime lowers the victim's perceived self- and social worth, both in the eyes of the victim and in society more generally. As one social psychologist, Kenworthy Bilz, explains, "[W]hen we are harmed by a criminal offender, there is an element of doubt about whether or not we deserved it, or whether *others* will think we deserved it."[31] But such doubts do not exist for a child victim: no one ever believes that a child remotely "deserves" to be victimized. All of which suggests that our willingness to punish such offenders will be qualitatively greater.

And so one major development has been the increased use of civil confinement provisions. These laws allow states to detain convicted sex offenders in civil facilities after the expiration of any prison term until

---

[30] Keith Soothill, *Sex Offender Recidivism*, 39 CRIME & JUSTICE 145, 150–151 (2010).

[31] Kenworthy Bilz, *The Puzzle of Delegated Revenge*, 87 B.U. L. REV. 1059, 1088 (2007).

such time as they no longer pose a threat. Since these laws are focused on potential harm, not past punishment, they are technically civil, not criminal, which has important implications for defendants. But despite their official "civil" status, they are clearly part of the criminal justice system's overall effort to regulate sexual offending.

At least twenty states and the federal government have currently passed some form of civil confinement statute for sex offenders.[32] These laws generally follow the same broad pattern. Prisoners convicted of and incarcerated for certain enumerated violent sexual crimes (or in some cases just arrested or found not guilty by reason of mental insanity) are examined by mental health experts shortly before release to determine whether the inmate is a "sexually violent predator" (SVP), or some similar term. Although there is some variation in how states define an SVP, the offender generally needs to have been convicted or charged with certain sexual offenses, and he must exhibit some sort of "mental abnormality" or "personality disorder" that indicates a greater risk of future offending. The latter requirement is one imposed by the Supreme Court, which has held that a state cannot civilly confine one of its citizens unless he both poses a threat to himself or to others *and* possess some sort of mental defect.[33] A few examples of SVP definitions are the following:

Fl. Stat. § 394.912:

5. "Mental abnormality" means a mental condition affecting a person's emotional or volitional capacity which predisposes the person to commit sexually violent offenses. . . .

9. "Sexually violent offense" means:

   a. Murder of a human being while engaged in sexual battery . . . ;

   b. Kidnapping of a child under the age of 13 and, in the course of that offense, committing:

      1. Sexual battery; or

      2. A lewd, lascivious, or indecent assault or act upon or in the presence of the child;

   c. Committing the offense of false imprisonment upon a child under the age of 13 and, in the course of that offense, committing:

      1. Sexual battery; or 1.

---

[32] As of 2010, the twenty states are: Arizona, California, Florida, Illinois, Iowa, Kansas, Massachusetts, Minnesota, Missouri, Nebraska, New Hampshire, New Jersey, New York, North Dakota, Pennsylvania, South Carolina, Texas, Virginia, Washington, and Wisconsin. See http://www.atsa.com/civil-commitment-sexually-violent-predators.

[33] *Kansas v. Hendricks*, 521 U.S. 346 (1997).

2. A lewd, lascivious, or indecent assault or 2. act upon or in the presence of the child;

d. Sexual battery. . . . ;

e. Lewd, lascivious, or indecent assault or act upon or in presence of the child. . . . ;

f. An attempt, criminal solicitation, or conspiracy . . . of a sexually violent offense; . . .

h. Any criminal act that, either at the time of sentencing for the offense or subsequently during civil commitment proceedings under this part, has been determined beyond a reasonable doubt to have been sexually motivated.

10. "Sexually violent predator" means any person who:

a. Has been convicted of a sexually violent offense; and

b. Suffers from a mental abnormality or personality disorder that makes the person likely to engage in acts of sexual violence if not confined in a secure facility for long-term control, care, and treatment.

NJ Stat. 30:4–27.26:

"Likely to engage in acts of sexual violence" means the propensity of a person to commit acts of sexual violence is of such a degree as to pose a threat to the health and safety of others.

"Mental abnormality" means a mental condition that affects a person's emotional, cognitive or volitional capacity in a manner that predisposes that person to commit acts of sexual violence.

"Sexually violent offense" means:

a. aggravated sexual assault; sexual assault; aggravated criminal sexual contact; kidnapping . . . ; criminal sexual contact; felony murder . . . if the underlying crime is sexual assault; an attempt to commit any of these enumerated offenses; or a criminal offense with substantially the same elements as any offense enumerated above, entered or imposed under the laws of the United States, this State or another state; or

b. any offense for which the court makes a specific finding on the record that, based on the circumstances of the case, the person's offense should be considered a sexually violent offense.

"Sexually violent predator" means a person who has been convicted, adjudicated delinquent or found not guilty by reason of insanity for commission of a sexually violent offense, or has been charged with a sexually violent offense but found to be incompetent to stand trial, and suffers from a mental abnormality or personality disorder that makes the person likely to engage in acts of sexual violence if not confined in a secure facility for control, care and treatment.

Unlike with other provisions we've seen, there is not much variation in how these statutes are written, since they were all mostly adopted around the same time and clearly drew on common templates.[34] The exact list of offenses vary, as does the precise definition of the mental abnormality, but the contours of these laws are quite similar.

Once an inmate is classified as an SVP, a judicial hearing is held to determine whether he should be civilly confined. The following excerpt provides a concise summary of the standard sort of process SVP classification requires:

> Although SVP commitment procedures vary from state to state, they follow a common basic pattern exhibited in California. In California, an incarcerated individual is identified as a potential SVP by the Department of Corrections and Rehabilitation [DOC].... DOC then determines whether the individual has committed a violent sexual offense. If DOC finds that the inmate is "likely to be a sexually violent predator," then the individual is referred to the Department of Mental Health.... The inmate is then evaluated by two psychiatric professionals. The designated psychiatrists must explain that the purpose of their examination is evaluative and not focused on treatment. But "[i]t is not required that the person [being examined] appreciate or understand that information." If the psychiatrists agree that the individual is an SVP, then DMH must forward a request for commitment to the county in which the individual was originally committed. If the county's prosecuting officer agrees with DMH's assessment, a petition of commitment is filed with the superior court of the relevant county.
>
> Once the commitment petition is filed, the superior court judge is required to determine whether probable cause exists that the inmate is an SVP. Upon such a finding, the state may initiate a commitment proceeding against the inmate. This proceeding takes the form of a trial, in which the accused individual is entitled to counsel and to psychiatrists to perform an evaluation on the individual's behalf. In California, the accused may demand a jury trial, and the standard of proof is beyond a reasonable doubt. Other states, and the federal SVP statute,

---

[34] See, for example, the list of statutory provisions given in Table 1 of Holly A. Miller, Amy E. Amenta, and Mary Alice Conroy, *Sexually Violent Predator Evaluations: Empirical Evidence, Strategies for Professionals, and Research Directions*, 29 L. & HUMAN BEHAVIOR 29 (2005).

require only a bench trial and proof by clear and convincing evidence.[35]

If the SVP is ordered to be held, he is handed over to the Department of Health or a similar civil authority, and he is confined in some sort of secure facility: a stand-alone secure hospital, a secure wing of a mental facility, or a separate wing of a prison. Once confined, SVPs face the risk of lengthy stays. Civil confinement statutes are open-ended, allowing the SVP to be detained until he no longer poses a risk, with no maximum term listed. True, SVPs are generally entitled to annual hearings on whether they still qualify as SVPs, but as long as they are not reclassified, they can be detained indefinitely, a concern frequently voiced about such laws.

> **Question:** What incentives do doctors (who make diagnoses) and judges (who ultimately rule on release decisions) face? What costs do they face when they release an SVP who later re-offends (false negatives)? What costs do they face when they continue to detain an SVP who is actually no longer a risk (false positives)? Can you think of any procedures that might mitigate some of these problems?

As of 2006, about 3,600 SVPs were held in civil facilities. Turnover is generally slow. Between 2003 and 2011, Virginia designated about 350 sexual offenders as SVPs; 57 were released from prison without being sent to a secure civil center, but only 21 of the remaining 300 confined SVPs have ever been released. In South Carolina, the number of confined SVPs rose from 94 to 157 between 2008 and 2012, as prosecutors began to aggressively fight release orders (which had previously numbered about ten per year). Civil confinement is a particularly expensive approach—some data suggest that the average cost of civil confinement could be as much as *four times* that of incarceration, and the relative differences in marginal costs could be even larger.[36] The budgetary pressures have grown strong enough that some states have debated whether to increase the standard prison sentence for SVPs in order to minimize the need to rely on more-expensive civil confinement. Keep this

---

[35] John L. Schwab, *Due Process and the "Worst of the Worst": Mental Competence in Sexually Violent Predator Civil Commitment Proceedings*, 112 COLUM. L. REV. 912, 917–918 (2012).

[36] See Monica Davey & Abby Goodnough, "Doubts Rise as States Hold Sex Offenders After Prison," NY TIMES (March 4, 2007), available on-line http://www.nytimes.com/2007/03/04/us/04civil.html. Recall the differences between average and marginal costs of incarceration: the average cost simply divides the total amount spent by the total number of prisoners, while the marginal cost is the cost of one additional prisoner. These need not be the same, since one additional prisoner does not require any extra buildings, extra guards, etc. One study suggests that the marginal cost of a prisoner is half the average cost.

There is at least a plausible argument that the marginal cost of another civil commitment is greater than that of another incarceration. SVPs require treatment and therapy, which work only if therapist-patient ratios are sufficiently low. So each new SVP is much more likely to trigger the need to hire more staff than each new general inmate; and if no new staff is hired, each new SVP is more likely to degrade the overall quality of care provided to other SVPs, thus either increasing the time each must spend confined or increasing the risk of reoffending upon release, both of which must be counted as marginal costs.

debate in mind as you read on—as you will quickly realize, its implications reach beyond fiscal policy to strike at the very heart of the justification for civil confinement.

Question: See why?

Civil confinement laws have been subjected to numerous legal challenges, but I want to focus on two related ones here: the short-term question of whether they violate *ex post facto* clauses for SVPs who commit their offenses before the passage of the civil confinement law, and the more durable question of the due process requirements on how a state defines "mental abnormality." The common question that ties these two issues together is this: is civil confinement *punishment*, or is it something different? In *Hendricks v. Kansas*, the Court holds that civil confinement is not punishment, but as a result of that there are limits on how it can be imposed.

Kansas v. Hendricks
521 U.S. 346 (1997)

■ JUSTICE THOMAS delivered the opinion of the Court.

In 1994, Kansas enacted the Sexually Violent Predator Act, which establishes procedures for the civil commitment of persons who, due to a "mental abnormality" or a "personality disorder," are likely to engage in "predatory acts of sexual violence." The State invoked the Act for the first time to commit Leroy Hendricks, an inmate who had a long history of sexually molesting children, and who was scheduled for release from prison shortly after the Act became law. Hendricks challenged his commitment on, inter alia, "substantive" due process, double jeopardy, and ex post facto grounds.

Kansas argues that the Act's definition of "mental abnormality" satisfies "substantive" due process requirements. We agree. Although freedom from physical restraint "has always been at the core of the liberty protected by the Due Process Clause from arbitrary governmental action," that liberty interest is not absolute. Accordingly, States have in certain narrow circumstances provided for the forcible civil detainment of people who are unable to control their behavior and who thereby pose a danger to the public health and safety.

A finding of dangerousness, standing alone, is ordinarily not a sufficient ground upon which to justify indefinite involuntary commitment. We have sustained civil commitment statutes when they have coupled proof of dangerousness with the proof of some additional factor, such as a "mental illness" or "mental abnormality." These added statutory requirements serve to limit involuntary civil confinement to those who suffer from a volitional impairment rendering them dangerous beyond their control. The Kansas Act is plainly of a kind with these other civil commitment statutes. . . .

[W]e have never required state legislatures to adopt any particular nomenclature in drafting civil commitment statutes. Rather, we have traditionally left to legislators the task of defining terms of a medical nature that have legal significance. As a consequence, the States have, over the years, developed numerous specialized terms to define mental health concepts. Often, those definitions do not fit precisely with the definitions employed by the medical community. Legal definitions, . . . which must "take into account such issues as individual responsibility . . . and competency," need not mirror those advanced by the medical profession.

[Hendricks also argues that the statute is punitive and thus his confinement under it violates both ex post facto and double jeopardy restrictions, since his triggering offense occurred before the statute was passed.] The thrust of Hendricks' argument is that the Act establishes criminal proceedings; hence confinement under it necessarily constitutes punishment. We are unpersuaded by Hendricks' argument that Kansas has established criminal proceedings.

The categorization of a particular proceeding as civil or criminal "is first of all a question of statutory construction." We must initially ascertain whether the legislature meant the statute to establish "civil" proceedings. If so, we ordinarily defer to the legislature's stated intent. Here, Kansas' objective to create a civil proceeding is evidenced by its placement of the Act within the Kansas probate code, instead of the criminal code. . . .

Although we recognize that a "civil label is not always dispositive," we will reject the legislature's manifest intent only where a party challenging the statute provides "the clearest proof" that "the statutory scheme [is] so punitive either in purpose or effect as to negate [the State's] intention" to deem it "civil." Hendricks, however, has failed to satisfy this heavy burden.

As a threshold matter, commitment under the Act does not implicate either of the two primary objectives of criminal punishment: retribution or deterrence. The Act's purpose is not retributive because it does not affix culpability for prior criminal conduct. Instead, such conduct is used solely for evidentiary purposes. . . . In addition, the Kansas Act does not make a criminal conviction a prerequisite for commitment-persons absolved of criminal responsibility may nonetheless be subject to confinement under the Act. An absence of the necessary criminal responsibility suggests that the State is not seeking retribution for a past misdeed.

Nor can it be said that the legislature intended the Act to function as a deterrent. Those persons committed under the Act are, by definition, suffering from a "mental abnormality" or a "personality disorder" that prevents them from exercising adequate control over their behavior. Such persons are therefore unlikely to be deterred by the threat of confinement. And the conditions surrounding that confinement do not suggest a punitive purpose on the State's part. The State has represented that an individual confined under the Act is not subject to the more restrictive conditions placed on state prisoners, but instead experiences essentially the same conditions as any involuntarily committed patient in the state mental institution. Because none of the parties argues that people institutionalized under the Kansas general civil commitment statute are subject to punitive conditions, even though they may be involuntarily confined, it is difficult to conclude that persons confined under this Act are being "punished."

Hendricks focuses on his confinement's potentially indefinite duration as evidence of the State's punitive intent. That focus, however, is misplaced. Far from any punitive objective, the confinement's duration is instead linked to the stated purposes of the commitment, namely, to hold the person until his mental abnormality no longer causes him to be a threat to others.

Finally, Hendricks argues that the Act is necessarily punitive because it fails to offer any legitimate "treatment." Without such treatment, Hendricks asserts, confinement under the Act amounts to little more than disguised punishment. [The Kansas Supreme Court agreed that treatment was essentially non-existent because the legislature purportedly did not think that SVPs were treatable; note that Kansas maintained that it thought Hendricks was treatable.] Absent a treatable mental illness, the Kansas court concluded, Hendricks could not be detained against his will.

Accepting the Kansas court's apparent determination that treatment is not possible for this category of individuals does not obligate us to adopt its legal conclusions. We have already observed that, under the appropriate circumstances and when accompanied by proper procedures, incapacitation may be a legitimate end of the civil law. Accordingly, the Kansas court's determination that the Act's "overriding concern" was the continued "segregation of sexually violent offenders" is consistent with our conclusion that the Act establishes civil proceedings especially when that concern is coupled with the State's ancillary goal of providing treatment to those offenders, if such is possible.

Where the State has "disavowed any punitive intent"; limited confinement to a small segment of particularly dangerous individuals; provided strict procedural safeguards; directed that confined persons be segregated from the general prison population and afforded the same status as others who have been civilly committed; recommended treatment if such is possible; and permitted immediate release upon a showing that the individual is no longer dangerous or mentally impaired, we cannot say that it acted with punitive intent. We therefore hold that the Act does not establish criminal proceedings and that involuntary confinement pursuant to the Act is not punitive. Our conclusion that the

Act is nonpunitive thus removes an essential prerequisite for both Hendricks' double jeopardy and ex post facto claims.

We hold that the Kansas Sexually Violent Predator Act comports with due process requirements and neither runs afoul of double jeopardy principles nor constitutes an exercise in impermissible ex post facto lawmaking. Accordingly, the judgment of the Kansas Supreme Court is reversed.

■ JUSTICE KENNEDY, concurring.

Notwithstanding its civil attributes, the practical effect of the Kansas law may be to impose confinement for life. At this stage of medical knowledge, although future treatments cannot be predicted, psychiatrists or other professionals engaged in treating pedophilia may be reluctant to find measurable success in treatment even after a long period and may be unable to predict that no serious danger will come from release of the detainee.

A common response to this may be, "A life term is exactly what the sentence should have been anyway," or, in the words of a Kansas task force member, "SO BE IT." The point, however, is not how long Hendricks and others like him should serve a criminal sentence. With his criminal record, after all, a life term may well have been the only sentence appropriate to protect society and vindicate the wrong. The concern instead is whether it is the criminal system or the civil system which should make the decision in the first place. If the civil system is used simply to impose punishment after the State makes an improvident plea bargain on the criminal side, then it is not performing its proper function. We should bear in mind that while incapacitation is a goal common to both the criminal and civil systems of confinement, retribution and general deterrence are reserved for the criminal system alone.

On the record before us, the Kansas civil statute conforms to our precedents. If, however, civil confinement were to become a mechanism for retribution or general deterrence, or if it were shown that mental abnormality is too imprecise a category to offer a solid basis for concluding that civil detention is justified, our precedents would not suffice to validate it.

■ JUSTICE BREYER, with whom JUSTICE STEVENS and JUSTICE SOUTER join, and with whom JUSTICE GINSBURG joins [in part], dissenting.

I agree with the majority that the Kansas Sexually Violent Predator Act's "definition of 'mental abnormality' " satisfies the "substantive" requirements of the Due Process Clause. Kansas, however, concedes that Hendricks' condition is treatable; yet the Act did not provide Hendricks (or others like him) with any treatment until after his release date from prison and only inadequate treatment thereafter. These, and certain other, special features of the Act convince me that it was not simply an effort to commit Hendricks civilly, but rather an effort to inflict further punishment upon him. The Ex Post Facto Clause therefore prohibits the

Act's application to Hendricks, who committed his crimes prior to its enactment.

Certain resemblances between the Act's "civil commitment" and traditional criminal punishments are obvious. Like criminal imprisonment, the Act's civil commitment amounts to "secure" confinement and "incarceration against one's will.". See Testimony of Terry Davis, SRS Director of Quality Assurance, (confinement takes place in the psychiatric wing of a prison hospital where those whom the Act confines and ordinary prisoners are treated alike). In addition, a basic objective of the Act is incapacitation, which, as Blackstone said in describing an objective of criminal law, is to "depriv[e] the party injuring of the power to do future mischief."

Moreover, the Act, like criminal punishment, imposes its confinement (or sanction) only upon an individual who has previously committed a criminal offense. And the Act imposes that confinement through the use of persons (county prosecutors), procedural guarantees (trial by jury, assistance of counsel, psychiatric evaluations), and standards ("beyond a reasonable doubt") traditionally associated with the criminal law.

These obvious resemblances by themselves, however, are not legally sufficient to transform what the Act calls "civil commitment" into a criminal punishment. Nor does the fact that criminal behavior triggers the Act make the critical difference. The Act's insistence upon a prior crime, by screening out those whose past behavior does not concretely demonstrate the existence of a mental problem or potential future danger, may serve an important noncriminal evidentiary purpose. Neither is the presence of criminal law-type procedures determinative. Those procedures can serve an important purpose that in this context one might consider noncriminal, namely, helping to prevent judgmental mistakes that would wrongly deprive a person of important liberty.

In this circumstance, with important features of the Act pointing in opposite directions, I would place particular importance upon those features that would likely distinguish between a basically punitive and a basically nonpunitive purpose. And I note that the Court, in an earlier civil commitment case, *Allen v. Illinois*, 478 U.S. 364 (1986), looked primarily to the law's concern for treatment as an important distinguishing feature. I do not believe that *Allen* means that a particular law's lack of concern for treatment, by itself, is enough to make an incapacitative law punitive. But . . . when a State believes that treatment does exist, and then couples that admission with a legislatively required delay of such treatment until a person is at the end of his jail term (so that further incapacitation is therefore necessary), such a legislative scheme begins to look punitive.

The *Allen* Court's focus upon treatment, as a kind of touchstone helping to distinguish civil from punitive purposes, is not surprising, for one would expect a nonpunitive statutory scheme to confine, not simply in order to protect, but also in order to cure. That is to say, one would expect a nonpunitively motivated legislature that confines because of a dangerous mental abnormality to seek to help the individual himself overcome that abnormality (at least insofar as professional treatment for the abnormality exists and is potentially helpful, as Kansas, supported by some groups of mental health professionals, argues is the case here). Conversely, a statutory scheme that provides confinement that does not reasonably fit a practically available, medically oriented treatment objective, more likely reflects a primarily punitive legislative purpose.

The [Kansas Supreme Court] found that, as of the time of Hendricks' commitment, the State had not funded treatment, it had not entered into treatment contracts, and it had little, if any, qualified treatment staff. Indeed, . . . [looking beyond the record] would reveal that Hendricks, according to the commitment program's own director, was receiving "essentially no treatment." It is therefore not surprising that some of the Act's official supporters had seen in it an opportunity permanently to confine dangerous sex offenders. . . .

Second, the Kansas statute, insofar as it applies to previously convicted offenders such as Hendricks, commits, confines, and treats those offenders after they have served virtually their entire criminal sentence. That time-related circumstance seems deliberate. The Act explicitly defers diagnosis, evaluation, and commitment proceedings until a few weeks prior to the "anticipated release" of a previously convicted offender from prison. But why, one might ask, does the Act not commit and require treatment of sex offenders sooner, say, soon after they begin to serve their sentences?

I recognize one possible counterargument. A State, wanting both to punish Hendricks (say, for deterrence purposes) and also to treat him, might argue that it should be permitted to postpone treatment until after punishment in order to make certain that the punishment in fact occurs. But any such reasoning is out of place here. Much of the treatment that Kansas offered here can be given at the same time as, and in the same place where, Hendricks serves his punishment. Hence, assuming, arguendo, that it would be otherwise permissible, Kansas need not postpone treatment in order to make certain that sex offenders serve their full terms of imprisonment, i.e., to make certain that they receive the entire punishment that Kansas criminal law provides.

Third, the statute, at least as of the time Kansas applied it to Hendricks, did not require the committing authority to consider the possibility of using less restrictive alternatives, such as postrelease supervision, halfway houses, or other methods that amici supporting Kansas here have mentioned. This Court has said that a failure to consider, or to use, "alternative and less harsh methods" to achieve a nonpunitive objective can help to show that legislature's "purpose . . . was to punish." And one can draw a similar conclusion here. Legislation that seeks to help the individual offender as well as to protect the public would avoid significantly greater restriction of an individual's liberty than public safety requires. Legislation that seeks almost exclusively to incapacitate the individual through confinement, however, would not necessarily concern itself with potentially less restrictive forms of incapacitation. I would reemphasize that this is not a case in which the State claims there is no treatment potentially available. Fourth, the laws of other States confirm, through comparison, that Kansas' "civil commitment" objectives do not require the statutory features that indicate a punitive purpose. I have found 17 States with laws that seek to protect the public from mentally abnormal, sexually dangerous individuals through civil commitment or other mandatory treatment programs. Ten of those statutes, unlike the Kansas statute, begin treatment of an offender soon after he has been apprehended and charged with a serious sex offense. Only seven, like Kansas, delay "civil" commitment (and treatment) until the offender has served his criminal sentence (and this figure includes the Acts of Minnesota and New Jersey, both of which generally do not delay treatment). Of these seven, however, six (unlike Kansas) require consideration of less restrictive alternatives. Only one State other than Kansas, namely Iowa, both delays civil commitment (and consequent treatment) and does not explicitly consider less restrictive alternatives. But the law of that State applies prospectively only, thereby avoiding ex post facto problems.

Civil confinement laws are highly controversial. Stephen Morse provides a strong normative and positive critique of such laws.

Stephen J. Morse, *Fear of Danger, Flight From Culpability*
4 Psych., Pub. Pol'y, & L. 250, 256–263 (1998)

Before *Hendricks*, our legal system maintained a satisfyingly strict distinction between criminal and civil confinement. Criminal confinement was justified for responsible, culpable offenders and limited by principles of desert and proportionality. In contrast, civil confinement was justified for nonresponsible, nonculpable agents and limited by an attempt to balance principles of liberty, safety, and dignity. Desert and proportionality were irrelevant.

Despite its constitutional and theoretical credentials, the civil-criminal distinction is neither logically nor practically required to guide confinement. One might adopt a purely preventive regime in which confinement is authorized for dangerousness alone, untied to culpability or nonresponsibility. This would be a scheme of "behavioral quarantine," analogous to medical quarantine to prevent the spread of infectious disease. If society decided that safety concerns trump the usual culpability and nonresponsibility limitations, only epistemological anxieties about accurate prediction would hinder such a regime. For now, however, the liberty interests enshrined in our constitutional law do not permit pure behavioral quarantine.

Leroy Hendricks starkly presented [a] problem. Although Hendricks manifested a condition that most mental health professionals consider a mental disorder, he was fully responsible according to even the most permissive cognitive standard for criminal responsibility. . . . [F]or decades there has been widespread agreement on theoretical and practical grounds that people with mental disorders that might contribute to the potential for dangerous conduct are not properly committable unless the mental disorder is quite severe and renders them not responsible for themselves. [Hendricks's disorder did not meet this standard.]

The Kansas sexual predator statute tried to fill the gap between traditional criminal and civil confinement for people like Hendricks who fit neither category. The problem is the nonresponsibility justification. Using criteria for mental abnormality, Kansas sought to bring the statute within the allegedly nonpunitive, civil confinement paradigm by implying that sexual predators were not responsible for their conduct. It is utterly paradoxical to claim that a sexually violent predator is sufficiently responsible to deserve the stigma and punishment of criminal incarceration, but that the predator is not sufficiently responsible to be permitted the usual freedom from involuntary civil commitment that even very predictably dangerous but responsible agents retain. . . .

An agent responsible enough to warrant criminal punishment is sufficiently responsible to avoid preventive detention. If the State seriously believes that any mental disability sufficiently compromises responsibility to warrant preventive detention, then such disability should surely be part of the criteria for the insanity defense. In effect, *Hendricks* jettisons culpability and nonresponsibility as predicates for confinement and declares open season on pure preventive detention without admitting or perhaps even recognizing that it is doing this. To support this assertion, I turn to an analysis of the criteria for mental abnormality in Kansas that the Supreme Court approved.

[I]n creating legal criteria, states are not bound by the conceptions and definitions of any discipline. Nothing, for example, prevents a state from defining "mental abnormality" differently from traditional psychiatric or psychological definitions of mental disorder. But . . . such definitions and findings should comport with reasonable standards for conceptual coherence and empirical understanding of behavior. My claim is that the Kansas standard for "mental abnormality," which was accepted without critical analysis by the Supreme Court, falls far short of [this] standard, suggesting that Kansas and a complicitous U.S.

Supreme Court filled the gap between criminal and civil confinement by a legal sleight of hand.

The Kansas statute defines a sexually violent predator generally as "any person who has been convicted of or charged with a sexually violent offense and who suffers from a mental abnormality or personality disorder which makes the person likely to engage in the predatory acts of sexual violence." A "mental abnormality" is defined as a "congenital or acquired condition affecting the emotional or volitional capacity which predisposes the person to commit sexually violent offenses in a degree constituting such person a menace to the health and safety of others."

These provisions together are vague and even incoherent definitions of abnormally produced sexual danger. The former, which attempts to satisfy the critical nonresponsibility criterion for justifiable civil commitment, simply requires that an abnormality must produce the potential sexual predation. The terms "personality disorder" and "mental abnormality" must therefore do all the work. Personality disorder is a recognized diagnostic category, but people with such disorders . . . rarely can avoid responsibility for their deeds. This is not a promising predicate for nonresponsibility. . . . Mental abnormality is not a recognized diagnostic term, . . . but as mentioned, a statutory term creates a legal criterion and need not precisely track terms from other disciplines, such as psychiatry. The issue is whether the statutory definition makes any rational sense on its own terms.

The definition states that a person is abnormal if any biological or environmental variable caused the person's emotional or volitional capacity to predispose the agent to engage in criminal sexual misconduct. But what else would predispose anyone to any conduct, sexual or otherwise, if not biological and environmental variables that affect emotional and volitional capacities? In other words, the definition is simply a description of the causation of any behavior. For example, mental abnormality might be defined as "a congenital or acquired condition . . . which predisposes the person": to contribute to a law review symposium issue devoted to the *Hendricks* case. . . . The content of abnormality in the definition is entirely parasitic on the requirement of "sexually violent offenses." Nothing else in the definition differentiates the sexual predator from any other person. All behavior, normal and abnormal alike, is the product of congenital or acquired conditions affecting emotional or volitional predispositions. If anyone who has a tendency to engage in sexual violence is abnormal, then the term "mental abnormality" is circularly defined and does no independent conceptual or causal work.

[Furthermore,] why any particular abnormality should excuse remains unexplained. Simply because a mental abnormality may be causally related to other behavior does not mean that the behavior should be excused. This is to confuse causation and excuse. Causation, even by an "abnormal" variable, is not an excusing condition. To believe otherwise is to commit what I have termed, "the fundamental psycholegal error."

What actual theory to hold potential predators nonresponsible might be implicit, however? [The only really viable option is] some type of control theory of excuse. Indeed, this was precisely the theory of nonresponsibility that the Supreme Court accepted as sufficient to justify the civil commitment of sexually violent predators generally. But what good reason is there to believe that volitional problems are well understood and that sexually violent predators specially lack the ability to control their sexual conduct? So-called volitional or control problems are generally and notoriously difficult conceptually to define and practically to apply. Moreover, what is there about sexual desires that makes them more "compelling" than other equally strong desires, such as the greed that may result in property crime? Why is the "Moneyphile" not as out of control as the person suffering from, say, "sexual sadism," a so-called paraphilia included in DSM-IV, which would surely satisfy Kansas's abnormality requirement?

Punishment Versus Prevention

The peculiarities of civil confinement for sex offenders shed some important light on the costs of our incoherence over how to balance the proper goals of punishment. As we discussed in Chapter 2, the goals of punishment can be lumped into two broad categories: punishment (just deserts) or public safety (deterrence, incapacitation, rehabilitation). Quite frequently we simply blur the two together. Consider three-strike laws and other recidivist-enhancement provisions. Part of their justification is that these offenders deserve more punishment, but much of it is that they need to be confined longer in the name of public safety. Perhaps ironically, such criminal detention actually requires *less* evidence of dangerousness and control than civil detention. Kansas could have easily passed a recidivist sex offender statute that confined Hendricks in prison for a very long time without having to make any showing whatsoever about mental abnormality or personality disorder.

At some level, then, the criminal justice system is frequently "piggybacking" forward-looking protection onto backwards-looking punishment. When the protection part is viewed alone, like for the civil confinement of SVPs, we either want (normatively) or at least require (legally-positively) some sort of concrete showing of dangerousness that we don't insist on when the protection part is quietly merged with the punishment part.

Such an approach encourages merger, but that should trouble us: what factors matter for punishment need not be the same ones that matter for protection. Consider, for example, the age of the offender, which (as long as the offender is an adult) may be irrelevant for punishment but highly relevant to protection. Or even the magnitude of harm, which may tell us a lot about how much to punish but very little about the risk of reoffending. Meshing competing and sometimes-contradictory justifications and motivations for sentencing into a single hybrid regime can lead to unsatisfying results.

These tensions have led Paul Robinson to argue that we should explicitly separate punishment from prevention by using short punitive prison sentences (for punishment) along with much more extensive use of civil confinement (for prevention). As he explains:

> [U]nder a segregated system, the community would be better off because such a system offers both more justice and increased protection from dangerous offenders. Giving the criminal justice system a better chance of doing justice is valuable for its own sake. It also creates greater moral credibility for the system, and thus greater long-term crime-control power. An explicit preventive detention system offers better protection, because it can directly consider a person's present dangerousness and more accurately predict who is dangerous. Such a system also enhances accuracy by allowing for periodic re-evaluations, in comparison with the present system's need to make a single prediction of dangerousness years in advance. Greater accuracy leads to more detention of the dangerous, better protection, and less detention of the nondangerous, thus saving resources.
>
> A segregated system also benefits the potential detainees for many of the same reasons. Better accuracy in prediction means less detention of nondangerous offenders. Periodic re-evaluation leads to detention limited to periods of actual dangerousness. Acknowledging the preventive nature of the detention also logically suggests a right to treatment, a right to nonpunitive conditions, and the application of the principle of minimum restraint, meaning greater freedom among those who are detained.[37]

Robinson acknowledges the risk that such a system could transform itself into an American-style civil-confinement gulag, but he also notes that it could also reduce our reliance on incarceration. He suggests, quite plausibly, that situations likes life sentences for minor repeat offenses— examples of which we have seen in *Andrade*, *Ewing*, and *Bordenkircher*— may be much harder to defend when the "future dangerousness" component is separated out from the punitive. He states:

> Life terms without the possibility of parole may be common and acceptable in a criminal justice system, in which horrible crimes

---

[37] Paul H. Robinson, *Punishing Dangerousness: Cloaking Preventive Detention as Criminal Justice*, 114 HARV. L. REV. 1429, 1455 (2001).

deserve severe punishment. But life commitment with no further dangerousness review for a property offense would be preposterous on its face in a civil preventive detention system.

It is also worth wondering what effect the greater cost of civil confinement would have on states' willingness to punish minor crimes, as least if local prosecutors bore some of the (state) costs of such lock-ups.

Predictive Accuracy

If we are going to rely more extensively on civil confinement, it is worth asking how accurately we can predict future dangerousness. In order to do this, though, we have to take a very brief detour through some easy (I swear!) statistics.

Two core statistics for any sort of diagnostic test, whether a test to detect cancer or the risk of recidivism, are the test's **false positive rate** and **false negative rate**.[38] "False positive" refers to people the test identifies as being "at risk" (of having cancer, of recidivating) but who in fact are not; "false negative" is the opposite, those people tagged as *not* being "at risk" but who in fact are. A simple example makes the concepts clear. Table 11–3 reports the results from a hypothetical risk assessment tool designed to determine if someone would recidivate within five years of release. The test is applied to 1000 people, and these are the results:

Table 11–3: Hypothetical Risk Assessment Outcomes

		Outcome	
		Did recidivate	Did not recidivate
Prediction	"Will recidivate"	100 (A)	200 (B)
	"Won't recidivate"	300 (C)	400 (D)

Within this sample, 400 will recidivate (A + C), while 600 will not (B + D). Among the 400 who will eventually recidivate, the test properly identifies 100 of them, so its true-positive rate is 0.25 (100/400) and its false negative rate is 0.75 (300/400). For the 600 who will not recidivate, the test properly identifies 400 as not posing a threat, for a true-negative rate of 0.67 (400/600) and thus a false-positive rate of 0.33 (200/600).[39]

False positive and false negative rates help us get a sense of how reliable a test is. In this case, the test does not do a good job of identifying recidivists who will recidivate, but it does do a decent job of identifying those who will not. In general, these values move in opposite directions:

---

[38] Sometimes you will see reports about a test's "accuracy rate," reported as a single number: "this test has an 85% accuracy rate." This statement is meaningless. The false positive rate is rarely if ever the same as the false negative rate—in fact, the two generally move in opposite directions—so a single number is an insufficient statistic.

[39] Note, somewhat confusingly, that the opposite of true positive is false negative. If someone is "at risk," he can either be correctly identified as being "at risk" (true positive) or incorrectly identified as "not at risk" (false negative).

the steps needed to reduce a test's false positive rate will generally push up its false negative rate. This is intuitive, since researchers lower the false positive rate by making the test more willing to tag people as (in this instance) recidivists, which means it is also more likely to also label non-recidivists as potential recidivists.[40]

But false positives and false negatives alone do not tell us the full implications of a positive or negative test result. For this, we also need the **baserate**, the underlying rate of the "disease" (here, future recidivism) in the population. Even a highly-accurate test can be highly imprecise on average if the base rate is too low.

Consider the following example, which closely tracks one from Ch. 3. Imagine we have a remarkably powerful test: its false-negative rate is 0% (so if someone is going to recidivate, the test accurately predicts this 100% of the time), and its false-positive rate is 1% (so it accidentally identifies only 1 out of every 100 future non-recidivists as a future recidivist). This test is significantly more accurate than any future-dangerousness tests currently deployed, and it seems like a positive result on a test should mean that the person is almost certainly going to recidivate. But it need not.

Two scenarios highlight the importance of base rates. In the first scenario, the base rate is very low: in a population of 100,000 people being released from prison, assume that only 0.1%, or 100 people, will actually recidivate. Apply our predictive test to this population. The test correctly predicts that all 100 future recidivists will in fact recidivate (the 0% false-negative rate). Of the remaining 99,900 non-recidivists, it mistakenly identifies 1% of them, or 999, as recidivists (the 1% false-positive rate). So the test identifies 1,099 people as future recidivists, but only 100 of them actually are. So a positive test result means that there is a 9.1% (100/1099) chance that the person will actually recidivate. That is a huge (almost-hundredfold) jump from the prior probability that any one person would recidivate (0.1%), but it still means that a positive test result implies the offender is much more likely than not a *non*-recidivist. Now change the base rate to 10%: 10,000 out of 100,000 will recidivate. Again, the test properly identifies all 10,000 future recidivists, and of the remaining 90,000 non-recidivists is mistakenly tags 1%, or 900, as future recidivists. So now a positive test result implies that there is a 91.7% (10,000/10,900) chance the offender will recidivate. Figure 11.4 summarizes these results.[41]

---

[40] Think of this trivial example: a test that labels every single person a recidivist has a 0% false-positive rate but a really high false-negative rate, and vice versa for a test that labels everyone as a non-recidivist.

[41] Introducing false negatives does not change this example in any interesting way: false negatives simply make a positive prediction less meaningful in obvious ways. Return to the example with a 10% base rate a 1% false positive rate, but assume the test also has a 5% false negative rate. Then from the 10,000 people who will actually recidivate, the test only makes that prediction in 95% (or 9,500) of the cases. So the total number of positive results is 10,400

Table 11–4: The Importance of Baserates

Baserate = 0.1%				Baserate = 10%			
Recidivists (n = 100)		Non-Recidivists (n = 99,900)		Recidivists (n = 10,000)		Non-Recidivists (n = 90,000)	
Right	Wrong	Right	Wrong	Right	Wrong	Right	Wrong
100	0	98,901	999	10,000	0	89,100	900
Predicted Recidivists	1,099			Predicted Recidivists	10,900		
Actual Recidivists	100			Actual Recidivists	10,000		
Percent correct	9.1%			Percent correct	91.7%		

The intuition here is simple. When the base rate is low, the pool of non-recidivists is much larger than the pool of recidivists. So even if the test rarely mis-identifies a non-recidivist (has a low false-positive rate), a small percent of a large number of non-recidivists can still be a (relatively) large absolute number. As the share of offenders who won't recidivate shrinks, there are fewer absolute mis-identifications for a given false positive rate, and the reliabiity of a positive result get stronger.

So we must ask what are the false positive and false negative rates for tests of sex offender recidivism, as well as what are the base rates. A recent meta-analysis of nine common risk-assessment tools suggests that the tests have fairly high false negative rates—they often fail to identify those who will commit future sex offenses—but low false positive rates, so they do not frequently misidentify low-risk people as high risk.[42] More specifically, the paper suggests that the false positive rate for sex offenders is 12% (with a confidence interval of 8% to 17%) and the false negative rate 66% (with a confidence interval of 49% to 80%). The base rate of sex offending in the sample is approximately 0.17.

Thus, if we have a pool of 10,000 sex offenders, 1,700 of them will reoffend. Of these 1,700, the test will correctly identify 34%, or 578, of them (false negative rate of 66%). Of the remaining 8,300 low-risk offenders, the test will incorrectly identify 12%, or 996, of them as future sex-offense recidivists. Thus the test yields 1,574 positives, of which 37% (578 out of 1,574) are true (future) recidivists.

(9,500 true positives plus 900 false positives), for a positive accuracy rate of 91.3% (9,500/10,400).

[42] Seena Fazel, Jay P. Singh, Helen Doll, & Martin Graham, *Use of Risk Assessment Instruments to Predict Violence and Antisocial Behaviour in 73 Samples Involving 24,827 People: Systematic Review and Meta-Analysis*, BRITISH MED. J. 2012: 345:e4692.

If we were to point to one of 10,000 at random and announce "I think you'll recidivate," we would be right 17% of the time. If we choose based on these tools, we will be right 37% of the time. So the tools are about twice as good as just guessing. But is that good enough for civil commitment?

There are two other concerns we should have with these sorts of diagnostic tools. First, even if you think the above average accuracy is acceptable, not all tests return identical results for the same subject. Table 11–5 recreates a table from a paper looking at the variation in results given by several risk assessment tools in a real case.[43] Predicted risks of future re-offending range from 0.39 to "medium to high" to the utterly impossible 1.00.[44] Perhaps a judge or mental health professional confronted with this array of outcomes could think of a way to synthesize the results into a meaningful "average," but that would require extensive information on the relative reliability of the various tests, which is often hard to come by. Classification will thus be a noisy process, and choosing the "right" test is a difficult normative question, since it forces us to explicitly balance the false negative/false positive error costs.

Table 11–5: Variation in Risk Assessment Predictions

Scale	Predicted Prob. Of Recidivism
Static-99	0.39 (within 5 years)
	0.45 (within 10 years)
	0.52 (within 15 years)
SORAG	1.00 (violent, within 7 years)
SVR-20	"Medium to High"
VRAG	1.00 (violent, within 7 years)
PCL-R	0.81 (general)
	0.37 (violent)
MnSOST-R	0.88 (if baserate = 0.35)
	0.78 (if baserate = 0.21)

---

[43] Scott I. Vrieze & William M. Grove, *Multidimensional Assessment of Criminal Recidivism: Problems, Pitfalls, and Proposed Solutions*, 22 PSYCHOL. ASSESS. 382 (2011).

[44] It is impossible that the risk of reoffending be 1.00. If nothing else, on any given day there is a non-zero risk the offender could die (getting hit by a car crossing the street), thus eliminating his ability to reoffend. Not to mention that the vagaries of human behavior are such that no model can predict behavior with absolute certainty—a chance encounter with minister, for example, could lead to an unexpected conversion and a rejection of criminal conduct, certainly of violent criminal conduct.

	0.70 (if baserate = 0.15)[45]
HCR-20	0.92

Second, assessment in a sterile clinical setting is different from that in an adversarial proceeding. One study, for example, took eighty-eight real cases that had been subjected to SVP review in Texas and gave them to a panel of independent exerts for evaluation.[46] The experts generally reached similar conclusions for each of the cases. That stood in stark contrast to what had happened in the trials themselves, with defense and prosecution experts consistently reaching significantly different conclusions—and with both partisan experts disagreeing with the independent experts too!

And the explanation for the independent/partisan split is not a simple state-expert-scores-them-high/defense-expert-scores-them-low story. To start with, in only forty-four of the eighty-eight cases were there both defense and state experts; in a majority of cases in Texas the defense does not bring its own expert to the hearing. And in the cases without a defense expert, the independent and state experts agreed much more than they did in the cases that involved a defense expert. That could imply that state experts change their scoring behavior when they know the hearing will be adversarial or, as the study's authors suggest, it could imply that the offenders in cases with dueling experts are simply harder to evaluate than the uncontested cases (which could explain *why* some cases are contested and others are not). The authors conclude that we still know very little about the reasons for field differences in outcomes, but that perhaps as much as 28% of the variation in outcomes is due to partisan allegiance. And there is no strong evidence that one party is more accurate more of the time.

And assuming that 28% number is correct, whether that is too high or too low is a difficult normative question. Accuracy is important, but it is not the only value the criminal justice system promotes: party control and party voice are important too, and imposing independent experts on the parties undermines these goals. We also lack evidence on what judges do in the conflicting cases; their decisions could mitigate—or aggravate—the problems raised by inter-rater disagreement.

So, to conclude: Civil confinement for sex offenders has been an increasingly popular policy, although its spread across states has slowed in recent years, and the total number of sex offenders civilly confined remains fairly small. But even if the numbers civilly confined remain low,

---

[45] The MnSOST-R attempts to account for the baserate issues discussed above by providing different predictions based on different assumptions about baserates. Ironically, despite the case being in Minnesota, and the MnSOST-R being a test designed *for* Minnesota, none of the hypothetical baserates match the baserate of sex offending in Minnesota itself.

[46] Katrina A. Rufino, Marcus T. Boccaccini, Samuel W. Hawes, & Daniel C. Murrie, *When Experts Disagreed, Who Was Correct? A Comparison of PCL-R Scores From Independent Raters and Opposing Forensic Experts*, 36 L. & HUMAN BEHAVIOR 527 (2012).

the ideas raised here are of increasing importance, especially since some states have already begun to wonder if they should expand civil commitment to violent offenders more broadly, although it is likely that the on-going budget problems that started in 2008 have discouraged such policies for now.

It is also worth asking if any concerns you have with civil confinement in turn shape your views on how prison sentences should be structured in the first place. If someone is opposed to civil confinement, what should he or she think about lengthening initial criminal sentences on incapacitation grounds? And shifting from the normative to the positive, how likely do you think it is that we could see the rise of civil confinement for non-sex offenders? Is there a rational line to draw between sex offenders and violent offenders in general? Normatively speaking, what sort of line *ought* we draw?

QUESTIONS

1. **Limits of confinement, Part I.** If civil confinement statutes are just about protection, why do they generally apply only to those with some sort of conviction or arrest? How early should be we allowed to act?

2. **Limits of confinement, Part II.** Is there any logical reason to limit SVP laws to *S*VPs? Why not non-*S* VPs in general? And why not non-V Ps, like serial burglars/thieves/embezzlers/drug dealers?

3. **Treatment and punishment.** Breyer argues that to remain non-criminal, civil confinement must focus on treatment, otherwise it becomes punitive. Is this right? What if someone catches a rare, highly virulent, incurable disease through no fault of his own and is quarantined/civilly committed. Is he being punished? Now here, Kansas conceded that treatment was possible. What if Kansas retracted that claim?

4. **Morse v. Robinson.** Is Morse right that a defendant who is responsible enough to deserve criminal punishment is likewise responsible enough to evade civil confinement? Would Robinson agree with this argument?

5. **Fundamental psycholegal error.** Even if you don't buy Morse's fundamental psycholegal error argument—and we saw its limitations when discussing determinism in Chapter 4—we still need to ask why the "abnormalities" of sex offenders deserve different treatment. Are they deserving of any unique treatment? If sex offending is *psychologically* abnormal, why isn't aggravated assault, or theft? To the extent that concerns about sexual abuse focus on the harms to the *victim*, does that tell us anything about the psychological state (and thus the permissible treatments) of the *offender*?

6. **Baserates, Part 1.** There are approximately 750,000 people listed on sex offender registries, or 0.2% of the population. Assume (arbitrarily, but for the sake of argument) that the list understates the extent of sex offending by a factor of 10, that there are really 7.5 million people, or 2% of the

population of 300 million, guilty of sex offenses (if often uncharged or unconvicted). If we were to test the whole population, and the test has a false positive rate of 5% and false negative rate of 10%, how likely is someone who tests positive to recidivate? Someone who tests negative? Concerns?

7. **Baserates, Part 2.** What if we restrict ourselves just to the 750,000 people on the registry, and what if the BJS numbers implying a 5% recidivism rate are correct? If we apply the same test, what happens? Might this be one reason why we focus on the previously-convicted, to minimize the baserate problem?

B.2. DOMESTIC RESTRAINING ORDERS

Domestic abuse is another area where we sometimes attempt to address potential criminal conduct civilly rather than criminally. Domestic abuse is a serious cause of criminal victimization, particularly among women. According to the 2010 National Crime Victimization Survey, approximately 400,000 of the 1.85 million acts of nonfatal violence against women (or approximately 22%) were caused by "intimates," who are defined as current or former boyfriends, girlfriends, or spouses; an additional 160,000 were caused by relatives (bringing the total to 30%).[47] For men, intimates were responsible for approximately 100,000 nonfatal acts of violence out of a total of 1.96 million, or only 5%, with relatives contributing another 110,000. And it is worth noting that these rates of violence reflect recent historical lows: between 1993 and 2008, female victimization by intimates declined by 53%, and male victimization (from a much lower baserate) by 54%.[48] For lethal violence, intimates were responsible for approximately 14% of all homicides in 2007. Tellingly, while women comprise only about 20% of all murder victims in general, in 2007 they comprised 70% (1,640 out of 2,340) of all domestic homicides. These homicides represent about 53% of the 3,115 women killed in 2007.[49]

Yet given the inherently close emotional (and financial) ties between victim and abuser, prosecuting domestic violence cases can be difficult. Jeannie Suk provides a brief overview of protection order law and explains how these orders address some of the potential problems with preventing domestic violence (or "DV").

Jeannie Suk, *Criminal Law Comes Home*
116 YALE L. J. 2, 13–22 (2006)

The civil protection order, the "grandmother of domestic violence law," has constituted a crucial step in the criminalization of DV. Since passage of Pennsylvania's Protection from Abuse Act in 1976, all the

---

[47] TRUMAN, VICTIMIZATION, supra note 27.

[48] SHANNAN CATALANO, ERICA SMITH, HOWARD SNYDER, AND MICHAEL RAND, FEMALE VICTIMS OF VIOLENCE (2009).

[49] Murder statistics from here: http://www.albany.edu/sourcebook/pdf/t31222010.pdf.

states have enacted protection order legislation, which they have amended and refined over the last thirty years. These statutes enable individuals to go directly to general-purpose civil court or family court to seek protection orders against their intimate partners.

In addition to enjoining violence against the victim, the civil protection order . . . typically prohibits contact with the victim and requires the subject of the order to vacate the shared home, even if he is the sole or joint owner of the property. The order may also address custody of children, visitation rights, and child support and other economic relief. On application by the victim, the civil court issues the order, usually ex parte on an emergency temporary basis, until the court holds a subsequent adversary hearing after which the order may be made permanent. In most states, the permanent order remains effective for one to three years and is subject to extension.

Because, for a long time, the criminal justice system was less than forthcoming in its response to DV, advocates looked to civil protection orders as an alternative to criminal law. Early advocates felt significant ambivalence about engaging with the state, which, they believed, embodied the patriarchy that condoned and legitimated violence against women. Many advocates thought the criminal system would remain crude or unresponsive. As an alternative to criminalization, the civil protection order was a prospective remedy designed to prevent future violence rather than to punish past conduct. As advocates conceived it, the protection order would empower women to bypass the criminal system and seek individualized protection from the courts.

The civil protection order, once envisioned as an alternative to criminal process, has now been subsumed by the criminalization strategy. Today, protection orders are primarily enforced through criminal misdemeanor charges. Almost every state has made the violation of a DV protection order a crime. Violations of orders are generally misdemeanors, but in some states they are felonies.

The protection order enables a particular mode of criminalization that is an important component of the criminalization of DV. It criminalizes conduct that is not generally criminal—namely presence at home—in order to punish or prevent the target criminal conduct. Presence at home is a proxy for DV. The protection order creates this proxy relation.

The advantages of using presence at home as a proxy are evidentiary and preventive. The problems with prosecuting DV are well known. Evidentiary difficulties may prevent convictions because victims are typically unwilling, often out of fear, to cooperate with the prosecution. Without victims' cooperation, criminal cases are weak and proof of guilt beyond a reasonable doubt at trial is elusive.

Prosecutions for protection order violations can be a way of "short-circuiting proof problems for the prosecution," and thus a more efficient and effective means of convicting and punishing domestic abusers. A violation of a protection order is far easier to prove than the target crime of DV. The testimony of the victim is generally less important. No physical injury need be shown. The existence of the protection order and the defendant's presence in the home, to which the arresting officer can usually bear witness, are sufficient to establish violation of the protection order. With a "no-contact" order, all that may need to be shown is that the defendant made a phone call to the protected party. Thus, one function of protection orders can be to relax or circumvent the burden of proof for DV.

Furthermore, using presence at home as a proxy is designed to prevent conduct that, though innocent itself, can lead to the target crime. The logic of this preventive goal is that by "isolat[ing] a convenient point in time from which it is predictable that some moral wrongs will occur, . . . such wrongs can thus be efficiently prevented by preventing the earlier, non-wrongful act." Prohibiting a person's presence at home via the protection order reduces the likelihood that he will have the opportunity to engage in DV.

Using presence at home as a proxy for DV differs from pretextual prosecution (of Al Capone fame), in which prosecutors suspect a defendant of a particular crime that they cannot easily prove in court and so strategically charge and convict him of an unrelated, less serious crime—for example, charging tax evasion when a defendant is suspected of murder. First, presence at home is not prohibited independent of DV in the way that tax evasion is prohibited independent of murder.

Second, whereas pretextual conduct is unrelated to its target crime, presence at home is not considered to be unrelated to the target crime. An alleged abuser's presence at home is causally associated with the potential for violence there. By contrast, tax evasion need not be related to murder.

Third, disapproval of an alleged abuser's presence at home does not actually function as a pretext or cover for real disapproval of the target conduct. Rather, underlying the association of presence in the home with violence is the view that an abuser's presence at home is itself threatening and causes fear and intimidation. Thus criminalization of his presence at home via the protection order is not a cover for combating violence; it is openly and candidly directed at DV.

Mediated through the crime of violating a court order, the criminal prohibition of a person's presence at home becomes legitimate as a way for the criminal law to reach domestic abusers. To prosecutors and courts, an abuser's presence in the home comes to seem interchangeable with DV.

Victims' resistance to criminal prosecution for domestic abuse does not just stem from fear of retaliation, although that is a major component. One survey of 207 urban African-American women who were victims of domestic violence found that 35% did not want to see their abusers prosecuted.[50] Their reasons ranged from feeling that the offense was "not that serious" (18 of the 64 women who did not favor prosecution) to the relationship is on-going (5 of the 64), with just one saying that fear of retaliation made her not want to press charges. Of course reasons given to interviewers need not be the real reasons driving their behavior—respondents may be lying to the interviewer or even to themselves—and the small-sample problem noted in the previous footnote may be important. But these results nonetheless suggest that the reasons for not wanting formal prosecution are multifaceted and complex.

Thus it may be that protection orders are not just about providing a means of indirect prosecution for hard-to-prove cases, as Suk explains. They may also provide a genuine intermediate sanction for those victims who feel that the full punishment is not appropriate. One may debate whether such preferences are rational or even acceptable; perhaps we should abolish the intermediate step to force victims to impose more serious sanctions on abusers. But that argument in turn raises an open empirical question: the absence of an intermediate step will induce some victims to seek full prosecution but others to seek no intervention at all, so the net effect on abuse is quite unclear. And in the presence of such uncertainty, to whose judgment should we defer?

Obviously, the major empirical question concerning orders is whether they are effective at reducing DV. One study of nearly 3,000 women in Seattle measured the probability a woman previously exposed to DV would report subsequent psychological or physical abuse to the police over a 17-month period in 1998 and 1999, comparing women who received temporary (generally 2-week long) or permanent restraining orders to those who received none.[51] Table 11–6 summarizes the basic findings, which report relative risk ratios; the numbers in parentheses underneath are the confidence interval ranges (roughly, how precise the estimates are). As always, if the ratio is less than one, the named group

---

[50] Arlene M. Weitz, *Prosecution of Batterers: Views of African American Battered Women*, 17 VIOL. & VICTIMS 19 (2002). These women represent about 22% of those the researchers attempted to reach, which is a fairly low response rate and raises serious questions about selection bias: how do those reached compare to those not reached? Many failed attempts, for example, were due to disconnected phone lines. This suggests that the women interviewed were in more stable (and perhaps more financial secure) environments, which is likely correlated with a desire to seek out prosecution, although the direction is unclear: are such women more personally financially secure and thus more willing to face the economic risks of going forward with an abuse prosecution, or are they more dependent on the earnings of their abuser and thus less willing to press charges?

[51] Victoria L. Holt, Mary A. Kernic, Thomas Lumley, Marsha E. Wolf, & Frederick P. Rivara, *Civil Protection Orders and Risk of Subsequent Police-Reported Violence*, 288 J. AM. MED. ASS'N 589 (2002).

(here, women with either temporary and permanent orders) are less likely to experience the risk than the reference group (here, women without orders); if the ratio is greater than one, then the named group is more likely to experience the risk.[52]

Table 11–6: Impact of Restraining Orders on Subsequent Psychological and Physical Abuse

	Temporary Order		Permanent Order	
	6 months	12 months	6 months	12 months
Physical Abuse	0.8 (0.2–3.4)	1.6 (0.6–4.4)	0.4 (0.1–1.1)	0.2 (0.1–0.8)
Psychol. Abuse	4.0 (2.2–7.2)	4.9 (2.8–8.6)	1.1 (0.5–2.3)	0.9 (0.5–1.7)

The results indicate that either sort of order seems to protect against physical abuse, but both—temporary in particular—appear to increase the risk of psychological abuse. Note, though, that the estimates are pretty imprecise, generally due to fairly small sample sizes.

In a somewhat related study, Radha Iyengar provides results indicating that state adoptions of mandatory arrest policies—which require police to arrest the abuser in all DV calls, even if the victim does not wish to press charges—are correlated with increases in intimate-partner homicides in those states.[53] She points to two possible causal explanations: first, that victims will be less likely to report instances of DV when they do not want their partners arrested, which in turn allows abusers act with more impunity, and second, that abusers may be more likely to engage in reprisal attacks for the arrest. The non-report issue does not shed any light on the impact of restraining orders, since by definition, these are given to women who are reporting their attacks. And while Iyengar focuses primarily on non-reporting, she notes that her results are also often consistent with reprisals playing a role as well. Thus her findings are certainly consistent with those in Table 11–6, which suggest that orders can sometimes lead to increased risks.

---

[52] The relative risk ratio that a woman with a temporary restraining order suffers an act of psychological abuse, when compared to a woman without an order at all, is 4.0 in Table 11–6. This means that the probability a woman with an order suffer abuse is four times that of a woman who doesn't have an order. For example, assume that 100 women have a temporary order, and 100 women have no order. If 80 women with an order suffer abuse, the risk of being abused for these women is 0.8. If 20 women without an order suffer abuse, their risk of abuse is 0.2. So the *relative* risk for women with a temporary order is 0.8/0.2 = 4.0. Note that the risk ratio cannot tell us the absolute level of risk. If 8 women with orders are abused to 2 without orders, the ratio is again 4.0, even though the absolute risks are one-tenth those in the first example.

[53] Radha Iyengar, *Does the Certainty of Arrest Reduce Domestic Violence? Evidence from Mandatory and Recommended Arrest Laws*, 93 J. PUB. ECON. 85 (2009).

Question: How should we take Iyengar's results into account? What policy implications flow from restraining orders leading to more violence (if that is the case)?

C. SHAME, RESTORATIVE JUSTICE, AND DRUG/ALTERNATIVE COURTS

The final set of sanctions moves away from direct state punishment and relies either on civilian actors to punish (shame) or rehabilitate (restorative justice), or on non-executive actors to rehabilitate (drug/treatment courts). These approaches are tied together by an intensive focus on the important role the offender's local community can play in reducing his future offending. Shame was briefly popular in the late 1990s and early 2000s but has basically faded from view, though it provides an illuminating segue into the arguments in favor of restorative justice (and it still pops up here and there). And unlike shaming sanctions, drug courts are currently quite popular (if somewhat controversial), although there are serious concerns about just how far we can expand them as a substitute for other sanctions (like prison).

C.1. SHAMING SANCTIONS

Shame has always been an important part of sanctioning in the United States. Many early, colonial punishments, such as the stocks and pillory, were explicitly built around shame. As the prison became the dominant form of serious punishment, however, shame faded; in many ways, the prison is the antithesis of shaming sanction, since it hides the offender away from his community (often at a great distance) rather than exposing him to its ridicule and scorn. Even the primary minor punishment, probation, tends to avoid shaming components.[54] None of which is to say that shame and social opprobrium do not attach to offenders, but the state no longer takes an active role of *promoting* that shame.[55] In fact, rules permitting certain types of criminal records to be sealed can be seen as trying to *prevent* social stigmatization.

In the 1990s, however, there was a resurgent interest in shame as a sanction by both academics and, perhaps to a much more muted extent, policy makers that picked up steam in the 1990s. The motivation was straight-forward: prison populations were increasingly expensive, and with crime rates falling cheaper alternatives were increasingly politically feasible. Yet the conventional alternatives to incarceration, probation or fines, were viewed by many as insufficient. Shaming sanctions provided

---

[54] Recall that this is a central aspect of the history of punishment set forth by Foucault, that as states matured they moved away from spectacular sanctions designed to shock and awe and towards more professionalized punishments conducted outside of public view and intended to regulate the offender rather than to cow the general public.

[55] A major common exception to this rule—the "perp walk"—is troubling, since it takes place *before* any conviction, and thus when state actors should still abide by the presumption of innocence.

a potentially viable alternative, since they were cheaper than prisons but possessed a "punitive" element that fines did not. Dan Kahan provides a succinct defense of shaming punishments:

> [W]hy do American jurisdictions rely so heavily on imprisonment? Criminal justice experts have long agreed that as many as half the persons in American prisons and jails—those serving relatively short terms of incarceration for petty theft, various forms of white collar crime, drunk driving, drug possession, and various other minor offenses—could be deterred as effectively, and at considerably less cost, by fines and community service. Why had the argument for alternative sanctions made such little headway as a practical political matter?
>
> The answer, I suggested, was that the conventional alternative sanctions are deficient along the expressive dimension of punishment. [M]embers of the public expect punishments not only to protect them from harm or to inflict . . . pain on offenders but also to express moral disapprobation. Because of the symbolic association of liberty with human worth in our society, taking away a person's freedom unambiguously signifies condemnation. Merely fining someone, however, seems to connote that we are attaching a price tag to that person's behavior. Community service creates a similar form of dissonance: because we ordinarily admire persons who restore dilapidated low-income housing, educate the retarded, furnish aid to the elderly, and the like, it's hard for members of society to believe that law genuinely means to condemn persons when it orders them to perform such services as criminal punishments.
>
> What shaming punishments mean . . . equips them to overcome this constraint on the political acceptability of conventional alternative sanctions. In a famous article, Harold Garfinkel described the conditions of "successful degradation ceremonies"—ritualized deprivations that, against the background of social norms, mark someone as a wrongdoer unentitled to the respect and consideration afforded virtuous members of the community. Shaming penalties, whether in the form of adverse publicity, stigmatizing forms of clothing or property markings, coerced gestures of contrition, or more ornate self-debasement rituals, all satisfy these conditions. Because shaming, unlike fines and community service, gratifies rather than disappoints the demand for denunciation, . . . substituting shame for imprisonment would not provoke the sort of popular resistance that had frustrated the alternative sanctions movement.

[There is also] an independent policy defense of shaming punishments[, based] on the relative value of shaming instead of incarcerating.... Like conventional alternatives such as fines and community service, shame, I speculated, would likely deter and incapacitate as or nearly as well as short terms of incarceration without imposing nearly so much cost on society or suffering on offenders. [S]hame is open to moral objections and anxieties of various sorts; but because I was proposing shaming as an alternative to prison, it struck me as a decisive rejoinder that shame was unquestionably less problematic than imprisonment along nearly every dimension of what constitutes just punishment. The best should not be permitted to be an enemy of the good, or even the less bad, when the less bad seems like the best we can do.[56]

Starting in the 1980s and 1990s, we did in fact see some judges rely increasingly on shaming sanctions to punish low-level offenders. Some examples:

- Some offenders had to wear t-shirts, bracelets, or placards that announced their crime ("I write bad checks!" or "DUI Convict").[57]
- Slumlords were forced to live in the buildings they managed or have their names displayed on banners in front of condemned homes.[58]
- Embezzlers, defrauders, and other white collar offenders were forced to publish apologies in local papers.[59]
- A man convicted of aggravated battery was forced to put a sign on his front yard reading "Warning! A Violent Felon Lives Here. Enter at Your Own Risk!"[60]
- Many different police departments published the faces of johns who solicited prostitutes on billboards, newspapers, and elsewhere. (**Question:** Why do police departments focus on johns, not the prostitutes?)

Such sanctions have always been controversial; in several of the examples cited above the trial court's shaming sanction was later reversed by a higher court that felt the conditions were too far removed

---

[56] Dan M. Kahan, *What's Really Wrong With Shaming Sanctions*, 84 TEX. L. REV. 2075, 2077–79 (2006). As the title of this paper makes clear, Kahan ultimately rejected the idea that shaming sanctions were a viable alternative, so the argument given here reflects one he once held (particularly in Dan M. Kahan, *What Do Alternative Sanctions Mean?*, 63 U. CHI. L. REV. 591 (1996)), but does not currently advance.

[57] Kahan, *Alternative Sanctions,* supra note 56 at 591.

[58] Dan M. Kahan & Eric A. Posner, *Shaming White Collar Criminals: A Proposal for Reform of the Federal Sentencing Guidelines*, 42 J. L. & ECON. 365, 367 (1999).

[59] *Id.*

[60] David R. Karp, *The Judicial and Judicious Use of Shame Penalties*, 44 CRIME & DELINQ. 277, 281 (1998).

from the goals of punishment. But not every appellate court has disagreed with such punishments. Perhaps the most detailed analysis of shaming sanctions by an appellate court came in the 9th Circuit's opinion in *United States v. Gementera*.

United States v. Gementera
379 F.3d 596 (9th Cir. 2004)

■ O'SCANNLAIN, CIRCUIT JUDGE:

We must decide the legality of a supervised release condition that requires a convicted mail thief to spend a day standing outside a post office wearing a signboard stating, "I stole mail. This is my punishment."

We first address Gementera's argument that the eight-hour sandwich board condition violates the Sentencing Reform Act. The Sentencing Reform Act affords district courts broad discretion in fashioning appropriate conditions of supervised release, while mandating that such conditions serve legitimate objectives. [T]o comply with this requirement, any condition must be "reasonably related" to "the nature and circumstances of the offense and the history and characteristics of the defendant." Moreover, it must be both "reasonably related" to and "involve no greater deprivation of liberty than is reasonably necessary" to "afford adequate deterrence to criminal conduct," "protect the public from further crimes of the defendant," and "provide the defendant with needed educational or vocational training, medical care, or other correctional treatment in the most effective manner." Accordingly, the three legitimate statutory purposes of deterrence, protection of the public, and rehabilitation frame our analysis.

Gementera first urges that the condition was imposed for an impermissible purpose of humiliation. He points to certain remarks of the district court at [a] first sentencing hearing:

> [H]e needs to understand the disapproval that society has for this kind of conduct, and that's the idea behind the humiliation. And it should be humiliation of having to stand and be labeled in front of people coming and going from a post office as somebody who has stolen the mail.

According to Gementera, these remarks, among others, indicate that the district court viewed humiliation as an end in itself and the condition's purpose. Reading the record in context, however, we cannot but conclude that the district court's stated rationale aligned with permissible statutory objectives. At [a] second sentencing hearing, when the sentence was amended to what is now before us, the court explained: "[U]ltimately, the objective here is, one, to deter criminal conduct, and, number two, to rehabilitate the offender so that after he has paid his punishment, he does not reoffend, and a public expiation of having offended is, or at least it should be, rehabilitating in its effect." Although, in general, criminal punishment "is or at least should be humiliating," the court emphasized that "[h]umiliation is not the point."

The court expressed particular concern that the defendant did not fully understand the gravity of his offense. Mail theft is an anonymous crime and, by "bring[ing] home to defendant that his conduct has palpable significance to real people within his community," the court aimed to break the defendant of the illusion that his theft was victimless or not serious. Moreover, "[i]t will also have a deterrent effect on both this defendant and others who might not otherwise have been made aware of the real legal consequences of engaging in mail theft."

Assuming the court articulated a legitimate purpose, Gementera asserts . . . that humiliation or so-called "shaming" conditions are not "reasonably related" to rehabilitation.

While our knowledge of rehabilitation is limited, we have nonetheless explicitly held that "a public apology may serve a rehabilitative purpose." Of course, for Gementera to prevail, introducing mere uncertainty about whether the condition aids rehabilitation does not suffice; rather, he must persuade us that the condition's supposed relationship to rehabilitation is unreasonable.

Reflecting upon [Gementera's] criminal history, the court expressed concern that he did not fully understand the consequences of his continued criminality, and had not truly accepted responsibility. The court also determined that Gementera needed to be educated about the seriousness of mail crimes in particular, given that they might appear to be victimless. . . . [T]he district court [thus] concluded that public acknowledgment of one's offense—beyond the formal yet sterile plea in a cloistered courtroom—was necessary to his rehabilitation.

It is true, of course, that much uncertainty exists as to how rehabilitation is best accomplished. Were that picture clearer, our criminal justice system would be vastly different, and substantially improved. By one estimate, two-thirds of the 640,000 state and federal inmates who will be released in 2004 will return to prison within a few years. The cost to humanity of our ignorance in these matters is staggering.

Gementera and amicus contend that shaming conditions cannot be rehabilitative because such conditions necessarily cause the offender to withdraw from society or otherwise inflict psychological damage, and they would erect a per se bar against such conditions. Though the district court had no scientific evidence before it, as Gementera complains, we do not insist upon such evidence in our deferential review. Moreover, the fact is that a vigorous, multifaceted, scholarly debate on shaming sanctions' efficacy, desirability, and underlying rationales continues within the academy. By no means is this conversation one-sided.

Criminal offenses, and the penalties that accompany them, nearly always cause shame and embarrassment. Indeed, the mere fact of conviction, without which state-sponsored rehabilitation efforts do not commence, is stigmatic. The fact that a condition causes shame or embarrassment does not automatically render a condition objectionable; rather, such feelings generally signal the defendant's acknowledgment of his wrongdoing. See Webster's Ninth New Collegiate Dictionary 1081 (1986) (defining shame as "a painful emotion caused by consciousness of guilt, shortcoming, or impropriety"). We have recognized that "the societal consequences that flow from a criminal conviction are virtually unlimited," and the tendency to cause shame is insufficient to extinguish a condition's rehabilitative promise, at least insofar as required for our flexible reasonable relation test.

While the district court's sandwich board condition was somewhat crude, and by itself could entail risk of social withdrawal and stigmatization, it was coupled with more socially useful provisions, including lecturing at a high school and writing apologies, that might loosely be understood to promote the offender's social reintegration. We see this factor as highly significant. In short, here we consider not a stand-alone condition intended solely to humiliate, but rather a comprehensive set of provisions that expose the defendant to social disapprobation, but that also then provide an opportunity for Gementera to repair his relationship with society—first by seeking its forgiveness and then by making, as a member of the community, an independent contribution to the moral formation of its youth.

Finally, we are aware that lengthier imprisonment was an alternative available to the court. The court, however, reasoned that rehabilitation would be better achieved by a shorter sentence, coupled with the additional conditions: "It would seem to me that he's better off with a taste of prison, rather than a longer prison sentence, and some form of condition of release that brings him face-to-face with the consequences of his crime." The judge's reasoning that rehabilitation would better be served by means other than extended incarceration and punishment is plainly reasonable. . . .

Accordingly, we hold that the condition imposed upon Gementera reasonably related to the legitimate statutory objective of rehabilitation. In so holding, we are careful not to articulate a principle broader than that presented by the facts of this case. With care and specificity, the district court outlined a sensible logic underlying its conclusion that a set of conditions, including the signboard provision, but also including reintegrative provisions, would better promote this defendant's rehabilitation and amendment of life than would a lengthier term of incarceration. By contrast, a per se rule that the mandatory public airing of one's offense can never assist an offender to reassume his duty of obedience to the law would impose a narrow penological orthodoxy not contemplated by the Guidelines' express approval of "any other condition [the district court] considers to be appropriate."

Gementera also urges that the sandwich board condition violates the [Eighth Amendment to the] Constitution. [The court considers whether shaming sanctions offend our "evolving standards of decency."] The parties have offered no evidence whatsoever, aside from bare assertion, that shaming sanctions violate contemporary standards of decency. But the occasional imposition of such sanctions is hardly unusual, particularly in our state courts. In the absence of any evidence to the contrary, and particularly in comparison with the reality of the modern prison, we simply have no reason to conclude that the sanction before us exceeds the bounds of "civilized standards" or other "evolving standards of decency that mark the progress of a maturing society."

Affirmed.

■ HAWKINS, CIRCUIT JUDGE, dissenting:

Conditions of supervised release must be reasonably related to and "involve no greater deprivation of liberty than is reasonably necessary" to deter criminal conduct, protect the public, and rehabilitate the offender. Clearly, the shaming punishment at issue in this case was intended to humiliate Gementera. And that is all it will do. Any attempt to classify the goal of the punishment as anything other than humiliation would be disingenuous.

There is precious little federal authority on sentences that include shaming components, perhaps indicative of a recognition that whatever legal justification may be marshaled in support of sentences involving public humiliation, they simply have no place in the majesty of an Article III courtroom. Some state courts have reviewed such sentences and the results have been mixed.

Although the majority opinion initially seems to accept the district court's retroactive justification for the punishment, it later as much as concedes that the sandwich board condition amounted to a shaming punishment. Admitting that the condition was "crude" and "could entail risk of social withdrawal and stigmatization," the majority nonetheless finds the condition acceptable because it was "coupled with more socially useful provisions." Put another way, the majority says that it is not considering "a stand-alone condition intended sole[l]y to humiliate, but rather a comprehensive set of conditions." But the majority cites to no provision in the Sentencing Reform Act and to no case law indicating that conditions on supervised release should be reviewed as a set and not individually, or that humiliation somehow ceases to be humiliation when combined with other punishment.

Although I believe that the sandwich board condition violates the Sentencing Reform Act and we should reverse the district court for that reason, I also believe that this is simply bad policy. A fair measure of a civilized society is how its institutions behave in the space between what it may have the power to do and what it should do. The shaming component of the sentence in this case fails that test. "When one shames another person, the goal is to degrade the object of shame, to place him lower in the chain of being, to dehumanize him."

To affirm the imposition of such punishments recalls a time in our history when pillories and stocks were the order of the day. To sanction such use of power runs the very great risk that by doing so we instill "a sense of disrespect for the criminal justice system" itself. I would vacate the sentence and remand for re-sentencing, instructing the district court that public humiliation or shaming has no proper place in our system of justice.

As the majority in *Gementera* indicates, academics have debated the efficacy of shame as a sanction, with little resolution. In the end, though, the use of punitive shaming sanctions never fully caught on. There have been some minor punishments here and there, but no fundamental shift toward shaming sanctions, even for non-violent offenses for which the political will may have been stronger.[61] The following passage from Kahan's *What's Wrong with Shaming Sanctions* illuminates some of the common criticisms that were leveled against shame as well as Kahan's take on what ultimately rendered it politically unviable.

Dan Kahan, *What's Wrong With Shaming Sanctions*
84 TEX. L. REV. 2075, 2079–2090 (2006)

My argument [in favor of shaming sanctions] provoked a torrent of criticism. Many of the arguments were practical and empirical in nature: that shaming punishments couldn't be expected to deter, for example, because most offenders don't value their reputations enough to be influenced by the threat of humiliation; or, alternatively, that shaming punishments would actually backfire because they would destroy offenders' reputations and feelings of self-esteem and thus simultaneously extinguish their incentive to protect their good standing and their opportunities to be reintegrated into law-abiding society. Others worried about the justice of shaming: purposefully degrading offenders, they argued, was cruel and illiberal. Still others fretted that shaming, because it depended for its effect on public condemnation, would activate preferences for debasement or other social dynamics that would threaten civility or order.

---

[61] The evidence here is more absence of evidence than evidence of absence: there is little data gathered on shaming sanctions, which makes it hard to "prove" that they are not widely used, but which suggests that they are not—since if they were, there would be more data on them.

Many of these arguments reflected highly contentious, and often mutually inconsistent, premises. But rather than try to pick at them in a fine-grained way, my instinct was to offer a sort of demurrer grounded in the pragmatic underpinnings of my own normative defense of shaming as an alternative to imprisonment. The potential dangers they detected in shame were not fanciful. But treating them as dispositive grounds for rejecting shame would result in the certainty of the even greater evils of imprisonment: the default punishment in the absence of an expressively viable alternative sanction.

It's obviously false, for example, to think that shaming uniquely enlists members of the public to visit condemnation on criminal wrongdoers. Imprisonment, every bit as much as shame, is a degradation ceremony. Imprisonment so evocatively expresses moral condemnation precisely because, in our society, liberty deprivation successfully marks someone as being unworthy of the respect we believe virtuous persons are due. As such, imprisonment clearly invites continued—indeed, usually permanent—shunning. Just as clearly, at least to anyone who keeps an eye on media coverage of white collar crimes in particular, imprisonment excites a conspicuous public appetite to demean those who engage in offenses for which prison is usually meted out.

Likewise, it is myopic to worry that shaming will vitiate the reputational stake a person has in resuming a law-abiding life, or the opportunities she'll have to do so. Nothing interferes with an offender's prospects for social reintegration nearly so much as a record of incarceration does! Precisely because we should worry about the impact of having been shamed on a person's reputational incentive to comply with the law ex post, moreover, it's naïve to suggest that the prospect of being shamed won't have a deterrent impact ex ante.

If we worry that shaming is cruel—and we should—then we should worry all the more about imprisoning rather than shaming, since the former is unquestionably more painful and degrading than the latter. All one has to do to confirm this is ask individual offenders, who typically opt for shaming as a condition of probation rather than go to jail.

Recognizing that I was in a state of persistent disagreement with persons of immense intelligence whose moral commitments I shared, I began to reflect on what mistake I must necessarily be making. There was some element of the expressive political economy of penal law I obviously wasn't getting. As a result of work that I have since done on the expressive dynamics of law and politics generally . . . , I think I now have a much better idea of what it was.

Beliefs about the efficacy of environmental regulations, gun control, public health laws, and the like are distributed in patterns—within and across issues—that map onto individuals' cultural worldviews. [I]ndividuals are naturally disposed to believe that policies that cohere with and are supported by others who hold their values also promote their interests. Indeed, once cultural worldviews are controlled for, education, income, party affiliation and other factors that might be thought to determine perceptions of whose interests these policies promote fade into insignificance.

Just as important as its power to explain political conflict, however, is the power of [this] theory to explain consensus. Individuals tend to favor policies that express their cultural values—both because they attach intrinsic value to what laws say, and because they are naturally disposed to believe that expressively congenial laws promote good consequences. Laws that manage to affirm diverse cultural worldviews simultaneously, then, are the ones most likely to overcome political conflict and generate broad scale support.

Generalizing, then, [this] account of expressive political economy suggests an important principle about the political acceptability of various laws and institutions. Call it the principle of expressive overdetermination. A law or policy can be said to be expressively overdetermined when it bears meanings sufficiently rich in nature and large in number to enable diverse cultural groups to find simultaneously affirmation of their values within it. Such a policy will enjoy widespread appeal in part because it satisfies the desire individuals have to see their worldviews endorsed (or at least not trampled upon) by law, and it is likely to strike them as advancing their material well-being.

Laws that lack expressive overdetermination—ones that bear meanings perceived as affirming the values of only some cultural perspectives and as denigrating others—are in a much more precarious position. Such laws will generate persistent resistance from powerful constituencies, who will see such laws as simultaneously assaulting their status and imperiling their material welfare. They are thus less likely to be adopted in the first place and, if they are adopted, are more vulnerable to being overturned.

The expressive overdetermination principle, I believe, is what was missing from my earlier account of shame as an alternative sanction. Simply stated, imprisonment is expressively overdetermined and shaming punishments are not.

More generally, the analysis of *What Do Alternative Sanctions Mean?* reflected too simplistic an understanding of the expressive political economy of penal law. My main claim was that the political acceptability of various forms of punishments turns on whether they express moral denunciation. There's obviously more to it, even from a purely expressive standpoint. [C]itizens are sensitive to whether institutions, policies, and laws affirm the values that construct their preferred way of life. It follows, then, that citizens will expect punishments not only to express condemnation but also to express condemnation in a way that coheres with, rather than assaults, their more basic cultural commitments.

Forms of punishment that unambiguously express condemnation can nevertheless do so in ways that affirm only some ways of life while denigrating others. An example is corporal punishment. Historically, the imposition of physical pain as a mode of punishment was characteristic of hierarchical relationships: it was the way that sovereigns disciplined subjects, masters disciplined slaves, parents disciplined children, and husbands disciplined wives. Persons of higher classes, in fact, were often exempt from corporal punishment. As [several scholars] have documented, this history imbued corporal punishment with social meanings that made it particularly congenial to the aristocratic South in the eighteenth and nineteenth centuries, and an anathema to the more egalitarian and individualistic Northern states, which during this time gravitated toward imprisonment as a mode of discipline more fitting for a "republic."

I'm persuaded that shaming punishments are afflicted with a similar social meaning tax. Like corporal punishments, they resonate with significations of hierarchy and community that assault the sensibilities of those who favor more egalitarian and individualistic forms of social organization.

In some sense, these meanings are out of keeping with the motivations behind and feel of shaming on the ground. In particular, shaming penalties often have a strong populist flavor; I think of the support for shaming rather than fining white collar offenders in general, and of Hoboken's experiment with ordering Manhattan yuppies convicted of public urination to scrub the city streets in particular, as examples. I also believe that shaming can very easily be appropriated by egalitarians to reinforce obligations—e.g., delinquent child support payments due to poor, single mothers—that typically go underenforced in a legal system that is more concerned with protecting the powerful.

But punishments mean not what a policy advocate would have them mean but what they do in fact mean to the public. . . . And for a sizable portion of the public, including many who hold the sorts of progressive sensibilities that otherwise incline them to support alternative sanctions, shaming does connote objectionable forms of social stratification and potentially suffocating impositions of communal norms. This is so, I think, in part because of the history of shaming. Like corporal punishment, shaming punishments occupied a conspicuous place in the penal tool kit of hierarchical regimes; indeed, shame played as large a part as the infliction of pain in many colonial corporal punishments—the stocks being a prime example. Shaming also played a role in enforcing conformity with communal norms, themselves often hierarchical, as Hawthorne's *The Scarlet Letter* famously illustrates.

I was also making some related mistakes about the expressive political economy of imprisonment. Again, my analysis of the political acceptability of imprisonment was too flat. An immensely rich and ambiguous institution, imprisonment not only condemns, but condemns in a multiplicity of registers that make it simultaneously agreeable to persons of diverse cultural outlooks: hierarchists can see it as supplying a delicious form of debasement for those who resist their proper place in the social order; communitarians, a fitting gesture of banishment for those who wrongfully renounce social obligation; individualists, a reciprocal deprivation of liberty for those who fail to respect the liberty of others; and egalitarians, a uniquely democratic metric of punishment for persons who enjoy value by virtue of their capacity for autonomy. Neither the ascendancy of imprisonment nor its stubborn persistence can be understood without an appreciation of the political advantages it has enjoyed over rival forms of punishment by virtue of its expressive overdetermination.

QUESTIONS

1. **Source of shame.** As a doctrinal or policy matter, how satisfying is it that the court in *Gementera* looks to the judge's rationale to determine whether the punishment is humiliating? Empirically, is this the right place to look? Even if we take a more subjective view, should we look to the subjective goals of the judge or the subjective impact on the defendant? Does this complicate all the more our discussion of what constitutes sentencing "disparities"?

2. **Drafting rules.** Does the ability of the district court in *Gementera* to justify his punishment in Round 2 point to a problem with having so many theories of punishment in play?

3. ***Ex ante* vs. *ex post*.** Shaming may lead to disassociation, but the fear of disassociation may deter. When deciding on the appropriateness of a sanction, should we look to its ex ante or ex post effects? Does this point to any problems with relying on courts to craft criminal sentencing policy?

4. **Public humiliation.** The dissent in *Gementera* is concerned with public humiliation. But what is the proper baseline—as the majority points out, prison is stigmatizing too. Against what standard should we evaluate "too" humiliating? Furthermore, what if a different outcome in *Gementera* resulted in generally longer prison sentences, as likely would have been the case for Gementera himself had he prevailed?

5. **Science in the courtroom.** Does it make sense in *Gemetera* for the court to cite Webster's for a scientific proposition that shame reflects acknowledgement of guilt?) Does this point to any concerns more generally with empirical evidence in the courtroom?

While punitive shame has not caught on, a close analog—restorative justice—has. Though fundamentally different in design, both are motived by a common underlying idea, namely that the community should be involved in dealing with the offender. With shaming sanctions, the community was called on to actively disassociate itself from the offender;

restorative justice moves in the opposite direction, calling on the community to figure out how to reintegrate an offender so he is less likely to offend again. Shaming sanctions were built on the idea of using the community to enforce outside sanctions on an offender, just like the police and prisons do. Restorative justice, on the other hand, seeks to use the community to help the offender police himself from within by reducing, rather than just deterring, his criminal impulses. So we want to turn our attention to restorative justice now.

C.2. RESTORATIVE JUSTICE

A substantial body of evidence indicates that informal social controls play a much bigger role in controlling crime than the threat of formal sanctions: it is less fear of arrest and incarceration that deters criminal conduct, but fear of scorn and opprobrium from friends and family. Thus traditional sanctions, incarceration in particular, represent a gamble. These punishments often weaken informal social controls, by distancing the offender from his social circle, stigmatizing him, and undermining generally pro-social developments like finding a job and a partner. The hope, then, is that fear of incarceration will deter or prevent more crime than it causes by impeding these social controls which, however weak they were before the offender committed his crime (their very weakness may explain why he committed the crime in the first place), will be weaker still upon release.

Restorative justice—which, as we will see, is an ambiguous, amorphous term—seeks to rectify this problem. If crime is often prevented by strong social ties, then its commission is indication of weakened ties; weakening these social bonds further, the theory goes, would be iatrogenic, so we should seek instead to make them stronger. Defining restorative justice broadly, it aims to bring together the offender, the victim, and other stakeholders to help the offender understand the harm he has caused, and to seek out an appropriate sanction that reintegrates the offender into the community, while also giving proper recognition to the victim's injury.

This section will start with an overview of what restorative justice is, then consider evidence about its effectiveness, and conclude by looking at some of the concerns that have been raised about it.

Mark S. Umbreit, Betty Vos, Robert B. Coates, & Elizabeth Lightfoot, *Restorative Justice in the Twenty-First Century: A Social Movement Full of Opportunities and Pitfalls*
89 MARQ. L. REV. 251, 254–270 (2005)

Most contemporary criminal justice systems focus on law violation, the need to hold offenders accountable and punish them, and other state interests. Actual crime victims are quite subsidiary to the process and generally have no legal standing in the proceedings. Crime is viewed as having been committed against the state, which, therefore, essentially owns the conflict and determines how to respond to it. The resulting criminal justice system is almost entirely offender driven.

Restorative justice offers a very different way of understanding and responding to crime. Instead of viewing the state as the primary victim in criminal acts and placing victims, offenders, and the community in passive roles, restorative justice recognizes crime as being directed against individual people. It is grounded in the belief that those most affected by crime should have the opportunity to become actively involved in resolving the conflict. Repairing harm and restoring losses, allowing offenders to take direct responsibility for their actions, and assisting victims to move beyond vulnerability towards some degree of closure stand in sharp contrast to the values and practices of the conventional criminal justice system with its focus on past criminal behavior through ever-increasing levels of punishment.

Instead of focusing upon the weaknesses or deficits of offenders and crime victims, restorative justice attempts to draw upon the strengths of these individuals and their capacity to openly address the need to repair the harm caused. Restorative justice denounces criminal behavior yet emphasizes the need to treat offenders with respect and to reintegrate them into the larger community in ways that can lead to lawful behavior.

The philosopher of law, Conrad Brunk, argues that on a theoretical level, retribution and restoration are not the polar opposites that many assume. He notes that both actually have much in common: a desire to vindicate by some type of reciprocal action and some type of proportional relationship between the criminal act and the response to it. Retributive theory and restorative theory, however, differ significantly in how to "even the score"—how to make things right. Retributive theory holds that the imposition of some form of pain will vindicate, most frequently deprivation of liberty and even loss of life in some cases. Restorative theory argues that "what truly vindicates is acknowledgement of victims' harms and needs, combined with an active effort to encourage offenders to take responsibility, make right the wrongs, and address the causes of their behavior."

The conventional criminal justice system focuses upon three questions: (1) What laws have been broken?; (2) Who did it?; and (3) What do they deserve? From a restorative justice perspective, an entirely different set of questions are asked: (1) Who has been hurt?; (2) What are their needs?; and (3) Whose obligations are these?

A wide range of restorative justice practices, programs, and policies are developing in communities throughout the United States and abroad. [Here] we briefly describe several different examples, followed by a more detailed presentation of a system-wide change effort.

In Orange County, California, a victim-offender mediation and conferencing program receives nearly one thousand referrals of juvenile offenders and their victims each year. This program is supported by a large government grant and provides much needed support, assistance, and restoration for victims of crime, while also holding these young people accountable to their communities. By diverting these cases from further penetration into the justice system, if the victim's needs are met, the county also benefits from a significant cost reduction in the already overcrowded court system.

In several United States cities, prosecuting attorney offices routinely offer choices for victims of crime to actively participate in the justice system, to participate in restorative dialogue with the offender and others affected by the crime, and to meet whatever other needs these individuals are facing. A program in Indianapolis works closely with the police department in offering family group conferencing services in which young offenders and their families meet the individuals they have victimized and work toward repairing the harm, resulting in a significant reduction in recidivism among these offenders.

Restorative justice dialogue responses are increasingly being offered to victims of severe and violent crime, driven by requests from victims for such opportunities. Departments of corrections in Texas, Ohio, Pennsylvania, and several other states have initiated statewide victim-offender mediation and dialogue programs through their victim services units. In such programs, victims of severe violence, including homicide, meet in facilitated dialogue with the offenders who have harmed them as part of their search for meaning and some measure of closure in the wake of trauma. A retired Wisconsin Supreme Court Justice facilitates dialogue groups in a state prison among prisoners and with several victims of severe violence in an effort to ingrain the full human impact of the prisoners' behavior upon victims and their communities.

* * *

As a means of providing an in-depth examination of restorative justice in practice, we have elected to turn our close-up lens on restorative justice dialogue. In so doing, we do not mean to imply that it is the best practice or the only practice worth examining. We selected it because it is the oldest, most widely practiced, and most thoroughly researched of the various processes that fall under the broad umbrella of restorative justice.

[W]e examine f]our general types of restorative justice dialogue.... These include victim-offender mediation, group conferencing, circles, and "other." All have in common the inclusion of victims and offenders in direct dialogue, nearly always face-to-face, about a specific offense or infraction; the presence of at least one additional person who serves as mediator, facilitator, convener, or circle keeper; and usually, advance preparation of the parties so they will know what to expect. The focus of the encounter nearly always involves naming what happened, identifying its impact, and coming to some common understanding, often including reaching agreement as to how any resultant harm would be repaired. Use of these processes can take place at any point in the justice process, including pre-arrest, pre-court referral, pre-sentencing, post-sentencing, and even during incarceration.

Victim-offender mediation (often called "victim-offender conferencing," "victim-offender reconciliation," or "victim-offender dialogue") usually involves a victim and an offender in direct mediation facilitated by one or sometimes two mediators or facilitators; occasionally, the dialogue takes place through a third party who carries information back and forth, a process known as shuttle mediation. In face-to-face meetings, support persons (such as parents or friends) for victims or offenders are often present. A 1999 survey of victim-offender mediation programs in the United States found that support persons, including parents in juvenile cases, were present in nearly nine out of ten cases.

Group conferencing (usually known as "family group conferencing," "community group conferencing," or "restorative group conferencing") routinely involves support persons for both victims and offenders as well as additional participants from the community. Many group conferencing programs rely on a script, though some are more open-ended. The number of support persons present can often range from ten to six to only a few, much like victim-offender mediation. Some group conferences can be quite large.

Circles are variously called "peacemaking circles," "restorative justice circles," "repair of harm circles," and "sentencing circles." The numbers and types of participants gathered for circles are similar to those gathered for conferences, though sometimes there is even wider community member participation as interested persons, additional circle-keepers, or facilitators. The process involves the use of a "talking piece" that is passed around the circle to designate who may speak.

"Other" refers to programs such as reparative boards and other community-based programs that invite victims and offenders to participate together in crafting an appropriate response to the offense.

Unlike guideline systems, and akin to indeterminate ones, restorative justice approaches generally have few procedural rules in place. This is perhaps intuitive, given that the goal is not to guide two adversarial parties to some sort of legal resolution but rather to help two (or more) people reach some sort of mutually satisfactory solution. As one commentator observes:

> Through victim-offender mediation, all parties involved may agree upon an appropriate response to the offense, which they

feel is just and fair. They are not restricted by formal legal requirements, and the response may be creative, innovative, and unknown to the formal criminal justice process. For instance, the offender may undertake to assist the victim in activities of daily life that are difficult for the victim, to accompany the victim to the authorities, or to compensate the victim by labor or other means. A friendly understanding or rapport between the parties may enable solutions that a court could not have imposed.[62]

Delaware's victim-offender mediation statute gives a good sense of how open-ended these provisions are. Del. Code Title XI, Ch. 95 consists of five sections, §§ 9501–9505. Section 9502 deals with the funding specifics, § 9503 the confidentiality of the proceedings, and § 9505 civil immunity for those running the mediations. The two remaining sections state:

§ 9501. Purpose.

(a) The General Assembly finds and declares that:

(1) The resolution of felony, misdemeanor and juvenile delinquent disputes can be costly and complex in a judicial setting where the parties involved are necessarily in an adversary posture and subject to formalized procedures; and

(2) Victim-offender mediation programs can meet the needs of Delaware's citizens by providing forums in which persons may voluntarily participate in the resolution of certain criminal offenses in an informal and less adversarial atmosphere.

(b) It is the intent of the General Assembly that each program established pursuant to this chapter:

(1) Stimulate the establishment and use of victim-offender mediation programs to help meet the need for alternatives to the courts for the resolution of certain criminal offenses, whether before or after adjudication;

(2) Encourage continuing community participation in the development, administration and oversight of local victim-offender mediation programs;

(3) Offer structures for victim-offender mediation which may serve as models for programs in other communities; and

---

[62] Gabriel Hallevy, *Therapeutic Victim-Offender Mediation Within the Criminal Justice Process—Sharpening the Evaluation of Personal Potential for Rehabilitation While Righting Wrongs Under the ADR Philosophy*, 16 HARV. NEGOT. L. REV. 65, 74 (2011).

(4) Serve a specific community or locale and resolve certain criminal offenses that arise within that community or locale.

§ 9504. Eligibility.

No offender shall be admitted to the program unless the Attorney General certifies that the offender is appropriate to the program, regardless of any criteria established under any program or this chapter.

Any person who voluntarily enters a mediation process at a victim-offender mediation program established under this chapter may revoke that person's consent, withdraw from mediation and seek judicial or administrative redress prior to reaching a written agreement. No legal penalty, sanction or restraint may be imposed upon the person for such withdrawal.

That is the extent of the formal, statutory rules. Such flexibility may seem surprising at first glance, but realize that indeterminate sentencing is equally permissive. Which, of course, begs the following question:

Question: Is there any clear reason why mediation should be subject to more formal rules than the imposition of incarceration?

According to Umbreit et al., the restorative justice movement began in the 1970s but remained relatively unimportant until the mid-1990s, at which point it started to gain more adherents. In 1994, the American Bar Association endorsed victim-offender mediation, and the National Organization for Victim Assistance came out in support of restorative justice in 1995. Looking more globally, the Council of Europe spoke out in favor of restorative justice in 1999, and the European Union in 2001.

Restorative justice programs have continued to grow in the US and, even more rapidly, in Europe, Australia, and New Zealand. Umbreit et al. note that Australia sought to incorporate restorative justice methods throughout its criminal justice system as early as 1988, and New Zealand put restorative justice principles at the forefront of its juvenile justice system in 1989.

But while increasingly popular, it is worth asking whether restorative justice is successful. There are two challenges to answering this question: defining what we mean by "successful," and then figuring out how to measure whether restorative justice practices accomplish these goals.

There are at least three ways to measure success for restorative justice approaches: (1) Does it reduce crime better than more traditional approaches? (2) Is it a cost-effective alternative to traditional sanctions?—perhaps crime is a bit higher, but the crime it does prevent is prevented so much more cheaply. And (3) regardless of its effect on crime rates, do restorative justice techniques leave victims feeling better than traditional approaches?

The problem we face in evaluating restorative justice techniques is one of selection bias. Restorative justice approaches can only work if all parties *want* to participate—regardless of whether mandatory mediation works, forced participation is contrary to the aims of restorative justice. Thus a defendant participates in a victim-offender mediation session only if the victim, the offender, the prosecutor, and the judge all agree that a session is acceptable.

So what does it mean if, say, we observe that offenders who enter restorative justice programs recidivate less than those who do not? It could mean that such programs are successful, and that we should expand them to cover even more defendants. But it could just mean that those offenders who qualify for restorative justice programs are less likely to recidivate whether they participate or not—that's *why* they seem like promising candidates. In other words, is the lower recidivism rate due to the program or does it simply reflect the traits that cause offenders to select/be selected into the program?

The solution is to randomly assign offenders into treatment programs: some get sent to mediation, others do not, but the choice is random. The next reading discusses the results from the randomized trials that have been conducted on mediation programs; the results are generally favorable, sometimes quite so.

But keep a question in the back of your mind. What does the pool of randomized offenders look like? These trials work by taking a pool of offenders *who qualify for mediation* and then randomly assigning some to mediation and others to a no-mediation "control" group. So:

Question: Assume the strongly-favorable results are correct. Does this mean that judges and other actors should expand the pool of eligible defendants, perhaps requiring participation by certain felons?

Lawrence W. Sherman & Heather Strang, *Restorative Justice: The Evidence*
13–23 (2007)

Restorative justice is a strategy that many people have advocated for responding to crime and intentional harm. Like many such strategies, it embraces a variety of forms with a single list of hypothesised outcomes. This report examines the available (and reliable) evidence on those hypotheses that has been produced to date, at least in the English language and within the scope of our search.

These hypotheses can be summed up as two major claims, one about procedures, and one about effectiveness. The procedural claim is that restorative justice (RJ) is seen by victims and offenders as a more humane and respectful way to process crimes than conventional justice (CJ). The effectiveness claim is that RJ is better than CJ in producing important results that we want from justice: less repeat offending, more repair of harm to victims, fewer crimes of vengeance by victims, more reconciliation and social bonding among families and friends affected by crime, and more offences brought to justice.

Promising evidence

A systematic review of tests of these hypotheses offers promising evidence in support of both claims, although with caveats. Victims and offenders who participate in RJ are generally quite pleased with its procedures, more so than with CJ. Some of that evidence may be due to self-selection bias, but other tests eliminated that bias by giving participants little or no choice. This preference is accompanied by strong evidence that RJ is at least as effective in producing the desired results of justice as CJ, often more so, and only rarely (if powerfully) counterproductive. There are also indications of possible cost savings.

Few advocates claim that RJ should ever be used when an offender denies having committed a crime. Rather, the effectiveness claim suggests that RJ will foster more offenders agreeing to accept responsibility for having caused harm criminally. The hypothesis is that RJ would thus help to bring more offenders and offences to justice, since fewer offenders will deny responsibility if offered the prospect of RJ than they do with CJ. In fact, offenders in five controlled tests in New York City and Canberra readily took responsibility for serious crimes and "declined to deny" their guilt-choosing instead the prospect of participation in deciding what should be done about their crimes.

Varieties of restorative justice

Most of the evidence we highlight is based on just one of the many varieties of restorative justice, . . . a process "whereby parties with a stake in a specific offence collectively resolve how to deal with the aftermath of the offence and its implications for the future". That variety is face-to-face conferences of offenders, victims and their supporters.

This method can substantially reduce repeat offending for some (but not all) kinds of crimes and offenders. It can reduce victims' desire for violent revenge against the offender. Victims also suffer less intense post-traumatic stress symptoms after face-to-face restorative justice, returning to work and normal life sooner than they do without it—which should, in turn, reduce the long-term severity and costs of such health problems as coronary heart disease.

"Indirect" restorative justice usually describes any process by which offenders and victims communicate only through third parties, but not face to face. These methods include "shuttle communication", in which a mediator or facilitator may carry messages by phone or in person between victims (or victims' representatives) and offenders (or their representatives). They also include one-way communications such as letters of apology from offender to victim, or letters describing a crime's impact from the victim to the offender. Perhaps the most indirect form of RJ is court-ordered restitution (which has become a substantial source of imprisonment in the US for offender failure to pay). Youth referral panels in the UK may also order restitution. When this form of RJ has been put to controlled tests, it has reduced recidivism in both adult and juvenile samples, but not consistently so.

Missing evidence

In assessing the prospects for a major expansion in the use of RJ, [our] review found no evidence of the kind that might be needed to roll out a national policy. That evidence about the effects of up-scaling RJ for widespread use—whether it would produce "collateral benefits" or harms for entire communities beyond those we can observe in studies limited to comparisons of individual cases—would include the following questions:

- Would broader use of RJ encourage more witnesses to come forward to help police solve more crimes, bringing more offences and offenders to justice by more public confidence in justice and the law?
- Would broader use of RJ encourage more offenders to accept responsibility for their offences, increasing offences brought to justice?
- If an entire community or basic command unit adopted RJ as the initial response to most crimes, would that policy weaken the general deterrent effects of the law—or strengthen compliance with the law by increasing its legitimacy?
- If RJ became more widely known and understood by the public through far more frequent use, would it attract even more victim and offender consent to participate than the substantial levels it has achieved in some pilot tests?

These and other questions about large-scale RJ could be answered with evidence generated by the scientific method, using communities as the unit of analysis. They cannot, however, be answered with evidence generated solely at the individual or case level in small-scale pilot tests. Thus the implication of this conclusion is that progress in evidence-based restorative justice is likely to depend on whether future testing of RJ is conducted on a neighbourhood-wide or community-wide basis.

The reasons why

One key question [we considered] is why RJ works when it does work. The short answer is that we cannot tell much from the available evidence, but there are some theories that could guide further analysis.

The modern revival of RJ has been long on theory, but shorter on tests of those theories. Even when RJ itself is subjected to rigorous testing, the theories that could explain its effects are often much harder to test. This situation is not uncommon in science, as in the case of antibiotics, which cure infections for reasons that are not fully understood. Yet there is no doubt that understanding the reasons why RJ works—or doesn't—could help improve predictions and policies about when to use it or not.

A central theory about RJ highlights a massive difference from the theory of conventional justice—and also explains why conventional justice fails to deter repeat convictions far more often than not. That theory, based on "defiance theory", is that:

- People who commit crimes often believe, or convince themselves, that they are not acting immorally.
- RJ engages such people in a moral discussion about whether crime is wrong.
- An RJ discussion can lead offenders to redefine themselves as law-abiders, and to agree that they are not the kind of people who would do immoral things.
- That discussion would lead to the conclusion that what they did was in fact immoral, and that they should therefore not repeat such behaviour. (Whether they do anyway remains the key empirical question about this theory.)

In contrast, criminal law doctrine presumes that people know they are doing wrong, and that only fear of punishment can stop them from repeating their crime. Thus punishment is required in order to deter them (and others) from doing such wrongs. While such neoclassical theory therefore centres on punishment, RJ centres on persuasion. The aim of punishment is to enhance fear of further punishment; the aim of persuasion is to enhance moral support for voluntary obedience of the law. A theory of obeying the law by persuasion is thus the ultimate commitment to a rule of law.

Predicting RJ effects on repeat crime by offenders

The question of repeat offending is often thought to be a small or limited part of the crime problem. UK evidence suggests otherwise. According to Home Office data, 76% of all persons sentenced for indictable offences in 2003 in England and Wales were people with prior convictions. If prior arrests had been used, the percentage of convicted criminals who had indications of prior crime would probably have been even higher. Based on people either caught or actually punished, then, most crime is repeat crime.

How can we tell how much crime RJ might prevent? A reliable prediction of how RJ will affect repeat offending by offenders attending conferences must first be based on unbiased evidence. Much of the evidence about RJ, even with very large sample sizes, is uninformative for this purpose because it is plagued with the bias of self-selection. This means that the kinds of offenders who complete RJ may be substantially different from those who do not, in ways that may predict their risk of repeat offending regardless of RJ. If people with lower risk of repeat offending are more likely to be offered, accept or complete RJ than people with higher risks of repeat offending, then the reason why RJ cases had less repeat offending would not be the result of RJ. The correlation with RJ would be what statisticians call a "spurious" association that reflects some third, underlying cause, rather than the effect of RJ. Much of the positive evidence on RJ suffers from this fatal flaw, especially the direct comparisons between RJ completers and RJ refusers.

Much of the evidence claiming that RJ does not reduce crime may suffer a different bias: the bias of measurement. Using police records on thousands of cases, for example, as the sole measure of the delivery of RJ may fail to detect an enormous variability in the content and intensity of the RJ experience. When RJ (or any programme) is rolled out quickly on a wide scale, there is a risk that many conferences will just "go through the motions" to "tick off a box", rather than treating each case as a kind of surgical procedure requiring careful advance planning, preparation and follow-up. With such heterogeneity of the RJ being delivered, the research is biased against finding any effect of "good practice" RJ, because no measurement was taken of the elements of good practice.

Randomised controlled trials (RCTs) provide the best opportunity to control both selection and measurement biases. RCTs generally remove selection bias because they first obtain consent and then assign RJ to some (but not all) of those consenting. RCTs also measure consistency of delivery of RJ, so it is clearer just what is being tested. Finally, the best RCTs analyse their data based on assignment rather than completion of RJ, so that any self-selection bias in completion is eliminated. While this procedure dilutes the effects of RJ, it maintains the capacity of the research to rule out spurious causes of a difference in repeat offending. RCTs are not the only kind of evidence that can help predict the effects of RJ on crime, but they are now available in greater abundance for RJ than for any other response to crime ever tested.

These controlled tests show that face-to-face RJ, consistently delivered by facilitators (mostly police officers) trained by the same Australian RJ training firm, has reduced repeat offending on three continents, for highly specific populations, all of which are identified by characteristics that existed before random assignment and are therefore considered by statisticians to be appropriate for subgroup analyses that produce . . . (see section 10):

- violent offenders under age 30 in Canberra . . . ;
- violent girls under 18 in Northumbria;
- male property offenders under 18 in Northumbria;

- property and violence offenders aged seven to 14 in Indianapolis.

Tests of other varieties of RJ, primarily court-ordered restitution or intervention of various descriptions, has also reduced crime among:

- violent families in Newfoundland and Labrador;
- adult male property and violence offenders diverted from prison in Winnipeg (and recidivism no worse than from jail for youth in Idaho);
- youth property offenders in Clayton County, Georgia;
- youth violence and property offenders in Washington, DC.

The rigorous RCT methods, however, have also found evidence that the same kind of RJ delivered by the same facilitators made little or no difference in repeat offending rates among police-selected samples of:

- property offenders under 18 in Canberra;
- violent males under 18 in Northumbria;
- property offenders under 18 in Bethlehem, Pennsylvania.

Most important, these same RCT methods have found that face-to-face RJ offered as a diversion from court causes a substantial increase in the frequency of arrests among a small sample of Aboriginals under 18 in Canberra arrested for property crimes, when compared with Aboriginals randomly assigned to court for similar offences. The Bethlehem findings, with many Hispanics in the sample, also veer close to significance . . . in the same direction.

These findings raise important "reason why" questions about the relationship between RJ and social "marginality", with both negative and positive implications. One question is whether offenders from deeply alienated social groups, such as Australian Aboriginals or American Hispanics, will react very badly to appeals for obedience to the laws of a government they perceive as illegitimate, if they do not believe their crimes to be wrong. The same question could be raised about Islamist radicals (who believe murder in the name of God to be moral) or certain Afro-Caribbean gangs (who may see violence as part of the moral rules of a business enterprise).

The other question is whether the emotional power of RJ could be customised to engage whatever authority structure may be effective inside such alienated groups. Mobilising older Aboriginal males to attend RJ conferences, for example, could increase the perceived legitimacy of the process among such offenders—changing their minds about the morality of obeying the law more than a white police officer or white crime victim might be able to.

Insight about other reasons RJ results, in general, vary widely among different kinds of offenders can be gained from a quasiexperimental (non-RCT) study of differences in repeat offending among offenders under age 18 in South Australia. This found, controlling for other predictors of recidivism, that the lowest repeat offending rates followed conferences during which offenders showed remorse, and in which agreements were reached by a clearly consensual process among the people in the room. Similar findings have been reported in long-term follow-up of juvenile cases in New Zealand.

The large magnitude of the RJ effects in this evidence—both good and bad—suggests that RJ is like a powerful drug that needs to be carefully tested for specific kinds of cases before it is put into general practice. Just as penicillin can cure infections, but cannot cure cancer or diabetes, RJ can reduce crime for some kinds of offenders but not others. And just as some people are so allergic to penicillin that it can almost kill them, some offenders may find RJ so enraging or humiliating that they are provoked into committing even more crime than they would have done without RJ. This evidence might be taken as a reason to ban RJ altogether, but only one such very strong reaction has been found to date, among a small sample of Australian youth.

All interventions in medicine, or agriculture, or public health (such as vaccination programmes) cause harm under some circumstances. Yet that is rarely sufficient reason to impose a complete ban on a treatment that offers benefits under some conditions. Instead, the usual response is to predict as reliably as possible when there will be harm, and then to apply limited prohibitions of the intervention under those specific circumstances. That approach has allowed antibiotics to save millions of lives. It could also allow restorative justice to prevent millions of crimes.

Predicting RJ effects on victims

The evidence on victims is far more consistent than it is on offenders. On average, in every test available, victims do better when they participate in RJ than when they do not. Victims may report dissatisfaction in the (very infrequent) cases when offenders refuse to accept responsibility, or if offenders fail to appear at a conference as agreed, or when offenders fail to complete outcome agreements. Yet the very high rate of offender attendance, remorse and apologies in RJ conferences far outweighs these exceptions, protecting victims from being "re-victimised" during the RJ. Instead, from Canberra to London to Indianapolis, victims who go to RJ conferences report that they are glad they went. The benefits they describe include less fear of the offender, less anger at the offender, and greater ability to get on their lives.

The reductions in anger at the offender extend to victims admitting they have less desire for physical revenge against the offender after RJ than before—a result confirmed in some tests by far higher levels of desire for vengeance among victims assigned to control group status than those assigned to an RJ conference.

In London, the effects of RJ on victims of burglary and robbery include large reductions in their post-traumatic stress symptoms.

Compared with victims willing to meet with willing offenders but who were not randomly assigned to RJ, victims who were assigned to (and completed) RJ reported greater ability to return to work, to resume normal daily activities, to sleep better at night and to stop their "racing thoughts". Long-term data on these victims may reveal how much RJ has improved their health, given other evidence that comparable levels of post-traumatic stress elevate risks of coronary heart disease. That, in turn, could potentially reduce National Health Service costs in an amount sufficient to justify spending on RJ as a disease prevention strategy for crime victims.

Could RJ reduce government spending?

Healthcare for crime victims is only one of several possible avenues by which RJ could reduce government spending. Perhaps the largest opportunity is in the reduction of the prison population, especially . . . in the area of short sentences. For somewhat less serious offences in which courts may be inclined to give a short custodial sentence, the addition of RJ could possibly tip the balance to keep them out of custody altogether. Even in robbery cases, London Crown Court judges have said that they had withheld a custodial sentence due to offender participation in RJ.

The possible substitution of RJ for prison is even more attractive if it would result in less crime. The reduction of reconvictions in Winnipeg with RJ as an alternative to prison provides evidence of that possibility. Even if there is merely no increase in crime, the cost savings could be achieved with zero impact on public safety. Evidence that in Boise, Idaho, youths did no worse with RJ than they did with eight days in jail is especially relevant to the debate over short sentences in the UK. At the pro rata cost of some £35,000 per year for each UK prison sentence, one offender kept out of prison for one year would cover the costs of more than 50 RJ conferences (at £25 per hour of police work for an average of 20 hours per conference, plus supervisory and overhead costs). That would equal one week of custody for each RJ conference.

Put another way, if only one in 50 RJ conferences prevented a year in custody, that alone could cover the costs of the conferences. The money for one year could thus be saved in one of two ways: by reducing sentence length, or by reducing the costs of repeat offending and reincarceration.

Another way that RJ could save money is in fees paid to lawyers by the government for appearances in court and at police stations. This would require many more defendants than at present to admit guilt in anticipation of a conditional caution involving RJ. Each admission of guilt—and diversion to RJ—could save thousands of pounds in legal fees for both defence and prosecution.

The Sherman and Strang reading makes something of a case for extending restorative justice techniques further. But other commentators have pointed out important limitations to expanding the scope of RJ. Kathleen Daly, for example, highlights several concerns:[63]

- Restorative justice techniques should only be used at sentencing, not at the trial phase. As Daly explains:

    The reason that established CJ is adversarial is that its adjudication process rests on a fundamental right of those accused to say they did not commit an offence and to defend themselves against the state's allegations of wrong-doing. [Surely] no one would wish to dispense with the right of citizens to defend themselves against the state's power to prosecute and punish alleged crime. The focus of RJ on the penalty (or post-penalty) phase can [thus] be viewed as a strength.

- RJ practices often rely on "thick social ties," and such ties "are not present in modern urban contemporary societies." This is perhaps a bit of an overstatement, but it does illuminate an important limitation: RJ will work better the stronger social ties are. And crime, sadly (but likely causally), tends to be concentrated in areas with high mobility.

    Question: Should we be concerned with how access to RJ will be distributed across various racial and social classes if it is delivered to communities best able to respond well to it?

- Daly also expresses concern about defendants possessing the necessary emotional maturity: "[E]ffective participation requires a degree of moral maturity and empathetic concern that many people, and especially young people, may not possess."

- RJ conferences score much higher on procedural fairness grounds than on real "restoration," where the latter is defined as remorse, spontaneous apology by the defendants, and general positive movement between defendant and victim. Daly hypothesizes that procedural fairness is predominantly in control of well-trained administrators, while restoration rests much more with the generally-more youthful and less predictable offenders and victims.

- Apologies can be hard to deliver sincerely. As one commentator cited by Daly points out:

    [T]here are "competing demands" placed on youthful offenders in the conference process: they are asked both to explain what happened . . . and to apologize for

---

[63] Kathleen Daly, *The Limits of Restorative Justice*, in HANDBOOK OF RESTORATIVE JUSTICE: A GLOBAL PERSPECTIVE (Dennis Sullivan & Larry Tifft, eds. 2006).

what they did. [The commentator] surmises that "offenders' speech act . . . may drift from apologetic discourse to mitigating accounts and back again." Victims may interpret what is said (and not said) as being insincere.

- RJ can likely be used only with a subset of victims, particularly those who experience low distress from the triggering offense. Daly again:

  > When comparing victim distress in 1998 with their recovery one year later, [a 1999 study found] startling results. Whereas 63 per cent of the moderate, 78 per cent of the low, and 95 per cent of the no distress victims had recovered in 1999, 71 per cent of the high distress victims had *not* recovered. Thus, for the most highly distressed victims, and RJ process may be of little held in recovering from crime.

  A fair limitation to consider, but not one that necessarily invalidates RJ. (Also note that Daly, unlike Sherman and Strang, is relying on a single study here, not a meta-analysis of *all* studies.) But certainly one that forces us to think carefully about where to apply it.

So how widespread are "restorative justice" techniques? It is hard to calculate a direct number, given the disagreement over terms. And, as Kathleen Daly points out, some processes classified as "restorative justice" are more-traditional approaches given a new marketing spin. At least in the United States, restorative justice programs appear to be popping up around the country, but CJ practices definitely remain the dominant norm, and even in the current "smart on crime" climate RJ practices do not often come up in discussion.

That said, the results from Sherman and Strang certainly suggest that it looks like a viable, if still not fully understood, alternative. Moreover, and perhaps arguably more important, restorative justice is an alternative that forces us to rethink the fundamental orientation of criminal justice. Look back on the "three questions" that Umbreit et al. discussed:

> The conventional criminal justice system focuses upon three questions: (1) What laws have been broken?; (2) Who did it?; and (3) What do they deserve? From a restorative justice perspective, an entirely different set of questions are asked: (1) Who has been hurt?; (2) What are their needs?; and (3) Whose obligations are these?

The shift from what laws/who broke/what deserve to who hurt/what needs/whose obligations is a qualitative, not quantitative, shift. All of the previous alternatives were focused on trying to accomplish the same basic goal, just in a cheaper or less collaterally-harmful way. RJ compels us to ask whether we are fundamentally asking the right question at all.

QUESTIONS

1. **Externalities.** Given the flexibility inherent in restorative justice techniques, don't we need *all* stakeholders present? If focusing just on defendant and victim, are there externality risks? On the other hand, might the more traditional system, relying on judicial and legislative sanctions, prioritize third parties too much, or ignore other externalities?

2. **Crime rates.** If restorative justice leads to more offending by lowering the perceived sanction, does that mean it shouldn't be adopted?

3. **Disparate treatment.** As long as defendants can opt in to restorative justice programs only with the blessing of the victim, should we be concerned that victims will focus on "impermissible" defendant traits when deciding whether to participate? If so, what if anything can the criminal justice system do to offset/rectify this?

We now want to turn our attention to what can be thought of as a variant of restorative justice: therapeutic justice. The idea here, most famously exemplified by drug courts, is less about reconciling the offender and victim, and more about focusing closely on the causes of the offender's behavior and trying to "cure" these problems. Like restorative justice, therapeutic justice reflects a move away from punishment and towards solving the underlying problem, but with much more of a focus on the individual behavioral failings thought to be responsible for the offending, rather than on the social networks that also regulate people's actions. But unlike rehabilitation, therapeutic courts work to keep the defendant *out* of prison. And unlike Restorative Justice, therapeutic courts in general, and drug courts in particular, are widely popular in the United States right now.

C.3. DRUG AND OTHER THERAPEUTIC COURTS

Over the past twenty-five years, we have seen the rise of various sorts of "problem-solving" courts, which adopt less-formal procedures in an effort to better target the underlying causes of crime. These courts tend to be less adversarial, viewing the goal as one of bringing the state and defense together to work out a plan that treats the root causes of the offender's behavior. Since the establishment in 1989 of the first drug court, in Miami-Dade County, the number of problem-solving courts has blossomed to approximately 3,000. As Michael Dorf and Jeffrey Fagan explain:

> Three institutional imperatives gave rise to the diffusion of drug courts. First was the docket pressure created by intensification

of the war on drugs in the 1980s. Second was the perception shared by the public and legal elites that the crush of drug cases led to a crisis in the courts, characterized by an ineffective system of punishment and a "revolving door" that recycled offenders without reducing either their drug use or criminality. Third was discomfort among some trial court judges with the restricted sentencing discretion in drug laws enacted during this same period, creating incentives for experimentation with sentencing alternatives. At the same time, the popular demand for punitive responses to control what was perceived as a runaway epidemic of drugs and collateral social problems focused the courts on solutions that blended judicial control with therapeutic interventions.

Drug courts provided a structure and philosophy that promised to resolve each of these tensions. Whereas the public at large tended to view drug-addicted criminals chiefly as a social menace, judges and other legal actors were more comfortable treating (nonviolent) offenses committed by drug addicts as a medical problem. Indeed, because drug courts emphasized both the individual responsibility of drug addicts and the disease model of addiction, they enabled persons with widely divergent views about drug policy to find common ground. They were, in short, an innovation well suited to the times.[64]

Another commentator draws attention to the strong link between drug and alcohol abuse on the one hand and criminal offending on the other and notes:

> Given the association between substance misuse and offending, success in drug treatment appears to have a measurable impact on lowering crime rates.
>
> For many years, the primary approach in the U.S. to reducing drug misuse and the criminal conduct attendant upon it has been to criminalize the unauthorized possession and distribution of controlled substances, and to rigorously enforce these prohibitions. This traditional criminal punishment-based approach has proven to be ineffective. More than eighty percent of drug-abusing offenders resume drug use within one year of release from prison, and well over ninety percent do so within three years. Even offenders who have received drug abuse treatment while incarcerated tend to exhibit a high rate of relapse, and those who receive no transitional care upon release appear to do no better than other drug abusing ex-offenders who receive no treatment while in prison.

---

[64] Michael C. Dorf & Jeffrey A. Fagan, *Forward: Problem-Solving Courts: From Innovation to Institutionalization*, 40 AM. CRIM. L. REV. 1501, 1501–1502 (2003).

In light of these failures, a number of advocates have called for an alternative medical approach to dealing with drug addiction. This approach views alcohol and other drug use disorders as diseases requiring treatment in the community rather than isolation and punishment. Critics of this strategy note, however, that success in treatment (measured as length of time to relapse) is directly related to the length of time that clients are retained in treatment. . . . Unfortunately, attrition rates for community-based substance abuse treatment are high. Depending upon the treatment modality, drop-out rates can run as high as ninety percent during the first year of treatment, which means that most clients who are "voluntarily" in treatment leave before obtaining a clinical "dose" sufficient to produce a measurably positive outcome.

Advocates of the drug court model and of many of the problem-solving court variations on that model point to the shortcomings of both the traditional criminal punishment approach and the medical alternative and argue that an integrated third way is necessary. In their view, combining the coercive aspects of the criminal system with the therapeutic tools in place within the community-based treatment system offers the best hope of retaining clients in treatment, thereby reducing relapse and, by extension, overall crime rates. This argument for deploying the coercive features of the criminal system to improve treatment outcomes has been widely adopted.[65]

Given their positioning as "third way" alternatives to purely punitive and purely medical approaches to the interaction between substance abuse and crime, drug and other therapeutic courts combine therapy/treatment alongside the threat of traditional punishment. In fact, in many cases defendants must plead guilty in order to enter the treatment court, giving the judge a powerful stick—the threat of incarceration on the original charges—with which to attempt to induce compliance with treatment. As a report from the Justice Policy Institute explains:

> While drug courts vary across localities and no drug court is exactly the same as the next, there are two main categories of drug courts: deferred prosecution programs (pretrial diversion method, or "pre plea") and post adjudication programs (post sentencing method). People who enter a deferred prosecution program are diverted into the drug court system before being convicted. They are not required to plead guilty, and are only prosecuted if they fail to complete the program. Alternatively, post adjudication ("post-plea") programs require participants to

---

[65] Richard C. Boldt, *The "Tomahawk" And The "Healing Balm": Drug Treatment Courts In Theory And Practice*, 10 U. MD. L.J. RACE, RELIGION, GENDER & CLASS 45, 46–49 (2010).

plead guilty to the charges against them, and have their sentences deferred or suspended while they are in the program. The sentence will be waived or reduced, and often the offense will be expunged from their record, if he or she completes the program. The case will be returned to court and the person will face sentencing on their previously entered guilty plea if he or she fails to satisfy the program requirements.

The original drug courts were almost solely pre plea, but according to the National Drug Court Institute, only about 7 percent of today's adult drug courts are diversionary or pre plea, compared to 59 percent that are post conviction and another 19 percent that work both with people who are pre plea or post plea. In total, 78 percent of all adult drug courts have a probationary or post plea condition.[66]

Thus while treatment courts reflect an attempt to attack the root causes of crime from more of a public-health perspective, they remain rooted in the criminal justice sphere. This tension often raises concerns at the same time that the flexibility of such approaches receives praise.

It helps to start by thinking a bit more about what exactly treatment or problem-solving courts really are. In a wide-ranging review of these institutions, Allegra McLeod points out that problem-solving courts are not monolithic in design, but rather can be classified into four broad categories of courts, each with different goals and approaches.

Allegra M. McLeod, *Decarceration Courts: Possibilities and Perils of a Shifting Criminal Law*
100 GEORGETOWN L. J. 1587, 1612–1637 (2012)

A. Therapeutic Jurisprudence Model

Specialized criminal courts adopting a therapeutic jurisprudence model are at work in every state in the country and increasingly in a wide range of foreign jurisdictions. In a certain respect, in the criminal law context a therapeutic jurisprudence model is a repackaging of a rehabilitative theory of sentencing that also borrows from restorative justice approaches, but therapeutic jurisprudence is farther reaching. The judge in a therapeutic specialized criminal court does not simply assign a sentence that aims to rehabilitate or serve a therapeutic or restorative function. Instead, the court proceedings themselves—whether through the judge's warm encouragement or "tough love"—are intended to promote therapeutic outcomes. The entire legal process—in fact, the entire institutional operation of the court as such—is to be reconceived on the therapeutic model. Accordingly, to the extent earlier critiques leveled against rehabilitative punishment and indeterminate

---

[66] JUSTICE POLICY INSTITUTE, ADDICTED TO COURTS: HOW A GROWING DEPENDENCE ON DRUG COURTS IMPACTS PEOPLE AND COMMUNITIES, 2–3 (2011).

sentencing may apply to a therapeutic jurisprudence model, they apply with even greater force because, on a therapeutic jurisprudence model, the rehabilitative or therapeutic ambition stretches beyond sentencing and punishment to nearly every aspect of the court proceedings.

Once a defendant opts into a specialized therapeutic criminal court, "all of the major players in the courtroom—judge, prosecutor, and defense attorney—explicitly acknowledge that the goal is to change [the defendant's] behavior, moving [the defendant] from addiction to sobriety and from a life of crime to law-abiding behavior." In contrast to the traditional adversarial model of the disengaged, dispassionate judge whose primary task is to decide cases fairly and impartially, therapeutic judges are active and engaged, invested in acquiring expertise regarding the problems they address. On a therapeutic model, the specialized criminal court judge—whether in a drug court, mental health court, therapeutic sex offense court, or another type of specialized therapeutic criminal court—engages in a direct, emotional, and frequently effusive manner with defendants, who are often referred to as the courts' "clients."

In Washington, D.C.'s Mental Health Diversion Court, for example, Judge Linda Kay Davis greets defendants by warmly asking them how they are doing and how they are feeling. She encourages them in their accomplishments and, for a sustained period of good behavior—clean drug tests and regular attendance of psychotherapy—she gives them a rose, a certificate, and a coin. In the spirit of therapeutic jurisprudence, Judge Davis asks defendants who fail drug tests or other court requirements "what the court can do to help" and extends and intensifies their period of court supervision.

The actual therapeutic or other effects of this engagement remain uncertain. Judge Davis, for instance, who was once a public defender at D.C.'s Public Defender Service, conducts her court in a therapeutic manner that appears eminently humane, though she has no formal psychotherapeutic expertise. Illustrating the bizarre quality and uncertain psychotherapeutic impact of merging judicial and therapeutic roles, one afternoon in mental health court, Judge Davis greeted a defendant/client with smiles and congratulations, telling the mentally ill defendant/client how "proud" she was of her, and how the defendant/client was "really doing well," about which the judge relayed "delight." But the clerk interrupted the exchange to point out to the judge that the day prior the defendant/client had tested positive for cocaine. Judge Davis then desisted in her praise, extended the defendant/client's term in the criminal supervisory program, issued a stern warning about noncompliance, and ordered the defendant/client to talk to the assigned therapist about the relapse. The mentally ill defendant/client looked visibly pleased at the judge's initial encouraging approval and then visibly distraught by the abrupt turn of events. The defendant/client reported to the judge directly (not through counsel) having difficulty finding an available individual therapist to comply with the court's orders as none were available, and she related that she was hanging out with drug users, which made it hard for her to resist using drugs. It appeared unclear whether the defendant/client understood that the role of the judge was distinct from that of a mental health care provider or other counselor. The judge listened in front of the full courtroom and then called the next defendant/client.

A therapeutic jurisprudence model . . . does little by itself to reduce reliance on criminal supervision and incarceration unless administered by a judge already inclined to reduce carceral sentencing and enable other positive interventions; and in fact, in the wrong judge's hands, a therapeutic approach may cause significant harm.

B. Judicial Monitoring Model

The defining characteristic of specialized criminal courts operating on a judicial monitoring model is that they rely primarily on judges to engage in monitoring of defendants or participants who may be asked to submit to urine tests and curfews and to attend court appointments as often as several times per week. The theoretical basis of the judicial monitoring model is that intensified judicially administered criminal surveillance will reduce future misconduct, at lesser cost than incarceration, and with greater efficacy than conventional probation or parole. As distinct from the therapeutic jurisprudence model, specialized criminal courts operating exclusively on a judicial monitoring model do not aim to generate therapeutic outcomes through courtroom proceedings. Instead, the judge is empowered to closely monitor defendants' compliance with court mandates in a manner akin to a probation or parole officer. On the judicial monitoring model, the court retains jurisdiction to monitor the defendant/participant during pretrial proceedings. And when the court assigns a non-carceral sentence, the judge mandates reporting back to the court on a regular basis.

The impetus for judicial monitoring courts arose largely due to an acute sense of the limits of conventional probation and other non-carceral forms of criminal supervision. Although probation is by far the most common criminal sanction in the United States, with caseloads of up to 1,000 probationers per officer, the degree of supervision is frequently minimal. Judicial monitoring aims to improve supervision by transferring authority to judges to monitor defendants. This transfer, it is hoped, will reduce recidivism and thereby reduce incarceration.

[A]s with the neo-rehabilitative approach of the therapeutic jurisprudence model, the judicial monitoring model is unconstrained by concerns of proportionality and operates without self-consciousness of its potentially punitive and overreaching, rather than purely deterrent, effects. Further, because a judicial monitoring model is frequently dominant in specialized courts where retributive responses are likely to be triggered—such as domestic violence and sex offense courts—the threat of punitive judicial overreaching in carrying out purportedly purely deterrent monitoring is of special concern. In other words, whereas the therapeutic approach tends to dominate in courts addressing more sympathetic cases—those involving drug addicts, veterans, or the mentally ill—the punitive excesses of judicial monitoring threaten to surface with particular force given that the model plays a central role in courts with less conventionally sympathetically received defendants.

C. Order Maintenance Model

The third widely occurring criminal law reformist model operative in specialized criminal courts seeks to advance order maintenance by convening local tribunals devoted to prosecutions of relatively minor quality-of-life crimes . . . that conventional criminal courts were otherwise inclined to ignore. The theoretical framework underlying the order maintenance model is largely derived from the broken windows approach to policing. The theory, as applied to specialized criminal courts, holds that, as a consequence of prosecuting public order offenses, crime overall will decline and, with it, more general reliance on criminal arrests and incarceration.

There are three supposed advantages to an order maintenance model of specialized criminal court administration, all of which fail to withstand close scrutiny. First, proponents suggest that these courts will increase potential offenders' perceptions of the criminal law's legitimacy and, hence, will increase law-abiding behavior overall. This is thought to be the case because the courts assign presumably more meaningful noncarceral sanctions. But order maintenance courts are often perceived as harsher and less legitimate than conventional courts in their response to public order violations.

A second purported advantage of an order maintenance model is that it will reduce reliance on conventional carceral sentencing, instead introducing more effective and beneficial intermediate sanctions, like community service. But when defendants fail to comply with intermediate sanctions, they are often punished with at least short-term incarceration. Indeed, empirical analyses establish that increased short-term incarceration is the unintended outcome of at least some courts operating on an order maintenance model.

Additionally, in a manner distinct from that of therapeutic courts, order maintenance courts widen the net of infractions addressed by criminal courts because they focus primarily on low-level misdemeanor offenses, which otherwise would receive less attention: disorderly conduct prosecutions are commonplace in order maintenance courts for pedicab drivers' obstruction of crosswalks or unlicensed vending of t-shirts or otherwise licit goods. Whether other beneficial effects on local neighborhoods follow from this net widening criminal law enforcement remains uncertain.

A final benefit noted by supporters of an order maintenance model, and of community courts in particular, involves the courts' revival of local democratic participation in criminal law administration. The local democratic potential of community courts is thought to derive from the involvement of community members in setting the courts' priorities, the local access to community court judges, and more general increased accessibility and transparency of the courts. Yet, the actual democratic potential of order maintenance community courts is unclear given that, as multiple studies indicate, only a small number of often relatively wealthy or unusually vocal individuals participate actively in community court programs. In fact, there is some evidence that these courts may serve to advance the interests of a moneyed minority interest group in furthering gentrification to improve property values.

D. Decarceration Model

A decarceration model is committed foremost to reducing reliance on incarceration and to a sociologically and empirically informed framework that links court participants to local social services and other institutions, shifting the management of socially disruptive conduct in part from criminal courts to other sectors. The ultimate aim of a decarceration model, as applied to specialized criminal courts, is to isolate those crimes for which conventional criminal law administration may be most fitting, contributing gradually to the de facto decriminalization of certain categories of conduct and enabling alternative non-carceral regulatory approaches to a range of social ills where criminalization remains appropriate. The basic premise underlying a decarceration model in the specialized courts context is that overcriminalization and overincarceration are in part structural problems, which specialized criminal courts may begin to address.

Courts operating predominately on a decarceration model circumvent some of the legislative impediments to changing substantive criminal law by working cooperatively with prosecutors, police, defense counsel, and elected officials at the local level to shift cases out of the conventional criminal courts. Without requiring legislative repeal of particular criminal statutes, these courts provide a venue for suspending or dropping criminal charges in drug cases, a range of misdemeanor cases, and, in some instances, even in cases involving more serious felony charges as well as in a range of matters involving mentally ill offenders and veterans. A decarceration approach seeks to locate alternative fora for responding to these matters, and then when the courts have obtained a certain measure of broad-based support, legislators are able to enact statutes that legitimize and institutionalize the decarceration regime. This method has proven to be more politically viable than seeking directly to decriminalize particular conduct, and alternative diversionary court approaches have garnered considerable public support.

In their day-to-day operations on a decarceration model, courts act as diversionary clearinghouses for social service resources, ensuring the assignment of individual defendants to those resources. Careful empirical monitoring tracks on an ongoing basis court outcomes to ensure that incarceration is actually reduced and to ascertain the effect of various alternative sanctions and services on participants and other relevant variables.

The theoretical framework that informs the decarceration model focuses on deploying social structures separate from criminal law administrative components—such as local neighborhood networks, business organizations, and mental health, public health, job training, and other social services—to reduce criminal offending and to foster socially constructive citizenship behaviors. The foundational idea is that social institutions outside the criminal law context are critical to the maintenance of social order and to organizing informal surveillance. Correspondingly, a shift away from current carceral practices will be enabled by bolstering opportunities for social integration and institutional involvement, particularly for those persons with otherwise limited access to such conventional social institutions. There is wide-ranging empirical and theoretical support for this structural approach.

The purpose of a decarceration approach—more conducive to adoption by conventional courts than reformist approaches that entail providing therapy in a courtroom context or transforming judges into probation officers, though certainly not typical of traditionally conceived courts—is to oversee the adequate provision of services to the class of defendants referred to those services and appearing before the diversionary courts, predominately by monitoring the service providers.

As McLeod's article makes clear, states and communities establish problem-solving courts to address several broad policy goals. Often a given court may address several of the four goals she lists at once. Consider the recent development of veterans' courts, the first of which was established in Buffalo, New York, in 2008, and which are intended to address offenses committed by veterans that are somehow related to their military service (generally due to PTSD). A real case-study can illuminate the multiple motives that are often at play in these courts.[67]

Staff Sgt. Brad Eifert suffered from PTSD as a result of service in Iraq, and once back home in the United States he suffered from depression, drank heavily, and contemplated suicide. After one particularly bad day, he ended up in a stand-off with the police; he fired nine shots at the officers, then threw down his gun and demanded that they shoot him. He initially faced five counts of assault with intent to kill a police officer, each of which had a maximum of life.

---

[67] http://www.nytimes.com/2011/07/18/us/18vets.html?pagewanted=all.

Ultimately, however, the case was transferred to a veteran's court. As the New York Times explains:

> On Aug. 2 [,2011], Mr. Eifert, having pleaded guilty to a single charge of carrying a weapon with unlawful intent, a felony, will officially enter the veterans court program. He separated from the Army on June 9. Twelve to 18 months from now, if he adheres to the strict regimen of treatment through the Veterans Affairs hospital in Battle Creek [Michigan] and supervision set by the court, the charge could be dismissed or reduced to a misdemeanor.

There are several reasons why more than eighty jurisdictions have established veterans courts. Some of them are moral. We as a society sent veterans to war, so we as a society bear some obligation to take into account the wounds—physical or psychological—that they suffered. There are also arguments that veterans are uniquely amenable to treatment, since they are familiar with highly regimented disciplinary regimes. In fact, veterans courts, like the one in which Eifert found himself, usually assign a military mentor to each defendant for just this purpose, to try to recreate some of the structure former soldiers were used to having in the military. Moreover, while veterans' courts are not "PTSD courts," PTSD is often a significant contributor to criminal conduct: judges may become experts on handling PTSD cases, avoiding the problem that judges in broader treatment courts may face in trying to understand a new disorder each day. These treatments may be more feasible for judges to manage as well.

A veteran's court therefore acts as a form of treatment court, as a form of monitoring court (via the mentor), and perhaps even as a form of decarceration court (by trying to link up veterans to non-criminal support structures that can help them manage the underlying causes of their offending). Not all courts are so multifaceted, but many often exhibit multiple goals or purposes.

Yet while McLeod's article raises interesting questions about the efficacy of problem-solving courts, it does not answer them directly. Whether they "succeed"—once we define what the means—is an empirical question. Although success is a particularly difficult term to nail down. Consider the following scenario:

Scenario: Joe and Kevin are both heavy abusers of illegally-obtained prescription pain killers. Both Joe and Kevin break into people's homes to steal things to either trade for drugs, or to sell for cash with which to buy drugs. Eventually both are arrested. Joe is diverted to a therapeutic drug court, while Kevin—due to nothing more than pure chance—ends up in a traditional court. Both Joe and Kevin plead guilty. For Joe, the guilty plea results in 18 months of treatment and intense judicial oversight; for Kevin, 18 months in prison.

Following discharge (for Joe) and release (for Kevin), both Joe and Kevin vow to clean up their lives. Both sincerely hope to stay off drugs, both attempt to reconnect with their families, and both attempt to find legitimate employment. Over the first several months, both Joe and Kevin remain drug-free. But staying off drugs is harder for Kevin, and in struggling with his addiction he focuses less on his family than Joe does, and his relationship with his wife and children sours, at times even resulting in violence; Joe's relationship, though challenged, remains much stronger, in part due to what he learned in the treatment program. And Kevin has a much harder time finding a job. While Joe lands a low-paying but steady job at a grocery store, Kevin is only able to find infrequent, off-book, below-minimum wage jobs; again, Joe's documented treatment history gives him a slight edge. Kevin's financial instability only adds to his marital problems, and it makes it harder for him to stay clean. Four months after release, Kevin relapses, returns to abusing prescription medications, and gets arrested once more for burglary. As he pleads guilty again, his wife files for divorce.

While more stable, Joe's life is still not easy. The grocery job is low-paying and tedious, and Joe and his family live paycheck to paycheck. Over time, the combination of stress and monotony wear on Joe, and the longer out of treatment he is, the harder it is for him to keep the temptation to abuse at bay. About two years after discharge, he too relapses and is eventually rearrested for a burglary. With much more reservation than Kevin's wife, Joe's wife too decides that divorce is the best option. And the grocery store fires Joe as he gets ready for another trial.

After two years, Joe and Kevin are in the same place: addicted to pain medication, unemployed, awaiting trial, and divorced. By their stories, is the drug court a failure?

The answer to that question is clearly a tricky one, and it cannot be answered without thinking carefully about what "success" means, as well as what sort of metrics of success the criminal justice system should concern itself with. Unfortunately, most of the empirical work on problem solving courts has chosen to focus on just one definition: reduced recidivism. This is clearly an important metric—perhaps even *the* most important metric for criminal courts—to consider; but it is just as essential to keep in mind that it is not the *only* one that matters.

Question: So, did the treatment program fail?

But taking reduced recidivism as our primary goal, what do the studies say? Not surprisingly, most work has focused on drug courts, and the results are not entirely clear-cut. A lot of studies indicate that defendants who are processed by drug courts recidivate less than those who follow a more traditional path, but in general the more methodologically reliable studies return weaker results.

Like with restorative justice programs above, the main challenge any such comparison faces is selection bias. If we simply compare the recidivism rates of those admitted to drug courts to those admitted to prison, we should expect to see a lower recidivism rate among the former group, even if drug courts have *no effect at all*. This is because we rarely randomly assign people to drug courts: judges and prosecutors divert those who they think are most promising, so the superior outcome for drug courts need not reflect the court itself but the sort of defendant chosen to participate. As the following reading indicates, drug courts do seem to have some positive effect, but not as strong as it may initially seem:

> Overall, this body of literature is methodologically weak with few randomized evaluations of each type of drug court and only a modest number of rigorous quasi-experimental evaluations of adult drug courts and juvenile drug courts. Of the 92 evaluations of adult drug courts, only 3 (3%) were randomized experiments, another 20 (22%) were rigorous quasi-experiments; thus, approximately 25% of evaluations were categorized as relatively rigorous. Evaluations of juvenile and DWI drug courts were somewhat more rigorous with a greater proportion of evaluations categorized into the two most rigorous categories, 35% and 32% for juvenile and DWI drug courts, respectively. However, only one (3%) uncompromised randomized experimental evaluation of a juvenile drug court has been conducted and four (14%) such evaluations have been conducted on DWI drug courts.
>
> [Mitchell et al. then list a few problem with many of the studies included in their meta-analysis. For many, the treatment group (those going to drug court) was not entirely comparable to the control group. Further, in a large number of studies the follow-up period was just 12 months, so little time to capture drawn-out relapse.]
>
> [The data] show a clear pattern of evidence favoring drug courts. . . . The general recidivism measure is both statistically significant for all three court types and moderate to small in size. . . . Relative to a 50% recidivism rate in the control group (a typical value), these translate into recidivism rates for the drug court of 37.6%, 42.2%, and 37.7%.
>
> [Mitchell et al. then note that these results are strongest for adult drug courts, and that the impact of juvenile drug court participation is almost nothing. They then report that only a few drug court evaluations measure actual drug use (via tests like urinalysis or via self-reports). The handful that do suggest that actual use does decline after participation more so than in

the control group, but the number of studies is too small to get statistically significant results.]

An important issue in drug court research is whether the effects last long-term. Assessing drug courts' long-term effect, however, is challenging. There are two inter-related issues. The first is whether the observed pattern of positive results reflects a suppression effect. Many of the outcomes are examined during the course of drug court participation. It is possible that drug courts suppress offending behavior while someone is active in the program but that this effect disappears post-program once behavioral contingencies are removed. The second issue is simply whether observed effects continue long-term, such as three years after post-program. [Results suggest that "the positive results do not appear to be simply a temporary suppression effect" and that the effects appear to persist to at least 36 months out.[68]

While the focus of empirical work has primarily been on drug courts, as problem solving courts have expanded so too has the empirical study of these other courts. Consider the following review of mental health courts:

> [Meta-analytic results suggest that mental-health courts (MHCs)] may be moderately effective treatments for reducing recidivism. The results also showed an MHC had the potential to positively impact clinical outcomes . . . and decreasing [sic] costly services such as psychiatric emergency room visits[,] but those findings were limited. It appears that MHCs seem to have the greatest impact on the reduction of recidivism among individuals who participate in those programs.
>
> This study also showed that the majority of participants in MHCs were white Caucasian males in their mid-30s. This finding is of concern given that among jail populations in the United States, as of midyear 2007, African-American males were the largest percentage (35.4%) of inmates in federal prisons, state facilities, or local jails. Additionally, some research suggests that psychiatric diagnoses are more prevalent in disadvantaged minority groups, and that schizophrenia is a common diagnosis found among MHC participants.
>
> A noticeable trend throughout this analysis was the considerable portion of individuals who opted not to participate in the mental health court program or who were deemed noncompliant and subsequently terminated. Unfortunately, there was not enough information contained within the studies

---

[68] Ojmarrh Mitchell, David B. Wilson, Amy Eggers, & Doris L. MacKenzie, *Assessing the Effectiveness of Drug Courts on Recidivism: A Meta-Analytic Review of Traditional and Non-traditional Drug Courts*, 40 J. CRIM. JUSTICE 60, 63–68 (2012).

to explore these trends empirically. It would be interesting to know more about the reasons individuals chose not to participate in the MHC program. It would also be helpful to know more about what precisely is meant by the term "noncompliance." Many studies reported that some participants were noncompliant but did not detail what this term meant or why the clients failed to fully participate in treatment.[69]

Drug courts and other problem-solving courts thus appear to "work," but it is easy to overstate their effectiveness. And their long-term effects remain fairly unclear.

Some Concerns with Problem Solving Courts

I want to conclude this section by considering several concerns that have been raised with problem-solving courts. We've already considered a few, such as whether they result in net-widening or increased risk of incarceration. Here I want to focus briefly on two more. First, can they be scaled up to any significant size? And second, how do they complicate the roles of defense attorneys and prosecutors in an adversarial system?

The moderate effect of drug courts noted above serves to only amplify a major concern that people have raised with problem-solving courts: they are very hard to bring up to scale. As Mark Kleiman points out:

> The question of whether drug courts can be scaled up enough to make a measurable dent in crime remains open; with fewer than 100,000 drug court slots to serve at least two million drug-involved offenders, drug courts have not yet reached the relevant scale. Their capacity to grow is limited both by the number of judges interested in playing the nontraditional role of a drug-court judge and by the profligate use drug courts make of scarce resources.[70]

Not surprisingly, Kleiman has been a leading proponent of HOPE, which was designed to avoid these sorts of scaling problems (and is discussed in more detail above). Unlike drug courts, HOPE relies much more extensively on the threat of immediate punishment to encourage the defendant to monitor himself. As a result, a single judge with access to only a handful of prison cells can monitor a large number of defendants, apparently quite successfully.

Furthermore, as Allegra McLeod points out in her article, drug courts focus only on individual drug users, not on the broader social and structural problems that lead to drug abuse in the first place. Given that such courts are more resource-intensive than more-traditional approaches, it is even more important to keep one eye on the opportunity

---

[69] Christine M. Sarteschi, Michael G. Vaughn, & Kevin Kim, *Assessing the Effectiveness of Mental Health Courts: A Quantitative Review*, 39 J. CRIM. JUSTICE 12, 17–18 (2011).

[70] MARK A. R. KLEIMAN, WHEN BRUTE FORCE FAILS (2009).

costs of scaling them up, such as diverting resources that could be used to tackle these root causes.

After all, showing that drug courts reduce recidivism does not necessarily imply that they do so *cost-effectively*. In a meta-analysis of drug court analyses published in 2011, for example, the General Accounting Office identified eleven studies that contained enough data to run cost-benefit analyses, eight of which reported positive net benefits and three negative net benefits.[71] Values ranged from net gains of almost $48,000 to net losses of more than $7,000. Of course, as always, comparison groups matter: the largest net benefit came from comparing the cost of drug court treatment to the cost of incarceration, while lower estimates compared drug court treatment to less-costly probation alternatives.

Thus drug courts and other problem-solving courts may always remain niche players in the criminal justice system. Which is not to say that they may not be quite useful in that niche: if drug courts are generally better for defendants than incarceration or a more-traditional probationary period, then the fact that they result in better expected outcomes for 70,000 to 100,000 defendants is nothing to scoff at. If anything, the inability to scale up drug courts may be less a condemnation of such courts and more a commentary on the sheer scope of our prison system (and the extent of drug abuse as well).

A second major concern with problem-solving courts is how lawyers should conceive of their roles when working in them. Our system is generally adversarial, and our codes of ethics require vigorous advocacy. But problem-solving courts are distinctly non-adversarial—or at least distinctly *less*-adversarial than traditional courts—and thus may force lawyers to rethink what exactly their roles should be. The excerpt below, written by Daniel Richman in response to a piece by William Simon, addresses some of these concerns.

Daniel Richman, *Professional Identity: Comment on Simon*
40 AM. CRIM. L. REV. 1609 (2003)

Lord Brougham[,] the icon of zealous advocacy, . . . saw it as his duty to "save [his royal] client by all means and expedients and at all hazards and costs to other persons and, among them, to himself." The question is, how comfortable would he be in a drug treatment court? Could he do his job? How well would he do it? Would he want to? And should we care if he couldn't and wouldn't?

---

[71] U.S. GOVERNMENT ACCOUNTABILITY OFFICE, ADULT DRUG COURTS: STUDIES SHOW COURTS REDUCE RECIDIVISM, BUT DOJ COULD ENHANCE FUTURE PERFORMANCE MEASURE REVISION EFFORTS (2011).

When defining the "key components" of drug courts, the Justice Department's Drug Court Program Office noted, "To facilitate an individual's progress in treatment, the prosecutor and defense counsel must shed their traditional adversarial courtroom relationship and work together as a team." After ensuring that, before entering a treatment program, a defendant understands his rights, the nature of the program, and the consequences of his failure, defense counsel's main job is to ensure that, once signed up, he stays until graduation.

While they don't deny the relief that drug courts offer from the rote and seemingly futile narcotics dispositions in regular criminal courts, defense counsel familiar with drug courts have had ethical qualms (at the very least) about the roles they are expected to play in these innovative regimes. Particularly in those jurisdictions in which an eligible defendant cannot enter the program until he has entered a guilty plea, defenders face an enormous counseling challenge. To raise or even take the time to investigate legal claims may foreclose the client's entry into the program. But to advise a client ill-suited to the program's rigors to waive any potential legal claims and expose himself to sanctions and ultimately a stiff sentence is also irresponsible. And knowing a client's suitability at this early juncture may be difficult indeed.

Another ethical dilemma, we are told, arises once a client enters the program. A client is alleged to have failed several drug tests and is threatened with a sanction. In her role as team-player seeking to further an ultimate therapeutic goal, the defense lawyer is expected to encourage her client to be truthful when inquiry is made at the status hearing. But as one defender has noted, providing such advice and "allowing the court to impose whatever sanction it chose" "would seem to be less than satisfactory" under the ethical rules.

Before one confronts the ethical issues relating to drug court defense work, one should ask: "Compared to what?" The reality (however regrettable) of our criminal justice system is that the alternative to therapeutic monitoring after a quick guilty plea is not a full-blown trial, but just a quick guilty plea. From his nineteenth-century vantage point, Lord Brougham would doubtless find scant difference between ordinary twenty-first-century criminal courts and innovative twenty-first-century drug courts. . . . Yet the dissonance between professional ideology and drug court practice bears special attention because the very premises of drug courts are said to be at odds with standard notions of zealous advocacy.

Even within this conventional model, Simon suggests, the zealous advocate can comfortably (and ethically) function within the drug treatment court regime. The key is to avoid falling victim to the Warren Court's blind allegiance to process and confusing the duty of zealous advocacy with the "duty" to assert every possible legal right regardless of the client's interests. Defendants have simply been given an expanded range of choices, and "the lawyer's role remains to help him make the choice that best serves his interests among the options open to him."

Simon has two answers to those who complain that they cannot ethically counsel a client about the drug treatment court option in the absence of fuller information: "[I]t's not unusual for lawyers to advise clients in highly uncertain situations." And, in any event, this uncertainty should diminish over time, as drug courts develop longer track records. Though beleaguered defenders ill-equipped to assess a client's treatment prospects at all—let alone in the short time they have to do so—may not be satisfied with these responses, Simon has a point. The sad reality is that much of what goes on in our criminal courts occurs at high speed, under conditions of frightful uncertainty. Perhaps the drug court calculus now seems more indeterminate than that in other courts, but that may change. On the other hand, given that the human frailties of a non-repeat player (as opposed to a court's sanctioning norms) may be the determining factor in case outcomes, Simon's confidence seems overstated.

Simon's response to concerns about confidentiality once a client has entered the program is to suggest that, at least in the drug court context, information control may not be a fundamental part of the lawyer's duty of zealous advocacy. That duty can appropriately be re-envisioned in this context as a charge to hold the program to its commitments and to force it "to justify actions adverse to the client in terms of the program's values and experiences."

I suspect that many defenders imbued with traditional conceptions of zealous advocacy would not be persuaded by this. Drug treatment courts—particularly those with post-adjudication populations—operate in the shadow of criminal sanctions, and often quite harsh ones. Indeed, shadow is probably the wrong word since in many jurisdictions (to switch metaphors) those harsh sanctions are always on the table. And to the extent that they are, a vision of advocacy that would strive simply to make sure the state explained its recourse to such sanctions is quite a departure from traditional conceptions.

Simon makes only a tentative effort to harmonize the role for defenders envisioned by many drug court proponents with traditional conceptions of advocacy. Rightly so. Diversity in program specifics is too great and the whole enterprise too new for him to press this point. In any event, it would be odd for someone who has so cogently pressed us to think beyond traditional conceptions to stay within that frame.

Simon's key move is to remind us that in many cases, but particularly in the therapeutic drug court context, some degree of paternalism is not only unavoidable, but appropriate. To exalt client "autonomy" for its own sake, and to think of the lawyer's role as trying to make the client master of his own fate at every single moment in time, is to be willfully blind to the disabilities under which clients labor, and the role that a well-designed program can play in enhancing clients' long-term ability to make choices for themselves. Having made this move away from a narrow conception of client autonomy, Simon recognizes that he has imposed on the defender a greater personal moral responsibility for her actions than is envisioned by traditional notions of advocacy. Indeed he embraces this responsibility, making a virtue out of necessity—since defenders will inevitably have to make rationing choices that optimally will rest on some assessment of the community's interest. And then another critical move: Conceptions of public values need not rest on the Warren Court paradigm of the defender confronting the state. If state power is exercised and tempered by community-controlled courts, institutional accountability can replace zealous advancement of a client's legal rights as the means by which public values are advanced. To the extent that drug courts are catch-basins for "quality of life" policing policies imposed on communities, this move does not work. But where these courts are organically situated in and responsive to the communities they serve, Simon's move has considerable allure.

Simon provides the basis for a nice response to those who wonder why the person at the side of the drug court defendant as he moves through his therapeutic regime should be a lawyer, and not some other sort of professional. To be sure, the short and sufficient answer to this question is that criminal defendants get lawyers, and the state will pay for them if (as is usually the case) the defendant is indigent. Drug courts just find a more useful role for those lawyers to play, and one that the state probably would not adequately fund if left for other professionals. But this short answer doesn't suggest why lawyers are well suited to play this role, as opposed to, say, social workers. Simon does suggest why. At its best, the team that monitors a defendant's progress will not simply be a selection of people with therapeutic expertise, one of whom is assigned to look after the defendant particularly. It will, like all optimal teams, draw on the "mutually complementary" capacities of a diverse set of professionals and will be more effective for the rich deliberations that the interaction of different disciplines will produce. Tied to a profession committed to discovering and opposing abuses of power, the drug court defender will bring a unique and helpful perspective to the problem-solving team.

Simon thus gracefully brings us to see the defender working in a problem-solving team as acting in the finest traditions of the legal profession, and benefiting from an association with the more adversarial elements of that profession. But the harmonization of role and professional identity that Simon envisions may be frightfully hard, and perhaps impossible, to institutionalize. Just as drug treatment courts exist (and flourish) in the shadow of a highly coercive system, so must defenders in drug courts work, far more than Simon admits, in the shadow of the adversarial ideology that keeps their colleagues going in regular criminal court.

In the Bronx Treatment Court, for example (according to a recent report), defendants must enter a guilty plea before they will be admitted into the program. "In agreeing to the plea charge, the defendant also agrees to an alternative incarcerative sentence if he or she fails to complete treatment." These alternative sentences are typically for one to three years, but are two to six years for defendants pleading guilty to B-level felonies. "These alternative sentences are fairly long" because, we are told, "the district attorney's office considers the treatment court more lenient with offenders, so that failing in the court implies consistent disregard for the court's authority and should be punished more severely."

It is thus not simply that the defender's contribution is enhanced by her professional connection to those ready to take up the adversarial arms forged by the Warren Court. She must also be ready at short notice to take up those arms herself. While in the context of a treatment program, certain sanctions may have obvious (or at least possible) therapeutic value, the same cannot be said about the criminal penalties faced by defendants who do not make it through the program. [T]he defender must . . . be ready to fend off harsh penalties with the very adversarial tools that may have provoked them.

Where does this leave us? The defender in drug treatment court should strive to play the facilitative role necessary for therapeutic collaboration. But she will have to be ready to embrace her inner Lord Brougham. This sounds like a bad Halloween skit, or at least a recipe for professional and personal confusion. Yet translated to an institutional context it is rather a suggestion that the experimentalism so characteristic of the drug court project be pursued as much in defender organizations as in the drug courts they serve.

QUESTIONS

1. **Pleas as preconditions.** The JPI argues that conviction should not be a condition for treatment, and that poor communities often lack access to treatment except through drug courts. Is this a fair concern? Is this a problem the criminal justice system can fix? Does it matter that drug courts were often created by the judiciary itself, not by legislators? After all, the latter have much more ability to take into account criminal and public health issues than courts.

2. **Proper evaluative baseline.** The story of Judge Davis's interaction with the mentally ill defendant is perhaps somewhat troubling. But what would the interaction have looked like in a traditional setting? Is our concern that this defendant would never have been in court but for the therapeutic option? Or, put differently, as long as we are going to require some sort of criminal justice intervention, how do we evaluate what is good or bad about therapeutic courts? What is the relevant baseline? Is it some ideal non-criminal, truly therapeutic mental health system theoretical

optimum, or should be have a much less appealing traditional criminal justice approach baseline?

3. **Net-widening.** Some have raised concerns about net-widening effects. But is net-widening necessarily bad here? And given that drug courts are costly to scale up, how serious a concern is net-widening? How many minor cases are making it into the limited number of drug court spots?

4. **Changing goals.** How could each type of non-decarceration court remodel itself as a decarceration court?

5. **Veterans' courts.** While many offending veterans suffer from PTSD, most veterans with PTSD do not offend. What does this suggest about the appeal of treating soldiers with PTSD differently? And why does military-based PTSD merit special treatment: might a child raised in a violent, high-crime urban housing project suffer from PTSD as an adult? How about an immigrant from a war-torn country?

CHAPTER 12
PAROLE AND RE-ENTRY

There are currently about 1.5 million people in prison, and almost all of them will eventually return to society, and most of them fairly quickly. Each year over 600,000 people leave prison, most (70%) onto parole.[1] To put that number in global perspective, every year more people are *released* from US prisons than the total number *serving time* in *all* European countries, by over 25%.[2] There are several million inmates now living outside of prisons (exact numbers are surprisingly hard to come by), most of whom are surely struggling with the challenges of making their way in society.

This chapter looks at the law and policy of re-entry, perhaps one of the most important and widely-debated issues in criminal justice policy right now, if only because of the sheer volume of returning prisoners. Most of the chapter will focus on parole. It starts by summarizing the points made in Chapter 10 about the challenges prisoners face when leaving prison, and it then examines what sort of support can best help released inmates avoid future re-offending. Once we have a sense of what we may *want* to do, the chapter turns its attention to what we in fact *do* do. After providing a brief history of parole, the chapter considers two major legal issues: (1) what procedures are used to determine who gets parole, and what rights do inmates have in the parole process, and (2) what sorts of restrictions can we place on the behavior of those paroled, and how well do the restrictions we employ advance the goals (what goals?) of parole? The discussion of parole will conclude by considering the relationship between parole policies and prison growth. Many have argued that our seemingly increased willingness to violate people on parole back to prison a major cause of prison growth, but the data suggests this may not be the case. After looking at parole, the chapter will conclude by briefly discussing three other broad tools that are available, but rarely used, to release prisoners and to help with re-entry: commutation, pardon, and amnesty.

Throughout this chapter, keep in mind the following results from a recent BJS study on recidivism.[3] Of 404,638 parolees released in 30 states in 2005, 68% were rearrested within three years and 77% within five years (with property offenders the most re-arrested, at 82%). In a slightly smaller sample of states, 45% of parolees were sentenced to prison or jail on a new charge within five years of release, with over half

---

[1] About 30 to 40 "releases" come from executions and another 3,500 from death by other (mostly natural) causes.

[2] In 2011, European prisons and jails held approximately 505,000 inmates. US prisons (not jails) released over 688,000 inmates that year. See http://www.idcr.org.uk/wp-content/uploads/2010/09/WPPL-9-22.pdf and http://www.bjs.gov/content/pub/pdf/p11.pdf (Table 13).

[3] http://www.bjs.gov/content/pub/pdf/rprts05p0510.pdf.

of those (more than 28%) heading back to prison. All told, about 55% of parolees had returned to prison on either a new charge or "technical" violation within five years.

So, is parole a failure? That more than two-thirds are re-arrested and over one-half returned to prison within five years may seem quite high at first. But keep in mind that 100% of those in the survey had been arrested and sent to prison at least once before. And we don't say that chemotherapy is a "failure" because a fraction of cancer patients still die following treatment. What,then, is an "acceptable" success rate? And what, even, should we count as "success"? Is recidivism the only relevant metric? These statistics indicate that we can, and should, think carefully about how to improve parole practices, but when doing so you should think carefully about what constitutes a successful or failed program or approach.

A. THE CHALLENGES OF RE-ENTRY

A.1. THE BASIC PROBLEM

As we discussed in Chapter 10, returning prisoners face a wide array of obstacles. Their available hours and wages are lower (from an already-low baseline), their health is worse, their relationships frayed. And all these problems exist before we get to the ones the government itself imposes, such as restricting access to public housing, food stamps, and other forms of support that returning prisoners may need as they try to get their lives back on track.

As a reminder, here are some of the key facts presented in Chapter 10:

- Unemployment rates are substantially higher: 62% of New York State parolees are unemployed, and as many as 80% of California's.[4]

- The wages of those who have never been to prison are about 20% lower than those who have, weeks worked are 45% fewer, and annual income is about 60% smaller.[5]

- HIV rates of prisoners are three times the national average, and prisoners are at elevated risks for diseases such as tuberculosis and Hepatitis.[6]

---

[4] https://www.parole.ny.gov/program_stats.html (last visited November 1, 2014); Mediha Fejzagic DiMartino, "Parolees Struggling to Find Jobs," The (San Bernardino) Sun Times, August 29, 2009 (citing the California Research Bureau).

[5] BRUCE WESTERN, PUNISHMENT AND INEQUALITY, at 116 Table 5.2 (2007).

[6] See, e.g., Andrew P. Wilper, Steffie Woolhandler, J. Wesley Boyd, Karen E. Lasser, Danny McCormick, David H. Bor, & David U. Himmelstein, *The Health and Health Care of US Prisoners: Results of a Nationwide Survey*, 99 AM. J. PUB. HEALTH 666 (2009).

- The rate of mental health problems in prisons appears to be about five times that in the overall US population.[7]
- Similarly, drug use and abuse among inmates seems to be about five time the national average (and likely skewed more towards heavier, non-marijuana, drugs).
- Children of incarcerated parents are about 10% more likely to engage in antisocial behavior than similarly-situated peers.

Now, of course, it is important to be careful when using these statistics: as Chapter 10 took pains to point out, comparing prisoners to national averages, as opposed to the average conditions in the (generally disadvantaged) neighborhoods from which prisoners disproportionately come, will overstate the negative effects of prison. But it remains true that stints in prison leave offenders more socially and financially precarious and in an overall worse off condition. Furthermore, since they are generally returned to the same environment in which they committed the crime that got them incarcerated, released inmates find themselves immediately subject to the same situational and contextual pressures that contributed to their offending in the first place. So while re-entry needs to focus on helping returnees confront the reduced opportunities and increased challenges they face, it also needs to impose rules that prevent backsliding from occurring in high-risk environments. As we will see, these goals are often in tension, something the parole system has frequently struggled with.

A.2. What Seems to Work

Before looking at how criminal justice actors regulate (or at least try to regulate) the behavior of released inmates, it is useful to first consider what is known about the forces that lead offenders to successfully desist from criminal conduct. But even before looking at *this* issue, though, it is important to realize that the very term "desistance" is a tricky one to pin down—and if we can't define what desistance *is*, how can we hope to know when we've accomplished it? So let's start with that: what is desistance?

A simple question demonstrates how complicated "desistance" can be:

Question: Bob has been committing various property and low-level violent crimes since he was 15. His behavior has been driven in part by anger-management problems, but also by persistent drug (heroin and cocaine) use which started when he was 15. He has tried to get clean, but he has inevitably relapsed,

---

[7] Doris J. James & Lauren E. Glaze, Mental Health Problems of Prison and Jail Inmates (2006).

in part because he lives in an economically depressed area and finds the frustration of unemployment too hard to deal with.

Now 34, he has just been released from prison for the fourth time, and he vows to himself "no more crime!" At the start he maintains his promise, but two weeks after release he is out with friends and smokes some marijuana. After that, he remains relatively clean, abstaining fully from cocaine and heroin, though occasionally using marijuana. Yet he struggles to find work. More sober than before, he is able to hold down some part-time jobs, but the economy is weak and he is repeatedly laid off. After a year, he commits some petty theft to make rent. And with his anger problem untreated, he still gets in the occasional fist-fight, though substantially less frequently than when he was using harder drugs. Has Bob desisted? Is his post-release behavior "successful" or "a failure"? If he did desist, at which point did it happen?

Our standard view of "desistance" is "cessation," but that is likely too stringent a definition. Changing behavior is hard enough under the best of circumstances, and most released offenders are not operating under the "best of circumstances" once freed from prison. Perhaps we should try to adopt more nuanced, complex views of what constitutes (at least partial) success.

John Sampson and Robert Laub provide a good summary of how to think about desistance and what it means, and what *that* means for evaluating whether our programs work or not:

> A clear and precise definition of desistance cannot be developed that is separate from a clear and precise research question. Developing a definition of desistance for the sake of having a definition is not worth the effort. Currently, there is no agreed-upon definition of desistance. Some definitions are vague. For example, Shover defined desistance as the "voluntary termination of serious criminal participation." Other definitions are arbitrary. For instance, Farrington and Hawkins defined desistance as having no convictions between ages twenty-one and thirty-two following a conviction before age twenty-one. Others are so idiosyncratic to a study or a data set that they are hard to defend. For example, Warr defined desistance as reporting smoking marijuana during the year preceding wave 5 interviews in the National Youth Survey but not reporting any such incidents in the year preceding wave 6. Other definitions do not sound like desistance at all. Clarke and Cornish write, "Desistance is, in any case, not necessarily permanent and may simply be part of a continuing process of lulls in the offending of persistent criminals . . . or even, perhaps, of a more casual drifting in and out of particular crimes." Finally, some researchers do not define desistance but purport to study it!

Weitekamp and Kerner have tried to disentangle the various components of desistance. They define termination as the time when the criminal or delinquent behavior stops permanently. In contrast, suspension is defined as a break in offending behavior. These authors also view desistance as a process (not an event) by which frequency of offending decelerates and exhibits less variety.... Weitekamp and Kerner recommend abandoning the notion of "spontaneous remission" in the study of desistance, arguing that the concept is unclear and theoretically barren. In a similar vein, Loeber and LeBlanc tried to disentangle desistance by specifying four components of the term: a slowing down in the frequency of offending (deceleration); a reduction in the variety of offending (specialization); a reduction in the seriousness of offending (de-escalation); and remaining at a certain level of seriousness in offending without escalating to more serious acts (reaching a ceiling).[8]

So what helps lead offenders down the vaguely-defined path of desistance? The following excerpt from a 2005 National Research Council report on parole programs highlights several key pathways away from crime, in particular marriage, employment, and the individual desire to change.

National Research Council, *Parole, Desistance From Crime, and Community Integration*
21–28 (2007)

In addition to the cessation or reduction of criminal activities, the concept of desistance as a process generally also encompasses positive outcomes in terms of individuals' behavior and integration into society. "[The] successful establishment of bonds with conventional others and participation in conventional activities are major contingencies on the path that leads to termination of a criminal career." More recently, [two criminologists] have argued that "desistance is a process characterized by particular behavioral states or markers" that is marked by the assumption of "adult occupational and family roles." Along similar lines, [another criminologist] has contended that desistance is only possible when ex-offenders "develop a coherent, prosocial identity for themselves." Thus, desistance is also generally viewed in terms of social integration or reintegration.

Marriage

Family and work seem to be especially important in the desistance process. The association of marriage with lower crime among men has been widely reported in both quantitative and qualitative studies.

---

[8] John H. Laub & Robert J. Sampson, *Understanding Desistance from Crime*, 28 CRIME & JUSTICE 1, 8–9 (2001).

Marriage, especially strong marital attachment, has thus been identified as a significant factor in desistance for men.

Recent research has extended this finding to women, but the researchers find the effects for marriage are less robust for women than they are for men. They find marriage reduces offending for males, especially for those men with a low propensity to marry. They find that marriage reduces offending for females, but only for those with a moderate propensity to marry.

A change in criminal behavior may not necessarily result from marriage alone; rather, a change may occur in response to an enduring attachment that emerges from entering into a good marriage. From this perspective, the growth of social bonds is like an investment process. As the investment in social bonds grows, the incentive for avoiding crime increases because more is at stake. Empirical support for the idea of marriage as an investment process comes from research findings that early marriages characterized by social cohesiveness led to a growing preventive effect.

Marriage also influences desistance because it often leads to significant changes in everyday routines. It is well known that life-styles and routine activities are a major source of variation in exposure to crime and victimization. For example, participation in unstructured socializing activities with peers increases the frequency of deviant behaviors among those ages 18 to 26. Marriage has the potential to radically alter routine activities, especially with regard to one's peer group. As Osgood and Lee have argued, marriage entails obligations that tend to reduce leisure activities outside of the family. It is reasonable to assume that married people will spend more time together than with their same-sex peers. There is supporting empirical evidence that the transition to marriage is followed by a decline in time spent with friends and with exposure to delinquent peers. Marriage, therefore, has the potential to cut off an ex-offender from peers at risk of re-offending. [It also "may transform the identity of the offender in ways that allow a life of greater responsibility as a spouse and parent."]

[Another study] found that conventional marriages inhibited continuity in criminal activity generally for both whites and nonwhites. However, the researchers found that conventional marriage did not appear to significantly inhibit violent arrests among nonwhites. They also found that common-law marriages increased crime (both violent and nonviolent) for nonwhites, but was insignificant for whites.

[A further study] also found that while marriage reduces offending, cohabitation increases it. This finding is important in light of the fact that by 2002, only 48 percent of black families were headed by married couples, down from 70 percent during the 1960s, and that one factor influencing this decline is the rise of incarceration rates, among black men since 1980. It would be important, therefore, to study the effects of marriage on reentry outcomes among a contemporary population of released prisoners. Data on the effects of marriage on this reentering population are needed.

Work

Like marriage, strong ties to work can lead to desistance from crime. One study using longitudinal data found that job stability was strongly related to desistance from crime. In a similar vein, a study using qualitative data showed that acquiring a satisfying job was an important contingency in the lives of men who desisted from crime. However, as in the case of marriage, the nature of the relationship between work and desistance is not known: it is possible that "selection effects" are affecting that link: some factor or factors that predispose persons to find and remain in stable employment may also predispose them to desist from crime.

One of the most convincing attempts to counteract selection bias comes from an analysis of data from a national work experiment that drew participants from poor urban neighborhoods in nine U.S. cities. Overall, the people who were given jobs through the experiment showed no reduction in crime relative to those in a control group. However, age significantly interacted with employment to affect the timing of illegal earnings and arrest. Participants aged 27 or older were more likely to desist when provided with even marginal employment. For younger participants, the experimental job treatment had no effect on desistance. The[se] findings . . . are important because the experimental nature of the data addresses the selectivity issue that has plagued much of the research on desistance. [T]his study provides more refined estimates of the effects of work as a turning point in the lives of offenders. Unfortunately, data for this study were collected from 1975–1979. Given changes in labor markets since the 1970s and current employment prospects for uneducated whites and minorities, the finding that work is a turning point may also be outdated.

More recently, [two researchers], in their evaluation of the Opportunities to Succeed (OPTS) Program, found that full-time employment among releasees increased with greater interaction with case managers and with higher levels of participation in drug treatment programs and that an increase in levels of employment was a predictor of reductions in drug dealing, violent crime, and property crime.

[Several researchers] note[ ] that there have been few rigorous studies of recent, employee-focused reentry models. New models of work programs for releasees . . . focus on providing coordinated services both before and after an inmate is released. Evaluations of such models show results that are only somewhat positive.

There are multiple pathways and factors involved in desistance from crime, including marriage and work, as noted above. Transformation of personal identify—that is, cognitive change as a precursor to behavioral change—has also been documented. Reduced exposure to delinquent peers fosters desistance from crime for youthful offenders. Perhaps the most obvious and simplest pathway to desistance from crime is aging: offending declines with age for all offenses. However, in spite of the evidence to date, interventions designed to help men and women desist from criminal behavior have been slow to target these factors, with the exception of those related to employment—job readiness, training, and placement programs. Such programs are easier to implement than programs concerned with marriage and family and peer associations.

One factor that appears to increase desistance from crime is reduced consumption of illegal drugs. The Federal Bureau of Prisons Office of Research and Evaluation evaluated its residential drug treatment program, which includes a transitional component that keeps former prisoners engaged in treatment as they return to their home communities. A rigorous research design included three methodologies to account for selection bias. More than 2,000 individuals were included in the research. After 3 years, treatment subjects were significantly less likely to be rearrested or have their parole revoked, than the control subjects (52% and 44%) and less likely to use drugs (58% and 50%). These results mean reduction in recidivism of about 16 percent. Arrests for all offenders also showed differences. Employment rates showed no differences. Moreover, in a 12-year follow-up of a sample of cocaine-dependent releasees, [several researchers] found that men who were continually abstinent for at least 5 years reported less past year involvement in crime, unemployment, and abuse of other substances than those who continued to use cocaine.

Other factors have also been proposed as important in the desistance process. With regard to education, [two researchers] found that education decreases arrest and incarceration, based on prisoner, arrest, and self-report data. Other factors for which there is little or mixed evidence include residential change, religion, criminal justice sanctions, criminal justice supervision (probation and parole), and a wide range of correctional and community interventions.

The Process of Individual Change

Processes of desistance have emerged that are common across a variety of problem behavior areas, including crime. First, the decision to stop appears to be preceded by a variety of negative consequences, both formal and informal, such as a prison sentence or the loss of a job. Second, multiple processes appear to be involved in sustaining and reinforcing the decision to change. Research on alcoholism, smoking, and obesity show commonalities in a process of three basic stages of behavior change: motivation and commitment, initial behavior change, and maintenance of change. Given this pattern, a realistic goal for ex-offenders, especially for high-rate offenders released from prison, is not zero offending, but reduced offending (reduced in terms of frequency and seriousness) and increased lengths of nonoffending periods. Empirical research on desistance has consistently demonstrated that this goal can be achieved.

There appears to be an important distinction between lapses (slips) and relapse, and much could be learned about the processes of change if more were known about which slips lead to relapses and which do not. There is some evidence to suggest that the determinants of lapses are different from the determinants of relapses. For instance, lapses are more commonly associated with situational factors, and relapses are related to individual factors such as negative emotional states or stress events. It would also be valuable to know more about the timing of lapses in the change process, how this process applies to desistance from crime, and how it operates in a context of severe official sanctions, such as reincarceration, which typically are not part of the dynamics of behavioral change for addictive disorders.

What is most important from this perspective is that the goal of desistance programs is not necessarily zero offending, but less offending and less serious offending. Less crime does not mean no crime: it is important for policy makers and program administrators to have realistic goals and to have forms of punishments and rewards available that will support those realistic goals.

There is also evidence that peer groups and social stability can help determine whether a released inmate is more or less likely to (continue to) desist from crime. The NRC report notes that juveniles who are separated from delinquent peers appear more likely to desist from crime. Moreover, stable residency appears to lead to more stable outcomes:

> Sampson and Laub underscored the importance of family in inhibiting offending during individuals' childhood years. Yet, the potential effects of parents or other relatives have not received much empirical attention within the context of adulthood. This is probably because for most adults relationships with friends and significant others become more important, and familial effects on adult behaviors become less proximate. However, offenders returning from prison are often devoid of social networks and/or ties, and parents and other family members can be (and often are) one of their few available resources that may facilitate successful reentry. Living with a parent or other relative may provide indirect control over offenders' behavior because even though the strength of the attachment between parent and child or between family members may weaken during the offender's incarceration, it could also strengthen more quickly than potential attachments between offenders and other prosocial individuals. Parents and other relatives also have a vested interest in seeing their family member succeed, and so they may be willing to assist parole authorities in the supervision (direct control) of the offender.

Although it is likely that some offenders' parents are poor and some parents or other relatives exhibit antisocial tendencies themselves, it is also true that even people who are deviant themselves can be good parents and "bad parents" are good parents much of the time. In addition, parole authorities often restrict offenders from living with individuals (other than parents and spouses) who are also under supervision or have a criminal history. Prosocial ties (such as between an offender and his or her law-abiding relative) can inhibit offending by bringing new resources to the offender and/or altering or expanding social networks. For all these reasons, it is reasonable to expect that offenders who live with their parents or other relatives will be less likely to recidivate.

Parole authorities not only have the power to restrict who offenders live with but also to direct where offenders live. Released offenders can be placed in halfway houses or homeless shelters, or referred to inpatient treatment programs. These referrals or placements can occur as the result of community sanctions for violations of conditions of postrelease supervision or as a part of case-management plans designed to address offenders' reentry needs. Regardless of how offenders are placed in residential programming, involvement in the program can formally control offenders' behavior by structuring their routines, increasing supervision over their behaviors, and limiting opportunities to violate the terms of their release.

In contrast to offenders who live in the aforementioned residential situations, offenders who are homeless or have absconded are in situations that lack supervision, assistance, and/or prosocial associations. Offenders living in these situational contexts often have fewer ties to conventional others and/or less to lose by deviating from (or further from) supervision. For those offenders in these situations, conformity may be less likely.

Offenders' residential mobility may also influence the level of control over their behavior. The inability to find and maintain stable housing can inhibit the forming of prosocial networks and decrease involvement in conventional activities. Residential instability may also weaken offenders' stake in conformity or attachment to their community. Findings from related studies suggest that offenders who move more often are more likely to recidivate.[9]

Note, too, that these pathways overlap. Familial stability may contribute to employment opportunities. The labor market, after all,

---

[9] Benjamin Steiner, Matthew D. Makarios, & Lawrence F. Travis III, *Examining the Effects of Residential Situations and Residential Mobility on Offender Recidivism*, 20 CRIME & DELINQ. 1, 4–5 (2011).

operates primarily through social ties. We find jobs by knowing the people who have jobs, or at least knowing the people who know the people. Thus a returning inmate with weakened social ties may experience less direct social oversight, but he also will find it harder to land a job due to his inability to tap into any sort of social connection to available work.

Question: Tricky Cause and Effect: One study purports to show that each move by a parolee in Georgia increases the risk of rearrest by 25%.[10] What are the potential "correlation does not imply causation" problems with this claim?

Thus a pattern emerges, namely one of stability: social stability, marital stability, employment stability. The law can try to help inmates lead more-stable lives, or it can impose restrictions that disrupt them. Thus we turn to that issue now: what does re-entry look like for the typical inmate?

QUESTIONS

1. **Proper sanction.** If we are going to define desistance as something other than complete cessation, how should we structure parole punishments? The traditional sanction is that parole violations, particularly the commission of a new offense, leads to reincarceration. Does that make sense?

2. **Recidivists and first time offenders.** Continuing the previous question, do you see any potential distributional problems with trying to distinguish between "lapse" and "relapse" for parolees?

3. **Deceleration and de-escalation.** If parole is reoriented towards managing desistance rather than demanding cessation, we'd need to focus on deceleration (fewer offenses) and de-escalation (less-serious offenses). What challenges does this pose for the parole officer?

B. THE PROCESS OF PAROLE

This section considers three issues. First, it provides a brief overview of the history of parole. Second, it turns to the more formalist/legal issues surround parole: do inmates have a right to parole? What sort of procedures protections do they get in the parole process? What sort of limits exist for the conditions that can be put on parole? And third, it looks to what is taking place on the ground, in terms of what sort of restrictions are in fact placed on parolees, and what sort of support are they given. The core question, of course, is whether these restrictions and assistance comport at all with the factors thought to successfully lead inmates out of crime. As we will see, the picture is generally pretty grim.

---

[10] T. Meredith, J. C. Speir, & S. Johnson, *Developing and Implementing Automated Risk Assessments in Parole*, 9 JUSTICE RES. & POL'Y 1 (2007).

B.1. A Brief History of Parole

The excerpt below by Joan Petersilia, one of the nation's leading experts on parole, provides a succinct history of parole in the US. Started initially as a carrot to encourage good behavior and training for post-release success, it became a central component of the rehabilitory goals that defined corrections in the US for over a century. Just like a patient sees a specialist for as long as it takes to get well, so too with inmates: they should remain confined until "cured," whether that is quick or not. But in the 1970s parole came under sustained attack from the left and right alike. And while rumors of its death are greatly exaggerated—a majority of states still use parole-based systems—it has changed significantly since its heyday during the rehabilitative era. That said, with rehabilitation making a seeming comeback, parole too could find itself more in favor, especially in an era of tight finances when "tough choices" have to be made.

Joan Petersilia, *Parole and Prisoner Re-Entry in the United States*
Perspectives 36–40 (Summer 2000)

Parole comes from the word French word *parol*, referring to "word" as in giving one's word of honor or promise. It has come to mean an inmate's promise to conduct him or herself in a law-abiding manner and according to certain rules in exchange for release. In penal philosophy, parole is part of the general 19th-century trend in criminology from punishment to reformation. Chief credit for developing the early parole system is usually given to Alexander Maconochie, who was in charge of the English penal colony at Norfolk Island, 1,000 miles off the coast of Australia, and to Sir Walter Crofton, who directed Ireland's prisons.

By 1865, American penal reformers were well aware of the reforms achieved in the European prison systems. . . . Zebulon Brockway, a Michigan penologist, is given credit for implementing the first parole system in the U.S. He proposed a two-pronged strategy for managing prison populations and preparing inmates for release: indeterminate sentencing coupled with parole supervision. He was given a chance to put his proposal into practice in 1876 when he was appointed superintendent at a new youth reformatory, the Elmira Reformatory in New York. He instituted a system of indeterminacy and parole release, and is commonly credited as the father of both in the United States. His ideas reflected the tenor of the times—a belief that criminals could be reformed, and that every prisoner's treatment should be individualized.

Indeterminate sentencing and parole spread rapidly through the United States. In 1907, New York became the first state to formally adopt all the components of a parole system: indeterminate sentences, a system for granting release, post-release supervision and specific criteria for parole revocation. By 1927, only three states (Florida, Mississippi and

Virginia) were without a parole system, and by 1942, all states and the federal government had such systems.

The percentage of U.S. prisoners released on parole rose from 44 percent in 1940 to a high of 72 percent in 1977, after which some states began to question the very foundations of parole, and the number of prisoners released in this fashion began to decline.

Parole, it seemed during the first half of the 20th century, made perfect sense. First, it was believed to contribute to prisoner reform, by encouraging participation in programs aimed at rehabilitation. Second, the power to grant parole was thought to provide corrections officials with a tool for maintaining institutional control and discipline. The prospect of a reduced sentence in exchange for good behavior encouraged better conduct among inmates. Finally, release on parole, as a "back end" solution to prison crowding was important from the beginning.

The tremendous growth in parole as a concept, however, did not imply uniform development, public support or quality practices. As [one scholar] wrote, "it is doubtful whether parole ever really operated consistently in the United States either in principle or practice." Moreover, [that scholar] notes that parole-as-rehabilitation was never taken very seriously, and from its inception, prison administrators used parole primarily to manage prison crowding and reduce inmate violence.

Despite its expanded usage, parole was controversial from the start. A Gallup poll conducted in 1934 revealed that 82 percent of U.S. adults believed that parole was not strict enough and should not be as frequently granted. Today, parole is still unpopular, and a recent survey shows that 80 percent of Americans favor making parole more difficult to obtain. A comparable percentage is opposed to granting parole a second time to inmates who have previously been granted parole for a serious crime. On the other hand, the public significantly underestimates the amount of time inmates serve, so their lack of support for parole reflects that misperception.

Nonetheless, over time, the positivistic approach to crime and criminals—which viewed the offender as "sick" and in need of help—began to influence parole release and supervision. The rehabilitation ideal, as it came to be known, affected all of corrections well into the 1960s, and gained acceptance for the belief that the purpose of incarceration and parole was to change the offender's behavior rather than simply to punish. [As] the rehabilitative ideal evolved, indeterminate sentencing in tandem with parole acquired a newfound legitimacy. It also gave legitimacy and purpose to parole boards, which were supposed to be composed of "experts" in behavioral change, and it was their responsibility to discern that moment during confinement when the offender was rehabilitated and thus suitable for release.

Regardless of criticisms, the use of parole release grew, and instead of using it as a special privilege to be extended to exceptional prisoners, it began to be used as a standard mode of release from prison, routinely considered upon completion of a minimum term of confinement. What had started as a practical alternative to executive clemency, and then came to be used as a mechanism for controlling prison growth, gradually developed a distinctively rehabilitative rationale incorporating the promise of help and assistance as well as surveillance).

The pillars of the American corrections systems—indeterminate sentencing coupled with parole release, for the purposes of offender rehabilitation—came under severe attack and basically collapsed during the late 1970s and early 1980s. [A]ttacks on indeterminate sentencing and parole release seem to have centered on three major criticisms. First, there was little scientific evidence that parole release and supervision reduced subsequent recidivism.

Second, parole and indeterminate sentencing were challenged on moral grounds as unjust and inhumane, especially when imposed on unwilling participants. Research showed there was little relationship between in-prison behavior, participation in rehabilitation programs and post-release recidivism. If that was true, then why base release dates on in-prison performance? Prisoners argued that not knowing their release dates held them in "suspended animation" and contributed one more pain of imprisonment.

Third, indeterminate sentencing permitted authorities to utilize a great deal of uncontrolled discretion in release decisions, and these decisions were often inconsistent and discriminatory. Since parole boards had a great deal of autonomy and their decisions were not subject to outside scrutiny, critics argued that it was a hidden system of discretionary decision-making and led to race and class bias in release decisions.

It seemed as if no one liked indeterminate sentencing and parole in the early 1980s, and the time was ripe for change. [Reformers] advocated a system with less emphasis on rehabilitation and the abolition of indeterminate sentencing and discretionary parole release. Liberals and conservatives endorsed the proposals. The political left was concerned about excessive discretion that permitted vastly different sentences in presumably similar cases, and the political right was concerned about the leniency of parole boards. A political coalition resulted, and soon incapacitation and "just deserts" replaced rehabilitation as the primary goal of American prisons.

With that changed focus, the indeterminate sentencing and parole release came under serious attack, and calls for "abolishing parole" were heard in state after state. In 1976, Maine became the first state to eliminate parole. The following year, California and Indiana joined Maine in establishing determinate sentencing legislation and abolishing discretionary parole release. As noted, by the end of 1998, 14 states had abolished discretionary parole release for all inmates. Additionally, in 21 states parole authorities are operating under what might be called a sundown provision, in that they have discretion over a small or diminished parole eligible population. Today, just fifteen states have given their parole boards full authority to release inmates through a discretionary process.

One of the presumed effects of eliminating parole or limiting its use is to increase the length of prison term served. After all, parole release is widely regarded as "letting them out early." Time served in prison has increased in recent years, but it is attributed to the implementation of Truth-in-Sentencing Laws rather than the abolition of parole boards. BJS data reveal no obvious relationship between type of release (mandatory vs. parole board) and actual length of time spent in prison prior to release. For all offense types combined the mean (average) time served in prison for those released from state prison in 1996 through "discretionary" (parole) methods was 25 months served; whereas for those released "mandatorily," the average (mean) time served in prison was 24 months.

As Petersilia's overview makes clear, the use of parole has waxed and waned over the years. Yet while many states have abolished parole or imposed truth in sentencing laws, it is worth noting that a slim majority of states still rely on indeterminate sentencing and parole boards, and even states with truth in sentencing laws do not necessarily apply TIS standards to *all* offenses. So for all the criticism it has received, discretionary parole release remains largest form of release today. The most recent data, from 2013,[11] reports that of the 430,000 parolees released that year, 184,000 were under discretionary regimes, to only 110,000 under mandatory policies.[12] Moreover, as "smart on crime" techniques gain in popularity (including the use of actuarial risk-release models), and as states continue to look for ways to rein in or reduce prison populations and correctional spending, support for discretionary parole may be increasing.

B.2. RIGHTS AND PROCEDURES AT PAROLE

We can break parole down into three stages: the initial grant of parole, the conditions imposed on parolees and how they are monitored, and how (or whether) parole is revoked if any of the conditions are not met. We will look at each of these in turn. We will start, though, by first briefly considering what parole boards look like.

---

[11] ERINN J. HERBERMAN, AND THOMAS P. BONCZAR, PROBATION AND PAROLE IN THE UNITED STATES, 2013 App. Table 5 (2014).

[12] **Discretionary parole releases** are what people generally think of when they hear "parole": a board evaluates an inmate to decide if he is ready for release. **Mandatory parole releases** are those that are used in truth-in-sentencing and similar contexts, in which the inmate is automatically paroled after serving a certain fraction of his sentence (such as 85% under the standard TIS regime).

B.2.a. THE PAROLE BOARD

States vary widely in the design and composition of their parole boards and parole procedures. At least fifteen states and the federal government have eliminated discretionary release, which greatly curtails the powers of and need for parole boards, and Kansas recently abolished its parole board altogether and moved its responsibilities directly into the state department of correction (though how big a change this will be in practice is not clear).[13] But most states still have parole boards, and these parole boards still retain significant power.

Though powerful, however, there is little consensus about what a parole board should look like:

> Most states provide certain statutory requirements for parole board membership. Many state statutes provide relatively narrow requirements for board members. For instance, in South Dakota, the board is required to have three attorneys. New York law requires that each member of its parole board have at least a bachelor's degree and five years work experience in the fields of "criminology, administration of criminal justice, law enforcement, sociology, law, social work, corrections, psychology, psychiatry or medicine." However, most states do not have strict requirements, resulting in underqualified board appointees.
>
> Provisions for judicial immunity and deficient release guidelines both illustrate parole board members' lack of accountability. First, much like judges and executive officials making discretionary decisions, state parole board members are generally given absolute judicial immunity against damages suits brought under 42 U.S.C. § 1983. Thus, despite the distinct due process implications of parole board hearings—especially parole revocation hearing—board members' decisions are insulated from liability. Second, parole release guidelines in states that have maintained their boards' release authority are inconsistent and often do not provide sufficient criteria to ensure accountability for release decisions.
>
> In most states, parole board members are nominated by the governor and approved with the advice and consent of the state senate. Aside from this common similarity, however, the state laws governing parole board appointments . . . are disparate. For example, the number of members on state parole boards may range from three members to nineteen. Most state statutes require that parole board members serve in their capacity full-time. Additionally, parole board members serve terms ranging from three to six years. The requirements for removing parole board members also vary from state to state. Whereas one state

---

[13] http://rightoncrime.com/2011/04/kansas-abolishes-its-parole-board/.

may allow removal only for cause, another state may offer very little protection for parole board members and remind them that they serve at the pleasure of the Governor. This threat of removal introduces a "political element" into the parole process. Parole board members seeking to serve another term are likely to act in accordance with the goals of the administration so they can ensure reappointment. Parole boards also face pressure from sources beyond the political sphere. Members are "prone to bend to community pressure in connection with decisions to award or deny parole to notorious criminals."

Some states do not specify any particular requirements for parole board membership. Other states use vague and expansive language without mentioning any specific criteria. A few states provide only that parole board members should reflect "a cross section of the racial, sexual, economic, and geographic features of the population of the state." Some states, on the other hand, require parole board members to meet more rigorous requirements for appointment such as extensive experience in certain disciplines or a Bachelor's degree. In certain states, statutes provide that the board must consist of a person who has been the victim of a crime.

As a result of these disparate requirements, the makeup of parole boards is extremely different from state to state. For example, in Kentucky, the nine-member parole board has two attorneys, one retired teacher, and six members with a background in criminal justice and corrections. On the other hand, each member of Utah's five-member parole board has received a Juris Doctorate.[14]

As Bing points out, not only do boards vary in how they are composed, but in what they are asked to do:

> Currently, all fifty states have parole boards in some fashion. However, sixteen states have cancelled the release authority of their boards. Congress passed the Violent Crime Control and Law Enforcement Act of 1994 which, inter alia, provides funding for additional state prisons for states that meet certain criteria. One of these criterion, called "truth-in-sentencing," requires that States enact laws that require persons convicted of violent crimes "to serve not less than 85 percent" of the prison sentence. One effect of the "truth-in-sentencing" requirement has been the diminution of the importance of parole boards in certain states. Eight states abolished parole board release during the same year a truth-in-sentencing law was passed. Nevertheless, these states retain their parole boards to make decisions regarding

---

[14] Stefan J. Bing, *Reconsidering State Parole Board Membership Requirements in Light of Model Penal Code Sentencing Revisions*, 100 KY L. J. 871, 872–877 (2012).

persons sentenced "prior to the effective date of the law that eliminated parole board release." Moreover, in addition to establishing the date of release, parole boards supervise felons after their release from incarceration.[15]

A 2008 survey of forty-four state releasing agencies/parole boards yielded the following findings.

Susan C. Kinnevy & Joel M. Caplan, *National Surveys of State Paroling Authorities: Models of Service Delivery*
74 Federal Probation (2010)

The concept of parole has been around for more than a century in the United States and the goals and activities of parole agencies have evolved over time as social and political environments changed. Throughout the history of parole, calls for reform and new parole models have been voiced by prominent criminologists; however, no attempts were made to identify existing commonalities among state paroling authorities (i.e., parole boards). They are often nonchalantly categorized by authors of published articles and reports using binary descriptors that meet their literary needs. For example, two categorizations commonly referenced in the literature are *discretionary* parole, by which paroling authorities decide releases for eligible inmates on a case-by-case basis, and *mandatory* parole, by which judges or statutes define parole release as a function of an inmate's sentence. *Indeterminate and determinate* sentencing structures have also been used repeatedly to describe paroling authorities. Other less common descriptors include *casework* and *surveillance* models, *summary parole and regular parole* models, and *part-time parole boards and full-time parole boards*.

This exploratory study assumed that paroling authorities (Pas) are more complex in terms of their structures and operations than their traditional references, which only describe one aspect of parole and are not exhaustive. The limited attention given to parole models may be attributable to the fact that reasonable people can disagree over which label best characterizes a particular agency or jurisdiction. However, this explanation does not account for the absence of models that aggregate shared attributes of PAs among different states rather than debate experts' preferences. A census of contemporary paroling authority (PA) attributes must be identified first before new models can be developed or existing models improved. Heeding calls for reform of parole is difficult when the system of independent agencies is greatly unknown in the broader context of the nation.

---

[15] *Id.* at 872–873.

Overview of Parole in the U.S.: Key Findings from the APAI Survey

Most paroling authorities . . . consist of members appointed by the governor and who serve an average of five years. They are most often independent agencies or affiliated with the Department of Corrections. A majority of state PAs have the authority to make final release decisions and make those decisions within a mixed determinate and indeterminate sentencing structure. Over half the PAs require interviews with parole-eligible offenders prior to release, with most interviews conducted in-person by a panel of PA members. A minimum of three panel members and three votes are needed to decide release.

The top three sources of input considered by PAs in their release decision-making process are from the victim, the offender's family and the district attorney. Other factors that impact most heavily on the decision to release are crime severity, crime type, and offender criminal history, respectively. The most frequently cited factor in delayed release is a delay in program completion. Program completion is a prerequisite for release in most states; almost all PAs report that they do not have enough available programs. Most states do give time off credits (TOC), the most common one being statutory good time.

More than half of PAs have full authority over supervision and most have the power to set conditions of supervision for all their offenders across crime categories. More than half the PAs also have the authority to terminate supervision prior to maximum sentence for all offenders across crime categories. The most often cited responses to violations of supervision are outpatient and inpatient treatment programs, electronic monitoring, and house arrest. Most PAs can approve motions to revoke parole and over half can issue arrest warrants. Almost all PAs have the authority to manage or adjudicate violations, although only 75 percent can set the time to serve for revocation.

Over 90 percent of PAs can revoke supervision for all offenders across crime categories. Most PAs include both revocation options that return offenders to prison with or without treatment and non-revocation options that place offenders in intermediate sanctions or community-based facilities. Management of community-based facilities usually resides with the states' correctional authority. With regard to instruments used to guide the parole process, the most commonly cited are Static-99, LSI-R, and instruments developed in-house. However, the only instruments that are routinely validated are those developed in-house.

The most easily produced and regularly published statistic by PAs is the number of offenders paroled in a given calendar year. Other statistics seem to be difficult to produce, apparently because the PAs are not always the entity that manages statistics. Only 29 PAs provided recidivism rates, with averages ranging from 25.1 percent calculated for one year to 4.28 percent calculated for over three years. The offender population used to calculate rates varied too much to report a pattern. The events used to calculate recidivism were generally those that resulted in incarceration. Only 19 PAs reported having secure facilities that can be used in place of incarceration.

[*Ed. note*: the tables below summarize the findings of the survey in more compact form than in the original report. Note that the numbers often do not add up to forty-four (the total number of surveyed states), due to various under-reporting issues with the survey. The survey divided up its analysis into four categories: structural differences (how the board was structured and the powers that it has), pre-release differences (how it decides who to release), post-release supervision differences (how it supervises releases), and post-release revocation differences (how it decides whose parole to revoke).]

Structural Differences

Terminate before max time	Can set minimum time	Authority to release offenders	Board Membership	Number of States
Yes	Yes	Yes	Full time	2
Yes	Yes	Yes	Part time	1
Yes	Yes	Yes	Mixed time	3
Yes	No	Yes	Full time	11
Yes	No	Yes	Part time	6
Yes	No	Yes	Mixed time	3
No	Yes	Yes	Full time	1
No	Yes	Yes	Part time	1
No	No	Yes	Full time	7
No	No	Yes	Mixed time	3
No	No	No	Part time	1
No	No	No	Mixed time	1

Pre-Release Differences

Time off credits available	Program completion required	Use assessment model	Number of states
Yes	Yes	Yes	24
Yes	Yes	No	4

Yes	No	Yes	3
Yes	No	No	2
No	Yes	Yes	9
No	Yes	No	2

Post-Release Supervision Differences

Assessment models used to set levels	Assessment models used to set conditions	Set conditions for parole	Full authority over parolees	Number of states
Yes	Yes	Yes	Yes	13
Yes	Yes	Yes	No	6
Yes	No	Yes	Yes	2
Yes	No	Yes	No	1
No	Yes	Yes	No	1
No	No	Yes	Yes	4
No	No	Yes	No	5

Post-Release Revocation Differences

Risk assessment tool for revocation	Authority to revoke supervision	Number of states
Yes	Yes	12
No	Yes	31
No	No	1

As the survey indicates, there is a wide range in how parole boards are designed. Which leads to a perhaps some obvious, but challenging, questions:

QUESTIONS

1. **Optimal design:** Which set of options seemed to be the "best"? Does your answer depend on what the goals of punishment are?

2. **Locus of variation:** Putting aside truth-in-sentencing laws, which apply a unique set of rules to specific violent offenses, does it make sense that rules vary *across* states but generally not across *offenses* or *offenders*? Would it make more sense to apply one set of rules (say, using actuarial

models but limited authority over parolees) for one set of offenses but a different set of rules for another?

As the Bing reading points out, sixteen states and the federal government have abolished discretionary parole release. In 2013, 4 states released no inmates via discretionary parole, and another 11 used discretionary release for only a small fraction of their parolee population.[16] Yet these states are still releasing inmates every year onto parole—over 110,000 via mandatory parole alone—only according to substantially more fixed schedules, not the discretionary choices of a parole board. Whatever the new(ish) restrictions on it, parole remains a core aspect of our sentencing regimes.

B.2.b. GRANTING PAROLE

As noted above, there are two broad means by which states grant parole: discretionary releases and mandatory releases. In a discretionary release regime, parole board members decide whether an inmate qualifies for parole once he is eligible for release (which is determined by the sentence initially imposed by the judge). In a mandatory regime, inmates are released according to a much more fixed schedule based on the initial sentence and some number of good-time credits awarded by the prison. In these latter cases, the inmate is still subjected to post-release supervision and monitoring, just like the "traditional" parolee, but the board has much less discretion—in many cases, arguably none—to determine when that release takes place.

In this section, we will focus primarily on discretionary parole regimes, since (1) the legal issues are more intriguing, and (2) it remains the dominant policy in the country, despite over thirty years of efforts to rein in parole's use. To get a sense for how discretionary parole grants are determined, we start by looking at the limitations the Constitution imposes on parole hearings, and we then turn to what procedural protections state statutes create. We will then briefly consider what power parole boards have.

B.2.b.i. *Constitutional and Statutory Protections*

The constitutional law of parole hearings, at least, is easy to summarize: in *Greenholtz v. Inmates of Neb. Penal & Corr. Complex* (excerpted below), the Supreme Court held as long as parole is discretionary, inmates have no right to the state's mercy and thus no right to any sort of due process protections over how parole is determined. Whether this is *sound*, either doctrinally or policy-wise, is a much more complex issue, but the law is at least straightforward in this instance.

---

[16] HERBERMAN AND BONCZAR, supra note 11 at App. Table 5.

Greenholtz v. Inmates of Neb. Penal & Corr. Complex
442 U.S. 1 (1979)

■ CHIEF JUSTICE BURGER delivered the opinion of the Court.

We granted certiorari to decide whether the Due Process Clause of the Fourteenth Amendment applies to discretionary parole-release determinations made by the Nebraska Board of Parole, and, if so, whether the procedures the Board currently provides meet constitutional requirements. [Inmates in Nebraska claimed that the state's parole procedures—which consisted of an initial review of documentation and an informal interview followed by a second hearing if the inmates was considered to be a viable candidate for parole—were insufficient and challenged them under the Due Process clause.]

The Due Process Clause applies when government action deprives a person of liberty or property; accordingly, when there is a claimed denial of due process we have inquired into the nature of the individual's claimed interest. [T]o determine whether due process requirements apply in the first place, we must look not to the "weight" but to the *nature* of the interest at stake. This has meant that to obtain a protectible right a person clearly must have more than an abstract need or desire for it. He must have more than a unilateral expectation of it. He must, instead, have a legitimate claim of entitlement to it.

There is no constitutional or inherent right of a convicted person to be conditionally released before the expiration of a valid sentence. The natural desire of an individual to be released is indistinguishable from the initial resistance to being confined. But the conviction, with all its procedural safeguards, has extinguished that liberty right: [G]iven a valid conviction, the criminal defendant has been constitutionally deprived of his liberty.

Decisions of the Executive Branch, however serious their impact, do not automatically invoke due process protection; there simply is no constitutional guarantee that all executive decisionmaking must comply with standards that assure error-free determinations. This is especially true with respect to the sensitive choices presented by the administrative decision to grant parole release.

A state may, as Nebraska has, establish a parole system, but it has no duty to do so. Moreover, to insure that the state-created parole system serves the public-interest purposes of rehabilitation and deterrence, the state may be specific or general in defining the conditions for release and the factors that should be considered by the parole authority. It is thus not surprising that there is no prescribed or defined combination of facts which, if shown, would mandate release on parole. Indeed, the very institution of parole is still in an experimental stage. In parole releases, like its siblings probation release and institution rehabilitation, few certainties exist. In each case, the decision differs from the traditional mold of judicial decisionmaking in that the choice involves a synthesis of record facts and personal observation filtered through the experience of the decisionmaker and leading to a predictive judgment as to what is best both for the individual inmate and for the community. This latter conclusion requires the Board to assess whether, in light of the nature of the crime, the inmate's release will minimize the gravity of the offense, weaken the deterrent impact on others, and undermine respect for the administration of justice. The entire inquiry is, in a sense, an "equity" type judgment that cannot always be articulated in traditional findings.

Respondents suggest two theories to support their view that they have a constitutionally protected interest in a parole determination which calls for the process mandated by the Court of Appeals. First, they claim that a reasonable entitlement is created whenever a state provides for the *possibility* of parole. Alternatively, they claim that the language in Nebraska's statute creates a legitimate expectation of parole, invoking due process protections.

In support of their first theory, respondents rely heavily on *Morrissey v. Brewer* [see below], where we held that a parole-revocation determination must meet certain due process standards They argue that the ultimate interest at stake both in a parole-revocation decision and in a parole determination is conditional liberty and that since the underlying interest is the same the two situations should be accorded the same constitutional protection.

The fallacy in respondents' position is that parole *release* and parole *revocation* are quite different. There is a crucial distinction between being deprived of a liberty one has, as in parole, and being denied a conditional liberty that one desires. The parolees in *Morrissey* . . . were at liberty and as such could "be gainfully employed and [were] free to be with family and friends and to form the other enduring attachments of normal life." The inmates here, on the other hand, are confined and thus subject to all of the necessary restraints that inhere in a prison.

A second important difference between discretionary parole *release* from confinement and *termination* of parole lies in the nature of the decision that must be made in each case. As we recognized in *Morrissey*, the parole-revocation determination actually requires two decisions: whether the parolee in fact acted in violation of one or more conditions of parole and whether the parolee should be recommitted either for his or society's benefit. The first step in a revocation decision thus involves a wholly retrospective factual question.

The parole-release decision, however, is more subtle and depends on an amalgam of elements, some of which are factual but many of which are purely subjective appraisals by the Board members based upon their experience with the difficult and sensitive task of evaluating the advisability of parole release. Unlike the revocation decision, there is no set of facts which, if shown, mandate a decision favorable to the individual. The decision turns on a discretionary assessment of a multiplicity of imponderables, entailing primarily what a man is and what he may become rather than simply what he has done.

That the state holds out the *possibility* of parole provides no more than a mere hope that the benefit will be obtained. To that extent the general interest asserted here is no more substantial than the inmate's hope that he will not be transferred to another prison, a hope which is not protected by due process.

Respondents' second argument is that the Nebraska statutory language itself creates a protectible expectation of parole. They rely on the section which provides in part:

"Whenever the Board of Parole considers the release of a committed offender who is eligible for release on parole, it shall order his release unless it is of the opinion that his release should be deferred because:

"(a) There is a substantial risk that he will not conform to the conditions of parole;

"(b) His release would depreciate the seriousness of his crime or promote disrespect for law;

"(c) His release would have a substantially adverse effect on institutional discipline; or

"(d) His continued correctional treatment, medical care, or vocational or other training in the facility will substantially enhance his capacity to lead a law-abiding life when released at a later date."

Respondents emphasize that the structure of the provision together with the use of the word "shall" binds the Board of Parole to release an inmate unless any one of the four specifically designated reasons are found. In their view, the statute creates a presumption that parole release will be granted, and that this in turn creates a legitimate expectation of release absent the requisite finding that one of the justifications for deferral exists.

It is axiomatic that due process "is flexible and calls for such procedural protections as the particular situation demands." The function of legal process, as that concept is embodied in the Constitution, and in the realm of factfinding, is to minimize the risk of erroneous decisions.

Procedures designed to elicit specific facts, such as those required in *Morrissey* [and other parole and probation cases] are not necessarily appropriate to a Nebraska parole determination. Merely because a statutory expectation exists cannot mean that in addition to the full panoply of due process required to convict and confine there must also be repeated, adversary hearings in order to continue the confinement. However, since the Nebraska Parole Board provides at least one and often two hearings every year to each eligible inmate, we need only consider whether . . . additional procedures . . . are required under [our Constitutional] standards. . . .

[In the appellate case that led to this opinion, the Circuit Court imposed several additional procedural requirements on the Nebraska parole board.] Two procedures mandated by the Court of Appeals are particularly challenged by the Board: the requirement that a formal hearing be held for every inmate, and the requirement that every adverse parole decision include a statement of the evidence relied upon by the Board.

The requirement of a hearing . . . in all cases would provide at best a negligible decrease in the risk of error. At the Board's initial interview hearing, the inmate is permitted to appear before the Board and present letters and statements on his own behalf. He is thereby provided with an effective opportunity, first, to insure that the records before the Board are in fact the records relating to his case; and, second, to present any special considerations demonstrating why he is an appropriate candidate for parole. Since the decision is one that must be made largely on the basis of the inmate's files, this procedure adequately safeguards against serious risks of error and thus satisfies due process.

Next, we find nothing in the due process concepts as they have thus far evolved that requires the Parole Board to specify the particular "evidence" in the inmate's file or at his interview on which it rests the discretionary determination that an inmate is not ready for conditional release. The Board communicates the reason for its denial as a guide to the inmate for his future behavior. To require the parole authority to provide a summary of the evidence would tend to convert the process into an adversary proceeding and to equate the Board's parole-release determination with a guilt determination. The Nebraska statute contemplates, and experience has shown, that the parole-release decision is, as we noted earlier, essentially an experienced prediction based on a host of variables. The Nebraska procedure affords an opportunity to be heard, and when parole is denied it informs the inmate in what respects he falls short of qualifying for parole; this affords the process that is due under these circumstances. The Constitution does not require more.

So ordered.

■ JUSTICE POWELL, concurring in part and dissenting in part.

I agree with the Court that the respondents have a right under the Fourteenth Amendment to due process in the consideration of their release on parole. I do not believe, however, that the applicability of the Due Process Clause to parole-release determinations depends upon the particular wording of the statute governing the deliberations of the parole board, or that the limited notice of the final hearing currently given by the State is consistent with the requirements of due process.

A substantial liberty from legal restraint is at stake when the State makes decisions regarding parole or probation. Although still subject to limitations not imposed on citizens never convicted of a crime, the parolee enjoys a liberty incomparably greater than whatever minimal freedom of action he may have retained within prison walls, a fact that the Court recognized in *Morrissey v. Brewer*. . . .

In principle, it seems to me that the Due Process Clause is no less applicable to the parole-release determination than to the decisions by state agencies at issue in the [parole- and probation-revocation] cases. Nothing in the Constitution requires a State to provide for probation or parole. But when a State adopts a parole system that applies general standards of eligibility, prisoners justifiably expect that parole will be granted fairly and according to law whenever those standards are met. This is so whether the governing statute states, as here, that parole "shall" be granted unless certain conditions exist, or provides some other standard for making the parole decision. Contrary to the Court's conclusion, I am convinced that the presence of a parole system is sufficient to create a liberty interest, protected by the Constitution, in the parole-release decision.

The Court today, however, concludes that parole release and parole revocation "are quite different," because "there is a . . . difference between losing what one has and not getting what one wants." I am unpersuaded that this difference, if indeed it exists at all, is as significant as the Court implies. Release on parole marks the first time when the severe restrictions imposed on a prisoner's liberty by the prison regimen may be lifted, and his behavior in prison often is molded by his hope and expectation of securing parole at the earliest time permitted by law. Thus, the parole-release determination may be as important to the prisoner as some later, and generally unanticipated, parole-revocation decision.

I am unconvinced also by the Court's suggestion that the prisoner has due process rights in the context of parole revocation but not parole release because of the different "nature of the decision that must be made in each case." It is true that the parole-revocation determination involves two inquiries: the parole board must ascertain the facts related to the prisoner's behavior on parole, and must then make a judgment whether or not he should be returned to prison. But unless the parole board makes parole release determinations in some arbitrary or random fashion, these subjective evaluations about future success on parole also must be based on retrospective factual findings.

■ JUSTICE MARSHALL, with whom JUSTICE BRENNAN and JUSTICE STEVENS join, dissenting in part.

My disagreement with the Court's opinion extends to both its analysis of respondents' liberty interest and its delincation of the procedures constitutionally required in parole release proceedings. I must register my opinion that *all* prisoners potentially eligible for parole have a liberty interest of which they may not be deprived without due process, regardless of the particular statutory language that implements the parole system.

First, the Court finds a difference of constitutional dimension between a deprivation of liberty one has and a denial of liberty one desires. While there is obviously some difference, it is not one relevant to the established constitutional inquiry. Whether an individual currently enjoys a particular freedom has no bearing on whether he possesses a protected interest in securing and maintaining that liberty.

The Court's second justification for distinguishing between parole release and parole revocation is based on the "nature of the decision that must be made in each case." The majority apparently believes that the interest affected by parole release proceedings is somehow diminished if the administrative decision may turn on "subjective evaluations." Yet the Court nowhere explains why the *nature of the decisional process* has even the slightest bearing in assessing the *nature of the interest* that this process may terminate.

But even assuming the subjective nature of the decisionmaking process were relevant to due process analysis in general, this consideration does not adequately distinguish the processes of granting and revoking parole. Contrary to the Court's assertion that the decision to revoke parole is predominantly a " 'retrospective factual question,' " *Morrissey* recognized that only the first step in the revocation decision can be so characterized. "[The] second step, deciding what to do about the violation once it is identified, *is not purely factual but also predictive and discretionary. . .*"

[The dissent then challenges the claim that parole is merely a "hope" by looking at how extensively it is granted.]

As the Court observed in *Morrissey*:

"During the past 60 years, the practice of releasing prisoners on parole before the end of their sentences has become an integral part of the penological system. . . . Rather than being an *ad hoc* exercise of clemency, parole is an established variation on imprisonment of convicted criminals."

Indeed, the available evidence belies the majority's broad assumptions concerning inmate expectations, at least with respect to the federal system, and there is no suggestion that experience in other jurisdictions is significantly different.

[E]xperience in the federal system has led both judges and legislators to expect that inmates will be paroled substantially before their sentences expire. Insofar as it is critical under the Court's due process analysis, this understanding would certainly justify a similar expectation on the part of the federal inmates. Hence, I believe it is unrealistic for this Court to speculate that the existence of a parole system provides prisoners "no more than a mere hope" of release.

I also cannot subscribe to the Court's assessment of the procedures necessary to safeguard respondents' liberty interest.

To begin with, the Court focuses almost exclusively on the likelihood that a particular procedure will significantly reduce the risk of error in parole release proceedings. Yet *Mathews* advances *three* factors to be considered in determining the specific dictates of due process:

"First, the private interest that will be affected by the official action; second, the risk of an erroneous deprivation of such interest through the procedures used, and the probable value, if any, of additional or substitute procedural safeguards; and finally, the Government's interest, including the function involved and the fiscal and administrative burdens that the additional or substitute procedural requirement would entail."

By ignoring the other two factors set forth in *Mathews,* the Court skews the inquiry in favor of the Board. For example, the Court does not identify any justification for the Parole Board's refusal to provide inmates with specific advance notice of the hearing date or with a list of factors that may be considered. Nor does the Board demonstrate that it would be unduly burdensome to provide a brief summary of the evidence justifying the denial of parole. To be sure, these measures may cause some inconvenience, but the Constitution recognizes higher values than speed and efficiency. . . .

QUESTIONS

1. **The need for parole?** Is the majority in *Greenholtz* correct that discretionary parole is just something that the state voluntarily provides? Especially at the time that the opinion came down, when all states used parole, and often quite heavily, could the sentencing regimes in place function without parole grants? Note that the dissent points out that in the federal system at the time, a majority of inmates served only about 1/3 of their terms.

2. **Parole decisions vs. judicial decisions.** The majority argues that parole decision differ from "the traditional mold of judicial decisionmaking in that the choice involves a synthesis of record facts and personal observation filtered through the experience of the decisionmaker and leading to a predictive judgment as to what is best both for the individual inmate and for the community." Does this make sense? What sort of decisions do judges "traditionally" make? Is the majority tipping its hand about some sort of unstated—perhaps even unrealized—assumptions concerning the normative goals of punishment, and how they may differ from those of parole?

3. **Subjective decisionmaking.** Is the majority's claim that parole grant decisions require less procedure because they rest on more subjective decisions normatively appealing (leaving aside whether revocations are equally subjective)? Might such hearings require *more* procedural

protection—and if so, why? And is the majority right that these findings are more "equitable" in nature and thus ones that "cannot always be articulated in traditional findings"?[17]

4. **Empirical constitutional rights.** The dissent argues that prevailing rates of parole undermine the majority's claim that an inmate simply has a "mere hope" of parole: its extensive use essentially creates an expectation. How appealing of a normative-doctrinal position is this for the Court to take? What potential problems can arise?

5. **The obvious loop-hole.** How can states easily evade *Greenholtz*'s due process obligations?

As *Greenholtz* makes clear, the *Constitution* does not impose any obligations on the state about how it makes parole determinations, but state *statutes* can do so. Statutes vary, however, in how they go about doing this. Some obligations (or their absence) can be established explicitly, others implicitly by how the hearing is established or managed.

Iowa, for example, provides more procedures than the bare minimum dictated by *Greenholtz*. The board is generally required to allow the inmate to review all allegations made against him and his disciplinary record, and for information which he cannot be shown due to confidentiality concerns he is at least informed of the nature of the information and the number of such reports. He is granted "ample opportunity to express views and present materials," though the Board can cut that time short for inmates with little chance of success (such as those who have served only a small fraction of long sentences). And New York requires that an inmate denied parole be informed of why in some detail, and that such a report cannot be merely "conclusory."

Another way in which states are providing structure is via actuarial risk assessment. Colorado, for example, requires that the board use the Colorado Actuarial Risk Assessment Scale; Alaska, North Dakota, and Pennsylvania that the boards use the LSI-R (one of the most widely-used actuarial scales); and Iowa that the board use a scale of its choice. In none of these states is the scale binding. In Colorado, for example, the statute simply states that the board *may* grant parole, thus not creating any right or expectation of parole for the inmate.[18] Yet such scales surely exert some influence on parole boards—if nothing else, there is psychological evidence that people respond strongly to quantified measures of things—and thus influence the decisions parole boards make.

---

[17] The majority argues that the "Board [must] assess whether, in light of the nature of the crime, the inmate's release will minimize the gravity of the offense, weaken the deterrent impact on others, and undermine respect for the administration of justice. The entire inquiry is, in a sense, an "quity" type judgment that cannot always be articulated in traditional findings."

[18] See, e.g., *Reggans v. Owens*, 2006 WL 5044960 (D. Colo. 2006).

B.2.b.ii. What Parole Boards Consider

Those are the formal rules that guide parole boards. But it is worth thinking about what factors parole boards actually put weight on. Despite the statutory requirements under which they operate, parole board members continue to wield significant discretion over the decision to grant or deny parole, so it is not immediately clear that they will follow what the statutes dictate.

Joel M. Caplan, *What Factor Affect Parole: A Review of Empirical Research*
71 FED. PROBATION 16, 16–19 (2007)

As American criminal justice policies and practices became more punitive in the 1970s, parole board discretion was simultaneously limited or eliminated. Much of the empirical research on parole release decisions during this time was conducted in an effort to create objective, actuarial models and guidelines for determining releases from prison. These models were supposed to be immune from subjective or indiscriminate feelings towards inmates by parole board members.

However, a detailed review of the empirical literature on parole release decision-making suggests that despite guidelines, parole release decisions remained irregularly applied and were primarily a function of institutional behavior, crime severity, criminal history, incarceration length, mental illness, and victim input. Even the structure of parole boards themselves can be an overriding factor in release decisions. For example, during [one] 1986 study of parole decision making in Colorado, at least two board members made the majority of release decisions; in 2000, only one board member in Colorado was required to decide parole release. With only one decision-maker, parole is more dependent on the individual board member's education, background, and philosophy. Despite the nuances of parole board policies or structures, a review of parole decision-making literature to date reveals that parole release decisions are primarily a function of institutional behavior, crime severity, criminal history, incarceration length, mental illness, and victim input.

Institutional Behavior

Many empirical studies on parole board decision-making found institutional conduct to be significantly associated with release decisions. [A 1982 study in Pennsylvania] identified institutional behavior as the single most important variable predicting release. Institutional behavior was used to make judgments about risk of future crime, risk of future dangerousness, and prognosis for supervision and rehabilitation. [The study] further identified five broad categories of crime causes that were identified by parole interviewers as important when deciding parole releases: a) personal dispositions, b) drugs, c) alcohol, d) money, and e) environment. Inmates whose crimes were believed to be caused by the first three categories consistently received less favorable prognoses for supervision and rehabilitation and were less likely to be released on parole. [Several other studies] also found that institutional conduct and predictions of future conduct were among the strongest factors associated with parole release and revocation in Oklahoma, Connecticut, Texas, and Nebraska. . . .

[A 2000 study interviewed inmates about why they thought their parole requests had been denied.] In contrast to inmate expectations, [the study] found that instead of good institutional behavior being a major consideration for release, only misbehavior and noncompliance with required treatment programs were taken into account by parole board members and served as reasons to deny parole.

In results similar to prior research, [a sophisticated 1999 study] also found that institutional recommendations by prison staff had the most significant influence on parole board reviewers deliberating whether to grant or deny inmates a full parole board hearing. Criminal history and education level were also found to be significant factors.

The relative insignificance of crime severity when deciding parole release is notable in several of the above studies.

Crime Severity, Criminal History, and Incarceration Length

The New Jersey Parole Act of 1979 attempted to limit parole discretion through presumptive parole—mandating release upon first eligibility unless the parole board found preponderant evidence of future recidivism. [A study was] conducted [in 1999] to determine if parole board decision-making complied with this 1979 law, and whether factors such as plea bargaining, aggravation, or type of crime affected these decisions.

Results indicated that the type of crime for which an inmate was incarcerated was the most influential factor in parole release decisions, while the presence or absence of plea bargaining had no effect. According to the restrictions of the 1979 parole act, the type of crime itself should not influence decision behavior. However, [the study] found a significant difference between violent and nonviolent crime categories. "A sexual assault conviction practically guaranteed parole denial," stated [the study], "regardless of crime particulars, institutional record, or defendant factors."

Furthermore, cases rated "too severe" in sentence length produced odds favoring parole release, while cases rated "too lenient" produced odds that favored parole denial. Based on her results, [the study's author] suggested that New Jersey parole hearing officers applied a correction in cases where the crime and sentence received were perceived as incongruent. This is consistent with findings from other studies. . . .

Mental Illness

Several studies have found mental illness to have a negative effect on an inmate's chances for parole release. [The 1982 study] found that older inmates were generally rated (or perceived to be) more mentally disturbed, which negatively influenced judgments about usefulness of counseling progress, prognosis for supervision, and parole release. [A 2004 study] found that board members interpret knowledge of a woman's mental health as relevant to determinations of violence, and that women who had been diagnosed with a mental disorder were significantly less likely to be released on parole compared to men. [A 1994 study] concluded that inmates without a history of psychiatric hospitalization while incarcerated were 30 times more likely to be granted parole than inmates with a history of psychiatric hospitalization, when controlling for a number of factors, including race, prison infractions, prior imprisonments and violence of offense.

Victim Input

[Only a few studies] have directly and empirically studied the influence of outside victims on parole release decisions. [The studies all found that victim input reduced the likelihood of parole being granted. In some cases, the victim's gender mattered as well, as did the victim's decision to send letters vs. appearing at the hearing (with the latter being more likely to result in a parole denial).]

Discussion

A review of the empirical literature on parole release decision-making highlights four important points regarding this topic. First, much of the scholarly research on parole release decision-making is more than 20 years old and may be irrelevant to contemporary parole board policies and practices in U.S. states with discretionary parole release. Second, institutional behavior, incarceration length, crime severity, criminal history, mental illness, and victim input are among the most influential factors affecting parole release for parole-eligible inmates. Furthermore, victim input against parole release remains highly significant in explaining the denial of parole for parole-eligible inmates when controlling for other significantly influential factors. Regarding victim input, however, the external validity of these studies is limited due to their sampling designs. For example, non-violent inmates, input from non-victims, and input in favor of parole release are understudied. And finally, an inmate's education, gender, and age may also have a significant influence on parole release dispositions.

This review of empirical research is intended to improve understanding of the dynamics of parole release decision-making and to inform initiatives to make parole processes more effective and efficient by, for example, encouraging evaluations and detailed assessments of current parole practices in the United States. [A 2000 study] warned that when the factors inmates believe affect release decisions are different from the factors that parole boards consider, inmates will not only be confused and angry, but will be less likely to conform to requirements for institutional control. "Each parole case that is deferred or set back becomes another story, duly embellished," wrote [the author of the study], "that makes its rounds throughout the prison population, fueling suspicion, resentment, and fear of an unbridled discretionary system of power, control, and punishment." Future research and evaluation regarding parole release decision-making at a general policy level can result in a more transparent and equitable system for both victims and inmates.

The obvious way to restrict the way in which parole boards make decisions is to require them to use actuarial devices, and to adhere to the determination that the instrument provides. As will we saw above, a growing number of states are moving in this direction, with at least 36 states requiring their parole boards to consult an actuarial device as part of their deliberations over release. Since we've discussed actuarial models in depth before (see Chapter 3), I won't belabor the point here. But it is useful to keep a few concerns in mind:

1. Are we using the right models? One study points out that desistance is often tied to successful program completion, so perhaps a model that looks at probability-of-completing-the-program is better than one that looks at risk-of-reoffending. Obviously these are correlated, but by focusing on the latter question we may include variables that aren't entirely on-point, throwing off the precision of the model.

2. Are we focused on the right thing? Models will generally draw our attention to what is quantifiable. So whether an inmate recidivates is objectively measurable (**Question:** only *sort of* objectively measurable: why only sort of?), while whether he, say, has a "more productive" life while on parole, even if he ultimately "fails" in the sense of returning to prison, is not. And while recidivism has been the traditional measure of success, it need not be the only one.

B.3. CONDITIONS OF PAROLE

Once a parole board decides to release an inmate, it then has the ability to impose certain conditions on him, ranging from abstaining from drugs or alcohol to refusing to associate with known felons to waiving his Fourth Amendment right to be free of warrantless searches. Some of these conditions are mandated by statute for all inmates, but other conditions are imposed on a case-by-case basis by the parole board.

The types of conditions that a board can impose are limited both by state and federal constitutions as well as by the parole statute itself. As we saw in Chapter 11's discussion of probation conditions, which applies equally to parole restrictions, state statutes likely do most of the work. Courts strike down provisions that seem too attenuated from any real theory of punishment, they police provisions to make sure they are not unconstitutionally vague, and they subject restrictions that trigger constitutionally protected rights to closer review. Courts are generally fairly deferential to parole boards, but not absolutely. Federal circuit courts, for example, are split as to whether bans on "pornography" for released sex offenders are unconstitutionally vague or overbroad.[19]

In general, parolees face two sorts of conditions. One set, defined by statute, applies to all parolees. The second set are "special conditions" that parole boards can impose on individual parolees as they see fit. Such conditions need to be tied to the goals of parole, such as rehabilitation and crime prevention, but again boards generally have a lot of latitude when it comes to imposing such limitations.

The following reading looks at the sorts of conditions parole boards impose. As quickly becomes clear, over time the number of such conditions has grown significantly.

Lawrence F. Travis, III, and James Stacey, *A Half Century of Parole Rules: Conditions of Parole in the United States, 2008*
38 J. CRIM. JUSTICE 604, 604–607 (2010)[20]

Many observers suggest that the number and breadth of parole conditions, coupled with a punitive and risk-control orientation among parole agencies impede successful reentry. This article reports the results of a national survey of parole conditions imposed on offenders released from prison in the United States. These conditions define the offenses of one-third of those admitted to prison each year.

Changing perceptions of parole conditions

Michael Jacobson observes that current conditions of parole make it virtually impossible for many offenders released from prison successfully to complete their supervision. He notes, "Given all the social, economic, and health deficits of those coming out of prison, it becomes less than surprising that so many parolees are sent back to prison for rule violations. When one combines these problems with conditions that are routinely set for parole—no drug use, having a permanent address, having or actively pursuing employment, keeping all reporting and treatment appointments—a recipe for failure results."

---

[19] Laura A. Napoli, *Demystifying "Pornography": Tailoring Special Release Conditions Concerning Pornography and Sexually Oriented Expression*, 11 U.N.H.L. REV. 69 (2013).

[20] Lawrence F. Travis, III, and James Stacey, *A Half Century of Parole Rules: Conditions of Parole in the United States, 2008*, 38 J. CRIM. JUSTICE 604, 604–607 (2010).

[One scholar] briefly traced the changes in perceptions of parole conditions and parole revocation over the past four decades [, noting that] "Violations and revocation of probation and parole have been topics of discussion among corrections practitioners for decades. The nature of those discussions has often revealed a great deal about the critical issues facing corrections at the time." In the 1970's attention focused on due process protections during revocation hearings. In the next decade, with an emphasis on "risk control," some argued that revocation based on rule violations was evidence of successful risk control and public protection. In the 1990s, critics saw revocations as a source of prison crowding. In the current context, proponents of reentry view parole conditions and relatively high rates of revocation as obstacles to offender reintegration. Most observers call for a reduction in parole revocation rates, especially revocation for violations of "technical" conditions of parole.

Changes in parole and parole conditions in the United States

[A survey of parole conditions in 1956] concluded that parole conditions were often too numerous, too vague, and too unrealistic to be of any real value. [The survey's author] noted that the rules of parole were not uniform across the various jurisdictions. [A follow-up study] repeated this survey thirteen years later [in 1969]. [That study] reported that most jurisdictions had increased the number of parole conditions and that, in general, parole conditions suffered serious defects including redundancy, impracticality, and a lack of uniformity. In short, in his opinion, things had not improved over time.

[A subsequent survey of conditions in place in 1982] echoed many of conclusions [from the 1956 and 1969 surveys]. However, it appeared that the number of conditions imposed on parolees might have been decreasing after the 1969 study. [The 1982 survey] observed, "In the majority of the categories of parole rules employed in this study, the states dropping parole conditions outnumber those which have added parole conditions." They identified 139 separate conditions, with a mean of 14.8 conditions imposed per parole jurisdiction.

Yet thirteen years later, [a 1996 study] again surveyed standard parole conditions[, t]his time using a slightly different classification, but again, it appeared that the trend was towards a reduction in the absolute number of standard conditions of parole, and in the average number of conditions imposed on parolees. [The 1996 study] reported 76 distinct conditions with a mean of 11.5 conditions imposed per jurisdiction.

The research reported here represents the fourth iteration of [the] original survey of parole conditions conducted in 1956. As with the previous reviews, this one was conducted 13 years after the previous review and, in total, the surveys cover 52 years of parole conditions from 1956 through 2008.

As part of a rehabilitative focus in American corrections, parole supervision represented a continuation of care post-incarceration and included a variety of treatment requirements as part of the parole process. [The 1956 and 1969 surveys] reported a relatively high number of parole jurisdictions requiring participation in drug, alcohol, or psychological treatment programs. By the time [of the 1982 survey], treatment requirements were being reduced, perhaps being replaced by special conditions of supervision related to treatment needs. By the 1995 review, there was a discernible movement away from treatment requirements towards conditions aimed at strengthening surveillance and limiting the risk of new crime. Reflecting a general movement towards a "penal harm" approach to corrections, parole conditions reflected risk control, correctional management, and punishment more than treatment or rehabilitation.

In the past ten to fifteen years, there has been a resurgence of interest in "treatment," if not rehabilitation. Parole is increasingly lumped into the broader category of "Prisoner Re-entry," with an emphasis on programming and treatment continuing after release from incarceration. To the extent that current thinking about "best correctional practices" includes support for integrated programming spanning imprisonment and the return to society, parole conditions can be expected to expand to include program participation.

Findings

A total of 127 separate conditions* of parole were identified, with a mean of 18.6 conditions and a median of 19.5 for each jurisdiction ranging from a low of 10 to a high of 24 conditions. These are substantially greater numbers than those reported [in the 1996 survey], and represent almost as many total conditions of supervision, and a greater average number of standard conditions than reported [in the 1982 survey].

In the years between 1982 and 2008, a number of new conditions of parole have been added including restrictions on the possession and use of caller identification, police radio scanner, or surveillance equipment (North Dakota, Utah, and Wyoming), and a requirement that the parolee submit to a polygraph examination when asked (Illinois, Kansas, Washington, and Wisconsin). Ten states added a specific condition prohibiting parolees from absconding supervision.

Fifteen types of conditions were imposed on parolees in half or more of American paroling jurisdictions in 2008. The most common conditions in 2008, imposed in at least forty jurisdictions, were: comply with the law, restrictions on changing residence, prohibition on weapons possession, requirement of regular reporting, restrictions on out of state travel, allowing home and work visits by the parole officer, and restrictions on possession/use of controlled substances. All jurisdictions required that parolees comply with the law. This is the first time since 1956 that a

---

* *Ed note*: The authors of the study look only at *standard* conditions, the ones that are applied to all inmates upon release. Individual offenders may face more—perhaps many more—*special* conditions tailored for their specific circumstances.

single condition was required in all jurisdictions. While all jurisdictions restricted out of state travel in 1982, the specific restrictions varied across jurisdictions.

Other conditions imposed in at least three-quarters of the jurisdictions in 2008 require parolees to maintain employment or educational program participation, report any arrest, comply with medical/drug testing, make a "first arrival" report (making contact with the supervising officer soon after release from prison), and pay fees and restitution, and prohibitions against contact with undesirable associates. The remaining conditions imposed in over half of the jurisdictions included obeying the instructions/directions of the supervising officer, controls on the consumption of alcohol, and avoidance of undesirable associates or locations.

Several types of conditions were imposed in five or fewer jurisdictions. These least common conditions of supervision banned borrowing money, possession of caller identification/scanner/surveillance equipment, and opening a checking account. Others required the parolee to earn a G.E.D. and comply with court orders, notifying an employer of prior conviction, avoid contact with victims, placed restrictions on marriage, and limits on remaining away from the parolee's residence overnight. Finally, still other "conditions," including various notifications to the parolee about denial of bail, loss of credit for time served if revoked, calculation of release date, and restrictions on civil rights were imposed in fewer than five jurisdictions. Permission to use/possess knives required for employment, requirements to sign the parole order, carry identification papers, sit for an identification photograph, and notice that conditions of release may be changed were similarly imposed in fewer than five jurisdictions.

Table 1 compares standard conditions imposed in at least half (26) of parole jurisdictions across the three [most recent] survey years. Some of the parole conditions in effect in 2008 experienced growth in the sense that they are now required in more jurisdictions while others have been rescinded over the intervening years. The table includes eighteen types of standard parole conditions imposed by half of all jurisdictions in at least one of the survey years. The table reveals a generally [u-shaped] evolution of parole conditions in that half of the conditions were more or less common in 1982 and 2008 than in 1995.

Table 1
Changes in standard conditions of parole, 1982 – 2008

Standard Condition	1982	1995	2008
Comply with the law	96%	90%	100%
Change residence	92%	79%	98%
Possess firearm/dangerous weapon	92%	90%	96%
Maintain employment/education program	73%	81%	94%
Report regularly	94%	33%	87%
Permit home/work visits And searches	42%	61%	87%
Out of state travel	100%	88%	87%
Use controlled substances	63%	88%	81%
Change employment	87%	81%	79%
Pay fees/restitution	N/A	46%	79%
Report arrest/questioning By law enforcement	50%	63%	71%
Make first arrival report	75%	58%	63%
Submit to medical/drug test	N/A	40%	63%
Undesirable associates/locations	50%	N/A	60%
Alcohol use	44%	42%	54%
Obey P.O. instructions	N/A	23%	54%
Give written/oral information	N/A	55%	N/A
Waive extradition	50%	N/A	N/A

Discussion

In the current study, it appears that the general growth in the number and types of parole conditions reflects at least four separate trends and the multiple purposes served by parole conditions.

First, the recent emphasis on "re-entry" and the problems of prisoner reintegration with society may have supported an increase in "treatment" conditions including requirements that parolees participate in educational/employment programs (imposed in 49 of jurisdictions) and drug/alcohol/psychological programs (imposed in 19 jurisdictions). Second, a review of current parole conditions indicates a continuation of efforts to enhance the crime control/crime prevention effectiveness of supervision. Many conditions have been added or expanded that strengthen supervision, such as requirements that changes in employment (40 jurisdictions) be reported, that officer visits to parolee's homes and work locations (45 jurisdictions) be allowed, that parolees waive extradition, and similar conditions aimed at strengthening surveillance and control of parolee behavior. Third, some of these conditions represent the development of changes in technology (requirements that the parolee submit to drug/medical testing or limits on communications technology) and changes in criminal justice practice (requirements that parolees pay fees). Finally, it would appear that many "conditions" have been added to parole that actually represent notice of applicable statutes or policies (such as conditions that bail may be denied, or that time served credit will not be awarded if parole is revoked).

A large number of parole conditions that cover a range of behaviors and circumstances constitute an "arsenal of the prosecutor." Conditions enable the parole authority to revoke liberty and re-imprison the parolee for any failure to obey. More numerous and comprehensive conditions increase the probability that a parolee will violate at least some constraint. If we seek to reduce the rate of "technical" failures on parole, we might do well to minimize the number and extent of parole conditions. The current tension around parole revocation reflects this reality.

The contemporary debate about "technical" violations of parole and, by extension, standard conditions of supervision hinges on the purposes and requirements of parole supervision. Some argue that parolees returned to prison for violating the "technical" conditions of parole represent an unnecessary and perhaps unfair imprisonment of parolees for behaviors that would not bring a similar punishment for persons not under supervision. Further, the imprisonment of those found to have violated parole conditions disrupts reintegration into society and thus successful re-entry by release offenders.

Alternatively, the fact that offenders will be supervised and can be returned to custody before they might commit a serious crime is often given as a rationale for discretionary parole release. We have no data with which to assess how restricting the capacity to supervise parolees might reduce the willingness of parole authorities to grant discretionary release. We also face serious limitations in our ability to assess the crime control and public safety implications of current parole rules and revocation practices.

Even technical violators of parole may not really be "technical violators." [A 2006 study examined] over 38,000 offenders released from prison in 15 states in 1994. [It] compared rearrest rates for offenders under each of three release conditions; discretionary release to supervision, mandatory release to supervision, and unsupervised release. In general, [it] found only slight differences in rearrest across the three groups. Importantly, when discussing "technical violators," [it] reported ". . . very few individuals (340 in the original sample) were rearrested only for a technical violation, and arguably many of those involved an underlying crime."

Question: Why include a parole condition for something that is already illegal? In other words, what does "obey the law" accomplish as a *parole* restriction? *Everyone*, even those with no criminal history at all, are subject to that rule.

In many instances, the conditions make sense: abstain from drinking, get a job (if possible), attend anger management sessions. But in many instances the parole conditions seem to set the parolee up to fail. This is likely not intentional, but it is easy to see how a vicious cycle can develop. When a parolee subject to a host of conditions fails, it is logical that many people will think "we need to monitor him more, restrict his behavior more, to keep him from failing again." The new conditions can then lead to more failure, and thus to more demands for closer monitoring and control. Of course, people could also see the failure and think that what is needed is a newer, better approach; but the one-way ratchet in conditions is at least *understandable*, even if it isn't necessarily *effective*.

The growing number of conditions, along with shrinking budgets have not just affected parolees, but parole *officers* as well, who find themselves increasingly focused on simply trying to monitor compliance, rather than taking on a more social-worker type goals. As one scholar explains:

> Parole supervision styles generally fall into either casework or surveillance approaches. The social casework approach, which emphasizes assisting parolees with problems, counseling, and working to make sure they succeed, has long predominated. But this style has shifted over the past 30 years to one of surveillance, which emphasizes law enforcement and the close monitoring of parolees to catch them if they fail and return them to prison.
>
> Public rejection of leniency in corrections, loss of faith in the efficacy of treatment, and tightening state budgets are primarily responsible for contemporary parole practices that sacrifice casework and treatment to focus on risk management and administrative efficiency. In the 1970s, parole officers handled caseloads averaging 45 offenders; today it is up to 70 or more. Significantly larger caseloads give parole officers very little time to focus on parolees as individuals and to provide counseling or referrals to community agencies. As a result, officers have little choice but to concentrate on surveillance and the impersonal monitoring of their clients. [One observer] explained that:
>
>> The emphasis on surveillance of community offenders results in a trend to violate releases [parolees] for minor technical violations, as administrators and parole boards do not want to risk keeping offenders in the community. If these minor violators later commit a serious crime, those deciding to allow them to continue in the community despite technical violations could face criticism or even legal action. This "risk-free" approach represents an "invisible policy" not passed by legislatures or formally adopted by correctional agencies. However, these actions have a tremendous impact on prison populations, cost, and community stability.

[A] 1997 [study] suggested that a strictly surveillance-oriented style of parole was not effective at reducing recidivism. [It argued] that a balanced role of both social worker and law enforcer provides the best results for parolees, parole officers, and society. According to parole and probation officer surveys and interviews, casework functions were reported to be the most effective in assisting parolees, while surveillance functions were ideal for catching those who violate conditions of supervision.

Line-level parole officers generally believe that the most effective functions they perform are to help those under their supervision. [A] study of Texas parole officers . . . showed an overwhelming desire for more treatment resources; greater seniority and smaller caseloads were among the most powerful factors in predicting which parole officers would emphasize treatment resources. An earlier study . . . showed that orientation to rehabilitation was rather high among Alabama parole officers, and that punitiveness was inversely related to amount of client contact and directly predicted by size of caseloads. [Another study] also found considerable support for rehabilitation, even among officers given reduced caseloads in a program designed to stress control and surveillance rather than the provision of treatment services. A more recent study . . . showed that parole officers believe that a balanced supervisory style should be the goal, and that current caseloads are forcing more of a surveillance approach. Officers who were surveyed for this study estimated that they spend about 54 percent of their time engaged in what experts classify as casework activities. However, these same officers perceived themselves as more surveillance oriented on a 10-point continuum). When the pendulum of public support gains momentum toward surveillance and risk-management, it is clearly difficult for parole officers to resist.[21]

Moreover, the conditions imposed on parolees by parole boards are not the only restrictions that parolees face. Other statutory provisions restrict their options even more, such as denying released inmates access to public housing and other forms of public assistance, and even going so far as to deny them the right to vote. Consider the following list of restrictions and challenges that returning prisoners face, compiled by Joan Petersilia.[22]

1. **Publicly available criminal records.** By 1999, nearly 60 million people had criminal records, and these records are publicly available in a majority of states. Employers are often unwilling to hire former felons, so such availability

---

[21] Joel M. Caplan, *Parole System Anomie: Conflicting Models of Casework and Surveillance*, 70 FED. PROBATION 32, 34–35 (2006).

[22] JOAN PETERSILIA, WHEN PRISONERS COME HOME 105–137 (2003).

acts as a significant barrier to employment, and thus desistance. In fact, survey data suggests that employers feel more comfortable hiring someone with a long history of unemployment than with any sort of criminal record.

2. **Employment restrictions.** Although employers rarely can refuse to hire felons across the board, they are often not permitted to hire them for certain jobs. Petersilia points out that felons are banned not just jobs like medicine and law, but also real estate. Furthermore, even when not legally banned from a job, a felon may find that licensing boards generally deny former convicts licenses. In New York State, for example, the most popular training program in prisons is barber school, but the licensing board for barbers in New York refuses to issue licenses to felons. As the number of professions with licensing requirements continues to grow, such barriers will multiply as well.

   Other restrictions can be more indirect: employment may require ID like a driver's license, but a federal law requires states to revoke licenses of those convicted of a wide range of drug offenses.[23] Or an employer who wishes to hire a former felon may not be able to acquire the necessary insurance, or in a few instances may face a greater risk of liability (including punitive damages) if that employee (rather than one without a record) commits a crime.

3. **Housing.** One challenge inmates face upon release is finding a place to live. As we noted at the start of this chapter, residential stability and proximity to family could be important forms of support for desistance. But some laws deny public housing to certain offenders (generally those convicted of sex or drug offenses). And family members who let parolees live with them run the risk of losing their access to public housing as well. In fact, if one person living in a public housing unit commits a crime, the *entire family* can be evicted. And that's before we even get to the host of residency restrictions imposed on sex offenders, which we discuss below.

4. **Welfare benefits.** The federal government, as part of its welfare reform under President Clinton, passed a law that banned drug offenders—but *only* drug offenders—from receiving federal welfare benefits for life. Congress also authorized states to test all welfare recipients more

---

[23] One peculiar aspect of federal involvement in re-entry is an intense focus on punishing drug offenders. Thus federal benefits may be denied to a drug offender but not to, say, a murderer.

aggressively for drug abuse.[24] The collateral costs of such restrictions can be severe, especially when applied to drug-dealing female offenders, who frequently are supporting children (who now lose their benefits as well). As Petersilia puts it bluntly:

> One wonders how the children in these fragile family units are to survive when their parents return home. They will no longer be able to receive financial subsidies for housing and food, and the parent's criminal record will make it very difficult to get a job. Without access to welfare benefits, these vulnerable families are left with virtually no safety net.[25]

5. **Felony disenfranchisement.** 48 states deny felons the right to vote while in prison, and 24 deny them the right to vote while on parole or probation; 11 states impose permanent limits on voting (7 for some felons, 4 for *all* felons).[26] The concern with such laws from a pragmatic perspective is that they disproportionately target Democratic voters, since felons are more likely to be poor, and they over-represent minority populations. Of course, there are obvious moral concerns one can raise as well, although the rebuttals to these should be clear as well. It is worth noting, though, that no other democracy disenfranchises released offenders.

6. **Fees.** Another effective restriction, which has grown in popularity since Petersilia wrote her review, is the use of fees. Over the past few decades, states and counties have been imposing an increasing number of fees on those convicted of crimes or released onto parole to cover the costs of running the criminal justice system. Given that most defendants are poor—somewhere around 80% to 90% of defendants are eligible for indigent defense—these fees can be very hard to pay back, and with late fees they can continue to grow. Such fees increase the risk of being returned to prison for violating parole.[27] They also run the risk of triggering adverse events like homelessness and a

---

[24] Florida recently required all welfare recipients to undergo drug testing, but it has quickly become clear that sufficiently few welfare recipients are using drugs that whatever savings come from denying drug users benefits are swamped by the costs of testing all those who are not using.

[25] *Id.* at 126.

[26] See http://www.brennancenter.org/sites/default/files/legacy/d/download_file_48642.pdf.

[27] According to the Supreme Court, people cannot be incarcerated simply because of their inability to pay a fine. *Williams v. Illinois*, 399 U.S. 235 (1970). Yet it appears that parolees are re-incarcerated for just this reason, whether due to judicial ignorance of the Court's holding or the defendant's unawareness of his ability to contest revocation of parole due to poverty—both of which reflect the general inadequate nature of the representation indigent defendants often receive.

general inability to provide for oneself or family, and they increase the general stress under which parolees find themselves—both of which in turn increase the probability the parolee recidivates, either out of necessity or an inability to regulate behavior when operating under extreme stress.

These fees can be sizable. The Brennan Center cites one case from Pennsylvania, in which a woman convicted of a drug charge paid a $500 in fines, $325 in restitution, and $2,464 in fees, including charges for the ride in the police car, substance abuse education classes (in general, not for her), court costs, and so on.[28] Her fees were nearly triple her sanctions!

Aside: The Conditions for Sex Offenders

The post-release restrictions we place on sex offenders have become uniquely harsh, so it is worth taking a moment to briefly examine how we manage them upon release. Sex offenders face two types of restrictions that no other sort of parolee faces: the requirement to register (and sometimes announce) their status as a sex offender, and often stringent restrictions on where they can live.

Let's start with sex offender registries. The logic behind the registries is fairly clear. If sex offenders are, as the claim goes, uniquely undeterrable, then it falls to the potential victims to engage in self-protection efforts. By forcing sex offenders to publicly list where they are—and in some cases to announce their status to neighbors—potential victims (most notably children, through their parents) can make sure to avoid the offenders.

Over the years, the federal government has sought to shape how states design their registries:

> In 1994, Congress passed the Jacob Wetterling Crimes against Children and Sexually Violent Offender Registration Act ("Wetterling"), which required states, the District of Columbia, and the principle territories to create sex offender registries containing information about convicted sex offenders for use by law enforcement. The act required convicted sex offenders to register their addresses with local law enforcement agencies upon the completion of their custodial sentence in order to assist the authorities in monitoring offenders and apprehending known recidivists. Although Wetterling required states to establish sex offender websites, it left discretion to the states regarding which offenders to register, what information would be posted, and who could access the websites. This lack of

---

[28] REBEKAH DILLER, ALICIA BANNON, AND MITALI NAGRECHA, CRIMINAL JUSTICE DEBT: A BARRIER TO REENTRY 9 (2010).

guidance resulted in an inconsistent patchwork of state run sex offender databases that was not capable of tracking sex offenders across state lines.

In 1996, . . . Congress passed Megan's Law, which required that states make their sex offender databases available to the public so that citizens could be aware of dangerous sexual predators near them and take appropriate measures to protect themselves. This law, however, did not solve the problem of inconsistency among state databases that limited their utility in tracking the movements of sex offenders.

In 2006, Congress passed The Adam Walsh Child Protection and Safety Act (AWA. . . . Title I of the AWA, the Sex Offender Registration and Notification Act (SORNA), created the first comprehensive national system of registration for sex offenders with certain uniform, minimum standards of data (twenty data requirements in total) that must be included (i.e., name, address, social security number, date of birth, photograph, place of employment, license plate number, etc.). It establishes a baseline of information that must be included, thereby giving jurisdictions some flexibility, within limits set forth in SORNA, to supplement that information with additional information to suit the needs of the citizens living in those jurisdictions.

Among other things, the law separates sex offenders into three tiers based mainly on their crime of conviction and sometimes elevated by past criminal sexual convictions, and establishes the frequency and length of time for which sex offenders in each tier must remain in the registration system. SORNA also created a separate prosecutable offense for failure to comply with these registration requirements. Tier III offenders, deemed the most dangerous and most likely to recidivate, applies to those convicted of aggravated sexual assault, contact offenses against children younger than 13 years, kidnapping of minors (unless committed by a parent or guardian), and attempts or conspiracies associated with any of these offenses. Tier III offenders must provide quarterly, in-person reports to confirm or update their registration information for the rest of their lives. Tier II offenders are those convicted of sex trafficking, coercion and enticement, transportation with intent to engage in criminal sexual activity, abusive sexual conduct, use of a minor in a sexual performance, solicitation of a minor to practice prostitution, and production or distribution of child pornography. Tier II offenders must provide semi-annual, in-person reports for 25 years. Tier I is a catch-all, covering any other "sex offense" . . . not covered by the higher tiers, such as possession of child pornography, most misdemeanors sex crimes, and minor sexual assaults against adults. Tier I offenders are those deemed the least dangerous and least likely to recidivate. They must provide annual, in-person updates of their whereabouts for 15 years. Both tier III juvenile sex offenders and tier I sex offenders can get their registration terms reduced by several years by fulfilling [a] "clean record" requirement. . . .[29]

A recent 50-state survey of sex offender registration laws, compiled by Margaret Love, the former US Pardon Attorney, attempted to sum them up thusly:

> But getting all of the state laws condensed into a few categories turned out to be a considerably more complex task than we imagined, in part because we had to fill in a lot of gaps, and in part because of the extraordinary variety and complexity of the laws themselves.
>
> It is risky to try to generalize about the results of our study, However, we found that registration laws seem to fall into three general categories:
>
> - 18 states provide a single indefinite or lifetime registration period for all sex offenses, but a substantial portion of these allow those convicted of less serious offenses to return to court after a specified period of time to seek removal;
> - 19 states and the District of Columbia have a two-tier registration system, which requires serious offenders and recidivists to register for life but automatically excuses those convicted of misdemeanors and other less serious offenses from the obligation to register after a specified period of time, typically 10 years;
> - 13 states and the federal system have a three-tier system, requiring Tier III offenders to register for life, and Tier I and Tier II offenders to register for a term of years, generally 15 and 25 years.
>
> Most states require recidivists to register for life. About half the states have shorter terms or special termination provisions for juveniles. Successful completion of deferred adjudication avoids registration in many states.
>
> Most of the states that authorize discretionary relief after a period of years specify the criteria that are to be considered by

---

[29] JOHN G. MALCOLM, THE SEX OFFENDER REGISTRATION AND NOTIFICATION ACT: A SENSIBLE AND WORKABLE LAW THAT HELPS KEEP US SAFE, available on-line at http://www.fed-soc.org/publications/detail/an-exchange-over-the-sex-offender-registration-and-notification-act-sorna.

courts, and require that there be no intervening convictions of any kind.[30]

A comparison of Love's summary with SORNA's requirements makes it clear that most states are not in compliance with SORNA, despite the fact that Congress set a 2009 deadline. According to the Department of Justice, only seventeen states are currently substantially in compliance with the law.[31] Some states are struggling to enact and adopt its rules.

But others are simply refusing to comply. After all, sex offender registration is a distinctly state function, so Congress can't actually *require* the states to adopt the provisions in SORNA. In this case, Congress decided to forego the traditional carrot ("adopt this law in exchange for grant money") and chose to use a stick instead: states not in compliance with SORNA can lose up to 10% of the grant money they receive from the Federal Government's Byrne Justice Assistance Grants.[32]

The key question, of course, is whether such registries actually reduce sex offending. There has been surprisingly little work on this topic, but two recent empirical papers return fairly bleak results. As one of them explains:

> This paper evaluates the effectiveness of such registries from two angles. First, I use variation across states in sex offender registration laws to explore whether the introduction of sex offender registration or community notification changes sex offense rates and whether offenders who are released into states with registration laws are less likely to recidivate. Second, I use variation across census blocks in Washington, D.C., to evaluate whether the presence of a registered sex offender in a block leads to higher rates of sex offense there. The first analysis addresses directly the effectiveness of sex offender registries. The second addresses the potential effectiveness of registries by considering whether where offenders live is predictive of where they offend.
>
> I find little evidence to support the effectiveness of sex offender registries, either in practice or in potential. Rates of sex offense do not decline after the introduction of a registry or public access to a registry via the Internet, nor do sex offenders appear to recidivate less when released into states with registries. The

---

[30] http://ccresourcecenter.org/2015/05/14/50-state-survey-of-relief-provisions-affecting-sex-offender-registration/.

[31] http://www.smart.gov/sorna.htm.

[32] Some perspective: in 2014, the federal government awarded about $300 million through the Byrne program, while in 2006 (the last year for which data are available) state and local governments spent $173 *billion* on law enforcement. So Byrne grants are on the order of 0.2% of law enforcement spending; a 10% cut in those grants, a 0.02% hit to total state and local budgets.

data from Washington, D.C., indicate that census blocks with more offenders do not experience statistically significantly higher rates of sexual abuse, which implies that there is little information one can infer from knowing that a sex offender lives on one's block.

More recent work by Prescott and Rockoff* . . . uses data across states and exploits the variation in timing of the start of registration to attempt to determine the effectiveness of sex offender registries. [T]hey find mixed results for the effects of registration. They attempt to separate out the effects of registration and notification on the relationship between offenders and victims, on deterrence, and on recidivism. They find that the number of sex offenses committed against known victims (relatives or others with a prior relationship with the offender) was reduced after registries were implemented. They find no effect on sex offenses committed against strangers. In terms of recidivism, the authors find that registered offenders may actually be more likely to recidivate when subject to community notification. They find no evidence that the registration requirement deters first-time offenders but do find evidence that registration itself (separate from community notification) reduces the recidivism of registered sex offenders—likely because of the increased information the registries provide to the police. When looking at arrests rather than incidents, they find no significant effect of registration or notification.[33]

In short, registries might have some gains, but by and large they seem to have little positive effect, and may even have some iatrogenic effects that at least partially offset what few gains they have. Moreover, the empirical studies here are looking only at short-run impacts and not the longer-run disruptive effects registries might have on desistance.

The second major restriction we place on sex offenders concerns where they can live. These residency rules hold that registered sex offenders cannot live within some distance, usually between 500 and 2000 feet, of places like parks, schools, etc., where children are likely to be. The harshest attempt, in Georgia, included a 1000-foot ban around all bus stops, effectively rendering the *entire state* off limits. This outcome was desired by the legislators, although a court ultimately struck down the bus-stop part of the law.

---

* *Ed note*: This is the second recent paper: J.J. Prescott and Jonah E. Rockoff, *Do Sex Offender Registration and Notification Laws Affect Criminal Behavior?* 54 J. L. & ECON. 161 (2011).

[33] Amanda Y. Agan, Sex Offender Registries: Fear without Function? 54 J. L. & Econ. 207, 208–209 (2011).

These laws were motivated by fears of stranger attacks: if we keep potential offenders away from children, they won't victimize again. Unfortunately, such a perspective is inconsistent with the data, as a policy paper from the Association for the Treatment of Sexual Abusers explains:

> [R]esearch has indicated that the majority of sexual abuse is perpetrated by someone known to the victim, such as a family member, acquaintance, teacher, coach or friend. According to the US Bureau of Justice Statistics, 93% of children were sexually abused by someone known to them, such as a family member or acquaintance. . . . [A]pproximately 60% of offenses take place in the victim's home or the home of someone known to them. Therefore, policies based on "stranger danger" do not adequately address the reality of sexual abuse.
>
> Research shows that residing close to schools or daycare centers does not increase risk to sexually reoffend. [One research team] compared the proximity of recidivists and non-recidivists to schools and daycares . . . in Florida. Those who lived within 1,000, 1,500, or 2,500 feet of schools or daycare centers did not reoffend more frequently than those who lived farther away. The Minnesota Department of Corrections . . . investigated the characteristics of 224 sexual reoffense crimes and the authors concluded that residence restrictions would not have prevented even one re-offense. Most of the offenses involving children were committed not by strangers, but by sexual offenders who were closely acquainted with their victims, such as parents, caretakers, paramours of the mother, babysitters, or friends of the family. The repeat offender was a neighbor of the victim in only about 4% of the cases. Sexual assaults that occurred within a mile of the offender's residence also typically involved adult victims, and none of the crimes took place in or near a school, daycare center, or park.[34]

Not only are residency requirements based on an erroneous model about how sex offenders encounter their victims, but they may actually aggravate the risk of recidivism by those on whom they are employed. The ATRA report notes that successful treatment of sex offenders requires "supportive environments that focus on improving psychosocial functioning in order to reduce the likelihood of recidivism. Support services should include access to housing, employment opportunities, prosocial support persons, mental health treatment, and transportation." Not surprisingly, residency restrictions cut against these:

> The unintended consequences of residence restrictions include transience, homelessness, instability, and other obstacles to

---

[34] ASSOCIATION FOR THE TREATMENT OF SEXUAL ABUSERS, SEXUAL OFFENDER RESIDENCY RESTRICTIONS 2 (2014).

community reentry that may actually compromise, rather than promote, public safety. Offenders are often pushed to areas that are more rural (the higher the population density, the more likely neighborhoods include schools, parks, etc.) which often leads to diminished access to specialized treatment and close monitoring by law enforcement professionals, as well as disproportionally clustering offenders in areas with more compliant housing.

Employment and housing disruption, as well as separation from supportive and/or dependent family members, can hinder effective treatment and may interfere with the overall goal of reducing recidivism and re-victimization. In fact, unemployment, unstable housing, and lack of support are associated with increased criminal recidivism. Thus, residence restrictions, aimed at improving community safety may inadvertently create an environment in which offenders are at an increased risk to reoffend.[35]

In some cases, sex offenders have been forced to live under bridges (with state support), clustered in run-down hotels on the edges of towns, or find themselves homeless (but denied access to homeless shelters) or living in their cars due to the inability to find anyplace legal to live. Not surprisingly, the rate of abscondment by sex offenders has risen. All of this makes it even harder to provide offenders with treatment, and it makes their lives more stressful and thus more at risk of relapse. Furthermore, many simply fail to comply with the law, leaving them at risk of being returned to prison:

> Researchers have continued to document the difficulties in monitoring and enforcement of residence restrictions. . . . In Ohio, 31% to 45% of sex offenders were in violation of residence restrictions. Roughly half of sex offenders maintained a residence within a restricted zone in Florida and Texas, and noncompliance rates were even higher in New York. The enforcement of these laws becomes particularly difficult with the enactment of community-level restrictions, and several states have passed legislation that allows judges and local authorities to determine the size and nature of residence restrictions.
>
> Discretion to monitor and enforce residence restrictions varies by state, community, and community supervision officer. Individual agents will differ in their perspectives and approaches. For instance, agents who support residence restriction legislation are more likely to enforce restrictions. The extent to which agents align with the culture and goals of their

---

[35] *Id.* at 3.

agency can certainly influence discretionary strategies of monitoring and enforcement.[36]

Given all this, it is not surprising that the empirical work on residency requirements—a topic that has not actually received that much statistical attention—generally finds that they have no effect on recidivism rates by sex offenders. If anything, it is perhaps somewhat surprising that the results do not find that restrictions are *positively* correlated with reoffending (either via a sex or non-sex crime).[37]

———

In the end, many of the restrictions we place on returning inmates reflect a tension between short-run public safety and longer-run desistance and rehabilitation. Many of the rules are intended to deny the parolee the ability to commit crimes right away: without a car, there's no getaway; without drinking, there's a lower chance of alcohol-fueled aggression; denied access to public housing, there's less of a chance of victimizing residents. But many of these rules impede desistance and rehabilitation. Limited employment opportunities, or even denying access to a car, blocks offenders from the benefits of employment; residency restrictions push parolees toward temporary housing or homeless, adding to stress and undermining social capital; and so on. During the crime boom and the years after, the primary focus was on the short run. Perhaps one benefit of low crime rates and the shift towards being "smart" rather than "tough" on crime will be a growing interest in aiding longer-run desistance.

QUESTIONS

1. **Winners and losers.** As conviction records have become more widely accessible, some people have won, and others have lost. Among young black men, who do you think have gained the most? Does this complicate the normative arguments of groups such as "Ban the Box" which want to make it harder for employers to know about prior criminal records?

2. **Partial solutions.** Obviously knowledge of prior records is important in *some* cases: we don't want people convicted of sex crimes against children working in daycares, or those with histories of theft in banks. How could we design a prior-record system that balances these concerns against re-entry goals?

3. **Disenfranchisement.** Some studies have argued that Florida went for Bush rather than Gore in the 2000 election because so many likely-Democratic black voters were ineligible to vote due to a prior conviction. The studies make these claims by imputing to felons the voting behavior of similar non-felons (same race, age, socio-economic status, education). Do you

———

[36] Beth M. Huebner et al., *The Effect and Implications of Sex Offender Residence Restrictions*, 13 CRIMINOLOGY & PUB. POL'Y 139, 156 (2014).

[37] *Id.* at 142–143.

see any concerns with this approach? How does this shape your views of state-level (as opposed to individual-level) studies that show little difference in voting outcomes between states that disenfranchise heavily and those that do not?

4. **Punishment theories and collateral consequences.** Are these collateral consequences consistent with retribution as a normative goal? With rehabilitation? With incapacitation? With deterrence? If yes, in most cases? Some cases? And even if a good (or satisfactory) *theoretical* match, are there any policy concerns with how well the consequences advance that particular theory?

5. **Post-conviction bail.** One nascent trend in the United States is towards "post-conviction bail," in which convicts are required to post a bond to a private bail-bondsman, who then ensures that the offender completes all aspects of his punishment, including any fines and post-release treatment programs. Can you justify such a practice? Does your answer turn on whether the sanction is (county-funded) probation or (perhaps state-funded) parole?

6. **Poorly reasoned residency restrictions.** Sex offenders are not allowed to live near schools. Sex offenders are, like all parolees, required to find a job. Can you see something illogical here? Does this suggest that we might be operating in a time more of moral panic than of real crime control when it comes to sex offenses?

When talking through question 4, it should become clear that many of the conditions we impose on parolees seem unlikely to facilitate "success," no matter which theory we turn to for a definition. But the sheer volume of people leaving prison each year has made the challenge of reentry—and the need to ensure greater levels of success—an issue of increasing importance for numerous reformers. Consider the following arguments from Joan Petersilia about how to best reform our parole system.[38] She argues that successful reintegration requires change in four key areas:

1. Alter the in-prison experience. Provide more education, work, and rehabilitation opportunities. Change the prison environment to promote life skills rather than violence and domination.

2. Change prison release and revocation practices. Institute a system of discretionary parole release that incorporates parole release guidelines. These parole guidelines should be based primarily on recidivism prediction.

3. Revise post-prison services and supervision. Incorporate better parole supervision classification systems, and target

---

[38] PETERSILIA, PRISONERS COME HOME, supra note 22 at 171–220.

services and surveillance to those with high need and risk profiles.

4. Foster collaborations with the community and enhance mechanisms of informal social control. Develop partnerships with service providers, ex-convicts, law enforcement, family members, victim advocates, and neighborhoods to support the offender.[39]

Those are fairly broad and lofty goals, so it is worth looking the twelve specific proposals she makes for accomplishing them:

1. Encourage prison officials to embrace re-integration as the goal of confinement. Reintegration programs should start almost immediately upon *entry* for most inmates, and such a holistic view requires administrators to be committed to the idea of reintegration.

2. Prisons need treatment, work, and education tracks to prep inmates for re-entry. These programs should not be viewed as perks to be awarded or withheld but as core functions of the prison. And a growing body of rigorous empirical research can help administrators know which programs are proven to be effective. That said, Petersilia warns of some limitations: the effects of the proven programs are moderate, so we don't want to oversell their effectiveness; most programs are evaluated using poor methodology, so the research base can be hard for administrators to understand; and sometimes even effective programs are not necessarily *cost* effective.

3. Inmates should be encouraged to take on personal responsibility through "parallel universe" concepts. Simply learning how to read, etc., is of little use if the inmate doesn't understand *why* the skill is useful. "Parallel Universe" models attempt to make inmate life mirror the outside world as much as possible: they take on work-related and non-work related activities at appropriate times, learn relapse-prevention strategies, earn chances to make choices and be held accountable for those choices, and can earn benefits for good conduct.

4. "Prisoners should participate in comprehensive pre-release planning." Prison life is not outside life, and prisoners, especially those who have been in for a while, need help learning skills like filling out job applications, learning how to ride the bus or acquire a driver's license, and what legal restrictions they face on parole. Some also argue that inmates need training on how to adopt more "pro-social"

---

[39] *Id.* at 171–172.

attitudes to help them integrate better into the wider population.

5. Bring back discretionary parole, based on risk (of recidivism) analysis. Not only does the abolition of parole eliminate a major carrot for encouraging inmate behavior/release-planning, but it makes it harder to states to prioritize the confinement of violent offenders. The development of actuarial models creates the opportunity to bring back release without all the concerns of abuse of discretion.

6. Ask victims about timing of release and whether special parole conditions are needed. This can be seen as a simple moral good in and of itself, or as a way to ensure victims feel heard. It's also often the case that victims can provide the most information about the nature of the crime and its consequences.

7. Take advantage of technological advances to better monitor high-risk, violent releasees. The nature of tracking technology improves every year (ankle bracelets, smartphone apps, etc.), and it gives us more and more opportunities to allow felons to live more cheaply outside of prison while minimizing their risk of reoffending.

8. Provide treatment and work programs to all parolees who want them.

9. Neighborhood supervision should be adopted by parole offices. "Neighborhood supervision" is built on the idea that parole officers should be more involved in the parolee's community, acting as a mediator between the returning inmate and his new environment, offering employment, social, and treatment support as needed.

10. Rely more extensively on re-entry courts. See Chapter 11 above for a longer discussion of such courts (and the potential limitations of such a proposal).

11. Use more dynamic, goal-oriented parole terms. In many states, parole terms are roughly one-size-fits-all. Instead, states should make the term reflect the seriousness of the underlying offense, and they should allow the conditions, or lengths of the term, to be modified or reduced as the parolee demonstrates continued success.

12. Allow parolees to earn back forfeited rights. Some states now offer "certificates of rehabilitation," which restore to parolees certain social rights (like the ability to vote) that they had lost thanks to a felony conviction.

A report by the Urban Institute in 2008 echoed many of these suggestions, and it also added a few of its own. In particular, it suggested that states front-load supervision resources (since the risk of reoffending is greatest early on), work to develop strategies that balance surveillance and treatment, attempt to leverage informal social controls to shape behavior, and use HOPE-like swift-and-sure punishments—in a graduated manner—to deal with parole failures.

QUESTIONS

1. **The relevant metric.** Both Petersilia and the Urban Institute focus on recidivism as the primary metric of "success." Is this correct? What other metrics might be relevant? How would we measure "success" in these cases? Would it change the sort of pre-release and release policies we should employ?

2. **Technocorrections and net-widening.** Petersilia's reforms touch on the use of "technocorrections." In her case, she focuses on tracking and monitoring via ankle bracelets and other forms of GPS tracking. But technological advances allow us to control parolee behavior in other ways. Ignition interlocks, for example, require people to breathe into a sensor before their cars will let them drive, effectively thwarting DUIs. Are these efficient advances, or are there also net-widening concerns here—and if so, are they necessarily *bad* concerns?

C. VIOLATING PAROLE

As noted above, acccording to a 2014 study by the BJS, of a sample of about 400,000 state prisoners released onto parole in 2005 (out of a total of nearly 500,000 conditional that year), approximately 76% were rearrested within five years, 55% were reconvicted, and 55% were readmitted to prison on either a new charge or due to a parole violation.[40] In this section we consider the rules that govern parole revocations, and then we consider exactly *why* people are failing parole—is it more "technical" administrative failures or new substantive offenses—and look at the impact, if any, parole violations have had on overall prison growth.

C.1. RIGHTS AND PROCEDURES AT VIOLATION HEARINGS

A prisoner may have no right to parole, and thus few process claims for how (or whether) it is granted, but that changes once he is freed from prison. As a parolee, he *does* have a liberty interest in *remaining* free, and thus the government is legally required to provide some procedural protections in the revocation process. The Supreme Court laid out its basic view in *Morrissey v. Brewer*, and then discussed the more limited

---

[40] Matthew R. Durose, Alexia D. Cooper, & Howard N. Snyder, Recidivism of Prisoners Released in 30 States in 2005: Patterns from 2005 to 2010 (2014). Note that the sample sizes are slightly different for each measure: 30 states for arrests, 23 for reconvictions, and 29 for readmissions.

issue of a right to counsel in *Gagnon v. Scarpell*. The two cases are excerpted here.

Morrissey v. Brewer
408 U.S 471 (1972)

■ CHIEF JUSTICE BURGER delivered the opinion of the Court.

We granted certiorari in this case to determine whether the Due Process Clause of the Fourteenth Amendment requires that a State afford an individual some opportunity to be heard prior to revoking his parole.

Before reaching the issue of whether due process applies to the parole system, it is important to recall the function of parole in the correctional process.

During the past 60 years, the practice of releasing prisoners on parole before the end of their sentences has become an integral part of the penological system. Rather than being an *ad hoc* exercise of clemency, parole is an established variation on imprisonment of convicted criminals. Its purpose is to help individuals reintegrate into society as constructive individuals as soon as they are able. . . . It also serves to alleviate the costs to society of keeping an individual in prison. The essence of parole is release from prison, before the completion of sentence, on the condition that the prisoner abide by certain rules during the balance of the sentence.

To accomplish the purpose of parole, those who are allowed to leave prison early are subjected to specified conditions for the duration of their terms.

The enforcement leverage that supports the parole conditions derives from the authority to return the parolee to prison to serve out the balance of his sentence if he fails to abide by the rules. In practice, not every violation of parole conditions automatically leads to revocation. Yet revocation of parole is not an unusual phenomenon, affecting only a few parolees. It has been estimated that 35%–45% of all parolees are subjected to revocation and return to prison. Sometimes revocation occurs when the parolee is accused of another crime; it is often preferred to a new prosecution because of the procedural ease of recommitting the individual on the basis of a lesser showing by the State.

Implicit in the system's concern with parole violations is the notion that the parolee is entitled to retain his liberty as long as he substantially abides by the conditions of his parole. The first step in a revocation decision thus involves a wholly retrospective factual question: whether the parolee has in fact acted in violation of one or more conditions of his parole. Only if it is determined that the parolee did violate the conditions does the second question arise: should the parolee be recommitted to prison or should other steps be taken to protect society and improve chances of rehabilitation? The first step is relatively simple; the second is more complex. The second question involves the application of expertise by the parole authority in making a prediction as to the ability of the individual to live in society without committing antisocial acts. This part of the decision, too, depends on facts, and therefore it is important for the board to know not only that some violation was committed but also to know accurately how many and how serious the violations were. Yet this second step, deciding what to do about the violation once it is identified, is not purely factual but also predictive and discretionary.

If a parolee is returned to prison, he usually receives no credit for the time "served" on parole. Thus, the returnee may face a potential of substantial imprisonment.

We begin with the proposition that the revocation of parole is not part of a criminal prosecution and thus the full panoply of rights due a defendant in such a proceeding does not apply to parole revocations. Parole arises after the end of the criminal prosecution, including imposition of sentence. Supervision is not directly by the court but by an administrative agency, which is sometimes an arm of the court and sometimes of the executive. Revocation deprives an individual, not of the absolute liberty to which every citizen is entitled, but only of the conditional liberty properly dependent on observance of special parole restrictions.

We turn, therefore, to the question whether the requirements of due process in general apply to parole revocations. Whether any procedural protections are due depends on the extent to which an individual will be "condemned to suffer grievous loss." Once it is determined that due process applies, the question remains what process is due. It has been said so often by this Court and others as not to require citation of authority that due process is flexible and calls for such procedural protections as the particular situation demands. [I]t is a recognition that not all situations calling for procedural safeguards call for the same kind of procedure.

We turn to an examination of the nature of the interest of the parolee in his continued liberty. The liberty of a parolee enables him to do a wide range of things open to persons who have never been convicted of any crime. The parolee has been released from prison based on an evaluation that he shows reasonable promise of being able to return to society and function as a responsible, self-reliant person. Subject to the conditions of his parole, he can be gainfully employed and is free to be with family and friends and to form the other enduring attachments of normal life. Though the State properly subjects him to many restrictions not applicable to other citizens, his condition is very different from that of confinement in a prison. He may have been on parole for a number of years and may be living a relatively normal life at the time he is faced with revocation. The parolee has relied on at least an implicit promise that parole will be revoked only if he fails to live up to the parole conditions. In many cases, the parolee faces lengthy incarceration if his parole is revoked.

We see, therefore, that the liberty of a parolee, although indeterminate, includes many of the core values of unqualified liberty and its termination inflicts a "grievous loss" on the parolee and often on others. It is hardly useful any longer to try to deal with this problem in terms of whether the parolee's liberty is a "right" or a "privilege." By whatever name, the liberty is valuable and must be seen as within the protection of the Fourteenth Amendment. Its termination calls for some orderly process, however informal.

Turning to the question what process is due, we find that the State's interests are several. The State has found the parolee guilty of a crime against the people. That finding justifies imposing extensive restrictions on the individual's liberty. Release of the parolee before the end of his prison sentence is made with the recognition that with many prisoners there is a risk that they will not be able to live in society without committing additional antisocial acts. Given the previous conviction and the proper imposition of conditions, the State has an overwhelming interest in being able to return the individual to imprisonment without the burden of a new adversary criminal trial if in fact he has failed to abide by the conditions of his parole.

Yet, the State has no interest in revoking parole without some informal procedural guarantees. Although the parolee is often formally described as being "in custody," the argument cannot even be made here that summary treatment is necessary as it may be with respect to controlling a large group of potentially disruptive prisoners in actual custody. Nor are we persuaded by the argument that revocation is so totally a discretionary matter that some form of hearing would be administratively intolerable. A simple factual hearing will not interfere with the exercise of discretion.

This discretionary aspect of the revocation decision need not be reached unless there is first an appropriate determination that the individual has in fact breached the conditions of parole. The parolee is not the only one who has a stake in his conditional liberty. Society has a stake in whatever may be the chance of restoring him to normal and useful life within the law. Society thus has an interest in not having parole revoked because of erroneous information or because of an erroneous evaluation of the need to revoke parole, given the breach of parole conditions. And society has a further interest in treating the parolee with basic fairness: fair treatment in parole revocations will enhance the chance of rehabilitation by avoiding reactions to arbitrariness.

We now turn to the nature of the process that is due, bearing in mind that the interest of both State and parolee will be furthered by an effective but informal hearing. In analyzing what is due, we see two important stages in the typical process of parole revocation.

(a) Arrest of Parolee and Preliminary Hearing. The first stage occurs when the parolee is arrested and detained, usually at the direction of his parole officer. The second occurs when parole is formally revoked. There is typically a substantial time lag between the arrest and the eventual determination by the parole board whether parole should be revoked. Additionally, it may be that the parolee is arrested at a place distant from the state institution, to which he may be returned before the final decision is made concerning revocation. Given these factors, due process would seem to require that some minimal inquiry be conducted at or reasonably near the place of the alleged parole violation or arrest and as promptly as convenient after arrest while information is fresh and sources are available. Such an inquiry should be seen as in the nature of a "preliminary hearing" to determine whether there is probable cause or reasonable ground to believe that the arrested parolee has committed acts that would constitute a violation of parole conditions.

In our view, due process requires that after the arrest, the determination that reasonable ground exists for revocation of parole should be made by someone not directly involved in the case.

This independent officer need not be a judicial officer. The granting and revocation of parole are matters traditionally handled by administrative officers. It will be sufficient, therefore, in the parole revocation context, if an evaluation of whether reasonable cause exists to believe that conditions of parole have been violated is made by someone such as a parole officer other than the one who has made the report of parole violations or has recommended revocation.

With respect to the preliminary hearing before this officer, the parolee should be given notice that the hearing will take place and that its purpose is to determine whether there is probable cause to believe he has committed a parole violation. The notice should state what parole violations have been alleged. At the hearing the parolee may appear and speak in his own behalf; he may bring letters, documents, or individuals who can give relevant information to the hearing officer. On request of the parolee, person who has given adverse information on which parole revocation is to be based is to be made available for questioning in his presence. However, if the hearing officer determines that an informant would be subjected to risk of harm if his identity were disclosed, he need not be subjected to confrontation and cross-examination.

The hearing officer shall have the duty of making a summary, or digest, of what occurs at the hearing in terms of the responses of the parolee and the substance of the documents or evidence given in support of parole revocation and of the parolee's position. Based on the information before him, the officer should determine whether there is probable cause to hold the parolee for the final decision of the parole board on revocation. Such a determination would be sufficient to warrant the parolee's continued detention and return to the state correctional institution pending the final decision.

(b) The Revocation Hearing. There must also be an opportunity for a hearing, if it is desired by the parolee, prior to the final decision on revocation by the parole authority. This hearing must be the basis for more than determining probable cause; it must lead to a final evaluation of any contested relevant facts and consideration of whether the facts as determined warrant revocation. The parolee must have an opportunity to be heard and to show, if he can, that he did not violate the conditions, or, if he did, that circumstances in mitigation suggest that the violation does not warrant revocation. The revocation hearing must be tendered within a reasonable time after the parolee is taken into custody. A lapse of two months, as respondents suggest occurs in some cases, would not appear to be unreasonable.

We cannot write a code of procedure; that is the responsibility of each State. Most States have done so by legislation, others by judicial decision usually on due process grounds. Our task is limited to deciding the minimum requirements of due process. They include (a) written notice of the claimed violations of parole; (b) disclosure to the parolee of evidence against him; (c) opportunity to be heard in person and to present witnesses and documentary evidence; (d) the right to confront and cross-examine adverse witnesses (unless the hearing officer specifically finds good cause for not allowing confrontation); (e) a "neutral and detached" hearing body such as a traditional parole board, members of which need not be judicial officers or lawyers; and (f) a written statement by the factfinders as to the evidence relied on and reasons for revoking parole. We emphasize there is no thought to equate this second stage of parole revocation to a criminal prosecution in any sense. It is a narrow inquiry; the process should be flexible enough to consider evidence including letters, affidavits, and other material that would not be admissible in an adversary criminal trial.

We do not reach or decide the question whether the parolee is entitled to the assistance of retained counsel or to appointed counsel if he is indigent.

We have no thought to create an inflexible structure for parole revocation procedures. The few basic requirements set out above, which are applicable to future revocations of parole, should not impose a great burden on any State's parole system. Control over the required proceedings by the hearing officers can assure that delaying tactics and other abuses sometimes present in the traditional adversary trial situation do not occur. Obviously a parolee cannot relitigate issues determined against him in other forums, as in the situation presented when the revocation is based on conviction of another crime.

Reversed and remanded.

■ JUSTICE DOUGLAS, dissenting in part.

Procedural due process requires the following.

If a violation of a condition of parole is involved, rather than the commission of a new offense, there should not be an arrest of the parolee and his return to the prison or to a local jail. Rather, notice of the alleged violation should be given to the parolee and a time set for a hearing. The hearing should not be before the parole officer, as he is the one who is making the charge and "there is inherent danger in combining the functions of judge and advocate." Moreover, the parolee should be entitled to counsel. As the Supreme Court of Oregon said in *Perry v. Williard*, "A hearing in which counsel is absent or is present only on behalf of one side is inherently unsatisfactory if not unfair. Counsel can see that relevant facts are brought out, vague and insubstantial allegations discounted, and irrelevancies eliminated."

The hearing required is not a grant of the full panoply of rights applicable to a criminal trial. But confrontation with the informer may . . . be necessary for a fair hearing and the ascertainment of the truth. The hearing is to determine the fact of parole violation. The results of the hearing would go to the parole board—or other authorized state agency—for final action, as would cases which involved voluntary admission of violations.

The rule of law is important in the stability of society. Arbitrary actions in the revocation of paroles can only impede and impair the rehabilitative aspects of modern penology.

I would not prescribe the precise formula for the management of the parole problems. We do not sit as an ombudsman, telling the States the precise procedures they must follow. I would hold that so far as the due process requirements of parole revocation are concerned:

(1) the parole officer—whatever may be his duties under various state statutes—in Iowa appears to be an agent having some of the functions of a prosecutor and of the police; the parole officer is therefore not qualified as a hearing officer;

(2) the parolee is entitled to a due process notice and a due process hearing of the alleged parole violations including, for example, the opportunity to be confronted by his accusers and to present evidence and argument on his own behalf; and

(3) the parolee is entitled to the freedom granted a parolee until the results of the hearing are known and the parole board—or other authorized state agency—acts.

I would reverse the judgments and remand for further consideration in light of this opinion.

The next year, in *Gagnon v. Scarpelli*, 411 U.S. 778 (1973), the Court addressed directly the issue of whether indigent parolees (and probationers, since Gagnon was on probation) were entitled to state-provided counsel. It's answer was ambiguous: sometimes. As the Court explained:

> The introduction of counsel into a revocation proceeding will alter significantly the nature of the proceeding. If counsel is provided for the probationer or parolee, the State in turn will normally provide its own counsel; lawyers, by training and disposition, are advocates and bound by professional duty to present all available evidence and arguments in support of their clients' positions and to contest with vigor all adverse evidence and views. The role of the hearing body itself, aptly described in *Morrissey* as being "predictive and discretionary" as well as factfinding, may become more akin to that of a judge at a trial, and less attuned to the rehabilitative needs of the individual probationer or parolee. In the greater self-consciousness of its quasi-judicial role, the hearing body may be less tolerant of marginal deviant behavior and feel more pressure to reincarcerate than to continue nonpunitive rehabilitation. Certainly, the decisionmaking process will be prolonged, and the financial cost to the State—for appointed counsel, counsel for the State, a longer record, and the possibility of judicial review—will not be insubstantial.
>
> In some cases, these modifications in the nature of the revocation hearing must be endured and the costs borne because, as we have indicated above, the probationer's or parolee's version of a disputed issue can fairly be represented only by a trained advocate. But due process is not so rigid as to require that the significant interests in informality, flexibility, and economy must always be sacrificed.
>
> We thus find no justification for a new inflexible constitutional rule with respect to the requirement of counsel. We think, rather, that the decision as to the need for counsel must be made on a case-by-case basis in the exercise of a sound discretion by the state authority charged with responsibility for administering the probation and parole system. Although the presence and participation of counsel will probably be both undesirable and constitutionally unnecessary in most revocation hearings, there will remain certain cases in which fundamental fairness—the touchstone of due process—will require that the State provide at its expense counsel for indigent probationers or parolees.
>
> It is neither possible nor prudent to attempt to formulate a precise and detailed set of guidelines to be followed in

determining when the providing of counsel is necessary to meet the applicable due process requirements. The facts and circumstances in preliminary and final hearings are susceptible of almost infinite variation, and a considerable discretion must be allowed the responsible agency in making the decision. Presumptively, it may be said that counsel should be provided in cases where, after being informed of his right to request counsel, the probationer or parolee makes such a request, based on a timely and colorable claim (i) that he has not committed the alleged violation of the conditions upon which he is at liberty; or (ii) that, even if the violation is a matter of public record or is uncontested, there are substantial reasons which justified or mitigated the violation and make revocation inappropriate, and that the reasons are complex or otherwise difficult to develop or present. In passing on a request for the appointment of counsel, the responsible agency also should consider, especially in doubtful cases, whether the probationer appears to be capable of speaking effectively for himself. In every case in which a request for counsel at a preliminary or final hearing is refused, the grounds for refusal should be stated succinctly in the record. [*Id.* at 788–790.]

As always, the Supreme Court sets the minimum bar, and states remain free to grant parolees even more procedural protections than those laid out in *Morrissey* and *Gagnon*. So, two examples: Wisconsin, for example, has created a statutory right to counsel in all revocation cases, going beyond the requirements of *Gagnon*. And since *Morrissey* is silent as to who needs to hear the revocation, states vary there as well: Colorado requires a single parole board member to preside over the revocation proceeding, Louisiana at least three members of the boards, and Wisconsin requires an administrative law judge.

When talking about the HOPE program above, we noted that some critics have argued that formal procedures do not necessarily work in the state's—or *parolee's*—favor. Consider a parolee contemplating whether to smoke marijuana on a given Tuesday. Under the traditional parole system, even if he fails a drug test on Thursday his preliminary hearing may be weeks in the future and his final hearing months after that, and he may make bail during the interim (though the standards for post-conviction bail are less favorable than those pre-conviction). Under HOPE, he would be admitted to prison that very Thursday and would not be released until the start of the next week: revocation is swift and certain (and, ideally, fair—as HOPE spreads beyond Hawaii, it is being renamed "Swift, Certain, and Fair").[41] Those who commit crimes, as we've noted several times before, are more likely discount the future more heavily, so the immediacy and certainty of HOPE may serve as a

---

[41] No other state name starts with H, so the acronym doesn't travel very well.

greater deterrent—but it works only if the procedural rights parolees face are lower.

Of course, HOPE-like procedures cannot work everywhere and in all circumstances: they are best applied to situations in which violations can be easily and objectively detected (such as via a drug test), and in which the violations do not mandate more-extensive re-incarceration, either for moral or pragmatic reason.

QUESTIONS

1. **Pretextual revocations.** The Court in *Morrisey* notes that a parole revocation isn't entitled to the same protections as a new criminal case. But it also notes that many parolees have their parole revoked in lieu of new charges for a new offense *because revocation* is easier. If the parole revocation is being used as a pretext to lock up the parolee for a new crime, shouldn't he get more protections? Isn't this especially true if the time the parolee faces for revocation is longer than the time he'd likely serve if convicted of the new substantive offense (such as when the new offense is a less serious crime)?

2. **Appointed counsel.** Is the Court's argument that the defendant could be better off without a lawyer an accurate one? Is the problem with lawyers, or with court procedures? Does our recent experiment with drug- and other problem-solving courts affect your answer at all?

3. **Expanding HOPE.** Besides drug offenses, what other sorts of crimes are amenable to swift-certain-fair procedures like those in HOPE?

C.2. TECHNICAL VIOLATIONS

When someone commits a new, substantive offense, the argument for returning the offender to prison is perhaps fairly strong. But what about "technical" violations, which generally refer to instances where the parolee violates either a non-criminal provision (like failing to get a job) or a drug provision (testing positive for drugs or skipping a drug test)? Many commentators lately have argued that we are returning a lot of people to prison on "purely" technical violations, and that this reflects a needless and mindless punitiveness that we should rein in. But two related questions should immediately come to mind: First, how serious are these cases? Are technical violators serious offenders who are returned to prison via technical violations simply because those are easier to prove? And, second, how many true technical violators are returning to prison? As the follow passage makes clear, the impact of true technical violators appears to be overstated:

> Not all parole violations are created equal: some parolees return to prison after committing new, serious offenses, others after more "technical" violations such as failing drug tests or failing to satisfy other more-regulatory conditions of parole. Most of the datasets on prison admissions gathered by the Bureau of Justice

Statistics record that an admission is due to parole revocation, but rarely why parole was revoked. The exceptions here are the periodic Survey of Inmates in State Correctional Facilities and the Survey of Inmates in Federal Correctional Facilities. The most recent wave of the survey, conducted in 2004, interviewed a nationally-representative sample of 14,499 inmates in state prisons across the country. Among the hundreds of questions it asked each inmate was whether that inmate had had parole revoked and, if so, why.

Table 3 summarizes the 2004 Survey's results for its questions about what, if anything, an inmate did to trigger a parole revocation. The first column gives the percentage of all inmates reporting the various reasons for revocation, the second column the percentage of all inmates who were admitted for violating parole.

Table 3: Reasons for Returning to Prison

Reason	% All Inmates	% Violated Inmates
New arrest/offense	10.1%	68.3%
Failed drug test	1.5%	9.3%
Drug possession	1.0%	5.9%
Failed to take drug test	0.4%	2.3%
Failed to report to drug/alcohol treatment	0.4%	2.2%
Failed to report for other counseling	0.4%	2.3%
Failed to report to parole officer	2.7%	17.1%
Left jurisdiction without permission	0.7%	4.3%
Failed to find/maintain employment	0.2%	1.0%
Failed to pay fines	0.3%	1.7%
Contact with known felons	0.2%	1.1%
Possession of gun	0.3%	1.7%
Other reason	1.6%	10.3%

These statistics demonstrate that drug-related technical violations—failing a drug test, failing to take a drug test, or failing to report to treatment—play minimal roles in overall admissions, and even fairly minor roles within the pool of parole revocations. And Table 3 actually overstates the role of technical violations since . . . inmates often reported multiple reasons for being violated back. And revocation for a new offense—arguably the least technical of all violations—is reported by 26% of those who also failed a drug test, 29% of those who also failed to report to a drug test, 31% of those who also failed to report to treatment, 36% of those who also failed to report to other treatment, and so on. Moreover, for over half of those who reported both a new offense violation and a drug test violation, the new offense was something more serious than a drug crime—either a violent or property offense. Only 22% of those who reported failing parole due to both a technical drug violation and a new offense reported that the new offense was a drug crime.

Furthermore, new drug offenses do not appear to be triggering parolee violations at a significant rate. Among those violated back for a new offense, a drug offense was the top new charge in only 20.3% of the cases. Violent and property offenses comprised 60.3% of all revoking new offenses: 37.5% violent, 22.8% property.[42]

In other words, only a fairly small percent of "technical" parole revocations were purely technical. Of those who returned to prison due to a parole revocation, over two-thirds—68.3%—came back for new crime (making up slightly more than 10% of all prison admissions). And these new offenses were generally violent or property crimes, thus not, say, a drug charge tied to the drugs that led to a drug-test failure (which would feel like a technical violation-related new offense). Even among those who did not return for a new offense (which, of course, does not mean they didn't *commit* a new offense), many of the cases involved multiple technical violations, not just one. So whatever impact parole violations have had on prison growth—the topic we turn to next—it has been primarily through the impact of substantive, not technical, violations.

C.3. THE IMPACT OF PAROLE VIOLATIONS ON PRISON GROWTH

The boom in incarceration that began in the late 1970s has, perhaps not surprisingly, been accompanied by a boom in parole releases. From 107,691 in 1978, the number of people conditionally released almost *pentupled* to nearly 506,000 in 2007, though that number had declined to slightly under 400,000 by 2013 (which is still more than triple the 1978 level). Even as many states "abolish" parole and adopt truth-in-

---

[42] John F. Pfaff. *The War on Drugs and Prison Growth: Limited Importance, Limited Legislative Options*, 52 HARV. J. ON LEGIS. 173, 190–191 (2015).

sentencing laws that require certain violent offenders to serve a minimum of 85% of their sentences, parole remains the dominant form of release, with about 70% of all releases consistently being onto some form of parole or supervised release.

At the same time, the number of parole *violations* back to prison has risen, from almost 24,000 in 1978 to 253,000 in 2008, though dropping to about 164,000 in 2013. That's a remarkably steep *ten-fold* increase (though keep the baseline in mind), which is sharp enough to lead many to argue that revocations have played a major role in driving up prison populations. The following reading, however, points out that this is actually a difficult argument to make, not just empirically, but conceptually.

John F. Pfaff, *The War on Drugs and Prison Growth: Limited Importance, Limited Legislative Options*
52 HARV. J. ON LEGIS. 173, 190–191 (2015)

That people posit a link between parole revocations and prison growth is understandable. Consider Figure 3A, which plots the number of prisoners released onto parole and the number of parolees violated back to prison for all fifty states except California.* As the prison population rose, so too do did the number of parole releases and parole revocations: between 1978 and 2012, prison populations grew by 376%, parole releases by 339%, and parole revocations by 606%. Parole revocations rose much more quickly than the population as a whole, which at first glance implies that they may have played a role in pushing populations up—although, as always, base rates matter.

Figures 3B and 3C, however, quickly complicate that simple narrative. Figure 3B plots both annual releases (whether onto parole or otherwise) as a percent of total prison population and annual parole releases as a percent of all releases. What Figure 3B shows is that about 45% to 50% of the total prison population is consistently released each year, and that parole releases are consistently about 70% of all releases. In other words, as prison populations marched steadily upwards from the 1980s into the 2010s, a relatively constant fraction of inmates was released each year, and a relatively constant fraction of those released were released onto parole.[43]

Figure 3C then attempts to estimate the extent to which the risk of parole revocation changes over time, by computing—roughly—the

---

* *Ed. note*: During this time, California became an extreme outlier in the extent to which it relied on parole releases and revocations to manage its outsized prison population. Given its size and extreme behavior, it throws off nationally-aggregated statistics.

[43] Both the share of releases and parole's share of those releases declines somewhat in the mid-1990s, which is likely due to the adoption of parole-restricting policies such as Truth-in-Sentencing Laws in the wake of the Violent Crime Control Act of 1994. Note, though, that both rebound a bit in the 2000s and the total drop for each is about five points.

fraction of a year's parole releases that are revoked the following year. For example, the y-axis measures, say, the number of parole revocations in 1990 divided by the number of parole releases in 1989; the lag is used to capture the fact that parole revocations are not immediate. This rough estimate of the risk of revocation does trend upwards from the late 1970s to the early 1990s, but over the course of the 1990s and 2000s it is generally stable, if somewhat noisy.

Taken together, then, these figures tell an interesting story: while parole revocations have risen, this rise seems to be the result of prison growth, not its cause. As prison populations have risen, a relatively constant fraction of prisoners have been released in general, and released onto parole in particular. And at least since the 1990s, the risk that these parolees would be violated back to prison has remained fairly constant as well. These results strongly suggest that at least from the 1990s on, prison growth has driven up parole revocations, not the other way around.

The claim that growth is causing revocations rather than revocations driving growth is further supported by Figure 3D, which plots the percent of prison admissions that are parole revocations. As admissions grew over the course of the prison boom, the share of parole revocations in each admissions cohort has been fairly stable, again at least since the early 1990s. And even before then, it only rose by about ten percentage points over fifteen years. In other words, while admissions rose by 28% between 1994 and 2012, the share of admissions due to parole revocations rose by about one percentage point, from 25.7% to 26.7%. Note, too, that prison growth appears to be driven entirely by admissions, not by time served; that parole violations are not driving up admissions implies that they are not driving up prison populations overall.

Figure 3A: Parole Releases and Parole Revocations

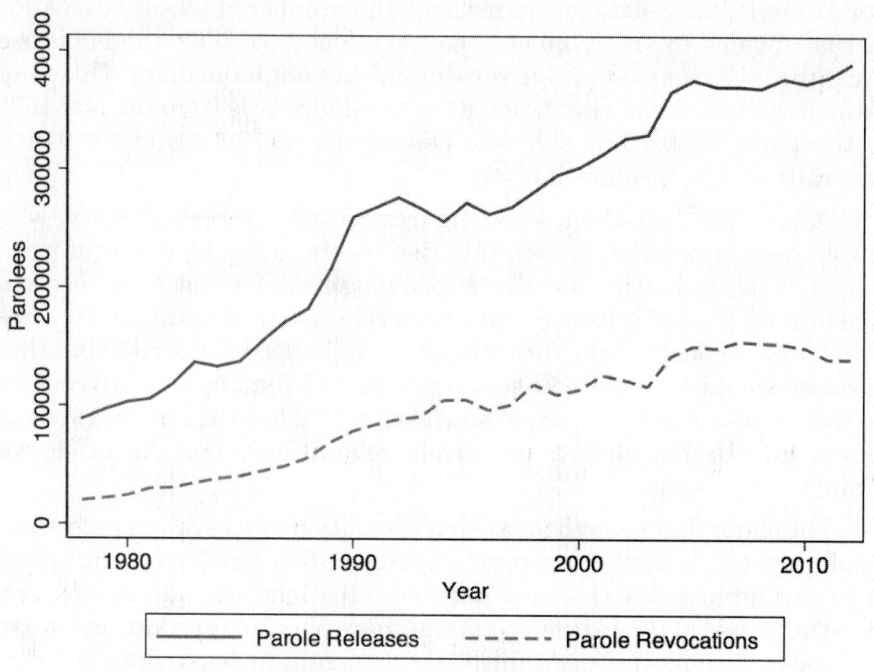

Note: Data from NPS, excluding California.

Figure 3B: Parole and Release Shares

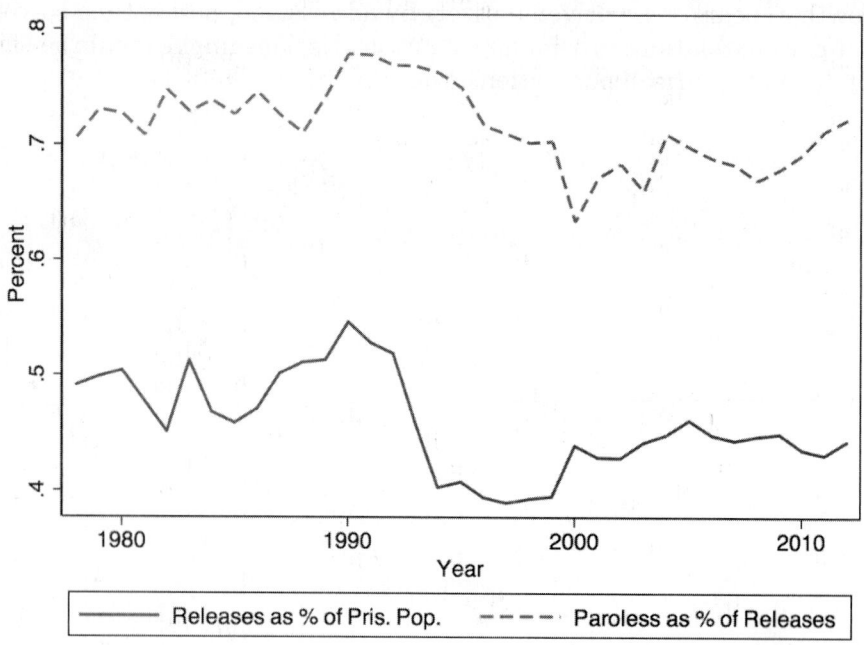

Note: Data from NPS, excluding California.

Figure 3C: Percent of Parole Releases Resulting in Revocations

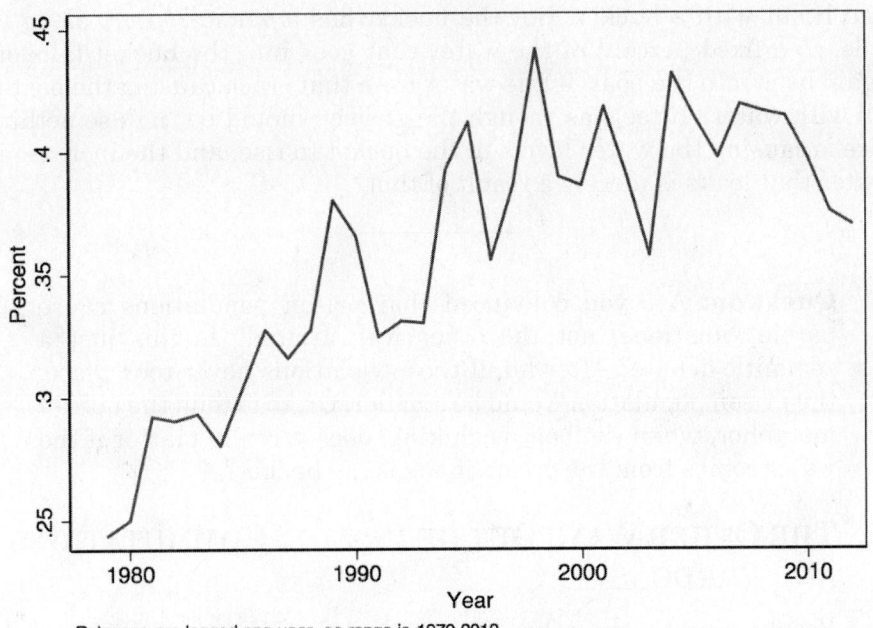

Releases are lagged one year, so range is 1979-2012.

Note: Data from NPS, excluding California.

Figure 3D: Parole Revocations as Percent of All Admissions

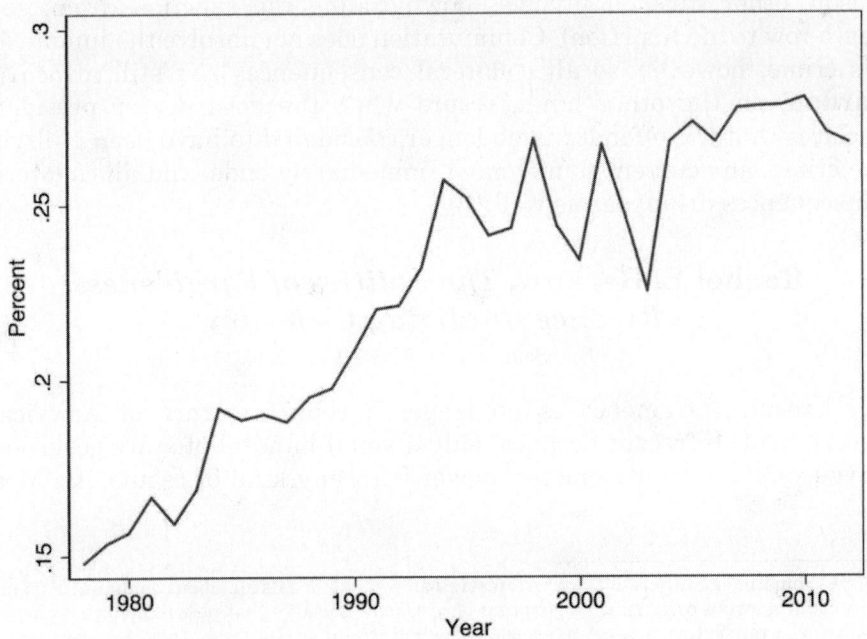

Note: Data from NPS, excluding California.

The argument here can be summarized with a simple metaphor. Assume there is a boat filling up with water, and someone is trying to bail it out with a bucket. But the bucket has a vertical crack along its side, so a fixed percent of the water that goes into the bucket falls out again back into the boat. Is the water from that crack causing the boat to fill with water? It feels as though the answer should be "no"; something else is causing the water levels in the bucket to rise, and the increase in water that leaks is merely a result of that.

Question: Are you convinced that prison populations cause parole violations, not the other way around? Is this just a semantic debate? After all, if those violations never took place, the prison population would be smaller. Or, to extend the bucket metaphor, when the boat is sinking, does it really matter if the water comes from the ocean or the leaky bucket?

D. THE OTHER WAYS OUT OF PRISON: COMMUTATIONS AND PARDONS

Besides parole, the other major ways that inmates can either be released from prison early, or at least released from the collateral costs of conviction, are via commutation or pardon. **Commutation** occurs when the inmate's punishment is replaced with something less severe. In most cases, commutations occur when the inmate is released early from prison; other times it involves downgrading the sanction (from, say, death row to life in prison). Commutation does not absolve the inmate for his crime, however, so all collateral consequences can still attach. A **pardon**, on the other hand, occurs when the governor or president declares that the offender is no longer considered to have been guilty of the crime: any current punishment immediately ends, and all collateral consequences disappear as well.[44]

Rachel E. Barkow, *The Politics of Forgiveness: Reconceptualizing Clemency*
21 Fed. Sent. Rpt'r 153, 153–155 (2009)

Executive clemency is no longer a robust feature of American government. In recent decades, only a small handful of state governors have exercised their clemency power with any kind of regularity. Most

---

[44] Sometimes authors include **amnesties** as well when talking about commutations and pardons. Amnesties occur when a governor or president declares that he will not press charges against a certain category of offender, such as when President Jimmy Carter declared that the US government would not prosecute anyone who had escaped to Canada to avoid the draft. Amnesty, however, is less a back-end change in sentencing and more a front-end decision by the executive about how to deploy his enforcement, not sanctioning, resources.

governors, like recent presidents, have rarely used their power to commute sentences and have issued pardons sporadically and erratically.

In an era with more than seven million people either serving time in prison or under some form of supervised release, the question of how to reinvigorate clemency has become an urgent one. Commutation through executive clemency is often the only hope for correcting a sentence after it has been imposed by a judge because parole has been abolished or dramatically curtailed in many jurisdictions, and judicial sentencing reduction power after a sentence has been handed down is weak or nonexistent in most places. Even after an offender has served his or her sentence in full, clemency is important because the collateral consequences of conviction do not end with release from prison. The executive's power to pardon is often the only means by which offenders can remove or limit legal restrictions to enable them to reenter and reintegrate into society.

The dilemma is that the pressing need for robust clemency is equaled by the difficulty of achieving it. Politicians remain afraid of soft-on-crime accusations or facing a Willie Horton-style advertisement should an individual on the receiving end of a pardon or commutation go on to commit another crime. And in a legal era that calls for transparency and regularity of process, an unfettered and undisclosed clemency power has been under attack by legal reformers and scholars.

Recent decades have seen a precipitous drop in the number of clemency requests being granted by state executives and the president. The number of pardons has decreased, and commutations are particularly rare, with the president and the vast majority of states governors granting only a handful of commutations in the past decade—all while the number of people being sentenced escalates at a rapid rate.

But the general pattern masks some notable exceptions. First, individual governors have bucked this trend, granting a high number of clemency requests in a variety of cases even when facing reelection or with the goal of seeking a higher office. Former Arkansas Governor Mike Huckabee, for example, stands out for having granted clemency (pardons and commutations) to more than 1,000 individuals in his time as governor, many of which occurred in his first term in office. Former Maryland Governor Robert E[h]rlich similarly granted a high number of pardons and commutations. Virginia Governor Timothy Kaine is also granting clemency requests at a rapid clip. In only his first fourteen months in office, he granted nine commutations and restored the rights of 768 individuals.

Huckabee and Kaine's approach to clemency seems to have been driven in part by their religious faith and moral convictions. Ehrlich's view was that he had a constitutional duty to take pardon seriously. Notably, none of them have appeared to have suffered politically for their clemency decisions.

Second, some governors have targeted specific populations for relief or granted only a narrow form of relief. In Colorado, Governor Bill Ritter established a new board to review clemency applications of juveniles who were tried as adults and imprisoned in adult facilities. This may or may not signal a greater willingness to grant clemency, but it does show the governor's interest in giving these cases greater scrutiny. Other governors have also been willing to give relief on a more targeted basis. In particular, some governors have focused on restoring voting rights for offenders who have served their sentences. In Florida, for example, Governor Charlie Crist urged the state's parole commission to reinstate the voting rights of 600,000 offenders who had completed their sentences. Governor Tom Vilsack of Iowa, before leaving office, issued an executive order reinstating rights to those felons who had completed their sentences. Governor Beshear of Kentucky has pushed for legislation to restore rights to felons.

The experience of Governors Huckabee, Ehrlich, and Kaine shows two things. First, it demonstrates that some executives have an incentive to pardon, out of a sense of either faith or duty. Second, using the themes of redemption and forgiveness as tenets of religious faith or constitutional duty can, in turn, offer a competing political narrative that may shield governors who exercise their pardon power from attack. Governors Huckabee and Kaine were explicit in the role that religion played in their executive decisions, and their decisions to forgive offenders and give them a second chance fit well within a faith-based narrative. For his part, Ehrlich relied on his constitutional duty to ensure that errors were corrected in criminal cases and that just sentences were meted out.

Another lesson from the aforementioned examples is that governors could increase clemency grants with less political risk if they were to approach clemency in a more surgical fashion, focusing on forms of relief that are not as vulnerable to political attack. Pardons issued after an offender has served a sentence in full and has lived in society for some number of years without reoffending are certainly less risky than commutations that set someone free before the end of the judicially imposed sentence. To take the sliding scale concept further, it is also less risky to grant a former felon only a modest form of relief by reinstating his or her right to vote but granting no other relief.

Taking this lesson a bit further, governors can narrow not simply the forms of relief they make available, but the types of offenders whom they deem eligible. It is less politically risky to show mercy on first-time offenders and/or those who have committed nonviolent offenses. In this regard, drug cases may be particularly good candidates for more clemency grants because narcotics laws frequently impose mandatory sentences that are harsher than the specific facts of a case warrant. A more generous approach to clemency for those who were very young when they committed their offense might also be feasible, as Governor Ritter's efforts seem to indicate, because these offenders can be very sympathetic figures whose claims of rehabilitation may be seen as more believable than most because of the maturation that comes with getting older. At the opposite end of the spectrum, clemency for elderly inmates is viable for similar reasons. These offenders can plausibly argue that age has given them the wisdom to see how wrong their crimes were. Moreover, these claims can be bolstered by data; ex-convicts over the age of fifty-five have a much lower recidivism rate than eighteen- to fortynine-year-olds.

Of course, the narrower the approach, the less valuable clemency is at checking legislative and prosecutorial overreaching and ensuring individualized justice. Moreover, most of the narrower approaches to clemency still come with risks. It takes just one offender who benefited from a pardon or commutation to reoffend to call into question an executive's judgment. Nonviolent or elderly offenders may be less likely to commit additional crimes, but some of them undoubtedly will. And while voters might respect governors who pardon as part of their religious faith, that may not be a sufficient defense if someone pardoned goes on to commit a particularly heinous crime.

It is this risk of the one bad apple that serves as the greatest deterrent for an executive deciding whether to use his pardon or commutation powers. In the nine states with a more robust clemency practice, the governor can shift the blame to the clemency board if someone pardoned reoffends. The problem with the independent agency model as a cure-all is that not every state with a pardon board as part of the process has seen an increase in clemency grants.

Barkow is right to draw our attention to the risks of the "one bad apple." One of the 1,000-plus inmates whose sentences Huckabee commuted was Maurice Clemmons, who had been sentenced to 100 years for a crime spree. In 2009, nine years after his sentence was commuted, Clemmons executed four police officers in a coffee shop in Tacoma, Washington.[45] Huckabee's name was being raised as a contender for the 2012 Republican presidential nomination, and immediately pundits began to wonder what this one crime—committed by one of over 1,000 commutations—would do to his chances.

Much of criminal justice operates in a "low information, high salience" world: people know very little about the day-to-day operations of things, and they only learn about the highly salient—but thus non-representative—outcomes. The Clemmons case is a good example of that. The crime was shockingly salient, making national news, but Clemmons represented less than 0.1% of all those whose sentences Huckabee

---

[45] http://www.nytimes.com/2009/12/01/us/politics/01huckabee.html?pagewanted=all&_r=0.

commuted. To judge his commutation record, or his political aspirations overall, on this one case seems fundamentally unjust. But politicians rationally fear such predictable backlashes, and this fear explains to some extent why politicians often remain tougher on crime than their constituents: polls make respondents think about the "average" case, while politicians are keenly attuned to the costly outlier.

At least for now, there is no real indication that clemency is on the rise. In the wake of the 2008 financial crisis, several governors commuted sentences of some non-violent offenders in an effort to cut correctional budgets. But there's been no groundswell of support for executive action of this sort. It's true that prison populations have fallen somewhat in the 2010s, but clemency is not playing a role in that—front-end decision-making by prosecutors (whose decisions *not* to prosecute could perhaps be seen as a form of clemency) is the main driver there.

QUESTIONS

1. **Political costs.** Barkow points out that Huckabee (at least until 2009), Ehrlich, and Kaine didn't suffer any political costs from their commutations. Does this mean that it is safe for other governors to do so as well?

2. **Is clemency anti-democratic?** Dan Markel has argued that mercy is, in many way, inherently anti-democratic, since it flies in the face of equal protection before the laws: some people are granted mercy, and others are not, often for arbitrary reasons. That seems unfair to the offenders who are not granted mercy, and it can also be seen as unfair to the *victims* whose attackers *are*. Is this a convincing reason to eliminate clemency?

3. **Clemency and accountability.** Barkow argues that clemency could be appealing in drug cases where mandatory minimum often impose particularly harsh, seemingly unjust sentences (though more in the federal than in the state system). Could this be an argument *against* clemency? What does clemency allow the legislature to avoid? What concerns might we have with clemency as a corrective?

APPENDIX

STATISTICAL GLOSSARY

The purpose of this Appendix is to provide slightly more detailed explanations for some of the statistical concepts discussed in the book. The terms here are arranged in alphabetical order, not in the order in which they first appear in the book, so that this is an easy resource whenever you need to look up any of the concepts.

1. **Complex evidence base.** Sometimes the evidence base is really complicated: some studies say longer prison sentences lead to less crime, others to more crime, still others say no effect. What are we to do in such a situation?

    The standard legal (and, sadly, social scientific) solution has been to rely on the string cite: the author lists a bunch of articles, notes that some contradict others, makes some *ad hoc* argument about why one of the branches is more credible than the others, and draws some rough approximation of what the favored studies say. Fortunately, this sort of informal resolution is starting to come under sustained attack.

    Its limitations are clear. The reviewer may miss important articles, and his assessment of quality may be accidentally or cynically biased by his prior beliefs. Someone who genuinely believes that prisons reduce crime may find articles that reach contrary conclusions methodologically weak mostly because of their *conclusions,* not their actual methodology.

    The solution that is becoming increasingly popular, though still too-rarely used, is the **systematic review** or the **meta-analysis**. These reviews develop rigorous algorithms to scour all relevant on-line databases to try to gather every article, employ fairly objective and transparent (we hope) guidelines to assess quality, and then attempt to synthesize the findings of the high-quality to see what they collectively say. This approach is revolutionizing how knowledge is generated in medicine and the biosciences, and it is slowly—slowly—spreading to the social sciences.

    For lawyers, the main takeaway is that when the evidence base is muddy—and more often than not that will be the case—be wary of the informal conclusion drawn from the informal string cite.

2. **Endogeneity.** This is one of the more important statistical concepts to keep in mind. A relationship is **endogenous** if

each variable causally affects the other. The relationship between rain and a windowsill plant is *not* endongeous: the amount of rain influences how much the plant grows, but the growth of the plant has no impact on the amount rain. But if we replace "windowsill plant" with "Amazon rain forest," the relationship becomes endogenous, since rain makes the forest grow, but the size of the forest shapes global weather patterns.

How does this relate to crime? Many criminal justice issues are endogenous. More police, for example, reduce crime, but cities tend to hire more police when crime goes up. Sending more people to prison reduces crime, but states generally send more people to prison when crime rates are rising. Kids with delinquent peers are more likely to commit crime, but kids who are more likely to commit crime are more likely to hang out with out delinquent children.

This can make it very hard to understand the relationship we are interested in. Crudely speaking, when you run a statistical model of an endogenous relationship without properly "correcting" for it, the result you get back is sort of an average of the two effects. If we want to know the effect of police on crime, but we fail to properly account for the fact that crime rates also influence the number of police, then our results will average both the effect of police on crime (negative, since more police lead to less crime) *and* the effect of crime on police (positive, since more crime leads to more police). So we'll get a number that isn't negative enough: if the true relationship is –10, we'll get back –4, or maybe even +3. (There are complex statistical ways to address this problem, which are beyond the scope of this book.)

3. **Meta-analysis:** See complex evidence base.

4. **Moderating** and **mediating effects.** A **moderating** variable is one that may alter the relationship between two others over time. For example, being male makes it much more likely that someone is going to commit a crime. But over time, as a person ages, the magnitude of that effect weakens, so that a man in his fifties may more likely to offend than a woman in her fifties, but that gap is smaller than when they were both in their twenties. In this context, age is a moderating variable.

A **mediating** variable is tied somewhat to the idea of spurious correlation (defined below). A mediating variable is one that explains why a correlation may exist. If we observe that children of offenders offend more, it could be because of other background factors that are correlated with the parent being an offender, such as living in a high-crime neighborhood.

5. **Omitted variable bias.** Here's a simple example that can demonstrate what omitted variable bias is. Assume someone has a dataset of military combat deaths and runs a regression to test the extent to which being male predicts being killed in combat, and the model finds a strong effect. Does this mean that men are inherently more likely to be killed than women (because they are bigger risk-takers, or more-obvious targets due to their larger size, or more likely to suffer medical complications)?

Here, there is an obvious variable missing from the model: is the solider in a front-line combat unit. In general, only men can serve in these units, and these units are much more likely to come under fire. So is the effect the author identified the effect of being male, or is it really the effect of being in a combat unit, which is highly correlated with being male?

This is the problem of omitted variable bias. Being in a combat unit is highly correlated with being male (our explanatory variable) and with being killed (the dependent variable we are trying to understand). This leads to bias: in this case, the model is going to overstate the effect of being male, because it attributes to "male" the impact of being in a combat unit, which is highly correlated with maleness. If we added in a variable for "being in combat unit," the effect of "male" would likely drop substantially.

We can think of a lot of criminal justice examples of omitted variable bias. What if a researcher tried to understand the impact of education on the likelihood that a juvenile was arrested, but he excluded any measure of the kids' poverty status? Or tried to measure the impact of incarceration on crime but excluded whether the state was socially conservative? In these cases, the excluded term is correlated with both the proposed explanatory variable (education, incarceration) and the outcome variable (individual offending, state crime rates).

Now for the bias to exist, *both* correlations are needed: the excluded term needs to be correlated with both the included explanatory variable and with the outcome variable. If either correlation is weak, then the problem isn't so strong. This is a good thing. No model can include *all* relevant variables, so the question to ask is whether it includes all the ones that are *sufficiently correlated*.

Let's assume that a researcher wants to understand the impact of education on juvenile criminal offending, and so she runs a regression of kids' education on whether they were ever arrested for a crime, and she finds a fairly strong effect: more education, less offending. But assume, too, that the model doesn't include any measure the poverty status of the children (maybe because the data simply weren't available, or the researcher didn't think to include them).

How does this exclusion—this **omitted variable**—shape our willingness to accept the researcher's findings? In short, if we think that poverty is correlated with education (which is likely) and with offending (which is likely), then we have a problem.

6. **Present value.** The idea of present value is to figure out how much something in the future is worth today. No one is indifferent between being offered $1 today versus $1 a year from now: we all prefer immediate consumption, so we'd take the $1 today. But how about $1 today vs. $1.05 a year from now? $2 a year from now? $10? At some point, with enough compensation, we'll give up consumption today for more in the future. The degree of compensation we demand is our **discount rate**. The higher the discount rate—the more someone needs to be compensated to give up consumption today—the more impatient someone is.

So what does it mean to have a discount rate of 10%? That means to give up consumption today, the person needs to get 10% back in the next period (let's assume a year). So he'd give up $1 today for 1*(1.10) = $1.10 next year. And he needs that compensation for each period. So if he had to wait two years to get paid back, he'd demand 1*(1.10)*(1.10) = $1.21. Any amount above this, he'll give up consumption today; below, he won't.

Note that we can reverse this too. If someone offers to pay you $5 in five years, how much is that worth? It's just 5/[1.1*1.1*1.1*1.1*1.1] = $3.42. To see why, just flip it around. If someone had to give up $3.42 today, what's the minimum amount he'd need to be compensated if he was going to be paid back five years from now? 3.42*(1.1)*(1.1)*(1.1)*(1.1)*(1.1) = $5. So $3.42 today is equal to $5 in 5 years, or $5 in five years is equal to $3.42 today.

Note too that this applies to costs as well. A cost today hurts more than a cost tomorrow, since we discount the impact of that cost the same way. This is why people downplay future risks, since they put less weight on them. A $5 cost in 5 years is viewed today as only costing $3.42.

So think back to Easterbrook's argument about the present value of prison sentences. He states that with a 10% discount rate, a 50-year prison sentence has a present value of 9.91 years (assuming—and he admits this is impossible—that all 9.91 years could be served immediately). How did he compute this? Well, at 10%, the first year in prison (assuming it is served a year from when the plea bargain takes place) "costs" only $1/1.1 = 0.91$ years today. The second year, even further into the future, costs only $1/(1.1*1.1) = 0/83$ years today. And so on and so on. Add up all these costs, and they come to 9.91 years. Note how large the discounts get. The fiftieth year in prison "costs" only 0.008 years today. This is why very long sentences do not deter: those future years are given almost no weight when people decide how to act today.

7. **Spurious correlation.** A spurious correlation is one that exists between two terms not because one is influencing the other, but because both are being influenced by some underlying third factor. For example, as noted in Ch. 1, those who commit crimes are more likely to smoke. Yet if we insisted that no one smoke, it likely wouldn't reduce crime. It's not the smoking that's causing the crime, nor is it the crime that's causing smoking. Evidence suggests that impulsiveness and a relative lack of forward-thinking causes people both to smoke and to be more likely to engage in crime. If we ignore the spuriousness, we could get very bad policy recommendations.

INDEX

References are to Pages

ACTUARIAL MODELS
    Generally, 131
See also Discretion, this index

AGE OF OFFENDERS
Elderly offenders
    Prison life of, 239
    Recidivism, 771
Lifecycle trends in offending, 21
Sex of offender relevance compared, 234
Youthful offenders
    Generally, 2, 233 et seq.
    Death penalty, 233, 395
    DGN factors compared, 233
    Guidelines criteria, 26
    Juvenile justice system, 234
    Life sentences, 233

AGGRAVATING FACTORS
Constitutional limitations on sentencing use, 190
Death Penalty, this index
Factual proof of, 113, 205
Prior Criminal History, this index
Statutory enumeration, 245

ALCOHOL
See Drugs and Alcohol, this index

ALTERNATIVES TO INCARCERATION
    Generally, 587 et seq.
Asset Forfeitures, this index
Boot camps, 616
Domestic Batterers, this index
Drug and Other Therapeutic Courts, this index
Fines and Fees, this index
Parol. See Re-Entry After Incarceration, this index
Probation, this index
Recidivism impacts of custodial vs noncustodial sanctions, 582
Restorative Justice, this index
Sex Offenders, this index
Shaming Sanctions, this index

ANCHORING OF PERCEPTIONS
    Generally, 11, 62
Plea bargaining, 464, 471

ASSET FORFEITURES
    Generally, 608
Civil vs criminal forfeiture, 609
Equitable sharing of seized assets, 612
Federal law, 612
Moral hazard problem, 616
Offsets against criminal justice budgets, 615
Proof issues, 610

BAIL
Conditions of parole, bond requirements, 749
Gender effects, 232
Racial discrimination, 106

BEHAVIORALISM
See Offender Traits, this index

BOOT CAMPS
Alternatives to incarceration, 616

CAPITAL CASES
See Death Penalty, this index

CHILD ABUSE AND NEGLECT
Risk factors for criminal behavior, 18

COMMUTATIONS
Re-entry after incarceration, 768

CONFIRMATION BIAS
Why we sentence, 12

CONFLICTING INTERESTS
See Moral Hazard Problem, this index

CONSECUTIVE VS CONCURRENT SENTENCES
Comparative law, 474
Constitutional limitations, 368

CONSEQUENTIALIST THEORIES
    Generally, 57
See also Utilitarian Theories of Punishment, this index

CONSTITUTIONAL LAW
Actuarial models use, equal protection tensions, 139
Aggravating factors, 190
Conditions of parole, constitutional restrictions, 731
Consecutive vs concurrent sentences, 368
Death Penalty, this index
Discretionary punishment powers, constitutional limitations, 1
Disproportionate sentencing, Eighth Amendment limitations, 254
Grants of parole, constitutional protections, 718
Guidelines, this index
Habitual-offender laws, 206
Plea bargaining, death penalty cases, 436
Prior criminal history evidence use, 202
Probation, supervision conditions, 595
Procedures at Sentencing Stage, this index
Racial bias claims, Eighth Amendment challenges, 391
Right to counsel
    Parole hearings, 761

779

Plea bargaining, 439
Sentencing factors vs elements of crimes, elimination of the distinction, 145, 301 et seq.
Sex offenders, alternatives to incarceration, 627
Shaming sanctions, 655
Three-strike laws, 206, 255
Victim statements, 182
Violating parole, 753

COSTS
See also Moral Hazard Problem, this index
Alternatives to incarceration, costs and fees assessments, 606
Death penalty, costs of application, 427
Electronic monitoring, 608
Guidelines use, costs impacts, 286
Hate crimes statutes, 177
Incarceration
    Costs at county and state levels, 429
    Police service costs compared, 97
Plea bargaining
    Costs considerations, 469
    Discounting future costs, 462
Restorative justice, costs advantages, 674
Truth-in-sentencing laws, costs constraints, 262

COUNTIES
See State vs County Responsibilities, this index

CRIMINAL HISTORY
See Prior Criminal History, this index

DEATH PENALTY
Generally, 375 et seq.
Administration, legal and practical problems, 407 et seq.
Age-based challenges, 233, 395
Aggravating circumstances findings, 380, 396
Anti-Terrorism and Effective Death Penalty Act, 402
Arbitrariness, USSC jurisprudence, 376, 381
Commutations, 406
Costs of application at county and state levels, 427
Deterrence justification, 421
Discretion challenges, 375
Eligible crimes, legislative rules, 397
Error rates in capital cases, 407
Evidence of DGN factors, use in court, 226
Evolving standards of decency arguments, 397
Federal legislative rules, 400
Governors' roles, 406
Innocence issue, 407
Judicial review and systemic problems, 384
Legislative rules
    Generally, 397
    Anti-Terrorism and Effective Death Penalty Act, 402
    Application standards, 398
    Eligible crimes, 397
    Federal, 400
    Special sentencing issues, 399
Life-without-parole alternatives, 295
Mandatory death sentences, 378
National consensus arguments, 397
Plea bargaining in shadow of, 436
Political support, 430
Prosecutors, moral hazard, 428
Retributivist theory, 417
Scope of application, 426
USSC cases, 375 et seq.
Victim statements
    Generally, 182
    Execution impact statements, 188

DEFENDANTS
Age of Offenders, this index
Domestic Batterers, this index
Offender Traits, this index
Rights of Offenders, this index
Sex Offenders, this index
Offense Traits, this index

DEFENSE ATTORNEYS
Drug courts, representation conflicts, 691
Plea Bargaining, this index
Restorative justice, representation conflicts, 681
Right to counsel
    Parole hearings, 761
    Plea bargaining, 439
Sentencing roles
    Generally, 81, 99
    Assigned counsel systems, 100
    Constituencies affecting sentencing policies, 82
    Public defender systems, 100

DESERT THEORISTS
See Just Deserts Theorists, this index

DESISTANCE FROM CRIME
Generally, 565, 699

DETERMINATE VS INDETERMINATE SENTENCING
Generally, 260
Constitutional limits, 321
Guidelines, determinate sentencing as, 264
Release decisions under indeterminate sentencing, 710
Statutory mandates, 264

DETERRENCE THEORY OF PUNISHMENT
Generally, 37, 38
Death penalty, 421
Determinism and, 226
Efficacy, 51
Federal guidelines, 65
Hate crime punishments, 176
Immutable offender characteristics, 210
Incapacitation compared, 197

Incarceration effects on crime rates, 574, 578, 581
Mandatory penalties, 292
Marginal deterrence hypothesis, 293
Mutable offender characteristics, 242
Political pressures from left and right, 50
Proportionality, 63
Recidivist sentencing, 194, 196
Rehabilitation theory vs, 59
Sex offenders
    Alternatives to incarceration, 619
    Civil commitment, 636
Specific effects of incarceration, 581
Specific-deterrence, 140
Youth as mitigating factor, 234

DETOUR PROSECUTIONS
Prosecutors, 95

DEVELOPMENTAL (DGN) FACTORS
See Offender Traits, this index

DISCRETION IN SENTENCING
    Generally, 131 et seq.
Actuarial model compared
    Generally, 131 et seq., 295
    Advantages, 132
    Equal protection tensions, 139
    Limitations, 135, 141
    Parole decisions, 138, 730
    Predictive efficacy, 133
    Sex offenders, 132
Clinical risk assessment
    Generally, 132
    Actuarial model compared, 134
Death penalty, constitutional limitations, 375
Drug courts, 122
Judicial vs prosecutorial discretion, policy, 112, 299
Lawlessness of allocations of, 375
Legislative restrictions, 131
Limitations of actuarial model, 135, 141
Predictive efficacy of actuarial models, 133
Probation enforcement policies, 590
Punishment implications of discretionary powers, 1
Sex offender sentencing, 132
Structured sentencing laws reforms, 299

DOMESTIC BATTERERS
    Generally, 619, 644
Civil protection orders
    Generally, 644
    Criminal law enforcement, 645
    Efficacy, 647
Incidence of domestic violence, 644
Mandatory arrest policies, 648
Victim protections, 644

DRUG AND OTHER THERAPEUTIC COURTS
    Generally, 677 et seq.
Advocates' arguments for, 679
Confidentiality issues, 693
Decarceration model, 684
Defense attorneys' roles, 691
Deferred prosecution programs, 679
Effectiveness concerns, 690
Judicial monitoring model, 682
Legislative vs prosecutorial discretion, 122
Mental-health courts, 689
Mentally ill offenders, 684
Order maintenance model, 683
Pleas as preconditions, 695
Post adjudication programs, 679
Probationer participation, 686
Problem-solving courts, 680, 685
Promise of, 678
Recidivism studies, 687
Therapeutic jurisprudence model, 680
Treatment courts, 680, 686
Veterans' courts, 685

DRUGS AND ALCOHOL
Addictions as mutable characteristics, 243
Cocaine convictions, Fair Sentencing Act, 367
Offender Traits, this index
Prison inmates, 562
Testing, probation conditions, 592

EFFECTS OF INCARCERATION
    Generally, 537 et seq.
Assaults, 543
Collateral costs of incarceration on the inmate, 549
Community impacts, 569
Concentrated incarceration, public health implications, 571
Crime rates, 574
Criminogenic effects, 140
Death in Custody Reporting Act, 543
Deterrence theory, 574, 578, 581
Diary of a prisoner, 537
Drugs and alcohol in prison, 562
Employment limitations of released inmates, 549, 739
Family life impacts, 565
Federal oversight of prison conditions
    Generally, 545
    Prison Litigation Reform Act, 547
General deterrence and incapacitation, 578
Health impacts, 552
Homicides, 543
Individual effects, 581
Inmates, effects on, 537, 548
Licensing laws restrictions on released inmates, 551, 739
Medical care, 552
Mental health impacts, 559
Neighborhood incarceration rates, 570
Prison Litigation Reform Act, 547
Probation compared, 599
Public health implications of concentrated incarceration, 571
Recidivism
    Generally, 140
    Impacts of custodial vs noncustodial sanctions, 582

Security levels, 544
Sexual assaults, 543
Specific effects, 581
Specific-deterrence effects, 140
Total effect on crime rates, 574
Urban pockets of intense incarceration, 570
Visitation difficulties, 567

ELDERLY OFFENDERS
Prisoners, 239
Recidivism, 771

ELECTRONIC MONITORING
Costs and fees assessments, 608

ELEMENTS OF OFFENSES
Sentencing factors vs, elimination of the distinction, 145, 301 et seq.

FAIR SENTENCING ACT
Cocaine convictions, 367

FAMILIAL OFFENDING
Risk factors for criminal behavior, 17

FINES AND FEES
Generally, 602
Ability to pay disparities
    Generally, 604
    European systems, 606
Condemnation effects, 604
Costs and fees assessments, 606
Enforcement disparities, 605
European fines systems, 602
Moral hazard problem, 608
Probation, payment requirements, 592
Rate setting practices, 603
Recidivism, fee responsibilities exacerbating, 741
Restitution incidence compared, 605

GENDER
See Offender Traits, this index

GENETIC (DGN) FACTORS
See Offender Traits, this index

GOVERNORS' ROLES IN SENTENCING
Generally, 81, 114
Clemency grants, 770
Commutation powers
    Generally, 768
    Death penalty commutations, 406
Constituencies affecting sentencing policies, 82
Pardon powers, 114, 768

GUIDELINES
Generally, 264 et seq.
Age considerations, 26
Alleged related offenses, federal guidelines, 284
Charge-offense approach, 284
Complexity of federal guidelines, 280
Costs impacts, 286
Determinate sentencing laws as, 264
Federal guidelines
    Adoption, 275
    Alleged related offenses, 284
    Complexity, 280
    Constitutionality, 65, 344 et seq., 358
    Fair Sentencing Act, 367
    Goal of federal approach, 280
    Real offense sentencing, 281, 287, 449
    Reasonableness review, 362
    Retributivist vs utilitarian approach, 279
    Special verdicts applying, 280
    State guidelines compared, 275, 283
Historical background, 112, 261
Impacts of, 286
Judicial establishment, 1
Legislative enactment, 122
Legislative purposes, 105
Parole board release guidelines, 712
Plea bargaining
    Guidelines-based sentencing impacting, 471
    Guidelines for prosecutors, 442
Practice, use of guidelines in, 266
Presumptive guidelines, 261
Presumptive vs voluntary, constitutionality, 339, 358
Probation conditions, 598
Race and sex factors impacts, 286
Real offense sentencing
    DOJ directive, 449
    Federal guidelines, 281, 287
Reasonableness review of federal guideline applications, 362
Retributivist vs utilitarian approach, 279
Special verdicts applying federal guidelines, 280
State guidelines
    Generally, 63, 265
    Federal guidelines compared, 275, 283
    USSC review, 337
Truth-in-sentencing laws affects, 299
Voluntary vs presumptive, constitutionality, 339, 358

HABITUAL-OFFENDER LAWS
See also Recidivism, this index
Sentencing use, 206

HARM
Offense Traits, this index
Victims, this index

HATE CRIMES
Generally, 170
Costs, 177
Harm levels analysis, 175
Historical background, 170
Motive
    Generally, 177, 316
    Proof of, 174
Prejudice fueling behavior, 174
Proof of motive, 174
Retaliation issues, 176
Sexual assaults as, 177

Statistics, 176
Victim characteristic factors, 174

HUMAN BEHAVIOR MODELS
Generally, 6
See also Risk, this index

IMPRISONMENT
See Incarceration, this index

IMPULSIVENESS
Risk factors for criminal behavior, 16

INCAPACITATION THEORY OF PUNISHMENT
Generally, 38, 44
Age factors, 26, 37
Deterrence compared, 197
Drug court programs, 122
Federal guidelines, 65
General effects of incarceration, 581
Hate crime punishments, 176
Immutable offender characteristics, 210
Incarceration effects on crime rates, 574, 578
Mandatory minimums, 295
Mutable offender characteristics, 242
Prior criminal history, 197
Prison growth implications, 505
Recidivist sentencing, 197
Rehabilitation theory vs, 59, 197
Sex offenders, civil commitment, 636
Specific effects of incarceration, 581
Three-strike laws, 47, 206
Youth as mitigating factor, 234

INCARCERATION
Alternatives to Incarceration, this index
Costs at county and state levels
    Generally, 429
    See also Moral Hazard Problem, this index
Criminogenic effects, 140
Effects of Incarceration, this index
Police service costs compared, 97
Prison Growth Factors, this index
Re-Entry After Incarceration, this index

INDETERMINATE SENTENCING
See Determinate vs Indeterminate Sentencing, this index

JUDGES' ROLES IN SENTENCING
Generally, 81, 103
Bias, explicit and implicit, 106, 113
Constituencies affecting sentencing policies, 82
Discretionary powers
    Legislative limitations on, 103
    Prosecutorial discretion vs as policy matter, 112, 299
    Punishment implications, 1
Legislative limitations on discretionary powers, 103
Leniency, accounting for, 113
Motives, theoretical analyses, 104
Political accountability, 104
Sex-based disparities in sentencing, 110

JUST DESERT THEORISTS
Generally, 35, 57
See also Retributivist Theory of Punishment, this index
Sex offenders, civil commitment, 636

JUVENILES
See Age of Offenders, this index

LEGISLATURES' ROLES IN SENTENCING
Generally, 81, 121 et seq.
See also Politics of Punishment, this index
Constituencies affecting sentencing policies, 82
Discretionary powers, punishment implications, 1
Guidelines, this index
Partisan political pressures within, 126
Prosecutor power frictions, 122
Suburban over-representation factors, 127

LOCAL CRIME CONTROL
See also Moral Hazard Problem, this index
State crime control disconnect, 97

MANDATORY MINIMUMS
See Procedures at Sentencing Stage, this index

MENTAL ILLNESS
Deinstitutionalization and prison growth, 484, 496
Mental-health courts, 689
Neurological factors. See Offender Traits, this index
Parole grants, mental illness obstacles, 729

MICRO- VS MACRO-PUNISHMENT
Generally, 89

MINORS
See Age of Offenders, this index

MISDEMEANOR/FELONY DECISIONS
See Moral Hazard Problem, this index

MITIGATING FACTORS
Employment history, 74
Factual proof of, 113, 205
First offenders, 191
Statutory enumeration, 245
Youth, 234

MORAL HAZARD PROBLEM
Asset forfeitures, 616
Assigned counsel programs, 101
California's Realignment Program, 98, 299, 512
Fines and fees as alternatives to incarceration, 608
Gubernatorial responsibilities, 114
Prison growth rates, county prosecutors impacting, 490
Prosecutors

Death penalty cases, 428
Misdemeanor/felony decisions, 92, 97, 299
Urban communities, excessive punishments in, 518

MOTIVE
Generally, 170 et seq.
See also Hate Crimes, this index
Judges', theoretical analyses, 104
Proof of, 174

NEUROLOGICAL (DGN) FACTORS
See Offender Traits, this index

NORMATIVE GOALS OF PUNISHMENT
See Why We Punish, this index

OFFENDER TRAITS
Generally, 189 et seq.
See also Offense Traits, this index
Addictions as more mutable characteristics, 243
Age of Offenders, this index
Alcohol and drug use as more mutable characteristics, 242
Anchoring, behaviorist analysis, 11
Behavioral genetics evidence, 226
Behavioralism, 10, 16
Behavioralist critiques, 10
Brain dysfunction, 213
Compatibilism, 219
Compatibilist/determinist tensions, 223
Consequentialist concerns with repeat-offender enhancements, 194
Controllable and uncontrollable, 189
Crimes of passion, 223
Criminal history. See Prior Criminal History, this index
Determinism and free will questions, 218
Deterrence principles in a deterministic world, 226
Developmental genetic, and neurological (DGN) factors
Generally, 210 et seq.
Admissibility of evidence, 226
Age, 233
Challenge of using DGN evidence, 216
Connection between DGN and crime, 211
Environmental interactions with DGN factors, 217, 225
Judicial attitudes towards DGN evidence, 230
Normative importance of DGN evidence, 217
Situationalism and DGN evidence, 27, 226
Diminished responsibility questions, 221
Domestic Batterers, this index
Free will questions, 218
Gender. Sex of offender as factor, below
Habitual-offender laws, 206
Hate Crimes, this index
Human behavior models, 6
Immutable characteristics, 209 et seq.
Implications of determinism, 224
Insanity defense, 224
IQ tests reliability, 214
Irresistible impulse test, 225
Motive, this index
Mutable characteristics, 242
Offense trait distinctions, 145, 189
Persistent felony offenders, 342
Prior Criminal History, this index
Psychophysiological factors, 213
Race Discrimination, this index
Rational actor model, 6
Rational addiction as more mutable characteristics, 244
Rationality vs causation tensions, 223
Recidivism, this index
Risk, this index
Salience, behaviorist analysis, 11
Sex of offender as factor
Generally, 230
Age of offender factor compared, 234
Guidelines, 286
Judicial sentencing disparities, 110
Sex Offenders, this index
Three-strike laws, 206
Utility maximization, 10
Violence potential factors affecting punishment, 2

OFFENSE TRAITS
Generally, 145 et seq.
See also Offender Traits, this index
Absolute vs relative severity, 152
Child pornography, quantitative severity, 161
Cocaine, quantitative severity
Generally, 166
Fair Sentencing Act, 367
Consequences as measurement of severity, 146
Differences across groups as to qualitative severity, 152, 155
Domestic Batterers, this index
Drug offenses, quantitative severity, 159
Economic vs physical harm, perceived seriousness, 147
Elements of crimes vs sentencing factors, elimination of the distinction, 145, 301 et seq.
Escalating crime-distrust model of punitiveness, 153
Harm
Objective harm vs subjective impact, 177
Quantitative severity and harm analysis, 164
Victims, this index
Wrongfulness vs harmfulness, relative importance, 147, 152
Hate Crimes, this index
Moral decline model of punitiveness, 153
Moral gravity, 147
Motive, this index
Multidimensional vs unidimensional view of severity, 148

Objective harm vs subjective impact, 177
Offender trait distinctions, 145, 189
Physical vs economic harm, perceived seriousness, 147
Punishment theories and severity rankings, 151
Punitiveness attitudes, 152
Qualitative severity, 146 et seq.
Quantifiability issues, 156, 163
Quantitative severity, 155 et seq.
Racial-animus model of punitiveness, 153
Relative vs absolute severity, 152
Retributivists, qualitative severity, 151
Sentencing factors vs elements of crimes, elimination of the distinction, 145, 301 et seq.
Seriousness, definitions of term, 146
Severity
    Generally, 145 et seq.
    Qualitative, 146
    Quantitative, 155
Sex Offenders, this index
Sliding scales of quantitative severity, 165
Survey studies of qualitative severity, 148
Theft, quantitative severity, 156
Unidimensional vs multidimensional view of severity, 148
Victimless crimes, qualitative severity, 147
Violent crimes, qualitative severity, 147
Wrongfulness vs harmfulness, relative importance, 147, 152

OVERCRIMINALIZATION PROBLEM
Generally, 95, 684

PARDONS
Governors' roles in sentencing, 114
Re-entry after incarceration, 768

PAROLE BOARDS' ROLES IN SENTENCING
Generally, 81, 116
See also Re-Entry After Incarceration, this index
Authorities of parole boards, 715
Caseload pressure, 120
Conditions of parole. See Re-Entry After Incarceration, this index
Constituencies affecting sentencing policies, 82
Costs and fees assessments, 608
Death penalty, life-without-parole alternatives, 295
Design and composition variations, 712
Discretionary parole systems, 714, 718
Discretionary powers, punishment implications, 1, 117
False positive problem, 118
Grants of parole. See Re-Entry After Incarceration, this index
Incentives for decisions, 117
Judicial immunity, 712
Legislative limitations on discretionary powers, 103
Mandatory minimums, 262
Mandatory parole systems, 714, 718
Political pressures, 118
Qualifications and salaries, 117
Racial discrimination, 121
Re-entry as parolee. See Re-Entry After Incarceration, this index
Reincarceration decisions, 119
Release guidelines, 712
Truth-in-Sentencing Laws, this index
Violation of parole. See Re-Entry After Incarceration, this index

PLEA BARGAINING
Generally, 433
Anchoring of perceptions, 464, 471
Arguments for and against, 454, 474
Bans, legislative, 448
Charge bargaining vs sentence bargaining. 84, 434
Charge stacking, 437, 464
Coercion argument, 456
Comparative law, 472
Constitutionality, death penalty cases, 436
Contracts of enslavement view, 459
Contractual view, 458
Costs considerations, 469
Death penalty cases, 436
Defense attorney pressures, 103
Denial mechanisms, 462
Discounting future costs, 462
Discounts, plea, 453
Discretionary powers, punishment implications, 1
Distributional justice view, 459
Drug court participation, pleas as preconditions, 695
Externalities, 467
Fact bargaining, DOJ directive, 449
Federal level regulation, 449
Feeney Amendment, 450
Guidelines-based sentencing and, 471
Guidelines for prosecutors, 442
Information access, 470
Innocence claims, unconscionable pleas, 457
International comparison of plea bargaining policy, 472
Judicial review, limitations of, 436
Market failure challenges, 455
Non-judicial regulation, 442
Prohibitions, legislative, 448
Proportional plea bargaining, 442
Rate, plea, 433
Real offense sentencing, DOJ directive, 449
Right of effective assistance of counsel, 439
Risk tolerance and distribution, 463
Sentence bargaining vs charge bargaining, 84, 434
Sentencing differentials, three sources, 456
Shadow of the trial principle, 459
Stacking of charges, 437, 464
Structured sentencing, 471
Substantive law, 434 et seq.

Trial penalty principle, 441, 456
Truth-in-sentencing laws affects on
    prosecutor policies, 299
Unconscionable pleas, 457

POLICE ROLES IN SENTENCING
    Generally, 81, 84 et seq.
Case file control, implications of, 89
Constituencies affecting sentencing
    policies, 82
Domestic violence, mandatory arrest, 648
Incarceration costs, policing costs
    compared, 97
Incentives and goals, 87
Legalistic-style agencies, 88
Prosecutors interaction, 85
Service-style agencies, 88
Suburbanization of law enforcement
    priorities, 128
Watchman-style departments, 88

POLITICS OF PUNISHMENT
    See also Tough on Crime Politics,
        this index
County vs state political accountability
    levels, 92
Death penalty, political support for, 430
Deterrence, political pressures from left
    and right, 50
Judges, political accountability, 104
Legislatures, partisan political pressures
    within, 126
Parole boards, political pressures, 118
Prison growth factors, political theories,
    484, 498 et seq.
Prosecutors, political accountability, 92
Punishment theory, political aspects, 79
Sentencing commissions, political cover
    functions, 131
State vs county political accountability
    levels, 92

PRIOR CRIMINAL HISTORY
    Generally, 190 et seq.
    See also Recidivism, this index
Arguments for recidivist-based
    punishment, 194
Consequentialist concerns with repeat-
    offender enhancements, 194
Conservation of resource issues, 195
Constitutionality of history evidence use,
    202
Evidence, reliability of, 202
Habitual-offender laws, 206
Heuristic biases, 195
Incapacitation vs rehabilitation theories,
    197
Justifications for sentencing use, 196
Prior acquittals as factor, 199
Reliability of evidence, 202
Respect for the law factors, 196
Social stigma factors, 196
Theoretical justifications, 190
Three-strike laws, 206
Utilitarian vs retributivist theories, 190

PRISON GROWTH FACTORS
    Generally, 479 et seq.
Balanced budget provisions, 507
California's Realignment Program as
    response, 98, 299, 512
Capacity increases, incarceration rate
    impacts, 485
Census factors, 513
Commutations, increases to alleviate, 512
Comparative law, 527
Crime rates impacting, 491
Crime theory of, 481
Deinstitutionalization of mentally ill, 484,
    496
Demographic theory, 483
Diffuse responsibility, 517
Drug offenses, 493
Economic factors, 485
Economic theory, 482
Empirical understanding of, 486
Federal challenges to overcrowding, 485
Fiscal capacity, 507
Geography, 517
Incarceration rates, 479
Interest groups, 507
International law comparison, 527
Moral hazard problem of county
    prosecutors, 490
Nothing works theory, 504
Overcrowding, federal challenges to, 485
Political theories, 484, 498 et seq.
Politicians, 511, 513
Private prisons, 506
Prosecutors' actions affecting, 487
Punitiveness, perception and reality of,
    523
Race, 517
Rural welfare, 513
Sentencing commissions, 511
Social changes, 498, 504
State interest groups, 507
Tough on Crime Politics, this index
Victims' rights movement, 505
Violating parole reincarcerations, 763

PROBATION
    Generally, 588
Access to services, 592
Caseload sizes, 592
Civil disabilities, 592
Constitutional limitations on supervision
    conditions, 595
Contracts of probation, 592
Costs and fees assessments, 608
Discretionary enforcement, 590
Drug and Other Therapeutic Courts, this
    index
Drug testing, 592
Employment requirements, 592
Fine payment requirements, 592
Funding, 591
Growth of community corrections
    populations, 591
Guidelines, 598
Historical background, 589

Incarceration compared, punitive effects, 599
Piling up of supervision conditions, 593
Presentence investigations, 590
Rearrests for violations, 598
Recidivism issues, 599
Resources available to programs, 590
Restitution requirements, 592, 595
Shaming Sanctions, this index
Supervision conditions
    Generally, 592
    Constitutional limitations, 595
    Piling up of, 593
Violation rearrests, 598

PROCEDURES AT SENTENCING STAGE
Generally, 249
Aggravated felonies, constitutional limits, 307
Alleged related offenses, federal guidelines, 284
Charge-offense approach, guidelines, 284
Consecutive vs concurrent sentences
    Comparative law, 474
    Constitutional limits, 368
Constitutional law
    Generally, 300 et seq.
    Aggravated felonies, 307
    Applicability at sentencing stage, 249
    Consecutive vs concurrent sentences, 368
    Determinate vs indeterminate sentencing, 321
    Drafting rules, 304, 321
    Element/sentencing factor distinction, 145, 301 et seq.
    Fact finding mandates, 327 et seq.
    Federal guidelines, 344 et seq., 358
    Presumptive vs voluntary guidelines, 339, 358
    Reliance on USSC rulings, 321
    State guidelines, USSC review, 337
    Structured sentencing, 301 et seq.
Death Penalty, this index
Determinate vs Indeterminate Sentencing, this index
Disproportionate sentencing, Eighth Amendment limitations, 254
Drafting rules, constitutional limits, 304, 321
Due process, 251, 337
Eighth Amendment limitations, 254
Element of crime/sentencing factor distinction, 145, 301 et seq.
Fact finding, constitutional mandates, 327 et seq.
Federal and state court impositions of substantive rules, 254
Guidelines, this index
Historical background, 143
Law-based regimes, 249
Legislative developments, 260 et seq.
Mandatory minimums
    Generally, 262, 288
    Critiques, 290
Persistent felony offenders, 342
Plea Bargaining, this index
Presumptive vs voluntary guidelines, 339, 358
Proportionality review, 259
Protections, 249
Race and sex factors impacts guidelines, 286
Real offense sentencing, federal guidelines, 281, 287
State constitutional case law favorable to defendants, 257
Structured Sentencing, this index
Substantive rules, 253
Victim statements. See Victims, this index

PROSECUTORS' SENTENCING ROLES
Generally, 91, 89 et seq.
Charge bargaining, 84
Constituencies affecting sentencing policies, 82
County vs state political accountability, 92
Death penalty cases, moral hazard, 428
Detour prosecutions, 95
Discretionary powers
    Judicial discretion vs as policy matter, 112, 299
    Punishment implications, 1, 92
    Structured sentencing laws, 299
Legislature power frictions, 122
Misdemeanor/felony decisions, 92, 97, 299
Moral Hazard Problem, this index
Overcriminalization problem, 95
Performance measures, 95, 98
Plea Bargaining, this index
Police interaction, 85
Political accountability, county vs state, 92
Pretextual charging, 94, 122
Prison growth, prosecutors' actions affecting, 487
Specificity of charging decisions, 91

RACIAL DISCRIMINATION
Bail-setting, 106
Bias, explicit and implicit, 106, 113
Cocaine sentencing
    Generally, 166
    Fair Sentencing Act, 367
Death penalty adjudications, racial bias challenges, 387
Eighth Amendment racial bias challenges, 391
Guideline impacts, 286
Parole boards, 121
Punishment theory, racial aspects, 78
Sentencing Reform Act of 1984, 106

RATIONAL ACTOR MODEL
Generally, 6, 13

REAL OFFENSE SENTENCING
See Guidelines, this index

RE-ENTRY AFTER INCARCERATION

Generally, 697 et seq.
Challenges of, 698 et seq.
Clemency grants, 770
Commutations, 768
Conditions of parole
    Generally, 730 et seq.
    Bond requirements, 749
    Changing perceptions of, 731
    Constitutional restrictions, 731
    Federal restraints, 739
    Sex offenders, 741
    Statutory restrictions, 731
    Supervision styles, 737
    Technical violations, 736
    Violating parole, below
Constitutional law
    Conditions of parole, 731
    Grants of parole, 718
    Violating parole, 753
Desistance from criminal conduct, 699
Drug abstinence, importance in the desistance process, 704
Employment limitations of released inmates, 549, 739
Federal restraints on parolees, 739
Felony disenfranchisement, 740, 748
Grants of parole
    Generally, 718 et seq.
    Actuarial devices to control, 138, 730
    Conditions of parole, above
    Constitutional protections, 718
    Discretionary parole systems, 714, 718
    Mandatory parole systems, 714, 718
    Mental illness obstacles, 729
    Presumptive parole systems, 728
    Statutory protections, 718
    Victim inputs affecting, 729
Halfway houses, 706
Housing challenges, 739
Incarceration conditions challenges, 698 et seq.
Indeterminate sentencing and release decisions, 710
Licensing laws restrictions, 551, 739
Marriage, importance in the desistance process, 701
Mental illness obstacles to grants of parole, 729
Pardons, 768
Parole, re-entry subject to
    Generally, 707 et seq.
    Authority of parole boards, 715
    Conditions of parole, above
    Design and composition of parole boards, 712
    Eliminating parole, impacts, 711
    Grants of parole, above
    Historical background, 708
    Presumptive parole systems, 728
    Pretextual revocations, 761
    Public assistance access of parolees, 738
    Recidivism impacts, 710
    Recidivism statistics, 697
    Residence restrictions, 706
    Revocation hearings, 757
    Rights and procedures, 711
    Success vs failure rates, 698
    Supervision styles, 737
    Technical violations, 736, 761
    Three stages of, 711
    Violating parole, below
Peer groups. importance in the desistance process, 705
Presumptive parole systems, 728
Process of individual change, 704
Public assistance access of parolees, 738
Recidivism, this index
Residence, parole restrictions, 706, 746
Rights and procedures at parole, 711
Sex offenders, conditions of parole, 741
Social stability, importance in the desistance process, 705
Statutory protections
    Conditions of parole, 731
    Grants of parole, 718
Success vs failure rates of parole programs, 698
Technical violations of parole, 736, 761
Violating parole
    Generally, 752 et seq.
    Constitutional rights, 753
    Impact of parole violations on prison growth, 763
    Pretextual revocations, 761
    Revocation hearings, 757
    Right to counsel, 761
    Rights and procedures at violation hearings, 752
    Technical violations, 761
Work, importance in the desistance process, 703

RECIDIVISM

See also Prior Criminal History, this index
Bureau of Justice Statistics, 697
Custodial vs noncustodial sanctions impacting, 582
Desistance from criminal conduct, 699
Drug courts efficacy, recidivism studies, 687
Elderly offenders, 771
Fee charge responsibilities exacerbating, 741
Impacts of custodial vs noncustodial sanctions, 582
Incarceration's effect on, 140
Magnitude statistics, 198
Parole programs impacting, 710
Parole surveillance effectiveness, 738
Prior Criminal History, this index
Probation violations, recidivism issues, 599
Rates studies, 715
Re-Entry After Incarceration, this index
Sex offenders
    Generally, 638, 742

Alternatives to incarceration, 621

REHABILITATION THEORY OF PUNISHMENT
Generally, 38
Crime rates, effects of incarceration, 574
Decline of, 504
Deterrence theory vs, 59
Effects of incarceration on crime rates, 574
General effects of incarceration, 581
Immutable offender characteristics, 210
Incapacitation theory vs, 59
Incarceration effects on crime rates, 574
Limitations, 56
Mutable offender characteristics, 242
Prison growth implications of perceived failure of, 505
Sex offenders, civil commitment, 636
Shaming sanctions, 653
Specific effects of incarceration, 581
Why we punish, 48
Youth as mitigating factor, 234

RESTITUTION
Fines incidence compared, 605
Probation requirements, 592, 595
Victims' needs, 179

RESTORATIVE JUSTICE
Generally, 661 et seq.
Acceptances levels, 676
Costs advantages, 674
Defense attorneys' conflicts, 681
Definitional problems, 661
Dialogues, 663
Disparate treatment concerns, 677
Effectiveness, 667
Effects on victims, 673
Externality risks, 677
Group conferencing, 664
Mediation, victim-offender, 665
Peacemaking circles, 664
Retribution and restoration compared, 662
Shaming sanctions compared, 660
Social controls as alternative to incarceration, 661
Victims' roles
  Generally, 662
  Effects on victims, 673

RETRIBUTIVIST THEORY OF PUNISHMENT
Generally, 57
Death penalty cases, 417
Emotive retributivism, 419
Federal guidelines, 65
Objective vs subjective retributivism, 61
Offense traits, qualitative severity, 151
Prison growth implications, 505
Restoration and retribution compared, 662
Revenge and retributivism, 418
Sex offenders, alternatives to incarceration, 619
Three-strike laws, 60

Utilitarian theories distinguished
  Generally, 37, 57
  Consequentialism, 38
  Federal guidelines, 279
  Harm analysis, 165
  Prior criminal history, 190
  Victim statements, 182

RIGHTS OF OFFENDERS
Constitutional Law, this index
Parol hearings. See Re-Entry After Incarceration, this index
Procedures at Sentencing Stage, this index

RISK
Clinical risk assessment
  Generally, 132
  Actuarial model compared, 134
Criminal behavior risk factors
  Generally, 13 et seq.
  Child abuse and neglect, 18
  Early risk factors, 15
  External factors, 27
  Familial offending, 17
  Impulsiveness theory, 16
  Lifecycle trends in offending, 21
  Recidivism risks, predicting, 138
Plea bargaining, risk tolerance and distribution, 463
Restorative justice, externality risks, 677
Sex offenders, recidivism risks, 638

SENTENCING COMMISSIONS
Generally, 81, 129
Constituencies affecting sentencing policies, 82
Guidelines, this index
Political cover functions, 131
Prisons, rise of, 511

SENTENCING FACTORS
Elements of crimes distinguished, 145, 301 et seq.

SENTENCING GUIDELINES
See Guidelines, this index

SENTENCING REFORM ACT
See also Guidelines, this index
Racial discrimination, 106
Shaming sanctions, 652

SEX OF OFFENDER
See Offender Traits, this index

SEX OFFENDERS
Alternatives to incarceration
  Generally, 618 et seq.
  Constitutionality, 627
Child victimization rates, 620
Civil confinement
  Generally, 619 et seq.
  Critique, 633
Conditions of parole, 741
Deterrence theory, 619
Hate crimes, sexual assaults as, 177
Mental abnormality disorder findings, 623

Personality disorder findings, 623
Public perceptions of child abuse incidence, 621
Rates of civil confinement, 642
Recidivism, this index
Registration requirements, 619, 643, 741
Residency restrictions, 619
Retribution theory, 619
Sentencing, discretionary and actuarial model compared, 132
Sexually violent predator status determinations, 623
Theories supporting civil commitment, 636
Treatment and punishment, 643

SHAMING SANCTIONS
Generally, 649 et seq.
Constitutionality, 655
Efficacy critique, 656
Ex ante or ex post effects, 660
Forms of shaming penalties, 650
Historical background, 649
Rehabilitative theory, 653
Restorative justice compared, 660
Sentencing Reform Act challenge, 652

SITUATIONALISM
Offender traits, 27, 226

SOCIAL SCIENCE EVIDENCE
Proper use in sentencing, 34

SPECIFICITY OF CHARGING DECISIONS
Prosecutors, 91

STATE ATTORNEYS GENERALS
Roles in sentencing, 114

STATE VS COUNTY RESPONSIBILITIES
See also Moral Hazard Problem, this index
Crime control, state/local disconnect, 97
Death penalty costs, 427
Incarceration costs, 429
Political accountability levels, 92
Prison growth, 490

STATISTICAL GLOSSARY
Generally, 773

STRUCTURED SENTENCING
Constitutional limits, 301 et seq.
Determinate vs Indeterminate Sentencing, this index
Guidelines, this index
Plea bargaining, 471
Prosecutorial discretion, 299
Three-Strike Laws, this index

THEORIES OF PUNISHMENT
See Why We Punish, this index

THERAPEUTIC COURTS
See Drug and Other Therapeutic Courts, this index

THREE-STRIKE LAWS
Generally, 206, 262
Constitutionality, 255
Incapacitation theory, 47, 206
Retributivists, 60
Zero-tolerance drug policies compared, 78

TOUGH ON CRIME POLITICS
Escalating crime-distrust model, 153
Identity politics and, 499
International attitudes compared, 530
Legislative incentives, 439
Punitiveness, perception and reality of, 523
Voter pandering, 2
Wariness about, 511

TRAITS AFFECTING SENTENCING
Age of Offenders, this index
Domestic Batterers, this index
Elements of crimes vs. elimination of the distinction, 145, 301 et seq.
Offender Traits, this index
Offense Traits, this index
Sex Offenders, this index

TRUTH-IN-SENTENCING (TIS) LAWS
Costs constraints, 262
Federal financial incentives and TIS adoptions, 297
Felony/misdemeanor distinctions, 296
Guidelines effects, 299
Parole boards discretion, legislative limitations, 103, 143
Plea bargaining effects, 299
Sentencing decision impacts, 296

UTILITARIAN THEORIES OF PUNISHMENT
Generally, 37
Retribution distinguished. See Retributivist Theory of Punishment, this index
Why We Punish, this index

UTILITY MAXIMIZATION
Offender traits, 10

VICTIMS
Generally, 177 et seq.
Children, sex offenses against, 620
Comparative law, 474
Death penalty, execution impact statements, 182, 188
Domestic Batterers, this index
Hate crimes, victim characteristic factors, 174
Objective harm vs subjective impact, 177
Parole grants, victim inputs affecting, 729
Prison growth, victims' rights movement affecting, 505
Restitution needs, 179
Restorative Justice, this index
Roles in sentencing, 177 et seq.
Sentencing statements
Generally, 178
Arguments for, 180

Constitutionality, 182
Criticisms, 181
Death penalty, execution impact statements, 182, 188
Emotional impacts on fact finders, 183
Problematic variation, 182
Retributivist and utilitarian theories distinguished, 182
State laws, 178

Sex offenses against children, 620

WHY WE PUNISH
Generally, 37 et seq.
Comparative studies, 71
Confirmation bias, behaviorist analysis, 12
Consensus, reaching, 63
Consequentialist theory, 57
Deterrence Theory of Punishment, this index
Incapacitation Theory of Punishment, this index
Normative goals, 37 et seq.
Political aspects of punishment theory, 79
Politics of Punishment, this index
Positive theories, 70
Punitive vs rehabilitative tensions, 48, 129
Racial aspects of punishment theory, 78
Rehabilitation Theory of Punishment, this index
Retributivist Theory of Punishment, this index
Tough on Crime Politics, this index
Utilitarian punishment theories, 37

WRONGFULNESS
Generally, 146
Harmfulness compared, relative importance, 147, 152